Women's America

WOMEN'S AMERICA

Refocusing the Past

FIFTH EDITION

Edited by

Linda K. Kerber
University of Iowa

Jane Sherron De Hart
University of California, Santa Barbara

*22⁷ -
246
271 - 282
259 - 62*

New York Oxford
Oxford University Press
2000

Oxford University Press

Oxford   New York
Athens   Auckland   Bangkok   Bogotá   Buenos Aires   Calcutta
Cape Town   Chennai   Dar es Salaam   Delhi   Florence   Hong Kong   Istanbul
Karachi   Kuala Lumpur   Madrid   Melbourne   Mexico City   Mumbai
Nairobi   Paris   São Paulo   Singapore   Taipei   Tokyo   Toronto   Warsaw

and associated companies in

Berlin   Ibadan

Published by Oxford University Press, Inc.,
198 Madison Avenue, New York, New York 10016
http://www.oup-usa.org

Library of Congress Cataloging-in-Publication Data
Women's America : refocusing the past / edited by Linda K. Kerber,
Jane Sherron De Hart. — 5th ed.
p.   cm.
Includes bibliographical references.
ISBN 0-19-512180-5 (cloth : alk. paper). — ISBN 0-19-512181-3 (pbk. : alk. paper)
1. Women—United States—History—Sources.   2. Women—Employment—
United States—History—Sources.   3. Women in politics—United
States—History—Sources.   4. Women—Health and hygiene—United
States—History—Sources.   5. Feminism—United States—History—
Sources.   I. Kerber, Linda K.   II. De Hart, Jane Sherron.
HQ1426.W663   2000
305.4'0973—dc21   99-18726
                                                                            CIP

Printing (last digit): 10 9 8 7 6 5 4 3 2 1

Printed in the United States of America
on acid-free paper

For

Dorothy Haber Kaufman

and

Ruby Sherron De Hart

who read each successive edition
as if it were the first.

Acknowledgments

Preparing each new edition of *Women's America* extends our own education. The energy and skill with which historians have been writing about the history of women and gender has made the challenge of choosing among this new work especially difficult. We are grateful to five anonymous reviewers who offered shrewd criticism, and to the wise advice of Alice Kessler-Harris, Gail Bederman, Eileen Boris, Laura Edwards, Estelle Freedman, Vivian Hart, Elaine Tyler May, Maureen Murphy Nutting, and Barbara Ransby. When it came time to seek out photographs, Coline Jenkins-Sahlins, Erika Gottfried, and Marilyn Wandrus responded with enthusiasm and generosity.

We owe special thanks to Alexandra Epstein for the graphs. Dan Gomes of the University of California, Santa Barbara and Rachel Bohlmann and Charles Hawley of the University of Iowa took on difficult challenges with verve and creativity. We are also grateful to Jillian Dowling, who worked on earlier stages of the book. At the Obermann Center for Advanced Studies at the University of Iowa, Jay Semel and Lorna Olson provided indispensable support, and Katie Adams and Rachel Warden made it possible for us almost to meet our deadlines. In New York, Georges Borchardt and DeAnna Heindel have offered important advice. At Oxford University Press, Stacie Caminos has kept us on time and in order, Pamela Montgomery LaBarbiera was a sensitive copy-editor, and Christine D'Antonio managed the stages of production with a keen eye and quick reflexes.

This new edition marks the beginning of a new collaboration with our editor, Gioia Stevens. We are grateful for her generous encouragement and for her help in reassessing and reconceptualizing *Women's America*.

Linda K. Kerber   Jane Sherron De Hart
University of Iowa   *University of California, Santa Barbara*

CONTENTS

III THE MANY FRONTIERS OF INDUSTRIALIZING
   AMERICA, 1880–1920

Women's America

INTRODUCTION

Gender and the New Women's History

Jane Sherron De Hart
Linda K. Kerber

One of the most effective ways in which dominant groups maintain their power is by depriving the people they dominate of the knowledge of their own history. The Martiniquian psychiatrist Frantz Fanon, a leader of the Algerian resistance against the French in the 1950s, understood this well. In *The Wretched of the Earth,* his classic attack on colonialism, Fanon observed that "colonialism is not satisfied merely with holding a people in its grip . . . [but] by a kind of perverted logic, it turns to the past of an oppressed people, and distorts, disfigures and destroys it." Lacking an appreciation of their own historical experience and the dignity, even glory, of the actions of their own people, the colonized are encouraged to think that they have no alternative to oppressive conditions. "The effect consciously sought . . . [is] to drive into the natives' heads the idea that if the settlers were to leave, they would at once fall back into barbarism, degradation and bestiality."[1]

Throughout history, certain women have understood this. When, in 1404, Christine de Pizan undertook to write the earliest modern chronicle of the lives of great women of the past, she explained to her readers that she hoped to bring them "out of the ignorance which so blinds your own intellect." Although they knew "for a certainty" from their own experience that women were capable of virtue and fortitude, they were vulnerable to "philosophers" who defined women as trivial. Pizan described her contemporaries as "valiant women" who, denied a knowledge of their own history, had been "abandoned . . . exposed like a field without a surrounding hedge, without finding a champion to afford them an adequate defense. . . . Where is there a city so strong which could not be taken immediately if no resistance were forthcoming . . . ?" To provide women with their history was to build "a city wall, strongly constructed and well founded."[2]

WOMEN'S HISTORY AS A FIELD OF RESEARCH

A fictional woman in Jane Austen's novel *Northanger Abbey* (1818) complains that she reads history only a little, "as a duty, but it tells me little that does not either vex or weary me. The quarrels of popes and kings, with wars or pestilences, in every page; the men all so good for nothing, and hardly any women at all."[3] As recently as ten years

3

ago, students in high school and college history classes could examine the index of their American history survey texts and reach the same conclusion.

In mid-nineteenth-century America, women activists self-consciously created a historical archive. Fearing that women would be denied knowledge of their own history, knowing that the actions of women were little regarded by historians, and predicting that pioneering activists on behalf of women's rights would die before their experiences had been recorded, Elizabeth Cady Stanton and Susan B. Anthony energetically collected evidence of the women's movement of their own time. The rich collection of documents that they published—six large volumes, entitled *History of Woman Suffrage*—was intended to be "an arsenal of facts" for the next generation of activists and historians.[4] But most historians ignored it. Ralph Henry Gabriel's *The Course of American Democratic Thought*, the standard text widely used throughout the 1940s and 1950s in college history courses, failed to cite a single work by a woman, not even the massive *History of Woman Suffrage*. "[I]f women were doing any thinking . . . ," the historian Mary Beard acidly observed in 1946, "it is difficult to find out from this treatise what it was."[5] In 1933 she herself edited a documentary collection, *America Through Women's Eyes,* in which she argued that an accurate understanding of the past required that women's experience be analyzed with as much care as historians normally devote to the experience of men. Our perspective and our goals in this book are similar to hers. We offer essays that we not only enjoy reading and rereading but that represent some of the best work done during the past three decades in which women's history emerged as a research field.

Surveying those decades, the historian Gerda Lerner suggested that the writing of women's history can be arranged in four stages of development, each stage more complex and sophisticated than the last, but all useful and necessary.[6] The first stage she called "compensatory history," in which the historian wanders, like Diogenes with a lantern, seeking to identify women and their activities. In the decade of the 1970s, some historians began to search for women whose work and experiences deserved to be more widely known. The accomplishments of these women ranged from feats of exploration and endurance to scientific discoveries, artistic achievements, and humanitarian reforms. They included such pioneers as Amelia Earhart, the pilot whose solo flight across the Atlantic in 1933 dramatically demonstrated women's courage and daring; Alice Hamilton, the social reformer and physician whose innovative work in the 1920s on lead poisoning and other toxins made her a world authority on industrial disease and a strong critic of American industry; Maria Goeppert-Mayer, the brilliant theoretical physicist whose research on the structure of the atom and its nucleus won her the Nobel Prize; and Zora Neale Hurston, the novelist and folklorist who mastered African-American folk idiom and depicted independent black women. One result of this search has been the publication of *Notable American Women,* four volumes of fascinating biographies of 1,800 remarkable individuals.[7]

"The next level of conceptualizing women's history," Lerner suggested, has been "contribution history." In this stage, historians describe women's contribution to topics, issues, and themes that have already been determined to be important. The main actors in the historical narrative remain men; women are subordinate, "helping" or "contributing" to the work of male activists. If the tone of "compensatory history" is delighted discovery of previously unknown women, the tone of contributory history can often be reproachful: how is it that men did not acknowledge women's help? Still, the work of contributory history can be very important in connecting women to major movements in the past: the women of Hull House "contribute" to Progressive reforms, the women in cotton factories in Lowell, Massachusetts, are an important part of the story of the industrialization of America. Pioneering historians in the late 1920s and 1930s, among them Julia Cherry Spruill, Mary Beard, and Caroline Ware, wrote important books that firmly established women's participation in and contribution to significant developments in American history: frontier settlement, abolition, urbanization and industrialization, populism and progressivism.

It could be said that a third stage of women's history—which developed as a vigorous field of study and research in the 1970s and 1980s—is to move past a recounting of women's "contributions" and to seek to test familiar generalizations and to rewrite the historical narrative. Things we thought we "knew" about American history turn out to be more complex than we had suspected. For example, most textbooks suggest that the frontier meant opportunity for Americans, "a gate of escape from the bondage of the past." But it was men who more readily found on the frontier compensation for their hard work; many women found only drudgery. (In fact, women were more likely to find economic opportunity in cities than on the frontier.) Other generalizations turn out to be equally suspect. We have often assumed that American slaves were provided with at least adequate diets, but the generalization holds better for male slaves than for pregnant women and nursing mothers; for them, the slaves' diet meant semistarvation. The new women's history challenges us to re-examine the social relations of the sexes, to *reconstruct* many historical generalizations, and to *reconfigure* the historical narrative.

Finally, women's history challenges us to understand that gender itself is a social construction. Historians increasingly ask questions about how people construct meaning for their historical experience, and how difference between the sexes operates to shape the construction of meaning. Women's history also suggests a more complex understanding of traditional categories of historical interpretation. Conventional periodization has used presidential administrations or wars as major guideposts in organizing our description of the past: the Revolutionary Era, the Age of Jackson, the Civil War, the Eisenhower Years. Conventional interpretations have tended to emphasize the accomplishments of men, whether they be presidents, generals, farmers, or ranch hands. But all men had women for contemporaries, and women experienced the same great social phenomena that men did.

This book is divided into three major chronological sections. Because dates that mark major turning points in traditional historical accounts do not automatically coincide with those dates that mark significant changes in the lives of American women, women's history challenges us to re-examine conventional periodization. Our sections are generally congruent with familiar periodization; they also reflect changing realities in women's experience. The dividing date between traditional and industrial America is 1820, by which time forces were in motion that would erode the domestic economy of an agrarian society, slowly transforming women's lives in the process. The long period of industrialization that followed 1820 may conveniently be broken at 1880, by which time large-scale industries in which women were employed were firmly established. By this time, too, women's rights leaders had come to recognize that suffrage would not be granted by the courts on the basis of a fresh interpretation of the Constitution, and they demanded a specific constitutional amendment. The second major period ends at 1920, when the necessary ingredients for emancipation were present. Gerda Lerner has identified these as "urbanization; industrialization with technology permitting society to remove food preparation and care of the sick from the home; the mechanization of heating and laundry; spread of health and medical care sufficient to lower infant mortality and protect maternal health; birth control; . . . and availability of education on all levels to all children."[8] These conditions existed in varying measure by 1920, which was also the year of the passage of the Equal Suffrage Amendment, the first year in which women attended large state universities in numbers comparable to men, and the first year in which more women were working in factories and white-collar jobs than in domestic service.

It should be noted, however, that industrialization was never a uniform process occurring simultaneously in all of the United States. Industrialized areas in the East and upper Midwest coexisted with frontier conditions in the West. There, encounters between Anglos, Native Americans, and Hispanics accentuated disparities just as had earlier contact in the East among British immigrants, Native Americans, and Africans. Frontiers, moreover, were not confined to borderlands where Anglo-Americans encountered other peoples. For immigrants coming from the shtetls of Eastern Europe, settling in New York involved crossing frontiers. So did the movement of women into new occupational categories that had previously been inhabited exclusively by men. Frontiers could also be intellectual ones, as the first group of college students in newly established elite women's colleges discovered when they were given access to the same curriculum provided men in long-established institutions such as Harvard University. Because so many different kinds of frontiers were crossed in the long period of industrialization between 1820 and 1920, we have headed that section "The Many Frontiers of Industrializing America." However historical experience is periodized, women shared in that experience. The history of industrialization is a history that involves female workers quite as much as it does male. Like their male counterparts, most women workers relied on their wages for their own support and that of their families. In the first factory labor force—the mill hands of Samuel Slater's first textile factory in Pawtucket, Rhode Island, in 1790—women and children actually outnumbered men. Extensively employed in manufacturing by the nineteenth century, they worked in a wide variety of trades as bookbinders, printers, shoemakers, seamstresses, laundresses, glass painters, button makers. In the twentieth century they worked in shipyards, airplane factories, and automobile plants turning out the military equipment essential to allied victory in two world wars.

Women were at the forefront of working-class protest. Women weavers in Pawtucket, Rhode Island, who walked off work in 1824 were among the first American workers to strike against low wages and long hours; a significant number of strikes by women workers followed in the 1830s.[9] Women at the textile mills in Lowell, Massachusetts, in the 1840s were the first industrial workers in the nation to demand state regulation of the length of the workday. In the twentieth century, large-scale strikes organized by men in mines and railroads had their counterparts in large-scale strikes organized by women in textile mills and garment factories.[10]

Similarly, enslaved workers—primarily Africans but also, in the early centuries, Indians—were as likely to be women as men. Enslaved women workers were to be found in the fields, toiling alongside men, in the same jobs.

THE DIFFERENT HISTORICAL EXPERIENCE OF WOMEN AND MEN

The historical experience of the two sexes, for all its similarities, was in many important ways profoundly different. Difference itself is a comparative term. As legal scholar Martha Minow writes, "I am no more different from you than you are from me. A short person is different only in relation to a tall one." While making distinctions helps people cope with complexity, descriptions of difference usually carry with them unstated assumptions of value and hierarchy. As Minow puts it, "Women are compared to the unstated norm of men, 'minority' races to white, handicapped persons to the able-bodied, and 'minority' religions to 'majorities.'"[11] Difference, therefore, is not a neutral term.

Differences among women are also multiple. Differences of culture, nationality, and historical memory are exacerbated by distinctions of race, class, ethnicity, and sexual preference. Because women are apt to live with men—husbands, fathers, sons—who share their racial, class, and ethnic identities, commonalities with women who don't share that identity are often obscured. Because each of these differences carries with it implications of hierarchy, further distancing can develop. Affluent women may feel superior to poor women; white women may feel hostile to black women; Asian-American women may feel that they have little in common with Hispanic women.

Hispanic women, who are often identified as a single ethnic group, are in fact people of many nationalities: Puerto Ricans, Cubans, Mexicans, Brazilians—to name a few. Moreover, most are of Central American Indian descent and share the gene pool of North American Indians. They learned to speak Spanish—hence the name "Hispanic"— only because their original land was conquered by Spain. "Hispanic" women differ from each other not only with respect to ethnicity but also class. Affluent women who are part of the Miami Cuban community may feel that they have little in common with migrant agricultural workers from Mexico. By the same token, Asian-American women who came from such countries as China, Japan, the Philippines, Korea, Thailand, or Vietnam are separated by diverse heritages, various languages, and disparate economic resources. So are white women who are separated by multiple ethnic backgrounds, religious affiliations, and class positions.

Differences in sexual preference further divide women, stigmatizing lesbians and obscuring the commonalities they share with heterosexual women. Even those heterosexual women who reject negative stereotypes of homosexuals may view their lesbian counterparts with ambivalence. Women who are able to tolerate same-sex relationships as long as they remain discreetly hidden are often uncomfortable with open displays of homosexual preference and distance themselves from the women involved. Lesbians who have struggled for self-validation and a life-style that allows them to express same-sex love, affection, and sexuality feel no less alienated from women whose discomfort is a measure of their identification with a system that has stigmatized and oppressed other women.

That the factors which women share with men and which separate them from other women have been so powerful and persistent should not blind us to fundamental divergence in the historical experience of women and men. Gender differences in life cycles and family experiences have been a central factor in that divergence. Employment patterns of white women in a large New England textile factory make this clear. As young single women at the turn of the century, they went into the mill to supplement family income, often allowing brothers to improve their job prospects by staying in school; as wives, they withdrew when children were born and returned as mothers of small children when the perilous state of family finances required them to do so. As mothers of grown children, they returned to stay. Thus family responsibilities were a crucial factor not only in determining at what stage in their life cycle women were gainfully employed but also in explaining why their employment patterns differed from those of male workers.

Once in the work force, the jobs to which women were assigned, the wages they were paid, the opportunities for unionization they encountered, and the relationship they forged with governmental regulators all reinforced fundamental differences between the sexes. Even when they entered the factory together, with comparable skills, men and women were assigned by management to different tasks at markedly different pay scales. Despite the low wages, which should have made them ripe recruits for unionization, most unions were loath to organize women workers. In part because women lacked the leverage that unions afforded skilled male workers, federal and state governments reluctantly agreed to regulate women's hours, wages, and working conditions long before they regulated men's.

Most people, male and female, particularly if they were white and middle class, understood difference to mean advantage. They assumed that women were spared heavy physical labor and fierce competitive pressures. Excused from primary responsibility for family support, wives and daughters could spend most of their adult lives at home rather than in the work force, devoting their time to such congenial tasks as caring for children, doing charitable deeds, and socializing with friends. Those who were employed outside the home were thought to work for "pin money," which they could use to indulge their whims as consumers.

Recent research makes clear that most of these "advantages" were class-specific and illusory. Exhausting labor performed in hazardous conditions characterized many women's jobs. Responsibility for supporting other family members was not limited to men, especially among the working class. Unmarried women often returned their wages to their parents, who relied on daughters' wages for essentials. Most adult women— whether they were single, widows, or wives—worked to feed and shelter themselves, their children, other members of their families. Their expenditure of money was rarely capricious; in fact they accepted low wages in nonunionized jobs because they were so likely to be in desperate need.

The notion that the home protected working-class housewives from the competitive pressures of the marketplace and all housewives from real work was also an illusion. The home has always been less a haven than a workplace. It was the site of housework—heavy physical labor and unremitting toil—work that was no less strenuous for all the denial that it was work at all since it was performed for love of family rather than wages. Even the middle-class housewife who enjoyed the conveniences of nineteenth-century town life and possibly a servant to help with the laundry and cooking struggled with an exhausting array of tasks that included washing, starching, ironing, sorting, and putting away laundry; scrubbing, sweeping, and dusting floors, walls, windows, furniture, and accessories; growing, pickling, preserving, and baking food; sewing, mending, and knitting clothes, towels, pillowcases, quilts, curtains, carpets, and rugs; birthing, nursing, tending, instructing, and disciplining children. According to one harried antebellum housewife, every day was "hurry, hurry, hurry, and drive, drive, drive."[12] For rural women the workload was even heavier. There were farm-related chores to perform and raw materials such as soap and cloth to produce in addition to core household tasks. Through much of the nineteenth century rural black women were enslaved; after the Civil War most lived in sharecropping families in which the level of subsistence was scarcely higher and the physical work load almost as heavy, although the psychological conditions were generally better. Reflecting on the workload of her mother's generation, a nineteenth-century daughter spoke for millions when she lamented that her mother had been robbed of "her health, her strength, and her life."[13] In some respects, little has changed. In the 1980s, a farm woman in northern Iowa told an interviewer, "I plant the garden, I feed the chickens, I sell the eggs, I put up a year's worth of vegetables. I don't have *time* to work!"[14]

Although twentieth-century technology has lightened the onerous physical burden, the equation of homemaking with leisure remains an illusion carefully nurtured by the advertising industry. From the introduction of the electrical washing machine in the 1920s—"an entire new day will be added to your week"—to the dishwashers, ranges, and microwave ovens of the 1990s that will do the work "whether you are at home or not," promises of relief from drudgery through the purchase of new products have been accompanied by new expectations that entailed more work.[15] Laundry—and there was more of it—had to be done more frequently; cooking demanded more creativity; clothing necessitated hours spent shopping; child care involved properly sterilized bottles, regular feeding schedules, greater attention to toilet training, nutrition, hygiene, and properly supervised play. If the nature of housework had changed, the time spent doing it did not. In 1960, nonemployed urban women were spending 55 hours per week in house-work—three hours more than rural homemakers in the 1920s. Fully employed women in the 1980s each week pack an additional 25 hours of work—housework—into evenings and weekends. While there is evidence to suggest that some younger men may be doing more, the gender disparity in terms of housework is likely to persist well into the twenty-first century.[16]

If women seldom found the home that tranquil center of repose depicted in popular literature, they had equal difficulty finding in it the much celebrated "haven" from the competitive pressures of a "heartless world." We have long understood that severe downturns in the market have enormous economic and psychic impact on family life. During the Great Depression of the 1930s, for example, many homemakers were thrust into the work force, joining the long lines of men desperate for work. Refusing to sit by passively when their families lacked basic necessities, others opened their homes to boarders and applied their sewing skills to piecework—measures that wives of laborers had long used to supplement family income even in periods of prosperity. Resorting to the home production that had engaged their grandmothers, middle- and working-class women alike raised and canned vegetables and patched, mended, and recycled clothes in order to keep cash outlays at a minimum.

What historians have only begun to appreciate is the extent to which in more prosperous times such enterprise and frugality benefited not only the household economy but the national economy as well. By helping out husbands in shops, buying in bulk, taking in boarders, doing piecework, taking in wash, peddling goods on the street, scavenging for food and fuel, wives in laboring-class households throughout the nineteenth and early twentieth century managed to transform a husband's wages below subsistence level into subsistence wages. Because of such efforts, business employing those husbands were able to stay afloat in an undercapitalized and volatile economy. Among the emerging middle class where a husband's income was sufficient for maintenance, it was the value of the wife's labor that frequently provided the kind of savings and investments that buffered the family against market vicissitudes and fueled economic growth in an industrializing nation. In sum, even in the nineteenth century, the boundaries between home and market, domestic sphere and public sphere, were far more permeable than once assumed.

GENDER AS A SOCIAL CONSTRUCTION

The adverse economic implications for women associated with the old perception that housework was not real work suggest that in this instance, as in many others, difference has meant disadvantage. Women's historians have not only documented this disadvantage, but have sought to explain it. The factors involved in this explanation are very complex and still imperfectly understood. The explanation traditionally offered has been a variant of biological essentialism. As Supreme Court Justice David Brewer put it in 1908, "The two sexes differ in the structure of the body, in the functions to be performed by each, in the amount of physical strength, in the capacity for long continuing labor . . . , [in] the self reliance which enables one to assert full rights, and in the capacity to maintain the struggle for subsistence." Woman's "physical structure and a proper discharge of her maternal functions" place her at a disadvantage in that struggle, he continued, and justify legislation to protect her.[17]

Justice Brewer's statement reveals a common confusion of sex and gender. To the extent that his view of difference is based on anatomical and hormonal features that differentiate males and females biologically, he is talking about *sexual* difference. When, however, he speaks of "the self-reliance that enables . . . [men] to assert full rights," "the capacity [of men] to maintain the struggle for subsistence," and the "proper discharge of [woman's] maternal functions," he is referring to *gender* difference. The assumption that men are self-reliant and that women are not, that men struggle for subsistence and women do not, that women nurture their children and men cannot, reflects the ways in which Justice Brewer and most of his generation understood the implications of being male or female.

In antebellum America, for example, white southern males, whether members of the low-country planter class or the backcountry working class, identified masculinity with a concept of personal honor, in defense of which duels were fought and fists flew. In the cities of the North, many young working-class males shared their southern counterparts' obsession with physical prowess and bellicosity. So synonymous were masculinity and toughness for those New Yorkers known as "Bowery boys" that when the Bowery boy was represented on stage, he was immediately recognizable by his swaggering gait and aggressive persona. Although the black abolitionist Frederick Douglass would not have been comfortable with the flamboyant aggressiveness and virility flaunted by the Bowery boys as a badge of working-class masculinity, the identification of force and power with manhood was a concept he well understood. In *Narrative of the*

Life of Frederick Douglass (1845), Douglass's autobiographical account of his life as a slave and his escape to freedom, the author prefaced a description of his brutal fight with the vicious slave breaker Covey with a single sentence: "You have seen how a man was made a slave; you shall see how a slave was made a man."

Not all social groups defined masculinity in this fashion, even in antebellum America. Although aggressiveness, self-reliance, and competitiveness were cultivated in most boys because these traits were needed in the work world of adult males, families whose values were shaped by evangelical Protestantism emphasized that manliness also involved self-restraint, moral self-discipline, and sobriety. These qualities became even more important in the new urban bourgeois culture of the late nineteenth century. A bureaucratized corporate capitalism would require of the middle class a model of masculinity different from the rougher, more "macho" ideal characteristic of the frontier. A "real" man, while projecting a virile and, if necessary, tough demeanor, also needed to be a "team player"—an attribute cultivated in boyhood games and team sports. Indeed, competitive sports, virility, and masculinity have become so intertwined in the twentieth century . . . that "the boy or man who dislikes competitive sports or virile postures has little choice but to affect 'manly' interests and behavior and to hope these affectations will not be exposed."[18] To behave otherwise was to risk being called a "sissy" or a "queer." Such labels reflected popular assumptions that "real" men were sportsmen and that nonathletes, whether heterosexual or not, were males who wished to have sexual relations only with males, were effeminate, and/or wished to be women. In other words, sex refers to biological differences that are unchanging; gender involves the *meaning* that a particular society and culture attach to sexual difference. Because that meaning varies over time and among cultures, gender differences are both socially constructed and subject to change. Definitions of what is masculine and feminine are learned as each society instructs its members from infancy through adulthood as to what behavior and personality attributes are appropriate for males and females of that generation.

Sexuality is also socially constructed. Anatomical and hormonal characteristics set certain boundaries within which we operate. Within those boundaries socially constructed scripts provide cues as to how we respond sexually—what or who arouses our desire. How sexual preference is first determined or chosen—and when—is a matter experts do not fully understand. But here, too, culture plays a part. It is helpful, writes historian Carroll Smith-Rosenberg, to "view sexual and emotional impulses as part of a continuum or spectrum. . . . At one end of the continuum lies committed heterosexuality, at the other uncompromising homosexuality; between, a wide latitude of emotions and sexual feelings."[19] Where we place ourselves on that continuum and whether we move within it is affected by cultural norms as well as a strong biological component.

Sexuality has its own history. Conceptions of sexuality, attitudes as to how sexual feelings should be expressed, with whom, and where, have been continually reshaped by the changing nature of the economy and politics. In the seventeenth century, for example, women were believed to be more lustful and carnal than men. Female sexuality was seen as a source of power and corruption to be feared and controlled. By the nineteenth century, when sexual restraints had to be internalized, sexuality was redefined. Women—at least white, native-born, middle- and upper-class women—were viewed as having weaker sexual desires than men. Sensuality was attached to poor or "darker" women—who, by definition, "invited" male advances.

As we begin to uncover the history of sexuality, we can better understand what part sexuality played in women's subordination. We can also see how women tried to devise ways to enhance sexual control and expression. In the nineteenth century, for example, some married women used the concept of women as passionless to reduce the frequency of sexual intercourse so as to reduce the likelihood of pregnancy and enhance sexual pleasure. Women who wished to express themselves sexually as well as emotionally in single-sex relationships constructed life-styles that opened up new realms of freedom. Indeed, we are just beginning to understand the ways in which these private relationships sustained the public activism of women such as Jane Addams or Lillian Wald.

Like gender and sexuality, race, too, is a social construction, despite the fact that we have long believed it to be an indisputable biological marker. Indeed, it was not until the nineteenth century that the idea of race was fully conceptualized in the way we understand it: human beings connected to or separated from other human beings by virtue of physical characteristics that are presumably genetic, such as skin pigmentation, hair texture, proportion, facial structure, and so on. In fact, however, there are no genetic characteristics possessed by all blacks but not non-blacks; similarly, there is no gene or cluster of genes common to all whites but not to non-whites. It is law and custom that are critical determinants of how individuals are classified with respect to race. In colonial Virginia, for example, a child born of a black mother and white father was classified as black. In the wake of American Revolution, the legal definition changed so that a person was defined as black if he or she had a black parent or grandparent; anyone less than one-quarter black was white. In practice, however, even a more distant black member in one's family tree resulted in the classification "black." In 1910, Virginians changed the law to define as black anyone who was one-sixteenth black. Twenty years later, the state adopted the notorious "one-drop" law, which defined as black anyone with one drop of African blood, however that might have been determined.

Mexican Americans have also been subject to changing classifications. In the early nineteenth century, the term referred to nationality, not to race. Those persons who lived in Mexico might be white, Native American, black, or Asian. Once land that had originally belonged to Mexico became a part of the Southwestern United States, "Mexican" became a racial category. In 1855, the California legislature defined Mexicans as people with Spanish and Indian blood. Called a "mixed breed," they were seen as an indolent, cowardly people—an inferior "mongrel" race. Yet in the twentieth century, the Supreme Court determined that Mexican Americans were "white."

Just how arbitrary and confusing racial classification could become is illustrated in the case of people from India. Uniformly classified as Caucasian by anthropologists, which should have earned them the designation "white," many were dark-skinned and therefore regarded by the American public as "non-white." In a 1922 Supreme Court decision, *United States* v. *Thind*,[20] the justices, reasoning that "the average well informed white American would learn with some degree of astonishment that the race to which he belongs is made up of such heterogenous elements," concluded that common knowledge rather than science prevailed. Bhagat Singh Thind, the plaintiff in the case, was not, as he claimed, "white." That a concept with no scientific significance that has been understood in such varied and often irrational ways retains such force as a source of meaning, identity, and (dis)advantage is a reminder of how powerfully social constructions function in how we organize and understand our social world.

Class is yet another category that is socially constructed. Differences in wealth and property are transformed into class by a set of institutional practices that allows a small propertied elite to retain property within that group. For example, the practice of restricting marriages to people within the same propertied group assured the retention of wealth within that group. Arranged marriages served this function, as did the internalization of cultural definitions of who might be a suitable marriage partner. Consider the example of Eliza Lucas, who at the age of 17 ran her father's South Carolina plantation while he served as royal governor of Antigua, a small island in the Caribbean. Rejecting the first two suitors her father selected, she made her own decision as to whom to marry. She chose a wealthy planter, Charles Pinckney—a choice consistent with the marital strategy of her class.

Miscegenation laws that prohibited racial intermarriage and, therefore, transmission of property to heirs of "mixed blood" have been a device designed to preserve property of a particular racial group. The interpenetration of class and race was most evident in the South, where, in the decades after the Civil War, lynching and other forms of terror were often directed at black men who managed to secure some degree of economic independence. When race and class intersected, as it did for those black women who had the financial resources to purchase a ticket entitling them to sit in the "Ladies" car of the train, race trumped class. Women such as Ida Wells Barnett and Charlotte Hawkins Brown suffered the humiliation of being physically ejected—a reminder of how spatial segregation can reinforce social distinctions. For upper-class Mexican American women, on the other hand, class could trump race. When marriage brought with it significant property, Anglo suitors, eager to consolidate their own class position, could easily be persuaded that the young woman was of "pure" Spanish ancestry. Such practices exemplify the meaning of the phrase "money whitens."

Understanding how differences associated with gender, sexuality, race, and class interacted—and continue to interact—in the lives of women to privilege as well as to exclude and oppress is key to understanding the varied experiences of American women. The place to begin is with gender.

GENDER AND ITS IMPLICATIONS

Understanding the difference between sex and gender provides a key to understanding the differences in men's and women's historical experience. In the workplace, for example, women and men were assigned jobs that reflected the employers' beliefs about the kind of work each sex should do. In a society whose understanding of gender included the conviction that women's primary obligations were familial and their basic talents domestic, female wage earners were persistently channeled into jobs that corresponded with the kind of work done in the domestic sphere or with characteristics long associated with women.

In the preindustrial domestic economy, women did both heavy physical labor—hauling water, slaughtering chickens—and skilled tasks—spinning, weaving, nursing. When women sought new avenues through which to gain economic independence they followed these chores into the marketplace. As slaves and as "hired help" they toiled on other people's farms; as "mill girls" they tended dangerous spinning machinery for twelve hours a day; as packinghouse workers they labored amid stench and slime. Upwardly mobile women laid claim to the teaching and nursing professions by emphasizing that the personality characteristics and skills required for such work were precisely those believed to be unique to the female sex. Thus nursing, considered in pre-Civil War years an occupation no respectable woman would enter, was eventually touted as a profession eminently suited to women. Providence, after all, had endowed the fairer sex with that "compassion which penetrate[s] the heart, that instinct which divines and anticipates the wants of the sick, and the patience which pliantly bends to all their caprices."[21] As the economy grew more complex, middle-class women infiltrated the ranks of librarians and secretaries. These occupations had been primarily male, but, like teaching and nursing, were redefined so as to emphasize the nurturing, service-oriented qualities ascribed to women—with a corresponding decrease in pay. Newer industries provided new job titles but old work categories. Receptionists and social workers were hired by employers still convinced that the tasks required in these jobs were consistent with the personality characteristics and skills traditionally associated with women. New white-collar jobs were also segregated by race, even in the North where segregation was not officially practiced. White women were overwhelmingly hired as stewardesses on national airlines until after the civil rights legislation of the 1960s. Because gender rather than individual talent or capability has been the primary consideration, the result of this kind of stereotyping has been to segregate women into certain kinds of work, whether in the professions or in industry. Most women workers are employed as waitresses, salespersons, secretaries, nurses, and teachers.

Once a form of work has been identified with women, it has invariably become associated with low pay and minimal prestige. "Theoretically, the market treats men and women neutrally, judging only the characteristics of their labor," writes the historian Alice Kessler-Harris. "In the world of economists, the wage is rooted in the play of supply and demand." In practice, she continues, "the wage is neither neutral nor natural, but reveals a set of social constructs . . . that convey messages about the nature of the world, and about . . . men and women and . . . the relations between them."[22] Low pay was appropriate for people assumed to be marginal workers, whose place was in the home where purity and virtue could be protected and family duties fulfilled. In this way the home subsidized the factory.

Gender was embedded not only in economic relations but in legal relations as well. In the legal tradition English colonists brought to America, the husband was understood to be the head of the family and to represent it in its dealings with the world. Upon marriage, the woman lost her separate civil identity; it was assumed that she had voluntarily forsworn the claim to make choices at odds with those of her husband. In a powerful legal fiction, man and wife were understood to be one person; the married woman was the *feme covert*, "covered" with her husband's legal identity for virtually all purposes except crime.[23] All personal property she brought to the marriage became her husband's; he could sell her jewelry, gamble away her money. He could not sell her real estate unless she consented, but he could decide how it was to be used: whether land was to be farmed, rented out, planted in corn or vegetables, whether trees on it were to be cultivated or cut down. Since married women did not own property they could not make legal contracts affecting it; they could not buy and sell without their husband's consent. A married woman could not decide whether their children were to be kept at home or apprenticed or, if apprenticed, who their masters would be. She could not sign a contract independently; not until she was a widow could she leave a will. So powerful was the fiction that husband and wife are one person that marital rape was inconceivable. Indeed, marital rape was not outlawed anywhere in the world until 1978, when New York State passed a statute prohibiting forced sexual intercourse whether by a stranger, an acquaintance, or a spouse. As of 1990, only nine states have followed New York's lead. Congress attempted to remedy the situation in 1990s, offering block grants to all states that would outlaw marital rape, but the recent date of the incentive, 1993, is a reminder of what a long struggle it has been to rid the law of remnants of coverture and obtain for women the bodily integrity that men enjoy.[24]

Gender also defined political relationships. In Anglo-American tradition the right to participate in political activities—voting, office-holding, jury duty—was conditioned on the holding of property. Since married women could not direct the use of their property, it seemed to follow that they could be neither jurors, nor voters, nor officeholders. That politics was considered a male domain, that women were not political beings, is an understanding as old as Western civilization. Aristotle, whose classic work provided the basic terms by which westerners have understood politics, said that men alone realized themselves as citizens. It is no accident that the civic *virtue* he extolled derives from the same root as the word *virile*. Women, Aristotle maintained, realized themselves only within the confines of the household. Their relationship to the world of politics, like their legal status, was derivative—through fathers, husbands, and sons.

This derivative relationship forced women to carve out a political role that rested upon their ability to influence those who held political power. A time-honored tradition, this use of influence was employed in the interests of a wide range of important social issues and philanthropic causes in the years before 1920. Women found that the wielding of influence benefited their communities and enlarged their political skills. The uses of influence continued to be exploited by American women even after they got the vote. As primary adviser to Al Smith, governor of New York and presidential candidate in the 1920s, Belle Moskowitz had enormous impact both on the policies of his administration and on the politics of the Democratic party. But she was uncomfortable claiming power for herself and never ran for political office. Mary McLeod Bethune, a prominent African-American educator, was equally adept in the uses of influence. As president of the National Association of Colored Women and the National Council of Negro Women, Bethune met Eleanor Roosevelt. The first lady, admiring the effectiveness with which this forceful, articulate black woman championed the needs of her people, used her own influence to secure for Bethune appointments to a number of positions, notably in the National Youth Administration. From her position within the administration, Bethune in turn organized the Federal Council on Negro Affairs, a group of black leaders who worked effectively to focus the attention of the media as well as the administration on the desperate problems facing blacks in the Depression.

The gendering of politics forced women to clothe their political claims in domestic language. Deflecting male hostility to their entry into the political arena, they argued that women should have the vote in order to elect city officials who would see to it that rotting garbage was removed from homes, decaying meat taken out of markets, and polluted water purified; otherwise, the best efforts of mothers to assure their children clean homes and wholesome food were to no avail. Women in the nuclear disarmament movement also used gendered language, naming their organization "Mothers Strike for Peace."

THE DIFFICULTIES OF UNDERSTANDING GENDER AS A SYSTEM

Economics, law, politics—each, as we have seen, was permeated by assumptions, practices, and expectations that were deeply gendered. So widely shared were these assumptions, practices, and expectations and so much a part of the ordinary, everyday experience that they acquired an aura of naturalness, rightness, even inevitability. Common sense dictated that "this is simply the way things are." But "common sense," as anthropologist Clifford Geertz has shrewdly observed, "is not what the mind cleared of cant spontaneously apprehends; it is what the mind filled with presuppositions . . . concludes."[25] The consequence of comprehending the world in this way—whether in the nineteenth century or in our own time—is that it obscures the workings of a system in which economic, political, and cultural forces interact and reinforce each other in ways that benefit one group and disadvantage the other. Unable to recognize the system, failing to understand that what shapes and defines our lives has been constructed piece by interlocking piece over time by other human beings, we constantly reproduce the world we know believing we have no other choice. As a result the inequities persist, becoming more difficult to challenge because they, too, seem as natural and inevitable as the system that has produced them.

To develop a way of looking that allows one to "see" economic and social relationships, which are presumed to be neutral and natural, as socially constructed arrangements which in fact benefit one group at the expense of others is always a difficult task. That task is made even more difficult by the fact that language itself has embedded within it the values, norms, and assumptions of the dominant group. Consequently it reflects and re-creates reality as it is perceived by that group. Using language that is not one's own to expose unequal relationships or to create an alternative to those relationships challenges the ingenuity and analytical abilities of even the most clearheaded and imaginative thinkers.

Analytical skills, however, are not inborn. They are developed slowly and painfully within an educational process that values and encourages those skills as contrasted, for example, with simple memorization or rote learning. Throughout history, women have been explicitly excluded from the intellectual community. Prior to the seventeenth century when most people were illiterate, elite families in which sons learned to read and write rarely provided such opportunities for their daughters. A major literacy gap existed until well into the nineteenth century throughout the world and, in many underdeveloped countries, persists today. At the time of the American Revolution, when it has been estimated that 70 percent of the men in Northern cities could read, only 35 percent of their female counterparts could do so. Slaves were denied by law access to instruction in reading and writing lest they learn about alternatives to slavery. Not until the second half of the nineteenth century were white women admitted to major state universities. Between 1870 and 1890 a few elite colleges were founded that were designed to provide upper middle-class young women an education equivalent to that which their brothers were receiving at Harvard, Yale, and Princeton universities. These new women's colleges reluctantly admitted a few black students. It was left to black women with meager resources in a rigidly segregated society—notably Mary McLeod Bethune and Charlotte Hawkins Brown—to develop their own institutions. Because public schools served black children so badly, these private institutions often began not as colleges, but as elementary or secondary schools and later grew into larger and higher-level colleges. Only in recent generations have women in substantial numbers been able to acquire not only a basic education, but the rigorous training that would facilitate their ability to analyze and question the social and cultural arrangements within which they lived.

Another consequence of women's educational deprivation was their ignorance of history and, therefore, their lack of an intimate acquaintance with other historical actors—male or female—who had faced challenges that in some way resembled their own. Lacking a history of their own, they had few models—heroes to emulate or strategies to adopt. The lack of a history in which women were actors made it particularly difficult for even educated women to envision a world other than one in which men— their experiences and needs—were the norm. Marginality in the past thus confirmed and reinforced marginality in the present.

Understanding economic and social relationships that benefit one sex at the expense of another, developing language with which to critique those hierarchical relationships and articulate an alternative vision, and forging the group solidarity necessary to realize that vision, have been the tasks of feminism. The term *feminism* came into use in the United States around 1910 at a time when women were engaged in the fight for suffrage as well as a host of other reforms. As historian Nancy Cott has pointed out, feminism included suffrage and other measures to promote women's welfare that had emerged out of the nineteenth-century women's movement.[26] However, feminism encompassed a wider range of fundamental changes, amounting to a revolution in the relation of the sexes. "As an *ism* (an ideology)," Cott notes, "feminism presupposed a set of principles not necessarily belonging to every woman—nor limited to women."[27] In other words, not all women would oppose a sex hierarchy that privileged men as a group nor would they feel compelled to struggle for sexual equality. Some men would, joining feminist women in their efforts to dismantle a system that conferred on one sex the power to define the other. While this system has been partially dismantled—the goal of suffrage was realized in law in 1920[28]—the wider revolution remains to be accomplished.

RETHINKING THE SOCIAL CONSTRUCTION OF GENDER

Embracing the goals of their feminist predecessors and enriched by current scholarship on gender, contemporary feminists seek to reconstruct social relations between the sexes. To do so, they believe, requires change in both public life and private behavior. This double agenda has a long history.

In 1848, when American feminists drafted their first manifesto, Elizabeth Cady Stanton demanded change in both law and custom. She called for legal change in the form of property rights for married women and voting rights for all women. Recognizing the ways in which women's self-esteem and autonomy were undermined, she also urged women to work for wide-ranging cultural change, such as equal standards of sexual behavior and equal roles in churches.

When twentieth-century feminists began to understand gender as a social construction, they too realized that the feminist revolution had to be waged in personal life as well as public life; in home as well as in workplace; in the most intimate relationships as well as the most remote. "It must be womanly as well as manly to earn your own living, to stand on your own feet," observed the feminist Crystal Eastman shortly after the national suffrage amendment was passed in 1920. "And it must be manly as well as womanly to know how to cook and sew and clean and take care of yourself in the ordinary exigencies of life. . . . [T]he second part of this revolution will be more passionately resisted than the first. Men will not give up their privilege of helplessness without a struggle. The average man has a carefully cultivated ignorance about household matters . . . a sort of cheerful inefficiency."[29] But it was fifty years before Eastman's insights became an agenda for action.

Feminists of the 1970s captured national attention with bitter criticisms of parents who gave nurses' kits to their daughters and doctors' bags to their sons and of guidance counselors who urged mathematically talented girls to become bookkeepers and boys to become engineers. Feminists condemned stereotypes that fit children to conventional roles in their adult life and encouraged the publication of books and toys designed to demonstrate to both boys and girls that they need not shape their aspirations to gendered stereotypes. (The popular TV show, record, and book, *Free to Be You and Me*, encapsulated these themes.) Feminists also urged a new set of private decisions in the family, so that both sexes would share more equitably the burdens and pleasures associated with earning a living, maintaining a household, and rearing a family. But gender stereotypes turned out to be more resilient than many had anticipated; socialization is a lifetime process.

Feminists themselves had to wrestle with a culture that maintained a hierarchy of values, reserving strength, competence, independence, and rationality for men and nurture, supportiveness, and empathy for women. Questioning both the hierarchy and the dualisms embedded in this gendering of values, feminists argued that these should be viewed as shared human qualities that are not sex-specific.

Sexual hierarchy was not the only cultural hierarchy that posed problems. There were also hierarchies of race and class. White feminists in the 1970s were criticized for promoting a vision of feminism that ignored black women and assumed that all women who were impatient with contemporary culture were white and middle-class. The upwardly mobile vision was a contested vision; the priorities of women of different classes and races did not necessarily converge. Many black women supported many elements of the agenda of middle-class white feminists of the 1970s—equal pay for equal work, access to jobs—but they disagreed on priorities. They were skeptical of those who placed the needs of middle-class women ahead of the needs of working women. Middle-class white women, the employers of domestic workers, were markedly more enthusiastic about the elimination of quotas for female students in law and medical schools than they were about the establishment of minimum wage and social security protection for domestic workers. The first generation of white radical feminists fought vigorously for the repeal of all abortion laws and for safe access to birth control; for black feminists the need for access to abortion was only one of a wide range of medical services for which many black women struggled.

Differences in sexual preference also posed problems for this generation of feminists. Challenges to traditional gender arrangements have always inspired charges of sexual deviance from those seeking to discredit the movement and trivialize grievances; the 1960s were no exception. Concerned about the movement's image, many feminists, rejecting the charge, attempted to push lesbians out of sight. They insisted that equality, not sexual preference, was the issue. Lesbian feminists disagreed, arguing that autonomy in sexual matters involved more than access to reproductive control. In time, tensions eased as many heterosexual feminists accepted the legitimacy of lesbian involvement and the validity of their contention that straight/gay divisions also constituted a form of cultural hierarchy that reinforced male supremacy.

THE COMPLEXITY OF CREATING EQUALITY

Recognizing the magnitude of cultural and personal change required if each woman was to realize her full human potential, feminists of the 1970s simultaneously challenged the institutions and the laws that denied women equal treatment. They launched a barrage of test cases in state and federal courts challenging practices of unequal responsibility for jury service, unequal benefits for dependents, unequal age requirements for drinking and marriage. In 1971, in an Idaho case testing who was to be the administrator of a will, feminists persuaded the Supreme Court for the first time in American history to treat discrimination on the basis of sex as a denial of equal protection under the law.[30] But the Supreme Court was reluctant to build on this precedent in subsequent cases. The Court's refusal to apply as strict a standard to sex discrimination as to racial discrimination prompted feminists to try to insert a ban on sex discrimination in the Constitution. The Equal Rights Amendment, passed overwhelmingly by Congress in 1972, failed to garner the last three states necessary for the three-quarter majority required for ratification. A contributing factor in its failure was basic disagreement on whether equality under law requires equality of military obligation.

Lobbying vigorously with both Congress and the executive branch, feminists won guarantees of equal pay for equal work, equal employment opportunities, equal access to credit and to education.[31] Building on the tactics and achievements of the civil rights movement, feminists secured major gains in the 1960s and 1970s. In the process, however, they discovered that guarantees of equality in a system structured with men's needs as the norm does not always produce a gender-neutral result. In many professions, for example, there is enormous pressure to demonstrate mastery of one's field in the early stages of a career, precisely when the physical hazards of childbearing are relatively minimal. Although the standard appears to be gender-neutral, it presents young women with excruciating choices that do not confront their male peers.

Nowhere was the challenge of achieving gender-neutrality in the workplace greater than on the matter of pregnancy. Aware of the long history of discrimination against pregnant employees, feminists successfully attacked regulations that prevented women from making their own decisions about whether and how long to work when pregnant. But initial legislative "solutions" raised new complexities challenging the assumption that equality always requires identical treatment. If employers could no longer fire pregnant women, they could still exclude from the company's disability program those temporarily unable to work during some portion of their pregnancy or at childbirth. Pregnancy, according to the Supreme Court, was not temporary disability but a "voluntary physical condition."[32] Outraged at the Court's ruling, feminists and their allies demanded congressional action that would require pregnancy and childbirth be treated like any other physical event that befalls workers. Responding in 1978 with model legislation mandating *equal* treatment in the workplace, Congress required employers to give physically disabled pregnant workers the same benefits given to other disabled workers. The problem, however, was not yet resolved.

If employers denied disability leave to all employees as a matter of company policy, federal legislation mandating equal treatment for both sexes with respect to pregnancy disability would, in effect, penalize female employees unable to work because of pregnancy-related illness. Equality, in this instance, seemed to require *special* treatment. Law makers in California and a few other states agreed and required employers to provide pregnant workers disability coverage even if no other illnesses were covered. Employers complained that this constituted "preferential treatment" for women. Some feminists, aware of the ways in which legislation designating women as a special class of employees because of their reproductive capacity had penalized female workers in the past, questioned whether such legislation was in the best interests of women. Would it reinforce sexist stereotypes of men as "natural" breadwinners and women as "natural" childbearers and rearers, making employers reluctant to hire married women of childbearing age and further marginalizing women as workers? Wouldn't it be better strategy to concentrate on extending disability benefits to workers of both sexes? Other feminists were untroubled. Pregnancy is unique to women, they argued, and calls for "special treatment" in recognition of that uniqueness. Such legislation, they insisted, acknowledges reality at a time when growing numbers of women become pregnant within one year of their employment.

Writing for the majority in a 1987 decision upholding a controversial California law on pregnancy disability benefits, Justice Thurgood Marshall went to the heart of the equality/difference dilemma. He noted that "while federal law mandates the same treatment of pregnant and non-pregnant employees, it would be violating the spirit of the law to read it as barring preferential treatment of pregnancy." The California law, he reasoned, "promotes equal employment opportunities because it allows women as well as men to have families without losing their jobs."[33]

The difficulty of determining what is fair treatment for pregnant women dramatically illustrates the complexities involved in reconciling equality and sexual difference. Part of the difficulty has to do with the meaning of equality. Is equality to be thought of, as it has been throughout American history, as equality of opportunity? Or is equality to be defined as equality of results? In either case, do the methods used to achieve equality demand the same treatment or different treatment? The stakes in this debate are high, as the debate over pregnancy in the workplace illustrates, because childbearing impacts so directly on women's struggle for economic independence.

Childbearing is only one aspect of sexual difference that complicates efforts to achieve equality between the sexes. Closely related are other issues surrounding reproduction. In the first half of the twentieth century, access to birth control was the contested issue. Feminists argued that the right to choose if and when to bear children was the foundation on which authentic equality between men and women must rest. The debate was intense and emotionally charged because reproductive issues involve sexuality, ethical and religious values, medical technology, constitutional rights to privacy, as well as matters of economic dependence, physical vulnerability, and state power. In the second half of the twentieth century, particularly in the wake of the Supreme Court's decision in *Roe* v. *Wade* (1973), these issues were fought out over policies governing access to abortion. Issues of race, class, and gender intersected. For many white middle-class feminists, preserving abortion rights was a top priority. Advocates of birth control, they saw abortion as a measure of last resort. Without that option, women's efforts to plan their lives, to set priorities, and to make choices were severely constrained, and constrained in ways that men's were not. For poor women and women of color who had been the subject of involuntary sterilization and who lacked access to a wide range of medical services, abortion was only one among many essential needs, and not necessarily the most pressing one. For many other women, abortion was not an essential need at all. Believing that the fetus is a human being from the moment of conception and that motherhood is women's key reason for being, they denied any connection between equality and access to abortion. They rejected the feminist contention that denying women access to abortion is a way in which men use the power of the state to reinforce their own power over women. Whether the state should permit and/or fund abortions for teen-age victims of incest is the most dramatic of the issues in conflict.

Incest is only one aspect of the larger problem of sexual violence that feminists contend is the ultimate expression of male dominance. Sexual violence, they insist, is violence, not sex, and it is a public, not a private, matter. Rape crisis centers, battered women's shelters, and "Take Back the Night" marches are expressions of their insistence that government respond to male violence against women. Feminists also attack directly the notion that female victims of violence are in some measure to blame by virtue of provocative dress and behavior or prior sexual experience. In the late 1970s they convinced policymakers that sexual harassment was a form of economic discrimination and that those who maintained workplaces were legally obliged to take action to prevent it.

Feminists also exposed the link between sexual violence and pornography. Many of them argued that material that objectifies women and equates violence against them with sexual pleasure is an invasion of their civil liberties. This interpretation represents a radical reformulation of traditional civil liberties arguments and a willingness on the part of some feminists to entertain reconsideration of the boundaries of protected speech. Other feminists strenuously object. They argue that some pornography can give people pleasure and enable them to learn about their sexuality, that causes of male violence against women are multiple, and that the likely effects of real-world enforcement of restrictions on pornography would serve neither the interests of women nor the cause of free speech. They fear, for example, that laws would be so vaguely written as to ensnare sexually explicit material that all feminists would agree should not be censored.

THE ANGUISH OF FUNDAMENTAL CHANGE

Reconciling equality and difference, equity and justice, involves feminists in a task as consequential as any in human history. Relationships assumed to be the result of choice, even of love, were now exposed as hierarchical relationships involving power and control. Such exposures are always traumatic. "All the decent drapery of life is . . . rudely torn off," complained the British legislator Edmund Burke when revolutionaries in France challenged the divine right of kings two hundred years ago. "When ancient opinions and rules of life are taken away, the loss cannot possibly be estimated. From that moment we have no compass to govern us; nor can we know distinctly to what port we steer."[34]

Even those in the vanguard of change can appreciate its difficulty; old habits are hard to break even for those determined to break them. For those who are not the initiators, challenges to long-standing beliefs and behaviors, whether issued now or in the past, can be, at best, unwelcome and, at worst, profoundly threatening. Feminism is no exception. Demands for equality in terms of power, resources, and prestige are usually seen as redistributive. Giving one party its share of the pie may result in a smaller share for the others. Even individuals who believe in equality in the abstract may find themselves loath to share power and privileges in practice, especially when their own lives are affected intimately. Moreover, new governmental policies designed to provide women equal protection in the law, equity in the workplace, and parity in politics were only part of what feminists were about. Cultural values as well as social institutions were under scrutiny. Even the definition of family was being tampered with as the 1980 White House Conference on Families made clear. Family had always meant that members were related by blood, marriage, or adoption. The term was now being applied to two mothers with children or an unmarried heterosexual couple who were childless; "anybody living under the same roof that provides support for each other *regardless* of blood, marriage, or adoption" seemed to qualify. To recognize these arrangements as multiple family forms, which many feminists did, was to legitimate people who, from the viewpoint of traditionalists, were living "illegitimate lifestyles."[35]

From this perspective it is hardly surprising that gender changes that feminists saw as expanding options for women and men alike, were seen by traditionalists as rejecting cherished beliefs and practices—"neuterizing society."[36] Women who believe they have lived useful and admirable lives by the old rules often regard feminists' attacks on traditional gender roles as an attack on a way of life they have mastered—and hence an attack on them personally. They fear that "a woman who has been a good wife and homemaker for decades" will be "turned out to pasture with impunity" by "a new, militant breed of women's liberationist" prepared to sacrifice justice for equality.[37] At issue are not just economic security and personal identity of individuals but the larger social order. Convinced that biological differences between the sexes dictate "natural" roles, traditionalists see the maintenance of these roles as socially and morally necessary—a source of stability in a world of flux. Thus feminist insistence that women should be able to seek fulfillment in the public world of work and power as well as in the private world of home and family is viewed by traditionalists as an egocentric demand that places personal gratification above familial duty. "Feminists praise self-centeredness and call it liberation," observed activist Connie Marshner.[38] By the same token, the demand that women themselves be the ultimate judge of whether and when to bear children is seen by some not as a legitimate desire to ensure a good life for those children who are born but as an escape from maternal obligations that threatens the future of the family and ultimately, therefore, society itself.

To suggest that some women find feminism an essential part of their identity and that other women define themselves and their lives in terms of traditionalism is not to suggest that the ideological history of women is bipolar. It embraces many variants. Nor do we suggest that there is little on which the two groups agree. Traditionalist women may be as suspicious of male-controlled institutions as feminists. Traditionalists may also be as vocal and publicly active on behalf of their goals. Feminists may be just as dedicated to family as traditionalists. Both groups identify with "sisterhood" and see "women's issues" as special ones, although they do not consistently agree on what they are or how they should be addressed. Partisans of these issues may unite or divide along class, occupational, or political lines. But no matter where they fall on the ideological spectrum, *all* women are a part of women's history.

"Woman has always been acting and thinking . . . at the center of life," wrote Mary Beard a half century ago;[39] but the significance of women's activities has, until recent years, often been discounted and rarely been understood. The scholarship of the past decades has spotlighted much that has lain in the shadows of history unnoticed and unappreciated. As we have examined that scholarship, we find ourselves less impressed by gender-based constraints—which were very real—than by the vigor and subtlety with which women have defined the terms of their existence. These creative experiences show how the private lives of historical persons can help us understand the rich complexities of change. To study women's history, then, is to take part in a bold enterprise that can eventually lead us to a new history, one that, by taking into account both sexes, should tell us more about each other and, therefore, our collective selves.

NOTES

1. Frantz Fanon, *The Wretched of the Earth*, translated by Constance Farrington (New York, 1963), p. 170.

2. Christine de Pizan, *The Book of the City of Ladies*, translated by Earl Jeffrey Prichards (New York, 1982), pp. 6–8, 10–11.

3. Jane Austen, *Northanger Abbey and Persuasion*, ed. John Davie, (London, 1971), pp. 97–99.

4. Elizabeth Cady Stanton, Susan B. Anthony and Matilda Joslyn Gage, *History of Woman Suffrage*, vol. 1. (New York, 1881), pp. 7–8.

5. Mary R. Beard, *Woman as Force in History: A Study in Traditions and Realities* (New York, 1946), pp. 59–60.

6. "Placing Women in History: Definitions and Challenges," *Feminist Studies* III (1975):5–14; reprinted in Gerda Lerner, *The Majority Finds Its Past: Placing Women in History* (New York, 1979), pp. 145–59.

7. Edward T. James, Janet Wilson James, and Paul Boyer, eds. *Notable American Women, 1607–1950: A Biographical Dictionary*, 3 vols. (Cambridge, Mass., 1971); and Barbara Sicherman and Carol Hurd Green, eds., *Notable American Women: The Modern Period* (Cambridge, Mass., 1980).

8. Lerner, *The Majority Finds Its Past*, pp. 49–50.

9. Alice Kessler-Harris, *Out to Work: A History of Wage-Earning Women in the United States* (New York, 1982), p. 40.

10. For detailed essays on the wave of garment workers' strikes of the early twentieth century, see Joan M. Jensen and Sue Davidson, eds., *A Needle, A Bobbin, A Strike: Women Needleworkers in America* (Philadelphia, 1984), pp. 81–182.

11. Martha Minow, "The Supreme Court—1986 Term. Foreword: Justice Engendered," *Harvard Law Review* 101 (1987):13. Minow points out that "'Minority' itself is a relative term. . . . Only in relation to white Westerners are [people of color] minorities."

12. Quoted from Harriet Beecher Stowe in Jeanne Boydston, *Home and Work: Housework, Wages, and the Ideology of Labor in the Early Republic* (New York, 1991), chap. 4.

13. George S. Merriam, ed., *Reminiscences and Letters of Caroline C. Briggs* (New York, 1897), pp. 21–23. Quoted in Boydston, *Home and Work*, chap. 4.

14. See Deborah Fink, *Open Country, Iowa: Rural Women, Tradition and Change* (Albany, N.Y., 1986), pp. 62–65.

15. Quoted in Susan Strasser, *Never Done: A History of American Housework* (New York, 1982), pp. 268, 278.

16. Joann Vanek, "Time Spent in Housework," *Scientific American* 231 (1974):116–20.

17. *Mueller* v. *Oregon*, 208 U.S. 412.

18. Mark C. Carnes and Clyde Griffin, eds., *Meanings for Manhood: Constructions of Masculinity in Victorian America* (Chicago, 1990), p. 203.

19. Carroll Smith-Rosenberg, "The Female World of Love and Ritual: Relations between Women in Nineteenth Century America," *Signs: Journal of Women in Culture and Society* 1 (1975):29–30.

20. On *United States* v. *Thind*, see Ian F. Haney Lopez, "White by Law," in *Critical Race Theory: The Cutting Edge*, edited by Richard Delgado (Philadelphia, 1995), pp. 542–550.

21. For purposes of these calculations, predominantly female occupations were defined as those hiring 70% or more women; predominantly male occupations were defined as those hiring 30% or less women. The calculations were made by Jennifer Lettieri on the basis of materials supplied by the U.S. Department of Labor, Bureau of Labor Statistics. See especially *Employment and Earnings* (Washington, D.C., January 1989), pp. 183–88.

22. Alice Kessler-Harris, *A Woman's Wages* (Lexington, Ky., 1990).

23. If, however, she committed a crime under his direction or surveillance, it was understood that he was the culprit. In most elements of criminal law, however, even married women were understood to have independent moral and ethical responsibilities; women could be charged with murder or treason.

24. New York Penal Law, Sec. # 130.00 1978. *McKinney's Consolidated Laws of New York Annotated* (St. Paul, 1987). For a basic review of the laws, see Herma Hill Kay, ed., *Sex-Based Discrimination* (St. Paul, 1988), pp. 239–62; and Raquel Kennedy Bergen, *Wife Rape: Understanding the Response of Survivors and Service Providers* (Thousand Oaks, Calif., 1996), p. 150. Remaining states enacted laws against marital rape in 1993 in order to qualify for funds under the Violence Against Women Act, which was finally passed in 1994. See U.S. Statutes at Large 108 (1994): 1796.

25. Clifford Geertz, *Local Knowledge: Further Essays in Interpretive Anthropology* (New York, 1983), p. 84.

26. Nancy F. Cott, *The Grounding of Modern Feminism* (New Haven, 1987), pp. 13–16.

27. Ibid., p. 3.

28. But in a segregated South, poll taxes and other devices barred black women (as well as men) from voting; not until the civil rights revolution of the 1950s and 1960s did the suffrage slowly and irregularly become available.

29. "Now We Can Begin," in Blanche Weisen Cook, ed., *Crystal Eastman on Women and Revolution* (New York, 1978), pp. 54–55. Originally published in *The Liberator* (December 1920).

30. *Reed* v. *Reed* 404 U.S. 71 (1971).

31. Equal Pay Act of 1963; Equal Credit Opportunity Act of 1974; Title VII of the Civil Rights Act of 1964; Title IX of the Educational Amendments Act of 1974.

32. *Geduldig* v. *Aiello* 417 U.S. 484 (1974); and *General Electric* v. *Martha Gilbert* 97 S. Ct. 401 (1976).

33. *California Federal Savings and Loan Association* v. *Guerra* 479 U.S. 272 (1987). "Promoting equal employment opportunities" requires new child care policies. Giving men and women equal access to a workplace that lacks provisions for child care is not gender neutral in its results when over 50% of these women have children under six. Working mothers, whatever the ages of their children and whatever their income level, currently spend 25 hours per week on domestic work compared with only 11 hours spent by their male partners. With less time and energy available for the kind of job-related activities and training programs that would improve their economic position, many are penalized with respect to both pay and promotion. Others who accept low-paying jobs for which they are overqualified because the hours or location allow them to more easily integrate wage work and family responsibilities find themselves similarly immobilized. For women who are single parents and heads of household, the penalties are especially severe.

34. Edmund Burke, *Reflections on the Revolution in France* (London, 1910), pp. 74–75.

35. Paul Weyrich, "Debate with Michael Lerner," speech presented at the Family Forum II conference, Washington, D.C., July 28, 1982. Quoted in Rebecca Klatch, *Women of the New Right* (Philadelphia, 1987), pp. 125–26.

36. Phyllis Schlafly, *The Power of the Positive Woman* (New Rochelle, N.Y., 1977), p. 25.

37. Ibid., p. 81.

38. Connaught Marshner, *The New Traditional Woman* (Washington, D.C., 1982), pp. 1, 3–4, 12. See also Klatch, *Women of the New Right*, p. 129.

39. Mary R. Beard, ed., *America Through Women's Eyes* (New York, 1933), pp. 4–5.

I

TRADITIONAL AMERICA
1600–1820

Many American histories treat the colonial period as a time when government and order were imposed upon a wilderness. The important subjects tend to be Indian wars, international trade, the establishment of legislatures, and rivalries between British colonies and those of other nations. The first woman mentioned is usually Pocahontas, the innocent Indian princess who allegedly saved the life of the hero of Jamestown, Captain John Smith. The second woman who appears is often Anne Hutchinson, who was banished from Massachusetts Bay Colony for heresy. Both met premature and unpleasant deaths. Unaccustomed to the climate of England, where she had been taken to be shown to Queen Anne, Pocahontas died of pneumonia. Hutchinson was massacred by Indians during a raid on her lonely dwelling in what is now Westchester County, New York. The reader who concludes from these examples that women were not very important in colonial America, and that the few women whom we remember are likely to have been troublesome and to have come to a bad end, may be pardoned.

But if we pose Mary Beard's question and ask, What did colonial America look like, seen through women's eyes? the picture changes. More constructive than troublesome, women were among the founders of virtually every colony. Indeed, a settlement counted itself as having passed the stage of a temporary camp only after it had attracted a reasonable complement of women. A sex ratio approaching 100 (that is, 100 women to every 100 men) was taken to be evidence that the settlement was here to stay. Once founded, communities were maintained in large part by women's labor. The productivity of housekeepers is not easily measured, but over fifty years ago Julia Cherry Spruill established the complexity of the tasks performed in frontier households.[1]

It may be that America seemed to European women less radical a change from the Old World than it did to men. The terrors of the ocean crossing and of the wilderness were shared by all. In the farming communities Europeans established along the eastern seaboard daily tasks proceeded in the manner of England, whether the agricultural laborer were farmer or farmer's wife. The rituals of childbirth were transmitted intact from Old World to New, although it may well have been that the rate of survival of mother and infant was better in the American countryside, where the dangers of infection were far fewer than in the towns and cities of Europe. By contrast, the innovations

The wyfe of an Herowan of Secotan.

This portrait of a Carolina Algonquin woman at her home settlement Secoton was drawn in the summer of 1585 by John White, the official artist of the Roanoke Expedition. His drawings are important representations of Algonquin life before extensive European contact. The woman, who looks skeptically at the viewer, is the wife of a leading male chief or counselor. Her body is decorated with gray, brown, and blue tattoos on the face, neck, arms, and legs. Women's tattoos simulated elaborate necklaces and other ornamentation; men used body paint for ceremonial purposes. (Courtesy of The British Museum. See Also Paul Hulton, America 1585: The Complete Drawings of John White *[Chapel Hill: University of North Carolina Press and British Museum Publications, 1984], pp. 66–67)* that made the colonies most distinctive from the Old World—especially governmental institutions like town meetings and provincial legislatures—were settings from which women were barred.

For African women, however, America meant violence and vulnerability. Slavery and the slave trade to the Americas had long been established by the Spanish and the Dutch when Virginians bought their first African slaves in 1619. In an era in which white working people often sold their labor for a term of years, African workers seem at first to have been treated not very differently from European indentured servants. But although white women servants were not generally required to do field labor, black women were. By the mid-seventeenth century, Africans were increasingly being treated as property. In 1662 the system was solidified: a Virginia law established that the children of an enslaved woman and an English man should follow "the condition of the mother," not the father. This rule made slaves out of mixed-race children and prevented the gradual erosion of slavery.

New England was largely settled by Protestant dissenters, and in the earliest days of their formation, radical Protestant groups often welcomed women as equals to men— not only in their moral selves, but also in some of their social roles. In the earliest days of Puritan settlement, women as well as men signed covenants establishing new churches; women as well as men made public professions of faith when they joined. (By the second generation of settlement, however, women's profession of faith was likely to be made privately, or read out loud by the minister.) Peripheral churches retained participatory, even disruptive roles for women longer; among the Quakers it was established that women could prophesy, that women would speak in public, and that women would have a significant role in the institutional decisions of the community. (Besides meetings for worship, Quakers held separate meetings of men and women to maintain the community; men and women had separate responsibilities and voted separately. If a new meeting house were to be built, the women's meeting and the men's meeting had to agree on the site.) Among Baptists and Methodists in the eighteenth century, radical evangelical faith also could translate into shared governance and public participation.

But despite repeated quotation of St. Paul's rule that "in Christ there is neither man or woman," believers of every faith were very conscious of gender distinctions. Anne Hutchinson's heresy was compounded by the fact that it was formulated by a woman. Many of the questions in her trial were grounded in the objection that she had stepped out of her proper place. For women, Puritans had special expectations and understood there to be special punishments. When dissenting women like Mary Dyer were delivered of malformed infants, John Winthrop saw no reason to be surprised at the divine punishment. Witchcraft, too, was a religious heresy; it, too, was gender specific, a woman's crime. Although witchcraft accusations normally arose in places where the entire community was troubled, the accusers were usually teen-aged girls, and the "witches" usually women. And as Baptist and Methodist communities became more solidly established, more "mainstream," they narrowed the space they offered "disorderly" women.[2]

English colonists brought with them English legal practices, including the English system of domestic law. The old law of domestic relations began from the principle that at marriage the husband controlled the physical body of the wife. (There was no concept of marital rape in American statutes until the mid-1970s.) If he controlled her body, then he could easily force her into agreement with him on every other aspect of their lives. There followed from this premise the elaborate system of coverture. The practice of coverture transferred a woman's civic identity to her husband at marriage, giving him the use and direction of her property throughout the marriage. "Covered" by her husband's civil identity, the married woman could not execute a contract without his signature (although a husband could manage the family's property without asking her consent). Without his agreement, she could not buy, sell, or trade; she could not apprentice her children or execute a valid will (until she was a widow). Some women, shrewd or wealthy—or both—nevertheless managed to control property after marriage through prenuptial agreements or marriage settlements.

When the United States purchased the Louisiana Territory, it acquired vast expanses of land that had been ruled by Spanish and French law, systems not marked by coverture, in which the property husbands and wives brought to their marriage became "community property." Although husbands were "head and master" of their households and had wide discretion in their use of family property, married women could keep separate property in their own names and pass it on to whomever they chose as heirs. These practices were not erased when the land passed to the United States; Louisiana, Texas, New Mexico, Arizona, Idaho, Nevada, California, and Washington remained community property states, offering significant legal advantages to married women deep into the twentieth century.

By treating married women as "covered" by their husbands' civic identity, by placing sharp constraints on the extent to which married women controlled their bodies and their property, the English law of domestic relations ensured that—with a few exceptions, like the obligation to refrain from treason—married women's obligations to their husbands and families overrode their obligations to the state. The right to participate in the political system was conditioned on holding property outright. Since married women could not hold property outright, it seemed logical to colonists that political rights be granted only to men. (Even this logic would not have explained the practice of excluding single women and widows from political rights.) Since girls could not grow up to be legislators or ministers or lawyers, little care was taken to provide them with any but the most elementary forms of schooling. "How many female minds, rich with native genius and noble sentiment, have been lost to the world, and all their mental treasures buried in oblivion?" mourned one writer.[3]

Like it or not, women were part of the community. What they chose to do or not to do set constraints on men's options. The Revolutionary army, lacking an effective quartermaster corps, was dependent on women for nursing, cooking, and cleaning. The army, in turn, could not march as quickly as Washington would have liked because provision had to be made for the "woemin of the army." The task of the recruiting officer was eased when men could rely on their female relatives to keep family farms and mills in operation, fend off squatters, and protect family property by their heavy labor, often at grave physical risk. We have no simple calculus for measuring the extent to which women's services made it possible for men to act in certain ways during the Revolution, but it is clear that women's work provided the civilian context in which the war was carried on.

When the war was over and the political structure of the new nation was being reshaped in federal and state constitutions, legislators made many radical changes in the system of government they had inherited from England. The new republic promised to protect "life, liberty and property," but under the old law a married woman was deprived of her property and had none to protect. Coverture was theoretically incompatible with revolutionary ideology and with the newly developing liberal commercial society. But patriot men carefully sustained it. Every free man, rich or poor, white or black, gained something from the system of domestic relations already in place; they had no need or desire to rethink it. Yet women did have distinctive political interests. For example, if women had had the vote in 1789, they might well have used it to claim independent property rights for themselves or to claim custody of their children in the event of divorce. Almost certainly they would have used the vote to establish pensions for widows of veterans. But women's distinctive needs continued to be discounted as trivial. It was left to women of succeeding generations to accomplish for themselves what the Revolution had not.

NOTES

1. Julia Cherry Spruill, *Women's Life and Work in the Southern Colonies* (Chapel Hill, N.C., 1938).

2. For Methodists, see Donald Mathews, *Religion in the Old South* (Chicago, 1977), chs. 1 and 2; for Baptists, see Susan Juster, *Disorderly Women: Sexual Politics and Evangelicalism in Revolutionary New England* (Ithaca, N.Y., 1994).

3. Clio [pseud.], "Thoughts on Female Education," *Royal American Magazine*, Jan. 1774, pp. 9–10.

SARA EVANS
The First American Women

The first American women were Native American women. The religious, economic, and political roles that they played within their own societies prior to the arrival of Europeans suggest that Europeans and Native Americans held dramatically different ideas about what women and men should be and should do. The difficulty that Europeans had in understanding the alternative gender realities to which they were exposed tells us how strong is the impulse to view established gender definitions in one's own culture as natural rather than socially constructed.

Note the importance Evans attaches to Native American women's religious functions. How did the sexual division of labor within Native American tribes she describes affect women's economic importance in a subsistence economy? To what extent did the Iroquois provide the authors of American constitutions with a democratic model?

According to the Iroquois, the creation of the earth began when a woman came from heaven and fluttered above the sea, unable to find a resting place for her feet. The fish and animals of the sea, having compassion on her, debated in council about which of them should help her. The tortoise offered his back, which became the land, and the woman made her home there. A spirit noticed her loneliness and with her begot three children to provide her company. The quarrels of her two sons can still be heard in the thunder. But her daughter became the mother of the great nations of the Iroquois.[1]

Women appear frequently at the cosmic center of native American myths and legends, tales that are undoubtedly very ancient. The history of women on the North American continent began 20,000 years ago with the migration of people from the Asian continent across the land bridge that now is the Bering Strait. These early ancestors of contemporary native Americans gradually created a great diversity of cultures as they adapted to varied environmental circumstances and conditions over time. The archaeological record indicates that 2,000 years ago some North American cultures lived nomadically, hunting and gathering

plants and animals. Others settled in villages and subsisted on domesticated plants as well as wild resources. Still others built complex, hierarchically organized societies centered in relatively large cities or towns. In these latter groups, archaeological remains reveal widespread trade relations and religious systems uniting people over vast areas of the continent. When the first Europeans reached North America in the fifteenth and sixteenth centuries, there were some 2,000 native American languages in use, a cultural diversity that made Europe look homogeneous.[2]

GATHERERS AND NURTURERS, TRADERS AND SHAMANS

Among the peoples of North America whose tribes lived in the woods, along the rivers, and on the edges of the plains, women were essential to group survival. In a subsistence economy, daily life revolved around finding food for the next meal or, at the most, the next season. Women's work as gatherers and processors of food and as nurturers of small children was not only visible to the whole community, but it also shaped ritual life and processes of community decision making.

Women's activities were sharply divided from those of men in most Indian societies. Women gathered seeds, roots, fruits, and other wild plants. And in horticultural groups they cultivated crops such as corn, beans, and squash. Women were also typically responsible for cooking, preserving foods, and making household utensils and furnishings. In addition, they built and maintained dwellings, such as earth or bark lodges and tepees, and associated household facilities like storage pits, benches, mats, wooden racks, and scaffolds. In groups that moved on a seasonal basis, women were often responsible for transporting all household goods from one location to the next.

Male activities in many groups centered on hunting and warfare. After the hunts, Indian women played an important role in processing the hides of deer or buffalo into clothing, blankets, floor coverings, tepees, or trade goods; preserving the meat; and manufacturing a variety of bone implements from the remains of the animals.

Indian societies differed in their definitions of which tasks were appropriate for women or men and in their degree of flexibility or rigidity. In some groups people would be ridiculed and shamed for engaging in tasks inappropriate for their gender, while other groups were more tolerant. Sometimes men and women performed separate, but complementary tasks. Among the Iroquois, for example, men cleared the fields so women could plant them. In other cases men and women performed the same tasks but the work was still segregated on the basis of sex. For example, many Plains Indian tribes divided the task of tanning hides according to the animal, some being assigned exclusively to women, others to men.

These differences shaped the relationships among women and between women and men. Societies with a clear sexual division of labor and cooperative modes of production, for example, encouraged gender solidarity. The Pawnee, a Plains society, lived in lodges large enough for several families, or about fifty people. Women shared cooking responsibilities among themselves, alternating between those on the north and those on the south sides of the lodge. Among the Hidatsa, another Plains group, female labor was organized by the household of female kin while male activities,

ranging from individual vision quests to sporadic hunting parties, were organized by age and by village. Groups of female kin built and maintained their homes, gathered seeds and edible plants, raised crops, and processed the meat and skins of animals killed by the men.[3]

In Iroquois society, where men were frequently away for prolonged periods of time, women farmed in a highly organized way. A white woman adopted in 1758 by the Seneca (one of the six tribes of the Iroquois Confederacy) described their work:

> In the summer season, we planted, tended, and harvested our corn, and generally had all of our children with us; but had no master to oversee or drive us, so that we could work as leisurely as we pleased. . . . We pursued our farming business according to the general custom of Indian women, which is as follows: In order to expedite their business, and at the same time enjoy each other's company, they all work together in one field, or at whatever job they may have on hand. In the spring, they choose an old active squaw to be their driver and overseer, when at labor, for the ensuing year. She accepts the honor, and they consider themselves bound to obey her.
>
> When the time for planting arrives, and the soil is prepared, the squaws are assembled in the morning, and conducted into a field where each plants one row. They then go into the next field and plant once across, and so on till they have gone through the tribe.[4]

As they gathered, cultivated, and produced food, tools, and housing, some women also actively participated in trade. Algonkian women on the Atlantic coast traded with whites from the earliest days. In 1609 John Juet, Henry Hudson's first mate, recorded an incident in New York Harbor: "There came eight and twentie Canoes full of men, women and children to betray us: but we saw their intent, and suffered none of them to come abord us. . . . They brought with them Oysters and Beanes, whereof we bought some."[5] In later years many observers noted both transactions with women and the high proportion of trade goods that were particularly interesting to women. Far to the northwest, on the Alaskan coast, the Tlingit built their economy on fishing for plentiful salmon and on trading with neighboring groups. Tlingit women not only dried and processed the salmon but they were also entrusted with managing and dispensing the family wealth. White traders were continually struck by the skill and sophistication of these women, who frequently stepped in to cancel unwise deals made by their husbands. These shrewd dealings paid off in that society where status could be gained by impressive displays of gift-giving.[6]

Religious myths and rituals offered women additional sources of power and status in their villages and tribes as they reflected in a symbolic realm the relations between people and nature.[7] In most North American Indian creation myths, females played critical roles as mediators between supernatural powers and earth. Many horticultural societies ritually celebrated the seasonal powers of Earth Mother—whose body produced the sacred foods of corn, beans, and squash. Groups primarily oriented to hunting more frequently conceptualized sacred powers as male, but in some cases the Keeper of the Game appeared as a woman. She observed humans' failures to address proper ritual prayers to the spirits of the animals and to treat the animal world on which they depended with proper respect; she could also inflict punishments of disease and famine.

American Indians perceived their world as sacred and alive. Power and mystery infused all living things, inspiring awe and fear. Women, like men, sought spiritual understanding and power by engaging in individual quests for visions. Quests involved a period of seclusion, fasting, and performance of prescribed rituals. Women's quests drew on the fasting and seclusion accompanying menstruation.

In most societies menstruating women were believed to be dangerously powerful, capable of harming crops or hunts and draining the spiritual powers of men. To avoid such harm they withdrew to menstrual huts outside the villages. Did women interpret this experience in terms of pollution and taboo, seeing it as a banishment, as many observers assumed? More likely they welcomed the occasional respite from daily responsibilities as an opportunity for meditation, spiritual growth, and the company of other women. The power that visions conferred allowed some women to serve as herbalists, midwives, medicine women, and shamans.

Marriage practices in some societies granted women considerable control in choosing their partners. In others, marriages were arranged by elders (often women) as a means of building economic alliances through kinship. Divorce, on the other hand, was common

and easy to accomplish. A woman could simply leave her husband or, if the house was hers, she could order him out on grounds of sterility, adultery, laziness, cruelty, or bad temper. Women's autonomy often had a further sexual dimension: Although the male-dominated groups prized female chastity, most Indian groups encouraged sexual expressiveness and did not enforce strict monogamy. Female power in marital and sexual relations could also be shaped by the proximity of a woman to her own kin.

Women's political power was rooted in kinship relations and economics. The scale of clan and village life meant that people knew one another primarily through kinship designators (daughter, husband, mother's brother, grandmother), and in many cases the most important level of sociopolitical organization was the local kin group. It seems likely that female power was most salient at the level of the village group, where it would shape many facets of daily life. In many tribes, however, there were some (often transitory or temporary) public forums, such as a council of elders, where decisions could be made for the community as a whole. Women held proportionately few of these public roles, but a recent reevaluation of ethnographic evidence shows that despite most scholars' belief that women had no significant political roles, there were numerous female chiefs, shamans, and traders.[8]

Iroquois women represented the apex of female political power. The land was theirs; the women worked it cooperatively and controlled the distribution of all food whether originally procured by women or by men. This gave them essential control over the economic organization of their tribe; they could withhold food at any point—in the household, the council of elders, war parties, or religious celebrations.[9] The Iroquois institutionalized female power in the rights of matrons, or older women, to nominate council elders and to depose chiefs. As one missionary wrote: "They did not hesitate, when the occasion required, to 'knock off the horns' as it was technically called, from the head of a chief and send him back to the ranks of the warriors. The original nomination of the chiefs also always rested with them."[10] When the council met, the matrons would lobby with the elders to make their views known. Though women did not sit

Their ripe corne

Their greene corne.

Corne newly sprong

Their sitting at meate

the place of solemne prayer

The house wherin the Tombe of their Herounds standeth.

SECOTON

A Ceremony in their prayers wth strange testure and songs danssng abowt posts carued on the topps lyke mens faces.

This *drawing* depicts the settlement of Secoton, the home of the Algonquin woman *pictured* on *page 26. The Secoton system of successive planting is illustrated by, from top to bottom, a field of ripe corn, a field of green corn, and newly planted corn. (Courtesy of the British Museum. See also Paul Hulton,* America 1585: The Complete Drawings of John White *[Chapel Hill: University of North Carolina Press and British Museum Publications, 1984], pp. 66–67)* in formal or public positions of power, as heads of households they were empowered *as a group*. This, in turn, reflected their considerable autonomy within their households.[11]

GENDER AND CHANGE: THE IMPACT OF EUROPEAN CONTACT

When Europeans began to invade the Americas in the 1500s, the most devastating assault on Indian life initially came from the unseen bacteria and viruses Europeans brought with them. Within a century raging epidemics of typhoid, diphtheria, influenza, measles, chicken pox, whooping cough, tuberculosis, smallpox, scarlet fever, strep, and yellow fever reduced the population of Mexico to only 5 to 10 percent of its former level of 25 million. The population of the northern areas which later became the United States suffered similar fates.[12]

As cultural, economic, and military contacts grew, the differences between women and men in each group began to change. In some cases women appropriated new sources of wealth and power; in others they lost both skills and autonomy. These various changes were shaped by the sexual division of labor in indigenous cultures, the demographic composition of European colonizers, and the nature of the economic relations between Indians and Europeans.

For example, when the Aztec empire fell before the superior military technology of the Spanish, women were booty in the military victory. The demographic facts of a dense Indian population and Spanish conquerors who were almost exclusively male shaped a continuing sexual interaction between Spanish men and Indian women. Seeking stability, the Spanish soon began to encourage marriages with Christianized Indian women. These Indian mothers of the mestizo (mixed-bloods) were historically stigmatized both by a racial caste system and by association with illegitimacy. Nevertheless, they fashioned for their children a new culture blending Christianity and the Spanish language with cultural concepts and practices from their Indian heritage. Contemporary Mexican culture is the result of their creative survival.[13]

On the Atlantic coast of North America, by contrast, English colonizers emigrated in family groups, and sexual liaisons with Indians were rare. Algonkian Indian women quickly seized the opportunity to trade for European goods such as metal kettles, tools, and needles and put them to use in their daily work. Although quick to appropriate European technology, they and their people actively resisted European domination. They fought back militarily, politically, and culturally. One key form of resistance was the Indian insistence on continuing women's prominent roles in politics, religious ritual, and trade despite the inability of Englishmen to recognize or deal with them.[14]

The impact of Europeans was more indirect for inland Indians. The European market for furs represented an opportunity for tribes eager to procure European trade goods. In all likelihood the men's increased emphasis on hunting and warfare sharpened the separation of men's and women's lives. The Iroquois, for example, quickly became dependent on trade goods and lost traditional crafts such as making pottery, stone axes, knives, and arrowheads. Yet by the 1640s they had depleted the beaver supply and had to compete with neighboring tribes for hunting grounds. One result of their longer and longer hunting expeditions was that the village itself became a female space. As hunters, traders, and fighters, men had to travel most of the year while women stayed at home, maintaining villages and cornfields generation after generation.[15] One consequence, then, of the fur trade in the first two centuries after contact was increased power for Iroquois women as they controlled local resources and local affairs.

Lacking a similar strong base in highly productive local agriculture, however, women in other tribes did not gain the power and influence that Iroquois women did. Among the Montagnais-Naskapi in the upper St. Lawrence valley, the fur trade gradually shifted the economic balance toward dependence on income provided by the men's trap lines or wages.[16] In some tribes, polygamy increased when a single hunter could provide more carcasses than a single woman could process.[17]

One group of Indian women—those who married fur traders—created an altogether new cultural and economic pattern. European fur traders, principally the French and later the English and Dutch, were almost exclusively male. As they traveled thousands of miles inland, traders depended on the Indians for their immediate survival and for long-term trade relations; thus, they began to marry Indian women. Indeed, Indian women provided the knowledge, skills, and labor that made it possible for many traders to survive in an unfamiliar environment. On the basis of such relationships, over the course of two centuries a fur trade society emerged, bound together by economics, kinship, rituals, and religion.[18]

Essentially traders adopted an indigenous way of life. Indian women prepared hides, made clothing and moccasins; manufactured snowshoes; prepared and preserved foods such as pemmican—a buffalo meat and fat mixture that could be carried on long trips; caught and dried fish; and gathered local fruits and vegetables such as wild rice, maple sugar, and berries. Stories abound of trading posts saved from starvation by the fishing or gathering or snaring skills of Indian women.

Indian women's ability to dress furs, build canoes, and travel in the wilderness rendered them invaluable to traders. A Chipewyan guide argued that the Hudson's Bay Company's failed expeditions were caused by a lack of women:

> in case they meet with success in hunting, who is to carry the produce of their labour? Women . . . also pitch our tents, make and mend our clothing, keep us warm at night; and, in fact, there is no such thing as travelling any considerable distance, or for any length of time, in this country, without their assistance.[19]

Indian women were active participants in the trade itself: They served as interpreters on whose linguistic and diplomatic abilities much depended. They trapped small animals and sold their pelts, as did many of their sisters who remained in traditional Indian society.

There is considerable evidence that some marriages between Indian women and fur traders resulted in long-lasting and apparently caring alliances. William McNeil, ship captain for the Hudson's Bay Company, mourned the loss of his Haida wife in childbirth: "The deceased has been a good and faithful partner for me for twenty years and we had twelve children together . . . [she] was a most kind mother to her children, and no Woman could have done her duty better, although an Indian."[20]

Despite their importance, many Indian women involved in the fur trade were ex-ploited. As guides or as wives, they lived in a social and economic structure organized around the needs of male European traders.[21] When they decided to return to Europe, traders were notorious for abandoning wives of many years, sometimes simply passing them on to their successors. Such practices contributed to the increased reluctance of Indian women to have any relations with white men. According to observers in the early nineteenth century, the fertility of traders' wives, who commonly had eight to twelve children, was sharply higher than that of traditional Indian women, who bore only four children on average. Traders did not observe traditional practices that restricted fertility, such as lengthy hunting expeditions and ritually prescribed abstinence. And unlike their traditional sisters who had virtual control over their offspring, traders' wives experienced the assertion of patriarchal authority most painfully when their children—especially their sons—were sent away to receive a "civilized education."[22]

The daughters of such marriages eventually replaced Indian women as the wives of traders. Their mothers' training in language and domestic skills and their ongoing relations with Indian kin fitted them to continue the role of "women-in-between" and their marriages settled into more permanent, lifelong patterns. At the same time, these mixed-blood, or metis, daughters lacked many of the sources of power and autonomy of their Indian mothers. They were less likely to choose their marriage partners and they married at a much younger age. Also, they did not have strong kinship networks to which to escape if their marriages proved unhappy or abusive. The absorption of European norms meant a far more polarized notion of men's public and women's private spheres along with the explicit subordination of women in both. The ultimate burden for the Indian wives of European traders came with the arrival of increased numbers of white women to the wilderness in the nineteenth century. Indian and mixed-blood wives experienced a growing racial prejudice that was not abated by even the highest degree of acculturation.[23]

The fur trade collapsed in the middle of the nineteenth century, as did the society that had grown up around it. Sizable towns in the Great Lakes region were populated by metis people who spoke a common language used in trade, shared the Catholic religion, and grounded their lives in the economics of the fur trade. The disappearance of the fur trade and the emergence of reservation policies in the United States forcing persons of Indian descent to register as Indians defined out of existence a people whose unique culture was built on the lives and activities of Indian "women-in-between."

By contrast, in the sixteenth and seventeenth centuries a very different set of circumstances strengthened the influence of women in some tribes on the Great Plains while marginalizing their power in others. These changes were less a product of trading relationships than of new technologies and economic possibilities inadvertently introduced by Europeans. Navaho women, for example, owned and managed livestock, enabling them to develop broad social and economic powers and a position of high prestige based on their economic independence. Sheep and goats, originally introduced by Spanish explorers, rapidly became the principal livestock, greatly expanding women's resources.[24]

Farther north, the introduction of horses in the early 1700s transformed the technology of hunting and, therefore, the Indians' way of life on the Plains.[25] Nomadic tribes previously had traveled slowly, depending principally on women's gathering for subsistence and engaging in highly organized collective hunts that often failed. Early in the eighteenth century, however, Plains tribes gained access to horses descended from those brought by early Spanish explorers. Horses enabled bands of hunters to range over a far wider territory and transformed buffalo hunting. An individual hunter could ride into a herd, choose as prey the largest rather than the weakest animals, and shoot his arrows at point-blank range. The consequence for the material life of Plains people was sudden, unprecedented wealth: more meat protein than they could consume, with plentiful hides for tepees, clothing, and finally, for trade.

More individualized hunting styles placed a premium on skill and prowess while encouraging the accumulation of wealth. The fact that a single hunter could easily supply several women with hides to dress and meat to cure encouraged polygamy. And the chronic shortage of horses led to institutionalized raiding and continuous intertribal warfare. The lifestyle that emerged under such circumstances has become in some respects the center of American mythology about the Indian. Mythical images of warlike braves galloping across the Plains in full headdress or engaging in rituals like the famed sundance leave little place for Indian women except as passive squaws waiting in the background.

The myths themselves reflect the heightened emphasis on male domination and concurrent loss of female power that accompanied the social and economic revolution brought by the use of horses. Certainly men's and women's life experiences diverged substantially. Frequently women traveled with hunting parties, charged with the care of tepees, children, food preparation, and clothing manufacture, as well as the processing of the huge carcasses. Though the women continued to do the bulk of the work, the romance and daring of war and hunting dominated the ritual life of the group. Male bonding grew with such ritual occasions and the development of military societies.[26]

By the nineteenth century the Lakota culture had incorporated an emphasis on sexual differences into all aspects of daily life. Cultural symbols sharply emphasized the distinction between aggressive maleness and passive femaleness. The sexual division of labor defined these differences concretely.[27] Extreme distinctions in demeanor, personality, and even language flowed from this rigid division. Men went on vision quests, directed religious rituals, and served as shamans and medicine men. Though women were economically dependent, their work remained essential to group survival, and their importance found ritual expression in female societies and in some women's individual visions that gave them access to sacred powers. The most important female society was made up of quill and beadwork specialists devoted to the mythic Double Woman Dreamer. The Lakota believed that dreams of the Double Woman caused women to behave in aggressive masculine ways: "They possessed the power to cast spells on men and seduce them. They were said to be very promiscuous, to live alone, and on occasion to perform the Double Woman Dreamer ceremony publically."[28]

The Double Woman Dreamer enabled the Lakota and other Plains Indians to incorporate specific social roles for women whose behavior violated feminine norms. Another was the widespread role of a "warrior woman" or "manly hearted woman" who acted as a man in both hunting and warfare. The manly hearted woman is a parallel role to the male "berdache," a man who could assume the dress and roles of a woman and was presumed to have special powers. Thus, although women lost both economic and cultural power as Plains tribes began using horses to hunt, to some degree women and men could move outside the boundaries of strictly defined feminine and masculine roles.

This fluidity allowed a few women quite literally to live the lives of men. In some societies manly hearted women were noticed very young and raised with extreme favoritism and license. In others the shift in gender roles received validation at a later age through dreams or visions. A trader on the Upper Missouri River told the story of one such woman, a member of the Gros Ventres captured at the age of 12.

> Already exhibiting manly interests, her adopted father encouraged these inclinations and trained her in a wide variety of male occupational skills. Although she dressed as a woman throughout her life, she pursued the role of a male in her adult years. She was a proficient hunter and chased big game on horseback and on foot. She was a skilled warrior, leading many successful war parties. In time, she sat on the council and ranked as the third leading warrior in a band of 160 lodges. After achieving success in manly pursuits, she took four wives whose hide-processing work brought considerable wealth to her lodge.[29]

WHAT THE EUROPEANS THOUGHT THEY SAW

At the time of the American Revolution, the existence of Indian societies, and in particular the highly democratic Iroquois Confederacy, provided for white Americans a living proof of the possibility of self-rule. Their virtues furnished a useful contrast to the corruption and tyranny against which Americans saw themselves struggling. For example, Thomas Jefferson wrote that the Europeans "have divided their nations into two classes, wolves and sheep." But for the Indians, "controls are in their manners and their moral sense of right

and wrong." As a result, Indians "enjoy . . . an infinitely greater degree of happiness than those who live under European governments."[30]

What the founding fathers did not explore, however, was that the Iroquois model included considerably more political and economic power for women than any Europeans considered possible. Many white observers overlooked the cultural complexity of Indian societies and the great range of women's economic, social, and religious roles. From the sixteenth to the nineteenth century both male and female writers persisted in describing Indian women—if they described them at all—as slaves, degraded and abused. A sixteenth-century Jesuit outlined the many tasks of Montagnais-Naskapi women, contrasted them with the observation that "the men concern themselves with nothing but the more laborious hunting and waging of war," and concluded that "their wives are regarded and treated as slaves."[31] An English fur trader, exploring the Canadian forests in the 1690s, described the status of Cree women: "Now as for a woman they do not so much mind her for they reckon she is like a Slead dog or Bitch when she is living & when she dies they think she departs to Eternity but a man they think departs to another world & lives again."[32]

Similarly, Europeans failed to comprehend women's political power. Early contacts with the coastal Algonkians, for example, produced elaborate descriptions of villages, tribes, and occasional confederacies headed by "chiefs" or "kings." Because Europeans looked for social organizations similar to the cities and states they knew, they could not imagine that the most significant political and economic unit of these people was the matrilineal-matrilocal clan in which women had considerable power and autonomy.[33]

What these observers saw was a division of labor in which women performed many tasks that European culture assigned to men. They were especially outraged to see women chopping wood, building houses, carrying heavy loads, and engaging in agriculture—jobs that in their view constituted the very definition of manly work. Missionaries, for example, persistently defined their goal as civilizing the Indians, by which they meant not only urging them to accept Christian doctrine and sacraments but also to adopt a way of life based on female domesticity and male-dominated, settled agriculture. Not surprisingly, their ideas met sharp resistance.

Iroquois women by the late eighteenth century, for example, were eager to obtain information about the agricultural practices of Quaker missionaries, but they wanted to use it themselves. When Quakers insisted on teaching men, the women ridiculed them as transvestites. "If a Man took hold of a Hoe to use it the Women would get down his gun by way of derision & would laugh & say such a warrior is a timid woman."[34]

In the long run, the Iroquois example held deep implications not only for self-rule but also for an inclusive democracy that sanctioned female participation. The latter, however, was something that revolutionary founding fathers could not fathom. Their definitions of "public" and "private," "masculine" and "feminine" did not allow them to see the more fluid, democratic, and simply different realities of Indian life. Yet over the course of American history, an understanding of public, political life built on an inclusive definition of citizenship proved to be a powerful idea, one capable of subverting even the ancient hierarchies of gender.

NOTES

1. Louis Hennepin, *A Description of Louisiana*, trans. John Gilmary Shea (New York: John G. Shea, 1880), pp. 278–80, in *The Colonial and Revolutionary Periods*, vol. 2 of *Women and Religion in America*, ed. Rosemary Radford Reuther and Rosemary Skinner Keller (San Francisco: Harper & Row, 1983), pp. 20–21.

2. See Carolyn Niethammer, *Daughters of the Earth: The Lives and Legends of American Indian Women* (New York: Collier Books, 1977); Ferdinand Anton, *Women in Pre-Columbian America* (New York: Abner Scham, 1973); and Gary B. Nash, *Red, White, and Black: The Peoples of Early America* (Englewood Cliffs, N.J.: Prentice-Hall, 1974). . . .

3. Janet D. Spector, "Male/Female Task Differentiation among the Hidatsa: Toward the Development of an Archeological Approach to the Study of Gender," in *The Hidden Half: Studies of Plains Indian Women*, ed. Patricia Albers and Beatrice Medicine (Washington, D.C.: University Press of America, 1983), pp. 77–99.

4. James Seaver, *Life of Mary Jemison: Deh-he-wamis* (1880), pp. 69–71, quoted in Judith Brown, "Economic Organization and the Position of Women among the Iroquois," *Ethnohistory* 17 (1970):151–67, quote on p. 158. . . .

5. Quoted in Robert Grumet, "Sunksquaws, Shamans, and Tradeswomen: Middle Atlantic Coastal Algonkian Women during the 17th and 18th Centuries," in *Women and Colonization: Anthropological Perspectives*, ed. Mona Etienne and Eleanor Leacock (New York: Praeger, 1980), p. 57.

6. Laura F. Klein, "Contending with Colonization: Tlingit Men and Women in Change," in Etienne and Leacock, *Women and Colonization*, pp. 88–108.

7. This section draws heavily on Jacqueline Peterson and Mary Druke, "American Indian Women and Religion," in Reuther and Keller, *Women and Religion*, pp. 1–41; see also Niethammer, *Daughters*, chap. 10.

8. Grumet, "Sunksquaws, Shamans, and Tradeswomen," pp. 43–62; see also Niethammer, *Daughters*, chap. 6.

9. Brown, "Economic Organization"; Diane Rothenberg, "The Mothers of the Nation: Seneca Resistance to a Quaker Intervention," in Etienne and Leacock, *Women and Colonization*, pp. 66–72.

10. Quoted in Brown, "Economic Organization," p. 154.

11. . . . [S]ee Elizabeth Tooker, "Women in Iroquois Society," in *Extending the Rafters: Interdisciplinary Approaches to Iroquois Studies*, ed. Michael K. Foster, Jack Campisi, and Marianne Mithun (Albany: State University of New York Press, 1984), pp. 109–23; . . . and Daniel K. Richter, "War and Culture: the Iroquois Experience," *William and Mary Quarterly* 40 (1983):528–59.

12. . . . See Henry Dobyns, "Estimating Aboriginal American Population: An Appraisal of Techniques with a New Hemispheric Estimate," *Current Anthropology* 7 (1966):395–412; . . . and Russell Thornton, *American Indian Holocaust and Survival: A Population History since 1492* (Norman: University of Oklahoma Press, 1987); . . .

13. See June Nash, "Aztec Women: The Transition from Status to Class in Empire and Colony," in Etienne and Leacock, *Women and Colonization*, pp. 134–48.

14. Niethammer, *Daughters*, chaps. 5–6.

15. Anthony F. C. Wallace, *The Death and Rebirth of the Seneca* (New York: Alfred A. Knopf, 1970), p. 28.

16. Leacock, "Montagnais Women and the Jesuit Program for Colonization," in Etienne and Leacock, *Women and Colonization*, p. 27. . . .

17. . . . See Carol Devens, "Separate Confrontations: Gender as a Factor in Indian Adaptation to European Colonization in New France," *American Quarterly* 38 (1986):461–80.

18. See Sylvia Van Kirk, "*Many Tender Ties*": *Women in Fur Trade Society in Western Canada, 1700–1850* (Winnipeg: Watson & Dwyer, 1980); Jennifer S. Brown, *Strangers in the Blood: Fur Trade Company Families in Indian Country* (Vancouver: University of British Columbia Press, 1980); . . .

19. Quoted in Van Kirk, "*Many Tender Ties*," p. 63.

20. Ibid., p. 33.

21. Ibid., p. 88.

22. Ibid., chap. 4.

23. [Ibid.,] . . . p. 145. See also chaps. 5–10.

24. Niethammer, *Daughters*, pp. 127–29.

25. Alan Klein, "The Political-Economy of Gender: A 19th Century Plains Indian Case Study," in

Albers and Medicine, *The Hidden Half*, pp. 143–73; Niethammer, *Daughters*, pp. 111–18.

26. See Klein, "The Political-Economy of Gender."

27. See, for example, quote from Geo. Sword, *Manuscript Writings of Geo Sword*, vol. 1 (ca. 1909), quoted in Raymond J. DeMallie, "Male and Female in Traditional Lakota Culture," in Albers and Medicine, *The Hidden Half*, p. 238.

28. Ibid., pp. 241–47, quote from p. 245; also Niethammer, *Daughters*, pp. 132–37.

29. In Beatrice Medicine, "Warrior Women—Sex Role Alternatives for Plains Indian Women," in Albers and Medicine, *The Hidden Half*, p. 273, see also pp. 267–80.

30. Thomas Jefferson quoted in Bruce Johnasen, *Forgotten Founders: Benjamin Franklin, the Iroquois and the Rationale for the American Revolution* (Ipswich, Mass.: Gambit, 1982), pp. 112, 114.

31. Quoted in Leacock, "Mantagnais Women," in Etienne and Leacock, *Women and Colonization*, p. 27.

32. Quoted in Van Kirk, *"Many Tender Ties,"* p. 17.

33. Grumet, "Sunksquaws, Shamans, and Tradeswomen."

34. "Journal of William Allinson of Burlington" (1809) quoted in Rothenberg, "Mothers of the Nation," in Etienne and Leacock, *Women and Colonization*, p. 77.

LAUREL THATCHER ULRICH
The Ways of Her Household

One of the greatest barriers to an accurate assessment of women's role in the community has been the habit of assuming that what women did was not very important. Housekeeping has long been women's work, and housework has long been regarded as trivial. Laurel Thatcher Ulrich shows, however, that housekeeping can be a complex task and that real skill and intelligence might be exercised in performing it. The services house-keepers perform, in traditional as well as contemporary America, are an important part of the economic arrangements that sustain the family and need to be taken into account when describing any community or society. Note the differences Ulrich finds between rural and urban women, and between middle-class and impoverished women.

By English tradition, a woman's environment was the family dwelling and the yard or yards surrounding it. Though the exact composition of her setting obviously depended upon the occupation and economic status of her husband, its general outlines were surprisingly similar regardless of where it was located. The difference between an urban "houselot" and a rural "homelot" was not as dramatic as one might suppose.

If we were to draw a line around the house-wife's domain, it would extend from the kitchen and its appendages, the cellars, pantries, brewhouses, milkhouses, washhouses, and butteries which appear in various combinations in household inventories, to the exterior of the house, where, even in the city, a mélange of animal and vegetable life flourished among the straw, husks, clutter, and muck. Encircling the pigpen, such a line would surround the garden, the milkyard, the well, the hen-house, and perhaps the orchard itself—though husbands pruned and planted trees and eventually supervised the making of cider, good housewives strung their wash between the trees and in season harvested fruit for pies and conserves.

The line demarking the housewife's realm

would not cross the fences which defined out-lying fields of Indian corn or barley, nor would it stretch to fishing stages, mills, or wharves, but in berry or mushroom season it would extend into nearby woods or marsh and in spells of dearth or leisure reach to the shore. Of necessity, the boundaries of each woman's world would also extend into the houses of neighbors and into the cartways of a village or town. Housewives commanded a limited domain. But they were neither isolated nor self-sufficient. Even in farming settlements, families found it essential to bargain for needed goods and services. For prosperous and socially prominent women, interdepend-ence took on another meaning as well. Pros-perity meant charity, and in early New England charity meant personal responsibility for nearby neighbors. . . .

. . . For most historians, as for almost all antiquarians, the quintessential early Ameri-can woman has been a churner of cream and a spinner of wool. Because home manufactur-ing has all but disappeared from modern housekeeping, many scholars have assumed that the key change in female economic life has been a shift from "production" to "consump-tion," a shift precipitated by the industrial rev-olution.[1] This is far too simple, obscuring the variety which existed even in the preindustrial world. . . .

. . . Beatrice Plummer, Hannah Grafton, and Magdalen Wear lived and died in New England in the years before 1750. One of them lived on the frontier, another on a farm, and a third in town. Because they were real women, however, and not hypothetical examples, the ways of their households were shaped by per-sonal as well as geographic factors. A careful examination of the contents of their kitchens and chambers suggests the varied complexity as well as the underlying unity in the lives of early American women.

Let us begin with Beatrice Plummer of New-bury, Massachusetts.[2] Forgetting that death brought her neighbors into the house on Jan-uary 24, 1672, we can use the probate inven-tory which they prepared to reconstruct the normal pattern of her work.

With a clear estate of £343, Francis Plum-mer had belonged to the "middling sort" who were the church members and freeholders of the Puritan settlement of Newbury. As an immigrant of 1653, he had listed himself as a "linnen weaver," but he soon became a farmer as well.[3] At his death, his loom and tackling stood in the "shop" with his pitchforks, his hoes, and his tools for smithing and carpentry. Plummer had integrated four smaller plots to form one continuous sixteen-acre farm. An additional twenty acres of salt marsh and meadow provided hay and forage for his small herd of cows and sheep. His farm provided a comfortable living for his family, which at this stage of his life included only his second wife, Beatrice, and her grandchild by a previous marriage. . . .

The house over which Beatrice presided must have looked much like surviving dwellings from seventeenth-century New England, with its "Hall" and "Parlor" on the ground floor and two "chambers" above. A space designated in the inventory only as "another Roome" held the family's collection of pots, kettles, dripping pans, trays, buckets, and earthenware. . . . The upstairs chambers were not bedrooms but storage rooms for foodstuffs and out-of-season equipment. The best bed with its bolster, pillows, blanket, and coverlet stood in the parlor; a second bed occu-pied one corner of the kitchen, while a cup-board, a "great chest," a table, and a backless bench called a "form" furnished the hall. More food was found in the "cellar" and in the "dairy house," a room which may have stood at the coolest end of the kitchen lean-to.[4]

The Plummer house was devoid of orna-ment, but its contents bespeak such comforts as conscientious yeomanry and good huswifery afforded. On this winter morning the dairy house held four and a half "flitches" or sides of bacon, a quarter of a barrel of salt pork, twenty-eight pounds of cheese, and four pounds of butter. Upstairs in a chamber were more than twenty-five bushels of "English" grain—barley, oats, wheat, and rye. (The Plummers apparently reserved their Indian corn, stored in another location, for their ani-mals.) When made into malt by a village spe-cialist, barley would become the basis for beer. Two bushels of malt were already stored in the house. The oats might appear in a variety of dishes, from plain breakfast porridge to "flum-mery," a gelatinous dish flavored with spices and dried fruit.[5] But the wheat and rye were almost certainly reserved for bread and pies. The fine hair sieves stored with the grain in the hall chamber suggest that Beatrice Plummer was particular about her baking, preferring a finer flour than came directly from the miller. A "bushell of pease & beans" found near the grain and a full barrel of cider in the cellar are the only vegetables and fruits listed in the inventory, though small quantities of pickles, preserves, or dried herbs might have escaped notice. Perhaps the Plummers added variety to their diet by trading some of their abundant supply of grain for cabbages, turnips, sugar, molasses, and spices. . . .

Since wives were involved with early-morning milking, breakfast of necessity featured prepared foods or leftovers—toasted bread, cheese, and perhaps meat and turnips kept from the day before, any of this washed down with cider or beer in winter, with milk in summer. Only on special occasions would there be pie or doughnuts. Dinner was the main meal of the day. Here a housewife with culinary aspirations and an ample larder could display her specialities. After harvest Beatrice Plummer might have served roast pork or goose with apples, in spring an eel pie flavored with parsley and winter savory, and in summer a leek soup or gooseberry cream; but for ordinary days the most common menu was boiled meat with whatever "sauce" the season provided—dried peas or beans, parsnips, turnips, onions, cabbage, or garden greens. A heavy pudding stuffed into a cloth bag could steam atop the vegetables and meat. The broth from this boiled dinner might reappear at supper as "pottage" with the addition of minced herbs and some oatmeal or barley for thickening. Supper, like breakfast, was a simple meal. Bread, cheese, and beer were as welcome at the end of a winter day as at the beginning. . . .

Preparing the simplest of these meals required both judgment and skill. . . . The most basic of the housewife's skills was building and regulating fires—a task so fundamental that it must have appeared more as habit than craft. Summer and winter, day and night, she kept a few brands smoldering, ready to stir into flame as needed. The cavernous fireplaces of early New England were but a century removed from the open fires of medieval houses, and they retained some of the characteristics of the latter. Standing inside one of these huge openings today, a person can see the sky above. Seventeenth-century housewives did stand in their fireplaces, which were conceived less as enclosed spaces for a single blaze than as accessible working surfaces upon which a number of small fires might be built. Preparing several dishes simultaneously, a cook could move from one fire to another, turning a spit, checking the state of the embers under a skillet, adjusting the height of a pot hung from the lug-pole by its adjustable trammel. The complexity of firetending, as much as anything else, encouraged the one-pot meal.[6]

The contents of her inventory suggest that Beatrice Plummer was adept not only at roasting, frying, and boiling but also at baking, the most difficult branch of cookery. Judging from the grain in the upstairs chamber, the bread which she baked was "maslin," a common type made from a mixture of wheat and other grains, usually rye. She began with the sieves stored nearby, carefully sifting out the coarser pieces of grain and bran. Soon after supper she could have mixed the "sponge," a thin dough made from warm water, yeast, and flour. Her yeast might have come from the foamy "barm" found on top of fermenting ale or beer, from a piece of dough saved from an earlier baking, or even from the crevices in an unwashed kneading trough. Like fire-building, bread-making was based upon a self-perpetuating chain, an organic sequence which if once interrupted was difficult to begin again. Warmth from the banked fire would raise the sponge by morning, when Beatrice could work in more flour, knead the finished dough, and shape the loaves, leaving them to rise again.

Even in twentieth-century kitchens with standardized yeast and thermostatically controlled temperatures, bread dough is subject to wide variations in consistency and behavior. In a drafty house with an uncertain supply of yeast, bread-making was indeed "an art, craft, and mystery." Not the least of the problem was regulating the fire so that the oven was ready at the same time as the risen loaves. Small cakes or biscuits could be baked in a skillet or directly on the hearth under an upside-down pot covered with coals. But to produce bread in any quantity required an oven. Before 1650 these were frequently constructed in dooryards, but in the last decades of the century they were built into the rear of the kitchen fireplace, as Beatrice Plummer's must have been. Since her oven would have had no flue, she would have left the door open once she kindled a fire inside, allowing the smoke to escape through the fireplace chimney. Moving about her kitchen, she would have kept an eye on this fire, occasionally raking the coals to distribute the heat evenly, testing periodically with her hand to see if the oven had reached the right temperature. When she determined that it had, she would have scraped out the coals and inserted the bread—assuming that it had risen enough by this time or had not risen too much and collapsed waiting for the oven to heat.[7]

Cooking and baking were year-round tasks. Inserted into these day-by-day routines were seasonal specialities which allowed a housewife to bridge the dearth of one period with the bounty of another. In the preservation calendar, dairying came first, beginning with the first calves of early spring. In colonial New England cows were all-purpose creatures, raised for meat as well as for milk. Even in new settlements they could survive by browsing on rough land; their meat was a hedge against famine. But only in areas with abundant meadow (and even there only in certain months) would they produce milk with sufficient butterfat for serious dairying.[8] Newbury was such a place.

We can imagine Beatrice Plummer some morning in early summer processing the milk which would appear as cheese in a January breakfast. Slowly she heated several gallons with rennet dried and saved from the autumn's slaughtering. Within an hour or two the curd had formed. She broke it, drained off the whey, then worked in a little of her own fresh butter. Packing this rich mixture into a mold, she turned it in her wooden press for an hour or more, changing and washing the cheesecloth frequently as the whey dripped out. Repacking it in dry cloth, she left it in the press for another thirty or forty hours before washing it once more with whey, drying it, and placing it in the cellar or dairy house to age. As a young girl she would have learned from her mother or a mistress the importance of thorough pressing and the virtues of cleanliness. . . .

The Plummer inventory gives little evidence of the second stage of preservation in the housewife's year, the season of gardening and gathering which followed quickly upon the dairy months. But there is ample evidence of the autumn slaughtering. Beatrice could well have killed the smaller pigs herself, hold-

ing their "hinder parts between her legs," as one observer described the process, "and taking the snout in her left hand" while she stuck the animal through the heart with a long knife. Once the bleeding stopped, she would have submerged the pig in boiling water for a few minutes, then rubbed it with rosin, stripped off the hair, and disemboweled it. Nothing was lost. She reserved the organ meats for immediate use, then cleaned the intestines for later service as sausage casing. Stuffed with meat scraps and herbs and smoked, these "links" were a treasured delicacy. The larger cuts could be roasted at once or preserved in several ways.[9] . . .

Fall was also the season for cider-making. The mildly alcoholic beverage produced by natural fermentation of apple juice was a staple of the New England diet and was practically the only method of preserving the fruit harvest. With the addition of sugar, the alcoholic content could be raised from five to about seven percent, as it usually was in taverns and for export. . . .

Prosaic beer was even more important to the Plummer diet. Although some housewives brewed a winter's supply of strong beer in October, storing it in the cellar, Beatrice seems to have been content with "small beer," a mild beverage usually brewed weekly or bi-weekly and used almost at once. Malting—the process of sprouting and drying barley to increase its sugar content—was wisely left to the village expert. Beatrice started with cracked malt or grist, processing her beer in three stages. "Mashing" required slow steeping at just below the boiling point, a sensitive and smelly process which largely determined the success of the beverage. Experienced brewers knew by taste whether the enzymes were working. If it was too hot, acetic acid developed which would sour the finished product. The next stage, "brewing," was relatively simple. Herbs and hops were boiled with the malted liquid. In the final step this liquor was cooled and mixed with yeast saved from last week's beer or bread. Within twenty-four hours—if all had gone well—the beer was bubbling actively.[10]

. . . A wife who knew how to manage the ticklish chemical processes which changed milk into cheese, meal into bread, malt into beer, and flesh into bacon was a valuable asset, though some men were too churlish to admit it. After her husband's death, Beatrice married a man who not only refused to provide her with provisions, but insisted on doing his own cooking. He took his meat "out of ye pickle" and broiled it directly on the coals, and when she offered him "a cup of my owne Sugar & Bear," he refused it. When the neighbors testified that she had been a dutiful wife, the Quarterly Court fined him for "abusive carriages and speeches." Even the unhappy marriage that thrust Beatrice Plummer into court helps to document the central position of huswifery in her life.[11]

Beatrice Plummer represents one type of early American housewife. Hannah Grafton represents another.[12] Chronology, geography, and personal biography created differences between the household inventories of the two women, but there are obvious similarities as well. Like Beatrice Plummer, Hannah Grafton lived in a house with two major rooms on the ground floor and two chambers above. At various locations near the ground-floor rooms were service areas—a washhouse with its own loft or chamber, a shop, a lean-to, and two cellars. The central rooms in the Grafton house were the "parlour," with the expected featherbed, and the "kitchen," which included much of the same collection of utensils and iron pots which appeared in the Plummer house. Standing in the corner of the kitchen were a spade and a hoe, two implements useful only for chipping away ice and snow on the December day on which the inventory was taken, though apparently destined for another purpose come spring. With a garden, a cow, and three pigs, Hannah Grafton clearly had agricultural responsibilities, but these were performed in a strikingly different context than on the Plummer farm. The Grafton homelot was a single acre of land standing just a few feet from shoreline in the urban center of Salem.[13]

Joshua Grafton was a mariner like his father before him. His estate of £236 was modest, but he was still a young man and he had firm connections with the seafaring elite who were transforming the economy of Salem. When he died late in 1699, Hannah had three living children—Hannah, eight; Joshua, six; and Priscilla, who was just ten months.[14] This young family used their space quite differently than had the Plummers. The upstairs chambers which served as storage areas in the New-

bury farmhouse were sleeping quarters here. In addition to the bed in the parlor and the cradle in the kitchen, there were two beds in each of the upstairs rooms. One of these, designated as "smaller," may have been used by young Joshua. It would be interesting to know whether the mother carried the two chamber pots kept in the parlor upstairs to the bedrooms at night or whether the children found their way in the dark to their parents' sides as necessity demanded. But adults were probably never far away. Because there are more bedsteads in the Grafton house than members of the immediate family, they may have shared their living quarters with unmarried relatives or servants.

Ten chairs and two stools furnished the kitchen, while no fewer than fifteen chairs, in two separate sets, crowded the parlor with its curtained bed. The presence of a punch bowl on a square table in the parlor reinforces the notion that sociability was an important value in this Salem household. Thirteen ounces of plate, a pair of gold buttons, and a silver-headed cane suggest a measure of luxury as well—all of this in stark contrast to the Plummers, who had only two chairs and a backless bench and no discernible ornamentation at all. Yet the Grafton house was only slightly more specialized than the Newbury farmhouse. It had no servants' quarters, no sharp segregation of public and private spaces, no real separation of sleeping, eating, and work. A cradle in the kitchen and a go-cart kept with the spinning wheels in the upstairs chamber show that little Priscilla was very much a part of this workaday world.

How then might the pattern of Hannah Grafton's work have differed from that of Beatrice Plummer? Certainly cooking remained central. Hannah's menus probably varied only slightly from those prepared in the Plummer kitchen, and her cooking techniques must have been identical. But one dramatic difference is apparent in the two inventories. The Grafton house contained no provisions worth listing on that December day when Isaac Foot and Samuel Willard appeared to take inventory. Hannah had brewing vessels, but no malt; sieves and a meal trough, but no grain; and a cow, but no cheese. What little milk her cow gave in winter probably went directly into the children's mugs. Perhaps she would continue to breast-feed Priscilla until spring brought a more secure supply.... Trade, rather than manufacturing or agriculture, was the dominant motif in her meal preparations.

In colonial New England most food went directly from processer or producer to consumer. Joshua may have purchased grain or flour from the mill near the shipbuilding center called Knocker's Hole, about a mile away from their house. Or Hannah may have eschewed bread-making altogether, walking or sending a servant the half-mile to Elizabeth Haskett's bakery near the North River. Fresh meat for the spits in her washhouse may have come from John Cromwell's slaughterhouse on Main Street near the Congregational meetinghouse, and soap for her washtubs from the soap-boiler farther up the street near the Quaker meetinghouse.[15] Salem, like other colonial towns, was laid out helter-skelter, with the residences of the wealthy interspersed with the small houses of carpenters or fishermen. Because there was no center of retail trade, assembling the ingredients of a dinner involved many transactions. Sugar, wine, and spice came by sea; fresh lamb, veal, eggs, butter, gooseberries, and parsnips came by land. Merchants retailed their goods in shops or warehouses near their wharves and houses. Farmers or their wives often hawked their produce door to door.[16] ...

In such a setting, trading for food might require as much energy and skill as manufacturing or growing it. One key to success was simply knowing where to go. Keeping abreast of the arrival of ships in the harbor or establishing personal contact with just the right farmwife from nearby Salem village required time and attention. Equally important was the ability to evaluate the variety of unstandardized goods offered. An apparently sound cheese might teem with maggots when cut.[17] Since cash was scarce, a third necessity was the establishment of credit, a problem which ultimately devolved upon husbands. But petty haggling over direct exchanges was also a feature of this barter economy.

Hannah Grafton was involved in trade on more than one level. The "shop" attached to her house was not the all-purpose storage shed and workroom it seems to have been for Francis Plummer. It was a retail store, offering door locks, nails, hammers, gimlets, and other hardware as well as English cloth, pins, needles, and thread. As a mariner, Joshua Grafton may well have sailed the ship which brought these goods to Salem. In his absence, Hannah was not only a mother and a housewife but, like many other Salem women, a shopkeeper as well.

There is another highly visible activity in the Grafton inventory which was not immediately apparent in the Plummer's—care of clothing. Presumably, Beatrice Plummer washed occasionally, but she did not have a "washhouse." Hannah did. The arrangement of this unusual room is far from clear. On December 2, 1699, it contained two spits, two "bouldishes," a gridiron, and "other things." Whether those other things included washtubs, soap, or a beating staff is impossible to determine. ...

But on any morning in December the washhouse could ... have been hung with the family wash. Dark woolen jackets and petticoats went from year to year without seeing a kettle of suds, but linen shifts, aprons, shirts, and handkerchiefs required washing. Laundering might not have been a weekly affair in most colonial households, but it was a well-defined if infrequent necessity even for transient seamen and laborers. One can only speculate on its frequency in a house with a child under a year. When her baby was only a few months old, Hannah may have learned to hold little Priscilla over the chamber pot at frequent intervals, but in early infancy, tightly wrapped in her cradle, the baby could easily have used five dozen "clouts" and almost as many "belly bands" from one washing to another. Even with the use of a "pilch," a thick square of flannel securely bound over the diaper, blankets and coverlets occasionally needed sudsing as well.[18]

Joshua's shirts and Hannah's own aprons and shifts would require careful ironing. Hannah's "smoothing irons" fitted into their own heaters, which she filled with coals from the fire. As the embers waned and the irons cooled, she would have made frequent trips from her table to the hearth to the fire and back to the table again. At least two of these heavy instruments were essential. A dampened apron could dry and wrinkle while a single flatiron replenished its heat.

As frequent a task as washing was sewing. Joshua's coats and breeches went to a tailor, but his shirts were probably made at home. Certainly Hannah stitched and unstitched the tucks which altered Priscilla's simple gowns and petticoats as she grew. The little dresses which the baby trailed in her go-cart had once clothed her brother. Gender identity in childhood was less important in this society than economy of effort. It was not that boys were seen as identical to girls, only that all-purpose garments could be handed from one child to another regardless of sex, and dresses were more easily altered than breeches and more adaptable to diapering and toileting. At eight years of age little Hannah had probably begun to imitate her mother's even stitches, helping with the continual mending, altering, and knitting which kept this growing family clothed.[19]

In some ways the most interesting items in the Grafton inventory are the two spinning wheels kept in the upstairs chamber. Beatrice Plummer's wheel and reel had been key components in an intricate production chain. The Plummers had twenty-five sheep in the fold and a loom in the shed. The Graftons had neither. Children—not sheep—put wheels in Hannah's house. The mechanical nature of spinning made it a perfect occupation for women whose attention was engrossed by young children. This is one reason why the ownership of wheels in both York and Essex counties had a constancy over time unrelated to the ownership of sheep or looms. In the dozen inventories taken in urban Salem about the time of Joshua Grafton's death, the six nonspinners averaged one minor child each, the six spinners had almost four. Instruction at the wheel was part of the almost ritualistic preparation mothers offered their daughters.[20] Spinning was a useful craft, easily picked up, easily put down, and even small quantities of yarn could be knitted into caps, stockings, dishcloths, and mittens.

. . . a cluster of objects in the chamber over Hannah Grafton's kitchen suggests a fanciful but by no means improbable vignette. Imagine her gathered with her two daughters in this upstairs room on a New England winter's day. Little Priscilla navigates around the end of the bedstead in her go-cart while her mother sits at one spinning wheel and her sister at the other. Young Hannah is spinning "oakum," the coarsest and least expensive part of the flax. As her mother leans over to help her wind the uneven thread on the bobbin, she catches a troublesome scent from downstairs. Have the turnips caught on the bottom of the pot? Has the maid scorched Joshua's best shirt? Or has a family servant returned from the wharf and spread his wet clothes by the fire? Hastening down the narrow stairs to the kitchen, Hannah hears the shop bell ring. Just then little Priscilla, left upstairs with her sister, begins to cry. In such pivotal but unrecorded moments much of the history of women lies hidden.

The third inventory can be more quickly described.[21] Elias Wear of York, Maine, left an estate totaling £92, of which less than £7 was in household goods—including some old pewter, a pot, two bedsteads, bedding, one chest, and a box. Wear also owned a saddle, three guns, and a river craft called a gundalow. But his wealth, such as it was, consisted of land (£40) and livestock (£36). It is not just relative poverty which distinguished Elias Wear's inventory from that of Joshua Grafton or Francis Plummer. Every settlement in northern New England had men who owned only a pot, a bed, and a chest. Their children crowded in with them or slept on straw. These men and their sons provided some of the labor which harvested barley for farmers like Francis Plummer or stepped masts for mariners like Joshua Grafton. Their wives and their daughters carded wool or kneaded bread in other women's kitchens. No, Elias Wear was distinguished by a special sort of frontier poverty.

His father had come to northern New England in the 1640s, exploring and trading for furs as far inland in New Hampshire as Lake Winnipesaukee. By 1650 he had settled in York, a then hopeful site for establishing a patrimony. Forty years later he died in the York Massacre, an assault by French and Indians which virtually destroyed the town, bringing death or captivity to fully half of the inhabitants. Almost continuous warfare between 1689 and 1713 created prosperity for the merchant community of Portsmouth and Kittery, but it kept most of the inhabitants of outlying settlements in a state of impecunious insecurity.[22]

In 1696, established on a small homestead in the same neighborhood in which his father had been killed, Elias Wear married a young widow with the fitting name of Magdalen. When their first child was born "too soon," the couple found themselves in York County court owning a presentment for fornication. Although New England courts were still sentencing couples in similar circumstances to "nine stripes a piece upon the Naked back," most of the defendants, like the Wears, managed to pay the not inconsequential fine. The fifty-nine shillings which Elias and Magdalen pledged the court amounted to almost half of the total value of two steers. A presentment for fornication was expensive as well as inconvenient, but it did not carry a permanent onus. Within seven years of their conviction Elias was himself serving on the "Jury of Tryalls" for the county, while Magdalen had proved herself a dutiful and productive wife.[23]

Every other winter she gave birth, producing four sons—Elias, Jeremiah, John, and Joseph—in addition to the untimely Ruth. A sixth child, Mary, was just five months old when her father met his own death by Indians in August of 1707 while traveling between their Cape Neddick home and the more densely settled York village. Without the benefits of a cradle, a go-cart, a spinning wheel, or even a secure supply of grain, Magdalen raised these six children. Unfortunately, there is little in her inventory and nothing in any other record to document the specific strategies which she used, though the general circumstances of her life can be imagined.

Chopping and hauling for a local timber merchant, Elias could have filled Magdalen's porridge pot with grain shipped from the port of Salem or Boston. During the spring corn famine, an almost yearly occurrence on the Maine frontier, she might have gone herself with other wives of her settlement to dig on the clam flats, hedging against the day when relief would come by sea.[24] Like Beatrice Plummer and Hannah Grafton, she would have spent some hours cooking, washing, hoeing cabbages, bargaining with neighbors, and, in season, herding and milking a cow. But poverty, short summers, and rough land also made gathering an essential part of her work. We may imagine her cutting pine splinters for lights and "cattails" and "silkgrass" for beds. Long before her small garden began to produce, she would have searched out a wild "sallet" in the nearby woods, in summer turning to streams and barrens for other delicacies congenial to English taste—eels, salmon, berries, and plums. She would have embarked on such excursions with caution, however, remembering the wives of nearby Exeter who took their children into the woods for strawberries "without any Guard" and narrowly avoided capture.[25] . . .

. . . The Wears probably lived in a single-story cottage which may or may not have been subdivided into more than one room. A loft above provided extra space for storage or sleeping. With the addition of a lean-to, this house could have sheltered animals as well as humans, especially in harsh weather or in periods of Indian alarm. Housing a pig or a calf in the next room would have have simplified Magdalen's chores in the winter. If she managed to raise a few chickens, these too would have thrived better near the kitchen fire.[26]

Thus, penury erased the elaborate demarcation of "houses" and "yards" evident in yeoman inventories. It also blurred distinctions between the work of a husbandman and the work of his wife. At planting time and at harvest Magdalen Wear undoubtedly went into the fields to help Elias, taking her babies with her or leaving Ruth to watch them as best she could.[27] A century later an elderly Maine woman bragged that she "had dropped corn many a day with two governors: a judge in her arms and a general on her back."[28] None of the Wear children grew up to such prominence, but all six of them survived to adulthood and four married and founded families of their own. Six children did not prevent Magdalen Wear from remarrying within two years of her husband's death. Whatever her assets—a pleasant face, a strong back, or lifetime possession of £40 in land—she was soon wed to the unmarried son of a neighboring millowner.[29]

Magdalen Wear, Hannah Grafton, and Beatrice Plummer were all "typical" New England housewives of the period 1650–1750. Magdalen's iron pot represents the housekeeping minimum which often characterized frontier life. Hannah's punch bowl and her hardware shop exemplify both the commerce and the self-conscious civilization of coastal towns. Beatrice's brewing tubs and churn epitomize home manufacturing and agrarian self-sufficiency as they existed in established villages. Each type of housekeeping could be found somewhere in northern New England in any decade of the century. Yet these three women should not be placed in rigidly separate categories. Wealth, geography, occupation, and age determined that some women in any decade would be more heavily involved in one aspect of housekeeping than another, yet all three women shared a common vocation. Each understood the rhythms of the seasons, the technology of fire-building, the persistence of the daily demands of cooking, the complexity of home production, and the dexterity demanded from the often conflicting roles of housekeeper, mother, and wife.

The thing which distinguished these women from their counterparts in modern America was not, as some historians have suggested, that their work was essential to survival. "Survival," after all, is a minimal concept. Individual men and women have never needed each other for mere survival but for far more complex reasons, and women were essential in the seventeenth century for the very same reasons they are essential today—for the perpetuation of the race.... Nor was it the narrowness of their choices which really set them apart. Women in industrial cities have lived monotonous and confining lives, and they may have worked even harder than early American women. The really striking differences are social.

... [T]he lives of early American housewives were distinguished less by the tasks they performed than by forms of social organization which linked economic responsibilities to family responsibilities and which tied each woman's household to the larger world of her village or town.

For centuries the industrious Bathsheba has been pictured sitting at a spinning wheel—"She layeth her hands to the spindle, and her hands hold the distaff." Perhaps it is time to suggest a new icon for women's history. Certainly spinning was an important female craft in northern New England, linked not only to housework but to mothering, but it was one enterprise among many. Spinning wheels are such intriguing and picturesque objects, so resonant with antiquity, that they tend to obscure rather than clarify the nature of female economic life, making home production the essential element in early American huswifery and the era of industrialization the period of crucial change. Challenging the symbolism of the wheel not only undermines the popular stereotype, it questions a prevailing emphasis in women's history.

An alternate symbol might be the pocket. In early America a woman's pocket was not attached to her clothing, but tied around her waist with a string or tape. (When "Lucy Locket lost her pocket, Kitty Fisher found it.") Much better than a spinning wheel, this homely object symbolizes the obscurity, the versatility, and the personal nature of the housekeeping role. A woman sat at a wheel, but she carried her pocket with her from room to room, from house to yard, from yard to street. The items which it contained would shift from day to day and from year to year, but they would of necessity be small, easily lost, yet precious. A pocket could be a mended and patched pouch of plain homespun or a rich personal ornament boldly embroidered in crewel. It reflected the status as well as the skills of its owner. Whether it contained cellar keys or a paper of pins, a packet of seeds or a baby's bib, a hank of yarn, or a Testament, it characterized the social complexity as well as the demanding diversity of women's work.

NOTES

1. [See] William H. Chafe, *Women and Equality: Changing Patterns in American Culture* (New York: Oxford University Press, 1977), p. 17; ... and Nancy F. Cott, *The Bonds of Womanhood* (New Haven and London: Yale University Press, 1977), p. 21.

2. Unless otherwise noted, the information which follows comes from the Francis Plummer will and inventory, *The Probate Records of Essex County* (hereafter *EPR*) (Salem, Mass.: Essex Institute, 1916–1920), II:319–22.

3. Joshua Coffin, *A Sketch of the History of Newbury, Newburyport, and West Newbury* (Boston, 1845; Hampton, N.H.: Peter E. Randall, 1977), p. 315.

4. Abbott Lowell Cummings, *The Framed Houses of Massachusetts Bay*, 1625–1725 (Cambridge, Mass., and London: Harvard University Press, 1979), pp. 29–32.

5. Darrett B. Rutman, *Husbandmen of Plymouth* (Boston: Beacon Press, 1967), pp. 10–11. ... *Records and Files of the Quarterly Courts of Essex County, Massachusetts* (hereafter *ECR*) (Salem, Mass.: Essex Institute, 1911–1975), III:50; ... Massachusetts Historical Society (hereafter MHS) *Collections*, 5th Ser., I:97; and Jay Allen Anderson, "A Solid Sufficiency: An Ethnography of Yeoman Foodways in Stuart England" (Ph.D. diss., University of Pennsylvania, 1971), pp. 171, 203–04, 265, 267, 268.

6. Cummings, *Framed Houses*, pp. 4, 120–22; ... Jane Carson, *Colonial Virginia Cookery* (Charlottesville: University Press of Virginia, 1968), p. 104; ...

7. Carson, *Colonial Virginia Cookery*, pp. 104–06.

8. Anderson, "Solid Sufficiency," pp. 63, 65, 118; ... New Hampshire Historical Society *Collections*, V (1837), p. 225.

9. Anderson, "Solid Sufficiency," pp. 99–108, 120–32.

10. Sanborn C. Brown, *Wines and Beers of Old New England* (Hanover, N.H.: University Press of New England, 1978). ...

11. ECR, IV:194–95, 297–98.

12. Unless otherwise noted, the information which follows comes from the Joshua Grafton will and inventory, Manuscript Probate Records, Essex County Probate Court, Salem, Mass. (hereafter Essex Probate), vol. CCCVII, pp. 58–59.

13. "Part of Salem in 1700," pocket map in James Duncan Phillips, *Salem in the Seventeenth Century* (Boston: Houghton Mifflin, 1933), H-6.

14. Sidney Perley, *The History of Salem, Massachusetts* (Salem, 1924), I:435, 441.

15. Phillips, *Salem in the Seventeenth Century*, pp. 328, 314, 318, 317; and James Duncan Phillips, *Salem in the Eighteenth Century* (Boston: Houghton Mifflin, 1937), pp. 20–21.

16. [See] Karen Friedman, "Victualling Colonial Boston," *Agricultural History* XLVII (July 1973): 189–205, and . . . Benjamin Coleman, *Some Reasons and Arguments Offered to the Good People of Boston and Adjacent Places, for the Setting Up Markets in Boston* (Boston, 1719), pp. 5–9.

17. . . . *The Salem Witchcraft Papers*, ed. Paul Boyer and Stephen Nissenbaum (New York: Da Capo Press, 1977), I:117–29.

18. [See] . . . e.g., *Province and Court Records of Maine* (hereafter *MPCR*) (Portland: Maine Historical Society, 1928–1975), IV:205–06; . . . and Essex Probate, CCCXXI:96. . . .

19. Susan Burrows Swan, *Plain and Fancy: American Women and Their Needlework, 1700–1850* (New York: Holt, Rinehart and Winston, 1977), pp. 18–19, 34–38.

20. "Letter-Book of Samuel Sewall," MHS *Collections*, 6th Ser., I:19. . . .

21. Unless otherwise noted, the information which follows comes from the Elias Wear will and inventory, Manuscript Probate Records, York County Probate Court, Alfred, Me., . . . II:26.

22. Charles Clark, *The Eastern Frontier* (New York: Alfred A. Knopf, 1970), pp. 67–72.

23. *MPCR*, IV:91–92, 175, 176, 206, 263, 307, 310.

24. Maine Historical Society *Collections*, IX:58–59, 457, 566; MHS *Collections*, 6th Ser., I:126–65, 182–84, 186–89; . . .

25. Cotton Mather, *Decennium Luctuosum* (Boston, 1699), reprint Charles H. Lincoln, ed., *Narratives of the Indian Wars* (New York: Charles Scribner's Sons, 1913), pp. 266–67.

26. Richard M. Candee, "Wooden Buildings in Early Maine and New Hampshire: A Technological and Cultural History, 1600–1720" (Ph.D. diss., University of Pennsylvania, 1976), pp. 18, 42–48. . . .

27. . . . MHS *Proceedings* (1876), p. 129. Also see *ECR*, II:372–73, 22, 442; . . .

28. Sarah Orne Jewett, *The Old Town of Berwick* (Berwick, Me.: Old Berwick Historical Society, 1967), n.p., . . .

29. Sybil Noyes, Charles Thornton Libby, and Walter Goodwin Davis, *A Genealogical Dictionary of Maine and New Hampshire* (Portland, Me.: Southworth-Anthoensen Press, 1928), pp. 726, 729.

DOCUMENTS: The Law of Domestic Relations: Marriage, Divorce, Dower

Examples from Colonial Connecticut

Each American colony developed its own code of laws. There were major variations from colony to colony, but the thirteen Atlantic seaboard colonies that would eventually rebel against England were governed by English law and the modifications their legislatures made in it. Marriage is the result of private choice, but it is also a public act and has important legal implications for women. In seventeenth- and eighteenth-century English law and practice, the great legal theorist William Blackstone wrote, "husband and wife are one person in law, that is, the very being or legal existence of the woman is suspended during the marriage, or at least is incorporated and consolidated into that of the husband; under whose wing, protection, and *cover*, she performs every thing; and is therefore called . . . a *feme covert*." This doctrine of "unity of person" underlay a complex system of law of domestic relations; when an English woman married, her husband became the owner of all the movable things she possessed and of all the property or wages she might earn during their marriage. He also received the right to manage and collect the rents and profits on any real estate she owned; if they had a child, the child could not inherit the dead mother's lands until after the death of the father.

French law and Spanish law both derived from Roman law, a considerably different legal tradition than the Anglo-Saxon tradition from which the English common law had developed. Roman law recognized the husband and wife to be separate persons, who could each continue to own separately the property they brought to the marriage, who were co-owners of the property they acquired during their marriage, and who passed the property down evenly to their heirs. The husband, however, was "the head and master" of the household, with broad powers over wife and children and over the use of the property during the duration of the marriage. In practice, women living under community property rules were only slightly better situated than those who lived under English legal systems. The concept of "community property" was unknown in the English colonies and the states that succeeded them, but when as a result of the Louisiana Purchase in 1803 the United States absorbed thousands of people who were already engaged in complex property and commercial relationships, it seemed wisest to maintain established property law. Community property continued to be the norm not only in Louisiana but in other states that developed from French or Spanish settlement—California, New Mexico, Arizona, Texas.

All colonies placed in their statutes a law regulating marriage. This step reflected a concern that marriage be celebrated publicly in order to guard against bigamy. Connecticut did not forbid interracial marriage, but many other colonies did. Laws also defined incest; note the large number of relatives prohibited from marrying in the statute

The Public Statute Laws of the State of Connecticut (Hartford, 1808) I:236, 239–40, 477–81.

from colonial Connecticut that follows. In the course of the next century the list of pro-hibited relatives was gradually reduced. Note that the Connecticut marriage law included a provision against cross-dressing.

AN ACT FOR REGULATING AND ORDERLY CELEBRATING OF MARRIAGES. . . . 1640, WITH REVISIONS 1672, 1702

Forasmuch as the ordinance of marriage is honourable amongst all; so it is meet it should be orderly and decently solemnized:

Be it therefore enacted . . . That no persons shall be joined in marriage, before the purpose or intention of the parties proceeding therein, hath been sufficiently published in some pub-lic meeting or congregation on the Lord's day, or on some public fast, thanksgiving, or lec-ture-day, in the town, parish, or society where the parties, or either of them do ordinarily reside; or such purpose or intention be set up in fair writing, upon some post or door of their meeting-house, or near the same, in public view, there to stand so as it may be read, eight days before such marriage.

. . . And in order to prevent incestuous and unlawful marriages, be it further enacted, That no man shall marry . . . his grand-father's wife, wife's grandmother, father's sister, mother's sister, father's brother's wife, mother's brother's wife, wife's father's sister, wife's mother's sister, father's wife, wife's mother, daughter, wife's daughter, son's wife, sister, brother's wife, son's daughter, daughter's daughter, son's son's wife, daughter's son's wife, wife's son's daughter, wife's daughter's daughter, brother's daughter, sister's daugh-ter, brother's son's wife, sister's son's wife.

And if any man shall hereafter marry, or have carnal copulation with any woman who is within the degrees before recited in this act, every such marriage shall be . . . null and void; And all children that shall hereafter be born of such incestuous marriage or copulation, shall be forever disabled to inherit by descent, or by being generally named in any deed or will, by father or mother. . . .

And that if any man shall wear women's apparel, or if any woman shall wear men's apparel, and be thereof duly convicted; such offenders shall be corporally punished or fined at the discretion of the county court, not exceeding *seventeen* dollars . . .

Early America was a divorceless society. South Carolina boasted that it granted no divorce until 1868. Most colonies followed the British practice of treating marriage as a moral obli-gation for life. Occasional special dissolutions of a marriage were granted by legislatures in response to individual petitions or by courts of equity, but these were separations from bed and board, which normally did not carry with them freedom to marry again.

The Puritan settlers of Massachusetts and Connecticut were unusual in treating mar-riage as a civil contract, which might be broken if its terms were not carried out. Con-necticut enacted the earliest divorce law in the colonies. It made divorce available after a simple petition to the superior court under certain circumstances. People who did not fit these circumstances were able to present special petitions to the legislature. Normally a divorce in Connecticut implied that the innocent party had the right to marry again.

Most petitioners for divorce in early America were women. On what grounds might Connecticut women petition for divorce?

AN ACT RELATING TO BILLS OF DIVORCE, 1667

Be it enacted . . . that no bill of divorce shall be granted to any man or woman, lawfully mar-ried, but in case of adultery, or fraudulent con-tract, or wilful desertion for three years with total neglect of duty; or in case of seven years absence of one party not heard of: after due enquiry is made, and the matter certified to the superior court, in which case the other party may be deemed and accounted single and unmarried. And in that case, and in all other cases afore-mentioned, a bill of divorce may be granted by the superior court to the aggrieved party; who may then lawfully marry or be married again.

Perhaps no statutes were more important to women in the first 250 years after settlement of the English colonies than the laws protecting their claims to dower. The "widow's dower" should be distinguished from the dowry a bride might bring with her into marriage. "The widow's dower" or the "widow's third" was the right of a widow to use one-third of the real estate that her husband held at the time of his death. She was also entitled to one-third of the personal property he had owned, after the debts were paid. It was an old English tradition that he might leave her more in his will, but he could not leave her less. If a man died without a will, the courts would ensure that his widow received her "thirds."

It is important to note that she only had the right to use the land and buildings. She might live on this property, rent it out, farm the land, and sell the produce. But she could not sell or bequeath it. If the real estate was simply the family home and her children were adults, she had a claim only to a *portion* of the house. (Occasionally husbands wrote that they intended the widow to have the "best" bedroom, a sign that they could not always trust their own sons to care well for their mothers.) After the widow's death the property reverted to her husband's heirs, who normally would be their children, but in the event of a childless marriage was likely to revert to his brothers or nephews.

In Lousiana law, community property was acquired during the marriage; the wife had her own separate claim to the property she brought to the marriage. "Dotal" property, or dowry, was intended to help with the expenses of the marriage; the husband could manage this property and spend its income, but at the end of the marriage it was restored to the wife or her heirs, thus keeping it in her own family line of succession. She also kept her own "paraphernalia"—personal clothing and other items—which she could trade as a merchant without her husband's consent or dispose of in her own will.

In the Connecticut statute, printed below, note the provisions protecting the widow's interests. Normally colonial courts were scrupulous about assigning the widow's portion. Observe, however, that widows could not claim dower in "movable" property, which might represent a larger share of their husband's wealth than real estate. As time passed and the American economy became more complex, it became increasingly likely that a man's property would not be held in the form of land. If the land were heavily mortgaged, the widow's prior right to her "third" became a barrier to creditors seeking to collect their portion of a husband's debts. By the early nineteenth century courts were losing their enthusiasm for protecting widows' thirds.

By the middle of the century the married women's property acts began to reformulate a definition of the terms by which married women could claim their share of the property of wife and husband. But between 1790 and 1840, when the right to dower was more and more laxly enforced and the new married women's property acts had not yet been devised, married women were in a particularly vulnerable position. See Keziah Kendall, pp. 198–200.

AN ACT CONCERNING THE DOWRY OF WIDOWS, 1672

That there may be suitable provision made for the maintenance and comfortable support of widows, after the decease of their husbands, Be it enacted . . . that every married woman, living with her husband in this state, or absent elsewhere from him with his consent, or through his mere default, or by inevitable providence; or in case of divorce where she is the innocent party, that shall not before marriage be estated by way of jointure in some houses, lands, tenements or hereditaments for term of life . . . shall immediately upon, and after the death of her husband, have right, title and interest by way of dower, in and unto one third part of the real estate of her said deceased husband, in houses and lands which he stood possessed of in his own right, at the time of his decease, to be to her during her natural life: the remainder of the estate shall be disposed of according to the will of the deceased. . . .

And for the more easy, and speedy ascertaining such rights of dower, It is further enacted, That upon the death of any man possessed of any real estate . . . which his widow . . . hath a right of dower in, if the person, or persons that by law have a right to inherit said estate, do not within sixty days next after the death of such husband, by three sufficient freeholders of the same county; to be appointed by the judge of probate . . . and sworn for that purpose, set out, and ascertain such right of dower, that then such widow may make her complaint to the judge of probate . . . which judge shall decree, and order that such woman's dowry shall be set out, and ascertained by three sufficient freeholders of the county . . . and upon approbation thereof by said judge, such dower shall remain fixed and certain. . . .

And every widow so endowed . . . shall maintain all such houses, buildings, fences, and inclosures as shall be assigned, and set out to her for her dowry; and shall leave the same in good and sufficient repair.

CAROL BERKIN
African American Women in Colonial Society

There was much in the slave experience that women and men shared. Denied any legal ability to control the conditions of their lives, both men and women labored according to their masters' demands. Both women and men were vulnerable to brutal punishment and to the separation of families; neither men nor women had any choice but to accept marginal food and clothing. Enslaved men and women were part of the productive system of the colonial economy; they were found on tobacco plantations, in rice fields, in urban households in Charleston and Savannah, and, though in fewer numbers, throughout farms and towns in the North.

But women also did reproductive work. By this we mean not only the actual bearing and nurturing of children but also the domestic work within slave quarters that fed husbands, fathers, and children and gave them the strength to persevere at the productive work of the masters' economy. As childbearing women, they were physically vulnerable in ways that men were not; indeed, slaves suffered a heavy proportion of deaths due to Sudden Infant Death Syndrome because of the malnutrition and over-work of mothers.* The law did not protect enslaved women against rape or seduction. Because the children of enslaved women followed "the condition of the mother," the legal system actually offered advantages to men of the master class who seduced or raped them. In the lives of slave women, economics and biology intersected in complex, forceful, and sorrowful ways.

Still, as Carol Berkin shows, enslaved women built strong bonds of family and com-munity. Note the wide range of work that slave women did. Compare and contrast the work they did on plantations and in cities, North as well as South. Consider the per-vasiveness of slavery throughout the colonies.

Mary came to Virginia aboard the *Margrett and John* in the spring of 1622, soon after the Powhatan Indians launched an attack on the English tidewater settlers. She entered a com-munity still reeling from the violent death of 350 colonists killed in a single morning. That the slaughter took place on Good Friday added to the horror these colonial survivors felt, but the day carried no special meaning for Mary. She was, after all, neither English nor Christian. She was one of a handful of Africans brought against her will to this struggling Chesapeake colony.

We can say very little about Mary; her age when she arrived in Virginia, her physical appearance, her temperament, her abilities are all unknown. Yet her experiences before arriv-ing in Virginia could not have differed greatly from those of other Africans wrenched from their homeland and carried to America. The accounts we have of the brutality of the slave traders, from both black and white witnesses, of the painful forced march to the Atlantic coast of Africa in which women and men were chained together, of the humiliation of brand-ing, and of the horrors of the "middle passage" allow us to envision her distress even if we lack her personal testimony on such matters. The knowledge we have of her adjustment to America—mastering a foreign tongue, adapt-ing to a new climate, to strange clothing and food, a new physical environment, and a cul-ture whose customs and values were alien—make the loneliness and isolation of her situa-

tion certain even if it is undocumented. Her circumstances, then, are more vivid than her personality.

Mary was taken to Richard Bennett's large tobacco plantation on the south side of the James River. Here she witnessed the full con-sequences of hostile relations between the English and the Indians, for only five of the fifty-seven servants who worked Bennett's Warresquioake plantation had survived the Good Friday assault. Although her English master needed every able-bodied worker he could muster, Bennett may not have set Mary to work in the tobacco fields. His culture iden-tified agriculture with masculinity, and in these earliest decades of Chesapeake society, some masters may have been unwilling to overturn the gendered division of labor they held to be natural. Mary surely demurred from such notions, for in most West African soci-eties women dominated agriculture. These very different traditions produced a surpris-ing harmony in the matter of slave importa-tion. Faced with demands for captives, African villages preferred to surrender up their males and protect their female agriculturists; faced with a need for fieldworkers, Europeans pre-ferred to purchase men.

What we do know of Mary's life in the colonies is that she had good fortune. Despite the scarcity of Africans of either sex in the Chesapeake, one of Warresquioake's five lucky survivors of the Good Friday attack was a black man named Antonio. Mary took him

*Michael P. Johnson, "Smothered Slave Infants: Were Slave Mothers at Fault?" *Journal of Southern History* 47 (1981): 495–509.

as her husband, in fact if not in English law. In a society where early deaths routinely interrupted marriages, Mary and Antonio enjoyed a forty-year relationship. Together they made the transition from bound service to freedom, although how and when is unclear, and together they raised four children, whom they baptized in the Christian faith.

Like most freed servants, Mary and her husband—known in their freedom as Mary and Anthony Johnson—migrated from Bennett's plantation, seeking arable land of their own. The Johnsons settled on the Pungoteague River, in a small farming community that included black and white families. By mid-century, they had accumulated an estate of over 250 acres on which they raised cattle and pigs. In 1653, their good luck was threatened by a fire which ravaged their plantation and brought the Johnson family close to ruin. Mary's neighbors responded with sympathy, and local authorities helped by granting the Johnsons' petition that Mary and her two daughters be exempt from local taxes for their lifetimes.

This considerate act by the courts is the first concrete evidence that race set Mary and her family apart from their English neighbors. In seventeenth-century Virginia, taxes were assessed on people rather than on possessions, and Virginia's taxable citizens were those "that worke in the grounde." Such a definition was intended to exempt the wives and daughters of Virginia planters, whose proper occupation was domestic. By the time of the Johnsons' devastating fire, however, the earlier unity of gender had been severed by race and "Negro women" were denied this exemption. And yet the racial distinction was not so rigid, the practice was not so uniform that Mary's neighbors could not embrace her as a proper woman if they chose. . . .

In the 1660s, the Johnsons, like other eastern shore colonists, pulled up stakes and moved to Maryland in search of fresh land. The Johnsons may have arranged to have someone else finance their move, for they were claimed as the headrights of two wealthy planters. They were not, however, claimed as servants. Instead, Anthony was a tenant, leasing a 300-acre farm in Somerset County, Maryland, which he named Tonies Vineyard. Anthony and Mary's now grown sons and daughters soon joined them in Maryland,

establishing farms nearby. Thus when Anthony died shortly after the move, Mary Johnson was surrounded by her family.

In 1672, when Mary sat down to write her will, a new generation of Johnsons was making its mark in this farming community. But a new generation of English colonists was making their task harder. Bad signs were everywhere: in a new colonial policy that forbade free blacks to employ white indentured servants, and in the Virginia and Maryland laws that lengthened terms for servants without indenture, a category to which almost every new African immigrant belonged. Mary's grandchildren, to whom she lovingly willed her cows and their calves, would grow to adulthood in a strikingly biracial society, for the number of African immigrants was rapidly growing. But few of these Africans would enter the world of free men and women as Mary and Anthony had done. The society that had once found room for "Mary a Negro," to become the matriarch of a comfortable family, could spare no such space for Mary's descendants. If it was accidental, it is apt that when Mary's grandson John died in 1706, the Johnson family disappeared from the historical record. . . .

In 1623 Mary Johnson was one of only twenty-three Africans in Virginia. By 1650, she was one of perhaps three hundred. . . . In the decade of Mary Johnson's death, the African population in the Chesapeake began to rise sharply, reaching 3,000 in Virginia by 1680 and continuing to grow until, by 1700, the colony had almost 6,000 black settlers. African population growth in Maryland was no less dramatic: in 1658 there were only 100 blacks in four Maryland counties, but by 1710 the number had risen to over 3,500, or almost one-quarter of the local population. Nearly 8,000 of Maryland's 43,000 colonists that year were black. Yet the mass involuntary migration of Africans had only begun. Between 1700 and 1740, 54,000 blacks reached the Chesapeake, the overwhelming majority imported directly to these colonies from Biafra and Angola rather than coming by way of the West Indies. Immigrants from the west, or "windward," coast of Africa poured into South Carolina as well. By the time of the American Revolution, over 100,000 Africans had been brought to the mainland colonies. For the overwhelming majority, their destination was the plantation fields of the upper and lower South.

The relentless demand for cheap agricultural labor spurred this great forced migration. As the English economy improved in the 1680s and 1690s, the steady supply of desperate young men and women willing to enter indentured servitude in the colonies dwindled. . . . Planters were forced to abide by customs that prevented labor after sunset, allotted five hours' rest in the heat of the day during the summer months, and forbade work on Saturday, Sunday, and many religious holidays. On the other hand, local courts would not acknowledge or uphold any claims to such "customary rights" by African servants . . .

Slavery—as a permanent and inheritable condition—developed unevenly across the colonies and within individual colonies. In the Chesapeake, the laws that sharply distinguished black bound labor from white were accompanied by laws that limited the economic and social opportunity of free blacks. Together, these laws established race as a primary social boundary. The process began before the greatest influx of Africans to the region. The 1672 law forbidding free black planters to purchase the labor of white servants squeezed those planters out of the competitive tobacco market. This disarming of African Americans in the economic sphere was echoed in Chesapeake laws that forbade blacks to carry or possess firearms or other weapons. In 1691, Chesapeake colonial assemblies passed a series of laws regulating basic social interaction and preventing the transition from servitude, or slavery, to freedom. Marriage between a white woman and a free black man was declared a criminal offense, and the illegitimate offspring of interracial unions were forced into bound service until they were thirty years old. A master could still choose to manumit a slave, but after 1691 he was required to bear the cost of removing the freed woman or man from the colony. Such laws discouraged intimacy across racial lines and etched into social consciousness the notion that African origins were synonymous with the enslaved condition. By 1705, political and legal discrimination further degraded African immigrants and their descendants, excluding them from officeholding, making it a criminal offense to strike a white colonist under any circumstances, and denying them the right to testify in courts of law. While Mary Johnson had never enjoyed the rights of citizenship available to her husband, Anthony, eighteenth-century African-American men of the Chesapeake lost their legal and political identity as well. Thus, the history of most African Americans in the Chesapeake region, as in the lower South, is the history of women and men defined by slavery, even in their freedom.

Much of a newly arrived slave woman's energy was devoted to learning the language of her masters, acquiring the skills of an agriculture foreign to her, and adjusting to the climate and environment of the Chesapeake. Weakened by the transatlantic voyage, often sick, disoriented, and coping with the impact of capture and enslavement to an alien culture, many women as well as men died before they could adjust to America. Until well into the eighteenth century, a woman who survived this adjustment faced the possibility of a lifetime as the solitary African on a farm, or as the solitary woman among the planter's African slaves. . . .

Under such circumstances, African women found it difficult to re-create the family and kinship relations that played as central a part in African identity as they did in Native American identity. In fact, the skewed sex ratio—roughly two to one into the early eighteenth century—and the wide scattering of the slave population, as much as the heterogeneity of African cultures and languages, often prevented any satisfactory form of stable family. Until the 1740s, those women and men who did become parents rarely belonged to the same master and could not rear their children together. The burden of these problems led many African-born women to delay childbearing until several years after their arrival in America. Most bore only three children, and of these, only two were likely to survive. With twice as many male slaves as female, delayed childbearing, and high mortality among both adults and infants, there was no natural increase among the Chesapeake slaves in the late seventeenth or early eighteenth century.

There was little any Chesapeake slave woman could do to rectify the circumstances of her personal life. While women of any race or class in colonial society lacked broad control over their person or their actions, the restraints of slavery were especially powerful. A woman deprived of physical mobility and unable to allocate the use of her time could take few effective steps to establish her own social world.

Although Mary Johnson may never have worked the fields at Warresquioake plantation, the slave women who came to the Chesapeake after 1650 were regularly assigned to field labor. Organized into mixed-sex work gangs of anywhere from two to a rare dozen laborers, slave women and men worked six days a week and often into the night. Daylight work included planting, tending, and harvesting tobacco and corn by hand, without the use of draft animals. In the evening, male and female slaves stripped the harvested tobacco leaves from stems or shucked and shelled corn. The crops were foreign to most African-born slave women, but the collective organization of workers was not. Indeed, slaves resisted any effort to deny them this familiar, cooperative form of labor.

By the middle of the eighteenth century, slave women on the largest Chesapeake plantations would wake to a day of labor that segregated them from men. As the great planters shifted from cultivation by the hoe to the plow, and as they branched out into wheat and rye production, lumbering, milling, and fishing, they reinstituted a gendered division of labor. Male slaves were assigned to the new skilled and semi-skilled tasks. While men plowed and mastered crafts, women remained in the fields, left to hoe by hand what the plows could not reach, to weed and worm the tobacco, and to carry the harvested grain to the barns on their heads or backs. When new tasks were added to women's work repertoire, they proved to be the least desirable: building fences, grubbing swamps in the winter, cleaning seed out of winnowed grain, breaking new ground too rough for the plow, cleaning stables, and spreading manure.

If many male slaves were drawn out of the fields and into the workshops or iron mills, few black women in their prime were assigned to domestic duty in the planter's house or taught housewifery skills. Instead, throughout the eighteenth century, young girls not yet strong enough for field labor and elderly women past their productive years in the hoeing gang were assigned to cleaning, child care, and other domestic tasks in the planter's home. Thus, much of the work done by Chesapeake slave women in 1750 differed little from the work done by slave women a half century earlier.

Slave women's work may have remained constant, but other aspects of their lives did not. By 1750, some of these women had the opportunity to create stable families and to participate in a cohesive slave community. These opportunities were linked to changes in the size of plantations and in the composition of their labor forces. Throughout the eighteenth century, great plantations developed, and the number of slaves on these plantations grew, too, ending the isolation the earliest generations had experienced. Many of these slaves were native-born rather than "saltwater," and their energies were not drained by the efforts of adjustment and acculturation. As English-speakers, they shared a common language, and in Christianity, many shared a common religion as well. Both were factors in helping creole slaves begin to create a distinctive community. The gradual equalization of the sex ratio among creoles also helped, and, so did the lower mortality rate. Finally, the evolution of this slave community and slave culture in the Chesapeake was aided by a growing opportunity for slaves to live away from the intrusive eyes of their white masters. The retreat from contact was mutual: many white colonists sought relief from the alien impact of Africanisms by creating separate slave quarters. In these slave quarters blacks acquired a social as well as a physical space in which to organize everyday domestic activities, establish rituals, and develop shared values and norms. Most important, they were able to establish families through which to sustain and uphold this shared culture. . . .

Black women delivered their children in the company of other women, just as English colonists continued to do throughout most of the eighteenth century, and midwives saw the mother through these births. The differences are perhaps more telling than the similarities, however. African nursing customs, retained by many slave women, produced wider intervals between children than English weaning patterns. Slave women bore an average of nine children, giving birth every twenty-seven to twenty-nine months. The power of masters to separate wives and husbands—through hiring-out practices or sales—led to wide gaps in many slave women's childbearing histories. Conception and birth cycles in King William Parish, Virginia, reveal other ways in which race interposed upon gender. Two-thirds of the black births in King William Parish occurred between February and July, while

Although white masters seem to have hesitated to require field work of indentured white women servants, they felt no hesitancy in requiring enslaved women to work in the fields at heavy labor. In this rare eyewitness testimony, Benjamin Henry Latrobe's watercolor documents the practice in late-eighteenth-century Virginia. He gave it the ironic title "An Overseer doing his duty." Watercolor, ink, and ink wash on paper, 1798. Papers of Benjamin Henry Latrobe. (Courtesy of the Maryland Historical Society, Baltimore, Maryland)

white women bore their children in the fall and early winter months. For black women, this meant that the most disabling months of pregnancy often fell in the midst of heavy spring planting chores. Perhaps this accounts for the greater risk of childbirth for slave mothers and the higher infant mortality rate among slave children. . . .

Thus, after 1750, a Chesapeake slave woman might be able to live out her life in the company of her family, as Mary Johnson had done. Yet she knew that powerful obstacles stood in her way. Husbands often lived on other plantations. Children between the ages of ten and fourteen, especially sons, were commonly sold. Sisters and brothers were moved to different slave quarters. And on a master's death, slaves were often dispensed along with other property to his heirs. A master who

might never separate a family during his lifetime thought it his obligation to his survivors to divide them at his death. Hard times could prompt a master to sell a slave woman's family members in order to provide for his own. A planter's widow might keep her family intact by hiring out her slave's sons or daughters. Even the wedding celebration of a planter's daughter might mean the tragic separation of a slave woman and her own young daughter, sent to serve in the bride's new home. In the 1770s, the westward expansion of agriculture into the Piedmont and beyond led to mass dispersal of slave families among the new farms and plantations. Slave women, and their men, could succeed in creating effective family structures despite the many demands of slavery, but they could not ensure their permanence. . . .

The planters of the Lower South also relied on an African slave-labor force. Indeed, the slave-based agriculture of this region developed with remarkable speed in the early eighteenth century. . . . Despite clear laws against slaveholding, the Georgia settlers were, as one observer put it, "stark Mad after Negroes." Illegal sale of slaves took place right under the nose of colonial authorities, eventually forcing the ban to be lifted. Between 1751 and 1770, the slave population of Georgia rose from 349 to 16,000; these slaves were imported directly from Africa or purchased from traders in South Carolina.

In the region's showplace city, Charleston, a largely creole population of African Americans swelled to over half the population, filling positions as house servants, boatmen, dockworkers, and artisans of all kinds. The highly acculturated Charleston slave women shared little in common with their rural sisters, for the slaves who worked the large rice plantations had almost no contact with white society. The plantation slave society that developed was the product of an isolation more pronounced than in the Chesapeake. And because of the steady importation of Africans throughout the eighteenth century, this community differed significantly from the creole-dominated world of the Chesapeake slaves. West African traditions shaped the rice and indigo culture in fundamental ways. Plantation slaves spoke Gullah, a language which combined English and several West African dialects, and they preserved the African custom of naming children for the day of the week on which they were born. Chesapeake girls and boys came to recognize themselves in the diminutives of English names—Lizzie, Betty, or Billy—but among slave children in the Lower South names like Quaco, Juba, and Cuba linked them to their African past.

Like Chesapeake slave women, Lower South women worked the fields. But as rice growers, the women of Carolina and Georgia labored under a task system rather than in gangs. This system assigned specific tasks to each slave but did not regulate the time in which it was to be completed. Thus, slaves on the rice plantations controlled the pace of their workday. The task system did provide a measure of autonomy, but no slave who worked the rice plantations would call their occupation an enviable one. "The labor required for the cultivation [of rice] is fit only for slaves," wrote one frank observer, "and I think the hardest work I have seen them engaged in." The most grueling of all the tasks was the pounding of grain with mortar and pestle—and this was a woman's job. It was also the deadliest; mortality rates were higher in the Lower South than in the Chesapeake, and the women who beat the rice were more likely to die than the men who spent hours stooping in the stagnant rice-paddy waters.

By the middle-of the eighteenth century, each slave was responsible for a quarter of an acre. Other activities on the plantation—pounding the rice, making fences, and later, in tidal rice cultivation, digging critical irrigation systems—were tasked as well. . . . The task system was not designed-to-accommodate the women and men who worked in the rice fields or paddies, of course. Its logic lay in the fact that effective rice cultivation did not require the constant supervision of workers. Yet the task system allowed slaves to develop a lively domestic or internal economy. South Carolina and Georgia slaves were given land on which to grow a variety of crops, including corn, potatoes, tobacco, peanuts, melons, and pumpkins, all of which they marketed. This agriculture within an agriculture quickly became entrenched, despite efforts by lawmakers to curtail it. By 1751 Lower South authorities were fighting a staying action, insisting that slaves could sell their rice, corn, or garden crops only to their own masters. These restrictions were ignored. Slave women and men continued to sell everything from corn to catfish, baskets, canoes, and poultry products. But here, unlike in the Piedmont, slave agriculture reflected the community's active African tradition, for Low Country slaves grew tania, bene, peppers, and other African crops. When local slave crops reached Charleston, slave women took charge of their marketing. These female traders were known for their shrewdness in bargaining with customers of both races, to whom they hawked poultry, eggs, and fruit at sometimes shocking prices. Slave women willingly paid their masters a fee for the privilege of selling the pies, cakes, handicrafts, or dry goods they made or brokered, for any profits after the fee was met belonged to them. These women drew on a West African tradition of female traders not unlike the female market-town traders of England. . . .

Slavery in the North was an accepted tradition but not a widespread habit. The Dutch had employed slave labor extensively when New York was New Netherlands, using African labor to compensate for the scarcity of colonists from Holland. The small farmers of New England, on the other hand, had little practical use for slave labor, and where slaves were employed it was often because of their master's close tie to the transatlantic slave trade. For example, the merchant-landowners of Rhode Island who made their riches in trade liked to flaunt their prosperity by retaining anywhere from five to forty slaves. One merchant magnate boasted a holding of 238 slaves. But the majority of New England slaves, like the slaves of the middle colonies, were found in the cities, where shortages of white labor in artisan shops, on the docks, and in household or personal service were a periodic problem. The greatest influx of African slaves to Pennsylvania, for example, came during the Seven Years War, when the flow of English and other European servants was seriously disrupted. By mid-century, roughly 10 percent of the population of Boston, Philadelphia, and New York was black, although only one out of every five families owned a slave.

A slave woman in these Northern cities spent her days engaged in housework—cooking, cleaning, washing and ironing, tending the fires and the gardens, and looking after her master's children. She passed her nights sleeping in the garret or the kitchen. She might be hired out to nurse the sick, to put in a neighbor's garden, to preserve food or wait on tables for a special occasion, but few urban slave women were ever hired out to learn a craft. Colonial artisans considered their shops a male domain. Ironically, the "black mammy" so often associated with plantation life was not an authentic figure of the colonial South, but she could be found in the fashionable homes of Philadelphia and New York. Slaves in the countryside also did housework, but more of their time was spent tending larger gardens, raising poultry, milking cows, and spinning cloth than in cooking, cleaning, or serving as personal maids to farm family members. At harvest time, these women were assigned to fieldwork.

As they worked in the wheat fields of southern Pennsylvania or in the kitchens of Boston, Northern slave women experienced constant, intimate contact with white society. Whether their owners were kind or callous, their values and customs were ever present, and a solitary black servant, working, eating, sleeping in a crowded Pennsylvania farmhouse, or in the close quarters of a merchant's home, lacked the steady reinforcement of her African heritage. Not surprisingly, Northern slave women were more likely to acculturate than their sisters in the plantation South.

Urban slave women had little hope of creating a family that could remain intact. Slaveholdings were too small for a woman to choose a husband from the household, and few urban colonists were willing to shoulder the costs of raising a slave child in their midst. Rural slaveholders could set a slave's child to work in the garden or field, but in the cities youngsters were simply a drain on resources and living space. At least one master preferred to sell his pregnant slave rather than suffer having her child underfoot. Other masters solved the problem of an extra mouth to feed by selling infants—or, in one case, giving his slave's baby away. Slave women who dared to start or add to their families were sometimes separated from the men who fathered their children. In Boston, a pregnant woman and her husband chose to commit suicide rather than endure the dissolution of their family. Urban slave women who were allowed to keep their children often lost them quickly. Communicable diseases and cramped quarters combined in deadly fashion in every household in eighteenth-century colonial cities, but black infant mortality rates were two to three times higher than white.

A slave woman's life—like a slave man's—could be enriched by a family, an independent culture and community, and the autonomous spaces created by the task system or wrested from the gang-labor system of the Chesapeake. In a sense, these were all forms of resistance to enslavement. But there were other forms of resistance as well—rebellion, suicide, murder, escape, self-mutilation, disobedience, the destruction of tools and equipment, arson, theft of supplies, feigned illness, feigned pregnancy, and feigned ignorance or stupidity. Colonial English society rarely assumed that slaves were docile or content, and slaveholders preferred to rely on repressive laws, a show of force, and harsh reprisals rather than a belief in the passivity or contentedness of their slaves ...

The work demanded of Northern slave women was less grueling than the work done with mortar and pestle in the Carolinas or with hoes and hands in the Chesapeake tobacco fields. Indeed, slavery in the North was generally less brutal than in the Southern colonies. Yet enslaved women in the middle colonies and New England also resisted, ran away, and rebelled. Here, too, women fled their master's home, determined to reunite with their husband or children. And here, too, women participated in the rare but violent uprisings of slaves seeking to overthrow their oppressors.

When authorities moved against participants in the 1712 Slave Revolt in New York City, several women were among those arrested and convicted. And when a slave presented the first petition for freedom to the newly formed state legislature of Massachusetts in 1782, she was a woman. The woman, Belinda, pressed these Revolutionaries to make good on their state constitution's pledge to discontinue slavery, stating her case with eloquence: "I have not yet enjoyed the benefits of creation . . . I beg freedom."

DOCUMENTS: The Law of Slavery

> *"According to the condition of the mother . . . "*

The system of slavery relied heavily on marking differences of status (slave or free)—by visible bodily difference (black or white). Free blacks and enslaved mulattoes undermined the simplicity of these signals, displaying in their very beings the fact that it was power, not nature, that placed any particular individual in one status or another.

How to interpret the status of children whose fathers were white and whose mothers were black? Might they make a claim for free status or support from their free parent? Could white fathers be obliged to take responsibility for such children? In Spanish colonies in South America, a complex system of godparenting made it possible for white fathers to maintain a wide variety of relationships with their mixed-blood children.

The Virginia Law of 1662 established a different set of rules for the English colony; Maryland passed a similar statute two years later. How does the 1662 law challenge traditional English inheritance practices? What do the two sections of the law reveal about how Virginia legislators wished to shape interracial sexual relations? What are the implications of the law for children whose fathers were free black men and whose mothers were enslaved?

WHEREAS some doubts have arrisen whether children got by any Englishman upon a negro woman should be slave or free, *Be it therefore enacted and declared by this present grand assembly,* that all children borne in this country shalbe held bond or free only according to the condition of the mother, *And* that if any christian shall committ fornication with a negro man or woman hee or shee soe offending shall pay double the [usual] fines. . . . *

*NOTE: The usual fine for fornication was 500 pounds of tobacco.

Assembly of Virginia, Act XVI, December 1691, in William Waller Hening, *The Statutes at Large: Being a Collection of All the Laws of Virginia, from the First Session of the Legislature, in the Year 1619,* 13 vols. (New York: R & W & G Bartow, 1823), 2:170.

"For prevention of that abominable mixture . . ."

By the late seventeenth century, Virginia and Maryland attempted to punish interracial sexual relations, even among free men and women. What relationships does the Virginia law of 1691 make illegal? What does it prescribe for interracial children? Why did the legislators think the law would be self-enforcing? A restatement of the statute in 1705 also punished ministers for officiating at interracial marriages.

[1691] . . . for prevention of that abominable mixture and spurious issue which hereafter may encrease in this dominion, as well by negroes, mulattoes, and Indians intermarrying with English, or other white women, as by their unlawful accompanying with one another, *Be it enacted* . . . that . . . whatsoever English or other white man or woman being free shall intermarry with a negroe, mulatto or Indian man or woman bond or free shall within three months after such marriage be banished and removed from this dominion forever. . . .

And be it further enacted . . . That if any English woman being free shall have a bastard child by any negro or mulatto, she pay the sume of fifteen pounds sterling, within one moneth after such bastard child shall be born, to the Church wardens of the parish . . . and in default of such payment she shall be taken into the possession of the said Church wardens and disposed of for five yeares, and the said fine of fifteen pounds, or whatever the woman shall be disposed of for, shall be paid, one third part to their majesties . . . and one other third part to the use of the parish . . . and the other third part to the informer, and that such bastard child be bound out as a servant by the said Church wardens untill he or she shall attaine the age of thirty yeares, and in case such English woman that shall have such bastard child be a servant, she shall be sold by the said church wardens, (after her time is expired that she ought by law to serve her master) for five yeares, and the money she shall be sold for divided as is before appointed, and the child to serve as aforesaid.

[1705] *And be it further enacted,* That no minister of the church of England, or other minister, or person whatsoever, within this colony and dominion, shall hereafter wittingly presume to marry a white man with a negro or mulatto woman; or to marry a white woman with a negro or mulatto man, upon pain of forfeiting or paying, for every such marriage the sum of ten thousand pounds of tobacco; one half to our sovereign lady the Queen . . . and the other half to the informer. . . .

Assembly of Virginia, Act XVI, April 1691, in William Waller Hening, *The Statutes at Large: Being a Collection of All the Laws of Virginia, from the First Session of the Legislature, in the Year 1619,* 13 vols. (New York: R & W & G Bartow, 1823), vol. 3, pp. 86–87; and Assembly of Virginia, Chap. XLIX, Sec. XX, October 1705 in Hening, vol. 3, p. 453.

MARY BETH NORTON
"Searchers Again Assembled": Gender Distinctions in Seventeenth-Century America

The story that Mary Beth Norton tells is one that demonstrates that gender is a a social as well as a biological construction. It is very rare that newborn is hermaphrodite, or intersexed, displaying "some combination of 'female' and 'male' reproductive and sexual features." Later in life, hormonal abnormalities may mask clear distinctions between male and female. In our own time, "sexual reassignment" surgery is generally performed while an intersexed child is an infant; for adults, hormonal treatments, sometimes accompanied by surgery, can be used to clarify the gender identity of an individual.*

In one seventeenth-century Virginia community, the presence of a person who dressed as man and also as a woman, who behaved alternately like a woman and like a man, and whose physical formation was vulnerable to multiple interpretations was deeply disconcerting. How did T. Hall's neighbors respond to gossip that this person's sex was unclear? What authority did women claim in assessing the situation? What authority did men claim? What does the struggle to mark T. Hall's gender identity suggest about the structure of community life and the roles of men and women?

On April 8, 1629, a person named Hall was brought before the General Court of the colony of Virginia. Hall was not formally charged with a crime, although witnesses alluded to a rumor about fornication. Yet Hall's case is one of the most remarkable to be found in the court records of any colony. If no crime was involved, why was Hall in court?

Hall had been reported to the authorities for one simple reason: people were confused about Hall's sexual identity. At times Hall dressed as a man; at other times, evidently, as a woman. What sex was this person? other colonists wanted to know. The vigor with which they pursued their concerns dramatically underscores the significance of gender distinctions in seventeenth-century Anglo-America. The case also provides excellent illustrations of the powerful role the community could play in individuals' lives and of the potential influence of ordinary folk, both men and women, on the official actions of colonial governments.

The Hall case offers compelling insights into the process of defining gender in early American society. Hall was an anomalous individual, and focusing on such anomalies can help to expose fundamental belief systems. Since in this case sex was difficult to determine, so too was gender identity. Persons of indeterminate sex, such as the subject of this discussion, pose perplexing questions for any society. The process through which the culture categorizes these people is both complex and revealing. The analysis here will examine the ways in which seventeenth-century Virginians

*Suzanne Kessler, "The Medical Construction of Gender: Case Management of Intersexed Infants." *Signs: Journal of Women in Culture and Society* XVI (1990): 3–26.

attempted to come to grips with the problems presented to them by a sexually ambiguous person.[1] ...

Describing my usage of personal pronouns and names is essential to the analysis that follows. The other historians who have dealt with the case have referred to Hall as "Thomas" and "he," as do the court records (with one significant exception). Yet the details of the case, including Hall's testimony, make such usage problematic. Therefore the practice here shall be the following: when Hall is acting as a female, the name "Thomasine" and the pronoun "she" will be used. Conversely, when Hall is acting as a male, "Thomas" and "he" are just as obviously called for. In moments of ambiguity or generalization (as now) "Hall," or the simple initial "T" will be employed (the latter as an ungendered pronoun).

Thomasine Hall was born "at or neere" the northeastern English city of Newcastle upon Tyne.[2] As the name suggests, Hall was christened and raised as a girl. At the age of twelve, Thomasine went to London to stay with her aunt, and she lived there for ten years. But in 1625 her brother was pressed into the army to serve in an expedition against Cadiz. Perhaps encouraged by her brother's experience (or perhaps taking his place after his death, for that expedition incurred many casualties), Hall subsequently adopted a new gender identity. Thomas told the court that he "Cut of[f] his heire and Changed his apparell into the fashion of man and went over as a souldier in the Isle of Ree being in the habit of a man."[3] Upon returning to Plymouth from army service in France, probably in the autumn of 1627, Hall resumed a feminine identity. Thomasine donned women's clothing and supported herself briefly by making "bone lace" and doing other needlework. That she did so suggests that Thomasine had been taught these valuable female skills by her aunt during her earlier sojourn in London.

Plymouth was one of the major points of embarkation for the American colonies, and Hall recounted that "shortly after" arriving in the city Thomasine learned that a ship was being made ready for a voyage to Virginia. Once again, Hall decided to become a man, so he put on men's clothing and sailed to the fledgling colony. Thomas was then approxi-

mately twenty-five years old, comparable in age to many of the immigrants to Virginia, and like most of his fellows he seems to have gone to the Chesapeake as an indentured servant.

By December, Hall was settled in Virginia, for on January 21, 1627/8, a man named Thomas Hall, living with John and Jane Tyos (T's master and mistress), was convicted along with them for receiving stolen goods from William Mills, a servant of one of their neighbors. According to the testimony, Hall and the Tyoses had encouraged Mills in a series of thefts that began before Christmas 1627. Some of the purloined items—which included tobacco, chickens, currants, a shirt, and several pairs of shoes—were still in the possession of Hall and the Tyoses at the time their house was searched by the authorities on January 14. Although Thomas Hall is a common name (indeed, John Tyos knew another Thomas Hall, who had arrived with him on the ship Bona Nova in 1620), a significant piece of evidence suggests that T and the man charged with this crime were one and the same. William Mills had difficulty carrying the currants, which he piled into his cap during his initial theft. Since that was clearly an unsatisfactory conveyance, when Mills was about to make a second foray after the desirable dried fruits he asked his accomplices to supply him with a better container. Thomas Hall testified that Jane Tyos then "did bring a napkin unto him and willed him to sowe it & make a bagg of it to carry currants." It is highly unlikely that an ordinary male servant would have had better seamstressing skills than his mistress, but Thomasine was an expert at such tasks.[4]

Although thus far in Hall's tale the chronology and the sequence of gender switches have been clear—for T specifically recounted the first part of the tale to the Virginia General Court, and the timing of the thefts and their prosecution is clearly described in court testimony—the next phase of the story must be pieced together from the muddled testimony of two witnesses and some logical surmises.

A key question not definitively answered in the records is: what happened to raise questions in people's minds about Hall's sexual identity? Two possibilities suggest themselves. One is that John and Jane Tyos, who obviously recognized that Hall had "feminine" skills shortly after T came to live with them, spoke of that fact to others, or perhaps visitors to their plantation observed Hall's activities and drew their own conclusions. Another possibility is that, after traveling to Virginia as a man, Hall reverted to the female clothing and role that T appears to have found more comfortable. The court records imply that Hall did choose to dress as a woman in Virginia, for Francis England, a witness, reported overhearing a conversation in which another man asked T directly: why do you wear women's clothing? T's reply—"I goe in weomans aparell to gett a bitt for my Catt"—is difficult to interpret and will be analyzed later. In any event, a Mr. Stacy (who cannot be further identified) seems to have first raised the issue of T's anomalous sexual character by asserting to other colonists that Hall was "as hee thought a man and woeman." Just when Mr. Stacy made this statement is not clear, but he probably voiced his opinion about a year after T arrived in the colony.

In the aftermath of Mr. Stacy's statement, a significant incident occurred at the home of Nicholas Eyres, perhaps a relative of Robert Eyres, who had recently become John Tyos's partner. "Uppon [Mr Stacy's] report," three women—Alice Longe, Dorothy Rodes, and Barbara Hall—scrutinized Hall's body. Their action implied that T was at the time dressed as a woman, for women regularly searched other women's bodies (often at the direction of a court) to look for signs of illicit pregnancy or perhaps witchcraft. They never, however, performed the same function with respect to men—or anyone dressed like a man. Moreover, John Tyos both then and later told Dorothy Rodes that Hall was a woman. Even so, the female searchers, having examined Hall, declared that T was a man. As a result of the disagreement between Tyos and the women about T's sex, T was brought before the commander of the region, Captain Nathaniel Basse, for further examination.[5]

Questioned by Mr. Basse, T responded with a description of a unique anatomy with ambiguous physical characteristics. (The text of the testimony is mutilated, and the remaining fragments are too incomplete to provide a clear description of T's body.) Hall then refused to choose a gender identity, instead declaring that T was "both man and woeman." Captain Basse nevertheless decided that Hall was female and ordered T "to bee putt in weomans apparell"—thus implying that T was, at

that moment at least, dressed as a man. The three women who had previously searched T's body were shaken by the official ruling that contradicted their own judgment; after being informed of the commander's decision, they reportedly "stood in doubte of what they had formerly affirmed."

John Tyos then sold Hall, now legally a maidservant named Thomasine, to John Atkins, who was present when Captain Basse questioned T. Atkins must have fully concurred with Mr. Basse's decision; surely he would not have purchased a female servant about whose sex he had any doubts. Yet on February 12, 1628/9, questions were again raised about T, for Alice Longe and her two friends went to Atkins's house to scrutinize Thomasine's body for a second time. They covertly examined her while she slept and once more decided that the servant was male. But Atkins, though summoned by the searchers to look at his maid's anatomy, was unable to do so, for Hall's "seeming to starre as if shee had beene awake" caused Atkins to leave without viewing her body.

The next Sunday, the three women returned with two additional female helpers.[6] On this occasion, the searchers had the active cooperation and participation of John Atkins, who ordered Thomasine to show her body to them. For a third time the women concluded that Hall was a man. Atkins thereupon ordered his servant to don men's clothing and informed Captain Basse of his decision.

By this time not only Hall but also everyone else was undoubtedly confused. Since Hall was now deemed to be male, the next curiosity-seekers to examine T's body were also male. One of them was Roger Rodes, probably the husband of Dorothy, who had joined in all the previous searches of Hall's body. Before forcefully throwing Thomas onto his back and checking his anatomy, Roger told Hall, "thou hast beene reported to be a woman and now thou art proved to bee a man, i will see what thou carriest." Like the female searchers before them, Roger and his associate Francis England concluded that T was male.

A rumor that Hall "did ly with a maid of Mr Richard Bennetts called greate Besse" must have added considerably to the uncertainty. Hall accused Alice Longe, one of the persistent female searchers, of spreading the tale. She denied the charge, blaming the slander instead on an unnamed male servant of John Tyos's. If the story was true, what did it imply about Hall's sexual identity? Whether Hall was male or female would obviously have a bearing on the interpretation of any relationship with Bennett's maid Bess. Clearly, Virginians now had reason to seek a firm resolution of the conflict. Since Captain Basse, the local commander, had been unable to find an acceptable solution, there was just one remaining alternative—referring the dilemma to the General Court.

That court, composed of the governor and council, was the highest judicial authority in the small colony. The judges heard from Hall and considered the sworn depositions of two male witnesses (Francis England and John Atkins), who described the events just outlined. Remarkably, the court accepted T's own self-definition and, although using the male personal pronoun, declared that Hall was "a man and a woeman, that all the Inhabitants there may take notice thereof and that hee shall goe Clothed in mans apparell, only his head to bee attired in a Coyfe and Crosecloth with an Apron before him." Ordering Hall to post bond for good behavior until formally released from that obligation, the court also told Captain Basse to see that its directives were carried out. Since most court records for subsequent years have been lost (they were burned during the Civil War), it is impossible to trace Hall's story further.

What can this tale reveal about gender definitions and the role of the community in the formative years of American society? Six different but related issues emerge from the analysis of Hall's case.

First, the relationship of sexual characteristics and gender identity. All those who examined T, be they male or female, insisted T was male. Thus T's external sex organs resembled male genitals. Roger Rodes and Francis England, for example, pronounced Thomas "a perfect man" after they had "pulled out his members." Still, T informed Captain Basse "hee had not the use of the mans parte" and told John Atkins that "I have a peece of an hole" (a vulva). Since T was identified as a girl at birth, christened Thomasine, and raised accordingly, T probably fell into that category of human beings who appear female in infancy but at puberty develop what seem to be male genitalia. Such

individuals were the subjects of many stories in early modern Europe, the most famous of which involved a French peasant girl, Marie, who suddenly developed male sex organs while chasing pigs when she was fifteen, and who in adulthood became a shepherd named Germain. It is not clear whether early Virginians were aware of such tales, but if they understood contemporary explanations of sexual difference, the narrative of Marie-Germain would not have surprised them. Women were viewed as inferior types of men, and their sexual organs were regarded as internal versions of male genitalia. In the best scientific understanding of the day, there was just one sex, and under certain circumstances women could turn into men.[7]

What, then, in the eyes of Virginia's English residents, constituted sufficient evidence of sexual identity? For the male and female searchers of T's body, genitalia that appeared to be normally masculine provided the answer. But that was not the only possible contemporary response to the question. Leaving aside for the moment the persons who saw T as a combination of male and female (they will be considered later), it is useful to focus on those who at different times indicated that they thought T was female. There were three such individuals, all of them men: Captain Nathaniel Basse, who ordered T to wear women's clothing after T had appeared before him; John Atkins, T's second master, who purchased Thomasine as a maidservant and referred to T as "shee" before bowing to the contrary opinion of the female searchers and changing the pronoun to "him"; and, most important of all, T's first master, John Tyos.

It is not clear from the trial record why Captain Basse directed T to dress as a woman, for T asserted a dual sexual identity in response to questioning and never claimed to be exclusively female. Perhaps the crucial fact was T's admission that "hee had not the use of the mans parte." Another possibility was that Mr. Basse interpreted T's anatomy as insufficiently masculine. As was already indicated, the partial physical description of T included in this portion of the record survives only in fragmentary form and so is impossible to interpret, especially in light of the certainty of all the searchers.

John Atkins acquired T as a servant after Captain Basse had issued his order, and he at first accepted Thomasine as a woman, referring to how "shee" seemed to awaken from sleep. Yet Atkins changed his mind about his servant after he and the five women subjected T's body to the most thorough examination described in the case record. It involved a physical search by the women, then questioning by Atkins, followed by an order from Atkins to Hall to "lye on his backe and shew" the "peece of an hole" that T claimed to have. When the women "did againe finde him to bee a man," Atkins issued the directive that contradicted Captain Basse's, ordering T to put on men's clothes. For Atkins, Hall's anatomy (which he saw with his own eyes) and the women's testimony were together decisive in overriding his initial belief that T was female, a belief presumably based at least in part on his presence at Mr. Basse's interrogation of T.

Unlike Atkins, John Tyos had purchased T as Thomas—a man. And for him the interpretive process was reversed. After just a brief acquaintance with Thomas, John and his wife learned that he had female skills. Approximately a year later Tyos "swore" to Dorothy Rodes that Hall "was a woman," a conclusion that contradicted the opinion of the female searchers. It also seemingly flew in the face of what must have been his own intimate knowledge of Hall's physical being. The lack of space in the small houses of the seventeenth-century Chesapeake is well known to scholars.[8] It is difficult to imagine that Tyos had never seen Hall's naked body—the same body that convinced searchers of both sexes that T was male. So why would Tyos insist that T was Thomasine, even to Dorothy Rodes, who forcefully asserted the contrary? The answer must lie not in T's sexual organs but in T's gender—that is, in the feminine skills and mannerisms that would have been exhibited by a person born, raised, and living as a female until reaching the age of twenty-two, and which would have been immediately evident to anyone who, like John Tyos, lived with T for any length of time.

Thus, for these colonists, sex had two possible determinants. One was physical: the nature of one's genitalia. The other was cultural: the character of one's knowledge and one's manner of behaving. The female and male searchers used the former criterion, John Tyos, the latter. John Atkins initially adopted the second approach, but later switched to the first. Nathaniel Basse may have agreed with

Tyos, or he may have refused to interpret T's anatomy as unambiguously as did the searchers: it is not clear which. But it is clear that two quite distinct tests of sexual identity existed in tandem in early Virginia. One relied on physical characteristics, the other on learned, gendered behavior. On most occasions, of course, results of the two tests would accord with each other. Persons raised as females would physically appear to be females; persons raised as males would look like other males. Hall acted like a woman and physically resembled a man. Thus in T's case the results of the two independent criteria clashed, and that was the source of the confusion.

Second, the importance of clothing. Many of the key questions about Hall were couched in terms of what clothing T should wear, men's or women's. Captain Basse and John Atkins did not say to T, "you are a man," or "you are a woman," but instead issued instructions about what sort of apparel T was to put on. Likewise, although the General Court declared explicitly that Hall was both male and female, its decision also described the clothing T was to wear in specific detail. Why was clothing so important?

The answer lies in the fact that in the seventeenth century clothing was a crucial identifier of persons. Not only did males and females wear very different garb, but persons of different ranks also were expected to reveal their social status in their dress. In short, one was supposed to display visually one's sex and rank to everyone else in the society. Thus, ideally, new acquaintances would know how to categorize each other even before exchanging a word of greeting. In a fundamental sense, seventeenth-century people's identity was expressed in their apparel. Virginia never went so far as Massachusetts, which passed laws regulating what clothing people of different ranks could wear, but the Virginia colonists were clearly determined to uphold the same sorts of rules.[9]

Clothing, which was sharply distinguished by the sex of its wearer, served as a visual trope for gender. And gender was one of the two most basic determinants of role in the early modern world (the other was rank, which was never at issue in Hall's case—T was always a servant). People who wore skirts nurtured children; people who wore pants did not. People who wore aprons could take no role in governing the colony, whereas other people could, if they were of appropriate status. People who wore headdresses performed certain sorts of jobs in the household; people who wore hats did other types of jobs in the fields. It is hardly surprising, therefore, that Virginians had difficulty dealing with a person who sometimes dressed as a man and other times as a woman—and who, on different occasions, did both at the direction of superiors. Nor, in light of this context, is it surprising that decisions about T's sexual identity were stated in terms of clothing.[10]

Third, the absence of a sense of personal privacy throughout the proceedings. To a modern sensibility, two aspects of the case stand out. First, seventeenth-century Virginians appear to have had few hesitations about their right to examine the genitalia of another colonist, with or without official authorization from a court and regardless of whether that activity occurred forcibly, clandestinely, or openly. The physical examinations were nominally by same-sex individuals (women when T was thought to be female, men when T had been declared to be male), with one key exception: John Atkins joined the women in scrutinizing the body of his maidservant. A master's authority over the household, in other words, extended to the bodies of his dependents. If a master like Atkins chose to search the body of a subordinate of either sex, no barrier would stand in his way.

Second, Hall seems not to have objected to any of the intrusive searches of T's body nor to the intimate questioning to which T was subjected by Captain Basse and the General Court. Hall too appears to have assumed that T's sexual identity was a matter of concern for the community at large. Such an attitude on Hall's part was congruent with a society in which the existing minimal privacy rights were seen as accruing to households as a unit or perhaps to their heads alone. Subordinates like Hall neither expected nor received any right to privacy of any sort.

Fourth, the involvement of the community, especially women, in the process of determining sexual identity. One of the most significant aspects of Hall's story is the initiative taken throughout by Hall's fellow colonists. They not only brought their doubts about Hall's sex to the attention of the authorities, they also refused to accept Captain Basse's determination that Hall was female. Both men and women joined in the effort to convince Virginia's leaders that T was male. Nearly uniformly rejecting T's self-characterization as "both" (the only exception outside the General Court being Mr. Stacy), Virginians insisted that Hall had to be either female or male, with most favoring the latter definition. They wanted a sexual category into which to fit T, and they did not hesitate to express their opinions about which category was the more appropriate.

Women in particular were active in this regard. Three times groups of women scrutinized T's body, whereas a group of men did so only once. After each examination, women rejected T as one of their number. Because of the vigorous and persistent efforts of female Virginians, Hall was deprived of the possibility of adopting unambiguously the role with which T seemed most comfortable, that of Thomasine. Here Hall's physical characteristics determined the outcome. Accustomed to searching the bodies of other females, women thought T did not physically qualify as feminine—regardless of the gendered skills T possessed—and they repeatedly asserted that to any man who would listen. For them, T's anatomy (sex) was more important than T's feminine qualities (gender).

Male opinion, on the other hand, was divided. The three male searchers of T's body—Roger Rodes, Francis England, and John Atkins—agreed with the women's conclusion. Other men were not so sure. John Tyos and Nathaniel Basse thought T more appropriately classified as a woman, while Mr. Stacy and the members of the General Court said T displayed aspects of both sexes. It seems plausible to infer from their lack of agreement about T's sex that men as a group were not entirely certain about what criteria to apply to create the categories "male" and "female." Some relied on physical appearance, others on behavior.

Moreover, the complacency of the male searchers can be interpreted as quite remarkable. They failed to police the boundaries of their sex with the same militance as did women. That T, if a man, was a very unusual sort of man indeed did not seem to bother Rodes, Atkins, and England. For them, T's physical resemblance to other men was adequate evidence of masculinity, despite their knowledge of T's feminine skills and occasional feminine dress. That opinion was, however, in the end overridden by the doubts of higher-ranking men on the General Court, who were not so willing to overlook T's peculiarities.

Fifth, the relationship among sex, gender, and sexuality. Twice, and in quite different ways, the case record raises issues of sexuality rather than of biological sex or of gendered behavior. Both references have been alluded to briefly: the rumor of Thomas's having committed fornication with "greate Besse," and T's explanation for wearing women's clothing—"to gett a bitt for my Catt."

A judgment about T's body would imply a judgment about T's sexuality as well. Yet was it possible to reach a definitive conclusion about T's sexuality? If T were Thomas, then he could potentially be guilty of fornicating with the maidservant Bess; if T were Thomasine, then being in the same bed with Bess might mean nothing—or it could imply "unnatural" acts, the sort of same-sex coupling universally condemned when it occurred between men. The rumor about Bess, which for an ordinary male servant might have led to a fistfight (with the supposed slanderer, Tyos's servant), a defamation suit, or a fornication presentment, thus raised perplexing questions because of T's ambiguous sexual identity, questions that had to be resolved in court.[11]

T's phrase "to gett a bitt for my Catt," as reported by Francis England, was even more troubling. What did it mean, and was that meaning evident to England and the members of the General Court? As an explanation for wearing female apparel, it could have been straightforward and innocent. One historian reads it literally, as indicating that Hall wore women's clothing to beg scraps for a pet cat. Hall might also have been saying that because T's skills were feminine, dressing as a woman was the best way for T to earn a living, "to get a bit (morsel) to eat." But some scholars have read erotic connotations into the statement. Could T, speaking as a man, have been saying that wearing women's clothing allowed T to get close to women, to—in modern slang—"get a piece of pussy" by masquerading as a female?[12]

There is another more likely and even more intriguing erotic possibility. Since Hall had served in the English army on an expedition to France, T could well have learned a contemporary French slang phrase—"pour avoir une bite pour mon chat"—or, crudely put in English, "to get a penis for my cunt." Translating the key words literally into English equivalents (bite=bit, chat=cat) rather than into their metaphorical meanings produced an answer that was probably as opaque and confusing to seventeenth-century Virginians as it has proved to be to subsequent historians.[13] Since much of Francis England's testimony (with the exception of his report of this statement and the account of his and Roger Rodes's examination of T's anatomy) duplicated John Atkins's deposition, England could have been called as a witness primarily to repeat such a mysterious conversation to the court.

If T was indeed employing a deliberately misleading Anglicized version of contemporary French slang, as appears probable, two conclusions are warranted. First, the response confirms T's predominantly feminine gender, for it describes sexual intercourse from a woman's perspective. In light of the shortage of women in early Virginia, it moreover would have accurately represented T's experience: donning women's garb unquestionably opened sexual possibilities to Thomasine that Thomas lacked. Second, at the same time, Hall was playing with T's listeners, answering the question about wearing women's apparel truthfully, but in such an obscure way that it was unlikely anyone would comprehend T's meaning. In other words, Hall was having a private joke at the expense of the formal and informal publics in the colony. Hall's sly reply thus discloses a mischievous aspect of T's character otherwise hidden by the flat prose of the legal record.

Sixth, the court's decision. At first glance, the most surprising aspect of the case is the General Court's acceptance of Hall's self-definition as both man and woman. By specifying that T's basic apparel should be masculine, but with feminine signs—the apron and the coif and cross-cloth, a headdress commonly worn by women at the time—Virginia officials formally recognized that Hall contained elements of both sexes. The elite men who sat as judges thereby demonstrated their ability to transcend the dichotomous sexual categories that determined the thinking of ordinary Virginians. But their superficially astonishing verdict becomes explicable when the judges' options are analyzed in terms of contemporary understandings of sex and gender.

First, consider T's sexual identity. Could the court have declared Hall to be female? That alternative was effectively foreclosed. Women had repeatedly scrutinized T's anatomy and had consistently concluded that T was male. Their initial determination that T was a man (in the wake of Mr. Stacy's comment that T was both) first brought the question before Captain Basse. Subsequently, their adamant rejection of Captain Basse's contrary opinion and their ability to convince John Atkins that they were correct, coupled with the similar assessment reached by two men, were the key elements forcing the General Court to consider the case. A small community could not tolerate a situation in which groups of men and women alternately stripped and searched the body of one of its residents, or in which the decisions of the local commander were so openly disobeyed. Declaring T to be female was impossible; ordinary Virginians of both sexes would not accept such a verdict.

Yet, at the same time, could anyone assert unconditionally that Hall was sexually a man? Francis England, Roger Rodes, John Atkins, and the five female searchers thought so, on the basis of anatomy; but John Tyos, who was probably better acquainted with T than anyone else, declared unequivocally that Hall was a woman. And T had testified about not having "the use of the mans parte." Hall, in other words, revealed that although T had what appeared to be male genitalia, T did not function sexually as a man and presumably could not have an erection. To Captain Basse and the members of the General Court, that meant that (whatever T's physical description) Hall would not be able to father children or be a proper husband to a wife.

. . . The ability to impregnate a woman was a key indicator of manhood in seventeenth-century Anglo-America. Childless men were the objects of gossip, and impotence served as adequate grounds for divorce. A person who could not father a child was by that criterion alone an unsatisfactory male. T had admitted being incapable of male orgasm. Given that admitted physical incapacity and its implications, declaring Hall to be a man was as impossible as declaring T to be a woman.[14]

Second, consider T's gender identity. In seventeenth-century Anglo-America, as in all other known societies, sexual characteristics carried with them gendered consequences. In Hall's life history those consequences were especially evident, because what T did and how T did it were deeply affected by whether T chose to be Thomas or Thomasine.

Whenever Hall traveled far from home, to France in the army or to Virginia, T became Thomas. Men had much more freedom of movement than did women. Unlike other persons raised as females, Hall's unusual anatomy gave T the opportunity to live as a male when there was an advantage to doing so. Even though T seemed more comfortable being Thomasine—to judge by frequent reversions to that role—the option of becoming Thomas must have been a welcome one. It permitted Hall to escape the normal strictures that governed early modern English women's lives and allowed T to pursue a more adventurous lifestyle.[15]

Thus whether T chose to be male or female made a great difference in T's life. As Thomas, Hall joined the army and emigrated to the colonies; as Thomasine, Hall lived quietly in London with an aunt, did fancy needlework in Plymouth, and presumably performed tasks normally assigned to women in Virginia. T's most highly developed skills were feminine ones, so T was undoubtedly more expert at and familiar with "women's work" in general, not just seamstressing.

It was, indeed, Hall's feminine skills that convinced some men that T was female; and those qualities, coupled with Hall's physical appearance, must have combined to lead to the court's decision. T's gender was feminine but T's sex seemed to be masculine—with the crucial exception of sexual functioning. Given T's sexual incapacity, all indications pointed to a feminine identity—to Thomasine. But Virginia women's refusal to accept T as Thomasine precluded that verdict. On the other hand, the judges could not declare a person to be male who had admitted to Captain Basse an inability to consummate a marriage. Ordinary men might possibly make a decision on the basis of physical appearance alone, but the members of the General Court had a responsibility to maintain the wider social order. If they said Hall was a man, then Thomas theoretically could marry and become a household head once his term of service was complete. That alternative was simply not acceptable for a person of T's description.

So, considering sex (incompletely masculine) and gender (primarily feminine), the Virginia General Court's solution to the dilemma posed by Hall was to create a unique category that combined sex and gender for T alone. Unable to fit Hall into the standard male/female dichotomy, the judges preferred to develop a singular definition that enshrined T's dual identity by prescribing clothing that simultaneously carried conflicting messages.

The court's decision to make Hall unique in terms of clothing—and thus gender identity—did not assist the community in classifying or dealing with T. After the verdict, Virginians were forced to cope with someone who by official sanction straddled the dichotomous roles of male and female. By court order, Hall was now a dual-sexed person. T's identity had no counterpart or precedent; paradoxically, a society in which gender—the outward manifestation of sex—served as a fundamental dividing line had formally designated a person as belonging to both sexes. Yet at the same time it was precisely because gender was so basic a concern to seventeenth-century society that no other solution was possible.

Hall's life after the court verdict must have been lonely. Marked as T was by unique clothing, unable to adopt the gender switches that had previously given T unparalleled flexibility in choosing a way of life, Hall must have had a very difficult time. T, like other publicly marked deviants—persons branded for theft or adultery or mutilated for perjury or forgery—was perhaps the target of insults or assaults. The verdict in T's case, in its insistence that T be constantly clothed as both sexes rather than alternating between them, was therefore harsh, though it nominally accorded with T's own self-definition. Hall's identity as "both" allowed movement back and forth across gender lines. The court's verdict had quite a different meaning, insisting not on the either/or sexual ambiguity T had employed to such great advantage, but rather on a definition of "both" that required duality and allowed for no flexibility.

It is essential to re-emphasize here what necessitated this unusual ending to a remarkable case: the opinions and actions of the female neighbors of John Tyos and John Atkins. Captain Nathaniel Basse, confronted with basically the same information that the General Court later considered, concluded that Hall should be dressed and treated as a woman. In a sexual belief system that hypothesized that women were inferior men, any inferior man—that is, one who could not function adequately in sexual terms—was a woman. Thus, charged the women at an Accomack cow pen in 1637, John Waltham "hade his Mounthly Courses as Women have" because his wife had not become pregnant.[16] Undoubtedly the General Court's first impulse would have been the same as Captain Basse's: to declare that T, an inferior man, was female and should wear women's clothing. But Virginia women had already demonstrated forcefully that they would not accept such a verdict. Hall's fate therefore was determined as much by a decision reached by ordinary women as it was by a verdict formally rendered by the elite men who served on the General Court.

NOTES

1. Anthropologists have been in the forefront of the investigation of the various relationships of sex and gender. A good introduction to such work is Sherry Ortner and Harriet Whitehead, eds., *Sexual Meanings: The Cultural Construction of Gender and Sexuality* (New York: Cambridge University Press, 1981). . . . For an account of how contemporary American society handles sexually ambiguous babies at birth, see Suzanne J. Kessler, "The Medical Construction of Gender: Case Management of Intersexed Infants," *Signs*, XVI (1990), 3–26.

2. Unless otherwise indicated, all quotations and details in the account that follows are taken from the record in the case, *Va Ct Recs*, 194–95.

3. The expedition in which Thomas took part was an ill-fated English attack on the Isle de Ré during the summer of 1627. The troops who futilely tried to relieve the French Protestants besieged in the city of La Rochelle embarked on July 10, 1627; most of them returned to Plymouth in early November.

4. *Va Ct Recs*, 159, 162–64 (quotation 163). Yet it is possible that the Thomas Hall in this case was the other man, the one who came to Virginia in 1620. (For him, see Virginia M. Meyer and John F. Dorman, eds., *Adventurers of Purse and Person Virginia 1607–1624/5*, 3d ed. [Richmond: Order of First Families of Virginia, 1987]. The Virginia muster of 1624/5 [ibid., 42] lists Thomas Hall and John Tyos as residents of George Sandys's plantation in James City. . . .

5. Little can be discovered about the three women. . . .

6. The two newcomers were the wife of Allen Kinaston and the wife of Ambrose Griffen. . . .

7. The best discussion of the one-sex model of humanity and its implications is Thomas Laqueur, *Making Sex: Body and Gender from the Greeks to Freud* (Cambridge, Mass.: Harvard University Press, 1990). See 126–30 for an analysis of Marie-Germain. . . .

8. See Lois Green Carr et al., *Robert Cole's World: Agriculture & Society in Early Maryland* (Chapel Hill: University of North Carolina Press, 1991), 90–114, on "the standard of life" in the early Chesapeake.

9. See *Mass Col Recs*, IV, pt 1, 60–61, IV, pt 2, 41–42. . . .

10. Laqueur observes, in *Making Sex*, 124–25, that "in the absence of a purportedly stable system of two sexes, strict sumptuary laws of the body attempted to stabilize gender—woman as woman and man as man—and punishments for transgression were quite severe." A relevant recent study is Marjorie Garber, *Vested Interests: Cross-Dressing and Cultural Anxiety* (New York: Routledge, 1991).

11. A good general discussion of the colonists' attitudes toward sexuality is John D'Emilio and Estelle B. Freedman, *Intimate Matters: A History of Sexuality in America* (New York: Harper & Row, 1988), 1–52, especially (on the regulation of deviance) 27–38.

12. Brown interprets the statement literally in her "Gender and the Genesis of Race and Class System," I, 88. The suggestion that the phrase might have meant "earning a living" is mine, developed after consulting the *OED* (q.v. "bit"). Katz speculates that T's phrase had the erotic meaning suggested here, though he recognizes that such an interpretation is problematic (*Gay/Lesbian Almanac*, 72).

13. I owe the identification of the probable French origin of this phrase to Marina Warner and, through her, to Julian Barnes, whom she consulted (personal communication, 1993). My colleague Steven Kaplan, a specialist in the history of early modern France (and scholars he consulted in Paris), confirmed that "bite" and "chat" were used thus in the late sixteenth century and that the interpretation appears plausible.

14. On the importance of marital sexuality in the colonies: D'Emilio and Freedman, *Intimate Matters*, 16–27.

15. See, on this point, Rudolf M. Dekker and Lotte C. van de Pol, *The Tradition of Female Transvestism in Early Modern Europe* (London: Macmillan, 1989).

16. Susie M. Ames, ed., *County Court Records of Accomack-Northampton, Virginia, 1632–1640* (American Legal Records, VII), (Washington, D.C., 1954), p. 85.

DOCUMENT: The Trial of Anne Hutchinson, 1637

"What law have I broken?"

The Antinomian heresy threw the Puritan colony of Massachusetts Bay into turmoil for years and forced its leaders to reconsider the nature of their experiment. Antinomians placed greater emphasis on religious feeling than did orthodox Puritans. They tended to be suspicious (*anti*) of law (*nomos*) or formal rules and came close to asserting that individuals had access to direct revelation from the Holy Spirit. They criticized ministers who seemed to argue that it was possible to *earn* salvation by good deeds rather than leaving it to God freely to decide who was to be saved by their faith, a distinction between the "covenant of works" and a "covenant of faith" which they thought separated authentic Puritans from ones who remained too close to the Anglican Church. The close relationship between church and state in Massachusetts Bay meant that challenge to the ministers was quickly interpreted as challenge to established authority of all kinds.

The leader of the dissenters was Anne Hutchinson, a woman who had come to the colony in 1634, four years after its founding, and who commanded great respect for her competence as a midwife. At meetings held in her home after Sunday church services she summarized, discussed, and criticized ministers' sermons. The meetings became very popular; soon she was holding separate gatherings for men as well as for women. Women who followed Hutchinson were often those who respected her medical knowledge and also shared her criticisms of the ministers. The men who came to the meetings were often those who were critical of the Puritan leadership on political and economic as well as religious grounds. Rumor spread that criticism of the governor and council as well as ministers was voiced in the Hutchinson home, and she was challenged, first by a convocation of ministers and then, in November 1637, by the General Court of the Colony. Her trial was conducted by the governor of the colony, John Winthrop. He was joined in his questioning by the deputy governor and other members of the legislature; at the end they handed down the very heavy sentence of banishment from the colony.

Hutchinson's secular trial before the General Court was followed by an examination before a board of ministers, who handed down the heaviest sentence in their arsenal, excommunication. When Hutchinson was held up to public ridicule and exiled, explicit dissent by women was firmly squelched in the Puritan community. In Winthrop's memoir of the events, published in 1644, miscarriages suffered by Hutchinson and her closest colleague, Mary Dyer, were offered as evidence of God's "displeasure against their opinions and practises, as clearly as if he had pointed with his finger, in causing the two fomenting women in the time of the height of the Opinions to produce

Excerpted from "Examination of Mrs. Anne Hutchinson before the court at Newton, 1637," in David D. Hall, ed., *The Antinomian Controversy, 1636–1638: A Documentary History* (Middletown, Conn.: Wesleyan University Press, 1968), pp. 312–16. Copyright © 1968 by David D. Hall. Reprinted by permission of the editor. Notes have been renumbered.

out of their wombs, as before they had out of their braines, such monstrous births as no Chronicle . . . hardly ever recorded the like."*

Hutchinson and her husband fled to Rhode Island, where Roger Williams offered toleration to dissenters; several years later they moved on to the forests of what is now Westchester County, north of New York City. Hutchinson died at the hands of Indians in 1643.

In reading this excerpt from Anne Hutchinson's trial in 1637, note the extent to which criticism of her religious and political behavior merge with the complaint that she is challenging gender roles. Note also the shrewdness with which Hutchinson defends her actions; at one point she challenges Winthrop that if he thinks it "not lawful for me to teach women . . . why do you call me to teach the court?"

NOVEMBER 1637

The Examination of Mrs. Ann Hutchinson at the Court at Newtown

Mr. Winthrop, governor. Mrs. Hutchinson, you are called here as one of those that have troubled the peace of the commonwealth and the churches here; you are known to be a woman that hath had a great share in the promoting and divulging of those opinions that are causes of this trouble, and to be nearly joined not only in affinity and affection with some of those the court had taken notice of and passed censure upon, but you have spoken divers things as we have been informed very prejudicial to the honour of the churches and ministers thereof, and you have maintained a meeting and an assembly in your house that hath been condemned by the general assembly as a thing not tolerable nor comely in the sight of God nor fitting for your sex, and notwith standing that was cried down you have continued the same, therefore we have thought good to send for you to understand how things are, that if you be in an erroneous way we may reduce you that so you may become a profitable member here among us, otherwise (if you be obstinate in your course that then the court may take such course that you may trouble us no further) therefore I would intreat you to express whether you do not hold and assent in practice to those opinions and factions that have been handled in court already, that is to say, whether you do not justify Mr. Wheelwright's sermon and the petition.

Mrs. Hutchinson. I am called here to answer before you but I hear no things laid to my charge.

Gov. I have told you some already and more I can tell you.

Mrs. H. Name one, Sir.

Gov. Have I not named some already?

Mrs. H. What have I said or done?

Gov. Why for your doings, this you did harbour and countenance those that are parties in this faction that you have heard of.

Mrs. H. That's matter of conscience, Sir.

Gov. Your conscience you must keep or it must be kept for you. . . . Say that one brother should commit felony or treason and come to his other brother's house, if he knows him guilty and conceals him he is guilty of the same. It is his conscience to entertain him, but if his conscience comes into act in giving countenance and entertainment to him that hath broken the law he is guilty too. So if you do countenance those that are transgressors of the law you are in the same fact.

Mrs. H. What law do they transgress?

Gov. The law of God and of the state.

Mrs. H. In what particular?

Gov. Why in this among the rest, whereas the Lord doth say honour thy father and thy mother.

Mrs. H. Ey Sir in the Lord.

Gov. This honour you have broke in giving countenance to them. . . .

Mrs. H. What law have I broken?

Gov. Why the fifth commandment.

Mrs. H. I deny that for [Mr. Wheelwright] saith in the Lord.

Gov. You have joined with them in the faction.

Mrs. H. In what faction have I joined with them?

Gov. In presenting the petition[1]. . . .

Mrs. H. But I had not my hand to the petition.

Gov. You have councelled them.

Mrs. H. Wherein?

Gov. Why in entertaining them.

Mrs. H. What breach of law is that Sir?

Gov. Why dishonouring of parents.

Mrs. H. But put the case Sir that I do fear the Lord and my parents, may not I entertain them that

---

*John Winthrop, *A Short Story of The Rise, Reign, and Ruine of the Antinomians, Familists & Libertines,* in David D. Hall, ed. *The Antinomian Controversy, 1636–1638: A Documentary History* (Middletown, Conn.: Wesleyan University Press, 1968), p. 214.

fear the Lord because my parents will not give me leave?

Gov. If they be the fathers of the commonwealth, and they of another religion, if you entertain them then you dishonour your parents and are justly punishable.

Mrs. H. If I entertain them, as they have dishonoured their parents I do.

Gov. No but you by countenancing them above others put honor upon them.

Mrs. H. I may put honor upon them as the children of God and as they do honor the Lord.

Gov. We do not mean to discourse with those of your sex but only this; you do adhere unto them and do endeavour to set forward this faction and so you do dishonour us.

Mrs. H. I do acknowledge no such thing neither do I think that I ever put any dishonour upon you.

Gov. Why do you keep such a meeting at your house as you do every week upon a set day?

Mrs. H. It is lawful for me so to do, as it is all your practices and can you find a warrant for yourself and condemn me for the same thing? [I]t was in practice before I came therefore I was not the first.

Gov. For this, that you appeal to our practice you need no confutation. If your meeting had answered to the former it had not been offensive, but I will say that there was no meeting of women alone, but your meeting is of another sort for there are sometimes men among you.

Mrs. H. There was never any man with us.

Gov. Well, admit there was no man at your meeting and that you was sorry for it, there is no warrant for your doings, and by what warrant do you continue such a course?

Mrs. H. I conceive there lyes a clear rule in Titus, that the elder women should instruct the younger[2] and then I must have a time wherein I must do it.

Gov. All this I grant you, I grant you a time for it, but what is this to the purpose that you Mrs. Hutchinson must call a company together from their callings to come to be taught of you?

Mrs. H. Will it please you to answer me this and to give me a rule for then I will willingly submit to any truth. If any come to my house to be instructed in the ways of God what rule have I to put them away?

Gov. But suppose that a hundred men come unto you to be instructed will you forbear to instruct them?

Mrs. H. As far as I conceive I cross a rule in it.

Gov. Very well and do you not so here?

Mrs. H. No Sir for my ground is they are men.

Gov. Men and women all is one for that, but suppose that a man should come and say Mrs. Hutchinson I hear that you are a woman that God hath given his grace unto and you have knowledge in the word of God I pray instruct me a little, ought you not to instruct this man?

Mrs. H. I think I may.—Do you think it not lawful for me to teach women and why do you call me to teach the court?

Gov. We do not call you to teach the court but to lay open yourself.

Mrs. H. I desire you that you would then set me down a rule by which I may put them away that come unto me and so have peace in so doing.

Gov. You must shew your rule to receive them.

Mrs. H. I have done it.

Gov. I deny it because I have brought more arguments than you have.

Mrs. H. I say, to me it is a rule.

Mr. Endicot. You say there are some rules unto you. I think there is a contradiction in your own words. What rule for your practice do you bring, only a custom in Boston.

Mrs. H. No Sir that was no rule to me but if you look upon the rule in Titus it is a rule to me. If you convince me that it is no rule I shall yield.

Gov. . . . . [T]his rule crosses that in the Corinthians.[3] But you must take it in this sense that elder women must instruct the younger about their business, and to love their husbands and not to make them to clash.

Mrs. H. I do not conceive but that it is meant for some publick times.

Gov. Well, have you no more to say but this?

Mrs. H. I have said sufficient for my practice.

Gov. Your course is not to be suffered for, besides that we find such a course as this to be greatly prejudicial to the state, besides the occasion that it is to seduce many honest persons that are called to those meetings and your opinions being known to be different from the word of God may seduce many simple souls that resort unto you, besides that the occasion which hath come of late hath come from none but such as have frequented your meetings, so that now they are flown off from magistrates and ministers and this since they have come to you, and besides that it will not well stand with the commonwealth that families should be neglected for so many neighbours and dames and so much time spent, we see no rule of God for this, we see not that any should have authority to set up any other exercises besides what authority hath already set up and so what hurt comes of this you will be guilty of and we for suffering you.

Mrs. H. Sir I do not believe that to be so.

Gov. Well, we see how it is we must therefore put it away from you, or restrain you from maintaining this course.

Mrs. H. If you have a rule for it from God's word you may.

Gov. We are your judges, and not you ours and we must compel you to it.

Mrs. H. If it please you by authority to put it down I freely let you for I am subject to your authority.

NOTES

1. The petition the Antinomian party presented to the General Court in March 1637.

2. Titus 2.3, 4, 5.
3. 1 Corinthians 14.34, 35.

CAROL F. KARLSEN
The Devil in the Shape of a Woman: The Economic Basis of Witchcraft

Puritan ministers stressed the equality of each soul in the eyes of God and the responsibility of each believer to read the Bible. They urged women as well as men toward literacy and taking responsibility for their own salvation. One distinguished minister, Cotton Mather, writing at the end of the seventeenth century, observed that since women came close to the experience of death in repeated childbirth, their religiosity was likely to be greater than that of men. In being "helpmeets" to their husbands, women were encouraged to strengthen their ability to be competent and capable. There was much in Puritan thought that could be appealing to women.

But, as we have seen in the case of Anne Hutchinson, the Puritan community was unforgiving to women who failed to serve the needs of godly men in their strictly hierarchical community. Lurking in their imagination—as it lurked throughout the Judeo-Christian tradition—was the cautionary biblical story of Eve, who, by her disobedience, brought evil into the world. (Puritans paid no attention to other elements of that complicated tale: Eve's disobedience, after all, was in quest of Knowledge; the biology of birth is reversed, with Eve emerging from Adam's body.) Witchcraft prosecutions were endemic throughout the Puritan colonies in America and exploded into the famous outbreak in Salem, Massachusetts, in 1692, during which nearly 200 people, three-quarters of them women, were accused, and 20 people, nearly three-quarters of them women, were executed. Carol Karlsen argues that an older view of women as a necessary evil had been only superficially superseded by a new view of women as a necessary good.

Anthropologists have long understood that communities define as witches people whose behavior enacts the things the community most fears; witchcraft beliefs, wrote Monica Hunter Wilson, are "the standardized nightmare of a group, and . . . the comparative analysis of such nightmares . . . [is] one of the keys to the understanding of society."* If the most cherished values of the Puritan community were hierarchy and order,

*Quoted in Karlsen, p. 181.

then it was an easy step to the condemnation of those who did not accept—or in some cases could not accept—their place in it. In what ways do the women described in the following essay fail to fit the values of the Puritan community?

Most observers now agree that witches in the villages and towns of late sixteenth- and early seventeenth-century England tended to be poor. They were not usually the poorest women in their communities, one historian has argued; they were the "moderately poor." Rarely were relief recipients suspect; rather it was those just above them on the economic ladder, "like the woman who felt she ought to get poor relief, but was denied it."[1] This example brings to mind New England's Eunice Cole, who once berated Hampton selectmen for refusing her aid when, she insisted, a man no worse off than she was receiving it.[2]

Eunice Cole's experience also suggests the difficulty in evaluating the class position of the accused. Commonly used class indicators such as the amount of property owned, yearly income, occupation, and political offices held are almost useless in analyzing the positions of women during the colonial period. While early New England women surely shared in the material benefits and social status of their fathers, husbands, and even sons, most were economically dependent on the male members of their families throughout their lives. Only a small proportion of these women owned property outright, and even though they participated actively in the productive work of their communities, their labor did not translate into financial independence or economic power. Any income generated by married women belonged by law to their husbands, and because occupations open to women were few and wages meager, women alone could only rarely support themselves. Their material condition, moreover, could easily change with an alteration in their marital status. William Cole, with an estate at his death of £41 after debts, might be counted among the "moderately poor," as might Eunice Cole when he was alive. But the refusal of the authorities to recognize the earlier transfer of this estate from husband to wife ensured, among other things, that as a widow Eunice Cole was among the poorest of New England's poor. . . .

Despite conceptual problems and sparse evidence, it is clear that poor women, both the destitute and those with access to some resources, were surely represented, and very probably overrepresented, among the New England accused. Perhaps 20 percent of accused women . . . were either impoverished or living at a level of bare subsistence when they were accused.[3] Some, like thirty-seven-year-old Abigail Somes, worked as servants a substantial portion of their adult lives. Some supported themselves and their families with various kinds of temporary labor such as nursing infants, caring for sick neighbors, taking in washing and sewing, or harvesting crops. A few, most notably Tituba, the first person accused during the Salem outbreak, were slaves. Others, like the once-prosperous Sarah Good of Wenham and Salem, and the never-very-well-off Ruth Wilford of Haverhill, found themselves reduced to abject poverty by the death of a parent or a change in their own marital status.[4] Accused witches came before local magistrates requesting permission to sell family land in order to support themselves, to submit claims against their children or executors of their former husbands' estates for nonpayment of the widow's lawful share of the estate, or simply to ask for food and fuel from the town selectmen. Because they could not pay the costs of their trials or jail terms, several were forced to remain in prison after courts acquitted them. The familiar stereotype of the witch as an indigent woman who resorted to begging for her survival is hardly an inaccurate picture of some of New England's accused.

Still, the poor account for only a minority of the women accused. Even without precise economic indicators, it is clear that women from all levels of society were vulnerable to accusation. . . . Wives, daughters, and widows of "middling" farmers, artisans, and mariners were regularly accused, and (although much less often) so too were women belonging to the gentry class. The accused were addressed as Goodwife (or Goody) and as the more honorific Mrs. or Mistress, as well as by their first names.

Prosecution was a different matter. Unless they were single or widowed, accused women from wealthy families—families with estates valued at more than £500—could be fairly confident that the accusations would be ignored by the authorities or deflected by their husbands through suits for slander against their accusers. Even during the Salem outbreak, when several women married to wealthy men were arrested, most managed to escape to the safety of other colonies through their husbands' influence. Married women from moderately well-off families—families with estates valued at between roughly £200 and £500—did not always escape prosecution so easily, but neither do they seem, as a group, to have been as vulnerable as their less prosperous counterparts. When only married women are considered, women in families with estates worth less than £200 seem significantly overrepresented among convicted witches—a pattern which suggests that economic position was a more important factor to judges and juries than to the community as a whole in its role as accuser.[5]

Without a husband to act on behalf of the accused, wealth alone rarely provided women with protection against prosecution. Boston's Ann Hibbens, New Haven's Elizabeth Godman, and Wethersfield's Katherine Harrison, all women alone, were tried as witches despite sizable estates. In contrast, the accusations against women like Hannah Griswold of Saybrook, Connecticut, Elizabeth Blackleach of Hartford, and Margaret Gifford of Salem, all wives of prosperous men when they were accused, were simply not taken seriously by the courts.[6] . . .

Economic considerations, then, do appear to have been at work in the New England witchcraft cases. But the issue was not simply the relative poverty—or wealth—of accused witches or their families. It was the special position of most accused witches vis-à-vis their society's rules for transferring wealth from one generation to another. To explain why their position was so unusual, we must turn first to New England's system of inheritance.

Inheritance is normally thought of as the transmission of property at death, but in New England, as in other agricultural societies, adult children received part of their father's accumulated estates prior to his death, usually at the time they married.[7] Thus the inheritance

system included both pre-mortem endowments and post-mortem distributions. While no laws compelled fathers to settle part of their estates on their children as marriage portions, it was customary to do so. Marriages were, among other things, economic arrangements, and young people could not benefit from these arrangements unless their fathers provided them with the means to set up households and earn their livelihoods. Sons' portions tended to be land, whereas daughters commonly received movable goods and/or money. The exact value of these endowments varied to a father's wealth and inclination, but it appears that as a general rule the father of the young woman settled on the couple roughly half as much as the father of the young man.[8]

Custom, not law, also guided the distribution of a man's property at his death, but with two important exceptions. First, a man's widow, if he left one, was legally entitled "by way of dower" to one-third part of his real property, "to have and injoy for term of her natural life." She was expected to support herself with the profits of this property, but since she held only a life interest in it, she had to see that she did not "strip or waste" it.[9] None of the immovable estate could be sold, unless necessary for her or her children's maintenance, and then only with the permission of the court. A man might will his wife more than a third of his real property—but not less. Only if the woman came before the court to renounce her dower right publicly, and then only if the court approved, could this principle be waived. In the form of her "thirds," dower was meant to provide for a woman's support in widowhood. The inviolability of dower protected the widow from the claims of her children against the estate and protected the community from the potential burden of her care.

The second way in which law determined inheritance patterns had to do specifically with intestate cases.[10] If a man died without leaving a will, several principles governed the division of his property. The widow's thirds, of course, were to be laid out first. Unless "just cause" could be shown for some other distribution, the other two-thirds were to be divided among the surviving children, both male and female.[11] A double portion was to go to the eldest son, and single portions to his sisters and younger brothers. If there were no sons, the law stipulated that the estate was to be shared equally by the daughters. In cases where any or all of the children had not yet come of age, their portions were to be held by their mother or by a court-appointed guardian until they reached their majorities[12] or married. What remained of the widow's thirds at her death was to be divided among the surviving children, in the same proportions as the other two-thirds.

Although bound to conform to laws concerning the widow's thirds, men who wrote wills were not legally required to follow the principles of inheritance laid out in intestate cases. Individual men had the right to decide for themselves who would ultimately inherit their property. . . . [T]he majority seem to have adhered closely (though not always precisely) to the custom of leaving a double portion to the eldest son. Beyond that, New England men seem generally to have agreed to a system of partible inheritance, with both sons and daughters inheriting.

When these rules were followed, property ownership and control generally devolved upon men. Neither the widow's dower nor, for the most part, the daughter's right to inherit signified more than access to property. For widows, the law was clear that dower allowed for "use" only. For inheriting daughters who were married, the separate but inheritance-related principle of coverture applied. Under English common law, "feme covert" stipulated that married women had no right to own property—indeed, upon marriage, "the very being or legal existence of the woman is suspended."[13] Personal property which a married daughter inherited from her father, either as dowry or as a post-mortem bequest, immediately became the legal possession of her husband, who could exert full powers of ownership over it. A married daughter who inherited land from her father retained title to the land, which her husband could not sell without her consent. On her husband's death such land became the property of her children, but during his life her husband was entitled to the use and profits of it, and his wife could not devise it to her children by will.[14] The property of an inheriting daughter who was single seems to have been held "for improvement" for her until she was married, when it became her dowry.[15]

This is not to say that women did not benefit when they inherited property. A sizable inheritance could provide a woman with a materially better life; if single or widowed, inheriting women enjoyed better chances for an economically advantageous marriage or remarriage. But inheritance did not normally bring women the independent economic power it brought men.

The rules of inheritance were not always followed, however. In some cases, individual men decided not to conform to customary practices; instead, they employed one of several legal devices to give much larger shares of their estates to their wives or daughters, many times for disposal at their own discretion. Occasionally, the magistrates themselves allowed the estate to be distributed in some other fashion. Or, most commonly, the absence of male heirs in families made conformity impossible. In all three exceptions to inheritance customs, but most particularly the last, the women who stood to benefit economically also assumed a position of unusual vulnerability. They, and in many instances their daughters, became prime targets for witchcraft accusations.

Consider first the experience of witches who came from families without male heirs. . . . [T]hese histories begin to illuminate the subtle and often intricate manner in which anxieties about inheritance lay at the heart of most witchcraft accusations.

KATHERINE HARRISON

Katherine Harrison first appears in the Connecticut colonial records in the early 1650s, as the wife of John Harrison, a wealthy Wethersfield landowner.[16] Her age is unknown[17] and her family background is obscure. We know that she called John, Jonathan, and Josiah Gilbert, three prominent Connecticut Valley settlers, her cousins, but her actual relationship to them is ambiguous.[18] . . . She may have been the daughter or niece of Lydia Gilbert, who was executed as a witch in Hartford in 1654, but we can be reasonably certain only that the two women were members of the same Connecticut family.[19] . . .

It has been said that Katherine Harrison was first tried as a witch in October 1668.[20] If so, then she must have been acquitted, because she was indicted in the Court of Assistants in Hartford on 25 May 1669, on the same charge.[21] The jury was unable to agree upon a verdict, however, and the court adjourned to the next session. Meantime, Harrison was supposed to remain in jail, but for some reason she was released in the summer or early fall, and she returned home to Wethersfield. Shortly thereafter, thirty-eight Wethersfield townsmen filed a petition, complaining that "shee was suffered to be at libertie," since she "was lately prooved to be Deaply guiltie of *suspicion* of Wichcrafte" and that "the Juerie (the greater part of them) judged or beleaved that she was guilty of such high crimes" and "ought to be put to death." Among the petition's signers were several of the town's most prominent citizens, including John Blackleach, Sr., who had "taken much paines in the prosecution of this cause from the beginninge," and John Chester, who was then involved in a legal controversy with Harrison concerning a parcel of land.[22] When the Court of Assistants met again in October, all of the jury members found her guilty of witchcraft.[23]

The Hartford magistrates, however, were reluctant to accept the verdict. Perhaps remembering how accusations had gotten out of hand during the Hartford outbreak seven years before, they put Harrison back in prison and appealed to local ministers for advice on the use of evidence. The response was ambiguous enough to forestall execution.[24] At a special session of the Court of Assistants the following May, the magistrates reconsidered the verdict, determined that they were not able to concur with the jury "so as to sentance her to death or to a longer continuance in restraynt," and ordered Harrison to pay her fees and leave the colony for good.[25]

If witnesses testifying against her in her 1669 trial can be believed, Katherine Harrison's neighbors had suspected that she was a witch sixteen or eighteen years earlier. Elizabeth Simon deposed that as a single woman, Harrison was noted to be "a great or notorious liar, a Sabbath breaker and one that told fortunes"—and that her predictions frequently came to pass. Simon was also suspicious of Harrison for another reason: because she "did often spin so great a quantity of fine linen yarn as the said Elizabeth did never know nor hear of any other woman that could spin so much."[26] Other witnesses testified to the more recent damage she did to individuals and their property. Harrison was also a healer, and although many of her neighbors called upon her skills, over the years some of them came

to suspect her of killing as well as curing.[27] Or so they said in 1668–69; she was not formally accused of any witchcraft crimes until after her husband's death.

John Harrison had died in 1666, leaving his wife one of the wealthiest, if not *the* wealthiest woman in Wethersfield. In his will he bequeathed his entire estate of £929 to his wife and three daughters. Rebecca, age twelve, was to have £60, and his two younger daughters, eleven-year-old Mary and nine-year-old Sarah, were to have £40 each. The remaining £789 was to go to his widow.[28] Unlike many widows in colonial New England, Katherine Harrison chose not to remarry. Instead she lived alone, managing her extensive holdings herself, with the advice and assistance of her Hartford kinsman, Jonathan Gilbert.

In October 1668, not long after her adversaries began gathering their witchcraft evidence against her, Harrison submitted a lengthy petition to "the Fathers of the Comonweale" asking for relief for the extensive vandalism of her estate since her husband's death. Among other damage, she spoke of oxen beaten and bruised to the point of being "altogether unserviceable"; of a hole bored into the side of her cow; of a three-year-old heifer slashed to death; and of the back of a two-year-old steer broken. Her corn crop was destroyed, she said, "damnified with horses, they being staked upon it," and "30 poles of hops cutt and spoyled." Twelve of her relatives and neighbors, she said, including Jonathan and Josiah Gilbert, could testify to the damage done. The response of the court went unrecorded, but there is no indication that provision was made for the "due recompense" Harrison requested or that her grievances were even investigated.[29]

The Court of Assistants also seems to have been unsympathetic to another petition Harrison submitted in the fall of 1668, in which she complained that the actions of the magistrates themselves were depleting her estate.[30] Indeed, the local court had recently fined her £40 for slandering her neighbors, Michael and Ann Griswold—a fine greatly in excess of the normal punishment in such cases.[31] The exact circumstances of the incident are unknown, but the Griswolds were among Harrison's witchcraft accusers, and she apparently considered Michael Griswold central in the recruiting of additional witnesses against her, for she said that "the sayd Michael Griswold would Hang her though he damned a thousand soules," adding that "as for his own soule it was damned long agoe." Griswold, a member of Wethersfield's elite, but not as wealthy as Harrison, sued her for these slanderous remarks and for calling his wife Ann "a savadge whore."[32] Besides levying the fine, the court ordered Harrison to confess her sins publicly.[33] She made the required confession, but she appealed the exorbitant fine.

Harrison's petition, which she filed within the month, was a peculiar mixture of justification for her actions, concession to the magistrates' insistence on deference in women, determination in her convictions, and desperation in her attempt to salvage her estate. Acknowledging herself to be "a female, a weaker vessell, subject to passion," she pleaded as the source of her frustration and anger the vicious abuse to which she had been subjected since her husband's death. She admitted her "corruption," but pointed out that it was well known that she had made "a full and free confession of [her] fault" and had offered "to repair the wound that [she] had given to [the Griswolds'] names by a plaster as broad as the sore, at any time and in any place where it should content them." At the same time, she indicated Michael Griswold for being less interested in the reparation of his name than in her estate and did not hesitate to call the fine oppressive, citing the laws of God and the laws of the commonwealth as providing "that noe mans estate shal be deminished or taken away by any colony or pretence of Authority" in such an arbitrary manner. In her final statements, however, she returned to a more conciliatory stance: "I speake not to excuse my fault," she said, "but to save my estate as far as Righteousness will permit for a distressed Widow and Orphanes."[34]

Fear of losing her estate is a recurring theme in the records of Harrison's life during this period. Almost immediately after her husband's death in 1666, she petitioned the court to change the terms of her husband's will. Arguing that the bequests to the children were "inconsiderate" (by which she probably meant inconsiderable), she asked that the magistrates settle on her eldest daughter £210, and £200 on each of her younger daughters, reserving the house and lot for herself during her lifetime.[35] Since her husband had left her full ownership

of most of his estate, she could simply have given her daughters larger portions, but she must have felt that the court's sanction rendered the inheritances less vulnerable. Several months later, she appealed directly to Connecticut's governor, John Winthrop, Jr., requesting that Hartford's John and Jonathan Gilbert, and John Riley of Wethersfield, be appointed overseers of her estate.[36] Winthrop must not have granted her request, because in 1668 Harrison signed over the rest of the estate she had inherited from her husband to her daughters and appointed Jonathan and John Gilbert her daughters' guardians.[37] By the following year, her neighbors reported, she had "disposed of great part of her estate to others in trust."[38]

In June 1670, Katherine Harrison moved to Westchester, New York, to begin her life anew. Her reputation for witchcraft followed her, however, in the form of a complaint, filed in July by two of her new neighbors, that she had been allowed to resettle in Westchester. Noting that suspicion of her in Connecticut "hath given some cause of apprehension" to the townspeople, in order to "end their jealousyes and feares" a local New York magistrate told her to leave the jurisdiction.[39] Harrison refused. Before any action could be taken against her, her eldest daughter was fortuitously betrothed to Josiah Hunt, a son of Thomas Hunt, one of the men who had protested her presence in Westchester. The elder Hunt became a supporter and appeared in court on her behalf, with his son and three other influential men. Though she was required to give security for her "Civill carriage and good behaviour," the General Court of Assizes in New York ordered "that in regard there is nothing appears against her deserving the continuance of that obligacion shee is to bee releast from it, and hath Liberty to remaine in the Towne of Westchester where shee now resides, or any where else in the Government during her pleasure."[40]

Evidently Harrison continued to live with recurring witchcraft suspicion, but after 1670 there is no further evidence of official harassment.[41] Early in 1672, she reappeared in Hartford to sue eleven of her old Connecticut Valley neighbors, in most cases for debt, and to release her "intrusted overseer" Jonathan Gilbert from his responsibilities for her estate (although he continued to act as guardian to her two younger daughters).[42] A month later, she signed at least some of her remaining Wethersfield land over to Gilbert.[43] After that, she fades from view. She may have returned to Connecticut for good at that time, for some evidence suggests that she died at Dividend, then an outlying section of Wethersfield, in October 1682.[44]

SUSANNA MARTIN

Born in England in 1625, Susanna North was the youngest of three daughters of Richard North. Her mother died when Susanna was young and her father subsequently remarried. The family migrated to New England in or just prior to 1639, the year in which Richard North was listed as one of the first proprietors of Salisbury, Massachusetts. Susanna's sister Mary had married Thomas Jones and was living in Gloucester by 1642. Of her sister Sarah we know only that she married a man named Oldham, had a daughter named Ann, and died before the child was grown. In August 1646, at the age of twenty-one, Susanna married George Martin, a Salisbury man whose first wife had recently died. In June of the following year, she gave birth to her son Richard, the first of nine children. One of these children, a son, died in infancy.[45] . . .

Early in 1668, less than a year after the birth of her last child, Susanna Martin's father died, leaving a modest estate of about £150. As the only surviving children, the then forty-three-year-old Susanna and her sister Mary anticipated receiving a major portion of the property, to posses either immediately or after the death of their stepmother, Ursula North. They were disappointed. According to the will probated shortly after he died, Richard North had voided all previous wills and written a new one—*nearly two decades* before his death. In this document, dated January 1649, he left all but £22 of his estate directly to his wife. Twenty-one pounds was to be divided among Mary Jones, Susanna Martin, and Ann Bates (Sarah Oldham's daughter). Susanna's share was 20 shillings and the cancellation of a £10 debt George Martin owed his father-in-law. Listed as witnesses to this will were Thomas Bradbury of Salisbury and Mary Jones's daughter, Mary Winsley.[46] But the will raised problems. In 1649, Ann Bates was still Ann Oldham (she did not marry Francis Bates until

1661) and the Mary Winsley listed as witness to the will was still Mary Jones, at most eleven or twelve years old when it was allegedly written.[47] Despite the obvious irregularities, Thomas Bradbury and Mary Winsley attested in court that this was indeed Richard North's last will and testament.

Whether Susanna Martin and her sister saw or protested this will when it was probated cannot be determined. Susanna, at least, may have had more pressing concerns on her mind. In April 1669, a bond of £100 was posted for her appearance at the next Court of Assistants "upon suspicion of witchcraft." That was the same day that George Martin sued William Sargent for slandering his wife. According to George Martin, Sargent had not only said that Susanna "was a witch, and he would call her witch," but also accused her of having "had a child" while still single and of "wringing its neck" shortly after. George Martin also sued William Sargent's brother Thomas for saying "that his son George Marttin was a bastard and that Richard Marttin was Goodwife Marttin's imp."[48] . . .

Meanwhile, the magistrates bound Susanna Martin over to the higher court to be tried for witchcraft. Although the records have not survived, she must have been acquitted, because several months later she was at liberty. In October 1669, George Martin was again bound for his wife's appearance in court, not for witchcraft this time but for calling one of her neighbors a liar and a thief.[49]

By April 1671, George and Susanna Martin (Susanna's sister Mary Jones would later join them) were involved in what would become protracted litigation over the estate of Susanna's father. Ursula North had died a month or two before, leaving a will, dated shortly after her husband's death, that effectively disinherited her two stepdaughters by awarding them 40 shillings apiece. She left the rest of the original North estate first to her grandaughter, Mary Winsley, and secondarily to Mary and Nathaniel Winsley's only child, Hepzibah.[50]

The exact sequence of the numerous court hearings that followed is less clear. Evidently, Susanna and George Martin initiated legal proceedings against Mary and Nathaniel Winsley in April 1671, for unwarranted possession of the North estate. . . . In October 1672, the General Court responded, giving

Susanna Martin liberty to sue for her inheritance a second time at the local level.

In April 1673, the recently widowed Mary Jones and George Martin, acting for his wife, sued Nathaniel Winsley "for withholding the inheritance of housing, lands and other estate . . . under color of a feigned or confused writing like the handwriting of Mr. Thomas Bradbury and seemingly attested by him, and Mary Winsly." The court declared the case nonsuited, and again Susanna Martin appealed to the General Court, requesting that the case be reheard at the local level. The General Court consented in May 1673, and the following October, Susanna and George Martin instituted proceedings against the Winsleys for the third time. Again the county court decided for the defendants, and the Martins appealed to the Court of Assistants. For a while it looked as though things were finally going their way. The higher court, which "found for the plaintiff there being no legall prooffe of Richard North's will," ordered that "the estate the said North left be left to the disposall of the county court." . . .

[In 1674] Susanna, George, and Mary appealed a final time to the General Court, this time for "a hearing of the whole case" by the highest court itself. The magistrates agreed to hear the case, remitting the usual court fees, as they had done before, on the basis of Susanna's pleas of poverty. But in October 1674, after "perusall of what hath binn heard and alleadged by both parties," the court found for Nathaniel Winsley.[51] In what Susanna Martin and Mary Jones believed was a flagrant miscarriage of justice, they had lost what they considered their rightful inheritances.

For almost the next two decades, Susanna Martin's name rarely appears in the public records of the colony. Her sister Mary died in 1682, followed by her husband George in 1686.[52] Early in 1692, she was again accused of witchcraft, this time by several of the possessed females in Salem. They claimed that her apparition "greviously afflected" them, urging them to become witches themselves. Summoned before the court as witnesses against her were eleven men and four women, all old neighbors of the now sixty-seven-year-old widow.[53]

Unnerved by neither the agonies of the possessed or the magistrates' obvious belief in her guilt, Martin insisted that she was innocent. To Cotton Mather, she "was one of the most impudent, scurrilous, wicked Creatures in the World," who had the effrontery to claim "that she had lead a most virtuous and holy life."[54] Years of living as a reputed witch had left Martin well-versed on the subject of the Devil's powers. "He that appeared in sam[uel]s shape, a glorifyed saint," she said, citing the Bible in her own defense, "can appear in any ones shape." She laughed at the fits of her young accusers, explaining: "Well I may at such folly." When asked what she thought the possessed were experiencing, she said she did not know. Pressed to speculate on it, she retorted: "I do not desire to spend my judgment upon it" and added (revealing what must have been her long-standing opinion of the magistrates' bias), "my thoughts are my own, when they are in, but when they are out they are anothers."[55] . . .

Susanna Martin was found guilty of witch-craft and was one of five women executed on 19 July 1692. One week later, another Salisbury woman was indicted on the same charge. She was Mary Bradbury, the now elderly wife of the man Susanna Martin believed had written her father's "will" nearly twenty-five years before. Mary Bradbury was sentenced to hang too, but friends helped her to escape. No explicit connection between the accusations of the two women is discernible. Rumors circulated, however, that because Thomas Bradbury had friends in positions of authority, there had been little real effort to capture his fugitive wife.[56] . . .

These . . . short histories . . . suggest the diverse economic circumstances of witches in early New England. . . . The . . . women featured in these histories were either (1) daughters of parents who had no sons (or whose sons had died), (2) women in marriages which brought forth only daughters (or in which the sons had died), or (3) women in marriages with no children at all. These patterns had significant economic implications. Because there were no legitimate male heirs in their immediate families, each of these . . . women stood to inherit, did inherit, or were denied their apparent right to inherit substantially larger portions of their fathers' or husbands' accumulated estates than women in families with male heirs. Whatever actually happened to the property in question—and in some cases we simply do not know—these women were aberrations in a society with an inheritance system designed to keep property in the hands of men.

These . . . cases also illustrate fertility and mortality patterns widely shared among the families of accused witches. A substantial majority of New England's accused females were women without brothers, women with daughters but no sons, or women in marriages with no children at all (see Table 1). Of the 267 accused females, enough is known about 158 to identify them as either having or not having brothers or sons to inherit: only 62 of the 158 (39 percent) did, whereas 96 (61 percent) did not. More striking, *once accused*, women without brothers or sons were even more likely than women with brothers or sons to be tried, convicted, and executed: women from families without male heirs made up 64 percent of the females prosecuted, 76 percent of those who were found guilty, and 89 percent of those who were executed.

These figures must be read with care, however, for two reasons. First, eighteen of the sixty-two accused females who *had* brothers or sons to inherit were themselves daughters and granddaughters of women who did not. It appears that these eighteen females, most of whom were young women or girls, were accused because their neighbors believed that their mothers and grandmothers passed their witchcraft on to them. Therefore they form a somewhat ambiguous group. Since they all had brothers to inherit, it would be inaccurate to exclude them from this category in Table 1, yet including them understates the extent to which inheritance-related concerns were at issue in witchcraft accusations. At the same time, the large number of cases in which the fertility and mortality patterns of witches' families are unknown (109 of the 267 accused females in New England) makes it impossible to assess precisely the proportion of women among the accused who did not have brothers or sons.

Table 2 helps clarify the point. It includes as a separate category the daughters and granddaughters of women without brothers or sons and incorporates the cases for which this information is unknown. Although inclusion of the unknowns renders the overall percentages meaningless, this way of representing the available information shows clearly the particular vulnerability of women without brothers or sons. Even if *all* the unknown cases involved women from families *with* male heirs—a highly unlikely possibility—women from families without males to inherit would still form a majority of convicted and executed witches. Were the complete picture visible, I suspect that it would not differ substantially from that presented earlier in Table 1—which is based on data reflecting 60 percent of New England's witches and which indicates that women without brothers and sons were more vulnerable than other women at all stages of the process.

Numbers alone, however, do not tell the whole story. More remains to be said about what happened to these inheriting or potentially inheriting women, both before and after they were accused of witchcraft.

It was not unusual for women in families without male heirs to be accused of witchcraft shortly after the deaths of fathers, husbands, brothers, or sons. Katherine Harrison [and] Susanna Martin . . . exemplify this pattern. So too does elderly Ann Hibbens of Boston, whose execution in 1656 seems to have had a profound enough effect on some of her peers to influence the outcome of subsequent trials for years to come. Hibbens had three sons from her first marriage, all of whom lived in England; but she had no children by her husband William Hibbens, with whom she had come to Massachusetts in the 1630s. William died in 1654; Ann was brought to trial two years later. Although her husband's will has not survived, he apparently left a substantial portion (if not all) of his property directly to her: when she wrote her own will shortly before her execution, Ann Hibbens was in full possession of a £344 estate, most of which she bequeathed to her sons in England.[57]

TABLE 1. Female Witches by Presence or Absence of Brothers or Sons, New England, 1620–1725 (A)

Action	Women without Brothers or Sons	Women with Brothers or Sons	Total
Accused	96 (61%)	62 (39%)	158
Tried	41 (64%)	23 (36%)	64
Convicted	25 (76%)	8 (24%)	33
Executed	17 (89%)	2 (11%)	19

TABLE 2. Female Witches by Presence or Absence of Brothers or Sons, New England, 1620–1725 (B)

Action	Women without Brothers or Sons	Daughters and Granddaughters of Women without Brothers or Sons	Women with Brothers or Sons	Unknown Cases	Total
Accused	96 (36%)	18 (7%)	44 (16%)	109 (41%)	267
Tried	41 (48%)	6 (7%)	17 (20%)	22 (26%)	86
Convicted	25 (56%)	0 (0%)	6 (13%)	12 (27%)	45
Executed	17 (61%)	0 (0%)	2 (7%)	9 (32%)	28

Similarly, less than two years elapsed between the death of Gloucester's William Vinson and the imprisonment of his widow Rachel in 1692. Two children, a son and a daughter, had been born to the marriage, but the son had died in 1675. Though William Vinson had had four sons (and three daughters) by a previous marriage, the sons were all dead by 1683. In his will, which he wrote in 1684, before he was certain that his last son had been lost at sea, William left his whole £180 estate to Rachel for her life, stipulating that she could sell part of the lands and cattle if she found herself in need of resources. After Rachel's death, "in Case" his son John "be Living and returne home agayne," William said, most of the estate was to be divided between John and their daughter Abigail. If John did not return, both shares were to be Abigail's.[58] . . .

In other cases, many years passed between the death of the crucial male relative and the moment when a formal witchcraft complaint was filed.

. . . Mary English of Salem was charged with witchcraft seven years after she came into her inheritance. Her father, merchant William Hollingworth, had been declared lost at sea in 1677, but at that time Mary's brother William was still alive. Possibly because the younger William was handling the family's interests in other colonies, or possibly because the father's estate was in debt for more than it was worth, the magistrates gave the widow Elinor Hollingworth power of attorney to salvage what she could. With her "owne labor," as she put it, "but making use of other mens estates," the aggressive and outspoken Mistress Hollingworth soon had her deceased husband's debts paid and his wharf, warehouse, and tavern solvent again.[59] She had no sooner done so, however, than she was accused of witchcraft by the wife of a Gloucester mariner.[60] Though the magistrates gave little credence to the charge at the time, they may have had second thoughts later. In 1685, her son William died, and Elinor subsequently conveyed the whole Hollingworth estate over to Mary English, who was probably her only surviving child.[61]

Elinor Hollingworth had died by 1692, but Mary English was one of the women cried out upon early in the Salem outbreak. Her husband, the merchant Philip English, was accused soon after. Knowing their lives were in grave danger, the Englishes fled to the safety of New York. But as one historian of witchcraft has pointed out, flight was "the legal equivalent of conviction."[62] No sooner had they left than close to £1200 of their property was confiscated under the law providing attainder for witchcraft.[63]

Not all witches from families without male heirs were accused of conspiring with the Devil *after* they had come into their inheritances. On the contrary, some were accused prior to the death of the crucial male relative, many times before it was clear who would inherit. . . . [O]ne of these women . . . was Martha Corey of Salem, who was accused of witchcraft in 1692 while her husband was still alive. Giles Corey had been married twice before and had several daughters by the time he married the widow Martha Rich, probably in the 1680s. With no sons to inherit, Giles's substantial land holdings would, his neighbors might have assumed, be passed on to his wife and daughters. Alice Parker, who may have been Giles's daughter from a former marriage, also came before the magistrates as a witch in 1692, as did Giles himself. Martha

Corey and Alice Parker maintained their innocence and were hanged. Giles Corey, in an
apparently futile attempt to preserve his whole
estate for his heirs, refused to respond to the
indictment. To force him to enter a plea, he
was tortured: successively heavier weights
were placed on his body until he was pressed
to death.[64]

What seems especially significant here is
that most accused witches whose husbands
were still alive were, like their counterparts
who were widows and spinsters, over forty
years of age—and therefore unlikely if not
unable to produce male heirs. Indeed, the fact
that witchcraft accusations were rarely taken
seriously by the community until the accused
stopped bearing children takes on a special
meaning when it is juxtaposed with the anomalous position of inheriting women or potentially inheriting women in New England's
social structure.

Witches in families without male heirs
sometimes had been dispossessed of part or all
of their inheritances before—sometimes long
before—they were formally charged with
witchcraft. Few of these women, however,
accepted disinheritance with equanimity.
Rather, like Susanna Martin, they took their
battles to court, casting themselves in the role
of public challengers to the system of male
inheritance. In most instances, the authorities
sided with their antagonists. . . .

. . . The property of women in families
without male heirs was vulnerable to loss in a
variety of ways, from deliberate destruction by
neighbors (as Katherine Harrison experienced)
to official sequestering by local magistrates. In
nearly every case, the authorities themselves
seem hostile or at best indifferent to the property claims of these women. One final example deserves mention here, not only because it
indicates how reluctant magistrates were to
leave property in the control of women, but
because it shows that the property of convicted
witches was liable to seizure even without the
benefit of an attainder law.

Rebecca Greensmith had been widowed
twice before her marriage to Nathaniel Greensmith. Her first husband, Abraham Elsen of
Wethersfield, had died intestate in 1648, leaving an estate £99. After checking the birth dates
of the Elsens' two children, three-year-old
Sarah and one-year-old Hannah, the court initially left the whole estate with the widow.

When Rebecca married Wethersfield's Jarvis
Mudge the following year, the local magistrates
sequestered the house and land Abraham Elsen
had left, worth £40, stating their intention to
rent it out "for the Use and Benefit of the two
daughters."[65] The family moved to New London shortly after, but Jarvis Mudge died in 1652
and Rebecca moved with Hannah and Sarah to
Hartford. Since Rebecca was unable to support
herself and her two daughters, the court
allowed her to sell the small amount of land
owned by her second husband (with whom she
had had no children) "for the paing of debts and
the Bettering the Childrens portyons."[66]

Sometime prior to 1660, Rebecca married
Nathaniel Greensmith. During the Hartford
outbreak, Rebecca came under suspicion of
witchcraft. After Nathaniel sued his wife's
accuser for slander, Nathaniel himself was
named. Both husband and wife were convicted and executed.[67]

Respecting Nathaniel's £182 estate, £44 of
which was claimed by the then eighteen-year-
old Sarah and seventeen-year-old Hannah
Elsen, the court ordered the three overseers "to
preserve the estate from Waste" and to pay
"any just debts," the only one recorded being
the Greensmiths' jail fees. Except for allowing
the overseers "to dispose of the 2 daughters,"
presumably to service, the magistrates postponed until the next court any decision concerning the young women's portions. First,
however, they deducted £40 to go "to the Treasurer for the County."[68] No reason was given
for this substantial appropriation and no
record of further distribution of the estate has
survived.

Aside from these many women who lived or
had lived in families without male heirs, there
were at least a dozen other witches who,
despite the presence of brothers and sons,
came into much larger shares of estates than
their neighbors would have expected. In some
cases, these women gained full control over
the disposition of property. We know about
these women because their fathers, husbands,
or other relatives left wills, because the women
themselves wrote wills, or because male relatives who felt cheated out of their customary
shares fought in the courts for more favorable
arrangements.

Grace Boulter of Hampton, one of several
children of Richard Swain, is one of these

women. Grace was accused of witchcraft in 1680, along with her thirty-two-year-old daughter, Mary Prescott. Twenty years earlier, in 1660, just prior to his removal to Nantucket, Grace's father had deeded a substantial portion of his Hampton property to her and her husband Nathaniel, some of which he gave directly to her.[69]

Another witch in this group is Jane James of Marblehead, who left an estate at her death in 1669 which was valued at £85. While it is not clear how she came into possession of it, the property had not belonged to her husband Erasmus, who had died in 1660, though it did play a significant role in a controversy between her son and son-in-law over their rightful shares of both Erasmus's and Jane's estates. Between 1650 and her death in 1669, Jane was accused of witchcraft at least three times by her Marblehead neighbors. . . .[70]

Looking back over the lives of these many women—most particularly those who did not have brothers or sons to inherit—we begin to understand the complexity of the economic dimension of New England witchcraft. Only rarely does the actual trial testimony indicate that economic power was even at issue. Nevertheless it is there, recurring with a telling persistence once we look beyond what was explicitly said about these women as witches. Inheritance disputes surface frequently enough in witchcraft cases, cropping up as part of the general context even when no direct link between the dispute and the charge is discernible, to suggest the fears that underlay most accusations. No matter how deeply entrenched the principle of male inheritance, no matter how carefully written the laws that protected it, it was impossible to insure that all families had male offspring. The women who stood to benefit from these demographic "accidents" account for most of New England's female witches.

The amount of property in question was not the crucial factor in the way these women were viewed or treated by their neighbors, however. Women of widely varying economic circumstances were vulnerable to accusation and even to conviction. Neither was there a direct line from accuser to material beneficiary of the accusation: others in the community did sometimes profit personally from the losses sustained by these women . . . , but only rarely did the gain accrue to the accusers themselves.

Indeed, occasionally there was no direct temporal connection: in some instances several decades passed between the creation of the key economic conditions and the charge of witchcraft; the charge in other cases even anticipated the development of those conditions.

Finally, inheriting or potentially inheriting women were vulnerable to witchcraft accusations not only during the Salem outbreak, but from the time of the first formal accusations in New England at least until the end of the century. . . . The Salem outbreak created only a slight wrinkle in this established fabric of suspicion. If daughters, husbands, and sons of witches were more vulnerable to danger in 1692 than they had been previously, they were mostly the daughters, husbands, and sons of inheriting or potentially inheriting women. As the outbreak spread, it drew into its orbit increasing numbers of women, "unlikely" witches in that they were married to well-off and influential men, but familiar figures to some of their neighbors nonetheless. What the impoverished Sarah Good had in common with Mary Phips, wife of Massachusetts's governor, was what Eunice Cole had in common with Katherine Harrison. . . . However varied their backgrounds and economic positions, as women without brothers or women without sons, they stood in the way of the orderly transmission of property from one generation of males to another.

NOTES

1. Alan Macfarlane, *Witchcraft in Tudor and Stuart England: A Regional and Comparative Study* (New York, 1970), pp. 149–51. See also Keith Thomas, *Religion and the Decline of Magic* (New York, 1971), pp. 457, 520–21, 560–68.

2. See Trials for Witchcraft in New England (unpaged), dated 5 September 1656 (manuscript volume, Houghton Library, Harvard University, Cambridge, Mass.).

3. Relying on very general indicators (a married woman who worked as a servant, a widow whose husband had left an estate of £39, and so forth), I was able to make rough estimates about the economic position of 150 accused women. Twenty-nine of these women seem to have been poor. . . .

4. For Abigail Somes, see *The Salem Witchcraft Papers: Verbatim Transcripts of the Legal Documents of the Salem Witchcraft Outbreak of 1692*, 3 vols., ed. Paul Boyer and Stephen Nissenbaum (New York, 1977), 3:733–37 (hereafter cited as *Witchcraft Papers*). For Tituba, see *Witchcraft Papers* 3:745–57. Documents relating to Ruth Wilford are in *Witchcraft Papers*

2:459; 3:961; *The Probate Records of Essex County, Massachusetts, 1635–1681*, 3 vols. (Salem, 1916–20), 3:93–95 (hereafter cited as *Essex Probate Records*).

5. Most families in seventeenth-century New England had estates worth less than £200. However, since only a very small proportion of convicted witches who were married seem to have come from families with estates worth *more* than £200, it seems reasonable to conclude that married women from families with less than £200 estates were overrepresented among the accused. Nearly all of the convictions of married women from families with estates worth more than £200 occurred during the Salem outbreak. . . .

6. For accusations against Hannah Griswold and Margaret Gifford, see Norbert B. Lacy, "The Records of the Court of Assistants of Connecticut, 1665–1701" (M.A. thesis, Yale University, 1937), pp. 6–7 (hereafter cited as "Conn. Assistants Records"); and *Records and Files of the Quarterly Courts of Essex County, Massachusetts*, 9 vols. (Salem, 1912–75), 7:405; 8:23 (hereafter cited as *Essex Court Records*).

7. This discussion of the inheritance system of seventeenth-century New England is drawn from the following sources: *The Book of the General Lawes and Libertyes Concerning the Inhabitants of the Massachusetts*, ed. Thomas G. Barnes (facsimile from the 1648 edition, San Marino, Calif., 1975); *The Colonial Laws of Massachusetts. Reprinted from the Edition of 1672, with the Supplements through 1686*, ed. William H. Whitmore (Boston, 1887); John D. Cushing, comp., *The Laws and Liberties of Massachusetts, 1641–91: A Facsimile Edition*, 3 vols. (Wilmington, Del., 1976); *Massachusetts Province Laws, 1692–1699*, ed. John D. Cushing (Wilmington, Del., 1978); *New Hampshire Probate Records; Essex Probate Records: A Digest of the Early Connecticut Probate Records*, vol. 1, ed. Charles W. Manwaring (Hartford, 1904) (hereafter cited as *Conn. Probate Records*); Marylynn Salmon, *Women and the Law of Property in Early America* (Chapel Hill, 1986); George L. Haskins, "The Beginnings of Partible Inheritance in the American Colonies," in *Essays in the History of American Law*, ed. David H. Flaherty (Chapel Hill, 1969); Edmund S. Morgan, *The Puritan Family: Religion and Domestic Relations in Seventeenth-Century New England* (1944; reprint New York, 1966).

8. See Morgan, *The Puritan Family*, pp. 81–82.

9. Barnes, *Book of the General Lawes*, pp. 17–18. . . .

10. Since only a small proportion of men left wills during the colonial period, intestacy law played a significant role in determining inheritance practices. See Salmon, *Women and the Law of Property*, p. 141.

11. Barnes, *The Book of the General Lawes*, p. 53.

12. Young women officially came of age in New England when they reached 18; young men when they reached 21.

13. William Blackstone, *Commentaries on the Laws of England*, 4 vols. (Oxford, 1765–69), 1:433.

14. Once widowed, a woman who inherited land from her father (or who had bought land with her husband in both of their names) could make a will of her own, as could a single woman who came

into possession of land. . . . See Salmon, *Women and the Law of Property*, pp. 144–45 and passim.

15. Evidence suggests that in seventeenth-century New England, daughters of fathers who died relatively young (and possibly most sons) did not normally come into their inheritances until they married. If daughters had received their shares when they came of age, we would expect to find probate records for single women who died before they had the opportunity to marry. Though there are many existing intestate records and wills for single men who died in early adulthood, I have located only one record involving a young, single woman.

16. Wethersfield Land Records (manuscript volume, Town Clerk's Office, Town Hall, Wethersfield, Conn.) 1:19, 38.

17. Given the ages of her children, Katherine Harrison had to have been between her late twenties and her mid-fifties when she was first accused of witchcraft in 1668. I suspect that she was in her forties.

18. See Wethersfield Land Records 2:149; Katherine Harrison to John Winthrop, Jr., undated letter (probably early 1667), and Katherine Harrison's Testimony, undated document (probably October 1669), in the Winthrop Papers, Massachusetts Historical Society, Boston (hereafter cited as Winthrop Papers). . . .

19. Samuel Wyllys Papers: Depositions on Cases of Witchcraft, Assault, Theft, Drunkenness and Other Crimes, Tried in Connecticut, 1663–1728 (manuscript volume, Archives, History and Genealogy Unit, Connecticut State Library, Hartford, doc. 15) (hereafter cited as Wyllys Papers).

20. See Sherman W. Adams and Henry R. Stiles, *The History of Ancient Wethersfield*, 2 vols. (New York, 1904), 1:682; and Lacy, "Conn. Assistants Records," p. 12.

21. Lacy, "Conn. Assistants Records," p. 13.

22. Petition for the Investigation of Katherine Harrison, Recently Released after Imprisonment, Signed by John Chester and Thirty-Eight Other Citizens of Wethersfield (Manuscript Collections, Connecticut Historical Society, Hartford [hereafter cited as Petition for the Investigation of Katherine Harrison]) (emphasis mine). See also Order about Katherine Harrison's Land, in the Winthrop Papers. . . .

23. Lacy, "Conn. Assistants Records," pp. 13–14, 18–19.

24. "The Answers of Some Ministers to the Questions Propounded to Them by the Honored Magistrates," dated 20 October 1669, Samuel Wyllys Papers, Supplement: Depositions on Cases of Witchcraft Tried in Connecticut, 1662–1693, photostat copies of original documents from the Wyllys Papers, Annmary Brown Memorial Brown University Library, Providence, R.I. . . .

25. Lacy, "Conn. Assistants Records," p. 23. . . .

26. Wyllys Papers Supplement, p. 11.

27. Depositions submitted against Harrison in 1668 and 1669 are in the Wyllys Papers, docs. 6–17; Wyllys Papers Supplement, pp. 46–63. . . . For Harrison's response to these accusations, see Katherine Harrison's Testimony, Winthrop Papers.

28. Manwaring, *Conn. Probate Records* 1:206.

29. "A Complaint of Severall Greevances of the Widdow Harrison's," Wyllys Papers Supplement, p. 53.

30. "The Declaration of Katherine Harrison in Her Appeal to This Court of Assistants," dated September 1668, in Connecticut Archives, Crimes and Misdemeanors, 1st ser. (1662–1789) (manuscript volume, Archives, History and Genealogy Unit, Connecticut State Library, Hartford), vol. 1 (pt. 1):34 (hereafter cited as Crimes and Misdemeanors).

31. Connecticut Colonial Probate Records 56:80; Records of the Colony of Connecticut, Connecticut Colonial Probate Records, County Court, vol. 56, 1663–77 (Archives, History and Genealogy Unit, Connecticut State Library, Hartford, 56:79–81 (hereafter cited as Connecticut Colonial Probate Records).

32. Ibid., pp. 78–79. For the Griswolds as accusers, see Katherine Harrison's Testimony, Winthrop Papers.

33. Connecticut Colonial Probate Records 56:80.

34. "The Declaration of Katherine Harrison," Crimes and Misdemeanors, 1 (pt. 1):34.

35. Manwaring, *Connecticut Probate Records*, p. 206.

36. Katherine Harrison to John Winthrop, Jr., "Letter," Winthrop Papers.

37. Wethersfield Land Records 2:149.

38. Petition for the Investigation of Katherine Harrison.

39. See "The Cases of Hall and Harrison," in *Narratives of the Witchcraft Cases, 1648–1706*, ed. Charles Lincoln Burr (New York, 1914), pp. 48–49.

40. Ibid., pp. 48–52.

41. See Samuel D. Drake, *Annals of Witchcraft in New England* (New York, 1869), pp. 133–34.

42. Connecticut Colonial Probate Records 56:118; Wethersfield Land Records 2:249.

43. Wethersfield Land Records 2:210.

44. See Gilbert Collection.

45. See Joseph Merrill, *History of Amesbury, Including the First Seventeen Years of Salisbury.* . . . (Haverhill, Mass., 1880), pp. 11–13, 28; *Vital Records of Salisbury* . . . (Topsfield, Mass., 1915), pp. 151, 415.

46. *Essex Probate Records* 2:125–27.

47. James Savage, *A Genealogical Dictionary of the First Settlers of New England,* 4 vols. (Boston, 1860–62), 1:138; 4:483.

48. See *Essex Court Records* 4:129, 133.

49. *Essex Court Records* 4:184, 187, 239.

50. *Essex Probate Records* 2:223–24.

51. See *Records of the Governor and Company of the Massachusetts Bay in New England,* 6 vols., ed. Nathaniel B. Shurtleff (Boston, 1853–54), 5:6, 26–27.

52. Savage, *Genealogical Dictionary* 2:566. . . . When he died, George Martin left an estate valued at £75, most of which he left to Susanna "during her Widowhood."

53. See *Witchcraft Papers* 2:549–79.

54. Cotton Mather, *The Wonders of the Invisible World* (1693; facsimile of the 1862 London edition, Ann Arbor, Mich., 1974), p. 148.

55. *Witchcraft Papers* 2:551.

56. *Witchcraft Papers* 1:115–29.

57. Ann Hibbens' will is reprinted in *New England Historical and Genealogical Register,* vol. 6 (1852), pp. 287–88.

58. See *Witchcraft Papers* 3:880–81.

59. *Essex Probate Records* 3:191–93.

60. *Essex Court Records* 7:238.

61. *New England Historical and Genealogical Register,* vol. 3 (1849), p. 129.

62. Marion L. Starkey, *The Devil in Massachusetts* (New York, 1949), p. 185.

63. *Witchcraft Papers* 3:988–91.

64. For Martha and Giles Corey and Alice Parker, see *Witchcraft Papers* 1:239–66; 2:623–28, 632–33; 3:985–86, 1018–19.

65. Manwaring, *Conn. Probate Records* 1:7–8.

66. *Records of the Particular Court of Connecticut, 1639–1663, Collections of the Connecticut Historical Society,* vol. 22 (1928), p. 119.

67. Ibid., p. 258.

68. Manwaring, *Conn. Probate Records* 1:121–22.

69. Norfolk Deeds (manuscript volume, Registry of Deeds, Essex County Courthouse, Salem, Mass.), 1:116, 154.

70. *Essex Probate Records* 1:314–16; 2:160; *Essex Court Records* 1:199, 204, 229; 2:213; 3:292, 342, 413.

CORNELIA HUGHES DAYTON

Taking the Trade:
Abortion and Gender Relations in an
Eighteenth-Century New England Village

Some pregnancies end spontaneously, probably because of an abnormality in the fetus or in the way it is implanted in the womb. Colonial Americans made little distinction between spontaneous and induced abortion; no law attempted to regulate the practice. Efforts to end pregnancies by the use of herbs like savin were generally understood to be efforts to "restore" the regular menstrual cycle. Experienced midwives had impressive records of safe deliveries that are comparable to pre-penicillin twentieth-century experience; Martha Ballard of rural Maine brought some 900 women safely through childbirth in the late eighteenth century.*

In the course of the eighteenth century, male physicians were increasingly involved with midwifery, a practice that had been monopolized by women. Men were also more likely than women midwives to use instruments; indeed only men were trained in the use of the first forceps. In the following essay, Cornelia Hughes Dayton carefully reconstructs the narrative of the abortion and death of Sarah Grosvenor in a Connecticut village in 1742. How does Dayton interpret the meaning of abortion for Sarah Grosvenor and her friends? If it was not illegal, why did they seek to keep it secret? In what ways does Dayton think that relations between young women and young men changed in the mid-eighteenth century? In what ways does Dayton think that relations between young people and their parents changed? How was the memory of Sarah Grosvenor's death transmitted in the histories of the town?

In 1742 in the village of Pomfret, perched in the hills of northeastern Connecticut, nineteen-year-old Sarah Grosvenor and twenty-seven-year-old Amasa Sessions became involved in a liaison that led to pregnancy, abortion, and death. Both were from prominent yeoman families, and neither a marriage between them nor an arrangement for the support of their illegitimate child would have been an unusual event for mid-eighteenth-century New England. Amasa Sessions chose a different course; in consultation with John Hallowell, a self-proclaimed "practitioner of physick," he coerced his lover into taking an abortifacient. Within two months, Sarah fell ill. Unbeknownst to all but Amasa, Sarah, Sarah's sister Zerviah, and her cousin Hannah, Hallowell made an attempt to "Remove her Conseption" by a "manual opperation." Two days later Sarah miscarried, and her two young relatives secretly buried the fetus in the woods. Over the next month, Sarah struggled against a "Malignant fever" and was attended by several physicians, but on September 14, 1742, she died.[1]

Most accounts of induced abortions among seventeenth- and eighteenth-century

*Laurel Thatcher Ulrich, "'The Living Mother of a Living Child': Midwifery and Mortality in Post-Revolutionary New England," *William and Mary Quarterly* 3rd Ser., XLVI (1989): 27–48.

Excerpted from "Taking the Trade: Abortion and Gender Relations in an Eighteenth-Century New England Village" by Cornelia Hughes Dayton in *William and Mary Quarterly*, 3rd Ser., 48 (1991):19–49. Notes have been edited.

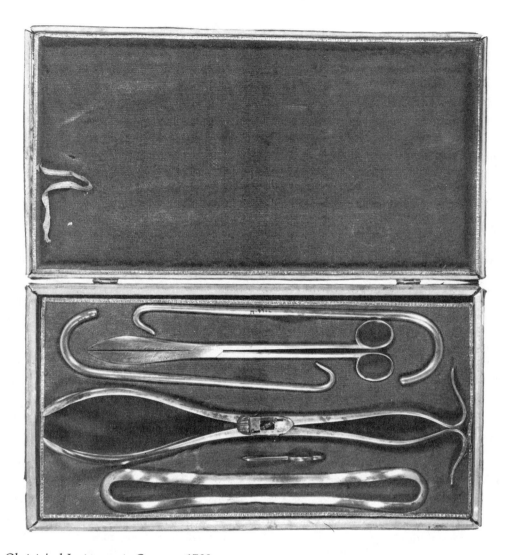

Obstetrical Instruments Case, ca. 1780.
The case includes forceps, a double lever, two double blunt hooks, and a perforator. Perhaps no technological invention in traditional America had more direct connection to women's lives than these. Hooks were used to dismember and remove a fetus that had died during delivery. Skillfully employed, forceps could be lifesaving. Professional training in the use of instruments was monopolized by male physicians, to whom the middle class turned in the late eighteenth and early nineteenth centuries. Advances in medical technology were accompanied by the exclusion of mid-wives from advanced training and, increasingly, from the birthing room itself. (Division of Medical Sciences, National Museum of American History, Smithsonian Institution)

whites in the Old and New Worlds consist of only a few lines in a private letter or court record book; these typically refer to the taking of savin or pennyroyal—two common herbal abortifacients. While men and women in diverse cultures have known how to perform abortions by inserting an instrument into the uterus, actual descriptions of such operations are extremely rare for any time period. Few accounts of abortions by instrument have yet been uncovered for early modern England, and I know of no other for colonial North America.[2] Thus the historical fragments recording events in a small New England town in 1742 take on an unusual power to illustrate how an abortion was conducted, how it was talked about, and how it was punished.

We know about the Grosvenor-Sessions case because in 1745 two prominent Windham County magistrates opened an investigation into Sarah's death. Why there was a three-year gap between that event and legal proceedings, and why justices from outside Pomfret initiated the legal process, remain a mystery. In November 1745 the investigating magistrates offered their preliminary opinion that Hallowell, Amasa Sessions, Zerviah Grosvenor, and Hannah Grosvenor were guilty of Sarah's murder, the last three as accessories. From the outset, Connecticut legal officials concentrated not on the act of abortion per se, but on the fact that an abortion attempt had led to a young woman's death.[3]

The case went next to Joseph Fowler, king's attorney for Windham County. He dropped charges against the two Grosvenor women, probably because he needed them as key witnesses and because they had played cover-up roles rather than originating the scheme. A year and a half passed as Fowler's first attempts to get convictions against Hallowell and Sessions failed either before grand juries or before the Superior Court on technical grounds. Finally, in March 1747, Fowler presented Hallowell and Sessions separately for the "highhanded Misdemeanour" of to destroy both Sarah Grosvenor's health and "the fruit of her womb."[4] A grand jury endorsed the bill against Hallowell but rejected a similarly worded presentment against Sessions. At Hallowell's trial before the Superior Court in Windham, the jury brought in a guilty verdict and the chief judge sentenced the physician to twenty-nine lashes and two

hours of public humiliation standing at the town gallows. Before the sentence could be executed, Hallowell managed to break jail. He fled to Rhode Island; as far as records indicate, he never returned to Connecticut. Thus, in the end, both Amasa Sessions and John Hallowell escaped legal punishment for their actions, whereas Sarah Grosvenor paid for her sexual transgression with her life.

Nearly two years of hearings and trials before the Superior Court produced a file of ten depositions and twenty-four other legal documents. This cache of papers is extraordinarily rich, not alone for its unusual chronicle of an abortion attempt, but for its illumination of the fault lines in Pomfret dividing parents from grown children, men from women, and mid-eighteenth-century colonial culture from its seventeenth-century counterpart.

The depositions reveal that in 1742 the elders of Pomfret, men and women alike, failed to act as vigilant monitors of Sarah Grosvenor's courtship and illness. Instead, young, married householders—kin of Sarah and Amasa—pledged themselves in a conspiracy of silence to allow the abortion plot to unfold undetected. The one person who had the opportunity to play middleman between the generations was Hallowell. A man in his forties, dogged by a shady past and yet adept at acquiring respectable connections, Hallowell provides an intriguing and rare portrait of a socially ambitious, rural medical practitioner. By siding with the young people of Pomfret and keeping their secret, Hallowell betrayed his peers and elders and thereby opened himself to severe censure and expulsion from the community.

Beyond depicting generational conflict, the Grosvenor-Sessions case dramatically highlights key changes in gender relations that reverberated through New England society in the eighteenth century. One of these changes involved the emergence of a marked sexual double standard. In the mid-seventeenth century, a young man like Amasa Sessions would have been pressured by parents, friends, or the courts to marry his lover. Had he resisted, he would most likely have been whipped or fined for the crime of fornication. By the late seventeenth century, New England judges gave up on enjoining sexually active couples to marry. In the 1740s, amid shifting standards of sexual behavior and growing concern over the evidentiary impossibility of establishing paternity, prosecutions of young men for premarital sex ceased. Thus fornication was decriminalized for men, but not for women. Many of Sarah Grosvenor's female peers continued to be prosecuted and fined for bearing illegitimate children. Through private arrangements, and occasionally through civil lawsuits, their male partners were sometimes cajoled or coerced into contributing to the child's upkeep.[5]

What is most striking about the Grosvenor-Sessions case is that an entire community apparently forgave Sessions for the extreme measures he took to avoid accountability for his bastard child. Although he initiated the actions that led to his lover's death, all charges against him were dropped. Moreover, the tragedy did not spur Sessions to leave town; instead, he spent the rest of his life in Pomfret as a respected citizen. Even more dramatically than excusing young men from the crime of fornication, the treatment of Amasa Sessions confirmed that the sexually irresponsible activities of men in their youth would not be held against them as they reached for repute and prosperity in their prime.

The documents allow us to listen in on the quite different responses of young men and women to the drama unfolding in Pomfret. Sarah Grosvenor's female kin and friends, as we shall see, became preoccupied with their guilt and with the inevitability of God's vengeance. Her male kin, on the other hand, reacted cautiously and legalistically, ferreting out information in order to assess how best to protect the Grosvenor family name. The contrast reminds us yet again of the complex and gendered ways in which we must rethink conventional interpretations of secularization in colonial New England.

Finally, the Grosvenor case raises more questions than it answers about New Englanders' access to and attitudes toward abortion. If Sarah had not died after miscarriage, it is doubtful that any word of Sessions's providing her with an abortifacient or Hallowell's operation would have survived into the twentieth century. Because it nearly went unrecorded and because it reveals that many Pomfret residents were familiar with the idea of abortion, the case supports historians' assumptions that abortion attempts were far from rare in colonial America.[6] We can also infer from the case that the most dangerous

abortions before 1800 may have been those instigated by men and performed by surgeons with instruments.[7] But both abortion's frequency and the lineaments of its social context remain obscure. . . .

Perhaps the most intriguing question centers on why women and men in early America acted *covertly* to effect abortions when abortion before quickening was legal. The Grosvenor case highlights the answer that applies to most known incidents from the period: abortion was understood as blameworthy because it was an extreme action designed to hide a prior sin, sex outside of marriage.[8] Reading the depositions, it is nearly impossible to disentangle the players' attitudes toward abortion itself from their expressions of censure or anxiety over failed courtship, illegitimacy, and the dangers posed for a young woman by a secret abortion. Strikingly absent from these eighteenth-century documents, however, is either outrage over the destruction of a fetus or denunciations of those who would arrest "nature's proper course." Those absences are a telling measure of how the discourse about abortion would change dramatically in later centuries.

THE NARRATIVE

Before delving into the response of the Pomfret community to Sarah Grosvenor's abortion and death, we need to know just who participated in the conspiracy to cover up her pregnancy and how they managed it. . . .

The chronicle opens in late July 1742 when Zerviah Grosvenor, aged twenty-one, finally prevailed upon her younger sister to admit that she was pregnant. In tears, Sarah explained that she had not told Zerviah sooner because "she had been taking [the] trade to remove it."[9] "Trade" was used in this period to signify stuff or goods, often in the deprecatory sense of rubbish and trash. The *Oxford English Dictionary* confirms that in some parts of England and New England the word was used to refer to medicine. In Pomfret trade meant a particular type of medicine, an abortifacient, thus a substance that might be regarded as "bad" medicine, as rubbish, unsafe and associated with destruction. What is notable is that Sarah and Zerviah, and neighboring young people who also used the word, had no need to explain to one another the meaning of "taking the trade."

Perhaps only a few New Englanders knew how to prepare an abortifacient or knew of books that would give them recipes, but many more, especially young women who lived with the fear of becoming pregnant before marriage, were familiar with at least the *idea* of taking an abortifacient.

Sarah probably began taking the trade in mid-May when she was already three-and-a-half-months pregnant.[10] It was brought to her in the form of a powder by Amasa.[11] Sarah understood clearly that her lover had obtained the concoction "from docter hollowel," who conveyed "directions" for her doses through Amasa. Zerviah deposed later that Sarah had been "loath to Take" the drug and "Thot it an Evil," probably because at three and a half months she anticipated quickening, the time from which she knew the law counted abortion an "unlawful measure."[12] At the outset, Sarah argued in vain with Amasa against his proposed "Method." Later, during June and July, she sometimes "neglected" to take the doses he left for her, but, with mounting urgency, Amasa and the doctor pressed her to comply. "It was necessary," Amasa explained in late July, that she take "more, or [else] they were afraid She would be greatly hurt by what was already done." To calm her worries, he assured her that "there was no life [left] in the Child" and that the potion "would not hurt her." Apparently, the men hoped that a few more doses would provoke a miscarriage, thereby expelling the dead fetus and restoring Sarah's body to its natural balance of humors.

Presumably, Hallowell decided to operate in early August because Sarah's pregnancy was increasingly visible, and he guessed that she was not going to miscarry. An operation in which the fetus would be removed or punctured was now the only certain way to terminate the pregnancy secretly.[13] To avoid the scrutiny of Sarah's parents, Hallowell resorted to a plan he had used once before in arranging a private examination of Sarah. Early one afternoon he arrived at the house of John Grosvenor and begged for a room as "he was weary and wanted Rest." John, Sarah's thirty-one-year-old first cousin, lived with his wife, Hannah, and their young children in a homestead only a short walk down the hill but out of sight of Sarah's father's house. While John and Hannah were busy, the physician sent one of the little children to fetch Sarah.

The narrative of Sarah's fateful meeting with Hallowell that August afternoon is best told in the words of one of the deponents. Abigail Nightingale had married and moved to Pomfret two years earlier, and by 1742 she had become Sarah's close friend. Several weeks after the operation, Sarah attempted to relieve her own "Distress of mind" by confiding the details of her shocking experience to Abigail. Unconnected to the Grosvenor or Sessions families by kinship, and without any other apparent stake in the legal uses of her testimony, Abigail can probably be trusted as a fairly accurate paraphraser of Sarah's words.[14] If so, we have here an unparalleled eyewitness account of an eighteenth-century abortion attempt.

This is how Abigail recollected Sarah's deathbed story:

> On [Sarah's] going down [to her cousin John's], [Hallowell] said he wanted to Speake with her alone; and then they two went into a Room together; and then sd. Hallowell told her it was necessary that something more should be done or else she would Certainly die; to which she replyed that she was afraid they had done too much already, and then he told her that there was one thing more that could easily be done, and she asking him what it was; he said he could easily deliver her. but she said she was afraid there was life in the Child, then he asked her how long she had felt it; and she replyed about a fortnight; then he said that was impossible or could not be or ever would; for that the trade she had taken had or would prevent it; and that the alteration she felt Was owing to what she had taken. And he farther told her that he verily thought that the Child grew to her body to the Bigness of his hand, or else it would have Come away before that time. and that it would never Come away, but Certainly Kill her, unless other Means were used.[15] On which she yielded to his making an Attempt to take it away; charging him that if he could perceive that there was life in it he would not proceed on any Account. And then the Doctor openning his portmantua took an Instrument out of it and Laid it on the Bed, and she asking him what it was for, he replyed that it was to make way; and that then he tryed to remove the Child for Some time in vain putting her to the Utmost Distress, and that at Last she observed he trembled and immediately perceived a Strange alteration in her body and thought a bone of the Child was broken; on which she desired him (as she said) to Call in some body, for that she feared she was a dying, and instantly swooned away.

With Sarah's faint, Abigail's account broke off, but within minutes others, who would testify later, stepped into the room. Hallowell reacted to Sarah's swoon by unfastening the door and calling in Hannah, the young mistress of the house, and Zerviah, who had followed her sister there. Cold water and "a bottle of drops" were brought to keep Sarah from fainting again, while Hallowell explained to the "much Surprized" women that "he had been making an Attempt" to deliver Sarah. Despite their protests, he then "used a further force upon her" but did not succeed in "Tak[ing] the Child . . . away." Some days later Hallowell told a Pomfret man that in this effort "to distroy hir conception" he had "either knipt or Squeisd the head of the Conception." At the time of the attempt, Hallowell explained to the women that he "had done so much to her, as would Cause the Birth of the Child in a Little time." Just before sunset, he packed up his portmanteau and went to a nearby tavern, where Amasa was waiting "to hear [the outcome of] the event." Meanwhile, Sarah, weak-kneed and in pain, leaned on the arm of her sister as the young women managed to make their way home in the twilight.

After his attempted "force," Hallowell fades from the scene, while Zerviah and Hannah Grosvenor become the key figures. About two days after enduring the operation, Sarah began to experience contractions. Zerviah ran to get Hannah, telling her "she Tho't . . . Sarah would be quickly delivered." They returned to find Sarah, who was alone "in her Father's Chamber," just delivered and rising from the chamber pot. In the pot was "an Untimely birth"—a "Child [that] did not Appear to have any Life In it." To Hannah, it "Seemed by The Scent . . . That it had been hurt and was decaying," while Zerviah later remembered it as "a perfect Child," even "a pritty child." Determined to keep the event "as private as they Could," the two women helped Sarah back to bed, and then "wr[ap]ed . . . up" the fetus, carried it to the woods on the edge of the farmstead, and there "Buried it in the Bushes."

. . . [A]bout ten days after the miscarriage, Sarah grew feverish and weak. Her parents consulted two college-educated physicians who hailed from outside the Pomfret area. Their visits did little good, nor were Sarah's symptoms—fever, delirium, convul-

sions—relieved by a visit from Hallowell, whom Amasa "fetcht" to Sarah's bedside. In the end, Hallowell, who had decided to move from nearby Killingly to more distant Providence, washed his hands of the case. A few days before Sarah died, her cousin John "went after" Hallowell, whether to bring him back or to express his rage, we do not know. Hallowell predicted "that She woul[d] not live."

Silence seems to have settled on the Grosvenor house and its neighborhood after Sarah's death on September 14. It was two and a half years later that rumors about a murderous abortion spread through and beyond Pomfret village, prompting legal investigation. The silence, the gap between event and prosecution, the passivity of Sarah's parents—all lend mystery to the narrative. But despite its ellipses, the Grosvenor case provides us with an unusual set of details about one young couple's extreme response to the common problem of failed courtship and illegitimacy. To gain insight into both the mysteries and the extremities of the Grosvenor-Sessions case, we need to look more closely at Pomfret, at the two families centrally involved, and at clues to the motivations of the principal participants. Our abortion tale, it turns out, holds beneath its surface a complex trail of evidence about generational conflict and troubled relations between men and women.

THE POMFRET PLAYERS

In 1742 the town of Pomfret had been settled for just over forty years. Within its central neighborhood and in homesteads scattered over rugged, wooded hillsides lived probably no more than 270 men, women, and children.[16] During the founding decades, the fathers of Sarah and Amasa ranked among the ten leading householders; Leicester Grosvenor and Nathaniel Sessions were chosen often to fill important local offices.

Grosvenor, the older of the two by seven years, had inherited standing and a choice farmstead from his father, one of the original six purchasers of the Pomfret territory. When the town was incorporated in 1714, he was elected a militia officer and one of the first selectmen. He was returned to the latter post nineteen times and eventually rose to the highest elective position—that of captain—in the local trainband. Concurrently, he was appointed many times throughout the 1710s and 1720s to ad hoc town committees, often alongside Nathaniel Sessions. But unlike Sessions, Grosvenor went on to serve at the colony level. Pomfret freemen chose him to represent them at ten General Assembly sessions between 1726 and 1744. Finally, in the 1730s, when he was in his late fifties, the legislature appointed him a justice of the peace for Windham County. Thus, until his retirement in 1748 at age seventy-four, his house would have served as the venue for petty trials, hearings, and recordings of documents. After retiring from public office, Grosvenor lived another eleven years, leaving behind in 1759 an estate worth over £600.[17]

Nathaniel Sessions managed a sizable farm and ran one of Pomfret's taverns at the family homestead. Town meetings were sometimes held there. Sessions was chosen constable in 1714 and rose from ensign to lieutenant in the militia—always a step behind Leicester Grosvenor. He could take pride in one exceptional distinction redounding to the family honor: in 1737 his son Darius became only the second Pomfret resident to graduate from Yale College, and before Sessions died at ninety-one he saw Darius elected assistant and then deputy governor of Rhode Island.[18]

The records are silent as to whether Sessions and his family resented the Grosvenors, who must have been perceived in town as more prominent, or whether the two families . . . enjoyed a close relationship that went sour for some reason *before* the affair between Sarah and Amasa. Instead, the signs (such as the cooperative public work of the two fathers, the visits back and forth between the Grosvenor and Sessions girls) point to a long-standing friendship and dense web of interchanges between the families. Indeed, courtship and marriage between a Sessions son and a Grosvenor daughter would hardly have been surprising.

What went wrong in the affair between Sarah and Amasa is not clear. Sarah's sisters and cousins knew that "Amasy" "made Sute to" Sarah, and they gave no indication of disapproving. The few who guessed at Sarah's condition in the summer of 1742 were not so much surprised that she was pregnant as that the couple "did not marry." It was evidently routine in this New England village, as in others, for courting couples to post banns for their nuptials soon after the woman discovered that she was pregnant.

Amasa offered different answers among his Pomfret peers to explain his failure to marry his lover. When Zerviah Grosvenor told Amasa that he and Sarah "had better Marry," he responded, "That would not do," for "he was afraid of his parents . . . [who would] always make their lives [at home] uncomfortable." Later, Abigail Nightingale heard rumors that Amasa was resorting to the standard excuse of men wishing to avoid a shotgun marriage—denying that the child was his.[19] Hallowell, with whom Amasa may have been honest, claimed "the Reason that they did not marry" was "that Sessions Did not Love her well a nough for [he] saith he did not believe it was his son and if he Could Cause her to gitt Red of it he would not Go near her again." Showing yet another face to a Grosvenor kinsman after Sarah's death, Amasa repented his actions and extravagantly claimed he would "give All he had" to "bring Sarah . . . To life again . . . and have her as his wife."

The unusual feature of Amasa's behavior was not his unwillingness to marry Sarah, but his determination to terminate her pregnancy before it showed. Increasing numbers of young men in eighteenth-century New England weathered the temporary obloquy of abandoning a pregnant lover in order to prolong their bachelorhood or marry someone else. What drove Amasa, and an ostensibly reluctant Sarah, to resort to abortion? Was it fear of their fathers? Nathaniel Sessions had chosen Amasa as the son who would remain on the family farm and care for his parents in their old age. An ill-timed marriage could have disrupted these plans and threatened Amasa's inheritance.[20] For his part, Leicester Grosvenor may have made it clear to his daughter that he would be greatly displeased at her marrying before she reached a certain age or until her older sister wed. Rigid piety, an authoritarian nature, an intense concern with being seen as a good household governor—any of these traits in Leicester Grosvenor or Nathaniel Sessions could have colored Amasa's decisions.

Perhaps it was not family relations that proved the catalyst but Amasa's acquaintance with a medical man who boasted about a powder more effective than the herbal remedies that were part of women's lore. Hallowell himself had fathered an illegitimate child fifteen years earlier, and he may have encouraged a rakish attitude in Amasa, beguiling the younger man with the promise of dissociating sex from its possible consequences. Or the explanation may have been that classic one: another woman. Two years after Sarah's death, Amasa married Hannah Miller of Rehoboth, Massachusetts. Perhaps in early 1742 he was already making trips to the town just east of Providence to see his future wife.[21]

What should we make of Sarah's role in the scheme? It is possible that she no longer loved Amasa and was as eager as he to forestall external pressures toward a quick marriage. However, Zerviah swore that on one occasion before the operation Amasa reluctantly agreed to post banns for their nuptials and that Sarah did not object.[22] *If* Sarah was a willing and active participant in the abortion plot all along, then by 1745 her female kin and friends had fabricated and rehearsed a careful and seamless story to preserve the memory of the dead girl untarnished.

In the portrait drawn by her friends, Sarah reacted to her pregnancy and to Amasa's plan first by arguing and finally by doing her utmost to protect her lover. She may have wished to marry Amasa, yet she did not insist on it or bring in older family members to negotiate with him and his parents. Abigail Nightingale insisted that Sarah accepted Amasa's recalcitrance and only pleaded with him that they not "go on to add sin to sin." Privately, she urged Amasa that there was an alternative to taking the trade—a way that would enable him to keep his role hidden and prevent the couple from committing a "Last transgression [that] would be worse then the first." Sarah told him that "she was willing to take the sin and shame to her self, and to be obliged never to tell whose Child it was, and that she did not doubt but that if she humbled her self on her Knees to her Father he would take her and her Child home." Her lover, afraid that his identity would become known, vetoed her proposal.[23]

According to the Pomfret women's reconstruction, abortion was not a freely chosen and defiant act for Sarah. Against her own desires, she reluctantly consented in taking the trade only because Amasa "So very earnestly perswaided her." In fact, she had claimed to her friends that she was coerced; he "would take no denyal." Sarah's confidantes presented her as being aware of her options, shrinking from abortion as an unnatural and immoral deed, and yet finally choosing the strategy consistent

with her lover's vision of what would best protect their futures. Thus, if Amasa's hubris was extreme, so too was Sarah's internalization of those strains of thought in her culture that taught women to make themselves pleasing and obedient to men.

While we cannot be sure that the deponents' picture of Sarah's initial recoil and reluctant submission to the abortion plot was entirely accurate, it is clear that once she was caught up in the plan she extracted a pledge of silence from all her confidantes. Near her death, before telling Abigail about the operation, she "insist[ed] on . . . [her friend's] never discovering the Matter" to anyone. Clearly, she had earlier bound Zerviah and Hannah on their honor not to tell their elders. Reluctant when faced with the abortionist's powder, Sarah became a leading co-conspirator when alone with her female friends.

One of the most remarkable aspects of the Grosvenor-Sessions case is Sarah and Amasa's success in keeping their parents in the dark, at least until her final illness. If by July Sarah's sisters grew suspicious that Sarah was "with child," what explains the failure of her parents to observe her pregnancy and to intervene and uncover the abortion scheme? Were they negligent, preoccupied with other matters, or willfully blind? . . .

In terms of who knew what, the events of summer 1742 in Pomfret apparently unfolded in two stages. The first stretched from Sarah's discovery of her pregnancy by early May to some point in late August after her miscarriage. In this period a determined, collective effort by Sarah and Amasa and their friends kept their elders in the dark.[24] When Sarah fell seriously ill from the aftereffects of the abortion attempt and miscarriage, rumors of the young people's secret activities reached Leicester Grosvenor's neighbors and even one of the doctors he had called in. It is difficult to escape the conclusion that by Sarah's death in mid-September her father and stepmother had learned of the steps that had precipitated her mortal condition and kept silent for reasons of their own.

Except for Hallowell, the circle of intimates entrusted by Amasa and Sarah with their scheme consisted of young adults ranging in age from nineteen to thirty-three. Born between about 1710 and 1725, these young people had grown up just as the town attracted enough settlers to support a church, militia, and local market. They were second-genera-tion Pomfret residents who shared the gener-ational identity that came with sitting side by side through long worship services, attending school, playing, and working together at chil-dren's tasks. By 1740, these sisters, brothers, cousins, courting couples, and neighbors, in their visits from house to house—sometimes in their own households, sometimes at their parents'—had managed to create a world of talk and socializing that was largely exempt from parental supervision.[25] In Pomfret in 1742 it was this group of young people in their twenties and early thirties, not the cluster of Grosvenor matrons over forty-five, who mon-itored Sarah's courtship, attempted to get Amasa to marry his lover, privately investi-gated the activities and motives of Amasa and Hallowell, and, belatedly, spoke out publicly to help Connecticut juries decide who should be blamed for Sarah's death.

That Leicester Grosvenor made no public move to punish those around him and that he avoided giving testimony when legal proceed-ings commenced are intriguing clues to social changes underway in New England villages in the mid-eighteenth century. Local leaders like Grosvenor, along with the respectable yeomen whom he represented in public office, were increasingly withdrawing delicate family prob-lems from the purview of their communities. Slander, illegitimacy, and feuds among neigh-bors came infrequently to local courts by mid-century, indicating male householders' grow-ing preference for handling such matters privately.[26] Wealthy and ambitious families adopted this ethic of privacy at the same time that they became caught up in elaborating their material worlds by adding rooms and acquir-ing luxury goods.[27] . . . But all the fine accou-trements in the world would not excuse Justice Grosvenor from his obligation to govern his household effectively. Mortified no doubt at his inability to monitor the young people in his extended family, he responded, ironically, by extending their conspiracy of silence. The best way for him to shield the family name from scandal and protect his political reputation in the county and colony was to keep the story of Sarah's abortion out of the courts.

THE DOCTOR

John Hallowell's status as an outsider in Pom-fret and his dangerous, secret alliance with the

town's young adults may have shaped his des-tiny as the one conspirator sentenced to suffer at the whipping post. Although the physician had been involved in shady dealings before 1742, he had managed to win the trust of many patients and a respectable social standing. Tracking down his history . . . tells us some-thing of the uncertainty surrounding personal and professional identity before the advent of police records and medical licensing boards. It also gives us an all-too-rare glimpse into the fashion in which an eighteenth-century coun-try doctor tried to make his way in the world.

Hallowell's earliest brushes with the law came in the 1720s. In 1725 he purchased land in Killingly, a Connecticut town just north of Pomfret and bordering both Massachusetts and Rhode Island. Newly married, he was probably in his twenties at the time. Seven months before his wife gave birth to their first child, a sixteen-year-old Killingly woman charged Hallowell with fathering her illegiti-mate child. Using the alias Nicholas Hallaway, he fled to southeastern Connecticut, where he lived as a "transient" for three months. He was arrested and settled the case by admitting to paternity and agreeing to contribute to the child's maintenance for four years.[28]

Hallowell resumed his life in Killingly. Two years later, now referred to as "Dr.," he was arrested again; this time the charge was counterfeiting. Hallowell and several confed-erates were hauled before the governor and council for questioning and then put on trial before the Superior Court. Although many Killingly witnesses testified to the team's sus-pect activities in a woodland shelter, the charges against Hallowell were dropped when a key informer failed to appear in court.[29]

Hallowell thus escaped conviction on a serious felony charge, but he had been tainted by stories linking him to the criminal subcul-ture of transient, disorderly, greedy, and man-ually skilled men who typically made up gangs of counterfeiters in eighteenth-century New England.[30] After 1727 Hallowell may have given up dabbling in money-making schemes and turned to earning his livelihood chiefly from his medical practice. Like two-thirds of the male medical practitioners in colonial New England, he probably did not have college or apprentice training, but his skill, or charm, was not therefore necessarily less than that of any one of his peers who might have inherited a library of books and a fund of knowledge from a physician father. All colonial practitioners, as Richard D. Brown reminds us, mixed learned practices with home or folk remedies, and no doctor had access to safe, reliable pharmacological preparations or antiseptic surgical procedures.[31]

In the years immediately following the counterfeiting charge. Hallowell appears to have made several deliberate moves to portray himself as a sober neighbor and reliable physician. At about the time of his second marriage, in 1729, he became a more frequent attendant at the Killingly meetinghouse, where he renewed his covenant and presented his first two children for baptism. He also threw himself into the land and credit markets of northeastern Connecticut, establishing himself as a physician who was also an enterprising yeoman and a frequent litigant.[32]

These activities had dual implications. On the one hand, they suggest that Hallowell epitomized the eighteenth-century Yankee citizen—a man as comfortable in the courtroom and countinghouse as at a patient's bedside; a man of restless energy, not content to limit his scope to his fields and village; a practical, ambitious man with a shrewd eye for a good deal.[33] On the other hand, Hallowell's losses to Boston creditors, his constant efforts to collect debts, and his farflung practice raise questions about the nature of his activities and medical practice. He evidently had clients not just in towns across northeastern Connecticut but also in neighboring Massachusetts and Rhode Island. Perhaps rural practitioners normally traveled extensively, spending many nights away from their wives and children. It is also possible, however, either that Hallowell was forced to travel because established doctors from leading families had monopolized the local practice or that he chose to recruit patients in Providence and other towns as a cover for illicit activities.[34] Despite his land speculations and his frequent resort to litigation, Hallowell was losing money. In the sixteen years before 1742, his creditors secured judgments against him for a total of £1,060, while he was able to collect only £700 in debts.[35] The disjunction between his ambition and actual material gains may have led Hallowell in middle age to renew his illicit money-making schemes. By supplying young men with potent abortifacients and dabbling in

schemes to counterfeit New England's paper money, he betrayed the very gentlemen whose respect, credit, and society he sought.

What is most intriguing about Hallowell was his ability to ingratiate himself throughout his life with elite men whose reputations were unblemished by scandal. Despite the rumors that must have circulated about his early sexual dalliance, counterfeiting activities, suspect medical remedies, heavy debts, and shady business transactions, leading ministers, merchants, and magistrates welcomed him into their houses. . . .

Lacking college degree and family pedigree, Hallowell traded on his profession and his charm to gain acceptability with the elite. In August 1742 he shrewdly removed himself from the Pomfret scene, just before Sarah Grosvenor's death. In that month he moved, possibly without his wife and children, to Providence, where he had many connections. Within five years, Hallowell had so insinuated himself with town leaders such as Stephen Hopkins that fourteen of them petitioned for mitigation of what they saw as the misguided sentence imposed on him in the Grosvenor case.[36]

Hallowell's capacity for landing on his feet, despite persistent brushes with scandal, debt, and the law, suggests that we should look at the fluidity of New England's eighteenth-century elite in new ways.[37] What bound sons of old New England families, learned men, and upwardly mobile merchants and professionals in an expanded elite may partly have been a reshaped, largely unspoken set of values shared by men. We know that the archetype for white New England women as sexual beings was changing from carnal Eve to resisting Pamela and that the calculus of accountability for seduction was shifting blame solely to women.[38] But the simultaneous metamorphosis in cultural images and values defining manhood in the early and mid-eighteenth century has not been studied. The scattered evidence we do have suggests that, increasingly, for men in the more secular and anglicized culture of New England, the lines between legitimate and illegitimate sexuality, between sanctioned and shady business dealings, and between speaking the truth and protecting family honor blurred. Hallowell's acceptability to men like minister Ebenezer Williams and merchant Stephen Hopkins hints at how changing sexual and moral standards shaped the economic and social alliances made by New England's male leadership in the 1700s.

WOMEN'S TALK AND MEN'S TALK

If age played a major role in determining who knew the truth about Sarah Grosvenor's illness, gender affected how the conspiring young adults responded to Sarah's impending death and how they weighed the issue of blame. Our last glimpse into the social world of eighteenth-century Pomfret looks at the different ways in which women and men reconstructed their roles in the events of 1742.

An inward gaze, a strong consciousness of sin and guilt, a desire to avoid conflict and achieve reconciliation, a need to confess—these are the impulses expressed in women's intimate talk in the weeks before Sarah died. The central female characters in the plot, Sarah and Zerviah Grosvenor, lived for six weeks with the daily fear that their parents or aunts might detect Sarah's condition or their covert comings and goings. Deposing three years later, Zerviah represented the sisters as suffering under an intensifying sense of complicity as they had passed through two stages of involvement in the concealment plan. At first, they were passive players, submitting to the hands of men. But once Hallowell declared that he had done all he could, they were left to salvage the conspiracy by enduring the terrors of a first delivery alone, knowing that their failure to call in the older women of the family resembled the decision made by women who committed infanticide.[39] While the pain and shock of miscarrying a five-and-one-half-month fetus through a possibly lacerated vagina may have been the experience that later most grieved Sarah, Zerviah would be haunted particularly by her stealthy venture into the woods with Hannah to bury the shrouded evidence of miscarriage.[40]

The Grosvenor sisters later recalled that they had regarded the first stage of the scheme—taking the trade—as "a Sin" and "an Evil" not so much because it was intended to end the life of a fetus but because it entailed a protracted set of actions, worse than a single lie, to cover up an initial transgression: fornication. According to their religion and the traditions of their New England culture, Sarah and Zerviah knew that the proper response to the sin of "uncleanness" (especially when it led to its visible manifestation, pregnancy) was to confess, seeking to allay God's wrath and cleanse oneself and one's community. Dire were the consequences of hiding a grave sin, so the logic and folklore of religion warned.[41] Having piled one covert act upon another, all in defiance of her parents, each sister wondered if she had not ventured beyond the pale, forsaking God and in turn being forsaken. . . .

. . . [V]isions of judgment and of their personal accountability to God haunted Sarah and Zerviah during the waning days of summer—or so their female friends later contended. Caught between the traditional religious ethic of confession, recently renewed in revivals across New England, and the newer, status-driven cultural pressure to keep moral missteps private, the Grosvenor women declined to take up roles as accusers. By focusing on their own actions, they rejected a portrait of themselves as helpless victims, yet they also ceded to their male kin responsibility for assessing blame and mediating between the public interest in seeing justice done and the private interests of the Grosvenor family. Finally, by trying to keep the conspiracy of silence intact and by allowing Amasa frequent visits to her bedside to lament his role and his delusion by Hallowell, Sarah at once endorsed a policy of private repentance and forgiveness *and* indicated that she wished her lover to be spared eventual public retribution for her death.

Talk among the men of Pomfret in the weeks preceding and following Sarah's death centered on more secular concerns than the preoccupation with sin and God's anger that ran through the women's conversations. Neither Hallowell nor Sessions expressed any guilt or sense of sin, as far as the record shows, *until* Sarah was diagnosed as mortally ill.[42] Indeed, their initial accounts of the plot took the form of braggadocio, with Amasa (according to Hallowell) casting himself as the rake who could "gitt Red" of his child and look elsewhere for female companionship, and Hallowell boasting of his abortionist's surgical technique to Sarah's cousin Ebenezer. Later, anticipating popular censure and possible prosecution, each man "Tried to Cast it" on the other. The physician insisted that "He did not do any thing but What Sessions Importuned him to Do," while Amasa exclaimed "That he could freely be Strip[p]ed naked provided he could bring Sarah . . . To life again . . . , but Doct Hallowell had Deluded him, and Destroyed her."[43] While this sort of denial and buck-passing seems very human, it was the antithesis of the New England way—a religious way of life that made confession its central motif. The Grosvenor-Sessions case is one illustration among many of how New England women continued to measure themselves by "the moral allegory of repentance and confession" while men, at least when presenting themselves before legal authorities, adopted secular voices and learned self-interested strategies.[44]

For the Grosvenor men—at least the cluster of Sarah's cousins living near her—the key issue was not exposing sin but protecting the family's reputation. In the weeks before Sarah died, her cousins John and Ebenezer each attempted to investigate and sort out the roles and motives of Amasa Sessions and John Hallowell in the scheme to conceal Sarah's pregnancy. Grilled in August by Ebenezer . . . , Hallowell revealed that "Sessions had bin Interseeding with him to Remove her Conseption." On another occasion, . . . Hallowell was more specific. He "[did] with her [Sarah] as he did . . . because Sessions Came to him and was So very earnest . . . and offered him five pounds if he would do it." "But," Hallowell boasted, "he would have twenty of[f] of him before he had done."[45] . . .

John and Ebenezer, deposing three or four years after these events, did not . . . explain why they did not act immediately to have charges brought against the two conspirators. Perhaps these young householders were loath to move against a male peer and childhood friend. More likely, they kept their information to themselves to protect John's wife, Hannah, and their cousin Zerviah from prosecution as accessories. They may also have acted, in league with their uncle Leicester, out of a larger concern for keeping the family name out of the courts. Finally, it is probable that the male cousins, partly because of their own complicity and partly because they may have believed that Sarah had consented to the abortion, simply did not think that Amasa's and Hallowell's actions added up to the murder to their relative.

Three years later, yet another Grosvenor cousin intervened, expressing himself much more vehemently than John or Ebenezer ever had. In 1742, John Shaw at age thirty-eight may have been perceived by the younger Grosvenors as too old—too close to the age when men took public office and served as grand jurors—to be trusted with their secret. Shaw seems to have known nothing of Sarah's taking the trade or having a miscarriage until 1745 when "the Storys" suddenly surfaced. Then Hannah and Zerviah gave him a truncated account. Shaw reacted with rage, realizing that Sarah had died not of natural causes but from "what Hollowell had done," and he set out to wring the truth from the doctor. Several times he sought out Hallowell in Rhode Island to tell him that "I could not look upon him otherwise Than [as] a Bad man Since he had Destroyed my Kinswoman." When Hallowell countered that "Amasa Sessions . . . was the Occasion of it," Shaw's fury grew. "I Told him he was like old Mother Eve When She said The Serpent beguild her, . . . [and] I Told him in my Mind he Deserved to dye for it."

Questioning Amasa, Shaw was quick to accept his protestations of sincere regret and his insistence that Hallowell had "Deluded" him. Shaw concluded that Amasa had never "Importuned [Hallowell] . . . to lay hands on her" (that is, to perform the manual abortion). Forged in the men's talk about the Grosvenor-Sessions case in 1745 and 1746 appears to have been a consensus that, while Amasa Sessions was somewhat blameworthy "as concerned in it," it was only Hallowell—the outsider, the man easily labeled a quack—who deserved to be branded "a Man of Death." Nevertheless, it was the stories of *both* men and women that ensured the fulfillment of a doctor's warning to Hallowell in the Leicester Grosvenor house just before Sarah died: "The Hand of Justice [will] Take hold of [you] sooner or Later."[46]

THE LAW

The hand of justice reached out to catch John Hallowell in November 1745. . . . *Something* had caused Zerviah and Hannah Grosvenor to break their silence. Zerviah provided the key to the puzzle, as she alone had been present at the crucial series of incidents leading to Sarah's death. The only surviving account of Zerviah's belated conversion from silence to public confession comes from the stories told by Pomfret residents into the nineteenth century. In Ellen Larned's melodramatic prose, the "whispered" tale recounted Zerviah's increasing discomfort thus: "Night after night, in her solitary chamber, the surviving sister was awakened by the rattling of the rings on which her bed-curtains were suspended, a ghostly knell continuing and intensifying till she was convinced of its preternatural origin; and at length, in response to her agonized entreaties, the spirit of her dead sister made known to her, 'That she could not rest in her grave till her crime was made public.'"[47]

Embellished as this tale undoubtedly is, we should not dismiss it out of hand as a Victorian ghost story. In early modern English culture, belief persisted in both apparitions and the supernatural power of the guiltless victim to return and expose her murderer.[48] Zerviah in 1742 already fretted over her sin as an accomplice, yet she kept her pledge of silence to her sister. It is certainly conceivable that, after a lapse of three years, she could no longer bear the pressure of hiding the acts that she increasingly believed amounted to the murder of her sister and an unborn child. Whether Zerviah's sudden outburst of talk in 1745 came about at the urging of some Pomfret confidante, or perhaps under the influence of the revivals then sweeping Windham County churches, or indeed because of her belief in nightly visitations by her dead sister's spirit, we simply cannot know.[49]

The Pomfret meetinghouse was the site of the first public legal hearing into the facts behind Sarah Grosvenor's death. We can imagine that townsfolk crowded the pews over the course of two November days to watch two prominent county magistrates examine a string of witnesses before pronouncing their preliminary judgment. The evidence, they concluded, was sufficient to bind four people over for trial at the Superior Court: Hallowell, who in their opinion was "Guilty of murdering Sarah," along with Amasa Sessions, Zerviah Grosvenor, and Hannah Grosvenor as accessories to that murder.[50] The inclusion of Zerviah and Hannah may have been a ploy to pressure these crucial, possibly still reluctant, witnesses to testify for the crown. When Joseph Fowler, the king's attorney, prepared a formal indictment in the case eleven months later, he dropped all charges against Zerviah and Hannah. Rather than stand trial, the two women traveled frequently during 1746 and

1747 to the county seat to give evidence against Sessions and Hallowell.

The criminal process recommenced in September 1746. A grand jury empaneled by the Superior Court at its Windham session first rejected a presentment against Hallowell for murdering Sarah "by his Wicked and Diabolical practice." Fowler, recognizing that the capital charges of murder and accessory to murder against Hallowell and Sessions were going to fail before jurors, changed his tack. He presented the grand jury with a joint indictment against the two men not for outright murder but for endangering Sarah's health by trying to "procure an Abortion" with medicines and "a violent manual opperation"; this time the jurors endorsed the bill. When the Superior Court trial opened in November, two attorneys for the defendants managed to persuade the judges that the indictment was faulty on technical grounds. However, upon the advice of the king's attorney that there "appear reasons vehemently to suspect" the two men "Guilty of Sundry Heinous Offenses" at Pomfret four years earlier, the justices agreed to bind them over to answer charges in March 1747.[51]

Fowler next moved to bring separate indictments against Hallowell and Sessions for the "highhanded misdemeanour" of endeavoring to destroy Sarah's health "and the fruit of her womb." This wording echoed the English common law designation of abortion as a misdemeanor, not a felony or capital crime. A newly empaneled grand jury of eighteen county yeomen made what turned out to be the pivotal decision in getting a conviction: they returned a true bill against Hallowell and rejected a similarly worded bill against Sessions.[52] Only Hallowell, "the notorious physician," would go to trial.[53]

On March 20, 1747, John Hallowell stepped before the bar for the final time to answer for the death of Sarah Grosvenor. He maintained his innocence, the case went to a trial jury of twelve men, and they returned with a guilty verdict. The Superior Court judges, who had discretion to choose any penalty less than death, pronounced a severe sentence of public shaming and corporal punishment. Hallowell was to be paraded to the town gallows, made to stand there before the public for two hours "with a rope visibly hanging about his neck," and then endure a public whipping of twenty-nine lashes "on the naked back."[54]

Before the authorities could carry out this sentence, Hallowell escaped and fled to Rhode Island. From Providence seven months after his trial, he audaciously petitioned the Connecticut General Assembly for a mitigated sentence, presenting himself as a destitute "Exile." As previously noted, fourteen respected male citizens of Providence took up his cause, arguing that this valued doctor had been convicted by prejudiced witnesses and hearsay evidence and asserting that corporal punishment was unwarranted in a misdemeanor case. While the Connecticut legislators rejected these petitions, the language used by Hallowell and his Rhode Island patrons is yet another marker of the distance separating many educated New England men at mid-century from their more God-fearing predecessors. Never mentioning the words "sin" or "repentance," the Providence men wrote that Hallowell was justified in escaping the lash since "every Person is prompted [by the natural Law of Self-Preservation] to avoid Pain and Misery."[55]

In the series of indictments against Hallowell and Sessions, the central legal question became who had directly caused Sarah's death. To the farmers in their forties and fifties who sat as jurors, Hallowell clearly deserved punishment. By recklessly endangering Sarah's life he had abused the trust that heads of household placed in him as a physician.[56] Moreover, he had conspired with the younger generation to keep their dangerous activities secret from their parents and elders.

Several rationales could have been behind the Windham jurors' conclusion that Amasa Sessions ought to be spared the lash. Legally, they could distinguish him from Hallowell as not being *directly* responsible for Sarah's death. Along with Sarah's male kin, they dismissed the evidence that Amasa had instigated the scheme, employed Hallowell, and monitored all of his activities. Perhaps they saw him as a native son who deserved the chance to prove himself mature and responsible. They may have excused his actions as nothing more than a misguided effort to cast off an unwanted lover. Rather than acknowledge that a culture that excused male sexual irresponsibility was responsible for Sarah's death, the Grosvenor family, the Pomfret community, and the jury men of the county persuaded themselves that Sessions had been ignorant of the potentially deadly consequences of his actions.

MEMORY AND HISTORY

No family feud, no endless round of recriminations followed the many months of deposing and attending trials that engaged the Grosvenor and Sessions clans in 1746 and 1747. Indeed, as Sarah and Amasa's generation matured, the ties between the two families thickened. . . . In 1775 Amasa's third son, and namesake, married sixteen-year-old Esther Grosvenor, daughter of Sarah's brother, Leicester, Jr.[57]

It is clear that the Grosvenor clan was not willing to break ranks with their respectable yeoman neighbors and heap blame on the Sessions family for Sarah's death. It would, however, be fascinating to know what women in Pomfret and other Windham County towns had to say about the outcome of the legal proceedings in 1747. Did they concur with the jurors that Hallowell was the prime culprit, or did they, unlike Sarah Grosvenor, direct their ire more concertedly at Amasa, insisting that he too was "a Bad man"? Nearly a century later, middle-class New England women would organize against the sexual double standard. However, Amasa's future career tells us that female piety in the 1740s did not instruct Windham County women to expel the newly married, thirty-two-year-old man from their homes.[58]

Amasa, as he grew into middle age in Pomfret, easily replicated his father's status. He served as militia captain in the Seven Years' War, prospered in farming, fathered ten children, and lived fifty-seven years beyond Sarah Grosvenor. His handsome gravestone, inscribed with a long verse, stands but twenty-five feet from the simpler stone erected in 1742 for Sarah.

After his death, male kin remembered Amasa fondly; nephews and grandsons recalled him as a "favorite" relative, "remarkably capable" in his prime and "very corpulent" in old age. Moreover, local story-telling tradition and the published history of the region, which made such a spectacular ghost story out of Sarah's abortion and death, preserved Amasa Sessions's reputation unsullied: the *name* of Sarah's lover was left out of the tale.[59]

If Sarah Grosvenor's life is a cautionary tale in any sense for us in the late twentieth century, it is as a reminder of the historically distinctive ways in which socialized gender roles, community and class solidarity, and legal culture combine in each set of generations to excuse or make invisible certain abuses and crimes against women. The form in which Sarah Grosvenor's death became local history reminds us of how the excuses and erasures of one generation not unwittingly become embedded in the narratives and memories of the next cultural era.

NOTES

1. The documentation is found in the record books and file papers of the Superior Court of Connecticut: *Rex* v. *John Hallowell et al.,* Superior Court Records, Book 9, pp. 113, 173, 175, and Windham County Superior Court Files, box 172, Connecticut State Library, Hartford. Hereafter all loose court papers cited are from *Rex* v. *Hallowell,* Windham Country Superior Court Files, box 172, unless otherwise indicated....

2. ...On the history of abortion practices see ... Angus McLaren, *Reproductive Rituals: The Perception of Fertility in England from the Sixteenth Century to the Nineteenth Century* (London, 1984), chap. 4; Linda Gordon, *Woman's Body, Woman's Right: A Social History of Birth Control in America* (New York, 1976), pp. 26–41, 49–60. ...

For specific cases indicating use of herbal abortifacients in the North American colonies, see Julia Cherry Spruill, *Women's Life and Work in the Southern Colonies* (New York, 1972: orig. pub. Chapel Hill, N.C., 1938), pp. 325–26; Roger Thompson, *Sex in Middlesex: Popular Mores in a Massachusetts County, 1649–1699* (Amherst, Mass., 1986), pp. 11, 24–26, 107–8, 182–83. I have found two references to the use of an abortifacient in colonial Connecticut court files.

3. Abortion before quickening (defined in the early modern period as the moment when the mother first felt the fetus move) was not viewed by the English or colonial courts as criminal. No statute law on abortion existed in either Britain or the colonies. To my knowledge, no New England court before 1745 had attempted to prosecute a physician or other conspirators for carrying out an abortion.

On the history of the legal treatment of abortion in Europe and the United States see ... James C. Mohr, *Abortion in America: The Origins and Evolution of National Policy, 1800–1900* (New York, 1978); Michael Grossberg, *Governing the Hearth: Law and the Family in Nineteenth-Century America* (Chapel Hill, N.C., 1985), chap. 5; and Carroll Smith-Rosenberg, "The Abortion Movement and the AMA, 1850–1880," in *Disorderly Conduct: Visions of Gender of Victorian America* (New York, 1985), pp. 217–244.

4. Indictment against John Hallowell, Mar. 1746/47.

5. The story of the decriminalization of fornication for men in colonial New England is told most succinctly by Carol F. Karlsen, *The Devil in the Shape of a Woman: Witchcraft in Colonial New England* (New York, 1987), pp. 194–96, 198–202, 255. Laurel

Thatcher Ulrich describes a late eighteenth-century Massachusetts jurisdiction in *A Midwife's Tale: The Life of Martha Ballard, Based on Her Diary, 1785–1812* (New York, 1990), 147–60. ... A partial survey of fornication prosecutions in the Windham County Court indicates that here, too, the local JPs and annually appointed grand jurymen stopped prosecuting men after the 1730s. The records for 1726–31 show that fifteen men were prosecuted to enjoin child support and twenty-one single women were charged with fornication and bastardy, while only two women brought civil suits for child maintenance. Nearly a decade ahead, in the three-year period 1740–42, no men were prosecuted while twenty-three single women were charged with fornication and ten women initiated civil paternity suits.

6. For a recent summary of the literature see Brief for American Historians as *Amicus Curiae* Supporting the Appellees 5–7, *William L. Webster et al.* v. *Reproductive Health Services et al.,* 109 S. Ct. 3040 (1989).

7. In none of the cases cited in n. 2 above did the woman ingesting an abortifacient die from it....

8. Married women may have hidden their abortion attempts because the activity was associated with lewd or dissident women.

9. Deposition of Zerviah Grosvenor. [All direct quotations from witnesses come from Depositions (see n. 1).] ... Hallowell's trade may have been an imported medicine or a powder he mixed himself, consisting chiefly of oil of savin, which could be extracted from juniper bushes found throughout New England.

10. So her sister Zerviah later estimated....

11. After she was let into the plot, Zerviah more than once watched Amasa take "a paper or powder out of his pockett" and insist that Sarah "take Some of it." ...

12. ... "Unlawful measure" was Zerviah's phrase for Amasa's "Method." Concerned for Sarah's well-being, she pleaded with Hallowell not to give her sister "any thing that should harm her"; Deposition of Zerviah Grosvenor. At the same time, Sarah was thinking about the quickening issue. She confided to a friend that when Amasa first insisted she take the trade, "she [had] feared it was too late"....

13. Hallowell claimed that he proceeded with the abortion in order to save Sarah's life. If the powder had had little effect and he knew it, then this claim was a deliberate deception. On the other hand, he may have sincerely believed that the potion had poisoned the fetus and that infection of the uterine cavity had followed fetal death. Since healthy babies were thought at that time to help with their own deliveries, Hallowell may also have anticipated a complicated delivery if Sarah were allowed to go to full term—a delivery that might kill her....

14. Hearsay evidence was still accepted in many eighteenth-century Anglo-American courts. ... Sarah's reported words may have carried special weight because in early New England persons on their deathbeds were thought to speak the truth.

15. Twentieth-century obstetrical studies show an average of six weeks between fetal death and spontaneous abortion; J Robert Willson and Elsie

Reid Carrington, eds., *Obstetrics and Gynecology*, 8th ed. (St. Louis, Mo., 1987), p. 212. Hallowell evidently grasped the link between the two events but felt he could not wait six weeks, either out of concern for Sarah's health or for fear their plot would be discovered.

16. I am using a list of forty heads of household in the Mashamoquet neighborhood of Pomfret in 1731, presuming five persons to a household, and assuming a 2.5 percent annual population growth. See Ellen D. Larned, *History of Windham County, Connecticut* (Worcester, Mass., 1874), vol. I, p. 342, and Bruce C. Daniels, *The Connecticut Town: Growth and Development, 1635–1790* (Middletown, Conn., 1979), pp. 44–51. Pomfret village had no central green or cluster of shops and small house lots around its meeting-house. No maps survive for early Pomfret apart from a 1719 survey of proprietors' tracts. See Larned, *History of Windham County* (1976 ed.), I, foldout at p. 185.

17. ...Larned, *History of Windham County*, I:200–202, 208–9, 269, 354, 343–44....

18. Larned, *History of Windham County*, I:201, 204, 206, 208–9, 344; Ellen D. Larned, *Historic Gleanings in Windham County, Connecticut* (Providence, R. I., 1899), pp. 141, 148–49....

19. ...Contradicting Amasa's attempt to disavow paternity were both his investment in Hallowell's efforts to get rid of the fetus and his own ready admission of paternity privately to Zerviah and Sarah.

20. Two years later, in Feb. 1744 (nine months before Amasa married), the senior Sessions deeded to his son the north part of his own farm for a payment of £310. Amasa, in exchange for caring for his parents in their old age, came into the whole farm when his father died in 1771. Pomfret Land Records, III:120; Estate Papers of Nathaniel Sessions, 1771, Pomfret Probate District. On the delay between marriage and "going to housekeeping" see Ulrich, *A Midwife's Tale*, pp. 138–44.

21. Francis G. Sessions, comp, *Materials for a History of the Sessions Family in America* (Albany, N.Y., 1890), p. 60; Pomfret Vit. Rec., I:29. All vital and land records cited hereafter are found in the Barbour Collection, Connecticut State Library.

22. The banns never appeared on the meeting-house door....

23. ...I have argued elsewhere that this is what most young New England women in the eighteenth century did when faced with illegitimacy. Their parents did not throw them out of the house but instead paid the cost of the mother and child's upkeep until she managed to marry. Dayton, *Women Before the Bar.* ch. 4.

24. In Larned's account, the oral legend insisted that Hallowell's "transaction" (meaning the abortion attempt) and the miscarriage were "utterly unsuspected by any ... member of the household" other than Zerviah. *History of Windham County.* I:363.

25. The famous "bad books" incident that disrupted Jonathan Edwards's career in 1744 involved a similar group of unsupervised young adults ages twenty-one to twenty-nine. See Patricia J. Tracy, *Jonathan Edwards, Pastor: Religion and Society in Eighteenth-Century Northampton* (New York, 1980), pp.

160–64. The best general investigation of youth culture in early New England is Thompson's *Sex in Middlesex*, pp. 71–96....

26. Helena M. Wall, *Fierce Communion: Family and Community in Early America* (Cambridge, Mass., 1990); Bruce H. Mann, *Neighbors and Strangers: Law and Community in Early Connecticut* (Chapel Hill, N.C., 1987).

27. ...For recent studies linking consumption patterns and class stratification see ... T. H. Breen, "'Baubles of Britain': The American and Consumer Revolutions of the Eighteenth Century," *Past and Present* 119 (May 1988): 73–104....

28. Killingly Land Records, II:139; *Rex* v. *John Hallowell and Mehitable Morris*, Dec. 1726, Windham County Court Records, Book I:43, and Windham County Court Files, box 363....

29. Hallowell was clearly the mastermind of the scheme, and there is little doubt that he lied to the authorities when questioned.... The case is found in Charles Hoadley, ed., *Public Records of the Colony of Connecticut*, 15 vols. (Hartford, Conn., 1873), vol. VII, p. 118.

30. The authority on counterfeiting in the colonies is Kenneth Scott... *Counterfeiting in Colonial America* [(New York, 1957),] esp. pp. 125, 35, 10, 36. See also Scott's more focused studies, *Counterfeiting in Colonial Connecticut* (New York, 1957) and *Counterfeiting in Colonial Rhode Island* (Providence, R.I., 1960).

For an illuminating social profile of thieves and burglars who often operated in small gangs, see Daniel A. Cohen, "A Fellowship of Thieves: Property Criminals in Eighteenth-Century Massachusetts," *Journal of Social History* XXII (1988):65–92.

31. Richard D. Brown, "The Healing Arts in Colonial and Revolutionary Massachusetts: The Context for Scientific Medicine," in Publications Col. Soc. Mass., *Medicine in Colonial Massachusetts 1620–1820* (Boston, 1980), esp. pp. 40–42....

32. Between 1725 and 1742, Hallowell was a party to twenty land sales and purchases in Killingly....

33. For example, in early 1735 Hallowell made a £170 profit from the sale of a sixty-acre tract with mill and mansion house that he had purchased two months earlier. Killingly Land Rec., IV:26, 36.

34. For a related hypothesis about the mobility of self-taught doctors in contrast to physicians from established medical families see Christianson, "Medical Practitioners of Massachusetts," in Col. Soc. Mass., *Medicine in Colonial Massachusetts*, p. 61....

35. These figures apply to suits in the Windham County Court record books, 1727–42. Hallowell may, of course, have prosecuted debtors in other jurisdictions.

36. The petition's signers included Hopkins, merchant, assembly speaker, and Superior Court justice, soon to become governor; Daniel Jencks, judge, assembly delegate, and prominent Baptist; Obadiah Brown, merchant and shopkeeper; and George Taylor, justice of the peace, town schoolmaster, and Anglican warden. Some of the signers stated that they had made a special trip to Windham to be "Earwitnesses" at Hallowell's trial....

37. For discussions of the elite see Jackson Turner Main, *Society and Economy in Colonial Connecticut* (Princeton, N.J., 1985), esp. pp. 317–66. . . .

38. Laurel Thatcher Ulrich, *Good Wives: Image and Reality in the Lives of Women in Northern New England, 1650–1750* (New York, 1982), pp. 103–5, 113–17.

39. See Ulrich, *Good Wives*, pp. 195–201. . . .

40. Burying the child was one of the key dramatic acts in infanticide episodes and tales, and popular beliefs in the inevitability that "murder will out" centered on the buried corpse. . . . For more on "murder will out" in New England culture, see David D. Hall, *Worlds of Wonder, Days of Judgment: Popular Religious Belief in Early New England* (New York, 1989), pp. 176–78. . . .

41. Hall, *Worlds of Wonder*, pp. 172–78.

42. . . . Abigail Nightingale recalled a scene when Sarah "was just going out of the world." She and Amasa were sitting on Sarah's bed, and Amasa "endeavour[ed] to raise her up &c. He asked my thought of her state &c. and then leaning over her used these words: poor Creature, I have undone you[!]"; Deposition of Abigail Nightingale.

43. . . . For discussions of male and female speech patterns and the distinctive narcissistic bravado of men's talk in early New England, see Robert St. George, "'Heated' Speech and Literacy in Seventeenth-Century New England," in David Grayson Allen and David D. Hall, eds., *Seventeenth-Century New England*, Publications of the Colonial Society of Massachusetts, LXIII (Boston, 1984), pp. 305–15. . . .

44. On the centrality of confession see Hall, *Worlds of Wonder*, pp. 173, 241. . . . On the growing gap between male and female piety in the eighteenth century see Mary Maples Dunn, "Saints and Sisters: Congregational and Quaker Women in the Early Colonial Period," *American Quarterly* XXX (1978): 582–601. . . .

45. Deposition of Ebenezer Grosvenor; Deposition of John Grosvenor.

46. . . . Shaw here was reporting Dr. [Theodore?] Coker's account of his confrontation with Hallowell during Sarah's final illness. . . .

47. Larned reported that, according to "the legend," the ghostly visitations ceased when "Hallowell fled his country." *History of Windham County*, I:363.

48. For mid-eighteenth-century Bristol residents who reported seeing apparitions and holding conversations with them see Jonathan Barry, "Piety and the Patient: Medicine and Religion in Eighteenth Century Bristol," in Roy Porter, ed., *Patients and Practitioners: Lay Perceptions of Medicines in Pre-Industrial Society* (Cambridge, [Eng.,] 1985), p. 157.

49. None of the depositions produced by Hallowell's trial offers any explanation of the three-year gap between Sarah's death and legal proceedings. . . .

50. Record of the Inferior Court held at Pomfret, Nov. 5–6, 1745. . . .

51. Indictment against Hallowell, Sept. 4, 1746; Indictment against Hallowell and Sessions, Sept. 20, 1746: Pleas of Hallowell and Sessions before the adjourned Windham Superior Court, Nov. [18], 1746; Sup. Ct. Rec., bk. 12, pp. 112–17, 131–33.

52. Sup. Ct. Rec., bk. 12, pp. 173, 175; Indictment against John Hallowell, Mar. 1746/47; *Rex* v. *Amasa Sessions*, Indictment, Mar. 1746/47, Windham Sup. Ct. Files, box 172. See William Blackstone, *Commentaries on the Laws of England* (Facsimile of 1st ed. of 1765–69) (Chicago, 1979), I:125–26, IV:198.

53. Larned, *History of Windham County*, I:363.

54. Even in the context of the inflation of the 1740s, Hallowell's bill of costs was unusually high: £110.2s6d. Sessions was hit hard in the pocketbook too; he was assessed £83.14s.2d. in costs.

55. Petition of John Hallowell, Oct. 1747, Conn. Archives, Crimes and Misdemeanors, Ser. I, IV: 108. . . .

56. Note Blackstone's discussion of the liability of "a physician or surgeon who gives his patient a portion . . . to cure him, which contrary to expectation kills him." *Commentaries*, IV:197.

57. Pomfret Vit. Rec., II:67.

58. Carroll Smith-Rosenberg, "Beauty, the Beast and the Militant Woman: A Case Study in Sex Roles and Social Stress in Jacksonian America," *American Quarterly* XXIII (1971):562–84. . . .

59. Sessions, *Sessions Family*, pp. 31, 35; Larned, *History of Windham County*, I:363–64.

DOCUMENTS: Supporting the Revolution

"The ladies going about for money exceeded everything . . ."

This broadside of 1780 announced a women's campaign to raise contributions for patriot soldiers. Organized and led by Esther DeBerdt Reed, wife of the president of Pennsylvania, and by Benjamin Franklin's daughter Sarah Franklin Bache, the campaign was large and effective. "Instead of waiting for the Donations being sent the ladys of each Ward go from dore to dore and collect them," wrote one participant. Collecting contributions this way invited confrontation. One loyalist wrote to her sister, "Of all absurdities, the ladies going about for money exceeded everything; they were so extremely importunate that people were obliged to give them something to get rid of them."* The campaign raised $300,000 in paper dollars in inflated war currency. Rather than let George Washington merge it with the general fund, the women insisted on using it to buy materials for making shirts so that each soldier might know he had received an extraordinary contribution from the women of Philadelphia. The broadside itself is an unusually explicit justification for women's intrusion into politics.

On the commencement of actual war, the Women of America manifested a firm resolution of contribute . . . to the deliverance of their country. Animated by the purest patriotism, they are sensible of sorrow at this day, in not offering more than barren wishes for the success of so glorious a Revolution. They aspire to render themselves more really useful; and this sentiment is universal from the north to the south of the Thirteen United States. Our ambition is kindled by the fame of those heroines of antiquity, who have rendered their sex illustrious, and have proved to the universe, that, if the weakness of our Constitution, if opinion and manners did not forbid us to march to glory by the same paths as the Men, we should at least equal, and sometimes surpass them in our love for the public good. I glory in all that which my sex has done great and commendable. I call to mind with enthusiasm and with admiration, all those acts of courage, of constancy and patriotism, which history has transmitted to us: The people favoured by Heaven, preserved from destruction by the virtues, the zeal and the resolution of Deborah, of Judith, of Esther! The fortitude of the mother of the Macchabees, in giving up her sons to die before her eyes: Rome saved from the fury of a victorious enemy by the efforts of Volumnia, and other Roman Ladies: So many famous sieges where the Women have been seen forgetting the weakness of their sex, building new walls, digging trenches with their feeble hands, furnishing arms to their defenders, they themselves darting the missile weapons on the enemy, resigning the ornaments of their apparel, and their fortune, to fill the public treasury, and to hasten the deliverance of their country; burying themselves under its ruins; throwing themselves into the flames rather than submit to the disgrace of humiliation before a proud enemy.

Born for liberty, disdaining to bear the irons of a tyrannic Government, we associate ourselves to the grandeur of those Sovereigns, cherished and revered, who have held with so much splendour the scepter of the greatest States, The Batildas, the Elizabeths, the Maries,

---

*Mary Morris to Catharine Livingston, June 10 [1780], Ridley Family Papers, Massachusetts Historical Society, Boston; Anna Rawle to Rebecca Rawle Shoemaker, June 30, 1780, in *Pennsylvania Magazine of History and Biography* 35 (1911):398.

Excerpted from *The Sentiments of an American Woman* ([Philadelphia]: John Dunlap, 1780).

the Catharines, who have extented the empire of liberty, and contented to reign by sweetness and justice, have broken the chains of slavery, forged by tyrants in times of ignorance and barbarity. . . .

We know that at a distance from the theatre of war, if we enjoy any tranquility, it is the fruit of your watchings, your labours, your dangers. . . . Who, amongst us, will not renounce with the highest pleasure, those vain ornaments, when she shall consider that the valiant defenders of America will be able to draw some advantage from the money which she may have laid out in these. . . . The time is

arrived to display the same sentiments which animated us at the beginning of the Revolution, when we renounced the use of teas, however agreeable to our taste, rather than receive them from our persecutors; when we made it appear to them that we placed former necessaries in the rank of superfluities, when our liberty was interested; when our republican and laborious hands spun the flax, prepared the linen intended for the use of our soldiers; when [as] exiles and fugitives we supported with courage all the evils which are the concomitants of war. . . .

Sarah Osborn, "The bullets would not cheat the gallows . . ."

Sarah Osborn was eighty-one years old when Congress made it possible for dependent survivors of Revolutionary war veterans to claim their pensions. She testified to her own service as well as to her husband's in the following deposition, sworn before the Court of Common Pleas in Wayne County, New Jersey, in 1837. Osborn's husband was a commissary guard; like many thousands of women, Osborn traveled with him, cooking and cleaning for troops at a time when there was no formal quartermaster corps and in which cleanliness was virtually the only guard against disease. Her account tells of working when the army was at West Point in 1780; of the long expedition south, marching proudly on horseback into Philadelphia, and then continuing to Yorktown. Osborn is the only one of the "women of the army" who has left us a narrative of her experiences. At Yorktown she brought food to soldiers under fire. When she told George Washington that she did not fear the bullets because they "would not cheat the gallows," she was conveying her understanding that her challenge to royal authority was congruent with his; if the soldiers risked being hanged for treason, so would she.

[In the march to Philadelphia in 1781?] Deponent was part of the time on horseback and part of the time in a wagon. Deponent's . . . husband was still serving as one of the commissary's guard. . . . They continued their march to Philadelphia, deponent on horseback through the streets. . . . Being out of bread, deponent was employed in baking the afternoon and evening . . . they continued their march . . . [at Baltimore she] embarked on

board a vessel and sailed . . . until they had got up the St. James River as far as the tide would carry them. . . . They . . . marched for Yorktown. . . . Deponent was on foot. . . . Deponent took her stand just back of the American tents, say about a mile from the town, and busied herself washing, mending, and cooking for the soldiers, in which she was assisted by the other females; some men washed their own clothing. She heard the roar of the artillery for a num-

---

Excerpted from John C. Dann, ed., The *Revolution Remembered: Eyewitness Accounts of the American Revolution* (Chicago: University of Chicago Press, 1980), pp. 240–45.

DEBORAH SAMPSON

Drawn by Joseph Stone Framingham 1797

Women like Sarah Osborn, who served in an informal quartermaster corps, were not the only women on or near Revolutionary War battlefields. In 1782, Deborah Sampson, who was already notable in her community of Middleborough, Massachusetts for her height and strength, adopted men's clothing and the name of Robert Shurtleff. She enlisted for service with the Fourth Massachusetts Regiment. Like many young women from impoverished families, Deborah Sampson had been bound out to domestic service as a young teenager; when her term was up she taught school briefly in Middleborough, and joined the First Baptist Church there. She was expelled from the church before her enlistment. She served with her regiment in New York and possibly in Pennsylvania until she was wounded at a battle near Tarrytown, New York.

After her return to Massachusetts, she married and bore three children, but the fame of her exploits persisted. After a fictionalized biography was published by Herman Mann, she went on a wide-ranging speaking tour, perhaps the first American woman to undertake such an enterprise, and applied for the pensions to which her wartime service entitled her. These were awarded slowly and grudgingly, and she died impoverished in 1827. (Joseph Stone, "Deborah Sampson Garrett," oil on paper, courtesy of the Rhode Island Historical Society) ber of days. . . . Deponent's . . . husband was there throwing up entrenchments, and deponent cooked and carried in beef, and bread, and coffee (in a gallon pot) to the soldiers in the entrenchment.

On one occasion when deponent was thus employed carrying in provisions, she met General Washington, who asked her if she "was not afraid of the cannonballs?"

She replied, "No, the bullets would not cheat the gallows," that "It would not do for the men to fight and starve too."

They dug entrenchments nearer and nearer to Yorktown every night or two till the last. While digging that, the enemy fired very heavy till about nine o'clock next morning, then stopped, and the drums from the enemy beat excessively. Deponent was a little way off in Colonel Van Shaick's or the officers' marquee and a number of officers were present. . . .

The drums continued beating, and all at once the officers hurrahed and swung their hats, and deponent asked them, "What is the matter now?"

One of them replied, "Are not you soldier enough to know what it means?"

Deponent replied, "No."

They then replied, "The British have surrendered."

Deponent, having provisions ready, carried the same down to the entrenchments that morning, and four of the soldiers whom she was in the habit of cooking for ate their breakfasts.

Deponent stood on one side of the road and the American officers upon the other side when the British officers came out of the town and rode up to the American officers and delivered up [their swords, which the deponent] thinks were returned again, and the British officers rode right on before the army, who marched out beating and playing a melancholy tune, their drums covered with black handkerchiefs and their fifes with black ribbands tied around them, into an old field and there grounded their arms and then returned into town again to await their destiny. . . . The British general at the head of the army was a large, portly man, full face, and the tears rolled down his cheeks as he passed along.

Rachel Wells, "I have Don as much to Carrey on the Warr as maney . . ."

Rachel Wells was probably sixty-five years old when she wrote the following words. She had bought loan office certificates from the state of New Jersey during the Revolution: subsequently she had moved to Philadelphia, but returned to Bordentown, New Jersey, after the war. In an effort to curb speculation, the New Jersey legislature decided that only state residents had a claim on interest payments; Rachel Wells's claim on her money was turned down because she had not been in the state at the war's end in 1783. She appealed directly to the Continental Congress. Although her petition was tabled, it remains—despite its bad spelling—as perhaps the most moving witness to the Revolution left to us by a woman. What did Rachel Wells think had been her contribution to the Revolution? What did she think the government owed to her?

Rachel Wells, Petition to Congress, May 18, 1786, Microfilm Papers of the Continental Congress, National Archives, Washington, D.C., microfilm M247, roll 56, item 42, vol. 8, pp. 354–55.

To the Honnorabell Congress I rachel do make this Complaint Who am a Widow far advanced in years & Dearly have ocasion of ye Interst for that Cash I Lent the States. I was a Sitisen in ye jersey when I Lent ye State a considerable Sum of Moneys & had I justice dun me it mite be Suficant to suporte me in ye Contrey whear I am now, near burdentown. I Leved hear then . . . but Being . . . so Robd by the Britans & others i went to Phila to try to get a Living . . . & was There in the year 1783 when our assembley was pleasd to pas a Law that No one Should have aney Interest that Livd out of jearsey Stats . . .

Now gentelmen is this Liberty, had it bin advertised that he or She that Moved out of the Stat should Louse his or her Interest you mite have sum plea against me. But I am Innocent Suspected no Trick. I have Don as much to Carrey on the Warr as maney that Sett now at ye healm of government. . . . your asembly Borrowed £300 in gould of me jest as the Warr Comencd & Now I Can Nither git Intrust nor principall Nor Even Security. . . . My dr Sister . . . wrote to me to be thankfull that I had it in my Power to help on the Warr which is well enough but then this is to be Considerd that others gits their Intrust & why then a poor old widow to be put of[f]. . . . I hartely pity others that ar in my Case that Cant Speak for themselves. . . .

god has Spred a plentifull table for us & you gentlemen are ye Carvers for us pray forgit Not the Poor weaklings at the foot of the Tabel ye poor Sogers has got Sum Crumbs That fall from their masters tabel. . . . Why Not Rachel Wells have a Little intrust?

if She did not fight She threw in all her mite which bought ye Sogers food & Clothing & Let Them have Blankets & Since that She has bin obligd to Lay upon Straw & glad of that. . . .

THE REPUBLICAN MOTHER AND THE WOMAN CITIZEN: CONTRADICTIONS AND CHOICES IN REVOLUTIONARY AMERICA

Linda K. Kerber

"I expect to see our young women forming a new era in female history," wrote Judith Sargent Murray in 1798. Her optimism was part of a general sense that all possibilities were open in the post-Revolutionary world. The experience of war had given words like *independence* and *self-reliance* personal as well as political overtones; among the things that ordinary people had learned from wartime had been that the world could, as the song played during the British surrender at Yorktown put it, turn upside down. The rich could quickly become poor; wives might suddenly have to manage farms and businesses; women might even, as the famous Deborah Sampson Gannett had done, shoulder a gun. Revolutionary experience taught that it was useful to be prepared for a wide range of unusual possibilities; political theory taught that republics rested on the virtue of their citizens. The stability and competence on which republican government relied required a highly literate and politically sophisticated constituency. Maintaining the republic was an intellectual and educational as well as a political challenge.

Murray herself, born into an elite family in Salem, Massachusetts, had felt the dislocations of the Revolution severely. Widowed, remarried to a Universalist minister of modest means, she understood what it was to be thrown on her own resources. "I would give my daughters every accomplishment which I thought proper," she wrote,

> and to crown all, I would early accustom them to habits of industry and order. They should be taught with precision the art economical; they should be enabled to procure for themselves the necessaries of life; independence should be placed within their grasp. . . . The SEX

This essay has been revised for the 5th edition of *Women's America*. It is drawn from *Women of the Republic: Intellect and Ideology in Revolutionary America* (Chapel Hill, N.C.: University of North Carolina Press, 1980), chs. 7 and 9; and *No Constitutional Right to Be Ladies: Women and the Obligations of Citizenship* (New York: Hill and Wang, 1998), introduction and ch. 1 © Linda K. Kerber.

should be taught to depend on their own efforts, for the procurement of an establishment in life.[1]

The model republican woman was competent and confident. She could resist the vagaries of fashion; she was rational, independent, literate, benevolent, and self-reliant. Nearly every writer who described this paragon prepared a list of role models, echoing the pantheon of heroines admired by the fund-raising women of Philadelphia in 1780 (see pp. 107–8). There were women of the ancient world, like Cornelia, the mother of the Gracchi; rulers like Elizabeth of England and the Empress Catherine the Great of Russia; and a long list of British intellectuals: Lady Mary Wortley Montagu, Hannah More, Mary Wollstonecraft, and the historian Catherine Macaulay. Those who believed in these republican models demanded that their presence be recognized and endorsed and that a new generation of young women be urged to find in them patterns for their own behavior.

The Revolutionary years had brought some women close to direct criticism of polit- ical systems. Women had signed petitions, they had boycotted imported tea and tex- tiles, they had made homespun and "felt nationly," as one young woman put it. In some places they had signed oaths of loyalty to patriot or loyalist forces. Rachel Wells bought £300 of government bonds to support the war and had a keen sense of her own contri- bution: "I did my Posabels every way . . . Ive Don as much to help on this war as Though I had bin a good Soger," she told the New Jersey legislature.[2] Women were citizens of the new republic. They could be naturalized; they were required to refrain from trea- son on pain of punishment; if single, they paid taxes. Women could develop their own agendas; when Abigail Adams wrote the now-famous letter in which she urged her hus- band and his colleagues in the Continental Congress to "remember the ladies," she urged that domestic violence should be on the republican agenda: "Put it out of the power of our husbands to use us with impunity," she demanded. "Remember all men would be tyrants if they could."[3]

Expressions of women's desire to play a frankly political role were regularly cam- ouflaged in satire, a device that typically makes new ideas and social criticism seem less threatening and more palatable. In 1791, for example, a New Jersey newspaper pub- lished a pair of semiserious satires in which women discuss the politics of excise taxes and national defense. "Roxana" expresses a feminist impatience:

> In fifty quarto volumes of ancient and modern history, you will not find fifty illustrious female names; heroes, statesmen, divines, philosophers, artists, are all of masculine gender. And pray what have they done during this long period of usurpation? . . . They have written ten thousand unintelligible books. . . . They have been cutting each other's throats all over the globe.[4]

Some years later, the students at Sarah Pierce's famous school for girls in Litchfield, Connecticut, prepared a "Ladies Declaration of Independence" for the Fourth of July. Alongside the frivolous phrasing is earnest comment on the unfilled promises of the republic. Less than ten years after that, Elizabeth Cady Stanton would use the same tech- nique. "When in the Course of Human Events," the Litchfield declaration begins,

> it becomes necessary for the Ladies to dissolve those bonds by which they have been sub- jected to others, and to assume among the self styled Lords of Creation that separate and equal station to which the laws of nature and their *own talents* entitle them, a decent respect

to the opinions of mankind requires, that they should declare the causes which impel them to the separation.

We hold these truths to be self evident. That all *mankind* are created equal.

The Litchfield women wished to change "social relations." They complained about men who "have undervalued our talents, and disparaged our attainments; they have combined with each other, for the purpose of excluding us from all participation in Legislation and in the administration of Justice."[5]

As these young women understood, American revolutionaries had brilliantly and radically challenged the laws governing the relationship between ruler and ruled, subjects and the king. Republican ideology was antipatriarchal. It voiced the claim of adult men to be freed from the control of kings and political "fathers" in an antique monarchical system. "Is it in the interest of a man to be a boy all his life?" Tom Paine asked in *Common Sense*, the great political manifesto of the era.

But the men who modeled the new American republic after the war remodeled it in their own image. They did not eliminate the political father immediately or completely. George Washington quickly became the "Father of his Country"; at the Governor's Palace in Williamsburg, Virginia, the life-size portrait of George III was quickly replaced by a life-size portrait of George Washington in a similar pose. American revolutionary men understood that two major elements of prerevolutionary social and political life—the system of slavery and the system of domestic relations—directly clashed with the egalitarian principles of the Revolution. But they kept both systems in place. By embedding the three-fifths compromise and the Fugitive Slave Law in the federal Constitution of 1787, the founders actually strengthened and stabilized the system of slavery. And they left virtually intact the old English law governing relations between husbands and wives.

In traditional English practice, at marriage a husband gained access to the body of his wife; it followed that he could easily pressure her into agreement with him on all other matters. A married woman was understood to be "covered" by her husband's civic identity, as though they were walking together under an umbrella that the husband held. There were relatively few constraints on what he could do with her body and her property, though she was nearly always guaranteed the use of one-third of their combined real estate and the ownership of one-third of the moveable property throughout her widowhood. The rules of coverture made it seem logical that fathers be the guardians of the children and that husbands manage the property that wives brought to marriage and earned during it. So long as she was married, she could not make a contract without his permission; she could not make a will until she was a widow. She could not make choices—for example, about to whom a child was to be apprenticed—that challenged the choices made by her husband. The revolutionary republic promised to protect "life, liberty and property," but under the old law a married woman was deprived of her property and had none to protect. Coverture was theoretically incompatible with revolutionary ideology and with the newly developing liberal commercial society. But patriot men carefully sustained it. Recognizing that husbands could easily pressure the electoral choices of married women, legislators concluded not that husbands should be controlled, but that women—unmarried as well as married—should not vote.

Yet the fact of women's citizenship in a democratic republic contained deep within it an implicit challenge to coverture. Patriot men rarely spoke about this issue, but their actions speak for them. In England, the killing of a husband by a wife was *petit treason*, analogous to regicide, although the killing of a wife by a husband was murder. The penalties for *petit treason* were worse than those for murder. The concept was not much enforced in colonial America, but it remained in the statutes. It was the only element of the old law of domestic relations that legislators of the early republic eliminated. Legislators were conscious of what they intended; they carefully retained the concept of *petit treason* for the killing of the master by a slave. With that single exception, neither the Revolutionary government under the Articles of Confederation nor the federal government of the Constitution directly challenged the legal system of coverture.[6] Every free man, rich or poor, white or black, gained something from the system of domestic relations already in place; they had no need to renegotiate it.

The best introduction to the old system of thinking about relations between women and men is to read the treatises on which judges and lawyers relied. They even continued to refer to the body of law of domestic relations by its traditional name, "the law of baron et feme"—not "husband and wife" or "man and woman" but "lord and woman." The same treatises that described the law of baron and feme invariably went on to laws of parent and child, master and servant.

In an era before law schools were attached to universities, and when prospective lawyers "read law" as apprentices in the offices of practitioners, Tapping Reeve conducted perhaps the most respected legal training in the nation. Students came from all over the country to study in his Litchfield, Connecticut, home; among them were Reeve's own brother-in-law Aaron Burr and, years later, John C. Calhoun from South Carolina. There were also future U.S. congressmen and senators, judges and Supreme Court justices. Reeve's treatise on the law of baron and feme, first published in 1816, was reprinted with up-to-date annotations in 1846, a testament to its continued vitality. Reeve offers us pithy accounts of what the early generations of American jurists took to be the common sense of the matter of relations between men and women. Nothing that he wrote would have surprised his contemporaries.

To follow the law of marriage, as Reeve delicately spun out its implications, is to watch the playing out of a stacked deck. Reeve began his book with the forthright statement that "the husband, by marriage, acquires an absolute title to all the personal property of the wife." Husbands also gained extensive power over her real estate; wives gained no advantages "in point of property" from marriage.

Once these asymmetrical property relations were established, personal implications wound their way throughout the law. The husband's control of all property gave him such coercive power over the wife that she could not defy him. Instead of revising the law to remove its coercive elements, jurists simply ensured that the coerced voices would not speak. Husbands were responsible for crimes committed by their wives in their presence or with their approval—except in the case of treason, a crime so severe that responsibility for it overrode obligation to the husband, or in the event that a wife kept a brothel with the husband's knowledge, since keeping a brothel "is an offense of which the wife is supposed to have the principal management."[7] Before married women signed away their right to dower property, judges were supposed to question them privately about whether their husbands had coerced them, although the law offered no protection against continued coercion. A wife could not normally make contracts in her own name;

if she did, her husband was bound "to fulfill the contract of his wife, when it is such an one as wives in her rank of life usually purchase. . . . If however, she were to purchase a ship or yoke of oxen, no such presumption would arise, for wives do not usually purchase ships or oxen."[8]

This system of marriage presupposed the husband's right to sexual access to the wife's body. When Reeve explained why it was logical that wives could not enter into contracts, his reason was not only that wives did not control property that could serve as a guarantee; it was that wives could not enter into contracts involving their own labor. "The right of the husband to the person of his wife," Reeve observed, " . . . is a right guarded by the law with the utmost solicitude; if she could bind herself by her contracts, she would be liable to be arrested, taken in execution, and confined in a prison; and then the husband would be deprived of the company of his wife, which the law will not suffer." If a husband were banished from the realm, however, then his wife "could contract, could sue and be sued in her own name; for, in this case, . . . he was already deprived of the company of his wife, and her confinement in prison would not deprive him of his wife to any greater extent than was already the case."[9]

That the system of marriage contradicted the basic tenets of republican thinking was obvious. But women who named the contradictions invited extraordinary hostility and ridicule. Among the most persistent themes was the link of female intellectual activity and political autonomy to an unflattering masculinity. "From all we read, and all we observe, we are authorized in supposing that there is a *sex of soul*," announced the Boston minister John Gardiner. "Women of masculine minds, have generally masculine manners. . . . Queen Elizabeth understood Latin and Greek, swore with the fluency of a sailor, and boxed the ears of her courtiers. . . . Mrs. Macaulay, the author of a dull democratic history, at a tolerably advanced age, married a boy." A "mild, dove-like remper is so necessary to Female beauty, is so natural a part of the sex," reflected Parson Mason Locke Weems wistfully. "A masculine air in a woman frightens us."[10]

When women addressed political issues, the attacks were similar. A good example of this response appears in a newspaper letter written in 1790 by a Marylander who signed himself as "Philanthropos." Warning against literal interpretations of the phrase "All mankind are born equal," "Philanthropos" thought the principle of equality could be "taken in too extensive a sense, and might tend to destroy those degrees of subordination which nature seems to point out," including the subordination of women to men. If women were inept, they were also somehow too effective.

> A Female Orator, in haranguing an Assembly, might like many crafty politicians, keep her *best argument* for last, and would then be sure of the victory—Men would be exposed to temptations too great for their strength, and those who could resist a bribe, offered in the common way, might reasonably yield to what it would be hardly possible for a *man* to refuse.

Selections from Mary Wollstonecraft's *Vindication of the Rights of Woman* were published in the American press shortly after the book appeared in 1792. She had borne one illegitimate daughter (Fanny Imlay) and lived with William Godwin before marrying him; after marriage she maintained lodgings in another house so that she could be free to write. Once her life history became generally known, it could be used to link intellectual women to political feminism and to aggressive sexuality, as the Federalist writer

Timothy Dwight did in his bitter "Morpheus" essays, which ran in a Boston newspaper in 1802. In a dream sequence in "Morpheus," Wollstonecraft has arrived in America and sets out to teach its inhabitants wisdom.

> Women . . . are entitled to all the rights, and are capable of all the energies, of men. I do not mean merely mental energies. If any dispute remained on this subject, I have removed it entirely by displaying, in my immortal writings, all the mental energy of LOCKE and BACON. I intend bodily energies. They can naturally run as fast, leap as high, and as far, and wrestle, scuffle, and box with as much success, as any of the . . . other sex.
>
> That is a mistake (said an old man) . . .
>
> It is no mistake, (said the Female Philosopher).
>
> . . . Why then, (said the senior again), are women always feebler than men?
>
> Because (said MARY) they are educated to be feeble; and by indulgence . . . are made poor, puny, baby-faced dolls; instead of the manly women, they ought to be.
>
> *Manly women!* (cried the wag). Wheu! a manly woman is a hoyden, a non descript.
>
> Am I a hoyden (interrupted MARY, with spirit.)
>
> You used to be a strumpet.

Wollstonecraft tells him that she was not a strumpet but a sentimental lover, "too free to brook the restraints of marriage." Her interlocutor responds, "We call them strumpets here, Madam—no offense, I hope," and then argues that when a woman claims the rights of men and the character of a manly woman, she necessarily forgoes what he calls women's "own rights" to "refined consideration." The implication is that Wollstonecraft can be insulted with impunity.

> Still (said the senior) you ought to remember that she is a woman.
>
> *She* ought to remember it (said the young man.)

Thus political behavior, like abstract thought, continued to be specifically proscribed as a threat to sensual attractiveness.

Only the Republican Mother was spared this hostility. The concept was a variant of the argument for the improved education of women that republicans such as Judith Sargent Murray and Wollstonecraft herself had demanded. It defended education for women not only for their autonomy and self-realization but also so that they could be better wives, rational household managers, and better mothers for the next generation of virtuous republican citizens—especially sons. In a widely reprinted speech, "Thoughts upon Female Education," originally given at the new Young Ladies Academy of Philadelphia, the physician and politician Benjamin Rush addressed the issue directly: "The equal share that every citizen has in the liberty and the possible share he may have in the government of our country make it necessary that our ladies should be qualified to a certain degree, by a peculiar and suitable education, to concur in instructing their sons in the principles of liberty and government." The Republican Mother was an educated woman who could be spared the criticism normally directed at the intellectually competent woman because she placed her learning at her family's service.

It was commonly believed that republican government was fragile and rested on the presence of virtuous citizens. The Republican Mother was also a Republican Wife.[11]

She chose a virtuous man for her husband; she condemned and corrected her husband's lapses from civic virtue; she educated her sons for it. The creation of virtuous citizens required wives and mothers who were well informed, "properly methodical," and free of "invidious and rancorous passions." The word *virtue* was derived from the Latin word for, man, with its connotations of virility. Political action was ideologically marked as masculine; as we have seen, if political voice required independent property holding, it was legally marked masculine as well. Virtue in a woman required another theater for its display. To that end, writers created a mother who had a political purpose and argued that her domestic behavior had a direct political function in the republic.

As one college orator put it,

> Let us then figure to ourselves the accomplished woman, surrounded by a sprightly band, from the babe that imbibes the nutritive fluid, to the generous youth. . . . Let us contemplate the mother distributing the mental nourishment to the fond smiling circle . . . watching the gradual openings of their minds . . . see, under her cultivating hand, reason assuming the reins of government, and knowledge increasing gradually to her beloved pupils. . . . Yes, ye fair, the reformation of a world is in your power. . . . It rests with you to make this retreat [from the corruptions of Europe] doubly peaceful, doubly happy, by banishing from it those crimes and corruptions, which have never yet failed of giving rise to tyranny, or anarchy. While you thus keep our country virtuous, you maintain its independence.[12]

Defined this way, the educated woman ceased to threaten the sanctity of marriage; the intellectual woman need not be masculine.

The ideology of Republican Motherhood was deeply ambivalent. On the one hand, it was a progressive ideology, challenging those who opposed women in politics by the proposal that women could—and should—play a political role through influencing their husbands and raising patriotic children. Within the dynamic relationships of the private family—between husbands and wives, mothers and children—it allocated an assertive role to women. Those who shared the vision of the Republican Mother usually insisted upon better education, clearer recognition of women's economic contributions, and a strong political identification with the republic. This ideology could complement the "fertility transition" under way in the postwar republic, a rapid fall in birthrates that would continue into our own time, and that was first found in urban areas that had experienced commercial and industrial as well as political revolution. Free women, the historian Susan Klepp has recently suggested, "applied egalitarian ideas and a virtuous, prudent sensibility to their bodies and to their traditional images of self as revolutions inspired discussion and debate. . . . On the household level, restricted fertility and high rates of literacy or years of education were persistently linked: the higher the educational attainment of women, the lower fertility rates."[13]

The idea that a mother can perform a political function represents the recognition that a citizen's political socialization takes place at an early age, that the family is a basic part of the system of political communication, and that patterns of family authority influence the general political culture. Most premodern political societies—and even some fairly modern democracies—maintain unarticulated, but nevertheless very firm, social restrictions that seem to isolate the family's domestic world from politics. The willingness of the American woman to overcome this ancient separation brought her into the political community.[14] In this sense, Republican Motherhood was an important and progressive invention congruent with revolutionary politics and the demographic transition. It altered the female domain in which most women had lived out their lives; it justified women's claims for participation in the civic culture. The ideology was strong enough to rout "Philan-thropos" and "Morpheus" by redefining female political behavior as valuable rather than abnormal, as a source of strength to the republic rather than an embarrassment. The ideology would be revived as a rallying point for many twentieth-century women reformers, who saw their committment to honest politics, efficient urban sanitation, and pure food and drug laws as an extension of their responsibilities as mothers.

But Republican Motherhood flourished in the context of coverture. The old law of domestic relations hemmed it in at every turn. Republican motherhood could legitimize only a minimum of political sophistication and interest. It was an extension into the republic of conservative traditions, stretching back at least as far as the Renaissance, that put narrow limits on women's assertiveness.[15] Captured by marriage, which not only secured their intimate relations but also their relationship to the public authority, for most of their lives most women had no alternative but to perform the narrow political role they managed to claim for themselves. Just as white planters claimed that democ-racy in the antebellum South necessarily rested on the economic base of black slavery, so male egalitarian society was said to rest on the moral base of deference among a class of people—women—who would devote their efforts to service by raising sons and dis-ciplining husbands to be virtuous citizens of the republic. The learned woman, who might very well wish to make choices as well as to influence attitudes, was a visible threat to this arrangement. Women were to contain their political judgments within their homes and families; they were not to bridge the world outside and the world within. The Republican Wife was not to tell her husband for whom to vote. She was a citizen but not really a constituent.

Restricting women's politicization was one of a series of conservative choices that Americans made in the postwar years as they avoided the full implications of their own Revolutionary radicalism. By these decisions Americans may well have been spared the agony of the French cycle of revolution and counterrevolution, which spilled more blood and produced a political system more regressive than had the American war. Never-theless, the impact of these choices was to leave race equality to the mercies of a bloody century that stretched from the Civil War through Reconstruction and lynching into the civil rights movement of our own time. And the impact of these choices was also to leave in place the system by which marriage stood between women and civil society. For most of the history of the United States, deep into the twentieth century, the legal traditions of marriage would be used to deny women citizens juries drawn from a full cross-section of the community, deny them control over their own property and their own earnings, sometimes deny them custody of their children, even deny them their rights as citizens should they marry a foreign man.

The "new era in female history" that Judith Sargent Murray had predicted remained to be created by women, fortified by their memories and myths of female strength dur-ing the trials of war, politicized by their resentment of male legislators slighting the issues of greatest significance to women. The promises of the republic remained to be fulfilled; remembering the Revolution helped to keep confidence alive. "Yes, gentle-men," said Elizabeth Cady Stanton to the New York legislature in 1854, "in republican America . . . we, the daughters of the revolutionary heroes of '76 demand at your hands the redress of our grievances—a revision of your State constitution—a new code of laws." Stanton understood that the traditions of coverture positioned domesticity against civic activism, motherhood against citizenship. Not until 1992 did the U.S. Supreme Court rule that as a general principle, "Women do not lose their constitutionally protected liberty when they marry."[16]

NOTES

1. Murray's newspaper essays were reprinted in a collected edition, *The Gleaner*, III (Boston, 1798). These comments appear in III, pp. 189; 167–68. See also Sheila L. Skemp, *Judith Sargent Murray: A Brief Biography with Documents* (Boston, 1998).

2. "Rachel Wells Petition for Relief," Nov 15, 1785, New Jersey Archives, Trenton.

3. Abigail Adams to John Adams, Mar. 31, 1776, *Adams Family Correspondence* (Cambridge, Mass., 1963), I: 370. See Nancy F. Cott, "Passionlessness: An Interpretation of Victorian Sexual Ideology, 1790–1850," *Signs: Journal of Women in Culture and Society* 4 (1978): 219–36.

4. *Burlington* (N.J.) *Advertiser*, Feb 1, 1791.

5. Miss Pierce's School Papers, 1849, Litchfield His. Soc., Litchfield, Conn.

6. See, for example, "An Act for Annulling the Distinction between the Crimes of Murder and Petit Treason," March 16, 1785, in Asahel Stearns et al., eds., *The General Laws of Massachusetts* . . . I (Boston, 1823), p. 188.

7. Tapping Reeve, *The Law of Baron and Femme, Parent and Child, Guardian and Ward, Master and Servant, and of the Powers of the Courts of Chancery* (New Haven, 1816; Burlington, 1846), ch. v, p. 73.

8. Reeve, ch. vi, pp. 78–79.

9. Reeve, ch. viii, pp. 98–99.

10. *New-England Palladium*, Sept. 18, 1801; Parson Mason Locke Weems, *Hymen's Recruiting Sergeant* (Philadelphia, 1800).

11. Jan Lewis, "The Republican Wife: Virtue and Seduction in the Early Republic," *William and Mary Quarterly* ser. 3, vol. 44 (1987):689–721.

12. *New York Magazine*, May 1795, pp. 301–5.

13. Susan E. Klepp, "Revolutionary Bodies: Women and the Fertility Transition in the Mid-Atlantic Region, 1760–1820," *Journal of American History* vol. 85 (1998), pp. 916, 915 (I have reversed the order of the sentences).

14. See Gabriel Almond and Sidney Verba, *The Civic Culture* (Princeton, 1963), pp. 377–401.

15. Elaine Forman Crane emphasizes this dimension; see *Ebb-Tide in New England: Women, Seaports, and Social Change, 1630–1800* (Boston, 1998), ch. 6.

16. *Planned Parenthood of Pennsylvania* v. *Casey* 112 S. Ct. 2791 (1992).

II

The Many Frontiers of Industrializing America 1820–1880

To Americans who lived through it, the Civil War was the most traumatic experience of the nineteenth century. The years from 1830 to 1860 have come to be called the *antebellum* period, as though their importance derives from what they preceded rather than what they encompassed. Other familiar labels—the Jacksonian era, the Rise of the Common Man, Freedom's Ferment—suggest the difficulty historians have had in characterizing the period.

In these years the American economy was transformed by the industrial revolution. Railroads and steamboats linked distant parts of the country and simplified economic interaction; during the Civil War the control of transportation networks would be an important ingredient in the North's success. The cotton gin ensured the profitability of the crop and reinforced the system of slave labor in the South. Steam-powered spinning and weaving equipment was placed in northern factories and tended by a new class of wage workers. The distinctive economies of North and South fostered a political dialogue that became increasingly acerbic over the years. The position of legislators on issues as disparate as tariffs or free speech could be linked to the economic interests of their sections and to the distinctive regional cultures. By 1860 institutions that had helped connect the two cultures—political parties, churches, economic networks—had broken down completely.

It has been relatively easy for historians to see that economic and political developments affected men's lives. The right to vote and hold office was extended to virtually every white man, whether or not he held property; after the Civil War it was extended to black men in many parts of the country. Congress was a national forum for debate among male political leaders; by the 1850s speeches made there were rapidly diffused to the public by cheap newspapers, printed by newly efficient presses and distributed by railroads throughout the nation. A host of new careers opened to men as politicians, journalists, teachers, capitalists, physicians, and reformers. The expansion of the physical boundaries of the country, by treaty and by war, opened new frontiers and created new opportunities for farmers, merchants, civic promoters, and land speculators.

When we look at these developments through women's eyes, we find that women's lives also changed markedly. The transportation revolution, for example, had

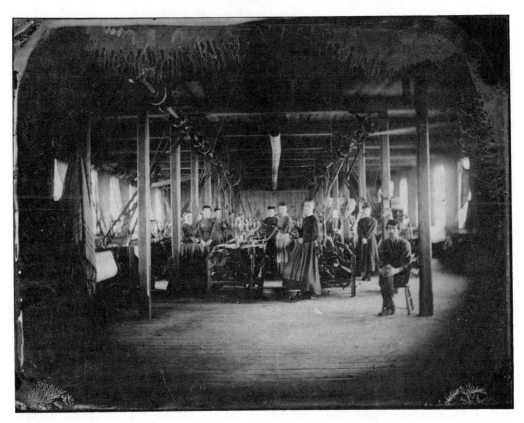

Women at textile machinery in a New England mill, approximately 1850. (Courtesy of George Eastman House)

special significance for women. Single women rarely traveled in the colonial period; long trips meant nights in unfamiliar taverns and lodging houses where accommodations were uncertain and safety could not be assured. The railroad changed that. In the three weeks between January 5 and January 26, 1855, Antoinette Brown and Ernestine Rose spoke at women suffrage meetings in eleven different counties in upstate New York.[1]

The women who traveled to raise funds for abolition societies and women's seminaries could not have played that role a century before. After the Civil War Elizabeth Cady Stanton and Susan B. Anthony traveled a regular lyceum circuit throughout the North and Midwest, speaking on behalf of women's rights.

Improvements in the printing technology and distribution of newspapers meant that women as well as men were no longer dependent on local sources of information and political guidance. Even if one's town lacked a temperance society or an abolitionist organization, one could still subscribe to a temperance or abolitionist newspaper. A person who did so was reaching out, past the local notables—ministers, politicians, lawyers—who had shaped opinion in the colonial period, to make contact with a larger political community. Abolition newspapers like the *National Anti-Slavery Standard* (which was, for a time, edited by a woman, Lydia Maria Child) and women's rights newspapers like *Una* or *The Revolution* could come straight to a woman's mailbox, enlarging her political world.

Although women could travel more freely and read more widely, in other ways the new industrial economy constrained their lives. As Gerda Lerner has pointed out, many of the new opportunities for men came in a form that closed options for women. When additional men were granted suffrage, for example, "women's political status, while legally unchanged, . . . deteriorated relative to the advances made by men." When new medical schools offered formal training only to men, "the process of professionalization . . . proceeded in such a way as to institutionalize an exclusion of women. . . . The status differential between male and female practitioners was more obviously disadvantageous and underscored women's marginality."[2]

The historian David Potter urged us to ask whether established generalizations about the past apply to women as accurately as they apply to men. We often find that they do not. Several traditional pictures must be refocused. For example, the great religious revival of the early part of the century is often described as though it affected both men and women with equal force. But careful examination of church records has suggested that women were already church members when the revival began; the new recruits were most likely to be sons and husbands of women who had long since been "saved." Seen in this light, the Second Great Awakening may be better understood as an occasion on which women acted as a catalyst for church recruitment.[3]

Although the experience of slavery has long received attention from historians, the distinctive experience of female slaves has been little examined until recently. Work roles on the plantation were defined by gender as well as by race. Women were especially vulnerable to sexual exploitation and to debilitating chronic ailments incidental to childbearing.

In free households female work—including taking in boarders, washing their clothes, and cooking for them—might account for as much income as working-class husbands gained from their own employment. If the husband's work was seasonal or erratic, the steady income from taking in boarders could be crucial to the family's survival. The story of the work done by women who took in boarders ought not to be relegated to the obligatory chapters on "home and family life." As Sharon Block shows, many "free" laborers were indentured or apprentices, and many indentured and enslaved girls and women worked in domestic service. Housework is central to the history of American labor.

Traditional interpretations of industrialization require refinement. Familiar accounts are likely to ignore the dependence of early factories on piecework done by women in their homes or on women for their actual labor force. Even Alexander Hamilton recognized that a crucial factor in the development of new factories was that their owners could count on a steady supply of female workers at low rates of pay. The "feminization of poverty" long predated the twentieth century; women were among the poorest workers. But they were also among the first self-conscious laborers in the United States; in Lowell, Massachusetts, some 2,000 women supported an unsuccessful strike in 1834.

Viewed through women's eyes, antebellum America looks different. The common school movement looms even larger than in traditional accounts. As Kathryn Kish Sklar's essay suggests, the story of the building of public schools does not begin and end with

Horace Mann and Henry Barnard. The work of Emma Willard and Catharine Beecher also requires attention. A history of education in antebellum America needs to explain how the great gap in literacy between men and women was closed during those years, and it must also find room for the large number of women who worked, even briefly, as schoolteachers at wage rates so low that planners could think it feasible to construct enough classrooms to educate every child in America.

The frontier has traditionally been treated as a metaphor for unbounded opportunity. New scholarship in the last decade has emphasized the multicultural complexities of frontiers, and their capacity to be sites of tension, rivalry, and violence. The experience of married women in the trans-Mississippi West was likely to be one of hardship encountered at the urging of their husbands, not out of their own initiative and choice. Malcolm Rohrbough explores the complexity of gender relations during the California Gold Rush.

Finally, in the middle years of the nineteenth century women pressed at the limits of the ways in which nonvoting citizens could influence the political order. In antislavery petition campaigns, in lobbying to persuade legislatures to reform laws dealing with married women's property rights and child custody, in responding to the crisis of the Civil War, in pressing charges against former Confederates who tried physically to intimidate them, in volunteering as teachers for freedmen's schools, women expressed political opinions and sought to shape political events. Some, like Catharine Beecher and Sarah Josepha Hale, began to formulate an interpretation of the republican community that suggested women could play an important part in it without voting; others, like Elizabeth Cady Stanton and Sojourner Truth, insisted that women's political rights ought to be the same as those of men.[4] But whatever particular solutions they proposed, whether suffragist or not, the way in which women's citizenship was displayed was a significant element on the American political scene.

NOTES

1. "Announcement by Susan B. Anthony," Jan. 5, 1855, *The Selected Papers of Elizabeth Cady Stanton and Susan B. Anthony* (New Brunswick, N.J., 1997), p. 291.
2. Gerda Lerner, *The Majority Finds Its Past: Placing Women in History* (New York, 1979), pp. 18, 20.
3. "American Women and the American Character" (1962), in *History and American Society: Essays of David M. Potter*, ed. Don E. Fehrenbacher (New York, 1979), p. 279; Mary P. Ryan, "A Woman's Awakening: Evangelical Religion and the Families of Utica, New York, 1800–1840," *American Quarterly* 30 (1978): 602–23; see also Catherine A. Brekus, *Strangers & Pilgrims: Female Preaching in America 1740–1845* (Chapel Hill, N.C., 1998), esp. pp. 343–46.
4. For Sojourner Truth's politics, see Carleton Mabee, *Sojourner Truth: Slave, Prophet, Legend* (New York, 1993), esp. chap. 15.

DOCUMENTS: The Testimony of Slave Women

> ## *Maria Perkins, "I am quite heartsick . . ."*

Because masters understood the connection between literacy and rebelliousness, slaves were rarely taught to read and write. This anguished letter from Maria Perkins is unusual because it was written by an enslaved woman. We do not know whether Perkins's husband Richard managed to persuade his master to buy her and keep the family together. If a trader did buy Maria Perkins or her child, the likelihood of permanent separation was great. Scottsville, mentioned in the letter, is a small town near Charlottesville; Staunton is some forty miles away.

Charlottesville, Oct. 8th, 1852

Dear Husband I write you a letter to let you know my distress my master has sold albert to a trader on Monday court day and myself and other child is for sale also and I want you to let [me] hear from you very soon before next cort if you can I don't know when I don't want you to wait till Christmas I want you to tell dr Hamelton and your master if either will buy me they can attend to it know and then I can go afterwards. I don't want a trader to get me they asked me if I had got any person to buy me and I told them no they took me to the court houste too they never put me up a man buy the name of brady bought albert and is gone I don't know where they say he lives in Scottesville my things is in several places some is in staunton and if I should be sold I don't know what will become of them I don't expect to meet with the luck to get that way till I am quite heartsick nothing more I am and ever will be your kind wife Maria Perkins.

Maria Perkins to Richard Perkins, October 8, 1852, Ulrich B. Phillips Collection, Yale University Library, New Haven.

> ## *Rose, "Look for some others for to 'plenish de earth"*

Letters like Maria Perkins's are very rare. Most firsthand evidence of the experience of being a slave comes from narratives prepared by ex-slaves after they were free. Some accounts were published by abolitionist societies before the Civil War; some people were interviewed by agents of the Freedmen's Bureau after the war. A large group of elderly ex-slaves was interviewed in the 1930s as part of the Federal Writers' Project. One of these speakers we know only as Rose.

Manuscript Slave Narrative Collection, Federal Writers' Project, 1941, vol. 17, Texas Narratives, part 4, pp. 174–78, Library of Congress, Washington, D.C.

Abolitionists accused masters of breeding slaves as they did cattle. Masters denied these charges and claimed that high birth rates among slave women should be taken as evidence of high levels of nutrition and good treatment. In Brazil, for example, where the treatment of slaves was more brutal, fewer children survived. There was some truth to this defense. But slave women lacked the normal legal protections against sexual coercion. It has long been known that Sally Hemings, one of Thomas Jefferson's slaves, was the half-sister of Jefferson's wife, Martha Wayles. In his own lifetime, Jefferson's political opponents had claimed that he had fathered at least one of Sally Hemings' children; family tradition among the descendants of Sally Hemings confirmed the point. In 1998, DNA tests established that the contemporary descendant of Eston Hemings Jefferson carries the same Y chromosome as that carried in Thomas Jefferson's own lineage.[*]

We are unlikely to know the emotional quality of the relationship between Sally Hemings and Thomas Jefferson; we do not know whether and to what extent it rested on coercion. But it is certain that Jefferson owned Hemings, and that she had no free choice in the matter. When Federalists denounced Jefferson for hypocritical denunciations of miscegenation, they were on the mark.

As Rose's moving narrative shows, on the average plantation, the line between "forced breeding" and "strong encouragement" could be a thin one.

What I say am de facts. If I's one day old, I's way over 90, and I's born in Bell Country, right here in Texas, and am owned by Massa William Black. He owns mammy and pappy, too. Massa Black has a big plantation but he has more niggers dan he need for work on dat place, 'cause he am a nigger trader. He trade and buy an sell all de time.

Massa Black am awful cruel and he whip de cullud folks and works 'em hard and feed dem poorly. We'uns have for rations de cornmeal and milk and 'lasses and some beans and peas and meat once a week. We'uns have to work in de field every day from daylight till dark and on Sunday we'uns do us washin'. Church? Shucks, we'uns don't know what dat mean.

I has de correct mem'randum of when de war start. Massa Black sold we'uns right den. Mammy and pappy powerful glad to get sold, and dey and I is put on de block with 'bout ten other niggers. When we'uns gits te de tradin' block, dere lots of white folks dere what come to look us over. One man shows de intres' in pappy. Him named Hawkins. He talk to pappy and pappy talk to him and say, "Dem my woman and chiles. Please buy all of us and have mercy on we'uns." Massa Hawkins say,

"Dat gal am a likely lookin' nigger, she am portly and strong, but three am more dan I wants, I guesses."

De sale start and 'fore long pappy a put on de block. Massa Hawkins wins de bid for pappy and when mammy am put on de block, he wins de bid for her. Den dere am three or four other niggers sold befo' my time comes. Den massa Black calls me to de block and de auction man say, "What am I offer for dis portly, strong young wench. She's never been 'bused and will make de good breeder."

I wants to hear Massa Hawkins bid, but him say nothin'. Two other men am biddin' 'gainst each other and I sho' has de worryment. Dere am tears comin' down my cheeks 'cause I's bein' sold to some man dat would make sep'ration from my mammy. One man bids $500 and de auction man ask, "Do I hear more? She am gwine at $500.00." Den someone say, $525.00 and de auction man say, "She am sold for $525.00 to Massa Hawkins." Am I glad and 'cited! Why, I's quiverin' all over.

Massa Hawkins takes we'uns to his place and it am a nice plantation. Lots better am dat place dan Massa Black's. Dere is 'bout 50 niggers what is growed and lots of chillen. De first thing massa do when we'uns gits home am

*Dinitia Smith and Nicholas Wade, "DNA Test Finds Evidence of Jefferson Child by Slave," *New York Times*, Nov. 1, 1998, p. A1.

give we'uns rations and a cabin. You mus' believe dis nigger when I says dem rations a feast for us. Dere plenty meat and tea and coffee and white flour. I's never tasted white flour and coffee and mammy fix some biscuits and coffee. Well, de biscuits was yum, yum, yum to me, but de coffee I doesn't like.

De quarters am purty good. Dere am twelve cabins all made from logs and a table and some benches and bunks for sleepin' and a fireplace for cookin' and de heat. Dere am no floor, jus' de ground.

Massa Hawkins am good to he niggers and not force 'em work too hard. Dere am as much diff'ence 'tween him and old Massa Black in de way of treatment as 'twixt de Lawd and de devil. Massa Hawkins 'lows he niggers have reason'ble parties and go fishin', but we'uns am never tooken to church and has no books for larnin'. Dere am no edumcation for de niggers.

Dere am one thing Massa Hawkins does to me what I can't shunt from my mind. I knows he don't do it for meanness, but I allus holds it 'gainst him. What he done am force me to live with dat nigger, Rufus, 'gainst my wants.

After I been at he place 'bout a year, de massa come to me and say, "You gwine live with Rufus in dat cabin over yonder. Go fix it for livin'." I's 'bout sixteen year old and has no larnin', and I's jus' igno'mus chile. I's thought dat him mean for me to tend de cabin for Rufus and some other niggers. Well, dat am start de pestigation for me.

I's took charge of de cabin after work am done and fixes supper. Now, I don't like dat Rufus, 'cause he a bully. He am big and 'cause he so, he think everybody do what him say. We'uns has supper, den I goes here and dere talkin', till I's ready for sleep and den I gits in de bunk. After I's in, dat nigger come and crawl in de bunk with me 'fore I knows it. I says, "What you mean, you fool nigger?" He say for me to hush de mouth. "Dis am my bunk, too," he say.

"You's teched in de head. Git out," I's told him, and I puts de feet 'gainst him and give him a shove and out he go on de floor 'fore he knows what I's doin'. Dat nigger jump up and he mad. He look like de wild bear. He starts for de bunk and I jumps quick for de poker. It am 'bout three feet long and when he comes at me I let him have it over de

head. Did dat nigger stop in he tracks? I's say he did. He looks at me steady for a minute and you's could tell he thinkin' hard. Den he go and set on de bench and say, "Jus wait. You thinks it am smart, but you's am foolish in de head. Dey's gwine larn you somethin'."

"Hush yous big mouth and stay 'way from dis nigger, dat all I wants," I say, and jus' sets and hold dat poker in de hand. He jus' sets, lookin' like de bull. Dere we'uns sets and sets for 'bout an hour and den he go out and I bars de door.

De nex' day I goes to de missy and tells her what Rufus wants and missy say dat am de massa's wishes. She say, "Yous am de portly gal and Rufus am de portly man. De massa wants you-uns for to bring forth portly chillen."

I's thinkin' 'bout what de missy say, but say to myse'f, "I's not gwine live with dat Rufus." Dat night when him come in de cabin, I grabs de poker and sits on de bench and says, "Git 'way from me, nigger, 'fore I busts yous brains out and stomp on dem." He say nothin' and git out.

De nex' day de massa call me and tell me, "Woman, I's pay big money for you and I's done dat for de cause I wants you to raise me chillens. I's put yous to live with Rufus for dat purpose. Now, if you doesn't want whippin' at de stake, yous do what I wants."

I thinks 'bout massa buyin' me offen de block and savin' me from bein' sep'rated from my folks and 'bout bein' whipped at de stake. Dere it am. What am I's to do? So I 'cides to do as de massa wish and so I yields.

When we'uns am given freedom, Massa Hawkins tells us we can stay and work for wages or share crop de land. Some stays and some goes. My folks and me stays. We works de land on shares for three years, den moved to other land near by. I stay with my folks till they dies.

If my mem'radum am correct, it am 'bout thirty year since I come to Fort Worth. Here I cooks for white folks till I goes blind 'bout ten year ago.

I never marries, 'cause one 'sperience am 'nough for dis nigger. After what I does for de massa, I's never wants no truck with any man. De Lawd forgive dis cullud woman, but he have to 'scuse me and look for some others for to 'plenish de earth.

SHARON BLOCK

Lines of Color, Sex, and Service: Sexual Coercion in the Early Republic

A long tradition of describing Northern society as "free" and Southern society as "slave" has had the unfortunate effect of making distinctions seem far more clear in retrospect than they were in experience. Manumission was gradual in most Northern states, and that meant that a mixture of slavery, indentured labor, and freedom persisted throughout the first half of the nineteenth century. The abolitionist Sojourner Truth [see pp. 211–13] was born into slavery as Isabella Van Wagenen in New York in the late 1790s. As a child she was sold twice; when she married it was under a New York state law that recognized marriages between slaves. When she became free on July 4, 1827, according to New York state law she owed no further service, but her children, born after 1799, were bound to service for as much as a decade longer. "Indentured," writes the historian Nell Painter, "the children could not follow Isabella into freedom. . . . When Sojourner Truth became an abolitionist, some of her children were not free."*

Children of poor families were put out to bound labor during the early republic; burdened by their work, they were also vulnerable to the power and authority of their masters. This included, as we see in the essay that follows, vulnerability to sexual coercion—a term Sharon Block uses to mark a wider range of experience than is suggested by the simple term rape. The essay that follows is based on a close reading of a Pennsylvania court record and on one of the great autobiographies of the nineteenth century, Harriet Jacobs' *Incidents in the Life of a Slave Girl*. Writing under a pseudonym after years as a fugitive, supported in her project by the abolitionist writer and editor Lydia Maria Child, Jacobs herself became invisible to historians. For many years her narrative was treated as fiction. Not until 1987, when historian Jean Fagan Yellin published an edition identifying virtually all the individuals and substantiating virtually all the events, has it been possible to understand the narrative as nonfiction. It is compelling reading.**

In what ways did Rachel Davis and Harriet Jacobs try to avoid the power of their masters? In whom did they find allies? In what ways were the experiences of these young women similar? What difference did slavery make?

---

*Nell Irvin Painter, *Sojourner Truth: A Life, A Symbol* (New York: W. W. Norton, 1996), p. 23.

**Harriet A. Jacobs, *Incidents in the Life of a Slave Girl: Written by Herself*, ed. Jean Fagan Yellin (Cambridge, Mass.: Harvard University Press, 1987).

Excerpted from "Lines of Color, Sex, and Service: Comparative Sexual Coercion in Early America," by Sharon Block, in Martha Hodes, ed., *Sex, Love, Race: Crossing Boundaries in North American History* (New York: New York University Press, 1999).
Note: First names are used for all actors in incidents of sexual coercion because first names more easily distinguish men from women and eliminate confusion in identifying members of the same family.

Rachel Davis was born a free white child in the Pennsylvania mountains in 1790. She was fourteen years old when she became an indentured servant to William and Becky Cress in Philadelphia County. By the time Rachel was fifteen, William had begun making sexual overtures to her. After months of continuing sexual assaults, William's wife, Becky, suspected that her husband was having a sexual relationship with their servant. Ultimately, Becky demanded that Rachel be removed from the house. William continued to visit Rachel at her new home, again trying to have sex with her. In 1807, Rachel's father found out what had occurred and initiated a rape prosecution against William, who was found guilty and sentenced to ten years in prison.[1]

Harriet Jacobs was born an enslaved black child in Edenton, North Carolina, in 1813. In 1825, she became a slave in James and Mary Norcom's household. By the time Harriet was sixteen, James had begun making sexual overtures toward her. After months of continuing sexual assaults, James's wife, Mary, suspected that her husband was having a sexual relationship with their slave. Ultimately, Mary demanded that Harriet be removed from the house. James continued to visit Harriet at her new home, again trying to have sex with her. In 1835, Harriet became a runaway slave, and spent the next seven years a fugitive, hiding in her free grandmother's attic crawlspace.[2]

If we were to focus on the conclusions to these stories, we would frame a picture of the contrasting consequences for masters who sexually coerced black and white women: the master of the white servant was sent to prison, while the black slave imprisoned herself to escape her abuser. But these opposing ends tell only part of the story. Until their conclusions, both women engaged in nearly parallel struggles with masters, mistresses, and unwanted sexual overtures. This contrast between the laborers' similar experiences and their stories' opposing conclusions suggests that the practice of sexual coercion and the classification of the criminal act of rape were differently dependent on status and race.

. . . Rachel had an opportunity for institutional intervention that was unequivocally denied to Harriet. Enslaved women in early America did not have access to legal redress against white men who raped them. While no colonial or early republic statute explicitly excluded enslaved women from being the victims of rape or attempted rape, many mid-Atlantic and Southern legislatures set harsh punishments for black men's sexual assaults on white women, thus implicitly privileging white women as victims of rape.[3] At the same time, enslaved people could only be witnesses against non-white defendants, so an enslaved woman could not testify against a white man who had raped her.[4] Accordingly, no historian has recorded a conviction of a white man for the rape of a slave at any point from 1700 to the Civil War, let alone a conviction of a master for raping his own slave. Rape in early America was a crime whose definition was structured by race.[5]

Even though the early American legal system segregated Rachel Davis and Harriet Jacobs into incomparable categories, their own presentations told nearly parallel stories of sexual coercion. In both women's stories, their masters attempted to control the parameters and meanings of sexual acts. Thus, rape in these situations was not just an act of power, it was also the power to define an act. Servants and slaves could not only be forced to consent, but this force was refigured as consent. At the same time, neither Harriet Jacobs nor Rachel Davis presented herself as an abject victim of her master's will.

Rather than a clear demarcation between the rape of slaves and the rape of servants, these narratives suggest that black and white laboring women interpreted and experienced a master's sexual coercion in strikingly similar ways. The parallels in these two stories, however, stopped at the courtroom door, where a racially based legal system ended the women's comparable negotiations of personal interactions.

CREATING MASTERY:
THE PROCESS OF COERCION

How did a master sexually coerce a servant or slave in early America? A master did not have to rely on physical abilities to force his dependents into a sexual act. Instead, he might use the power of his position to create opportunities for sexual coercion, backing a woman into a corner where capitulation was her best option. A servant or enslaved woman often recognized this manipulation and tried to negotiate her way around her master's overtures rather than confront him with direct resistance. But that compromise came at a high price . . . negotiation implied willingness, and a woman's willingness contrasted with the early American legal and social code that rape consisted of irresistible force. Despite its surface counterintuitiveness, it was precisely women's attempts to bargain their way out of sexual assaults that made these sexual encounters seem consensual.[6]

Both Harriet Jacobs and Rachel Davis drew direct links between their status and their masters' sexual assaults on them. Each explained how her master had forced her into situations where he could sexually coerce her without being discovered. Rachel described how William ordered her to hold the lantern for him one night in the stable, where he "tried to persuade me to something." In the most blatantly contrived incident, when they were reaping in the meadow, William "handed me his sickle & bad me to lay it down. He saw where I put it." Later that night, William asked Rachel,

> where I put them sickles. I asked if he did not see—he said no, I must come & show him. I told him I cd go with my sister, or by myself. he said that was not as he bad me. I went. Before we got quite to sickles, he bad me stop—I told him I was partly to the sickles—he bad me stop—I did—he came up & threw me down. . . . I hallowed—he put his hand over my mouth . . . he pulled up my cloathes, & got upon me . . . he did penetrate my body. I was dreadfully injured.

According to Rachel's statement, William had forced her to accompany him into a dark field on a contrived search for a purposefully lost farm implement so that he could rape her. William's authority to control where she went and what she did was integral to his ability to force Rachel to have sex with him.

Harriet Jacobs was even more explicit about the connections between James Norcum's mastery and his ability to force her into sexually vulnerable positions. It seemed to Harriet that he followed her everywhere—in her words, "my master met me at every turn"—trying to force her to have sex with him. As William did with Rachel, James structured Harriet's work so that she was often alone with him. He ordered Harriet to bring his meals to him so that while she watched him eat he could verbally torture her with the consequences of refusing his sexual overtures. Harriet further recalled that "when I suc-

ceeded in avoiding opportunities for him to talk to me at home, I was ordered to come to his office, to do some errand." Tiring of Harriet's continued resistance, James ordered his four-year-old daughter to sleep near him, thus requiring that Harriet also sleep in his room in case the child needed attention during the night. James repeatedly used his position as a master who controlled his slave's labor to manipulate Harriet into sexually vulnerable situations.[7] Controlling a woman's daily routine, her work requirements, and her physical presence—in other words, control over her labor and her body—gave men in positions of mastery access to a particular means of sexually coercive behavior.

Each woman also recalled how she had challenged her master's right to force her into a sexual relationship. Rachel recounted how she had "resisted" and "cried" when William tried to pull her into a darkened bedroom after sending the rest of the servants to bed, and how she threatened that she would tell his wife what he was doing. When these forms of resistance did not end his overtures, Rachel tried to carry out her master's orders in ways that might prevent her own sexual vulnerability. Rachel's description of being raped in the dark field began by recollecting that she had suggested that William could find the sickle himself, and then offered to find it on her own or with her sister. Ultimately, William resorted to his position as a master—"he said that was not as he bad me"—and issued a direct order for Rachel to accompany him. Rachel portrayed an interactive relationship with William: she may not have been able to override her master's orders, but she forced him to change their content. Rather than sex in the bedroom while the other children slept and his wife was away, Rachel forced William to order her into the dark field, thereby disrupting his original attempts at a seamless consensual interaction.

Harriet Jacobs's story contained similar efforts to avoid her master's sexual overtures that forced him to refigure his behavior. When Mary Norcum's suspicions made her husband revert to physical gestures instead of words to convey his sexual desires to Harriet, Harriet responded by letting "them pass, as if I did not understand what he meant." When James realized that Harriet could read, he wrote her notes that expressed his sexual intentions. But

Harriet repeatedly pretended "'I can't read them, sir.'" Overall, "by managing to keep within sight of people, as much as possible during the day time, I had hitherto succeeded in eluding my master." Harriet forced James into baldly claiming his right for sexual access as a privilege of mastery: according to Harriet, James began constantly "reminding me that I belonged to him, and swearing by heaven and earth that he would compel me to submit to him" because "I was his property; that I must be subject to his will in all things." Like Rachel Davis, Harriet Jacobs engaged in an exchange of maneuvers with her master where each tried to foil the other's plans and counterplans. Despite her master's legal property in her body, Harriet did not portray herself as utterly powerless. By playing into his image of her as too stupid to understand his signs and too illiterate to read his notes, Harriet used her own position as a slave to avoid her master's sexual overtures, forcing him to raise the stakes of his desires toward her.[8]

Because he did not receive unquestioned acquiescence from a servant or slave, a master had to create situations in which his laborers had little choice but to have sexual relations with him. Rachel's attempted refusal to go alone into a dark field with her master and Harriet's feigned ignorance of her master's intentions forced each man to modify his route to sexual interactions. By not consenting to a master's more subtle attempts at sexual relations, a servant or slave might force her master into more overtly coerced sexual acts. Ironically, this compelled a master to enact his laborer's interpretation of his overtures. Rather than the sexual offers that the masters first proposed, the men were forced to use coercion to carry out their sexual plans. Theoretically, a master could coerce through his physical prowess, but most masters did not have to rely exclusively on fists or whips to commit rape. Instead, they could rely on the strength of their mastery.

Beyond the unadorned physical power that could compel a woman into a sexual act, a master had an array of indirect means to force a dependent to have sex with him that simultaneously denied her resistance to him. . . . Harriet characterized her master as "a crafty man, [who] resorted to many means to accomplish his purposes. Sometimes he had stormy, terrific ways, that made his victims

tremble; sometimes he assumed a gentleness that he thought must surely subdue." James promised Harriet that if she would give in to him sexually, "I would cherish you. I would make a lady of you." The possibility of a better life that transcended her racial and labor status was more than a bribe to induce Harriet's consent. It created a fiction that Harriet could voluntarily choose to have sexual relations with her master. By switching between the threats of physical harm and the gifts of courtship, James undercut the appearance of a forced sexual interaction. By theoretically allowing space for Harriet's consent to his sexual overtures, James was redefining coercion into consensual sexual relations.[9]

Similarly, William's verbal narration of consensual relations overlay his forceful attempts at sex. While he had Rachel trapped underneath his body, William told her that "he wd have the good will of me." William's modification of the classic legal description of rape as a man having carnal knowledge of a woman "against her will" verbally created a consensual act even as he used force to have sexual relations.[10] In the same incident, William called Rachel by her family nickname, telling her, "Nate you dear creature, I must fuck you." Even while forcing Rachel to have sex with him, William used terms of endearment toward her. William's presentation of an affectionate and therefore consensual sexual relationship with Rachel differentiated his actions from the brutality that early Americans would most easily recognize as rape.

Thus, the process of master–servant and master–slave sexual coercion was not exclusively tied to racial boundaries. Harriet Jacobs's and Rachel Davis's similarly recounted experiences suggest that their sexual interactions were more directly shaped by lines of status and dependency. These patterns would be repeated as masters and their servants or slaves struggled to control public perceptions of what had occurred.

CREATING MASTER NARRATIVES: THE PROCESS OF PUBLICITY

Given these different versions of events, how did families, other household members, and communities interpret evidence of a possibly coercive sexual interaction? How did assaulted women portray what had happened to them? Harriet Jacobs's and Rachel Davis's narratives show that the process of publicizing a master's sexual overtures was again structured by the woman's position as his personally dependent laborer. Words—the power to speak them and the power to construct their meaning—became the prize in a struggle among masters, mistresses, and the assaulted servant or slave.

After attempting sexual overtures toward their laborers, masters had to contend with the possibility that the women would tell others about their masters' behavior. Harriet Jacobs's and Rachel Davis's masters attempted to threaten their laborers into silence about their sexual interactions. Harriet wrote that her master "swore he would kill me, if I was not as silent as the grave."[11] Similarly, William told Rachel that if she told "any body, he wd be the death of me." When Rachel threatened to tell his wife what William had been doing, "he sd if I did, I shd repent." By demanding her silence, each master tried to dictate the parameters of his sexual interactions with his servant or slave without outside interference that might contradict his interpretation or stop his sexual pursuit.

But both women also believed that their masters were afraid of the damage that they could do by publicizing their sexual behavior. Besides his threats of physical violence, William promised Rachel a "gown if she would not tell" what he had done, and on another occasion, "begged [Rachel] not to tell" her new mistress because "it wd be the Ruin of him." Harriet similarly believed that her master "did not wish to have his villainy made public." Instead, he "deemed it prudent to keep up some outward show of decency." From each woman's vantage point, then, her master's concern about his public image again allowed her some room for negotiation: he needed his servant or slave to conceal their sexual interactions. But by not telling anyone about her master's sexual assaults, a woman increased the likelihood that their sexual relationship would not appear to be a rape. This double-edged sword made the servant or slave an unwilling accomplice in the masking of her own sexual coercion.[12]

If pressuring his servant or slave into silence through bribes or threats did not silence her, a master might try to control her description of their sexual interaction. William Cress enacted an elaborate punishment scene that forced Rachel Davis to claim responsibility for anything that may have passed between them. After Rachel's complaints to her mistress prompted Mary to confront her husband about Rachel's allegations, William immediately challenged Rachel. "'Well Rachael,'" William accused, "'what are this you have been scraping up about me?,'" denying even in his question the possibility of his own misdeeds. When Rachel could not present a satisfactory answer, William employed the power of physical correction allowed to him as her master to reform her story. According to Rachel, he "whipt me dreadfully & he said . . . that he never had such a name before. . . . I fell down—he damned me, & bad me beg his pardon. I said I did not know how—he bad me go on my knees . . . he bad me go to house & tell" his wife that she (Rachel) had lied. By whipping Rachel, William attempted to disprove her story of sexual assault: his wife had said that if Rachel's assertions of sexual relations between herself and William "was lies" as William claimed, "he ought to whip" Rachel for her dishonesty. This whipping was not just a punishment unfairly inflicted, it was a punishment that retroactively attempted to define the sexual interactions between a servant and a master. Once subjugated, Rachel was required to deny that William had forced her to have sex with him. Rachel's younger sister, also a servant to William, believed this new version of events: she admitted that "I do remember D[efendant] whipping my sister—it was for telling so many lies." William was using his position as master to rewrite the sexual act that had taken place between them.

Rachel ended her description of this incident by stating that after William had beaten her, "he went to church that day & I showed my back to [my] Sister." Those final words on her master's brutal punishment (a whipping that prevented Rachel from lying on her side for three weeks) revealed the irony of the situation: while William continued to appear as a publicly reverent and virtuous patriarch, Rachel secretly bore the signs of his sins, visible only to those most intimate with her. In the process of sexual coercion, force did not have a solely physical purpose: masters also used force to create an image of consent.

Harriet Jacobs also noted the discrepancy between her master's public image and private behavior, telling her readers how he had preserved his image at her expense. When Harriet's mistress confronted Harriet with suspicions of her husband's sexual improprieties, Harriet swore on a Bible that she had not had a sexual relationship with her master. When Mary questioned her husband, however, James contradicted Harriet's statements. And just like Rachel's mistress, Harriet's mistress "would gladly have had me flogged for my supposed false oath." But unlike William Cress, James Norcum did not allow Harriet to be whipped because "the old sinner was politic. The application of the lash might have led to remarks that would have exposed him" to his family and community.[13]

In Rachel's and Harriet's narratives, their mistresses—the wives of their abusers—played important roles in the categorization of the sexually abusive relationship. Each woman had to deal with a mistress who ultimately took her displeasure at her husband's sexual relationship out on her servant or slave. Each mistress also used her position of secondary mastery to create a temporary alliance with her servant or slave. Once this alliance outlived its usefulness, it became another tool with which the mistress could assist in redefining or denying the sexual relationship between the master and the slave or servant.

In both women's stories, the masters' wives did not immediately take their hostility at their sexually aggressive husbands out on the objects of their husbands' overtures. When Rachel and William came back from retrieving the "lost" sickle, his wife, Becky, asked "where he had been—he said, after the sickles, with nate (so they called me in family) she sd it was very extraordinary, no body else could go." Perhaps Becky suspected some sort of sexual liaison between her husband and their servant, and her pointed questions let her husband know her of her suspicions. When Becky heard William trying to kiss Rachel in the cellar, she "said she had caught him & he wd deceive her no longer," but William denied any wrongdoing and Becky left in tears. These verbal confrontations apparently did not alter William's behavior; he continued to force himself sexually upon Rachel. Finally, Rachel's mistress "saw something was the matter with me, & asked what it was. I told her." After questioning her husband had little visible effect, Becky turned to Rachel to find out about

her husband's actions. This temporary alliance brought Rachel some protection from William's retribution, if not from his sexual overtures: when William heard that Rachel had told another relative some of what he had done to her, "he whipt me again, but not so bad—his wife wd not let him & said, he was in Fault."

Similarly, Harriet Jacobs believed that her mistress suspected James's illicit behavior: "She watched her husband with unceasing vigilance; but he was well practised in means to evade it." After Mary heard that her husband planned to have Harriet sleep in his room, she began questioning Harriet, who told her how James had been sexually harassing her. Harriet claimed that Mary, like most slave mistresses "had no compassion for the poor victim of her husband's perfidy. She pitied herself as a martyr." But Harriet also admitted that Mary "spoke kindly, and promised to protect me," ordering Harriet to sleep with her, rather than with James. This protective kindness also allowed Mary to try to obtain the "truth" of Harriet and James's relationship out of Harriet while Harriet slept: "she whispered in my ear, as though it was her husband who was speaking to me, and listened to hear what I would answer." When Harriet did not provide any self-incriminating information, Mary confronted her husband, but Mary's interventions did not end James's sexual overtures toward Harriet.[14]

If mistresses could not personally control their husbands' behavior, how could they stop the sexual relationship between master and laborer that was making a mockery of their marital vows? Theoretically, mistresses could turn to the legal system to petition for a divorce from their husbands. By the early nineteenth century, most states had divorce laws that allowed wives to apply for divorce on the grounds of their husbands' adultery, but women's petitions for divorce were more commonly based on charges of desertion.[15] Furthermore, proving adultery with a slave might be difficult without firsthand witnesses to the sexual interactions, since the slave was limited in her ability to testify against the white man. Married women also had a vested interest in their husbands' social and economic standing. Divorce or incarceration would most probably result in a woman's economic downturn from the loss of her husband's labor.

Ultimately, Rachel Davis's and Harriet Jacobs's mistresses concentrated their energies on removing their laborers from the household. Instead of bringing charges against her husband or applying for a divorce on the grounds of adultery, Becky Cress told Rachel Davis that she must "leave the house." Rachel recalled that "they then hired me out." Rachel's mistress may have ultimately recognized that her husband was (at best) complicit in his sexual relations with Rachel, but she also recognized that she, as his wife, was in a poor position to mandate a reform in his behavior. She could, however, as a mistress, remove the more disposable partner in the sexual relationship, and so she ordered Rachel to leave their home. Whether or not Becky believed Rachel's story of rape, she did not hold Rachel entirely innocent of wrongdoing. At the very least, she spread blame equally between her servant and her husband, with much of the resulting punishment falling on the more vulnerable of the two parties. As Rachel stated, "Before I was hired out, [my mistress] used me very bad & said she would knowck me down if I came to table to eat." Because William was a master—both of Rachel and of his household—his wife could enact only limited direct retribution against him. She could watch his behavior, confront him, and let him know her displeasure, but ultimately, it was easier to remove the object of his overtures than publicly to accuse him of wrongdoing.

Mary Norcum demanded that Harriet Jacobs leave the house once she learned that Harriet was pregnant, believing that conception was proof of their slave's sexual relationship with her husband. Harriet was not the only slave who was reputed to have been kicked out of her house because of a sexual relationship with the master. Recalling a story told to her by her grandmother about another slave, Harriet wrote that "her mistress had that day seen her baby for the first time, and in the lineaments of its fair face she saw a likeness to her husband. She turned the bondswoman and her child out of doors, and forbade her ever to return." In both of these examples, the mistress felt herself in sexual competition with the slave—even if the slave were not a willing competitor for the master's affections.[16]

Thus, while a wife's place in the household hierarchy may have proscribed her options, it did not leave her entirely at her hus-band's mercy. By forcing her husband to prove his marital loyalty by whipping the laborer for telling untruths about his sexual conduct, each mistress tried to create her own version of household sexual alliances. When mistresses could not force husbands to modify their behavior, these wives turned to regulating their servant's or slave's actions: first, by using them as the source of incriminating information, and later, as a problem that could be eliminated. Mistresses would not permanently join forces with slave or servant women to overthrow the household patriarch; they might want to change their husbands' behavior, but these wives did not wish publicly to condemn or disassociate themselves from their husbands through divorce or other legal action.

The silencing of sexual coercion was more profound in Harriet Jacobs's autobiography than it was in Rachel Davis's court-ordered testimony specifically about rape. Harriet's representation of her conflict with her master centered on the power to create a singular version of reality through the privilege of public speech. Throughout her narrative, Harriet insisted that her master sexually assaulted her only with words, never with his body. She wrote that he "tried his utmost to corrupt the pure principles my grandmother had instilled. He peopled my mind with unclean images." Harriet silenced her own description of her master's actions by calling the sexual degradation of slavery "more than I can describe." Harriet's versions of her master's verbal actions may have stood in for the literally unspeakable physical sexual abuse she suffered at his hands. By describing only James's speech, Harriet turned his possibly physical assaults on her into verbal assaults that no reader could expect her to control.[17]

In a personal letter written a few years before the publication of *Incidents in the Life of a Slave Girl* in 1861, Harriet hinted that she had indeed concealed the extent of James's actions. While she had tried to give a "true and just" account of her life in slavery, she admitted that "there are somethings I might have made plainer I know—Woman can whisper—her cruel wrongs into the ear of a very dear friend—much easier than she can record them for the world to read." In this passage, Jacobs drew a distinction between the private version of her pain and the version she chose to present for public consumption. Victorian woman-hood's emphasis on modesty and respectabil-ity as well as the established genre of sexual euphemism popularized in sentimental novels probably encouraged Harriet Jacobs to present a sanitized version of her master's assaults on her. But her decision may also have reflected a personal need to distance herself from painful events, and a difficulty in telling others about her suffering that was shared by other vic-tims—black and white—of a master's sexual harassment.[18]

Both Harriet and Rachel first told those closest to them about their masters' unwel-come sexual overtures. Harriet originally hes-itated to tell Molly Horniblow, her grand-mother and closest living relative, how James was treating her. Harriet "would have given the world to have laid my head on my grand-mother's faithful bosom, and told her all my troubles," but James's threats and her own fear of her grandmother's reaction made her stay silent. When Harriet eventually did talk to her grandmother, she told her only some of her difficulties: "I talked with my grandmother about it, and partly told her my fears. I did not dare to tell her the worst." Harriet also told her uncle about some of her suffering. He told another relative that "you don't know what a life they lead her. She has told me something about it, and I wish [her master] was dead, or a better man." Harriet's recollection of inter-actions with her grandmother and her uncle emphasized that neither relative knew the en-tire story of her master's abuses. Just as the reader was given a sanitized version in the public transcript of Harriet's life, her hesitancy to confess the full extent of sexual coercion was reiterated in Harriet's personal interactions. Her inability to confess "the worst" of her experiences may have maintained Harriet's image of sexual purity and self-identity, but it was at the cost of denying the full spectrum of her master's assaults on her.[19]

Similarly, Rachel eventually told people close to her—one of her sisters (a servant in another household), her aunt, and her new mistress—about what William was doing to her. She recounted that she was hesitant to tell the whole story even to them. Rachel told her new mistress "something of what passed in the meadow, but not the worst of it. I told my sis-ter Becky . . . the whole of it." Like Harriet's claim that it was easier to tell a close friend

than to proclaim one's victimization publicly, Rachel had an easier time confessing her prob-lems to her sister than to her new mistress. When Rachel spoke with her aunt, Elizabeth Ashton, she again refrained from disclosing the full extent of William's coercion. Elizabeth told the court that Rachel had explained how William had isolated her in the cellar, had told her to go to bed with him when his wife was away, had cornered her in the barn, and had forced her to go with him to retrieve the sickle in the meadow. But Rachel stopped short of telling her aunt that William had succeeded in raping her, that his manipulative maneuvers had led to forced sexual intercourse. Elizabeth specified under cross-examination that "*I did not understand from her that he had fully effected his purpose in the meadow.*"[20] By minimizing the extent of her master's abuse of her, Rachel cre-ated a public version of her master's actions that denied that she had been raped.

The victims of sexual coercion were not the only people who purposefully avoided discus-sions of sexual assaults. Elizabeth Ashton did not know that William had raped Rachel partly because, as she told the court, "I did not enquire whether he obtained his will in the meadow." When Rachel's sister told her own mistress that "Mr Cress wanted to be gret [great] with her sis-ter Rachael," the mistress replied, "I wanted to hear no more." When this sister eventually told their father what had happened, Jacob Davis recalled that she "did not tell me directly, she did not tell me the worst—I did not think it was so bad." A voluntary conspiracy of silence—from the servant who had difficulty discussing what had happened, to the other women who wanted neither to hear nor tell the full extent of William's abuse of Rachel—worked to deny the sexual coercion that William committed on his servant.

Similarly, Harriet Jacobs's fellow slaves were hesitant to volunteer verbal or physical assistance. Harriet believed that while her friends and relatives knew that she was being sexually abused, they were unable to speak of it. Harriet recalled that "the other slaves in my master's house noticed" her changed behavior as a result of her master's treatment, but "none dared to ask the cause. . . . They knew too well the guilty practices under that roof; and they were aware that to speak of them was an offence that never went unpunished." Har-riet's fellow slaves' silence, necessary for their own self-preservation, limited their ability to help Harriet resist their master's overtures. By controlling potential allies, a master enmeshed his original acts of sexual coercion in an ever-widening coercive web that structured his victim's possibilities for support or redress.[21]

By not telling others what had happened to her, Harriet was at the mercy of other people's versions of events. James's wife, Mary, went to the house of Harriet's free grandmother to tell her that Harriet was pregnant with James's baby. Molly Horniblow then turned on Harriet, apparently believing Mary's story that Harriet had consented to the relationship: "'I had rather see you dead than to see you as you now are,'" she told her granddaughter. "'You are a disgrace to your dead mother. . . . Go away . . . and never come to my house, again.'" Because Harriet had consistently denied or downplayed her master's sexual attempts on her, her grandmother believed Mary's story that Harriet had voluntarily had sexual relations with James. Later, Harriet's grandmother learned that Harriet had chosen to become pregnant with another man's baby to try to force her sexually abusive master to leave her alone or sell her. Once her grandmother understood "the real state of the case, and all I had been bearing for years. . . . She laid her old hand gently on my head, and murmured, 'Poor child! Poor child!'" Harriet's inability to speak about her master's sexual coercion temporarily isolated Harriet from the woman who was most able to support her. When Harriet ultimately received her grandmother's forgiveness, she also gained an ally in her fight against her master's sexual demands.[22]

Both Harriet and Rachel believed that an independently powerful figure outside of the household could counterbalance their masters' attempts at dominance. When Rachel's aunt questioned "why she did not go to a Squire to complain" about her master's sexual assaults, Rachel replied "she did not dare—she a bound girl & her father absent." After telling her sister what had happened, her sister "advised her to stay there & be a good girl. . . . I thought nothing could be done, as my father was away." Rachel herself told the court that "I did not know if I went to a Justice, he wd take notice of it. Enough people knew it, but waited till my Father came back." Without a patriar-

chal figure beside her, Rachel would not directly confront her master, and did not believe herself entitled to legal justice, a belief encouraged (or at least not contradicted) by the women in whom she confided. For Rachel, her father's support was crucial to her ability to receive public redress for her master's sexual assaults on her.

Enslaved women ordinarily did not have access to the protection offered by a patriarchal figure. Harriet Jacobs's observed that enslaved men "strive to protect wives and daughter from the insults of their masters. . . . [but] Some poor creatures have been so brutalized by the lash that they will sneak out of the way to give their masters free access to their wives and daughters." Although Harriet Jacobs did not have a waiting patriarchal figure to whom she could turn for protection, supporters outside of the household were still crucial to her limited redress. Harriet repeatedly spoke of her free grandmother's respect in the community, of how James "dreaded" this woman's "scorching rebuke," so that "her presence in the neighborhood was some protection to me." Ultimately, her grandmother's home became a partial refuge from James's pursuit. Harriet also spoke of her white lover's assistance in combatting her master's "persecutions" of her through his "wish to aid me." Harriet partly justified her decision to have sexual relations with this man (pseudonymously referred to as "Mr. Sands") because she was "sure my friend, Mr. Sands, would buy me . . . and I thought my freedom could be easily obtained from him." While Harriet could not hope for institutional retribution against her master, she could hope that her new lover would help provide freedom from her master.[23]

Both Harriet Jacobs and Rachel Davis fought similar battles against the veil of silence surrounding their masters' treatment of them. Both were confronted by relatives and neighbors who had limited authority over another household's problems. Both women turned to another powerful figure—father or free grandmother and elite white lover, respectively—to rescue them from their masters' sexual abuse. When Rachel finally told her father about her master's sexual assaults, Jacob Davis successfully encouraged the local legal system to begin a criminal prosecution. But neither Harriet Jacobs's ultimate confession to her grand-mother nor her involvement with a white lover could lead to legal intervention. The legal system marked an irreversible disjuncture in the two women's experiences.

EPILOGUE: CREATING RAPE: THE LEGAL PROCESS

Following the process of sexual coercion has led us back to this essay's opening, as Harriet Jacobs's and Rachel Davis's parallel stories reach diametrically opposed conclusions: while Rachel's master was convicted of rape and served a substantial jail sentence, there is no evidence that Harriet's master was ever subject to legal repercussions for his behavior. When a master tried to define coercive sex as consensual sex, both servants and slaves could negotiate with his terms and battle against his actions. But when the legal system defined enslaved women outside the judicial parameters of rape, there was little room for negotiation. The parallels in Harriet Jacobs's and Rachel Davis's stories ended with the legal distinction of criminal behavior. Rachel Davis may not have had easy access to criminal justice—her master was convicted of rape several years after he had first assaulted her. Yet she ultimately received legal protections that were denied to Harriet Jacobs.

We need to understand not only the legal history of rape, but the social history of sexual coercion. By taking seriously the possibility that white and black women in early America could have some experiences in common, we can begin to reassemble the complicated interactions of race, gender, and social and economic status in American history. Certainly the comparative possibilities are not exhausted with these two stories. Historians could compare the sexual experiences of free and enslaved African American women or white and black free servants. Were similar strategies used outside of households, in any relationship between a powerful man and a less powerful woman? In all of these comparisons, we should think carefully about how sex was coerced and how the crime of rape was defined. If we frame our investigations using solely the legal judgment of rape, we not only miss much of the story, we again replace women's experiences—much as their coercers had tried to do—with external categorizations.

Instead, by interrogating the multiple and contested meanings of sexual coercion, we can better understand the historical relationships of social and sexual power.

NOTES

1. "Commonwealth v. William Cress, Feb. 1808," Pennsylvania Court Papers, 1807–1809, Historical Society of Pennsylvania, Philadelphia, Pa. Unless otherwise noted, all quotations regarding Rachel Davis are from these documents. For the criminal prosecution of William Cress, see "Commonwealth v. William Cress, Philadelphia, Feb. 15, 1808," Pennsylvania Oyer and Terminer Docket, 1778–1827, 261, 262, 263, 265, Pennsylvania Historic and Museum Commission, Harrisburg, Pa.

2. Harriet Jacobs, *Incidents in the Life of a Slave Girl Written by Herself*, ed. Jean Fagan Yellin (1861; reprint, Cambridge, Mass.: Harvard University Press, 1987).

3. For examples of statutes specifying the crime of black-on-white rape, see John D. Cushing, ed., *The Earliest Printed Laws of Pennsylvania 1681–1713* (Wilmington, Del.: Michael Glazier, 1978), 69; B.W. Leigh, ed., *The Revised Code of the Laws of Virginia* (n.p., 1819), 585–86. See also Peter Bardaglio, "Rape and the Law in the Old South: 'Calculated to Excite Indignation in Every Heart,'" *Journal of Southern History* 60 (1994): 756–58.

4. See Thomas D. Morris, "Slaves and the Rules of Evidence in Criminal Trials," *Chicago-Kent Law Review* 68 (1993): 1209–39.

5. For further discussion of the cultural definitions of rape in early America, see Sharon Block, *He Said I Must: Coerced Sex in Early America* (Chapel Hill, OIEAHC at University of North Carolina Press, forthcoming).

6. Much of the following discussion about resistance's reformulation into consent was inspired by Ellen Rooney, "'A Little More than Persuading': Tess and the Subject of Sexual Violence," in *Rape and Representation*, eds. Lynn A. Higgins and Brenda R. Silver (New York: Columbia University Press, 1991), 87–114, and the fictional exploration of twentieth-century household sexual coercion in J.M. Redmann's three-book series culminating in *The Intersection of Law and Desire* (New York: W. W. Norton, 1995).

7. Jacobs, *Incidents*, 28, 27, 31–32. See also p. 41.

8. Ibid., 31, 32, 28, 27.

9. Ibid., 27, 35.

10. Italics added.

11. Jacobs, *Incidents*, 28. See also 32.

12. Ibid., 29.

13. Ibid., 34, 35.

14. Ibid., 31, 33, 34.

15. On divorce in the antebellum South, see Jane Turner Censer, "'Smiling Through Her Tears': Ante-bellum Southern Women and Divorce," American *Journal of Legal History* 25 (1981): 24–47; for

Pennsylvania, see Merril D. Smith, *Breaking the Bonds: Marital Discord in Pennsylvania, 1730–1830* (New York: New York University Press, 1991); Thomas Meehan, "'Not Made out of Levity': Evolution of Divorce in Early Pennsylvania," *Pennsylvania Magazine of History and Biography* 92 (1968): 441–64.

    16. Jacobs, Incidents, 59, 122.

    17. Ibid., 27–28.

    18. Harriet Jacobs to Amy Post, June 21, 1857, in Jacobs, *Incidents,* 242. For a discussion of African

American women's psychological reactions to systemic sexual exploitation, see Darlene Clark Hine, "Rape and the Inner Lives of Black Women in the Middle West: Preliminary Thoughts on the Culture of Dissemblance," *Signs* 14 (1989), 265–277.

    19. Jacobs, *Incidents,* 28, 38, 25.

    20. Underlining in original.

    21. Jacobs, *Incidents,* 28.

    22. Ibid., 56, 57.

    23. Ibid., 29, 54–55.

JEANNE BOYDSTON
The Pastoralization of Housework

Having read fiction and advice literature directed to women in the years before the Civil War, in 1966 the historian Barbara Welter identified a pervasive stereotype, which she called the "Cult of True Womanhood." Women were encouraged to cultivate the virtues of domesticity, piety, purity, and submissiveness. Home was referred to as women's "proper sphere" and understood to be a shelter from the outside world in which men engaged in hard work and cutthroat competition. Other historians agreed that men's and women's spheres of activity were separated and suggested that this separation was somehow linked to the simultaneous growth of capitalism and industrialization. Historian Gerda Lerner argued, by contrast, that stressing the shelter of home was a way by which middle-class women distinguished themselves from mill girls, and so maintained class boundaries.

How does Jeanne Boydston describe the relationship between home and work in antebellum America? How does she describe the relationship between women's work and men's work? What does she think were the uses of the ideology of separate spheres? How do the middle-class households described by Boydston differ from the households in which Harriet Jacobs and Rachel Davis lived?

In the colonial period, family survival had been based on two types of resources: the skills of the wife in housewifery, and the skills and property of the husband in agriculture. Both sets of skills involved the production of tangible goods for the family—such items as furnishings, food, and fabrics. Both were likely to involve some market exchange, as husbands sold grain and wives sold eggs or cheese, for example. And both involved services directly to the household. By the early nineteenth century, however, husbands' contributions to their households were focused disproportionately on market exchange—on the cash they brought into the family—while their direct activities in producing both goods and services for the family had vastly decreased.

The meaning of this shift has often been misread, interpreted as an indication that households were no longer dependent on goods and services provided from within but had instead become reliant upon the market for their survival. . . . [But] consumerism was sharply curtailed by the amount of available cash. Choices constantly had to be made: to purchase a new cloak or try to refurbish the old one for another season, to hire a woman to help with the wash or lay aside some money to buy a house. In these patterns of mundane decisions lay the essential economic character of antebellum households: they were in fact "mixed economies"—economic systems that functioned on the bases of both paid and unpaid labor and were dependent upon both. They required paid labor for the cash to purchase some goods and services. Equally, they depended on unpaid labor in the household to process those commodities into consumable form and to produce other goods and services directly without recourse to the cash market. . . .

[The] antebellum era was the last period during which most adult women shared the experience of having been, at some point in their lives, paid household workers. To an extent never repeated, even middle-class wives were likely to have worked as hired "help" in their youth. . . . [It is therefore possible to make a rough calculation] of the cost to a family to replace the unpaid labor of the wife by purchasing it on the market. . . . [1]

In northeastern cities in 1860, a woman hired both to cook and to do the laundry earned between $3 and $4 a week. Seamstresses and maids averaged two-and-a-half dollars a week. On the market, caring for children was at the lower end of the pay scale, seldom commanding more than $2 a week. If we assume that a woman did the full work of a hired cook and child's nurse, and also spent even an hour a day each sewing and cleaning (valued at about three cents an hour apiece), the weekly price of her basic housework would approximate $4.70. Even if we reduce this almost by half to $3 a week (to allow for variations in her work schedule and for the presence of assistance of some sort), taken at an average, this puts the price of a wife's basic housework at about $150 dollars a year. . . . [2]

To this should be added the value of goods a wife might make available within the family for free or at a reduced cost. Among poorer households, this was the labor of scavenging. A rag rug found among the refuse was worth half

a dollar in money saved, an old coat, several dollars. Flour for a week, scooped from a broken barrel on the docks, could save the household almost a dollar in cash outlay.[3] In these ways, a wife with a good eye and a quick hand might easily save her family a dollar a week— or $50 or so over the course of the year. In households with more cash, wives found other ways to avoid expenditures. By shopping carefully, buying in bulk, and drying or salting extra food, a wife could save ten to fifty percent of the family food budget . . . this could mean a saving of from 40 cents to over $2 a week. Wives who kept kitchen gardens or chickens . . . could . . . produce food worth a quarter a week (the price of 1/4 bushel of potatoes in New York in 1851).[4]

But there was also the cash that working-class wives brought into the household, by their needlework, or vending, or by taking in boarders, running a grocery or a tavern from her kitchen, or working unpaid in her husband's trade. A boarder might pay $4 a week into the family economy. Subtracting a dollar and a half for food and rent, the wife's labor-time represented $2.50 of that amount, or $130 a year. . . . [5]

The particular labor performed by a given woman depended on the size and resources of her household. . . . Yet we can estimate a general market price of housework by combining the values of the individual activities that made it up: perhaps $150 for cooking, cleaning, laundry, and childrearing; another $50 or so saved through scavenging or careful shopping, another $50 or so in cash brought directly into the household. This would set the price of a wife's labor-time among the laboring poor at roughly $250 a year beyond maintenance. . . . In working-class households with more income, where the wife could focus her labor on money-saving and on taking in a full-time boarder, that price might reach over $500 annually. . . . These shifts in the nature of a wife's work, and in the value of that work, as a husband's income increased seems not to have been entirely lost on males, who advised young men that if they meant to get ahead, they should "get married". . . . [6]

But husbands were not the sole beneficiaries of the economic value of housework, or of its unique invisibility. Employers were enabled by the presence of this sizeable but uncounted labor in the home to pay both men and women wages which were, in fact, below the level of subsistence. The difference was critical to the development of industrialization in the antebellum Northeast. . . . [7] Occasionally, mill owners acknowledged that the wages they paid did not cover maintenance. One agent admitted: "So long as they can do my work *for what I choose to pay them,* I keep them, getting out of them all I can. . . . [H]ow they fare outside my walls I don't know, nor do I consider it my business to know. They must look out for themselves. . . ."[8]

Even when employers paid high enough salaries to provide present security for a family, they seldom provided either the income or the job security to ensure a household's well-being against the erratic boom-and-bust cycles of business and the unemployment consequent upon those cycles. . . . Women's unremunerated labor in the household provided the needed "safety net," enabling middle-class families to maintain some degree of both material stability and healthfulness in a volatile economic environment. . . . Put simply, a wife was a good investment for a man who wanted to get ahead.

THE PASTORALIZATION OF HOUSEWORK

The culture of the antebellum Northeast recognized the role of wives in the making of contented and healthy families. Indeed, the years between the War of 1812 and the Civil War were a period of almost unabated celebration of women's special and saving domestic mission. "Grant that others besides woman have responsibilities at home. . . ." wrote the Reverend Jesse Peck in 1857, "[s]till we fully accord the supremacy of domestic bliss to the wife and mother. . . ."[9]

As recent historians have recognized, this glorification of wife and motherhood was at the heart of one of the most compelling and widely shared belief systems of the early nineteenth century: the ideology of gender spheres. An elaborate set of intellectual and behavioral conventions, the doctrine of gender spheres expressed a worldview in which both the orderliness of daily social relations and the larger organization of society derived from and depended on the preservation of an all-encompassing gender division of labor. Consequently, in the conceptual and emotional

universe of the doctrine of spheres, males and females existed as creatures of naturally and essentially different capacities. As the Providence-based *Ladies Museum* explained in 1825:

> Man is strong—woman is beautiful. Man is daring and confident—woman is diffident and unassuming. Man is great in action—woman i[n] suffering. Man shines abroad—woman at home. Man talks to convince—woman to persuade and please. Man has a rugged heart—woman a soft and tender one. Man prevents misery—woman relieves it. Man has science—woman taste. Man has judgment—woman sensibility. Man is a being of justice—woman of mercy.

These "natural" differences of temperament and ability were presumed to translate into different social roles and responsibilities for men and women. Clearly intended by the order of nature to "shine at home," Woman was deemed especially ill-equipped to venture into the world of nineteenth-century business, where "cunning, intrigue, falsehood, slander, [and] vituperative violence" reigned and where "mercy, pity, and sympathy, are vagrant fowls." . . . [10]

[T]he ideology of gender spheres was partly a response to the ongoing chaos of a changing society—an intellectually and emotionally comforting way of setting limits to the uncertainties of early industrialization. . . . The traits that presumably rendered Woman so defenseless against the guiles and machinations of the business world not only served to confine her to the home as her proper sphere but made her presence there crucial for her family, especially for her husband. Even the most enthusiastic boosters of economic expansion agreed that the explosive opportunism of antebellum society created an atmosphere too heady with competition and greed to engender either social or personal stability. However great his wisdom or strong his determination, to each man must come a time

> when body, mind, and heart are overtaxed with exhausting labor; when the heavens are overcast, and the angry clouds portend the fearful storm; when business schemes are antagonized, thwarted by stubborn matter, capricious man, or an inauspicious providence; when coldness, jealousy, or slander chills his heart, misrepresents his motives, or attacks his reputation; when he looks with suspicion on all he sees, and shrinks

from the frauds and corruptions of men with instinctive dread.... [11]

Whatever the proclivities or ambitions of individual women, the presumed contrasts between the sexes permitted Woman-in-the-abstract to be defined as the embodiment of all that was contrary to the values and behaviors of men in the marketplace, and thus, to the marketplace itself. Against its callousness, she offered nurturance. Against its ambition, she pitted her self-effacement and the modesty of her needs. Against its materialism, she held up the twin shields of morality and spiritual solace. If business was a world into which only men traveled and where they daily risked losing their souls, then wherever Woman was, was sanctuary. And Woman was in the Home.

The contrast between Man and Woman melted easily into a contrast between "workplace" and "home" and between "work" as Man engaged in it and the "occupations" of Woman in the home. Most writers of prescriptive literature did acknowledge that women were involved in activities of some sort in their households. For example, T. S. Arthur worried that a woman would be unable to keep the constant vigilance required to be a good mother if she also had to attend to "the operations of the needle, the mysteries of culinary science, and all the complicated duties of housekeeping." His language is revealing, however: housework consisted of "mysteries" and "duties"; it was a different order of activity from the labor that men performed. Indeed, some observers cautioned that the wife and mother should deliberately stay clear of employments which might seem to involve her in the economy.... William Alcott was among this group. Noting that a woman "... has duties to perform to the sick and to the well—to the young and to the aged; duties even to domestic animals," Alcott nevertheless cautioned that "[v]ery few of these duties are favorable to the laying up of much property, and some are opposed to it. So that while we commend industry—of the most untiring kind, too—we would neither commend nor recommend strong efforts to lay up property." The advice was not only consistent with, but reflected a critical aspect of the ideology of spheres: to the extent that workers in the household identified themselves with the labor of the marketplace, the function of the home as a place of psychological refuge would be undermined.[12]

Thus, the responsibilities of wives in their households were generally described in the prescriptive literature less as purposeful activities required and ordered by the welfare of their individual families than as emanations of an abstract but shared Womanhood. As Daniel C. Eddy explained:

> Home is woman's throne, where she maintains her royal court, and sways her queenly authority. It is there that man learns to appreciate her worth, and to realize the sweet and tender influences which she casts around her; there she exhibits the excellences of character which God had in view in her creation.

Underscoring the essentially passive nature of women's functions, Eddy concluded: "Her life should be a calm, holy, beautiful walk...."[13]

... The consequence of this conflation of ideology with behavior was to obscure both the nature and the economic importance of women's domestic labor. It was not only Woman-in-the-abstract who did not labor in the economy, but also, by extension, individual women. It was not only Woman-in-the-abstract, but presumably, real women who guided the on-going functions of the home through the effortless "emanations" of their very being, providing for the needs of their families without labor, through their very presence in the household. As romantic narrative played against lived experience, the labor and economic value of housework ceased to exist in the culture of the antebellum Northeast. It became work's opposite: a new form of leisure....

William Alcott's description of the wife's labors in *The Young Wife* provides a striking illustration of the pastoralization of housework in descriptions of the antebellum home:

> Where is it that the eye brightens, the smile lights up, the tongue becomes flippant, the form erect, and every motion cheerful and graceful? Is it at home? Is it in doing the work of the kitchen? Is it at the wash-tub—at the oven—darning a stocking—mending a coat—making a pudding? Is it in preparing a neat table and table cloth, with a few plain but neat dishes? Is it in covering it with some of nature's simple but choice viands? Is it in preparing the room for the reception of an

absent companion? Is it in warming and lighting the apartments at evening, and waiting, with female patience, for his return from his appointed labor? Is it in greeting him with all her heart on his arrival?[14]

Clearly, Alcott was quite familiar with the types of work performed by women in their own families, and his description is all the more interesting on this account: cooking, baking, washing clothes, mending and darning, serving meals, building fires, attending to lamps—it is a surprisingly accurate catalogue. It is also incomplete, of course. Missing from this picture is the making of the soap that the wash might be done, the lugging and heating of the water, the tiresome process of heating and lifting cast-iron irons, the dusting and sweeping of rooms, the cleaning of the stove, and the making of the stocking and the coat now in need of repair.

Even the domestic tasks which Alcott acknowledges, however, are not to be contemplated as true work, a point which is made explicit in his identification of only the husband's employments as "labor." With "labor," indeed, the wife's activities have no truck, for there is no labor here to perform. . . . the food appears virtually as a gift of nature, and the compliant fires and lamps seem to light and tend themselves. . . . All is ordered, and the ordering of it is not only *not* burdensome or tiring, but the certain vehicle of good health and a cheerful disposition. Far from labor, housework is positively regenerating. . . .

The pastoralization of housework, with its emphasis on the sanctified home as an emanation of Woman's nature, required the articulation of a new way of seeing (or, more exactly, of *not* seeing) women as actors, capable of physical exertion. Most specifically, this applied to women as laborers, but the "magical extraction" of physical activity from the concept of Womanhood in fact proceeded in much larger terms and was most apparent in the recurrent celebrations of female "influence." Typically invoked as the female counterpart to the presumably *male* formal political power,[15] the concept of indirect womanly "influence" supplanted notions of women as direct agents, and thus as laborers. [In an article entitled "Woman's Offices and Influences," J. H. Agnew argued that] the contrast between presumably male "power" (physical as well as

moral) and female "influence" could be drawn quite explicitly:

> We may stand in awe, indeed, before the exhibition of *power*, whether physical or moral, but we are not won by them to the love of truth and goodness, while *influence* steals in upon our hearts, gets hold of the springs of action, and leads us into its own ways. It is the *inflowing* upon others from the nameless traits of character which constitute woman's idiosyncracy. Her heart is a great reservoir of love, the water-works of moral influence, from which go out ten thousand tubes, conveying the ethereal essences of her nature, and diffusing them quietly over the secret chambers of man's inner being.

Woman does not herself *act*. Rather, she "gets hold of the springs of action." An idiosyncrasy in the human order, she is not so much a physical as an ethereal being. Agnew concluded: "Let man, then, exercise power; woman exercise influence. By this she will best perform her offices, discharge her duties." It is the crowning touch on the pastoralization of housework: the home is not the setting of labor, but of "offices" and "duties." Therefore, what is required for the happy home is not a worker, but rather "a great reservoir of love."[16]

The pastoralization of household labor became a common feature of antebellum literature, both private and published. . . . [It] shaped much of the fiction of the period. In a piece entitled "The Wife" (published in the *Ladies' Literary Cabinet* in July of 1819 and included in *The Sketch Book* the following year), Washington Irving described the plight of a young couple forced by the husband's disastrous speculations to give up their fashionable life in the city and move to a modest country cottage. One might anticipate numerous headaches and a good deal of hard work in such a move, especially for the wife, but such was not the case for Irving's "Wife." Mary goes out to the cottage to spend the day "superintending its arrangement," but the substance of that process remains a mystery, for the packing and unpacking, cleaning, hanging of curtains, arranging of furniture, putting away of dishes, sorting of clothes, and adjusting of new domestic equipment which one might expect to be required under such circumstances remain undisclosed in the text. Indeed, all we learn is that, when next encountered by the narrator, Mary "'seems in better spirits than I have ever known.'" Transformed into a creature who is far more sylvan nymph than human female, Mary greets her husband and the narrator "singing, in a style of the most touching simplicity.... Mary came tripping forth to meet us; she was in a pretty rural dress of white, a few wild flowers were twisted in her fine hair, a fresh bloom was on her cheek, her whole countenance beamed with smile— I have never seen her look so lovely." To complete the pastoral scene, nature has obligingly provided "'a beautiful tree behind the cottage'" where the threesome picnic on a feast of wild strawberries and thick sweet cream.[17] ...

In both its briefer and its more extended forms in fiction and in exposition, in prescription and in proscription, the pastoralization of housework permeated the culture of the antebellum Northeast. Often, it was expressed simply as a truism, as when the Reverend Hubbard Winslow reminded his Boston congregation that "[t]he more severe manual labors, the toils of the fields, the mechanics, the cares and burdens of mercantile business, the exposures and perils of absence from home, the duties of the learned professions devolve upon man...." [H]e considered women's occupations to be of a "more delicate and retired nature." That same year, the shocked and angered Congregational clergy of Massachusetts drew upon the same assumptions and the same imagery of Womanhood to denounce the abolitionist activities of Sarah and Angelina Grimké. Reminding their female congregants that "the power of woman is in her dependence," the clergy spoke of the "unobtrusive and private" nature of women's "appropriate duties" and directed them to devote their energies to "those departments of life that form the character of individuals" and to embodying "that modesty and delicacy which is the charm of domestic life...."[18]

As we have seen, working class husbands appear to have embraced the view that paid labor was economically superior to unpaid labor. They shared, too, a tendency to pastoralize the labor of their wives. The speeches of early labor activists, for example, frequently invoked both the rhetoric of the ideology of spheres and pastoral images of the household, implying a sharp contrast between "the odious, cruel, unjust and tyrannical system" of the factory, which "compels the operative

Mechanic to exhaust his physical and mental powers," with the presumably rejuvenating powers of the home. Discouraging women from carrying their labor "beyond the home," working men called upon women to devote themselves to improving the quality of life within their families.... [A]s William Sylvis put it, it was the proper work of woman "to guide the tottering footsteps of tender infancy in the paths of rectitude and virtue, to smooth down the wrinkles of our perverse nature, to weep over our shortcomings, and make us glad in the days of our adversity, ..."[19]

African-American newspapers of the antebellum Northeast also reflected and reaffirmed the pastoral conventions of women's domestic labor. The Rights of All compared women to ornamental creatures of nature, "as various in decorations as the insects, the birds, and the shells...." In 1842, The Northern Star and Freeman's Advocate approvingly reprinted an article from the Philadelphia Temperance Advocate in which wives were described as deities "who preside over the sanctities of domestic life, and administer its sacred rights...." That this perception ill fit the experiences of those female readers whose home was also their unpaid workplace, as well as those women who worked for money in someone else's home, appears not to have disturbed the paper's editors. Rather than as a worker, Woman was represented as a force of nature— and presumably one intended for man's special benefit: "The morning star of our youth— the day star of our manhood—the evening star of our age."[20]

For both middle-class and working-class men, the insecurities of income-earning during the antebellum period struck at the very heart of their traditional roles as husbands and fathers. Particularly since the late eighteenth century, manhood had been identified with wage-earning—with the provision of the cash necessary to make the necessary purchases of the household. In the context of the reorganization of paid work in the antebellum Northeast, the growing dependency of households on cash, and the roller-coaster business cycles against which few families could feel safe, that identification faced almost constant challenge. And as it was challenged, it intensified.

By the antebellum period, the late-eighteenth century association of manhood with wage-earning had flowered into the cult of the male "breadwinner." A direct response to the unstable economic conditions of early industrialization, this association crossed the lines of the emerging classes, characterizing the self-perceptions and social claims of both laboring and middle-class men.

Among laboring men, the identification of manhood with wage-earning melded easily with the traditional emphasis on the "manliness" of the crafts. . . . General Trades' Union leader Ely Moore warned that the unchecked industrial avarice of employers would create a class of "breadless and impotent" workers. When they struck for higher wages in 1860, the shoemakers of Massachusetts linked the encroachments of capital with an attack upon their manhood; in the "Cordwainers' Song," they called upon each other to "stand for your rights like men" and "Resolve by your fathers' graves" to emerge victorious and "like men" to "hold onto the last!"[21] Gender also provided the language for belittling the oppressor, for working men often expressed their rage—and reaffirmed the importance of their own manhood—by impugning the masculinity of their employers. The "Mechanic" sneered at "[t]he employers and those who hang on their skirts."[22]

In the midst of the upheavals of the antebellum economy, however, it was not only employers who threatened the old artisan definitions of manhood. Because an entire way of life was being undermined, so the dangers seemed to arise from everywhere in the new social order—including from wage-earning women themselves. In fact, women seldom directly imperiled men's jobs. The young women who went to Lowell were entering an essentially new industry. Moreover, in their families and hired out on an individual basis, carding, spinning, fulling, and even, to some extent, weaving had long been a part of women's work. . . .

But if wage-earning women did not directly challenge men's jobs, their very presence in the new paid labor force may have underscored the precariousness of men's position as wage-earners. Particularly given the post-Revolutionary emphasis on the importance of women's remaining in the home to cultivate the private virtues, females who were visible as outworkers and operatives may have seemed to bespeak an "unnaturalness" in society—an inability of wage-earning men to establish proper households. Like the witches of the seventeenth century, wage-earning women became symbols of the threats posed to a particular concept of manhood—in this instance, a concept that identified male claims to authority and power with the status of sole wage-earner. As they grappled with the precariousness of their own positions, laboring-class men focused their anxieties on the women who were their wives, daughters, and sisters, as well as on the men who were their employers.

They expressed these anxieties in two forms. First, wage-earning men complained that women were taking jobs—and thus the proper masculine role—away from men. An 1836 report of the National Trades Union charged that because women's wages were so low, a woman's "efforts to sustain herself and family are actually the same as tying a stone around the neck of her natural protector, Man, and destroying him with the weight she has brought to his assistance." Not uncommonly, working men suggested that women did not really need to work for money and castigated "the girl, or the woman, as the case may be, who being in a condition to live comfortably at home by proper economy" selfishly took work from the truly needy. In 1831, the *Working Man's Advocate* called upon "those females who . . . are not dependent on their labor for a living" to withdraw from paid work so that men might have the jobs.[23]

At the same time, working men organized to call for "the family wage"—a wage packet for the male "breadwinner" high enough to permit his wife and children to withdraw from paid work. As Martha May has pointed out, the family wage "promised a means to diminish capitalists' control over family life, by allowing workingmen to provide independently for their families." But the demand for the family wage also signalled the gendering of the emerging class system, and, in this, the gendering of early industrial culture. Identifying the husband as the proper and "natural" wage-earner, the family wage ideal reinforced a distinctive male claim to the role of "breadwinner." By nature, women were ill-suited to wage-earning, many laboring-class men insisted. The National Trades' Union called attention to Women's "physical organization" and "moral sensibilities" as evidence of her unfitness for paid labor, and the anonymous "mechanic" focused on "the fragile character

of a girl's constitution, [and] her peculiar liability to sickness."[24] Presumably, only men
had the constitution for regular, paid labor.

It is tempting to see in the antebellum ideology of spheres a simple extension of the Puritan injunction to wives to be keepers at home
and faithful helpmates to men. Certainly, the
two sets of beliefs were related. The colonists
brought with them a conviction that men and
women were socially different beings, so created by God and so designated in the order of
nature. Both were meant to labor, but they
were meant to labor at different tasks. Perhaps
even more important, they were meant to
occupy quite different stations in social life
and to exercise quite different levels of control
over economic life. . . . "Labor" may have been
a gender-neutral term in colonial culture, but
"authority" and "property" were masculine
concepts, while "dependence" and "subordination" were clearly feminine conditions. . . .

The origins of the antebellum gender culture were as much in the particular conditions
of early industrialization as in the inherited
past, however. . . . [T]he specific character of
the nineteenth-century gender culture was dictated less by transformations in women's
experience than by transformations in men's.
To be sure, the principle of male dominance
persisted into the nineteenth century. . . . Social
power in the antebellum Northeast rested
increasingly on the ability to command the
instruments of production and to accumulate
and reinvest profits. From these activities
wives were legally barred, as they were from
formal political processes that established the
ground rules for the development of industrial
capitalism. While most men were also eliminated from the contest on other grounds (race,
class, and ethnicity, primarily), one had to be
male to get into the competition at all. . . .

With the demise of the artisan system, and
so of a man's hopes to pass along a trade to
his sons, the practical grounds on which a
laboring man might lay claim to the role of
male head-of-household had altered. Increasingly, it was less his position as future benefactor of the next generation than his position
as the provider of the present generation (that
is, the "breadwinner") that established a man's
familial authority.

For men of the emerging middle class, the
stakes were equally high but somewhat different. Many of these were the sons and grand-

sons of middling farmers, forebears who, while
not wealthy, had established their adulthood
through the ownership of land, and whose role
within the family had been centrally that of the
"father." Their power residing in their control
of inheritance to the next generation—these
were men who might have been described with
some degree of accuracy as "patriarchs." But
by the second decade of the nineteenth century
middling farms throughout much of the
Northeast were scarcely capable of supporting
the present generation; much less were they
sizeable or fertile enough to establish patriarchal control of the family. Simultaneously, the
emergence of an increasingly industrialized
and urbanized society rendered the inheritance of land a less useful and less attractive
investment in the future for sons. Even successful businessmen and professionals experienced diminishing control over their sons' economic futures. A son might still read the law
with his father, but new law schools, like medical schools, foreshadowed the time when specialized education, rather than on-the-job
training with his father or his father's friends,
would offer a young man the best chance for
success. . . .

Early industrialization preserved the principle of male dominance, then, but in a new
form: the "husband" replaced the "father."
Men claimed social authority—and indeed
exercised economic control—not because they
owned the material resources upon which subsequent generations would be founded, but
because they owned the resources upon which
the present generations subsisted. More important, they had established hegemony over the
definition of those resources. In the gender culture of the antebellum Northeast, subsistence
was purchased by wages—and men were the
wage-earners.

Early industrialization had simultaneously redefined the paradigm that guided the
social and economic position of women. . . .
[T]he paradigm of womanhood shifted from
"goodwife" to "mother"—that is, from
"worker" to "nurturer." . . . [W]hat-ever cultural authority women gained as "mothers"
was at the direct cost of a social identity in the
terms that counted most in the nineteenth century—that is, as workers. As Caroline Dall
noted in 1860, most Americans cherished "that
old idea, that all men support all women. . . ."
Dall recognized this to be "an absurd fiction,"

but it was a fiction with enormous social consequences. Even when women did enter paid work, their preeminent social identity as "mothers" (in distinct contrast to "workers") made their status as producers in the economy suspect: the predisposition to consider women "unfit" helped to justify underpaying them.[25]

In all of this, the pastoralization of housework implicitly reinforced both the social right and the power of husbands and capitalists to claim the surplus value of women's labor, both paid and unpaid. It accomplished this by rendering the economic dimension of the labor invisible, thereby making pointless the very question of exploitation: one cannot confiscate what does not exist. Since the ideology of spheres made the non-economic character of housework a simple fact of nature, few observers in the antebellum Northeast felt compelled to argue the point.

The ideology of spheres did not affect all women in the same way, of course. Insisting that the domestic ideal was founded in the nature of Woman (and not in the nature of society), prescriptive writers saw its embodiments everywhere—from the poorest orphan on the streets, to the mechanic's daughter, to the merchant's wife. But their models transparently were meant to be the women of the emerging middle class. It was, after was, after all, in the middle classes that women had presumably been freed from the necessity for labor that had characterized the colonial helpmate; there, that mothers and wives had supposedly been enabled to express their fullest capacities in the service of family formation. In celebrations of middle-class "Motherhood" lay the fullest embodiments of the marginalization of housewives as workers.

But if middle-class women were encased in the image of the nurturant (and nonlaboring) mother, working-class women found that their visible inability to replicate that model worked equally hard against them. As historian Christine Stansell has vividly demonstrated, the inability (or unwillingness) of working-class women to remain in their homes—that is, their need to go out into the streets, as vendors, washerwomen, prostitutes, or simply as neighbors helping a friend out—provided the excuse for a growing middle-class intrusion into working-class households, as reformers claimed that women who could

not (or did not wish to) aspire to middle-class standards were defined as poor mothers.[26]

In addition to its specific implications for women, the ideology of spheres, and the pastoralization of housework which lay at the heart of that ideology, both represented and supported larger cultural changes attendant upon the evolution of early industrial capitalism. The transition of industrialization was not purely material: it was ideological as well, involving and requiring new ways of viewing the relationship of labor to its products and of the worker to his or her work. In its denial of the economic value of one form of labor, the pastoralization of housework signalled the growing devaluation of labor in general in industrial America. Artisans were discovering, and would continue to discover, what housewives learned early in the nineteenth century: as the old skills were debased, and gradually replaced by new ones, workers' social claims to the fruits of their labor would be severely undercut. Increasingly, productivity was attributed, not to workers, but to those "most wonderful machines."[27] It was in part against such a redefinition that the craft workers of New York and the shoemakers of Lynn, Massachusetts, struggled.[28]

The denial of the economic value of housework was also one aspect of a tendency, originating much earlier but growing throughout the eighteenth and nineteenth centuries, to draw ever-finer distinctions between the values of different categories of labor, and to elevate certain forms of economic activity to a superior status on the grounds of the income they produced. As with housework, these distinctions were rarely founded on the actual material value of the labor in question. Rather, they were based on contemporary levels of power and wealth, and served to justify those existing conditions. An industrialist or financier presumably deserved to earn very sizeable amounts of money, because in accumulating capital he had clearly contributed more labor and labor of a more valuable kind to society than had, for example, a drayman or a foundry worker. . . .

Finally, the ideology of spheres functioned to support the emergence of the wage system necessary to the development of industrial capitalism. The success of the wage system depends upon a number of factors—among them the perception of money as a neutral index of economic value and the acceptance of the wage as representing a fair "livelihood." The devaluation of housework was a part of a larger process of obscuring the continuation of and necessity for barter-based exchanges in the American economy. In this, it veiled the reliance of the family on resources other than those provided through paid labor and heightened the visibility of the wage as the source of family maintenance.

But how did women respond to the growing devaluation of their contributions as laborers in the family economy? . . . [I]n their private letters and diaries, wives quietly offered their own definition of what constituted the livelihood of their families, posing their own perception of the importance of conservation and stewardship against the cash-based index of the marketplace and easily integrating the family's periodic needs for extra cash into their understanding of their own obligations.

Nevertheless, among the public voices affirming that Woman was meant for a different sphere than Man, and that the employments of Woman in the home were of a spiritual rather than an economic nature, were the voices of many women. In *Woman in America,* for example, Mrs. A. J. Graves declared: ". . . home is [woman's] appropriate sphere of action; and . . . whenever she neglects these duties, or goes out of this sphere . . . she is deserting the station which God and nature have assigned to her." Underscoring the stark contrast between Woman's duties in the household and Man's in "the busy and turbulent world," Graves described the refuge of the home in terms as solemn as any penned by men during the antebellum period: " . . . our husbands and our sons . . . will rejoice to return to its sanctuary of rest," she averred, "there to refresh their wearied spirits, and renew their strength for the toils and conflicts of life."[29]

Graves was not unusual in her endorsement of the ideology of spheres and of the pastoralization of housework. Even those women who most championed the continuing importance of women's household labor often couched that position in the language of spheres. No one more graphically illustrates this combination than Catharine Beecher, at once probably the most outspoken defender of the importance of women's domestic labor and one of the chief proponents of the ideology of female domesticity. . . . Beecher was clear and insistent that housework was hard work, and she did not shrink from suggesting that its demands and obligations were very similar to men's "business." In her *Treatise on Domestic Economy,* Beecher went so far as to draw a specific analogy between the marriage contract and the wage labor contract:

> No woman is forced to obey any husband but the one she chooses for herself; nor is she obliged to take a husband, if she prefers to remain single. So every domestic, and every artisan or laborer, after passing from parental control, can choose the employer to whom he is to accord obedience, or, if he prefers to relinquish certain advantages, he can remain without taking a subordinate place to any employer.

Nevertheless, Beecher regularly characterized women's work in the home as the occupation merely of administering "the gentler charities of life," a "mission" chiefly of "self-denial" to "lay up treasures, not on earth, but in heaven." This employment she contrasts with the "toils" of Man, to whom was "appointed the out-door labor—to till the earth, dig the mines, toil in the foundries, traverse the ocean, transport the merchandise, labor in manufactories, construct houses . . . and all the heavy work. . . ."[30]

Beecher's apparently self-defeating endorsement of a view that ultimately discounted the value of women's labor arose from many sources, not the least of which was her own identification with the larger middle-class interests served by the ideology of spheres. Beecher enjoyed the new standing afforded middle-class women by their roles as moral guardians to their families and to societies, and based much of her own claim to status as a woman on the presumed differences between herself and immigrant and laboring-class women. For example, she ended an extended discussion of "the care of Servants" in *The American Woman's Home* with the resigned conclusion that "[t]he mistresses of American families, whether they like it or not, have the duties of missionaries imposed upon them by that class from which our supply of domestic servants is drawn."[31]

But, also like many women in antebellum America, Catharine Beecher was sharply aware of the power difference between males and females. It was a theme to which she constantly returned in her writings, especially in her discussions of women's rights. . . . In her *Essay on Slavery and Abolitionism,* Beecher was quite explicit about the reasons why a woman might cloak herself and her positions in the language of dependency and subordination:

> [T]he moment woman begins to feel the promptings of ambition, or the thirst for power, her aegis of defence is gone. All the sacred protection of religion, all the generous promptings of chivalry, all the poetry of romantic gallantry, depend upon woman's retaining her place as dependent and defenceless, and making no claims. . . .

It was much the same point that Elizabeth Ellet would later make in her *The Practical Housekeeper:* since men had many more alternatives than women, the smart woman made it her "policy" to create an appearance of domestic serenity.[32]

But it would be a mistake to read women's endorsement of the pastoralization of housework purely as a protective strategy. Women were not immune from the values of their communities, and many wives appear to have shared the perception of the larger society that their work had separated from the economic life of the community and that it was, in fact, not really work at all.

Those misgivings were nowhere more evident than in the letter that Harriet Beecher Stowe wrote to her sister-in-law, Sarah Beecher, in 1850. It was the first opportunity Harriet had had to write since the Stowes had moved to Brunswick, Maine, the spring before. Since her arrival with the children, she explained, she had "made two sofas—or lounges—a barrel chair—divers bedspreads—pillowcases—pillows—bolsters—matresses . . . painted rooms . . . [and] revarnished furniture." She had also laid a month-long siege at the landlord's door, lobbying him to install a new sink. Meanwhile, she had given birth to her eighth child, made her way through the novels of Sir Walter Scott, and tried to meet the obligations of her increasingly active career as an author—all of this while also attending to the more mundane work of running a household: dealing with tradespeople, cooking, and taking care of the children. From delivery bed to delivery cart, downstairs to the kitchen, upstairs to the baby, out to a neighbor's, home to stir the stew, the image of Stowe flies through these pages like the specter of the sorcerer's apprentice.

Halfway through the letter, Stowe paused. "And yet," she confided to her sister-in-law, "I am constantly pursued and haunted by the idea that I don't do anything."[33] It is a jarring note in a letter—and a life—so shaped by the demands of housework. That a skilled and loving mother could impart dignity and a sense of humane purpose to a family otherwise vulnerable to the degradations of the marketplace, Stowe had no doubt. But was that really "work"? She was less certain. In that uncertainty, to borrow Daniel Eddy's words, lay "a world of domestic meaning"—for housewives of the antebellum era, and for women since.

Notes

1. See Luisella Goldschmidt-Clermont, *Unpaid Work in the Household: A Review of Economic Evaluation Methods* (Geneva, 1982).
2. See Edgar Martin, *The Standard of Living in 1860: American Consumption Levels on the Eve of the Civil War* (Chicago, 1942), p. 177; and Faye Dudden, *Serving Women: Household Service in Nineteenth-Century America* (Middletown, Conn., 1983), p. 149.
3. This is calculated on the basis of an average weekly budget for a working-class family of five, as itemized in the New York *Daily Tribune,* May 27, 1851. See also Martin, *Standard of Living,* p. 122.
4. The New York *Daily Tribune,* May 27, 1851.
5. Martin, *Standard of Living,* p. 168.
6. Grant Thorburn, *Sketches from the Note-book of Lurie Todd* (New York, 1847), p. 12.
7. See Alice Kessler-Harris and Karen Brodlin Sacks, "The Demise of Domesticity in America," *Women, Households, and the Economy,* ed. Lourdes Beneria and Catherine R. Stimpson (New Brunswick, N.J., 1987), p. 67.
8. Quoted in Norman Ware, *The Industrial Worker, 1840–1860: The Reaction of American Industrial Society to the Advance of the Industrial Revolution* (New York, 1924; reprinted Gloucester, Mass., 1959), p. 77.
9. Jesse T. Peck, *The True Woman; or, Life and Happiness at Home and Abroad* (New York, 1857), p. 245.
10. *The Ladies Museum,* July 16, 1825, p. 3; Henry Ward Beecher, *Lectures to Young Men, on Various Important Subjects* (Boston, 1846), pp. 87, 91.
11. Peck, *The True Woman,* pp. 242–43.
12. *The Mother's Rule: or, The Right Way and the Wrong Way,* ed. T. S. Arthur (Philadelphia, 1856), p. 261; William A. Alcott, *The Young Wife, or, Duties of Woman in the Marriage Relation* (Boston, 1837), p. 149.
13. Daniel C. Eddy, *The Young Woman's Friend; or the Duties, Trials, Loves, and Hopes of Woman* (Boston, 1857), p. 23.
14. Alcott, *The Young Wife,* pp. 84–85.
15. For an excellent discussion of the concept of female "influence," see Lori D. Ginzburg, *Women and the Work of Benevolence: Morality and Politics in the Northeastern United States, 1820–1885* (New Haven, Conn., 1990).

16. J. H. Agnew, "Women's Offices and Influence," *Harper's New Monthly Magazine* 17:no. 3 (Oct. 1851):654–57, quote on p. 657.

17. Washington Irving, "The Wife," *Ladies Literary Cabinet*, July 4, 1819, pp. 82–84. Quotations are from Washington Irving, *The Sketch Book of Geoffrey Crayon, Gent.* (New York, 1961), pp. 34–36.

18. "Pastoral Letter of the Massachusetts Congregationalist Clergy" (1837) in *Up From the Pedestal: Selected Writings in the History of American Feminism*, ed. Aileen S. Kraditor (Chicago, 1968), pp. 51–52; Reverend Hubbard Winslow, *A Discourse Delivered in the Bowdoin Street Church* (Boston, 1837), p. 8.

19. *The Man*, May 13, 1835; *Life, Speeches, Labors, and Essays of William H. Sylvis*, ed. James C. Sylvis (Philadelphia, 1872), p. 120.

20. *The Rights of All*, June 12, 1829; *The Northern Star and Freeman's Advocate*, Dec. 8, 1842, and Jan. 2, 1843.

21. Moore is quoted in Sean Wilentz, *Chants Democratic: New York City and the Rise of the American Working Class, 1788–1850* (New York, 1986), p. 239. The "Cordwainers' Song" is printed in Alan Dawley, *Class and Community: The Industrial Revolution in Lynn* (Cambridge, Mass., 1976), pp. 82–83.

22. "A Mechanic," *Elements of Social Disorder: A Plea for the Working Classes in the United States* (Providence, R.I., 1844), p. 96.

23. Quoted in John Andrews and W. D. P. Bliss, *A History of Women in Trade Unions*, vol. 10 of *Report on Condition of Woman and Child Earners in the United States*, Senate Doc. 645, 61st Cong., 2d Sess. (Washington, D.C., 1911; reprint ed. New York, 1974), p. 48; "Mechanic," *Elements of Social Disorder*, p. 45; *Working Man's Advocate*, June 11, 1831.

24. Martha May, "Bread Before Roses: American Workingmen, Labor Unions and the Family Wage," in *Women, Work, and Protest: A Century of U.S.*

Women's Labor History, ed. Ruth Milkman (Boston, 1985), p. 4; vol. 6 of *A Documentary History of American Industrial Society*, ed. John R. Commons et al. (New York, 1958), p. 281; "Mechanic," *Elements of Social Disorder*, p. 42.

25. Caroline Dall, *"Woman's Right to Labor"; or, Low Wages and Hard Work* (Boston, 1860), p. 57.

26. Christine Stansell, *City of Women: Sex and Class in New York, 1789–1860* (New York, 1986), pp. 193–216.

27. The phrase is from the title of Judith McGaw's study, *Most Wonderful Machine: Mechanization and Social Change in Berkshire Papermaking, 1801–1885* (Princeton, 1987).

28. See Wilentz, *Chants Democratic;* and Dawley, *Class and Community*, cited in n. 21 above.

29. Mrs. A. J. Garves, *Woman in America: Being an Examination into the Morals and Intellectual Condition of American Female Society* (New York, 1841), p. 156.

30. Catharine E. Beecher, *A Treatise on Domestic Economy, for the Use of Young Ladies at Home, and at School* (Boston, 1841), p. 26; Beecher, *An Essay on Slavery and Abolitionism, with Reference to the Duty of American Females* (Philadelphia, 1837), p. 128; Catharine E. Beecher and Harriet Beecher Stowe, *The American Woman's Home, or Principles of Domestic Science* (Hartford, Conn., 1975), p. 19.

31. Beecher and Stowe, *The American Woman's Home*, p. 327.

32. Beecher, *Essay on Slavery and Abolitionism*, pp. 101–2; *The Practical Housekeeper; a Cyclopaedia of Domestic Economy*, ed. Mrs. [Elizabeth] Ellet (New York, 1857), p. 17.

33. Harriet Beecher Stowe to Sarah Buckingham Beecher, Dec. 17 [1850], The Schlesinger Library, Radcliffe College, Cambridge, Mass.

MALCOLM J. ROHRBOUGH

Duty, Adventure, and Opportunity: Women in the California Gold Rush

The United States gained control of California during the Mexican War. While the Treaty of Guadaloupe Hidalgo was being finalized, gold was discovered by workmen on the estate of John Sutter in the Sierra Nevada foothills. Sutter tried to keep it a secret, but news leaked out; rumors had reached the East Coast by the fall, and by December large gold rocks were on display at the War Department in Washington D.C. At the time there were some 13,000 people of European descent in California; perhaps half were "Californios," of Mexican or Spanish descent. The native population was some ten times as large. Within the single calendar year 1849, the Gold Rush became a men's adventure; some 80,000 migrants arrived, all expecting instant wealth. The migration put breathtaking pressure on Indians and on Californios; when California was admitted as a state as part of the Compromise of 1850, its population was already close to 200,000.

The Gold Rush is generally treated as an important event in the political and economic history of the United States. At the outset, speculators occasionally earned as much in a week as they had once earned in a year. It is also an important event in the history of American expansion and in the tension between North and South; the addition of a new free state in 1850 was accomplished by concessions to the interests of slaveholders, including the passage of a Fugitive Slave Law.

But as Malcolm Rohrbough argues, the Gold Rush profoundly destabilized relations between men and women, as tens of thousands of men left their families to seek adventure and riches far from home. They had been accustomed to a family economy in which, as Jeanne Boydston has explained, married women's household management and domestic production had stretched the purchasing power of money. Now men conceded to their wives authority to manage households, farms, and business enterprises; in California they formed all-male working communities. Some women made their way west to California; they did not expect to change gender roles, but some found opportunities that would not have existed in settled communities.

In what ways did the Gold Rush place gender relations in midcentury United States under stress? In what ways did the migration offer opportunities to women?

The gold rush had begun as a predominantly male phenomenon, with its economic and psychological center located in the remote camps in the Sierra. During the first two full years, however, the emergence and growth of cities and towns set the stage for the participation of women in the Gold Rush. Women participated in the California Gold Rush for the same reasons men did: out of a sense of duty to their families, because they, too, wanted to pursue California's golden opportunities, and because they sought adventure. . . .

MOTIVES

Duty came first. The question was, of course, whose duty to whom. Most women accepted the idea of duty to their husbands and families, but many of these also voiced their own opinions about what represented an appropriate duty and under what circumstances it was appropriate. Markedly different ideas of duty soon emerged. On one side, many family members thought it was the duty of

spouses and mothers and sisters to prevent men from going to California, . . . Their trust was a sacred one, they were told; they must preserve the family and remind men of their solemn obligations at home.

This view of a woman's duty to her family was enforced by the community at large and its institutions. In his sermon "The Duties of Females in Reference to the California Gold Excitement," the Reverend James H. Davis warned that the "duty" of a woman to persuade men everywhere, especially within her own family, to remain at home followed from the nature of the gold mania itself as "the emblem of human depravity." The enterprise was immoral, for it elevated the specter of Mammon and gold above spiritual things. This made women responsible, for "if any of these young men should die in their exile, you could never forgive yourself for having consented to their departure." . . .

Whatever they might be told was women's duty in relation to the Gold Rush and however they acted upon it in the deliberations over the prudence of the journey, however, once preparations for departure were actively underway, some women began to consider whether they themselves should not also go to California.

They had strong arguments to back them up. They emphasized duty to their husbands: a wife belonged at her husband's side. They also cast their requests in forms that stressed their potential contributions to the economic advantages that would accrue from the trip. With the support of a woman, a man could devote himself exclusively to the amassing of gold that was the reason for the voyage to California. "Oh Charles I wish you would send for me or come after me," wrote Maria Tuttle to her husband. "How much I would like to go to California. My ambition does not in the least abate. I would be willing to share with you almost any difficulties I could become independent and live in easy but plain circumstances."[1]

Most men resisted these calls for their spouses to accompany them. Their counterarguments were equally strong, equally rooted in American values at midcentury: it was a dangerous and expensive journey to a distant place whose reputation ranged from unknown to uncivilized (that is, Mexican and Catholic), with no physical amenities and little society. A woman's responsibility was to remain within the family and do the myriad chores of domestic service, nurturing children and caring for the elderly, that demanded regular attention, chores broadened and heightened by the departures of men for the gold fields.

Even as many men and women struggled to come to terms with the idea of duty, others already had begun to think in terms of opportunity. The interest in the presence of women in California—by which the 49ers meant Euro-American women—began with the first plans to go to the gold fields. The character of early arrangements quickly suggested that the emigrations would be not only large, but also almost entirely male. The scarcity of women would make them a valuable addition to such parties, opening opportunities for them and for the entrepreneurs who were already hatching schemes to benefit from the migration west.

Finally, although it was judged to be unseemly for a woman to pursue adventure, some noted its appeal, especially when they were actually on the trail west. The idea of

leaving the limitations of the past and confronting the opportunities of the future in a new physical and social setting affected women as well as men. Emeline Day, who went west to join her husband in 1853, wrote one month after leaving home, "I do not regret my course. I am happy & contented. If I could return I would not."[2] . . .

After all, for two hundred years, women had participated in the great adventure that was the emigration toward new lands in the West, and sometimes these departures had carried them long distances and into new kinds of country, across the mountains into Kentucky, for example, or down the Ohio River into the Northwest Territory. No one had seemed especially alarmed by this, or by the departure of women with their families for Oregon in the 1840s.

Indeed, not everyone was alarmed at the idea when some of the first notices that offered ship accommodation to those heading for the gold fields also tendered similar arrangements to women at the same price. A North Carolina company organized in Raleigh "for gathering gold" sought one hundred "sober, moral, respectable citizens." The cost was two hundred dollars for each member, including wives and children, "payable into the common fund by the first of March." "Respectable single ladies will be admitted into the Company on the same Terms," the company notice continued. "Separate accommodations will be allotted to the females." The organizers emphasized the scarcity of women in California and added the comment, "a few of the stout hearted and lovely girls and widows, of the Old North State, would assuredly find the enterprise a princely speculation—in immediately getting rich husbands in this fine country." The people most needed in California, the notice continued, were "wives, sempstresses, house-keepers, milliners, tailors." But "wives stand at the head of those most wanted, Just think of that!" Respectable single women "would go off like hot cakes—not for husbands and tobacco, but for husbands and gold!"[3] . . .

Although their accommodations may have been marginally better—especially on shipboard—women do not seem to have experienced special difficulties in making the trip to California. To the women as well as the men, the voyages in ships seemed long and tedious, but they had the usual degree of service and safety. Women passengers included the wives of ships' captains, the wives of company officers, and the wives of military officers stationed in California. Because the greater cost of a sea voyage created a clear distinction between those who could afford such accommodations and those who could not, the latter group had to go by land.

The overland expedition across half the continent, beginning with the infinite spaces of the Great Plains and ending with high passes in the Sierra Nevada, seemed to many totally unlike anything that women were prepared to endure and certainly not something that they would enjoy. . . .

Arkansas newspapers followed in detail the journey of Miss Mary E. Conway, who went to California with her father. . . . Noted the correspondent to the Little Rock papers, "there are many here who will be happy to learn that she stands the trip bravely, and is still sparkling and bright through all the dangers and privations of such a journey." Miss Conway apparently had surmounted the dangers of the continent without infringing on those ladylike qualities that were appropriate to her qualities as a woman.[4]

WOMEN IN CALIFORNIA

Up to a point, women's experiences in California seemed much like men's, many and varied. Like many of the male 49ers, women often settled in cities and towns, in their roles as wives, when married, and in search of the economic advantages that urban places offered, when single. . . .

Margaret DeWitt was married in April 1848 and left at once for California with her husband Alfred. Once arrived in San Francisco, Margaret became responsible for managing the household of an extended family of her husband's male relatives that sometimes reached twelve persons. She immediately sought to hire a servant to assist her. Alfred had preferred a man, but Margaret wanted a woman "and a nice American servant." She soon employed "a nice Irish woman." The Irish woman, Margaret wrote, "has been 10 years in America and came out with her husband who is going to the mines—and she wanted a good home was willing to come for Sixty dollars a month." She considered herself

fortunate. In other households, servants demanded and received one hundred dollars a month. Furthermore, she wrote, "This woman is a good washer and ironer which is a great thing." Margaret spent much time dealing with the problem of servants and their conditions of employment.[5]

Margaret DeWitt saw her continued presence in California as part of the duty she owed her husband. She missed her mother, father, sister, and friends, and she wrote constantly of her adjustments to the new world of San Francisco, especially those necessary to keep house for Alfred and his bachelor brothers. She regretted her inexperience as a wife and constantly expressed her determination to make Alfred happy. Lodged in and responsible for a household of bachelors, she seemed acutely conscious of her married status and her duty to make all male members of the extended family content.[6] . . .

Margaret DeWitt was an acute and interested observer of other housekeeping establishments among the new arrivals in San Francisco, as well as of her own. By the fall of 1849, she noted, many of the first families to arrive in response to the Gold Rush had begun to break up. The men moved to the towns or to the diggings in the gold country, and the women returned to the East. The reason was cost, Margaret continued, for "it was so very expensive and difficult to get along without several servants and that besides the high wages cost a great deal."[7] . . .

In addition to household management, Margaret also took on the universal occupation of women in families—that of nurse. Alfred was often ill, and whenever he was confined to his bed, Margaret became a full-time caretaker.[8] . . . Certainly California and the Gold Rush made little difference to Margaret's sense of her domestic world, except for the initial scarcity and high cost of servants.

For those women who sought active employment, urban Gold Rush California offered a wide range of opportunities. The employment chances exemplified by Margaret DeWitt's Irish woman highlight one dimension of the rising demand for services. As the new waves of 49ers prospered in the cities, towns, and even the diggings, they sought to use a portion of their new-found wealth to hire servants, who were both scarce and expensive. . . .

Henry Packer wrote from Sacramento in the fall of 1850 describing the continuing employment opportunities for women: "Women's time is much more valuable than men's. A woman can get $150.00 per month for house work, while hundreds of men are now employed upon the levee, which is being constructed to prevent another overflow of the city, at $75.00 per month." . . .

For women with capital to invest and for those who sought employment with a greater degree of independence, the most profitable option was owning or running a boardinghouse. Emeline Day crossed the plains to California in 1853. After her husband returned to Ohio, she managed a rooming house in Sacramento "in partnership with a Mr. Ward." For three months' work, she received one hundred and eighty-four dollars, plus room and board. Of the work she wrote, "I have enjoyed the labor, am content and happy. I have done all the work for from twelve to fifteen and sometimes as high as thirty persons."[9]

Day's generally optimistic views about her work disguised the long, varied, and continuous demands associated with providing lodging and meals for miners and transients. Mary Ballou's account of her boardinghouse, dated from the fall of 1852, suggests the range of activities and the primitive conditions under which she worked. "Now I will try to tell you what my work is in this Boarding House," she began.

Well sometimes I am washing and Ironing sometimes I am making mince pie and Apple pie and squash pies. Sometimes frying mince turnovers and Donuts. I make Buiscuit and now and then Indian jonny cake and then again I am making minute puding filled with rasons and Indian Bake pudings and then again a nice Plum Puding and then again I am Stuffing a Ham of pork that cost forty cents a pound. Sometimes I am . . . making gruel for the sick now and then cooking oisters sometimes making coffee for the French people strong enough for a man to walk on that has Faith as Peter had. Three times a day I set my Table which is about thirty feet in length and do all the little fixings about it such as filling pepper boxes and vinegar cruits and mustard pots and butter cups. Sometimes I am feeding my chickens and then again I am scareing the Hogs out of my kitchen and Driving the mules out of my Dining room. . . . Sometimes I take my fan and try to fan myself but I work so hard that my Arms pain me so severely that I kneed some-

one to fan me so I do not find much comfort anywhere.

Mary Ballou had other work, too. She took care of children (including nursing them), made soap, and sewed. Amid the wide range of economic opportunities for women, she wrote, "I would not advise any Lady to come out here and suffer the toil and fatigue that I have suffered for the sake of a little gold neither do I advise any one to come."[10] Yet the experiences of both Day and Ballou into the 1850s suggest that employment for women in the service sectors of the cities and towns probably lasted longer than the chances for individual miners in the gold fields.

Some of these economic opportunities for women lay in the thriving entertainment industry. Here, the activities of "fancy" girls from the dance halls—who "would not be noticed in Gods Country but here they are very handsome indeed"—often drew expressions of outrage. Prostitutes were traditional targets of middle-class scorn, and the hostility spread out to include women who performed in other occupations. The 49ers routinely encountered the "Shocking Sight" of women tending bar in San Francisco or women running the gaming tables.[11] One Argonaut described women's roles in these operations in a San Francisco public house as follows:

Add to this, the "Bankers" who are generally women chosen for their *attractive* powers—and you will not wonder that the poor Devil who has been so long away from Civilization becomes reckless, and forgits in the excitement, every thing but the Present—and if he escapes this, the next building, whose doors are always open contains allurements still harder to resist. The front room contains a "Bar" which is tended by girls, who will mix your "Toddy"—chat and laugh, and Drink too, with every one who invited them and then invite you into the Parlor whose doors are always open—here you will find girls dressed in the most magnificent apparel, dancing, walzing, Playing the Piano, or guitar In lounging on the sofa, and sipping, her wine (which costs 15 dollars per Botle) at the expense of the poor Devel, on whose shoulder she leans, until he, half Drunk, or crazy, follows her to chambers and awakes the next morning, to find himself worse off, perhaps, than the one who got "fleeced" at the other house.[12]

Within the camps and the gold fields themselves, women appeared in a variety of

roles within an almost exclusively male setting, roles that seem to have defied traditional
categories. Among these were women who
mined (generally although not exclusively
alongside their husbands); women who lived
alone in mining camps and pursued their own
independent businesses, especially boardinghouses, laundries, restaurants, or bake shops;
and women who lived and worked on the surrounding farms and ranches. Of the occupations in demand, the two most lucrative were
washing and cooking. These were two areas
where 49ers would pay high prices on a continuing basis for services. Louise A. K. S.
Clapp, writing under the pseudonym of
"Dame Shirley," wrote with high admiration
of the washerwoman in Rich Bar. This woman
cleared one hundred dollars a week washing
clothes, the fabled one ounce of gold dust a
day, and she did so in 1851, when returns in
the diggings were only half that sum. According to Dame Shirley, Mrs. R. (for so she called
her) drew the unbounded admiration of the
men in Rich Bar for the skill with which she
performed her services and for the profit she
made. "Such women ain't common, I tell you,"
sighed one man. "If they were, a man might
marry, and make money by the operation."[13]

Women who mined in the diggings
reflected the presence of families as mining
units. Just as 49ers joined together in small
companies to live and wash, so family groups
could realize the same advantages in labor and
living. Reports of women in the gold fields
appeared almost as soon as news of gold itself,
and their presence seemed worthy of comment
in the first great migration to California.
"Thousands of men (and even women) are
digging and washing out from the earth, pure
Virgin Gold in vast amounts," reported a
"Correspondent in the Gold Diggings."[14]
Whole families—husbands, wives, and children—dug and washed. And finally, within a
year, rumors surfaced of a woman who disguised herself as a man to join her husband in
the mines.[15] This traditional story, retold in
contemporary terms, had accompanied men
into battle, on crusades, and even on hunting
expeditions for a thousand years. That women
mined openly alongside their husbands could
not prevent its appearance.

At the same time that they might profit
from economic advantages created by the
Gold Rush, some women also suffered loneli-

ness and isolation. The scarcity of women that
created opportunities for their employment
also reduced contact with other women. Far
from their families, they found fewer women
for friends and confidants. Social constraints
made women less mobile than men, and they
found it more difficult to travel. Men spent
much time and emotional energy in search of
male companions in whom they could repose
trust; to the extent that women searched for
female companions with whom they could do
the same—there is no reason to suppose they
were less interested in such contacts—they
had a much smaller group on which to draw.
Accordingly, ties with family often increased
in importance.

Lydia Burns scrawled her feelings from
the mining town of Placerville to Polly, her distant married sister. Polly's recent letter "was
like a drop of water to a thirsty soul when all
hope is gone it gives new life to the drooping
spirits and cheer me here in a strange land not
friendless but far from home." Lydia worked
in a "publick house" where she earned fifty
dollars a month.[16] . . . She had "meny very
kind friends here but know kind Sister or
Brother." As a single woman in a mining
camp, even in 1854, she had many admirers.
She continued:

> I have had meny chances to change my name but
> dide not except I dont know but I mite been bet-
> ter off and then I mite been worse some times I
> think I will Merry the first chance and then I am
> afraide they may not be kind to me and then I
> shall wish I hade remained Single. . . . This is A
> very pleasant Country but I find meny Sade and
> loanly hours but I truy to drive them away by
> thinking Their is better dayes acoming you wrote
> for me to write if I was ever Coming home I doant
> know I want to see you all once more but dont
> knoe as I shall ever get means ever to come it
> coast a greateale for clothes here.[17]

Lydia Burns's ambivalence about marriage
suggests that the larger number of choices in
California for women did not guarantee happiness.

LUCY STODDARD WAKEFIELD

No more than Lydia Burns was Lucy Stoddard
Wakefield a representative woman in the California gold fields. So varied were the places
and duties that each was simply one among
several. But this woman was surely more independent and probably more successful than

most. The context of the Gold Rush provided a series of new opportunities for her talents.

Lucy Stoddard Wakefield and her husband left New Haven, Connecticut, for California in the spring of 1849. She had long been unhappy in her marriage. As one of her relatives put it, her life was "wretched & miserable pride forbade her to complain of her own choice & stir the stink among her Friends, although he was in the constant habit of tentelizing and insulting her feelings with abusive epithets & jealous aspersions of all her connections."[18] On the way west across the plains, the two agreed to end their marriage. The image of the couple from New Haven discussing such arrangements as the wagon train moved ever farther from the structure and institutions of the East raises the question of whether the dry air of the plains and the thin air of the mountains lent itself to plain speaking and an ease in managing those issues so burdened with baggage in their university town in New England.

Once arrived in California, Lucy Stoddard Wakefield divorced her husband and made her way directly to the mining town of Placerville, where she went into the business of baking pies. It was a product always in demand. "I have been toiling hard for the last two and a half years and am still doing an almost incredible amount of work averaging about 20 dozen pies weekly with my own hands without any one to fetch so much as a bucket of water," she wrote friends. Her life contrasted in almost every way with that of her acquaintances in the East, "people who have so little to do that they do not know how to dispose of either themselves or their time." She knew full well how to use her time on a daily basis in toil so prolonged and severe that she could not "stand up another minute." She rose early, before light, and brought a first batch of pies from the ovens at daylight; a second group she baked in the afternoon to cater to miners leaving the town after errands. Two hundred and forty pies at a dollar each produced a substantial weekly income, which she dispersed in expenses and rent. She worked fourteen hours a day. On the other side of this endless drudgery lay a degree of independence she had never known. Freed from the demands of her husband, she worked for herself, set her own hours, made her own business decisions, and kept what she earned.

When her friends in New Haven inquired whether a friend should come West, she wrote of women's lot in California: "There is no way for a woman to make money except by hard work of some sort." If a woman were willing to come to California and work hard, she might profit from the opportunities associated with the Gold Rush. "I have no doubt she might take home over and above her expenses coming, while here, and going home, $3000, in three years, but they would be three years of toil, hardship, and in some respects severe privations, . . ."

Wakefield may have gone on to do things she never could have done in New England, but she still carried with her New England views of other groups. Placerville had "few women and those generally of the most ordinary class of Dutch, Irish or western women. I know of no women from the Eastern States not any one recently from N York State, and fortunately for the lazy southrons very few of them." Her prolonged stay in Placerville only seemed to confirm such ideas. Scorned and ignored by her friends in New Haven after her divorce, she continued to exhibit New England values.

In late 1851, her relative, Leslie Bryson, visited her in Placerville. His account of their meeting and her life offers an additional perspective on a woman making a living independently in a mining town. Bryson thought Wakefield markedly superior to her former husband "in every point of view and uncongeniality of feeling, taste, and everything else seems to me to have been the difficulty between them." In Placerville, she worked "alone but actively in making pies." Within the town, she "commands the respect and admiration of all good people in the country she dwells."

What struck Bryson most forcibly about Wakefield's nature was what he interpreted as its masculine character. Her hard work had "imparted to her additional strength of mind her knowledge of human nature far exceeds that of any woman I have ever met, her talents appear to me of A higher order than I supposed them to be at Home Her head is Masculine rather than Feminine." He concluded from these forceful qualities that she was ill equipped to be a good wife, a view reinforced by her determination: "she vaunts her disregard for the opinion of others." In her comments about the family, she spoke "with no measured freedom." Bryson concluded that "from all I have seen and heard of her in California I respect her more than I ever did at home." His respect arose from a range of accomplishments that she never had a chance to do "at home." In a California Gold Rush town, she had the opportunity to strike out on her own, indifferent to the views of her friends in New Haven and unaffected by the other women in Placerville, with whom she felt a degree of common cause. Lucy Stoddard Wakefield well could have penned the words written by Dame Shirley, "I like this wild and barbarous life."[19]

NOTES

1. Maria to Charles Tuttle, February 23, 1850, Letters, Bancroft Library, University of California, Berkeley; hereafter cited as BAN. A newspaper account of a woman's experiences in the first months of the Gold Rush, dated April 1848, was reprinted in the Raleigh Star & N. Carolina Gazette, March 7, 1849.

2. Emeline Day, journal, April 14, 21, 1853, BAN. Two contrasting journals both dating from 1852 are those of Algeline Ashley (excited about the trip across the plains) and Mary Stuart Bailey (distraught by separation from her friends), both in [Huntington Library, San Marino, California; hereafter cited as] HEH.

3. *Raleigh Register*, February 3, 1849.

4. Little Rock *Arkansas Banner*, September 25, 1849, Bieber Coll., HEH.

5. Margaret DeWitt to her father and mother, July 30 1849, May 15, 1850, DeWitt Papers, BAN.

6. Margaret DeWitt to her father and mother, August 28, 1849, ibid.

7. Margaret DeWitt to her father and mother, September 28, November 28, 1849, ibid. In a letter to her father: "I will bring my letter to a close, and I dare say you will be glad—for I believe gentlemen do not care much to read what ladies write especially if they have no more to say than I." November 30, 1849.

8. Margaret DeWitt to her father and mother, August 14, 1850, ibid.

9. Emeline Day, journal, October 2, 1853, BAN.

10. Mary B. Ballou to "My Dear Selden," October 30, 1852, quoted in Nancy Woloch, ed., *Early American Women* (Belmont, Calif.: Wadsworth, 1992), 272.

11. Benjamin Baxter, journal, August 10, 1850, HEH; William A. Brown to his father, July 25, 1850, the Brown Letters, HEH; C. C. Mobley, diary, November 1, 1850, HEH.

12. Anon to Lizzie, October 15, 1853, HEH.

13. Clapp, *The Shirley Letters*, 39.

14. Newburyport, Massachusetts, *Herald*, December 14, 1849, Bieber Coll., HEH.

15. North Carolina *Fayetteville Observer*, January 8, 1850, ibid.

16. Lydia Burns to Polly Burns Hall, September 18, 1853, the Burns Letters, HEH.

17. Lydia Burns to Polly Burns Hall, June 1854, ibid.

18. The story of Lucy Stoddard Wakefield lies in two documents: Wakefield to Lucius and Rebecca, September 18, 1851, Letter, HEH; and Leslie Bryson to "Friend Stoddard," December 3, 1851, Letter, HEH. Bryson was a merchant/speculator in San Francisco; he was one of the first to import Chinese labor under contract.

19. Louise A. K. S. Clappe ["Dame Shirley"], *The Shirley Letters from California Gold Mines: 1851–1852*, Richard E. Oglesby, ed. (Salt Lake City: Peregrine Smith Books, 1985), 198.

DOCUMENT: Working Conditions in Early Factories, 1845

> *"She complained of the hours for labor being too many . . ."*

The textile factories of the first wave of industrialization might not have been built at all had their owners not believed they could count on a steady supply of cheap female labor. The history of industrialization as it affected both men and women needs to be understood in the context of the segmented labor market that women entered. Women were a major part of the first new work force that was shaped into "modern" work patterns: long, uninterrupted hours of labor in a mechanized factory with little or no room for individual initiative.

One of the earliest mill towns was Lowell, Massachusetts, where factory owners began recruiting young, unmarried women to work in six textile mills in 1823. Rural young women already toiled at home at farm labor and also at "outwork," goods that could be made at home and sold for cash. Compared to the work they had done at home, mill work at first seemed to pay well and to offer new opportunities. The Lowell mills developed a system of boardinghouses, which assured families that girls would live in wholesome surroundings. Letters sent home and fiction published by young women in the first wave of employment often testified to their pride in the financial independence that their new work brought.

Work in the mills was strictly segregated by sex: men were supervisors and skilled mechanics; women attended the spinning and weaving machinery. Women's wages ranged from one-third to one-half that of men; the highest-paid woman generally earned less than the lowest-paid man. Employers responded to economic downturns in the 1830s by adjusting their expenses. Women's wages in the Lowell mills dropped; piece rates forced increases in production without increases in pay. Mills established stricter discipline: those who were insubordinate were fired, workers who did not fulfill their year-long contracts were blacklisted. But boardinghouse life meant that the factory women developed strong support networks; when their wages were cut and work hours lengthened in the 1830s, those who lived together came together in opposition to the owners and staged some of the earliest industrial strikes in American history. In 1836, 1,500 women walked out in protest, claiming their inheritance as "Daughters of the Revolution." One manifesto stated: "As our fathers resisted unto blood the lordly avarice of the British ministry, so we, their daughters, never will wear the yoke which has been prepared for us."*

In January 1845, led by the indomitable worker Sarah Bagley, the Female Labor Reform Association organized a petition drive throughout the region, which forced the

---

*Thomas Dublin, *Women at Work* (New York: Columbia University Press, 1979), p. 98.

Excerpted from "The First Official Investigation of Labor Conditions in Massachusetts," in vol. 8 of *A Documentary History of American Industrial Society*, ed. John R. Commons, Ulrich B. Phillips, Eugene A. Gilmore, Helen L. Sumner, and John B. Andrews (Cleveland, 1910), pp. 133–142.

Massachusetts legislature to hold the first public hearings on industrial working conditions ever held in the United States. On February 13, 1845, Eliza Hemmingway and Sarah Bagley had their chance to testify. What did they think it was important for the legislators to know?

... The first petitioner who testified was Eliza R. Hemmingway. She had worked 2 years and 9 months in the Lowell Factories ... Her employment is weaving—works by the piece. ... and attends one loom. Her wages average from $16 to $23 a month exclusive of board. She complained of the hours for labor being too many, and the time for meals too limited. In the summer season, the work is commenced at 5 o'clock, a.m., and continued till 7 o'clock, p.m., with half an hour for breakfast and three quarters of an hour for dinner. During eight months of the year, but half an hour is allowed for dinner. The air in the room she considered not to be wholesome. There were 293 small [oil] lamps and 61 large lamps lighted in the room in which she worked, when evening work is required. These lamps are also lighted sometimes in the morning. About 130 females, 11 men, and 12 children (between the ages of 11 and 14) work in the room with her ... The children work but 9 months out of 12. The other 3 months they must attend school. Thinks that there is no day when there are less than six of the females out of the mill from sickness. Has known as many as thirty. She herself, is out quite often, on account of sickness. ...

She thought there was a general desire among the females to work but ten hours, regardless of pay. ... She knew of one girl who last winter went into the mill at half past 4 o'clock, a.m. and worked till half past 7 o'clock, p.m. She did so to make more money. She earned from $25 to $30 per month. There is always a large number of girls at the gate wishing to get in before the bell rings. ... They do this to make more wages. A large number

come to Lowell to make money to aid their parents who are poor. She knew of many cases where married women came to Lowell and worked in the mills to assist their husbands to pay for their farms. ...

Miss Sarah G. Bagley said she had worked in the Lowell Mills eight years and a half ... She is a weaver, and works by the piece. ... She thinks the health of the operatives is not so good as the health of females who do housework or millinery business. The chief evil, so far as health is concerned, is the shortness of time allowed for meals. The next evil is the length of time employed—not giving them time to cultivate their minds. ... She had presented a petition, same as the one before the Committee, to 132 girls, most of whom said that they would prefer to work but ten hours. In a pecuniary point of view, it would be better, as their health would be improved. They would have more time for sewing. Their intellectual, moral and religious habits would also be benefited by the change. ...

On Saturday the 1st of March, a portion of the Committee went to Lowell to examine the mills, and to observe the general appearance of the operatives. ... [The Committee concluded:] Not only is the interior of the mills kept in the best order, but great regard has been paid by many of the agents to the arrangement of the enclosed grounds. Grass plats have been laid out, trees have been planted ... everything in and about the mills, and the boarding houses appeared, to have for its end, health and comfort. ... The [average hours of work per day throughout the year was 11½; the workday was longest in April, when it reached 13½ hours].

KATHRYN KISH SKLAR
Catharine Beecher:
Transforming the Teaching Profession

In the following essay Kathryn Kish Sklar describes the merger of economic and ideological concerns in the career of Catharine Beecher. By publicizing the appropriateness of teaching as a career for women, Beecher facilitated the entry of many women into the profession. In the process she also developed her own career, traveling widely, speaking in public frequently, and publishing popular books. Beecher made use of the familiar ideology that stressed women's "natural" docile and nurturing qualities and has been called the "Cult of True Womanhood." It was said, for example, that women had a duty to be teachers because their natural role as mothers suited them to the care of young children.

Within a single generation women replaced men in the ranks of teachers and were entrusted with classes that included boys as well as girls. It has been estimated that approximately one out of five white women in antebellum Massachusetts was a schoolteacher at some time in her life. Once the profession of teaching was "feminized" it would remain so; in 1970 more than 85 percent of the nation's elementary school teachers were women.

For the next decade and a half Catharine Beecher maintained the pace of life that she began in the summer of 1843. She sought out people ... who were either themselves wealthy or could open doors to the wealth of other evangelical individuals and groups. She toured constantly in both East and West, raising funds, seeking sites for schools and seminaries, and recruiting teachers to occupy them. Her *Treatise [on Domestic Economy]* made her nationally known, and her frequent speaking tours kept her immediately in the public view. By the end of the 1840s she was one of the most widely known women in America.

Over the course of the decade, as she met with greater and greater success in promoting the primacy of women in American education, Catharine's public and private lives converged. Finally she had found a role commensurate with her personal needs and desires, and much of her achievement during

this decade may have arisen from that congruence. As she traveled about the country advocating a special role for her sex, she became the living embodiment of that role. This new consistency in Catharine's life lent conviction to her activities and greatly enhanced her powers of persuasion....

Catharine returned to Cincinnati in the fall of 1843.... She spent the winter striving to create a national organization to promote "the cause of popular education, and as intimately connected with it, the elevation of my sex by the opening of a profession for them as educators of the young." All that winter and spring she corresponded with prominent individuals in the East and West, soliciting their endorsement of such an organization.[1] ...

... in the winter of 1845 she visited almost every major city in the East, delivering a standard speech and organizing local groups of church women to collect and forward funds and proselytize her views.[2]

Catharine's addresses were subsequently published in three volumes by Harpers. The first was entitled *The Evils Suffered by American Women and American Children: The Causes and the Remedy;* it was followed by *The Duty of American Women to Their Country;* and lastly, by *An Address to the Protestant Clergy of the United States.* These addresses clarified the ideas Catharine had evolved over the course of the last two decades. Now however like a practiced evangelist she played expertly upon the feelings and fears of her audience and ultimately brought them to commit themselves to her vision of a nation redeemed by women. The full meaning of Catharine's exhortation was not revealed until halfway through her addresses. First she gained her audiences' sympathy for the sufferings of masses of American children under cruel teachers and in degenerate environments. She quoted from several reports to state legislatures that described "the comfortless and dilapidated buildings, the un-hung doors, broken sashes, absent panes, stilted benches, gaping walls, yawning roofs, and muddy moldering floors," of contemporary schools and "the self-styled teachers, who lash and dogmatize in these miserable tenements of humanity." Many teachers were "low, vulgar, obscene, intemperate," according to one report to the New York State legislature, "and utterly incompetent to teach anything good." [3]

To remedy this situation Catharine then proposed a national benevolent movement, similar to the temperance movement or the missionary boards, to raise money for teachers and schoolrooms. Yet Catharine's plan went even beyond the contemporary benevolent models. Her chief goal was to "elevate and dignify" her sex, and this goal was inextricably bound to her vision of a more consolidated society. The united effort of women in the East, combined with the moral influence of women in the West, would create homogeneous national institutions, Catharine asserted. The family, the school, and the social morality upon which these institutions were based would everywhere be similar. Sectional and ethnic diversities would give way to national unity as the influence of women increased.

To make her image of a unified society more understandable to her audience, she explained that it was a Protestant parallel to the Catholic pattern of close interaction between social and religious forms. Protestant women should have the same social support for their religious and moral activities as Catholic nuns received from their society. She related the stories of many women she had known who were willing to sacrifice themselves to socially ameliorative efforts, but who had been rebuffed by public opinion and restricted to quiet domestic lives. "Had these ladies turned Catholic and offered their services to extend that church, they would instantly have found bishops, priests, Jesuits and all their subordinates at hand, to counsel and sustain; a strong *public sentiment* would have been created in their favor; while abundant funds would have been laid at their feet," she said.[4] Her plan envisioned a similar kind of cultural support for Protestant women. A web of interlocking social institutions, including the family, the school, and the church, would form a new cultural matrix within which women would assume a central role.

The ideological basis of Catharine's social theory was self-denial. The Catholic church's employment of self-denying women initially attracted Catharine to it as a model for her own plan. Yet Catharine emphasized that her notion of self-denial was different from the Catholic one. The Catholics had "a selfish and ascetic self-denial, aiming mainly to save *self* by inflictions and losses," Catharine said, whereas she advocated self-denial not as the means of personal salvation, but as the means of social cohesion.[5] . . . Self-denial was an inclusive virtue that could be practiced by wealthy and poor, converted and unconverted, by persons of all ages and both sexes. As the ideological basis of a national morality it was especially congenial to Catharine since women could be both the embodiment and the chief instructors of self-denial. It made possible an expanded cultural role for women as the exemplars and the teachers of a national morality.

To support this cultural role for women Catharine advocated three corollary ideas, each of which pointed toward a more consolidated American society. First, she said, women should abolish class distinctions among themselves and form one united social group. Catharine Beecher had earlier defended class distinctions as a part of the natural order of God's universe, but such divisions were no longer endorsed in her public writings. This change in her views was prompted in part by a visit she made to Lowell, Massachusetts, where she went to look for teachers. Catharine did not believe the Lowell owners' claims that factory work was a means of self-improvement for the women operatives. She concluded that at Lowell and in New York City women were deliberately exploited. "Work of all kinds is got from poor women, at prices that will not keep soul and body together," Catharine wrote, "and then the articles thus made are sold for prices that give monstrous profits to the capitalist, who thus grows rich on the hard labors of our sex."[6] Rather than participate in this kind of class exploitation, Catharine suggested women should donate their services to the cause of education. Although they might still be poor, their economic sacrifice would transcend class lines and benefit the whole nation instead of a self-interested class of businessmen.

While economic factors oppressed working-class women, social custom suppressed upper-class women. "The customs and prejudices of society forbid" educated young women from engaging in socially useful employments. Their sufferings were just as keen as those of working-class women, Catharine said, the only difference being that their spirits were starved instead of their bodies. "A little working of muslin and worsted, a little light reading, a little calling and shopping, and a great deal of the high stimulus of fashionable amusement, are all the ailment their starving spirits find," Catharine wrote. "The influence and the principle of *caste*," she maintained, must cease to operate on both these groups. Her solution was to secure "a proper education for all classes, and make productive labor honorable, by having all classes engage in it."[7]

The specific labor Catharine endorsed for both groups was teaching. Working-class women should leave the factories and seize the opportunity to go to the West as missionary teachers. Their places in the factories should be taken by men. Upper-class women, Catharine said, should do whatever they could to contribute to the "proper education" of American children. Whether by teaching themselves, or by raising funds, or by supervising schools in their community, all well-to-do women could do some productive labor for education. By their efforts, moreover, the public attitude toward the teaching profession could be changed. Teaching is regarded "as the most wearying drudgery, and few resort to it except from necessity," Catharine said, but by elevating the teaching profession into a "true and noble" one, and by making it the special "profession of a woman," women would be freed from the caste principles that suppressed them and enter into a new casteless, but elevated condition.[8] In effect Catharine would eliminate the extremes of class identity and fortify a middle-class social order.

The second corollary to the new social role Catharine described for women was that of fostering the nation's social conscience. Young women teachers in the West would be in the vanguard of settlement, and from them the character of the place would take its shape. "Soon, in all parts of our country, in each neglected village, or new settlement, the Christian female teacher will quietly take her station, collecting the ignorant children around her, teaching them habits of neatness, order and thrift; opening the book of knowledge, inspiring the principles of morality, and awakening the hope of immortality," she said.[9] . . . Catharine cited several examples of western settlement where the female teacher preceded the minister. Thus she asserted that a woman could be chiefly responsible for setting the moral tone of the community. A community could coalesce around women rather than the church.

The promotion of national unity was a third aspect of the new social role Catharine was defining for women. The special esteem in which American women were held meant that their united actions would have a nationwide effect. "It is the pride and honour of our country," she said, "that woman holds a commanding influence in the domestic and social circle, which is accorded to the sex in no other nation, and such as will make her wishes and efforts, if united for a benevolent and patriotic object, almost omnipotent." Women thus had the power to shape the character of the whole nation, and that character, Catharine said, would be one of a united nation rather than a collection of sections.[10] . . .

At the end of each address Catharine presented to her audience her plan for practical action. A committee of clergymen led by [Calvin] Stowe would, as soon as sufficient funds were raised for a salary, "appoint one man who shall act as an agent," giving his full time to the organization. The committee would also appoint "a Board of Managers, consisting of men from each of the principal Protestant denominations from each of the different sections of the country." In addition, local committees of women would raise funds "to aid in educating and locating missionary teachers." In the West such committees could aid in providing schools for those sent out. In both places the committees could publicize the cause. Lastly Catharine revealed how "every woman who feels an interest in the effort can contribute at least a small sum to promote it" by immediately purchasing Catharine's *Treatise on Domestic Economy* and her *Domestic Receipt Book,* since half the profits from the sale of these books was to be given to the cause.[11]

Catharine Beecher apparently misled her audience when she claimed that "the copyright interest in these two works is held by a board of gentlemen appointed for the purpose." Her original contract with Harper & Brothers, still preserved by Harper & Row, gave Catharine full control of the profits and did not mention a "board of gentlemen." Catharine's contract gave her 50 percent of the net profits, so she was correct in representing to her audience the fact that only half the price went to the publisher. But when she said that "Half the profits (after paying a moderate compensation to the author for the time and labour of preparing them, the amount to be decided by the above gentlemen) will be devoted to this object," she misrepresented the flow of power and profit between herself and the "gentlemen." For neither Stowe nor any of the other named Cincinnati clergymen would have been capable of questioning Catharine's use of the money that came to her from Harpers. Catharine had a reputation in her family of being "clever" to deal with financially, and it was extremely unlikely that Calvin Stowe would have crossed swords with his sister-in-law on financial issues. Later, when a salaried agent was found for the organization, he received his funds from the money he himself raised, not from the profits of Catharine's books.

Catharine's tactics in presenting herself and her cause to the public made her an enor-

mously successful publicist. She sent circulars signed by Calvin Stowe to county newspapers and small-town clergymen throughout the East and West, asking for the names of women who might be willing to serve as missionary teachers and for the names of towns and villages where such teachers would be welcomed. The Catholic analogy and the ideology of self-denial made her efforts newsworthy, and to make the work of county editors easier she dispatched articles, such as the one entitled "Education at the West—Sisters of Charity," for newspapers to print alongside Stowe's circular.[12] The primary targets for Catharine's fund-raising efforts were the local groups of church women she organized in every city and town she visited.[13] She asked each group to make at least a hundred-dollar donation, this being the amount necessary to train and locate one teacher.

Catharine's efforts gained the endorsement of the most prominent American educators. Horace Mann, Henry Barnard, Thomas Burrowes, Samuel Lewis, and Gorham Abbot lent their support, and with each new endorsement by a national figure, Catharine's local fund-raising became more successful.[14] Catharine's tactic in each city was to plead her cause with the town's most eminent personage and, having gained his or her endorsement, to use it to build a substantial and active local committee. In this way she even drew into her cause those who traditionally opposed evangelical projects and especially opposed the Beecher family. . . .

By the spring of 1846 Catharine had delivered her addresses in most of the major cities of the East. Everywhere she called upon women to "save" their country from ignorance and immorality, and everywhere women responded. In Boston the Ladies Society for Promoting Education at the West donated several thousand dollars over the course of the decade to Catharine Beecher and her cause, and in other cities similar groups of women were organized by her into active proponents of her ideas on women and education. She corresponded with these groups constantly, relating her recent advances in other cities and exhorting her followers on to greater efforts. In a typical five-week period early in 1846 Catharine spoke in Pittsburgh, Baltimore, Washington, D.C., Philadelphia, New York City, Troy, Albany, and Hartford. She retraced her steps often, sometimes staying only one night in a place—long enough to deliver a public speech, encourage her old supporters, and welcome new ones. She traveled like a candidate for political office, moving quickly from one city to another, thereby promoting a large amount of newspaper coverage of her arrivals and departures.[15] . . .

In Albany in the spring of 1847 and in Hartford in the fall Catharine collected two groups of thirty-five young women for one month's training before they were sent to locations . . . in the West. The local women's committees provided room and board for Catharine and her young women. Catharine lectured the prospective teachers on how to meet all the difficulties that were to face them in the West: how to overcome the lack of books and proper schoolrooms; how to train children to good moral habits "when all domestic and social influences tend to weaken such habits"; how to impart spiritual training "without giving occasion for sectarian jealousy and alarm"; and how to preserve their health "from the risks of climate and dangers of overexertion and excessive care." Catharine also lectured on the ways in which they could influence the community outside the schoolroom. They learned how to teach "the laws of health by the aid of simple drawings on the blackboard so that the children could copy them on slates to take home and explain to their parents," and how to teach certain branches of "domestic economy" so that parents would "be willing to adopt these improvements." Most of all they learned how to be moral examples that the rest of the community could imitate.[16]

Most of the seventy young women were New Englanders; only three came from New York and one from Pennsylvania. More than half of them went to Illinois and Indiana, seven crossed the Mississippi into Iowa, and a few went to Wisconsin, Michigan, Kentucky, and Tennessee. Each of them was expected to act as "a new source of moral power" in her community, and the reports they made at the end of the year revealed how seriously they took this charge.[17] . . .

The letters Catharine received from these teachers testified to the effectiveness of her training and to the tenacity of purpose she instilled. One woman went West to join a constituency that had migrated from North Car-

olina, Tennessee, and Germany and was met with a log cabin classroom holding forty-five pupils ranging in age from six to eighteen, and a community of hostile parents. "They seem desirous to have their children educated, but they differed so much about almost every thing, that they could not build a schoolhouse," she wrote Catharine.

> I was told, when I came, that they would not pay a teacher for more than three months in a year. At first, they were very suspicious, and watched me narrowly; but, through the blessing of my heavenly Father, I have gained their good will and confidence, so that they have provided me a good frame schoolhouse, with writing-desks and a blackboard, and they promise to support me all the year around.

Having proved herself in their eyes, she succeeded next in drawing both parents and children to a Sunday school. Then, because the nearest church was seven miles away and the people did not go to it, she persuaded them "to invite the nearest clergyman to preach" in her schoolhouse the next Sunday. This New England woman, though unused to frontier conditions, decided to stay on in the place even though she had to board "where there are eight children and the parents and only two rooms in the house," and she went without simple amenities such as candles and a place to bathe.[18] . . . Developments shaping the teaching profession at this precise moment made the field especially receptive to Catharine Beecher's view that it properly belonged to women. Although female teachers began to replace men in some eastern states in the 1830s, the utility of that shift was not apparent to most state and local boards of education until 1840. What had begun as an improvised economic measure had by then proved to be a pedagogic as well as a fiscal improvement, and as these obvious benefits were discovered by state and local boards of education from 1840 to 1880, women gradually replaced their male predecessors in the teaching profession. By 1888, 63 percent of American teachers were women, and in cities women constituted 90 percent of the teaching force.[19]

Although it is impossible to measure completely Catharine Beecher's impact on the profession, her publicizing in behalf of women did at least facilitate an otherwise confused transition period in the nation's schools. For the traditionally higher value attached to male labor blinded many communities to the advantages of female teachers, and as late as 1850 the state of Indiana viewed the female teacher as the exception rather than the rule.[20] The West was, on the whole, slower to employ women as teachers, perhaps because it attracted ample numbers of ambitious men who, typically, would teach for a brief period or even a few years before locating more lucrative commercial employment.[21] These male teachers were usually paid twice as much as female teachers, and a male teacher frequently brought fewer pedagogic talents to the job than a woman. In New York, one of the earliest states to shift to women teachers, the state board of regents in 1838 still assumed that teachers should be male, and they failed to approve the governor's request that normal schools be attached to female academies because they concluded that men, rather than women, needed the normal training.[22] Therefore it was far from obvious to the American public that teaching was a woman's profession.

On the other hand the shift to women teachers was well enough along by 1843 to provide a solid factual basis for Catharine Beecher's claims on their behalf. In Massachusetts, the first state to promote the employment of women as teachers, women outnumbered men three to two in 1837 and two to one in 1842.[23] Many school districts had since the 1820s routinely employed women to teach the summer session, although they believed men were needed to "manage" the older boys present at the winter school session. Some New York districts learned in the 1820s that they could, with the state subsidy of half a teacher's salary, employ a woman to teach full-time and thus not have to bear any of the cost themselves.[24] As a leading educator pointed out later in the century, "the effective reason" women were employed in schools was that they were "cheaper than men." If they had not been cheaper, "they would not have replaced nine-tenths of the men in American public schools."[25]

The need for such educational economies became more critical in the 1830s and 1840s, when immigration and internal migration increased the population of many areas, but did not immediately increase the tax base. By reducing the school costs by hiring women, a district could accommodate its larger numbers of children without taxing itself at a higher rate.[26]

Three basic assumptions were used to justify these lower salaries for women: women, unlike men, did not have to support a family; women were only working temporarily until they married; and the free workings of the economic marketplace determined cheaper salaries for women. Women do not "expect to accumulate much property by this occupation; if it affords them a respectable support and a situation where they can be useful, it is as much as they demand," wrote the state superintendent of Ohio in 1839. He therefore urged "those counties who are in the habit of paying men for instructing little children" to hire women since "females would do it for less than half the sum and generally much better than men can."[27]

Catharine chose to exploit the short-term gains that these discriminatory practices brought to women, and her publicity on behalf of female teachers emphasized their willingness to work for less money. "To make education universal, it must be moderate in expense," Catharine wrote in a petition to Congress in 1853 for free normal schools for female teachers, "and women can afford to teach for one-half, or even less, the salary which men would ask, because the female teacher has only to sustain herself; she does not look forward to the duty of supporting a family, should she marry; nor has she the ambition to amass a fortune." Catharine also insisted that women's employment as teachers would not create a "celibate class" of women, but that their employment was only temporary, and would in fact prepare them to be better wives and mothers. By defining teaching as an extension of the duties of the home, Catharine presented her idea in a form most likely to gain widespread public support. "It is ordained by infinite wisdom, that, as in the family, so in the social state, the interests of young children and of women are one and the same," Catharine insisted.[28]

Since the profession had lower pay and status than most men qualified to teach could get elsewhere, since the economics of education called for even lower pay in the 1830s and 1840s, and since the schoolroom could be seen as functionally akin to the home, both public sentiment and economic facts supported

Catharine Beecher's efforts to redefine the gender of the American teacher.

NOTES

1. Catharine Beecher, *Educational Reminiscences and Suggestions* (New York, 1874), p. 101. Hereafter cited as CB, *Reminiscences.* . . .

2. CB, "Memoranda," 3 Oct. 1844 to 7 June 1845, Beecher-Stowe Collection, Radcliffe College, Cambridge, Mass.

3. CB, *The Evils Suffered by American Women and American Children: The Causes and the Remedy* (New York, 1846), p. 29.

4. CB, *An Address to the Protestant Clergy of the United States* (New York, 1846), p. 29.

5. Ibid., pp. 22–23; CB, *The Evils Suffered,* p. 16.

6. CB, "Memoranda," 29 Nov. to 4 Dec. 1844; CB, *The Evils Suffered,* pp. 6–9.

7. CB, *The Evils Suffered,* pp. 11–14.

8. Ibid., p. 11.

9. Ibid., pp. 9–10.

10. Ibid., p. 11.

11. CB, *The Duty of American Women to Their Country* (New York, 1845), pp. 112–31.

12. CB to Judge Lane, 26 July 1845, Ebenezer Lane Papers, Rutherford B. Hayes Library, Fremont, Ohio. . . .

13. CB, *Reminiscences,* p. 115.

14. Samuel Lewis was the state superintendent of schools for Ohio; Gorham Abbot, the brother of Jacob Abbot, was the director of a fashionable school for girls in New York City. CB also appealed to Rufus Choate, then the director of the Smithsonian Institution, and Mrs. James K. Polk, the nation's first lady, for their endorsements. See CB to The Hon. Rufus Choate, 29 Aug. 1846, Harriet Beecher Stowe Collection, Clifton Waller Barrett Library, University of Virginia; CB to Mrs. James K. Polk [1847], Hillhouse Family Papers, box 27, Sterling Memorial Library.

15. CB, "Memoranda," 21 Mar. to 27 Apr. 1846. Charles H. Foster, *An Errand of Mercy, The Evangelical United Front, 1790–1837* (Chapel Hill, 1960), p. 136, describes the traditional support New England women gave to education. . . .

16. William Slade, "Circular to the Friends of Popular Education in the United States," 15 May 1847, Increase Lapham Papers, State Historical Society of Wisconsin, Madison.

17. *First Annual Report of the General Agent of the Board of National Popular Education* (Hartford, 1848), pp. 15, 22–26.

18. CB, *The True Remedy for the Wrongs of Women* (Boston, 1851), pp. 163, 167.

19. Thomas Woody, *A History of Women's Education in the United States* (New York, 1929), 1:499.

20. Richard G. Boone, *A History of Education in Indiana* (New York, 1892), p. 142.

21. Michael Katz, *The Irony of Early School Reform: Innovation in Mid-Nineteenth Century Massachusetts* (Cambridge, Mass., 1968), pp. 57–58. . . .

22. Elsie Garland Hobson, "Educational Legislation and Administration in the State of New York from 1772 to 1850," *Supplementary Educational Monographs* 3, no. 1 (Chicago, 1918), p. 75.

23. Woody, *History of Women's Education,* 1:497.

24. Hobson, "Educational Legislation," p. 66.

25. . . . Charles William Eliot, "Wise and Unwise Economy in Schools," *Atlantic Monthly,* no. 35 (June 1875):715, quoted in Katz, *Irony of Early School Reform,* p. 58.

26. Katz, *Irony of Early School Reform,* pp. 56–58.

27. Woody, *History of Women's Education,* 1:491.

28. Petition appeared in *Godey's Lady's Book* (January 1853): 176–77. . . .

SUELLEN HOY
Agatha O'Brien and the Sisters of Mercy: A Community of Nuns in Early Chicago

Immigration to the United States accelerated dramatically in the antebellum years; employers welcomed unskilled laborers and harsh times in Europe, especially the Irish famine, drew men and women from Ireland and Germany. Many were Catholic, a minority faith in the United States, and one that most Protestants viewed with skepticism if

Written especially for *Women's America* by Suellen Hoy. © 1999 by Suellen Hoy.

not outright hostility (despite the support that the Catholic King of France had offered during the Revolutionary War). Some Catholic gender traditions were in sharp contrast to those of the Protestant Reformation: a celibate clergy and celibate religious communities of women were singled out for attack. Lurid anti-Catholic propaganda circulated widely—in 1834 an anti-Catholic mob in Boston burned an Ursuline convent, convinced that a Protestant woman was being held against her will. Anti-Catholicism was part of the platform of the nativist Know-Nothing Party, which flourished in the 1850s.

Yet most Catholic immigrants were quietly absorbed into the American population. Among them were religious communities of women. Although many had been part of cloistered communities in Europe, those were rarely replicated in the United States; most women religious devoted themselves to active forms of social service as well as to prayer and contemplation. What commonalities did Sister Agatha and her colleagues share with the teachers whom Sklar described in the previous essay? Note that Protestant families sometimes sent their children to Catholic academies.

Sister Agatha O'Brien, who led the first community of nuns in frontier Chicago, entered the Sisters of Mercy in Ireland in 1843 when she was twenty-one years old. She was one of seventeen children born in County Carlow to the wife of a barrelmaker. Educated but poor, she began religious life as a lay sister (a nun without dowry), working in the convent kitchen. Within a year she had volunteered to join the first group of Sisters of Mercy to emigrate to the United States; they were headed for Pittsburgh. The Irish-born Bishop Michael O'Connor, who had invited them and crossed the Atlantic with them, recognized O'Brien's potential. He recommended that she take the habit and be professed as a choir nun, a position for an educated woman. He did not want her talent restricted to cooking and cleaning only "because her father happened to be a poor man in Ireland." Later he would remark that Sister Agatha was "capable of ruling a nation."[1]

In September 1846, after less than two years in Pittsburgh, she and four companions arrived in Chicago. It was a primitive Western outpost of less than 20,000 people. During the next decade, as the population expanded to encompass thousands of desperate emigrants fleeing Ireland's Great Famine, these five Mercy pioneers remained the city's only community of Catholic sisters. Residing in a convent at Wabash and Madison, they offered the church's welcome to destitute newcomers, who were often despised for their filth, faith, and ignorance. (Chicago's St. Vincent de Paul Society was not founded until 1857.) Inspired by their Irish founder, Catherine McAuley,

who had encouraged her sisters to follow St. Paul's example and "go into the middle of a perverse world," they took to the streets to tend the poor, the sick, and the illiterate. Always on the move, they became known in Chicago as the "walking nuns."

Sister Agatha, as Superior, set the pace. By midcentury the number of nuns had grown from 5 to 44. In a handful of her letters from the early 1850s, there is a constant, even monotonous refrain. Over and again she wrote that she had "not one moment to spare," that "my hands are full," that "time is real precious here." In 1851, to her brother, Charles, she explained:

> We are very busy here; we have two free schools in which there are about two hundred children and a select school with about forty—two orphan asylums, with children from one year up to ten, all these we have to support and educate and take care of; we also have a hospital for the sick in which there are generally from twenty to thirty patients, so from this you may infer how arduous and laborious our duties are.

Sister Agatha neglected to mention that her expanding community was also volunteering at a dispensary opened by Rush Medical College, teaching Sunday School at several city parishes, running a small employment bureau for working women, and holding night classes for illiterate adults.

Like the well-known settlement workers who opened Hull House in Chicago forty years later (see pp. 315–18), this antebellum community of women religious, who were without family responsibilities and lived among the neediest, could direct their energy and enthusiasm to larger enterprises. Not all were aimed solely at Catholics. In 1851, Sister Agatha told a friend in Pittsburgh that she had "so much to do with Protestants." She said that "almost all the children in the select school [St. Xavier's Academy]" were Protestant, that Protestants visited the sisters "constantly," and that they had "some very warm friends among them."[2] No doubt it is for this reason that Catherine Beecher, a mid-nineteenth-century Protestant reformer, found the work of Catholic sisters in the Midwest both impressive and threatening. In 1851, Beecher looked with envy at the Catholic Church, which had "posts of competence, usefulness, and honor . . . for women of every rank and of every description of talents." Catholic nuns were Beecher's direct competitors; when Beecher had to give up a school in Cincinnati because she could not make it financially self-sustaining, nuns took it over and under their care and management the school flourished.[3]

Chicago's first Sisters of Mercy were mostly immigrants or the daughters of immigrants. The majority, though not all, were Irish. Sister Agatha once observed that the members of her community were "Irish, American, German and French . . . a mixture of many nations, but all one with respect to religion." Committed to one another and to the poor who lived nearby, they gave Chicagoans a powerful example of how single women might live useful, Christian lives. In fact, during the nineteenth century and well into the twentieth, communal life—particularly one with a public dimension—would provide an attractive and popular alternative to the life choices available to most women.

As the Sisters of Mercy's numbers and reputation for service grew, Sister Agatha was beseiged by invitations from "clergymen . . . throughout the state [who] are continually crying out for the Sisters to form new missions." When she opened houses in Chicago or away from the city (i.e., Galena, 1848), she did so with relative ease and "no trouble":

I always place at the head one on whom I can rely. I never drive or torment her but treat them [sic] kindly and give them to understand that I place confidence in them, & in no instance have I ever found them to betray me.

Collegial, solicitous, and energetic, Sister Agatha appears to have been admired in life. She most certainly was admired in death.

The cholera epidemic of 1854, which had devastating effects on Chicago, did not spare the Mercy convent. After a full day of nursing the sick on July 7, Sister Agatha became ill. She died the next day; she was thirty-two years old. By July 11, three more nuns had also become cholera victims.

Six months later, in December 1854, when the Sisters of Mercy opened a second academy in the city, they called it "St. Agatha's" in tribute to their spirited leader. She had not only offered a dramatic personal example of how religious life in America could be transforming, but she and her colleagues had won for Catholics and their church increased tolerance and respectability. Sister Agatha O'Brien had "succeeded by her zeal and wisdom," according to an obituary in the 1855 Metropolitan Catholic Almanac. She had laid the foundation for many charitable and educational enterprises; Mercy Hospital and St. Xavier University thrive at the turn of the twenty-first century. By trusting in Providence and responding generously to those in need, she and her community of women religious had established in early Chicago a workable model for effecting social and religious change.

NOTES

1. Mother Mary Austin Carroll, *Leaves From the Annals of the Sisters of Mercy in Four Volumes* (New York, 1889), vol. III, p. 245.

2. Quotations from Sister Agatha O'Brien are from letters written on Nov. 12, 1850; Feb. 7, June 28, Sept. 4, Nov. 12, 1851.

3. Catharine E. Beecher *The True Remedy for the Wrongs of Woman* (Boston, 1851), p. 51.

CARROLL SMITH-ROSENBERG

The Female World of Love and Ritual: Relations between Women in Nineteenth-Century America

Women's associations with each other have traditionally been ignored by historians. One reason for this has been a fascination with public life; only women who were powerful in the same fashion as men or whose lives were intertwined with the lives of powerful men attracted the historical spotlight. The world of women was treated as wholly private or domestic, encompassing only family responsibilities. Women's diaries and letters were used primarily as a source of illustrative anecdote.

Carroll Smith-Rosenberg has read the letters and diaries of women in a strikingly original way. She evaluates nineteenth-century American society in much the same way an anthropologist might observe a distant culture. She describes relations between women as intellectually active, personally rewarding, mutually supportive, and socially creative. Smith-Rosenberg offers a radically new account of the relationship between the sexes in Victorian America. What revision does she suggest ought to be made in our traditional understanding of Victorian sexuality?

The female friendship of the nineteenth century, the long-lived, intimate, loving friendship between two women, is an excellent example of the type of historical phenomena which most historians know something about, which few have thought much about, and which virtually no one has written about.[1] It is one aspect of the female experience which consciously or unconsciously we have chosen to ignore. Yet an abundance of manuscript evidence suggests that eighteenth- and nineteenth-century women routinely formed emotional ties with other women. Such deeply felt, same-sex friendships were casually accepted in American society. Indeed, from at least the late eighteenth through the mid-nineteenth century, a female world of varied and yet highly structured relationships appears to have been an essential aspect of American society. These relationships ranged from the supportive love of sisters, through the enthu-siasms of adolescent girls, to sensual avowals of love by mature women. It was a world in which men made but a shadowy appearance.[2]

Defining and analyzing same-sex relationships involves the historian in deeply problematical questions of method and interpretation. This is especially true since historians, influenced by Freud's libidinal theory, have discussed these relationships almost exclusively within the context of individual psychosexual developments or, to be more explicit, psychopathology.[3] Seeing same-sex relationships in terms of a dichotomy between normal and abnormal, they have sought the origins of such apparent deviance in childhood or adolescent trauma and detected the symptoms of "latent" homosexuality in the lives of both those who later became "overtly" homosexual and those who did not. Yet theories concerning the nature and origins of same-sex relationships are frequently contradictory or based on questionable or arbitrary data. In recent years such hypotheses have been subjected to criticism both from within and without the psychological professions. Historians who seek to work within a psychological framework, therefore, are faced with two hard questions: Do sound psychodynamic theories concerning the nature and origins of same-sex relationships exist? If so, does the historical datum exist which would permit the use of such dynamic models?

I would like to suggest an alternative approach to female friendships—one which would view them within a cultural and social setting rather than from an exclusively individual psychosexual perspective. Only by thus altering our approach will we be in the position to evaluate the appropriateness of particular dynamic interpretations. Intimate friendships between men and men and women and women existed in a larger world of social relations and social values. To interpret such friendships more fully they must be related to the structure of the American family and to the nature of sex-role divisions and of male-female relations both within the family and in society generally. The female friendship must not be seen in isolation; it must be analyzed as one aspect of women's overall relations with one another. The ties between mothers and daughters, sisters, female cousins and friends, at all stages of the female life cycle constitute the most suggestive framework for the historian to begin an analysis of intimacy and affection between women. Such an analysis would not only emphasize general cultural patterns rather than the internal dynamics of a particular family or childhood; it would shift the focus of the study from a concern with deviance to that of defining configurations of legitimate behavioral norms and options.[4]

This analysis will be based upon the correspondence and diaries of women and men in thirty-five families between the 1760s and the 1880s. These families, though limited in number, represented a broad range of the American middle class, from hard-pressed pioneer families and orphaned girls to daughters of the intellectual and social elite. It includes families from most geographic regions, rural and urban, and a spectrum of Protestant denominations ranging from Mormon to orthodox Quaker. Although scarcely a comprehensive sample of America's increasingly heterogeneous population, it does, I believe, reflect accurately the literate middle class to which the historian working with letters and diaries is necessarily bound. It was involved an analysis of many thousands of letters written to women friends, kin, husbands, brothers, and children at every period of life from adolescence to old age. Some collections encompass virtually entire life spans; one contains over 100,000 letters as well as diaries and account books. It is my contention that an analysis of women's private letters and diaries which were never intended to be published permits the historian to explore a very private world of emotional realities central both to women's lives and to the middle-class family in nineteenth-century America.[5]

The question of female friendships is peculiarly elusive; we know so little or perhaps have forgotten so much. An intriguing and almost alien form of human relationship, they flourished in a different social structure and amidst different sexual norms. Before attempting to reconstruct their social setting, therefore, it might be best first to describe two not atypical friendships. These two friendships, intense, loving, and openly avowed, began during the women's adolescence and, despite subsequent marriages and geographic separation, continued throughout their lives. For nearly half a century these women played a central emotional role in each other's lives, writing time and again of their love and of the pain of separation. Paradoxically to twentieth-century minds, their love appears to have been both sensual and platonic.

Sarah Butler Wister first met Jeannie Field Musgrove while vacationing with her family at Stockbridge, Massachusetts, in the summer of 1849.[6] Jeannie was then sixteen, Sarah fourteen. During two subsequent years spent together in boarding school, they formed a deep and intimate friendship. Sarah began to keep a bouquet of flowers before Jeannie's portrait and wrote complaining of the intensity and anguish of her affection.[7] Both young women assumed nom de plumes, Jeannie a female name, Sarah a male one; they would use these secret names into old age.[8] They frequently commented on the nature of their affection: "If the day should come," Sarah wrote Jeannie in the spring of 1861, "when you failed me either through your fault or my own, I would forswear all human friendship, thenceforth." A few months later Jeannie commented: "Gratitude is a word I should never use toward you. It is perhaps a misfortune of such intimacy and love that it makes one regard all kindness as a matter of course, as one has always found it, as natural as the embrace in meeting."[9]

Sarah's marriage altered neither the frequency of their correspondence nor their desire to be together. In 1864, when twenty-nine, married, and a mother, Sarah wrote to Jeannie: "I shall be entirely alone [this coming week]. I can give you no idea how desperately I shall want you...." After one such visit Jeannie, then a spinster in New York, echoed Sarah's longing: "Dear darling Sarah! How I love you & how happy I have been! You are the joy of my life.... I cannot tell you how much happiness you gave me, nor how constantly it is all in my thoughts.... My darling how I long for the time when I shall see you...." After another visit Jeannie wrote: "I want you to tell me in your next letter, to assure me, that I am your dearest.... I do not doubt you, & I am not jealous but I long to hear you say it once more & it seems already a long time since your voice fell on my ear. So just fill a quarter page with caresses & expressions of endearment. Your silly Angelina." Jeannie ended one letter: "Goodbye my dearest, dearest lover—ever your own Angelina." And another, "I will go to bed ... [though] I could write all night—A thousand kisses—I love you with my whole soul—your Angelina."

When Jeannie finally married in 1870 at the age of thirty-seven, Sarah underwent a period of extreme anxiety. Two days before Jeannie's marriage Sarah, then in London, wrote desperately: "Dearest darling—How incessantly have I thought of you these eight days—all today—the entire uncertainty, the distance, the long silence—are all new features in my separation from you, grievous to be borne.... Oh Jeannie. I have thought & thought & yearned over you these two days. Are you married I wonder? My dearest love to you wherever and *who*ever you are."[10] Like many other women in this collection of thirty-five families, marriage brought Sarah and Jeannie physical separation; it did not cause emotional distance. Although at first they may have wondered how marriage would affect their relationship, their affection remained

unabated throughout their lives, underscored by their loneliness and their desire to be together.[11]

During the same years that Jeannie and Sarah wrote of their love and need for each other, two slightly younger women began a similar odyssey of love, dependence and—ultimately—physical, though not emotional, separation. Molly and Helena met in 1868 while both attended the Cooper Institute School of Design for Women in New York City. For several years these young women studied and explored the city together, visited each other's families, and formed part of a social network of other artistic young women. Gradually, over the years, their initial friendship deepened into a close intimate bond which continued throughout their lives. The tone in the letters which Molly wrote to Helena changed over these years from "My dear Helena," and signed "your attached friend," to "My dearest Helena," "My Dearest," "My Beloved," and signed "Thine always" or "thine Molly."[12]

The letters they wrote to each other during these first five years permit us to reconstruct something of their relationship together. As Molly wrote in one early letter:

> I have not said to you in so many or so few words that I was happy with you during those few so incredibly short weeks but surely you do not need words to tell you what you must know. Those two or three days so dark without, so bright with firelight and contentment within I shall always remember as proof that, for a time, at least—I fancy for quite a long time—we might be sufficient for each other. We know that we can amuse each other for many idle hours together and now we know that we can also work together. And that means much, don't you think so?

She ended: "I shall return in a few days. Imagine yourself kissed many times by one who loved you so dearly."

The intensity and even physical nature of Molly's love was echoed in many of the letters she wrote during the next few years, as, for instance in this short thank-you note for a small present: "Imagine yourself kissed a dozen times my darling. Perhaps it is well for you that we are far apart. You might find my thanks so expressed rather overpowering. I have that delightful feeling that it doesn't matter much what I say or how I say it, since we shall meet so soon and forget in that moment that we were ever separated. . . . I shall see you soon and be content."[13]

At the end of the fifth year, however, several crises occurred. The relationship, at least in its intense form, ended, though Molly and Helena continued an intimate and complex relationship for the next half-century. The exact nature of these crises is not completely clear, but it seems to have involved Molly's decision not to live with Helena, as they had originally planned, but to remain at home because of parental insistence. Molly was now in her late twenties. Helena responded with anger and Molly became frantic at the thought that Helena would break off their relationship. Though she wrote distraught letters and made despairing attempts to see Helena, the relationship never regained its former ardor—possibly because Molly had a male suitor.[14] Within six months Helena had decided to marry a man who was, coincidentally, Molly's friend and publisher. Two years later Molly herself finally married. The letters toward the end of this period discuss the transition both women made to having male lovers—Molly spending much time reassuring Helena, who seemed depressed about the end of their relationship and with her forthcoming marriage.[15]

It is clearly difficult from a distance of 100 years and from a post-Freudian cultural perspective to decipher the complexities of Molly and Helena's relationship. Certainly Molly and Helena were lovers—emotionally if not physically. The emotional intensity and pathos of their love becomes apparent in several letters Molly wrote Helena during their crisis: "I wanted so to put my arms round my girl of all the girls in the world and tell her . . . I love her as wives do love their husbands, as *friends* who have taken each other for life—and believe in her, as I believe in my God. . . . If I didn't love you do you suppose I'd care about anything or have ridiculous notions and panics and behave like an old fool who ought to know better. I'm going to hang on to your skirts. . . . You can't get away from [my] love." Or as she wrote after Helena's decision to marry: "You know dear Helena, I really was in love with you. It was a passion such as I had never known until I saw you. I don't think it was the noblest way to love you." The theme of intense female love was one Molly again expressed in a letter she wrote to the man Helena was to marry: "Do you know sir, that until you came along I believe that she loved me almost as girls love their lovers. *I know I loved her so.* Don't you wonder that I can stand the sight of you." This was in a letter congratulating them on their forthcoming marriage.[16]

The essential question is not whether these women had genital contact and can therefore be defined as heterosexual or homosexual. The twentieth-century tendency to view human love and sexuality within a dichotomized universe of deviance and normality, genitality and platonic love, is alien to the emotions and attitudes of the nineteenth century and fundamentally distorts the nature of these women's emotional interaction. These letters are significant because they force us to place such female love in a particular historical context. There is every indication that these four women, their husbands and families—all eminently respectable and socially conservative—considered such love both socially acceptable and fully compatible with heterosexual marriage. Emotionally and cognitively, their heterosocial and their homosocial worlds were complementary.

One could argue, on the other hand, that these letters were but an example of the romantic rhetoric with which the nineteenth century surrounded the concept of friendship. Yet they possess an emotional intensity and a sensual and physical explicitness that is difficult to dismiss. Jeannie longed to hold Sarah in her arms; Molly mourned her physical isolation from Helena. Molly's love and devotion to Helena, the emotions that bound Jeannie and Sarah together, while perhaps a phenomenon of nineteenth-century society, were not the less real for their Victorian origins. A survey of the correspondence and diaries of eighteenth- and nineteenth-century women indicates that Molly, Jeannie, and Sarah represented one very real behavioral and emotional option socially available to nineteenth-century women.

This is not to argue that individual needs, personalities, and family dynamics did not have a significant role in determining the nature of particular relationships. But the scholar must ask if it is historically possible and, if possible, important, to study the intensely individual aspects of psychosexual dynamics. Is it not the historian's first task to explore the social structure and the world view which made intense and sometimes sensual female love both a possible and an acceptable emotional option? From such a social perspective a new and quite different series of questions suggests itself. What emotional function did such female love serve? What was its place within the hetero-and homosocial worlds which women jointly inhabited? Did a spectrum of love-object choices exist in the nineteenth century across which some individuals, at least, were capable of moving? Without attempting to answer these questions it will be difficult to understand either nineteenth-century sexuality or the nineteenth-century family.

Several factors in American society between the mid-eighteenth and the mid-nineteenth centuries may well have permitted women to form a variety of close emotional relationships with other women. American society was characterized in large part by rigid gender-role differentiation within the family and within society as a whole, leading to the emotional segregation of women and men. The roles of daughter and mother shaded imperceptibly and ineluctably into each other, while the biological realities of frequent pregnancies, childbirth, nursing, and menopause bound women together in physical and emotional intimacy. It was within just such a social framework, I would argue, that a specifically female world did indeed develop, a world built around a generic and unself-conscious pattern of single-sex or homosocial networks. These supportive networks were institutionalized in social conventions or rituals which accompanied virtually every important event in a woman's life, from birth to death. Such female relationships were frequently supported and paralleled by severe social restrictions on intimacy between young men and women. Within such a world of emotional richness and complexity devotion to and love of other women became a plausible and socially accepted form of human interaction.

An abundance of printed and manuscript sources exists to support such a hypothesis. Etiquette books, advice books on child rearing, religious sermons, guides to young men and young women, medical texts, and school curricula all suggest that late eighteenth- and most nineteenth-century Americans assumed the existence of a world composed of distinctly male and female spheres, spheres determined by the immutable laws of God and nature.[17] The unpublished letters and diaries of Americans during this same period concur, detailing the existence of sexually segregated worlds inhabited by human beings with different values, expectations, and personalities. Contacts between men and women frequently partook of a formality and stiffness quite alien to twentieth-century America and which today we tend to define as "Victorian." Women, however, did not form an isolated and oppressed subcategory in male society. Their letters and diaries indicate that women's sphere had an essential integrity and dignity that grew out of women's shared experiences and mutual affection and that, despite the profound changes which affected American social structure and institutions between the 1760s and the 1870s, retained a constancy and predictability. The ways in which women thought of and interacted with each other remained unchanged. Continuity, not discontinuity, characterized this female world. Molly Hallock's and Jeannie Field's words, emotions, and experiences have direct parallels in the 1760s and the 1790s.[18] There are indications in contemporary sociological and psychological literature that female closeness and support networks have continued into the twentieth century—not only among ethnic and working-class groups but even among the middle class.[19]

Most eighteenth- and nineteenth-century women lived within a world bounded by home, church, and the institution of visiting—that endless trooping of women to each other's homes for social purposes. It was a world inhabited by children and by other women.[20] Women helped each other with domestic chores and in times of sickness, sorrow, or trouble. Entire days, even weeks, might be spent almost exclusively with other women.[21] Urban and town women could devote virtually every day to visits, teas, or shopping trips with other women. Rural women developed a pattern of more extended visits that lasted weeks and sometimes months, at times even dislodging husbands from their beds and bedrooms so that dear friends might spend every hour of every day together.[22] When husbands traveled, wives routinely moved in with other women, invited women friends to teas and suppers, sat together sharing and comparing the letters they had received from other close women friends. Secrets were exchanged and cherished, and the husband's return at times viewed with some ambivalence.[23]

Summer vacations were frequently organized to permit old friends to meet at water spas or share a country home. In 1848, for example, a young matron wrote cheerfully to her husband about the delightful time she was having with five close women friends whom she had invited to spend the summer with her; he remained at home alone to face the heat of Philadelphia and a cholera epidemic.[24] Some ninety years earlier, two young Quaker girls commented upon the vacation their aunt had taken alone with another woman; their remarks were openly envious and tell us something of the emotional quality of these friendships: "I hear Aunt is gone with the Friend and wont be back for two weeks, fine times indeed I think the old friends had, taking their pleasure about the country . . . and have the advantage of that fine woman's conversation and instruction, while we poor young girls must spend all spring at home. . . . What a disappointment that we are not together. . . ."[25]

Friends did not form isolated dyads but were normally part of highly integrated networks. Knowing each other, perhaps related to each other, they played a central role in holding communities and kin systems together. Especially when families became geographically mobile women's long visits to each other and their frequent letters filled with discussions of marriages and births, illness and deaths, descriptions of growing children, and reminiscences of times and people past provided an important sense of continuity in a rapidly changing society.[26] Central to this female world was an inner core of kin. The ties between sisters, first cousins, aunts, and nieces provided the underlying structure upon which groups of friends and their network of female relatives clustered. Although most of the women within this sample would appear to be living within isolated nuclear families, the emotional ties between nonresidential kin were deep and binding and provided one of the fundamental existential realities of women's lives.[27] Twenty years after Parke Lewis Butler moved with her husband to Louisiana, she sent her two daughters back to Virginia to attend school, live with their grandmother and aunt, and be integrated back into Virginia society.[28] The constant letters between Maria Inskeep and Fanny Hampton,

sisters separated in their early twenties when Maria moved with her husband from New Jersey to Louisiana, held their families together, making it possible for their daughters to feel a part of their cousins' network of friends and interests.[29] The Ripley daughters, growing up in western Massachusetts in the early 1800s, spent months each year with their mother's sister and her family in distant Boston; these female cousins and their network of friends exchanged gossip-filled letters and gradually formed deeply loving and dependent ties.[30]

Women frequently spent their days within the social confines of such extended families. Sisters-in-law visited each other and, in some families, seemed to spend more time with each other than with their husbands. First cousins cared for each other's babies—for weeks or even months in times of sickness or childbirth. Sisters helped each other with housework, shopped and sewed for each other. Geographic separation was borne with difficulty. A sister's absence for even a week or two could cause loneliness and depression and would be bridged by frequent letters. Sibling rivalry was hardly unknown, but with separation or illness the theme of deep affection and dependency reemerged.[31]

Sisterly bonds continued across a lifetime. In her old age a rural Quaker matron, Martha Jefferis, wrote to her daughter Anne concerning her own half-sister, Phoebe: "In sister Phoebe I have a real friend—she studies my comfort and waits on me like a child. . . . She is exceedingly kind and this to all other homes (set aside yours) I would prefer—it is next to being with a daughter." Phoebe's own letters confirmed Martha's evaluation of her feelings. "Thou knowest my dear sister," Phoebe wrote, "there is no one . . . that exactly feels [for] thee as I do, for I think without boasting I can truly say that my desire is for thee."[32]

Such women, whether friends or relatives, assumed an emotional centrality in each other's lives. In their diaries and letters they wrote of the joy and contentment they felt in each other's company, their sense of isolation and despair when apart. The regularity of their correspondence underlies the sincerity of their words. Women named their daughters after one another and sought to integrate dear friends into their lives after marriage.[33] As one young bride wrote to an old friend shortly after her marriage: "I want to see you and talk with you and feel that we are united by the same bonds of sympathy and congeniality as ever."[34] After years of friendship one aging woman wrote of another: "Time cannot destroy the fascination of her manner . . . her voice is music to the ear. . . ."[35] Women made elaborate presents for each other, ranging from the Quakers' frugal pies and breads to painted velvet bags and phantom bouquets.[36] When a friend died, their grief was deeply felt. Martha Jefferis was unable to write to her daughter for three weeks because of the sorrow she felt at the death of a dear friend. Such distress was not unusual. A generation earlier a young Massachusetts farm woman filled pages of her diary with her grief at the death of her "dearest friend" and transcribed the letters of condolence other women sent her. She marked the anniversary of Rachel's death each year in her diary, contrasting her faithfulness with that of Rachel's husband who had soon remarried.[37]

These female friendships served a number of emotional functions. Within this secure and empathetic world women could share sorrows, anxieties, and joys, confident that other women had experienced similar emotions. One mid-nineteenth-century rural matron in a letter to her daughter discussed this particular aspect of women's friendships: "To have such a friend as thyself to look to and sympathize with her—and enter into all her little needs and in whose bosom she could with freedom pour forth her joys and sorrows—such a friend would very much relieve the tedium of many a wearisome hour. . . ." A generation later Molly more informally underscored the importance of this same function in a letter to Helena: "Suppose I come down . . . [and] spend Sunday with you quietly," she wrote Helena " . . . that means talking all the time until you are relieved of all your latest troubles, and I of mine. . . ."[38] These were frequently troubles that apparently no man could understand. When Anne Jefferis Sheppard was first married, she and her older sister Edith (who then lived with Anne) wrote in detail to their mother of the severe depression and anxiety which they experienced. Moses Sheppard, Anne's husband, added cheerful postscripts to the sisters' letters—which he had clearly not read—remarking on Anne's and Edith's contentment. Theirs was an emotional world to which he had little access.[39]

This was, as well, a female world in which hostility and criticism of other women were discouraged, and thus a milieu in which women could develop a sense of inner security and self-esteem. As one young woman wrote to her mother's longtime friend: "I cannot sufficiently thank you for the kind unvaried affection & indulgence you have ever shown and expressed both by words and actions for me. . . . Happy would it be did all the world view me as you do, through the medium of kindness and forbearance."[40] They valued each other. Women, who had little status or power in the larger world of male concerns, possessed status and power in the lives and worlds of other women.[41]

An intimate mother-daughter relationship lay at the heart of this female world. The diaries and letters of both mothers and daughters attest to their closeness and mutual emotional dependency. Daughters routinely discussed their mother's health and activities with their own friends, expressed anxiety in cases of their mother's ill health and concern for her cares.[42] Expressions of hostility which we would today consider routine on the part of both mothers and daughters seem to have been uncommon indeed. On the contrary, this sample of families indicates that the normal relationship between mother and daughter was one of sympathy and understanding.[43] Only sickness or great geographic distance was allowed to cause extended separation. When marriage did result in such separation, both viewed the distance between them with distress.[44] Something of this sympathy and love between mothers and daughters is evident in a letter Sarah Alden Ripley, at age sixty-nine, wrote her youngest and recently married daughter: "You do not know how much I miss you, not only when I struggle in and out of my mortal envelop and pump my nightly potation and no longer pour into your sympathizing ear my senile gossip, but all the day I muse away, since the sound of your voice no longer rouses me to sympathy with your joys or sorrows. . . . You cannot know how much I miss your affectionate demonstrations."[45] A dozen aging mothers in this sample of over thirty families echoed her sentiments.

Central to these mother-daughter relations is what might be described as an apprenticeship system. In those families where the daughter followed the mother into a life of traditional domesticity, mothers and other older women carefully trained daughters in the arts of housewifery and motherhood. Such training undoubtedly occurred throughout a girl's childhood but became more systematized, almost ritualistic, in the years following the end of her formal education and before her marriage. At this time a girl either returned home from boarding school or no longer divided her time between home and school. Rather, she devoted her energies on two tasks: mastering new domestic skills and participating in the visiting and social activities necessary to finding a husband. Under the careful supervision of their mothers and of older female relatives, such late-adolescent girls temporarily took over the household management from their mothers, tended their young nieces and nephews, and helped in childbirth, nursing, and weaning. Such experiences tied the generations together in shared skills and emotional interaction.[46]

Daughters were born into a female world. Their mother's life expectations and sympathetic network of friends and relations were among the first realities in the life of the developing child. As long as the mother's domestic role remained relatively stable and few viable alternatives competed with it, daughters tended to accept their mother's world and to turn automatically to other women for support and intimacy. It was within this closed and intimate female world that the young girl grew toward womanhood.

One could speculate at length concerning the absence of that mother-daughter hostility today considered almost inevitable to an adolescent's struggle for autonomy and self-identity. It is possible that taboos against female aggression and hostility were sufficiently strong to repress even that between mothers and their adolescent daughters. Yet these letters seem so alive and the interest of daughters in their mothers' affairs so vital and genuine that it is difficult to interpret their closeness exclusively in terms of repression and denial. The functional bonds that held mothers and daughters together in a world that permitted few alternatives to domesticity might well have created a source of mutuality and trust absent in societies where greater options were available for daughters than for mothers. Furthermore, the extended female network—a daughter's close ties with her own older sisters, cousins, and aunts—may well have permitted a diffusion and a relaxation of mother-daughter identification and so have aided a daughter in her struggle for identity and autonomy. None of these explanations are mutually exclusive; all may well have interacted to produce the degree of empathy evident in those letters and diaries.

At some point in adolescence, the young girl began to move outside the matrix of her mother's support group to develop a network of her own. Among the middle class, at least, this transition toward what was at the same time both a limited autonomy and a repetition of her mother's life seemed to have most frequently coincided with a girl's going to school. Indeed education appears to have played a crucial role in the lives of most of the families in this study. Attending school for a few months, for a year, or longer, was common even among daughters of relatively poor families, while middle-class girls routinely spent at least a year in boarding school.[47] These school years ordinarily marked a girl's first separation from home. They served to wean the daughter from her home, to train her in the essential social graces, and, ultimately, to help introduce her into the marriage market. It was not infrequently a trying emotional experience for both mother and daughter.[48]

In this process of leaving one home and adjusting to another, the mother's friends and relatives played a key transitional role. Such older women routinely accepted the role of foster mother; they supervised the young girl's deportment, monitored her health and introduced her to their own network of female friends and kin.[49] Not infrequently women, friends from their own school years, arranged to send their daughters to the same school so that the girls might form bonds paralleling those their mothers had made. For years Molly and Helena wrote of their daughters' meeting and worried over each other's children. When Molly finally brought her daughter east to school, their first act on reaching New York was to meet Helena and her daughters. Elizabeth Bordley Gibson virtually adopted the daughters of her school chum, Eleanor Custis Lewis. The Lewis daughters soon began to write Elizabeth Gibson letters with the salutation "Dearest Mama." Eleuthera DuPont, attending boarding school in Philadelphia at roughly the same time as the Lewis girls, developed a parallel relationship with her mother's friend, Elizabeth McKie Smith. Eleuthera went to the same school and became a close friend of the Smith girls and eventually married their first cousin. During this period she routinely called Mrs. Smith "Mother." Indeed Eleuthera so internalized the sense of having two mothers that she casually wrote her sisters of her "Mamma's" visits at her "mother's" house—that is, at Mrs. Smith's.[50]

Even more important to this process of maturation than their mother's friends were the female friends young women made at school. Young girls helped each other overcome homesickness and endure the crises of adolescence. They gossiped about beaux, incorporated each other into their own kinship systems, and attended and gave teas and balls together. Older girls in boarding school "adopted" younger ones, who called them "Mother."[51] Dear friends might indeed continue this pattern of adoption and mothering throughout their lives; one woman might routinely assume the nurturing role of pseudo-mother, the other the dependency role of daughter. The pseudomother performed for the other woman all the services which we normally associate with mothers; she went to absurd lengths to purchase items her "daughter" could have obtained from other sources, gave advice and functioned as an idealized figure in her "daughter's" imagination. Helena played such a role for Molly, as did Sarah for Jeannie. Elizabeth Bordley Gibson bought almost all Eleanor Parke Custis Lewis's necessities—from shoes and corset covers to bedding and harp strings—and sent them from Philadelphia to Virginia, a procedure that sometimes took months. Eleanor frequently asked Elizabeth to take back her purchases, have them redone, and argue with shopkeepers about prices. These were favors automatically asked and complied with. Anne Jefferis Sheppard made the analogy very explicitly in a letter to her own mother written shortly after Anne's marriage, when she was feeling depressed about their separation: "Mary Paulen is truly kind, almost acts the part of a mother and trys to aid and *comfort me,* and also to *lighten my new cares.*"[52]

A comparison of the references to men and women in these young women's letters is striking. Boys were obviously indispensable to the elaborate courtship ritual girls engaged in. In these teenage letters and diaries, however, boys appear distant and warded off—an effect produced both by the girl's sense of bonding and by a highly developed and deprecatory whimsy. Girls joked among themselves about the conceit, poor looks or affectations of suitors. Rarely, especially in the eighteenth and early nineteenth centuries, were favorable remarks exchanged. Indeed, while hostility and criticism of other women were so rare as to seem almost tabooed, young women permitted themselves to express a great deal of hostility toward peer-group men.[53] When unacceptable suitors appeared, girls might even band together to harass them. When one such unfortunate came to court Sophie DuPont she hid in her room, first sending her sister Eleuthera to entertain him and then dispatching a number of urgent notes to her neighboring sister-in-law, cousins, and a visiting friend who all came to Sophie's support. A wild female romp ensued, ending only when Sophie banged into a door, lacerated her nose, and retired, with her female cohorts, to bed. Her brother and the presumably disconcerted suitor were left alone. These were not the antics of teenagers but of women in their early and mid-twenties.[54]

Even if young men were acceptable suitors, girls referred to them formally and obliquely: "The last week I received the unexpected intelligence of the arrival of a friend in Boston," Sarah Ripley wrote in her diary of the young man to whom she had been engaged for years and whom she would shortly marry. Harriet Manigault assiduously kept a lively and gossipy diary during the three years preceding her marriage, yet did not once comment upon her own engagement nor indeed make any personal references to her fiancé— who was never identified as such but always referred to as Mr. Wilcox.[55] The point is not that these young women were hostile to young men. Far from it; they sought marriage and domesticity. Yet in these letters and diaries men appear as an other or out group, segregated into different schools, supported by their own male network of friends and kin, socialized to different behavior, and coached to a proper formality in courtship behavior. As a consequence, relations between young women and men frequently lacked the spontaneity and emotional intimacy that characterized the young girls' ties to each other.

Indeed, in sharp contrast to their distant relations with boys, young women's relations with each other were close, often frolicsome, and surprisingly long lasting and devoted. They wrote secret missives to each other, spent long solitary days with each other, curled up together in bed at night to whisper fantasies and secrets.[56] In 1862 one young woman in her early twenties described one such scene to an absent friend: "I have sat up to midnight listening to the confidences of Constance Kinney, whose heart was opened by that most charming of all situations, a seat on a bedside late at night, when all the household are asleep & only oneself & one's confidante survive in wakefulness. So she has told me all her loves and tried to get some confidences in return but being five or six years older than she, I know better. . . ."[57] Elizabeth Bordley and Nelly Parke Custis, teenagers in Philadelphia in the 1790s, routinely secreted themselves until late each night in Nelly's attic, where they each wrote a novel about the other.[58] Quite a few young women kept diaries, and it was a sign of special friendship to show their diaries to each other. The emotional quality of such exchanges emerges from the comments of one young girl who grew up along the Ohio frontier:

> Sisters CW and RT keep diaries & allow me the inestimable pleasure of reading them and in turn they see mine—but O shame covers my face when I think of it; theirs is so much better than mine, that every time. Then I think well now I *will* burn mine but upon second thought it would deprive me the pleasure of reading theirs, for I esteem it a very great privilege indeed, as well as very improving, as we lay our hearts open to each other, it heightens our love & helps to cherish & keep alive that sweet soothing friendship and endears us to each other by that soft attraction.[59]

Girls routinely slept together, kissed and hugged each other. Indeed, while waltzing with young men scandalized the otherwise flighty and highly fashionable Harriet Manigault, she considered waltzing with other young women not only acceptable but pleasant.[60]

Marriage followed adolescence. With increasing frequency in the nineteenth century, marriage involved a girl's traumatic removal from her mother and her mother's network. It involved, as well, adjustment to a husband, who, because he was male came to marriage with both a different world view and vastly different experiences. Not surprisingly, marriage was an event surrounded with supportive, almost ritualistic, practices. (Weddings are one of the last female rituals remaining in twentieth-century America.) Young women routinely spent the months preceding their marriage almost exclusively with other women—at neighborhood sewing bees and quilting parties or in a round of visits to geographically distant friends and relatives. Ostensibly they went to receive assistance in the practical preparations for their new home—sewing and quilting a trousseau and linen—but of equal importance, they appear to have gained emotional support and reassurance. Sarah Ripley spent over a month with friends and relatives in Boston and Hingham before her wedding; Parke Custis Lewis exchanged visits with her aunts and first cousins throughout Virginia.[61] Anne Jefferis, who married with some hesitation, spent virtually half a year in endless visiting with cousins, aunts, and friends. Despite their reassurance and support, however, she would not marry Moses Sheppard until her sister Edith and her cousin Rebecca moved into the groom's home, met his friends, and explored his personality.[62] The wedding did not take place until Edith wrote to Anne: "I can say in truth I am entirely willing thou shouldst follow him even away in the Jersey sands believing if thou are not happy in thy future home it will not be any fault on his part. . . ."[63]

Sisters, cousins, and friends frequently accompanied newlyweds on their wedding night and wedding trip, which often involved additional family visiting. Such extensive visits presumably served to wean the daughter from her family of origin. As such they often contained a note of ambivalence. Nelly Custis, for example, reported homesickness and loneliness on her wedding trip. "I left my Beloved and revered Grandmamma with sincere regret," she wrote Elizabeth Bordley. "It was sometime before I could feel reconciled to traveling without her." Perhaps they also functioned to reassure the young woman herself, and her friends and kin, that though marriage might alter it would not destroy old bonds of intimacy and familiarity.[64]

Married life, too, was structured about a host of female rituals. Childbirth, especially the birth of the first child, became virtually a *rite de passage,* with a lengthy seclusion of the woman before and after delivery, severe restrictions on her activities, and finally a dramatic reemergence.[65] This seclusion was supervised by mothers, sisters, and loving friends. Nursing and weaning involved the advice and assistance of female friends and relatives. So did miscarriage.[66] Death, like birth, was structured around elaborate unisexed rituals. When Nelly Parke Custis Lewis rushed to nurse her daughter who was critically ill while away at school, Nelly received support, not from her husband, who remained on their plantation, but from her old school friend, Elizabeth Bordley. Elizabeth aided Nelly in caring for her dying daughter, cared for Nelly's other children, played a major role in the elaborate funeral arrangements (which the father did not attend), and frequently visited the girl's grave at the mother's request. For years Elizabeth continued to be the confidante of Nelly's anguished recollections of her lost daughter. These memories, Nelly's letters make clear, were for Elizabeth alone. "Mr. L. knows nothing of this," was a frequent comment.[67] Virtually every collection of letters and diaries in my sample contained evidence of women turning to each other for comfort when facing the frequent and unavoidable deaths of the eighteenth and nineteenth centuries.[68] While mourning for her father's death, Sophie DuPont received elaborate letters and visits of condolence—all from women. No man wrote or visited Sophie to offer sympathy at her father's death.[69] Among rural Pennsylvania Quakers, death and mourning rituals assumed an even more extreme same-sex form, with men or women largely barred from the deathbeds of the other sex. Women relatives and friends slept with the dying woman, nursed her, and prepared her body for burial.[70]

Eighteenth- and nineteenth-century women thus lived in emotional proximity to each other. Friendships and intimacies followed the biological ebb and flow of women's lives. Marriage and pregnancy, childbirth and weaning, sickness and death involved physical and psychic trauma which comfort and sympathy made easier to bear. Intense bonds of love and intimacy bound together those women who, offering each other aid and sympathy, shared such stressful moments.

These bonds were often physical as well as emotional. An undeniably romantic and even sensual note frequently marked female relationships. This theme, significant throughout the stages of a woman's life, surfaced first during adolescence. As one teenager from a struggling pioneer family in the Ohio Valley wrote in her diary in 1808: "I laid with my dear R[ebecca] and a glorious good talk we had until about 4[A.M.]—O how hard I do *love* her...."[71] Only a few years later Bostonian Eunice Callender carved her initials and Sarah Ripley's into a favorite tree, along with a pledge of eternal love, and then waited breathlessly for Sarah to discover and respond to her declaration of affection. The response appears to have been affirmative.[72] A half-century later urbane and sophisticated Katherine Wharton commented upon meeting an old school chum: "She was a great pet of mine at school & I thought as I watched her light figure how often I had held her in my arms—how dear she had once been to me." Katie maintained a long intimate friendship with another girl. When a young man began to court this friend seriously, Katie commented in her diary that she had never realized "how deeply I loved Eng and how fully." She wrote over and over again in that entry: "Indeed I love her!" and only with great reluctance left the city that summer since it meant also leaving Eng with Eng's new suitor.[73]

Peggy Emlen, a Quaker adolescent in Philadelphia in the 1760s, expressed similar feelings about her first cousin, Sally Logan. The girls sent love poems to each other (not unlike the ones Elizabeth Bordley wrote to Nellie Custis a generation later), took long solitary walks together, and even haunted the empty house of the other when one was out of town. Indeed Sally's absences from Philadelphia caused Peggy acute unhappiness. So strong were Peggy's feelings that her brothers began to tease about her affection for Sally and threatened to steal Sally's letters, much to both girls' alarm. In one letter that Peggy wrote the absent Sally she elaborately described the depth and nature of her feelings: "I have not words to express my impatience to see My Dear Cousin, what would I not give just now for an hours sweet conversation with her, it seems as if I had a thousand things to say to thee, yet when I see thee, everything will be forgot thro' joy.... I have a very great friendship for several Girls yet it dont give me so much uneasiness at being absent from them as from thee.... [Let us] go and spend a day down at our place together and there unmolested enjoy each others company."[74]

Sarah Alden Ripley, a young, highly educated woman, formed a similar intense relationship, in this instance with a woman somewhat older than herself. The immediate bond of friendship rested on their atypically intense scholarly interests, but it soon involved strong emotions, at least on Sarah's part. "Friendship," she wrote Mary Emerson, "is fast twining about her willing captive the silken hands of dependence, a dependence so sweet who would renounce it for the apathy of self-sufficiency?" Subsequent letters became far more emotional, almost conspiratorial. Mary visited Sarah secretly in her room, or the two women crept away from family and friends to meet in a nearby woods. Sarah became jealous of Mary's other young friends. Mary's trips away from Boston also thrust Sarah into periods of anguished depression. Interestingly, the letters detailing their love were not destroyed but were preserved and even reprinted in a eulogistic biography of Sarah Alden Ripley.[75]

Tender letters between adolescent women, confessions of loneliness and emotional dependency, were not peculiar to Sarah Alden, Peggy Emlen, or Katie Wharton. They are found throughout the letters of the thirty-five families studied. They have, of course, their parallel today in the musings of many female adolescents. Yet these eighteenth- and nineteenth-century friendships lasted with undiminished, indeed often increased, intensity throughout the women's lives. Sarah Alden Ripley's first child was named after Mary Emerson. Nelly Custis Lewis's love for and dependence on Elizabeth Bordley Gibson only increased after her marriage. Eunice Callender remained enamored of her cousin Sarah Ripley for years and rejected as impossible the suggestion by another woman that their love might some day fade away.[76] Sophie DuPont and her childhood friend, Clementina Smith, exchanged letters filled with love and dependency for forty years while another dear friend, Mary Black Couper, wrote of dreaming that she, Sophie, and her husband were all united in one marriage. Mary's letters to Sophie are filled with avowals of love and indications of ambivalence toward her own husband. Eliza Schlatter, another of Sophie's intimate friends, wrote to her at a time of crisis: "I wish I could be with you present in the body as well as the mind & heart—I would turn your *good husband out of bed*—and snuggle into you and we would have a long talk like old times in Pine St.—I want to tell you so many things that are not *writable*...."[77]

Such mutual dependency and deep affection is a central existential reality coloring the world of supportive networks and rituals. In the case of Katie, Sophie, or Eunice—as with Molly, Jeannie, and Sarah—their need for closeness and support merged with more intense demands for a love which was at the same time both emotional and sensual. Perhaps the most explicit statement concerning women's lifelong friendships appeared in the letter abolitionist and reformer Mary Grew wrote about the same time, referring to her own love for her dear friend and lifelong companion, Margaret Burleigh. Grew wrote, in response to a letter of condolence from another woman on Burleigh's death: "Your words respecting my beloved friend touch me deeply. Evidently ... you comprehend and appreciate, as few persons do ... the nature of the relation which existed, which exists, between her and myself. Her only surviving niece ... also does. To me it seems to have been a closer union than that of most marriages. We know there have been other such between two men and also between two women. And why should there not be. Love is spiritual, only passion is sexual."[78]

How then can we ultimately interpret these long-lived intimate female relationships and integrate them into our understanding of Victorian sexuality? Their ambivalent and romantic rhetoric presents us with an ultimate puzzle: the relationship along the spectrum of human emotions between love, sensuality, and sexuality.

One is tempted, as I have remarked, to compare Molly, Peggy, or Sophie's relationships with the friendships adolescent girls in the twentieth century routinely form—close friendships of great emotional intensity. Helene Deutsch and Clara Thompson have both described these friendships as emotionally necessary to a girl's psychosexual development. But, they warn, such friendships might shade into adolescent and postadolescent homosexuality.[79]

It is possible to speculate that in the twentieth century a number of cultural taboos evolved to cut short the homosocial ties of girl hood and to impel the emerging women of thirteen or fourteen toward heterosexual relationships. In contrast, nineteenth-century American society did not taboo close female relationships but rather recognized them as a socially viable form of human contact—and, as such, acceptable throughout a woman's life. Indeed it was not these homosocial ties that were inhibited but rather heterosexual leanings. While closeness, freedom of emotional expression, and uninhibited physical contact characterized women's relationships with each other, the opposite was frequently true of male-female relationships. One could thus argue that within such a world of female support, intimacy, and ritual it was only to be expected that adult women would turn trustingly and lovingly to each other. It was a behavior they had observed and learned since childhood. A different type of emotional landscape existed in the nineteenth century, one in which Molly and Helena's love became a natural development.

Of perhaps equal significance are the implications we can garner from this framework for the understanding of heterosexual marriages in the nineteenth century. If men and women grew up as they did in relatively homogeneous and segregated sexual groups, then marriage represented a major problem in adjustment. From this perspective we could interpret much of the emotional stiffness and distance that we associate with Victorian marriage as a structural consequence of contemporary sex-role differentiation and gender-role socialization. With marriage both women and men had to adjust to life with a person who was, in essence, a member of an alien group.

I have thus far substituted a cultural or psychosocial for a psychosexual interpretation of women's emotional bonding. But there are psychosexual implications in this model which I think it only fair to make more explicit. Despite Sigmund Freud's insistence on the bisexuality of us all or the recent American Psychiatric Association decision on homosexuality, many psychiatrists today tend explicitly or implicitly to view homosexuality as a totally alien or pathological behavior—as totally unlike heterosexuality. I suspect that in essence they may have adopted an explanatory model similar to the one used in discussing schizophrenia. As a psychiatrist can speak of schizophrenia and of a borderline schizophrenic personality as both ultimately and fundamentally different from a normal or neurotic personality, so they also think of both homosexuality and latent homosexuality as states totally different from heterosexuality. With this rapid dichotomous model of assumption, "latent homosexuality" becomes the indication of a disease in progress—seeds of a pathology which belie the reality of an individual's heterosexuality.

Yet at the same time we are well aware that cultural values can affect choices in the gender of a person's sexual partner. We, for instance, do not necessarily consider homosexual-object choice among men in prison, on shipboard or in boarding schools a necessary indication of pathology. I would urge that we expand this relativistic model and hypothesize that a number of cultures might well tolerate or even encourage diversity in sexual and nonsexual relations. Based on my research into this nineteenth-century world of female intimacy, I would further suggest that rather than seeing a gulf between the normal and the abnormal we view sexual and emotional impulses as part of a continuum or spectrum of affect gradations strongly affected by cultural norms and arrangements, a continuum influenced in part by observed and thus learned behavior. At one end of the continuum lies committed heterosexuality, at the other uncompromising homosexuality; between, a wide latitude of emotions and sexual feelings. Certain cultures and environments permit individuals a great deal of freedom in moving across this spectrum. I would like to suggest that the nineteenth century was such a cultural environment. That is, the supposedly repressive and destructive Victorian sexual ethos may have been more flexible and responsive to the needs of particular individuals than those of mid-twentieth century.

NOTES

1. The most notable exception to this rule is now eleven years old: William R. Taylor and Christopher Lasch, "Two 'Kindred Spirits': Sorority and Family in New England, 1839–1846," *New England Quarterly* 36 (1963):25–41. . . . I do not . . . accept the Taylor-Lasch thesis that female friendships developed in the mid-nineteenth century because of geographic mobility and the breakup of the colonial family. I have found these friendships as frequently in the eighteenth century as in the nine-

teenth and would hypothesize that the geographic mobility of the mid-nineteenth century eroded them as it did so many other traditional social institutions. . . .

2. I do not wish to deny the importance of women's relations with particular men. Obviously, women were close to brothers, husbands, fathers, and sons. However, there is evidence that despite such closeness relationships between men and women differed in both emotional texture and frequency from those between women. . . . I have discussed some aspects of male-female relationships in two articles: "Puberty to Menopause: The Cycle of Femininity in Nineteenth-Century America," Feminist Studies 1 (1973):58–72, and, with Charles Rosenberg, "The Female Animal: Medical and Biological Views of Women in 19th Century America," Journal of American History 59 (1973):331–56.

3. See Freud's classic paper on homosexuality, "Three Essays on the Theory of Sexuality," in The Standard Edition of the Complete Psychological Works of Sigmund Freud, trans. James Strachey (London: Hogarth Press, 1953), 7:135–72. The essays originally appeared in 1905. . . .

4. . . . [S]ee Charles Rosenberg, "Sexuality, Class and Role," American Quarterly 25 (1973): 131–53.

5. See, e.g., the letters of Peggy Emlen to Sally Logan, 1768–72, Wells Morris Collection, Box 1, Historical Society of Pennsylvania; and the Eleanor Parke Custis Lewis Letters, Historical Society of Pennsylvania, Philadelphia.

6. Sarah Butler Wister was the daughter of Fanny Kemble and Pierce Butler. In 1859 she married a Philadelphia physician, Owen Wister. The novelist Owen Wister is her son. Jeannie Field Musgrove was the half-orphaned daughter of constitutional lawyer and New York Republican politician David Dudley Field. Their correspondence (1855–98) is in the Sarah Butler Wister Papers, Wister Family Papers, Historical Society of Pennsylvania.

7. Sarah Butler, Butler Place, S.C., to Jeannie Field, New York, Sept. 14, 1855.

8. See, e.g., Sarah Butler Wister, Germantown, Pa., to Jeannie Field, New York, Sept. 25, 1862, Oct. 21, 1863; or Jeannie Field, New York, to Sarah Butler Wister, Germantown, July 3, 1861, Jan. 23 and July 12, 1863.

9. Sarah Butler Wister, Germantown, to Jeannie Field, New York, June 5, 1861, Feb. 29, 1864; Jeannie Field to Sarah Butler Wister, Nov. 22, 1861, Jan. 4 and June 14, 1863.

10. Sarah Butler Wister, London, to Jeannie Field Musgrove, New York, June 18 and Aug. 3, 1870.

11. See, e.g., two of Sarah's letters to Jeannie: Dec. 21, 1873, July 16, 1878.

12. This is the 1868–1920 correspondence between Mary Hallock Foote and Helena, a New York friend (the Mary Hallock Foote Papers are in the Manuscript Division, Stanford University). . . . In many ways these letters are typical of those women wrote to other women. Women frequently began letters to each other with salutations such as "Dearest," "My Most Beloved," "You Darling Girl," and signed them "tenderly" or "to my dear dear

sweet friend, good-bye." . . . She was by no means unique. See, e.g., Annie to Charlene Van Vleck Anderson, Appleton, Wis., June 10, 1871, Anderson Family Papers, Manuscript Division, Stanford University; Maggie to Emily Howland, Philadelphia, July 12, 1851, Howland Family Papers, Phoebe King Collection, Friends Historical Library, Swarthmore College; Mary Jane Burleigh to Emily Howland, Sherwood, N.Y., Mar. 27, 1872, Howland Family Papers, Sophia Smith Collection, Smith College; Mary Black Couper to Sophia Madeleine DuPont, Wilmington, Del.: n.d. [1834] (two letters), Samuel Francis DuPont Papers, Eleutherian Mills Foundation, Wilmington, Del. . . . in general the correspondence (1838–49) between Rebecca Biddle of Philadelphia and Martha Jefferis, Chester County, Pa., Jefferis Family Correspondence, Chester County Historical Society, West Chester, Pa.; Phoebe Bradford Diary, June 7 and July 13, 1832, Historical Society of Pennsylvania; . . . the Sarah Alden Ripley Correspondence, Schlesinger Library, Radcliffe College; . . . Anne Sterling Biddle Family Papers, Friends Historical Society, Swarthmore College; Harriet Manigault Wilcox Diary, Aug. 7, 1814, Historical Society of Pennsylvania; . . . Mrs. O. J. Wister and Miss Agnes Irwin, eds., Worthy Women of Our First Century (Philadelphia: J. B. Lippincott & Co., 1877), p. 195.

13. Mary Hallock [Foote] to Helena, n.d. [1869–70], n.d. [1871–72], Folder 1, Mary Hallock Foote Letters, . . .

14. Mary Hallock [Foote] to Helena, Sept. 15 and 23, 1873, n.d. [Oct. 1873], Oct. 12, 1873.

15. Mary Hallock [Foote] to Helena, n.d. [Jan. 1874], n.d. [Spring 1874].

16. Mary Hallock [Foote] to Helena, Sept. 23, 1873; Mary Hallock [Foote] to Richard, Dec. 13, 1873. Molly's and Helena's relationship continued for the rest of their lives. . . .

17. . . . [S]ee Barbara Welter, "The Cult of True Womanhood: 1820–1860," American Quarterly 18 (Summer 1966):151–74; Anne Firor Scott, The Southern Lady: From Pedestal to Politics, 1830–1930 (Chicago: University of Chicago Press, 1970), chaps. 1–2; Smith-Rosenberg and Rosenberg.

18. See, e.g., the letters of Peggy Emlen to Sally Logan, 1768–72. . . .

19. See, [e.g.,] Elizabeth Botts, Family and Social Network (London: Tavistock Publications, 1957); . . .

20. This pattern seemed to cross class barriers. . . . See Ann McGrann, Philadelphia, to Sophie M. DuPont, Philadelphia, July 3, 1834, Sophie Madeleine DuPont Letters, Eleutherian Mills Foundation.

21. [See, e.g.,] Harriet Manigault Diary, June 28, 1814, and passim; . . .

22. [See, e.g.,] . . . Ann Sterling Biddle Papers, passim, . . .

23. [See, e.g.,] Phoebe Bradford Diary, Jan. 13, Nov. 16–19, 1832, Apr. 26 and May 7, 1833; . . .

24. Lisa Mitchell Diary, 1860s, passim, Manuscript Division, Tulane University; . . . Jeannie McCall, Cedar Park, to Peter McCall, Philadelphia, June 30, 1849, McCall Section, Cadwalader Collection, Historical Society of Pennsylvania.

25. Peggy Emlen to Sally Logan, May 3, 1769.

26. For a prime example of this type of letter, see Eleanor Parke Custis Lewis to Elizabeth Bordley Gibson, Passim; . . .

27. Place of residence is not the only variable significance in characterizing family structure. Strong emotional ties and frequent visiting and correspondence can unite families that do not live under one roof. . . .

28. Eleanor Parke Custis Lewis to Elizabeth Bordley Gibson, Apr. 20 and Sept. 25, 1848.

29. Maria Inskeep to Fanny Hampton Correspondence, 1823–60, Inskeep Collection, Tulane University Library.

30. Eunice Callender, Boston, to Sarah Ripley [Stearns], Sept. 24 and Oct. 29, 1803, Feb. 16, 1805, Apr. 29 and Oct. 9, 1806, May 26, 1810.

31. Sophie DuPont filled her letters to her younger brother Henry (with whom she had been assigned to correspond while he was at boarding school) with accounts of family visiting (see, e.g., Dec. 13, 1827, Jan. 10 and Mar. 9, 1828, Feb. 4 and Mar. 10, 1832). . . . Mary B. Ashew Diary, July 11 and 13, Aug. 17, Summer and Oct. 1858. . . .

32. Martha Jefferis to Anne Jefferis Sheppard, Jan. 12, 1845; Phoebe Middleton to Martha Jefferis, Feb. 22, 1848. . . .

33. Rebecca Biddle to Martha Jefferis, 1838–49, passim; Martha Jefferis to Anne Jefferis Sheppard, July 6, 1846; Anne Jefferis Sheppard to Rachael Jefferis, Jan. 16, 1865; Sarah Foulke Farquhar [Emlen] Diary, Sept. 22, 1813, Friends Historical Library, Swarthmore College; . . .

34. Sarah Alden Ripley to Abba Allyn, n.d. . . .

35. Phoebe Bradford Diary, July 13, 1832.

36. Mary Hallock [Foote] to Helena, Dec. 23 [1868 or 1869]; Phoebe Bradford Diary, Dec. 8, 1832; Martha Jefferis and Anne Jefferis Sheppard letters, passim.

37. Martha Jefferis to Anne Jefferis Sheppard, Aug. 3, 1849; Sarah Ripley [Stearns] Diary, Nov. 12, 1808, Jan. 8, 1811. . . .

38. Martha Jefferis to Edith Jefferis, Mar. 15, 1841; Mary Hallock Foote to Helena, n.d. [1874–75?]; . . .

39. Anne Jefferis Sheppard to Martha Jefferis, Sept. 29, 1841.

40. Frances Parke Lewis to Elizabeth Bordley Gibson, Apr. 29, 1821.

41. [See, e.g.,] Mary Jane Burleigh, Mount Pleasant, S.C., to Emily Howland, Sherwood N.Y., Mar. 27, 1872, Howland Family Papers; . . .

42. [See, e.g.,] Harriet Manigault Diary, Aug. 15, 21, and 23, 1814, Historical Society of Pennsylvania; . . .

43. Mrs. S. S. Dalton, "Autobiography" (Circle Valley, Utah, 1876), pp. 21–22, Bancroft Library, University of California, Berkeley; Sarah Foulke Emlen Diary, Apr. 1809; Louisa G. Van Vleck, Appleton, Wis., to Charlena Van Vleck Anderson, Göttingen, n.d. [1875], . . .

44. Abigail Brackett Lyman, Boston, to Mrs. Abigail Brackett (daughter to mother), n.d. [1797], June 3, 1800; Sarah Alden Ripley wrote weekly to her daughter, Sophy Ripley Fisher, after the latter's

marriage (Sarah Alden Ripley Correspondence, passim); Phoebe Bradford Diary, Feb. 25, 1833, passim, 1832–33; Louisa G. Van Vleck to Charlena Van Vleck Anderson, Dec. 15, 1873, July 4, Aug. 15 and 29, Sept. 19, and Nov. 9, 1875. . . . Daughters evidently frequently slept with their mothers—into adulthood (Harriet Manigault [Wilcox] Diary, Feb. 19, 1815; Eleanor Parke Custis Lewis to Elizabeth Bordley Gibson, Oct. 10, 1832). Daughters also frequently asked mothers to live with them and professed delight when they did so. . . . We did find a few exceptions to this mother-daughter felicity (M. B. Ashew Diary, Nov. 19, 1857, Apr. 10 and May 17, 1858). Sarah Foulke Emlen was at first very hostile to her step-mother (Sarah Foulke Emlen Diary, Aug. 9, 1807), but they later developed a warm supportive relationship.

45. Sarah Alden Ripley to Sophy Thayer, n.d. [1861].

46. [See, e.g.,] Mary Hallock Foote to Helena [Winter 1873] (no. 52); Jossie, Stevens Point, Wis., to Charlena Van Vleck [Anderson], Appleton, Wis., Oct. 24, 1870; Pollie Chandler, Green Bay, Wis., to Charlena Van Vleck [Anderson], Appleton, n.d. [1870]; Eleuthera DuPont to Sophie DuPont, Sept. 5, 1829; . . .

47. . . . Sarah Foulke Emlen Journal, Sarah Ripley Stearns Diary, Mrs. S. S. Dalton, "Autobiography."

48. Maria Revere to her mother [Mrs. Paul Revere], June 13, 1801, Paul Revere Papers, Massachusetts Historical Society. In a letter to Elizabeth Bordley Gibson, Mar. 28, 1847, Eleanor Parke Custis Lewis from Virginia discussed the anxiety her daughter felt when her granddaughters left home to go to boarding school. . . .

49. . . . [See, e.g.,] the letters and diaries of three generations of Manigault women in Philadelphia: Mrs. Gabrielle Manigault, her daughter, Harriet Manigault Wilcox, and granddaughter, Charlotte Wilcox McCall. . . . Mrs. Henry Middleton, Charleston, S.C., to Mrs. Gabrielle Manigault, n.d. [mid 1800s]; Harriet Manigault Diary, vol. 1; Dec. 1, 1813, June 28, 1814; Charlotte Wilcox McCall Diary, vol. 1, 1842, passim. All in Historical Society of Philadelphia.

50. Frances Parke Lewis, Woodlawn, Va., to Elizabeth Bordley Gibson, Philadelphia, Apr. 11, 1821, Lewis Correspondence; Eleuthera DuPont, Philadelphia, to Victorine DuPont Bauday, Brandywine, Dec. 8, 1821, Jan. 31, 1822; Eleuthera DuPont, Brandywine, to Margaretta Lammont [DuPont], Philadelphia, May 1823.

51. [See, e.g.,] Sarah Ripley Stearns Diary, Mar. 9 and 25, 1810; Peggy Emlen to Sally Logan, Mar. and July 4, 1769; . . . Deborah Cope, West Town School, to Rest Cope, Philadelphia, July 9, 1828, Chester County Historical Society, West Chester, Pa.; . . .

52. Anne Jefferis Sheppard to Martha Jefferis, Mar. 17, 1841.

53. [See, e.g.,] Peggy Emlen to Sally Logan, Mar. 1769, Mount Vernon, Va.; . . .

54. Sophie M. DuPont and Eleuthera DuPont, Brandywine, to Victorine DuPont Bauday, Philadelphia, Jan. 25, 1832.

55. Sarah Ripley [Stearns] Diary and Harriet Manigault Diary, passim.

56. [See, e.g.,] Sophie Madeleine DuPont to Eleuthera DuPont, Dec. 1827; Clementina Beach Smith to Sophie Madeleine DuPont, Dec. 26, 1828; Sarah Faulke Emlen Diary, July 21, 1808, Mar. 30, 1809; . . .

57. Jeannie Field, New York, to Sarah Butler Wister, Germantown, Apr. 6, 1862.

58. Elizabeth Bordley Gibson, introductory statement to the Eleanor Parke Custis Lewis Letters [1850s], Historical Society of Pennsylvania.

59. Sarah Foulke [Emlen] Diary, Mar. 30, 1809.

60. Harriet Manigault Diary, May 26, 1815.

61. Sarah Ripley [Stearns] Diary, May 17 and Oct. 2, 1812; Eleanor Parke Custis Lewis to Elizabeth Bordley Gibson, Apr. 23, 1826; . . .

62. Anne Jefferis to Martha Jefferis, Nov. 22 and 27, 1840, Jan. 13 and Mar. 17, 1841; Edith Jefferis, Greenwich, N.J., to Anne Jefferis, Philadelphia, Jan. 31, Feb. 6 and Feb. 1841.

63. Edith Jefferis to Anne Jefferis, Jan. 31, 1841.

64. Eleanor Parke Custis Lewis to Elizabeth Bordley, Nov. 4, 1799. . . .

65. [See, e.g.,] Mary Hallock to Helena DeKay Gilder [1876] (no. 81); n.d. (no. 83), Mar. 3, 1884; Mary Ashew Diary, vol. 2, Sept.–Jan. 1860; . . .

66. [See, e.g.,] Fanny Ferris to Anne Biddle, Nov. 19, 1811; Eleanor Parke Custis Lewis to Elizabeth Bordley Gibson, Nov. 4, 1799, Apr. 27, 1827; . . .

67. Eleanor Parke Custis Lewis to Elizabeth Bordley Gibson, Oct.–Nov. 1820, passim.

68. [See, e.g.,] Emily Howland to Hannah, Sept. 30, 1866; Emily Howland Diary, Feb. 8, 11, and 27, 1880; Phoebe Bradford Diary, Apr. 12 and 13, and Aug. 4, 1833; . . .

69. Mary Black [Couper] to Sophie Madeleine DuPont, Feb. 1827 [Nov. 1, 1834], Nov. 12, 1834, two letters [late Nov. 1834]; Eliza Schlatter to Sophie Madeleine DuPont, Nov. 2, 1834.

70. For a few of the references to death rituals in the Jefferis papers see: Martha Jefferis to Anne Jefferis Sheppard, Sept. 28, 1843, Aug. 21 and Sept. 25, 1844, Jan. 11, 1846, Summer 1848, passim; . . . This is not to argue that men and women did not mourn together. Yet in many families women aided and comforted women and men, men. . . .

71. Sarah Foulke [Emlen] Diary, Dec. 29, 1808.

72. Eunice Callender, Boston, to Sarah Ripley [Stearns], Greenfield, Mass., May 24, 1803.

73. Katherine Johnstone Brinley [Wharton] Journal, Apr. 26, May 30, and May 29, 1856, Historical Society of Pennsylvania.

74. A series of roughly fourteen letters written by Peggy Emlen to Sally Logan (1768–71) has been preserved in the Wells Morris Collection, Box 1, Historical Society of Pennsylvania (see esp. May 3 and July 4, 1769, Jan. 8, 1768).

75. . . . The eulogistic biographical sketch appeared in Wister and Irwin (n. 12 above). . . .

76. See Sarah Alden Ripley to Mary Emerson, Nov. 19, 1823. Sarah Alden Ripley routinely, and one must assume ritualistically, read Mary Emerson's letters to her infant daughter, Mary. Eleanor Parke Custis Lewis reported doing the same with Elizabeth Bordley Gibson's letters, passim. Eunice Callender, Boston, to Sarah Ripley [Stearns], Oct. 19, 1808.

77. Mary Black Couper to Sophie M. DuPont, Mar. 5, 1832. The Clementina Smith–Sophie DuPont correspondence is in the Sophie DuPont Correspondence. The quotation is from Eliza Schlatter, Mount Holly, N.J., to Sophie DuPont, Brandywine, Aug. 24, 1834. . . .

78. Mary Grew, Providence, R.I., to Isabel Howland, Sherwood, N.Y., Apr. 27, 1892, Howland Correspondence, Sophia Smith Collection, Smith College.

79. Helena Deutsch, *Psychology of Women* (New York: Grune & Stratton, 1944), 1: chaps. 1–3; Clara Thompson, *On Women*, ed. Maurice Green (New York: New American Library, 1971).

JAMES C. MOHR

Abortion in America

If we observe nineteenth-century society through women's eyes, surely no experience was as widely shared as the experience of childbirth. The biological act of maternity created powerful bonds among women as they coped with the experience of childbirth.

Until the twentieth century, most births took place at home, where the birthing mother was likely to be surrounded by her mother, sisters, and cousins, a midwife and other experienced women, and her woman friends. The "female world of love and ritual" that Carroll Smith-Rosenberg describes "formed across the childbirth bed," writes historian Judith Walzer Leavitt. "When women had suffered the agonies of watching their friends die, when they had helped a friend recover from a difficult delivery, or when they had participated in a successful birthing they developed a closeness that lasted a lifetime." Leavitt finds that these circles of friendly support made significant choices. "The collectivity of women gathered around the birthing bed made sure that birth attendants were responsive to their wishes. They made decisions about when and if to call physicians to births that midwives were attending; they gave or withheld permission for physicians' procedures; and they created the atmosphere of female support in a room that might have contained both women and men." Leavitt argues that when in the twentieth century birthing moved to hospitals, much of this support evaporated; the reforms in hospital practices demanded by feminists since the 1970s have been an effort to reclaim what had been lost.*

During the centuries before reliable fertility control measures made it possible for women to set limits on reproduction, most married women and many unmarried women had to bear the physical and psychological burden of repeated pregnancies, childbirths, and postpartum recoveries. The cost in terms of time, energy, dreams, and bodies was high. If we observe nineteenth-century society through women's eyes, surely no statistic was as significant as the one that marked the decline in the average number of children borne by each woman. Childbirth was a time of terror.

During the early nineteenth century, a sharp decline took place in the birth rates; the decline was particularly marked in urban areas. No innovations in birth control technology appeared in this period; the decline was the result of choices—later marriage, abstinence from sexual intercourse—to limit the number of times women faced childbirth. In the mid-eighteenth century, the average rural woman could expect to face childbirth eight or nine times; by the early nineteenth century that number had dropped to six and in some urban areas to four. Except for occasional "baby booms," birth rates in the United States have fallen steadily and continue to stabilize in our own time.

When unsuccessful in avoiding pregnancies, many women attempted to abort them. The methods of the times were dangerous, but until the 1840s, the women were rarely censured by the community if fetal movement had not been felt. The vigorous attack on abortion after 1840 may well have been a response to the growing willingness of married women to attempt it. After 1840, an act that had been dealt with in a biological context was given ideological overtones.

What does the debate on abortion policy reveal about public attitudes toward women and their place in the family and in society? How had attitudes changed since Sarah Grosvenor's time? (See pp. 90–106.)

*Judith Walzer Leavitt, "Under the Shadow of Maternity: American Women's Responses to Death and Debility Fears in Nineteenth-Century Childbirth," *Feminist Studies* 12(1986):129–54.

ABORTION IN AMERICA 1800–1825

In the absence of any legislation whatsoever on the subject of abortion in the United States in 1800, the legal status of the practice was governed by the traditional British common law as interpreted by the local courts of the new American states. For centuries prior to 1800 the key to the common law's attitude toward abortion had been a phenomenon associated with normal gestation known as quickening. Quickening was the first perception of fetal movement by the pregnant woman herself. Quickening generally occurred near the midpoint of gestation, late in the fourth or early in the fifth month, though it could and still does vary a good deal from one woman to another. The common law did not formally recognize the existence of a fetus in criminal cases until it had quickened. After quickening, the expulsion and destruction of a fetus without due cause was considered a crime, because the fetus itself had manifested some semblance of a separate existence: the ability to move. The crime was qualitatively different from the destruction of a human being, however, and punished less harshly. Before quickening, actions that had the effect of terminating what turned out to have been an early pregnancy were not considered criminal under the common law in effect in England and the United States in 1800.[1]

Both practical and moral arguments lay behind the quickening distinction. Practically, because no reliable tests for pregnancy existed in the early nineteenth century, quickening alone could confirm with absolute certainty that a woman really was pregnant. Prior to quickening, each of the telltale signs of pregnancy could, at least in theory, be explained in alternative ways by physicians of the day. Hence, either a doctor or a woman herself could take actions designed to restore menstrual flow after one or more missed periods on the assumption that something might be unnaturally "blocking" or "obstructing" her normal cycles, and if left untreated the obstruction would wreak real harm upon the woman. Medically, the procedures for removing a blockage were the same as those for inducing an early abortion. Not until the obstruction moved could either a physician or a woman, regardless of their suspicions, be completely certain that it was a "natural"

blockage—a pregnancy—rather than a potentially dangerous situation. Morally, the question of whether or not a fetus was "alive" had been the subject of philosophical and religious debate among honest people for at least 5000 years. The quickening doctrine itself appears to have entered the British common law tradition by way of the tangled disputes of medieval theologians over whether or not an impregnated ovum possessed a soul.[2] The upshot was that American women in 1800 were legally free to attempt to terminate a condition that might turn out to have been a pregnancy until the existence of that pregnancy was incontrovertibly confirmed by the perception of fetal movement.

An ability to suspend one's modern preconceptions and to accept the early nineteenth century on its own terms regarding the distinction between quick and unquick is absolutely crucial to an understanding of the evolution of abortion policy in the United States. However doubtful the notion appears to modern readers, the distinction was virtually universal in America during the early decades of the nineteenth century and accepted in good faith. Perhaps the strongest evidence of the tenacity and universality of the doctrine in the United States was the fact that American courts pointedly sustained the most lenient implications of the quickening doctrine even after the British themselves had abandoned them. . . .

Because women believed themselves to be carrying inert non-beings prior to quickening, a potential for life rather than life itself, and because the common law permitted them to attempt to rid themselves of suspected and unwanted pregnancies up to the point when the potential for life gave a sure sign that it was developing into something actually alive, some American women did practice abortion in the early decades of the nineteenth century. One piece of evidence for this conclusion was the ready access American women had to abortifacient information from 1800 onward. A chief source of such information was the home medical literature of the era.

Home medical manuals characteristically contained abortifacient information in two different sections. One listed in explicit detail a number of procedures that might release "obstructed menses" and the other identified a number of specific things to be avoided in a suspected pregnancy because they were thought to bring on abortion. Americans probably consulted William Buchan's Domestic Medicine more frequently than any other home medical guide during the first decades of the nineteenth century.[3] Buchan suggested several courses of action designed to restore menstrual flow if a period was missed. These included bloodletting, bathing, iron and quinine concoctions, and if those failed, "a teaspoonful of the tincture of black hellebore [a violent purgative] . . . twice aday in a cup of warm water." Four pages later he listed among "the common causes" of abortion "great evacuations [and] vomiting," exactly as would be produced by the treatment he urged for suppressed menses. Later in pregnancy a venturesome, or desperate, woman could try some of the other abortion inducers he ticked off: "violent exercise; raising great weights; reaching too high; jumping, or stepping from an eminence; strokes [strong blows] on the belly; [and] falls."[4] . . .

Like most early abortion material, Buchan's . . . advice harked back to almost primordial or instinctual methods of ending a pregnancy. Bloodletting, for example, was evidently thought to serve as a surrogate period; it was hoped that bleeding from any part of the body might have the same flushing effect upon the womb that menstrual bleeding was known to have. This primitive folk belief lingered long into the nineteenth century, well after bleeding was abandoned as medical therapy in other kinds of cases, and it was common for abortionists as late as the 1870s to pull a tooth as part of their routine.[5] . . .

In addition to home medical guides and health manuals addressed to women, abortions and abortifacient information were also available in the United States from midwives and midwifery texts.[6] . . .

Herbal healers, the so-called Indian doctors, and various other irregular practitioners also helped spread abortifacient information in the United States during the early decades of the nineteenth century. Their surviving pamphlets, of which Peter Smith's 1813 brochure entitled "The Indian Doctor's Dispensary" is an example, contained abortifacient recipes that typically combined the better-known cathartics with native North American ingredients thought to have emmenagogic properties. For "obstructed menses" Smith recommended a concoction he called "Dr.

Reeder's chalybeate." The key ingredients were myrrh and aloes, combined with liquor, sugar, vinegar, iron dust, ivy, and Virginia or seneca snakeroot.[7] A sweet-and-sour cocktail like that may or may not have induced abortion, but must certainly have jolted the system of any woman who tried one. . . .

Finally, and most importantly, America's regular physicians, those who had formal medical training either in the United States or in Great Britain or had been apprenticed under a regular doctor, clearly possessed the physiological knowledge and the surgical techniques necessary to terminate a pregnancy by mechanical means. They knew that dilation of the cervix at virtually any stage of gestation would generally bring on uterine contractions that would in turn lead to the expulsion of the contents of the uterus. They knew that any irritation introduced into the uterus would have the same effect. They knew that rupturing the amniotic sac, especially in the middle and later months of pregnancy, would usually also induce contractions and expulsion, regardless of whether the fetus was viable. Indeed, they were taught in their lecture courses and in their textbooks various procedures much more complex than a simple abortion, such as in utero decapitation and fetal pulverization, processes they were instructed to employ in lieu of the even more horribly dangerous Caesarean section. Like the general public, they knew the drugs and herbs most commonly used as abortifacients and emmenagogues, and also like the general public, they believed such preparations to have been frequently effective.[8] . . .

This placed great pressure on physicians to provide what amounted to abortion services early in pregnancy. An unmarried girl who feared herself pregnant, for example, could approach her family doctor and ask to be treated for menstrual blockage. If he hoped to retain the girl and her family as future patients, the physician would have little choice but to accept the girl's assessment of the situation, even if he suspected otherwise. He realized that every member of his profession would testify to the fact that he had no totally reliable means of distinguishing between an early pregnancy, on the one hand, and the amenorrhea that the girl claimed, on the other. Consequently, he treated for obstruction, which involved exactly the same procedures he would have used to induce an early abortion, and wittingly or unwittingly terminated the pregnancy. Regular physicians were also asked to bring to a safe conclusion abortions that irregulars or women themselves had initiated. . . . And through all of this the physician might bear in mind that he could never be held legally guilty of wrongdoing. No statutes existed anywhere in the United States on the subject of abortion, and the common law . . . considered abortion actionable only after a pregnancy had quickened. No wonder then that Heber C. Kimball, recalling his courtship with a woman he married in 1822, claimed that she had been "taught . . . in our young days, when she got into the family way, to send for a doctor and get rid of the child"; a course that she followed.[9]

In summary, then, the practice of aborting unwanted pregnancies was, if not common, almost certainly not rare in the United States during the first decades of the nineteenth century. A knowledge of various drugs, potions, and techniques was available from home medical guides, from health books for women, from midwives and irregular practitioners, and from trained physicians. Substantial evidence suggests that many American women sought abortions, tried the standard techniques of the day, and no doubt succeeded some proportion of the time in terminating unwanted pregnancies. Moreover, this practice was neither morally nor legally wrong in the eyes of the vast majority of Americans, provided it was accomplished before quickening.

The actual number of abortions in the United States prior to the advent of any statutes regulating its practice simply cannot be known. But an equally significant piece of information about those abortions can be gleaned from the historical record. It concerns the women who were having them. Virtually every observer through the middle of the 1830s believed that an overwhelming percentage of the American women who sought and succeeded in having abortions did so because they feared the social consequences of an illegitimate pregnancy, not because they wanted to limit their fertility per se. The doctor who uncovered the use of snake root as an abortifacient, for example, related that in all of the many instances he heard about "it was taken by women who had indulged in illegitimate love. . . ."[10]

In short, abortion was not thought to be a means of family limitation in the United States, at least on any significant scale, through the first third of the nineteenth century. This was hardly surprising in a largely rural and essentially preindustrial society, whose birthrates were exceeding any ever recorded in a European nation.[11] One could, along with medical student [Thomas] Massie, be less than enthusiastic about such an "unnatural" practice as abortion, yet tolerate it as the "recourse . . . of the victim of passion . . . the child of nature" who was driven by "an unrelenting world" unable to forgive any "deviation from what they have termed virtue."[12] Consequently, Americans in the early nineteenth century could and did look the other way when they encountered abortion. Nothing in their medical knowledge or in the rulings of their courts compelled them to do otherwise, and, as Massie indicated, there was considerable compassion for the women involved. It would be nearly midcentury before the perception of who was having abortions for what reasons would begin to shift in the United States, and that shift would prove to be one of the critical developments in the evolution of American abortion policy.

A final point remains to be made about abortion in the United States during the first decades of the nineteenth century. Most observers appeared to consider it relatively safe, at least by the medical standards of the day, rather than extremely dangerous. . . . This too must have reassured women who decided to risk an abortion before quickening. According to the lecture notes of one of his best students, Walter Channing told his Harvard classes that abortion could be troublesome when produced by external blows, because severe internal hemorrhage would be likely, but that generally considered, "abortion [was] not so dangerous as commonly supposed."[13]

The significance of these opinions lay less in whether or not they were accurate than in the fact that writers on abortion, including physicians, saw no reason to stress the dangers attendant to the process. Far from it. They were skeptical about poisons and purgatives, but appear to have assessed physically induced abortions as medically acceptable risks by the standards of the day, especially if brought on during the period of pregnancy when both popular belief and the public courts condoned them anyhow. Here again was a significant early perception that would later change. That change, like the shift in the perception of who was having abortions for what purposes, would also have an impact on the evolution of American abortion policy. . . .

THE SOCIAL CHARACTER
OF ABORTION IN AMERICA 1840–1880

Before 1840 abortion was perceived in the United States primarily as a recourse of the desperate, especially of the young woman in trouble who feared the wrath of an overexacting society. After 1840, however, evidence began to accumulate that the social character of the practice had changed. A high proportion of the women whose abortions contributed to the soaring incidence of that practice in the United States between 1840 and 1880 appeared to be married, native-born, Protestant women, frequently of middle- or upper-class status. The data came from disparate sources, some biased and some not, but in the end proved compelling.

Even before the availability of reliable evidence confirmed that the nation's birthrates were starting to plummet, observers noticed that abortion more and more frequently involved married women rather than single women in trouble. Professor Hugh L. Hodge of the University of Pennsylvania, one of the first physicians in the United States to speak out about abortion in anything approaching a public forum, lectured his introductory obstetrics students in 1839 that abortion was fast becoming a prominent feature of American life. Hodge still considered women trying "to destroy the fruit of illicit pleasure" to be the ones most often seeking abortions, but he alerted his students to the fact that "married women, also, from the fear of labor, from indisposition to have the care, the expense, or the trouble of children, or some other motive" were more and more frequently requesting "that the embryo be destroyed by their medical attendant." Hodge attributed a good deal of this activity to the quickening doctrine, which allowed "women whose moral character is, in other respects, without reproach; mothers who are devoted, with an ardent and self-denying affection, to the children who already constitute[d] their family [to be] perfectly indifferent respecting the foetus in the utero."[14] . . .

Opinion was divided regarding the social status of the women who accounted for the great upsurge of abortion during the middle period of the nineteenth century. While most observers agreed "all classes of society, rich and poor" were involved to some extent, many thought that the middle and upper classes practiced abortion more extensively than the lower classes.[15] The Michigan State Medical Society in 1859 declared that abortion "pervade[d] all ranks" in that state.[16] The Medical Society of Buffalo pointed out that same year "now we have ladies, yes, *educated and refined ladies*" involved as well.[17] On the other hand, court cases revealed at least a sprinkling of lower-class women, servant girls, and the like. . . .

Although the going price for an abortion varied tremendously according to place, time, practitioner, and patient, abortions appear to have been generally quite expensive. Regular physicians testified repeatedly throughout the period that the abortion business was enormously lucrative. Those doctors pledged not to perform abortions bitterly resented men like the Boston botanic indicted for manslaughter in an abortion case in 1851, who posted $8000 bond and returned to his offices, at a time when the average university professor in the United States earned under $2000 per year.[18] . . .

When women turned from regulars to the commercial abortionists, the prices were still not cheap. Itinerants and irregulars generally tried to charge whatever they judged the traffic would bear, which could vary anywhere from $5 to $500. During the 1840s, for example, Madame Restell charged $5 for an initial visit and diagnosis, then negotiated the price of the operation "according to the wealth and liberality of the parties." In a case for which she was indicted in 1846 she asked a young woman about "her beau's circumstances" before quoting a figure, and then tried to get $100 when she found out the man was a reasonably successful manufacturer's representative. The man thought that was too costly, and only after extensive haggling among go-betweens was a $75 fee agreed upon.[19] . . .

Despite the apparent gradual leveling of prices, however, the abortion business remained a profitable commercial venture well into the 1870s. Anthony Comstock, the single-minded leader of a massive anti-obscenity campaign launched in the United States during the 1870s, kept meticulous and extensive records of all of the people he helped arrest while operating as a special agent of the Post Office Department. Between 1872 and 1880 Comstock and his associates aided in the indictment of 55 persons whom Comstock identified as abortionists. The vast majority were very wealthy and posted large bonds with ease. . . .

. . . abortion entered the mainstream of American life during the middle decades of the nineteenth century. While the unmarried and the socially desperate continued to have recourse to it as they had earlier in the century, abortion also became highly visible, much more frequently practiced, and quite common as a means of family limitation among white, Protestant, native-born wives of middle- and upper-class standing. These dramatic changes, in turn, evoked sharp comment from two ideologically opposed groups in American society, each of which either directly or indirectly blamed the other for the shift in abortion patterns. On one side of the debate were the antifeminists, led by regular physicians, and on the other side were the nation's feminists. Both groups agreed that abortion had become a large-scale and socially significant phenomenon in American life, but they disagreed over the reasons why.

Before examining the two chief explanations put forward by contemporaries for the striking shifts in the incidence and the character of abortion in the United States after 1840, two observations may be worth making. First, it is never easy to understand why people do what they do even in the most straightforward of situations; it is nearly impossible to know with certainty the different reasons, rational and irrational, why people in the past might have taken such a psychologically loaded action as the termination of a suspected pregnancy. Second, most participants on both sides of the contemporary debate over why so many American women began to practice abortion after 1840 actually devoted most of their attention to the question of why American women wanted to limit their fertility. This confirmed that abortion was important between 1840 and 1880 primarily as a means of family limitation, but such discussions offer only marginal help in understanding why so many American women turned to abortion itself as a means toward that end.

Cultural anthropologists argue that abortion has been practiced widely and frequently in preindustrial societies at least in part because "it is a woman's method [of limiting fertility] and can be practiced without the man's knowledge."[20] This implies a sort of women's conspiracy to limit population, which would be difficult to demonstrate in the context of nineteenth-century America. Nonetheless, there is some evidence, though it must be considered carefully, to suggest that an American variant of this proposition may have been at least one of the reasons why abortion became such a common form of family limitation in the United States during the period. A number of physicians, as will become evident, certainly believed that one of the keys to the upsurge of abortion was the fact that it was a uniquely female practice, which men could neither control nor prevent. . . .

Earlier in the century observers had alleged that the tract literature and lectures of the women's rights movement advocated family planning and disseminated abortifacient information.[21] In 1859 Harvard professor Walter Channing reported the opinion that "women for whom this office of foeticide, unborn-child-killing, is committed, are strong-minded," and no later writer ever accused them of being weak-minded.[22] . . .

The most common variant of the view that abortion was a manifestation of the women's rights movement hinged upon the word "fashion." Over and over men claimed that women who aborted did so because they cared more about scratching for a better perch in society than they did about raising children. They dared not waste time on the latter lest they fall behind in the former. Women, in short, were accused of being aggressively self-indulgent. Some women, for example, had "the effrontery to say boldly, that they have neither the time nor inclination to nurse babies"; others exhibited "self-indulgence in most disgusting forms"; and many of the women practicing abortion were described as more interested in "selfish and personal ends" or "fast living" than in the maternity for which God had supposedly created them.[23] . . . For this reason, some doctors urged that feticide be made a legal ground for divorce.[24] A substantial number of writers between 1840 and 1880, in other words, were willing to portray women who had abortions as domestic subversives. . . .

Notwithstanding the possibility that recourse to abortion sometimes reflected the rising consciousness of the women who had them, and notwithstanding the fact that some males, especially regular physicians, were distinctly uneasy about the practice because of what its ultimate effects upon the social position of women might be, the relationship between abortion and feminism in the nineteenth century nevertheless remained indirect and ironical. This becomes evident when the arguments of the feminists themselves are analyzed. One of the most forceful early statements of what subsequently became the feminist position on abortion was made in the 1850s in a volume entitled *The Unwelcome Child*.[25] The author, Henry C. Wright, asserted that women alone had the right to say when they would become pregnant and blamed the tremendous outburst of abortion in America on selfishly sensual husbands. Wright's volume was more interesting than other similar tracts, however, because he published a large number of letters from women detailing the circumstances under which they had sought abortions.

One of Wright's letters was from a woman who had her first abortion in 1841, because her one-year-old firstborn was sick and her husband was earning almost nothing. She "consulted a lady friend, and by her persuasion and assistance, killed" the fetus she was carrying. When she found herself pregnant again shortly thereafter she "consulted a physician. . . . He was ready with his logic, his medicines and instruments, and told me how to destroy it. After experimenting on myself three months, I was successful. I killed my child about five months after conception." She steeled herself to go full term with her next pregnancy and to "endure" an addition to her impoverished and unhappy household. When pregnant again she "employed a doctor, to kill my child, and in the destruction of it . . . ended my power to be a mother." The woman's point throughout, however, was that abortion "was most repulsive" to her and her recourse to it "rendered [her] an object of loathing to [her]self." Abortion was not a purposeful female conspiracy, but an undesirable necessity forced by thoughtless men. As this woman put it: "I was the veriest slave alive."[26] . . .

The attitudes expressed by Wright's correspondents in the 1840s and 1850s became the basis of the official position of American feminists toward abortion after the Civil War. As Elizabeth Cady Stanton phrased it, the practice was one more result of "the degradation of woman" in the nineteenth century, not of woman's rising consciousness or expanding opportunities outside the home.[27] . . . The remedy to the problem of abortion in the United States, in their view, was not legalized abortion open to all but "the education and enfranchisement of women" which would make abortion unnecessary in a future world of egalitarian respect and sexual discretion.[28] In short, most feminists, though they agreed completely with other observers that abortion was endemic in America by midcentury, did not blame the increase on the rising ambitions of women but asserted with Matilda E. J. Gage "that this crime of 'child murder,' 'abortion,' 'infanticide,' lies at the door of the male sex."[29] The *Woman's Advocate* of Dayton, Ohio, put it even more forcefully in 1869: "Till men learn to check their sensualism, and leave their wives free to choose their periods of maternity, let us hear no more invectives against women for the destruction of prospective unwelcome children, whose dispositions, made miserable by unhappy ante-natal conditions, would only make their lives a curse to themselves and others."[30] . . .

Despite the blame and recrimination evoked by the great upsurge of abortion in the United States in the nineteenth century, some of which was directed at women and some at men, it appears likely that most decisions to use abortion probably involved couples conferring together, not just men imposing their wills or women acting unilaterally, and that abortion was the result of diffuse pressures, not merely the rising consciousness of women or the tyrannical aggressions of men. American men and women wanted to express their sexuality and mutual affections, on the one hand, and to limit their fertility, on the other. Abortion was neither desirable nor undesirable in itself, but rather one of the few available means of reconciling and realizing those two higher priorities. And it seems likely that the man and woman agreed to both of those higher priorities in most instances, thus somewhat mooting in advance the question of which one was more responsible for the decisions that made abortion a common phenomenon in mid-nineteenth-century America.[31]

Court records provide one source of evidence for the mutuality of most abortion decisions. Almost every nineteenth-century abortion case that was written up, whether in the popular press, in medical journals, or in the official proceedings of state supreme courts, involved the agreement of both the man and the woman. There is no record of any man ever having sued any woman for aborting his child. . . .

Perhaps the best evidence for the likely mutuality of most abortion decisions is contained in the diary that Lester Frank Ward, who later became one of America's most famous sociologists, kept as a newlywed in the 1860s. Though Ward was unique in writing down the intimate decisions that he and his wife had to make, the couple seemed otherwise typical young Americans, almost as Tocqueville might have described them, anxious for further education and ambitious to get ahead quickly. Both Ward and his wife understood that a child would overburden their limited resources and reduce the probability of ever realizing either their individual goals of self-improvement or their mutual goals as a couple. They avoided pregnancy in pre-marital intercourse, then continued to avoid it after their marriage in August 1862. Not until early in 1864 did Lizzie Ward become pregnant. In March, without consulting her husband, she obtained "an effective remedy" from a local woman, which made her very sick for two days but helped her to terminate her pregnancy. She probably took this action after missing three or four periods; it was still early enough in gestation that her husband did not realize she was pregnant but late enough that lactation had begun. Ward noted in his diary that "the proof" she had been pregnant was "the milk" that appeared after the abortion.[32]

Anti-feminists might have portrayed Lizzie Ward's action as diabolical, a betrayal of duty. Feminists might have viewed it as the only recourse open to a female who wanted both to further her own education and to remain on good terms with an ambitious spouse who would certainly have sacrificed his wife's goals to child-rearing, while he pursued his own. But the decision was really the result of a pre-existing consensus between the two of them. Though Ward had not been party to the process in a legal or direct sense, which may go some distance toward confirming the role of abortion as a more uniquely female method of family limitation than contraception, he was clearly delighted that his wife was "out of danger" and would not be having a child. After this brush with family responsibility, the Wards tried a number of new methods of contraception, which they presumably hoped would be more effective than whatever they had been using to avoid pregnancy before Lizzie had to resort to abortion. These included both "pills" and "instruments." Not until the summer of 1865, after Ward had obtained a decent job in Washington, did the couple have a baby.[33]

Abortion had been for the Wards what it apparently also was for many other American couples: an acceptable means toward a mutually desirable end, one of the only ways they had to allow themselves both to express their sexuality and affection toward each other with some degree of frequency and to postpone family responsibilities until they thought they were better prepared to raise children. The line of acceptability for most Americans trying to reconcile these twin priorities ran just about where Lizzie Ward had drawn it. Infanticide, the destruction of a baby after its birth, was clearly unacceptable, and so was abortion after quickening, though that was a much grayer area than infanticide. But abortion before quickening, like contraception itself, was an appropriate and legally permissible method of avoiding unwanted children. And it had one great advantage, as the Wards learned, over contraception: it worked. As more and more women began to practice abortion, however, and as the practice changed from being invisible to being visible, from being quantitatively insignificant to being a systematic practice that terminated a substantial number of pregnancies after 1840, and from being almost entirely a recourse of the desperate and the socially marginal to being a commonly employed procedure among the middle and upper classes of American society, state legislators decided to reassess their policies toward the practice. Between 1840 and 1860 law-makers in several states began to respond to the increase of abortion in American life.

NOTES

1. The quickening doctrine went back to the thirteenth century in England. . . . On quickening in

the common law see Cyril C. Means, Jr., "The Law of New York concerning Abortion and the Status of the Foetus, 1664–1968: A Case of Cessation of Constitutionality," *New York Law Forum* XIV, no. 3 (Fall 1968): 419–426.

2. Ibid., pp. 411–19, and John T. Noonan, Jr., "An Almost Absolute Value in History," in John T. Noonan, Jr., ed., *The Morality of Abortion* (Cambridge, Mass., 1970), pp. 1–59. . . .

3. . . . Buchan's volume was published in Philadelphia as early as 1782, where it went through many editions. . . . This remarkably successful book continued to be reprinted in America through 1850.

4. Buchan, *Domestic Medicine*, pp. 400, 403–4.

5. See, for example, Frederick Hollick, *Diseases of Women, Their Causes and Cure Familiarly Explained: With Practical Hints for Their Prevention, and for the Preservation of Female Health: For Every Female's Private Use* (New York, 1849), p. 150. . . .

6. . . . [See] George Ellington, *The Women of New York, or the Under-World of the Great City* (New York, 1869), pp. 399–400.

7. Peter Smith, "The Indian Doctor's Dispensary, Being Father Peter Smith's Advice Respecting Diseases and Their Cure; Consisting of Prescriptions for Many Complaints: And a Description of Medicines, Simple and Compound, Showing Their Virtues and How to Apply Them," [1813] reproduced in J. U. Lloyd, ed., *Bulletin of the Lloyd Library of Botany, Pharmacy and Materia Medica* (1901), Bull. #2, Reproduction Series #2, pp. 46–47.

8. John Burns, *Observations on Abortion: Containing an Account of the Manner in Which It Takes Place, the Causes Which Produce It, and the Method of Preventing or Treating It* (Troy, N.Y., 1808), pp. 73–81. . . .

9. Heber C. Kimball in the *Journal of Discourses*, 26 vols. (Liverpool, 1857), V:91–92.

10. Thomas Massie, "An Experimental Inquiry into the Properties of the Polygala Senega," in Charles Caldwell, ed., *Medical Theses, . . .* (Philadelphia, 1806), p. 203.

11. . . . William Petersen's widely used *Population* (New York, 3rd ed., 1975), p. 15, labels [the U.S. population from 1800 to 1830 as] the "underdeveloped" type and identifies its characteristics as a mixed economy, high fertility rates, falling mortality rates, and very high rates of population growth.

12. Massie, "Polygala Senega," p. 204.

13. John G. Metcalf, student notebooks written while attending Dr. Walter Channing's lectures of midwifery at Harvard Medical School, 1825–1826 (Countway Library, Harvard Medical School), entry for Dec. 27, 1825. . . .

14. Hugh L. Hodge in Francis Wharton and Moreton Stillé, *Treatise on Medical Jurisprudence* (Philadelphia, 1855), p. 270.

15. "Report on Criminal Abortion," *Transactions of the American Medical Association* XII (1859):75.

16. E. P. Christian, "Report to the State Medical Society on Criminal Abortions," *Peninsular & Independent Medical Journal* II:135.

17. "Criminal Abortions," *Buffalo Medical Journal and Monthly Review* XIV (1859):249.

18. *Boston Medical and Surgical Journal* XLIV, no. 14 (May 7, 1851):288. . . . Worthington Hooker, *Physician and Patient . . .* (New York, 1849), passim, and especially pp. 405–8. The estimate on income is from Colin B. Burke, "The Quiet Influence" (Ph.D. diss, Washington University of St. Louis, 1973):69, Table 2.19.

19. A Physician of New-York, *Trial of Madame Restell, For Producing Abortion on the Person of Maria Bodine, . . .* (New York, 1847), pp. 3–4, 10.

20. Kingsley Davis and Judith Blake, "Social Structure and Fertility: An Analytical Framework," *Economic Development and Cultural Change* IV, no. 3 (April 1956):230.

21. Hooker, *Physician and Patient*, p. 93; James Reed, *From Private Vice to Public Virtue: The Birth Control Movement and American Society since 1830* (New York, 1978), chaps. 1–5.

22. Walter Channing, "Effects of Criminal Abortion," *Boston Medical and Surgical Journal* LX (Mar. 17, 1859):135.

23. E. M. Buckingham, "Criminal Abortion," *Cincinnati Lancet & Observer* X (Mar. 1867):141; Channing, "Effects of Criminal Abortion," p. 135; J. C. Stone, "Report on the Subject of Criminal Abortion," *Transactions of the Iowa State Medical Society* I (1867):29; J. Miller, "Criminal Abortion," *The Kansas City Medical Record* I (Aug. 1884):296.

24. [See] H. Gibbons, Sr., "On Feticide," *Pacific Medical and Surgical Journal* (San Francisco) XXI, no. 3 (Aug. 1879):97–111; . . .

25. Henry C. Wright, *The Unwelcome Child; or, the Crime of an Undesigned and Undesired Maternity* (Boston, 1860). The volume was copyrighted in 1858.

26. Ibid., pp. 65–69.

27. E[lizabeth] C[ady] S[tanton], "Infanticide and Prostitution," *Revolution* I, no. 5 (Feb. 5, 1868):65.

28. Ibid. For the same point reiterated see "Child Murder," in ibid. I, no. 10 (Mar. 12, 1868):146–47. . . .

29. Ibid. I, no. 14 (Apr. 9, 1868):215–16.

30. E. V. B., "Restellism, and the N.Y. Medical Gazette," *Woman's Advocate* (Dayton, Ohio) I, no. 20 (Apr. 8, 1869):16. . . .

31. Carl N. Degler is one of those who have argued persuasively that nineteenth-century American women were very much aware of their own sexuality and desirous, morality books notwithstanding, of expressing it: "What Ought To Be and What Was: Women's Sexuality in the Nineteenth Century," *American Historical Review* LXXIX, no. 5 (Dec. 1974):1467–90.

32. Lester Ward, *Young Ward's Diary*, Bernhard J. Stern, ed. (New York, 1935), p. 140.

33. Ibid., pp. 150, 152–53, 174.

DOCUMENTS: Claiming Rights I

> *Sarah and Angelina Grimké: The Connection between Religious Faith, Abolition, and Women's Rights*

Sarah and Angelina Grimké were the first, and it seems likely the only, women of a slaveholding family to speak and write publicly as abolitionists. They were the first women agents of the American Anti-Slavery Society to tour widely and to speak to audiences of men and women. They were the first women who, from within the abolitionist movement, defended their rights *as women* to free speech. They were sustained in their work by a deep religious devotion, and their writings are examples of the spirit in which many women's rights advocates developed a wide-ranging critique of the relationship between the state, churches, and families.

The Grimké sisters grew up in Charleston, South Carolina. Their father was a distinguished legislator and judge; although he gave his daughters a traditional female education (lacking Greek, Latin, and philosophy), when he trained his sons for the law he included his daughters in the exercises. Both young women were sensitive to the injustices of slavery; as a young woman Sarah broke the law against teaching slaves to read and Angelina held prayer meetings for the family's slaves. When she was twenty-four years old Sarah accompanied her father to Philadelphia, where he sought medical treatment; after his death she returned there in 1821 to live among Quakers, who impressed her by their piety, simplicity, and refusal to hold slaves. In 1829 Angelina joined her; both joined a Quaker meeting. Sarah committed herself to boycott products made in slavery; Angelina joined the Philadelphia Female Antislavery Society. When reformers faced violence from proslavery mobs in the summer of 1835, William Lloyd Garrison wrote strong editorials in *The Liberator* denouncing what he called a "reign of terror." Angelina Grimké responded with a letter complimenting him on his fortitude: "The ground on which you stand is holy ground," she wrote, "never—never surrender it." Garrison surprised her by printing her letter; thus encouraged, Angelina went on to write *An Appeal to the Christian Women of the South*. The pamphlet sold widely in the North and made her reputation, but it was burned in Charleston.

When the American Anti-Slavery Society organized a group of "Agents" to travel and speak on slavery, Angelina and Sarah Grimké were among them. They began in late 1836, speaking to women in private parlors in New York City; by the turn of the year no private room was big enough and they held their sessions in a Baptist church. They involved themselves in founding women's antislavery societies and organizing women's antislavery petitions to Congress; they published their speeches as pamphlets. In mid-1837 they moved on to Boston, where an intense debate among factions of abolitionists was already under way. Sarah wrote a series of essays that appeared first in newspapers and then as a pamphlet, *Letters on the Equality of the Sexes and the Condition of Women.*

In the summer of 1837, the Congregational ministers of Massachusetts published a "Pastoral Letter" attacking them as unwomanly. In the past they had offered their criticism of slavery in the context of religious faith; now they claimed that as moral individuals, women had as much right to take political positions as men. Though even some of their allies—including Theodore Dwight Weld, whom Angelina would soon marry—sought to dissuade them, they were forthright in their response. The term "feminist" had not yet been invented—it would be devised in the 1910s—but the ingredients of the concept were already present in the ideas of the Grimké sisters.*

ANGELINA GRIMKÉ, APPEAL TO THE CHRISTIAN WOMEN OF THE SOUTH (1836)

. . . Sisters in Christ I feel an interest in *you*, and often has the secret prayer arisen on your behalf, Lord "open thou their eyes that they may see wondrous things out of thy Law"—It is then, because I *do feel* and *do pray* for you, that I thus address you upon a subject about which of all others, perhaps you would rather not hear any thing; but, "would to God ye could bear with me a little in my folly, and indeed bear with me, for I am jealous over you with godly jealousy." Be not afraid then to read my appeal; it is *not* written in the heat of passion or prejudice, but in that solemn calmness which is the result of conviction and duty. It is true, I am going to tell you unwelcome truths, but I mean to speak those *truths in love*, and remember Solomon says, "faithful are the *wounds* of a friend." I do not believe the time has yet come when *Christian women* "will not endure sound doctrine," even on the subject of slavery, if it is spoken to them in tenderness and love, therefore I now address you. . . .

We must come back to the good old doctrine of our forefathers who declared to the world, "this self evident truth that *all* men are created equal, and that they have certain *inalienable* rights among which are life, *liberty*, and the pursuit of happiness." It is even a greater absurdity to suppose a man can be legally born a slave under *our free Republican* Government, than under the petty despotisms of barbarian Africa. If then, we have no right to enslave an African, surely we can have none to enslave an American; if it is a self evident truth that *all* men, every where and of every color are born equal, and have an *inalienable right to liberty*, then it is equally true that *no* man can be born a slave, and no man can ever *rightfully* be reduced to *involuntary* bondage and held as a slave, however fair may be the claim of his master or mistress through will and title-deeds. . . .

But perhaps you will be ready to query, why appeal to *women* on this subject? *We* do not make the laws which perpetuate slavery. No legislative power is vested in *us; we* can do nothing to overthrow the system, even if we wished to do so. To this I reply, I know you do not make the laws, but I also know that *you are the wives and mothers, the sisters and daughters of those who do;* and if you really suppose *you* can do nothing to overthrow slavery, you are greatly mistaken. You can do much in every way: four things I will name. Ist. You can read on this subject. 2d. You can pray over this subject. 3d. You can speak on this subject. 4th. You can *act* on this subject. I have not placed reading before praying because I regard it more important, but because, in order to pray aright, we must understand what we are praying for; it is only then we can "pray with the understanding and the spirit also."

1.   Read then on the subject of slavery. Search the Scriptures daily, whether the things I have told you are true. Other books and papers might be a great help to you in this investigation, but they are not necessary. . . .

2. Pray over this subject. When you have entered into your closets, and shut to the doors, then pray to your father, who seeth in

---

*See Gerda Lerner, *The Grimké Sisters from South Carolina: Rebels Against Slavery* (Boston, 1967), and *The Public Years of Sarah and Angelina Grimké: Selected Writings 1835–1839*, ed. Larry Ceplair (New York, 1989). The selections that follow are taken from the Ceplair edition, pp. 37–38, 54–56, 220–23, 268–69, 211, 216.

secret, that he would open your eyes to see whether slavery is *sinful,* and if it is, that he would enable you to bear a faithful, open and unshrinking testimony against it, and to do whatsoever your hands find to do . . .

3. Speak on this subject. It is through the tongue, the pen, and the press, that truth is principally propagated. Speak then to your relatives, your friends, your acquaintances on the subject of slavery; be not afraid if you are conscientiously convinced it is *sinful,* to say so openly, but calmly, and to let your sentiments be known. If you are served by the slaves of others, try to ameliorate their condition as much as possible; never aggravate their faults, and thus add fuel to the fire of anger already kindled in a master and mistress's bosom. . . .

4. Act on this subject. Some of you *own* slaves yourselves. If you believe slavery is *Sinful,* set them at liberty, "undo the heavy burdens and let the oppressed go free." If they wish to remain with you, pay them wages,if not let them leave you. Should they remain teach them, and have them taught the common branches of an English education; they have minds and those minds, *ought to be improved.* So precious a talent as intellect, never was given to be wrapt in a napkin and buried in the earth. It is the *duty* of all, as far as they can, to improve their own mental faculties, because we are commanded to love God with *all our minds,* as well as with all our hearts, and we commit a great sin, if we *forbid or prevent* that cultivation of the mind in others, which would enable them to perform this duty. Teach your servants then to read &c, and encourage them to believe it is their *duty* to learn, if it were only that they might read the Bible.

But some of you will say, we can neither free our slaves nor teach them to read, for the laws of our state forbid it. Be not surprised when I say such wicked laws *ought to be no barrier* in the way of your duty, and I appeal to the Bible to prove this position. What was the conduct of Shiphrah and Puah, when the king of Egypt issued his cruel mandate, with regard to the Hebrew children? "*They* feared *God,* and did *not* as the King of Egypt commanded them, but saved the men children alive." Did these *women* do right in disobeying that monarch? "*Therefore* (says the sacred text,) *God dealt well* with them, and made them houses."

SARAH M. GRIMKÉ, LETTERS ON THE EQUALITY OF THE SEXES AND THE CONDITION OF WOMEN (1837)

LETTER VIII: "ON THE CONDITION OF WOMEN IN THE UNITED STATES"
During the early part of my life, my lot was cast among the butterflies of the *fashionable* world; and of this class of women, I am constrained to say, both from experience and observation, that their education is miserably deficient; that they are taught to regard marriage as the one thing needful, the only avenue to distinction; hence to attract the notice and win the attentions of men, by their external charms, is the chief business of fashionable girls. They seldom think that men will be allured by intellectual acquirements, because they find, that where any mental superiority exists, a woman is generally shunned and regarded as step-ping out of her "appropriate sphere," which, in their view, is to dress, to dance, to set out to the best possible advantage her person, to read the novels which inundate the press, and which do more to destroy her character as a rational creature, than any thing else. . . .

There is another and much more numerous class in this country, who are withdrawn by education or circumstances from the circle of fashionable amusements, but who are brought up with the dangerous and absurd idea, that *marriage* is a kind of preferment; and that to be able to keep their husband's house, and render his situation comfortable, is the end of her being. Much that she does and says and thinks is done in reference to this situation; and to be married is too often held up to the view of girls as the sine qua non of human happiness and human existence. . . . I do long to see the time, when it will no longer be necessary for women to expend so many precious hours in furnishing "a well spread table," but that their husbands will forego some of the accustomed indulgences in this way, and encourage their wives to devote some portion of their time to mental cultivation, even at the expense of having to dine sometimes on baked potatoes, or bread and butter. . . .

There is another way in which the general opinion, that women are inferior to men, is manifested, that bears with tremendous effect on the laboring class, and indeed on almost all who are obliged to earn a subsistence, whether it be by mental or physical exertion—I allude to the disproportionate value set on the time and labor of men and of women. A man who is engaged in teaching, can always, I believe, command a higher price for tuition than a woman—even when he teaches the same branches, and is not in any respect superior to the woman. This I know is the case in boarding and other schools with which I have been acquainted, and it is so in every occupation in which the sexes engaged indiscriminately. As for example, in tailoring, a man has twice, or three times as much for making a waistcoat or pantaloons as a woman, although the work done by each may be equally good. In those employments which are peculiar to women, their time is estimated at only half the value of that of men. A woman who goes out to wash, works as hard in proportion as a wood sawyer, or a coal heaver, but she is not generally able to make more than half as much by a day's work. . . .

There is another class of women in this country, to whom I cannot refer, without feelings of the deepest shame and sorrow. I allude to our female slaves. Our southern cities are whelmed beneath a tide of pollution; the virtue of female slaves is wholly at the mercy of irresponsible tyrants, and women are bought and sold in our slave markets, to gratify the brutal lust of those who bear the name of Christians. In our slave States, if amid all her degradation and ignorance, a women desires to preserve her virtue unsullied, she is either bribed or whipped into compliance, or if she dares resist her seducer, her life by the laws of some of the slave States may be, and has actually been sacrificed to the fury of disappointed passion. Where such laws do not exist, the power which is necessarily vested in the master over his property, leaves the defenceless slave entiely at his mercy, and the sufferings of some females on this account, both physical and mental, are intense.

LETTER XV: MAN EQUALLY GUILTY WITH WOMAN IN THE FALL

. . . In contemplating the great moral reformations of the day, and the part which they are bound to take in them, instead of puzzling themselves with the harassing, because unnecessary inquiry, how far they may go without overstepping the bounds of propriety, which separate male and female duties, they will only inquire, "Lord, what wilt thou have us do?" They will be enabled to see the simple truth, that God has made no distinction between men and women as moral beings; that the distinction now so much insisted upon between male and female virtues is as absurd as it is unscriptural, and has been the fruitful source of much mischief—granting to man a license for the exhibition of brute force and conflict on the battle field; for sternness, selfishness, and the exercise of irresponsible power in the circle of home—and to woman a permit to rest on an arm of flesh, and to regard modesty and delicacy, and all the kindred virtues, as peculiarly appropriate to her. Now to me it is perfectly clear, that WHATSOEVER IT IS MORALLY RIGHT FOR A MAN TO DO, IT IS MORALLY RIGHT FOR A WOMAN TO DO; and that confusion must exist in the moral world, until woman takes her stand on the same platform with man, and feels that she is clothed by her Maker with the *same rights,* and, of course, that upon her devolve the *same duties.*

PASTORAL LETTER:
THE GENERAL ASSOCIATION
OF MASSACHUSETTS TO THE
CHURCHES UNDER THEIR CARE

III.—We invite your attention to the dangers which at present seem to threaten the female character with wide spread and permanent injury.

The appropriate duties and influence of women are clearly stated in the New Testament. Those duties and that influence are unobtrusive and private, but the sources of mighty power. When the mild, dependant [sic], softening influence of woman upon the sternness of man's opinion is fully exercised, society feels the effects of it in a thousand forms. The power of woman is in her dependence, flowing from the consciousness of that weakness which God has given her for her protection, and which keeps her in those departments of life that form the character of individuals and of the nation. There are social influences which females use in promoting piety and the great objects of Christian benevolence which we cannot too highly commend. We appreciate the unostentatious prayers and efforts of woman in advancing the cause of religion at home and abroad; in Sabbath schools; in leading religious inquirers to the pastors for instruction; and in all such associated effort as becomes the modesty of her sex; and earnestly hope that she may abound more and more in these labors of piety and love.

But when she assumes the place and tone of man as a public reformer, our care and protection of her seem unnecessary; we put ourselves in self-defence against her; she yields the power which God has given her for protection, and her character becomes unnatural. If the vine, whose strength and beauty is to lean upon the trellis and half conceal its clusters, thinks to assume the independence and the overshading nature of the elm, it will not only cease to bear fruit, but fall in shame and dishonor into the dust. We cannot, therefore, but regret the mistaken conduct of those who encourage females to bear an obtrusive and ostentatious part in measures of reform, and countenance any of that sex who so far forget themselves as to itinerate in the character of public lecturers and teachers. We especially deplore the intimate acquaintance and promiscuous conversation of females with regard to things "which ought not to be named"; by which that modesty and delicacy which is the charm of domestic life, and which constitutes the true influence of woman in society is consumed, and the way opened, as we apprehend, for degeneracy and ruin . . .

SARAH M. GRIMKÉ, RESPONSE TO "THE PASTORAL LETTER . . ."

The motto of woman, when she is engaged in the great work of public reformation should be,—"The Lord is my light and my salvation; whom shall I fear? The Lord is the strength of my life; of whom shall I be afraid?" She must feel, if she feels rightly, that she is fulfilling one of the important duties laid upon her as an accountable being, and that her character, instead of being "unnatural," is in exact accordance with the will of Him to whom, and to no other, she is responsible for the talents and the gifts confided to her. As to the pretty simile, introduced into the "Pastoral Letter," "If the vine whose strength and beauty is to lean upon the trellis work, and half conceal its clusters, thinks to assume the independence and the overshadowing nature of the elm," & c. I shall only remark that it might well suit the poet's fancy, who sings of sparkling eyes and coral lips, and knights in armor clad; but it seems to me utterly inconsistent with the dignity of a Christian body, to endeavor to draw such an anti-scriptural distinction between men and women. Ah! how many of my sex feel in the dominion, thus unrighteously exercised over them, under the gentle appellation of *protection,* that what they have leaned upon has proved a broken reed at best, and oft a spear.

Thine in the bonds of womanhood,

Sarah M. Grimké.

Keziah Kendall, "What I have suffered, I cannot tell you"

We know nothing more about "Keziah Kendall" than what she revealed in this letter, which historians Dianne Avery and Alfred S. Konefsky discovered among the papers of Simon Greenleaf, a prominent Harvard law professor. It has not been possible to locate the author in the usual places—tax lists, land records, church lists—but whether the name is real or fictional, the issues addressed in the letter are authentic. "Kendall" had been dismayed by what she heard when she attended a public lyceum lecture on women's rights given by Greenleaf early in 1839. At a time when the legal disabilities of inherited common law were increasingly being questioned—in Massachusetts, the abolitionists Sarah and Angelina Grimké had only recently delivered a forthright series of lectures on the rights of women—Greenleaf devoted his lecture to the claim that American women were well protected by American law as it stood. He argued that excluding women from politics saved society from "uproar" and impropriety; that constraints on married women's use of their property was merely a technicality because in a happy marriage all property became part of "a common fund . . . it can make but little difference . . . by whose name it is called." And he insisted that except for "restriction in *political* matters" there were no significant "distinctions between the legal rights of unmarried women, and of men."

"Keziah Kendall" was unpersuaded. The farm that she and her sisters inherited was a substantial one; she and her sisters were wealthy rural women. Describing her own anxieties as the older sister of a flighty girl and her own tragic ordeal as the fiancée of a man with high ethical commitments, "Kendall" demanded that Greenleaf offer another lecture, acknowledging the "legal wrongs" of women.

What are "Kendall's" objections to the law as she experienced it? What connections does she draw between paying taxes, voting, and officeholding? Why does she blame Massachusetts property law for her fiancé's death? Why is she worried about her sister's forthcoming marriage?

Keziah Kendall to Simon Greenleaf [1839?] I take the liberty to write to you on the subject of the Lyceum lecture you delivered last Feb. but as you are not acquainted with me I think I will introduce myself. My name is Kezia Kendall. I live not many miles from Cambridge, on a farm with two sisters, one older, one younger than myself. I am thirty two. Our parents and only brother are dead—we have a good estate—comfortable house—nice barn, garden, orchard & c and money in the bank besides. Jemima is a very good manager in the house, keeps everything comfortable—sees that the milk is nicely prepared for market— looks after everything herself, and rises before day, winter and summer,—but she never had any head for figures, and always expects me to keep all accounts, and attend to all business concerns. Keranhappuck, (who is called Kerry) is quite young, only nineteen, and as she was

---

Letter from Keziah Kendall to Simon Greenleaf (undated). Box 3, Folder 10, Simon Greenleaf Papers, Harvard Law School Library. Excerpted from Diane Avery and Alfred S. Konefsky. "The Daughters of Job: Property Rights and Women's Lives in Mid-Nineteenth-Century Massachusetts," *Law and History Review*, X (Fall 1992): 323–56. Notes have been renumbered and edited.

a little girl when mother died, we've always petted her, and let her do as she pleased, and now she's courted. Under these circumstances the whole responsibility of our property, not less than twenty five thousand dollars rests upon me. I am not over fond of money, but I have worked hard ever since I was a little girl, and tried to do all in my power to help earn, and help save, and it would be strange if I did not think more of it than those who never earned anything, and never saved anything they could get to spend, and you know Sir, there are many such girls nowadays. Well— our milkman brought word when he came from market that you were a going to lecture on the legal rights of women, and so I thought I would go and learn. Now I hope you wont think me bold when I say, I did not like that lecture much. I dont speak of the manner, it was pretty spoken enough, but there was nothing in it but what every body knows. We all know about a widow's thirds,[1] and we all know that a man must maintain his wife, and we all know that he must pay her debts, if she has any—but I never heard of a yankee woman marrying in debt. What I wanted to know, was good reasons for some of those laws that I cant account for. I do hope if you are ever to lecture at the Lyceum again, that you will give us some. I must tell my story to make you understand what I mean. One Lyceum lecture that I heard in C. stated that the Americans went to war with the British, because they were taxed without being represented in Parliament. Now we are taxed every year to the full amount of every dollar we possess—town, county, state taxes—taxes for land, for movables, for money and all. Now I dont want to go representative or any thing else, any more than I do to be a "constable or a sheriff," but I have no voice about public improvements, and I dont see the justice of being taxed any more than the "revolutionary heroes" did. You mention that woman here, are not treated like heathen and Indian women—we know that—nor do I think we are treated as Christian women ought to be, according to the Bible rule of doing to others as you would others should do unto you. I am told (not by you) that if a woman dies a week after she's married that her husband takes all her personal property and the use of her real estate as long as he lives[2]—if a man dies his wife can have her thirds—this does not come up to the Gospel rule. Now the young fellow that is engaged to our Kerry, is a pleasant clever fellow, but he is not quite one and twenty, and I dont s'pose he ever earned a coat in his life. Uncle told me there was a way for a woman to have her property trustee'd,[3] and I told it to Kerry—but she, poor girl has romantic notions owing to reading too many novels,[4] and when I told her of it, she would not hear of such a thing—"What take the law to keep my property away from James before I marry him—if it was a million of dollars he should have it all." So you see I think the law is in fault here—to tell you the truth I do not think young men are near so careful about getting in debt as girls, and I have known more than one that used their wife's money to pay off old scores. . . . I had rather go to my mantua maker[5] to borrow twenty dollars if I needed it, than to the richest married woman I know.

Another thing I have to tell you—when I was young I had a lover, Jos. Thompson, he went into business in a neighboring town, and after a year or two while I was getting the wedding things—Joe failed, he met with misfortunes that he did not expect,—he could have concealed it from me and married, but he did not—he was honorable, and so we delayed. He lived along here two or three years, and tried all he could to settle with his creditors, but some were stiff and held out, and thought by and by we would marry, and they should get my property. Uncle said he knew if we were married, there were those who would take my cattle and the improvement of my land. Joseph used to visit me often those years, but he lost his spirits and he could not get into business again, and he thought he must go to sea. I begged him not to, and told him we should be able to manage things in time, but he said no— he must try his luck, and at least get enough to settle off old scores, and then he would come here and live and we would make the best of what I had. We parted—but it pleased God he should be lost at sea. What I have suffered, I cannot tell you. Now Joe was no sailor when I engaged with him, and if it had been a thing known that I should always have a right to keep possession of my own, he need never have gone to sea, and we might have lived happily together, and in time with industry and economy, he might have paid off all. I am one that cant be convinced without better reasons than I have heard of, that woman are dealt with by the "gospel rule." There is more might than right in such laws as far as I can see—if you see differently, do tell us next time you lecture. Another thing—you made some reflections upon women following the Anti's. . . . Women have joined the Antislavery societies, and why? women are kept for slaves as well as men—it is a common cause, deny the justice of it, who can! To be sure I do not wish to go about lecturing like the Misses Grimkie, but I have not the knowledge they have, and I verily believe that if I had been brought up among slaves as they were, and knew all that they know, and felt a call from humanity to speak, I should run the venture of your displeasure, and that of a good many others like you.[6] [See pp. 193–97] I told Uncle that I thought your lecture was a onesided thing—and he said, "why Keziah, Squire Greenleaf is an advocate, not a judge, you must get him to take t'other side next time." Now I have taken this opportunity to ask you to give us a remedy for the "legal wrongs" of women, whenever you have a chance. The fathers of the land should look to these things—who knows but your daughter may be placed in the sad situation I am in, or the dangerous one Kerry is in. I hear you are a good man, to make it certain—do all the good you can, and justify no wrong thing.

Yours with regard
Keziah Kendall.

NOTES

1. She is, of course, referring to a widow's dower rights. [See "The Law of Domestic Relations" pp. 51–52.]
2. "Kendall" was correct in her understanding of a husband's rights in his wife's personal property if she should die as early as "a week after she's married." But under the common law he would not inherit a life interest in her real estate unless they were parents of a child.
3. This is a reference to the equitable device of placing the woman's property in a trust before marriage for the purpose of avoiding the husband's common law rights in her property as well as protecting it from the husband's creditors. Under the trust agreement, the trustee would be obligated to manage the property for the benefit of the married woman.
4. "Kendall" shared a widely held distrust of romantic novels.
5. In the early republic, mantua makers [i.e., skilled dressmakers] were often economically independent women.
6. "Kendall" is probably referring here to the "Pastoral Letter" issued by the Congregationalist ministers in the summer of 1837 denouncing the public lecturing of the Grimké sisters. [See pp. 196–97.]

GERDA LERNER

The Meanings of Seneca Falls, 1848–1998

In the familiar photographs, like the one reprinted on page 260, Elizabeth Cady Stanton comes to us as she appeared in her fifties and older—a plump, matronly woman with graying hair and a kindly face. But in 1848, when she wrote the great manifesto that set the agenda for the American women's movement for 150 years, she was thirty-three years old, and the one photograph we have of her from that time shows her to be slight and thin, her dark hair hanging in limp ringlets. Did she look tired because she was the mother of three boys under six? Her future—and ours—lay before her.

As Keziah Kendall and Sarah and Angelina Grimké had done, many people in the 1830s and 1840s had begun to criticize the way American law and custom defined gender relations. The 1848 *Declaration of Sentiments* (see pp. 207–9) gathered these complaints into a manifesto and offered an agenda for change that would shape a women's rights movement deep into our own time. But the Declaration itself has its own history, emerging out of the specific social conditions in western New York state, out of political and religious arguments, and out of the personal experiences of the women and men who wrote its words and signed their names to it.

The meticulous research of Judith Wellman has enabled us to know the class position, religious affiliation, kin relations, and political sympathies of many of the singers at Seneca Falls. Two-thirds of the signers were women; the signers' ages stretched from fourteen-year old Susan Quinn to sixty-eight-year-old George Pryor. Most came with another family member: wives with husbands, mothers with daughters, sisters with brothers. (Daniel Anthony was there, but his daughter Susan would not meet Stanton for another three years.) Seventy percent came from the immediate locality of Seneca Falls and neighboring Waterloo, an area that had seen substantial dislocation from a farm region to a manufacturing town, where a substantial group of men had broken with the Democratic and Whig parties to join the abolitionist Free Soilers, and where dissidents from the Quaker Genesee Yearly Meeting formed their own society of Friends devoted to egalitarian gender relations and abolition. Legislative battles over married women's property acts made women's rights especially visible in New York.*

The Declaration of Sentiments, Stanton's indictment of the relations between men and women in her own society, is still stunning in its energy, its precision, and its foresight. In the essay that follows, written for the quincentenary of the Seneca Falls convention, the distinguished historian Gerda Lerner reflects on the meaning of the Declaration for its time and for our own.

In 1848, according to Karl Marx and Frederick Engels, "a specter [was] haunting Europe—the specter of communism." In that same year, the upstate New York village of Seneca Falls hosted a gathering of fewer than three hundred people, earnestly debating a Declaration of Sentiments to be spread by newsprint and oratory. The Seneca Falls Woman's Rights Convention marked the beginning of the woman's rights movement.

The specter that haunted Europe developed into a mighty movement, embracing the globe, causing revolutions, wars, tyrannies and counterrevolutions. Having gained state power in Russia, China and Eastern Europe, twentieth-century communism, in 1948, seemed more threatening a specter than ever before. Yet, after a bitter period of "cold war," which pitted nuclear nations against one another in a futile stalemate, it fell of its own weight in almost all its major centers.

The small spark figuratively ignited at Seneca Falls never produced revolutions, usurpation of power or wars. Yet it led to a transformation of consciousness and a movement of empowerment on behalf of half the human race, which hardly has its equal in human history.

Until very recently, the Seneca Falls convention of 1848 was not recognized as significant by historians, was not included in history textbooks, not celebrated as an important event in public schools, never mentioned in the media or the press. In the 1950s, the building where it was held, formerly the Wesleyan chapel, was used as a filling station. In the 1960s, it housed a laundromat. It was only due to the resurgence of modern feminism and the

*Judith Wellman, "The Seneca Falls Women's Rights Convention: A Study of Social Networks," *Journal of Women's History* 3 (1991):9–37.

advances of the field of Women's History that the convention has entered the nation's consciousness. The establishment of Women's History Month as a national event during the Carter administration and its continuance through every administration since then has helped to educate the nation to the significance of women's role in history. Still, it took decades of struggle by women's organizations, feminist historians and preservationists to rescue the building at Seneca Falls and finally to persuade the National Park Service to turn it into a historic site. . . . This history of "long forgetting and short remembering" has been an important aspect of women's historic past, the significance of which we only understood as we began to study women's history in depth.

Elizabeth Cady Stanton, the great communicator and propagandist of nineteenth-century feminism, has left a detailed account of the origins of the Seneca Falls convention both in her autobiography and in the monumental *History of Woman Suffrage*. The idea for such a meeting originated with her and with Lucretia Mott, when they both attended the 1840 World Antislavery Convention in London, at which representatives of female antislavery societies were denied seating and voting rights. Outraged by this humiliating experience, Stanton and Mott decided in London that they would convene a meeting of women in the United States to discuss their grievances as soon as possible. But her responsibilities as mother of a growing family intervened, and Stanton could not implement her plan until 1848, when Lucretia Mott visited her sister Martha Wright in Waterloo, a town near Seneca Falls. There, Stanton met with her, her hostess Jane Hunt and their friend Mary Ann McClintock. Stanton wrote: "I poured out that day the torrent of my long accumulating discontent with such vehemence and indignation that I stirred myself, as well as the rest of the party, to do or dare anything." The five drafted an announcement for a "Woman's Rights Convention" to be held at Seneca Falls on the nineteenth and twentieth of July, and placed the notice in the local paper and the abolitionist press.

The five women who issued the call to the Seneca Falls convention were hardly as naive and inexperienced as later, somewhat mythical versions of the events would lead one to believe. Lucretia Mott was an experienced and highly acclaimed public speaker, a Quaker minister and longtime abolitionist. She had attended the founding meeting of the American Antislavery Society in 1833, which admitted women only as observers. She was a founder of the Philadelphia Female Anti-Slavery Society and its long-term president. The fact that she was announced as the principal speaker at the Seneca Falls convention was a distinct drawing card.

Elizabeth Cady Stanton's "long accumulating discontent" had to do with her struggle to raise her three children (she would later have four more) and run a large household in the frequent absences of her husband Henry, a budding lawyer and Free Soil politican. Still, she found time to be involved in the campaign for reform of women's property rights in New York state, where a reform bill was passed just prior to the convention, and she had spoken before the state legislature.

Martha Wright, Jane Hunt and Mary Ann McClintock were all separatist Quakers, long active in working to improve the position of women within their church. All of them were veterans of reform and women's organizations and had worked on antislavery fairs.

The [region] where they held their convention . . . had for more than two decades been the center of reform and utopian movements, largely due to the economic upheavals brought by the opening of the Erie Canal and the ensuing competition with western agriculture, which brought many farmers to bankruptcy. Economic uncertainty led many to embrace utopian schemes for salvation. The region was known as the "burned-over" district, because so many schemes for reforms had swept over it in rapid succession, from the evangelical revivalism of Charles Grandison Finney, to temperance, abolition, church reform, Mormonism and the chiliastic movement of William Miller, who predicted the second coming of Christ with precision for October 12, 1843 at three A.M. The nearly one million followers of Miller had survived the uneventful passing of that night and the similarly uneventful revised dates of March or October 1844, but their zeal for reform had not lessened.

The men and women who gathered in the Seneca Falls Wesleyan chapel were not a national audience; they all came from upstate New York and represented a relatively narrow spectrum of reform activists. Their local background predisposed them to accept radical pronouncements and challenging proposals. Most of them were abolitionists, the women having been active for nearly ten years in charitable, reform, and antislavery societies. They were experienced in running petition campaigns and many had organized antislavery fund-raising fairs. Historian[s] Nancy Isenberg [and Judith Wellman] who [have] analyzed the origins and affiliations of those attending the convention, showed that many were religious dissidents, Quakers, who just two months prior had separated from their more traditional church and would shortly form their own group, New York Congregationalist Friends. Another dissident group were Wesleyan Methodists who had been involved in a struggle within their church about the role of women and of the laity in church governance. Yet another group came from the ranks of the temperance movement. Among the men in attendance several were local lawyers with Liberty Party or Free Soil affiliations. Also present and taking a prominent part in the deliberations was Frederick Douglass, the former slave and celebrated abolitionist speaker, now editor of the *North Star.*

Far from representing a group of inexperienced housewives running their first public meeting, the majority of the convention participants were reformers with considerable organizational experience. For example, Amy Post and six other women from Rochester who came to Seneca Falls were able to organize a similar woman's rights convention in Rochester just two weeks later. One of the significant aspects of the Seneca Falls convention is that it was grounded in several organizational networks that had already existed for some time and could mobilize the energies of seasoned reform activists.

Most of the reformers attending had family, church and political affiliations in other areas of the North and Midwest. It was through them that the message of Seneca Falls spread quickly and led to the formation of a national movement. The first truly national convention on Woman's Rights was held in Worcester, Massachusetts in 1850. By 1860 ten national and many local woman's rights conventions had been organized.

THE DECLARATION OF SENTIMENTS

The first day of the Seneca Falls meeting was reserved to women, who occupied themselves with debating, paragraph by paragraph, the Declaration of Sentiments prepared by Elizabeth Cady Stanton. Resolutions were offered, debated and adopted. At the end of the second day, sixty-eight women and thirty-two men signed their names to a Declaration of Sentiments, which embodied the program of the nascent movement and provided a model for future woman's rights conventions. The number of signers represented only one third of those present, which probably was due to the radical nature of the statement. . . .

By selecting the Declaration of Independence for their formal model and following its preamble almost verbatim, except for the insertion of gender-neutral language, the organizers of the convention sought to base their main appeal on the democratic rights embodied in the nation's founding document. They also put the weight and symbolism of this revered text behind what was in their time a radical assertion: "We hold these truths to be self-evident: that all men and women are created equal."

The feminist appeal to natural rights and the social contract had long antecedents on the European continent, the most important advocate of it being Mary Wollstonecraft. Her work was well known in the United States, where the same argument had been well made by Judith Sargent Murray, Frances Wright, Emma Willard, Sarah Grimké and Margaret Fuller.

The second fundamental argument for the equality of woman was religious. As stated in the Declaration:

> Resolved, That woman is man's equal—was intended to be so by the Creator, and the highest good of the race demands that she should be recognized as such.

And one of the "grievances" is:

> He [man] has usurped the prerogative of Jehovah himself, claiming it as his right to assign to her a sphere of action, when that belongs to her conscience and her God.

The feminist argument based on biblical grounds can be traced back for seven hundred years prior to 1848, but the women assembled at Seneca Falls were unaware of that fact, because of the nonexistence of anything like Women's History. They did know the Quaker argument, especially as made in her public lectures by Lucretia Mott. They had read Sarah Grimké's *Letters on the Equality of the Sexes,* and several of the resolutions in fact followed her text. They knew the biblical argument by Ann Lee of the Shakers and they echoed the anti-slavery biblical argument, applying it to women.

The Declaration departed from precedent in its most radical statement:

> The history of mankind is a history of repeated injuries and usurpations on the part of man toward woman, having in direct object the establishment of an absolute tyranny over her.

The naming of "man" as the culprit, thereby identifying patriarchy as a system of "tyranny," was highly original, but it may have been dictated more by the rhetorical flourishes of the Declaration of Independence than by an actual analysis of woman's situation. When it came to the list of grievances, the authors departed from the text and became quite specific.

Woman had been denied "her inalienable right to the elective franchise"; she had no voice in the making of laws; she was deprived of other rights of citizenship; she was declared civilly dead upon marriage; deprived of her property and wages; discriminated against in case of divorce, and in payment for work. Women were denied equal access to education and were kept out of the professions, held in a subordinate position in Church and State and assigned by man to the domestic sphere. Man has endeavored to destroy woman's self-respect and keep her dependent.

They concluded that in view of the disfranchisement of one-half the people of this country

> ... we insist that [women] have immediate admission to all the rights and privileges which belong to them as citizens of these United States.

It has been claimed by historians, and by herself, that Stanton's controversial resolution advocating voting rights for women—the only resolution not approved unanimously at the convention—was her most important original contribution. In fact, Sarah and Angelina Grimké had advocated woman's right to vote and hold office in 1838, and Frances Wright had done so in the 1830s. It was not so much the originality, as the inclusiveness of the listed grievances that was important.

The Declaration claimed universality, even though it never mentioned differences among women. Future woman's rights conferences before the Civil War would rectify this omission and pay particular attention to the needs of lower class and slave women.

While grievances pertaining to woman's sexual oppression were not explicitly included in the Declaration of Sentiments, they were very much alive in the consciousness of the leading participants. Elizabeth Cady Stanton had already in 1848 begun to include allusions to what we now call "marital rape" in her letters and soon after the Seneca Falls convention made such references explicit, calling on legislatures to forbid marriage to "drunkards." She soon became an open advocate of divorce and of the right of women to leave abusive marriages. Later woman's rights conventions would include some of these issues among their demands, although they used carefully guarded language and focused on abuses by "drunkards." This was a hidden feminist theme of the mainstream woman's temperance movement in the 1880s and caused many temperance women to embrace woman suffrage. What we now call "a woman's right to her body" was already on the agenda of the nineteenth-century woman's rights movement.

It was the confluence of a broad-ranging programmatic declaration with a format familiar and accessible to reformers that gave the event its historical significance. The Seneca Falls convention was the first forum in which women gathered together to publicly air their own grievances, not those of the needy, the enslaved, orphans or widows. The achievement of a public voice for women and the recognition that women could not win their rights unless they organized, made Seneca Falls a major event in history.

RIGHTS AND EMANCIPATION

... It is useful to think of women's demands as encompassing two sets of needs: women's rights and women's emancipation.

Women's rights essentially are civil rights—to vote, to hold office, to have access to education and to economic and political power at every level of society on an equal basis with men. . . . These rights are demanded on the basis of a claim to *equality:* as citizens, as members of society, women are by rights equal and must therefore be treated equally. All of the rights here listed are based on the acceptance of the status quo; . . . These are essentially reformist demands.

Women's emancipation is freedom from oppressive restrictions imposed by reason of sex; self-determination and autonomy. Oppressive restrictions are biological restrictions due to sex, as well as socially imposed ones. Thus, women's bearing and nursing children is a biological given, but the assignment to women of the major responsibility for the rearing of children and for housework is socially imposed.

Self-determination means being free to decide one's own destiny, to define one's own social role. Autonomy means earning one's status, not being born into it or marrying it. . . . It means freedom to define issues, roles, laws and cultural norms on an equality with men. The demands for emancipation are based on stressing women's difference from men, but also on stressing women's difference from other women. They are radical demands, which can only be achieved by transforming society for men and women, equalizing gender definitions for both sexes, assigning the reproductive work of raising the next generation to both men and women, and reorganizing social institutions so as to make such arrangements possible.

Women, just like men, are placed in society as individuals *and* as citizens. They are both equal *and* different. The demand for women's emancipation always includes the demand for women's rights, but the reverse is not true. Generally speaking, women's rights have been won or improved upon in many parts of the world in the past 150 years. Women's emancipation has not yet been won anywhere.

The movement started at Seneca Falls . . . from the start embraced both [concepts]—by demanding legal, property, civil rights; and by demanding changes in gender-role definition and in woman's rights to her own body. As the nineteenth-century movement matured, there developed some tension between advocates of these two different sets of demands, with the mainstream focusing more and more

on legal and property rights, while radicals and outsiders, like sex reformers, birth control advocates, and socialist feminists, demanded more profound social changes.

. . . But the same distinctions and tensions . . . have appeared in [the twentieth-century women movement]. One wing focused mainly on women's rights—adoption of ERA, legal/political rights and representation and civil rights for women of different classes, races and sexual orientations. The other wing began as "radical women's liberation" and later branched off into many more specialized groups working on abortion rights; protection of women against violence and sexual harassment; the opening up to women of nontraditional occupations: self-empowerment and the creation of women's cultural institutions, ranging from lesbian groupings to women's music festivals and pop culture. The two informally defined wings of the movement often overlapped, sometimes collaborated on specific narrow issues, and recently have worked more and more on bridge-building. The Women's Studies movement has struggled long and hard to bridge the two wings and encompass them educationally. Further, new forms of feminism by women of color or women who define themselves as "different" from the majority in various ways have sprung up and served their own constituencies. Their existence has not weakened the movement, as its critics like to claim, but has strengthened it immensely by grounding it more firmly in different constituencies.

Let us not forget, ever, that when we talk about women's rights we talk about the rights of half the human race. No one expects all men to have the same interests, issues or demands. We should therefore never expect women to have one agenda, one set of issues or demands.

The women's rights demands first raised at Seneca Falls have in the United States been generally achieved for middle-class white women. They have been partially achieved for working-class women and women of color, but progress has been very uneven. . . .

The feminization of poverty and the increasing income gap between the rich and the poor have turned many legal gains won by women into empty shells. An example is the way in which legal restrictions on women's right to choose abortion have fallen more heavily on poor women than on the well-to-do. The uneven availability of child care for working mothers is another example.

The cultural transformation on which demands for woman's emancipation build, has been enormous. Many demands that seemed outrageous 150 years ago are now commonly accepted, such as a woman's right to equal guardianship of her children, to divorce, to jury duty, to acceptance in nontraditional occupations. Female police and fire officers and female military personnel are accepted everywhere without question. Women's participation in competitive sports is another area in which progress has been great, though it is far from complete. Many other feminist demands that seemed outrageously radical thirty years ago have become commonplace today—the acceptance of lesbians as "normal" members of the community; single motherhood; the criminal character of sexual harassment and marital rape. The acceptance of such ideas is still uneven and different in different places, but generally, the feminist program has been accepted by millions of people who refuse to identify themselves as "feminists." What critics decry as the splintering and diffusion of the movement is actually its greatest strength today.

It should also be recognized that the aims of feminism are transformative, but its methods have been peaceful reform, persuasion and education. For 150 years feminists have organized, lobbied, marched, petitioned, put their bodies on the line in demonstrations, and have overcome ancient prejudices by heroic acts of self-help. Whatever gains were won, had to be won step by step, over and over again. Nothing "was given" to women; whatever gains we made we have had to earn. And perhaps the most precious "right" we have won in these two centuries, is the right to know our own history, to draw on the knowledge and experience of the women before us, to celebrate and emulate our heroines and finally to know that "greatness" is not a sexual attribute.

WHAT MEANING DOES SENECA FALLS HOLD TODAY?

- It shows that a small group of people, armed with a persuasive analysis of grievances and an argument based on generally held moral and religious beliefs, can, if they are willing and able to work hard at organizing, create a transformative mass movement. The women who launched a small movement in 1848 had to build, county by county, state by state, the largest grassroots movement of the nineteenth century and then build it again in the twentieth century to transform the right to vote into the right to equal representation.

- Seneca Falls and the movement it spawned show that legal changes can be reversed, unless social and cultural transformations sustain them. Over the past 150 years all of the grievances listed at Seneca Falls have been resolved or at least dealt with, though new inequities and grievances arise in each generation. The "specter that haunted Europe" left some gains, but mostly bloodshed, terror and devastation in its wake, and most of the inequities it sought to adjust are still with us. Feminism has behind it a record of solid gains without the costs of bloody war and revolution.

Although the media and many politicians with monotonous frequency declare feminism to be dead, many of its goals have been accomplished and its momentum, worldwide, is steadily rising. The worldwide movement of women for their emancipation is irreversible. It will continue to live and grow, as long as women anywhere have "grievances" they can proclaim and as long as they are willing and able to organize to rectify them.

DOCUMENTS: Claiming Rights II

Declaration of Sentiments, 1848

The rhetoric of the Declaration of Sentiments was borrowed from the Declaration of Independence. Through its lines flowed the conviction that the Revolution had made implicit promises to women which had not been kept.

Seneca Falls, New York,
July 19–20, 1848

When, in the course of human events, it becomes necessary for one portion of the family of man to assume among the people of the earth a position different from that which they have hitherto occupied, but one to which the laws of nature and of nature's God entitle them, a decent respect to the opinions of mankind requires that they should declare the causes that impel them to such a course.

We hold these truths to be self-evident: that all men and women are created equal; that they are endowed by their Creator with certain inalienable rights; that among these are life, liberty, and the pursuit of happiness; that to secure these rights governments are instituted, deriving their just powers from the consent of the governed. Whenever any form of government becomes destructive of these ends, it is the right of those who suffer from it to refuse allegiance to it, and to insist upon the institution of a new government, laying its foundation on such principles, and organizing its powers in such form, as to them shall seem most likely to effect their safety and happiness. Prudence, indeed, will dictate that governments long established should not be changed for light and transient causes; and accordingly all experience hath shown that mankind are more disposed to suffer, while evils are sufferable, than to right themselves by abolishing the forms to which they were accustomed. But when a long train of abuses and usurpations, pursuing invariably the same object evinces a design to reduce them under absolute despotism, it is their duty to throw off such govern-ment, and to provide new guards for their future security. Such has been the patient sufferance of the women under this government, and such is now the necessity which constrains them to demand the equal station to which they are entitled.

The history of mankind is a history of repeated injuries and usurpations on the part of man toward woman, having in direct object the establishment of an absolute tyranny over her. To prove this, let facts be submitted to a candid world.

He has never permitted her to exercise her inalienable right to the elective franchise.

He has compelled her to submit to laws, in the formation of which she had no voice.

He has withheld from her rights which are given to the most ignorant and degraded men—both native and foreigners.

Having deprived her of this first right of a citizen, the elective franchise, thereby leaving her without representation in the halls of legislation, he has oppressed her on all sides.

He has made her, if married, in the eye of the law, civilly dead.

He has taken from her all right in property, even to the wages she earns.

He has made her, morally, an irresponsible being, as she can commit many crimes with impunity, provided they be done in the presence of her husband. In the covenant of marriage, she is compelled to promise obedience to her husband, he becoming, to all intents and purposes, her master—the law giving him power to deprive her of her liberty, and to administer chastisement.

He has so framed the laws of divorce, as

Declaration of Sentiments, in *History of Woman Suffrage*, edited by Elizabeth Cady Stanton, Susan B. Anthony, and Matilda Joslyn Gage, vol. 1 (New York: Fowler & Wells, 1881), pp. 70–71.

to what shall be the proper causes, and in case of separation, to whom the guardianship of the children shall be given, as to be wholly regardless of the happiness of women—the law, in all cases, going upon a false supposition of the supremacy of man, and giving all power into his hands.

After depriving her of all rights as a married woman, if single, and the owner of property, he has taxed her to support a government which recognizes her only when her property can be made profitable to it.

He has monopolized nearly all the profitable employments, and from those she is permitted to follow, she receives but a scanty remuneration. He closes against her all the avenues to wealth and distinction which he considers most honorable to himself. As a teacher of theology, medicine, or law, she is not known.

He has denied her the facilities for obtaining a thorough education, all colleges being closed against her.

He allows her in Church, as well as State, but a subordinate position, claiming Apostolic authority for her exclusion from the ministry, and, with some exceptions, from any public participation in the affairs of the Church.

He has created a false public sentiment by giving to the world a different code of morals for men and women, by which moral delinquencies which exclude women from society, are not only tolerated, but deemed of little account in man.

He has usurped the prerogative of Jehovah himself, claiming it as his right to assign for her a sphere of action, when that belongs to her conscience and to her God.

He has endeavored, in every way that he could, to destroy her confidence in her own powers, to lessen her self-respect, and to make her willing to lead a dependent and abject life.

Now, in view of this entire disfranchisement of one-half the people of this country, their social and religious degradation—in view of the unjust laws above mentioned, and because women do feel themselves aggrieved, oppressed, and fraudulently deprived of their most sacred rights, we insist that they have immediate admission to all the rights and privileges which belong to them as citizens of the United States.

In entering upon the great work before us, we anticipate no small amount of misconception, misrepresentation, and ridicule; but we shall use every instrumentality within our power to effect our object. We shall employ agents, circulate tracts, petition the State and National legislatures, and endeavor to enlist the pulpit and the press in our behalf. We hope this Convention will be followed by a series of Conventions embracing every part of the country.

The following resolutions were discussed by Lucretia Mott, Thomas and Mary Ann McClintock, Amy Post, Catharine A. F. Stebbins, and others, and were adopted:

WHEREAS, The great precept of nature is conceded to be, that "man shall pursue his own true and substantial happiness." Blackstone in his Commentaries remarks, that this law of Nature being coeval with mankind, and dictated by God himself, is of course superior in obligation to any other. It is binding over all the globe, in all countries, and at all times; no human laws are of any validity if contrary to this, and such of them as are valid, derive all their force, and all their validity, and all their authority, mediately and immediately, from this original; therefore;

Resolved, That such laws as conflict, in any way, with the true and substantial happiness of woman, are contrary to the great precept of nature and of no validity, for this is "superior in obligation to any other."

Resolved, That all laws which prevent woman from occupying such a station in society as her conscience shall dictate, or which place her in a position inferior to that of man, are contrary to the great precept of nature, and therefore of no force or authority.

Resolved, That woman is man's equal— was intended to be so by the Creator, and the highest good of the race demands that she should be recognized as such.

Resolved, That the women of this country ought to be enlightened in regard to the laws under which they live, that they may no longer publish their degradation by declaring themselves satisfied with their present position, nor their ignorance by asserting that they have all the rights they want.

Resolved, That inasmuch as man, while claiming for himself intellectual superiority, does accord to woman moral superiority, it is preeminently his duty to encourage her to speak and teach, as she has an opportunity, in all religious assemblies.

Resolved, That the same amount of virtue, delicacy, and refinement of behavior that is required of woman in the social state, should also be required of man, and the same transgressions should be visited with equal severity on both man and woman.

Resolved, That the objection of indelicacy and impropriety, which is so often brought against woman when she addresses a public audience, comes with a very ill-grace from those who encourage, by their attendance, her appearance on the stage, in the concert, or in feats of the circus.

Resolved, That woman has too long rested satisfied in the circumscribed limits which corrupt customs and a perverted application of the Scriptures have marked out for her, and that it is time she should move in the enlarged sphere which her great Creator has assigned her.

Resolved, That it is the duty of the women of this country to secure to themselves their sacred right to the elective franchise.

Resolved, That the equality of human rights results necessarily from the fact of the identity of the race in capabilities and responsibilities.

Resolved, therefore, That, being invested by the Creator with the same capabilities, and the same consciousness of responsibility for their exercise, it is demonstrably the right and duty of woman, equally with man, to promote every righteous cause by every righteous means; and especially in regard to the great subjects of morals and religion, it is self-evidently her right to participate with her brother in teaching them, both in private and in public, by writing and by speaking, by any instrumentalities proper to be used, and in any assemblies proper to be held; and this being a self-evident truth growing out of the divinely implanted principles of human nature, any custom or authority adverse to it, whether modern or wearing the hoary sanction of antiquity, is to be regarded as a self-evident falsehood, and at war with mankind.

At the last session Lucretia Mott offered and spoke to the following resolution:

Resolved, That the speedy success of our cause depends upon the zealous and untiring efforts of both men and women, for the overthrow of the monopoly of the pulpit, and for the securing to woman an equal participation with men in the various trades, professions, and commerce.

Married Women's Property Acts, New York State, 1848, 1860

Ironically, the first married women's property acts, passed in Mississippi in 1839 and in New York in 1848, were supported by many male legislators out of a desire to preserve the estates of married daughters against spendthrift sons-in-law. Four out of the five sections of the Mississippi act broadened the rights of married women over their own slaves.

Note the limits of the 1848 New York law and the ways in which women's rights were extended by the 1860 revision. In 1860 married women were also confirmed in the joint guardianship of their children.

The statutes were narrowly interpreted by most courts, not only in New York but in other states that established similar legislation. For example, although married women were authorized to "carry on any trade or business, and perform any labor or services on her sole or separate account," that authorization was regularly interpreted as applying only when her work was not done on family property. She could rarely make claims for her earnings within the family or against her husband's estate; deep into the twentieth century farm women had, for example, no legal claim to the "butter and egg money" that customary practice enabled them to claim because they did the hard work of the barn and chicken coop.

1848

The real and personal property of any female [now married and] who may hereafter marry, and which she shall own at the time of marriage, and the rents issues and profits thereof shall not be subject to the disposal of her husband, nor be liable for his debts, and shall continue her sole and separate property, as if she were a single female. . . .

It shall be lawful for any married female to receive, by gift, grant, devise or bequest, from any person other than her husband and hold to her sole and separate use, as if she were a single female, real and personal property, and the rents, issues and profits thereof, and the same shall not be subject to the disposal of her husband, nor be liable for his debts. . . .

1860

[The provisions of the law of 1848 were retained, and others were added:]
A married woman may bargain, sell, assign, and transfer her separate personal property, and carry on any trade or business, and perform any labor or services on her sole and sep-

arate account, and the earnings of any married woman from her trade . . . shall be her sole and separate property, and may be used or invested by her in her own name. . . .

Any married woman may, while married, sue and be sued in all matters having relation to her . . . sole and separate property . . . in the same manner as if she were sole. And any married woman may bring and maintain an action in her own name, for damages, against any person or body corporate, for any injury to her person or character, the same as if she were sole; and the money received upon the settlement . . . shall be her sole and separate property.

No bargain or contract made by any married woman, in respect to her sole and separate property . . . shall be binding upon her husband, or render him or his property in any way liable therefor.

Every married woman is hereby constituted and declared to be the joint guardian of her children, with her husband, with equal powers, rights, and duties in regard to them, with the husband. . . .

Laws of the State of New-York, Passed at the Seventy-First Session of the Legislature . . . (Albany, 1848), pp. 307–8; *Laws of the State of New York, Passed at the Eighty-Third Session of the Legislature* . . . (Albany, 1860), pp. 157–59.

NELL IRVIN PAINTER

Sojourner Truth's Defense of the Rights of Women (as reported in 1851; rewritten in 1863)

Sojourner Truth (ca. 1797–1883) is often equated with the phrase "ar'n't I a woman?" which symbolizes black women in American history and strong women of any race. Truth, who was born a slave named Isabella in New York's Hudson River Valley, was emancipated by state law in 1827, moved to New York City in 1828, worked in private households to gain her living, became an unorthodox Methodist, and made a reputation as an exhorter. In 1843 divine inspiration directed her to take the name Sojourner Truth and become an itinerant preacher. Addressing outdoor camp meetings on Long Island and up the Connecticut River Valley, she reached the utopian Northampton [Massachusetts] Association in the winter of 1843–1844, where she settled and met abolitionists like William Lloyd Garrison and Frederick Douglass.

In 1845 Douglass published his first autobiography, which became a best-seller in England and the United States and inspired Sojourner Truth. Unlike Douglass, Truth was illiterate, and she dictated her narrative to Olive Gilbert, a teacher from Connecticut. In 1850 Truth paid to have *The Narrative of Sojourner Truth* published and began traveling the reform lecture circuit, speaking against slavery and for women's rights. Wherever she appeared she sold her *Narrative*, which provided her material support.

A women's rights convention in Akron, Ohio, in 1851 furnished Truth an opportunity to address a sympathetic gathering and sell books. The 1851 report by one of Truth's close associates in the Salem *Antislavery Bugle* runs like this:

One of the most unique and interesting speeches of the Convention was made by Sojourner Truth, an emancipated slave. It is impossible to transfer it to paper, or convey any adequate idea of the effect it produced upon the audience. Those only can appreciate it who saw her powerful form, her whole-souled, earnest gestures, and listened to her strong and truthful tones. She came forward to the platform and addressing the President said with great simplicity:

May I say a few words? Receiving an affirmative answer, she proceeded; I want to say a few words about this matter. I am a woman's rights. [*sic*] I have as much muscle as any man, and can do as much work as any man. I have plowed and reaped and husked and chopped and mowed, and can any man do more than that? I have heard much about the sexes being equal; I can carry as much as any man, and can eat as much too, if I can get it. I am as strong as any man that is now. As for intellect, all I can say is, if a woman have a pint and man a quart—why cant she have her little pint full? You need not be afraid to give us our rights for fear we will take too much,—for we cant take more than our pint'll hold. The poor men seem to be all in confusion, and dont know what to do. Why children, if you have woman's rights give it to her and you will feel better. You will have your own rights, and they wont be so much trouble. I cant read, but I can hear. I have heard the bible and have learned that Eve caused man to sin. Well if woman upset the world, do give her a chance to set it right side up again. The Lady has spoken about Jesus, how he never spurned woman from him, and she was right. When Lazarus died, Mary and Martha came to him with faith and love and besought him to raise their brother. And Jesus wept—and Lazarus came forth. And how came Jesus into the world? Through God who created him and woman who bore him. Man, where is your part? But the women are coming up blessed be God and a few of the man are coming up with them. But man is in a tight place, the poor slave is on him, woman is coming on him, and he is surely between a hawk and a buzzard.

Sojourner Truth (ca. 1797–1883) Is better known in the twentieth century for words she did not utter—"ar'n't I a woman?"—than for her fierce and exemplary insistence on asserting her rights to speak and act publicly and to religious expression. (Courtesy of Photographs and Prints Division of The Schomburg Center for Research in Black Culture, The New York Public Library, Astor, Lenox and Tilden Foundations)

The same newspaper also ran a report of the speech given by Frances Dana Gage (1808–1884), who chaired the convention. Gage was a lecturer, journalist, and poet who published mainly in the antislavery and feminist press. A more radical feminist and abolitionist than Harriet Beecher Stowe, Gage was less well known. In 1851 Gage used Sojourner Truth as a character called Winna in a story she serialized in a feminist newspaper, but she did not describe Truth's 1851 speech until a good deal later. In the meanwhile, Truth continued speaking and selling her books.

In the nineteenth century, as today, authors commonly asked celebrities for blurbs to use as advertisement. After the phenomenal success of *Uncle Tom's Cabin* in 1851–1852 made Harriet Beecher Stowe famous, Truth visited her to request a blurb, which was forthcoming. In subsequent years, Stowe mentioned Truth to her friends privately, but she did not publish anything until the 1860s. Once the Emancipation Proclamation and the acceptance of black men into the Union Army made the Civil War into an acknowledged struggle over slavery, "the Negro" became a popular topic of discourse; then Stowe tapped into her recollections of Truth to shape an essay in the *Atlantic Monthly,* one of the most respectable periodicals of the time. "Sojourner Truth, the Libyan Sibyl" appeared in April 1863.

The publication of Stowe's article inspired Gage to write her own essay and invent the phrase, "ar'n't I a woman?" As long as the values of consumers of journalism were more attuned to the sentimentalism of Stowe than the radicalism of Gage, Stowe's "Libyan Sibyl" remained more popular, but at the end of the nineteenth century, the balance began to tip in Gage's favor.

Susan B. Anthony (Gage's friend since the 1850s) and Elizabeth Cady Stanton included Gage's report, not Stowe's, in *The History of Woman Suffrage,* where woman suffragists found a figure of Sojourner Truth that was useful against antagonists. In the mid-twentieth century American tastes changed, rejecting Stowe's quaint little exotic and embracing Gage's bold feminist. The 1851 report of Truth's speech, however, still seems too moderate to be useful as symbolism, even though it captures the historic—as opposed to the emblematic—Sojourner Truth. At least for the time being, a symbol rather than an individual black woman's utterance is what American culture demands.

DREW GILPIN FAUST

Enemies in Our Households: Confederate Women and Slavery

The Civil War profoundly disrupted and reshaped American society; more people died in it than in all America's subsequent wars put together. It tested the stability of the Union and the meaning of democracy; Confederates insisted that their vision of a republic, which rested on racial hierarchy and the subordination of blacks, sustained the same claims to self-determination that had been central to the principles of the Revolution of 1776. The war would involve civilians in novel ways.

Because soldiers were recruited as companies from the same locality, it was not impossible for women to dress as men and enlist; buddies kept their secrets. A conservative estimate is that some 400 women joined in this way. A handful of women crossed military lines as spies, some disguising their race or their gender in the process. Thousands more women were recruited as hospital workers in both North and South; late in the war the Union recruited hundreds of freedwomen for this service. The bureaucracy of the federal government was vastly expanded during the war, and the personnel shortage was solved by hiring, for the first time in U.S. history, women to work in the same offices as men doing similar work.

Throughout the nation, North and South, familiar patterns of gender relations were disrupted, in a manner not unlike what had happened when men left for the Gold Rush, but on a far greater and more frightening scale. In the South, as Drew Faust explains, the departure of white men for war meant that white women were challenged to assume authority and to stabilize slavery despite the loss of the usual forms of force that had kept it in place. They discovered that they were living "with enemies in our own households." How they responded to this challenge varied; they were often profoundly transformed by their experiences.

What challenges did elite women face at the beginning of the war? What were some of the ways in which they responded? What allies did they have? What forms of resistance to authority did slaves engage in? How did the disruptions of the war bring into question traditional relations between white women and men?

When slaveholding men departed for battle, white women on farms and plantations across the South assumed direction of the region's "peculiar institution." In the antebellum years white men had borne overwhelming responsibility for slavery's daily management and per-

From *Mothers of Invention: Women of the Slaveholding South in the American Civil War* by Drew Gilpin Faust. Copyright © 1996 by the University of North Carolina Press. Used by permission of the publisher. Notes have been renumbered and edited.

petuation. But as war changed the shape of southern households, it necessarily transformed the structures of domestic authority, requiring white women to exercise unaccustomed—and unsought—power in defense of public as well as private order. Slavery was, as Confederate vice-president Alexander Stephens proclaimed, the "cornerstone" of the region's society, economy, and politics. Yet slavery's survival depended less on sweeping dictates of state policy than on tens of thousands of individual acts of personal domination exercised by particular masters over particular slaves. As wartime opportunity encouraged slaves openly to assert their desire for freedom, the daily struggle over coercion and control on hundreds of plantations and farms became just as crucial to defense of the southern way of life as any military encounter. Women called to manage increasingly restive and even rebellious slaves were in a significant sense garrisoning a second front in the South's war against Yankee domination.[1] . . .

Although white southerners—both male and female—might insist that politics was not, even in the changed circumstances of wartime, an appropriate part of woman's sphere, the female slave manager necessarily served as a pillar of the South's political order. White women's actions as slave mistresses were crucial to Confederate destinies, for the viability of the southern agricultural economy and the stability of the social order as well as the continuing loyalty of the civilian population all depended on successful slave control.

. . . The very meaning of mastery itself was rooted in the concepts of masculinity and male power. From the outset, Confederate leaders were uneasy about the transfer of such responsibility to women. . . .

As support grew in the fall of 1862 for some official draft exemption for slave managers, the *Macon Daily Telegraph* demanded, "Is it possible that Congress thinks . . . our women can control the slaves and oversee the farms? Do they suppose that our patriotic mothers, sisters and daughters can assume and discharge the active duties and drudgery of an overseer? Certainly not. They know better." In October Congress demonstrated that it did indeed know better, passing a law exempt-

ing from service one white man on each plantation of twenty or more slaves. But the soon infamous [law] . . . triggered enormous popular resentment, both from nonslaveholders who regarded it as valuing the lives of the elite over their own and from smaller slaveholders who were not included in its scope.[2]

In an effort to silence this threatening outburst of class hostility and at the same time meet the South's ever increasing manpower needs, the Confederate Congress repeatedly amended conscription policy, both broadening the age of eligibility and limiting exemptions. . . . This erosion of the statutory foundation for overseer exemptions greatly increased the difficulty of finding men not subject to military duty who could, as the original bill had phrased it, "secure the proper police of the country." Women across the Confederacy would find themselves unable to obtain the assistance of white men on their plantations and farms.

Conscription policy reveals fundamental Confederate assumptions, for it represents significant choices made by the Confederate leadership, choices that in important ways defined issues of class as more central to Confederate survival than those of gender. . . . White women in slaveowning households found their needs relegated to a position of secondary importance in comparison with the demands of nonslaveholding men. These men could vote, and the Confederacy required their service on the battlefield; retaining their loyalty was a priority. Minimizing class divisions within the Confederacy was imperative—even if ultimately unsuccessful. Addressing emerging gender divisions seemed less critical, because women—even the "privileged" ladies of the slaveowning elite—neither voted nor wrote editorials nor bore arms.[3]

With ever escalating military manpower demands, however, white women came to assume responsibility for directing the slave system that was so central a cause and purpose of the war. Yet they could not forget the promises of male protection and obligation that they believed their due. Women's troubling experiences as slave managers generated a growing fear and resentment of the burdens imposed by the disintegrating institution. Ultimately these tensions did much to undermine women's active support for both slavery and the Confederate cause. And throughout the South eroding slave control and diminishing plantation efficiency directly contributed to failures of morale and productivity on the homefront.

UNPROTECTED AND AFRAID

Women agreed with the Georgia newspaper that had proclaimed them unfit masters. "Where there are so many negroes upon places as upon ours," wrote an Alabama woman to the governor, "it is quite necessary that there should be men who can and will control them, especially at this time." Faced with the prospect of being left with sixty slaves, a Mississippi planter's wife expressed similar sentiments. "Do you think," she demanded of Governor John Pettus, "that this woman's hand can keep them in check?" Women compelled to assume responsibility over slaves tended to regard their new role more as a duty than an opportunity. Like many southern soldiers, they were conscripts rather than volunteers. As Lizzie Neblett explained to her husband, Will, when he enlisted in the 20th Texas Infantry, her impending service as agricultural and slave manager was "a coercive one."[4]

Women's reluctance derived in no small part from a profound sense of their own incapacities. One Mississippi woman complained that she lacked sufficient "moral courage" to govern slaves; another believed "managing negroes . . . beyond my power." "Master's eye and voice," Catherine Edmondston remarked, "are much more potent than mistress'." . . . Slaves themselves frequently seemed to share their mistresses' views of their own incapacities. Ellen Moore of Virginia complained that her laborers "all think I am a kind of usurper & have no authority over them." As war and the promise of freedom encouraged increasing black assertiveness, white women discovered themselves in charge of an institution quite different from the one their husbands, brothers, fathers, and sons had managed before military conflict commenced.[5]

Female apprehensions about slave mastery arose from fears of this very rebelliousness and from a sense of the special threat slave violence might pose to white women. Keziah Brevard, a fifty-eight-year-old South Carolina widow, lived in almost constant fear of her sizable slave force. "It is dreadful to dwell on insurrections," she acknowledged. Yet "many an hour have I laid awake in my life thinking of our danger."[6] . . .

Early in the war, Mary Chesnut, who professed never to have had any fear of her slaves, felt compelled to reconsider her own safety when her cousin Betsey Witherspoon was smothered by her servants. An elderly widow who lived alone with her slaves, Witherspoon was well known as an ineffective and indulgent manager. Her murder underlined both the inadequacies and vulnerabilities of white women as slave masters; her fate was exactly what her South Carolina neighbor Keziah Brevard most feared. Another Carolina widow, Ada Bacot, contemplated Witherspoon's death and the prospects of her own slaves' loyalty with similar dismay. "I fear twould take very little to make them put me out of the way," she wrote.[7] . . .

. . . Reports of individual acts of violence proliferated as well. Ada Bacot was certain the fire in her neighbors' house was set by their slave Abel; Laura Lee was horrified when occupying troops released a Winchester slave convicted of murdering her mistress. In September 1862 the *Mobile Advertiser and Register* noted that a slave had succeeded in poisoning his master; the same month the *Richmond Enquirer* recorded the conviction of one Lavinia for torching her mistress's house.[8] . . .

By the middle years of the war, women had begun publicly to voice their fears, writing hundreds of letters to state and Confederate officials imploring that men be detailed from military service to control the slaves. A group of women living near New Bern petitioned North Carolina Governor Zebulon Vance for exemptions for the few men who still remained at home. "We pray your Excellency to consider that in the absence of all protection the female portion of this community may be subjected to a system of outrage that may be justly denominated the harrow of harrows more terrable to the contemplation of the virtuous maiden and matron than death." A petition to the Confederate secretary of war from a similar collection of "Ladies of the N.E. beat of Jas[per] County, Miss." sought male protection against an anticipated slave insurrection. If that was impossible, they requested arms and ammunition to defend themselves from "the demonic invasion" so that "we die with honor & innocence sustained."[9]

These women chose different euphemisms to express their anxieties—insult, outrage, "harrow of harrows," dishonor, stain, and molestation—but the theme was undeniably sexual. The Old South had justified white woman's subordination in terms of her biological difference, emphasizing an essential female weakness that rested ultimately in sexual vulnerability. In a society based on the oppression of a potentially hostile population of 4 million black slaves, such vulnerability assumed special significance. On this foundation of race, the white South erected its particular—and particularly compelling—logic of female dependence. Only the white man's strength could provide adequate and necessary protection. The very word *protection* was invoked again and again by Confederate women petitioning for what they believed [was] the fundamental right guaranteed them by the paternalistic social order of the South: "I feel unprotected and afraid," "unable to protect myself," "unable to stand up under her burden without the assistance of some white male to protect her." Denied such assurances of safety, many women would be impelled to question—even if implicitly—the logic of their willing acceptance of their own inferiority. In seeking, like the ladies of Jasper County, Mississippi, to protect themselves, Confederate women profoundly undermined the legitimacy of their subordination, demonstrating that they did not—indeed could not—depend on the supposed superior strength of white men.[10]

Significantly, the "demonic" invaders these Mississippi women most feared were not Yankees but rebellious slaves. In their terror of an insurgent black population, white southern women advanced their own definition of wartime priorities, one seemingly not shared by the Confederate leadership and government. "I fear the blacks more than I do the Yankees," confessed Mrs. A. Ingraham of besieged Vicksburg. . . . Living with slavery in wartime was, one Virginia woman observed, living with "enemies in our own households."[11]

The arrival of black soldiers in parts of the South represented the conjunction and culmination of these fears. Mary Lee of Winchester, Virginia, came "near fainting" when the troops appeared; she felt "more unnerved than by any sight I have seen since the war [began]."

These soldiers were at once men, blacks, and national enemies—her gender, racial, and political opposites, the quintessential powerful and hostile Other. Their occupying presence in Winchester reminded her so forcefully of her weakness and vulnerability that she responded with a swoon, an unwanted and unwonted display of the feminine impotence and delicacy she had struggled to overcome during long years of her own as well as Confederate independence.[12]

Yet women often denied or repressed these profound fears of racial violence, confronting them only in the darkest hours of anxious, sleepless nights. Constance Cary Harrison remembered that in the daytime, apprehensions about slave violence seemed "preposterous," but at night, "there was the fear . . . dark, boding, oppressive and altogether hateful . . . the ghost that refused to be laid."[13] . . .

Some women in fact regarded their slaves as protectors, hoping for the loyalty that the many tales of "faithful servants" would enshrine in Confederate popular culture and, later, within the myth of the Lost Cause. Elizabeth Saxon, in a typically rose-colored remembrance of slavery during the war, recalled in 1905 that "not an outrage was perpetrated, no house was burned. . . . [O]n lonely farms women with little children slept at peace, guarded by a sable crowd, whom they perfectly trusted. . . . [I]n no land was ever a people so tender and helpful." The discrepancy between this portrait and the anxieties of everyday life on Confederate plantations underscores how white southerners, both during the war and afterward, struggled to retain a view of slavery as a benevolent institution, appreciated by blacks as well as whites. During the war such "faithful servant" stories served to calm white fears. But examples of persisting white trust and confidence in slaves cannot be discounted entirely, nor can the stories themselves be uniformly dismissed as white inventions. There were in fact slaves who buried the master's silver to hide it from the enemy; there were slaves, like one Catherine Edmondston described, who drew knives to defend mistresses against Yankee troops. Such incidents reinforced white southerners' desire not to believe that men and women they thought they had known intimately—sometimes all their lives—had suddenly become murderers and revolutionaries.[14]

Much of the complexity of wartime relationships between white women and slaves arose because women increasingly relied on slaves' labor, competence, and even companionship at a time when slaves saw diminishing motivation for work or obedience. White women's dependence on their slaves grew simultaneously with slaves' independence of their owners, creating a troubling situation of confusion and ambivalence for mistresses compelled constantly to reassess, to interrogate, and to revise their assumptions as they struggled to reconcile need with fear. . . . Some slave mistresses, especially in isolated plantation settings, found that in changed wartime households, their closest adult connections were with female slaves. When Rhoda died in April 1862, her owner Anna Green wrote in despair to her sister. "I feel like I have lost my only friend and I do believe she was the most faithful friend I had [even] if she was a servant." Leila Callaway described the death from smallpox of her slave Susanna in almost identical terms. "Next to my own dear family Susanna was my warmest best friend." "I have no one now in your absence," she informed her husband, "to look to for protection." In the disruptions of the South's hierarchies of gender and race, Leila Callaway had invested a black woman with some of the responsibilities—emotional and otherwise—of the absent white man.[15]

. . . Maria Hawkins keenly felt the absence of her slave protector Moses and wrote to Governor Vance with a variation of the hundreds of letters to southern officials seeking discharge of husbands and sons. Hawkins requested Moses' release from impressment as a laborer on coastal fortifications. "He slept in the house, every night while at home, & protected everything in the house & yard & at these perilous times when deserters are committing depredations, on plantations every day, I am really so much frightened every night, that I am up nearly all night." In Hawkins's particular configuration of gender and racial anxieties, a black male protector was far preferable to no male at all.[16]

THE FRUITS OF THE WAR

Within the context of everyday life in the Confederacy, most women slaveholders confronted neither murderous revolutionaries nor the unfailingly loyal retainers of "moonlight and magnolias" tradition. Instead they faced complex human beings whose desires for freedom expressed themselves in ways that varied with changing means and opportunities as slavery weakened steadily under unrelenting northern military pressure.

Often opportunity was greatest in areas close to Union lines, and slave-owners in these locations confronted the greatest challenges of discipline. . . . Ada Bacot, widowed South Carolina plantation owner, believed her "orders disregarded more & more every day. I can do nothing so must submit, which is anything but pleasant." When she left Carolina for a nursing post at the Monticello Hospital in Charlottesville, however, she soon discovered "Virginia Negroes are not near so servile as those of S.C." . . . When an adolescent slave named William defied her order to clean up the dinner table in the house where she and the other nurses and doctors lodged, she called him to task. But the young slave was "so impertinent that I slaped him in the mouth before I knew what I did." His mother rushed from the kitchen to his defense, provoking Bacot to threaten both slaves with punishment. Unlike many Confederate slave managers, though, Bacot did not live in a world comprised exclusively of women. She turned for aid to the white male doctors who were also residents of the household, and they whipped both irate mother and insolent child.[17]

For many white women this physical dimension of slave control proved most troubling. . . .

Just as "paternalism" and "mastery" were rooted in concepts of masculinity, so violence was similarly gendered as male within the ideology of the Old South. Recourse to physical force in support of male honor and white supremacy was regarded as the right, even the responsibility, of each white man—within his household, on his plantation, in his community, and with the outbreak of war, for his nation. Women slave managers inherited a social order that depended on the threat and often the use of violence. Throughout the history of the peculiar institution, slave mistresses had in fact slapped, hit, and even brutally whipped their slaves—particularly slave women or children. But their relationship to this exercise of physical power was significantly different from that of their men. No gendered code of honor celebrated women's physical power or dominance. A contrasting yet parallel ideology extolled female sensitivity, weakness, and vulnerability. In the prewar years, exercise of the violence fundamental to slavery was overwhelmingly the responsibility and prerogative of white men. A white woman disciplined and punished as the master's subordinate and surrogate. Rationalized, systematic, autonomous, and instrumental use of violence belonged to men.

Ada Bacot surprised herself when she lashed out and slapped young William, and it was in just such moments of rage that many Confederate women embraced physical force. But for the kind of rationalized punishment intended to function as the mainstay of slave discipline, Bacot turned to men. Women alone customarily sought overseers, male relatives, or neighbors to undertake physical coercion of slaves, especially slave men. As white men disappeared to war, however, finding such help became increasingly difficult. . . .

As slaves grew more assertive in anticipation of their freedom, their female managers regarded physical coercion as at once more essential and more impossible. Some white women began to bargain with violence, trying to make slavery seem benign in hopes of retaining their slaves' service, if not their loyalty. Avoiding physical punishment even in the face of insolence or poor work, they endeavored to keep their slaves from departing altogether. . . . [In Texas,] Lizzie Neblett urged her part-time overseer not to beat a slave in response to his insubordination. "I told him not to whip Joe, as long as he done his work well . . . that he might run away & we might never get him & if he never done me any good he might my children." Lizzie worried as well that whipping might provoke violent retaliation against managers who possessed the obvious vulnerability of the Confederacy's white females. Many had, she noted, become "actually affraid to whip the negros."[18]

The Old South's social hierarchies had created a spectrum of legitimate access to violence, so that social empowerment was inextricably bound up with the right to employ physical force. Violence was all but required of white men of all classes, a cultural principle rendered explicit by the coming of war and conscription. Black slaves, by contrast, were forbidden the use of violence entirely, except

within their own communities, where the dominant society chose to regard it as essentially invisible. White women stood upon an ill-defined middle ground, where behavior and ideology often diverged.

The Civil War exacerbated this very tension . . . even on the homefront, women felt inadequate; their understanding of their gender undermined their effectiveness. Just as their inability to bear arms left Confederate women feeling "useless," so their inhibitions about violence made many females regard themselves as failures at slave management. As Lizzie Neblett wrote of her frustration in the effort to control eleven recalcitrant slaves, "I am so sick of trying to do a man's business when I am nothing but, a poor contemptible piece of multiplying human flesh tied to the house by a crying young one, looked upon as belonging to a race of inferior beings." The language she chose to describe her self-loathing is significant, for she borrowed it from the vocabulary of race as well as gender. Invoking the objective constraints of biology—"multiplying flesh"—as well as the socially constructed limitations of status—"looked upon as belonging to a race of inferior beings"—she identified herself not with the white elite, not with those in whose interest the war was being fought, but with the South's oppressed and disadvantaged. Increasingly, even though self-indulgently, she came to regard herself as the victim rather than the beneficiary of her region's slave society. Lizzie Neblett's uniquely documented experience with violence and slavery deserves exploration in some detail, for it illustrates not simply the contradictions inherent in female management, but the profound personal crisis of identity generated by her new and unaccustomed role.[19]

TROUBLED IN MIND

When her husband departed for war in the spring of 1863, Lizzie had set about the task of management committed to "doing my best" but was apprehensive both about her ignorance of agriculture and about the behavior she might expect from her eleven slaves. Their initial response to her direction, however, seemed promising. "The negros," she wrote Will in late April, "seem to be mightily stirred up about making a good crop."[20]

By harvest, however, the situation had already changed. "The negros are doing nothing," Lizzie wrote Will at the height of first cotton picking in mid-August. . . . Lizzie harbored few illusions about the long-term loyalty of her own black family. "I dont think we have one who will stay with us."[21]

After a harvest that fell well below the previous year's achievement, Lizzie saw the need for new managerial arrangements. Will had provided for a male neighbor to keep a general supervisory eye over the Neblett slave force, but Lizzie wrote Will in the fall of 1863 that she had contracted to pay a Mr. Meyers to spend three half-days a week with her slaves. "He will be right tight on the negroes I think, but they need it. Meyers will lay down the law and enforce it." But Lizzie emphasized that she would not permit cruelty or abuse.[22]

Controlling Meyers would prove in some ways more difficult than controlling the slaves. His second day on the plantation Meyers whipped three young male slaves for idleness, and on his next visit, as Lizzie put it, "he undertook old Sam." Gossip had spread among slaves in the neighborhood—and from them to their masters—that Sam intended to take a whipping from no man.[23] Will Neblett had, in fact, not been a harsh disciplinarian, tending more to threatening and grumbling than whipping. But Meyers regarded Sam's challenge as quite "enough." When Sam refused to come to Meyers to receive a whipping he felt he did not deserve, Meyers cornered and threatened to shoot him. Enraged, Meyers beat Sam so severely that Lizzie feared he might die. She anxiously called the doctor, who assured her that Sam had no internal injuries and that he had seen slaves beaten far worse.

Lizzie was torn over how to respond—to Meyers or to Sam. "Tho I pity the poor wretch," she confided to Will, "I don't want him to know it." To the other slaves she insisted that "Meyers would not have whipped him if he had not deserved it," and to Will she defensively maintained, "somebody must take them in hand[.] they grow worse all the time[.] I could not begin to write you . . . how little they mind me." She saw Meyers's actions as part of a plan to establish control at the outset: "he lets them know what he is . . . & then has no more trouble." But Lizzie's very insistence and defensiveness suggest that this was not, even in her mind, slave management in its ideal form.[24]

Over the next few days, Lizzie's doubts about Meyers and his course of action grew. Instead of eliminating trouble at the outset, as he had intended, the incident seemed to have created an uproar. Sarah, a cook and house slave, reported to Lizzie that Sam suspected the whipping had been his mistress's idea, and that, when well enough, he would run away until Will came home.[25]

To resolve the volatile situation and to salvage her reputation as slave mistress, Lizzie now enlisted another white man, Coleman, to talk reasonably with Sam. Coleman had been her dead father's overseer and continued to manage her mother's property. In the absence of Will and Lizzie's brothers at the front, he was an obvious family deputy, and he had undoubtedly known Sam before Lizzie had inherited him from her father's estate. Coleman agreed to "try to show Sam the error he had been guilty of." At last Sam spoke the words Coleman sought, admitting he had done wrong and promising no further insubordination.[26]

Two weeks after the incident, Lizzie and Sam finally had a direct and, in Lizzie's view at least, comforting exchange: Meyers had ordered Sam back to work, but Lizzie had interceded in response to Sam's complaints of persisting weakness. Taking his cue from Lizzie's conciliatory gesture and acting as well in accordance with Coleman's advice, Sam apologized for disappointing Lizzie's expectations, acknowledging that as the oldest slave he had special responsibilities in Will's absence. Henceforth, he promised Lizzie, he was "going to do his work faithfully & be of as much service to me as he could. I could not help," Lizzie confessed to Will, "feeling sorry for the old fellow[.] . . . he talked so humbly & seemed so hurt that I should have had him whipped so."[27]

Sam's adroit transformation from rebel into Sambo helped resolve Lizzie's uncertainties about the appropriate course of slave management. Abandoning her defense of Meyers's severity, even interceding on Sam's behalf against her own manager, Lizzie assured Sam she had not been responsible for his punishment, had indeed been "astonished" by it. Meyers, she reported to Will with newfound assurance, "did wrong" and "knows nothing" about the management of slaves. He "don't," she noted revealingly, "treat them as moral beings but manages by brute force." Henceforth, Lizzie concluded, she would not feel impelled by her sense of helplessness to countenance extreme severity. Instead, she promised Sam, if he remained "humble and submissive," she would ensure "he would not get another lick."[28]

The incident of Sam's whipping served as the occasion for an extended negotiation between Lizzie and her slaves about the terms of her power. In calling upon Meyers and Coleman, she demonstrated that, despite appearances, she was not in fact a woman alone, dependent entirely on her own resources. Although the ultimate responsibility might be hers, slave management was a community concern. Pushed toward sanctioning Meyers's cruelty by fear of her own impotence, Lizzie then stepped back from the extreme position in which Meyers had placed her. But at the same time she dissociated herself from Meyers's action, she also reaped its benefit: Sam's abandonment of a posture of overt defiance for one of apparent submission. Sam and Lizzie were ultimately able to join forces in an agreement that Meyers must be at once deplored and tolerated as a necessary evil whom both mistress and slave would strive ceaselessly to manipulate. Abandoning their brief tryouts as Simon Legree and Nat Turner, Lizzie and Sam returned to the more accustomed and comfortable roles of concerned paternalist and loyal slave. Each recognized at last that his or her own performance depended in large measure on a complementary performance by the other.

Lizzie's behavior throughout the crisis demonstrated the essential part gender identities and assumptions played in master-slave relations. . . .

Accustomed to occasional strikes against female slaves, Lizzie called on a male slave to whip the adolescent Tom, then, later, she enlisted a male neighbor to dominate the venerable Sam. Yet even this structured hierarchy of violence was becoming increasingly "disagreeable" to her as she acted out her new wartime role as "chief of affairs." In part, Lizzie knew she was objectively physically weaker than both black and white men around her. But she confessed as well to a "troubled . . . mind," to uncertainties about her appropriate relationship to the ultimate exertion of force upon which slavery rested. As wartime pressures weakened the foundations for the "moral" management that Lizzie preferred, what she referred to as "brute force" became simultaneously more attractive and more dangerous as an instrument of coercion.

Forbidden the physical severity that served as the fundamental prop of his system of slave management, Meyers requested to be released from his contract with Lizzie at the end of the crop year. Early in the agreement, Meyers had told Lizzie that he could "conquer" her slaves, "but may have to kill some one of them." It remained with Lizzie, he explained, to make the decision. In her moments of greatest exasperation, Lizzie was willing to consent to such extreme measures. "I say do it." But with calm reflection, tempered by Will's measured advice, considerations of humanity reasserted their claim. Repeatedly she interceded between Meyers and the slaves, protecting them from whippings or condemning Meyers when he disobeyed her orders and punished them severely. Yet despite her difficulties in managing Meyers and despite her belief that he was "deficient in judgment," Lizzie recognized her dependence on him and on the threat of force he represented. She was determined to "hold him on as long as I can." If he quit and the slaves found that no one was coming to replace him, she wrote revealingly, "the jig will be up." The game, the trick, the sham of her slave management would be over. Without a man—or a man part time for three half-days a week—without the recourse to violence that Meyers embodied, slavery was unworkable. The velvet glove of paternalism required its iron hand.[29]

Violence was the ultimate foundation of power in the slave South, but gender prescriptions carefully barred white women—especially those elite women most likely to find themselves responsible for controlling slaves—from purposeful exercise of physical dominance. Even when circumstances had shifted to make female authority socially desirable, it remained for many plantation mistresses personally unachievable. Lizzie's struggle with her attraction to violence and her simultaneous abhorrence of it embodied the contradictions that the necessary wartime paradox of female slave management imposed. Lizzie begged Will to hire out his slaves or even to "give your negros away and, I'll . . . work with my hands, as hard as I can, but my mind will rest." Lizzie wished repeatedly to die, to be a man, or to give up the slaves altogether—except, tellingly, for "one good negro to wait upon me." White women had reaped slavery's benefits throughout its existence in the colonial and antebellum South. But they could not be its everyday managers without in some measure failing to be what they understood as female. The authority of their class and race could not overcome the dependence they had learned to identify as the essence of their womanhood . . . [30]

Beginning her duties as slave manager with optimism and enthusiasm, Mary Bell [of Franklin, North Carolina] came ultimately to share with Lizzie Neblett a profound sense of failure and personal inadequacy. As she repeatedly told [her husband], Alf, "unless you could be at home," "unless you were at home," the system would not work. "You say," Mary Bell wrote her husband in December 1864, "you think I am a good farmer if I only had confidence in myself. I confess I have very little confidence in my own judgment and management. wish I had more. perhaps if I had I would not get so out of heart. Sometimes I am almost ready to give up and think that surely my lot is harder than anyone else."[31]

A growing disillusionment with slavery among many elite white women arose from this very desire to "give up"—to be freed from burdens of management and fear of black reprisal that often outweighed any tangible benefits from the labor of increasingly recalcitrant slaves. Few slaveowning women had seriously questioned the moral or political legitimacy of the system, although many admitted to the profound evils associated with the institution. Gertrude Thomas noted its "terribly demoralising influence upon our men and boys," and Mary Chesnut's vehement criticisms similarly fixed on the almost unrestricted sexual access slavery gave white men to black women. Yet her concerns, like those of Gertrude Thomas, lay with the impact of these social arrangements on whites and their families rather than on exploited slaves. White southern women readily embraced the racism of their era. Blacks were, Chesnut remarked, "dirty—slatternly—idle—ill smelling by nature." Slaves were unquestionably inferior beings "blest," as one North Carolina woman wrote, "in having a home among Anglo Saxons." Jane Howison Beale of Virginia had no doubt that blacks "were ordained of High Heaven to serve the white man and it is only in that capacity they can be happy useful and respected."[32]

Southern slave mistresses began to convince themselves, however, that an institution that they were certain worked in the interest of blacks did not necessarily advance their own. Confederate women could afford little contemplation of slavery's merits "in the abstract," as its prewar defenders had urged. Slavery's meaning did not rest in the detached and intellectualized realms of politics or moral philosophy. The growing emotional and physical cost of the system to slaveholding women made its own forceful appeal, and many slave mistresses began to persuade themselves that the institution had become a greater inconvenience than benefit. . . . Like Lizzie Neblett, many white women focused on slavery's trials and yearned for the peculiar institution—and all the troublesome blacks constrained within its bonds—magically to disappear . . . . But . . . many women who entertained such fantasies at the same time longed for just "one good negro to wait upon me." For white women, this would be emancipation's greatest cost.[33]

AN ENTIRE RUPTURE
OF OUR DOMESTIC RELATIONS

In the summer of 1862 a Confederate woman overheard two small girls "playing ladies." "Good morning, ma'am," said little Sallie to her friend. "How are you today?" "I don't feel very well this morning," four-year-old Nannie Belle replied. "*All my niggers have run away and left me.*"[34]

From the first months of the war, white women confronted yet another change in their households, one that a Virginia woman described as "an entire disruption of our domestic relations": the departure of their slaves. Sometimes, especially when Yankee troops swept through an area, the loss was total and immediate. Sarah Hughes of Alabama stood as a roadside spectator at the triumphant procession of hundreds of her slaves toward freedom. Her niece, Eliza Walker, en route to visit her aunt, described the scene that greeted her as she approached the Hughes plantation.

> Down the road [the Bluecoats] . . . came, and with them all the slaves . . . , journeying, as they thought, to the promised land. I saw them as they trudged the main road, many of the women with

babes in their arms ... old and young, men, women and children. Some of them fared better than the others. A negro woman, Laura, my aunt's fancy seamstress, rode Mrs. Hughes' beautiful white pony, sitting [on] the red plush saddle of her mistress. The Hughes' family carriage, driven by Taliaferro, the old coachman, and filled with blue coated soldiers and negroes, passed in state, and this was followed by other vehicles.

With the trusted domestics leading the way, Sarah Hughes's slaves had turned her world upside down.[35]

Usually the departure of slaves was less dramatic and more secretive, as blacks simply stole away one by one or in groups of two or three when they heard of opportunities to reach Union armies and freedom. In Middleburg, Virginia, Catherine Cochran reported, "Scarcely a morning dawned that some stampede was not announced—sometimes persons would awake to find every servant gone & we never went to bed without anticipating such an occurrence." In nearby Winchester, Mary Lee presided over a more extended dissolution of her slave force. Her male slaves were the first to leave in the spring of 1862. Emily and Betty threatened to follow, and Lee considered sending them off to a more secure location away from Federal lines in order to keep from losing them altogether. Having regular help in the house seemed imperative, though, even if it was risky. "I despise menial work," Lee confessed. But she had no confidence she would retain her property. "It is an uncomfortable thought, in waking in the morning, to be uncertain as to whether you will have any servants to bring in water and prepare breakfast. . . . I dread our house servants going and having to do their work." When Betty talked again of leaving in June 1863, Laura Lee, Mary's sister-in-law, locked up the clothes the black woman had packed in anticipation of departure. Laura was determined "not to lose them too, if I could help it." Temporarily thwarted, Betty left for good the next summer, and the Lees lost slave and clothing after all.[36]

By the time of her exile from Winchester in February 1865, Mary Lee was surprised that her household still enjoyed the services of a mother and daughter, Sarah and Emily, who, despite repeated threats and stormy confrontations, had not yet fled to freedom. Mary Lee entertained few illusions about the con-

tinuing loyalty of her slaves. Early in the war, she made it clear that "I have never had the least confidence in the fidelity of any negro." Her grief at their gradual disappearance was highly pragmatic; she mourned their lost labor but did not seem to cherish an ideal of master-slave harmony to be shaken by the slaves' choice of freedom over loyalty.[37]

A South Carolina woman, by contrast, became "miserably depressed" when her three most dependable house slaves fled. "If they felt as I do," she explained, "they could not possibly leave me." The Jones family of Georgia, devout Presbyterians, reflected the tenacity of their evangelical proslavery vision in their indignant feelings of betrayal at the departure of their human property. Eva Jones was distraught when three female slaves seized their freedom "without bidding any of us an affectionate adieu." Mary Jones felt deeply wounded by what she regarded as slaves' "ingratitude." Committed to a conception of slavery as a Christian institution founded in reciprocal rights and duties, she could understand blacks' desire for freedom only as an unjust failure to appreciate her dedicated performance of her obligations within the system. "My life long . . . I have been laboring and caring for them, and since the war have labored with all my might to supply their wants, and expended everything I had upon their support, directly or indirectly, and this is their return." Even the shock of the blacks' behavior did not help Mary Jones to understand that her construction of slavery as an institution of mutual benevolence was not shared by her slaves. With their sights set on freedom, the blacks felt no duty to abide by the terms of the system as the white South had defined them.[38] . . .

In their reactions to slaves' departures, women revealed—to themselves as well as to posterity—the extent of their dependence on their servants. In our day of automated housework and prepared foods, it is easy to forget how much skill nineteenth-century housekeeping required. Many slave mistresses lacked this basic competence, having left to their slaves responsibility for execution of a wide range of essential domestic tasks. . . . Many white women felt themselves entirely ignorant about how to perform basic functions of everyday life.[39]

A Louisiana lady who had "never even so

much as washed out a pocket handkerchief with my own hands" suddenly had to learn to do laundry for her entire family. Kate Foster found that when her house servants left and she took on the washing, she "came near ruining myself for life as I was too delicately raised for such hard work." . . . Lizzie Carter of Petersburg gained a new understanding of motherhood when she was left without a nurse. "I never knew before the trouble of children," she complained to her sister. Martha Horne of Missouri remembered after the war that "I had never cooked a meal when the negro women left, and had a hard time learning." . . . When Henrietta Barr's cook departed, she assumed her place in the kitchen. "(Although a confession is humiliating)," she confided to her diary, "I must say I do not in the smallest particular fill the situation as creditably as she did. I certainly do not think my forte lies in cooking."[40]

The forte of the southern lady did not seem to lie in slave management either. These women were beginning to feel they could live neither with slaves nor without them. "To be without them is a misery & to have them is just as bad," confessed Amelia Barr of Galveston. Women already frustrated "trying to do a man's business" and direct slaves now discovered that they often felt equally incompetent executing the tasks that had belonged to their supposed racial inferiors. Like Henrietta Barr, many regarded the situation as "humiliating." "It is such a degradation," Matthella Page Harrison of Virginia wrote as she anticipated the imminent flight of her slaves, "to be so dependent upon the servants as we are."[41]

The concept of female dependence and weakness was not simply a prop of southern gender ideology; in the context of war, white ladies were finding it to be all too painful a reality. Socialized to believe in their own weakness and sheltered from the necessity of performing even life's basic tasks, many white women felt almost crippled by their unpreparedness for the new lives war had brought. Yet as they struggled to cope with change, their dedication to the old order faltered as well. Slavery, the "cornerstone" of the civilization for which their nation fought, increasingly seemed a burden rather than a benefit. White women regarded it as a threat as well. In failing to guarantee what white women believed to be their most fundamental right, in

failing to protect women or to exert control over insolent and even rebellious slaves, Confederate men undermined not only the foundations of the South's peculiar institution but the legitimacy of their power as white males, as masters of families of white women and black slaves.

NOTES

1. Alexander Stephens, *Southern Confederacy* [Atlanta], March 13, 1861.

2. *Macon Daily Telegraph*, September 1, 1862, quoted in Clarence Mohr, *On the Threshold of Freedom: Masters and Slaves in Civil War Georgia* (Athens: University of Georgia Press, 1986), 221.

3. See *The Statutes at Large of the Confederate States of America, passed at the Third Session of the First Congress* (Richmond: R. M. Smith, 1863), 158, 213–14; James M. Mathews, ed., *The Statutes at Large of the Confederate States of America* (Richmond: R. M. Smith, 1862), 30; *Acts of Congress in Relation to the Conscription and Exemption Laws* (Houston: Texas Book and Job Printing House, 1862), 8 (quotation); *Southern Historical Society Papers 48* (1941): 104; Albert Burton Moore, *Conscription and Conflict in the Confederacy*, (New York: Macmillan, 1924), 83–113.

4. Mrs. B. A. Smith to Governor Shorter, July 18, 1862, Governor's Files, Alabama Dept. of Archives and History, Montgomery, Ala.; hereafter cited as ADAH; A Planter's Wife to Governor John J. Pettus, May 1, 1862, John J. Pettus Papers, Mississippi Dept. of Archives and History, Jackson, Miss.; hereafter cited as MDAH; see also Letitia Andrews to Governor John J. Pettus, March 28, 1863, Pettus Papers, MDAH, and Lizzie Neblett to Will Neblett, April 26, 1863, Lizzie Neblett Papers, Center for American History, University of Texas, Austin, Tex.; hereafter cited as UTA.

5. Lucy A. Sharp to Hon. John C. Randolph, October 1, 1862, Letters Received, Confederate Sec. of War; hereafter cited as LRCSW, S1000, RG 109, reel 72, M437, National Archives, Washington, D.C.; hereafter cited as NA; Sarah Whitesides to Hon. James Seddon, February 13, 1863, LRCSW, RG 109, reel 115, W136, NA; Catherine Edmondston, *Journal of a Secesh Lady: The Diary of Catherine Ann Devereux Edmondston, 1860–1866*, ed. Beth G. Crabtree and James W. Patton (Raleigh: North Carolina Department of Archives and History, 1979), 240; Frances Mitten to editors of the *Christian Index*, July 6, 1864, Thomas Watts, Governor's Papers, ADAH; Martha Fort to George Fort, October 7, 1861, Tomlinson Fort Papers, Special Collections, Woodruff Library, Emory Univ., Atlanta, GA; hereafter cited as EU; Amanda Walker to Secretary of War, October 31, 1862, LRCSW, RG 109, reel 79, W1106, NA.

6. Keziah Brevard Diary, November 28, 1860, April 4, 1861, December 29, 1860, South Caroliniana Library, University of South Carolina, Columbia, S.C.; hereafter cited as SCL.

7. C. Vann Woodward, ed., *Mary Chesnut's Civil*

War (New Haven: Yale University Press, 1981), 198–99; Ada Bacot Diary, September 21, 1861, SCL.

8. Laura Lee Diary, March 12, 1862, WM; Bacot Diary, February 27, 1861, SCL; *Mobile Advertiser and Register,* September 11, 1862; *Richmond Enquirer,* September 9, 1862.

9. Nancy Hall et al. to Governor Zebulon Vance, August 11, 1863, Zebulon Vance Papers, North Carolina Division of Archives and History, Raleigh, N.C.; hereafter cited as NCDAH; Miss Lettie Kennedy in behalf of the Ladies of the N.E. beat of Jas. County, Miss., September 15, 1862, LRCSW, RG 109, reel 56, K148, NA. See also Lida Sessums to Governor John J. Pettus, October 8, 1862, Pettus Papers, MDAH.

10. Lucy Watkins to Secretary of War Randolph, October 13, 1862, LRCSW, RG 109, reel 79, M1091, NA; Harriet Pipkin to S. Cooper, Adj Gen. and Insp Gen, series 12 (LR), box 18, H2636, NA; Mary Watts to Hon. James Seddon, May 15, 1863, LRCSW, RG 109, reel 116, W315, NA.

11. W. Maury Darst, "The Vicksburg Diary of Mrs. Alfred Ingraham," May 27, 1863, *Journal of Mississippi History* 44 (May 1982): 171; Catherine Broun Diary, May 11, 1862, Broun Family Papers, Woodson Research Center, Fondren Library, Rice Univ, Houston. Tex.; hereafter cited as RU.

12. Mary Greenhow Lee Diary, April 3, 1864, Winchester-Frederick County Historical Society, Handley Library, Winchester, Va.; hereafter cited as HL.

13. Constance Cary Harrison, "A Virginia Girl in the First Year of the War," *Century* 30 (August 1885): 606.

14. Elizabeth Saxon, *A Southern Woman's War Time Reminiscences* (Memphis: Pilcher, 1905), 33; Eugene D. Genovese, *Roll, Jordan, Roll: The World the Slaves Made* (New York: Pantheon, 1974), 99.

15. Anna Green to Martha Jones, April 16, 1862, Prescott-Jones Papers, Georgia Dept. of Archives and History, Atlanta, GA; hereafter cited as GDAH; Leila Callaway to Morgan Callaway, January 22, 19, 1863, Morgan Callaway Papers, EU.

16. Maria Hawkins to Governor Zebulon Vance, December 11, 1863, Vance Papers, NCDAH.

17. Edmondston, *Journal of a Secesh Lady,* 220; see also Octavia Stephens to Winston Stephens, July 15, 1862, Bryant-Stephens Papers, P.K. Yonge Library, University of Florida, Gainesville, Fla; hereafter cited as UFL; May, "Southern Elite Women," 255; and Bacot Diary, May 3, December 25, 1861, March 17, September 8, 1862, SCL.

18. Lizzie Neblett to Will Neblett, April 15, 1864, August 18, 1863, Neblett Papers, UTA.

19. Ibid., August 28, 1863, Neblett Papers, UTA. For a strikingly similar statement of female incapacity, see Carolina Pettigrew to Charles Pettigrew, June 19, 1862, Pettigrew Family Papers, Southern Historical College, University of North Carolina, Chapel Hill, N.C.; hereafter cited as SHC.

20. Lizzie Neblett to Will Neblett, April 26, 1863, Neblett Papers, UTA.

21. Ibid., August 18, 1863.

22. Ibid., November 17, 1863.

23. Ibid., November 23, 17, 1863.

24. Ibid., November 23, 1863.

25. Ibid., November 29, 1863.

26. Ibid.

27. Ibid., December 6, 1863.

28. Ibid.

29. Ibid., February 12, July 3, June 5, 1864.

30. Ibid., March 20, 1864, letter fragment [1864].

31. Mary Bell to Alfred Bell, November 24, December 16, 1864. See Elizabeth Fox-Genovese, *Within the Plantation Household: Black and White Women of the Old South* (Chapel Hill: University of North Carolina Press, 1988), 142, on women's desire for household slaves.

32. Ella Gertrude Clanton Thomas, *The Secret Eye: The Journal of Ella Gertrude Clanton Thomas, 1848–1889,* ed. Virginia Ingraham Burr (Chapel Hill: University of North Carolina Press, 1990), 236; Mary Chesnut quoted in Elisabeth Muhlenfeld, *Mary Boykin Chesnut: A Biography* (Baton Rouge: Louisiana State University Press, 1981), 109; Mary Brown to John B. Brown, June 20, 1865, W. Vance Brown Papers, NCDAH; Jane Howison Beale, *The Journal of Jane Howison Beale of Fredericksburg, Virginia, 1850–1862* (Fredericksburg: Historic Fredericksburg Foundation, 1979), 43.

33. Lizzie Neblett to Will Neblett, undated letter fragment [1864], Neblett Papers, UTA.

34. Betty Herndon Maury, *The Confederate Diary of Betty Herndon Maury, 1861–1863,* ed. Alice Maury Parmalee (Washington, D.C.: privately printed, 1938), 89.

35. Beale, *Journal,* June 1, 1862, 47; Eliza Kendrick Walker Reminiscences, 117–18, ADAH.

36. Catherine Cochran Reminiscences, March 1862, vol. 1, Virginia Historical Society, Richmond, Va.; hereafter cited as VHS; Mary Greenhow Lee Diary, June 29, July 15, 1862, HL; Laura Lee Diary, June 13, 1863, August 18, 1864, Manuscripts and Rare Books, Swem Library, College at William and Mary. Williamsburg, Va.; hereafter cited as WM. See also Sarah Fitch Poates Diary, July 6, 8, 23, November 1, 1863, Asa Fitch Papers, Dept. of Manuscripts, Library Cornell University, Ithaca, N.Y.; Hereafter cited as CU.

37. Mary Greenhow Lee Diary, March 22, 1862, HL.

38. Emma Mordecai Diary, May 6, 1865, Mordecai Family Papers, SHC; Genovese, *Roll, Jordan, Roll,* 105–6; Robert Manson Myers, ed., *The Children of Pride: A True Story of Georgia and the Civil War* (New Haven: Yale University Press, 1972), 1274, 1287, 1308.

39. On this point, see Fox-Genovese, *Within the Plantation Household,* 115, 128. See also Amanda Worthington Diary, April 25, 1863, MDAH.

40. George C. Rable, *Civil Wars: Women and the Crisis of Southern Nationalism* (Urbana: University of Illinois Press, 1989), 255; Kate Foster Diary, November 15, 1863, Manuscript Dept., Perkins Library, Duke University, Durham, N.C.; hereafter cited as DU; Lizzie Carter to her sister, March 23, 1863, W. Vance Brown Papers, NCDAH; Martha Horne, "War Experiences," in *Reminiscences of the Women of Missouri during the Sixties,* by Missouri Division, United Daughters of the Confederacy (Jefferson City, Mo.: Hugh Stephens, 192–), 43; *The Civil War Diary of Mrs. Henrietta Fitzhugh Barr, 1862–3,* ed. Sally Kiger Winn (Mari-

etta, Ohio: Marietta College Press, 1963), 25. See also Annie Harper Reminiscences, 46, MDAH; Emma Holmes, *The Diary of Miss Emma Holmes, 1861–1866*, ed. John Marszalek (Baton Rouge: Louisiana State University Press, 1979), 467; and Sarah Anne Grover Strickler Diary, August 12, 1862, Manuscripts Dept., Alderman Library, University of Virginia, Charlottesville, Va.; hereafter cited as UVA.

41. Amelia Barr to My Dear Jenny, March 3, [1866?], Amelia Barr Papers, UTA; Lizzie Neblett to Will Neblett, August 8, 1863, Neblett Papers, UTA; Matthella Page Harrison Diary, April 28, 1863, UVA.

DOCUMENTS: Counterfeit Freedom

> ## A. S. Hitchcock, "Young women particularly flock back & forth . . ."

Early in the Civil War, before the Emancipation Proclamation, the Union Army occupied the Sea Islands off the coast of Georgia; plantation owners fled and the army established base camps there. Although the Union forces expected former slaves to continue to work on their old plantations as contract laborers, freedpeople believed that the end of slavery should mean that they could travel freely and that they could choose other ways of supporting themselves.

How did the Union officials interpret the movement of women around the Islands?

A. S. HITCHCOCK, ACTING GENERAL SUPERINTENDENT OF CONTRABANDS TO PROVOST MARSHAL GENERAL OF THE DEPARTMENT OF THE SOUTH, AUGUST 25, 1864 In accordance with a request made by you at this office . . . concerning measures to be instituted to lessen the number of idle & dissolute persons hanging about the central Posts of the Department & traveling to & from between them . . . I write this note. . . .

Had I the control of the negroes the first thing I would endeavor to do, & the thing I think of most importance to be done, is to Keep all the people possible on the farms or plantations at *honest steady* labor. As one great means to this end, I would make it as difficult as possible for them to get to the centres of population.—Young women particularly flock back & forth by scores to Hilton Head, to Beaufort, to the country simply to while away their time, or constantly to seek some new excitement, or what is worse to live by lasciviousness. . . . I would allow no peddling around camps whatsoever. . . . All rationing I would stop utterly, & introduce the poor house system, feeding none on any pretense who would not go to the place provided for all paupers to live. . . . All

persons out of the poor house and running from place to beg a living I would treat as vagabonds, & also all persons, whether in town or on plantations, white or black, who lived without occupation should either go to the poor house or be put in a place where they *must work*—a work house or chain gang, & if women where they could wash iron & scrub for the benefit of the public. . . .

SEPTEMBER 6, 1864
GENERAL ORDERS NO. 130

Hilton Head, S.C. . . . The practice of allowing negro women to wander about from one plantation to another, and from one Post or District to another, on Government transports, for no other purpose than to while away their time, or visit their husbands serving in the ranks of the Army, is not only objectionable in every point of view, both to the soldiers and to themselves, but is generally subversive of moral restraint, and must be discontinued at once. All negro women, in future found wandering in this manner, will be immediately arrested, and compelled to work at some steady employment on the Plantations.

Excerpted from *Freedom: A Documentary History of Emancipation 1861–1867*, edited by Ira Berlin, Joseph P. Reidy, and Leslie S. Rowland, Ser. I, vol. 3, pp. 316–317. Reprinted with the permission of Cambridge University Press.

Roda Ann Childs, "I was more dead than alive"

In January 1865, before the Civil War was over, Congress and the states in the Union ratified the Thirteenth Amendment, putting an end to slavery and "involuntary servitude, except as punishment for crime whereof the party shall have been duly convicted." Once peace was established, it became clear that the states of the former Confederacy were quite creative in devising systems that maintained racial subordination (for example, broad definitions of what counted as "vagrancy" which, as crimes, could be punished by involuntary servitude). The Civil Rights Act of 1866 was designed to protect freedpeople; it promised "citizens of every race and color . . . full and equal benefit of all laws and proceedings for the security of person and property, as is enjoyed by white citizens. . . ." But the statute had been passed only over the veto of President Andrew Johnson, who denied that the states of the Confederacy had forfeited all civil rights and privileges by their rebellion. The Freedmen's Bureau was charged with protecting the rights of former slaves and assisting their transition to a market economy; it accomplished much, but it was always underfunded and understaffed, and many of its staff members were themselves deeply skeptical of freedpeople.

In a political climate marked by struggle between Congress and the President, the Ku Klux Klan and other vigilantes who wanted to intimidate freedpeople and take vengeance for their own defeat in war seized their opportunity. Not until 1871 did Congress pass the Ku Klux Klan Act, prescribing fines and imprisonment for those who went in disguise to terrorize others. The congressional committee that conducted a traveling inquiry into "the Condition of Affairs in the Late Insurrectionary States" filed a twelve-volume report. Its testimony of violence and intimidation, in excruciating detail, makes it clear that Roda Ann Childs's experience was replicated throughout the South.

Roda Ann Childs made her way to a Freedman's Bureau agent in Griffin, Georgia, to swear this affidavit; she signed it with her mark. There is no evidence that her case was pursued. What clue does she offer for why she was a target for mob violence?

[Griffin, GA] Sept. 25, 1866

Rhoda Ann Childs came into this office and made the following statement:

"Myself and husband were under contract with Mrs. Amelia Childs of Henry County, and worked from Jan. 1, 1866, until the crops were laid by, or in other words until the main work of the year was done, without difficulty. Then, (the fashion being prevalent among the planters) we were called upon one night, and my husband was demanded; I Said he was not there. They then asked where he was. I Said he was gone to the water mellon patch. They then Seized me and took me Some distance from the house, where they 'bucked' me down across a log, Stripped my clothes over my head, one of the men Standing astride my neck, and beat me across my posterior, two men holding my legs. In this manner I was beaten until they were tired. Then they turned me parallel with the log, laying my neck on a limb which projected from the log, and one man placing his foot upon my neck, beat me again on my hip and thigh. Then I was thrown

Excerpted from *Freedom: A Documentary History of Emancipation, 1861–1876*, edited by Ira Berlin, Joseph P. Reidy and Leslie S. Rowland, Ser. I, vol. 3, pp. 316–17. Reprinted with the permission of Cambridge University Press.

upon the ground on my back, one of the men Stood upon my breast, while two others took hold of my feet and stretched My limbs as far apart as they could, while the man Standing upon my breast applied the Strap to my private parts until fatigued into stopping, and I was more dead than alive. Then a man, Supposed to be an ex-con-federate Soldier, as he was on crutches, fell upon me and ravished me. During the whipping one of the men ran his pistol into me, and Said he had a hell of a mind to pull the trigger, and Swore they ought to Shoot me, as my husband had been in the 'God damned Yankee Army,' and Swore they meant to kill every black Son-of-a-bitch they could find that had ever fought against them. They then went back to the house, Seized my two daughters and beat them, demanding their father's pistol, and upon failure to get that, they entered the house and took Such articles of clothing as Suited their fancy, and decamped. There were concerned in this affair eight men, none of which could be recognized for certain.

her
Roda Ann × Childs
mark

TERA W. HUNTER
Reconstruction and the Meanings of Freedom

When the Civil War was ended at Appomatox, a long and complex struggle over its meaning had just begun. The Thirteenth Amendment technically ended slavery, but it left much room for interpretation about the meaning of servitude. It said nothing about equality, leaving resentful Southerners to conclude that the North would condone systems of racial hierarchy. Even after the passage of the Fourteenth Amendment, which provided that *All persons born or naturalized in the United States . . . are citizens of the United States and of the State wherein they reside,* the meanings of "citizenship" remained to be defined.

The aftermath of defeat is an internationally shared phenomenon. How did white southerners understand their defeat? What tensions marked postwar society? What would it mean to "reconstruct" the former Confederacy? Tera Hunter examines the experiences of freedpeople in the city of Atlanta, Georgia—Roda Ann Childs lived not far away. She finds that the process of rebuilding their lives could be quite different for men and for women. What opportunities did African American men have that African American women did not? What strategies might freedwomen use to stabilize their lives? In what ways did freedwomen participate in political life?

The Union victory at Appomattox in the spring of 1865 marked the official end of the war and inspired somber reflection, foot-stomping church meetings, and joyous street parades among the newly free. African Americans eagerly rushed into Atlanta in even greater

Excerpted from "Reconstruction and the Meanings of Freedom," ch. 2 of *To 'Joy My Freedom: Black Women's Lives and Labors after the Civil War* by Tera W. Hunter (Cambridge, Mass.: Harvard University Press, 1997). Copyright © 1997 by Tera W. Hunter. Reprinted by permission of the publisher. Notes have been numbered and edited.

numbers than before. Between 1860 and 1870, blacks in Atlanta increased from a mere nineteen hundred to ten thousand, more than doubling their proportion in the city's population, from 20 to 46 percent. Women made up the majority of this burgeoning population. . . .[1]

Wherever they came from, virtually all black women were compelled to find jobs as household workers once they arrived in the city. Some had acquired experience in such jobs as house slaves; others had worked in the fields or combined field and domestic chores. Whether or not they were working as domestics for the first time, black women had to struggle to assert new terms for their labor. The Civil War had exposed the parallel contests occurring in white households as the conflict on the battlefield, in the marketplace, and in the political arena unfolded. The war continued on the home front during Reconstruction after the Confederacy's military defeat. . . .

Just as black women and men in Atlanta had to reconstitute their lives as free people and build from the ground up, the city was faced with similar challenges. The legacy of physical desecration left by Sherman's invasion was everywhere. Tons of debris, twisted rails, dislodged roofs, crumbled chimneys, discharged cannon balls, and charred frame dwellings cluttered the streets.[2] Visitors to the city swapped remarks on the distinctive spirit of industry exemplified in the repair and rebuilding. . . . Atlanta aspired to construct a city in the New South in the image of established cities above the Mason-Dixon line.[3]

The capitalist zeal that impressed outsiders offered few benefits to the average person, however. Overwhelmed contractors could not keep up with demands, which added to housing shortages that sent prices for rents soaring beyond the means of most residents. . . .[4] Some builders took advantage of the shortage to offer makeshift huts and shanties to freedpeople at exorbitant prices.[5] Ex-slaves in more dire straits assembled scanty lodging that consisted of tents, cabins, and shanties made of tin, line, and cloth on rented parcels of land.[6] . . . The cost of food and other consumer goods likewise followed the pattern of scarcity, poor quality, and deliberate price gouging.[7]

The abrupt population growth and the inability of private charities or public coffers to relieve the migrants of want exacerbated postwar privation. Almost everyone in the city, regardless of race, shared the status of newcomer. It was not just African Americans who were migrating to the city in large numbers; so did many whites. In 1860, there were 7,600 whites living in Atlanta, ten years later there were 11,900.[8] White yeoman farmers fled to the city to find wage labor in the wake of the elimination of their rural self-sufficiency. White Northern and foreign industrial workers followed the prosperity promised by the railroad and construction boom.

Women and children, black and white, were particularly noticeable among the destitute sprawled over the desolate urban landscape. The indigent included elderly, single women, widows of soldiers, and wives of unemployed or underemployed men. White women seamstresses who numbered in the thousands during the war were reduced to poverty with the collapse of military uniform manufacturers.[9] Labor agents egregiously contributed to the disproportionate sex ratio among urban blacks by taking away men to distant agricultural fields, leaving the women and children deserted.[10] Those abandoned wandered the streets and scavenged for food, often walking between ten and forty miles per day. "Sometimes I gits along tolerable," stated a widow washerwoman with six children. "Sometimes right slim; but dat's de way wid everybody—times is powerful hard right now."[11]

The municipal government showed neither the capability nor the ambition to meet the needs of the poor. It allocated few resources for basic human services. Yet the Freedmen's Bureau, which was established by the federal government in 1865 to distribute rations and relief to ex-slaves, to monitor the transition to a free labor system, and to protect black rights, proved inadequate also. The bureau was preoccupied with stemming migration, establishing order, and restoring the economy, which led it to force blacks into accepting contracts without sufficient regard for the fairness of the terms. The federals evicted ex-slaves from contraband camps or pushed them further from the center of town to the edges—out of sight and out of mind.[12] Bureau officials urged their agents: "You must not issue rations or afford shelter to any person who can, and will not labor for his or her own support." . . .[13]

Ex-slaves who were evicted from the camps by the end of 1865 were more fortunate than they could appreciate initially. They escaped a smallpox epidemic in the city that devastated the enclaves. One missionary reported a horrifying scene she witnessed in the camps: "Men, women, and children lying on the damp ground suffering in every degree from the mildest symptoms to the most violent. The tents crowded, no fire to make them comfortable, and worse all the poor creatures were almost destitute of wearing apparel."[14] The dead who lay around the sick and suffering were buried in the ground half-naked or without clothes at all. . . .

African-American women and men were willing to endure the adversities of food shortages, natural disasters, dilapidated housing, and inadequate clothing in postwar Atlanta because what they left behind in the countryside, by comparison, was much worse. In the city at least there were reasons to be optimistic that their strength in numbers and their collective strategies of empowerment could be effective. In rural areas, however, their dispersion and separation by miles of uninhabited backwoods left them more vulnerable to elements intent on depriving them of life, liberty, and happiness. Abram Colby, a Republican legislator from Greene County, summed up the motivations for migration by stating that blacks went to Atlanta "for protection." He explained further: "The military is here and nobody interferes with us here . . . we cannot stop anywhere else so safely."[15]

African Americans moved to the city not only in search of safety, but also in search of economic self-sufficiency. Though most ex-slaves held dreams of owning farm land, many preferred to set up households in a city with a more diverse urban economy. In Atlanta they encountered an economy that was quickly recovering from the war and continuing to grow in the direction propelled by military demands and the promise of modernization. . . .[16]

Though the kaleidoscope of industry appeared to offer vast possibilities for workers, African Americans were slotted into unskilled and service labor. Black men filled positions with the railroads; as day workers, they groomed roads, distributed ballast, and shoveled snow off the tracks. As brakemen, they coupled and uncoupled stationary cars and ran along the roof of moving trains to apply the brakes, risking life and limb. Many others worked in rolling and lumber mills, mostly in

the lowest-paid positions as helpers to white men. Hotels employed black men as cooks, waiters, porters, bellhops, and barroom workers. A few ex-slaves worked in bakeries, small foundries, the paper mill, and candy factories. Slave artisans were high in number in the antebellum South, but in the postbellum era black men were rarely hired in skilled positions. They were able to benefit from the aggressive physical rebuilding of Atlanta, however, in the construction trades, as painters, carpenters, and brickmasons. Between 1870 and 1880, the proportion of black male shoemakers tripled to constitute the majority of the entire trade. A select few owned small businesses such as barber shops and grocery stores or worked in the professions as teachers and ministers.[17]

The range of job opportunities for black women was more narrow than for men. Black women were excluded from small manufacturing plants that hired white women, such as those that made candy, clothing, textiles, paper boxes, bookbinding, and straw goods. They were confined primarily to domestic labor in private homes as cooks, maids, and child-nurses. A few black women found related jobs in local hotels—a step above the same work performed in private households. Large numbers worked in their own homes in a relatively autonomous craft as laundresses, which had the advantage of accommodating family and community obligations. More desirable, yet less accessible, were skilled jobs outside domestic service as seamstresses or dressmakers. . . . Only a few black women were able to escape common labor and enter the professions as teachers.[18]

Reconstruction of the post-slavery South occurred on many levels. Just as the city's infrastructure had to be rebuilt for daily life to reach a new normalcy, so blacks had to rebuild their lives as free people by earning an independent living. Women's success or frustrations in influencing the character of domestic labor would define how meaningful freedom would be. Slave women had already demonstrated fundamental disagreements with masters over the principles and practices of free labor during the war. This conflict continued as workers and employers negotiated new terms. Even the most mundane and minute details of organizing a free labor system required rethinking assumptions about work that had previously relied on physical coercion. An employer acknowledged the trial-and-error nature of this process: "I had no idea what was considered a task in washing so I gave her all the small things belonging to the children taking out all the table cloths sheets counterpanes & c." The novice employer then decided in the same haphazard manner to pay the laundry worker 30 cents a day. But the laborer asserted her own understanding of fair work. "She was through by dinner time [and] appeared to work steady. I gave her dinner and afterwards told her that I had a few more clothes I wished washed out," the employer explained. "Her reply was that she was tired." The worker and employer held different expectations about the length of the work day and the quantity of the output of labor.[19]

African Americans labored according to their own sense of equity, with the guiding assumption that wage labor should not emulate slavery—especially in the arbitrariness of time and tasks. The experience of an ex-slave named Nancy illustrates this point. As some ex-slaves departed from their former masters' households, the burden of the work shifted to those who remained. Consequently, when the regular cook departed, Nancy's employer added cooking and washing to her previous child-care job, without her consent. Nancy faked illness on ironing days and eventually quit in protest against the extra encumbrance.[20] If workers and employers disagreed on the assignment of specific tasks, they also disagreed on how to execute them. Workers held to their own methods and preferences; employers held to theirs. . . .

If [a worker's] frustrations reached an intolerable level, she could exercise a new privilege as a free worker to register the ultimate complaint: she could quit and seek better terms for her work. Ex-slaves committed themselves to this precept of free labor with a firmness that vexed employers. "We daily hear of people who are in want of servants, and who have had in their employ in the last three or four months, a dozen different ones," stated a familiar news report. "The common experience of all is that the servants of the 'African-persuasion' can't be retained," it continued. "They are fond of change and since it is their privilege to come and go at pleasure, they make full use of the large liberty they enjoy."[21] . . .

African-American women decided to quit work over such grievances as low wages, long hours, ill treatment, and unpleasant tasks. Quitting could not guarantee a higher standard of living or a more pleasant work environment for workers, but it was an effective strategy to deprive employers of complete power over their labor. . . .

Employers did not share the same interpretations of labor mobility, however. They blamed the subversive influence of Yankees and "pernicious" Negroes for inciting "bad" work habits, or they explained quitting as a scientifically proven racial deficiency.[22] Whereas recently freed slaves often worked as much as they needed to survive and no more, white Southerners believed that if they refused to work as hard as slaves driven by fear they were mendicants and vagrants. "When a wench gets very hungry and ragged, she is ready to do the cooking for any sized family," a news report exclaimed. "But after she gets her belly well filled with provender, she begins to don't see the use of working all day and every day, and goes out to enjoy her freedom."[23]

Although many white Southerners resented the presence of the Freedmen's Bureau as the Northern overseer of Reconstruction, they readily sought its assistance to stem the revolving door of domestic workers. "What are persons to do when a 'freedman' that you hire as a nurse goes out at any time & against your direct orders?" one former master queried the bureau. "What must be done when they are hired and do only just what they please? orders being disregarded in every instance," he asked further. A bureau agent responded with an answer to alleviate the employer's frustrations and to teach him a lesson about the precepts of free labor. "Discharge her and tell her she dont suit you," the agent stated simply. "If you have a written contract with them and they quit you without good and sufficient cause—I will use all my power to have them comply," he reassured. But if these words provided comfort, the bureau agent made clear that the operative words were "without good and sufficient cause." He reiterated the employers' obligations and responsibilities to respect the liberties of workers: "You are expected to deal with them as Freemen and Freewomen. Individual exceptions there may be but as a whole where they are well treated they are faithful and work well."[24]

The federal government refused to return to white employers unilateral power to prohibit the mobility of black workers, leading employers to elicit the support of local laws. Quitting work became defined as "idleness" and "vagrancy"—prosecutable offenses. Southern state legislatures began passing repressive Black Codes in 1865 to obstruct black laborers' full participation in the marketplace and political arena. In 1866, the Atlanta City Council responded in a similar vein to stop the movement of household workers: it passed a law requiring employers to solicit recommendations from previous jobs in order to distinguish "worthy" from "worthless" laborers and to make it more difficult for workers to change jobs. Complaints continued long after the law took effect, which suggests its ineffectiveness.[25] . . .

Black women used the marginal leverage they could exercise in the face of conflict between employers to enhance their wages and to improve the conditions of work. When Hannah, "a cook & washer of the first character," was approached by Virginia Shelton in search of domestic help, she bargained for an agreement to match her needs. Hannah wanted to bring along her husband, a general laborer, and expected good wages for both of them. Shelton made an initial offer of $5 per month to Hannah and $10 per month to her husband. But the couple demanded $8 and $15, to which Shelton acceded. Shelton realized that it was worth making compromises with a servant she had traveled a long distance to recruit.[26]

Not all negotiations ended so pleasantly or in the workers' favor, however. . . . Domestic workers often complained of physical abuse by employers following disputes about wages, hours of work, or other work-related matters. . . . Samuel Ellison explained the argument that led to the death of his wife, Eliza Jane. Mrs. Ellison had argued with her employer, Mrs. L. B. Walton, about washing clothes. According to Ellison's husband, "My wife asked Mrs. Walton who would pay her for her washing extra clothes and which she was not bound to do by her contract." Walton's husband intervened and "abused" the laundress for "insulting" his wife. He left the house, returned and began another argument, insisting to Ellison, "shut up you God damn bitch." The fight ended when Walton shot Eliza Jane Ellison to death.[27]

African-American women like Ellison undoubtedly paid a high price for the simple desire to be treated like human beings. Incidents like this one made it apparent that freedom could not be secured through wage labor alone. The material survival of African Americans was critical, but they also needed to exercise their political rights to safeguard it. The political system had to undergo dramatic transformation to advance their interests, but here too they faced many obstacles.

The Ku Klux Klan, an anti-black terrorist organization founded by former Confederate soldiers in 1866, mounted the most bitter opposition to black rights. The KKK quickly became dominated by Democratic Party officials bent on preempting black participation in the electoral arena. The Klan sought to wrest economic and political power from the governing Republicans in order to restore it to the antebellum planter elite and to the Democrats. KKK members victimized Republican politicians like Abram Colby, whom they stripped and beat for hours in the woods. They harassed registered voters and independent landholders, ransacked churches and schools, intimidated common laborers who refused to bow obsequiously to planters, and tormented white Republicans sympathetic to any or all of the foregoing.[28]

African Americans' recalcitrance in commonplace disagreements with employers routinely provoked the vigilantes. Alfred Richardson, a legislator from Clarke County, suggested how labor relations continued to have strong political ramifications. The KKK assisted employers in securing the upper hand in conflicts with wage household workers. "Many times, you know, a white lady has a colored lady for cook or waiting in the house, or something of that sort," Richardson explained. "They have some quarrel, and sometimes probably the colored woman gives the lady a little jaw. In a night or two a crowd will come in and take her out and whip her." The Klan stripped and beat African Americans with sticks, straps, or pistol barrels when all else failed to elicit their compliance.[29]

If the KKK was determined to halt the reconstruction of a free labor system, it was most insistent about eliminating black political power. Though women were denied the right to vote in the dominant political system, they actively engaged in a grass-roots political culture that valued the participation of the entire community. Black women and children attended parades, rallies, and conventions; they voiced their opinions and cast their votes on resolutions passed at mass meetings. In the 1860s and 1870s, women organized their own political organizations, such as the Rising Daughters of Liberty Society, and stood guard at political meetings organized by men to allow them to meet without fear of enemy raids. They boldly tacked buttons on the clothing they wore to work in support of favorite candidates. They took time off from work to attend to their political duties, such as traveling to the polls to make sure men cast the right ballots. White housekeepers were as troubled by the dramatic absences of domestic workers on election day or during political conventions as were the planters and urban employers of men.[30] During an election riot in nearby Macon, a newspaper reported: "The Negro women, if possible, were wilder than the men. They were seen everywhere, talking in an excited manner, and urging the men on. Some of them were almost furious, showing it to be part of their religion to keep their husbands and brothers straight in politics."[31]

Whether they gave political advice and support to the men in their families and communities or carried out more directly subversive activities, black women showed courage in the face of political violence. Hannah Flournoy, a cook and laundress, ran a boardinghouse in Columbus well known as a gathering place for Republicans. When George Ashburn, a white party leader stalked by the KKK, looked to her for shelter she complied, unlike his other supporters in the town. Flournoy promised him, "You are a republican, and I am willing to die for you. I am a republican, tooth and toe-nail."[32] But neither Flournoy nor Ashburn could stop the Klan in its determination to take the life of freedom fighters. After Klansmen killed Ashburn, Flournoy escaped to Atlanta, leaving behind valuable property.

Republican activists like Ashburn and Flournoy were not the only victims of KKK violence. The Klan also targeted bystanders who happened to witness their misdeeds. In White County, Joe Brown's entire family was subjected to sadistic and brutal harassment because Brown had observed a murder committed by the Klan. "They just stripped me stark naked, and fell to beating us," Brown reported later. "They got a great big trace-chain, swung me up from the ground, and swung [my wife] up until she fainted; and they beat us all over the yard with great big sticks." The Klan continued its torture against his mother-in-law and sister-in-law. "They made all the women show their nakedness; they made them lie down, and they jabbed them with sticks." Indiscriminate in violating adults and children, the KKK lined up Brown's young daughters and sons "and went to playing with their backsides with a piece of fishing-pole."[33] . . .

Migrating to Atlanta certainly improved the personal safety of ex-slaves escaping the KKK and sexual assaults, but it did not ensure foolproof protection against bodily harm. Black women risked sexual abuse no matter where they lived. Domestics in white homes were the most susceptible to attacks. A year after the war ended, Henry McNeal Turner and other black men mounted the podium and wrote petitions to demand the cessation of sexual assaults upon black women. Freedom, they insisted, was meaningless without ownership and control over one's own body. Black men took great offense at the fact that while they were falsely accused of raping white women, white men granted themselves total immunity in the exploitation of black women. "*All we ask of the white man is to let our ladies alone,* and they need not fear us," Turner warned. "The difficulty has heretofore been *our ladies were not always at our disposal.*"[34] In Savannah, black men mobilized the Sons of Benevolence "for the protection of female virtue" in 1865.[35] In Richmond, African Americans complained to military authorities that women were being "gobbled up" off the streets, thrown into the jail, and ravished by the guards. In Mobile, black men organized the National Lincoln Association and petitioned the Alabama State Constitutional Convention to enact laws to protect black women from assault by white civilians and the police.[36]

Most whites refused to acknowledge the culpability of white men in abusing black women. "Rape" and "black women" were words that were never uttered in the same breath by white Southerners. Any sexual relations that developed between black women and white men were considered consensual, even coerced by the seductions of black women's lascivious nature. Rape was a crime defined exclusively, in theory and in practice, as perceived or actual threats against white female virtue by black men, which resulted in lynchings and castrations of numbers of innocent black men. But Z. B. Hargrove, a white attorney, admitted with rare candor that the obsession with black men raping white women was misplaced. "It is all on the other foot," as he put it. The "colored women have a great deal more to fear from white men."[37]

Black Atlantans during Reconstruction were subjected to other kinds of physical violence, especially at the hands of white civilians and police. . . . When Mary Price objected to being called a "damned bitch" by a white neighbor, Mr. Hoyt, he brought police officer C. M. Barry to her door to reprimand her. Price's mother, Barbara, pregnant at the time, intervened and spoke to the police: "I replied that I would protect my daughter in my own house, whereupon he pulled me out of the house into the street. Here he called another man and the two jerked and pulled me along [the street] to the guard house and throwed me in there." When a Freedmen's Bureau agent complained to the mayor and city council on the Prices' behalf, the complaint was rebuffed by a unanimous vote acquitting the policeman of all charges against him. Meanwhile, mother and daughter were arrested, convicted for using profane language, and forced to pay $350 each in fines and court costs. Only after it became clear that the Bureau would persist in its efforts to get justice for the Price women did the mayor have a change of heart and fine the offending policeman. Barry was one of the worst officers on the force, and the Freedmen's Bureau eventually forced the city council to fire him, though he was rehired a year later.[38]

African Americans not only had to ward off physical threats; they were also challenged by the existence of perfectly legal abuses that diminished the meaning of freedom. Ex-slaves defined the reconstruction of their families torn asunder by slavery and war as an important aspect of the realization of the full exercise of their civil rights. But former masters seized upon the misery of African Americans, with the assistance of the law, to prolong the conditions of slavery and deny them the prerogative of reuniting their families. The Georgia legislature passed an Apprentice Act in 1866, ostensibly to protect black orphans by providing them

with guardianship and "good" homes until they reached the age of consent at twenty-one. Planters used the law to reinstate bondage through uncompensated child labor.[39] Aunts, uncles, parents, and grandparents inundated the Freedmen's Bureau with requests for assistance in rescuing their children, though this same agency also assisted in apprenticing black minors. Martin Lee, for example, a former slave living in Florence, Alabama, wrote to the chief of the Georgia bureau for help in releasing his nephew from bondage. He had successfully reunited part of his extended family, but could not gain the release of his nephew despite the fact that he and the child's mother, Lee's sister, were both willing and able to take custody.[40]

If admitted enemies of black freedom recklessly disregarded the unity of black families through apprenticeships, some of their friends operated just as wantonly. The American Missionary Association (AMA) sometimes impeded parents and relatives who wished to reclaim their children. In 1866, the AMA started an orphanage that operated out of a tent. Soon afterward they opened the Washburn Orphanage in a building to accommodate the large number of homeless black children who were surviving on the streets on scant diets of saltpork and hardtack. But the asylum functioned as a temporary way station for children before apprenticing them out as domestic help to white sponsors. "I succeeded in getting a little girl from the orphans asylum by the name of Mary Jane Peirce," one eager patron of the orphanage exclaimed. "Her father and mother are both dead. She has a step mother and a little step brother." Peirce's new guardian minced no words in disclosing reckless disregard for the reunion of the child's family. "I am glad she will have no outside influence exherted upon her," the guardian admitted.[41] . . .

African Americans persisted in pursuing the reconstitution of family ties, despite the obstacles put in their way. [Rebeca] Craighead [the matron of the asylum,] recognized the persistence of these ex-slaves, yet she showed neither respect nor sensitivity toward the virtues of their ambition. "Somehow these black people have the faculty of finding out where their children are," she acknowledged.[42] Both the uncle, Martin Lee, who used official channels to retrieve his nephew, and the anonymous aunt, who relied on her own resources to "steal" her niece, displayed no small measure of resourcefulness in achieving their aims. Men no less than women, non-kin as well as kin, sought to recreate the family bonds that had been strained or severed by slavery and the Civil War.

Not all missionaries were as insensitive as Craighead; there were others, like Frederick Ayers, who fully appreciated the significance of family to ex-slaves. "The idea of 'freedom' of independence, of calling their wives and their children, and little hut their *own*, was a soul animating one, that buoyed up their spirits," he observed.[43] . . .

Broad understandings of kinship encouraged black women to assume responsibility for needy children other than their natural offspring. Silvey, for example, could hardly survive on the minimal subsistence she earned, yet she extended compassion to the youngsters lost or deserted by other ex-slaves. "She was hard put to it, to work for them all," observed her former owner, Emma Prescott. But "of course, as our means were all limited, we could not supply her enough to feed them. Her life, was anything but ease & it was a pitiful sight."[44] . . .

The most complicated family issues involved romantic relationships between women and men. For generations slaves had married one another and passed on the importance of conjugal obligations, despite the absence of legal protection. Marriages between slaves were long-term commitments, usually only disrupted by forcible separation or the death of a spouse. Emancipation offered new opportunities to reaffirm marital vows and to reunite couples who had previously lived "abroad" in the households of different masters. Even before the last shots of gunfire ending the Civil War, thousands of husbands and wives sought the help of Union officers and Northern missionaries to register their nuptials and to conduct wedding ceremonies.[45] The significance of formalizing these ties was articulated by a black soldier: "*I praise God for this day! The Marriage Covenant is at the foundation of all our rights.*"[46] Putting marriages on a legal footing bolstered the ability of ex-slaves to keep their families together, to make decisions about labor and education, and to stay out of the unscrupulous grasp of erstwhile masters.

The hardships of slavery and war that disrupted families, however, meant that in the postwar period spouses were not always reunited without problems and tensions. Slaves traveled long distances to reunite with spouses from whom they had been separated for years. They wrote love letters and mailed them to churches and to the Freedmen's Bureau, and retraced the routes of labor agents who had taken their partners away.[47] Emotional bonds were sometimes so intense that spouses would choose to suffer indefinitely if they could not be reunited with their lost loved ones. But affections undernourished by hundreds of miles and many years might be supplanted by other relationships. Many ex-slaves faced awkward dilemmas when spouses presumed to be dead or long-lost suddenly reappeared. Ex-slaves created novel solutions for the vexing moral, legal, and practical concerns in resolving marital relations disrupted by forces beyond their control. One woman lived with each of her two husbands for a two-week trial before making a decision. Some men felt obligated to two wives and stayed married to one wife while providing support to the other. In one case, perhaps unique, a wife resumed her relationship with her first husband, while the second husband, a much older man, was brought into the family as a "poor relation."[48]

The presence of children complicated marriages even further. Some spouses registered their marriages with the Freedmen's Bureau or local courts even when their spouses were dead or missing, in order to give legal recognition to their children. When both parents were present and unable to reconcile their differences, child custody became a point of contention. Madison Day and Maria Richardson reached a mutual agreement to separate after emancipation. The love between husband and wife may have changed, but the love that each displayed for their children did not. The Richardsons put the Freedmen's Bureau agent in a quandary in determining who should receive custody. "Neither husband nor wife seem to be in a condition to provide for the children in a manner better than is usual with the freedpeople," the agent noted. "Still both appear to have an affectionate regard for the children and each loudly demands them."[49] . . .

Sheer survival and the reconstruction of family, despite all the difficulties, were the highest priorities of ex-slaves in the postwar period. But the desire for literacy and education was closely related to their strategies for achieving economic self-sufficiency, political autonomy, and personal enrichment. By 1860, 5 percent of the slave population had defied the laws and learned to read and write. Some were taught by their masters, but many learned to read in clandestine sessions taught by other blacks. African Americans all over the South organized secret schools long before the arrival of Northern missionaries. When a New England teacher arrived in Atlanta in 1865, he discovered an ex-slave already running a school in a church basement.[50]

African Americans welcomed the support of New England teachers and the federal government in their education movement. But centuries of slavery had stirred the longing for self-reliance in operating schools and filling teaching staffs, with assistance, but without white control. Ex-slaves enthusiastically raised funds and donated in-kind labor for building, repairing, and maintaining school houses. They opened their spartan quarters to house teachers and shared vegetables from their gardens to feed them. Ex-slaves in Georgia ranked highest in the South in the amount of financial assistance donated to their own education.[51]

The education movement among African Americans in Georgia went hand in hand with the demand for political rights. In January 1865, black ministers formed the Savannah Education Association, which operated schools staffed entirely with black teachers. Despite the efforts of General Davis Tillson, the conservative head of the Freedmen's Bureau, to keep politics out of the organization, African Americans and more liberal white allies infused the group with political objectives. The name was changed to the Georgia Equal Rights and Education Association, explicitly linking equal rights in the political arena with the pursuit of education. The organization became an important training ground for black politicians and laypersons at the grass-roots level and functioned as the state's predecessor to the Republican Party.[52] . . .

African Americans' advocacy of universal public education did not fare well at the city level, because the municipal government was firmly controlled by Democrats and businessmen. William Finch, elected in 1870 as one of Atlanta's first black city councilmen, made universal education a hallmark of his election campaign. Finch attempted, but failed, to galvanize the support of the white working class on this issue. City Hall's cold reception shifted the burden of basic education for blacks to private foundations. Finch did succeed in getting the council to absorb two primary schools run by the AMA. After his short term in office and unsuccessful bid for reelection in December 1871, he continued to be a strong advocate of public education and helped to negotiate a deal in 1872 whereby the city would pay nominal costs for some blacks to receive secondary training at Atlanta University. No publicly funded high school for blacks would be created until a half-century later, however.[53]

Former slaves of all ages were undeterred in their goals to achieve literacy, regardless of the obstacles imposed by municipal and state governments. "It is quite amusing to see little girls eight or ten years old lead up full-grown women, as well as children, to have their names enrolled," remarked a missionary. "Men, women, and children are daily inquiring when the 'Free School' is to commence, and whether all can come[.] There is a large class of married women who wish to attend, if the schools are not too crowded."[54] Household workers figured prominently among this group of older, eager scholars. Their eagerness to learn was not diminished, although often interrupted, by the pressing demands of gainful labor. In fact, these obstacles may have increased the value of education in the eyes of the ex-slaves. Sabbath schools operated by black churches and evening classes sponsored by the Freedmen's Bureau and Northern missionaries afforded alternatives for those who could not sacrifice time during the day. But black women also inventively stole time away from work by carrying their books along and studying during spare moments—even fastening textbooks to backyard fences to glimpse their lessons as they washed clothes.[55]

As parents, working-class adults were especially committed to the education of their children. The story of Sarah J. Thomas, a young woman from Macon, whose mother was a cook and washerwoman, is a poignant illustration. Thomas wrote Edmund Asa Ware, president of Atlanta University, to gain his support in her plans to enroll in the secondary school. "I expected to come to Atlanta to morrow but I am dissappointed. The reason I can not come to morrow is this. You know how mothers are! I guess about their youngest children *girls* especially," she wrote. Mother Thomas was protective of her daughter and reluctant to send her away alone. "In order that I may *come* Mr. Ware! mother says can she get a place to work there in the family?" she asked. The younger Thomas boasted of her mother's fine skills and reputation and slipped in her salary history. She assured the president, surely swamped by requests for financial aid, that her matriculation depended upon parental supervision, not the need for money. "Mother says she dont mean not the least to work to pay for *my schooling?* father pays for that him self she dont have any thing to do with it she only want to be where she can see me."[56] The young scholar's astute strategizing swayed both her mother and the school's president; she entered Atlanta University and achieved a successful teaching career after graduation in 1875.

Clandestine antebellum activities and values had bolstered the exemplary efforts of African Americans to seek literacy and to build and sustain educational institutions after the war. Ex-slaves took mutual obligations seriously. Their belief in personal development was aided rather than hampered by ideals that emphasized broad definitions of kinship and community. Freedom meant the reestablishment of lost family connections, the achievement of literacy, the exercise of political rights, and the security of a decent livelihood without the sacrifice of human dignity or self-determination. Ex-slave women migrated to Atlanta, where they hoped they would have a better chance of fulfilling these expectations. They were faced with many challenges; uppermost among them were the white residents who were resentful of the abolition of slavery and persisted in thwarting the realization of the true meaning of freedom. Black women continued to struggle, resilient and creative, in pursuing their goals for dignity and autonomy. The character of the contest had already been cast, but the many guises of domination and resistance had yet to be exhausted as life in the New South unfolded.

NOTES

1. ... Franklin M. Garrett, *Yesterday's Atlanta* (Miami: E. A. Seeman, 1974), p. 38; Eric Foner, *Reconstruction: America's Unfinished Revolution, 1863–1877* (New York: Harper & Row, 1988), pp. 81–82; Leon

F. Litwack, *Been in the Storm So Long: The Aftermath of Slavery* (New York: Knopf, 1979), pp. 310–316; U.S. Department of the Treasury, Register of Signatures of Depositors in the Branches of the Freedman's Savings and Trust Company, Atlanta Branch, 1870–1874 (Microfilm Publication, M-544), National Archives (hereafter cited as Freedman's Bank Records). Frederick Ayer to George Whipple, 15 February 1866 (Georgia microfilm reels), American Missionary Association Archives, Amistad Research Center, Tulane University (hereafter cited as AMA Papers).

2. John Richard Dennett, *The South As It Is: 1865–1866*, ed. Henry M. Christman (New York: Viking, 1965), pp. 267–271; Sidney Andrews, *The South Since the War: As Shown by Fourteen Weeks of Travel and Observation in Georgia and the Carolinas* (Boston, 1866; reprint ed., New York: Arno, 1970), pp. 339–340; Don H. Doyle, *New Men, New Cities, New South: Atlanta, Nashville, Charleston, Mobile, 1860–1910* (Chapel Hill: University of North Carolina Press, 1990), p. 31.

3. Rebecca Craighead to [Samuel] Grant, 15 January 1866, Georgia, AMA Papers; Andrews, *South Since the War*, p. 340; Whitelaw Reid, *After the War: A Tour of the Southern States, 1865–1866* (London, 1866; reprint ed., New York: Harper & Row, 1965), p. 355; Doyle, *New Men*, pp. 34–35; Howard N. Rabinowitz, *Race Relations in the Urban South 1865–1890* (New York: Oxford University Press, 1978), pp. 5–17.

4. See James Michael Russell, *Atlanta, 1847–1890: City Building in the Old South and the New* (Baton Rouge: Louisiana State University Press, 1988), pp. 117–128.

5. Frederick Ayers to Rev. George Whipple, 15 February 1866, Georgia, AMA Papers.

6. See Rebecca Craighead to Rev. Samuel Hunt, 30 April 1866, Georgia, AMA Papers; E. T. Ayer to Rev. Samuel Grant, 3 February 1866, Georgia, AMA Papers; Harriet M. Phillips to Rev. Samuel Grant, 15 January 1866, Georgia, AMA Papers; *American Missionary* 13 (January 1869): 4; John T. Trowbridge, *The South: A Tour of Its Battle-Fields and Ruined Cities* (Hartford, 1866; reprint ed., New York: Arno, 1969), p. 453.

7. Frederick Ayers to Rev. George Whipple, 15 February 1866, Georgia, AMA Papers.

8. See Table 1 at the back of the book.

9. Gretchen Ehrmann Maclachlan, "Women's Work: Atlanta's Industrialization and Urbanization, 1879–1929" (Ph.D. diss., Emory University, 1992), p. 29.

10. H. A. Buck to General [Davis Tillson], 2 October 1865, Letters Recd., ser. 732, Atlanta, Ga. Subasst. Comr., Record Group 105: Bureau of Refugees, Freedmen, and Abandoned Lands (hereafter cited as BRFAL), National Archives (hereafter cited as NA), [FSSP A-5153]; Franklin Brown to Gen. Tillson, 30 July 1866, Unregistered Letters Recd., ser. 632, Ga. Asst. Comr., BRFAL, NA, [FSSP A-5327]; clipping from *Augusta Constitutionalist*, 16 February 1866, filed with Lt. Col. D. O. Poole to Brig. Gen. Davis Tillson, 19 February 1866, Unregistered Letters Recd., ser. 632, Ga. Asst. Comr., BRFAL, NA, [FSSP A-5447]. Citations for photo-

copied documents from the National Archives that were consulted at the Freedmen and Southern Society Project, University of Maryland, conclude with the designation "FSSP" and the project's document control number in square brackets: for example, [FSSP A-5447].

11. Quoted in Trowbridge, *South Tour,* pp. 453–454.

12. Jerry Thornbery, "The Development of Black Atlanta, 1865–1885" (Ph.D. diss., University of Maryland, 1977), pp. 48–53; Edmund L. Drago, *Black Politicians and Reconstruction in Georgia: A Splendid Failure* (Baton Rouge: Louisiana State University Press, 1982), pp. 113–116.

13. Brig. Genl. Davis Tillson to Captain George R. Walbridge, 12 March 1866, Letters Recd., ser. 732, Ga. Subasst. Comr., BRFAL, NA, [FSSP A-5153].

14. Rebecca Craighead to Rev. Samuel Hunt, 15 February 1866, Georgia, AMA Papers; see also F. Ayers to Rev. George Whipple, 15 February 1866, Georgia, AMA Papers.

15. Testimony of Abram Colby, 28 October 1871, in 42nd Congress, 2nd Session, House Report no. 22, pt. 6, *Testimony taken by the Joint Select Committee to Inquire into the Condition of Affairs in the Late Insurrectionary States* (Washington, D.C., 1872), vol. 2, p. 700 (hereafter cited as KKK Hearings). See also testimony of Alfred Richardson, 7 July 1871, KKK Hearings, vol. 1, p. 12.

16. Doyle, *New Men,* pp. 38–48, 151; Jonathan W. McLeod, *Workers and Workplace Dynamics in Reconstruction Era Atlanta* (Los Angeles: Center for Afro-American Studies, University of California), pp. 10–16.

17. McLeod, *Workers and Workplace,* pp. 24–31, 45, 61, 75, 81, 91, 94.

18. Ibid., pp. 77–92, 100–103; Thornbery, "Black Atlanta," pp. 191–225.

19. Entry of 27 May 1865, Ella Gertrude Clanton Thomas Journal, William R. Perkins Library, Duke University (hereafter cited as DU).

20. See entries for May 1865, Thomas Journal, DU.

21. Atlanta *Daily Intelligencer,* 25 October 1865.

22. Emma J. S. Prescott, "Reminiscences of the War," typescript, pp. 49–50, 55, Atlanta History Center (hereafter cited as AHC).

23. Atlanta *Daily New Era,* 27 February 1868.

24. Mr. J. T. Ball to Maj. Knox, 19 March 1866, Unregistered Letters Recd., ser. 2250, Meridian, Miss. Subasst. Comr., BRFAL, NA, [FSSP A-9423].

25. Alexa Wynell Benson, "Race Relations in Atlanta, As Seen in a Critical Analysis of the City Council Proceedings and Other Related Works, 1865–1877" (M.A. thesis, Atlanta University, 1966), pp. 43–44; Foner, *Reconstruction,* pp. 199–202; Theodore Brantner Wilson, *The Black Codes of the South* (University, Ala.: University of Alabama Press, 1965); Rabinowitz, *Race Relations,* pp. 34–35; Atlanta *Daily New Era,* 27 February 1868.

26. Virginia Shelton to William Shelton, 20 August 1866, Campbell Family Papers, DU. See also Ellen Chisholm to Laura Perry, 27 July 1867, Perry Family Papers, AHC.

27. Affidavit of Samuel Ellison, 16 Jan 1867 BRFAL, NA.

28. Foner, *Reconstruction,* pp. 425–444; see testimony of Abram Colby, 28 October 1871, KKK Hearings, vol. 2, pp. 699–702.

29. Testimony of Alfred Richardson, 7 July 1871, KKK Hearings, vol. 1, pp. 12, 18.

30. Foner, *Reconstruction,* pp. 87, 290–291; Elsa Barkley Brown, "Negotiating and Transforming the Public Sphere: African American Political Life in the Transition from Slavery to Freedom," *Public Culture* 7 (Fall 1994): 107–126; Thomas C. Holt, *Black Over White: Negro Political Leadership in South Carolina during Reconstruction* (Urbana: University of Illinois Press, 1977), pp. 34–35.

31. Macon *Georgia Weekly Telegraph,* 8 October 1872, as quoted in Edmund L. Drago, "Militancy and Black Women in Reconstruction Georgia," *Journal of American Culture* 1 (Winter 1978): 841.

32. Testimony of Hannah Flournoy, 24 October 1871, KKK Hearings, vol. 1, p. 533. On Ashburn's death see Drago, *Black Politicians,* pp. 145, 153.

33. Testimony of Joe Brown, 24 October 1871, KKK Hearings, vol. 1, p. 502.

34. Henry McNeal Turner's emancipation speech, 1 January 1866, Augusta, as quoted in Herbert G. Gutman, *The Black Family in Slavery and Freedom, 1750–1925* (New York: Pantheon Books, 1977), p. 388. See also Catherine Clinton, "Bloody Terrain: Freedwomen, Sexuality and Violence During Reconstruction," *Georgia Historical Quarterly* 76 (Summer 1992): 318; Atlanta *Weekly Defiance,* 24 February 1883.

35. Eliza Frances Andrews, *The War-Time Journal of a Georgia Girl, 1864–1865,* ed. Spencer Bidwell King, Jr. (Macon, Ga.: Arvidian Press, 1960), p. 349.

36. Gutman, *Black Family,* pp. 387–388.

37. Testimony of Z. B. Hargrove, 13 July 1871, KKK Hearings, vol. 1, p. 83. See also testimony of George B. Burnett, 2 November 1871, KKK Hearings, vol. 2, p. 949. See Jacquelyn Dowd Hall, *Revolt Against Chivalry: Jesse Daniel Ames and the Women's Campaign Against Lynching* (New York: Columbia University Press, 1974).

38. Affidavit of Barbara Price, 15 May 1867, Misc. Court Records, ser. 737, Atlanta, Ga. Subasst. Comr., BRFAL; Bvt. Maj. Fred. Mosebach to Mayor and City Council of Atlanta, 15 May 1867, and Bvt. Maj. Fred. Mosebach to Col. C. C. Sibley, 21 May 1867, vol. 99, pp. 49 and 53–54, Letters Sent, ser. 729, Atlanta, Ga. Subasst. Comr., BRFAL, NA, [FSSP A-5709]. See also James M. Russell and Jerry Thornbery, "William Finch of Atlanta: The Black Politician as Civic Leader," in Howard N. Rabinowitz, ed. *Southern Black Leaders of the Reconstruction Era* (Urbana: University of Illinois Press, 1982), pp. 317, 332.

39. The apprenticeship system was not entirely limited to the conscription of minors; young adults actively providing for themselves were also apprenticed. For example, a turpentine worker with a wife and child was defined as an orphan in North Carolina. See Foner, *Reconstruction,* p. 201.

40. Martin Lee to Mr. Tillson, 7 December 1866, in Ira Berlin et al., "Afro-American Families in the Transition from Slavery to Freedom," *Radical History Review* 42 (Fall 1988): 102–103.

41. Entry of 27 May 1865, Thomas Journal, DU. Evidence from ex-slave narratives suggests a pattern of exploitation of child laborers; they received little or no cash wages. See testimony of Nancy Smith, in George P. Rawick, ed., *The American Slave: A Composite Autobiography* (Westport, Conn.: Greenwood Press, 1941; 1972), *Georgia Narratives*, vol. 13, pt. 3, p. 302 (hereafter cited as WPA Ga. Narr.); testimony of Georgia Telfair, WPA Ga. Narr., vol. 13, pt. 4, p. 5.

42. Rebecca M. Craighead to Bvt. Brig. Gen. J. H. Lewis, 11 May 1866, Ga. Asst. Comr., C-69, 1867, Letters Recd., ser. 631, Ga. Asst. Comr., BRFAL, NA, [FSSP A-415].

43. F. Ayers to Rev. George Whipple, 15 February 1866, Georgia, AMA Papers.

44. Prescott, "Reminiscences of the War," p. 56, AHC. Prescott goes on to reveal that Silvey died penniless, without the help of former owners.

45. Gutman, *Black Family,* pp. 9–23; Berlin et al., "Afro-American Families," pp. 92–93.

46. Corporal Murray, as quoted in J. R. Johnson to Col. S. Lee, 1 June 1866, in Berlin et al., "Afro-American Families," p. 97.

47. For examples of these efforts see Wm. H. Sinclair to Freedmen's Bureau agent at Savannah, Ga., 12 September 1866, Unregistered Letters, ser. 1013, Savannah, Ga. Subasst. Comr., BRFAL, NA, [FSSP A-5762]; R. F. Patterson to Col. D. C. Poole, Letters Recd., ser. 732, Atlanta, Ga. Subasst. Comr., BRFAL, NA, [FSSP A-5704].

48. Gutman, *Black Family,* pp. 418–425.

49. 1st Lt. F. E. Grossmann to the Acting Assistant Adjutant General, 1 October 1866, in Berlin et al., "Afro-American Families," pp. 97–98. Gutman, *Black Family,* pp. 418–425.

50. James D. Anderson, *The Education of Blacks in the South, 1860–1935* (Chapel Hill: University of North Carolina Press, 1988), pp. 4–9, 16; Herbert G. Gutman, "Schools for Freedom: The Post-Emancipation Origins of Afro-American Education," in Herbert G. Gutman, *Power and Culture: Essays on the American Working-Class,* ed. Ira Berlin (New York: Pantheon, 1987), p. 294; Jacqueline Jones, *Soldiers of Light and Love: Northern Teachers and Georgia Blacks 1865–1873 Chapel Hill: University of North Carolina Press, 1980),* p. 59.

51. Gutman, "Schools for Freedom," pp. 286, 294; Jones, *Soldiers of Light and Love,* p. 62; Anderson, *Education of Blacks in the South,* pp. 4–32.

52. Drago, *Black Politicians,* pp. 27–28.

53. Russell and Thornbery, "William Finch of Atlanta," pp. 319, 322; Russell, *Atlanta,* p. 181.

54. Mrs. E. T. Ayers to Rev. Samuel Hunt, 1 September 1866, Georgia, AMA Papers.

55. Jennies Barium to Rev. Samuel Grant, 27 January 1866, Georgia, AMA Papers; Andrews, *South Since the War,* p. 338.

56. Sarah J. Thomas to Mr. [Edmund A.] Ware, 11 October 1869, Edmund A. Ware Papers, Robert W. Woodruff Library, Clarke Atlanta University.

DOCUMENTS: After the Civil War: Reconsidering the Law

Reconstruction Amendments, 1868, 1870

Until 1868, the United States Constitution made no explicit distinctions on the basis of gender. Of qualifications for voters, it said only that "the electors in each State shall have the qualifications requisite for electors of the most numerous branch of the State legislature" (Article I, section 2). Reformers merely needed to persuade each state legislature to change its own rules in order to enfranchise women in national elections.

The word *male* was introduced into the Constitution in section 2 of the Fourteenth Amendment, as part of a complex provision—never enforced—intended to constrain former Confederates from interfering with the civil rights of newly freed slaves. Suffragists were bitterly disappointed at the failure to include sex as a category in the Fifteenth Amendment. But until the test case of *Minor* v. *Happersett* (pp. 245–46), they clung to the hope that the first article of the Fourteenth Amendment would be interpreted broadly enough to admit women to the polls.

FOURTEENTH AMENDMENT, 1868

1. All persons born or naturalized in the United States, and subject to the jurisdiction thereof, are citizens of the United States and of the State wherein they reside. No State shall make or enforce any law which shall abridge the privileges or immunities of citizens of the United States; nor shall any State deprive any person of life, liberty, or property, without due process of law; nor deny to any person within its jurisdiction the equal protection of the laws.

2. Representatives shall be apportioned among the several States according to their respective numbers, counting the whole number of persons in each State, excluding Indians not taxed. But when the right to vote at any election for the choice of electors for President and Vice-President of the United States, Representatives in Congress, the executive and judicial officers of a State, or the members of the legislature thereof, is denied to any of the male inhabitants of such State, being twenty-one years of age and citizens of the United States, or in any way abridged, except for participation in rebellion, or other crime, the basis of representation therein shall be reduced in the proportion which the number of such male citizens shall bear to the whole number of male citizens twenty-one years of age in such State. . . .

FIFTEENTH AMENDMENT, 1870

The right of citizens of the United States to vote shall not be denied or abridged by the United States or by any State on account of race, color, or previous condition of servitude. . . .

Bradwell *v.* Illinois, *1873*

Although she could not practice in the courts until the end of her career, Myra Brad-well was perhaps the most notable female lawyer of the nineteenth century. She read law in the office of her husband, a prominent Chicago attorney and county judge. In 1868 she began to publish the *Chicago Legal News*, a weekly newspaper covering developments in courts and legislatures throughout the country. Because she had received a special charter from the state legislature under which she was permitted to act without the usual legal disabilities of a married woman, she ran the *News* as her own business. She wrote vigorous editorials, evaluating legal opinions and new laws, assessing proposed state legislation, and supporting progressive developments like prison reform, the establishment of law schools, and women's rights. She drafted bills improving married women's rights to child custody and to property, including the Illinois Married Woman's Property Act of 1869. Thanks in part to her own lobbying efforts, Illinois permitted women to own property and to control their own earnings.

It was only logical that Myra Bradwell should seek admission to the bar. Although she passed the entrance tests in 1869, although the Illinois Married Woman's Property Act permitted her to own property, and although the law that gave the state supreme court the power to license attorneys did not explicitly exclude women, her application was rejected by the Illinois Supreme Court on the grounds that she was a married woman, and therefore not a truly free agent. Appealing to the United States Supreme Court, her attorney argued that among the "privileges and immunities" guaranteed to each citizen by the Fourteenth Amendment was the right to pursue any honorable profession. "Intelligence, integrity and honor are the only qualifications that can be prescribed . . . the broad shield of the Constitution is over all, and protects each in that measure of success which his or her individual merits may secure."

The Court's decision came in two parts. Speaking for the majority and citing the most recent decision of the Supreme Court in the slaughterhouse cases, Justice Samuel F. Miller held that the right to practice law in the courts of any particular state was a right that had to be granted by the individual state; it was not one of the "privileges and immunities" of national citizenship. This judgment was supplemented by a concurring opinion, in which Justice Joseph P. Bradley offered an ideological justification for the Court's decision that was based on inherent differences between men and women and that was to be widely used thereafter to defend the exclusion of women from professional careers.

While her case was pending before the U.S. Supreme Court, Bradwell and Alta M. Hulett, another woman who had been refused admission to the bar even though she was otherwise qualified, successfully lobbied for a law that granted freedom of occupational choice to all Illinois citizens, both male and female. The bill was passed in 1872; a year later Alta Hulett was sworn in before the Illinois Bar. Bradwell did not think she should have to beg for admission, and she never formally applied for a license to practice law under the new statute. In the *Chicago Legal News* she observed that "having once complied with the rules and regulations of the court . . . [I] declined to . . . again ask for admission." In 1890, twenty years after her initial application, the Illinois Supreme Court admitted Bradwell to the bar. Two years before her death in 1894 she was admitted to practice before the U.S. Supreme Court, but she never did argue a case there.*

MR. JUSTICE JOSEPH P. BRADLEY

The claim of the plaintiff, who is a married woman, to be admitted to practice as an attorney and counselor at law, is based upon the supposed right of every person, man or woman, to engage in any lawful employment for a livelihood. The supreme court of Illinois denied the application on the ground that, by the common law, which is the basis of the laws of Illinois, only men were admitted to the bar, and the legislature had not made any change in this respect. . . .

The claim that, under the 14th Amendment of the Constitution, which declares that no state shall make or enforce any law which shall abridge the privileges and immunities of citizens of the United States, and the statute law of Illinois, or the common law prevailing in that state, can no longer be set up as a barrier against the right of females to pursue any lawful employment . . . assumes that it is one of the privileges and immunities of women as citizens to engage in any and every profession, occupation or employment in civil life.

It certainly cannot be affirmed, as a historical fact, that this has ever been established as one of the fundamental privileges and immunities of the sex. On the contrary, the civil law, as well as nature herself, has always recognized a wide difference in the respective spheres and destinies of man and woman. Man is, or should be, woman's protector and defender. The natural and proper timidity and delicacy which belongs to the female sex evidently unfits it for many of the occupations of civil life. The constitution of the family organization, which is founded in the divine ordinance, as well as in the nature of things, indi-

cates the domestic sphere as that which properly belongs to the domain and functions of womanhood. The harmony, not to say identity, of interests and views which belong or should belong to the family institution, is repugnant to the idea of a woman adopting a distinct and independent career from that of her husband. So firmly fixed was this sentiment in the founders of the common law that it became a maxim of that system of jurisprudence that a woman had no legal existence separate from her husband, who was regarded as her head and representative in the social state; and, notwithstanding some recent modifications of this civil status, many of the special rules of law flowing from and dependent upon this cardinal principle still exist in full force in most states. One of these is, that a married woman is incapable, without her husband's consent, of making contracts which shall be binding on her or him. This very incapacity was one circumstance which the supreme court of Illinois deemed important in rendering a married woman incompetent fully to perform the duties and trusts that belong to the office of an attorney and counselor.

It is true that many women are unmarried and not affected by any of the duties, complications, and incapacities arising out of the married state, but these are exceptions to the general rule. The paramount destiny and mission of woman are to fulfill the noble and benign offices of wife and mother. This is the law of the Creator. And the rules of civil society must be adapted to the general constitution of things, and cannot be based upon exceptional cases. . . .

*See also Frances Olsen, "From False Paternalism to False Equality: Judicial Assaults on Feminist Community, Illinois 1869–1895," *Michigan Law Review* 84 (1986):1518–43.

Comstock Law, 1873

This "Act for the Suppression of Trade in, and Circulation of Obscene Literature and Articles of Immoral Use" was passed at the urging of Anthony Comstock, the head of the New York Society for the Suppression of Vice. The first section prohibited the sale of the described materials in the District of Columbia and the territories; subsequent sections prohibited the sending of these materials through the mails or their importation into the United States. In the 1870s many states passed their own versions of the federal law.

The law reflected a widespread belief that both contraception and abortion were acts of interference with the natural order and with God's intentions. No distinction was made between drugs used for abortion and materials used for contraception; all were treated in the same terms as pornographic materials. Note the heavy penalties provided.

A century after the Comstock Law, its limitations on birth control information and on pornography had eroded. By 1973 the Supreme Court finally agreed on the definition of obscene material, that is, material unprotected as an exercise of free speech under the First Amendment: "the average person, applying contemporary community standards, would find that the work, taken as a whole, appeals to the prurient interest . . . [describes sexual conduct] in a patently offensive way . . . and . . . lacks serious literary, artistic, political, or scientific value" (*Miller v. California*, 413 U.S. 15 [1973]). In the 1980s some feminists began to argue that pornography ought to be defined not merely as obscenity but as "sexually explicit subordination of women"; that is, that pornography was not simply an expression of free speech, protected under the First Amendment, but an actual injury, to be protected against as a civil liberty. "Depictions of subordination tend to perpetuate subordination. The subordinate status of women in turn leads to affront and lower pay at work, insult and injury at home, battery and rape on the streets," observed a federal court in the course of evaluating an Indianapolis ordinance outlawing pornography in 1985 (*American Booksellers Association v. Hudnut*, 771 F.2d 323 [1985]). Although the Court refused to uphold the ordinance, the issue continues to be debated.

Be it enacted . . . That whoever, within the District of Columbia or any of the Territories of the United States . . . shall sell . . . or shall offer to sell, or to lend, or to give away, or in any manner to exhibit, or shall otherwise publish or offer to publish in any manner, or shall have in his possession, for any such purpose or purposes, any obscene book, pamphlet, paper, writing, advertisement, circular, print, picture, drawing or other representation, figure, or image on or of paper or other material, or any cast, instrument, or other article of an immoral nature, or any drug or medicine, or any article whatever, for the prevention of conception, or for causing unlawful abortion, or shall advertize the same for sale, or shall write or print, or cause to be written or printed, any card, circular, book, pamphlet, advertisement, or notice of any kind, stating when, where, how, or of whom, or by what means, any of

---

Public Laws of the United States of America, Passed at the Third Session of the Forty-Second Congress (Boston, 1873), p. 598.

the articles in this section . . . can be purchased or obtained, or shall manufacture, draw, or print, or in any wise make any of such articles, shall be deemed guilty of a misdemeanor, and on conviction thereof in any court of the United States . . . he shall be imprisoned at hard labor in the penitentiary for not less than six months nor more than five years for each offense, or fined not less than one hundred dollars nor more than two thousand dollars, with costs of court. . . .

Minor v. Happersett, 1875

In 1872 suffragists in a number of places attempted to test the possibilities of the first section of the Fourteenth Amendment. "The power to regulate is one thing, the power to prevent is an entirely different thing," observed Virginia Minor, president of the Woman Suffrage Association of Missouri, and she presented herself at the polls in St. Louis in 1872. When the registrar refused to permit her to register to vote, she and her husband sued him for denying her one of the "privileges and immunities of citizenship"; when they lost the case they appealed to the Supreme Court.

In a unanimous opinion the justices held that if the authors of the Constitution had intended that women should vote, they would have said so explicitly. The decision of the Court meant that woman suffrage could not be developed by way of a quiet reinterpretation of the Constitution but would require an explicit amendment to the Constitution or a series of revisions in the laws of the states.

MR. CHIEF JUSTICE MORRISON R. WAITE DELIVERED THE OPINION OF THE COURT:

The question is presented in this case, whether, since the adoption of the fourteenth amendment, a woman, who is a citizen of the United States and of the State of Missouri, is a voter in that State, notwithstanding the provision of the constitution and laws of the State, which confine the right of suffrage to men alone. . . . The argument is, that as a woman, born or naturalized in the United States and subject to the jurisdiction thereof, is a citizen of the United States and of the State in which she resides, she has the right of suffrage as one of the privileges and immunities of her citizenship, which the State cannot by its laws or constitution abridge.

There is no doubt that women may be citizens. They are persons, and by the fourteenth amendment "all persons born or naturalized in the United States and subject to the jurisdiction thereof" are expressly declared to be "citizens of the United States and of the State wherein they reside." But, in our opinion, it did not need this amendment to give them that position . . . sex has never been made one of the elements of citizenship in the United States. In this respect men have never had an advantage over women. The same laws precisely apply to both. The fourteenth amendment did not affect the citizenship of women any more than it did of men . . . Mrs. Minor . . . has always been a citizen from her birth, and entitled to all the privileges and immunities of citizenship.

If the right of suffrage is one of the necessary privileges of a citizen of the United States, then the constitution and laws of Missouri confining it to men are in violation of the Constitution of the United States, as amended, and consequently void. The direct question is,

88 U.S. 162.

therefore, presented whether all citizens are necessarily voters.

The Constitution does not define the privileges and immunities of citizens. For that definition we must look elsewhere. In this case we need not determine what they are, but only whether suffrage is necessarily one of them.

It certainly is nowhere made so in express terms. The United States has no voters in the States of its own creation. The elective officers of the United States are all elected directly or indirectly by state voters. . . . it cannot for a moment be doubted that if it had been intended to make all citizens of the United States voters, the framers of the Constitution would not have left it to implication. . . .

It is true that the United States guarantees to every State a republican form of government. . . . No particular government is designated as republican, neither is the exact form to be guaranteed, in any manner especially designated. . . . When the Constitution was adopted . . . all the citizens of the States were not invested with the right of suffrage. In all, save perhaps New Jersey, this right was only bestowed upon men and not upon all of them. . . . Under these circumstances it is certainly now too late to contend that a government is not republican, within the meaning of this guaranty in the Constitution, because women are not made voters. . . . If suffrage was intended to be included within its obligations, language better adapted to express that intent would most certainly have been employed. . . .

. . . For nearly ninety years the people have acted upon the idea that the Constitution, when it conferred citizenship, did not necessarily confer the right of suffrage. If uniform practice long continued can settle the construction of so important an instrument as the Constitution of the United States confessedly is, most certainly it has been done here. Our province is to decide what the law is, not to declare what it should be.

We have given this case the careful consideration its importance demands. If the law is wrong, it ought to be changed; but the power for that is not with us. . . . No argument as to woman's need of suffrage can be considered. We can only act upon her rights as they exist. . . .

BARBARA SICHERMAN
Reading *Little Women:* The Many Lives of a Text

Why should girls be learn'd and wise?
Books only serve to spoil their eyes.
The studious eye but faintly twinkles.
And reading paves the way to wrinkles.
—*John Trumbull, 1773*

Although there was much skepticism about whether advanced learning was good for women, the early republic was a time of a transformation of educational opportunity. A virtual revolution in literacy was under way, encouraged by the transition of the economy to a print culture and reinforced by a technology that made printed materials more

From *U.S. History as Women's History: New Feminist Essays*, edited by Linda K. Kerber, Alice Kessler-Harris, and Kathryn Kish Sklar. Copyright © 1995 by the University of North Carolina Press. Used by permission of the publisher. Notes have been renumbered and edited.

widely available and injected them into new areas of life. Reading was linked to rationality, upward mobility, and control of one's own life. Although literacy did not increase at the same rate for each class or each sex within each class, what might be called a "literacy gap" between free white men and women gradually closed during the years before the Civil War. As early as the 1780s, 80 percent of the white women of urban New England were literate; they seem to have been the most literate women in the Western world.

The gains were specific to region. The South lagged far behind; as late as 1850 one out of five white women in the South was illiterate. Literacy was denied slaves by law; free blacks lacked both opportunity and institutional support for extended study. Yet urban African Americans quickly narrowed the gap between the races after the Civil War.

In a world in which only a few thousand women were in a college or university in any given year, and in which even high school education was rare, most "higher" education was necessarily self-education. Women shaped their intellectual lives out of their own diary-keeping, letter-writing, and reading. They chose books that had meaning for their lives. One book came to have more meaning for more women than perhaps any other contemporary publication: Louisa May Alcott's *Little Women*. Barbara Sicherman examines this phenomenon.

What elements of *Little Women* did its first readers respond to? Did the meaning of Little Women change over time? What issues in women's lives did it address? How do you account for its continuing popularity? Did you read *Little Women* when you were young? Have you seen any of the films? What differences of emphasis have you seen between the films and the novel?

"I have read and re-read 'Little Women' and it never seems to grow old," fifteen-year-old Jane Addams confided to a friend.[1] Writing in 1876, Addams did not say why she liked *Little Women*. But her partiality was by no means unusual among women, and even some men, of her generation. Louisa May Alcott's tale of growing up female was an unexpected success when it appeared in the fall of 1868. Already a classic when Addams wrote, the book has been called "the most popular girls' story in American literature"; a century and a quarter after publication, there are twenty editions in print.[2]

The early history of this publishing phenomenon is full of ironies. Not the least of them is the author's expressed distaste for the project. When Thomas Niles Jr., literary editor of the respected Boston firm of Roberts Brothers, asked Alcott to write a *"girls' story,"* the author tartly observed in her journal: "I plod away, though I don't enjoy this sort of thing. Never liked girls or knew many, except my sisters, but our queer plays and experiences may prove interesting, though I doubt it."[3] After

delivering twelve chapters in June 1868, she claimed that both she and her editor found them *"dull."*[4] Niles assured her that he was "pleased—I ought to be more emphatic & say delighted,—so *please* to consider 'judgement' as favorable"; the following month he predicted that the book would "'hit.'"[5] Influenced perhaps by the verdict of "some girls" who had pronounced the manuscript "'splendid!'" Alcott reconsidered while correcting proof: "It reads better than I expected. Not a bit sensational, but simple and true, for we really lived most of it." Of the youngsters who liked it, she observed: "As it is for them, they are the best critics, so I should be satisfied."[6]

The informal "readers' report" was right on target. Published in early October 1868, the first printing (2,000 copies) of *Little Women, or, Meg, Jo, Beth and Amy* sold out within the month. A sequel appeared the following April, with only the designation *Part Second* differentiating it from the original. By the end of the year some 38,000 copies (of both parts) were in print, with another 32,000 in 1870. Nearly

200,000 copies had been printed by Roberts Brothers by January 1888, two months before Alcott's death.[7] Like it or not, with this book Alcott established her niche in the expanding market for juvenile literature.

Perhaps even more remarkable than *Little Women's* initial success has been its longevity. It topped a list of forty books compiled by the Federal Bureau of Education in 1925 that "all children should read before they are sixteen."[8] . . . On a [1976] bicentennial list of the best eleven American children's books, *Little Women, The Adventures of Tom Sawyer,* and *The Adventures of Huckleberry Finn* were the only nineteenth-century titles. Like most iconic works, *Little Women* has been transmuted into other media, into song and opera, theater, radio, and film. A comic strip even surfaced briefly in 1988 in the revamped *Ms.*[9]

Polls and statistics do not begin to do justice to the *Little Women* phenomenon. Reading the book has been a rite of passage for generations of adolescent and preadolescent females of the comfortable classes. It still elicits powerful narratives of love and passion.[10] In a 1982 essay on how she became a writer, Cynthia Ozick declared: "I read 'Little Women' a thousand times. Ten thousand. I am no longer incognito, not even to myself. I am Jo in her 'vortex'; not Jo exactly, but some Jo-of-the-future. I am under an enchantment: Who I truly am must be deferred, waited for and waited for."[11] Ozick's avowal encapsulates recurrent themes in readers' accounts: the deep, almost inexplicable emotions engendered by the novel; the passionate identification with Jo March, the feisty tomboy heroine who publishes stories in her teens; and— allowing for exaggeration—a pattern of multiple readings. Numerous women who grew up in the 1940s and 1950s report that they read the book yearly or more during their teens or earlier; some confide that they continue to read it as adults, though less frequently. Presumably for them, as for Jane Addams, the story did not grow old.

One of many intriguing questions about *Little Women* is how and why the "dull" book, the girls' story by a woman who claimed she never liked girls, captivated so many readers. An added irony is that Alcott, the product of an unconventional upbringing, whose eccentric transcendentalist father self-consciously tested his child-rearing theories on his daugh-

ters, took them to live in a commune, and failed utterly as a breadwinner, should write what many contemporaries considered the definitive story of American family life.[12] . . .

EARLY PUBLISHING AND MARKETING HISTORY

Alcott claimed that she kept on with *Little Women* because "lively, simple books are very much needed for girls, and perhaps I can supply the need."[13] . . . She may have regretted being channeled into one type of literature, but she was extremely well paid for her efforts, a source of considerable pride to a woman whose father was so feckless about money.[14]

Juvenile literature was entering a new phase in the 1860s at the very time Alcott was refashioning her career. . . . In contrast to the overtly religious antebellum stories, in which both sexes were expected to be good and domesticated, the new juvenile market was becoming increasingly segmented by gender. An exciting new adventure literature for boys developed after 1850, featuring escape from domesticity and female authority. Seeking to tap into a new market, Niles asked Alcott to write a "girls' story[.]" . . . Although people of all ages and both sexes read *Little Women,* the book evolved for the emerging female youth market, the "young adults" in the transitional period between childhood and adulthood that would soon be labeled adolescence.[15]

These readers had an unusual say in determining Jo's fate. Eager to capitalize on his experiment, Niles urged Alcott to add a chapter "in which allusions might be made to something in the future."[16] Employing a metaphor well suited to a writer who engaged in theatrical performances most of her life, the volume concludes: "So grouped the curtain falls upon Meg, Jo, Beth and Amy. Whether it ever rises again, depends upon the reception given to the first act of the domestic drama, called 'LITTLE WOMEN.'"[17] Reader response to Alcott's floater was positive but complicated her task. Reluctant to depart from autobiography, Alcott insisted that by rights Jo should remain a "literary spinster." But she felt pressured by readers to imagine a different fate for her heroine. The day she began work on the sequel, she observed: "Girls write to ask who the little women marry, as if that was the only end and aim of a woman's life. I *won't* marry

Jo to Laurie to please anyone." To foil her readers, she created a "funny match" for Jo—the middle-aged, bumbling German professor, Friedrich Bhaer.[18]

The aspect of the book that has frustrated generations of readers—the foreclosing of marriage between Jo and Laurie—thus represents a compromise between Alcott and her initial audience. Paradoxically, this seeming misstep has probably been a major factor in the story's enduring success. If Jo had remained a spinster, as Alcott wished, or if she had married the attractive and wealthy hero, as readers hoped, it is unlikely that the book would have had such a wide appeal. Rather, the problematic ending contributed to Little Women's popularity, the lack of satisfying closure helping to keep the story alive, something to ponder, return to, reread, perhaps with the hope of a different resolution. Alcott's refusal of the conventionally happy ending represented by a pairing of Jo and Laurie and her insistence on a "funny match" to the rumpled and much older professor effectively subvert adolescent romantic ideals. The absence of a compelling love plot has also made it easier for generations of readers to ignore the novel's ending when Jo becomes Mother Bhaer and to retain the image of Jo as the questing teenage tomboy.[19]

At the same time, an adolescent reader, struggling with her appearance and unruly impulses while contemplating the burdens of future womanhood, might find it reassuring that her fictional counterpart emerges happily, if not perhaps ideally, from similar circumstances. For Jo is loved. And she has choices. She turns down the charming but erratic hero, who consoles himself by marrying her pretty and vain younger sister, Amy. Professor Bhaer is no schoolgirl's hero, but Jo believes that he is better suited to her than Laurie. The crucial point is that the choice is hers, its quirkiness another sign of her much-prized individuality.[20] Jo gives up writing sensation stories because her prospective husband considers them unworthy, but she makes it clear that she intends to contribute to the support of their future family.

By marrying off the sisters in the second part, Alcott bowed to young women's interest in romance. The addition of the marriage to the quest plot enabled Little Women to touch the essential bases for middle-class female readers in the late nineteenth century. In this regard, it was unusual for its time. . . . The conjunction of quest and marriage plots helps to account for the book's staying power: it is difficult to imagine large numbers of adolescent female readers in the twentieth century gravitating to a book in which the heroine remained single.[21] Little Women took off with the publication of the second part in April 1869. A Concord neighbor called it "the rage in '69 as 'Pinafore' was in '68."[22] A savvy judge of the market, Niles urged Alcott to "'Make hay while the Sunshines'" and did everything he could to keep her name before the public.[23] Shortly after the appearance of Little Women, Part Second, Roberts Brothers brought out an augmented edition of her first critical success under the title, Hospital Sketches and Camp and Fireside Stories, and in succeeding years published An Old-Fashioned Girl (1870) and Little Men (1871), a sequel to Little Women. . . .

Reviewers stressed the realism of her characters and scenes; readers recognized themselves in her work. Thirteen-year-old Annie Adams of Fair Haven, Vermont, wrote St. Nicholas, the most prestigious of the new children's magazines, that she and her three sisters each resembled one of the March sisters (she was Jo): "So, you see, I was greatly interested in 'Little Women,' as I could appreciate it so well; and it seemed to me as if Miss Alcott must have seen us four girls before she wrote the story."[24] Girls not only read themselves into Little Women, they elaborated on it and incorporated the story into their lives. In 1872 the five Lukens sisters from Brinton, Pennsylvania, sent Alcott a copy of their home newspaper, "Little Things," which was modeled after "The Pickwick Portfolio" produced by the March sisters. Alcott responded with encouragement, asked for further details, and subscribed to the paper . . . She took their aspirations seriously, providing frank, practical advice about magazines, publishers, and authors' fees to these budding literary women.[25]

There was, then, a reciprocal relationship between the characters and home life depicted in Little Women and the lives of middle-class American girls. An unusual feature of this identification was the perception that author and heroine were interchangeable. Alcott's work was marketed to encourage the illusion not only that Jo was Alcott but that Alcott was Jo. When Alcott traveled in Europe in 1870, Niles encouraged her to send for publication

"'Jo's Letters from Abroad to the March's [sic] at Home'" . . .

Readers responded in kind. An ad for *Little Women* quotes a letter written by "Nelly" addressed to "Dear Jo, or Miss Alcott": "We have all been reading 'Little Women,' and we liked it so much I could not help wanting to write to you. We think *you* are perfectly splendid; I like you better every time I read it. We were all so disappointed about your not marrying Laurie; I cried over that part,— . . . Blurring the lines between author and character, the writer also requested a picture, wished the recipient improved health, and invited her to visit.[26]

The illusion that she was the youthful and unconventional Jo made Alcott a more approachable author. But the conflation of author and character had its risks. Young readers who formed an image of the author as Jo, a teenager for most of the novel, were startled by Alcott's appearance. When the Lukens sisters informed her that some "friends" had been disappointed in her picture, Alcott replied that she could not understand why people insisted Jo was young "when she is said to be 30 at the end of the book . . . After seeing the photograph it is hardly necessary to say that Jo and L.M.A. are *not* one, & that the latter is a tired out old lady of 42."[27]

With the publication of *Little Women, Part Second,* Alcott became a celebrity. Correspondents demanded her photograph and autograph seekers descended on her home while she "dodge[d] into the woods *à la* Hawthorne."[2] . . . Alcott also drew more serious admirers, some of whom, like the Lukens sisters, sought her literary advice. In the 1860s and 1870s authorship was the most respected female vocation—and the best paid. . . .

Alcott was a well-respected writer during her lifetime, an era of relatively inclusive and nonhierarchical definitions of literature. An American literature course taken by Jane Addams at Rockford Female Seminary in 1878–79 covered authors of domestic fiction, Alcott among them.[29] But her literary reputation transcended the category. A review of *Little Men* pronounced: "Even thus early in her brief history as a country and a nation, America can boast a long list of classics—Prescott, Irving, Hawthorne, Longfellow—and Time, the great sculptor will one day carve Miss Alcott's name among them."[30] . . .

A teenage girl contemplating a literary career could dream of becoming a published author who, like Alcott, might produce a beloved and immortal work. At a time when young women were encouraged, even expected, to take part in the literary activities that suffused middle-class domestic life, such success was not beyond imagining. From James S. Hart's [*Manual of American Literature* (1873)], a reader could learn that Alcott began writing for publication at sixteen and, by hard work and perseverance, became both famous and self-supporting by her pen in her late thirties.[31] The real female American success story was Alcott's, not Jo's.

There were, then, many reasons why a young woman seeking a literary career in the 1870s and early 1880s would look to Alcott as a model. Most important was the story that brought pleasure to so many. . . . The contrast with Martha Finley's *Elsie Dinsmore* (1867), a story in which strict obedience is exacted from children—to the point of whipping—is striking. In this first of many volumes, the lachrymose and devoutly religious heroine is put upon by relatives and by her father, who punishes her for refusing to play the piano on the Sabbath. Elsie holds fast to her principles but is otherwise self-abnegating in the extreme: it is difficult to imagine her even trying to have fun. . . .

The fictional world of *Little Women* is strikingly different. Despite the use of John Bunyan's *Pilgrim's Progress* as a framing device, an older Calvinist worldview that emphasized sin and obedience to the deity has been replaced by a moral outlook in which self-discipline and doing good to others come first.[32] Consonant with *Little Women's* new moral tone, so congenial to an expanding middle class, are its informal style and rollicking escapades. Aided by her love of the theater and influenced as well by her youthful idol, Charles Dickens, Alcott was a wonderful painter of dramatic scenes; some were heartbreaking, but many were high-spirited depictions of frolics, games, and theatrical productions.[33] She also had an ear for young people's language: her substitution of dialogue for the long passages of moralizing narrative that characterized most girls' books gave her story a compelling sense of immediacy. So did her use of slang, for which critics often faulted her, but which must have endeared her to young readers. Finally, the beautifully realized portrait of Jo March as tomboy, one of the first of its kind, spoke to changing standards of girlhood. Beginning in the 1860s, tomboys were not only tolerated but even admired—up to a point, the point at which they were expected to become women.[34] Perhaps it was fitting after all that it was Alcott, writing of her idiosyncratic childhood in the 1840s, who identified a new type of American girlhood for the 1870s.[35] . . .

JO AS A LITERARY
AND INTELLECTUAL MODEL

Reading Alcott became a necessary ritual for children of the comfortable classes. Growing up at a time and in a class that conferred leisure on its young, children devoted considerable time and energy to literary pursuits. *Little Women* was a way station en route to more adult books. But it was also a text that acquired its own cachet. Alcott was such an accepted part of childhood that even Theodore Roosevelt declared, "at the cost of being deemed effeminate," that he "worshiped" *Little Men, Little Women,* and *An Old-Fashioned Girl.*[36] . . .

Not all of Alcott's early readers focused on Jo; some were taken with the saga of the entire March family, which invited comparisons with their own. Charlotte Perkins Gilman, for example, who grew up in genteel poverty after her father abandoned the family, liked the fact that in Alcott . . . , "the heroes and heroines were almost always poor, and good, while the rich people were generally bad."[37] . . .

Jo March . . . fueled the literary aspirations of M. Carey Thomas, one of Alcott's early readers, during the critical years of early adolescence. In the fall of 1869, the year of *Little Women's* great success, Thomas and her cousin Frank Smith adopted the personae of Jo and Laurie, although as Quakers they should not have been reading fiction at all. At the ages of twelve and fifteen respectively, Thomas and Smith began addressing each other and signing their letters as Jo and Laurie; they meted out other roles to friends and relatives. . . .

When Thomas began a journal in 1870 at age thirteen, she did so in Jo's name. Declaring at the outset: "Ain't going to be sentimental/'No no not for Jo' (not Joe)," she had much in common with Alcott's heroine.[38] Both were "bookworms" and tomboys; both desired independence. Like Jo, Thomas wished to do something "splendid." In early adolescence her ambitions were still diffuse, but they centered on becoming a famous writer, a famous *woman* writer—"Jo (not Joe)." Her life was suffused with literature, with writing as well as reading: in addition to keeping a journal, she wrote poetry, kept a commonplace book, and complied lists of favorite books and poems, some of them annotated. As she gravitated to such champions of aestheticism as Algernon Charles Swinburne and Dante Gabriel Rossetti, by her early twenties she had outgrown Alcott and other writers who upheld morality in their art. But her close friend Bessie King acknowledged the importance of their childhood play in 1879, when Thomas took the audacious step of starting graduate study in Germany: "Somehow today I went back to those early days when our horizon was so limited yet so full of light & our path lay as plain before us. It all came of reading over Miss Alcott's books now the quintescence [sic] of Philistinism then a Bible. . . . Doesn't thee remember when to turn out a 'Jo' was the height of ambition"?[39]

At the time Thomas was so engaged with *Little Women,* she was already a feminist. Sensitive to any gender restriction or slight, whether from people she knew or from biblical or scientific sources, she resolved at fifteen to disprove female inferiority by advancing her own education.[40] Despite its inception as a domestic story, then, Thomas read *Little Women* as a female bildungsroman, as did many women after her. This has in many ways been the most important reading, the one that has made the book such a phenomenon for so many years.

With its secular recasting of *Pilgrim's Progress, Little Women* transforms Christian's allegorical search for the Celestial City into the quintessential female quest plot. In a chapter entitled "Castles in the Air," each of the March sisters reveals her deepest ambition. In its loving depictions of the sisters' struggles to attain their goals (Jo to be a famous writer, Amy an artist, and Meg mistress of a lovely house), *Little Women* succeeds in authorizing female vocation and individuality. Nor did Alcott rule out the possibility of future artistic creativity: although married and managing a large household and school, Jo has not entirely given up her literary dreams, nor Amy her artistic ones. Beth, who has no ambition other than "to stay at home safe with father and mother, and help take care of the family," dies because she can find no way of growing up; her mysterious illness may be read as a failure of imagination, her inability to build castles in the air.[41]

In Jo, Alcott creates a portrait of female creativity that was not traditionally available to women:

> Every few weeks she would shut herself up in her room, put on her scribbling suit, and "fall into a vortex," as she expressed it, writing away at her novel with all her heart and soul, for till that was finished she could find no peace. . . .
>
> She did not think herself a genius by any means; but when the writing fit came on, she gave herself up to it with entire abandon, and led a blissful life, unconscious of want, care, or bad weather, while she sat safe and happy in an imaginary world, full of friends almost as real and dear to her as any in the flesh. Sleep forsook her eyes, meals stood untasted, day and night were all too short to enjoy the happiness which blessed her only at such times, and made these hours worth living, even if they bore no other fruit. The divine afflatus usually lasted a week or two, and then she emerged from her "vortex" hungry, sleepy, cross, or despondent.[42]

Alcott's portrait of concentrated purpose—which describes her own creative practice—is as far removed as it could be from the ordinary lot of women, at least any adult woman. Jo not only has a room of her own; she also has the leisure—and the license—to remove herself from all obligation to others. Jo was important to young women like Thomas because there were so few of her—in literature or in life. . . .

More conventional readers of Thomas's era could find in Little Women practical advice on two subjects of growing concern to women: economic opportunities and marriage. Alcott was well qualified to advise on the former because of her long years of struggle in the marketplace. . . . Middle-class women's need to be able to earn a living is a central motif in Little Women, as it was in Alcott's life. . . . Mr. March's economic setback, like Bronson Alcott's, forces his daughters into the labor market. Their jobs (as governess and companion) are depicted as mainly unrewarding, although Jo's literary career is described with

loving particularity. . . . But although the March sisters marry, Marmee March, who wishes no greater joy for her daughters than a happy marriage, declares that it is better to remain single than to marry without love. Opportunities for self-respecting singlehood and women's employment went hand in hand, as Alcott knew.[43]

If Alcott articulated issues highly pertinent to young women of her era, Jo's continued appeal suggests not only the dearth of fictional heroines to foster dreams of glory but the continued absence of real-life models. Perhaps that is why Simone de Beauvoir was so attracted to Little Women, in which she thought she "caught a glimpse of my future self":

> I identified passionately with Jo, the intellectual. . . . She wrote: in order to imitate her more completely, I composed two or three short stories. . . . [T]he relationship between Jo and Laurie touched me to the heart. Later, I had no doubt, they would marry one another; so it was possible for maturity to bring the promises made in childhood to fruition instead of denying them: this thought filled me with renewed hope. . . . [I]n Little Women Jo was superior to her sisters, who were either more virtuous or more beautiful than she, because of her passion for knowledge and the vigor of her thinking. . . . I, too, felt I was entitled to consider my taste in reading and my scholastic success as tokens of a personal superiority which would be borne out by the future. I became in my own eyes a character out of a novel.[44]

De Beauvoir found in Jo a model of authentic selfhood, someone she could emulate in the present and through whom she could read—and invent—her own destiny. It was a future full of possibility, open rather than closed, intellectual and literary rather than domestic. By fictionalizing her own life, de Beauvoir could more readily contemplate a career as a writer and an intellectual, no matter how improbable such an outcome seemed to her family. . . . Although de Beauvoir later claimed that she first learned from Little Women that "marriage was not necessary," she responded to the romance as well as the quest plot. Her conviction that Jo and Laurie would marry some day and the "renewed hope" this belief gave her suggest the power of wish fulfillment and the reader's capacity to create her own text. There is no textual basis for this belief: Jo and Laurie each marry someone else; each is a parent by the end of the story. De

Beauvoir's reading is therefore not just a matter of filling in gaps but of rewriting the text. Her powerful commentary suggests the creativity of the reading experience and the permeability of boundaries between life and art: lives can be fictionalized, texts can be rewritten, art can become life and life art.

Not all women read with the intensity of Thomas or de Beauvoir. But there is considerable evidence that, from the time of her creation until the recent past, Jo March provided for young women of the comfortable classes a model of female independence and of intellectual and literary achievement. This is not the only way of reading *Little Women,* but it constitutes a major interpretive strand, particularly in the twentieth century. Testimony on this point began as soon as the book was published and persists today among women who grew up in the 1940s and 1950s.[45] Thomas, whose love relations were with women, never mentions the marriage plot, but for de Beauvoir, writing in the twentieth century, it was both important and compatible with a quest plot.

INFLECTIONS OF CLASS AND CULTURE

. . . For African American women, in the nineteenth century at least, class rather than race was probably the primary determinant of reading practices. Both Mary Church Terrell, a graduate of Oberlin College, and Ida B. Wells, the slave-born daughter of a carpenter and "a famous cook" who became a journalist and reformer, read Alcott. Terrell claimed that her books "were received with an acclaim among the young people of this country which has rarely if ever been equaled and never surpassed," while Wells observed: "I had formed my ideals on the best of Dickens's stories, Louisa May Alcott's, Mrs. A.D.T. Whitney's, and Charlotte Brontë's books, and Oliver Optic's stories for boys." Neither singled out *Little Women;* both seem to have read Alcott as part of the standard fare of an American middle-class childhood.[46]

For African American writer Ann Petry, [who died in 1997 at the age of 89,] *Little Women* was much more than that. On the occasion of her induction into the Connecticut Women's Hall of Fame, she noted her admiration for women writers who had preceded and set the stage for her—"'Think of Louisa May Alcott.'" *Little Women* was the first book

Petry "read on her own as a child." Her comments are reminiscent of those of de Beauvoir and other writers: "I couldn't stop reading because I had encountered Jo March. I felt as though I was part of Jo and she was part of me. I, too, was a tomboy and a misfit and kept a secret diary. . . . She said things like 'I wish I was a horse, then I could run for miles in this splendid air and not lose my breath.' I found myself wishing the same thing whenever I ran for the sheer joy of running. She was a would-be writer—and so was I."[47] . . .

Some working-class women found *Little Women* . . . banal. Dorothy Richardson, a journalist, suggests as much in *The Long Day,* an account of her life among the working class. In an arresting episode, Richardson ridicules the reading preferences of her fellow workers in a paper box factory. The plot of a favorite novel, Laura Jean Libbey's *Little Rosebud's Lovers; or, A Cruel Revenge,* is recounted by one of the workers as a tale of a woman's triumph over all sorts of adversity, including abductions and a false marriage to one of the villains. When Richardson summarizes *Little Women,* a coworker dismisses it: "'[T]hat's no story—that's just everyday happenings. I don't see what's the use of putting things like that in books. I'll bet any money that lady what wrote it knew all them boys and girls. They just sound like real, live people; and when you was telling about them I could just see them as plain as plain could be. . . . I suppose farmer folks likes them kind of stories. . . . They ain't used to the same styles of anything that us city folks are.'"[48]

The box makers found the characters in *Little Women* "real"—an interesting point in itself—but did not care to enter its narrative framework. Though they were not class conscious in a political sense, their awareness of their class position may account at least in part for their disinterest in a story whose heroines, despite economic reverses, had the leisure to pursue their interests in art, music, and literature and could expect to live in suburban cottages, conditions out of reach for most working-class women. Since *their* "everyday happenings" were poverty and exhausting work, the attraction of fictions about working girls who preserved their virtue and came into great wealth, either through marriage or disclosure of their middle- or upper-class origins, is understandable. Such denouements would have seemed just as likely—or unlikely—as a future in a suburban cottage. In the absence, in story or in life, of a female success tradition of moving up the occupational ladder, the "Cinderella tale" of marrying up was the nearest thing to a Horatio Alger story for working-class women.[49]

Reading practices depend on cultural as well as class location. It is a telling commentary on class in America that some Jewish immigrant women, who would be defined as working class on the basis of family income and occupation, not only enjoyed Little Women but also found in it a vehicle for envisioning a new and higher status.[50] For them, Alcott's classic provided a model for transcending their status as ethnic outsiders and for gaining access to American life and culture. It was a first step into the kind of middle-class family life rejected by Thomas and de Beauvoir. These immigrants found the book liberating and read it as a success story—but of a different kind.

In My Mother and I, Elizabeth G. Stern (1889–1954) charts the cultural distance a Jewish immigrant woman traveled from Russia and a midwestern urban ghetto to the American mainstream: she graduates from college, studies social work marries a professional man, and becomes a social worker and writer.[51] Little Women occupies a crucial place in the story. After the narrator comes across it in a stack of newspapers in a rag shop, the book utterly engrosses her: "I sat in the dim light of the rag shop and read the browned pages of that ragged copy of 'Little Women.' . . . [N]o book I have opened has meant as much to me as did that small volume telling in simple words such as I myself spoke, the story of an American childhood in New England. I had found a new literature, the literature of childhood." She had also found the literature of America: "I no longer read the little paper-bound Yiddish novelettes which father then sold. In the old rag shop loft I devoured the English magazines and newspapers." Of the books her teachers brought her from the public library, she writes:

Far more marvellous than the fairy stories were to me in the ghetto street the stories of American child life, all the Alcott and the Pepper books. The pretty mothers, the childish ideals, the open gardens, the homes of many rooms were as unreal to me as the fairy stories. But reading of them made my aspirations beautiful.

My books were doors that gave me entrance into another world. Often I think that I did not grow up in the ghetto but in the books I read as a child in the ghetto. The life in Soho passed me by and did not touch me, once I began to read.[52] . . .

Stern was not unique in reading Little Women as a vehicle for assimilation into American middle-class life or in conflating "American" and "middle class." More than half a century later, a Jewish male writer explored the novel's appeal as an "American" book:

[T]o me, a first generation American, raised in an Orthodox Jewish house-hold where more Yiddish was spoken than English, everything about Little Women was exotic. It was all so American, so full of a life I did not know but desperately hoped to be part of, an America full of promises, hopes, optimisms, an America where everyone had a chance to become somebody wonderful like Jo March—Louisa May Alcott who (I had discovered that the Marches and the Alcotts were almost identical) did become, with this story book that I adored, world famous.[53]

What had been realistic to the early middle- and upper-middle-class WASP readers of Little Women was "exotic" to Jewish immigrants a generation or two later. Could there be a better illustration of the importance of historical location in determining meaning? . . .

One of the Jewish immigrants for whom Alcott's success proved inspiring was Mary Antin, a fervent advocate of assimilation into American life. Alcott's were the children's books she "remember[ed] with the greatest delight" (followed by boys' adventure books, especially Alger's). Antin, who published poems in English in her teens and contemplated a literary career, lingered over the biographical entries she found in an encyclopedia. She "could not resist the temptation to study out the exact place . . . where my name would belong. I saw that it would come not far from 'Alcott, Louisa M.'; and I covered my face with my hands, to hide the silly, baseless joy in it."[54] We have come full circle. Eager to assimilate, Antin responded in ways reminiscent of Alcott's early native-born and middle-class readers who admired her success as an author. Antin, too, could imagine a successful American career for herself, a career for which Alcott was still the model.

CONCLUSION

Not all readers of Little Women read the same text. This is literally the case, since the story went through many editions. Not until 1880 did it appear in one volume, illustrated in this case and purged of some of its slang.[55] Since then there have been numerous editions and many publishers. I have been concerned here with the changing meaning of the story for different audiences and with historical continuities as well. For many middle-class readers, early and later, *Little Women* provided a model of womanhood that deviated from conventional gender norms, a continuity that suggests how little these norms changed in their essentials from the late 1860s to the 1960s. Reading individualistically, they viewed Jo as an intellectual and a writer, the liberated woman they sought to become. No matter that Jo marries and raises a family; such readers remember the young Jo, the teenager who is far from beautiful, struggles with her temper, is both a bookworm and the center of action, and dreams of literary glory while helping to support her family with her pen. These readers for the most part took for granted their right to a long and privileged childhood, largely exempt from the labor market. Jewish women who immigrated to the United States in their youth could not assume such a childhood. Nor were those raised in Orthodox Jewish households brought up on an individualistic philosophy. Their school experiences and reading—American books like *Little Women*—made them aware of different standards of decorum and material life that we tend to associate with class, but that are cultural as well. For some of these readers, *Little Women* offered a fascinating glimpse into an American world. Of course we know, as they did not, that the world Alcott depicted was vanishing, even as she wrote. Nevertheless, that fictional world, along with their school encounters, provided a vision of what life, American life, could be.

Can readers do whatever they like with texts? Yes and no. As we have seen, *Little Women* has been read in many ways, depending not only on when and by whom it was read but also on readers' experiences and aspirations. It has been read as a romance or as a quest, or both. It has been read as a family drama that validates virtue over wealth. It has been read as a how-to manual by immigrants who wanted to assimilate into American, middle-class life and as a means of escaping that life by women who knew its gender constraints too well. For many, especially in the

early years, *Little Women* was read through the life of the author, whose literary success exceeded that of her fictional persona.

At the same time, both the passion *Little Women* has engendered in diverse readers and its ability to survive its era and transcend its genre point to a text of unusual permeability.... Most important, readers' testimony in the nineteenth and twentieth centuries points to *Little Women* as a text that opens up possibilities rather than foreclosing them. With its multiple reference points and voices (four sisters, each distinct and recognizable), its depictions of joy as well as sorrow, its fresh and unlabored speech, Alcott's classic has something for almost everyone. For readers on the threshold of adulthood, the text's authorizing of female ambition has been a significant counterweight to more habitual gender prescriptions.

Little Women is such a harbinger of modern life, of consumer culture and new freedom for middle-class children, it is easy to forget that it was written just a few years after the Civil War, in the midst of Reconstruction and at a time of economic dislocation. For the most part, Alcott left such contemporary markers out of her story, another sign of the text's openness. The Civil War provides an important backdrop and a spur to heroism at home as well as on the battlefield, but it is primarily a plot device to remove Mr. March from the scene. Despite her family's support of John Brown, Alcott does not press a particular interpretation of the war. A final reason *Little Women* has survived so well, despite the chasm that separates Alcott's era from ours, is the virtual absence of references to outside events that would date her story and make it grow old.[56] That way each generation can invent it anew.

NOTES

Citations to the Alcott Family Papers (bMS Am 1130.8 and bMS Am 800.23) are by permission of the Houghton Library, Harvard University.

1. Addams to Vallie Beck, March 16, 1876, *The Jane Addams Papers*, edited by Mary Lynn McGree Bryan (Ann Arbor: University Microfilms International, 1984) (hereafter cited as *Addams Papers*), reel 1.

2. Frank Luther Mott, *Golden Multitudes: The Story of Best Sellers in the United States* (New York: Macmillan, 1947), p. 102: *Books in Print*, 1992–93.

3. May 1868, *The Journals of Louisa May Alcott*, edited by Joel Myerson and Daniel Shealy, associate ed. Madeleine B. Stern (Boston: Little, Brown, 1989),

pp. 165–66 (hereafter cited as *Journals*). On reading this entry in later years, Alcott quipped: "Good joke."

4. June [1868], *Journals*, p. 166.

5. Niles to Alcott, June 16, 1868 (#1) and July 25, 1868 (#2), bMS Am 1130.8, Alcott Family Papers, Houghton Library, Harvard University (all citations from Niles's letters are from this collection).

6. August 26 [1868], *Journals*, p. 166. . . .

7. For an account of Alcott's sales through 1909, by which time nearly 598,000 copies of *Little Women* had been printed by Roberts Brothers, see Joel Myerson and Daniel Shealy, "The Sales of Louisa May Alcott's Books," *Harvard Library Bulletin*, n.s., 1 (Spring 1990), esp. pp. 69–71, 86. Sales figures are unreliable for the twentieth century, in part because of foreign sales and the proliferation of editions after the expiration of copyright. Dorothea Lawrence Mann, "When the Alcott Books Were New," *Publishers' Weekly* 116 (September 28, 1929): 1619, claimed sales of nearly three million.

Sales, of course, are only part of the story: library use was high at the outset and remained so.

8. Mann, "When the Alcott Books Were New."

9. See Gloria T. Delamar, *Louisa May Alcott and 'Little Women': Biography, Critique, Publications, Poems, Songs, and Contemporary Relevance* (Jefferson, N.C.: McFarland and Co., 1990), p. 167 and passim.

10. For an intriguing analysis of well-loved texts that takes *Little Women* as a point of departure, see Catharine R. Stimpson, "Reading for Love: Canons, Paracanons, and Whistling Jo March," *New Literary History* 21 (Autumn 1990): 957–76.

11. "Spells, Wishes, Goldfish, Old School Hurts," *New York Times Book Review*, January 31, 1982, p. 24.

12. The classic biography is still Madeleine B. Stern, *Louisa May Alcott* (Norman: University of Oklahoma Press, 1950), which should be supplemented by Stern's extensive criticism on Alcott. See also Sarah Elbert, *A Hunger for Home: Louisa May Alcott and "Little Women"* (Philadelphia: Temple University Press, 1984), and Martha Saxton, *Louisa May: A Modern Biography of Louisa May Alcott* (New York: Avon Books, 1978).

13. June [1868], *Journals*, p. 166.

14. Niles told Alcott that her royalties were higher than any other Roberts Brothers author, including Harriet Beecher Stowe, whom he considered the American writer who could command the highest fees (Alcott possibly excepted). On the redirection of Alcott's career, see Richard H. Brodhead, "Starting Out in the 1860s: Alcott, Authorship, and the Postbellum Literary Field," in *Cultures of Letters: Scenes of Reading and Writing in Nineteenth-Century America* (Chicago: University of Chicago Press, 1993).

15. See Edward G. Salmon, "What Girls Read," *Nineteenth Century* 20 (October 1886): 515–29, and the ad for a series of "Books for Girls" whose intended audience was those "between eight and eighteen. . . . for growing-up girls, the mothers of the next generation." *American Literary Gazette and Publishers' Circular* (ALG) 17 (June 1, 1871): 88.

16. Niles to Alcott, July 25, 1868 (#2).

17. *Little Women* (New York: Random House/Modern Library, 1983), p. 290.

18. November 1, [1868], *Journals*, p. 167; Alcott

to Elizabeth Powell, March 20, [1869], in *The Selected Letters of Louisa May Alcott*, edited by Joel Myerson and Daniel Shealy, associate ed. Madeleine B. Stern (Boston: Little, Brown, 1987), p. 125 (hereafter cited as *SL*). Erin Graham, "Books That Girls Have Loved," *Lippincott's Monthly Magazine*, September 1897, pp. 428–32, makes much of Bhaer's foreignness and ungainliness.

19. Jo's standing as a tomboy was recognized— and even respected; an ad for *Little Men* noted that "when a girl, [Jo] was half a boy herself." ALG 17 (May 15, 1871): 49. For girls in early adolescence and/or for lesbian readers, the young Jo may have been the primary romantic interest.

20. A conversation with Dolores Kreisman contributed to this analysis.

21. For an analysis of changes in girls' stories as the heterosexual imperative became stronger, see Martha Vicinus, "What Makes a Heroine?: Nineteenth-Century Girls' Biographies," *Genre* 20 (Summer 1987): 171–87.

22. Frank Preston Stearns, *Sketches from Concord and Appledore* (New York: Putnam, 1895), p. 82.

23. Niles to Alcott, April 14, 1869 (#4).

24. Letter in *St. Nicholas*, February 1878, p. 300.

25. "Little Things," at first handwritten, then typeset on a small press, was part of a national phenomenon. See Paula Petrik, "The Youngest Fourth Estate: The Novelty Toy Printing Press and Adolescence, 1870–1886," in *Small Worlds: Children and Adolescents in America, 1850–1950*, edited by Elliott West and Paula Petrik (Lawrence: University Press of Kansas, 1992), pp. 125–42. Alcott's correspondence with the Lukens sisters, which extended over fourteen years, is reprinted in SL. . . . The Alcott sisters had their own Pickwick Club in 1849.

26. Letter from "Nelly," dated March 12, 1870, reproduced in Delamar, *Louisa May Alcott*, p. 146.

27. Alcott to the Lukens Sisters, October 2, 1874, SL, pp. 185–86. . . .

28. April [1869], *Journals*, p. 171.

29. "American Literature," [1878–79], *Addams Papers*, reel 27, frames 239–95.

30. Undated review of *Little Men* ("Capital" penciled in), bMS Am 800.23, Alcott Family Papers.

31. See, e.g., Louise Chandler Moulton, "Louisa May Alcott," *Our Famous Women* (1883; reprint, Hartford: A. D. Worthington, 1884), pp. 29–52, which was prepared with Alcott's assistance. Reports of Alcott's financial success appeared frequently in the press.

32. *The Ladies' Repository* ([December 1868], p. 472), while finding *Little Women* "very readable," pointedly observed that it was "not a Christian book. It is religion without spirituality, and salvation without Christ."

33. Alcott's depiction of home theatricals drew the wrath of some evangelicals. Niles to Alcott, October 26, 1868 (#3). . . .

34. On tomboys, see Sharon O'Brien, "Tomboyism and Adolescent Conflict: Three Nineteenth-Century Case Studies," in *Woman's Being, Woman's Place: Female Identity and Vocation in American History*, edited by Mary Kelley (Boston: G. K. Hall, 1979), pp. 351–72, which includes a section on Alcott. . . .

35. The Katy books of "Susan Coolidge," pen

name of Sarah Chauncey Woolsey, another Roberts Brothers author, are perhaps closest to Alcott's. But even Katy Carr, who begins as another Jo, an ambitious, harumscarum, and fun-loving girl, is severely punished for disobedience; only after suffering a broken back and several years of invalidism does she emerge as a thoughtful girl who will grow into "true womanhood."

36. Roosevelt, *An Autobiography* (1913; reprint, New York: De Capo Press, 1985), p. 17.

37. Gilman, *The Living of Charlotte Perkins Gilman* (1935; reprint, New York: Harper and Row, 1975), p. 35.

38. M. Carey Thomas Journal, June 20, 1870, *The Papers of M. Carey Thomas in the Bryn Mawr College Archives*, edited by Lucy Fisher West (Woodbridge, Conn.: Research Publications, 1982) (hereafter cited as MCTP), reel 1.

39. Elizabeth King Ellicott to Thomas, November 23, [1879], MCTP, reel 39.

40. See Marjorie Housepian Dobkin, ed., *The Making of a Feminist: Early Journals and Letters of M. Carey Thomas* (N.p.: Kent State University Press, 1979), pp. 66–67 and passim.

41. These remarks draw on Sicherman, "Reading and Ambition: M. Carey Thomas and Female Heroism," *American Quarterly* 45 (March 1993): 82–83.

42. *Little Women*, pp. 328–29.

43. On this subject, see Lee Virginia Chambers-Schiller, *Liberty, a Better Husband: Single Women in America: The Generations of 1780–1840* (New Haven: Yale University Press, 1984). In her next book, *An Old-Fashioned Girl*, Alcott ventures much further in envisioning a life of singlehood and lovingly depicts a community of self-supporting women artists.

44. Simone de Beauvoir, *Memoirs of a Dutiful Daughter*, translated by James Kirkup (1949; reprint, Cleveland: World Publishing Co., 1959), pp. 94–95. . . . According to Deirdre Bair, de Beauvoir had read Little Women by the time she was ten. Bair, *Simone de Beauvoir: A Biography* (New York: Summit Books, 1990), pp. 68–71.

45. These conclusions emerge from my reading and from discussions of *Little Women* with more than a dozen women. They were highly educated for the most part and mainly over fifty, but some women under thirty also felt passionately about the book. Most of my informants were white, but see n. 48 below.

46. Mary Church Terrell, *A Colored Woman in a White World* (1940; reprint, New York: Arno Press, 1980), p. 26; Alfreda M. Duster, ed., *Crusade for Justice: The Autobiography of Ida B. Wells* (Chicago: University of Chicago Press, 1970), pp. 7, 21–22. Wells observed that in her early years, she "never read a Negro book or anything about Negroes."

47. *The Middletown Press*, June 1, 1994, p. B1, and Ann Petry to author, letter postmarked July 23, 1994; I am grateful to Farah Jasmine Griffin for the *Middletown Press* reference. *Little Women* continues to play an important role in the lives of some young black women. A high school student in Jamaica, for example, rewrote the story to fit a local setting. And a young, African American academic felt so strongly about *Little Women* that, on learning about my proj-ect, she contended with some heat that Aunt March was unfair in taking Amy rather than Jo to Europe; she seemed to be picking up a conversation she had just left off. Comments like these and Petry's suggest the need for research on the interaction between race and class in African American women's reading practices.

48. Dorothy Richardson, *The Long Day: The Story of a New York Working Girl as Told by Herself* (1905; reprint, New York: Quadrangle Books, 1972), pp. 75–86 (quotation, p. 86). . . . *The Long Day*, which purports to be the story of an educated woman forced by circumstances to do manual labor, must be used with caution. It was initially published anonymously, and many scenes read like sensational fiction. Leonora O'Reilly, a feminist trade unionist, was so outraged at the book's condescension and its insinuations that working-class women were immoral that she drafted a blazing indictment. Leonora O'Reilly Papers, edited by Edward T. James, *Papers of the Women's Trade Union League and Its Principal Leaders* (Woodbridge, Conn.: Research Publications, 1981), reel 9.

49. Michael Denning, *Mechanic Accents: Dime Novels and Working-Class Culture in America* (London: Verso, 1987), pp. 197–200, analyzes *Little Rosebud's Lovers* as a "Cinderella tale." He suggests that stories read by the middle class tended to depict working-class women as victims (of seduction and poverty) rather than as triumphant.

50. I have discussed Jewish immigrants at some length because of the abundance of evidence, not because I view them as the only model for an alternative reading of *Little Women*.

51. *My Mother and I* (New York: Macmillan, 1917) is a problematic book. Some contemporaries reviewed it as autobiographical fiction, but recent critics have tended to view it as autobiography. Theodore Roosevelt must have considered it the latter when he lauded it as a "really noteworthy story" of Americanization in the foreword. . . . Moreover, the facts Stern gave out about her early life—including her status as an Eastern European Jewish immigrant—correspond with the narrator's history. Stern's older son, however, maintains that his mother was native born and Protestant and claimed her Jewish foster parents as her biological parents to hide her out-of-wedlock birth. T[homas] Noel Stern, *Secret Family* (South Dartmouth, Mass.: T. Noel Stern, 1988). Ellen M. Umansky, who generously shared her research materials with me, concludes in "Representations of Jewish Women in the Works and Life of Elizabeth Stern," *Modern Judaism* 13 (1993): 165–76: "[I]t may be difficult if not impossible to ever determine which of Stern's literary self representations reflected her own experiences" (p. 174). Sources that appear to substantiate Elizabeth Stern's foreign and Jewish birth are the U.S. Census for 1900 and for 1910, which both list her birthplace as Russia; the certificate of her marriage, which was performed by a prominent Orthodox rabbi in Pittsburgh; and Aaron Levin's will, which lists Stern as his oldest child.

Despite its contested status, I have drawn on *My Mother and I* because Stern's choice of *Little Women* as a critical marker of American aspirations is consistent with other evidence. The narrative's emphasis on the differences between immigrant and American culture comports with representations in less problematic works by Jewish immigrant writers. Moreover, whatever the facts of Stern's birth, she lived with the Jewish Levin family for many years.

52. *My Mother and I*, pp. 69–71.

53. Leo Lerman, "Little Women: Who's in Love with Miss Louisa May Alcott? I Am," *Mademoiselle*, December 1973, reprinted in Madeleine B. Stern, ed., *Critical Essays on Louisa May Alcott* (Boston: G. K. Hall, 1984), p. 113. See also Stephan F. Brumberg, *Going to America, Going to School: The Jewish Immigrant Public School Encounter in Turn-of-the-Century New York City* (New York: Praeger, 1986), pp. 121–22, 141.

54. Mary Antin, *The Promised Land* (Boston: Houghton Mifflin, 1912), pp. 257, 258–59.

55. Elaine Showalter, "*Little Women:* The American Female Myth," chap. 3 in *Sister's Choice: Tradition and Change in Women's Writing* (Oxford: Clarendon Press, 1991), pp. 55–56; Madeleine B. Stern to author, July 31, 1993. The English edition continued to be published in two volumes, the second under the title *Good Wives*.

56. Elizabeth Young, "Embodied Politics: Fictions of the American Civil War" (Ph.D. diss., University of California, Berkeley, 1993), reading *Little Women* in conjunction with *Hospital Sketches*, views it as a "war novel" (p. 108).

DOCUMENT: The Women's Centennial Agenda, 1876

Elizabeth Cady Stanton and Susan B. Anthony, "Guaranteed to us and our daughters forever"

The capstone of the celebration of the Centennial was a public reading of the Declaration of Independence in Independence Square, Philadelphia, by a descendant of a signer, Richard Henry Lee. Elizabeth Cady Stanton, who was then president of the National Woman Suffrage Association, asked permission to present silently a women's protest and a written Declaration of Rights. The request was denied. "Tomorrow we propose to celebrate what we have done the last hundred years," replied the president of the official ceremonies, "not what we have failed to do."

Led by suffragist Susan B. Anthony, five women appeared at the official reading, distributing copies of their declaration. After this mildly disruptive gesture they withdrew to the other side of Independence Hall, where they staged a counter-Centennial and Anthony read the following address. Compare it to the Declaration of Sentiments (pp. 207–9) of twenty-eight years before. Note the splendid oratorical flourish of the final paragraph.

July 4, 1876

While the nation is buoyant with patriotism, and all hearts are attuned to praise, it is with sorrow we come to strike the one discordant note, on this one-hundredth anniversary of our country's birth. When subjects of kings, emperors, and czars, from the old world join in our national jubilee, shall the women of the republic refuse to lay their hands with benedictions on the nation's head? Surveying America's exposition, surpassing in magnificence those of London, Paris, and Vienna, shall we not rejoice at the success of the youngest rival among the nations of the earth? May not our hearts, in unison with all, swell with pride at our great achievements as a people; our free speech, free press, free schools, free church, and the rapid progress we have made in material wealth, trade, commerce and the inventive arts? And we do rejoice in the success, thus far, of our experiment of self-government. Our faith is firm and unwavering in the broad principles of human rights proclaimed in 1776, not only as abstract truths, but as the corner stones of a republic. Yet we cannot forget, even in this glad hour, that while all men of every race, and clime, and condition, have been invested with the full rights of citizenship under our hospitable flag, all women still suffer the degradation of disfranchisement.

The history of our country the past hundred years has been a series of assumptions and usurpations of power over woman, in direct opposition to the

principles of just government, acknowledged by the United States as its foundation. . . .

And for the violation of these fundamental principles of our government, we arraign our rulers on this Fourth day of July, 1876,— and these are our articles of impeachment:

Bills of attainder have been passed by the introduction of the word "male" into all the State constitutions, denying to women the right of suffrage, and thereby making sex a crime—an exercise of power clearly forbidden in article 1, sections 9, 10, of the United States constitution. . . .

The right of trial by a jury of one's peers was so jealously guarded that States refused to ratify the original constitution until it was guaranteed by the sixth amendment. And yet the women of this nation have never been allowed a jury of their peers—being tried in all cases by men, native, and foreign, educated and ignorant, virtuous and vicious. Young girls have been arraigned in our courts for the crime of infanticide; tried, convicted, hanged—victims, perchance, of judge, jurors, advocates—while no woman's voice could be heard in their defense. . . .

Taxation without representation, the immediate cause of the rebellion of the colonies against

Excerpted from Susan B. Anthony, Declaration of Rights for Women by the National Woman Suffrage Association, in *History of Woman Suffrage*, edited by Elizabeth Cady Stanton, Susan B. Anthony, and Matilda Joslyn Gage, vol. 3 (Rochester, N.Y.: Susan B. Anthony, 1886), pp. 31–34.

Nora Blatch (Barney), Elizabeth Cady Stanton, Harriot Stanton Blatch (1886) (Courtesy Rhoda Jenkins/Coline Jenkins-Sahlin)

Elizabeth Jenkins-Sahlin (age 13), Rhoda Barney Jenkins, Coline Jenkins-Sahlin (1998) (Courtesy Joyce Dopkeen/New York Times)

"Mother believed in pushing," observed Rhoda Barney Jenkins, who became an architect. "You don't question a hurricane." Coline Jenkins-Sahlin has served as a member of the Greenwich, Connecticut, Representative Town Meeting and helped found Third Wave Television, a production company that makes programs on women's issues. "What they did was heroic," observes Elizabeth.

Great Britain, is one of the grievous wrongs the women of this country have suffered during the century. Deploring war, with all the demoralization that follows in its train, we have been taxed to support standing armies, with their waste of life and wealth. Believing in temperance, we have been taxed to support the vice, crime and pauperism of the liquor traffic. While we suffer its wrongs and abuses infinitely more than man, we have no power to protect our sons against this giant evil. . . .

Unequal codes for men and women. Held by law a perpetual minor, deemed incapable of self-protection, even in the industries of the world, woman is denied equality of rights. The fact of sex, not the quantity or quality of work, in most cases, decides the pay and position; and because of this injustice thousands of fatherless girls are compelled to choose between a life of shame and starvation. Laws catering to man's vices have created two codes of morals in which penalties are graded according to the political status of the offender. Under such laws, women are fined and imprisoned if found alone in the streets, or in public places of resort, at certain hours. Under the pretense of regulating public morals, police officers seizing the occupants of disreputable houses, march the women in platoons to prison, while the men, partners in their guilt, go free. . . .

Representation of woman has had no place in the nation's thought. Since the incorporation of the thirteen original States, twenty-four have been admitted to the Union, not one of which has recognized woman's right of self-government. On this birthday of our national liberties, July Fourth, 1876, Colorado, like all her elder sisters, comes into the Union with the invidious word "male" in her constitution. . . .

The judiciary above the nation has proved itself but the echo of the party in power, by upholding and enforcing laws that are opposed to the spirit and letter of the constitution. When the slave power was dominant, the Supreme Court decided that a black man was not a citizen, because he had not the right to vote; and when the constitution was so amended as to make all persons citizens, the same high tribunal decided that a woman, though a citizen, had not the right to vote. Such vacillating interpretations of constitutional law unsettle our faith in judicial authority, and undermine the liberties of the whole people.

These articles of impeachment against our rulers we now submit to the impartial judgment of the people. To all these wrongs and oppressions woman has not submitted in silence and resignation. From the beginning of the century, when Abigail Adams, the wife of one president and mother of another, said, "We will not hold ourselves bound to obey laws in which we have no voice or representation," until now, woman's discontent has been steadily increasing, culminating nearly thirty years ago in a simultaneous movement among the women of the nation, demanding the right of suffrage. In making our just demands, a higher motive than the pride of sex inspires us; we feel that national safety and stability depend on the complete recognition of the broad principles of our government. Woman's degraded, helpless position is the weak point in our institutions today; a disturbing force everywhere, severing family ties, filling our asylums with the deaf, the dumb, the blind; our prisons with criminals, our cities with drunkenness and prostitution; our homes with disease and death. It was the boast of the founders of the republic, that the rights for which they contended were the rights of human nature. If these rights are ignored in the case of one-half the people, the nation is surely preparing for its downfall. Governments try themselves. The recognition of a governing and a governed class is incompatible with the first principles of freedom. Woman has not been a heedless spectator of the events of this century, nor a dull listener to the grand arguments for the equal rights of humanity. From the earliest history of our country woman has shown equal devotion with man to the cause of freedom, and has stood firmly by his side in its defense. Together they have made this country what it is. Woman's wealth, thought and labor have cemented the stones of every monument man has reared to liberty.

And now, at the close of a hundred years, as the hour-hand of the great clock that marks the centuries points to 1876, we declare our faith in the principles of self-government; our full equality with man in natural rights; that woman was made first for her own happiness, with the absolute right to herself—to all the opportunities and advantages life affords for her complete development; and we deny that dogma of the centuries, incorporated in the codes of all nations—that woman was made for man—her best interests, in all cases, to be sacrificed to his will. We ask of our rulers, at this hour, no special privileges, no special legislation. We ask justice, we ask equality, we ask that all the civil and political rights that belong to citizens of the United States, be guaranteed to us and our daughters forever.

This photograph of a young woman, nonchalantly posed atop the framing of a Chicago skyscraper in 1920, conveys both personal daring and a challenge to gender roles. (Photograph by Connie Colliers, courtesy of the Carbis/Bettman Archive)

III

THE MANY FRONTIERS OF INDUSTRIALIZING AMERICA 1880–1920

Americans triumphantly celebrated the end of the nineteenth century. They had secured sectional unity between North and South and the benefits of continental expansion. The industrial revolution, dominated by the vision and organizational genius of a few hard-driving, ruthless entrepreneurs, had transformed a wilderness into a new landscape, crisscrossed by railroads and telegraph and telephone lines and dotted with foundries, factories, and mills. Sprawling cities and industrial centers lured native and immigrant alike with the promise of a new job and a fresh start. As the urban population increased from 15 million in 1880 to 45 million in 1910, America's farmers expanded their output not only to feed this nation's teeming cities but those of Europe as well. American technology provided its own "miracles." The Brooklyn Bridge, upon completion in 1883, was the longest suspension bridge in the world. Serving thousands of daily commuters between Brooklyn and Manhattan, it stood as a symbol not only of the technological achievements of the American people but of the emergence of a new nation—industrial, urban, and ethnically diverse.

Maturing as an economic power in an age of imperialism, America was fast becoming an international power as well. Competing with Europe in a worldwide quest for new trade outlets, the United States picked up new territories along with new markets. Acquisition of Alaska (1867) was followed by involvement in—and ultimately annexation of—Samoa (1872) and Hawaii (1898). After a "splendid little war" with Spain, this nation was left with Puerto Rico, Guam, and the Philippines. Eager to protect strategic interests in the Pacific, the United States acquired the right to construct an interoceanic canal to be owned by the new country of Panama but under American control. The Panama Canal, another triumph of American engineering, was one of many developments portending this nation's willingness to intervene in the affairs of other nations to the south in order to establish hemispheric dominance and protect American investments.

The economic expansion that had enabled, and indeed encouraged, this former British colony to create its own imperial system did not occur painlessly. The populist movement of the 1890s, for example, expressed the anger of agrarians who attacked the injustices of an economic system that victimized farmers while benefiting industrial, railroad, and banking interests. The growing socialist movement was but one expression of workers' discontent with an industrial order in which 5 percent of the population owned nearly half the nation's property while more than a third of its 76 million people in 1910 lived below the poverty line. Living conditions were no better than working conditions for the millions trapped in the poverty and misery of teeming urban ghettos. Cities, ill prepared to cope with rapid population growth, were governed inadequately and often dishonestly by politicians whose base of support lay in wards populated by immigrants inexperienced with American politics and grateful for services provided by the "machine."

Attempting to steer a middle course between radicalism and reaction, many Americans at the turn of the century turned to progressivism, participating in a multifaceted coalition of reformers that included insurgent intellectuals and university professors, Christian "social gospelers," women activists, investigative reporters, business and professional men, farmers, and laborers. A diverse lot dedicated to a variety of goals, progressives generally agreed on certain basic propositions. Government, particularly at the local and state level, must be made more democratic, honest, and efficient; monopolies must be controlled and big business made more responsive to the public interest; natural resources must be used more rationally; social conditions must be made more just and humane and the environment in which people lived and worked made safer. Extending to international affairs this same concern for order and reform, they agreed that in the wake of World War I the postwar world created must be progressive as well. Although their efforts to meet the needs of this new urban, industrial society were sometimes contradictory and not always successful, progressives laid the foundations of the modern welfare state.

The developments shaping American life between 1880 and 1920 were, in sum, many and complex: westward expansion and interracial and intercultural confrontation, immigration and economic exploitation, commercialization of agriculture and agrarian uprisings, industrialization and the emergence of organized labor, urbanization and the appearance of commercialized amusements, domestic reform and state formation, international expansion and involvement in world war. In the South there were racial adjustments as well. Crossing the frontier from slavery to freedom brought new efforts to preserve the old racial hierarchy on the part of whites and sustained resistance on the part of blacks.

Historians have customarily acknowledged that women were part of these developments. Familiar names in textbooks include Mary Elizabeth Lease, the Populist orator who urged hard-pressed farmers "to raise less corn and more hell"; Mary Harris ("Mother") Jones, the fiery labor agitator who became a symbol of defiance wherever strikers gathered; and, of course, Jane Addams, the humanitarian reformer whose settlement house work made her a relentless foe of economic exploitation and an equally determined advocate of governmental regulation and assistance. Yet even in studying Progressive-era reformers, most historians have focused on men, whether as civil service proponents, consumer protection advocates, municipal reformers, trustbusters, conservationists, trade unionists, or racial conciliators. Yet suppose we reverse this emphasis. Instead of seeing women as an ancillary group that was simply there, let us explore the difference that "being there" made.

We might begin by focusing on the growth of trade unions. It was originally assumed by male labor leaders and historians alike that women had little to do with the emergence of organized labor. Indeed, in the worker brotherhood, women, by definition, could not belong. Yet women proved to be formidable and courageous organizers as well as tireless proponents of state protection for women workers. Their efforts promoted unionization and legislative and judicial change.

Race relations afford another example. The story of the Southern quest for white supremacy is a grim one, replete with lynching, voter disfranchisement, and rigid segregation of everything from cemeteries to drinking fountains. It has traditionally been a white male story in which black male resisters such as Booker T. Washington and W. E. B. Du Bois are counterposed against white supremacists. But there was a female dimension to this resistance. Ida B. Wells's campaign against lynching and mob violence put her in grave personal danger, forcing her to flee the South. White women who made up the Association of Southern Women for the Prevention of Lynching eventually took up the fight against this most egregious form of mob violence. When black men were disenfranchised at the turn of the century, a largely elite network of black women forged interracial ties with white women activists to temper white supremacy and, after women gained the vote, to use the Nineteenth Amendment as a wedge to help black men reenter politics. Painting women, especially black women, into the picture alters our understanding of a pivotal era in the American South.

State formation provides still another example. For many years, women reformers were seen as only one group in a much larger coalition of progressive reformers whose demands for governmental action led to the formation of the regulatory state. But suppose for the moment we view progressivism as part of women's history, looking at the way in which men steadily moved from the domestic into the public sphere. The first stage of that process we can locate in the early years of the republic when women as "Republican Mothers" assumed a role that made their domestic domain of education and nurture into a schoolroom for the next generation of virtuous citizens. This acknowledgment of the mother's private domain as a public trust helped to establish women—in the ideal, at least—as public persons with public responsibilities, even if exercised within the privacy of the family. At an ever-accelerating pace between 1820 and 1880—the dates are approximations—women expanded that role into what might be called "Reformist Motherhood." Instead of influencing the public domain indirectly through the lives of their sons, women began to extend their role as nurturers and teachers of morals from the domestic sphere into the public sphere through church, missionary, and moral reform groups. Women sought to make the world conform more strictly to values taught in the home—sexual responsibility and restraint for men as well as women, self-discipline for those who used strong drink, charity and rehabilitation for those who were entrapped by poverty and crime, sympathy and justice for African Americans.

Between 1880 and 1920 a new role developed that might be called "Political Motherhood." Increasing numbers of women joined the Woman's Christian Temperance Union (WCTU), the Young Women's Christian Association (YWCA), the settlement house movement, the General Federation of Women's Clubs, the National Association of Colored Women, the Children's Aid Society, the National Child Labor Committee, the National Consumers' League, the Pure Food Association, and a host of others. (By 1920, for example, the WCTU had 800,000 members, the General Federation of Women's Clubs nearly one million.) Through these organizations and related activities, women enlarged still further their sphere in public life where once only men had acted. They worked to protect industrial workers, especially women and children, to clean up local politics as well as unsanitary slaughterhouses and polluted water supplies, to promote health, education, social welfare, juvenile justice, and mental hygiene. Even big business was no longer "off limits" to women, as Ida Tarbell proved when she exposed the corrupt practices used by John D. Rockefeller to create his oil empire. In their rejection of an individualism that, in the hands of such men, had become exploitative, and in their willingness to use government at all levels to create a more humane, caring community, women were thinking and acting in ways that were quintessentially progressive.

Moreover, they were behaving in ways that were highly political, even though they were still barred from voting. From petitions and personal appeals to legislators, they moved to more sophisticated ways of securing legislative action around the turn of the century. They conducted surveys that would provide supportive data for desired legislation, even participating, as did Florence Kelley, in the actual drafting of bills. In the suffrage campaign, women organized at the district and precinct level, forming one of the most effective single-issue pressure groups in U.S. history and, in the process, legitimating interest-group politics. And they developed a policy agenda focusing on the well-being of mothers and their families which, when successfully legislated, formed the basis for a nascent welfare state that some scholars have labeled maternalist. Among the first pieces of social legislation passed by Congress were mothers' pensions, protective labor legislation for women in industry, and maternal and infant medical care.

In transforming women's sphere from the private, family-oriented world of domesticity into the formerly male world of politics and government, a major change was occurring. "Motherhood" was becoming less a biological fact—birthing and nurturing children—and more a political role with ideological dimensions. Whether we label it "political motherhood," "public housekeeping," or "maternalist politics," women reformers had succeeded in redefining their responsibilities so that the nurture of children included the nation's children, obligation to family included other people's families, and responsibility for household included factories, city hall, and state house.

Through this exercise of taking women out of the progressive coalition and putting progressivism into women's history, we discover that female reformers were not merely one group among many in the progressive coalition. Women's perspectives and policy agendas shaped the nation's social policy agenda, and women's activism fueled state formation. In the first decades of the twentieth century, women, in short, were *active creators* of America's history, not incidental to it.

Document: Working for Racial Justice

> *Ida B. Wells, "Nobody . . . believes the old thread bare lie"*

Ida B. Wells was born during the Civil War to enslaved parents. After the war her parents remained in Holly Springs, Missisippi, where her father's work as a carpenter gave them hopes of rising into the middle class. Ida was educated in schools supported by the American Missionary Association; by the age of 16 she was studying at Shaw University [later Rust College] in Holly Springs. When both parents and a younger sibling died in the yellow fever epidemic of 1878, sixteen-year-old Ida refused to let her sisters and brothers be divided among relatives. She supported them by her work as a schoolteacher for six years. In 1883 she moved to Memphis, where a thriving black community seemed to offer more opportunities.

Railroad facilities in an increasingly segregated South were allocated in overlapping categories of race, class, and gender. When twenty-two-year-old Ida B. Wells bought a ticket for the "ladies" car on a Chesapeake and Ohio train in May 1884 and refused to exchange her seat for one in the "colored" car, where men and women sat together, she was physically pulled off the train. She sued the railroad and won. But she could not collect the $500 damages she was awarded; the state supreme court reversed the decision in 1887. She could not pursue the case all the way to the U.S. Supreme Court, but another challenge to segregation on public conveyances—*Plessy* v. *Ferguson*—would be lost in 1896, when the Supreme Court ruled that "separate but equal" facilities were enough to satisfy the "equal protection" clause of the Fourteenth Amendment.

When Wells wrote an account of her experience for a black-owned Memphis newspaper, she was asked to write more; when, in 1891, she criticized inadequate black schools and segregated education, she was fired from her teaching job. After that she would support herself by journalism. She was an editor of the Memphis *Free Speech* when three friends, young black struggling businessmen, were lynched. Wells's editorials denouncing the lynching urged the black community to move out of Memphis, urged whites of good will to control mob rule, and denounced the claim that black men deserved lynching because they threatened white women's virtue, arguing that the real threat was the economic challenge a middle-class black community could pose to white competitors.

Well's editorials put her in grave personal danger. She extended her editorials into powerful pamphlets and speeches publicizing the scale of mob violence in America. Between 1892 and 1895, years in which lynching was at its height but presidents and Congress refused to act and newspapers trivialized its horrors, Wells carried on a vigorous campaign demanding that the nation, which called itself democratic, cease encour-

Excerpted from "The Reason Why the Colored American Is Not in the World's Columbian Exposition" (1893), "Southern Horrors: Lynch Law in All Its Phases" (1892), and "A Red Record: Tabulated Statistics and Alleged Cases of Lynchings in the United States, 1892–1893–1894" (1895) by Ida B. Wells-Barnett, in *Selected Works of Ida B. Wells-Barnett*, edited by Trudier Harris (New York: Oxford University Press, 1991), pp. 17–19, 74–79, 145, and 226–32.

aging mob rule. During this period she moved to Chicago and married Ferdinand Barnett; they had four children. For the rest of her life Wells-Barnett worked for social justice for African Americans. Among her Chicago activities were the organization of an activist women's club and the Negro Fellowship League, a settlement house for migrant men. She also worked for woman suffrage, founding the first black women's suffrage association in Illinois and directly challenging white women's organizations to accept black women as colleagues.

Among Ida B. Wells's most bitter writings was her pamphlet distributed at the Chicago Columbian Exposition of 1893, which contrasted the beauty of the nation's presentation of itself at the world's fair against the terror with which all black Americans daily lived. She was bitterly disappointed in the refusal of the largest women's reform organization of her time, the Woman's Christian Temperance Union, and its long-term president, Frances Willard, to denounce lynching and to help create a multiracial women's movement against violence.

The selections that follow are taken from several pamphlets written between 1892 and 1895, the years of her most vigorous journalism. Most of the people lynched were men; most of the lynchers were men. On what grounds does Wells argue that white women were often complicit in lynching?

Lynch law flourishes most largely in the states which foster the convict lease system, and is brought to bear mainly against the Negro. The first fifteen years of his freedom he was murdered by masked mobs for trying to vote. Public opinion having made lynching for that cause unpopular, a new reason is given to justify the murders of the past 15 years. The Negro was first charged with attempting to rule white people, and hundreds were murdered on that pretended supposition. He is now charged with assaulting or attempting to assault white women. This charge, as false as it is foul, robs us of the sympathy of the world and is blasting the race's good name.

The men who make these charges encourage or lead the mobs which do the lynching. They belong to the race which holds Negro life cheap, which owns the telegraph wires, newspapers, and all other communication with the outside world. They write the reports which justify lynching by painting the Negro as black as possible, and those reports are accepted by the press associations and the world without question or investigation. The mob spirit has increased with alarming frequency and violence. Over a thousand black men, women and children have been thus sacrificed the past ten years. Masks have long since been thrown aside and the lynchings of the present day take place in broad daylight. The sheriffs, police and state officials stand by and see the work well done. The coroner's jury is often formed among those who took part in the lynching and a verdict, "Death at the hands of parties unknown to the jury" is rendered. As the number of lynchings have increased, so has the cruelty and barbarism of the lynchers. Three human beings were burned alive in civilized America during the first six months of this year (1893). Over one hundred have been lynched in this half year. They were hanged, then cut, shot and burned.

The following table published by the Chicago *Tribune* January, 1892, is submitted for thoughtful consideration.

1882, 52 Negroes murdered by mobs

1883, 39	"	"	"	"
1884, 53	"	"	"	"
1885, 77	"	"	"	"
1886, 73	"	"	"	"
1887, 70	"	"	"	"
1888, 72	"	"	"	"
1889, 95	"	"	"	"
1890, 100	"	"	"	"
1891, 169	"	"	"	"

Of this number

269 were charged with rape.

253	"	"	"	murder.
44	"	"	"	robbery.
37	"	"	"	incendiarism.
4	"	"	"	burglary.
27	"	"	"	race prejudice.
13	"	"	"	quarreling with white men.
10	"	"	"	making threats.
7	"	"	"	rioting.
5	"	"	"	miscegenation.
32	"	"	"	no reasons given.

This table shows . . . that only one-third of nearly a thousand murdered black persons have been even charged with the crime of outrage. This crime is only so punished when white women accuse black men, which accusation is never proven. The same crime committed by Negroes against Negroes, or by white men against black women is ignored even in the law courts. . . .

. . . Will Lewis, an 18 year old Negro youth was lynched at Tullahoma, Tennessee, August, 1891, for being "drunk and saucy to white folks."

The women of the race have not escaped the fury of the mob. In Jackson, Tennessee, in the summer of 1886, a white woman died of poisoning. Her black cook was suspected, and as a box of rat poison was found in her room, she was hurried away to jail. When the mob had worked itself to the lynching pitch, she was dragged out of jail, every stitch of clothing torn from her body, and she was hung in the public courthouse square in sight of everybody. Jackson is one of the oldest towns in the State, and the State Supreme Court holds its sittings there; but no one was arrested for the deed—not even a protest was uttered. The husband of the poisoned woman has since died a raving maniac, and his ravings showed that he, and not the poor black cook, was the poisoner of his wife. . . .

. . . In 1892 there were 241 persons lynched. . . . Of this number 160 were of Negro descent. Four of them were lynched in New York, Ohio and Kansas; the remainder were murdered in the South. Five of this number were females. . . .

. . . A lynching equally as cold-blooded took place in Memphis, Tennessee, March 1892. Three young colored men in an altercation at their place of business, fired on white men in self-defense. They were imprisoned for three days, then taken out by the mob and horribly shot to death. Thomas Moss, Will Stewart and Calvin McDowell were energetic business men who had built up a flourishing grocery business. This business had prospered and that of a rival white grocer named Barrett had declined. Barrett led the attack on their grocery which resulted in the wounding of three white men. For this cause were three innocent men barbarously lynched, and their families left without protectors. Memphis is one of the leading cities of Tennessee, a town of seventy-five thousand inhabitants! No effort whatever was made to punish the murderers of these three men. It counted for nothing that the victims of this outrage were three of the best known young men of a population of thirty thousand colored people of Memphis. They were the officers of the company which conducted the grocery. Moss being the President, Stewart the Secretary of the Company and McDowell the Manager. Moss was in the Civil Service of the United States as letter carrier, and all three were men of splendid reputation for honesty, integrity and sobriety. But their murders, though well known, have never been indicted, were not even troubled with a preliminary examination.

[In an editorial for *Free Speech,* May 21, 1892, Wells wrote:]

["]Nobody in this section of the country believes the old thread bare lie that Negro men rape white women. If Southern white men are not careful, they will over-reach themselves and public sentiment will have a reaction; a conclusion will then be reached which will be very damaging to the moral reputation of their women."

"The Daily Commercial" [a white-owned newspaper] of Wednesday following, May 25th, contained the following . . . [editorial]:

"Those negroes who are attempting to make the lynching of individuals of their race a means for arousing the worst passions of their kind are playing with a dangerous sentiment. The negroes may as well understand that there is no mercy for the negro rapist and little patience with his defenders. A negro organ printed in this city, in a recent issue publishes the following atrocious paragraph: 'Nobody in this section of the country believes the old thread-bare lie that negro men rape white women. . . .

"The fact that a black scoundrel is allowed to live and utter such loathsome and repulsive calumnies is a volume of evidence as to the wonderful patience of Southern whites. But we have had enough of it.

"There are some things that the Southern white man will not tolerate, and the obscene intimations of the foregoing have brought the writer to the very outermost limit of public patience. We hope we have said enough." . . .

Acting upon this advice, the leading citizens met in the Cotton Exchange Building the same evening, and threats of lynching were freely indulged, not by the lawless element upon which the deviltry of the South is usually saddled—but by the leading business men, in the leading business centre. Mr. Fleming, the business manager and owning a half interest the "Free Speech," had to leave town to escape the mob, and was afterwards ordered not to return; letters and telegrams sent me in New York where I was spending my vacation advised me that bodily harm awaited my return. Creditors took possession of the office and sold the outfit, and the "Free Speech" was as if it had never been.

The editorial in question was prompted by the many inhuman and fiendish lynchings of Afro-Americans which have recently taken place and was meant as a warning. Eight lynched in one week and five of them charged with rape! The thinking public will not easily believe freedom and education more brutalizing than slavery, and the world knows that the crime of rape was unknown during four years of civil war, when the white women of the South were at the mercy of the race which is all at once charged with being a bestial one.

Since my business has been destroyed and I am an exile from home because of that editorial, the issue has been forced, and as the writer of it I feel that the race and the public generally should have a statement of the facts as they exist. They will serve at the same time as a defense for the Afro-American Samsons who suffer themselves to be betrayed by white Delilahs. . . .

. . . [T]here are many white women in the South who would marry colored men if such an act would not place them at once beyond the pale of society and within the clutches of the law. The miscegenation laws of the South only operate against the legitimate union of the races; they leave the white man free to seduce all the colored girls he can, but it is death to the colored man who yields to the force and advances of a similar attraction in white women. White men lynch the offending Afro-American, not because he is a despoiler of virtue, but because he succumbs to the smiles of white women.

. . . The Southern white man says that it is impossible for a voluntary alliance to exist between a white woman and a colored man, and therefore, the fact of an alliance is a proof of force. In numerous instances where colored men have been lynched on the charge of rape, it was positively known at the time of lynching, and indisputably proven after the victim's death, that the relationship sustained between the man and woman was voluntary and clandestine, and that in no court of law could even the charge of assault have been successfully maintained. . . .

COLL-PETER THRUSH
AND ROBERT H. KELLER, JR.
The Life and Murder Trial of Xwelas, a S'Klallam Woman

The American West was by 1880 a territory of many cultures. Not only were there indigenous Indians and Mexican Americans, but also immigrants from Europe and even Asia. As different groups jostled for control of the land and its resources, intermarriage occurred, often between white men and Indian women. One such marriage occurred in the Pacific Northwest between Xwelas, a S'Klallam woman, and George Phillips, an immigrant Welsh barrel maker. What makes the story of this particular marriage worth telling is the fact that it was marked by a very contemporary problem—domestic violence. An estimated three to four million American women are battered each year by their husbands or partners.*

Because battering was long considered a personal rather than a social problem, women in such relationships had little recourse. Some, like Xwelas, finally took matters into their own hands and killed their abusers. Although Xwelas was convicted, she was, for reasons described by the authors, dealt with more leniently by the legal system than was usually the case. Other women were less fortunate. Only in recent decades has an expanded concept of self-defense been used by clients such as Xwelas. Developed by feminist lawyers in the 1980s, it made the claim that using force was not an unreasonable response to a pattern of abuse.

Xwelas's story is not simply one of domestic violence. It is also an illustration of how race can compound gender disadvantage. Revealed as well is a frontier experience more complex than the conventional story suggests.

Christmas Day, 1878. George Phillips, a Welsh immigrant cooper at the Langdon Lime Works on Orcas Island in Washington Territory, trudges along a forest trail with his teenage stepson, Mason Fitzhugh. Suddenly a gun explodes, lead shot ripping through underbrush beside the path and tearing into Phillips, who staggers backwards and cries to Fitzhugh for help. The boy eases his stepfather to the ground, but within moments Phillips is dead. As Mason Fitzhugh runs for help, he sees the killer standing in the brush along the trail. Shotgun in hand, a baby strapped to her back, the assailant is his mother and Phillips's wife, a woman known as Mary, but whose true name is Xwelas. She had fired the gun; she

*Current information about domestic violence is taken from the National Women's Abuse Prevent Project's "Domestic Violence Fact Sheets."

Excerpted from "'I See What I Have Done': The Life and Murder Trial of Xwelas, a S'Klallam Woman" by Coll-Peter Thrush and Robert H. Keller, Jr., in *Writing the Range: Race, Class, and Culture in the Women's West*, edited by Elizabeth Jameson and Susan Armitage (Norman, Okla.: University of Oklahoma Press, 1997), pp. 172–87. Reprinted by permission of the authors and *Western Historical Quarterly*. Notes have been renumbered and edited.

would be indicted for murder and she would eventually be tried and convicted by a court of white men. . . .

As a nineteenth-century native woman, Xwelas's life was both common and exceptional, and it offers insight into ethnic, gender, and legal relations in the Pacific Northwest. When Xwelas (pronounced hweh-LASS) was born in the 1830s, her people faced sudden and profound changes. She belonged to the S'Klallam, who lived along the northern coast of Washington's Olympic Peninsula, to the southwest of the San Juan Islands. . . . The S'Klallam had first encountered white explorers in July of 1788, when British officer Robert Duffin and his crew . . . reached the site of today's Port Townsend before being driven away by canoes manned by S'Klallam warriors. Spanish visitors were equally unwelcome during this early period of contact, but when George Vancouver sailed into S'Klallam territory in 1792, the tribe decided to ignore the whites altogether. . . .

A half-century later, new forces gave the S'Klallam, and surrounding native communities, little choice but to pay attention. Diseases such as smallpox began to ravage the coastal peoples, and deadly epidemics—along with a new economy, European trade goods that included alcohol, and massive immigration of white settlers—eroded the North Coast's traditional lifeways. Thus, Xwelas reached adulthood in a period of rapid social change and emotional turmoil. Not only were the S'Klallam forced to contend with the Euro-American settlers, but intertribal raiding and violence in the region may have also increased during the first half of the nineteenth century. Attacks by Vancouver Island tribes and bands from the south, together with the threat of slavery, depopulation due to disease, and the breakdown of traditional ways, could have encouraged a young Indian woman to seek relative refuge in marriage with a white man, miles from her home.[1]

Xwelas's marriage reveals an important dynamic. Her people and other Northwest native communities did not simply drown under a flood tide of immigrants, merchants, and missionaries. Rather, for several generations after Euro-American settlement, we find extensive cultural interdependence. Newcomers, whether British, Russian, Spanish, American, Hawaiian, or Asian, depended upon native knowledge for survival and for access to resources that fueled the new economies. Likewise, Indians came to depend upon immigrants for trade and protection. Alliances between Indians and whites proved necessary for both parties, one form of alliance being marriage. Before contact with Euro-Americans, different native communities had traditionally intermarried to strengthen bonds and prevent conflict; that practice extended to intermarriage with European and American male settlers after 1840.

One such marriage took place in the 1850s between E-yow-alth and Edmund Clare Fitzhugh. . . . Fitzhugh, a native of Virginia's Stafford County, had served in the Virginia legislature in 1846 and 1847 and had practiced law in California before coming to the Pacific Northwest in the early 1850s.[2] . . . Fitzhugh was an influential figure during the early years of Sehome. He became, among other things, superintendent of the Bellingham Bay Coal Company, Indian agent, county auditor, customs inspector, military aide to Governor Isaac I. Stevens, and territorial supreme court justice under President James Buchanan. His busy career did not escape scandal, however. According to one settler's diary, during Fitzhugh's tenure as judge, he allegedly shot and killed a man after a gambling dispute, then promptly tried and acquitted himself of the murder charge.[3]

But perhaps Fitzhugh's most glaring escapades involved his relations with women. Whenever Xwelas or other Indians visited the new white settlements around Bellingham Bay, they did not encounter neatly kept and morally upright communities following an ideal New England or midwestern model. In 1876, Phares B. Harrison, a "home missionary" to Sehome and its sister settlement of New Whatcom, found just the opposite and reacted with revulsion: "We have confronting us here heathenism—enlightened and benighted— civilized and legalized—in its most repulsive forms. . . . Drunkenness with its bloated impurities and crime, is not the most corrupting form of vice among us. Adultery, open, unconcealed, bold, and unblushing, in the cabins of the miners, and in *higher places,* in the Chinese quarters, resists the pure gospel of the Son of God."[4]

Part of this debauchery, in Christian missionary eyes, involved white men's liaisons with native women. In the early Northwest, eligible white brides were few and far between, encouraging the common practice of Caucasian men marrying Indian women, a pact often made for both sexual and economic reasons.[5] In Sehome and surrounding Whatcom County, the Lummi Indians had provided so many brides, or "kloochman," to white settlers that by the time E. C. Fitzhugh sought a partner, Lummi leader Chowitzit protested that too many young women had already married outside the tribe. Chowitzit referred Fitzhugh to the nearby Samish people to the south of Bellingham Bay. There, the Lummi presided over negotiations between Fitzhugh, "the tyee [chief] of Whatcom Falls," and S'ya-whom, the Samish headman. Following the traditions of his culture, in which romantic love played a lesser part in marriage than political diplomacy or social mobility, Chowitzit pointed out the advantages of a marriage alliance, while Fitzhugh spoke of his own wealth and how well he would be able to provide for a wife. In the end, S'ya-whom gave his sixteen-year-old daughter, E-yow-alth, to Fitzhugh, a man more than twenty years her senior. Throughout the nuptial negotiations, E-yow-alth's aunt, Xwelas, watched from the sidelines.[6]

Years later, Xwelas would remember traveling to visit her married niece on Bellingham Bay. The trip required five or six hours by canoe, following the shoreline below the storm-sculpted sandstone cliffs of the Chuckanut Mountains. On arriving for a visit not long after E-yow-alth's wedding, Xwelas learned that all was not well in the white man's household. Fitzhugh had become discontent with E-yow-alth, who had borne him a daughter named Julia, and he now began to entice his young wife's aunt. Eventually, Fitzhugh took Xwelas as his second wife. While multiple marriages would not have raised eyebrows among the Indian population, one might expect it to have done so among white society, particularly when involving a figure as public as Fitzhugh. Surprisingly, however, no recorded condemnation of his bigamy exists. And so Fitzhugh, took both E-yow-alth and Xwelas, now christened, respectively, Julie and Mary, to form a single family. Xwelas eventually gave birth to two sons named Mason and Julius.[7] Over time, even with two wives, Fitzhugh found that the appeal of

domestic life waned. Sometime in the late 1850s, he suddenly left Sehome for Seattle, taking daughter Julia with him. While Fitzhugh roamed, E-yow-alth and Xwelas rebuilt their lives. Xwelas would marry again, this time to William King Lear.

Lear, an immigrant from Alabama . . . settled among the few houses and shops clinging to a spit called Semiahmoo, twenty miles to the north of Bellingham Bay. A land speculator, Lear dispensed titles to lots on the spit and also served his clients as a storekeeper.[6] In the mid-1860s, he married Xwelas, now in her thirties. No details remain of their union, but sometime around 1866, Xwelas gave birth to William Jr., or "Billy." Not long after Billy's arrival, Lear abandoned his family and rushed back to Alabama when he learned that a relative had died [and] . . . did not return to Bellingham Bay for more than twenty years. . . . So, by her early thirties, Xwelas had been twice abandoned by white husbands. . . .

According to one report, Xwelas returned to her people near Port Townsend after King Lear left for the East. A single woman with children required support that the extended kinship systems of the S'Klallam community could provide. That she would marry yet a third time comes as no surprise; the S'Klallam allowed and even encouraged individuals to remarry, especially to continue useful alliances.[8] The social standing of Xwelas's third spouse, however, does come as a surprise. Rather than choosing a prominent figure in politics or business such as Fitzhugh or King Lear, she wedded a common laborer. Why? Perhaps, as a forty-year-old woman with three children fathered by two different men, Xwelas may have been considered "used merchandise" by potential white suitors and by tribal leaders looking for strategic marriage alliances. Or perhaps there may have been a romantic attraction between Xwelas and the Welsh cooper. For whatever reasons, Xwelas married George Phillips on 9 February 1878.[9]

As a poor immigrant barrel maker at a lime kiln in the rough-and-ready Orcas Island outpost of Langdon, George Phillips lacked any political or economic standing. Local histories cast him in a much less beneficient light than Xwelas's first two husbands, and by any standard, her marriage to Phillips seems to have been the worst of Xwelas's three marriages. Virtually every account of George Phillips mentions his alcoholism and his penchant for violent rages. His beatings of Xwelas often drew the attention of neighbors, although she was not incapable of defending herself. One account describes an argument between the couple in a canoe, in which Phillips hit Xwelas with a paddle. After a moment of silence, she asked if she could take over the rowing; after taking a few strokes, she then hit him with the oar. Such violence appears to have been a staple of the relationship.[10] [Nonetheless] . . . there were children . . . and Xwelas was pregnant once again at Christmas 1878.[11]

What exactly provoked the Yuletide killing of George Phillips? Some reports claimed that the family—George, the pregnant Xwelas, the infant Maggie, and Xwelas's eldest son, Mason Fitzhugh—had attended a "squaw dance," where Phillips's flirtations with another Indian woman provoked Xwelas's anger. According to this theory, she later ambushed and shot her husband out of jealousy.[12]

Xwelas herself described the events of that day during her trial. She and Phillips had gone to the house of a neighbor, William Shattuck, to drink and gamble, she said. She recalled that both she and her husband drank considerably, with Phillips "in very high spirits, laughing & singing songs." Eventually, he became so intoxicated that she asked for help escorting him home after finally persuading him to leave the party:

> After we had gone some distance George said, "[W]here were you last night, you old whore you, when I was hunting for you?" After some quarreling I called him a dog & he struck me with the oar on the cheek, then everything became dark and I fell forward. I then rose up & picked up the child when he punched me in the side with the oar. I then called him a dog & said, "don't you know I've got a child in my bowels?" He said he didn't care if he killed me; he'd get another woman, that I was whoring with Siwashes.[13]

According to Xwelas's testimony, her husband repeatedly threatened to kill her after they reached the Langdon settlement and their house in the late afternoon. "George told me to get my things and leave, calling me a slut. He demanded the key to the house & ere I could give it to him, he took the axe & broke open the door." Phillips then grabbed two guns from above the mantle and began loading them. Although Mason Fitzhugh assured her that George would sober up, Xwelas decided to spend the night in the woods. Putting baby Maggie on her back, she took a double-barreled shotgun and walked to a neighbor's root house. As her husband and Mason approached the building along the trail a short time later, Xwelas hid in the nearby brush. Then Maggie cried out "Papa," alerting Phillips:

> I raised up from behind the brush. George then rushed forward & grasped the gun by the middle of the barrel. We each tried to pull the gun from the other, & while we were thus struggling the gun went off shooting George. He staggered back calling for Mason. . . . Mason came [and] said to me, "Do you see what you have done?" I answered, "I see what I have done."[14]

The testimony of other witnesses quoted Xwelas as saying that she had feared for her life, but they contradicted her account of self-defense. Especially damaging were descriptions of how buckshot had ripped leaves and branches from the brush along the trail and how no one could have reached the point of firing from the path. To compound the issue, Phillips's body showed no powder burns, alerting jurors to the fact that he was killed from a distance.

Immediately after Phillips was killed, Mason Fitzhugh, who was near enough that wadding from the shotgun blast flew past him, dragged his stepfather's body into a barnyard and enlisted neighbors to keep the hogs away from the corpse.[15] After a hasty coroner's inquest the next day, Xwelas was indicted for murder. The Orcas Island sheriff immediately took her by boat across the water to Port Townsend, where she awaited a trial that would bring together the two driving personalities in Orcas Island politics and society— Colonel Enoch May and James Francis Tulloch.

Enoch May had complex relations with the Lummi and other original inhabitants of Orcas. He lived at North Beach where, according to his archrival, James Tulloch, he "had a band of the worst Indian characters always camped under the leadership of an outlaw Indian known as Old Tom to whose credit more than one murder was attributed. Here May posed as King of the Squaw Men, declaring that it was their last ditch [stand] and that he would fight to prevent settlement of the island by white families."[16] Despite their personal and political disagreements, testimony from Tulloch and May differed little regarding the death of George Phillips. Both men recalled Phillips's drinking, the fights between him and Xwelas, and the events of Christmas Day. Neighbors Henry Stone and William Shattuck, stepson Mason Fitzhugh, and other witnesses offered only slight variations on the same theme. The major contradiction in testimonies regarded Xwelas's claim that she and Phillips had struggled over the gun; witnesses reported that she had indeed fired from behind a screen of underbrush.[17]

Most of Xwelas's neighbors seemed sympathetic, inclined toward what modern courts would call an insanity defense. Henry Stone, like several other Orcas residents, recalled that

> George has at often times told me that the prisoner was not in her right mind. He has often come to my house and told me and my wife that his wife is crazy, and was getting worse every day; and he has told that he was afraid of her. I have seen indications of insanity in her, for instance, she publicly expresses her belief that the death of her two children [at the lime works] was a plot.[18]

Even Xwelas's son, Mason Fitzhugh, testified that his mother would at times act "as if she were not in her right mind and at other times she is all right."[19]

Judge Roger Greene instructed the jurors to weigh whether or not Xwelas understood the consequences of her action and whether or not that action was justified in the light of her husband's violence. Judge Greene also reminded jurors to consider Phillips's character and that he had attacked Xwelas with "the intention of destroying her unborn child."

By common notions of frontier justice, Xwelas should have been hanged. The jury might have doubted whether she was sane or whether her actions were justified, but that she had in fact killed George Phillips was never in question. During this period in the American West, no legal precedents existed that took into account as justification for homicide domestic violence against women.[20] Moreover, one would have expected the bias of white male jurisprudence to prevail over the interests of an Indian woman.

But Xwelas did not hang. When the two-day trial ended on 16 September 1879—almost ten months after the shooting—foreman Rufus Calhoun read the verdict: "We find the defen-

dant guilty of manslaughter and not guilty of murder." The jury recommended Xwelas to the mercy of Judge Greene, who sentenced her to two years in prison, less the ten months spent awaiting trial. In the case of *Washington Territory* v. *Mary Phillips*, the territorial justice system and Xwelas's neighbors had spent over sixteen hundred dollars to maintain due process of law, to bond witnesses, and to care for Xwelas's children, including the infant Tom, born while she was in the Port Townsend jail.[21] Finally, Xwelas herself was allowed to testify, as was her mixed-blood son Mason. Our conventional wisdom about intercultural relations, about the status of women, about the low value placed on Indian opinion, and about the whimsy of nineteenth-century justice tells us that a jury of white men should have been less forgiving in a case such as this. So why the lenient treatment?

One explanation of the verdict may have been pangs of conscience over convicting a mother with five surviving children, including an infant born in prison. A burgeoning northwest town with eager boosters, prolific newspapers, and a concern for its own image may have found a harsh sentence and the ensuing publicity to its detriment. But other factors emerge as well.

First, many local white men, perhaps even a majority at the time, had married or enjoyed liaisons with Indian women. Even Xwelas's defense attorney had once been a "squaw man."[22] Very possibly some of the jurors had been as well. Thus, while notions of racial and cultural superiority were central to territorial society, white male familiarity with native women could have favored Xwelas in the eyes of the jury.

Second, the presence of Xwelas's S'Klallam kin in the community could have influenced the jury's decision. During the 1870s, Native Americans of the Chimacum, S'Klallam, Lushootseed, Twana, and other tribal groups remained a familiar sight in Port Townsend and other northwest communities. Just as interracial marriages could provide alliances between racial groups, a fair trial and positive outcome for Xwelas could have been important in maintaining stable relations between whites and S'Klallams.[23]

Third, George Phillips's reputation could have prejudiced the jury. Had Xwelas killed Edmund Clare Fitzhugh, William King Lear, or another prominent civic figure, she more likely would have suffered a harsher sentence. But to ambush Phillips, a poor, alcoholic, abusive Welsh laborer, signified no great loss. Social class and national origin could be at least as important as race and gender in ordaining the relative value of human life in the West.

Ultimately, the legal decision probably rested on whether or not Xwelas understood her actions. Unfortunately, the most important psychological evidence, the opinions of doctors called to testify at her trial, has been lost. The foreman's note says nothing on this matter, but it may have been easier to dismiss Xwelas as a crazy Indian woman and to mete out a lesser sentence than to deal with the personal and political consequences of a more severe judgment.

Finally, the murder trial of Xwelas took place during a period in which legal and judicial standards, as they applied to Native Americans, were ill-defined and in a constant state of flux. For example, five years previously, in 1874, a mixed-blood Indian named Henry, or Harry, Fisk stood trial in Olympia for the murder of a Squaxin Indian shaman called Doctor Jackson. Fisk's primary defense for killing Jackson was that the shaman had caused Fisk's wife to become ill and that only Jackson's death could reverse the illness. While nineteenth-century American jurisprudence was not known for allowing shamanic self-defense as a justification for murder, the trial proceedings were marked by an attempt to understand native concepts of justice, and the all-white jury acquitted Fisk after only eight minutes of deliberation.[24]

Five years after Xwelas's trial, in 1884, the Stolo youth Louie Sam was abducted and lynched by a white mob near Sumas on the Canadian border for the murder of a prominent local shopkeeper named James Bell. According to at least one historian, another white settler named William Osterman was the more likely culprit. Nevertheless, local white thirst for vengeance was slaked when a mob strung up Louie Sam.[25] Considered alongside the trial of Xwelas, in which an Indian woman ironically benefited from a legal system largely created by and for white men, these cases illustrate the kaleidoscopic morass that was the legal status of nineteenth-century Native Americans.

After her conviction, Xwelas virtually disappears from the historical record. Her later life seems to have been removed from crisis or controversy; she lived with sons Billy Lear and Tom Phillips on the Lummi Reservation. She did not marry again, nor did she bear more children, and she seems to have withdrawn from the white world altogether. Sometime near the end of World War I, Mary Sehome Fitzhugh Lear Phillips—Xwelas—died in her tiny home on the reservation.[26] Only sixty years after her death, Xwelas is barely a ghost, her voice but a whisper. The evidence of her life is scattered, like the hand of winter.

The story of Xwelas sheds light on the realities of frontier experience in the Northwest, laying bare several assumptions about the region, its history, and its cultural legacy. First, Xwelas's tribal affiliations reveal the fluid nature of Native American societies of the Northwest Coast. Born among the S'Klallam, she lived with the Samish and with whites, returned for a time to the S'Klallam, and then died among the Lummi. In light of her life, we must question the concept of geographically and culturally distinct native tribes existing separate from each other. Instead, complex ties of kinship, political interdependence, and economic alliance wove the native communities together into a regional fabric.[27]

Second, the interdependence of white settlers and Indian residents also becomes clear through her story. Rather than a tide of immigrants erasing the native presence, on many levels—sexual, financial, political—Xwelas's life illustrates the continuing importance of Native Americans long after initial contact. In fact, it may have been the influential political and social presence of her S'Klallam kin that saved Xwelas from a murder conviction.

Finally, Xwelas's relationship to white men helps to shatter the myth that Christian pioneers . . . brought civilization and morality to a savage frontier. In many ways, it is the deserter Edmund Clare Fitzhugh, the profiteer William King Lear [and] the abusive George Phillips . . . who represent the . . . savage frontier.

NOTES

1. The best ethnography of the region is Wayne Suttles, *Coast Salish Essays* (Seattle: University of Washington Press, 1987). On the S'Klallam specifi-

cally, consult Erna Gunther, *Klallam Folk Tales*, University of Washington Publications in Anthropology, vol. 1, no. 4 (Seattle, 1925), and *Klallam Ethnography*, University of Washington Publications in Anthropology, vol. 1, no. 5 (Seattle, 1927). For intertribal raiding and violence during this era, see Robert H. Ruby and John A. Brown, *Indian Slavery in the Pacific Northwest* (Spokane: Arthur H. Clark, 1993), chap. 6. For Indian-white relations in the region, see Jerry Gorsline, ed., *Shadows of Our Ancestors: Readings in the History of Klallam-White Relations* (Port Townsend, Wash.: Empty Bowl Press, 1992). . . . See Robin Fisher, "Indian Warfare and Two Frontiers: A Comparison of British Columbia and Washington Territory during the Early Years of Settlement," *Pacific Historical Review* 50 (February 1981): 31–51.

2. Percival Jeffcoat, "Samish Chief Negotiates with Fitzhugh for Princess," *Bellingham* (Wash.) *Herald*, 13 October 1968. Although Jeffcoat was a respected local historian, we realize that relying on his undocumented newspaper accounts raises legitimate doubts.

3. *The Virginia General Assembly, July 30 1619 to January 11 1978: A Bicentennial Registry of Members*, comp. Cynthia Miller Leonard (Richmond: Virginia State Library, 1978).

4. Lottie Roeder Roth, *History of Whatcom County*, vol. 1 (Seattle: Pioneer Press, 1926), 38, 45–46; Percival R. Jeffcoat, "Why Samish Chief's Name Became Sehome," *Bellingham Herald*, 20 October 1968.

5. James F. Tulloch, *The James Francis Tulloch Diary, 1875–1910*, ed. Gordon Keith (Portland, Ore.: Binford & Mort, 1978), 11.

6. From Harrison's November 1876 correspondence with the American Home Mission Society. Correspondence held in the Amistad Research Center, Old U.S. Mint, New Orleans. Quoted in Robert H. Keller, Jr., "The Gospel Comes to Northwest Washington," *Pacific Northwest Forum* 10 (Winter 1985): 4. Emphasis in text.

7. For the mixing of trade and personal life as well as the active economic role of native women in the early Northwest, see Sylvia Van Kirk, *Many Tender Ties: Women in Fur-Trade Society, 1670–1870* (Norman: University of Oklahoma Press, 1980). For specific insights into the lives of Xwelas's peers, including her granddaughter Maggie Tom, consult Karen Jones-Lamb, *Native American Wives of San Juan Settlers* (n.p.: Bryn Tirion Publishing, 1994).

8. Jeffcoat, "Samish Chief Negotiates." For more information on S'Klallam and Lummi marriage traditions, see Wayne Suttles, "Central Coast Salish," in *Northwest Coast*, ed. Wayne Suttles, vol. 7 of *Handbook of North American Indians*, ed. William

C. Sturtevant (Washington, D.C.: Smithsonian Institution, 1990), 453–75.

9. Jeffcoat, "Why Samish Chief's Name."

10. Roth, *History*, 107–8.

11. Suttles, "Central Coast Salish."

12. John D. Carter, ed., *Washington's First Marriages of the 39 Counties* (Spokane: Eastern Washington Genealogical Society, 1980).

13. Pretrial affidavits in *Washington Territory* v. *Mary Phillips* file, case no. 1070, series 1, box 21, Washington Territorial Case Files, Third Judicial District, Jefferson County, Washington Territory, Washington State Archives: Northwest Region, Western Washington University, Bellingham (hereafter *Wash. Terr.* v. *Phillips*).

14. *Seattle Weekly Intelligencer*, 4 January 1879.

15. Affidavit of Mary Phillips, Orcas Island, 26 December 1878, *Wash. Terr.* v. *Phillips*.

16. *Testimony of Mary Phillips, Wash. Terr.* v. *Phillips*.

17. Pigs are voracious omnivores.

18. Testimonies in *Wash. Terr.* v. *Phillips*.

19. Stone testimony in *Wash. Terr.* v. *Phillips*.

20. Fitzhugh testimony in *Wash. Terr.* v. *Phillips*.

21. See Cynthia K. Gillespie, *Justifiable Homicide: Battered Women, Self-Defense, and the Law* (Columbus: Ohio State University Press, 1989), 45.

22. To put this monetary figure in context, consider that in 1880 streetcar operators in New York City earned less than twenty cents an hour, while coal miners earned approximately five hundred dollars a year for working twelve hours a day, six days a week.

23. Tulloch, *Diary*, 36.

24. For an account of nineteenth-century Port Townsend, see Ivan Doig's *Winter Brothers: A Season at the Edge of America* (New York: Harcourt Brace & Jovanovich, 1980).

25. Brad Asher, "The Shaman-Killing Case on Puget Sound, 1873: American Law and Salish Culture," paper presented at the Pacific Northwest History Conference at Western Washington University in Bellingham, 25 March 1994, copy in authors' possession.

26. Keith Thor Carlson, "The Lynching of Louis Sam: A Story of Cross-Cultural Confusion, Tri-National Relations, and Murder," paper presented at the Pacific Northwest History Conference at Western Washington University in Bellingham, 25 March 1994, copy in authors' possession.

27. Gordon Charles, informal interview conducted by Coll-Peter Thrush, Lummi Reservation, 18 May 1993, notes of interview in authors' possession.

PEGGY PASCOE
Ophelia Paquet, a Tillamook Indian Wife: Miscegenation Laws and the Privileges of Property

If Xwelas' marriage was fraught with peril, so was Ophelia Paquet's, but for a different reason. When her husband died in 1919, the county court recognized her as his widow—the Paquets had been married for thirty years—and appointed Ophelia to administer his estate. As there were no children, Ophelia stood to inherit her late husband's property. It was a just arrangement inasmuch as it was her money that had been used to purchase the land and pay taxes on it. John Paquet, Fred's disreputable brother, thought otherwise. Ultimately the court awarded the estate to him, leaving the sixty-five-year-old widow destitute.

Ophelia's story is a complicated one. It illuminates many issues: the purpose of miscegenation laws, the role of marriage in the transmission of property, the "invisibility" of married women's economic contributions, and the way race can compound gender disadvantage.

In what respects does John Paquet's victory illuminate the convergence of race and class? What parallels does Pascoe draw between the Paquet case and contemporary debates over same-sex marriage? How is the failure to count Ophelia's economic contribution to the marriage related to the "pastoralization" of housework that Jeanne Boydston discussed in part II?

Although miscegenation laws are usually remembered (when they are remembered at all) as a Southern development aimed at African Americans, they were actually a much broader phenomenon. Adopted in both the North and the South in the colonial period and extended to western states in the nineteenth century, miscegenation laws grew up with slavery but became even more significant after the Civil War, for it was then that they came to form the crucial "bottom line" of the system of white supremacy embodied in segregation.

The earliest miscegenation laws, passed in the South, forbade whites to marry African Americans, but the list of groups prohibited from marrying whites was gradually expanded, especially in western states, by adding first American Indians, then Chinese and Japanese (both often referred to by the catchall term "Mongolians"), and then Malays (or Filipinos). And even this didn't exhaust the list. Oregon prohibited whites from marrying "Kanakas" (or native Hawaiians); South Dakota proscribed "Coreans"; Arizona singled out Hindus; and Georgia prohibited whites from marrying "West" and "Asiatic" Indians.

Many states packed their miscegenation laws with multiple categories and quasi-mathematical definitions of "race." Oregon, for example, declared that "it shall not be lawful

From *New Viewpoints in Women's History: Working Papers from the Schlesinger Library 50th Anniversary Conference, March 4–5, 1994* edited by Susan Ware. Cambridge, Mass.: Arthur and Elizabeth Schlesinger Library on the History of Women in America, Radcliffe College (1994). Condensed and reprinted by permission of the author. Notes have been renumbered and edited.

within this state for any white person, male or female, to intermarry with any negro, Chinese, or any person having one fourth or more negro, Chinese, or Kanaka blood, or any person having more than one half Indian blood." Altogether, miscegenation laws covered forty-one states and colonies. They spanned three centuries of American history: the first ones were enacted in the 1660s, and the last ones were not declared unconstitutional until 1967.

Although it is their sexual taboos that have attracted most recent attention, the structure and function of miscegenation laws were . . . more fundamentally related to the institution of marriage than to sexual behavior itself. In sheer numbers, many more laws prohibited interracial marriage than interracial sex. And in an even deeper sense, all miscegenation laws were designed to privilege marriage as a social and economic unit. Couples who challenged the laws knew that the right to marry translated into social respectability and economic benefits, including inheritance rights and legitimacy for children, that were denied to sexual liaisons outside marriage. Miscegenation laws were designed to patrol this border by making so-called "miscegenous marriage" a legal impossibility. Thus criminal courts treated offenders as if they had never been married at all; that is, prosecutors charged interracial couples with the moral offense of fornication or other illicit sex crimes, then denied them the use of marriage as a defense.

Civil courts guarded the junction between marriage and economic privilege. From Reconstruction to the 1930s, most miscegenation cases heard in civil courts were ex post facto attempts to invalidate relationships that had already lasted for a long time. They were brought by relatives or, sometimes, by the state, after the death of one partner, almost always a white man. Many of them were specifically designed to take property or inheritances away from the surviving partner, almost always an African American or American Indian woman. By looking at civil law suits like these (which were, at least in appeals court records, more common than criminal cases), we can begin to trace the links between white patriarchal privilege and property that sustained miscegenation laws.

Let me illustrate the point by describing [a] sample case, *In re Paquet's Estate*, decided by the Oregon Supreme Court in 1921.[1] The Paquet case, like most of the civil miscegenation cases of this period, was fought over the estate of a white man. The man in question, Fred Paquet, died in 1919, survived by his 63-year-old Tillamook Indian wife, named Ophelia. The Paquet estate included 22 acres of land, some farm animals, tools, and a buggy, altogether worth perhaps $2500.[2] Fred and Ophelia's relationship had a long history. In the 1880s, Fred had already begun to visit Ophelia frequently and openly enough that he had become one of many targets of a local grand jury which periodically threatened to indict white men who lived with Indian women.[3] Seeking to formalize the relationship—and, presumably, end this harrassment—Fred consulted a lawyer, who advised him to make sure to hold a ceremony which would meet the legal requirements for an "Indian custom" marriage. Accordingly, in 1889, Fred not only reached the customary agreement with Ophelia's Tillamook relatives, paying them $50 in gifts, but also sought the formal sanction of Tillamook tribal chief Betsy Fuller (who was herself married to a white man); Fuller arranged for a tribal council to consider and confirm the marriage.[4] Afterwards Fred and Ophelia lived together until his death, for more than thirty years. Fred clearly considered Ophelia his wife, and his neighbors, too, recognized their relationship, but because Fred died without leaving a formal will, administration of the estate was subject to state laws which provided for the distribution of property to surviving family members.

When Fred Paquet died, the county court recognized Ophelia as his widow and promptly appointed her administrator of the estate. Because the couple had no children, all the property, including the land, which Ophelia lived on and the Paquets had owned for more than two decades, would ordinarily have gone to her. Two days later, though, Fred's brother John came forward to contest Ophelia for control over the property.[5] John Paquet had little to recommend him to the court. Some of his neighbors accused him of raping native women, and he had such an unsavory reputation in the community that at one point the county judge declared him "a man of immoral habits . . . incompetent to transact ordinary business affairs and generally untrustworthy."[6] He was, however, a "white" man, and under Oregon's miscegenation law, that was enough to ensure that he won his case against Ophelia, an Indian woman.

The case eventually ended up in the Oregon Supreme Court. In making its decision, the key issue for the court was whether or not to recognize Fred and Ophelia's marriage, which violated Oregon's miscegenation law.[7] The Court listened to—and then dismissed—Ophelia's argument that the marriage met the requirements for an Indian custom marriage and so should have been recognized as valid out of routine courtesy to the authority of another jurisdiction (that of the Tillamook tribe).[8] The Court also heard and dismissed Ophelia's claim that Oregon's miscegenation law discriminated against Indians and was therefore an unconstitutional denial of the Fourteenth Amendment guarantee of equal protection. The Court ingenuously explained its reasoning; it held that the Oregon miscegenation law did not discriminate because it "applied alike to all persons, either white, negroes, Chinese, Kanaka, or Indians."[9] Following this logic, the Court declared Fred and Ophelia's marriage void because it violated Oregon's miscegenation law; it ordered that the estate and all its property be transferred to "the only relative in the state," John Paquet, to be distributed among him, his siblings and their heirs.[10]

As the Paquet case demonstrates, miscegenation law did not always prevent the formation of interracial relationships, sexual or otherwise. Fred and Ophelia had, after all, lived together for more than thirty years and had apparently won recognition as a couple from many of those around them; their perseverance had even allowed them to elude grand jury crackdowns. They did not, however, manage to escape the really crucial power of miscegenation law: the role it played in connecting white supremacy to the transmission of property. In American law, marriage provided the glue which allowed for the transmission of property from husbands to wives and their children; miscegenation law kept property within racial boundaries by invalidating marriages between white men and women of color whenever ancillary white relatives like John Paquet contested them. . . . Property, so often described in legal sources as simple economic assets (like land and capital) was actually a much more expansive phenomenon, one which took various forms and

structured crucial relationships. . . . Race is in and of itself a kind of property.[12] As [legal scholar] Derrick Bell . . . explains, most whites did—and still do—"expect the society to recognize an unspoken but no less vested property right in their 'whiteness.'" "This right," Bell maintains, "is recognized and upheld by courts and the society like all property rights under a government created and sustained primarily for that purpose."[13]

As applied to the Paquet case, this theme is easy to trace, for, in a sense, the victorious John Paquet had turned his "whiteness" (the best—and perhaps the only—asset he had) into property, and did so at Ophelia's expense. This transformation happened not once but repeatedly. One instance occurred shortly after the county judge had branded John Paquet immoral and unreliable. Dismissing these charges as the opinions of "a few scalawags and Garibaldi Indians," John Paquet's lawyers rallied enough white witnesses who would speak in his defense to mount an appeal which convinced a circuit court judge to declare Paquet competent to administer the estate.[14] Another example of the transformation of "whiteness" into property came when the Oregon Supreme Court ruled that Ophelia Paquet's "Indianness" disqualified her from legal marriage to a white man; with Ophelia thus out of the way, John and his siblings won the right to inherit the property.

The second property relationship [is] illuminated by the etymological connection between the words "property" and "propriety." Miscegenation law played on this connection by drawing a sharp line between "legitimate marriage" on the one hand and "illicit sex" on the other, then defining all interracial relationships as illicit sex. The distinction was a crucial one, for husbands were legally obligated to provide for legitimate wives and children, but men owed nothing to "mere" sexual partners: neither inheritance rights nor the legitimacy of children accompanied illicit relationships.

By defining all interracial relationships as illicit, miscegenation law did not so much prohibit or punish illicit sex as it did create and reproduce it. Conditioned by stereotypes which associated women of color with hypersexuality, judges routinely branded long-term settled relationships as "mere" sex rather than marriage. Lawyers played to these assumptions by reducing interracial relationships to interracial sex, then distinguishing interracial sex from marriage by associating it with prostitution. Describing the relationship between Fred and Ophelia Paquet, for example, John Paquet's lawyers claimed that "the alleged 'marriage' was a mere commercial affair" that did not deserve legal recognition because "the relations were entirely meretricious from their inception."[15]

It was all but impossible for women of color to escape the legacy of these associations. Ophelia Paquet's lawyers tried to find a way out by changing the subject. Rather than refuting the association between women of color and illicit sexuality, they highlighted its flip side, the supposed connection between white women and legitimate marriage. Ophelia Paquet, they told the judge, "had been to the man as good a wife as any white woman could have been."[16] In its final decision, the Oregon Supreme Court came as close as any court of that time did to accepting this line of argument. Taking the unusual step of admitting that "the record is conclusive that [Ophelia] lived with [Fred] as a good and faithful wife for more than 30 years," the judges admitted that they felt some sympathy for Ophelia, enough to recommend—but not require—that John Paquet offer her what they called "a fair and reasonable settlement."[17] But in the Paquet case, as in other miscegenation cases, sexual morality, important as it was, was nonetheless still subordinate to channelling the transmission of property along racial ... lines. Ophelia got a judicial pat on the head for good behavior, but John and his siblings got the property.

Which brings me to the third form of property relationship structured by miscegenation laws—and, for that matter, marriage laws in general—and that is women's economic dependence on men. Here the problems started long before the final decision gave John Paquet control of the Paquet estate. One of the most intriguing facts about the Paquet case is that everyone acted as if the estate in question belonged solely to Fred Paquet. In fact, however, throughout the Paquet marriage, Fred had whiled away most of his time; it was Ophelia's basket-making, fruit-picking, milk-selling, and wage work that had provided the income they needed to sustain themselves. And although the deed to their land was made out in Fred Paquet's name, the couple had used Ophelia's earnings, combined with her proceeds from government payments to Tillamook tribal members, both to purchase the property and to pay the yearly taxes on it. It is significant ... that, although lawyers on both sides of the case knew this, neither they nor the Oregon Supreme Court judges considered it a key issue at the trial in which Ophelia lost all legal right to what the courts considered "Fred's" estate.

Indeed, Ophelia's economic contribution might never have been taken into account if it were not for the fact that in the wake of the Oregon Supreme Court decision, United States Indian officials found themselves responsible for the care of the now impoverished Ophelia. Apparently hoping both to defend Ophelia and to relieve themselves of the burden of her support, they sued John Paquet on Ophelia's behalf. Working through the federal courts that covered Indian relations and equity claims, rather than the state courts that enforced miscegenation laws, they eventually won a partial settlement. Yet their argument, too, reflected the assumption that men were better suited than women to the ownership of what the legal system referred to as "real" property. Although their brief claimed that "Fred Paquet had practically no income aside from the income he received through the labor and efforts of the said Ophelia Paquet," they asked the Court to grant Ophelia the right to only half of the Paquet land.[18] In the end, the Court ordered that Ophelia should receive a cash settlement (the amount was figured at half the value of the land), but only if she agreed to make her award contingent on its sale.[19] To get any settlement at all, Ophelia Paquet had to relinquish all claims to actual ownership of the land, although such a claim might have given her legal grounds to prevent its sale and so allow her to spend her final years on the property.

It is not even clear that she received any payment on the settlement ordered by the court. As late as 1928, John Paquet's major creditor complained to a judge that Paquet had repeatedly turned down acceptable offers to sell the land; perhaps he had chosen to live on it himself.[20]

Like any single example, the Paquet case captures miscegenation law as it stood at one moment, and a very particular moment at that, one that might be considered the high water mark of American courts' determination to structure both family formation and property transmission along racial dividing lines.

Today, most Americans have trouble remembering that miscegenation laws ever existed ... [and] are incredulous at the injustice and the arbitrariness of the racial classifications that stand out in [such] ... cases. [Yet] few ... notice that one of the themes raised in the Paquet case—the significance of marriage in structuring property transmission—not only remains alive and well, but has, in fact, outlived both the erosion of traditional patriarchy and the rise and fall of racial classifications in marriage law.

More than a generation after the demise of miscegenation laws ... the drawing of exclusionary lines around marriage [continues]. ... The most prominent—though hardly the only—victims are lesbian and gay couples, who point out that the sex classifications currently embedded in marriage law operate in much the same way that the race classifications embedded in miscegenation laws once did: that is, they allow courts to categorize same-sex relationships as illicit sex rather than legitimate marriage and they allow courts to exclude same-sex couples from the property benefits of marriage, which now include everything from tax advantages to medical insurance coverage.

Both these modern legal battles and the earlier ones fought by couples like Fred and Ophelia Paquet suggest ... that focusing on the connections between property and the political economy of marriage ... offer a revealing vantage point from which to study both the form and power of analogies between race and sex classifications in American law and the relationships between race and gender hierarchies in American history.

Notes

1. The Paquet case can be followed not only by reading the text of the appeals court decision, In re Paquet's Estate, 200 P 911 (Oregon 1921), but also in the following archival case files: Paquet v. Paquet, file No. 4268, Oregon Supreme Court, 1920; Paquet v. Henkle, file No. 4267, Oregon Supreme Court, 1920; and Tillamook County Probate file #605, all in the Oregon State Archives; and in U.S. v. John B. Paquet, Judgment Roll 11409, Register No. 8-8665, March 1925, National Archives and Records Administration, Pacific Northwest Branch.

2. Initial estimates of the value of the estate were much higher, ranging from $4500 to $12,500. I have relied on the figure of $2528.50 provided by court-appointed assessors. See Tillamook Country Probate file #605, Inventory and Appraisement, June 15, 1920.

3. Paquet v. Paquet, Respondent's brief, November 1, 1920, pp. 2–5.

4. Tillamook County Probate file #605, Judge A.M. Hare, Findings of Facts and Conclusions of Law, February 3, 1920; Paquet v. Paquet, Appellants Abstract of Record, September 3, 1920, pp. 10–16.

5. Paquet v. Paquet, Appellants Abstract of Record, September 3, 1920, p. 3.

6. Tillamook County Probate file #605, Judge A.M. Hare, Findings of Fact and Conclusions of Law, February 3, 1920.

7. Court records identify Fred Paquet as being of French Canadian origin. Both sides agreed that Fred was a "pure" or "full-blooded" "white" man and Ophelia was a "pure" or "full-blooded" "Indian" woman. Paquet v. Paquet, Appellant's First Brief, October 8, 1920, p. 1; Paquet v. Paquet; Respondent's brief, November 1, 1920, p. 2.

8. The question of legal jurisdiction over Indian tribes was—and is—a very thorny issue. Relations with Indians were generally a responsibility of the U.S. federal government, which, although it advocated assimilating Indian families into white middle-class molds, had little practical choice but to grant general recognition to tribally-determined marriages performed according to Indian custom. In the U.S. legal system, however, jurisdiction over marriage rested with the states rather than the federal government. States could, therefore, use their control over marriage as a wedge to exert some power over Indians by claiming that Indian-white marriages, especially those performed outside recognized reservations, were subject to state jurisdiction. In the Paquet case, for example, the court insisted that, because the Tillamook had never been assigned to a reservation and because Fred and Ophelia lived in a mixed settlement, Ophelia could not be considered part of a recognized tribe nor a "ward" of the federal government. As events would later show, both contentions were inaccurate: Ophelia was an enrolled member of the Tillamook tribe, which was under the supervision of the Siletz Indian Agency; the federal government claimed her as "a ward of the United States." See U.S. v. John B. Paquet, Bill of Complaint in Equity, September 21, 1923, p. 3.

9. In re Paquet's Estate, 200 P 911 at 913 (Oregon 1921).

10. In re Paquet's Estate, 200 P 911 at 914 (Oregon 1921).

11. Although the issue did not come up in the Paquet case, ... in miscegenation cases, not only the wife but also the children might lose their legal standing, for one effect of invalidating an interracial marriage was to make the children technically illegitimate. According to the law of most states, illegitimate children automatically inherited from their mothers, but they could inherit from their fathers only if their father had taken legal steps to formally recognize or adopt them. Since plaintiffs could rarely convince judges that fathers had done so, the children of interracial marriages were often disinherited along with their mothers.

12. Derrick Bell, "Remembrances of Racism Past," in Hill and Jones, *Race in America: The Struggle for Equality* (Madison: University of Wisconsin Press, 1992), 78. See also Bell, "White Superiority in America: Its Legal Legacy, Its Economic Costs," *Villanova Law Review* 33 (1988), 767–779.

13. *Paquet* v. *Henkle*, Respondent's brief, March 14, 1920, p. 6; *Paquet* v. *Henkle*, Index to Transcript, August 25, 1920, p. 3.

14. *Paquet* v. *Paquet*, Respondent's brief, November 1, 1920, p. 7. Using typical imagery, they added that the Paquet relationship was "a case where a white man and a full blooded Indian woman have chosen to cohabit together illictly [sic], to agree to a relation of concubinage, which is not only a violation of the law of Oregon, but a transgression against the law of morality and the law of nature" (p. 16).

15. *Paquet* v. *Paquet*, Appellant's First Brief, October 8, 1920, p. 2.

16. In re Paquet's Estate, 200 P 911 at 914 (Oregon 1921).

17. *U.S.* v. *John B. Paquet*, Bill of Complaint in Equity, September 21, 1923, pp. 4, 6–7.

18. *U.S.* v. *John B. Paquet*, Stipulation, June 2, 1924; *U.S.* v. *John B. Paquet*, Decree, June 2, 1924.

19. Tillamook County Probate file #605, J.S. Cole, Petition, June 7, 1928. Cole was president of the Tillamook-Lincoln County Credit Association.

20. For a particularly insightful analysis of the historical connections between concepts of "race" and "family," see Liu, "Teaching the Differences among Women in a Historical Perspective," *Women's Studies International Forum* 14 (1991): 265–276.

GLENDA GILMORE
Forging Interracial Links in the Jim Crow South

Anna Julia Cooper—an extraordinary woman in her own right—wrote in 1892, "the colored woman of today . . . is confronted by a woman question and a race problem."* Equality of the sexes, Cooper insisted, would mean that black women should not be passive and subordinate in their relationships with black men; and black men should not criticize women's efforts to obtain equal rights. Equality of the sexes, Cooper continued, meant sharing the leadership burden in the struggle against racism. A remarkable group of African-American women did just that.

Part of a small but growing black middle class in the South, they were prepared by education, professional training, and voluntary work to be the vanguard of their race. Following the disfranchisement of black men in the 1890s, they emerged not only as community activists, but as ambassadors to the white community and astute political strategists. Their political skills were put to the test when, during the most racist era in U.S. history, these black women attempted to forge links with elite white women in an interracial movement. At the forefront of the effort was a remarkable North Carolinian, Charlotte Hawkins Brown.

Glenda Gilmore illuminates Brown's search for fault lines in the system of white supremacy with great sensitivity and insight in the following essay. She also demon-

*Anna Julia Cooper, *A Voice from the South by a Black Woman of the South* (Xenia, Ohio: Aldine, 1892), p. 135.

strates just how Brown manipulated class, gender, and even her own identity in the interests of racial justice. In the end, Brown's generation fell short of their goal of racial and sexual equality. The odds against them were overwhelming. In the process, however, they created and nourished a tradition of activism that would emerge with new force and greater success in the 1960s.

Consider Brown's strategy. What were her options? What were the personal costs? Do you agree with Gilmore's characterization of her as a "political genius"?

In the segregated world of the Jim Crow South, laws told black and white people where to eat and where to sit. Undergirding those laws lay a complex web of custom. Its strands separated the races in places beyond the reach of legislation. Custom dictated, for example, which part of the sidewalk belonged to whites and which to blacks. When whites and blacks sometimes occupied the same space, custom demanded that African Americans behave in a subservient manner. Any breach of these codes by a black person could bring an instant response from a white person: a reprimand, a beating, a jail sentence, or even death at the end of a lyncher's rope.

Whites held two unshakable beliefs that gave them the courage and energy to structure such a complicated society, making good on its rules with violence and even murder. First, whites thought that they acted to protect white women from black men's sexual desires. Second, they firmly believed that African Americans should be excluded from the American democratic system. They spoke freely and acted openly against any extension of political rights to blacks. After the turn of the century, restrictive legislation prevented most southern black men from voting and segregation laws crowded the books. White men considered their work done. Henceforth, they thought, African Americans would be a permanent lower caste in southern society: physically separated and politically powerless.

But the white supremacists did not reckon with black women. From behind the borders of segregation and disfranchisement, African American women became diplomats to the white community. They built social service and civic structures that wrested some recognition and meager services from the expanding welfare state. Ironically, as black men were forced from the political sphere, the functions of government expanded, opening a new

space for black women to approach officials as good citizens intent on civic betterment.

One of their political strategies was to build contacts with white women. Meager and unequal as they were, these interracial connections often provided black women access to resources for their families, students, and neighbors. Charlotte Hawkins Brown personified such black women across the South who forged invisible careers in interracial politics.

As president of the North Carolina Association of Colored Women's Clubs, Charlotte Hawkins Brown began to direct African American women's formal civic experiences in the state in 1912 and continued to do so for twenty-five years. . . . No black man could claim prominence to equal hers in . . . the state during the period. Brown's work and racialist ideologies illustrate that the decade before woman suffrage constituted a critical period in defining the boundaries of race relations that would remain in place until the post–World War II era.

Charlotte Hawkins Brown's life also provides a parable of the possibilities and the personal costs of interracial cooperation. Her story is so interwoven with myth—fiction that she fashioned to outmaneuver racism—that it is difficult to separate the reality of her experience from the result of her self-creation. The difference between her lived life and her public persona reveals a great deal about her perception of southern whites' racial ideologies and the points at which she saw possibility. Charlotte Hawkins Brown invented herself, repeatedly and with brilliance, but at great personal cost.[1]

According to her account, she was born in Henderson, North Carolina, in 1883 to Caroline Frances Hawkins, the daughter of Rebecca and Mingo Hawkins. Her father was Edmund H. Hight, from "whom fate separated me at birth" and who "belonged to a family that had grown up on the adjoining plantation."[2] Brown characterized her grandmother, Rebecca Hawkins, as a "fair" woman "with blue eyes," the African American sister of her white master, "a great railroad captain whose vision and foresight built up the great Southern Railroad." Brown cast the white master as the Hawkins family's "protector."[3] About the time of my birth, colored people in large numbers were leaving for parts north," she remembered. Charlotte moved with her mother and brother to Cambridge, Massachusetts, where her mother married and the family lived in a large, handsome house near Harvard University.[4] Caroline Hawkins managed a hand laundry in the basement, and Charlotte attended the public schools of Cambridge. Whisked away from the South at an early age, Charlotte was "not conscious of the difference in color and took part in all the activities of my class."[5] She acquired a New England accent, which she kept all of her life.

Charlotte Hawkins's family insisted that she get a practical education and sent her to Massachusetts State Normal School in Salem. Alice Freeman Palmer, the wife of a Harvard professor and the first female president of Wellesley College, was a member of the state board of education that oversaw the school. One day a few months before she entered the normal school, as Charlotte Hawkins was pushing a baby carriage while reading a high school Latin textbook, she chanced to meet Palmer on the street. Hawkins was babysitting to raise money for a silk slip to wear under her new organdy graduation dress, but Palmer assumed that she was an impoverished student, overcoming all odds to get an education. Palmer mentioned Hawkins favorably to the principal of her high school when they next met, and the incident ended. Now, when Hawkins realized that Palmer was an overseer of her normal school, she wrote to her and reminded her of their chance meeting. Palmer responded by paying Hawkins's tuition.[6]

Several months before graduation, Charlotte Hawkins met a supervisor from the American Missionary Association (AMA) on a train. The AMA representative impressed upon Hawkins the needs of the South, and Hawkins left school to accept a position at a one-teacher school in Sedalia, North Carolina, near Greensboro in 1901.[7] The AMA funded the school for

two years, then withdrew support. For a year, Hawkins drew no salary, and she and the students survived on what they grew, the produce their parents donated, and a $100 county appropriation. Charlotte Hawkins returned to Cambridge and approached Alice Freeman Palmer for financial help, which Palmer promised to consider when she returned from Europe some months later. Palmer died in Europe, however, and Hawkins decided to name the school in her memory. With continuing county support and private contributions, Palmer Memorial Institute taught practical vocational skills to its students, and Hawkins became active in the North Carolina Teachers Association and in women's club work. In 1911, Hawkins married Edward S. Brown. But the marriage lasted only a few months since Edward said he could not remain in Sedalia and be "Miss Hawkins's husband."[8]

In the South, Brown tells us, she demanded the respect of whites and received it from the "quality people." She insisted upon being addressed as "Miss," "Mrs.," or, after she gained honorary degrees, "Doctor."[9] She refused to be Jim Crowed and reported that several times she was "put out of Pullman berths and seats during all hours of the night." . . . By 1920, with the support of prominent Greensboro whites, Brown built Palmer Memorial Institute into a sprawling complex. She was proud that the most powerful whites in Greensboro served on the Palmer board, including Lula McIver and Julius Cone, head of the huge Cone Mills.[10]

As Brown rendered it, the theme of her life story is challenge met through interracial cooperation. Brown shaped the narrative in two critical ways: she minimized the restrictions of race in her daily life and exaggerated whites' helpfulness at every critical juncture. She obscured the fact that she was illegitimate by making it seem as if her father, Edmund Hight, was separated from the family by slavery. Brown was born in 1883 and had an older brother, demonstrating that her mother had a long-term relationship with Hight. The Hight family continued to live near Henderson throughout the twentieth century. Brown's grandmother, Rebecca Hawkins, may have been the sister of railroad magnate Captain John Hawkins, Jr., but, far from acting as the family's protector, he retained no contact with his black relatives and was a Democrat of the white supremacist persuasion.[11]

Brown mythologized her birth to remind southern whites of slavery's legacy: their shared kinship with African Americans. At the same time, she drew whites as sympathetic figures, the "protectors" of their African American relatives. Such circumstances did exist in the South; they just did not happen to exist within Charlotte's immediate family. As whites created the fictional "good darky" who treasured the interpersonal relationships that sprang from the close association of whites and blacks during slavery, Brown created a fictional "good master" who realized the responsibilities of miscegenation and loved his family, white and black. She used this good master to assuage whites' guilt about slavery and to argue that even slaves and masters achieved interracial understanding. She did not have to fight whites who melded ancestral ties to romantic class mythologies; she could simply join them. She shared their aristocratic roots.

Brown had moved to Cambridge not "about the time of my birth" but at the age of six. Yet she claimed to have no memory of her early life in North Carolina, no firsthand recollection of discrimination against blacks in the South, indeed no racial consciousness while growing up, even though she spent a great deal of time in the South during her childhood, even entire summers. Brown remade herself as a New Englander. When asked how her name should appear on her high school diploma, she instantly dropped her North Carolina name—Lottie Hawkins— for the more genteel sounding "Charlotte Eugenia Hawkins," which she made up on the spot. She spoke in a manner that "combine[d] the mellow tones of the southern Negro and the quick clipped qualities of New England— people turn[ed] around to see who [was] speaking."[12]

By casting herself as a New Englander, Brown attempted to remain above the southern racial structure. In Greensboro, she occupied a place much like that of African diplomats to the United States—she was an exotic but North Carolina's own exotic. If whites accused her of being an outside agitator, Brown could fall back on her North Carolina roots. Then she presented herself as native stock, a female, black Ulysses who fought her

way back to the South and to her own people, where she belonged.

The story of the AMA's dispatch of Charlotte Hawkins to the South to save her people competes with another, more complicated parable that Brown merely hinted at and may have consciously avoided dwelling upon. Rather than seeing herself as a New England missionary to a foreign place, Brown may have construed her return to North Carolina as coming to terms with the realities of race in her own life. One night at a Cambridge meeting, she watched magic lantern slides of the race work being done by African Americans in the South. She was particularly struck by two educators, Joseph Price, the founder of Livingstone College, and Lucy Laney, the founder of Haines Institute in Augusta, Georgia. She noted that both Price and Laney were, like herself, very dark skinned. Price and Laney were also brilliant, and their faces on the screen moved Brown to feel that there was a place where she might belong: the South.[13] Brown never acknowledged publicly that she had any personal reason for wanting to leave New England, choosing rather to emphasize the missionary aspect of her return.

As the years passed, accounts of the relationship between Alice Freeman Palmer and Brown made it seem as if Palmer had sent Brown to the South to found the school and that they had enjoyed a close friendship. . . . Contemporary newspaper accounts, which relied on Brown's own promotional material, reported that Palmer's "efforts" had made the school possible and "until her death she was an ardent supporter of her namesake."[14]

Although Brown did not actually lie about Palmer's interest in her and the school, she embroidered the truth. Brown and Palmer spent less than fifteen minutes together in their lifetimes, and Palmer never promised that she would personally contribute to the school. Instead, Palmer had told Brown upon their second meeting that she was too busy at the moment but that after her return from Europe she would contact friends in Boston to encourage them to support the school. Why, then, when Palmer never returned, did Brown name the school Palmer Memorial Institute? Actually, Brown originally named the school Alice Freeman Palmer Settlement in order to gain support from Palmer's friends in Boston.[15]

Palmer, after a brilliant career, had died at a young age and was mourned by her friends, and a memorial to her could prompt contributions. . . .

Around 1910, Brown cannily began to play southern pride against northern dollars when she inspired white leaders in Greensboro to challenge their community to take over the financial support of Palmer.[16] In soliciting southern white support, Brown . . . most often called the school Sedalia rather than Palmer. For example, Brown named the group of students who sang African American spirituals the Sedalia Singers.[17] She understood the white southerners' sense of place, and since her school was the only thing in the crossroads of Sedalia, she did not encroach upon white territory in appropriating the name. The location of Palmer at Sedalia facilitated support from Greensboro whites. It was ten miles outside of the city, surrounded by sparsely populated farmland. Brown never permitted Palmer students to travel alone to Greensboro but instead brought them as a group, with the boys clad in coats and ties and the girls wearing hats and white gloves. Once in the city, they did not mingle with Greensboro's African Americans; rather, Brown negotiated special seating sections for her students at public events.[18]

Although Brown cloaked the curriculum at Palmer in vocational disguises and portrayed it to the press as an industrial school until the late 1930s, the institute offered mostly academic courses from its inception.[19] Booker T. Washington met Brown on a trip to Boston while she was still a student there and pronounced her "the only convert that he made in New England." If he believed her to be a convert, she outfoxed the Wizard himself.[20] . . . Brown never embraced Washington's vocational philosophy past the point of providing for the school's basic needs, but she portrayed the school as industrial, detailing "farm yields" in fund-raising letters.[21] An unidentified Palmer teacher explained the ruse this way: "[Brown] always had a college preparatory class . . . a cultural academic school. All the Negroes had to have that in order to get along in the South." Even though this teacher believed, along with Brown, that African Americans profited most from classical knowledge coupled with reinforcement of middle-class values, support for that sort of training did not exist. So Brown and her teachers posi-

tioned Palmer as a "vocational" school. Funding for industrial education "could always get through," the teacher recalled. Despite the vocational exterior, she continued, "you could teach anything you wanted when you got in your school. You came inside your class room and you taught them Latin and French and all the things you knew."[22] Although initially Brown's students were the poor children of the neighborhood, by 1920, Palmer functioned as an academic boarding school that drew students from counties across the state and included secondary grades.[23]

Notwithstanding her vocal cover, at times Brown argued that her approach to "cultural" instruction benefited whites as well as African Americans. She explained, "Recognizing the need of a cultural approach to life, believing absolutely in education through racial contacts, I have devoted my whole life to establish for Negro youth something superior to Jim Crowism." She tried to accomplish this "by bringing the two races together under the highest cultural environment that will increase race pride, mutual respect, confidence, sympathetic understanding, and interracial goodwill."[24]

Why did Brown repeatedly overdraw white understanding and support and minimize the restrictions that her color placed on her? Throughout her life, she operated by a simple rule: it is better to overestimate possibility than to underestimate it. Charlotte Hawkins Brown created a fictional mirror of civility in race relations and held it up to whites as a reflection of their better selves. From slavery, she drew compassion; from the loneliness of Cambridge, racial liberality among her schoolmates; from Alice Freeman Palmer's deferral, a legacy; and from frightened, pinched southern whites, chivalry of a sort. Brown was a political genius, especially suited for interracial work. Her renderings served her own purposes, but she did not . . . delude herself into thinking that they were true. Immune to her own romantic stories, Brown was the consummate pragmatist. So convinced was she of her mission and of her opponent's rigid character, that she could risk the heartbreak of gilding the lily. She expected nothing, received little, and turned that pittance into bounty.

But Charlotte Hawkins Brown was a double agent. When she refused to turn her head toward the "colored" waiting room, she must have felt the stares of its patrons burn into her consciousness. In the decade preceding 1920, Brown immersed herself in social welfare projects and political activity that she kept hidden from whites. After 1920, Brown acquired a national reputation for her interracial work and landed official positions in interracial organizations, success that brought her activities under public scrutiny. Until then, and thereafter when she could, Brown generally said one thing to whites and then did another if it suited her purposes.

Brown's double life left its mark on her. . . . Living her life as a diplomat to the white community, Brown could never be just Lottie Hawkins. African American women who chose to take up interracial work walked a tightrope that required them to be forever careful, tense, and calculating. One slip would end their careers; they worked without nets.

In Lula Martin McIver, Brown found an exception to her belief that the southern white woman stood at the center of the race "problem." Their first meeting represents a classic case of the Brown treatment. Constantly seeking funds for Palmer Memorial Institute, Brown decided in the spring of 1905 that she must approach prominent white men in Greensboro for support. In Greensboro, Brown had no magic key such as Alice Freeman Palmer's name. Sedalia was a crossroads, Palmer Institute tiny, and Brown unknown. She had no historic connections to white North Carolinians there, no reputation in the black community, no denominational bridge since she had converted to Congregationalism, a faith rare in the South among either African Americans or whites. She had only herself— the New England persona she so carefully cultivated—and courage.

In 1904, she had written a poignant letter to Charles McIver, president of the white women's normal college in Greensboro. It began, "This letter may come to you from a strange source, but it comes from one whose heart is in the educational and moral uplift of our people." It concluded by begging McIver to come to Palmer for a visit. A year later, Brown was still imploring him to the same end, touting the ease of the train ride and signing herself "Very Anxiously Yours."[25] Still McIver did not come. One morning Brown dressed carefully in her customary ankle-length dress, hat, and white gloves and set out

to call on him in Greensboro. She had no appointment. Most often Brown did not write or telephone ahead and risk refusal from those she wished to meet but simply appeared on their doorstep. That morning she knocked on the front door of the president's residence and found that he was away. His wife, Lula Martin McIver, invited Brown in, an unusual act in itself. Lula McIver was stunned by Brown's appearance at the door. "Her daring, her enthusiasm, her faith intrigued me," McIver recalled. The two women talked for over an hour and warmed toward each other. Soon, McIver was advising Brown on "the best way to win friends" and on how to raise money among the Greensboro elite for the school.[26]

When Lula McIver opened the door, Brown chanced upon a valuable connection that would prove enduring. Brown sat in the parlor of the state's foremost white female educational advocate. Graduated from the Moravian academy in Salem, Lula Martin had longed to become a doctor like her father. After she learned that the profession was virtually closed to women, she became an outspoken feminist. As an adolescent, she abandoned the Moravians for the Methodists upon reading that the early Moravian settlers chose wives by lottery. In 1885, strong-willed Lula Martin met Charles Duncan McIver, a dedicated young teacher, who supported her feminist ideas and called her a "most sensible" woman. They married in a ceremony that omitted the word "obey," and Lula refused a wedding ring, which she regarded as a "badge of slavery."[27]

The McIvers worked to build North Carolina's white public educational system one school at a time. While Charles traveled throughout the state promoting graded school education, Lula served as his advance team, preceding him to scrub courthouse venues speckled with tobacco juice, to set up chairs, to post flyers, and to raise a crowd. She was delighted when Charles became first president of the state-supported normal school for white women since both felt that educating women would be the key to building an effective public school system. She helped to found the Woman's Association for the Betterment of Public School Houses, and after Charles's death, she accepted a paying position as its field secretary.[28]

The subtleties of Lula McIver's racial ideology are elusive, but at the center of her thinking about race lay the strongly held belief that African Americans deserved a good education. For nearly a half century after they met, McIver continually raised money for Palmer Memorial Institute. Lula McIver attended meetings of black women's clubs in Greensboro. After the early death of Charles McIver in 1909, and to the eternal perplexity of Greensboro whites, each semester Lula McIver invited a male African American student from nearby North Carolina Agricultural and Technical College to board in the president's residence where she lived until her death. There, surrounded by young white women students, Lula McIver offered an object lesson in race relations.[29]

Both Brown and McIver realized the restrictions on their relationship in the Jim Crow South. For starters, McIver was a woman and thus not powerful in her own right. Moreover, as the normal school's maternal figurehead, she had to act circumspectly since all of her actions reflected upon the school, which was still in the minds of some a dangerous experiment that wasted state money to educate women. Given these restrictions, McIver could do three concrete things for Brown: influence prominent white Greensboro men to support her, introduce leading club women to Palmer's mission, and raise money. She did another intangible and invaluable thing for Brown: Lula McIver publicly referred to Charlotte Hawkins Brown as her friend.[30]

It appears that Lula McIver realized that her husband's influence would be more valuable than her own, and she urged Charles to write an "open letter of endorsement" for Palmer Memorial Institute shortly after she met Brown. Since Charles McIver served on the Southern Education Board, his vote of confidence carried weight in the North as well as the South. The letter went out in June 1905, but Charles McIver admitted in it that he had never been to Palmer.[31] He died four years later. Long after that, Brown named Charles D. McIver as her "first friend" in North Carolina.[32] There is no record that McIver ever made the trip to Sedalia or that Brown ever met him. With Lula McIver's help, Brown appropriated the memory of Charles McIver as she had that of Alice Freeman Palmer.

Local support of Palmer flowered around 1914 when Lula McIver brought a delegation of white women from across the state to visit the school. A member of the delegation wrote an account of the visit that appeared in the *Greensboro Daily Record* and encouraged white women to take an interest in Brown's work. Brown struck just the right note in her solicitation letter: Palmer, she said, "has conducted its work for the past 13 years without seeking very much help from our southern friends." She claimed friendship and a debt come due in the same breath.[33] The 1914 campaign was the beginning of a steady stream of white visitors to the school and financial support from white North Carolinians.[34] In 1917, Lula McIver conducted some of Greensboro's leading white businessmen on a tour of the school. Many of the men who had ignored Brown's previous appeals converted after that visit. E. P. Wharton recalled that Charlotte Brown had called on him around 1903 to obtain support for Palmer and that he was "ashamed of [him]self for losing sight" of Brown's work. He subsequently served for decades as a Palmer trustee. By 1920, the board of Palmer Memorial Institute included a Greensboro attorney, a banker, and an industrial magnate.[35] McIver sought no publicity for a trip she made to Boston with Charlotte Hawkins Brown two years later. There McIver called upon prominent white women, vouched for Brown's success, and asked for contributions to Palmer. When northern white women visited Palmer, they would not spend the night at the black school but stayed instead with Lula McIver.[36]

In 1919, Charlotte Hawkins Brown, with the endorsement of Lula McIver, published a remarkable novel, *Mammy.* On its face, the appearance of *Mammy* places Brown squarely in the accommodationist camp of African Americans, currying favor from whites by invoking the ties of slavery. The story tells of a loving black woman who nurses a white family and raises its children. Then, when the woman becomes old and ill, the family provides no help beyond an occasional visit to her drafty log cabin. Ultimately, they stand by as Mammy goes to the county home. Brown dedicated the book to "my good friend, Mrs. Charles Duncan McIver." She continued, "It is with gratitude I acknowledge her personal interest in the colored members of her household."[37]

What could Brown have hoped to accomplish by the publication of *Mammy?* At the time, she served as president of the statewide

Association of Colored Women's Clubs, refused Jim Crow seating, and was secretly organizing a campaign to interest the state's black women in woman suffrage. She had spent almost twenty years building her dignity in North Carolina. It was amazing that she would play the *Mammy* card now. A close reading of Brown's introduction and McIver's response to the dedication indicates that both saw *Mammy* as a tool to promote their agenda: interracial cooperation among women. Mammies represented the one point of contact between southern black and white women, and white women continually bragged about their love for their Mammies. But Brown's *Mammy* is not a tale of love rewarded; it is an indictment of white neglect of African Americans. Brown calls upon white women to remember their duty to black women and redefines that duty in new ways. It is no longer enough to be fond of ol' Mammy; white women must act on that affection.

McIver framed her endorsement of *Mammy* carefully. She said that today's white woman was not the person her mother was, for in her mother's day, there was "understanding and sympathy" between the races. The problem was the separation of the races since there could be no racial harmony without "knowledge of each other's problems and an active interest in solving them." McIver endorsed the concept of "racial integrity" but reminded white southerners that their "task [was the] training of the uncivilized African." Brown must have winced at that remark, but it preceded McIver's most important statement: "I verily believe that to the most intelligent southern white women we must look for leadership in keeping our 'ship of state' off the rocks of racial antagonism." She signed the piece, "Your friend, Lula Martin McIver."[38]

Interracial cooperation, association among black and white women to solve mutual problems, was the solution that *Mammy* endorsed. McIver did not propose that white women individually care for their mammies but that they enter the public sphere and provide leadership. Male sailors had steered the ship of state onto rocky racial shores. It was time for women to man the lifeboats and rescue government from the oppressive racial politics of the white supremacists. In the same month that *Mammy* appeared, the state's white and black women began to do just that by traveling to Memphis,

Tennessee, for a formal interracial summit. The state associations of women's clubs and the YWCAs sent forth those first intrepid female navigators.

Most of the black women who traveled to the Memphis interracial summit learned leadership skills in the National Association of Colored Women, but their experience in working with white women had come from two other sources as well: heretofore racially segregated groups that came together on the homefront in World War I and the interracial work of the Young Women's Christian Association (YWCA). During World War I organizational lines between women's groups of both races blurred when the Council of National Defense chose white women from each southern state to head committees to coordinate work on the homefront. In North Carolina, white women set up integrated county councils that included African American and white women, carefully chosen to represent clubs, YWCAs, and denominational social service programs.[39]

The work of the black YWCA centered on another upheaval of the time: African American migration from farm to town. Southern black women believed strongly in the YWCA's ability to reach poor young women who had moved to the city to find work. The national YWCA board determined that any southern African American branch must be supervised by an existing "central" YWCA. "Central" meant white. Once founded, the black YWCA must be overseen by a management committee of three white women and two black women. The rules mandated interracial "cooperation" of a sort. Despite these humiliating restrictions, two southern black women, Mary McCrorey of Charlotte, North Carolina, and Lugenia Burns Hope of Atlanta, founded Ys in their cities.[40]

On the train to Memphis, a group of white men pulled Brown out of the Pullman car and marched her past "southern white women passing for Christians" who were on their way to the Memphis meeting. The white women sat silent as the men forced Brown to the Jim Crow car.[41] Brown probably recognized among the fellow Memphis delegates North Carolina white women whom she had come to know over the past decade. Among them was the wife of the governor, Fanny Bickett. . . .

When Brown rose to address the white women, the frustration of a decade of interracial work erupted, and she shared the humiliation of being ousted from the Pullman car two nights before. She exhorted white women to fight lynching, to recognize the dignity of the African American woman, and to help black women. Brown ended on an ominous note: "You are going to reach out for the same hand that I am reaching out for but I know that the dear Lord will not receive it if you are crushing me beneath your feet."[42] Most of the white women were profoundly moved.

As it happened, the women's Memphis interracial meeting foundered on the spot that Lula McIver had warned of in *Mammy:* the shoal of politics. Two months before the meeting, a federal amendment had mandated woman suffrage and a month after the meeting women would vote for the first time. Just before Brown left for Tennessee, she had been secretly been organizing black women in North Carolina to register to vote. One faction of black women would not budge on the issue of suffrage at the Memphis meeting. A full year later, the white and black women still had not agreed on a statement of goals for an interracial movement. Brown, McCrorey, and Hope favored a version that included the controversial demand for protection of African American voting rights. Their language was blunt: "We believe that the ballot is the safe-guard of the Nation and that every citizen in the Nation should have the right to use it. We believe that if there is ever to be any justice before the law, the Negro must have the right to exercise the vote."[43] But the white women balked at the suffrage statement and the condemnation of lynching, both points "which the Negro women dared not leave out."[44] Whites suggested the wording, "We believe that the ballot is the safe-guard of the Nation, and that every *qualified* citizen in the Nation should have the right to use it."[45]

Interracial cooperation led straight into politics. As black and white women inched toward cooperation on a grass roots level, they came face-to-face with larger political forces. With a decade of women's interracial experience behind them, many African American women believed that the time had come to take a firm stand on suffrage. Black women looked to their white allies to support their right to vote, a gesture that underscores the success of interracial cooperation. Yet white women's confusion over black women's suf-

frage reveals the limits of voluntary interracial work. Upon the passage of woman suffrage, white women involved with interracial social service projects had to chose between gender and race. They could support black women's right to vote as women, or oppose their right to vote as *black* women. Charlotte Hawkins Brown called the question when she used the NACW to organize black women's voter registration drives in urban areas in the fall of 1920. Across the South, other black women did the same thing, reporting back to the National Association for the Advancement of Colored People (NAACP).

In Mobile, Alabama, registrars told black women that they must own property to vote, and when the black juvenile court officer challenged them, court officials fired her.[46] From Birmingham came the news that when a black teacher attempted to register, the registrar "called her an ugly name and ordered her out." Another teacher "answered every question asked her—ex post facto law, habeas corpus proceedings, etc." The frustrated registrar still would not yield and "tore up her card and threw it in her face."[47] Ultimately, in Birmingham, 225 black women succeeded in registering, although 4,500 made the attempt.[48]

It is impossible to judge Charlotte Hawkins Brown's success in the North Carolina registration campaign. Most registration books failed to survive, but those that exist show not only that black women succeeded in urban areas, but that voter registration increased for black men as well. Probably less than 1,000 black women registered in North Carolina that fall.[49] To judge the results of black women's drive for suffrage, however, one must look not just at the few thousand who managed to register in 1920, but at the heritage of interracial work upon which they built and at the example they set for those who followed. The number of black women who voted in 1920 may have been small, but their significance in the South's racial politics was large. For the first time since the nineteenth century in the South, black voters approached the registrars en masse. They assembled as the result of a coordinated, subversive campaign that crossed over the boundaries of voluntary interracial work to reintroduce black civil rights in electoral politics. By their presence at the polls, black women dared whites to use violence and won the dare. In 1921, white supremacy still stood, but black women had found faultlines in its foundations.

NOTES

1. Ceci Jenkins, incomplete notes for "The Twig Bender of Sedalia" ([1946]), unpublished biography of Charlotte Hawkins Brown, reel 1, #12, Brown Collection, Manuscript Collection, Schlesinger Library (SL). See also Stephen Birmingham, *Certain People: America's Black Elite* (Boston: Little, Brown, 1977).

2. "A Biography," reel 1, and "Some Incidents in the Life and Career of Charlotte Hawkins Brown Growing out of Racial Situations, at the Request of Dr. Ralph Bunche," reel 1, #2, both in Brown Collection, SL.

3. "Some Incidents," 1–2, reel 1, #2, ibid.

4. "A Biography," reel 1, ibid. The language of "A Biography" is closely echoed in Sadie L. Daniel, *Women Builders* (Washington, D.C.: Associated Publishers, 1970), 133–63.

5. "A Biography," 13, reel 1, Brown Collection, SL.

6. On Palmer, see Ruth B. Bordin, *Alice Freeman Palmer: The Evolution of a New Woman* (Ann Arbor: University of Michigan Press, 1993). On the Brown/Palmer relationship, see "A Biography," 16–18, reel 1, and Jenkins, "Twig Bender of Sedalia," reel 1, #7, both in Brown Collection, SL.

7. Daniel, *Women Builders*, 139; "A Biography," 19, reel 1, Brown Collection, SL.

8. Charlotte E. Hawkins to Dr. Buttrick, 31 Aug. 1904, folder 1005, box 111, series 1, subseries 1, General Education Board Collection, RAC. Mary Grinnell to Charlotte Hawkins Brown, 4 Oct. 1910, 8 Feb. 1911; H. F. Kimball to Charlotte Hawkins Brown, 12 June 1911; and J. G. Bright to Charlotte Hawkins Brown, 1 Aug. 1911, all on reel 2, #33; Mary T. Grinnell to Charlotte Hawkins Brown, 6 Aug. 1912, 17 Feb. 1913, reel 2, #34; and Charlotte Hawkins Brown Ebony Questionnaire, 16, reel 1, #11, all in Brown Collection, SL.

9. Brown wrote that it was a "big surprise" that the white people in the South refused to "use the term 'Miss'" when they addressed black women. She continued, "Naturally I was constantly being insulting and insulted which merited for me the name 'Yankee Huzzy.'" See "Some Incidents," 5, reel 1, #2, Brown Collection, SL. Leading whites in Greensboro referred to her as "Dr. Brown" after she received honorary degrees from Wilberforce, Lincoln, and Howard universities. See Junius Scales to Glenda Gilmore, 4 Jan. 1990, in author's possession.

10. Letterhead, Palmer Memorial Institute, C. Hawkins Brown to W. E. B. Dubois [*sic*], to June 1930, W. E. B. Du Bois Papers, reel 33, University of Massachusetts, Amherst.

11. Ruth Anita Hawkins Hughes, *Contributions of Vance County People of Color* (Raleigh: Sparks Press, 1988).

12. Jenkins, "Twig Bender of Sedalia," 1, reel 1, #7, Brown Collection, SL.

13. Ibid., insert B; "Some Incidents," 9, reel 1, #2, Brown Collection, SL.

14. Eva M. Young, "Palmer Memorial Institute Unique," *Charlotte Observer*, 10 Mar. 1940, folder 51, box 94–3, ibid.

15. Jenkins, "Twig Bender of Sedalia," E.F. 16, reel 1, #7, Brown Collection, SL.

16. Ibid., E.F. 16, E.F. 17; "Some Incidents," reel 1, #2, Brown Collection, SL.

17. For an example of the conflation of Sedalia and Palmer Institute, see *Palmer Memorial Institute: The Mission and the Legacy* (Greensboro: Women of Greensboro, [1981]).

18. The description here is from interviews and conversations with Dawn Gilmore, Brooks Gilmore, and Lois MacKenzie, the author's aunt, uncle, and mother, respectively. The author's grandfather, Clyde Manly Gilmore, was Brown's physician, and the author's mother, MacKenzie, was her attorney's secretary in the 1950s.

19. Brown transformed the institute in the late 1930s into a preparatory school for upper-class African Americans. By 1940, the school letterhead read: "The Charm School Idea of the Palmer Memorial Institute, Charlotte Hawkins Brown, President and Promoter." See C. Hawkins Brown to My Dear Friend, 20 Mar. 1940, folder 124, box 112–4, Washington Conservatory of Music Records, Moorland-Spingarn Research Center, Howard University (MRSC).

20. Jenkins, "Twig Bender of Sedalia," insert G, reel 1, #7, Brown Collection, SL.

21. Charlotte Hawkins Brown to Wallace Buttrick, 19 Dec. 1912, folder 1005, box 111, series 1, subseries 1, General Education Board Collection, Rockefeller Archive Center (RAC).

22. "Charlotte Hawkins Brown," Dannett Collection, uncataloged, LC. See also Sylvia G. L. Dannett, *Profiles of Negro Womanhood* (New York: M. W. Lads, 1964–66), 59–63. The notes for Dannett's biographical sketches often do not identify the interviewee and are fragmentary.

23. Map, "Palmer Memorial Institute—Sedalia—Enrol[l]ment—1920–1921," folder 1006, box 111, series 1, subseries 1, General Education Board Collection, RAC.

24. "Some Incidents," reel 1, #2, Brown Collection, SL.

25. Board, 1904, Correspondence G-M, box 14, and C. E. Hawkins to Dr. McIver, 13 Apr. 1905, file Southern Education Board, 1905, Correspondence, E-L, box 15, both in Charles D. McIver Collection, University Archives, Walter Clinton Jackson Library, University of North Carolina, Greensboro (WCJL).

26. Mrs. Charles D. McIver to editor of *Greensboro Daily News*, [ca. 1940], reel 1, #13, and Jenkins, "Twig Bender of Sedalia," reel 1, #7, both in Brown Collection, SL.

27. Rose Howell Holder, *McIver of North Carolina* (Chapel Hill: University of North Carolina Press, 1917), 63–67. See also Virginia T. Lathrop, "Mrs. McIver Believes Greatness of the Past Holds State's Hope for Present and Future," *News and Observer*, 6 Oct. 1940, Clipping File, vol. 94, reel 24, 371–72, North Carolina Collection, University of North Carolina, Chapel Hill (NCC).

28. James Leloudis, "'A More Certain Means of Grace': Pedagogy, Self, and Society in North Carolina, 1880–1920" (Ph.D. diss., University of North Carolina at Chapel Hill, 1989), and Pamela Dean, "Covert Curriculum: Class and Gender in a New South Women's College" (Ph.D. diss., University of North Carolina at Chapel Hill, 1995). On the association, see James Leloudis, "School Reform in the New South: The Woman's Association for the Betterment of Public School Houses in North Carolina, 1902–1919," *Journal of American History* 69 (March 1983): 886–909. See also Lula Martin McIver to Charles L. Coon, 4 Feb. 1909, folder 28, box 2, and Lula Martin McIver to Charles L. Coon, 25 Jan. 1910, folder 29, box 2, both in Coon Papers, Southern Historical Collection, University of North Carolina, Chapel Hill (SHC).

29. Sallie Waugh McBryan to Mrs. McIver, 22 Nov. 1913, file Correspondence, 1909–44, box 141, Lula Martin McIver Collection, WCJL; "Famous Landmark at WCUNC Razed," *Durham Morning Herald*, 26 Oct. 1952, Clipping File, vol. 94, reel 24, 343–44, NCC.

30. Lula Martin McIver to Charlotte Hawkins Brown, 6 Apr. 1920, reel 2, #41, Brown Collection, SL.

31. Charles D. McIver letter, 5 June 1905, reel 2, #30, Correspondence, 1902–6, ibid.

32. "Award Will Go to Dr. Brown," *Greensboro Daily News*, 10 Apr. 1947, Clipping File, vol. 18, reel 5, 239, NCC.

33. C. Hawkins Brown to My dear Sir [Professor Julius I. Foust], 25 May 1914, file General Correspondence, 1913–15, box 57, Foust Collection, WCJL.

34. Jenkins, "Twig Bender of Sedalia," 77, reel 1, #12, Brown Collection, SL.

35. E. P. Wharton to Charlotte Hawkins Brown, 12 Jan. 1917, reel 2, #37, Jan.–Apr. 1917; Mrs. Charles D. McIver to editor of *Greensboro Daily News*, n.d., reel 1 #13; and Jenkins, "Twig Bender of Sedalia," 78, reel 1, #12, all in Brown Collection, SL.

36. H. F. Kimball to Charlotte Hawkins Brown, 6 Nov. 1916, reel 2, #36, 1916, and "Notes," copy of notebook maintained by Charlotte Hawkins Brown, reel 1, #8, both in Brown Collection, SL; Annie L. Vickery to My Dear Mrs. McIver, 7 Mar. 1917, file Correspondence, 1909–44, box 141, Lula Martin McIver Collection, WCJL.

37. Charlotte Hawkins Brown, *Mammy* (Boston: Pilgrim Press, 1919).

38. Lula Martin McIver to Charlotte Hawkins Brown, 6 Apr. 1920, reel 2, #41, Brown Collection, SL.

39. Laura Holmes Reilley to D. H. Hill, 18 Oct. 1917, file Women's Committee, box 30, North Carolina Council of Defense, World War I Papers, 1903–33, pt. 2, Military Collection, North Carolina Department of Archives and History.

40. Mary J. McCrorey to Mrs. Hope, 7 May 1920; "Mrs. Hope of the Cleveland Meeting, 1920," 29 May 1920; "What the Colored Women Are Asking of the Y.W.C.A."; "To the National Board of the Young Women's Christian Association"; Minutes of the Cleveland Meeting, 1920; "Minutes of the meeting held in the offices of the South Atlantic Field Committee, Richmond, Virginia, 3 July 1920"; and Mary J. McCrorey to Mrs. Hope, 27 Jan. 1921, all in box 5, NU 14-C-5, Y.W.C.A., Neighborhood Union Papers, Special Collections, Robert Woodruff Library, Atlanta University, Atlanta, Georgia. Mary J. McCrorey to Charlotte Hawkins Brown, 2 Apr. 1920, reel 2, #41, Brown Collection, SL.

41. Jacquelyn Dowd Hall, *Revolt against Chivalry: Jessie Daniel Ames and the Women's Campaign against Lynching*, rev. ed. (New York: Columbia University Press, 1987), 93; "Some Incidents," reel 1, #2, Brown Collection, SL.

42. Brown address, folder 1, box 1, ibid.; Hall, *Revolt against Chivalry*, 93–94.

43. "First Draft," section 2, folder 1, box 1, ibid.

44. "Statement of Negro Women in Session, Mar. 26, 1921," folder 1, box 1.

45. Folder 1, box 1, ibid. (emphasis added).

46. W. E. Morton to NAACP, file Voting, 10–30 Nov. 1920, C284, National Association for the Advancement of Colored People Papers, Library of Congress.

47. H. M. Kingsley to NAACP, 9 Nov. 1920, file Voting, 1–9 Nov. 1920, C284, NAACP Papers.

48. Charles McPerson to NAACP, file Voting, 1–9 Nov. 1920, C284, NAACP Papers. For a summary of reports from across the South, see "Disfranchisement of Colored Americans in the Presidential Election of 1920" ([1920]), file Voting, Dec. 1920, C284, NAACP Papers.

49. Glenda E. Gilmore, *Gender and Jim Crow: Women and the Politics of White Supremacy in North Carolina, 1896–1920* (Chapel Hill: University of North Carolina Press, 1996), 219–224.

ANNELISE ORLECK
From the Russian Pale to Labor Organizing in New York City

The pale of Jewish settlement was a territory within Russia to which Jews were restricted during the eighteenth and nineteenth centuries and where they were frequently subjected to ferocious outbursts of anti-Semitic violence. Crossing from the pale to the teeming streets of Manhattan's Lower East Side was a frontier crossing of major proportions. Yet two million European Jews who came to the United States between 1880 and 1924 made it across, among them the remarkable young women who are the subjects of Orleck's lively and informative essay.

Like so many of their fellow immigrants, Rose Schneiderman, Fannia Cohn, Clara Lemlich, and Pauline Newman gravitated to one of the earliest industries to employ women—the garment industry. Based in New York City, the industry had long provided countless married women with piecework to take back to dimly lit tenements, where they often enlisted the help of grandmothers and children. By the turn of the century, much of the work had been transferred to sweatshops and factories that were notorious for their low wages and squalid working conditions. Because so many of the female employees were young, single women who presumably regarded their work as a temporary necessity until rescued by marriage, labor leaders usually assumed that the women were virtually unorganizable. Yet between 1909 and 1915, women garment workers in New York as well as in other cities exploded in labor militancy. By 1919, half of all women garment workers belonged to trade unions and many had joined the suffrage struggle as well. The role these four young women played in this process is the focus of Orleck's essay.

What experiences shaped their political consciousness and propelled their activism? As young girls forced to work and forego school and college, how did they educate themselves and for what purpose? Who were their allies and why were these alliances so necessary, yet so unstable? How was the balancing act required of the four with respect to male trade unionists and elite female reformers similar to that required of Charlotte Hawkins Brown, albeit in a different context? What attracted these young working women to suffrage? What is meant by the term "industrial feminists"?

Excerpted from "From the Russian Pale to the Lower East Side: The Cultural Roots of Four Jewish Women's Radicalism," "Coming of Age: The Shock of the Shops and the Dawning of Political Consciousness, 1900–1909," and "Audacity: The Uprising of Women Garment Workers, 1909–1915," prologue and chapters 1–2 of Annelise Orleck, *Common Sense and a Little Fire: Women and Working-Class Politics in the United States, 1900–1965* (Chapel Hill, N.C.: The University of North Carolina Press, 1995). Copyright © 1995 the University of North Carolina Press. Reprinted by permission of the author and publisher. The author has reversed the order of some of the pages, provided connecting sentences, and renumbered and edited notes.

During the summer of 1907, when New York City was gripped by a severe economic depression, a group of young women workers who had been laid off and were facing eviction took tents and sleeping rolls to the verdant Palisades overlooking the Hudson River. While rising rents and unemployment spread panic among the poor immigrants of Manhattan's Lower East Side, these teenagers lived in a makeshift summer camp, getting work where they could find it, sharing whatever food and drink they could afford, reading, hiking, and gathering around a campfire at night to sing Russian and Yiddish songs. "Thus we avoided paying rent or, worse still, being evicted," Pauline Newman later recalled. "Besides which, we liked living in the open—plenty of fresh air, sunshine and the lovely Hudson for which there was no charge."[1]

Away from the clatter of the shops and the filth of Lower East Side streets, the young women talked into the night, refreshed by what Newman called "the cool of the evening, glorious sunsets, the moon and stars." They shared personal concerns as well as shop-floor gripes—worries about love, about the future, and about the pressing problems of housing and food.

Their cliffside village meant more to Newman and her friends than a summer escape. They had created a vibrant alternative to the tenement life they found so oppressive, and their experience of it had set them to wondering. Perhaps the same sense of joy and comradeship could help workers transcend the drudgery of the garment shops and form the basis for effective organizing.[2]

At season's end, they emerged with strengthened bonds and renewed resolve to organize their communities around issues that the recent depression had brought into sharp relief: the need for stabilized rent and food prices, improved working conditions, and housing for the poor.[3]

The spirit of intimacy and solidarity that pervaded the summer of 1907 would inspire much of Pauline Newman's later organizing. Indeed, it became a model for the vision of change that Newman shared with her fellow Jewish immigrant radicals Fannia Cohn, Rose Schneiderman and Clara Lemlich. The four women moved to political struggle not simply by the need for better wages, hours and working conditions but also, in Newman's words,

by a need to ensure that "poverty did not deprive us from finding joy and satisfaction in things of the spirit."[4] This essay examines the early careers of these four remarkable organizers and the role they played in building a militant working women's movement during the first decades of the twentieth century.

For even as girls, these marginally educated immigrants wanted to be more than ... shop-floor drudges. They wanted lives filled with beauty—with friendships, books, art, music, dance, fresh air, and clean water. "A working girl is a human being," Newman would later tell a legislative committee investigating factory conditions, "with a heart, with desires, with aspirations, with ideas and ideals." That image nourished Newman, Schneiderman, Lemlich, and Cohn throughout their long careers. And it focused them on a single goal: to reshape U.S. society so that "working girls" like themselves could fulfill some of their dreams.[5]

The four women moved through strikingly different cultural milieus over the course of long careers that would carry them in different directions. Still, they each bore the imprint of the shared culture in which they were raised, first in Eastern Europe and then in New York City. That common experience gave them a particular understanding of gender, class, and ethnicity that shaped their later activism and political thought.

All four were born in the Russian-dominated pale of Jewish settlement during the last two decades of the nineteenth century. Rose Schneiderman was born in the Polish village of Saven in 1882; Fannia Cohn was born in Kletsk, Poland, in 1885; Clara Lemlich was born in the Ukrainian village of Gorodok in 1886; and Pauline Newman was born in Kovno, Lithuania, around 1890.[6]

They were ushered into a world swept by a firestorm of new ideas, where the contrasting but equally messianic visions of orthodox Judaism and revolutionary Socialism competed for young minds. The excitement of living in a revolutionary era imbued these young women with a faith in progress and a belief that political commitment gave life meaning. It also taught them, at an early age, that gender, class, and ethnicity were fundamental social categories and essential building blocks for political change. Being born into turbulence does not in itself make a child into a political activist. But the changes sweeping the Russian Empire toward the end of the nineteenth century shaped the consciousness of a generation of Eastern European Jews who contributed, in wildly disproportionate numbers, to revolutionary movements in Russia and to the labor and radical movements in the United States.[7]

The four were exposed to Marxist ideas at a tender age. As Eastern Europe shifted uneasily from feudalism to capitalism in the latter part of the nineteenth century, class analysis became part of the common parlance of young people in Jewish towns and villages. "Behind every other volume of Talmud in those years, there was a volume of Marx," one union organizer recalled of his small Polish town. Clara Lemlich grew up on revolutionary tracts and songs; Fannia Cohn considered herself a committed Socialist by the age of sixteen.[8]

Their awareness of ethnicity was even more keen. As Jews in Eastern Europe, the four learned young that ethnic identity was a double-edged sword. It was a source of strength and solace in their bitterly poor communities, but it also enabled Tsarist authorities to single Jews out and sow seeds of suspicion among their peasant neighbors. Jews living under Russian rule were made painfully aware of their status as permanent "others" in the land where they had lived for centuries. Clara Lemlich's family lived not far from Kishinev, where in 1903 the Tsar's government openly and unabashedly directed an orgy of anti-Jewish violence that shocked the world. In cosmopolitan Minsk, where she had gone to study, Fannia Cohn watched with dismay as the revolutionary populist organization she had joined began mouthing the same anti-Semitic conspiracy theories spewed by the government they despised. Frustration turned to fear when her brother was almost killed in yet another pogrom.[9]

Sex was just as distinct a dividing line as class and ethnicity. Eastern European Jews had observed a strict sexual division of labor for more than a thousand years. But by the late nineteenth century, as political and economic upheaval jolted long-accepted ways of thinking, sex roles too were being questioned. And so the four girls' understandings of gender were informed both by traditional Jewish conceptions of womanhood and by the challenges issued by new political movements.

In traditional Jewish society, mothers were also entrepreneurs. Clara Lemlich, Pauline Newman, and Rose Schneiderman were all raised by mothers who were skilled businesswomen. Jewish mothers' success in this role grew out of and reinforced a belief that women were innately suited to competition in the economic sphere. In contrast to the image of the sheltered middle-class housewife then dominant in the United States, Eastern European Jewish religious tradition glorified strong, economically sophisticated wives and mothers.

But as much as women's entrepreneurship was respected, a far higher premium was placed on study and prayer. And that, religious tradition dictated, could be performed only by men. A woman was expected to be pious, to read the vernacular Yiddish—rather than ancient Hebrew—translation of the Bible, and perhaps to attend women's services at the synagogue. But her primary religious role was as keeper of the home. Formal religious education was offered only to males.[10] Because Eastern European Jewish women had to fight for every scrap of education they received, many began to see education as the key to independence from all masters. This view would strongly influence their political organizing once in the United States.

The four emigrated as part of the mass movement that brought two million Jews from Eastern Europe to the United States between 1881 and 1924. Schneiderman came in 1890, Newman in 1901, Lemlich in 1903, and Cohn in 1904. Like most of their compatriots, they arrived in New York Harbor and settled on Manhattan's Lower East Side, the largest settlement of Eastern European Jews in the United States.[11] The newcomers were tantalized by the exciting diversions that New York life promised: libraries, theater, music, department stores, and amusement parks. But they had neither time nor money to indulge in such pleasures, for all of them soon found themselves laboring long hours to support their families.

At an age when most girls in the United States were still in grade school, immigrant working girls like Newman spent twelve- to fourteen-hour days in the harshest of atmospheres. Their bodies and minds reeled from the shock of the shops: the deafening noise, the brutal pace, and the rebukes of foremen. Some children were able to slough off the hardship with jokes and games. Others, realizing that they were destined to spend their youth in dank factories rather than in classrooms or schoolyards, grew swollen and withdrawn.

Clara Lemlich, like so many others, was quickly disillusioned by her first job in a New York garment shop: "I went to work two weeks after landing in this country. We worked from sunrise to set seven days a week. . . . Those who worked on machines had to carry the machines on their back both to and from work. . . . The shop we worked in had no central heating, no electric power. . . . The hissing of the machines, the yelling of the foreman, made life unbearable."[12]

Anger drove young women workers like Lemlich and Newman to band together. Untrained and largely unschooled, these young women were drawn to Socialism and trade unionism not because they felt an ideological affinity but because they had a desperate need to improve their working conditions. "I knew very little about Socialism," Lemlich recalled. "[But] the girls, whether Socialist or not, had many stoppages and strikes." Newman too found that for most young women workers, political understanding followed action rather than precipitating it: "We of the 1909 vintage knew nothing about the economics of . . . industry or for that matter about economics in general. All we knew was the bitter fact that, after working seventy and eighty hours in a seven day week, we did not earn enough to keep body and soul together." These assertions reveal much about the political development of the tens of thousands of women garment workers who would soon amaze New York and the nation with their militancy.[13]

Shop-floor culture fed the young women's emerging sense of political identity. Working alongside older men and women who discussed Socialism daily, they began to feel a sense of belonging to a distinct class of people in the world: workers. This allegiance would soon become as important to them as their Judaism. The shops also provided an opportunity for bonding with other women. Slowly, out of their workplace experiences, they began to develop a complex political identity in which class, gender and ethnicity overlapped. Young women workers were moved by the idea of sisterhood. It captured their own experiences in the sex-segregated shops where they worked. The majority of New York's garment workers were little more than girls, and the relationships they forged with factory friends were similar to those of schoolgirls—intense, melodramatic, and deeply loyal. They were teenage confidantes as well as fellow workers, and they relied on shop-floor rapport to soften the harshness of factory life.[14] For young immigrant women trying to build lives in a new land, such bonds were powerful and lasting. From these shop-floor friendships would soon evolve the ties of union sisterhood.[15]

Pauline Newman and her co-workers at the Triangle Shirtwaist Factory literally grew up together. Only twelve when she first came to Triangle, Newman was assigned to a corner known as "the kindergarten," where workers as young as eight, nine, or ten years old trimmed threads from finished garments. They labored, Newman later recalled, "from 7:30 A.M. to 6:30 at night when it wasn't busy. When the season was on we worked till 9 o'clock. No overtime pay." Their only taste of a normal childhood came through the songs and games they invented to help pass the time, the stories they told and the secrets they shared.[16]

By the early twentieth century, New York State had passed laws prohibiting night work for children. But little attempt was made to enforce them. On the rare occasions when an inspector showed up at her factory, Newman remembered, "the employers were always tipped off. . . . 'Quick,' they'd say, 'Into the boxes!' And we children would climb into the big box the finished shirts were stored in. Then some shirts were piled on top of us and when the inspector came—No children." In a way it was fun, Newman remembered. They thought they were playing a game like hide and seek.[17]

But it wasn't really a game. Children who had to help support their parents grew up quickly. Rose Schneiderman was thirteen when her mother begged United Hebrew Charities, an organization run by middle-class German Jews, to find her daughter a "respectable job" at a department store. Retail jobs were deemed more respectable than factory work because the environment was more pleasant and sexual harassment was thought to be less common. Deborah Schneiderman worried that factory work would sully Rose's reputation and make her less marriageable. A job as a fashionable salesgirl, she hoped, would usher Rose into the middle class. The single mother who had fed her children on charity food baskets and had been forced to place them in orphanages was grimly determined to help them escape poverty.

But then as now, pink-collar jobs paid significantly less than industrial work. Anxious to free her mother from the rigors of maintaining their tenement building, Schneiderman left her job in Ridley's department store for the harsher and more morally suspect conditions of an industrial shop. Making linings for caps and hats, she immediately raised her weekly income from $2.75 to $6. As the sole supporter of her family, the sixteen-year-old hoped to work her way up quickly to a skilled job in the cap trade.[18]

Clara Lemlich's family also relied on her wages, particularly because her father was unemployed. She aspired to the skilled position of draper, one of the highest-paid positions a woman could attain in the dressmaking trade. Despite terrible working conditions, many ambitious young women chose garment work over other jobs because it seemed to offer their greatest chance to acquire skills and command high wages. When these hopes were dashed, some young workers grew angry. That anger was fanned and channeled by older women in the shops who were itching to challenge the authority of the bosses.[19]

That is what happened to Rose Schneiderman, who, like many skilled women garment workers, was blocked from advancement by the unofficial gender hierarchy at her factory. Finding that all the highest-paid jobs in her cap-making shop were reserved for men, Schneiderman asked around about ways to break through those barriers. When she approached fellow worker Bessie Braut with her concerns, Schneiderman was initiated simultaneously into trade unionism, Socialism, and feminism. Schneiderman recalled, "Bessie was an unusual person. Her beautiful eyes shone out of a badly pockmarked face and the effect was startling. An outspoken anarchist, she made a strong impression on us. She wasted no time in giving us the facts of life—that the men in our trade belonged to a union and were, therefore, able to better their conditions. She added pointedly that it would be a good thing for the lining-makers to join a union along with the trimmers, who were all women."[20]

Schneiderman, Braut, and several other workers called on the secretary-treasurer of the United Cloth Hat and Cap Makers to request union recognition for their fledgling local of trimmers and lining makers. Within a few days they had enough signatures to win a charter for their local, and Schneiderman was elected secretary.[21]

Surprising even herself, the once-shy redhead soon found she could be an eloquent and fierce advocate for her fellow workers. In recognition of her growing reputation, the capmakers elected her to the Central Labor Union of New York. Deborah Schneiderman was disturbed by the turn Rose's life was taking. She warned Rose that if she pursued a public life she would never find a husband. No man wants a woman with a big mouth, her mother said.[22]

In the flush of excitement at the praise and warmth suddenly coming her way, young Rose did not stop to worry. In organizing, she had found both a calling and a world of friends. She had no intention of turning back. "It was such an exciting time," she wrote later. "A new life opened up for me. All of a sudden I was not lonely anymore. . . . It was the beginning of a period that molded all my subsequent life."[23]

Fannia Cohn, too, chose garment work as her path to a career. And like Schneiderman, Lemlich, and Newman, she found a community there. Unlike the others, however, she did not enter a garment factory looking for work that paid well. She was a comfortable middle-class woman in search of a trade ripe for unionizing.

Cohn arrived in New York in 1904 and moved in with her affluent cousins. There was little about her early days in the United States that was comparable to the hard-pressed scrambling for a living that the Schneidermans, Lemlichs, and Newmans experienced. "My family suggested that I complete my studies and then join the labor movement but I rejected this as I did not want to come into it from 'without' but from 'within.' I realized then that if I wanted to really understand the mind, the aspirations of the workers, I should experience the life of the worker in a shop."[24] In 1905, Fannia Cohn became a sleevemaker. For a year she moved from shop to shop until, in the "white goods" trade, she found the organizing challenge she was looking for.

Shops that manufactured white goods—underwear, kimonos, and robes—were considered particularly hard to organize. Production took place in tiny sweatshops, not large factories, and the manufacturing process had been broken down into small tasks that required little skill. The majority of white goods workers were immigrant girls under the age of fifteen. And because they came from a wide range of backgrounds—Jewish, Italian, Syrian, Turkish, and Greek—it was difficult for them to communicate with each other, let alone organize. As a result, these workers were among the lowest paid in the garment trades.

At twenty, Cohn was an elder in the trade. With her high school education and fluency in three languages, she was seen as a mother figure by many of the adolescents in the shops. She and a handful of older women workers began to operate as mentors, meeting with the girls in each shop and identifying potential leaders. Cohn taught her co-workers to read, write, and speak in public, hoping they would channel those skills into the union struggle. Cohn had already created the role that she would play throughout her career: an educator of younger workers.[25]

Education was a primary driving force in the metamorphosis of all four young women from shop workers to union organizers. From the isolated towns and restive cities of Eastern Europe, where gender, class, and ethnicity stymied Jewish girls' hopes for education, the lure of free public schooling in the United States beckoned powerfully. Having to drop out of school to work was more than a disappointment for many Jewish immigrant girls; it was their first great disillusionment with the dream of America. And they did not give that dream up easily.

"When I went to work," Rose Schneiderman remembered, "I was determined to continue my studies." Her only option was to attend one of the many night schools then open to immigrant workers in New York. Having carried with her from Poland the ideal of education as an exalted, liberating process, she was disgusted by the mediocre instruction she encountered and felt betrayed by teachers who seemed to be patronizing her. "I enrolled and went faithfully every evening for about four weeks. But I found that ... the instructor seemed more interested in getting one-hundred-percent attendance than in giving one-

hundred-percent instruction. He would joke and tell silly stories. . . . I soon realized I was wasting my time." Schneiderman left the evening school but did not stop studying. She asked older co-workers if she could borrow books that she had discussed with them in the shop. In the evenings, she read with her mother at home. Serializations of Emile Zola's *J'Accuse* and other contemporary writings in the Yiddish evening paper *Abendblatt* gave Rose a taste for literature. "I devoured everything I could get my hands on."[26]

Clara Lemlich was an equally avid reader. At the end of each twelve-hour day stitching shirtwaists, she would walk from her factory to the East Broadway branch of the New York Public Library. There she read the library's entire collection of Russian classics. "I was so eager to learn things," she later recalled. When she tired of solitary study, Lemlich joined a free night school on Grand Street. She returned home late each night, ate the dinner her mother had kept warm for her, then slept for just a few hours before rising again for work.[27]

Not surprisingly, young women like Schneiderman, Newman, and Lemlich turned to radical politics to fulfill their desire for a life of the mind. If no other school was available, then what Pauline Newman called "the school of solidarity" would have to do. Membership in the Socialist Party and in unions, tenant organizations, and benevolent societies provided immigrant women with an opportunity to learn and study that most would never have gotten otherwise. And as Newman put it, "Because they were hitherto deprived of any tutorship, they at once became ardent students."[28]

Pauline Newman was just fifteen when she first knocked on the doors of the Socialist Literary Society. Although women were not yet allowed to join, she was permitted to attend classes. The Literary Society was a revelation to the young worker. There she was introduced to the writings of Shakespeare, George Eliot, and Thomas Hardy and personally met writers like Jack London and Charlotte Perkins Gilman, who came to speak there. Gratitude, however, didn't stop her from joining a successful petition drive to admit women to the society.

For Newman—as for Clara Lemlich, who attended Marxist theory classes at the Socialist Party's Rand School—studying was more than a distraction from work. The "desire to get out of the shop," Newman wrote later, "to learn, to understand, became the dominant force in my life." But unlike many immigrants, who saw schooling as a ladder out of the working class, both she and Lemlich were committed to helping others rise with them. So Newman and Lemlich formed study groups that met during lunch hours and after work to share what they were learning with their friends.[29]

"We tried to educate ourselves," Newman remembered of her co-workers at the Triangle Shirtwaist Factory. "I would invite the girls to my room and we took turns reading poetry in English to improve our understanding of the language." Because they had to steal the time to study, the young women approached everything they read with a heightened sensitivity. And when something they were reading struck a chord of recognition, seemed to reflect on their own lives, the catharsis was not only emotional; it was political.[30]

The evolution of Lemlich's study group illustrates how study often led to union activity. Older workers, who were teaching Lemlich the craft of draping, invited her to join their lunchtime discussion groups to learn more about trade unionism. Soon Lemlich and a group of young women waistmakers formed their own study group. Discussion quickly escalated to action, and they decided to form a union.[31]

Skilled male workers in the shirtwaist trade had been trying to establish a union since 1900. But after five years the union had managed to attract only ten members. The problem, Lemlich told her male colleagues, was that women workers had to be approached by an organizer who understood their particular needs as women. They bristled at the suggestion that this young girl might know more about their business than they did. But years later, one conceded that the failure of the first waistmakers' union was due at least in part to their ham-fisted tactics: "We would issue a circular reading somewhat as follows: 'Murder the exploiters, the blood-suckers, the manufacturers. . . . Pay your dues. . . . Down with the Capitalists!'" Few women or men showed up at their meetings.[32]

During the spring of 1905 the union disbanded and reorganized as Local 25 of the ILGWU, with Clara Lemlich and a group of six young women from her waistmaking shop on the executive board. Taking their cue from Lemlich, the new union used women organizers to attract women workers. Lemlich addressed street-corner meetings in English and Yiddish and found Italian women to address the Italian workers. Soon, like Schneiderman, Newman, and Cohn, she realized that she had found a calling.[33]

In the progressive atmosphere of early-twentieth-century New York City, influential people quickly noticed the militant young working women. Older Socialists, trade unionists, and middle-class reformers offered their assistance. These benefactors helped the young organizers sharpen their arguments, provided financial assistance, and introduced them to politicians and public officials. The protégés recognized the importance of this informal mentoring and would later work to recreate such networks in the unions, schools, and training programs they built for young women workers. Schneiderman, Newman, Lemlich, and Cohn were keenly aware that young working women needed help from more experienced and more powerful allies. But they also worried that the voices of women workers might be outshouted in the clamorous process of building alliances. From these early days, they battled to preserve the integrity of their vision.

Pauline Newman found her first mentors in the Socialist Party, which she joined in 1906 at the age of fifteen. Older women, including former garment worker Theresa Serber Malkiel, took her on as a protégé. Newman quickly blossomed under their tutelage. Before long she was running street-corner meetings. Armed with a sonorous voice and the certitude of youth, she would take "an American flag and a soapbox and go from corner to corner," exhorting the gospel of Socialism in Yiddish and English. "I, like many of my friends and comrades, thought that socialism and socialism alone could and would someday fill the gap between rich and poor," Newman recalled. In a neighborhood crowded with sidewalk proselytizers, this child evangelist became one of the party's most popular street-corner attractions.[34]

In 1908, nine years before New York State gave women the vote, seventeen-year-old Newman was nominated by the Socialist Party to run for New York's Secretary of State. New-

Rose Schneiderman at a sewing machine, posed during the capmakers' strike of 1905. (Courtesy Rose Schneiderman Collection, Robert F. Wagner Labor Archives, New York University)

Rose Schneiderman addresses a street rally in New York. (Courtesy Brown Brothers, Sterling, Pennsylvania)

man used her campaign as a platform for suffrage. Her speeches were heckled by some Socialist men, and her candidacy provoked amused commentaries in New York City newspapers; some writers snickered at the prospect of a "skirted Secretary of State." It was a largely symbolic crusade, but Newman felt that she got people talking about the idea of women in government. The highlight of the campaign was her whistlestop tour with presidential candidate and Socialist leader Eugene V. Debs on his "Red Special" train.

The Socialist Party opened up a new world to Newman, who, after all, had never graduated from elementary school. Along with Debs, she met future Congressmen Meyer Berger and Morris Hillquit and leading Socialist intellectuals. Newman later wrote about the excitement of discussions that carried over from meetings and went into the night as she and her friends walked through Central Park, arguing till the sun came up. Those nights made her feel part of a historic moment.[35]

While Newman was being nurtured by the Socialist Party, Rose Schneiderman found her mentors in the United Cloth Hat and Cap Makers. At the union's 1904 convention she was elected to the General Executive Board; she was the first woman to win such a high-level post in the American labor movement. During the winter of 1904–5, Schneiderman's leadership skills were tested when owners tried to open up union shops to nonunion workers. The largely immigrant capmaker's union called for a general strike. The 1905 strike was a watershed event in Schneiderman's emerging career. Her role as the only woman leader in the union won attention from the press and lasting respect from male capmakers, including the future president of the union, Max Zaritsky, who became a lifelong friend and admirer.[36]

It also brought her to the attention of the newly formed Women's Trade Union League (WTUL), an organization of progressive middle- and upper-class women reformers founded in 1903 to help working women organize. Schneiderman had misgivings about the group because she "could not believe that men and women who were not wage earners themselves understood the problems that workers faced." But she trusted the League's best-known working-class member, Irish shirt-maker Leonora O'Reilly. And she could not ignore the favorable publicity that the WTUL won for the strikers. By March 1905, Schneiderman had been elected to the executive board of the New York WTUL. In 1906, the group elected her vice president.[37]

Schneiderman's entrance into the New York WTUL was an important turning point for both her and the organization. Three years after its founding, the WTUL remained dominated by affluent reformers who had dubbed themselves "allies" of the working class. Despite their genuine commitment to trade unionism, League leaders had credibility problems among women workers. Schneiderman had joined the League recognizing that working women lacked the education, the money, and the political clout to organize effectively without powerful allies. Still, she remained ambivalent for a variety of reasons.[38]

The progressive reformers who dominated the League tried to steer workers away from radical influences, particularly the Socialist Party. Yet Schneiderman and O'Reilly, the League's leading working-class organizers, were Socialist Party members and saw unionism as a potentially revolutionary tool. As a result, the pair often felt torn by competing loyalties. Socialists distrusted their work with upper-crust women reformers. Union men were either indifferent or openly hostile to working women's attempts to become leaders in the labor movement. And the League women often seemed to Schneiderman and O'Reilly to act out of a patronizing benevolence that had little to do with real coalition building. The two grew angry at what they saw as attempts by wealthy allies to manipulate them. In January 1906, Leonora O'Reilly announced the first of her many resignations from the League, claiming "an overdose of allies."[39]

There were a few deep friendships between affluent WTUL leaders and working women like Schneiderman, O'Reilly, and Pauline Newman, who joined the League in 1909. Such bonds created hope that intimacy was possible between women of different classes; but cross-class friendships were the exception rather than the rule. Working women like Newman never lost sight of the ways their class background separated them from wealthy reformers. Sisterhood was exhilarating, but outside the WTUL, their lives and political agendas diverged sharply.[40]

Consequently, these women's relations with most wealthy League supporters were marked by deep ambivalence inasmuch as WTUL backers wanted to distance the League from radical working-class activism and to stake out a decidedly middle ground in the struggle for women's rights that was then gathering steam.

Schneiderman tried to counterbalance such influences by encouraging male union leaders to play a more active role in the League, but she had little success. She told them that the WTUL could help the labor movement by successfully organizing women workers, whose low wages might otherwise exert a downward pressure on unionized male wages. A *women's* trade union league was needed, she insisted, because women workers responded to different arguments than did men workers. The League could focus on the particular concerns of women, such as the double shift—having to perform household chores after coming home from long days in the factory. Her suggestions were greeted with indifference.

Addressing the First Convention of American Women Trade Unionists, held in New York on July 14, 1907, Schneiderman reported that she "was very much surprised and not a little disappointed that the attention of men unionists was so small." The truth is, she told her audience, working women needed more than unions. They needed political power. "The time has come," she said firmly, "when working women of the State of New York must be enfranchised and so secure political power to shape their own labor conditions." The convention passed a suffrage resolution, one of the first prosuffrage statements by any organization representing American working-class women.[41]

Schneiderman confronted middle- and upper-class allies with equal frankness. She told the NYWTUL executive board that they were having little success organizing women workers because they approached their task like scholars, not trade unionists. They surveyed conditions in the women's trades, noting which had the lowest salaries, the longest hours, and the worst hygienic conditions. Then they established committees to study the possibilities for unionizing each trade. Finally they went into the shops to explain their findings to the working women. Schneiderman

suggested a simpler alternative: take their lead from women workers and respond to requests for aid from women workers who were already trying to organize. It was something they had never thought to do.[42]

Before long, requests for help were pouring in, mostly from immigrant Jewish women. In the dress trade, where Clara Lemlich was working, and in the white goods trade, where Fannia Cohn was organizing, women workers had launched a series of wildcat strikes. "It was not unusual for unorganized workers to walk out without having any direct union affiliation," Schneiderman later recalled.[43]

By 1907, long-simmering anger over speedups, wage cuts, and the requirement that employees pay for their own thread reached a boiling point. Foreshadowing its role in the decades to come, the Women's Trade Union League decided to champion women workers ignored by the male unions. The strike fever soon engulfed Brooklyn, where for two years Fannia Cohn had been struggling against male union leaders' indifference to organize white goods workers. So when three hundred workers in one shop decided to strike in 1908, they bypassed the UGW and called for help from Schneiderman and the WTUL.

Since the ethnic makeup of the Brooklyn white goods trade was far more diverse than any other in the garment industry, this strike raised a new challenge for Schneiderman: how to forge a sense of solidarity between working-class women of many religions and nationalities. Schneiderman decided that the best way to reach immigrant workers was through organizers who literally spoke their language.[44]

She decided to focus first on Italian workers because, after Jews, they comprised the single largest ethnic group in the garment trades. Recognizing the cultural as well as linguistic differences that separated her from Italian immigrant women, Schneiderman tried a strategy she would employ many times over the years to come: to identify and cultivate a leader from within the ranks of the workers. She began working with a Brooklyn priest on ways to approach young Italian women. She also got the League to hire an Italian-speaking organizer who assembled a committee of progressive New York Italians—including prominent women professionals and the editor of a popular evening paper *Bolatino de la Sera*—to popularize trade unionism among Italian women workers.[45]

The strategy proved successful. By 1909 enough workers had enlisted that the ILGWU finally recognized the Brooklyn white goods workers' union. The vast majority of its members were teenage girls; these young women elected their mentor, Fannia Cohn, then twenty-four, to the union's first executive board. Cohn, who stepped off the shop floor to a policy-making position, would remain a paid union official for the rest of her life.[46]

In 1909, Clara Lemlich—then in her twenties and on the executive board of ILGWU Local 25—enlisted Schneiderman's aid in her drive to organize shirt-waist makers. For the past three years, Lemlich had been zigzagging between small shops, stirring up trouble. Her first full-scale strike was at Weisen and Goldstein's Manhattan factory. Like the Triangle Shirtwaist Factory, where Newman worked, Weisen and Goldstein's was considered a model shop. The workrooms were modern and airy—a pleasant contrast to the dark basement rooms where most white goods workers labored. However, the advantages of working in a clean, new factory were offset by the strains of mechanization. In 1907 the workers at Weisen and Goldstein's went on strike to protest speedups.

Older male strikers proved critical to Lemlich's political education. Confused by an argument between workers at a strike meeting, Lemlich asked one to explain the difference between Socialist unionism and the "pure and simple trade unionism" of the American Federation of Labor (AFL). When the meeting ended, the man took Lemlich for a long walk. He explained Socialism in terms she could use with her fellow workers. "He started with a bottle of milk—how it was made, who made the money from it through every stage of its production. Not only did the boss take the profits, he said, but not a drop of that milk did you drink unless he allowed you to. It was funny, you know, because I'd been saying things like that to the girls before. But now I understood it better and I began to use it more often—only with shirtwaists."[47]

Lemlich returned to the picket line with a more sophisticated view of organizing. She became a regular at Socialist Party meetings and began attending classes at the Rand School. Through the Socialist Party she became friends with Rose Schneiderman, Pauline Newman, and other young women organizers. Both individually and in tandem, this group of radical young women organized strikes across the Lower East Side.

In 1909, after being fired from two more shops for leading strikes, Lemlich began working at the Leiserson shop. Brazenly, she marched uninvited into a strike meeting that had been called by the shop's older male elite—the skilled cutters and drapers. Warning them that they would lose if they attempted to strike without organizing the shop's unskilled women, Lemlich demanded their help in organizing women workers. They bridled at her nerve, but ultimately they helped her unionize the women.[48]

Lemlich's reputation as a leader grew rapidly during the fall of 1909 as stories of her bravery spread. During the Leiserson strike, which began that September, she was arrested seventeen times and had six ribs broken by club-wielding police and company guards. Without complaint, she tended to her bruises and returned to the line. By November 1909, when she stepped onto the stage in Cooper Union's Great Hall of the People to deliver the speech that would spark the largest women's strike the nation had yet seen, Lemlich was not the anonymous "wisp of a girl" that news accounts described. She was a battle-scarred veteran of the labor movement, well known among her fellow workers.[49]

Still, it is worth remembering that in this period, the four women activists were just barely adults. Newman, Schneiderman, and Lemlich still lived with their parents. During the Leiserson strike, Lemlich was so fearful that her parents would try to keep her home if they knew about her injuries that she hid her escapades and bruises from them. Later she explained the events to her grandson: "Like rain the blows fell on me. The gangsters hit me. . . . The boys and girls invented themselves how to give back what they got from the scabs, with stones and whatnot, with sticks. . . . Sometimes when I came home I wouldn't tell because if I would tell they wouldn't want me to go anymore. Yes, my boy, it's not easy. Unions aren't built easy."[50]

On November 23, 1909, New York City awoke to a general strike of shirtwaist makers, the largest strike by women workers the United States had ever seen. Overnight, between 20,000 and 40,000 workers—most of them teenage girls—silenced their sewing machines to protest the low wages, long hours, and dangerous working conditions. Though the magnitude of the strike amazed nearly everyone, including Schneiderman, Newman, Cohn, and Lemlich, the four knew that this was no spontaneous uprising: they had been organizing feverishly for almost three years and had noted a transformation in the working women they talked to, a growing sense of collective identity matched by an increasing militancy. They had laid the groundwork through a series of smaller strikes and had trained fellow workers to expect and respond to the violent and divisive tactics used by bosses to break the strike.

Despite their effectiveness, the strike was threatened by the escalation of police violence against the young women picketers. Two weeks after the strike call, Schneiderman and Dreier led ten thousand young waistmakers on a march to city hall to demand that Mayor George McClellan rein in the police. He promised an investigation but did little. One month into the strike, there had been 771 arrests, many made with undue force.[51]

WTUL leaders decided to try a different tack. They called a mass meeting of all the young women who had been attacked by police. The press and wealthy supporters were invited. One after another, adolescent girls rose to the stage to tell their stories. Mollie Weingast told a cheering crowd that when an officer tried to arrest her, she informed him that she had a constitutional right to picket. Minnie Margolis demanded that a policeman protect her from physical attack by her boss. When he refused, she took down his badge and precinct numbers. It was, she told the audience, an officer's job to protect her right to protest peacefully. Celie Newman, sixteen, said that police had manhandled her and dragged her into court, where her boss told a judge that she was an anarchist and should be deported. At another meeting earlier that week, seventeen-year-old Etta Ruth said that police had taunted her with lewd suggestions.[52]

Implying that picketers were little better than streetwalkers, employers often resorted to sexual innuendos to discredit the strikers. The workers clearly resented the manner in which middle-class standards of acceptable feminine behavior were used to manipulate

them even though they enjoyed none of the advantages of middle-class birth. Then as now, society offered a limited range of cultural images of working-class women. They were either "good" girls who listened docilely to fathers, employers, and policemen, or "bad" women whose aggressive behavior made them akin to prostitutes. By walking on picket lines and going public with their demands, they'd forfeited their claims to femininity and respectability—and thus to protection.[53]

Such women were shown little deference by police and company thugs, who attacked them with iron bars, sticks, and billy clubs. And they received little sympathy in court when they attempted to press charges. One young woman appeared in court with a broken nose, a bruised face, and a head swathed in bandages. Yet the judge dropped her assault charge against police. "You are on strike against God and nature," one magistrate told a worker. Only the League's decision to invite college students and wealthy women onto the picket lines ended the violence. Alva Belmont and Anne Morgan led a contingent of New York's wealthiest women in what newspapers dubbed "mink brigades," which patrolled the dirty sidewalks of the Lower East Side. Fearful of clubbing someone on the Social Register, police grew more restrained.[54]

The socialites' presence generated both money and press for the strikers. The move proved politically wise for the suffrage cause as well, because the constant proselytizing of suffrage zealot Alva Belmont, who often bailed strikers out of jail, got young workers talking about the vote. But rubbing elbows with the mink brigade did not blind workers to the class-determined limits of sisterhood. How far they were from the protected status of more affluent women was made abundantly clear by the violence they encountered at the hands of police and company guards and by the fact that the mink brigades were able to end police brutality simply by joining the picket lines.

Encounters in court and with feminist allies speeded the growth of group consciousness. Telling their stories in court, to reporters, and to sympathetic audiences of college and society women, the strikers grew more confident of their speaking abilities and of their capacity to interpret their world. They became more aware of the distribution of power in the United States. And finally, the violence directed against them intensified their bonds with one another.

For Schneiderman, Newman, and Lemlich, the 1909 shirtwaist uprising sped their maturation as organizers and political leaders. The strike breathed new life into a struggling immigrant labor movement and transformed the tiny ILGWU into a union of national significance. Still, it ended with mixed success for workers. Many won pay increases and union recognition; others did not. And the contracts hammered out by ILGWU negotiators left a devastating legacy, for without consulting the strikers, male union negotiators decided that safety conditions were less important than other issues. Their concessions would come back to haunt the entire labor movement two years later, when the Triangle Shirtwaist Factory burned.[55]

Flames from the volcanic 1909 uprising licked industrial cities from New York to Michigan. Within a matter of weeks, 15,000 women waistmakers in Philadelphia walked off their jobs. The spirit of militancy soon touched the Midwest. In 1910, Chicago women led a strike of 41,000 men's clothing makers. The following year, women workers and the wives of male workers played key roles in a bitter cloakmakers' strike in Cleveland. Meanwhile, in Muscatine, Iowa, young women button makers waged and won a long battle for union recognition. In 1912, corset makers in Kalamazoo, Michigan, launched a campaign for better working conditions that polarized their city and won national press attention. In 1913, a strike of underwear and kimono makers swept up 35,000 young Brooklyn girls and women. Finally, in 1915, Chicago dressmakers capped this period of women's labor militancy by winning recognition of their local union after years of struggle. They elected their organizer, Fannia Cohn, as the first woman vice president of a major American labor union.[56]

Cohn, Rose Schneiderman, Pauline Newman, and Clara Lemlich were at the center of a storm that by 1919 had brought half of all women garment workers into trade unions. Individually and in tandem, the four women participated in all of the major women's strikes between 1909 and 1915, arguably the most intense period of women's labor militancy in U.S. history. This wave of "uprisings" seemed to herald the birth of a working women's

movement on a scale never before seen. And it catapulted the four young women into positions of leadership, forcing them, in conjunction with colleagues, to articulate a clearly defined set of goals for the new movement.[57] In the passion and excitement of the years that followed, Schneiderman, Newman, Lemlich, and Cohn would begin to mature as political leaders and to forge a vision of political change that originated in their years on the shop floor. Pauline Newman would later describe this new brand of activism as politics of the 1909 vintage, fermented during a brief era of young women's mass protest. That description expresses the importance of the 1909 strike as both symbol and catalyst for a new working women's politics.

"Industrial feminism," the phrase coined in 1915 by scholar Mildred Moore to describe working women's militancy over the previous six years, evokes the same spirit but focuses more broadly. It simultaneously captures the interaction between women workers and feminist activists and recognizes the profound influence that the shop floor had on shaping working women's political consciousness. Industrial feminism accurately depicts the contours of an emerging political movement that by decade's end would propel the problems and concerns of industrial working women to the center of U.S. political discourse and make them players in the Socialist Party, the suffrage movement, and the politics of progressive reform.[58]

Industrial feminism was not a carefully delineated code of political thought. It was a vision of change forged in an atmosphere of crisis and awakening, as women workers in one city after another "laid down their scissors, shook the threads off their clothes and calmly left the place that stood between them and starvation." These were the words of former cloakmaker, journalist, and Socialist Party activist Theresa Malkiel, a partisan chronicler of women's labor militancy. Once an organizer, later a mentor for Newman, Lemlich, and Schneiderman, Malkiel told readers of the *New York Call* that they should not be surprised by the seemingly sudden explosion of young women workers' discontent. As hard as they might find it to take seriously the notion of a "girl's strike," she warned them, this was no outburst of female hysteria. "It was not . . . a woman's fancy that drove them to it," she wrote, "but an eruption of a long smoldering volcano, an overflow of suffering, abuse and exhaustion."[59]

Common sense, Pauline Newman would later say, dictated the most immediate goals of industrial feminists in the era of women's strikes. Given the dire realities of garment workers' lives, the first order of business had to be to improve their wages, hours, and working conditions. Toward that end the "girl strikers" of 1909–15 followed the most basic tenets of unionism. They organized, struck, and negotiated through their labor unions. But the "long-smoldering volcano" that Malkiel cautioned her readers to heed had been stirred to life by more than dissatisfaction over low wages and poor conditions.

The nascent political philosophy that began to take shape after the 1909 strike was more complex than the bread-and-butter unionism of AFL president Samuel Gompers. Why, young working women reasoned, should unions only negotiate hours and wages? They wanted to build unions that would also offer workers educational and cultural activities, health care, and maybe even a chance to leave the city and enjoy the open countryside.

Such ambitious goals derived largely from the personal experiences of industrial feminist leaders like Cohn, Schneiderman, Lemlich, and Newman. Political activism had enriched the four young women's lives, exposing them to more interesting people than they would have met had they stayed on the shop floor: writers, artists, professors, people with ideas. Through politics they had found their voices and a forum in which to raise them. The personal excitement and satisfaction they found in activism in turn shaped the evolution of their political vision: they wanted to create institutions that would provide some of the same satisfactions to any working woman who joined.

But alone, working women had none of the political or economic clout needed to open up such doors of opportunity. To build a successful movement, the four knew that they would have to win the support of more powerful allies. So they learned to build coalitions. From the time they left the shop floor until the end of their careers, they operated within a tense nexus of union men, progressive middle- and upper-class women, and the working women they sought to organize. These alliances shifted continuously, requiring the four women to perform a draining and politically hazardous balancing act. But each core group contributed an important dimension to the political education of the four organizers.

With their male counterparts and older women in the labor movement, they shared a class solidarity that would always remain at the heart of their politics. Traveling around the country, they met coal miners, loggers, and railroad workers who shared both their experiences of exploitation as laborers and their exhilaration in the economic and political strength that trade unions gave them.

From the middle- and upper-class women who joined them on the picket lines and lent them both financial and strategic support, they learned that trade union activism was not the only way to fight for improved work conditions. These allies would expose Newman, Cohn, Schneiderman, and Lemlich to a world of power and political influence, encouraging them to believe that through suffrage and lobbying, government could be put to work for their benefit.

Finally, as they began to think in terms of forging a national movement, they were forced to develop new techniques to reach women workers of different races, religions, and ethnicities. They learned from the women they sought to organize that just as women workers were best reached by women organizers, so Italian, Polish, and Hispanic immigrants and native-born black and white Protestant women were better reached by one of their own than by Jewish women steeped in the political culture of Eastern Europe and the Lower East Side. Though each of the four women had some success in bridging racial and ethnic divisions, they were forced to acknowledge their limitations. They could not do it all themselves; they had to nurture women shop-floor leaders from different backgrounds.

The work required to remain politically effective in this nexus of often-conflicting relationships yielded some real rewards, both strategically and personally. But sometimes the constant struggling wore on them. Conflicts and tensions were brought into sharp relief as the four exhausted themselves making speeches and giving pep talks to weary workers, when they themselves needed reassurance: although they had achieved recognition by the end of the 1909 strike, Schneiderman, Cohn, Newman, and Lemlich were still poor, uneducated, and young. Newman was only eighteen years old when the strike began, and Lemlich twenty-three. Even the elders in the circle, Cohn and Schneiderman, were only twenty-five and twenty-eight, respectively.

Letters between Newman and Schneiderman from that era reveal their vulnerability to slights and criticisms by male union leaders and female reformers. Life on "the battlefield," as Newman referred to it, was lonely. At an age when other women were contemplating marriage and family, they spent their nights in smoky union halls or the cheap, dingy hotel rooms that unions rented for their organizers. They sometimes questioned their life choices, for the reality of union work was far less glamorous than it had seemed in their shop-floor days. Indeed, Newman would quit several times before decade's end. Ultimately, though, their disillusionment did not drive the four women from the union movement. Instead, it fueled their desire to broaden the vision of U.S. trade unionism. When Schneiderman said "The working woman needs bread, but she needs roses, too," she was speaking from personal experience.[60]

Notes

1. Pauline Newman, "Letters to Hugh and Michael" (1951–69), Box 1, Folder 3, Pauline M. Newman Papers, Schlesinger Library, Radcliffe College, Cambridge, Mass. (hereafter cited as Newman Papers).

2. Ibid.

3. Ibid.; *New York Times*, November 2, 25, December 3, 26, 1907.

4. Newman, "Letters to Hugh and Michael."

5. "The Testimony of Miss Pauline M. Newman," in *Hearings of the New York State Factory Investigating Commission* (Albany: J. B. Lyons Printers, 1915), 2868–71.

6. My estimate of Newman's age is based on evidence suggesting that she was around eighteen years old at the time of the 1909 shirtwaist strike. Newman, like many Jews of her generation, never knew for sure how old she was. Her birthdate was recorded only on the flyleaf of the family Bible. After the Bible was lost in transit, she could only guess at her age.

7. For analyses of the position of Jews in Russian society at the turn of the century, see S. Ettinger, "The Jews at the Outbreak of the Revolution," in *The Jews in Soviet Russia since 1917*, ed. Lionel Kochan, 3d ed. (Oxford: Oxford University Press, 1978), 15–30; see also Salo Baron, *The Russian Jew under Tsars and Soviets* (New York: Macmillan, 1976).

8. Sidney Jonas, interview by author, Brooklyn, N.Y., August 10, 1980; Paula Scheier, "Clara Lemlich Shavelson: Fifty Years in Labor's Front Line," *Jewish Life*, November 1954; Ricki Carole Myers Cohen, "Fannia Cohn and the International Ladies' Garment Workers' Union" (Ph.D. diss., University of Southern California, 1976), 5.

9. Newman, "Letters to Hugh and Michael"; Cohen, "Fannia Cohn," chap. 1; Scheier, "Clara Lemlich Shavelson"; Fannia M. Cohn to "Dear Emma," May 15, 1953, Fannia M. Cohn Papers, Astor, Lenox, and Tilden Foundations, Rare Books and Manuscripts Division, New York Public Library (hereafter cited as Cohn Papers).

In March 1903, gangs organized by Russian police rampaged through the Ukrainian town of Kishinev, killing 51 Jewish men, women, and children, and wounding at least 495 others. Edward H. Judge, *Eastern Kishinev: Anatomy of a Pogrom* (New York: New York University Press, 1992).

10. See Charlotte Baum, Paula Hyman, and Sonya Michel, *The Jewish Woman in America* (New York: NAL/Dutton, 1977), 55–91; Mark Zborowski and Elizabeth Herzog, *Life Is with People* (New York: Schocken, 1962); Jack Kugelmass and Jonathan Bayarin, *From a Ruined Garden: The Memorial Books of Polish Jewry* (New York: Schocken Books, 1985).

11. The Lower East Side continued to receive Jewish immigrants from Eastern Europe into the 1920s. See Ettinger, "Jews at the Outbreak of Revolution," 19–22; Celia Heller, *On the Edge of Destruction* (New York: Schocken, 1980), 45–55; and Irving Howe, *World of Our Fathers* (New York: Harcourt Brace & Jovanovich, 1976), xix.

12. Clara Lemlich Shavelson to Morris Schappes, March 15, 1965, published in *Jewish Currents* 36, no. 10 (November 1982): 9–11.

13. Clara Lemlich, "Remembering the Waistmakers' General Strike, 1909," *Jewish Currents*, November 1982; Newman, "Letters to Hugh and Michael."

14. Much has been written about the importance of women's colleges to the various social reform movements of the Progressive Era. Stephen Norwood makes a similar argument for high schools. Norwood, *Labor's Flaming Youth: Telephone Workers and Labor Militancy, 1878–1923* (Urbana: University of Illinois Press, 1990).

15. Newman, "Letters to Hugh and Michael"; Pauline Newman, interview by Barbara Wertheimer, New York, N.Y., November 1976; Pauline Newman résumé, n.d., Newman Papers.

16. Pauline Newman, interview by author, New York, N.Y., February 9, 1984; Newman, interview by Wertheimer.

17. Joan Morrison and Charlotte Fox Zabusky, eds., *American Mosaic* (New York: E. P. Dutton, 1980).

18. See Rose Schneiderman, *All for One* (New York: Paul S. Eriksson, 1967), 35–42, and Susan Porter Benson, "The Customers Ain't God: The Work Culture of Department Store Saleswomen, 1890–1940," in *Working Class America*, ed. Michael Frisch and Daniel J. Walkowitz (Urbana: University of Illinois Press, 1983), 185–212.

19. Scheier, "Clara Lemlich Shavelson." See also Susan Glenn, *Daughters of the Shtetl: Work,*

Unionism and the Immigrant Generation (Ithaca: Cornell University Press, 1990), 122–31.

20. Schneiderman, *All for One*, 48.

21. Ibid., 48–50.

22. Ibid.

23. Ibid.

24. FMC to Selig Perlman, December 26, 1951, Box 5, Cohn Papers.

25. Information on the problems of organizing the white goods trade is located in Minutes of the Executive Board of the NYWTUL, February 28, August 22, and November 26, 27, 1907, Reel 1, Papers of the New York Women's Trade Union League, Tamiment Institute Library, New York University (hereafter cited as NYWTUL Papers); information on Cohn comes from Cohen, "Fannia Cohn," 11–21.

26. Schneiderman, *All for One*, 39–40.

27. Scheier, "Clara Lemlich Shavelson."

28. Pauline Newman, "The White Goods Workers' Strike," *Ladies' Garment Worker* 4, no. 3 (March 1913):1–4.

29. Scheier, "Clara Lemlich Shavelson"; Pauline Newman, Fragments 1958–61, Box 1, Newman Papers.

30. Newman, interview by Wertheimer; Newman, interview in Morrison and Zabusky, *American Mosaic*.

31. Scheier, "Clara Lemlich Shavelson."

32. Louis Levine [Lewis Lorwin], *The Women's Garment Workers: A History of the International Ladies' Garment Workers' Union* (New York: B. W. Huebsch, 1924), 148–49.

33. This information is pieced together from Scheier, "Clara Lemlich Shavelson"; Dora Smorodin, interview by author, Maplewood, N.J., March 12, 1991; and Levine, *Women's Garment Workers*, 148–49.

34. Newman, interview by Wertheimer; Newman, "Letters to Hugh and Michael."

35. Ibid.

36. Schneiderman, *All for One*, 58–60.

37. Ibid., 73–77; Minutes of the NYWTUL Executive Board, February 24, March 24, 1905. Reel 1, NYWTUL Papers.

38. Nancy Schrom Dye, *As Equals and as Sisters: Feminism, Unionism and the Women's Trade Union League of New York* (Columbia: University of Missouri Press, 1980), 110–22.

39. Ibid.; Minutes of the NYWTUL Executive Board, January 25, 1906, Reel 1, NYWTUL Papers.

40. Newman, interview by Wertheimer; Newman, interview by author, February 9, 1984, New York.

41. See also Alice Kessler-Harris, "Rose Schneiderman," in *American Labor Leaders*, ed. Warren Van Tine and Melvyn Dubofsky (Urbana: University of Illinois Press, 1987), 160–84.

42. Minutes of the NYWTUL Executive Board, February 24, 1905-February 1, 1909, Reel 1, NYWTUL Papers.

43. Schneiderman, *All for One*, 84.

44. Minutes of the NYWTUL Executive Board, February 28, August 22, November 26, 27, 1907, Reel 1, NYWTUL, Papers; Levine, *Women's Garment Workers*, 220.

45. Minutes of the NYWTUL Executive Committee, November 26, 27, 1907, Reel 1, NYWTUL Papers.

46. Levine, *Women's Garment Workers*, 220; Cohen, "Fannia Cohn," 36–43.

47. Scheier, "Clara Lemlich Shavelson."

48. Martha Schaffer, telephone interview by author, March 11, 1989; Joel Schaffer, Evelyn Velson, and Julia Velson, interview by author, Oakland, Calif., September 9, 1992.

49. Scheier, "Clara Lemlich Shavelson."

50. Clara Lemlich Shavelson, interview by Martha and Joel Schaffer, Los Angeles, Calif., February 2, 1974.

51. *New York Call*, November 30, December 4, 5, 6, 7, 8, 29, 1909.

52. *New York Call*, December 5, 7, 8, 1909.

53. *New York Call*, December 29, 1909. For complete coverage of day-to-day events on the picket line, see the *New York Times*, November 5, 6, and 14, 1909, and almost daily from November 23, 1909, through January 28, 1910.

54. Minutes of the New York Women's Trade Union League Membership Meeting, April 20, June 15, 1910, Reel 1, NYWTUL Papers.

55. See Meredith Tax, *The Rising of the Women: Feminist Solidarity and Class Conflict, 1880–1917* (New York: Monthly Review Press, 1980), pp. 230–240. Tax discusses the hierarchical union structure and the ways that union-appointed arbitrators undermined the women workers' control of the strike.

56. For information on the many women's strikes of the period, read the WTUL publication *Life and Labor*, which covered them all in some detail. The progressive magazine *The Survey* (1909–1914) also has good coverage of most of the strikes. See too, Pauline Newman, "The White Goods Workers' Strike," *Ladies' Garment Worker* 4, number 3 (March 1913):1–4; on the Chicago strike see Mari Jo Buhle, *Women and American Socialism, 1870–1920* (Urbana: University of Illinois Press, 1981), 194–198. On the Kalamazoo strike see Karen Mason, "Feeling the Pinch: The Kalamazoo Corset Makers' Strike of 1912," in *To Toil the Livelong Day: America's Women at Work*, ed. Carol Groneman and Mary Beth Norton (Ithaca: Cornell University Press, 1987), 141–60. On the 1915 strike see *Chicago Day Book* cited in Winifred Carsel, *A History of the Chicago Ladies' Garment Workers' Union* (Chicago: Normandie House, 1940).

57. Gladys Boone, *The Women's Trade Union Leagues* (New York: Columbia University Press, 1942), 112–14.

58. Mildred Moore, "A History of the Women's Trade Union League of Chicago" (M.A. thesis, University of Chicago, 1915), cited in Diane Kirkby, "The Wage-Earning Woman and the State: The National Women's Trade Union League and Protective Labor Legislation, 1903–1923," *Labor History* 28, no. 1 (Winter 1987):58–74.

59. Theresa Malkiel, "The Uprising of the 40,000," *New York Call*, December 29, 1909.

60. Pauline Newman, "From the Battlefield—Some Phases of the Cloakmakers' Strike in Cleveland," *Life and Labor*, October 1911.

DOCUMENT: Claiming an Education

> *Mary Tape, "What right! have you to bar my children out of the school because she is a chinese Descend. . . ."*

Until the passage of the Chinese Exclusion Act of 1882, political upheaval and dire poverty in China, contrasted with what appeared to be economic opportunities in the United States, drew thousands of Chinese to "Gold Mountain," their term for California. Those who came initially were men, only a few of whom brought families. For many immigrants, the promise of Gold Mountain proved elusive; the reality was a lifetime of hard work and daily prejudice. Among the women who arrived were merchants' wives whose feet were bound—a painful mark of female subordination in the old country. Impoverished young women also arrived, many of whom had been kidnapped, lured by promises of marriage, or sold by poor parents to procurers in China who supplied prostitutes to the large population of unmarried Chinese men on the West Coast. Considered the property of men in any case, women were not expected to have a public voice. There were, however, exceptions—women who demonstrated what an emancipated Chinese-American woman might become. Mary Tape was one of that number.

Brought up in an orphanage in Shanghai, Mary Tape immigrated to the United States with missionaries when she was eleven years old. She lived for five years at the Ladies' Relief Society outside of Chinatown in San Francisco. Fluent in English and westernized in dress, she married Joseph Tape, with whom she had four children, one of whom was a daughter, Mamie. Mamie's parents wanted her to have an education that would best prepare her for life in the United States. But the San Francisco school system, which was prepared to educate the children of European immigrants, resisted the inclusion of Asians.

Mamie Tape was denied entrance to a neighborhood school outside of Chinatown on the grounds that the association with Chinese children would be "very mentally and morally detrimental" to white children. The Tapes sued the Board of Education and won.

But the School Board circumvented the court's ruling by establishing a separate school for Chinese children in Chinatown. Furious, Mary Tape responded. Her letter, while revealing an imperfect command of English, communicates her sentiments perfectly. Compare her sense of injustice to that expressed by Keziah Kendall (pp. 198–200).

I see that you are going to make all sorts of excuses to keep my child out off the Public Schools. Dear sirs, Will you please to tell me! Is it a disgrace to be Born a Chinese? Didn't God make us all!!! What right! have you to bar my children out of the school because she is a chinese Descend. . . . You have expended a lot of the Public money foolishly, all because of a one poor little Child. Her playmates is all Caucasians ever since she could toddle around. If

Quoted in *Unbound Feet: A Social History of Chinese Women in San Francisco* by Judy Yung (Berkeley, Los Angeles, and London: University of California Press, 1995), p. 49.

Medical Examination at Ellis Island. "The day of the emigrants' arrival in New York was the nearest earthly likeness to the final day of Judgment, when we have to prove our fitness to enter Heaven." The words were those of a sympathetic journalist who shared the anxiety-ridden experience awaiting immigrants at the port of entry, usually Ellis Island. Failing the medical test could mean deportation. (Courtesy of Brown Brothers, Sterling, Pennsylvania).

Chinese women and children wait at the Immigration Station on Angel Island, near San Francisco. (Courtesy California Historical Society, FN-18240)

she is good enough to play with them! Then is she not good enough to be in the same room and studie with them? . . . It seems no matter how a Chinese may live and dress so long as you know they Chinese. Then they are hated as one. There is not any right or justice for them. . . . May you Mr. Moulder, never be persecuted like the way you have persecuted little Mamie Tape. Mamie Tape will never attend any of the Chinese schools of your making! Never!!! I will let the world see sir What justice there is When it is govern by the Race prejudice men!

KATHRYN KISH SKLAR
Florence Kelley and Women's Activism in the Progressive Era

Florence Kelley was a remarkable woman who lived in a period when attempts to address the problems created by industrialization and urbanization generated both the early social sciences and the foundation of the welfare state. Kathryn Sklar, Kelley's

Written expressly for *Women's America*. A revised version of this essay will appear in *Historical Encyclopedia of Chicago Women* (Chicago: Indiana University Press, 1999). Copyright © 1998 by Kathryn Kish Sklar.

biographer, provides in this authoritative and highly informative essay an account of a single individual that also illuminates the pursuit of social justice in which many progressive women of Kelley's generation were involved. Sklar reveals the factors that made it possible for these women to influence public policy even before they were allowed to vote. She also describes the changing political context that limited their influence following the Red Scare at the end of World War I.

What were the influences, personal and intellectual, that shaped Kelley's vision of social reform? What strategies did she employ in pursuit of that vision? What does Sklar mean when she says that Kelley used gender-specific legislation as a surrogate for class legislation? Precisely how did the Red Scare affect the political agenda of women's organizations? In what respects were at least three of the four significant features of women's power in the Progressive era that Sklar identified highly gendered? As we move into the 1930s and beyond, think about which of the features persist and which do not.

One of the most powerful women in American history deserves to be better known today. Florence Kelley (1859–1932) was well known to her contemporaries as a leading champion of social justice legislation. For most of the 1890s she lived in the nation's leading reform institution, Hull House, a social settlement founded in Chicago by Jane Addams in 1889. Between 1899 and 1932 she served as head of the National Consumers' League in New York City.

Living collectively with other women reformers in Chicago and New York, Florence Kelley was able to make the most of her talents; for four decades she occupied the vanguard of social reform. Her forceful personality flourished in the combative atmosphere generated by her struggles for social justice. Jane Addams's nephew, who resided with Kelley at Hull House, was awed by the way she "hurled the spears of her thought with such apparent carelessness of what breasts they pierced." He thought her "the toughest customer in the reform riot, the finest rough-and-tumble fighter for the good life for others, that Hull House ever knew: Any weapon was a good weapon in her hand—evidence, argument, irony or invective." Nevertheless, he said, those who were close to her knew she was "full of love."[1]

Kelley's career, like that of many of her reform contemporaries, was responding to profound changes in American social and economic life. Rapid industrialization was recasting the economy, massive immigration was reconstituting the working class, and sustained urbanization was making cities the

focus of social change.[2] In this context, college-educated women reformers often achieved what men and male-dominated organizations could not.

Florence Kelley's life helps us understand how women reformers accomplished their goals. Her reform career exemplified four significant features of women's power in the Progressive era: their access to higher education; their prominence in early social science; the political autonomy of their separate institutions; and their ability to challenge American traditions of limited government. Having experienced these ingredients of women's power in her own life before 1899, thereafter, as the General Secretary of the National Consumers' League, she integrated them into her strategies for pursuing social justice.[3]

WOMEN'S ACCESS TO HIGHER EDUCATION

When she graduated from Cornell University in 1882, Florence Kelley joined thousands of other young women in her generation who received college educations. Two changes in the 1860s and 1870s enabled white, middle-class women to attend college in sufficient numbers to become a sociological phenomenon. Elite women's colleges, such as Vassar, Smith, and Wellesley, began accepting students between 1865 and 1875, providing equivalents to elite men's colleges such as Harvard, Yale, and Princeton. And state universities, established through the allocation of public lands in the Morrill Act of 1862 and required to be "open for all," gradually made college educations accessible for the first time to large numbers of women in the nation's central and western states. By 1880 women, numbering forty thousand, constituted 33 percent of all enrolled students in higher education.[4] Though a small percentage of all women, they exercised an influence disproportionate to their numbers.

To Cornell Kelley brought a social conscience shaped by her family. Born into an elite Philadelphia family with Quaker and Unitarian political traditions, she grew up against the background of the Civil War and Reconstruction—dramas in which her father and her mother's aunt played major roles. Her father, William Durrah Kelley, one of the founders of the Republican Party, was reelected to fifteen consecutive terms in the U.S. Congress between 1860 and 1890. As a Radical Republican, he advanced the cause of black suffrage and tried to forge a biracial Republican Party in the South. Her mother's aunt, Sarah Pugh, served as president of the Philadelphia Female Anti-Slavery Society almost every year between 1838 and 1870. In the 1860s and 1870s, Pugh accompanied her close friend, Lucretia Mott, to early woman suffrage conventions. To young "Florrie," Sarah Pugh was conscience incarnate, a full-time reformer who lived her beliefs, never wearing slave-made cotton or eating slave-produced sugar.[5]

During six mostly schoolless years before she entered Cornell, Florence systematically read through her father's library, imbibing the fiction of Dickens and Thackeray, Louisa May Alcott and Horatio Alger; the poetry of Shakespeare, Milton, Bryon, and Goldsmith; the writings of James Madison; histories by Bancroft, Prescott, and Parkman; and the moral and political philosophy of Emerson, Channing, Burke, Carlyle, Godwin, and Spencer. These readings helped her reach out to her moody and distant father. For that purpose she also began reading government reports at the age of ten and, on trips to Washington, began using the Library of Congress by the time she was twelve.

A darker side of Kelley's childhood was shaped by her mother's permanent depression—caused by the death of five of her eight children before they had reached the age of six. Caroline Bonsall Kelley was a descendant of John Bartram, the Quaker botanist. Orphaned at the age of nine, she was raised in the Pugh family. With the death of her infants, Caroline developed a "settled, gentle melancholy" that threatened to envelop her daughter as long as she lived at home.[6] Florence grew up with two brothers, but no sisters survived. Keenly aware of the high social cost of infant mortality to nineteenth-century families, she developed a rage against human suffering that formed her lifelong career as a reformer.

WOMEN'S PROMINENCE IN EARLY SOCIAL SCIENCE

Like higher education, the newly emerging field of social science served as a critical vehicle by which middle-class women expanded the space they occupied within American civic life between 1860 and 1890. Social science leveled the playing field on which women interacted with men in public life. It offered tools of analysis that enhanced women's ability to investigate economic and social change, speak for the welfare of the whole society, devise policy initiatives, and oversee their implementation. Yet at the same time, social science also deepened women's gender identity in public life and attached their civic activism even more securely to gender-specific issues.[7]

Kelley's early commitment to social science as a tool for social reform built on a generation of women's presence in American social science. Women came with the civic territory that social science embraced. Caroline Dall had been a cofounder of the association in 1865, and other women were especially active in the American Social Science Association's (ASSA) department of education, public health, and social economy, which gave them clear but limited mandates for leadership.

The question of "After college, what?" was as pertinent to Florence Kelley as it was to other women graduates.[8] Barred from admission to graduate study at the University of Pennsylvania because she was a woman, she faced a very limited set of opportunities. First she threw her energies into the New Century Working Women's Guild, an organization that fostered middle-class aid for self-supporting women. She helped found the Guild, taught classes in history, and assembled the group's library. Then, remaining a dutiful daughter, in 1882 she accompanied her brother when his doctor prescribed a winter of European travel to cure temporary blindness. In

Europe she encountered M. Carey Thomas, a Cornell acquaintance, who had just completed a Ph.D. at the University of Zurich, the only European university that granted degrees to women. Thomas recommended that Kelley go to Zurich for graduate study.

Initially accompanied by her mother and younger brother, Kelley studied government and law at Zurich between 1883 and 1886. There she promptly befriended exiled socialist students from Russia and Germany. To the shocked amazement of her family and friends, in 1885 she married Lazare Wischnewetzky, a Russian, Jewish, socialist, medical student. She then gave birth to three children in three years.

Cloaked with her new personal identity as a European married woman, she stopped communicating with her family and began to forge a new political identity. Rejecting American public culture because it limited her opportunities for social service and because her father's career revealed so starkly that culture's tolerance of social injustice, she underwent a dramatic conversion to socialism, joined the German Social Democratic Party (SPD), and began to translate the writings of Friedrich Engels and Karl Marx. Outlawed in Germany, the SPD maintained its European headquarters in Zurich, where Kelley met many of its leaders. Since the death of Marx in 1885, Engels had become the chief theoretician of German socialism. Kelley's translation of his 1845 book, *The Condition of the Working Class in England,* is still the preferred scholarly version of that now-classic social science study. This project launched a close but troubled relationship with Engels that persisted until his death in 1895.[9]

When Kelley returned to the United States in 1886 with her small family, she searched without success for a political context capable of sustaining her newfound radicalism. Settling in New York City, within a year she was expelled from the Socialist Labor Party, predominantly a German-speaking immigrant group, for "incessant slander" against party leaders, whom she denounced for failing to recognize the importance of the writings of Marx and Engels.[10] Having reached a political dead-end, Kelley reoriented her use of social science as a vehicle for her activism. She resumed contact with her Philadelphia family and became a self-taught authority on child labor in the United States, as well as a sharp critic of state bureaus of labor, the agencies responsible for monitoring child labor. Writing articles on child labor that deployed both statistical and rhetorical power, she discovered that her most responsive publisher was the Woman's Temperance Publication Association, which printed her lengthy, hard-hitting pamphlet, *Our Toiling Children,* in 1889.

Lazare Wischnewetzky, meanwhile, never having managed to establish a medical practice, began battering her. After enduring this for more than a year, she borrowed money from a friend and fled with her children to Chicago. There she headed for the Woman's Temple, a twelve-story office building and hotel constructed by the Woman's Christian Temperance Union, where she was directed to an even more congenial place—Hull House, the nation's preeminent social settlement founded by Jane Addams and Ellen Gates Starr in 1889.

THE POLITICAL AUTONOMY OF WOMEN'S SEPARATE INSTITUTIONS

"We were welcomed as though we had been invited," Kelley later wrote about her arrival at Hull House. "We stayed."[11] Addams arranged for Kelley's children, Nicholas, Margaret, and John, age seven, six, and five, to live with the family of Henry Demarest Lloyd and his wife, Jessie Bross Lloyd. That winter Kelley cast her lot with Addams and Hull House, remaining until May 1, 1899, when she returned to New York as a figure who had achieved national renown as a reformer of working conditions for women and children.

Chicago and the remarkable political culture of the city's women opened opportunities to Kelley that she had sought in vain in Philadelphia, Germany, and New York. Exploiting those opportunities to the fullest, she drew on the strength of three overlapping circles of politically active women. The core of her support lay with the community of women at Hull House. This remarkable group helped her reconstruct her political identity within women's class-bridging activism, and provided her with an economic and emotional alternative to married family life. Partly overlapping with this nucleus were women trade unionists. By drawing women and men trade unionists into the settlement community, she achieved the passage of pathbreaking legislation. Toward the end of her years in Chicago, she worked with the circle of middle-class and upper-middle-class women who supported Hull House and labor reform.

Florence Kelley's life in Chicago began with her relationship with Jane Addams. Julia Lathrop, another Hull House resident, reported that Kelley and Addams "understood each other's powers" instantly and worked together in a "wonderfully effective way."[12] Addams, the philosopher with a deep appreciation of the unity of life, was better able to construct a vehicle for expressing that unity in day-to-day living than she was capable of devising a diagram for charting the future. And Kelley, the politician with a thorough understanding of what the future should look like, was better able to invoke that future than to express it in her day-to-day existence. Addams taught Kelley how to live and have faith in an imperfect world, and Kelley taught Addams how to make demands on the future.

At Hull House Kelley joined a community of college-educated women reformers who, like Addams and herself, sought work commensurate with their talents. Julia Lathrop, almost twenty years later the first director of the U.S. Children's Bureau, had joined the settlement before Kelley. Alice Hamilton, who arrived in 1897, developed the field of industrial medicine. These four, with Mary Rozet Smith, Jane Addams's life partner, became the settlement's main leaders. In addition to these women, Kelley forged close ties with Mary Kenney, a trade union organizer affiliated with the settlement, who lived nearby with her mother.

Since her father had lost most of his money before his death in 1890, Kelley had to support herself and her children. She first did so by working for the Illinois Bureau of Labor Statistics and the U.S. Department of Labor, collecting data for governmental studies of working conditions. A good example of the empowerment of her Hull House residence lay in her use of data collected for the U.S. Department of Labor, which in 1895 formed the basis of the maps published in *Hull House Maps and Papers*. She and four government "schedule men" collected responses to sixty-four questions on printed schedules from "each house, tenement, and room" in the ward surrounding Hull House.[13] From this data Carroll Wright, head of the Department of Labor, con-

structed scores of tables. But Kelley and Hull House associates, using only data about nationalities and wages in conjunction with residential information, created color-coded maps that displayed geographic patterns that told more than Wright's charts. Because the maps defined spatial relationships among human groups, they vividly depicted social and economic relationships: the concentration of certain ethnic groups in certain blocks; the relationship between poverty and race; the distances between the isolated brothel district and the rest of the ward; the very poor who lived in crowded, airless rooms in the rear of tenements and those with more resources in the front; and the omniscient observer and the observed. Expressing the democratic relationship among Hull House residents, *Hull House Maps and Papers* listed only "Residents of Hull House" as the volume's editors.

Kelley described the transformative effect of the Hull House community on her personal life in a letter to her mother a few weeks after her arrival. "In the few weeks of my stay here I have won for the children and myself many and dear friends whose generous hospitality astonishes me. It is understood that I am to resume the maiden name and that the children are to have it."[14] By joining a community of women, she had achieved a new degree of personal autonomy.

CHALLENGING TRADITIONS OF LIMITED GOVERNMENT

In the spring of 1892, Kelley used Hull House as a base to exert leadership within an anti-sweatshop campaign that had been launched in 1888 by the Illinois Woman's Alliance, a class-bridging coalition of women's organizations. At mass meetings that attacked the sweatshop system, Kelley shared the podium with Mary Kenney, Henry Demarest Lloyd, and other Chicago notables such as Reverend Jenkin Lloyd Jones, minister at All Souls' Unitarian Church, the most liberal pulpit in Chicago, and with young trade union organizers in the clothing industry such as Abraham Bisno.

Campaigns against sweatshops were widespread in American cities in the 1890s. These efforts targeted "predatory management" and "parasitic manufacturers" who paid such low wages to their workers as to require them to seek support from relief or charity, thereby indirectly providing employers with subsidies that enabled them to lower wages further.[15] Supported by trade unions, these campaigns used a variety of strategies to shift work from tenement sweatshops to factories. In factories, union organizing could more easily succeed in improving working conditions and raising wages to levels necessary to sustain life.

Outcries raised by anti-sweatshop campaigns prompted government inquiries, and in 1893, after intense lobbying in Springfield by Hull House residents and other well-known Chicago women, the passage of path-breaking legislation drafted by Florence Kelley. That year Governor John Peter Altgeld appointed Kelley to a position the new statute created: Chief Factory Inspector of Illinois. Nowhere else in the Western world was a woman trusted to enforce the labor legislation of a city, let alone of a large industrial region the size of Illinois. With eleven deputies, five of whom were required to be women, and a budget of $28,000, for the next three years Kelley enforced the act's chief clauses. The act banned the labor of children under fourteen years of age; it regulated the labor of children age fourteen to sixteen; it outlawed the production of garments in tenements; it prohibited the employment of women and minors for more than eight hours a day; and it created a state office of factory inspection.

The statute's eight-hour clause made it the most advanced in the United States, equaled only by an eight-hour law for all workers in Australia. The limitation of hours, whether through statutes or union negotiations with employers, was the second most important goal of the labor movement between 1870 and 1910, the first being the recognition of the right of workers to form unions. Skilled workers had acquired the eight-hour day for themselves in many trades by the 1890s, but since women were not admitted to most skilled occupations, their hours remained long, often extending to twelve or even fourteen hours a day. In the late 1880s more than 85 percent of female wage earners were between the ages of fourteen and twenty-five and only about 5 percent were married.[16] Excluded from access to skilled jobs and presumed to leave the paid labor force upon marriage, they were crowded into a few unskilled occupations, where they were easily

replaced, and employers exploited them by requiring long hours and paying low wages. Statutes that limited women's hours limited this exploitation. How to achieve such reduction of hours without reducing wages was a challenge that Kelley's office met by promoting the formation of unions among affected women workers, thereby helping them negotiate better wages for the hours they worked.

But the reduction of women's hours by statute had other beneficial effects: in many occupations it also reduced the hours of unskilled men, as was the case in garment-making sweatshops. In this and many other occupations, it proved impossible to keep men working longer than the legal limit of the working day for women. Therefore, hours statutes drove sweatshops out of business, since their profits could only be achieved through long hours. In the United States more than in other industrializing nations, the union movement consisted with few exceptions (miners being the chief exception) of skilled workers who shunned responsibility for the welfare of unskilled workers. Therefore, in the United States more than in elsewhere, gender-specific reforms like Kelley's 1893 legislation—undertaken by women for women—also had the effect of aiding all unskilled workers, men as well as women and children. In the United States, where labor movements were not as strong as they were elsewhere, gender-specific reforms accomplished goals that elsewhere were achieved under the auspices of class-specific efforts.[17]

In an era when courts nullified legislative attempts to intervene in the laissez-faire relationship between capital and labor, Kelley's enforcement of this new eight-hour law was inevitably challenged in the courts. In 1895 the Illinois Supreme Court found the eight-hour clause of the 1893 law unconstitutional because it violated women's right to contract their labor on any terms set by their employer. This setback made Kelley determined to change the power of state courts to overturn hours laws for women.

The high tide of Kelley's achievements between 1893 and 1896 ebbed quickly when Altgeld lost the election of 1896. His successor replaced her with a person who did not challenge the economic status quo, and she was unable to find work commensurate with her talents. German admirers came to her rescue.

For fifty dollars a month she provided a leading German reform periodical with assessments of recent American social legislation. She also worked in the Crerar Library, a reference library specializing in economic, scientific, and medical topics.

Needing to reach beyond the limits of Hull House activities, Kelley began to work more closely with Ellen Henrotin. Wife of a leading Chicago banker, Henrotin had supported Kelley's legislation in 1892, and spoke vigorously at a rally to defend the law in 1894, urging those in attendance to "agitate for shorter hours for women because it means in the end shorter hours for all workers, men and women."[18] Henrotin's organization in 1893 of thirty women's congresses at the Chicago World's Fair catapulted her into the presidency of the General Federation of Women's Clubs (GFWC; founded 1890) from 1894 to 1898. By 1897 the GFWC served as an umbrella organization for more than five hundred women's clubs, including the powerful Chicago Women's Club. Fostering the creation of over twenty state federations to coordinate those clubs, Henrotin moved the GFWC in progressive directions by establishing national committees on industrial working conditions and national health. In this way she directed the path of what was to become one of the largest grass-roots organizations of American women beyond the minimal goals of good government and civil service reform to the more challenging issues of social inequalities and social justice.

Reflecting her growing awareness of the potential power of women's organizations as a vehicle for her social justice agenda, in 1897 Kelley began to work closely with Henrotin in organizing an Illinois Consumers' League. They built on the example of the New York Consumers' League, which had been founded in 1891 to channel consumers' consciousness toward political action on behalf of workers who made the goods that consumers purchased.

THE NATIONAL CONSUMERS' LEAGUE AND NEW STRATEGIES FOR SOCIAL JUSTICE

Kelley's work with Henrotin helped her make the biggest career step of her life when, in 1899, she agreed to serve as Secretary of the newly formed National Consumers' League, a posi-

tion she held until her death in 1932. With a salary of $1,500 plus traveling and other expenses, the job offered financial stability and a chance to develop a more radical and more focused women's organization than the GFWC.

When she carried her formidable talents into the National Consumers' League in 1899, women's political culture gained a warrior with formidable rhetorical and organizational skills. She quickly made the National Consumers' League (NCL) into the nation's leading promoter of protective labor legislation for women and children. Between 1900 and 1904 she built sixty-four local consumer leagues—one in nearly every large city outside the South. Through a demanding travel schedule, which required her to spend one day on the road for every day she worked at her desk, Kelley maintained close contact with local leagues, urging them to implement the national organization's agenda and inspiring them to greater action within their states and municipalities. At the age of forty she had finally found a platform that matched her talents and goals.

In New York she lived until 1926 at Lillian Wald's nurses' settlement on Henry Street on Manhattan's Lower East Side. Her children moved east with her. Supported by aid from Jane Addams's life partner, Mary Rozet Smith, Nicholas Kelley graduated from Harvard in 1905 and then from Harvard Law School. Living in Manhattan, he became his mother's closest advisor. In a blow that caused Kelley to spend the rest of that year in retirement in Maine, her daughter Margaret died of heart failure during her first week at Smith College in 1905. After this bereavement Kelley maintained a summer home on Penobscot Bay, Maine, where she retreated for periods of intense work with a secretary each summer. John Kelley never found a professional niche, but remained close to his mother and joined her in Maine each summer.

THE WHITE LABEL CAMPAIGN: NEW WAYS OF EDUCATING MIDDLE-CLASS WOMEN ABOUT INDUSTRIAL WORKING CONDITIONS

The national branch of the Consumers' League was formed in 1898 to coordinate the efforts of previously existing leagues in New York, Brooklyn, Philadelphia, Boston, and Chicago, all of which had conducted campaigns against sweatshops. At a convention of the local leagues called to coordinate their anti-sweatshop efforts, Kelley proposed the creation of a consumers' label as a way of identifying goods made under fair conditions. Her proposal galvanized the convention into creating a national organization "for the express purpose of offering a Consumers' League Label" nationally, recognizing that local efforts against sweatshops could never succeed until all producers were "compelled to compete on a higher level," and agreeing that the label could be a means of achieving that goal.[19] The NCL awarded its label to manufacturers who obeyed state factory laws, produced goods only on their own premises, did not require employees to work overtime, and did not employ children under sixteen years of age. To enforce the label, however, factories had to be inspected. Local leagues had employed their own factory inspectors; Kelley became the league's national inspector.

In determining whether local factories qualified for the label, local league members had to educate themselves about local working conditions. They had to pose and answer questions new to middle-class women, though painfully familiar to union organizers: Did the manufacturer subcontract to home workers in tenements? Were children employed? Were state factory laws violated? Could workers live on their wages, or were they forced to augment their pay with relief or charitable donations? How far below the standard set by the consumers' label were their own state laws? Even more technical questions arose when leagues came into contact with factory inspectors, bureaus of labor statistics, state legislatures, and courts. Should the state issue licenses for home workers? What was the relationship between illiteracy in child workers and the enforcement of effective child labor laws? Was their own state high or low on the NCL's ranked list showing the number of illiterate child workers in each? Should laws prohibit the labor of children at age fourteen or sixteen? Should exceptions be made for the children of widows? How energetically were state factory laws enforced? How could local factory standards be improved? These questions, recently quite alien to middle-class women, now held the interest of thousands of the most politically active among them. This was no small accomplishment. State leagues

differed in the degree to which they worked with state officials, but wherever they existed they created new civic space in which women used their new knowledge and power to expand state responsibility for the welfare of women and children workers.

On the road steadily between 1900 and 1907, Kelley inspected workshops, awarded the label to qualified manufacturers, and strengthened local leagues. Her efforts were rewarded by the spectacular growth of NCL locals, both in number and location. The NCL's 1901 report mentioned thirty leagues in eleven states; by 1906 they numbered sixty-three in twenty states.

Flourishing local leagues sustained the national's existence, channeling money, ideas, and the support of other local groups into the national office. At the same time, locals implemented the national's agenda at the state level. Most league members were white, urban, northern, middle-class Protestants, but Jewish women held important positions of leadership. Catholic women became more visible after Cardinal James Gibbons of Baltimore consented to serve as vice president of a Maryland league and Bishop J. Regis Canevin of Pittsburgh encouraged members of that city's Ladies Catholic Benevolent Association to join. Two important reasons for the absence of black women from the NCL's membership and agenda were the league's focus on Northern urban manufacturing, and the residence of 90 percent of the nation's black population in the South, employed primarily in agriculture, in 1900.

10-HOUR LAWS FOR WOMEN: NEW USES OF SOCIAL SCIENCE

The work of educating her constituency being achieved by 1907, Kelley implemented a second stage of league work. With the use of social science data, the NCL overcame legal obstacles to the passage of state laws limiting women's hours. The overturning of Illinois's 1893 law by Illinois's Supreme Court in 1895 made Kelley determined to defend such laws before the U.S. Supreme Court. When an Oregon ten-hour law came before the court in 1907, she threw the resources of the NCL into its defense. This case, *Muller v. Oregon,* pitted the NCL and its Oregon branch against a laundry owner who disputed the state's ability to regulate working hours in

Two contrasting photographs intended by photojournalist Lewis Hine to reveal the class-based nature of childhood at the turn of the century. Middle-class girls (top) *are pushing a doll made by child laborers and their mother* (bottom). *(Photos courtesy of the Library of Congress. Caption and photoidentification by Miriam Formanek-Brunell,* Made to Play House: Dolls and the Commercialization of American Girlhood, 1830–1930 *[New Haven, 1993], p. 110.)*

non-hazardous occupations. For what became known as the "Brandeis Brief," Kelley's Research Director, Josephine Goldmark, gathered printed evidence from medical and other authorities (most of whom were British or European) to demonstrate that workdays longer than ten hours were hazardous to the health of women. Goldmark obtained the services of her brother-in-law, Louis D. Brandeis, a leading Boston attorney, who successfully argued the case on sociological rather than legal grounds, using the evidence that Goldmark had compiled. Thus at the same time that this case cleared the way for state hours laws for women, it also established the court's recognition of sociological evidence, a strategy that sustained the court's ruling against segregated schools in *Brown* v. *Board of Education* in 1954.

In the years immediately following the *Muller* decision, inspired by Kelley's leadership, and supported by other groups, local consumer leagues gained the passage in twenty states of the first laws limiting women's working hours. Also responding to the decision, nineteen other states revised and expanded their laws governing women's working hours.

The Supreme Court's 1908 opinion tried to block the possibility of extending such protections to men by emphasizing women's special legal status (they did not possess the same contractual rights as men) and their physiological difference from men (their health affected the health of their future children). Nevertheless, in 1917 Kelley and the NCL again cooperated successfully with the Oregon league in arguing another case on sociological grounds before the U.S. Supreme Court, *Bunting* v. *Oregon,* in which the Court upheld the constitutionality of hours laws for men in non-hazardous occupations. Viewing laws for women as an entering wedge for improving conditions for all working people, Kelley achieved that goal in the progression from *Muller* to *Bunting.* In this as in other aspects of her work with the League, though nominally focused on gender, her reforms had class-wide effects.

THE MINIMUM WAGE CAMPAIGN: NEW USES OF THE POWER OF WOMEN'S ORGANIZATIONS

As early as 1899, Florence Kelley had hoped "to include a requirement as to minimal wages" in the NCL's White Label. Australia and New Zealand had already organized wage boards as part of compulsory arbitration, but the path to an American equivalent did not seem clear until she and other Consumers' League members in 1908 attended the First International Conference of Consumers' Leagues, in Geneva, where they learned about the proposed British wage law of 1909, which that year implemented minimum wages for all workers in certain poorly paid occupations.

Almost immediately on her return, Kelley established her leadership in what became an enormously successful campaign for minimum wage laws for women in the United States. In her campaign she denounced the large profits made in three industries: retail stores, sweatshop garment making, and textile manufacturers. "Low wages produce more poverty than all other causes together," she insisted, urging that "goods and profits are not ends in themselves to which human welfare may continue to be sacrificed."[20]

Kelley argued that minimum wages would raise the standards in women's employment by recognizing their need to support themselves. "So long as women's wages rest upon the assumption that every woman has a husband, father, brother, or lover contributing to her support, so long these sinister incidents of women's industrial employment (tuberculosis, insanity, vice) are inevitable." She urged that "society itself must build the floor beneath their feet."[21]

Minimum wage legislation was much more difficult to achieve than maximum hours laws because, as one of Kelley's allies put it, wage legislation "pierces to the heart the classic claim that industry is a purely private affair."[22] For this reason, Kelley and the NCL were unaided in their efforts by their male-dominated equivalent, the American Association for Labor Legislation (AALL). When Kelley appealed in 1910 to their executive director, John Andrews, he loftily replied: "I question very seriously the wisdom of injecting the minimum wage proposal into the legislative campaign of this year, because I do not believe our courts would at the present time uphold such legislation, and I am afraid it would seriously jeopardize the splendid progress now being made to establish maximum working hours."[23] Two years later the AALL still opposed wage legislation as premature.

Kelley and the NCL were able to move ahead with this pathbreaking legislation because they could mobilize grass-roots support for it at local and state levels. The AALL had no local branches; instead, their power flowed from a network of male academic experts who advised politicians about legislation. If politicians were not ready to move, neither was the AALL. The NCL, by contrast, had in its sixty-four local branches enough political muscle to take the initiative and lead politicians where they otherwise wouldn't have gone.

In 1912 Massachusetts passed the first minimum wage law for women, followed in 1913 by eight additional states: California, Colorado, Minnesota, Nebraska, Oregon, Utah, Washington, and Wisconsin. By 1919 fourteen states and the District of Columbia and Puerto Rico had enacted minimum wage statutes for women. The success of these laws influenced the inclusion of a minimum wage for men *and* women in the Fair Labor Standards Act (FLSA) of 1938. In 1942, when the U.S. Supreme Court approved the constitutionality of the FLSA, the eight-hour day and the minimum wage become part of the social contract for most American workers. The class-bridging activism of middle-class women in the NCL forged the way with these fundamental reforms.

GAINS AND SETBACKS IN THE 1920s

At Henry Street, Kelley continued to benefit from the same consolidation of female reform talents that had sustained her efforts at Hull House in Chicago. The creation of the U.S. Children's Bureau in 1911 sprang from her discussions with Lillian Wald. The Children's Bureau was the only governmental agency in any industrial society that was headed and run by women. Kelley thought that her most important contribution to social change was the passage in 1921 of the Sheppard-Towner Maternity and Infancy Protection Act, which first allocated federal funds to health care. She was instrumental in the creation of the coalition that backed the act's passage, the Women's Joint Congressional Committee, and in the coalition's successful campaign for the bill in Congress. Although limited to a program administered by the Children's Bureau to combat infant and maternal mortality, Kelley thought the Sheppard-Towner Act marked the beginning of a national health care program.[24]

After this high point in 1921, however, the decade brought a series of reversals that threatened to undo her most of her achievements. In 1923 the U.S. Supreme Court in *Adkins* v. *Children's Hospital* found Washington, D.C.'s wage law for women unconstitutional. Many state wage boards continued to function during the 1920s and 1930s, however, providing ample evidence of the benefits of the law, but no new wage laws were passed. In 1926, Congress refused to allocate new funds for Sheppard-Towner programs, and responsibility for maternal and infant health returned to state and county levels.[25]

Just as important, by 1922 Kelley's strategy of using gender-specific legislation as a surrogate for class legislation had generated opposition from a new quarter—women who did not themselves benefit from gendered laws. The National Woman's Party (NWP), formed in 1916 by the charismatic leadership of Alice Paul and funded almost entirely by Alva Belmont, created a small coalition consisting primarily of professional women with some wage-earning women who worked in male-dominated occupations. Despite Kelley's strong objections over the damage they would do to gender-specific legislation, including the Sheppard-Towner Act, in 1921 the NWP proposed an Equal Rights Amendment to the U.S. Constitution (ERA). Although mainstream organizations such as the General Federation of Women's Clubs and the League of Women Voters continued to support gender-specific legislation, the NWP's proposed amendment undercut the momentum of such gendered strategies. In the 1920s most wage-earning women opposed the ERA because they stood to lose rather than benefit from it. By the 1970s changes in working conditions and protective labor laws meant that most wage-earning women stood to benefit from the amendment, and many more supported it.[26]

Even more damaging than these reversals, however, were the right-wing attacks launched by hyperpatriots against Kelley and other women reformers during the "red scare" of the 1920s. *The Woman Patriot* exemplified these attacks. Launched in 1916 and published twice a month, before the enactment of the woman suffrage amendment this newsletter was subtitled *Dedicated to the Defense of Womanhood, Motherhood, the Family and the State AGAINST Suffragism, Feminism and Socialism.* After 1920 the newsletter dropped its reference to suffrage, but continued its virulent attacks on the social agenda of women reformers. "SHALL BOLSHE-VIST-FEMINISTS SECRETLY GOVERN AMERICA?" their headlines screamed, referring to the Shep-pard-Towner Act. When *The Woman Patriot* referred to Kelley as "Mrs. Wischnewtzky" and called her "Moscow's chief conspirator," Kel-ley urged Addams to join her in a libel suit against them. Addams gently persuaded her to ignore the attacks. Kelley then wrote an impas-sioned series of autobiographical articles that established her lineage as an inheritor of Amer-ican ideals and a dedicated promoter of Amer-ican values.[27]

Attacks on women reformers in the 1920s were in part generated by supporters of Amer-ican military expansion in the aftermath of World War I, when Kelley and many other women reformers were actively promoting peace and disarmament. For example, *The Woman Patriot* characterized the support that women reformers were giving to disarmament as "an organized internationalist Bolshevist-Feminist plot to embarrass the Limitation of Armaments Conference." Government em-ployees joined the attack in 1924, when Lucia Maxwell of the Chemical Warfare Department of the Department of War issued a "Spider Web Chart" entitled "The Socialist-Pacifist Move-ment in America Is an Absolutely Fundamen-tal and Integral Part of International Social-ism." Depicting the connections between women's organizations and Congressional lob-bying for social legislation and for disarma-ment, the chart sought to characterize as "pacifist-socialist" most women's organiza-tions in the United States, including the Na-tional Consumers' League, the National League of Women Voters, the General Federa-tion of Women's Clubs, the Woman's Chris-tian Temperance Union, the National Congress of Mothers and Parent-Teachers Association, the National Women's Trade Union League, the American Home Economics Association, the American Association of University Wo-men, the National Council of Jewish Women, the Girls' Friendly Society, the Young Women's Christian Association, and the National Feder-ation of Business and Professional Women.[28]

Historians have not measured the effect of these attacks on the political agendas of women's organizations, but after these attacks the agendas of many women's organizations,

for example that of the League for Women Voters, shifted from social justice to good gov-ernment projects, from support for a Child Labor Amendment to the U.S. Constitution to advocacy for a city manager form of gover-nance.[29] Such a shift was in keeping with the demise of the Progressive movement after World War I. But that demise was hastened by the rise of "red scare" tactics in American polit-ical culture.

Florence Kelley did not live to see many of her initiatives incorporated into federal leg-islation in the 1930s. Faced with the collapse of the American economy in the Great Depres-sion of 1929–1939, policymakers drew heavily on the legacy of Progressive reforms initiated between 1890 and 1920. Florence Kelley's lega-cies, including the minimum wage and maxi-mum hours legislation incorporated in the Fair Labor Standards Act of 1938, were strong enough to survive the reversals of the 1920s. In 1933, with the inauguration of Franklin Delano Roosevelt, Kelley's protégé Frances Perkins became the first woman to serve as a cabinet member. Reflecting the power of women's organizations in shaping a new social contract for American working people, Perkins was appointed Secretary of Labor.[30]

But Kelley's legacy reaches beyond any specific policies. U.S. Supreme Court Justice Felix Frankfurter said in 1953 that the nation owed Kelley an "enduring debt for the con-tinuing process she so largely helped to initi-ate, by which social legislation is promoted and eventually gets on the statute books."[31] As Kelley shaped it during her long reform career between 1890 and 1930, that process relied heavily on women's organizations and their ability to act independently of the political sta-tus quo.

NOTES

1. James Weber Linn, *Jane Addams: A Biography* (New York, 1938) p. 138.

2. For an overview of social change in the Pro-gressive era, see Steven J. Diner, *A Very Different Age: Americans of the Progressive Era* (New York, 1998).

3. For more on Kelley before 1900, see Kathryn Kish Sklar, *Florence Kelley and the Nation's Work: The Rise of Women's Political Culture, 1830–1900* (New Haven, 1995). Specific page references are provided for quotations used below.

4. Mabel Newcomer, *A Century of Higher Edu-cation for American Women* (New York, 1959), 37, 46. See also Barbara Miller Solomon, "*In the Company of*

Educated Women": A History of Women and Higher Education in America (New Haven, 1985), 62–77.

5. For Kelley's childhood, see Kathryn Kish Sklar, ed., *The Autobiography of Florence Kelley: Notes of Sixty Years* (Chicago, 1986).

6. Sklar, *Autobiography of Florence Kelley,* 30.

7. Kathryn Kish Sklar, "Hull House Maps and Papers: Social Science as Women's Work in the 1890s," in Helene Silverberg, ed., *Gender and American Social Science: The Formative Years* (Princeton, 1998).

8. See Joyce Antler, "After College, What?: New Graduates and the Family Claim," *American Quarterly* 32 (Fall 1980), 409–34.

9. See Dorothy Rose Blumberg, "'Dear Mr. Engels': Unpublished Letters, 1884–1894, of Florence Kelley (Wischnewetzky) to Friedrich Engels," *Labor History* 5 (Spring 1964), 103–33.

10. Sklar, *Florence Kelley,* 129.

11. Sklar, *Autobiography of Florence Kelley,* 77.

12. Jane Addams, *My Friend Julia Lathrop* (New York, 1935), 77.

13. Residents of Hull House, *Hull House Maps and Papers* (New York, 1895).

14. FK to Caroline B. Kelley, Chicago, Feb. 24, 1892, Nicholas Kelley Papers, New York Public Library.

15. Kathryn Kish Sklar, "Two Political Cultures in the Progressive Era: The National Consumers' League and the American Association for Labor Legislation," in Linda K. Kerber, Alice Kessler-Harris and Kathryn Kish Sklar, eds., *U.S. History as Women's History: New Feminist Essays* (Chapel Hill, N.C., 1995), 58.

16. U.S. Commissioner of Labor, *Fourth Annual Report, Working Women in Large Cities* (Washington, D.C., 1889), 62–64.

17. For a full argument of this point, see Kathryn Kish Sklar, "The Historical Foundations of Women's Power in the Creation of the American Welfare State, 1830–1930," in Seth Koven and Sonya Michel, eds., *Mothers of a New World: Maternalist Politics and the Origins of Welfare States* (New York, 1993).

18. "Hit at Sweat Shops," *Chicago Tribune,* April 23, 1894; Sklar, *Florence Kelley,* p. 261.

19. Sklar, *Florence Kelley,* 309.

20. Florence Kelley, "Minimum Wage Boards," *American Journal of Sociology* 17 (Nov. 1911), 303–14.

21. Florence Kelley, "Ten Years from Now," *Survey,* March 26, 1910, 978–81.

22. Sklar, "Two Political Cultures," 60.

23. See, for example, John B. Andrews to Erich Stern, New York, Dec. 14, 1910, American Association for Labor Legislation Papers, Cornell University.

24. See Molly Ladd-Taylor, *Mother-Work: Women, Child Welfare, and the State, 1890–1930* (Urbana, Ill., 1994), 167–96.

25. See J. Stanley Lemons, *The Woman Citizen: Social Feminism in the 1920s* (Urbana, Ill., 1973), 169–76.

26. For the opposition of the progressive mainstream of the women's movement, see Kathryn Kish Sklar, "Why Did Most Politically Active Women Oppose the ERA in the 1920s?" in Joan Hoff-Wilson, ed., *Rights of Passage: the Past and Future of the ERA* (Bloomington, Ind., 1986).

27. *The Woman Patriot,* Vol. 5, no. 29, Nov. 1, 1921, 1. For the complete documents of this correspondence between Kelley and Addams, see Anissa Harper, "Pacifism vs. Patriotism in Women's Organizations in the 1920s: How Was the Debate Shaped by the Expansion of the American Military," in *Women and Social Movements in the United States, 1830–1930,* an Internet website edited by Kathryn Kish Sklar and Thomas Dublin, *http://womhist.binghamton.edu.* See also Nancy F. Cott, *The Grounding of Modern Feminism* (New Haven, 1987), 243–67.

28. The Spider Web Chart is reproduced in Helen Baker, "How Did the Women's International League for Peace and Freedom Respond to Right Wing Attacks in the 1920s?" in *Women and Social Movements* at *http://womhist.binghamton.edu.*

29. For example, see the furor aroused within the League of Women Voters over the proposed Child Labor Amendment to the U.S. Constitution in 1924, in Louise M. Young, *In the Public Interest: The League of Women Voters, 1920–1970* (New York, 1989), 97–98.

30. For Perkins see Susan Ware, *Beyond Suffrage: Women in the New Deal* (Cambridge, Mass., 1981), *passim.*

31. Felix Frankfurter, "Foreword," in Josephine Goldmark, *Impatient Crusader: Florence Kelley's Life Story* (Urbana, Ill., 1953), p. v.

DOCUMENT: Protective Legislation

> ## Muller *v.* Oregon, *1908*

The farmer's workday was sunrise to sunset. When the first factories were established in the early nineteenth century, they were operated for equally long hours. It was a particular interest of laborers and of progressive reformers to support enactment of limits on the workday. The ten-hour day was on the agenda of early labor unions, and the federal civil service adopted it shortly after the Civil War.

But in 1905 the United States Supreme Court refused to uphold a state law limiting the hours of bakers to ten hours a day. Ruling in *Lochner* v. *New York* (198 U.S. 45 [1905]), the Court held that such a law was not "a legitimate exercise of the police power of the State, but an unreasonable, unnecessary, and arbitrary interference with the right and liberty of the individual to contract in relation to his labor. . . ."

After the *Lochner* decision progressives were forced to conclude that it was impractical to support limitations on hours that applied to *all* workers. But it occurred to some that a special case might be made in defense of a limit on working hours for women.

When the constitutionality of the Oregon ten-hour law for women was challenged, Florence Kelley committed the National Consumers' League to its defense. As Kathryn Kish Sklar has explained (pp. 312–24), NCL's Research Director, Josephine Goldmark, prepared a pathbreaking brief, of which only two pages consisted of traditional abstract legal reasoning, and over one hundred pages offered sociological evidence. Her brother-in-law, the future Supreme Court Justice Louis D. Brandeis, argued the case in the U.S. Supreme Court.

In 1908 the Supreme Court upheld the constitutionality of the Oregon law, though making it clear that it was swayed primarily by the case made for women's physical vulnerability and couching the decision in terms of traditional sex roles. Fifteen years later, only five states lacked maximum hour legislation of some sort, although provisions varied widely.

Protective legislation for women had complex consequences. Obviously an eight-hour workday was vastly preferable to a longer one. But in the absence of a minimum wage, women living at the margin of subsistence found that limitations on the hours they could work cut their income or speeded up their piecework; some would not have chosen to trade time for money. Maximum hour legislation was often supplemented by restrictions against night work and "heavy" work (the latter often conveniently defined to include well-paying skilled work like iron molding), which further segregated women in the workplace and gave men an advantage in the competition for jobs. There is substantial evidence that male unions understood this when they supported protective legislation.*

---

*See Alice Kessler-Harris, *Out to Work: A History of Wage-Earning Women in the United States* (New York, 1982), pp. 201–5.

208 U.S. 412.

Compare the reasoning in *Muller* to that offered in the *Bradwell* case (pp. 242–43) more than thirty-five years before. What were the advantages of pressing the argument of female weakness? What were the disadvantages?

MR. JUSTICE DAVID J. BREWER:

. . . It may not be amiss, in the present case, before examining the constitutional question, to notice the course of legislation, as well as expressions of opinion from other than judicial sources. In the brief filed by Mr. Louis D. Brandeis for the defendant . . . is a very copious collection of all these matters. . . .

The legislation and opinions referred to . . . may not be, technically speaking, authorities, and in them is little or no discussion of the constitutional question presented to us for determination, yet, they are significant of a widespread belief that woman's physical structure, and the functions she performs in consequence thereof, justify special legislation restricting or qualifying the conditions under which she should be permitted to toil. . . .

That woman's physical structure and the performance of maternal functions place her at a disadvantage in the struggle for subsistence is obvious. This is especially true when the burdens of motherhood are upon her. Even when they are not, by abundant testimony of the medical fraternity continuance for a long time on her feet at work, repeating this from day to day, tends to injurious effects upon the body, and, as healthy mothers are essential to vigorous offspring, the physical well-being of woman becomes an object of public interest and care in order to preserve the strength and vigor of the race.

. . . Differentiated by these matters from the other sex, she is properly placed in a class by herself, and legislation designed for her protection may be sustained, even when like legislation is not necessary for men, and could not be sustained. It is impossible to close one's eyes to the fact that she still looks to her brother and depends upon him. . . . her physical structure and a proper discharge of her maternal functions—having in view not merely her own health, but the well-being of the race—justify legislation to protect her from the greed as well as the passion of man. The limitations which this statute places upon her contractual powers, upon her right to agree with her employer as to the time she shall labor, are not imposed solely for her benefit, but also largely for the benefit of all. Many words cannot make this plainer. The two sexes differ in structure of body, in the functions to be performed by each, in the amount of physical strength, in the capacity for long continued labor, particularly when done standing, the influence of vigorous health upon the future well-being of the race, the self-reliance which enables one to assert full rights, and in the capacity to maintain the struggle for subsistence. This difference justifies a difference in legislation, and upholds that which is designed to compensate for some of the burdens which rest upon her.

We have not referred in this discussion to the denial of the elective franchise in the State of Oregon, for while it may disclose a lack of political equality in all things with her brother, that is not of itself decisive. The reason runs deeper, and rests in the inherent difference between the two sexes.

For these reasons, and without questioning in any respect the decision in *Lochner* v. *New York,* we are of the opinion that it cannot be adjudged that the act in question is in conflict with the Federal Constitution, so far as it respects the work of a female in a laundry, and the judgment of the Supreme Court of Oregon is Affirmed.

ELLEN CAROL DUBOIS
Harriot Stanton Blatch and the Winning of Woman Suffrage

Campaigns to expand the suffrage require that voters who are reasonably content with the status quo be persuaded to welcome into the political arena new and unpredictable constituencies. It is perhaps no surprise that the expansion of the suffrage is likely to meet severe resistance. The campaign for woman suffrage involved intellectual challenge to established political theory. It involved national mass mobilization. It required brilliant street theater on a massive scale and, simultaneously, clever and delicate political maneuvering. Although the accomplishment of women's suffrage in 1920 is well known, the complexity of the work that was required is less appreciated than it deserves to be.

Elizabeth Cady Stanton's daughter Harriot married an English businessman, Harry Blatch, in 1882. At her marriage she lost her U.S. citizenship (see *Mackenzie* v. *Hare*, pp. 338–40); "the consequences," her biographer has written, "would haunt her for most of her life." For the next fourteen years Harriot lived in England, bearing two daughters and engaging herself in the work of suffragists and of Fabian socialists. After the death of her daughter Helen in 1896, Harriot and her daughter Nora divided their time between England and the United States. Nora entered Cornell University in 1901. Challenging the prejudice against women that she felt still infused the insitution, Nora was the first woman admitted into the civil engineering program. In homage to her grandmother, Nora and her friends organized Cornell's first woman suffrage society.

Ironically, many suffragists demanded the vote out of their deep skepticism of politics. They claimed that women were more pure than men; if women had the vote, they promised, in effect, to end partisanship. Harriot Blatch and her colleagues, however, understood that partisanship was the route to acquiring the vote and to using the vote once acquired.

Starting in 1910, the crucial task facing New York suffragism was to force the state legislature to pass a bill authorizing a voters' referendum on suffrage. For the next three years, Harriot lobbied and politicked tirelessly to this end. It would be easy to miss the importance of this part of the New York state suffrage campaign, sandwiched as it was between the dramatic modernization of the movement before 1910 and the spirited electoral drive conducted between 1913 and 1915. But Harriot understood these efforts were crucial to the victory of votes for women. Professional politicians held the fate of woman suffrage in their hands; they had the power to repeatedly delay, even permanently halt, the forward motion of women's demand for political equality. Moreover, in facing male political power head on, women effected the deeper cultural and psychological changes, the transformations of

Excerpted from Ellen Carol DuBois, *Harriot Stanton Blatch and the Winning of Woman Suffrage*, ch. 7, "Politics" (New Haven: Yale University Press, 1997). © 1997 Yale University. Notes have been renumbered and edited.

masculinity and femininity that were necessary if enfranchisement was ever going to signify the revolution in gender relations that suffragists had always said it would.

During her first session of concerted lobbying in Albany in 1910, Harriot concentrated on establishing her authority over the legislative campaign and assembling the necessary parliamentary knowledge. The next year, when Democrats took control of both houses, she was ready to move. The links to working women she had built through the Equality League helped her to address the prolabor forces in the Democratic party. Then, in 1912, when the Progressive bolt from the Republican party created a situation in which no party had full control, Harriot saw the first real possibility for passage. Finally, in 1913, reluctant state legislators were forced to accept the suffrage referendum and pass it on to the voters. It took Harriot four years of complex and sustained legislative lobbying to win this part of the suffrage battle.

From one perspective, her target was the New York legislature, but at least as often, she regarded the regular suffrage lobby, the conservative and circumspect group of mostly upstate women working under the rubric of the New York State Woman Suffrage Association, as the greater obstacle to progress. "The difficulties in the suffrage path, it seemed to me, were not so much the intricacies of amending State and Federal Constitutions," she wrote in her memoirs, "as that there did not seem to be a grain of political knowledge in the movement."[1] For over a decade, the state society had been sweeping into Albany, delivering its arguments at polite hearings, and allowing itself to be assured by friends in the legislature that the cause was slowly advancing. Its assumption was that its "educational" efforts would gradually create more and more support for suffrage until the legislature would pass the woman suffrage amendment out to the voters. Harriot believed this approach to be futile, a reflection of women's naïveté about the self-interest and negotiations over power that really moved politicians. "While all educational work is not necessarily political," she insisted, "all political work is educational. Every stroke on the political side educates."[2]

Even from the distance of so many years, her conviction of her political infallibility is irritating, and so it must have been to her con-

temporaries, who were as eager as she to get the state legislature moving on woman suffrage. Nonetheless, the Women's Political Union under her direction was indisputably the driving force in state suffrage politics in these years. It was not so much that Harriot's political instincts were always right, as that she was already functioning as a politician. In the face of disappointments and betrayals from individual legislators and entire parties, she was always ready to adapt to political circumstances, change tactics, negotiate with whom she must, and adjust her strategic direction. New York State was the most complex yet crucial political venue in the United States, and short of regarding the coming of woman suffrage as an inevitable force obliterating all political obstacles in its path, the centrality of Harriot's individual contribution must be recognized.

Harriot's own evaluation of her contribution to the woman suffrage movement centered on legislative politics; she experienced the 1913 legislative authorization of the suffrage referendum as a sweet and personal achievement. The political maneuvering and power-mongering, which women had traditionally repudiated as the unhappy consequences of the male monopoly of politics, challenged and invigorated her. Her reminiscences of this three-year campaign occupy almost a third of her autobiography, and her retrospective relish in remembering every parliamentary detail is evident; it is a good guess that she never felt more powerful or more the woman she wanted to be than in these years, when she was playing "the game of politics." . . .

What does it mean to say that Harriot Blatch was distinctly "political" when the singular goal of the movement within which she worked was political rights and had been for over half a century? A decade later, after the Nineteenth Amendment had been secured, Carrie Chapman Catt made a distinction between "voting," into which women had at last been admitted, and "politics," from which they remained largely excluded.[3] Even as organized suffragism was nearing its goal of political equality, it still held fast to the rhetorical framework which identified the existing practice of politics with men, self-servingness, and corruption and counterposed it with women, morality, and social welfare. There was something about politics that made it

harder for women to take than other male preserves, such as education or paid labor. Nor
was it simply that men defended their monopoly over political power with all the weapons
at their disposal, although that certainly was
the case. The politicization of woman suffrage
was as marked by women's hesitancy as men's
hostility.

A fundamental element of suffragist
aversion to practicing politics was women's
horror of political parties. Even for suffragists, female nonpartisanship still had the status of a first principle. Men were also critics of
excessive partisanship, but male and female
nonpartisanship had different meanings. Traditional political partisanship was male to the
core: to be a man you had to have a party.
Men who criticized party excesses were vulnerable to charges of being "unmanly." By
contrast, female nonpartisanship was compatible with, indeed constitutive of womanliness. . . . [4] Partisan politics seemed so in-
exorably "male" in the Victorian context
because it involved conflict, opposition, contest. "Women at war with each other make
particularly displeasing sounds, and their
attitudes lack dignity and grace," editorialized the *New York Times*.[5]

Women's nonpartisanship was therefore
more a statement about the system of gender
that established and monitored boundaries
between masculinity and femininity than an
informed critique of how political parties
thwarted the democratic will. Traditional
female nonpartisanship complemented and
reinforced male partisanship in a variety of
ways. Inasmuch as most women lived in intimate and dependent relations with men, their
proud female contempt for parties coexisted
with class and family associations that inclined
them toward a particular party. In New York,
these inclinations were largely Republican.
And when women did associate themselves
with overtly political campaigns (for instance,
when the Women's Municipal League advocated reform candidates for New York City
mayor in the late 1890s), their involvement
elevated their male allies by clothing their otherwise suspect political involvements in the
selfless concern with community welfare associated with women's reform activism.[6]

The process to which Harriot had dedicated herself—finding a practical route to the
realization of woman suffrage—led her to

engage with parties as the basic structure of
politics; but the character of New York politics
in these years made it necessary for her to deal
with both Republicans and Democrats, not to
count on one or the other. Thus, her approach
was neither nonpartisan in a traditionally
female way nor partisan in a traditionally male
way; she neither abjured the party system nor
pledged loyalty to a particular party (though
her own family inclinations were Democratic).
When she spoke of herself as "nonpartisan,"
she meant that she was willing and able to take
on opponents from any party; she did not mean
that she would have nothing to do with the
entire system of political parties. She recognized that parties were the necessary territory
through which anyone with a serious legislative objective must move. "Any determined
minority under the political system which we
have in the United States can work its will,"
Harriot was concluding, "if marshalled by
those who have at their command enthusiasm
and political understanding."[7]

Harriot considered herself "a born politician,"[8] and she had the lineage on both sides
for it. Her mother and Susan B. Anthony had
immersed themselves in men's politics more
than any other women of their generation.
"Taught by two such veteran campaigners as
my mother and Miss Anthony," she recalled,
"I realized that women must adopt their own
plan of action, shoulder the responsibility and
be willing to accept temporary defeat."[9] But
fundamentally she identified politics as masculine and associated her own deeply felt
political tendencies with her father. The masculine character of politics drew her to it; she
liked that the traditional practice of politics
embraced the aspiration for power straight-
forwardly, unqualified and unashamed. Yet it
was no simple task for her to claim this paternal inheritance. Men were contemptuous of
women in politics, a response to which Harriot was regularly exposed.[10] The hostility of
male politicians was like a gauntlet thrown in
her face, a challenge she felt bound to answer
and confident she could meet. She was driven
by the desire to demonstrate to men that she
was at least their equal in politics, hopefully
their better.

Harriot trusted in the system of honor by
which she believed that men conducted politics among themselves.[11] She fully expected
that she and other women would be better

treated once they forced themselves inside the world of men's politics than they were as excluded nonparticipants. She considered the chivalrous notion that women's dependence brought out men's best qualities absurd; men respected their equals, not their subordinates. Throughout her memoirs, she described politics as a "sport" she was determined to master, "a game that becomes infinitely more enjoyable the more evenly matched the opponents."[12] She believed in the rules. . . .

Having discovered that New York's pollwatching law did not specify that one had to be a voter to serve, Harriot made her first incursion into American politics as a pollwatcher in the important 1909 New York City mayoral elections. She secured Prohibition party credentials and served as a pollwatcher on the upper West Side; other Equality League members watched on the lower East Side and in the Bowery. At a postelection meeting of suffragists, Harriot riveted her audience with the details of her absorbing day inside a polling place. "We have lifted the veil, we have entered the holy of holies," she declared to a hushed audience, "and yet the Republic is going on."[13]

At one level, women pollwatchers represented a relatively traditional female suspicion of political corruption. (Harriot and her pollwatching partner, Alberta Hill, had two drunken election officials removed by the police.) But pollwatching also functioned as a challenge to the political divide between the sexes. Polling places were set up in saloons, tobacco shops, and bootblack parlors, generically male sites that excluded women. After a day at these polling places, women were no longer as mystified by politics or the men involved in it. A condescending ward heeler told Harriot that a polling place "is no place for a woman," but after her pollwatching experience, she "laughed for the polling place was nothing but a candy store." It was the men at her polling place that she found to be weak and hysterical; she reported that one of them had nearly fainted, finding "the strain [of counting the ballots] too much."[14] She concluded that pollwatching brought women "behind the scenes" in politics, where men's ignorance and weakness could be observed and their claims to political infallibility exposed.[15]

Pollwatching desanctified the male preserve of politics. Female pollwatching had

about it the air of a battle over the gender character of electoral culture. . . . "I was the only woman there," pollwatcher Elizabeth Ellsworth Cook told reporters. "But I'd got so used to being the only girl in a lot of my courses at Cornell that I didn't mind a bit."[16]

Pollwatching was more than a symbolic threat, of course. A year later at the 1910 election, politicians had suffragists arrested. Eventually, Tammany leaders found women's pollwatching so disruptive that they had the privilege eliminated. By the same token suffragists saw that pollwatching would be an essential element in their eventual victory. The care that California suffragists took in that state's historic 1911 voters' referendum to patrol the ballot count seems to have been the only thing that protected their tiny, four-thousand-vote lead.[17] In New York, Harriot continued to fight for reinstatement of the pollwatching privilege for women, and by the time woman suffrage came before New York voters in 1915, women were once again at the polls on election day.[18]

Having entered the sanctum sanctorum as a pollwatcher, Harriot was now ready to become even more involved in "men's" politics. A series of special elections for New York state legislators had been called in the winter of 1909–10, the most important of which was to replace the recently deceased state senator P. H. McCarren, Democratic boss of Brooklyn. The Equality League raised a small budget, opened a storefront, and demanded that all three candidates for the seat come out in favor of woman suffrage.[19] The league declared it could influence the votes of enough men to make a difference in a three-way race, and they held regular open-air meetings at the Brooklyn end of the Williamsburg Bridge. Right before the election, two of the three candidates declared their support for the woman suffrage referendum bill.[20]

The special elections of 1909–10 convinced Harriot that she had hit on the "true method of gaining woman suffrage." In early 1910, the Equality League formally announced its determination "to change the legislature from an indifferent body into one responsive to our ideas." "We intend to question candidates before elections, not after . . . but with a fixed purpose to work against the man who is against woman suffrage."[21] The new policy foreswore reliance on any "knight errant" to come to suffragists' aid. Women must force the situation using their own power on their own behalf. "When we get the majority in a district on our side and make the connection between public opinion and the representative in the legislature," the league predicted, "we have Woman Suffrage for the first time on its way to victory."[22]

Harriot began her legislative offensive early in the 1910 session. Aware that the fate of the woman suffrage bill was always settled after the suffragists had conducted their hearings and left town, she knew that suffragists needed a constant presence in Albany throughout the entire legislative session. She negotiated with Katherine Mackay for the initial funds to open an Albany office and to assemble a staff to assist her there.[23] Determined to regularize suffragists' relations with the legislature, Harriot hired a professional woman lobbyist. "The State suffragists have many friends among the legislators, and we have never needed a lobbyist," Ella Crossett, state suffrage president, told reporters.[24] Harriot regarded this opinion as self-defeating, and the establishment of a regular suffrage lobby as essential.[25]

Hattie Graham, the woman Harriot selected as lobbyist, conducted the first systematic canvass of New York legislators and discovered that most districts had not one legislator who believed that women deserved the vote. Even legislators who had prosuffrage friends or relatives could not be counted on for support. The assemblyman who represented the state suffrage president's district did not support the suffrage bill.[26]

Graham submitted detailed and nuanced reports to Harriot of her findings. She was attentive to personal circumstances, and much of what she reported had to do with emotional aspects of legislators' positions, on which suffrage lobbyists could play. Of one representative from Queens, she wrote: "Wife and daughter [are] suffragists. Does not know any other women in his district wishing to vote. . . . Regrets lack of education. . . . In talking with him you feel that he is a good businessman. . . . He is full of inconsistencies. Says woman's place is in the home. . . . Said women teachers should receive more pay than men to enable them to marry and support a house." And of another man from a nearby district: "He thinks women should not vote because his sister does

not want to. . . . On the 17th [of January] I introduced Mrs. Blatch and Mrs. [Helen Hoy] Greeley to him as experts who would furnish him with the information he desired. He refused to ask a single question, turned and walked to his seat where he sat and laughed. The next day he apologized. On the 17th of February I was told . . . that [he] was going to support our bill, that he was in favor of suffrage."[27]

The other woman who came to work in Albany with Harriot was a twenty-eight-year-old Barnard graduate named Caroline Lexow, who went on to become Harriot's close friend and her most reliable and indefatigable organizer. Caroline Lexow had the perfect background for the legislative side of suffrage work. She had strong paternal links to the political process, stronger even than Harriot's. Her father was Clarence Lexow, the attorney and state senator who had headed the eponymous Lexow Commission that tore into New York City police corruption in 1894, thus establishing the legitimacy of subsequent calls for basic municipal political reform. "Her gift, both by inheritance and the training of environment, lay supremely along political lines," Harriot wrote. "She loved the game of politics as much as I did."[28] . . .

In the winter of 1910, Harriot and Caroline Lexow set up political shop in Albany, and almost immediately Albany politicians began to close ranks against the acceleration of suffragist demands on them. Several legislators tried to set up new obstacles to bringing votes for women to the electorate. In the Assembly Charles Dana proposed that all constitutional amendments require a supermajority of two-thirds of the legislators before being passed on for ratification.[29] In the Senate, Republican Edgar Brackett proposed holding an "election" among women themselves to show how limited their support for their own enfranchisement was. Leaders of the state society seemed intrigued by the Brackett Bill, but Harriot was disgusted. She regarded it as a deliberate attempt to make woman suffrage look ludicrous. She and Caroline fought both proposals, neither of which made any headway in the legislature.[30]

Using Hattie Graham's legislative canvass, Harriot and Caroline Lexow identified suffragists' initial strategic problem. The bill to authorize the referendum was trapped in the Senate and Assembly judiciary committees, both of which refused to report it out for a full vote of the legislature. . . . Convinced that any report, including a negative one, would advance the cause, Harriot determined to find a way to break through this deadlock.[31]

"When we took up legislative action," she wrote in her memoirs, "I recognized fully our entire lack of knowledge of detail and determined to replace ignorance with the soundest of information." For help she arranged for a meeting with one of the most powerful politicians in the state, a man who not only lacked any sympathy for the cause but embodied backroom politics at its most sordid. James Wadsworth, Republican Speaker of the Assembly, was, in Harriot's words, "a past master in legislative procedure." She was oddly confident that he would give her the information she needed, even if it meant improving her chances in battling him in the legislature. She counted on his "sportsman's" instincts, hoping he "would probably enjoy instructing his enemy in skill." She convinced him to become her legislative mentor and to teach her how to force a recalcitrant committee to act. Wadsworth explained to her what kind of motion she needed to discharge the Judiciary Committee from the suffrage bill's consideration.[32]

With Wadsworth's help, Harriot got Republican state Senator Josiah Newcomb to secure a floor vote to discharge the referendum bill from the Assembly Judiciary Committee. In April 1910, the full Assembly voted—for the first time in fifteen years—on a measure affecting the fate of woman suffrage. Even though the discharge bill was defeated, Harriot was pleased. "I understand men pretty well because I had five brothers, all of them different," she told reporters. "All of these men will be all right as soon as they understand that they can't play with us and smooth us down any more. We must make them see that they must reckon with us as they do with men."[33]

The suffrage parade of May 1910 took place immediately after the adverse Assembly vote and was advertised as a "parade of protest against the Legislature for its indifference to our demands for woman suffrage."[34] Armed with the support of the numbers who turned out and with the newspaper coverage the parade received, Harriot returned to Albany to push for a vote of the state Senate to discharge the suffrage bill from its judiciary

committee. Although the move failed in the Senate as it had in the Assembly, Harriot was confident that ground had been gained, debate had begun, and suffragists were in a position to target recalcitrant legislators.

Harriot also continued her efforts on the electoral side of politics. In November 1910 the Equality League and the Equal Franchise Society joined together in a campaign against Artemus Ward, member of the Assembly Judiciary Committee, opponent of woman suffrage, and representative of the "banner Republican district" in New York City. William Ivins and Herbert Parsons, reform Republican leaders who were married to suffragists, tried to temper the suffragist campaign against Ward, but Harriot was determined.[35] The intensity with which Harriot and her allies worked against Assemblyman Ward suggests that they were engaged as much in learning the electoral process as in defeating a particular politician. In the campaign against Ward, the suffragists made use of every electoral technique, traditional and progressive. They organized torchlight parades, held open-air meetings, and even conducted "dirty tricks." On election eve, in front of a crowd, they had a horse Ward was using seized by the city because it was abused. Harriot researched Ward's abysmal, reactionary voting record in Albany, and suffragists canvassed 90 percent of the district's registered voters with information on Ward and instructions on how to split a ticket. Ward was not defeated, but his margin of victory was whittled down to a few hundred votes and Harriot trusted that the campaign would have "an important effect on the attitude of the incoming legislature."[36] The thrill of a full-fledged political campaign was one more factor in Harriot's decision to redirect her focus from recruitment and propaganda to politics. The rechristening of the Equality League as the Women's Political Union occurred a week and a half later.

The irony of Harriot's second year of sustained lobbying, before the legislature of 1911, was that just as she was moving away from her original trade union base, Democrats took over both houses of the state legislature for the first time in seventeen years. A new generation of Democratic political leaders—men like Robert Wagner, Al Smith, and Franklin Roosevelt—began to reformulate progressive aspirations in terms of Democrats' working-class and immigrant constituencies. Democrats were not traditionally supporters of woman suffrage, which they tended to regard as a hobby of elite ladies and a Republican issue. For this to change, Democrats would have to be led to rethink suffrage in the context of their traditional labor politics. And yet the deepening necessity of a labor-friendly suffrage movement occurred just at the moment that Harriot was shifting from the Equality League and into the Women's Political Union. At the legislative hearings on the referendum bill early in 1911, Harriot invited the eloquent and authoritative Leonora O'Reilly to speak on behalf of working women's need of the suffrage. She arranged for O'Reilly's expenses to be paid by Katherine Mackay and promised her a ten-minute slot at the hearings. On arrival in Albany, however, O'Reilly found herself relegated to the end of the proceedings and limited to a few minutes. Overlooking the insult, she spoke with great effect.[37] "I represent 50,000 women in this State and over 800,000 in the country who have mauled in the mill, fagged in the factory, and worn out behind the counter," she dramatically proclaimed. "We can only strangle the organizations that want to make our hours longer at the ballot box."[38]

The conflict between the elite direction in which Harriot was moving and the necessity of cultivating Democratic political support can be seen most starkly in connection with the complex question of immigrant wives and their citizenship rights. As the prospects for the enfranchisement of women became more likely, careful observers were beginning to notice that the woman suffrage proposal before the legislature would allow immigrant wives of citizens to vote without having to go through the naturalization process that was required of all other immigrants. Under American law the wife's citizenship followed that of the husband, and thus an immigrant woman automatically became a U.S. citizen on marrying one. So far, citizenship had had little independent meaning for women, but with the coming of woman suffrage this would change. A practice that had had its origins in women's dependence and subordination would suddenly bring meaningful rights instead. Harriot knew the rule of wives' dependent citizenship well. In 1907, an act of Congress had clarified what she had long feared, that as an American woman who was married to a man who was

not American, she could no longer claim to be a U.S. citizen.[39]

How Harriot responded to this curious legal juncture is telling: instead of supporting the original referendum bill because it granted political rights to women, she sought to have it modified so that it would not grant political rights to immigrants. Here her own inclinations coincided with that of her elite allies, who were not eager to bring more immigrant voters to the polls. Early in the session of 1911, the Women's Political Union submitted a new version of the enabling legislation for the woman suffrage referendum. The bill required that "women whose citizenship is derived solely from marriage with citizens" must go through a separate naturalization process in order to vote.[40]

Nativism was Harriot's democratic weak spot, as it had been her mother's. Suspicion of and contempt for old-world nationalities was the other side of her passionate Americanism. She was an active supporter of greater rights for African Americans, for they were Americans, but the unassimilated European immigrants with whom she came in contact throughout the New York campaign had no such claim on her sympathies. She favored "American" over "foreign" workers, as she had done during the shirtwaist strike.[41] And when disappointed in her hopes for popular support for woman suffrage, she was always ready to blame immigrant men. Up to the last vote of the legislature in 1913, this special clause regarding immigrant wives threatened Democratic votes for the enabling bill. In the end, it may even have cost woman suffrage crucial votes and contributed to the referendum's defeat in 1915.

Despite the energy and determination Harriot poured into the lobbying campaign during 1911, it was nearly impossible to get any political movement out of the new Democratic majority. Hopes for reform were starting out most inauspiciously. The leading demand for prolabor reform—a bill limiting the hours of working women to fifty-four—was being slowly gutted of all substance by powerful manufacturing interests.[42] Then, at the end of March, the legislature's attention was suddenly drawn to the conditions of the state's industrial workers, in particular its women. Late on a Saturday afternoon, at the end of a long work week, a deadly fire roared through the Triangle

Shirtwaist Company in New York City, the site of the great women's strike fewer than fifteen months before. Within a few hours, 146 garment workers, mostly women, had either burned, fallen, or jumped to their deaths. The intrinsic horror of the event was enormous. But against the background of the Democratic ascendancy in Albany, the fire had special political meaning, intensifying the political prominence of working-class women and deepening conflicts about who spoke for them and what was said on their behalf.

In the aftermath of the fire, class tensions among New York women activists became heightened. Socialists, angry at the degree to which they had been overshadowed by bourgeois women during the shirtwaist strike of 1909–10, made sure they held the first public protest after the fire.[43] At a giant memorial meeting sponsored by society suffragists Alva Belmont and Anne Morgan four days later, upper-class patrons entered the hall early through a separate entrance to avoid confrontations with angry socialists and trade unionists. Once inside, they listened uneasily to Rose Schneiderman give her famous, fierce speech on the inadequacy of charity and "good fellowship" in the face of the squandering of working-class lives.[44] Two weeks after the fire, the International Ladies Garment Workers Union held a mass funeral procession which drew over a hundred thousand solemn marchers, the great majority working-class women. Those elite suffragists who participated, including Harriot, walked through the soaking rain in plain dress.[45]

Many political forces were positioning themselves to make political capital out of the Triangle deaths. The Women's Political Union was definitely among these and was determined to draw a straight line from the deadliness of the fire to the weakness of the state's factory inspection laws to the political powerlessness of working women. A month after the fire, in conjunction with the city's annual Labor Day parade, the WPU held a Sunday afternoon meeting on the lower East Side to make these connections. "Uptown women" were there to hear Leonora O'Reilly as the featured speaker, along with WPU Executive Board member Florence Kelley. "Your condition is no better than slavery, and as long as this slavery lasts you have got to work in fire-trap factories," O'Reilly told her sympathetic

audience. "The only way out is through the ballot and the only way to be sure of a good ballot is to cast it yourselves."[46]

It was under these conditions—Democratic control of the legislature, the Triangle fire, and a well-organized suffrage presence in Albany—that working-class woman suffragism in New York can be said to have finally come into its own. Out of O'Reilly's concentrated focus on votes for women in the winter and spring of 1911, and perhaps directly out of the WPU East Side meeting on April 30, the Wage Earners Suffrage League was formed.[47] Like the now-deceased Equality League, it linked industrial and professional women, but it was led by the former rather than the latter. As O'Reilly proudly put it, the new league was "officered and controlled by women who work for wages."[48]

The primary goal of the WPU's East Side labor suffrage meeting was "to arouse the enthusiasm of the industrial women" for New York's second grand suffrage parade, the next Saturday, on May 6.[49] Perhaps inspired by the Triangle fire funeral procession, Harriot declared that this year, parade participants would not be allowed to ride in automobiles, protected from direct contact with the voting public: everyone would walk.[50] Everything was meant to highlight the link between labor and suffrage. The parade was led off by a series of floats depicting the history of women's labor, from the "home industry of our grandmothers' time" to the modern ranks of industrial and professional working women. The marchers were organized by trade and profession, to indicate the variety and complexity of twentieth-century women's work. Tradeswomen marched under signs of their crafts, college women in caps and gowns, and a hundred society women from the Equal Franchise Society walked under a hand-embroidered banner. The garment workers with their crimson banner draped in funeral black particularly drew applause.[51] Photos of the march show bands of women marching three and four abreast, many of them in simple dress and hats, with banners held aloft proclaiming, "Women Need Votes to End Sweat Shops" and "Suffrage Pioneers Gained for Married Working Women the Right to Their Wages."

By highlighting the working woman case for suffrage, the suffrage parade of 1911 was intended to put as much pressure as possible on the legislature. Three days after the march, dozens of members of the Women's Political Union reassembled, banners and all, at Albany. Harriot carried a banner that listed the names of legislators considered suffrage's major enemies along with the inscription, in Greek, "He who plots against the cause of women, may he miserably perish, both himself and his house." The suffragists tried to march right into the Assembly chamber itself but were stopped at the door, forced to relinquish their standards, and entered unarmed.[52] Nonetheless, slightly more than a week after the New York parade, the Senate Judiciary Committee, which had been eluding WPU pressure for months, voted to report out the suffrage measure affirmatively. Now the entire Senate was faced with the necessity of voting yea or nea on the referendum, a distressing prospect.[53]

For the next two months, the legislative opponents of suffrage succeeded in postponing the full Senate's vote authorizing a referendum. Robert Wagner particularly incurred Harriot's wrath by pushing the vote on the suffrage bill further and further back to the end of the session. While other suffragists left for their vacations, Harriot, Caroline, and a few other WPU stalwarts stayed upstate through the hot summer months, lobbying legislators during the week and following them to their districts on the weekends. In Syracuse, they pursued one man to his own doorstep, where they extracted a public promise that he would vote to discharge the suffrage bill from committee. In Schenectady, the Women's Political Union held rallies outside the gates of General Electric and American Locomotive.[54]

Finally, on July 12, the woman suffrage bill was forced onto the floor and the long delayed debate began. Popular and powerful Tammany figure Senator "Big Tim" Sullivan spoke movingly in favor of votes for women. "You can go down into my section of the city [the Bowery] . . . I think there are more women than men going to work [at 7:00 A.M.]. . . . [Woman suffrage] is going to come and you can't stop it. . . . It is a good proposition and I hope the bill is advanced." Despite his support the suffrage bill was defeated in the Senate by one vote.[55] Several Democrats who had pledged their support were absent from the chamber. Franklin Roosevelt was not present, thus avoiding having to take a stand on woman suffrage. Harriot never forgave him for the dodge.[56]

The legislative experience of 1911 left the Women's Political Union hungry for revenge.[57] The formation of a committee was announced, chaired by Eunice Dana Brannan, to raise a campaign fund of one hundred thousand dollars to defeat enemy legislators at the polls. Although "tricked by the politicians [and] treated with discourtesy," the women "mean to play politics in the masculine way," the *New York Times* reported ominously.[58] In October 1911, the WPU directed all its energies toward defeating two New York City Democrats, considered implacable enemies, running for reelection to the Assembly. "Each Democratic voter in the two districts was either personally canvassed or received a leaflet showing the legislative record of the candidate of his party and a card instructing him how to split his ticket against our enemy," the WPU reported—149,000 pieces of literature were distributed. One of the candidates, Ron Carew, was defeated; the other, Lewis Cuvillier, was returned to the legislature, his margin uncomfortably trimmed, now an even more adamant foe of the suffragists.[59]

NOTES

1. Harriot Stanton Blatch and Alma Lutz, *Challenging Years: The Memoirs of Harriot Stanton Blatch* (New York: G. P. Putnam's Sons, 1940), p. 93.

2. Ibid., p. 111.

3. Carrie Chapman Catt, "What Women Have Done with Suffrage," n.d., reel 7, Carrie Chapman Catt Papers, Manuscript Division, Library of Congress; quoted in Melanie Gustafson's unpublished paper "Partisan Women: Progressive, Republican and Democratic Women in the 1912 and 1916 Elections" (delivered at the 1995 meetings of the American Historical Association).

4. Susan B. Anthony and Ida H. Harper, eds., *History of Woman Suffrage*, v. 4 (Rochester: Susan B. Anthony, 1902), p. 280. Although the shock of betrayal by the Republican party in the 1860s had given birth to an independent woman suffrage movement, it was not until the 1890s that the "lesson" derived from this history was that all political parties were the movement's implacable enemies. In a fine discussion of suffrage nonpartisanship, Aileen Kraditor argues that it was the experiences of the 1890s with Populists and Republicans that generated suffragists' obdurate antiparty attitudes (*Ideas of the Woman Suffrage Movement, 1890–1920* [New York: Columbia University Press, 1965], ch. 8). For an excellent consideration of women's suspicion of parties after 1920, see Nancy Cott, *The Grounding of Modern Feminism* (New Haven: Yale University Press, 1987), pp. 99–114. Conversely, Lori Ginzberg shows that there was substantial interest in party politics

among women in the mid-nineteenth century (*Women and the Work of Benevolence: Morality, Politics, and Class in the Nineteenth-Century United States* [New Haven: Yale University Press, 1990]).

5. "Dissensions among Suffragists," *New York Times*, March 10, 1910, p. 8.

6. Gustafson, "Partisan Women." The pioneering discussions of gender and partisanship can be found in Michael McGerr, *The Decline of Popular Politics: The American North, 1865–1928* (New York: Oxford University Press, 1986), pp. 54–56, and Paula Baker, *Moral Frameworks of Public Life: Gender, Politics and the State in Rural New York, 1870–1930* (New York: Oxford University Press, 1991), ch. 2.

7. Blatch and Lutz, *Challenging Years*, p. 91.

8. "Mrs. Blatch's Address," unidentified and undated clipping (c. 1903) from Scrapbooks of Women's Club of Orange, New Jersey, v. 4, New Jersey Historical Society; thanks to Gail Malmgreen for this clipping.

9. Blatch and Lutz, *Challenging Years*, p. 127.

10. Ibid., p. 153.

11. The best account of the male system of honor by which Gilded Age politics were organized can be found in Baker, *Moral Frameworks of Public Life*.

12. Blatch and Lutz, *Challenging Years*, p. 111. Note the difference of language when she describes war, in her *Mobilizing Woman Power* (New York: Womans Press, 1918): "War is not a sport, it is a cold, hard science, demanding every energy of the nation for its successful pursuit" (p. 136).

13. Blatch and Lutz, *Challenging Years*, p. 116; "Women Watchers at Polls Praise Ballot Casters," *New York World*, November 21, 1909, n.p., Harriot Stanton Blatch Papers, Manuscript Division Library of Congress hereafter cited as HSB-LC; "The Active Suffrage Movement," *Review of Reviews*, December 1909, pp. 653–54. She could still remember the details thirty years later, when talking to Alma Lutz (Lutz, notes from interview with Blatch, June 15, 1939, Alma Lutz Papers, Vassar College, Poughkeepsie, New York).

14. "Fair Sex on Guard," *New York American*, November 3, 1909, n.p.

15. Lutz, notes from interview with Blatch, June 15, 1939.

16. "Miss Elizabeth Cook Watching at the Polls," *New York Sun*, November 21, 1909, n.p., HSB-LC.

17. "California Farmers Give Vote to Women," *New York Times*, October 13, 1911, p. 1. So close was the vote that the first reports in the *New York Times* were that the referendum lost ("Suffragists Gaining in California Vote," October 12, 1911, p. 3).

18. Women's Political Union Annual Report, 1913–14, p. 12, reel 3, HSB-LC.

19. "Want Suffrage Senator," *New York Times*, December 5, 1909, p. 11. The Independence League was also running a candidate.

20. "Women Complicate 7th District Fight," *Brooklyn Times*, December 9, 1909, n.p., HSB-LC; Equality League of Self-Supporting Women, *Enunciation of a Political Policy*, 1909, pp. 4–5.

21. Blatch, "Question the Candidates," *Woman's Journal*, January 15, 1910, p. 11.

22. Equality League, *Enunciation of a Political Policy*, p. 4.

23. "Mrs. Mackay Opens Campaign at Albany," *New York Times*, January 26, 1910, p. 4.

24. "Lobbyist Splits Ranks," *New York Times*, March 2, 1910, p. 5.

25. Blatch and Lutz, *Challenging Years*, p. 119.

26. Hattie Graham, manuscript report on 1910 New York legislature, HSB-LC. Graham also reported that the chairman of the Senate Judiciary Committee thought Blatch was "very wholesome to look at" but had no intention of supporting woman suffrage.

27. Ibid.

28. Blatch and Lutz, *Challenging Years*, p. 120.

29. "Warning from Mrs. Blatch," *New York Times*, March 5, 1910, p. 4.

30. Blatch and Lutz, *Challenging Years*, p. 122; "Memorial of the Woman Suffrage Legislative Committees of the Senate and Assembly," *Progress*, March 1910, p. 2.

31. Equal Franchise Society, "Report of the Legislative Committee," 1910, p. 11, reel 1, HSB-LC.

32. Blatch and Lutz, *Challenging Years*, pp. 111–13. Wadsworth, who became a U.S. senator, remained a staunch opponent of suffrage, and a failed effort to remove him from Congress was one of New York women's first major postsuffrage electoral offensives (Carrie Chapman Catt and Nettie Rogers Shuler, *Woman Suffrage and Politics: The Inner Story of the Suffrage Movement* [New York: Charles Scribner's Sons, 1923], p. 327).

33. *New York Sun*, March 1910, n.p., Harriot Stanton Blatch Papers, Vassar College, Poughkeepsie, New York.

34. Blatch and Lutz, *Challenging Years*, p. 129.

35. Ibid., pp. 135–36.

36. Ibid.; "Women Make It Hot for Artemus Ward," *New York Times*, November 6, 1910, p. 8.

37. "Gowns Scared Solons Away," *New York Globe*, Feburary 22, 1911, n.p., HSB-LC.

38. Anne Herenden, WPU secretary writing for Blatch, to O'Reilly, February 16, 1911, with O'Reilly's penned notes, Leonora O'Reilly Papers, Schlesinger Library, Cambridge, Massachusetts; hereafter cited as LOR-Mass.

39. Sophonisba P. Breckenridge, *Marriage and the Civic Rights of Women* (Chicago: University of Chicago Press, 1931), p. 20. Her situation was further complicated by the fact that Harry had no intention of renouncing his own nationality. In 1909, after she had reestablished residence in the United States, Harriot began proceedings to reinstate her claim to U.S. citizenship ("Prepares to Cast Her Vote," *New York Times*, December 11, 1909, p. 8). Four years later, a federal district court judge ruled that so long as her husband remained a British subject, she would as well ("Mrs. Blatch Never to Vote," *New York Times*, March 26, 1913, p. 4).

40. "Suffragists' Bill Already," *New York Times*, January 5, 1911, p. 2.

41. On this division, see Elinor Lerner, "American Feminism and the Jewish Question," in *Anti-Semitism in American History*, ed. David A. Gerber (Urbana: University of Illinois Press, 1986), and

Nancy Schrom Dye, *As Equals and as Sisters: Feminism, Unionism and the Women's Trade Union League of New York* (Columbia: University of Missouri Press, 1980), pp. 114–15.

42. Irwin Yellowitz, *Labor and the Progressive Movement in New York State, 1897–1916* (Ithaca: Cornell University Press, 1965).

43. "Faint in a Frenzy over Tales of Fire," *New York Times,* March 30, 1911, p. 1; Mari Jo Buhle, *Women and American Socialism, 1870–1920* (Urbana: University of Illinois Press, 1981), pp. 224–27. Two days later, the College Equal Suffrage League held a meeting at Cooper Union. "Public Indifference Held Responsible," *New York Times,* April 1, 1911, p. 3.

44. "Mass Meeting Calls for New Fire Laws," *New York Times,* April 3, 1911, p. 3.

45. "19000 Pay Tribute to the Fire Victims," *New York Times,* April 6, 1911, p. 1.

46. "Suffragists Sing New March Song," *New York Times,* May 1, 1911, p. 5; "Urging Women to Parade: East Side Invaded by the Suffrage Workers," *New York Sun,* n.d., n.p., reel 2, HSB-LC.

47. Lavinia Dock, "Suffrage on the East Side," *Woman Voter,* March 11, 1911, p. 3; Elinor Lerner, "Jewish Involvement in the New York City Woman Suffrage Movement," *American Jewish History,* v. 70, June 1981, pp. 442–61.

48. O'Reilly to Hettie Sherwin, May 12, 1913, reel 6, LOR-Mass. The organization of the WESL represents "the dream of my life come true," said O'Reilly ("Suffrage Demanded by Working Women," *New York Times,* April 23, 1912, p. 24).

49. Blatch to O'Reilly, April 19, 1911, reel 5, LOR-Mass.

50. "Parade Postponed," *Woman's Journal,* October 8, 1910, p. 165; "Suffragists Plan a Street Parade," *New York Times,* February 21, 1911, p. 5; "Suffragists March in Procession Today," *New York Times,* May 6, 1911, p. 13.

51. "Women of All Ranks in Suffrage Parade," *New York Times,* April 15, 1911, p. 13; "Women Parade and Rejoice at End," ibid., May 7, 1911, p. 1.

52. Typescript, "Political History of Women's Political Union," probably by Nora de Forest, p. 9, reel 1, HSB-LC.

53. Blatch and Lutz, *Challenging Years,* p. 143; Women's Political Union, Legislative Report, 1911–12, p. 8, HSB-LC; "Suffragists Off to Albany," *New York Times,* May 9, 1911, p. 11.

54. Women's Political Union, Legislative Report, 1911–12, p. 16.

55. Blatch and Lutz, *Challenging Years,* pp. 151–52.

56. "Legislative Doings and Legislators," *Woman Voter,* July 1911, p. 203; Savelle, *Ladies' Lib,* p. 30.

57. Eunice Dana Brannan, letter to the editor, *New York Times,* July 30, 1911, p. 8.

58. "$100,000 Campaign Fund for Suffrage," *New York Times,* May 17, 1911, p. 1.

59. Women's Political Union, 1911–12 Annual Report, pp. 23–24.

DOCUMENTS: Dimensions of Citizenship

> ## Mackenzie *v.* Hare, *1915*

The persistent expansion of Married Women's Property Laws and the development of support for suffrage makes it tempting to conclude that the practice of coverture—women's civic subordination to men—steadily dissolved over the course of the nineteenth and early twentieth centuries. But while it is true that some aspects of coverture eroded, others were sustained and even strengthened.

Although Chief Justice Morrison R. Waite had been right when he observed in *Minor v. Happersett* (1875) [pp. 245–46] "[t]here is no doubt that women may be citizens," he was wrong when he went on to claim that "sex has never been made one of the elements of citizenship. . . . [M]en have never had an advantage over women." According to the common law and early American practice, white women, like men, became citizens either by birth or by their own choice to be naturalized. But in 1855, following practices established in France by the conservative Code Napoleon (1804) and in Britain in 1844, the U.S. Congress extended the principle of marital unity to provide that "any woman who might lawfully be naturalized under the existing laws, married, or shall be married to a citizen of the United States shall be deemed and taken to be a citizen." That is, foreign women who married male citizens did not need to go through a naturalization process or even take an oath of allegiance. The law made no comment about foreign-born men who might marry American women; for the next fifty years, there was little consistency in how courts dealt with the cases that came before them. But when the principle of "marital unity" prevailed, women who were American citizens actually lost their citizenship, and in 1907, Congress passed a statute that explicitly provided that women take the nationality of their husbands.

Expatriation—the loss of citizenship—traditionally has been a very severe punishment, usually reserved for cases of treason. If a married woman had to assume the nationality of her husband, she might become the subject of a king or tsar in a political system that offered her even less protection than did the United States. She might even become stateless. If Americans claimed to base their political system on the "consent of the governed," could women's "consent" be arbitrarily denied? In time of war, the American woman who married, say, a German national, could overnight change her status from a citizen to an alien enemy. President Ulysses S. Grant's daughter lost her citizenship when she married an Englishman in 1874; it required a special act of Congress to reinstate her citizenship when she returned from England as a widow in 1898.

Ethel Mackenzie, who had been born in California, married Gordon Mackenzie, a British subject, in 1909—two years after the passage of the Citizenship Act of 1907. She was active in the woman suffrage movement in California, and when it was successful in 1911 she worked in the San Francisco voter registration drive. It is not surprising that she herself should try to register to vote. When the Board of Election Commissioners

239 U.S. 299.

denied her application, holding that upon her marriage to a British subject she had "ceased to be a citizen of the United States," she refused to let her husband apply for citizenship and instead challenged the law, claiming that Congress had exceeded its authority. She could not believe that Congress had actually *intended* to deprive her of the citizenship she understood to be her birthright. Why did the Supreme Court deny her claim? What "ancient principle of jurisprudence" did they rely on? Why did the Court think that the marriage of an American woman to a foreign man should be treated differently than the marriage of an American man to a foreign woman?

Mr. Justice McKenna:

... The question ... is, Did [Ethel Mackenzie] cease to be a citizen by her marriage? ... [Mackenzie contends] that it was not the intention [of Congress] to deprive an American-born woman, remaining within the jurisdiction of the United States, of her citizenship by reason of her marriage to a resident foreigner.... [She is trying to persuade the Court that the citizenship statute was] beyond the authority of Congress.... [She offered the] earnest argument ... that ... under the Constitution and laws of the United States, [citizenship] became a right, privilege and immunity which could not be taken away from her except as a punishment for crime or by her voluntary expatriation....

[But the Court concludes:] ... The identity of husband and wife is an ancient principle of our jurisprudence. It was neither accidental nor arbitrary and worked in many instances for her protection. There has been, it is true, much relaxation of it but in its retention as in its origin it is determined by their intimate relation and unity of interests, and this relation and unity may make it of public concern in many instances to merge their identity, and give dominance to the husband. It has purpose, if not necessity, in purely domestic policy; it has greater purpose and, it may be, necessity, in international policy.... Having this purpose, has it not the sanction of power?

... The law in controversy deals with a condition voluntarily entered into.... The marriage of an American woman with a foreigner has consequences ... [similar to] her physical expatriation.... Therefore, as long as the relation lasts it is made tantamount to expatriation. This is no arbitrary exercise of government.... It is the conception of the legislation under review that such an act [marriage to a foreign man] may bring the Government into embarrassments and, it may be, into controversies.... [Marriage to a foreign man] is as voluntary and distinctive as expatriation and its consequence must be considered as elected.

The decision in *Mackenzie* angered suffragists and energized them; American women needed suffrage to protect themselves against involuntary expatriation and statelessness. The repeal of the Citizenship Act of 1907 was high on the suffragists' agenda, and they turned to it as soon as suffrage was accomplished (see Equal Suffrage [Nineteenth] Amendment). The Cable Act of 1922 provided that "the right of a person to become a naturalized citizen shall not be denied to a person on account of sex or because she is a married woman," but it permitted American women who married foreigners to retain their citizenship only if they married men from countries whose subjects were eligible for U.S. citizenship—that is, not from China or Japan. American-born women who married aliens from China or Japan still lost their citizenship. American-born women who married aliens not from China or Japan were treated as naturalized citizens who would lose their citizenship should they reside abroad for two years. The Cable Act was extended by amendments well into the 1930s, but loopholes remained, and not all of it was made retroactive. As late as the 1950s, some American-born women were denied passports because they had married aliens before 1992. In 1998 the U.S. Supreme Court upheld a practice of different rules by which a child born abroad to an unmarried citizen man and a non-citizen woman, or an unmarried citizen woman and a non-citizen man, could claim citizenship. [*Miller* v. *Albright* 523 U.S. 420 (1998).]*

*This note draws on Candice Lewis Bredbenner, *A Nationality of Her Own: Woman, Marriage and the Law of Citizenship* (Berkeley: University of California Press, 1998) and Linda K. Kerber, *No Constitutional Right to Be Ladies: Women and the Obligations of Citizenship* (New York: Hill and Wang, 1998), ch. 1.

Equal Suffrage (Nineteenth) Amendment, 1920

When the Fourteenth and Fifteenth Amendments (p. 241) failed to provide for universal suffrage, a federal amendment was introduced into the Senate by S. C. Pomeroy of Kansas in 1868 and into the House by George W. Julian of Indiana in March 1869. Historian Ellen DuBois has observed, "Previously the case for suffrage had consistently been put in terms of the individual rights of all persons, regardless of their sex and race. Angered by their exclusion from the Fifteenth Amendment, women's rights advocates began to develop fundamentally different arguments for their cause. They claimed their right to the ballot not as individuals but as a sex. . . . The reason women should vote was not that they were the same as men but that they were different. That made for a rather thorough reversal of classic women's rights premises."*

Arguing for the vote on the basis of women's *difference* from men could be effective in strengthening women's sense of group consciousness, but it also was compatible with racist and nativist arguments that white women needed the vote to counteract the suffrage of black and immigrant men. The old alliance of woman suffrage and abolitionist activism eroded, even though voting rights for black men were increasingly threatened after Reconstruction. The suffrage efforts of 1870 to 1920 continued to display arguments from equality, but younger generations of activists were increasingly likely to emphasize difference—what one activist called "the mother instinct for government."

Woman suffrage was not accomplished easily. One scholar has counted 480 suffrage campaigns between 1870 and 1910, but only seventeen referenda were held, with only two successes. Stanton died in 1902; Anthony in 1906. But a new, younger generation adopted new strategies; Americans were inspired by the militancy of the British suffrage movement; in 1902 Carrie Chapman Catt was simultaneously president of the International Woman Suffrage Alliance and the National American Woman Suffrage Association. By 1910 it was clear that a reinvigorated movement was underway, using door-to-door campaigns, street-corner speakers, poll watchers on election day. For the first time, cross-class suffrage organizations, like New York's Equality League of Inde-

*Ellen Carol DuBois, "Outgrowing the Compact of the Fathers: Equal Rights, Woman Suffrage, and the United States Constitution 1820–1878," *Journal of American History* 74 (1987):848.

pendent Women, were mobilizing support for suffrage. Suffragists staged public parades that attracted tens of thousands of supporters.

Although many suffragists had claimed that when women got the vote there would be no more war, Catt swung NAWSA behind Woodrow Wilson and American support for the Allies and eventually support for American entry into World War I. In 1918, the House of Representatives passed the suffrage amendment, barely achieving the required two-thirds majority, but despite a personal appearance of President Wilson, it failed by only two votes to carry the Senate. As state after state fell into line, the number of congressmen dependent on women's votes increased; when a federal amendment was proposed in Congress, these men were likely to feel they had no choice but to support it. NAWSA targeted four senators in the fall elections; two of them failed to be re-elected. Energetic campaigns in the states to elect prosuffrage people to Congress worked. When the amendment came up in the new Congress, Anne F. Scott and Andrew Scott report, "224 of those voting yes came from suffrage states, and eighty from nonsuffrage states." It squeaked by in the Senate. It was ratified by thirty-five states by August 1920; after a bitter fight in Tennessee, it was ratified by a single vote, just in time to permit women to vote in the elections of 1920.

When Puerto Rican women attempted to register to vote in 1920, however, the U.S. Bureau of Insular Affairs decided that the Nineteenth Amendment did not automatically apply to U.S. territories. Suffragist groups mobilized in Puerto Rico, lobbying throughout the next decade both on the island and in Washington, D.C., with support from the National Women's Party. In 1929 the territorial legislature granted suffrage to women restricted by a literacy requirement; not until 1935 was universal suffrage established in Puerto Rico.

Many southern states had excluded African-American men from voting by using literacy tests, poll taxes, and intimidation; in those states black women could vote no more easily than black men, and suffrage was an empty victory. The state of Georgia effectively discouraged white women from voting as well by providing that any woman who did not choose to register to vote did not have to pay the poll tax. This law, which encouraged women—and their husbands—to see voting as an expensive extravagance, was upheld by the U.S. Supreme Court in 1937. [*Breedlove* v. *Suttles*, 302 U.S. 277]

Section 1. The right of the citizens of the United States to vote shall not be denied or abridged by the United States or by any State on account of sex.

Section 2. Congress shall have power to enforce this article by appropriate legislation.

Adkins *v.* Children's Hospital, *1923*

Minimum wage legislation was the counterpart to maximum hour laws. In 1918 Congress authorized the Wage Board of the District of Columbia to fix minimum wages for women and children in order to protect them "from conditions detrimental to their health and morals, resulting from wages which are inadequate to maintain decent standards of living."

This act was attacked, much as maximum hour legislation had been, as an interference with the right of the employer and employee to contract freely. Suit was brought against it by a hospital that employed many women at lower than minimum wages. Arguing for the Wage Board and on behalf of the Consumers' League was Felix Frankfurter, who used a Brandeis Brief researched by Molly Dewson that was a thousand pages long. He convinced Justices William Howard Taft and Oliver Wendell Holmes, Jr., that low wages and long hours were linked. In their dissenting opinion they stated that if Congress could regulate one it could regulate the other. Holmes also observed that the phrase "liberty of contract" did not appear in the Constitution.

The majority of the Court was not persuaded, however. The members of the majority distinguished between maximum hours legislation, which they saw as directly allied to health concerns, and minimum wage legislation, which they thought "simply and exclusively a price-fixing law." The majority also observed that the Nineteenth Amendment obviated the need for protective legislation for women. In taking that position, the Justices were endorsing the arguments of Alice Paul and the National Women's Party, who had no faith in protective labor legislation and who were lobbying for an Equal Rights Amendment.

The *Adkins* decision blocked progress in minimum wage legislation for fifteen years, until there was a new president (Franklin D. Roosevelt) and a new approach in Congress. In 1938 the Fair Labor Standards Act established a federal minimum wage for *both* men and women. However, women continued often to be paid less than men for the same jobs. In 1963 the Equal Pay Act prohibited different pay for men and women when their jobs require "equal skill, effort and responsibility and are performed under similar working conditions." The Court has ruled that jobs meriting equal pay must be substantially equal but not necessarily identical: "Dusting is dusting is dusting" said one court in ruling that the pay of maids and janitors must be equal. More recently, the definition of what constitutes "equal skill, effort and responsibility" has been broadened to a public debate over what constitutes "comparable worth."

MR. JUSTICE GEORGE SUTHERLAND DELIVERED THE OPINION OF THE COURT:

... the ancient inequality of the sexes, otherwise than physical, as suggested in the *Muller Case* has continued "with diminishing intensity." In view of the great—not to say revolutionary—changes which have taken place since that utterance, in the contractual, political and civil status of women, culminating in the Nineteenth Amendment, it is not unreasonable to

261 U.S. 525.

say that these differences have now come almost, if not quite, to the vanishing point. . . . we cannot accept the doctrine that women of mature age, . . . require or may be subjected to restrictions upon their liberty of contract which could not lawfully be imposed in the case of men under similar circumstances. To do so would be to ignore all the implications to be drawn from the present day trend of legislation, as well as that of common thought and usage, by which woman is accorded emancipation from the old doctrine that she must be given special protection or be subjected to special restraint in her contractual and civil relationships. . . . . . . What is sufficient to supply the necessary cost of living for a woman worker and maintain her in good health and protect her morals is obviously not a precise or unvarying sum. . . . The amount will depend upon a variety of circumstances: the individual temperament, habits of thrift, care, ability to buy necessaries intelligently, and whether the woman live alone or with her family. . . . It cannot be shown that well paid women safeguard their morals more carefully than those who are poorly paid. Morality rests upon other considerations than wages. . . .

LINDA GORDON

Black and White Visions of Welfare: Women's Welfare Activism, 1890–1945

Linda Gordon's essay is a collective biography of the remarkable generation of women activists. Florence Kelley was one of 145 reformers whose work Gordon analyzes. Gordon's essay reminds us of the power and importance of friendship networks and the special advantages of growing up in politically prominent families in the decades when women were disenfranchised. Gordon's findings also attest to the high professional attainments achieved in an era when many universities and professional programs were closed to women. The ability of the women in her sample to control their fertility at a time when birth control was not widespread is also noteworthy. So, too, are the differences that Gordon discovered between black and white women with respect to welfare issues.

What characteristics emerge from this collective profile? What are the issues about which black and white reformers differed? How are those differences explained? What views did they share? Was either group able to influence policy?

This essay. . . . set[s] up a comparison between black and white women welfare activists. . . . a comparison which serves to alter somewhat our understanding of what welfare is and to bring into better visibility gender and race (and class) influences on welfare thinking. The essay uses two kinds of data: written and oral history records of the thought of these activists, and a rudimentary collective biography of 145 black and white women who were

Excerpted from "Black and White Visions of Welfare: Women's Welfare Activism, 1890–1945" by Linda Gordon in *Journal of American History*, 78(2) (Sept. 1991): 559–590. Reprinted by permission of *Journal of American History*. Notes have been renumbered and edited.

national leaders in campaigns for public welfare between 1890 and 1945. . . . I include
reformers who sought regulatory laws, such
as the Pure Food and Drugs Act, compulsory
education, and anti-child labor regulations. I
do not include reformers who worked mainly
on labor relations, civil rights, women's rights,
or a myriad of other reform issues not centrally
related to welfare. . . . I make no claim to having created a representative sample or an
exhaustive list. . . . To bound my sample, I
included only those who were national leaders—officers of national organizations campaigning for welfare provision or builders of
nationally important institutions, such as hospitals, schools, or asylums. . . . These leaders
were not typical welfare activists; more typical were those who worked exclusively locally,
and their personal profiles might be quite different. But the national leaders had a great deal
of influence on the thinking of other women.
I included only activists prominent after 1890
because it was in the 1890s that such key
national organizations as the National Association of Colored Women began and that white
women welfare activists began a marked
emphasis on *public* provision. . . . I ended in
1945 because after that date, among white
women, there was a marked decline in such
agitation and among blacks a shift in emphasis to civil rights.

I identified sixty-nine black women as
national leaders in welfare reform. Separating
the white from the black women was not my
decision: the networks were almost completely
segregated. First, the national women's organizations were segregated; those that included
blacks, such as the Young Women's Christian
Association (YWCA), had separate white and
black locals. Second, since black women rarely
held government positions, they rarely interacted with white women officially. Third, the
national network of white women reformers
usually excluded black women even when
they could have been included.[1] . . . There
were important counterexamples, interracial
efforts of significant impact, particularly local
ones: in Chicago, for instance, white settlement
and charity workers joined black reformers in
campaigning for public services for dependent
children, establishing the Chicago Urban
League, and responding to the 1919 race riot.
In the South, . . . some white members of this
sample group worked with the Commission of

Interracial Cooperation, forming its Women's
Council, which had 805 country-level groups
by 1929.[2] The national YWCA became a forum
for communication between black and white
women. But these efforts were marked by serious and sometimes crippling white prejudice,
and the core networks of women remained
segregated.

While the black group was created in part
by white racism, it was also created from the
inside, so to speak, by personal friendships.
Often these relationships were born in schools
and colleges and continued thereafter,
strengthened by the development of black
sororities after 1908. The creation of national
organizations and networks extended relationships and ideas among these black women
leaders across regional boundaries. For example, the Phillis Wheatley Home for the protection of single black urban women, established
by Jane Hunter in Cleveland in 1911, spurred
the opening of similar homes in Denver, Atlanta, Seattle, Boston, Detroit, Chicago, Green-
ville, Winston-Salem, Toledo, and Minneapolis
by 1934. Mutual support was strong. . . . Friendships could be intense, despite distance; black
women early in the twentieth century, like
white women, sometimes spoke openly of their
strong emotional bonds.

The black women's network was made
more coherent by its members' common
experience as educators and builders of educational institutions. Education was the single
most important area of activism for black
women. The majority of women in this sample taught at one time or another, and 38 percent were educators by profession. For many,
reform activism centered around establishing
schools, from kindergartens through colleges,
such as Nannie Burroughs's National Training School for Women and Girls in Washington, D.C., or Lucy Laney's Haines Institute in
Augusta, Georgia, or Arenia Mallory's Saints
Industrial and Literary Training School in
Mississippi. In his 1907 report on economic
cooperation among Negro Americans, for
example, W. E. B. Du Bois counted 151
church-connected and 161 nonsectarian private Negro schools. Although he did not discuss the labor of founding and maintaining
these institutions, we can guess that women
contributed disproportionately.[3] . . .

The cause second to education was health.
Black hospitals, while primarily initiated by

black and white men, depended on crucial support from black women. Between 1890 and 1930, African Americans created approximately 200 hospitals and nurse-training schools, and women often took charge of the community organizing and fund-raising labor. . . . Many women's clubs made health work their priority. The Washington, D.C., Colored YWCA built a program around visiting the sick. The Indianapolis Woman's Improvement Club focused on tuberculosis, attempting to make up for the denial of service to blacks by the Indianapolis board of health, the city hospital, and the Marion County tuberculosis society. . . . Possibly the most extraordinary individual in black women's public health work was Modjeska Simkins, who used her position as director of Negro work for the anti-tuberculosis association of South Carolina to inaugurate a program dealing with the entire range of black health problems, including maternal and infant mortality, venereal disease (VD), and malnutrition as well as tuberculosis. Perhaps the most ingenious women's program was Alpha Kappa Alpha's Mississippi Health Project. These black sorority women brought health care to sharecroppers in Holmes County, Mississippi, for several weeks every summer from 1935 to 1942. Unable to rent space for a clinic because of plantation owners' opposition, they turned cars into mobile health vans, immunizing over 15,000 children and providing services such as dentistry and treatment for malaria and VD to 2,500–4,000 people each summer.[4]

These reformers were united also through their churches, which were centers of networking and of activism, in the North as well as the South. . . . The YWCA also drew many of these women together. Victoria Matthews's White Rose Mission influenced the YWCA, through its leader Grace Dodge, to bring black women onto its staff, which experience groomed many black women leaders.

And despite the fact that these were national leaders, they shared a regional experience. At least 57 percent were born in the South. More important, perhaps, two-thirds of these migrated to the northeast, midwest, and mid-Atlantic regions, thus literally spreading their network as they fled Jim Crow and sought wider opportunity.[5]

Most members of this network were married—85 percent. More than half of the married

women had prominent men as spouses, and their marriages sometimes promoted their leadership positions. Lugenia Burns Hope was the wife of John Hope, first black president of Atlanta University. . . . George Edmund Haynes, husband of Elizabeth, was a Columbia Ph.D., a professor at Fisk, an assistant to the secretary of labor from 1918 to 1921, and a founder of the Urban League. George Ruffin, husband of Josephine, was a Harvard Law graduate, a member of the Boston City Council, and Boston's first black judge. Most of the women, however, had been activists before marriage, and many led lives quite independent of their husbands. (Of these married women, 20 percent were widowed, divorced, or separated.)

Their fertility pattern was probably related to their independence. Of the whole group, 43 percent had no children; and of the married women, 34 percent had no children (there were no unmarried mothers).[6] (In comparison, 31 percent of the white married women in this sample were childless.) It thus seems likely that these women welfare activists used birth control, although long physical separations from their husbands may have contributed to their low fertility.[7] In their contraceptive practices these women may have been as modern as contemporary white women of comparable class position.

For most African-American women a major reason for being in the public sphere after marriage was employment, due to economic necessity; but for this group of women, economic need was not a driving pressure. A remarkable number had prosperous parents.[8] Crystal Fauset's father, although born a slave, was principal of a black academy in Maryland. Elizabeth Ross Haynes's father went from slavery to ownership of a fifteen hundred-acre plantation. Addie Hunton's father was a substantial businessman and founder of the Negro Elks. Mary Church Terrell's mother and father were successful in business. Most black women in the sample had husbands who could support them; 51 percent of the married women had high-professional husbands—lawyers, physicians, ministers, educators. The women of this network were also often very class-conscious, and many of the clubs that built their collective identity were exclusive, such as the sororities, the Chautauqua Circle, and the Twelve in Atlanta. The fact that about

40 percent were born outside the South provides further evidence of their high status, since the evidence suggests that the earlier northward migrants were the more upwardly mobile.[9] In all these respects, this group probably differed from typical local activists, who were less privileged. Yet even among this elite group only a tiny minority—12 percent—were not employed.[10] To be sure, this economic privilege was only relative to the whole black population; on average, the black women's network was less wealthy than the white women's. Even those who were born to middle-class status were usually newly middle-class, perhaps a generation away from slavery and without much cushion against economic misfortune. . . .

The black women's national network was made more homogeneous by educational attainment, high social status, and a sense of superiority to the masses that brought with it obligations of service. Of the black women, 83 percent had a higher education, comparable to the proportion of white women, and 35 percent had attended graduate school. These figures may surprise those unfamiliar with the high professional achievement patterns of black women between 1890 and 1945. The full meaning of the statistics emerges when one compares them with the average educational opportunities for blacks in the United States at this time. In the earliest year for which we have figures, 1940, only 1 percent of Afro-Americans, male and female, had four or more years of college. Moreover, only 41 percent of the women in this sample attended black colleges, whereas those colleges conferred 86 percent of all black undergraduate degrees in the period from 1914 to 1936.[11] Several women in this sample who were born into the middle class described learning for the first time in adulthood of the conditions of poverty in which most African Americans lived—an ignorance characteristic of prosperous whites but rarer among blacks. As Alfreda Duster, Ida Wells-Barnett's daughter, recalled, "It was difficult for me to really empathize with people who had come from nothing, where they had lived in cottages, huts in the South, with no floor and no windows and had suffered the consequences of the discrimination and the hardships of the South."[12] . . . [But] the high social status and prosperity common in this group should not lead us to forget the discrimination

and humiliation that they faced. Their high levels of skills and education were frustrated by lack of career opportunity. Sadie Alexander, from one of the most prominent black families in the United States, was the first black woman to get a Ph.D. degree from the University of Pennsylvania. But she could not get an appropriate job because of her color and was forced to work as an assistant actuary for a black insurance company. . . .

Moreover, this black activism was born in an era of radically worsening conditions for most Afro-American women, in contrast to the improving conditions for white women. The older women in this network had felt segregation intensify in their adult lifetimes; there was widespread immiseration and denial of what political power they had accumulated after the emancipation. In the 1920s the second Ku Klux Klan attracted as many as six million members. These experiences, so rarely understood by whites, further reinforced the bonds uniting black women and influenced their welfare visions.

The seventy-six white women, like the blacks, constituted a coherent network. Most of them knew each other, and their compatibility was cemented by a homogeneous class, religious, and ethnic base. Most had prosperous, many even prominent parents; virtually all were of north European, Protestant backgrounds, from the Northeast or Midwest. The nine Jewish members were hardly representative of Jewish immigrants: five had wealthy German-Jewish parents (Elizabeth Brandeis Raushenbush, Hannah Einstein, Josephine and Pauline Goldmark, and Lillian Wald). There were three Catholics (Josephine Brown, Jane Hoey, and Agnes Regan), but they were hardly typical of Catholics in the United States in the period: they were all native-born of prosperous parents. The shared Protestantism of the others was more a sign of similar ethnic background than of avid religious commitment, for few were churchgoers or intense believers, and churches did not organize their welfare activities.

The great majority (86 percent) were college-educated, and 66 percent attended graduate school. By contrast, in 1920 fewer than 1 percent of all American women held college degrees. It is worth recalling, however, that 83 percent of the black women were college-educated, and their disproportion to the black population as a whole was even greater. The white women had attended more expensive, elite schools; 37 percent had graduated from one of the New England women's colleges.

The white women had even more occupational commonality than the blacks. The great majority were social workers.[13] To understand this correctly we must appreciate the changing historical meanings of social work. Prior to the Progressive Era, the term did not refer to a profession but to a range of helping and reform activity; the word social originally emphasized the reform, rather than the charity, component. Here it is relevant that many had mothers active in social reform.... By contrast to the Afro-American women, very few were educators, a pattern that suggests that creating new educational institutions was no longer a reform priority for white women and that other professional jobs, especially governmental, were open to them.[14]

The whites had at least as much geographical togetherness as the black women. Sixty-eight percent worked primarily in the New England and mid-Atlantic states—hardly surprising since the national headquarters of the organizations they worked for were usually located there. Moreover, 57 percent had worked in New York City during the Progressive Era or the 1920s. New York City played a vanguard role in the development of public services and regulation in the public interest, and women in the network were influential in that city's welfare programs. New York City settlement houses specialized in demonstration projects, beginning programs on a small, private scale and then getting them publicly funded. The settlements initiated vocational guidance programs, later adopted by the public schools; they initiated use of public schools for after-hours recreation programs and public health nursing. Lillian Wald, head of the Henry Street Settlement, coordinated the city's response to the 1919 influenza epidemic. The settlements lobbied for municipal legislation regulating tenements and landlord-tenant relations and milk purity and prices. In 1917 the Women's City Club of New York City opened a Maternity Center in Hell's Kitchen, where they provided prenatal nursing care and education and housekeeping services for new mothers. Expanded to ten locations in Manhattan, this effort served as a model for the bill that eventually became the Sheppard-Towner Act. The Women's City Club provided an important meeting place for many of these women, and it can serve as an indicator of their prosperity: members had to pay substantial dues and an initiation fee, and the club purchased a mansion on Thirty-fifth Street and Park Avenue for $160,000 in 1917.[15]

Some of these white women had been active in party politics even before they had the vote. Some had been in the Socialist party, and many were active in the 1912 Progressive party campaign. Most, however, preferred nonpartisan public activism. During the late 1920s and 1930s they became more active in political parties and transferred their allegiances to the Democratic party. Here too New York was important, because the political figure who most attracted these women to the Democrats was Franklin D. Roosevelt, in his governorship and then his presidency. Several women who had been active in reform in the city, notably Belle Moskowitz, Rose Schneiderman, and Eleanor Roosevelt, took on statewide roles....

The black network also underwent a political realignment from Republican to Democratic, but with different meanings, largely associated with migration northward, because the southern Democratic party was essentially closed to blacks. Ironically, this transition was also in part effectuated by Eleanor Roosevelt, who became the symbol of those few white political leaders willing to take stands on racial equality. Nevertheless Eleanor Roosevelt did not create an integrated network, nor was she able to swing the white network to support the leading black demand during the Roosevelt administration: a federal antilynching law.

Women in both networks taught, mentored, even self-consciously trained each other. Among blacks this occurred in colleges, in white-run organizations such as the YWCAs, and in black organizations such as sororities, the National Association of Colored Women (NACW), and many local groups. A higher proportion of the white than of the black women worked in settlement houses—probably partly because so many of the white women were single. That experience strongly encouraged intergenerational connections and intimacy, because the younger or newer volunteers actually lived with their elders, seeing them in action. In the civic organizations, leaders groomed, protected, and promoted their protégés: Jane Addams did this with Alice Hamilton, Lillian Wald, and Florence Kelley; Sophonisba Breckinridge launched her student Grace Abbott's career by placing her at the head of the newly formed Immigrants' Protective League; the whole network campaigned for Abbott and then for Frances Perkins to become secretary of labor.[16] Such involvements continued when network members became federal or state officials, with other members as their employees. . . .

It is quite possible that black women's personal and professional support networks were just as strong; there is less evidence because, as several historians of African-American women have suggested, black women left fewer private papers than did white. Given this caveat, the white women's network does appear to differ in one measure of mutual dependence. The great majority of the white women were single—only 34 percent had ever been married, and only 18 percent remained married during their peak political activity (42 percent of those who ever married were divorced, separated, or widowed). Only 28 percent had children. In this respect they are probably quite different from many local welfare activists, a group that included less elite and more married women. Moreover, 28 percent were in relationships with other women that might have been called "Boston marriages" a few decades before.[17] (My figure is a conservative one since I counted only those women for whom I could identify a specific partner. It does not include such women as Edith Rockwood who lived until her death in 1953 with Marjorie Heseltine of the Children's Bureau and Louise Griffith of the Social Security Agency and who built and owned a summer house jointly with Marion Crane of the Children's Bureau.[18]) At the time these relationships were mainly not named at all, although Mary ("Molly") Dewson referred to her mate as "partner." Contemporaries usually perceived them as celibate.[19] Today some of these women might be called lesbian, but there is much controversy among historians as to whether it is ahistorical to apply the word to that generation, a controversy I wish to avoid here since it is not relevant to my argument. What is relevant is not their sexual activity but their dependence on other women economically, for jobs; for care in grief, illness, and old age; for vacation companionship; for every

conceivable kind of help. Despite their singleness, their efforts were very much directed to family and child welfare. It is remarkable to contemplate that so many women who became symbols of matronly respectability and asexual "social motherhood" led such unconventional private lives.

Moreover, they turned this mutual dependency into a political caucus. . . . The women's female bonding did not disadvantage them but brought them political power, and they got it without making the sacrifices of personal intimacy that men so often did. Privileged women that they were, several of them had country homes, and groups would often weekend together; we can be sure that their conversation erased distinctions between the personal and the political, between gossip and tactics.

In truth we do not know how different these white women's relationships were from black women's. Many black married women, such as Bethune and Charlotte Hawkins Brown, lived apart from their husbands (but so did several white women counted here as married, such as Perkins); and a few black women, such as Dean Lucy Slowe of Howard, lived in Boston marriages. Many blacks in this sample spoke critically not only of men but of marriage and feared its potential to demobilize women. Dorothy Height lamented that the "over-emphasis on marriage has destroyed so many people."[20]

Both white and black women, if single, experienced a sense of betrayal when a friend married; and both, if about to marry, feared telling their single comrades.[21] In time, particularly from the 1930s on, the white women's sense that marriage and activity in the public sphere were incompatible choices diminished, and more married activists appeared.[22] This change, however, only makes it the more evident that throughout the period, black women had greater willingness, necessity, or ability to combine marriage and public activism, through coping strategies that may have included informal marital separations.

The white women's friendship network was particularly visible among the most prominent women because they took it with them to their prominent and well-documented jobs. Their friendships transcended boundaries between the public and private sectors, between government and civic organization. . . .

The powerful settlement houses, Hull House and the Henry Street Settlement, for example, became virtually a part of municipal government and were able to command the use of tax money when necessary. When women gained governmental positions, there was as much extraagency as intraagency consultation and direction. In its first project, collecting data on infant mortality, the Children's Bureau used hundred of volunteers from this organizational network to help. In 1920, Florence Kelley of the National Consumers' League (NCL) listed investigations the Women's Bureau should undertake, and these were done. Mary Anderson of the Women's Bureau arranged for the NCL to draft a bill for protection of female employees for the state of Indiana, and Anderson herself wrote comments on the draft. . . .

Singleness did not keep these women from useful connections with men, however. These connections came with kinship and class, if not with marriage. Clara Beyer got her "in" to the network because Felix Frankfurter recommended her to administer the 1918 District of Columbia minimum wage law. She then brought in Elizabeth Brandeis, the daughter of Louis Brandeis, to share the job with her. Brandeis's two sisters-in-law, Josephine and Pauline Goldmark, were also active in this network. Sophonisba Breckinridge, Florence Kelley, Julia Lathrop, and Katherine Lenroot were daughters of senators or congressmen. Loula Dunn's father and two grandfathers had been in the Alabama legislature. . . . These women often learned politics in their households and knew where to get introductions and referrals to politically influential people when they needed them. When Beyer said, "It was my contacts that made [me] so valuable, that I could go to these people," she was speaking about both her women's network and her male connections.[23]

With these group characteristics in mind, I want to examine the welfare ideas of these two networks.

One major difference in the orientation of the two groups was that the whites, well into the Great Depression, more strongly saw themselves as helping others—people who were "other" not only socially but often also ethnically and religiously. The perspective of the white network had been affected particularly by large-scale immigration, the reconsti-

tution of the urban working class by people of non-WASP origin, and residential segregation, which grouped the immigrants in ghettos not often seen by the white middle class. Much has been written about the arrogance and condescension these privileged social workers showed their immigrant clients. Little has been done to discover the impact of the immigrant population on the reformers' own ideas. The black/white comparison suggests that ethnic difference between the white poor and white reformers not only discouraged identification but also slowed the reformers' development of a structural understanding of the origins of poverty, as opposed to one that blamed individual character defects, however environmentally caused. Thus into the 1940s, the great majority of the white women in this sample supported welfare programs that were not only means-tested but also "morals-tested," continuing a distinction between the worthy and the unworthy poor. They believed that aid should always be accompanied by expert supervision and rehabilitation so as to inculcate into the poor work habits and morals that they so often (or so the reformers believed) lacked. (And, one might add, they did not mind the fact that this set up a sexual double standard in which women aid recipients would be treated differently and more severely than men recipients.)[24]

In comparison, black women were more focused on their own kind. Despite the *relative* privilege of most of them, and there was criticism from blacks of the snobbery of some of these network members, there was less distance between helper and helped than among white reformers. There was less chronological distance, for all their privileges were so recent and so tenuous. There was less geographical distance, for residential segregation did not allow the black middle class much insulation from the black poor. Concentrating their efforts more on education and health, and proportionally less on charity or relief, meant that they dealt more often with universal needs than with those of the particularly unfortunate and sought to provide universal, not means-tested, services.

These were differences of degree, [however,] and should not be overstated. Most of the white women in this sample favored environmental analyses of the sources of poverty. Many black women's groups engaged in classic charity activity. . . . Black leaders shared with white ones the conviction that the poor needed training, to develop not only skills but also moral and spiritual capacities. Mary Church Terrell could sound remarkably like a white clubwoman.

> To our poor, benighted sisters in the Black Belt of Alabama we have gone and we have been both a comfort and a help to these women, through the darkness of whose ignorance of everything that makes life sweet or worth the living, no ray of light would have penetrated but for us.[25]

Like the Progressive Era white female reformers, the blacks emphasized the need to improve the sexual morals of their people. Fannie Barrier William declared that the colored people's greatest need was a better and purer home life—that slavery had destroyed home ties, the sanctity of marriage, and the instincts of motherhood.[26]

Concern for sexual respectability by no means represented one class or stratum imposing its values on another; for black as for white women it grew also from a feminist, or womanist, desire to protect women from exploitation, a desire shared across class lines. But this priority had profoundly different meanings for black women reformers. Not only were black women more severely sexually victimized, but combatting sexual exploitation was for blacks inseparable from race uplift in general, as white sexual assaults against black women had long been a fundamental part of slavery and racial oppression. Indeed, black activists were far in advance of white feminists in their campaigns against rape and their identification of that crime as part of a system of power relations, and they did not assume that only *white* men were sexual aggressors. The historian Darlene Clark Hine suggests that efforts to build recreational programs for boys also reflected women's strategies for protecting girls from assault. . . . Many of the earliest black urban institutions were homes designed to protect working women. . . . The problem of sex exploitation could not be removed from intrarace class differences that left some black women much more vulnerable than others, not only to assault but also to having their reputations smeared; black, like white, women defined their middle-class status in part by their sexual respectability. But their sexual

protection efforts were so connected to uplift for the whole race, without which the reformers could not enjoy any class privileges, that the victim blaming was a smaller part of their message than among whites.[27]

. . . Black women reformers could not easily separate their welfare from their civil rights agitation.[28] As Deborah White puts it. "The race problem . . . inherently included the problems of poverty."[29] Race uplift work was usually welfare work by definition, and it was always conceived as a path to racial equality. And black poverty could not be ameliorated without challenges to white domination. . . .

The greater emphasis on civil rights [however] never eclipsed uplift strategies. From the New Deal on, black government leaders were simultaneously trying to get more black women hired, protesting the passing over of qualified black applicants, and working to improve the qualifications and performance of black individuals. In 1943 Corinne Robinson of the Federal Public Housing Authority organized a skit, entitled *Lazy Daisy*, which called upon black government workers to shed slothful habits.[30] . . . To repeat: there was for these women no inherent contradiction between race uplift and antidiscrimination thinking.[31]

These black welfare activists were also militant in their critique of male supremacy, that militance, too, arising from their work for the welfare of the race. . . . Charlotte Hawkins Brown declared her own work and thoughts were just as important as Booker T. Washington's.[32] Moreover, their ambitions were just as great as those of the white women: Afro-Americans spoke of uplifting their race; white women described themselves as promoting the general welfare, but only because their focus on their own race was silent and understood. Whether or not these women should be called feminists (and they certainly did not call themselves that), they shared characteristics of the white group that has been called "social feminists"; their activism arose from efforts to advance the welfare of the whole public, not just women, in a context where, they believed, men did not or could not adequately meet the needs.

Black and white women welfare reformers also differed in their thinking about women's economic role. The white women, with few exceptions, tended to view married women's economic dependence on men as desirable, and their employment as a misfortune; they accepted the family wage system and rarely expressed doubts about its effectiveness, let alone its justice. There was substantial variation within this network and change over time in its members' views of the family wage. There was also substantial contradiction. Beginning in the 1890s, women social investigators repeatedly demonstrated that the family wage did not work, because most men did not earn enough, because some men became disabled, and because others were irresponsible toward their families. Sybil Lipschultz has shown that between two key Supreme Court briefs written by women in the white network—for *Muller* v. *Oregon* in 1908, and for *Adkins* v. *Children's Hospital* in 1923—the grounds for protective legislation changed considerably. The brief for *Muller* privileged sacred motherhood and treated women's wage labor as an anomaly that should be prevented; the brief for *Adkins* argued from women's weaker position in the labor market and the need for government to intervene because it was not an anomaly. Yet when the women's welfare network moved away from protective labor legislation toward public assistance or family policy, its recommendations presupposed that the desirable position for women was as domestic wives and mothers dependent on male earnings. The many unmarried women in the network viewed their own singleness as a class privilege and a natural condition for women active in the public sphere and felt that remaining childless was an acceptable price for it. They were convinced that single motherhood and employment among mothers meant danger. They feared relief to single mothers offered without counseling or employment offered to mothers other than temporarily, because they resisted establishing single-mother families as durable institutions.[33] They did not share the belief of many contemporary European socialists that aid to single mothers should be a matter of right, of entitlement. . . .

The U.S. supporters of mothers' pensions envisioned aid as a gift to the deserving and felt an unshakable responsibility to supervise single mothers and restore marriages and wives' dependency on husbands whenever possible. This "white" view was clearly a class perspective as well. A troubling question is unavoidable: Did these elite white women

believe that independence was a privilege of wealth to which poor women ought not aspire?

The black women reformers also held up breadwinner husbands and nonemployed wives as an ideal; black and white women spoke very similarly about the appropriate "spheres" of the two sexes, equally emphasizing motherhood.[34] The difference I am describing here is not diametric. Lucy D. Slowe, dean of women at Howard, believed that working mothers caused urban juvenile delinquency, and she called for campaigns to "build up public sentiment for paying heads of families wages sufficient to reduce the number of Negro women who must be employed away from home to the detriment of their children and of the community in general."[35]

[Yet] acceptance of married women's employment as a long-term and widespread necessity was much greater among blacks than among whites. Fanny Jackson Coppin had argued in the 1860s for women's economic independence from men, and women were active in creating employment bureaus. We see the greater black acknowledgment of single mothers in the high priority black women reformers gave to organizing kindergartens, then usually called day nurseries. . . .

In poor urban white neighborhoods the need for child care may have been nearly as great, and some white activists created kindergartens, but proportionally far fewer. Virtually no northern white welfare reformers endorsed such programs as long-term or permanent services until the 1930s and 1940s; until then even the most progressive, such as Kelley, opposed them even as temporary solutions, fearing they would encourage the exploitation of women through low-wage labor.[36]

Black women decried the effects of the "double day" on poor women as much as did white reformers. They were outspoken in their criticism of men who failed to support families. Burroughs wrote, "Black men sing too much 'I Can't Give You Anything But Love, Baby.'"[37] But their solutions were different. From the beginning of her career, Burroughs understood that the great majority of black women would work all their lives, and she had to struggle against continuing resistance to accepting that fact to get her National Training School funded. And most black women activists projected a favorable view of working women and women's professional aspirations. . . . This high regard for women's economic independence is also reflected in the important and prestigious role played by businesswomen in black welfare activity. One of the best-known and most revered women of this network was Maggie Lena Walker, the first woman bank president in the United States. Beginning work at age fourteen in the Independent Order of St. Luke, a mutual benefit society in Richmond, Virginia, that provided illness and burial insurance as well as social activity for blacks, in 1903 she established the St. Luke Penny Savings Bank. Walker became a very wealthy woman. She devoted a great deal of her money and her energy to welfare activity, working in the National Association for the Advancement of Colored People (NAACP), the National Association of Wage Earners, and local Richmond groups. . . .

These factors suggest considerable differences in orientation (among the numerous similarities) between white and black women activists. . . . First, black women claimed leadership in looking after the welfare of their whole people more than did comparable whites. Because of this assumption of race responsibility, and because for blacks welfare was so indistinguishable from equal rights, black women emphasized programs for the unusually needy less, and universal provision more, than did white women. Perhaps in part because education was so important a part of the black women's program, and because education developed for whites in the United States as a universal public service, blacks' vision of welfare provision followed that model. Among whites, a relatively large middle class encouraged reformers to focus their helping efforts on others and kept alive and relatively uncriticized the use of means and morals testing as a way of distributing help, continuing the division of the "deserving" from the "undeserving" poor. Among the black reformers, despite their relatively elite position, welfare appeared more closely connected with legal entitlements, not so different from the right to vote or to ride the public transportation system. Had their ideas been integrated into the white women's thinking, one might ask, would means testing and humiliating invasions of privacy have been so uniformly accepted in programs such as Aid to Families with Dependent Children (AFDC),

over which the white women's network had substantial influence?

Another difference is the black women's different attitude toward married women's employment. Most of the white women welfare reformers retained, until World War II, a distinctly head-in-the-sand and even somewhat contradictory attitude toward it: it was a misfortune, not good for women, children, or men; helping working mothers too much would tend to encourage it. Thus they were more concerned to help—sometimes to force—single mothers to stay home than to provide services that would help working mothers, such as child care or maternity leave. Black women were much more positive about women's employment. Despite their agreement that a male family wage was the most desirable arrangement, they doubted that married women's employment would soon disappear or that it could be discouraged by making women and children suffer for it. In relation to this race difference, it is hard to ignore the different marital status of the majority of the women in the two groups: Most of the black women had themselves had the experience of combining public-sphere activism with marriage, if less often with children.[38] Perhaps the fact that most of the white women had dispensed with marriage and family, probably largely by choice, made them see the choice between family and work as an acceptable one, oblivious to the different conditions of such "choice" among poorer women.

Third, black and white welfare reformers differed considerably about how to protect women from sexual exploitation. Black welfare reformers were more concerned to combine the development of protective institutions for women with an antirape discourse. Among whites, rape was not an important topic of discussion during this period, and in protective work for women and girls, male sexuality was treated as natural and irrepressible. It is not clear how the black activists would have translated antirape consciousness into welfare policy, had they had the power to do so, but it seems likely that they would have tried.

There were also substantial areas of shared emphases between white and black women. Both groups oriented much of their welfarist thinking to children, rarely questioning the unique responsibility of women for children's welfare. Neither group questioned sexual "purity" as an appropriate goal for unmarried women. Both groups used women's organizations as their main political and social channels. Both emphasized the promotion of other women into positions of leadership and jobs, confident that increasing the numbers of women at the "top" would benefit the public welfare. Both believed that improving the status of women was essential to advancing the community as a whole. At the same time, both groups, in the 1920s, were moving away from explicitly feminist discourse and muting their public criticisms of what we would today call sexism. Moreover they shared many personal characteristics: low fertility, relatively high economic and social status, very high educational attainment.

The white women's reform network—but not the black—had some influence on welfare policy, particularly in public assistance programs. . . . This influence was as much colored by race as by gender. The white women's influence supported the legacies in our welfare programs of means testing, distinguishing the deserving from the undeserving, moral supervision of female welfare recipients, failing to criticize men's sexual behavior, and discouraging women's employment. Black women's influence on federal welfare programs was negligible in this period; indeed, the leading federal programs—old-age insurance, unemployment compensation, workmen's compensation, and the various forms of public assistance such as AFDC—were expressly constructed to exclude blacks. It is not too late now, however, to benefit from a review of black women's welfare thought as we reconsider the kind of welfare state we want.

NOTES

1. Of the 69 black women, 5 held governmental positions: By contrast, 53% of the white women held federal government positions and 58% held state positions. The full list appears in *The Journal of American History*, 78 (1991) pp. 589–90.
2. Steven J. Diner, "Chicago Social Workers and Blacks in the Progressive Era," *Social Service Review*, 44 (Dec. 1970), 393–410; Jacquelyn Dowd Hall, *Revolt against Chivalry: Jessie Daniel Ames and the Women's Campaign against Lynching* (New York, 1979), 66.
3. W. E. B. Du Bois, ed., *Economic Cooperation among Negro Americans* (Atlanta, 1907), 80–88.
4. Modjeska Simkins's work is briefly summarized in Edward H. Beardsley, *A History of Neglect: Health Care for Blacks and Mill Workers in the Twentieth Century South* (Knoxville, 1987), 108–12. Susan L.

Smith, "The Black Women's Club Movement: Self-Improvement and Sisterhood, 1890–1915" (M.A. thesis, University of Wisconsin, Madison, 1986); Susan L. Smith, "Black Activism in Health Care, 1890–1950," paper delivered at the conference "Black Health: Historical Perspectives and Current Issues," University of Wisconsin, Madison, April 1990 (in Gordon's possession).
5. I could not identify birthplaces for all the women, and those with missing information include some likely to have been southern-born.
6. In the black population in general, 7% of all married women born 1840–1859 were childless, and 28% of those born 1900–1919 were childless. U.S. Department of Commerce, Bureau of the Census, *Historical Statistics of the United States: Colonial Times to 1970* (2 vols., Washington, 1975), I, 53.
7. Supporting my view of black women's use of birth control, see Jessie M. Rodrique, "The Black Community and the Birth-Control Movement," in *Passion and Power: Sexuality in History*, ed. Kathy Peiss and Christina Simmons (Philadelphia, 1989), 138–54.
8. I was able to identify 25% (17) with prosperous parents.
9. Anna Arnold Hedgeman, *The Trumpet Sounds: A Memoir of Negro Leadership* (New York, 1964), 25, 74.
10. For corroboration on the employment of well-to-do black women, see Roth, "Matronage," 180–81.
11. Charles S. Johnson, *The Negro College Graduate* (Chapel Hill, 1938), 18–20; U.S. Department of Commerce, Bureau of the Census, *The Social and Economic Status of the Black Population in the United States: An Historical View, 1790–1978* (Washington, 1979), 93.
12. Alfreda Duster interview by Greenlee, March 8–9, 1978, transcript, p. 9, Black Women Oral History Project; Hedgeman, *Trumpet Sounds*, 3–28.
13. Of the white women reformers, 78% had been social workers at some time; 68% had social work as their major reform area. I checked to see if the social work background could have been a characteristic of the less prominent women, but this was not the case. The most prominent two-thirds of the group were even more frequently social workers (84%).
14. Of the white women, 18% had held academic jobs at one time; 9% were mainly employed as educators. For only 1% was education their major reform area.
15. Lillian Wald, *Windows on Henry Street* (Boston, 1934); Mary Kingsbury Simkhovitch, *Neighborhood: My Story of Greenwich House* (New York, 1938); William W. Bremer, *Depression Winters: New York Social Workers and the New Deal* (Philadelphia, 1984); George Martin, *Madame Secretary: Frances Perkins* (Boston, 1976), 134–35; Elisabeth Israels Perry, "Training for Public Life: ER and Women's Political Networks in the 1920s," in *Without Precedent: The Life and Career of Eleanor Roosevelt*, ed. Joan Hoff-Wilson and Marjorie Lightman (Bloomington, 1984), 30.
16. On settlement house relationships, see Virginia Kemp Fish, "The Hull House Circle: Women's Friendships and Achievements," in *Gender, Ideology, and Action: Historical Perspectives on Women's Public Lives*, ed. Janet Sharistanian (Westport, 1986); and Kathryn Kish Sklar, "Hull House in the 1890s: A

Community of Women Reformers," *Signs*, 10 (Summer 1985), 658–77. Lela B. Costin, *Two Sisters for Social Justice: A Biography of Grace and Edith Abbott* (Urbana, 1983), 38–40; Martin, *Madame Secretary*, 233.

17. The singleness of the white women reformers was characteristic of other women of their race, class, and education in this period. In 1890, for example, over half of all women doctors were single. Of women earning Ph.D.'s between 1877 and 1924, three-fourths remained single. As late as 1920, only 12% of all professional women were married. See, for example, Carl N. Degler, *At Odds: Women and the Family in America from the Revolution to the Present* (New York, 1980), 385.

18. Mrs. Tilden Frank Phillips, memoir, Feb. 22, Feb. 26, 1953, folder 22, Edith Rockwood Papers (Schlesinges Library); will of Edith Rockwood, folder 20, ibid.

19. Blanche Wiesen Cook, "The Historical Denial of Lesbianism," *Radical History Review*, 20 (Spring/Summer 1979), 60–65.

20. Slowe lived with Mary Burrill, who is treated as a partner in letters to and from Slowe and in letters of condolence to Burrill after Slowe's death in 1937. See letters in box 90-1, Slowe Papers. Height interview, 52.

21. Duster interview, 11; Wendy Beth Posner, "Charlotte Towle: A Biography" (Ph.D. diss., University of Chicago School of Social Service Administration, 1986), 47, 77–78.

22. Mary Dewson to Clara Beyer, Oct. 12, 1931, folder 40, box 2, Clara Beyer Papers (Schlesinger Library); Ware interview, 40–42; Janice Andrews, "Role of Female Social Workers in the Second Generation: Leaders or Followers," 1989 (in Gordon's possession).

23. Vivien Hart, "Watch What We Do: Women Administrators and the Implementation of Minimum Wage Policy, Washington, D.C., 1918–1923," paper delivered at the Berkshire Conference on the History of Women, 1990, p. 31 (in Gordon's possession).

24. Linda Gordon, "What Does Welfare Regulate?" *Social Research*, 55 (Winter 1988), 609–30; Barbara Nelson, "The Origins of the Two-Channel Welfare State: Workmen's Compensation and Mothers' Aid," in *Women, the State, and Welfare*, ed. Linda Gordon, 123–57.

25. Mary Church Terrell, "Club Work among Women," *New York Age*, Jan. 4, 1900, p. 1.

26. Fannie Barrier Williams, "Opportunities and Responsibilities of Colored Women," in *Afro-American Encyclopaedia; or the Thoughts, Doings, and Sayings of the Race*, ed. James T. Haley (Nashville, 1896), 150.

27. White reformers' rhetoric about protecting women named prostitution, not rape, as the problem. See Ellen DuBois and Linda Gordon, "Seeking Ecstasy on the Battlefield: Nineteenth-Century Feminist Views of Sexuality," *Feminist Studies*, 9 (Spring 1993), 7–25; Lillian Wald, "The Immigrant Young Girl," in *Proceedings of the National Conference of Charities and Correction at the Thirty-sixth Annual Session Held in the City of Buffalo, N.Y., June 9th to 16th, 1909* (Fort Wayne, n.d), 264; Jane Edna Hunter, *A Nickel and a Prayer* (Cleveland, 1940); Marilyn Dell Brady, "Organizing Afro-American Girls' Clubs in Kansas in the 1920s," *Frontiers*, 9 (no. 2, 1987), 69–73; Debo-

rah Gray White, "Fettered Sisterhood: Class and Classism in Early Twentieth Century Black Women's History," paper delivered at the annual meeting of the American Studies Association, Toronto, Nov. 1989 (in Gordon's possession); Darlene Clark Hine, "Rape and the Inner Lives of Black Women in the Middle West: Preliminary Thoughts on the Culture of Dissemblance," *Signs*, 14 (Summer 1989), 912–20; Constance M. Greene, *The Secret City: A History of Peace Relations in the Nation's Capital* (Princeton, 1967), 144–46; Dorothy Salem, *To Better Our World: Black Women in Organized Reform, 1890–1920* (Brooklyn, 1990), 44–46; Anne Firor Scott, "Most Invisible of All: Black Women's Voluntary Associations," *Journal of Southern History*, 56 (February 1990), 15; Monroe M. Work, "Problems of Negro Urban Welfare," (from *Southern Workman*, Jan. 1924) in *Black Heritage in Social Welfare*, ed. Edyth L. Ross, 383–84; Darlene Clark Hine, "'We Specialize in the Wholly Impossible': The Philanthropic Work of Black Women," in *Lady Bountiful Revisited: Women, Philanthropy, and Power*, ed. Kathleen D. McCarthy (New Brunswick, 1990), 73.

28. Evelyn Brooks, "Religion, Politics, and Gender: The Leadership of Nannie Helen Burroughs," *Journal of Religious Thought*, 44 (Winter/Spring 1988), 7–22; Cheryl Townsend Gilkes, "Building in Many Places: Multiple Commitments and Ideologies in Black Women's Community Work," in *Women and the Politics of Empowerment*, ed. Ann Bookman and Sandra Morgen (Philadelphia, 1988), 53–76.

29. White, "Fettered Sisterhood," 5.

30. Corinne Robinson to Jeanetta Welch Brown, with script of "Lazy Daisy" enclosed, Sept. 22, 1943, folder 274, box 17, series 5, National Council of Negro Women Papers.

31. Era Bell Thompson, "A Message from a Mahogany Blond," *Negro Digest*, 9 (July 1950), 31.

32. White, "Fettered Sisterhood"; Sandra N. Smith and Earle H. West, "Charlotte Hawkins Brown," *Journal of Negro Education*, 51 (Summer 1982), 199.

33. Linda Gordon, *Heroes of Their Own Lives: The Politics and History of Family Violence*, Boston, *1880–1960* (New York, 1988), 82–115.

34. See, for example, Darlene Rebecca Roth, "Matronage: Patterns in Women's Organizations, Atlanta Georgia, 1890–1940," (Ph. D. diss., George Washington University, 1978), 87.

35. Lucy D. Slowe, "Some Problems of Colored Women and Girls in the Urban Process" [probably 1930s], folder 143, box 90–6, Slowe Papers.

36. The white reformers in the first decades of the twentieth century were campaigning hard for mothers' pensions and feared that daytime child care would be used as an alternative, forcing mothers into poor jobs. But they continued to see mothers' employment as a misfortune.

37. Paula Giddings, *When and Where I Enter: The Impact of Black Women on Race and Sex in America* (New York, 1984), 205.

38. Although many of the Afro-American women leaders were legally married, it does not necessarily follow that they lived their daily lives in close partnerships with their husbands or carried much domestic labor responsibility.

DOCUMENT: Controlling Reproduction

Margaret Sanger, "I resolved that women should have knowledge of contraception. . . ."

Nowhere does gender matter more than in the area of reproduction. The contrast between the high fertility of newly arriving immigrants and the low birth rate among old-stock Americans around the turn of the century prompted such leaders as Theodore Roosevelt to lament "race suicide" and to exhort women of the "proper sort" to perform their maternal functions in the selfless fashion dictated by time and tradition. Viewed through women's eyes, however, these population trends looked different, as this selection on the beginnings of the birth control movement dramatically illustrates. While a few radicals such as Emma Goldman saw contraception as a means of liberating women by restoring to them control over their own bodies and thereby lessening their economic dependence on men, it was Margaret Higgins Sanger whose name would become most closely linked with the crusade for birth control.

The factors that propelled Sanger—always a complex personality—to leadership were many. One of eleven children, she helped bury her mother, who died of tuberculosis. Young Margaret, however, was convinced that it was the passion of her father who lived to be eighty which was the real cause of her mother's death. A nursing career also shaped Sanger's thinking, as the following account suggests. Arrested under the Comstock Law (pp. 244–45) for publication of a newspaper advocating contraception, she fled in 1914 to England with her husband and three children. There she met the famous British psychologist and sex expert, Havelock Ellis, who further convinced her that sexual experience should be separated from reproduction, enabling couples to enhance the quality of their sexual relationship. Returning to New York, the Sangers continued their activities on behalf of birth control. The opening of the Brownsville clinic in 1916, recounted here, resulted in still further confrontation with authorities. The hunger strike of Sanger's sister, Ethel Byrne, a nurse at the clinic, was followed by Sanger's own trial. Convicted of "maintaining a public nuisance," she was sentenced to thirty days in the workhouse. Ever the iconoclast and rebel, she gave talks to other inmates on sex hygiene when the matrons were out of sight. Divorcing William Sanger, she subsequently married a wealthy oil man who contributed liberally to the American Birth Control League, which she founded in 1921.

Important financial aid would also come in later years from the wealthy feminist Katherine McCormick, who shared Sanger's commitment to research in contraception. In the early 1950s McCormick provided funds for experiments in endocrinology that led to the development of the birth control pill. At a time when few scientists thought an oral contraceptive was possible, the insistence of Sanger and McCormick that every

Excerpted from "Awakening and Revolt," "A 'Public Nuisance,'" and "Hunger Strike." chaps. 3, 12, and 13 of *My Fight for Birth Control* by Margaret Sanger (New York: Farrar & Reinhart, 1931). Copyright © 1931 by Margaret Sanger. Reprinted by permission of Grant Sanger. Cross-references have been adjusted.

Margaret Sanger, following a decision by the New York Court of Appeals in 1918. Although the court upheld her conviction, it interpreted the law in question more broadly, allowing physicians to provide contraceptives to married women "to cure or prevent (venereal) disease." (Photograph reprinted by permission of Planned Parenthood® Federation of America)

woman had the right to control her own body helped bring about a major breakthrough in medical technology. In 1960 "the pill" became available to the public. The timing was propitious, for it coincided with a period of sexual liberation that, while proving in some respects to be a mixed blessing for women, also coincided with new recognition of the intensity of their sexual drive and capacity for sexual pleasure.

Although Sanger saw the development of an oral contraceptive as another victory in a long and difficult struggle for reproductive freedom, others viewed the birth control movement differently. Arguments that limiting family size could not only free women's energies for social reform but prevent the world's poor from producing children they were unable to care for met with opposition from women themselves in the early years of Sanger's crusade. Some feared that birth control would contribute to promiscuity; others feared it would deny women the dignity that was theirs by virtue of motherhood. The Roman Catholic Church was unrelenting in its opposition, maintaining that the use of contraceptives is a sin. Among groups in the self-styled profamily movement of the present, Sanger is still being angrily attacked. Her contribution to the lives of modern American women remains a matter of political debate. Birth control is not only a technical way of spacing and limiting children so as to benefit both mother and child but is part of a larger debate about the extent to which women should be able to control their own reproductive lives.

AWAKENING AND REVOLT

Early in the year 1912 I came to a sudden realization that my work as a nurse and my activities in social service were entirely palliative and consequently futile and useless to relieve the misery I saw all about me. . . .

It is among the mothers here that the most difficult problems arise—the outcasts of society with theft, filth, perjury, cruelty, brutality oozing from beneath.

Ignorance and neglect go on day by day; children born to breathe but a few hours and pass out of life; pregnant women toiling early and late to give food to four or five children, always hungry; boarders taken into homes where there is not sufficient room for the family; little girls eight and ten years of age sleeping in the same room with dirty, foul smelling, loathsome men; women whose weary, pregnant, shapeless bodies refuse to accommodate themselves to the husbands' desires find husbands looking with lustful eyes upon other women, sometimes upon their own little daughters, six and seven years of age.

In this atmosphere abortions and birth become the main theme of conversation. On Saturday nights I have seen groups of fifty to one hundred women going into questionable offices well known in the community for cheap abortions. I asked several women what took place there, and they all gave the same reply: a quick examination, a probe inserted into the uterus and turned a few times to disturb the fertilized ovum, and then the woman was sent home. Usually the flow began the next day and often continued four or five weeks. Sometimes an ambulance carried the victim to the hospital for a curetage, and if she returned home at all she was looked upon as a lucky woman.

This state of things became a nightmare with me. There seemed no sense to it all, no reason for such waste of mother life, no right to exhaust women's vitality and to throw them on the scrap-heap before the age of thirty-five.

Everywhere I looked, misery and fear stalked—men fearful of losing their jobs, women fearful that even worse conditions might come upon them. The menace of another pregnancy hung like a sword over the head of every poor woman I came in contact with that year. The question which met me was always the same: What can I do to keep from it? or, What can I do to get out of this? Sometimes they talked among themselves bitterly.

"It's the rich that know the tricks," they'd say, "while we have all the kids." Then, if the women were Roman Catholics, they talked about "Yankee tricks," and asked me if I knew what the Protestants did to keep their families down. When I said that I didn't believe that the rich knew much more than they did I was laughed at and suspected of holding back information for money. They would nudge each other and say something about paying me before I left the case if I would reveal the "secret." . . .

I heard over and over again of their desperate efforts at bringing themselves "around"—drinking various herb-teas, taking drops of turpentine on sugar, steaming over a chamber of boiling coffee or of turpentine water, rolling down stairs, and finally inserting slippery-elm sticks, or knitting needles, or shoe hooks into the uterus. I used to shudder with horror as I heard the details and, worse yet, learned of the conditions *behind the reason* for such desperate actions.

. . . Each time I returned it was to hear that Mrs. Cohen had been carried to a hospital but had never come back, that Mrs. Kelly had sent the children to a neighbor's and had put her head into the gas oven to end her misery. Many of the women had consulted midwives, social workers and doctors at the dispensary and asked a way to limit their families, but they were denied this help, sometimes indignantly or gruffly, sometimes jokingly; but always knowledge was denied them. Life for them had but one choice: either to abandon themselves to incessant childbearing, or to terminate their pregnancies through abortions. Is it any wonder they resigned themselves hopelessly, as the Jewish and Italian mothers, or fell into drunkenness, as the Irish and Scotch? The latter were often beaten by husbands, as well as by their sons and daughters. They were driven and cowed, and only as beasts of burden were allowed to exist. . . .

They claimed my thoughts night and day. One by one these women, with their worried, sad, pensive and aging faces would marshal themselves before me in my dreams, sometimes appealingly, sometimes accusingly. I could not escape from the facts of their misery, neither was I able to see the way out of their problems and their troubles. . . .

Finally the thing began to shape itself, to become accumulative during the three weeks I spent in the home of a desperately sick woman living on Grand Street, a lower section of New York's East Side.

Mrs. Sacks was only twenty-eight years old; her husband, an unskilled worker, thirty-two. Three children, aged five, three and one, were none too strong nor sturdy, and it took all the earnings of the father and the ingenuity of the mother to keep them clean, provide them with air and proper food, and give them a chance to grow into decent manhood and womanhood.

Both parents were devoted to these children and to each other. The woman had become pregnant and had taken various drugs and purgatives, as advised by her neighbors. Then, in desperation, she had used some instrument lent to her by a friend. She was found prostrate on the floor amidst the crying children when her husband returned from work. Neighbors advised against the ambulance, and a friendly doctor was called. The husband would not hear of her going to a hospital, and as a little money had been saved in the bank a nurse was called and the battle for that precious life began.

. . . The three-room apartment was turned into a hospital for the dying patient. Never had I worked so fast, so concentratedly as I did to keep alive that little mother. . . .

. . . July's sultry days and nights were melted into a torpid inferno. Day after day, night after night, I slept only in brief snatches, ever too anxious about the condition of that feeble heart bravely carrying on, to stay long from the bedside of the patient. With but one toilet for the building and that on the floor below, everything had to be carried down for disposal, while ice, food and other necessities had to be carried three flights up. It was one of those old airshaft buildings of which there were several thousands then standing in New York City.

At the end of two weeks recovery was in sight, and at the end of three weeks I was preparing to leave the fragile patient to take up the ordinary duties of her life, including those, of wifehood and motherhood. . . .

But as the hour for my departure came nearer, her anxiety increased, and finally with trembling voice she said: "Another baby will finish me, I suppose."

"It's too early to talk about that," I said, and resolved that I would turn the question over to the doctor for his advice. When he came I said: "Mrs. Sacks is worried about having another baby."

"She well might be," replied the doctor, and then he stood before her and said: "Any more such capers, young woman, and there will be no need to call me."

"Yes, yes—I know, Doctor," said the patient with trembling voice, "but," and she hesitated as if it took all of her courage to say it, "what can I do to prevent getting that way again?"

"Oh ho!" laughed the doctor good naturedly, "You want your cake while you eat it too, do you? Well, it can't be done." Then, familiarly slapping her on the back and picking up his hat and bag to depart, he said: "I'll tell you the only sure thing to do. Tell Jake to sleep on the roof!"

With those words he closed the door and went down the stairs, leaving us both petrified and stunned.

Tears sprang to my eyes, and a lump came in my throat as I looked at that face before me. It was stamped with sheer horror. I thought for a moment she might have gone insane, but she conquered her feelings, whatever they may have been, and turning to me in desperation said: "He can't understand, can he?—he's a man after all—but you do, don't you? You're a woman and you'll tell me the secret and I'll never tell it to a soul."

She clasped her hands as if in prayer, she leaned over and looked straight into my eyes and beseechingly implored me to tell her something—something *I really did not know*. . . .

I had to turn away from that imploring face. I could not answer her then. I quieted her as best I could. She saw that I was moved by the tears in my eyes. I promised that I would come back in a few days and tell her what she wanted to know. The few simple means of limiting the family like *coitus interruptus* or the condom were laughed at by the neighboring women when told these were the means used by men in the well-to-do families. That was not believed, and I knew such an answer would be swept aside as useless were I to tell her this at such a time. . . .

The intelligent reasoning of the young mother—how to prevent getting that way again—how sensible, how just she had been—yes, I promised myself I'd go back and have a long talk with her and tell her more, and perhaps she would not laugh but would believe that those methods were all that were really known.

But time flew past, and weeks rolled into months. . . . I was about to retire one night three months later when the telephone rang and an agitated man's voice begged me to come at once to help his wife who was sick again. It was the husband of Mrs. Sacks, and I intuitively knew before I left the telephone that it was almost useless to go.

. . . I arrived a few minutes after the doctor, the same one who had given her such noble advice. The woman was dying. She was unconscious. She died within ten minutes after my arrival. It was the same result, the same story told a thousand times before—death from abortion. She had become pregnant, had used drugs, had then consulted a five-dollar professional abortionist, and death followed.

The doctor shook his head as he rose from listening for the heart beat. . . . The gentle woman, the devoted mother, the loving wife had passed on leaving behind her a frantic husband, helpless in his loneliness, bewildered in his helplessness as he paced up and down the room, hands clenching his head, moaning "My God! My God! My God!"

The Revolution came—but not as it has been pictured nor as history relates that revolutions have come. . . .

After I left that desolate house I walked and walked and walked; for hours and hours I kept on, bag in hand, thinking, regretting, dreading to stop; fearful of my conscience, dreading to face my own accusing soul. At three in the morning I arrived home still clutching a heavy load the weight of which I was quite unconscious.

. . . As I stood at the window and looked out, the miseries and problems of that sleeping city arose before me in a clear vision like a panorama: crowded homes, too many children; babies dying in infancy; mothers overworked; baby nurseries; children neglected and hungry—mothers so nervously wrought they could not give the little things the comfort nor care they needed; mothers half sick most of their lives—"always ailing, never failing"; women made into drudges; children working in cellars; children aged six and seven pushed into the labor market to help earn a living; another baby on the way; still another; yet another; a baby born dead—great relief; an older child dies—sorrow, but nevertheless relief—insurance helps; a mother's death—children scattered into institutions; the father, desperate, drunken; he slinks away to become an outcast in a society which has trapped him.

... There was only one thing to be done: call out, start the alarm, set the heather on fire! Awaken the womanhood of America to free the motherhood of the world! I released from my almost paralyzed hand the nursing bag which unconsciously I had clutched, threw it across the room, tore the uniform from my body, flung it into a corner, and renounced all palliative work forever.

I would never go back again to nurse women's ailing bodies while their miseries were as vast as the stars. I was now finished with superficial cures, with doctors and nurses and social workers who were brought face to face with this overwhelming truth of women's needs and yet turned to pass on the other side. They must be made to see these facts. I resolved that women should have knowledge of contraception. They have every right to know about their own bodies. I would strike out—I would scream from the housetops. I would tell the world what was going on in the lives of these poor women. *I would* be heard. No matter what it should cost. *I would be heard.* . . .

I announced to my family the following day that I had finished nursing, that I would never go on another case—and I never have.

I asked doctors what one could do and was told I'd better keep off that subject or Anthony Comstock would get me. I was told that there were laws against that sort of thing. This was the reply from every medical man and woman I approached. . . .

A "PUBLIC NUISANCE"

The selection of a place for the first birth control clinic was of the greatest importance. No one could actually tell how it would be received in any neighborhood. I thought of all the possible difficulties: The indifference of women's organizations, the ignorance of the workers themselves, the resentment of social agencies, the opposition of the medical profession. Then there was the law—the law of New York State.

Section 1142 was definite. It stated that *no one* could give information to prevent conception to *anyone* for any reason. There was, however, Section 1145, which distinctly stated that physicians (*only*) could give advice to prevent conception for the cure or prevention of disease. I inquired about the section, and was told

by two attorneys and several physicians that this clause was an exception to 1142 referring only to venereal disease. But anyway, as I was not a physician, it could not protect me. Dared I risk it?

I began to think of the doctors I knew. Several who had previously promised now refused. I wrote, telephoned, asked friends to ask other friends to help me find a woman doctor to help me demonstrate the need of a birth control clinic in New York. None could be found. No one wanted to go to jail. No one cared to test out the law. Perhaps it would have to be done without a doctor. But it had to be done; that I knew.

Fania Mindell, an enthusiastic young worker in the cause, had come on from Chicago to help me. Together we tramped the streets on that dreary day in early October, through a driving rainstorm, to find the best location at the cheapest terms possible . . .

Finally at 46 Amboy Street, in the Brownsville Section of Brooklyn, we found a friendly landlord with a good place vacant at fifty dollars a month rental; and Brownsville was settled on. It was one of the most thickly populated sections. It had a large population of working class Jews, always interested in health measures, always tolerant of new ideas, willing to listen and to accept advice whenever the health of mother or children was involved. I knew that here there would at least be no breaking of windows, no hurling of insults into our teeth; but I was scarcely prepared for the popular support, the sympathy and friendly help given us in that neighborhood from that day to this. . . .

With a small bundle of handbills and a large amount of zeal, we fared forth each morning in a house-to-house canvass of the district in which the clinic was located. Every family in that great district received a "dodger" printed in English, Yiddish and Italian. . . .

Women of every race and creed flocked to the clinic with the determination not to have any more children than their health could stand or their husbands could support. Jews and Christians, Protestants and Roman Catholics alike made their confessions to us, whatever they may have professed at home or in the church. Some did not dare talk this over with their husbands; and some came urged on by their husbands. Men themselves came after work; and some brought timid, embarrassed wives, apologetically dragging a string of little children. . . .

When I asked a bright little Roman Catholic woman what she would say to the priest when he learned that she had been to the Clinic, she answered indignantly: "It's none of his business. My husband has a weak heart and works only four days a week. He gets twelve dollars, and we can barely live on it now. We have enough children."

Her friend, sitting by, nodded a vigorous approval. "When I was married," she broke in, "the priest told us to have lots of children, and we listened to him. I had fifteen. Six are living. Nine baby funerals in our house. I am thirty-six years old now. Look at me! I look sixty."

As I walked home that night, I made a mental calculation of fifteen baptismal fees, nine funeral expenses, masses and candles for the repose of nine little souls, the physical suffering of the mother, and the emotional suffering of both parents; and I asked myself, "Was it fair? Is this the price of Christianity?" . . .

Ethel Byrne, who is my sister and a trained nurse, assisted me in advising, explaining, and demonstrating to the women how to prevent conception. As all of our 488 records were confiscated by the detectives who later arrested us for violation of the New York State law, it is difficult to tell exactly how many more women came in those days to seek advice; but we estimate that it was far more than five hundred. As in any new enterprise, false reports were maliciously spread about the clinic; weird stories without the slightest foundation of truth. We talked plain talk and give plain facts to the women who came there. We kept a record of every applicant. All were mothers; most of them had large families.

It was whispered about that the police were to raid the place for abortions. We had no fear of that accusation. We were trying to spare mothers the necessity of that ordeal by giving them proper contraceptive information. . . .

The arrest and raid on the Brooklyn clinic was spectacular. There was no need of a large force of plain clothes men to drag off a trio of decent, serious women who were testing out a law on a fundamental principle. My federal arrest, on the contrary, had been assigned to intelligent men. One had to respect the dignity of their mission; but the New York city officials seem to use tactics suitable only for crooks, bandits and burglars. We were not sur-prised at being arrested, but the shock and horror of it was that a *woman,* with a squad of five plain clothes men, conducted the raid and made the arrest. A woman—the irony of it!

I refused to close down the clinic, hoping that a court decision would allow us to continue such necessary work. I was to be disappointed. Pressure was brought upon the landlord, and we were dispossessed by the law as a "public nuisance." In Holland the clinics were called "public utilities."

When the policewoman entered the clinic with her squad of plain clothes men and announced the arrest of Miss Mindell and myself (Mrs. Byrne was not present at the time and her arrest followed later), the room was crowded to suffocation with women waiting in the outer room. The police began bullying these mothers, asking them questions, writing down their names in order to subpoena them to testify against us at the trial. These women, always afraid of trouble which the very presence of a policeman signifies, screamed and cried aloud. The children on their laps screamed, too. It was like a panic for a few minutes until I walked into the room where they were stampeding and begged them to be quiet and not to get excited. I assured them that nothing could happen to them, that I was under arrest but they would be allowed to return home in a few minutes. That quieted them. The men were blocking the door to prevent anyone from leaving, but I finally persuaded them to allow these women to return to their homes, unmolested though terribly frightened by it all.

. . . The patrol wagon came rattling through the streets to our door, and at length Miss Mindell and I took our seats within and were taken to the police station. . . .

HUNGER STRIKE

Out of that spectacular raid, which resulted in an avalanche of nation-wide publicity in the daily press, four separate and distinct cases resulted:

Mrs. Ethel Byrne, my sister, was charged with violating Section 1142 of the Penal Code, designed to prevent dissemination of birth control information.

Miss Fania Mindell was charged with having sold an allegedly indecent book entitled "What Every Girl Should Know" written by Margaret Sanger.

I was charged with having conducted a clinic at 46 Amboy Street, Brooklyn, in violation of the same section of the Penal Code.

Having re-opened the clinic, I was arrested on a charge of "maintaining a public nuisance," in violation of Section 1530 of the Penal Code.

The three of us were held for trial in the Court of Special Sessions, with bail fixed at $500 each. This meant that our cases would be decided by three judges appointed by the Mayor and not by a jury. . . .

My sister was found guilty, and on January 22 she was sentenced to thirty days in the Workhouse. A writ of habeas corpus as a means of suspending sentence during appeal was refused by Supreme Court Justice Callahan. She spent the night in jail.

Ethel Byrne promptly declared a hunger strike. I knew that she would not flinch. Quiet, taciturn, with a will of steel hidden by a diffident air, schooled by her long training as a professional nurse, she announced briefly that she would neither eat, drink, nor work until her release. Commissioner of Correction Burdette G. Lewis promptly announced that she would be permitted to see no one but her attorney.

While the newspapers were reporting—always on the front page—the condition of the hunger striker, plans were hastened for a monster mass meeting of protest, to be held in Carnegie Hall. Helen Todd acted as chairman, and Dr. Mary Halton was an additional speaker. The hall was crowded by a huge audience of all classes. The women patients of the Brownsville clinic were given places of honor on the platform. The salvos of applause which greeted me showed that intelligent opinion was strongly behind us, and did much to give me the courage to fight with renewed strength for the immediate release of Ethel Byrne.

This meeting was acclaimed by the press as a "triumph of women, for women, by women." The meeting was said to have struck the right note—that of being instructive and persuasive, instead of agitational.

In the meantime, Ethel Byrne's refusal to eat and drink was crowding all other news off the front pages of the New York papers. Her defiance was sharpening the issue between self-respecting citizens and the existing law, which was denounced on every street corner as hypocritical. In the subway crowds, on street-corners, everywhere people gathered, the case was discussed. "They are imprisoning a woman for teaching physiological facts!" I heard one man exclaim. . . .

"It makes little difference whether I starve or not," she replied, through her attorney, "so long as this outrageous arrest calls attention to the archaic laws which would prevent our telling the truth about the facts of life. With eight thousand deaths a year in New York State from illegal operations on women, one more death won't make much difference."

All this served to convince the now panic-stricken Mr. Lewis [Commissioner of Correction in charge of Blackwell's Island] that Mrs. Byrne was different, after all, from the alcoholics and drug addicts who had given him his previous experience, and with whom he had gallantly compared her. When she had gone 103 hours without food, he established a precedent in American prison annals. He ordered her forcibly fed. She was the first woman so treated in this country. . . .

The truth was that Mrs. Byrne was in a critical condition after being rolled in a blanket and having milk, eggs and a stimulant forced into her stomach through a rubber tube. I realized this as soon as I heard that she was "passive under the feeding." Nothing but loss of strength could have lessened the power of her resistance to such authority. Nothing but brutality could have reduced her fiery spirit to acquiescence. I was desperate; torn between admiration for what she was doing and misery over what I feared might be the result.

On January 31st, a committee headed by Mrs. Amos Pinchot, Jessie Ashley and myself went to Albany for the purpose of asking Governor Whitman to appoint a commission to investigate birth control and make a report to the state legislature. Governor Whitman, a wise, fair, intelligent executive and statesman, received us, and listened to our exposition of the economic and moral necessity for birth control; the medical theory behind its justification. He promised to consider appointing the commission. During the interview Miss Jessie Ashley introduced the subject of Mrs. Byrne's treatment on Blackwell's Island and the anxiety we felt about her condition. We tried to make him see the outrage committed by the state in making anyone suffer for so just a cause. The Governor offered Mrs. Byrne a pardon on condition that she would not continue to disseminate birth control information. . . .

When we left Albany that day, I had the promise of a provisional pardon for Mrs. Byrne, but best of all I had in my purse a letter from the Governor to the authorities at Blackwell's Island authorizing me to see her. I was shocked and horrified when, in the late afternoon of February 1st, I saw my sister. She was lying semi-conscious on a cot in a dark corner of the prison cell. . . .

There was not time to inform her of the conditions of her pardon, and moreover she was too ill to face the question. I still believe that I was right in accepting the conditions which the Governor imposed. There was no other course. I saw that she was dangerously ill, that nothing further was to be gained by her keeping on, and that her death would have been a terrible calamity. Her life was what mattered to me, regardless of her future activities. . . .

At any rate, by the time she was released the subject was a burning issue. Newspapers which previously had ignored the case, had to mention a matter important enough to bring the Governor of the State from Albany to New York.

JOAN JACOBS BRUMBERG

Fasting Girls: The Emerging Ideal of Slenderness in American Culture

Although anorexia nervosa is generally considered a modern disease, appetite control has long been an important dimension of female experience. Joan Jacobs Brumberg's pioneering study of anorexia nervosa traces changing cultural pressure on women to control their appetite. Exploring the links between food and femininity in the nineteenth century, Brumberg found that by 1890 thinness had become a way in which young privileged women could distance themselves from their working-class counterparts. More important, food preferences and thin bodies also sent moral and aesthetic messages. The young woman whose frail, delicate frame demonstrated her rejection of all carnal appetites more closely approached the Victorian ideal of femininity than did her more robust counterpart whose heavier physique signaled sexual craving. The twentieth century brought additional pressures to control body weight, according to Brumberg, with the development of scientific nutrition and the standard sizing of clothes. By 1920, fat had become a moral issue. Combined with social changes having to do with food and sexuality occurring in the 1960s, the stage was set for the epidemic of eating disorders evident in the 1980s and 1990s.

Within the first two decades of the twentieth century, even before the advent of the flapper, the voice of American women revealed that the female struggle with weight was under way and was becoming intensely personal. As early as 1907 an *Atlantic Monthly* article described the reaction of a woman trying on a dress she had not worn for over a year: "The

Reprinted by permission of the publishers from *Fasting Girls: The Emergence of Anorexia Nervosa as a Modern Disease* by Joan Jacobs Brumberg, Cambridge, Mass.: Harvard University Press. Copyright © 1988 by the President and Fellows of Harvard College. Notes have been renumbered and edited.

gown was neither more [n]or less than antici-pated. But I ... *the fault was on me* ... I was more! Gasping I hooked it together. The gown was hopeless, and I ... I am fat."[1] ... By the twentieth century ... overweight in women was not only a physical liability, it was a char-acter flaw and a social impediment.

Early in the century elite American women began to take body weight seriously as fat became an aesthetic liability for those who followed the world of haute couture. Since the mid-nineteenth century wealthy Americans—the wives of J. P. Morgan, Cor-nelius Vanderbilt, and Harry Harkness Fla-gler, for instance—had traveled to Paris to pur-chase the latest creations from couturier collections such as those on view at Maison Worth on the famed rue de la Paix. The cou-turier was not just a dressmaker who made clothes for an individual woman; rather, the couturier fashioned "a look" or a collection of dresses for an abstraction—the stylish woman. In order to be stylish and wear couturier clothes, a woman's body had to conform to the dress rather than the dress to the body, as had been the case when the traditional dressmaker fitted each garment.[2] ...

In 1908 the world of women's fashion was revolutionized by Paul Poiret, whose new sil-houette was slim and straight. ... Almost immediately women of style began to pur-chase new kinds of undergarments that would make Poiret's look possible; for example, the traditional hourglass corset was cast aside for a rubber girdle to retract the hips.

After World War I the French continued to set the fashion standard for style-conscious American women. In 1922 Jeanne Lanvin's che-mise, a straight frock with a simple bateau neckline, was transformed by Gabrielle Chanel into the uniform of the flapper. Chanel dropped the waistline to the hips and began to expose more of the leg: in 1922 she moved her hemlines to midcalf, and in 1926–27 the ideal hem was raised to just below the knee. In order to look good in Chanel's fashionable little dress, its wearer had to think not only about the appearance of her legs but about the smooth-ness of her form.[3] Women who wore the flap-per uniform turned to flattening brassieres constructed of shoulder straps and a single band of material that encased the body from chest to waist. In 1914 a French physician com-mented on the revised dimensions of women's

bodies: "Nowadays it is not the fashion to be corpulent; the proper thing is to have a slight, graceful figure far removed from embonpoint, and *a fortiori* from obesity. For once, the physi-cian is called upon to interest himself in the question of feminine aesthetics."[4]

The slenderized fashion image of the French was picked up and promoted by Amer-ica's burgeoning ready-to-wear garment industry.[5] Stimulated by the popularity of the Gibson girl and the shirtwaist craze of the 1890s, ready-to-wear production in the United States accelerated in the first two decades of the twentieth century. Chanel's chemise dress was a further boon to the garment industry. Because of its simple cut, the chemise was easy to copy and produce, realities that explain its quick adoption as the uniform of the 1920s. Accord-ing to a 1923 *Vogue*, the American ready-to-wear industry successfully democratized French fashion: "Today, the mode which origi-nates in Paris is a factor in the lives of women of every rank, from the highest to the lowest."[6]

In order to market ready-to-wear clothing, the industry turned in the 1920s to standard sizing, an innovation that put increased emphasis on personal body size and gave legitimacy to the idea of a normative size range. For women, shopping for ready-to-wear clothes in the bustling department stores of the early twentieth century fostered height-ened concern about body size.[7] With a dress-maker, every style was theoretically available to every body; with standard sizing, items of clothing could be identified as desirable, only to be rejected on the grounds of fit. (For women the cost of altering a ready-made gar-ment was an "add-on"; for men it was not.) Female figure flaws became a source of frus-tration and embarrassment, not easily hidden from those who accompanied the shopper or from salesclerks. Experiences in department-store dressing rooms created a host of new anxieties for women and girls who could not fit into stylish clothing. ...

Ironically, standard sizing created an un-expected experience of frustration in a market-place that otherwise was offering a continually expansive opportunity for gratification via purchasable goods. Because many manufac-turers of stylish women's garments did not make clothing in large sizes, heavy women were at the greatest disadvantage. In addition to the moral [disgrace] of overweight, the standardization of garment production precluded fat women's participation in the mainstream of fashion. This situation became worse as the century progressed. Fashion photography was professionalized, a development thatparalleled the growth of modern advertising, and models became slimmer both to compensate for the distortions of the camera and to accommodate the new merchandising canon—modern fashion was best displayed on a lean body.[8]

The appearance in 1918 of America's first best-selling weight-control book confirmed that weight was a source of anxiety among women and that fat was out of fashion. *Diet and Health with a Key to the Calories* by Lulu Hunt Peters was directed at a female audience and based on the assumption that most readers wanted to lose rather than gain weight.... "You should know and also use the word calorie as frequently, or more frequently, than you use the words foot, yard, quart, gallon and so forth. ... Hereafter you are going to eat calories of food. Instead of saying one slice of bread, or a piece of pie, you will say 100 calories of bread, 350 calories of pie."[9]

Peters' book was popular because it was personal and timely. Her 1918 appeal was related to food shortages caused by the exigencies of the war in Europe. Peters told her readers that it was "more important than ever to reduce" and recommended the formation of local Watch Your Weight Anti-Kaiser Classes. "There are hundreds of thousands of individuals all over America who are hoarding food," she wrote. "They have vast amounts of this valuable commodity stored away in their own anatomy." In good-humored fashion Peters portrayed her own calories counting as both an act of patriotism and humanitarianism:

> I am reducing and the money that I can save will help keep a child from starving ... [I am explaining to my friends] that for every pang of hunger we feel we can have a double joy, that of knowing we are saving worse pangs in some little children, and that of knowing that for every pang we feel we lose a pound. A pang's a pound the world around we'll say.[10]

But Peters showed herself to be more than simply an informative and patriotic physician. Confessing that she once weighed as much as 200 pounds, the author also understood that heavy women were ashamed of their bulk and unlikely to reveal their actual weight. Peters observed that it was not a happy situation for fat women. "You are viewed with distrust, suspicion, and even aversion," she told her overweight readers. ...

Peters' book was among the first to articulate the new secular credo of physical denial: modern women suffered to be beautiful (thin) rather than pious. Peters' language and thinking reverberated with references to religious ideas of temptation and sin. For the modern female dieter, sweets, particularly chocolate, were the ultimate temptation. Eating chocolate violated the morality of the dieter and her dedication to her ideal, a slim body. Peters joked about her cravings ("My idea of heaven is a place with me and mine on a cloud of whipped cream") but she was adamant about the fact that indulgence must ultimately be paid for. "If you think you will die unless you have some chocolate creams [go on a] *debauch*," she advised. "'Eat 10 or so' but then *repent* with a 50-calorie dinner of bouillon and crackers." (Italics added.)[11]

Although the damage done by chocolate creams could be mediated by either fasting or more rigid dieting, Peters explained that there was a psychological cost in yielding to the temptation of candy or rich desserts. Like so many modern dieters, Peters wrote about the issue of guilt followed by redemption through parsimonious eating: "Every supposed pleasure in sin [eating] will furnish more than its equivalent of pain [dieting]." But appetite control was not only a question of learning to delay gratification, it was also an issue of self-esteem. "You will be tempted quite frequently, and you will have to choose whether you will enjoy yourself hugely in the twenty minutes or so that you will be consuming the excess calories, or whether you will dislike yourself cordially for the two or three days you lose by your lack of will power." For Peters dieting had as much to do with the mind as with the body. "There is a great deal of psychology to reducing," she wrote astutely.[12] In fact, with the popularization of the concept of calorie counting, physical features once regarded as natural—such as appetite and body weight—were designated as objects of conscious control. The notion of weight control through restriction of calories implied that ... overweight resulted solely from lack of control; to be a fat woman constituted a failure of personal morality.

The tendency to talk about female dieting as a moral issue was particularly strong among the popular beauty experts, that is, those in the fashion and cosmetics industry who sold scientific advice on how to become and stay beautiful. Many early-twentieth-century beauty culturists, including Grace Peckham Murray, Helena Rubenstein, and Hazel Bishop, studied chemistry and medical specialties such as dermatology. The creams and lotions they created, as well as the electrical gadgets they promoted, were intended to bring the findings of modern chemistry and physiology to the problem of female beauty. Nevertheless, women could not rely entirely on scientifically achieved results. The beauty experts also preached the credo of self-denial: to be beautiful, most women must suffer.

Because they regarded fat women as an affront to their faith, some were willing to criminalize as well as medicalize obesity. In 1902 *Vogue* speculated, "To judge by the efforts of the majority of women to attain slender and sylph-like proportions, one would fancy it a crime to be fat." By 1918 the message was more distinct: "There is one crime against the modern ethics of beauty which is unpardonable; far better it is to commit any number of petty crimes than to be guilty of the sin of growing fat." By 1930 there was no turning back. Helena Rubenstein, a high priestess of the faith, articulated in *The Art of Feminine Beauty* the moral and aesthetic dictum that would govern the lives of subsequent generations of women: "An abundance of fat is something repulsive and not in accord with the principles that rule our conception of the beautiful.[13] . . .

In adolescence fat was considered a particular liability because of the social strains associated with that stage of life. In the 1940s articles with titles such as "What to Do about the Fat Child at Puberty," "Reducing the Adolescent," and "Should the Teens Diet?" captured the rising interest in adolescent weight control.[14] Women's magazines, reflecting the concerns of mothers anxious to save their daughters from social ostracism, for the first time promoted diets for young girls. According to the *Ladies' Home Journal:* "Appearance plays too important a part in a girl's life not to have her grow up to be beauty-conscious. Girls should be encouraged to take an interest

in their appearance when they are very young."[15] . . . Adolescent weight control was also promoted by popular magazines hoping to sell products to young women. . . . *Seventeen's* adoption of the cause of weight control confirmed that slimness was a critical dimension of adolescent beauty and that a new constituency, high school girls, was learning how to diet. From 1944 [when it was founded] to 1948, *Seventeen* had published a full complement of articles on nutrition but almost nothing on weight control. Following the mode of earlier home economists and scientific nutritionists, the magazine had presented basic information about food groups and the importance of each in the daily diet; balance but not calories had been the initial focus. In 1948, however, *Seventeen* proclaimed overweight a medical problem and began educating its young readers about calories and the psychology of eating. Adolescent girls were warned against using eating as a form of emotional expression (do not "pamper your blues" with food) and were given practical tips on how to avoid food bingeing. No mention was made of the new "diet pills" (amphetamines) introduced in the 1930s for clinical treatment of obesity. Instead, teenagers were encouraged to go on "sensible" and "well-rounded" diets of between 1,200 and 1,800 calories. By the 1950s advertisements for "diet foods" such as Ry-Krisp were offering assistance as they told the readership "Nobody Loves a Fat Girl."[16] Girls, much as adult women, were expected to tame the natural appetite.

Although adolescent girls were consistently warned against weight reduction without medical supervision, dieting was always cast as a worthwhile endeavor with transforming powers. "Diets can do wonderful things. When dispensed or approved by your physician . . . all you have to do is follow whither the chart leads."[17] The process of metamorphosis from fat to thin always provided a narrative of uplift and interest. "The Fattest Girl in the Class" was the autobiographical account of Jane, an obese girl who, after suffering the social stigma associated with teenage overweight, went on a diet and found happiness.[18] Being thin was tied to attractiveness, popularity with the opposite sex, and self-esteem—all primary ingredients in adolescent culture. Nonfiction accounts of "make-overs" became a popular formula in all the beauty magazines of the postwar period and provided a tanta-lizing fantasy of psychological and spiritual transformation for mature and adolescent women alike.[19]

The popularization of adolescent female weight control in the postwar era is a prime component of the modern dieting story and a critical factor in explaining anorexia nervosa as we know it today. . . . Since the 1960s the diet-ing imperative has intensified in two notice-able and important ways. . . . First, the ideal female body size has become considerably slimmer. After a brief flirtation with full-breasted, curvaceous female figures in the politically conservative postwar recovery of the 1950s, our collective taste returned to an ideal of extreme thinness and an androgynous, if not childlike, figure.[20] A series of well-known studies point to the declining weight since the 1950s of fashion models, Miss America con-testants, and *Playboy* centerfolds.[21] Neither bosoms, hips, nor buttocks are currently in fashion as young and old alike attempt to meet the new aesthetic standard. A Bloomingdale's ad posits, "Bean lean, slender as the night, nar-row as an arrow, pencil thin, get the point?"[22] It is appropriate to recall Annette Kellerman who, at 5 feet $3\frac{3}{4}$ inches and 137 pounds, epit-omized the body beautiful of 1918. Obviously, our cultural tolerance for body fat has dimin-ished over the intervening years.

Second, notably since the middle to late 1970s, a new emphasis on physical fitness and athleticism has intensified cultural pressures on the individual for control and mastery of the body. For women this means that fitness has been added to slimness as a criterion of perfection.[23] Experts on the subject, such as Jane Fonda, encourage women to strive for a lean body with musculature. The incredible popularity among women of aerobics, condi-tioning programs, and jogging does testify to the satisfactions that come with gaining phys-ical strength through self-discipline, but it also expresses our current urgency about the phys-ical body. Many who are caught up in the exer-cise cult equate physical fitness and slimness with a higher moral state. . . . Compulsive exercising and chronic dieting have [thus] been joined as twin obsessions. . . . [In the] 1980s clinical reports and autobiographical statements show a clear-cut pattern of anorexic patients who exercise with ritualistic intensity. How much one runs and how little one eats is

the prevailing moral calculus in present-day anorexia nervosa. . . .

The proliferation of diet and exercise reg-imens in the past decade, although an impor-tant context for understanding the increase in anorexia nervosa, is not the whole story. For a more complete explanation we must turn to some other recent social changes, keeping in mind that no one factor has caused the con-temporary problem. Rather, it is the nature of our economic and cultural environment, inter-acting with individual and family characteris-tics, which exacerbates the social and emo-tional insecurities that put today's young women at increasing risk for anorexia nervosa. Two very basic social transformations are rel-evant to the problem: one has to do with food; the other, with new expectations between the sexes.

Since World War II, and especially in the last two decades, middle-class Americans have experienced a veritable revolution in terms of how and what we eat, as well as how we think about eating.[24] The imperatives of an expand-ing capitalist society have generated extraor-dinary technological and marketing innova-tions, which in turn have transformed food itself, expanded our repertoire of foods, and affected the ways in which we consume them. Even though much contemporary food is char-acterized by elaborate processing and conser-vation techniques that actually reduce and flat-ten distinctive textures and flavors, the current array of food choices seems to constitute an endless smorgasbord of new and different tastes. [Since] the 1980s an individual in an urban center looking for a quick lunch [has been] able to choose from tacos with gua-camole and salsa, hummus and falafel in pita, sushi, tortellini, quiche, and pad thai—along with more traditional "American" fare such as hamburgers. Thirty years ago this diversified international menu was as unknown to most Americans as were many of the food products used to create it. . . . As a consequence of [the expansion of our food repertoire], we are faced with an abundance of food which, in our obe-sophobic society, necessitates ever greater self-control. . . . It is no wonder, then, that we talk so incessantly about food and dieting.

The food revolution is a matter of ideas and manners as much as technology and mar-kets. . . . In our society food is chosen and eaten not merely on the basis of hunger. It is a commonplace to observe that contemporary advertising connects food to sociability, status, and sexuality. In an affluent society, in particular, where eating appears to involve considerable individual choice, food is regarded as an important analogue of the self.

In the 1960s, for example, many young people in the counterculture gave up goods associated with their bourgeois upbringing and turned instead to a diet of whole grains, unprocessed foods, and no meat. This new diet made a statement about personal and political values and became a way of separating one generation from another. . . . In the 1980s, the extent to which the choice of cuisine dominates and defines the sophisticated life-style [among well-to-do urbanites] is reflected in a recent *New Yorker* cartoon, which shows a young professional couple after a dinner party given by friends. In complete seriousness they say to each other, "We could get close with David and Elizabeth if they didn't put béarnaise sauce on everything."[25] The anorectic is obviously not alone in her use of food and eating as a means of self-definition. There are many others who internalize the dictum "You are what you eat"—or, for that matter, what you don't eat.[26]

Along with the expansion of our food repertoire and our extraordinary attention to food selection, the eating context has changed. Eating is being desocialized. In American society today, more and more food is being consumed away from the family table or any other fixed center of sociability. This process began in the postwar period with the introduction of convenience foods and drive-in restaurants, precursors of the fast-food chains that now constitute a $45-billion-a-year industry. . . . Americans [now] eat everywhere—in the classroom; in theaters, libraries, and museums; on the street; at their desks; on the phone; in hot tubs; in cars while driving. . . . Signs saying "no food and drink," infrequent in other parts of the world, adorn our public buildings, a clear sign of our pattern of vagabond eating.[27]

On college and university campuses, where eating disorders are rampant, the situation is exaggerated. By the early 1970s most undergraduate students were no longer required to take any sit-down meals at fixed times in college dormitories. . . . Typically, students frequent a series of university cafeterias or commercial off-campus restaurants where they can obtain breakfast, lunch, or dinner at any time of the day. Some campus food plans allow unlimited amounts, a policy that fuels the behavior of the bulimic: "I used to go to Contract, eat a whole bunch of stuff, go to the bathroom, throw it up, come back, eat again, throw it up, eat again."[28] In addition, the availability of nearly any kind of food at any time contributes to a pattern of indiscriminate eating. Traditions of food appropriateness—that is, that certain foods are eaten at particular times of the day or in a certain sequence—disappear in this unstructured climate. Thus, an ice-cream cone, a carbonated soft drink, and a bagel constitute an easy popular "meal" that may be eaten at any time of day. Most colleges and the surrounding communities have made provisions to gratify student appetites no matter what the hour. Snack bars and vending machines adorn nearly every free alcove in classroom buildings and residence halls; pizza and Chinese food are delivered hot in the middle of the night.

In a setting where eating is so promiscuous, it is no wonder that food habits become problematic. This is not to say that our universities, on their own, generate eating-disordered students. They do, however, provide fertile ground for those who carry the seeds of disorder with them from home. In the permissive and highly individualized food environment of the post-1970 college or university, overeating and undereating become distinct possibilities.[29]

For those young women with either incipient or pronounced anorexia nervosa, the unstructured college life . . . often accentuates the anorectic's physical and emotional problems. [As one young anorectic explained]:

> I don't know any limits here at all. At home, I have my mom dishing out my food . . . But when I'm here it's a totally different story—I can't tell portion size at all. I always get so afraid afterwards, after eating. Oh my God did I eat that much or this much? So I just pass things up altogether and don't eat.[30]

The anorectic's preoccupation with appetite control is fueled by incessant talk about dieting and weight even among friends and associates who eat regularly. Diet-conscious female students report that fasting, weight control, and binge eating are a normal part of life on American college campuses.[31] . . . In our obesophobic society women struggle with food because, among other things, food represents fat and loss of control. For a contemporary woman to eat heartily, energetically, and happily is usually problematic (and, at best, occasional). As a result, some come to fear and hate their own appetite; eating becomes a shameful and disgusting act, and denial of hunger becomes a central facet of identity and personality. . . .

Among adolescents concerned with the transition to adulthood, an intense concern with appetite control and the body [also] operates in tandem with increasing anxiety over sexuality and the implications of changing sex roles. For sex is the second important arena of social change that may contribute to the rising number of anorectics. There are, in fact, some justifiable social reasons why contemporary young women fear adult womanhood. The "anorexic generations," particularly those born since 1960, have been subject to a set of insecurities that make heterosexuality an anxious rather than a pleasant prospect. Family insecurity, reflected in the frequency of divorce, and changing sex and gender roles became facts of life for this group in their childhood. . . . Although there is no positive correlation between divorced families and anorexia nervosa, family disruption is part of the world view of the anorexic generations. Its members understand implicitly that not all heterosexual relationships have happy endings.

As a consequence of these social changes, some young women are ambivalent about commitments to men and have adopted an ideal of womanhood that reflects the impact of post-1960 feminism. Although they generally draw back from an explicitly feminist vocabulary, most undergraduate women today desire professional careers of their own without forsaking the idea of marriage and a family. A 1985 study of college women by sociologist Mirra Komarovsky reveals that finding one's place in the world of work has become essential for personal dignity in this generation—yet a career without marriage was the choice of only 2 percent of the sample.[32] Convinced that individuality can be accommodated in marriage, these young women are interested in heterosexuality, but admit that "relationships with guys" are difficult even in college. Komarovsky describes conflict over dating rit-

uals (who takes the initiative and who pays), decision making as a couple, intellectual rivalries, and competition for entrance into graduate school. Unlike Mother, who followed Dad to graduate school and supported him along the way, today's undergraduate—whether she is a declared feminist or not—wants her own professional career both as a ticket to the good life and as a protection for herself in case of divorce.

Sexual activity also requires an extraordinary degree of self-protection in the modern world of AIDS. While premarital sex is acceptable (if not desirable), it is an understandable source of worry among female undergraduates. An advertisement in a 1986 issue of *Ms.*, aimed at selling condoms to young women, captured the current ambivalence about the physical side of heterosexuality: "Let's face it, sex these days can be risky business, and you need all the protection you can get. Between the fear of unplanned pregnancy, sexually transmitted diseases, and the potential side effects of many forms of contraception, it may seem like sex is hardly worth the risk anymore."[33] For some students the unprecedented privacy and freedom of modern university life generates as much fear as pleasure. It bears repeating that clinical materials suggest an *absence* [emphasis is the editor's] of sexual activity on the part of anorectics.

Even though feminine dependency is no longer in fashion, these same young women combine traditional expectations with a quest for equity and power. To be brainy and beautiful; to have an exciting $75,000-a-year job; to nurture two wonderful children in consort with a supportive but equally high-powered husband—these are the personal ambitions of many in the present college generation. In order to achieve this level of personal and social perfection, young women must be extremely demanding of themselves: there can be no distracting personal or avocational detours—they must be unrelenting in the pursuit of goals. The kind of personal control required to become the new Superwoman (a term popularized by columnist Ellen Goodman)[34] parallels the single-mindedness that characterizes the anorectic. In sum, the golden ideal of this generation of privileged young women and their most distinctive pathology appear to be flip sides of the same record.

My assertion that the post-1960 epidemic of anorexia nervosa can be related to recent social change in the realm of sexuality [and gender roles] is not an argument for turning back the clock.... [H]istorical investigation demonstrates that anorexia nervosa was latent in the economic and emotional milieu of the bourgeois family as early as the 1950s. It makes little sense to think a cure will be achieved by putting women back in the kitchen, reinstituting sit-down meals on the nation's campuses, or limiting personal and professional choices to what they were in the Victorian era. On the basis of the best current research on anorexia nervosa, we must conclude that the disease develops as a result of the intersection of external and internal forces in the life of an individual. External forces such as those described here do not, by themselves, generate psychopathologies, but they do give them shape and influence their frequency.

In the confusion of this transitional moment, when a new future is being tentatively charted for women but gender roles and sexuality are still constrained by tradition, young women on the brink of adulthood are feeling the pain of social change most acutely.[35] They look about for direction, but find little in the way of useful experiential guides. What parts of women's tradition do they want to carry into the future? What parts should be left behind? These are difficult personal and political decisions, and most young women are being asked to make them without benefit of substantive education in the history and experience of their sex. In effect, our young women are being challenged and their expectations raised without a simultaneous level of support for either their specific aspirations or for female creativity in general.

Sadly, the cult of diet and exercise is the closest thing our secular society offers women in terms of a coherent philosophy of the self.[36] This being the case, anorexia nervosa is not a quirk and the symptom choice is not surprising. When personal and social difficulties arise, a substantial number of our young women become preoccupied with their bodies and control of appetite. Of all the messages they hear, the imperative to be beautiful and good, by being thin, is still the strongest and most familiar. Moreover, they are caught,

often at a very early age, in a deceptive cognitive trap that has them believing that body weight is entirely subject to their conscious control. Despite feminist influences on the career aspirations of the present college-age generation, little has transpired to dilute the basic strength of this powerful cultural prescription that plays on both individualism and conformity. The unfortunate truth is that even when she wants more than beauty and understands its limitations as a life goal, the bourgeois woman still expends an enormous amount of psychic energy on appetite control as well as on other aspects of presentation of the physical self.

And what of the future? ...

We can expect to see eating disorders continue, if not increase, among young women in those postindustrial societies where adolescents tend to be under stress. For both young men and young women, vast technological and cultural changes have made the transition to adulthood particularly difficult by transforming the nature of the family and community and rendering the future unpredictable. According to psychologist Urie Bronfenbrenner and others, American adolescents are in the worst trouble: we have the highest incidence of alcohol and drug abuse among adolescents of any country in the world; we also have the highest rate of teenage pregnancy of any industrialized nation; and we appear to have the most anorexia nervosa.[37]

Although the sexually active adolescent mother and the sexually inactive adolescent anorectic may seem to be light-years apart, they are linked by a common, though unarticulated, understanding. For adolescent women the body is still the most powerful paradigm regardless of social class. Unfortunately, a sizable number of our young women—poor and privileged alike—regard their body as the best vehicle for making a statement about their identity and personal dreams. This is what unprotected sexual intercourse and prolonged starvation have in common. Taken together, our unenviable preeminence in these two domains suggests the enormous difficulty involved in making the transition to adult womanhood in a society where women are still evaluated primarily in terms of the body rather than the mind.

NOTES

1. "On Growing Fat," *Atlantic Monthly* (Mar. 1907):430–31.

2. Jo Ann Olian, *The House of Worth: The Gilded Age, 1860–1918* (New York: Museum of the City of New York, 1982); Jane Beth Abrams, "The Thinning of America: The Emergence of the Ideal of Slenderness in American Popular Culture, 1870–1930," B.A. thesis, Harvard University, 1983, chap. 2.

3. Michael Batterberry and Ariane Batterberry, *Mirror Mirror: A Social History of Fashion* (New York: Holt, Rinehart and Winston, 1977), pp. 289–97; Diane DeMarly, *The History of Haute Couture, 1850–1950* (New York: Holmes & Meier, 1980), pp. 81–83.

4. P. Rostaine, "How to Get Thin," *Medical Press and Circular* 149 (Dec. 23, 1914):643–44.

5. Stuart Ewen and Elizabeth Ewen, *Channels of Desire: Mass Images and the Shaping of American Consciousness* (New York: McGraw-Hill, 1982), pt. 4; Claudia Kidwell and Margaret C. Christman, *Suiting Everyone: The Democratization of Clothing in America* (Washington, D.C.: Smithsonian Institution Press, 1974).

6. *Vogue* (Jan. 1, 1923):63.

7. Lois W. Banner, *American Beauty* (New York: Random House, 1983), p. 262; Ewen and Ewen, *Channels of Desire*, pp. 193–98.

8. Banner, *American Beauty*, p. 287; Anne Hollander, *Seeing through Clothes* (New York: Viking Press, 1975).

9. Lulu Hunt Peters, *Diet and Health with a Key to the Calories* (Chicago: The Reilly & Britton Company, 1918), pp. 24, 39.

10. Ibid., pp. 12, 104, 110.

11. Ibid., pp. 85, 94.

12. Ibid., pp. 85, 93, 94.

13. "On Her Dressing Table," *Vogue* (Apr. 24, 1902):413; ibid. (July 1, 1918):78.

14. Mildred H. Bryan, "Don't Let Your Child Get Fat!" *Hygeia* 15 (1937):801–3; G. D. Schultz, "Forget That Clean-Plate Bogey!" *Better Homes and Gardens* 21 (Sept. 1942):24.

15. Louise Paine Benjamin, "I Have Three Daughters," *Ladies Homes Journal* 57 (June 1940):74.

16. "You'll Eat It Up at Noon," *Seventeen* (Sept. 1946):21–22; Irma M. Phorylles, "The Lost Waistline," ibid. (Mar. 1948):124; "Overweight?" ibid. (Aug. 1948):184.

17. Ibid.

18. "Fattest Girl in the Class," ibid. (Jan. 1948):21–22.

19. "Psychology of Dieting," *Ladies' Home Journal* (Jan. 1965):66.

20. Banner, *American Beauty*, pp. 283–85.

21. David M. Garner et al., "Cultural Expectations of Thinness in Women," *Psychology Reports* 47 (1980):483–91.

22. Rita Freedman, *Beauty Bound* (Lexington: Lexington Books, 1986), p. 150.

23. "Coming on Strong: The New Ideal of Beauty," *Time* (Aug. 30, 1983):71–77.

24. William Chafe, *The Unfinished Journey: America since World War II* (New York: Oxford University Press, 1986).

25. *New Yorker* (July 21, 1986):71.

26. "What's Your Food Status Because the Way You Live Has a Lot to Do with the Way You Eat," *Mademoiselle* (Sept. 1985):224–26; "Food as Well as Clothes, Today, Make the Man—As a Matter of Life and Style," *Vogue* (June 1985):271–73.

27. "Severe Growing Pains for Fast Food," *Business Week* (Mar. 22, 1985):225.

28. Greg Foster and Susan Howerin, "The Quest for Perfection: An Interview with a Former Bulimic," *Iris: A Journal about Women* [Charlottesville, Va.] (1986):21.

29. Before they even arrive on campus, during their senior year in high school and the summer before entering college, many girls began to talk about the "freshmen 10 or 15." This is the weight gain predicted as a result of eating starchy institutional food and participating in late-night food forays with friends.

30. Elizabeth Greene, "Support Groups Forming for Students with Eating Disorders," *Chronicle of Higher Education* (Mar. 5, 1986):1, 30.

31. K. A. Halmi, J. R. Falk, and E. Schwartz, "Binge-Eating and Vomiting: A Survey of a College Population," *Psychological Medicine* 11 (1981):697–706; R. L. Pyle et al., "The Incident of Bulimia in Freshman College Students," *International Journal of Eating Disorders* 2, 3 (1983):75–86.

32. Mirra Komarovsky, *Women in College: Shaping the New Feminine Identities* (New York: Basic Books, 1985), pp. 89–92, 225–300.

33. *Ms.* (Sept. 1986):n.p. The condom is called Mentor.

34. Ellen Goodman, *Close to Home* (New York: Fawcett Crest, 1979).

35. In *Theories of Adolescence* (New York: Random House, 1962), R. E. Muuss wrote: "Societies in a period of rapid transition create a particular adolescent period; the adolescent has not only the society's problem to adjust to but his [or her] own as well" (p. 164).

36. My view of this issue complements ideas presented in Robert Bellah et al., *Habits of the Heart: Individualism and Commitment in American Life* (New York: Harper & Row, 1986).

37. These data are synthesized in Urie Bronfenbrenner, "Alienation and the Four Worlds of Childhood," *Phi Delta Kappan* (Feb. 1986):434.

A sixteen-year-old girl leads children's march to the courthouse in Greenwood, Alabama, 1965. "You think we have problems in Greenwood? We can't even have a peaceful march to our court-house to talk about them." (Photography © by Bob Fitch/Black Star. See Worth Long et al., We'll Never Turn Back *[Washington, D.C.: Smithsonian Performing Arts, 1980], p. 68)*

I V

MODERN AMERICA
1920–2000

The years between 1920 and 2000 have, in the main, been years of crisis. Domestically, innovations in technology, management, and marketing transformed an industrial nation into a consumer society. But consumption did not automatically bring the good life that advertisers promised. In the early years after World War I Americans were plagued by tensions that erupted into strikes, attacks upon radicals, and indiscriminate accusations of communism. The climate of suspicion and anxiety brought out the uglier aspects of American society—the Ku Klux Klan enjoyed a brief rebirth. Conflict between generations underscored anxiety over the continuing erosion of Victorian moral standards. Although elements of progressivism persisted, successive Republican administrations pursued policies designed primarily to benefit American corporations on the assumption that the prosperity of the few would bring prosperity to the many. Whether the assumption was true or not, the collapse of corporate America brought collapse to all after the stock market crash of 1929.

The resulting depression crippled industry and left 20 percent of the labor force unemployed. In 1932, after the Hoover administration had failed to produce recovery, voters turned to Franklin Delano Roosevelt and the Democrats. Promising a "new deal" at a time when people were homeless and starving, Roosevelt launched a program of economic recovery and reform, much of it improvised, not all of it successful, and some of it far less radical and extensive than many critics had wished. The result, however, was that in its efforts to cope with economic disaster, the Roosevelt administration redefined the responsibility of the federal government to its citizens. Relief and work programs were provided, unemployment compensation and minimum wages and hours legislation passed, old-age pensions introduced, individual savings accounts insured, farm prices supported, farm ownership encouraged, farm and home mortgages guaranteed, rural houses electrified, and regional development and soil conservation promoted. The welfare state had arrived. Presidents of both parties would subsequently expand it, designing their own programs to benefit the American people. In the process other changes accelerated by international crises occurred: growth in the power of the presidency, in the size of the federal bureaucracy, and in the level of government spending.

If domestic events had occupied the attention of most Americans in previous years, Nazi aggression and Japan's attack upon Pearl Harbor in 1941 thrust their country into a new international role. Mobilized for total war along conventional lines, Americans were psychologically unprepared for their entry into the new atomic age as citizens of the strongest industrial and military power in world history. The implications of these new developments were scarcely understood when tensions between the United States and its former ally, the USSR, escalated into a "cold" war. The expansion of Russian hegemony in eastern Europe and the victory of Chinese communists in a bloody civil war convinced key policy makers that this nation would have to pursue a vigorous policy to "contain" communism throughout the world. If historians cannot agree on the process that led to cold war, they can agree that the persistent confrontations between East and West during the 1950s profoundly affected American life. Viewing North Korea's invasion of South Korea as proof of Russia's drive for world domination and convinced that the credibility of "containment" was at stake, the Truman administration sent troops to check communist aggression. In the United States there was another kind of warfare. Fearing domestic subversion, anticommunists during the McCarthy era purged government, organized labor, the entertainment industry, and schools and universities of communists—real and alleged. Dissent had become tantamount to disloyalty. By the mid-1950s it was axiomatic to some Americans that any critique of American foreign policy or American society—even if justified—was communist inspired. It was not surprising, therefore, that in the 1960s and 1970s blacks and women who wished to improve their social position should be accused of leftist and un-American sympathies. Many Americans, however, weary of conflict and crisis, had long since sought refuge in suburban privatism and the affluent consumerism of the postwar years.

The election of John Fitzgerald Kennedy in 1960 promised energy and optimism. The succeeding years exemplified both, but not in the manner anticipated. Blacks refused to be intimidated any longer by appeals to "gradualism" or threats of violence. They forced white America to address domestic problems too long deferred; they also provided insight, tactics, rhetoric, and impetus to a resurgent feminist movement. Through the vivid images conveyed to them by television, Americans faced a new and disorderly world. Blacks, Chicanos, Indians, students, women, and protesters against the Vietnam War—all confronted the nation in its living rooms. America seemed to be disintegrating. Convinced that protest had become anarchy, middle America elected Richard M. Nixon in 1968 and again in 1972. But the candidate of "law and order" became the president who put himself above the law. His successors tried to repair the damage done the nation's highest office. In some measure, they succeeded. However, they also faced overwhelming economic problems. These became so grave that the American people would elect a conservative to the presidency in 1980 and reelect him in 1984—one whose "old-fashioned values" kept him from supporting an amendment to give women equal rights under the Constitution. The time of social reform was over. The expansive mood of the 1960s disintegrated in the face of anxiety over unemployment, inflation, rising energy costs, and declining productivity. Foreign relations were no consolation. There were the embarrassment of Vietnam and the danger of Soviet aggression, the weakening ties with our allies, and a greater interdependence of the industrial nations and the Third World. Looking ahead to the remaining years of the century, a distinguished historian observed that this nation's vaunted capacity for self-renewal would be "sorely tested." Even the demise of the Cold War and the collapse of the Soviet Union did not bring an end to international tensions, as the Gulf War and the disintegration of the former Yugoslavia demonstrated. As the century drew to an end, globalization had tied the fate of our economy ever more closely to that of other nations, and the spread of nuclear weapons continued.

Recounting these successive decades in traditional fashion suggests the difficulty of specifying the impact on women's experience. During an era when international developments assumed increasing importance, women were simply not part of the inner councils that debated issues of national security. Women were, of course, included in other aspects of historical experience. As shoppers in the 1920s, they purchased new consumer goods; as discontented citizens, some even joined the Ku Klux Klan. As unemployed laborers and as wives and daughters of unemployed laborers and dispossessed farmers, they shared the economic problems of the Depression; as members of the Roosevelt administration, they shared in the search for solutions. As industrial workers and as members of the armed forces during World War II, women filled critical jobs in a time of labor shortages and contributed to an allied victory. We can even incorporate women into the Washington drama of the McCarthy era, recognizing that women were among the victims of repressive practices and homophobic attitudes, as the experiences of prison reformer Miriam Van Waters attest. Women were also among McCarthy's critics. Margaret Chase Smith was one of the first senators to denounce the "'know-nothing suspect everything' attitudes" that had transformed the Senate into a "forum of hate and character assassination."[1] The women participating in Women Strike for Peace also played a role in discrediting the inquisition, as Amy Swerdlow demonstrates in her account of their confrontation with the House Un-American Activities Committee.

Similarly, in the 1960s, women were part of the dissent that rocked the nation. As military personnel, they experienced the horrors of guerrilla welfare in Vietnam in the 1970s and were captured by Iraqi soldiers in the Gulf War in 1990. As U.S. Senators and Representatives, and even Secretary of State, they coped with the most pressing national and international problems of our age.

Including women, even in this cursory fashion, does not mean, however, that they experienced the events of the last eight decades in the same fashion as did their male counterparts. Gender mattered, as of course, did race, class, ethnicity and sexual preference. Consider the differing experiences of male and female industrial workers employed during World War II. For working-class men, wartime jobs provided a foundation on which to build a secure future in a post-war era of full employment. For working-class women, the jobs were only a temporary bonus that they forfeited to returning veterans. Some of those who lost their jobs were heads of households. Forced to return to low-paying jobs as domestics or waitresses, they never enjoyed the economic security experienced by their male counterparts.

Consider, too, the difference gender made for the young men and women in uniform with aspirations for future civilian employment that required advanced degrees. They could return to universities for professional degrees as one of their G.I. benefits. But the men and women who did so often wound up with different career trajectories. For example, newly trained male scientists went on to rewarding careers in universities, research institutes or the research and development divisions of large corporations;

women with Ph.D.s in science often found themselves either jobless or in positions inappropriate for their level of talent and training. The difference could be measured not only in economic terms but in psychological well-being. One Navy veteran, trained as a research botanist at the war's end, but never able to secure suitable employment, captured the years of frustration in the title of her autobiography, *Slam the Door Gently: The Making and Unmaking of a Female Scientist.*[2]

A third example concerns participation in the protest movements that transformed the 1960s into a decade of self-criticism and turmoil. Young white women as well as young women of color were deeply involved in these struggles, the former in Students for a Democratic Society (SDS), an organization of the New Left, and the latter in groups such as the Student Nonviolent Coordinating Committee (SNCC) and the United Mexican American Students (UMAS). Despite their common commitment to equality, men tended to assume leadership roles, while women found themselves fulfilling customary roles as secretaries, housekeepers, and sexual partners. That radical groups committed to equality should engage in such traditional practices seemed inconsistent to some of the women involved. But their efforts to raise the issue were rebuffed and ridiculed. So great were the disparities in the experience of men and women in these organizations that many women, while not abandoning the movement's original goals, ultimately organized on their own behalf, as their statements in this volume reveal.

Including women's experience, even when it differs in significant ways from that of men, does not in itself refocus history. But it begins the process of valuing the experience of both sexes. And it sets in motion the search for a new paradigm that will enable us to find a post in which, as Gerda Lerner suggests, both *"men and women* are the measure of significance."[3] It alerts us, too, to the ways in which gender provides clues to relationships of inequality even when no women are present.

NOTES

1. *Congressional Record*, 96 (June 1, 1950):7894–95.
2. Ruth Ann Bobrov Glater, *Slam the Door Gently: The Making and Unmaking of a Female Scientist* (Santa Barbara, Calif., 1997).
3. Gerda Lerner, *The Majority Finds Its Past: Placing Women in History* (New York, 1979), p. 180.

NANCY F. COTT

Equal Rights and Economic Roles: The Conflict over the Equal Rights Amendment in the 1920s

The vote achieved, former suffragists turned their attention to sex-based discrimination in the law. The proper strategy, as in suffrage, seemed to be a constitutional amendment affirming equal rights; men and women would have to be treated under the law as equals and as individuals. Suffragists who had struggled to pass legislation shortening hours and improving working conditions for women in industry had achieved that goal only because the Supreme Court was prepared to regard women as a special class of workers in need of governmental protection because of their childbearing role. (See *Muller* v. *Oregon*, pp. 325–26.) An equal rights amendment would invalidate sex-based labor laws, they feared, since comparable protection would not be extended to men. The ensuing debate was a critical one creating deep and lasting divisions. Unable to agree on a unified agenda for four decades, veterans of the first women's movement expended energy in internal conflict, thereby diluting their political effectiveness. Not surprisingly women's issues made little headway until the 1960s.

The debate over ERA was critical not only because of its long-term consequences, but because it highlighted differing views within feminism of the social significance of gender and the meaning of equality. Does equality require that men and women have the "same" rights and be subject to the "same" treatment or does equality require "different" rights? How should the law treat the difference created by women's unique reproductive system? With these questions in mind, Nancy Cott carefully assesses the initial debate over ERA, making clear the assumptions and limitations inherent in the arguments of each side.

THE CONFLICT OVER THE EQUAL RIGHTS AMENDMENT IN THE 1920s

Campaigning for ratification of the Equal Rights Amendment during the 1970s, feminists who found it painful to be opposed by other groups of women were often unaware that the first proposal of that amendment in the 1920s had likewise caused a bitter split between women's groups claiming, on both sides, to represent women's interests. The 1920s conflict itself echoed some earlier ideological and tactical controversies. One central strategic question for the women's rights movement in the late nineteenth century had concerned alliances: should proponents of "the cause of woman" ally with advocates for the rights for freed slaves, with temperance workers, or labor reformers, or a political party, or none of them? At various times different women leaders felt passionately for and against such alliances, not agreeing on what they meant for the breadth of the women's movement and for the priority assigned to women's issues.[1] The 1920s contest over the equal rights amendment reiterated that debate insofar as the National Woman's Party, which proposed the ERA, took a "single-issue" approach, and the opposing women's organizations were committed to maintaining multiple alliances. But in even more striking ways than it recapitulated nineteenth-century struggles the 1920s equal rights conflict also predicted lines of fracture of the later twentieth-century women's movement. The advantages or compromises involved in "multi-issue" organizing are matters of contemporary concern, of course. Perhaps more important, the 1920s debate brought into sharp focus (and left for us generations later to resolve) the question whether "equal rights"— a concept adopted, after all, from the male political tradition—matched women's needs. The initial conflict between women over the ERA set the goal of enabling women to have the same opportunities and situations as men against the goal of enabling women freely to be different from men without adverse consequences. As never before in nineteenth-century controversies, these two were seen as competing, even mutually exclusive, alternatives.

The equal rights amendment was proposed as a legal or civic innovation but the intrafeminist controversy it caused focused on the economic arena. Indeed, the connection between economic and political subordination in women's relation to men has been central in women's rights advocacy since the latter part of the nineteenth century. In the Western political tradition, women were historically excluded from political initiatives because they were defined as dependent—like children and slaves—and their dependence was read as fundamentally economic. Nineteenth-century advocates, along with the vote, claimed women's "right to labor," by which they meant the right for women to have their labor recognized, and diversified. They emphasized that women, as human individuals no less than men, had the right and need to use their talents to serve society and themselves and to gain fair compensation. Influential voices such as Charlotte Perkins Gilman's at the turn of the century stressed not only women's service but the necessity and warrant for women's economic independence. Gilman argued simultaneously that social evolution made women's

move "from fireside to factory" inevitable, and also that the move ought to be spurred by conscious renovation of outworn tradition.

By the 1910s suffragists linked political and economic rights, and connected the vote with economic leverage, whether appealing to industrial workers, career women or housewives. They insisted on women's economic independence in principle and defense of wage-earning women in fact. Since the vast majority of wage-earning women were paid too little to become economically independent, however, the two commitments were not identical and might in practice be entirely at odds.[2] The purpose to validate women's existing economic roles might openly conflict with the purpose to throw open economic horizons for women to declare their own self-definition. These tensions introduced by the feminist and suffrage agitation of the 1910s flashed into controversy over the equal rights amendment in the 1920s.

The ERA was the baby of the National Woman's Party, yet not its brainchild alone. As early as 1914, a short-lived New York City group called the Feminist Alliance had suggested a constitutional amendment barring sex discrimination of all sorts. Like the later NWP, the Feminist Alliance was dominated by highly educated and ambitious women in the arts and professions, women who believed that "equal rights" were their due while they also aimed to rejuvenate and reorient thinking about "rights" around female rather than only male definition. Some members of the Feminist Alliance surely joined the NWP, which emerged as the agent of militant and political action during the final decade of the suffrage campaign.[3]

A small group (engaging perhaps 5 percent of all suffragists), the NWP grew from the Congressional Union founded by Alice Paul and Lucy Burns in 1913 to work on the federal rather than the state-by-state route to woman suffrage. Through the 'teens it came to stand for partisan tactics (opposing all Democrats because the Democratic administration had not passed woman suffrage) and for flamboyant, symbolic, publicity-generating actions— large parades, pickets in front of the White House, placards in the Congress, hunger-striking in jail, and more. It gained much of its energy from leftwing radical women who were attracted to its wholesale condemnation of gender inequality and to its tactical adaptations from the labor movement; at the same time, its imperious tendency to work from the top down attracted crucial financial and moral support from some very rich women. When the much larger group, the National American Woman Suffrage Association, moved its focus to a constitutional amendment in 1916, that was due in no little part (although certainly not solely), to the impact of the NWP. Yet while imitating its aim, NAWSA's leaders always hated and resented the NWP, for the way it had horned in on the same pro-suffrage turf while scorning the NAWSA's traditional nonpartisan, educative strategy. These resentments festered into deep and long-lasting personal conflicts between leaders of the two groups.

Just after the 19th Amendment was ratified in August of 1920, the NWP began planning a large convention at which its members would decide whether to continue as a group and, if so, what to work for. The convention, held six months later and tightly orchestrated by chairman Alice Paul, brushed aside all other suggestions and endorsed an ongoing program to "remove all remaining forms of the subjection of women," by means of the elimination of sex discrimination in law.[4] At the outset, NWP leaders seemed unaware that this program of "equal rights" would be much thornier to define and implement than "equal suffrage" had been. They began surveying state legal codes, conferring with lawyers, and drafting numerous versions of equal rights legislation and amendments at the state and federal levels.

Yet the "clean sweep" of such an approach immediately raised a problem: would it invalidate sex-based labor legislation—the laws regulating women's hours, wages, and conditions of work, that women trade unionists and reformers had worked to establish over the past thirty years? The doctrine of "liberty of contract" between employer and employed had ruled court interpretations of labor legislation in the early twentieth century, stymying state regulation of the wages and hours of male workers. State regulation for women workers, espoused and furthered by many women in the NWP, had been made possible only by differentiating female from male wage-earners on the basis of physiology and reproductive functions. Now members of the NWP had to grapple with the question whether such legislation

was sex "discrimination," hampering women workers in the labor market. Initially, there was a great deal of sentiment within the NWP, even voiced by Alice Paul herself, that efforts at equal rights legislation should not impair existing sex-based protective labor legislation. However, there was also contrary opinion, which Paul increasingly heeded; by late November 1921 she had come to believe firmly that "enacting labor laws along sex lines is erecting another handicap for women in the economic struggle." Some NWP affiliates were still trying to draft an amendment that would preserve special labor legislation, nonetheless, and continued to introduce equal rights bills with "safeguards" in some states through the following spring.[5]

Meanwhile women leaders in other organizations were becoming nervous and distrustful of the NWP's intentions. Led by the League of Women Voters (successor to the NAWSA), major women's organizations in 1920 formed a national lobbying group called the Women's Joint Congressional Committee. The LWV was interested in eliminating sex discrimination in the law, but more immediately concerned with the extension of sex-based labor legislation. Moreover, the LWV had inherited NAWSA's hostility to Alice Paul. The first president of the LWV, Maud Wood Park, still smarted from the discomfiture that NWP picketing tactics had caused her when she headed the NAWSA's Congressional Committee from 1916 to 1920.[6] Other leading groups in the Women's Joint Congressional Committee were no less suspicious of the NWP. The National Women's Trade Union League since the mid-1910s had concentrated its efforts on labor legislation to protect women workers. Florence Kelley, director of the National Consumers' League, had been part of the inner circle of the NWP during the suffrage campaign, but on the question of protective labor laws her priorities diverged. She had spent three decades trying to get state regulation of workers' hours and conditions, and was not about to abandon the gains achieved for women.[7]

In December 1921, at Kelley's behest, Paul and three other NWP members met for discussion with her and leaders of the League of Women Voters, the National Women's Trade Union League, the Woman's Christian Temperance Union, and the General Federation of

Women's Clubs. All the latter objected to the new constitutional amendment now formulated by the NWP: "No political, civil or legal disabilities or inequalities on account of sex, or on account of marriage unless applying alike to both sexes, shall exist within the United States or any place subject to their jurisdiction." Paul gave away no ground, and all left feeling that compromise was unlikely. Each side already thought the other intransigent, though in fact debate was still going on within the NWP.[8]

By mid-1922 the National Consumers' League, the LWV, and the Women's Trade Union League went on record opposing "blanket" equal rights bills, as the NWP formulations at both state and federal levels were called. About the same time, the tide turned in the NWP. The top leadership accepted as definitive the views of Gail Laughlin, a lawyer from Maine, who contended that sex-based labor legislation was not a lamented loss but a positive harm. "If women can be segregated as a class for special legislation," she warned, "the same classification can be used for special restrictions along any other line which may, at any time, appeal to the caprice or prejudice of our legislatures." In her opinion, if "protective" laws affecting women were not abolished and prohibited, "the advancement of women in business and industry will be stopped and women relegated to the lowest, worst paid labor."[9] Since NWP lobbyists working at the state level were making little headway, a federal constitutional amendment appeared all the more appealing. In November 1923, at a grand conference staged in Seneca Falls, New York, commemorating the seventy-fifth anniversary of Elizabeth Cady Stanton's Declaration of Sentiments, the NWP announced new language: "Men and women shall have equal rights throughout the United States and every place subject to its jurisdiction." The constitutional amendment was introduced into Congress on December 10, 1923.[10]

In the NWP view, this was the logical sequel to the 19th Amendment. There were so many different sex discriminations in state codes and legal practices—in family law, labor law, jury privileges, contract rights—that only a constitutional amendment seemed effective to remove them. The NWP took the language of liberal individualism, enshrined in the catchphrase of "equal rights," to express its

feminism. As Alice Paul saw it, what women as a gender group shared was their subordination and inequality to men as a whole; the legal structure most clearly expressed this subordination and inequality, and therefore was the logical point of attack. The NWP construed this agenda as "purely feminist," that is, appealing to women as women, uniting women around a concern common to them regardless of the other ways in which they might differ. Indeed, at its founding postsuffrage convention the NWP leadership purposely bypassed issues it saw as less "pure," including birth control, the defense of black women's voting rights in the South, and pacifism, which were predictably controversial among women themselves.

The NWP posited that women could and would perceive self-interest in "purely" gender terms. Faced by female opponents, its leaders imagined a fictive or abstract unity among women rather than attempting to encompass women's real diversity. They separated the proposal of equal rights from other social and political issues and effects. Although the campaign for equal rights was initiated in a vision of inclusiveness—envisioned as a stand that all women could take—it devolved into a practice of exclusiveness. The NWP's "appeal for conscious sex loyalty" (as a member once put it) went out to members of the sex who could subordinate identifications and loyalties of class, ethnicity, race, religion, politics, or whatever else to a "pure" sense of themselves as women differentiated from men. That meant principally women privileged by the dominant culture in every way except that they were female.[11]

In tandem with its lobbying for an equal rights amendment, the NWP presented its opposition to sex-based labor legislation as a positive program of "industrial equality." It championed women wage-earners who complained of "protective" legislation as restrictive, such as printers, railroad conductors, or waitresses hampered by hours limitation, or cleaning women fired and replaced by men after the passage of minimum-wage laws. Only a handful of working-class women rose to support for the ERA, however.[12] Mary Anderson, former factory worker herself and since 1919 the director of the U.S. Women's Bureau, which was founded to guide and assist women workers, threw her weight into the fight against the amendment. Male trade unionists—namely leaders of the American Federation of Labor—also voiced immediate opposition to the NWP aims, appearing at the very first U.S. Senate subcommittee hearings on the equal rights amendment. Male unionists or class-conscious workers in this period put their faith in collective bargaining and did not seek labor legislation for themselves, but endorsed it for women and child workers. This differentiation derived partly from male workers' belief in women's physical weakness and veneration of women's "place" in the home, partly from presumptions about women workers being difficult to organize, and also from the aim to keep women from competing for men's jobs. Male unionists tended to view wage-earning women first as women—potential or actual wives and mothers—and only secondarily as workers. For differing reasons women and men in the labor movement converged in their support of sex-based legislation: women because they saw special protection necessary to defend their stake in industry and in union organizations, limited as it was; men to hold at bay women's demands for equal entry into male-controlled union jobs and organizations.[13]

The arguments against the equal rights amendment offered by trade unionists and by such women's organizations as the League of Women Voters overlapped. They assumed that an equal rights amendment would invalidate sex-based labor laws or, at least, destine them for protracted argument in the courts, where judges had shown hostility to any state regulation of employer prerogatives. They insisted that the greatest good for the greatest number was served by protective labor laws. If sex-based legislation hampered some—as the NWP claimed, and could be shown true, for instance, in the case of women linotypists, who needed to work at night—then the proper tactic was to exempt some occupations, not to eliminate protective laws whole. They feared that state welfare legislation in place, such as widows' pensions, would also be at risk. They contended that a constitutional amendment was too undiscriminating an instrument: objectionable sex discriminations such as those concerning jury duty, inheritance rights, nationality, or child custody would be more efficiently and accurately eliminated by specific bills for specific instances. Sometimes, opponents claimed that the ERA took an

unnecessarily federal approach, overriding states' rights, although here they were hardly consistent for many of them were at the same time advocating a constitutional amendment to prohibit child labor.

Against the ERA, spokeswomen cited evidence that wage-earning women wanted and valued labor legislation and that male workers, too, benefitted from limits on women's hours in factories where men and women worked at interdependent tasks. Before hours were legally limited, "we were 'free' and 'equal' to work long hours for starvation wages, or free to leave the job and starve!" WTUL leader Pauline Newman bitterly recalled. Dr. Alice Hamilton, pioneer of industrial medicine, saw the NWP as maintaining "a purely negative program, . . . holding down in their present condition of industrial slavery hundreds of thousands of women without doing anything to alleviate their lot."[14] Trade-unionist and Women's Bureau colleagues attacked the NWP's vision as callously class-biased, the thoughtless outlook of rich women, at best relevant to the experience of exceptional skilled workers or professionals. They regularly accused the NWP of being the unwitting tool (at best) or the paid servant of rapacious employers, although no proof of the latter was ever brought forward. They heard in the NWP program the voice of the ruling class and denounced the equal rights amendment as "class" legislation, by and for the bourgeoisie.[15]

Indeed, at the Women's Bureau Conference on Women in Industry in 1926, the NWP's opposition to sex-based labor legislation was echoed by the president of the National Association of Manufacturers, who declared that the "handful" of women in industry could take care of themselves and were not served by legislative "poultices." In this controversy, the positions also lent themselves to, and inevitably were colored by, male "allies" whose principal concerns dealt less with women's economic or legal protection or advancement than political priorities of their own. At the same conference the U.S. Secretary of Labor appointed by President Coolidge took the side of sex-based protective legislation, proclaiming that "The place fixed for women by God and Nature is a great place," and "wherever we see women at work we must see them in terms of motherhood." What he saw as the great danger of the age was the "increasing loss of the distinction between manliness and true femininity."[16]

Often, ERA opponents who supported sex-based labor legislation—including civic-minded middle-class women, social welfare reformers, government officials, and trade union men—appeared more concerned with workingwomen's motherhood than with economic justice. "Women who are wage earners, with one job in the factory and another in the home have little time and energy left to carry on the fight to better their economic status. They need the help of other women and they need labor laws," announced Mary Anderson. Dr. Hamilton declared that "the great inarticulate body of working women . . . are largely helpless, . . . [and] have very special needs which unaided they cannot attain. . . ."[17] Where NWP advocates had before their eyes women who were eager and robust, supporters of protective legislation saw women overburdened and vulnerable. The former claimed that protective laws penalized the strong; the latter claimed that the ERA would sacrifice the weak. The NWP looked at women as individuals and wanted to dislodge gender differentiation from the labor market. Their opponents looked at women as members of families—daughters, wives, mothers, and widows with family responsibilities—and believed that the promise of "mere equality" did not sufficiently take those relationships into account. The one side tacitly positing the independent professional woman as the paradigm, the other presuming the doubly burdened mother in industry or service, neither side distinguished nor addressed directly the situation of the fastest-growing sector of employed women, in white-collar jobs. At least half of the female labor force—those in manufacturing and in domestic and personal service—worked in taxing, menial jobs with long hours, unpleasant and often unhealthy conditions, very low pay, and rare opportunities for advancement. But in overall pattern women's employment was leaving these sectors and swelling in clerical, managerial, sales, and professional areas. White-collar workers were fewer than 18 percent of all women employed in 1900, but the proportion more than doubled by 1920 and by 1930 was 44 percent.[18]

The relation of sex-based legislation to women workers' welfare was more ambiguous and complicated than either side acknowledged. Such laws immediately benefitted far larger numbers of employed women than they hindered, but the laws also had a negative impact on women's overall economic opportunities, both immediately and in the long term. Sex segregation of the labor market was a very significant factor. In industries monopolizing women workers, where wages, conditions, and hours were more likely to be substandard, protective legislation helped to bring things up to standard. It was in more desirable crafts and trades more unusual for women workers, where skill levels and pay were likely to be higher—that is, where women needed to enter in order to improve their earnings and economic advancement—that sex-based protective legislation held women back. There, as a contemporary inquiry into the issue said, "the practice of enacting laws covering women alone appears to discourage their employment, and thereby fosters the prejudice against them." The segregation of women into low-paid, dead-end jobs that made protective laws for women workers necessary, was thus abetted by the legislation itself.[19]

By 1925, all but four states limited workingwomen's hours; eighteen states prescribed rest periods and meal hours; sixteen states prohibited night work in certain occupations; and thirteen had minimum wage regulations. Such regulation was passed not only because it served women workers, but also because employers, especially large corporate employers, began to see benefits in its stabilization of the labor market and control of unscrupulous competition. Although the National Association of Manufacturers, fixed on "liberty of contract," remained opposed, large employers of women accepted sex-based labor legislation on reasoning about "protection of the race," or could see advantages for themselves in it, or both. A vice-president of Filene's, a large department store in Boston, for instance, approved laws regulating the hours, wages, and conditions of women employees because "economies have been effected by the reduction of labor turnover; by reduction of the number of days lost through illness and accidents; and by increase in the efficiency of the working force as well as in the efficiency of management." He appreciated the legislation's maintaining standards as to hours, wages, and working conditions "throughout industry as a *whole,* thus preventing selfish interests from indulging in unfair competition by the exploitation of women. . . ."[20]

While the anti-ERA side was right in the utilitarian contention that protective laws meant the greatest good to the greatest number of women workers (at least in the short run), the pro-ERA side was also right that such laws hampered women's scope in the labor market and sustained the assumption that employment advantage was not of primary concern to women. Those who advocated sex-based laws were looking at the labor market as it was, trying to protect women in it, but thereby contributing to the perpetuation of existing inequalities. They envisaged wage-earning women as veritable beasts of burden. That group portrait supplanted the prior feminist image of wage-earning women as a vanguard of independent female personalities, as equal producers of the world's wealth. Its advocates did not see that their conception of women's needs helped to confirm women's second-class position in the economy. On the other hand, the ERA advocates who opposed sex-based "protections" were envisioning the labor market as it might be, trying to ensure women the widest opportunities in that imagined arena, and thereby blinking at existing exploitation. They did not admit to the vulnerabilities that sex-based legislation addressed, while they overestimated what legal equality might do to unchain women from the economic stranglehold of the domestic stereotype.

Women on both sides of the controversy, however, saw themselves as legatees of suffragism and feminism, intending to defend the value of women's economic roles, to prevent economic exploitation of women and to open the doors to economic opportunity. A struggle over the very word feminism, which the NWP had embraced, became part of the controversy. For "us even to use the word feminist," contended Women's Trade Union League leader Ethel Smith, "is to invite from the extremists a challenge to our authenticity." Detractors in the WTUL and Women's Bureau called the NWP "ultra" or "extreme" feminists. Mary Anderson considered herself "a good feminist" but objected that "over-articulate theorists were attempting to solve the working women's problems on a purely feministic basis with the working women's own voice far less ade-

quately heard." Her own type of feminist was moderate and practical, Anderson declared; the others, putting the "woman question" above all other questions, were extreme and abstract. The bitterness was compounded by a conflict of personalities and tactics dragged on from the suffrage years. Opponents of the ERA, deeply resenting having to oppose something called equal rights, maligned the NWP as "pernicious," women who "discard[ed] all ethics and fair play," an "insane crowd" who espoused "a kind of hysterical feminism with a slogan for a program."[21] Their critiques fostered public perception of feminism as a sectarian and impracticable doctrine unrelated to real life and blind to injustices besides sex inequality. By the end of the 1920s women outside the NWP rarely made efforts to reclaim the term feminist for themselves, and the meaning of the term was depleted.

Forced into theorizing by this controversy, not prepared as philosophers or legal theorists, spokeswomen on either side in the 1920s were grappling with definitions of women's rights as compared to men's that neither the legal nor economic system was designed to accommodate. The question whether equality required women to have the same rights as men, or different rights, could not be answered without delving into definitions. Did "equality" pertain to opportunity, treatment, or outcome?[22] Should "difference" be construed to mean separation, discrimination, protection, privilege— or assault on the very standard that the male was the human norm?[23]

Opponents of the ERA believed that sex-based legislation was necessary because of women's biological and social roles as mothers. They claimed that "The inherent differences are permanent. Women will always need many laws different from those needed by men"; "Women as such, whether or not they are mothers present or prospective, will always need protective legislation"; "The working mother is handicapped by her own nature."[24] Their approach stressed maternal nature and inclination as well as conditioning, and implied that the sexual division of labor was eternal.

The NWP's approach, on the other hand, presupposed that women's differentiation from men in the law and the labor market was a particular, social-historical, and not necessary or inevitable construction. The sexual division of labor arose from archaic custom, enshrined in employer and employee attitudes and written in the law. The NWP approach assumed that wives and mothers as well as unencumbered women would want and should have open access to jobs and professions. NWP proponents imagined that the sexual division of labor (in the family and the marketplace) would change if women would secure the same rights as men and have free access to wage-earning. Their view made a fragile potential into a necessary fact. They assumed that women's wage-earning would, by its very existence, challenge the sexual division of labor, and that it would provide the means for women's economic independence—although neither of these tenets was necessarily being realized.

Wage-earning women's experience in the 1910s and 1920s, as documented by the Women's Bureau, showed that the sexual division of labor was budged only very selectively and marginally by women's gainful employment. Most women's wages did not bring them economic independence; women earned as part of a plan for family support (as men did, though that was rarely stressed). Contrary to the NWP's feminist visions, in those places in the nation where the highest proportions of wives and mothers worked for pay, the sexual division of labor was most oppressively in place. To every child growing up in the region of Southern textile and tobacco mills, where wives and mothers worked more "jobs" at home and in the factory than any other age or status group—and earned less—the sexual division of labor appeared no less prescriptive and burdensome than it had before women earned wages.[25]

Critiques of the NWP and its ERA as "abstract" or "extreme" or "fanatical" represented the gap between feminist tenets and harsh social reality as an oversight of the NWP, a failure to adjust their sights. Even more sympathetic critics, such as one Southern academic, asked rhetorically, "Do the feminists see in the tired and haggard faces of young waitresses, who spend seventy hours a week of hard work in exchange for a few dollars to pay for food and clothing, a deceptive mask of the noble spirit within?" She answered herself, "Surely it is not an increasing army of jaded girls and spent women that pours every day from factory and shop that the leaders of the feminist movement seek. But the call for women to make all labor their province can mean nothing more. They would free women from the rule of men only to make them greater slaves to the machines of industry."[26] Indeed, the exploitation of female service and industrial workers at "cheap" wages cruelly parodied the feminist notion that gainful employment represented an assertion of independence (just as the wifely duties required of a secretary parodied the feminist expectation that wage-earning would challenge the sexual division of labor and reopen definitions of feminity). What such critics were observing was the distance between the potential for women's wage-earning to challenge the sexual division of labor, and the social facts of gender and class hierarchy that clamped down on that challenge.

Defenders of sex-based protective legislation, trying to acknowledge women's unique reproductive endowments and social obligations, were grappling with problems so difficult they would still be present more than half a century later. Their immediate resolution was to portray women's "difference" in merely customary terms. "Average American women prefer to make a home for husbands and children to anything else," Mary Anderson asserted in defense of her position. "They would rather fulfill this normal function than go into the business world."[27] Keeping alive a critique of the class division of wealth, protective legislation advocates lost sight of the need to challenge the very sexual division of labor that was the root of women's "handicap" or "helplessness." As compared to the NWP's emphasis on the historical and social construction of gender roles, advocates of sex-based protective legislation echoed customary public opinion in proposing that motherhood and wage-earning should be mutually exclusive. They easily found allies among such social conservatives as the National Council of Catholic Women, whose representatives testified against the ERA because it "seriously menaced . . . the unity of the home and family life" and contravened the "essential differences in rights and duties" of the two sexes which were the "result of natural law." Edging into plain disapproval of mothers of young children who earned, protective legislation supporters became more prescriptive, less flexible, than wage-earning mothers themselves, for whom cash recognition of their labor was very welcome. "Why should not a married woman work [for pay], if a single one does?" demanded a mill worker who came to the Southern Summer School for Women Workers. "What would men think if they were told that a married man should not work? If we women would not be so submissive and take everything for granted, if we would awake and stand up for our rights, this world would be a better place to live in, at least it would be better for the women. . . ."[28]

The onset of the Depression in many ways worsened the ERA controversy, for the one side thought protective legislation all the more crucial when need drove women to take any jobs available, and the other side argued that protective legislation prevented women from competing for what jobs there were. In the 1930s it became clear that the labor movement's and League of Women Voters' opposition to the equal rights amendment ran deeper than concern for sex-based legislation as an "entering wedge." The Fair Labor Standards Act of 1938 mandated wages and hours regulation for all workers, and the U.S. Supreme Court upheld it in 1941; but the labor movement and the LWV still opposed the ERA. Other major women's organizations, however—most importantly the National Federation of Business and Professional Women's Clubs and the General Federation of Women's Clubs—and the national platforms of both the Republican [Party] and the Democratic Party endorsed the ERA by 1944.[29]

We generally learn "winners'" history—not the history of lost causes. If the ERA passed by Congress in 1972 had achieved ratification by 1982, perhaps historians of women would read the trajectory of the women's movement from 1923 to the present as a steady upward curve, and award the NWP unqualified original insight. The failure of the ERA this time around (on new, but not unrelated, grounds) compels us to see the longer history of equal rights in its true complexity.[30] The ERA battle of the 1920s seared into memory the fact of warring outlooks among women while it illustrated the inevitable intermeshing of women's legal and political rights with their economic situations. If the controversy testified to the difficulty of protecting women in the economic arena while opening opportunities to them, even more fundamentally the debate brought into question the NWP's premise that the articulation of sex discrimination—or the call for equal rights—would arouse all women to mobilize as a group. What kind of a group were women when their occupational and social and other loyalties were varied, when not all women viewed "women's" interests, or what constituted sex "discrimination," the same way? The ideological dimensions of that problem cross-cut both class consciousness and gender identity. The debate's intensity, both then and now, measured how fundamental was the revision needed if policies and practices of economic and civic life deriving from a male norm were to give full scope to women—and to women of all sorts.

NOTES

1. A good introduction to the issue of alliances in the nineteenth-century women's movement, and an essential text on the mid-nineteenth-century split, is Ellen Carol DuBois, *Feminism and Suffrage: The Emergence of an Independent Women's Movement, 1848–1869* (Ithaca, N.Y.: Cornell, 1978).

2. See Leslie Woodcock Tentler, *Wage-Earning Women: Industrial Work and Family Life in the U.S., 1900–1930* (New York: Oxford University Press, 1979), chap. 1, on industrially employed women's wages, keyed below subsistence.

3. On feminists in the final decade of the suffrage campaign, see Nancy F. Cott, *The Grounding of Modern Feminism* (New Haven: Yale University Press, 1987), pp. 23–66.

4. For more detailed discussion of the February 1921 convention, see Nancy F. Cott, "Feminist Politics in the 1920s: The National Woman's Party," *Journal of American History* 71, no. 1 (June 1984).

5. Paul to Jane Norman Smith, Nov. 29, 1921, folder 110, J. N. Smith Collection, Schlesinger Library (hereafter SL). See NWP correspondence of Feb.–Mar. 1921 in the microfilm collection "The National Woman's Party, 1913–1974" (Microfilm Corp. of America), reels #5–7 (hereafter NWP with reel no.), and Cott, *Grounding*, pp. 66–74, 120–25, for more detail.

In Wisconsin, prominent NWP suffragist Mabel Raef Putnam put together a coalition which successfully lobbied through the first state equal rights bill early in 1921. This legislation granted women the same rights and privileges as men *except for* "the special protection and privileges which they now enjoy for the general welfare." . . .

6. Maud Wood Park, *Front Door Lobby*, ed. Edna Stantial (Boston: Beacon Press, 1960), p. 23.

7. Historians' treatments of women's organizations' differing views on the ERA in the 1920s include William N. O'Neill, *Everyone Was Brave* (Chicago: Quadrangle, 1969), pp. 274–94; J. Stanley Lemons, *The Woman Citizen: Social Feminism in the 1920s* (Urbana: University of Illinois Press, 1973), pp. 184–99; William Chafe, *The American Woman: Her*

Changing Social, Economic and Political Roles (New York: Oxford University Press, 1972), pp. 112–32; Sheila M. Rothman, Woman's Proper Place: A History of Changing Ideals and Practices, 1870 to the Present (New York: Basic Books, 1978), pp. 153–65; Susan Becker, Origins of the Equal Rights Amendment: American Feminism between the Wars (Westport, Conn.: Greenwood Press, 1981), pp. 121–51; Alice Kessler-Harris, Out to Work: A History of Wage-Earning Women in the U.S. (New York: Oxford University Press, 1982), pp. 194–95, 205–12; Judith Sealander, As Minority Becomes Majority (Westport, Conn.: Greenwood Press, 1983). Fuller documentation of my reading of both sides can be found in Cott, Grounding, pp. 122–29 and accompanying notes.

8. "Conference on So-Called 'Equal Rights' Amendment Proposed by the National Woman's Party Dec. 4, 1921," ts. NWTUL Papers, microfilm reel 2. . . .

9. NWP National Council minutes, Dec. 17, 1921, Feb. 14, 1922, Apr. 11, 1922, NWP #114. To the NWP inner circle Laughlin's point was borne out by a 1923 ruling in Wisconsin, where, despite the Equal Rights Bill, the attorney general declined to strike down a 1905 law which prohibited women from being employed in the state legislature. He likened the prohibition to an hours-limitation law, because legislative service required "very long and often unreasonable hours." Alice Paul read his decision as "an extremely effective argument against" drafting equal rights bills with exemptions for sex-based protective legislation. Anita L. Pollitzer to Mrs. Jane Norman Smith, Jan. 5, 1922, folder 110, and Paul to Jane Norman Smith, Feb. 20, 1923, folder 111, J. N. Smith Coll.

10. National Council Minutes, June 19, 1923, NWP #114. Before 1923 the ERA went through scores of drafts, recorded in part F, NWP #116. Versions akin to the suffrage amendment—e.g., "Equal rights with men shall not be denied to women or abridged on account of sex or marriage . . ."—were considered in 1922, but not until 1943 was the amendment introduced into Congress in the form "Equality of rights under the law shall not be denied or abridged by the United States or by any state on account of sex," modeled on the Nineteenth Amendment, which in turn was modeled on the Fifteenth Amendment.

11. Quotation from Edith Houghton Hooker, Editor's Note, Equal Rights (the NWP monthly publication), Dec. 22, 1928, p. 365. See Cott, Grounding, pp. 75–82.

12. The two most seen on NWP platforms were Josephine Casey, a former ILGWU organizer, suffrage activist, later a bookbinder, and Mary Murray, a Brooklyn Railway employee who had resigned from her union in 1920 to protest its acceptance of laws prohibiting night work for women.

13. Kessler-Harris, Out to Work, 200–5; and "Problems of Coalition-Building: Women and Trade Unions in the 1920s," in Women, Work and Protest, ed. Ruth Milkman (Boston: Routledge and Kegan Paul, 1985), esp. p. 132.

14. . . . More extensive documentation of the debate can be found in the notes in Cott, Grounding, pp. 325–26.

15. Kessler-Harris, Out to Work, pp. 189–94, reveals ambivalent assessments of labor legislation by ordinary wage-earning women.

16. Printed release from the National Association of Manufacturers, "Defend American Womanhood by Protecting Their Homes, Edgerton Tells Women in Industry," Jan. 19, 1926, in folder 1118, and ts. speech by James Davis, U.S. Secretary of Labor, Jan. 18, 1926, in folder 1117, Box 71, Mary Van Kleeck Collection, Sophia Smith Collection, Smith College.

17. Mary Anderson, "Should There Be Labor Laws for Women? Yes," Good Housekeeping, Sept. 1925. . . .

18. See Valerie K. Oppenheimer, The Female Labor Force in the U.S. (Westport, Conn.: Greenwood Press, 1976), pp. 3, 149; Lois Scharf, To Work and to Wed (Westport, Conn.: Greenwood Press, 1980), pp. 15–16: Winifred Wandersee, Women's Work and Family Values 1920–1940 (Cambridge Mass.: Harvard, 1981), p. 85, 89.

19. Elizabeth F. Baker, "At the Crossroads in the Legal Protection of Women in Industry," Annals of the American Academy of Political and Social Science 143 (May 1929):277. . . .
Recently historians have stressed the regressive potential of sex-based protective laws. See . . . Nancy Schrom Dye, As Equals and as Sisters: Feminism, Unionism and the Women's Trade Union League of New York (Columbia: University of Missouri Press, 1980), pp. 159–60; Olive Banks, Faces of Feminism: A Study of Feminism as a Social Movement (New York: St. Martin's, 1981), p. 115; Judith A. Baer, The Chains of Protection: The Judicial Response to Women's Labor Legislation (Westport, Conn.: Greenwood Press, 1978). . . .

20. T. K. Cory to Mary Wiggins, Nov. 10, 1922, folder 378, Consumers' League of Mass. Coll., SL. See n. 16, above.

21. Ethel M. Smith, "What Is Sex Equality and What Are the Feminists Trying to Accomplish?" Century Monthly Magazine 118 (May 1929):96. . . . Mary Anderson, Woman at Work: The Autobiography of Mary Anderson as Told to Mary N. Winslow (Minneapolis: University of Minnesota Press, 1951), p. 168.

22. There is a valuable discussion of differing meanings for "equality" between the sexes in Jean Bethke Elshtain, "The Feminist Movement and the Question of Equality," Polity 7 (Summer 1975): 452–77.

23. This is, of course, the set of issues that has preoccupied feminist lawyers in the 1980s. For a sense of the recent debate, see, e.g., Wendy Williams, "The Equality Crisis: Some Reflections on Culture, Courts, and Feminism," Women's Rights Law Reporter 7, no. 3 (Spring 1982):175–200; Nadine Taub, "Will Equality Require More Than Assimilation, Accommodation or Separation from the Existing Social Structure?" Rutgers Law Review 37 (1985):825–44; Lucinda Finley, "Transcending Equality Theory: A Way out of the Maternity and the Workplace Debate," Columbia Law Review 86, no. 6 (Oct. 1986):1118–82; and Joan Williams, "Deconstructing Gender," Michigan Law Review 87, no. 4 (Feb. 1989):797–845.

24. Florence Kelley, "Shall Women Be Equal before the Law?" (debate with Elsie Hill), *Nation* 114 (Apr. 12, 1922):421. . . .

25. Dolores Janiewski, *Sisterhood Denied: Race, Gender and Class in a New South Community* (Philadelphia: Temple University Press, 1985), pp. 30–32, 127–50; Table 26 (p. 134) shows less than 40% of Durham women above age 12 engaged only in unpaid housework.

26. Guion G. Johnson, "Feminism and the Economic Independence of Woman," *Journal of Social Forces* 3 (May 4, 1925):615; cf. Tentler, *Wage-Earning Women*, esp. pp. 25, 45–46, and Wandersee, *Women's Work*, on motivations and psychological results of women's wage-earning.

27. Mary Anderson quoted in unidentified newspaper clipping, Nov. 25, 1925, in folder 349, Bureau of Vocational Information Collection, SL. Cf. Ethel Smith's objection that the NWP's feminism required that "men and women must have exactly the same things, and be treated in all respects as if they were alike," as distinguished from her own view that "men and women must each have the things best suited to their respective needs, which are not all the time, nor in all things, alike." Smith, "What Is Sex Equality?", p. 96.

28. National Council of Catholic Women testimony at U.S. Congress (House of Representatives) subcommittee of Committee on the Judiciary, hearings, 1925, quoted in Robin Whittemore, "Equality vs. Protection: Debate on the Equal Rights Amendment, 1923–1937" (M.A. thesis, Boston University, 1981), p. 19; mill worker quoted in Mary Frederickson, "The Southern Summer School for Women Workers," *Southern Exposure* 4 (Winter 1977):73. See also Maurine Greenwald, "Working-Class Feminism and the Family Wage Ideal: The Seattle Debate on Married Women's Right to Work, 1914–1920," *Journal of American History* 76, no. 1 (June 1989):118–49.

29. For the history of the NWP in the 1930s and 1940s see Becker, *Origins of the Equal Rights Amendment*. On the initiatives of the National Federation of Business and Professional Women and other groups to forward the equal rights amendment, see Lemons, *Woman Citizen*, pp. 202–4, and the papers of Lena Madesin Phillips and Florence Kitchelt at SL.

30. Jane L. Mansbridge's astute analysis, *Why We Lost the ERA* (Chicago: University of Chicago Press, 1986), is essential reading on the failed 1970s campaign for ratification.

JACQUELYN DOWD HALL

Disorderly Women: Gender and Labor Militancy in the Appalachian South

In the 1920s Eleanor Roosevelt and other elite women continued the political activism that reformers and suffragists such as Florence Kelley had initiated. Working-class women had little choice but to continue the labor militancy exemplified by Schneiderman, Newman, Cohn, and Lemlich. This was especially true in the South. Unionization had never taken hold in the former states of the Confederacy as it had in heavily industrialized areas of the Northeast and Midwest. Moreover, working conditions had worsened as factory owners introduced new innovations designed to improve productivity. Southern textile mills, as employers of large numbers of poorly paid women, were especially vulnerable to strikes.

Jacquelyn Dowd Hall focuses on one of the many strikes exploding across the South in that tumultuous decade, exploring female activism in an essay that calls into question old stereotypes about southern workers as individualistic, docile, and "hard to

Excerpted from "Disorderly Women: Gender and Labor Militancy in the Appalachian South" by Jacquelyn Dowd Hall, in *Journal of American History* 73 (1986):354–82. Copyright © 1986 by Jacquelyn Dowd Hall. Condensed and reprinted by permission of the author. Notes have been renumbered and edited.

Women used suffrage for a wide range of political expressions. Here women of the Ku Klux Klan parade down Pennsylvania Avenue in 1928. (Photograph courtesy of the Library of Congress)

organize." In this important study, Hall illuminates the distinctive style of collective action that the women of Elizabethton, Tennessee, employed and the self-concepts and family networks on which that style relied.

In what respects did working conditions resemble those confronting the young immigrant women in New York's garment district about whom Orleck wrote? What were the critical differences? Were the factors that inspired and sustained resistance similar? How does Hall view the actions of Trixie Perry and Texas Bill?

The rising sun "made a sort of halo around the crown of Cross Mountain" as Flossie Cole climbed into a neighbor's Model T and headed west down the gravel road to Elizabethton, bound for work in a rayon plant. Emerging from Stoney Creek hollow, the car joined a caravan of buses and self-styled "taxis" brimming with young people from dozens of tiny communities strung along the creek branches and nestled in the coves of the Blue Ridge Mountains of East Tennessee. The caravan picked up speed as it hit paved roads and crossed the Watauga River bridge, passing beneath a sign advertising the county seat's new-found identity as a "City of Power." By the time Cole reached the factory gate, it was 7:00 A.M., time to begin another ten-hour day as a reeler at the American Glanzstoff plant.[1]

The machines whirred, and work began as usual. But the reeling room stirred with anticipation. The day before, March 12, 1929, all but seventeen of the 360 women in the inspection room next door had walked off their jobs. Now they were gathered at the factory gate, refusing to work but ready to negotiate. When 9:00 A.M., approached and the plant manager failed to appear, they broke past the guards and rushed through the plant, urging their co-workers out on strike. By 1:40 P.M. the machines were idle and the plant was closed.

The Elizabethton conflict rocked Carter County and made national headlines. Before March ended, the spirit of protest had jumped the Blue Ridge and spread through the Piedmont. Gastonia, Marion, and Danville saw the most bitter conflicts, but dozens of towns were shocked by an unexpected workers' revolt.[2]

The textile industry has always been a stronghold of women's labor, and women were central to these events. They were noted by contemporaries, sometimes as leaders, more often as pathetic mill girls or as "Amazons" providing comic relief.[3] In historical renditions they have dropped out of sight. The result has been thin description: a one-dimensional view of labor conflict that fails to take culture and community into account.

Elizabethton, of course, is not unusual in this regard. Until recently, historians of trade unionism, like trade unionists themselves, neglected women, while historians of women concentrated on the Northeast and the middle class. There were few scholarly challenges to the assumption that women workers in general and southern women in particular were "hard to organize" and that women as family members exercised a conservative pull against class cohesion. Instances of female militancy were seen and not seen.[4] Because they contradicted conventional wisdom, they were easily dismissed.

Recent scholarship has revised that formulation by unearthing an impressive record of female activism. But our task is not only to describe and celebrate but also to contextualize, and thus to understand. In Elizabethton the preindustrial background, the structure of the work force and the industry, the global forces that impinged on local events—these particularities of time and place conditioned women's choices and shaped their identities. Equally important was a private world traditionally pushed to the margins of labor history. Female friendships and sexuality, cross-generational

and cross-class alliances, the incorporation of new consumer desires into a dynamic regional culture—these too energized women's participation. Women in turn were historical subjects, helping to create the circumstances from which the strike arose and guiding by their actions the course the conflict took.

With gender at the center of analysis, unexpected dimensions come into view. Chief among them is the strike's erotic undercurrent, its sexual theme. The activists of Elizabethton belonged to a venerable tradition of "disorderly women," women who, in times of political upheaval, embody tensions that are half-conscious or only dimly understood.[5] Beneath the surface of a conflict that pitted workers and farmers against a new middle class in the town lay an inner world of fantasy, gender ideology, and sexual style.

The melding of narrative and analysis that follows has two major goals. The first is a fresh reading of an important episode in southern labor history, employing a female angle of vision to reveal aspects of the conflict that have been overlooked or misunderstood. The second is a close look at women's distinctive forms of collective action, using language and gesture as points of entry to a culture.

The Elizabethton story may also help to make a more general point. Based as it is on what Michel Foucault has termed "local" or "subjugated" knowledge, that is, perceptions that seem idiosyncratic, naive, and irrelevant to historical explanation, this study highlights the limitations of conventional categories.[6] The women of Elizabethton were neither traditionalists acting on family values nor market-oriented individualists, neither peculiar mountaineers nor familiar modern women. Their irreverence and inventiveness shatter stereotypes and illuminate the intricacies of working-class women's lives.

In 1925 the J. P. Bemberg Company of Barmen, Germany, manufacturer of high-quality rayon yarn by an exclusive stretch spinning process, began pouring the thick concrete floors of its first United States subsidiary. Three years later Germany's leading producer of viscose yarn, the Vereinigte Glanzstoff Fabriken, A.G., of Elberfeld opened a jointly managed branch nearby. A post-World War I fashion revolution, combined with protective tariffs, had spurred the American rayon industry's spectacular growth. As one industry publicist put it, "With long skirts, cotton stockings were quite in order; but with short skirts, nothing would do except sheer, smooth stockings. . . . It was on the trim legs of post-war flappers, it has been said, that rayon first stepped out into big business." Dominated by a handful of European giants, the rayon industry clustered along the Appalachian mountain chain. By World War II, over 70 percent of American rayon production took place in the southern states, with 50 percent of the national total in Virginia and Tennessee alone.[7]

When the Bemberg and Glanzstoff companies chose East Tennessee as a site for overseas expansion, they came to a region that has occupied a peculiar place in the American economy and imagination. Since its "discovery" by local-color writers in the 1870s, southern Appalachia has been seen as a land "where time stood still." Mountain people have been romanticized as "our contemporary ancestors" or maligned as "latter-day white barbarians." Central to both images is the notion of a people untouched by modernity. In fact, as a generation of regional scholars has now made clear, the key to modern Appalachian history lies not in the region's isolation but in its role as a source of raw materials and an outlet for investment in a capitalist world economy.[8]

Frontier families had settled the fertile Watauga River Valley around Elizabethton before the Revolution. Later arrivals pushed farther up the mountains into the hollows carved by fast-falling creeks. Stoney Creek is the oldest and largest of those creek-bed communities. Here descendants of the original settlers cultivated their own small plots, grazed livestock in woods that custom held open to all, hunted and fished in an ancient hardwood forest, mined iron ore, made whiskey, spun cloth, and bartered with local merchants for what they could not produce at home.

In the 1880s East Tennessee's timber and mineral resources attracted the attention of capitalists in the United States and abroad, and an era of land speculation and railroad building began. The railroads opened the way to timber barons, who stripped away the forests, leaving hillsides stark and vulnerable to erosion. Farmers abandoned their fields to follow the march of the logging camps. Left behind, women and children did their best to pick up the slack.[9] But by the time Carter County was "timbered out" in the 1920s, farm families had crept upward to the barren ridge lands or grown dependent on "steady work and cash wages." Meanwhile, in Elizabethton, the county seat, an aggressive new class of bankers, lawyers, and businessmen served as brokers for outside developers, speculated in land, invested in homegrown factories, and looked beyond the hills for their standards of "push, progress and prosperity."[10]

Carter County, however, lacked Appalachia's grand prize: The rush for coal that devastated other parts of the mountains had bypassed that part of East Tennessee. Nor had county farmers been absorbed into the cotton kingdom, with its exploitative credit system and spreading tenancy. To be sure, they were increasingly hard pressed. As arable land disappeared, farms were divided and redivided. In 1880 the average rural family had supported itself on 140 acres of land; by 1920 it was making do on slightly more than 52 acres. Yet however diminished their circumstances, 84.5 percent still owned their own land.[11] The economic base that sustained traditional expectations of independence, production for use, and neighborly reciprocity tottered but did not give way.

The coming of the rayon plants represented a coup for Elizabethton's aspiring businessmen, who wooed investors with promises of free land, tax exemptions, and cheap labor. But at first the whole county seemed to share the boomtown spirit. Men from Stoney Creek, Gap Creek, and other mountain hamlets built the cavernous mills, then stayed on to learn the chemical processes that transformed the cellulose from wood pulp and cotton linters (the short fibers that remain on cotton seeds after longer, spinnable fibers are removed) into "artificial silk." Women vied for jobs in the textile division where they wound, reeled, twisted, and inspected the rayon yarn. Yet for all the excitement it engendered, industrialization in Carter County retained a distinctly rural cast. Although Elizabethton's population tripled (from 2,749 in 1920 to 8,093 in 1930), the rayon workers confounded predictions of spectacular urban growth, for most remained in the countryside, riding to work on chartered buses and trains or in taxis driven by neighbors and friends.

Women made up approximately 37 percent of the 3,213 workers in the mills. Most were under twenty-one, but many were as young as twelve, or more commonly, fourteen. By contrast, the work force contained a large proportion of older, married men. Those men, together with a smaller number of teenage boys, dominated the chemical division, while young women processed the finished yarn.[12]

Whether married or single, town- or country-bred, the men who labored in the rayon plants followed in the footsteps of fathers, and sometimes grandfathers, who had combined farming with a variety of wage-earning occupations. To a greater extent than we might expect, young women who had grown up in Elizabethton could also look to earlier models of gainful labor. A search of the 1910 manuscript census found 20 percent (97/507) of women aged fourteen and over in paid occupations. The largest proportion (29.6 percent) were cooks and servants. But close behind were women in what mountain people called "public work": wage-earning labor performed outside a household setting. For rayon workers from the countryside it was a different story. Only 5.2 percent of adult women on Stoney Creek were gainfully employed (33/638). Nineteen of these were farmers. The rest—except for one music teacher—were servants or washerwomen.[13]

These contrasts are telling, and from them we can surmise two things. The first is that industrialization did not burst upon a static, conflict free "traditional" world. The women who beat a path to the rayon plants came from families that had already been drawn into an economy where money was a key to survival. The second is that the timber industry, which attracted Carter County's men, undermined its agricultural base, and destroyed its natural resources, created few opportunities for rural women. No wonder that farm daughters in the mills counted their blessings and looked on themselves as pioneers.

Whether they sought work out of family need or for more individualistic reasons, these "factory girls" saw their jobs as a hopeful gamble rather than a desperate last resort, and they remembered the moment with astounding precision. "I'll never forget the day they hired me at Bemberg," said Flossie Cole. "We went down right in front of it. They'd come out and they'd say, 'You and you and you,' and they'd hire so many. And that day I was standing there and he picked out two or three more and

he looked at me and he said, 'You.' It thrilled me to death." She worked 56 hours that week and took home $8.16.[14]

Such pay scales were low even for the southern textile industry, and workers quickly found their income eaten away by the cost of commuting or of boarding in town. When the strike came it focused on the issue of Glanzstoff women's wages, which lagged behind those at the older Bemberg plant. But workers had other grievances as well. Caustic chemicals were used to turn cellulose into a viscous fluid that was then forced through spinnerets, thimble-shaped nozzles pierced with tiny holes. The fine, individual streams coagulated into rayon filaments in an acid bath. In the chemical division men waded through water and acid, exposed all day to a lethal spray. Women labored under less dangerous conditions, but for longer hours and less pay. Paid by the piece, they complained of rising production quotas and what everyone referred to as "hard rules."[15]

Women in particular were singled out for petty regulations, aimed not just at extracting labor but at shaping deportment as well. They were forbidden to wear makeup; in some departments they were required to purchase uniforms. Most galling of all was company surveillance of the washroom. According to Bessie Edens, who was promoted to "forelady" in the twisting room, "men could do what they wanted to in their own department," but women had to get a pass to leave the shop floor. "If we went to the bathroom, they'd follow us," Flossie Cole confirmed, "'fraid we'd stay a minute too long." If they did, their pay was docked; one too many trips and they lost their jobs.[16]

Complaints about the washroom may have had other meanings as well. When asked how she heard that a strike was brewing, Nettie Reece cited "bathroom gossip."[17] As the company well knew, the women's washroom, where only a forelady, not a male supervisor could go, might serve as a communications center, a hub of gossip where complaints were aired and plans were formulated.

The German origins of the plant managers contributed to the tension. Once the strike began, union organizers were quick to play on images of an "imported Prussian autocracy." The frontier republicanism of the mountains shaded easily into post-World War I Americanism as strikers demanded their rights as "natural-born American citizens" oppressed by a "latter day industrialism." In that they had much in common with other twentieth-century workers, for whom the democratic values articulated during the war became a rallying cry for social justice at home. The nationality of the managers helped throw those values into sharp relief.[18]

The strike came on March 12, 1929, led by women in Glanzstoff inspection department, by what one observer called "girls in their teens [who] decided not to put up with the present conditions any longer." The county court immediately issued injunctions forbidding all demonstrations against the company. When strikers ignored the injunctions, the governor sent in the National Guard. The strikers secured a charter from the American Federation of Labor's United Textile Workers union (UTW). Meeting in a place called the Tabernacle, built for religious revivals, they listened to a Baptist preacher from Stoney Creek warn: "The hand of oppression is growing on our people. . . . You women work for practically nothing. You must come together and say that such things must cease to be." Each night more workers "came forward" to take the union oath.[19]

Meanwhile, UTW and Federal Conciliation Service officials arrived on the scene. On March 22 they reached a "gentlemen's agreement" by which the company promised a new wage scale for "good girl help" and agreed not to discriminate against union members. The strikers returned to work, but the conflict was far from over. Higher paychecks never materialized; union members began losing their jobs. On April 4 local businessmen kidnapped two union organizers and ran them out of town. Eleven days later the workers responded with what most observers agreed was a "spontaneous and complete walkout."[20]

This time the conflict quickly escalated. More troops arrived, and the plants became fortresses, with machine guns on the rooftops and armed guardsmen on the ground. The company sent buses manned by soldiers farther up the hollows to recruit new workers and escort them back to town. Pickets blocked narrow mountain roads. Houses were blown up; the town water main was dynamited. An estimated 1,250 individuals were arrested in confrontations with the National Guard.[21]

As far as can be determined, no women were involved in barn burnings and dynamitings—what Bessie Edens referred to as "the rough . . . stuff" that accompanied the second strike. Men "went places that we didn't go," explained Christine Galliher. "They had big dark secrets . . . the men did." But when it came to public demonstrations women held center stage. At the outset "hundreds of girls" had ridden down main street "in buses and taxis, shouting and laughing at people who watched them from windows and doorsteps." Now they blocked the road at Gap Creek and refused soldiers' orders that they walk twelve miles to jail in town. "And there was one girl that was awful tough in the bunch. . . . She said, 'No, by God. We didn't walk out here, and we're not walking back!' And she sat her hind end down in the middle of the road, and we all sat down with her. And the law used tear gas on us! . . . And it nearly put our eyes out, but we still wouldn't walk back to town." In Elizabethton after picket duty, women marched down the "Bemberg Highway . . . draped in the American flag and carrying the colors"—thereby forcing the guardsmen to present arms each time they passed. Inventive, playful, and shrewd, the women's tactics encouraged a holiday spirit. They may also have deflected violence and garnered community support.[22]

Laughter was among the women's most effective weapons. But beneath high spirits the terms of battle had begun to change. Local organizers were hobbled by a national union that lacked the resources and commitment to sustain the strike. Instead of translating workers' grievances into a compelling challenge, the UTW pared their demands down to the bone. On May 26, six weeks after the strike began, the union agreed to a settlement that made no mention of wages, hours, working conditions, or union recognition. The company's only concession was a promise not to discriminate against union members. The workers were less than enthusiastic. According to one reporter, "It took nine speeches and a lot of question answering lasting two and a half hours to get the strikers to accept the terms."[23]

The press, for the most part, greeted the settlement as a workers' victory, or at least a satisfactory resolution of the conflict. Anna Weinstock, the first woman to serve as a federal conciliator, was credited with bringing the company to the bargaining table and was pictured as the heroine of the event. "SETTLED BY

A Woman!" headlined one journal. "This is the fact that astounds American newspaper editors." "Five feet five inches and 120 pounds of femininity; clean cut, even features"—and so on, in great detail. Little was made of Weinstock's own working-class origins. She was simply a "new woman," come to the rescue of a backward mountain folk. The strikers themselves dropped quickly from view.[24]

From the outside, the conflict at Elizabethton looked like a straightforward case of labor-management strife. But it appeared quite different from within. Everyone interviewed put the blame for low wages on an alliance between the German managers and the "leading citizens" of the town. Preserved in the oral tradition is the story of how the "town fathers" promised the company a supply of cheap and unorganized labor. Bessie Edens put it this way: They told the company that "women wasn't used to working, and they'd work for almost nothing, and the men would work for low wages. That's the way they got the plant here." In this version of events the strike was part of a long-term struggle, with development-minded townspeople on one side and workers, farmers, and country merchants on the other.[25]

Workers' roots in the countryside encouraged resistance and helped them to mobilize support once the strike began. "These workers have come so recently from the farms and mountains . . . and are of such independent spirit," Alfred Hoffman observed, "that they 'Don't care if they do lose their jobs' and cannot be scared." Asked by reporters what would happen if strike activity cost them their jobs, one woman remarked, "I haven't forgotten how to use a hoe," while another said, "We'll go back to the farm."[26] Such threats were not just bravado. High levels of farm ownership sustained cultural independence. Within the internal economy of families, individual fortunes were cushioned by reciprocity; an orientation toward subsistence survived side by side with the desire for cash and store-bought goods.

Stoney Creek farmers were solidly behind the sons and daughters they sent to the factories, as were the small shopkeepers who relied on farmers for their trade. In county politics Stoney Creekers had historically marshaled a block vote against the town. In 1929 Stoney Creek's own J.M. Moreland was county sheriff, and he openly took the strikers' side. A strike leader in the twisting room ran a country store and drove his working neighbors into town. "That's why he was pretty well accepted as their leader," said a fellow worker. "Some of them were cousins and other relations. Some of them traded at his store. Some of them rode in his taxi. All intertwined."[27]

The National Guard had divided loyalties. Parading past the plants, the strikers "waved to and called the first names of the guardsmen, for most of the young men in uniforms [were friends of] the men and girls on strike." Even when the local unit was fortified by outside recruits, fraternizing continued. Nettie Reece, like a number of her girlfriends, met her future husband that way; she saw him on the street and "knew that was mine right there." Some guardsmen went further and simply refused to serve. "The use of the National Guard here was the dirtiest deal ever pulled," one protested. "I turned in my equipment when I was ordered to go out and patrol the road. I was dropped from the payroll two weeks later."[28]

In this context of family-and community-based resistance, women had important roles to play. Farm mothers nurtured the strikers' independence simply by cleaving to the land, passing on to their children a heritage at odds with the values of the new order and maintaining family production as a hedge against the uncertainties of a market economy. But the situation of farm mothers had other effects as well, and it would be a mistake to push the argument for continuity too far. As their husbands ranged widely in search of wage labor, women's work intensified while their status—now tied to earning power—declined. The female strikers of Elizabethton saw their mothers as resourceful and strong but also as increasingly isolated and hard pressed. Most important, they no longer looked to their mothers' lives as patterns for their own.[29]

The summer after the strike, Bessie Edens attended the Southern Summer School for Women Workers, a workers' education project in North Carolina, where she set the group on its ear with an impassioned defense of women's rights:

It is nothing new for married women to work. They have always worked. . . . Women have always worked harder than men and always had to look up to the man and feel that they were weaker and inferior. . . . If we women would not be so submissive and take every thing for granted, if we would awake and stand up for our rights, this world would be a better place to live in, at least it would be better for the women.

Some girls think that as long as mother takes in washings, keeps ten or twelve boarders or perhaps takes in sewing, she isn't working. But I say that either one of the three is as hard work as women could do. So if they do that at home and don't get any wages for it, why would it not be all right for them to go to a factory and receive pay for what they do?

Edens had been the oldest of ten children. She had dreamed of going to nursing school, but her poverty-stricken parents had opposed her plan. At fifteen, she had gone to work as a servant. "Then I'd come back when Momma had a baby and wait on her, and help if she needed me in any way." Asked fifty years later about a daughter's place on a hardscrabble farm, Edens replied: "The girls were supposed to do housework and work in the fields. They were supposed to be slaves."[30]

Bessie Edens was unusual in her articulation of a working-class feminism. But scattered through the life histories written by other students are echoes of her general themes. Read in the context of farm daughters' lives—their first-hand exposure to rural poverty, their yearnings for a more expansive world—these stories reflect the "structure of feeling" women brought to the rayon plants and then to the picket line and union hall.[31] Women such as Edens, it seems, sensed the devaluation of women's handicraft labor in the face of cheap consumer goods. They feared the long arm of their mothers' fate, resented their fathers' distant authority, and envied their brothers' exploits away from home. By opting for work in the rayon plants, they struck out for their own place in a changing world. When low wages, high costs, and autocratic managers affronted their dignity and dashed their hopes, they were the first to revolt.

The Elizabethton story thus presents another pattern in the female protest tradition. In coal-mining communities a rigid division of labor and women's hardships in company towns have resulted, paradoxically, in the notable militancy of miners' wives. By contrast, tobacco factories have tended to employ married women, whose job commitments and associational lives enable them to assume leadership roles in sustained organizing drives. In yet other circumstances, such as the early New England textile mills or the union insurgency of the 1920s and 1930s, single women initiated independent strikes or provided strong support for male-led, mixed-sex campaigns. Where, as in Elizabethton, people were mobilized as family and community members rather than as individual workers, non-wage-earning women could provide essential support. Once in motion, their daughters might outdo men in militancy, perhaps because they had fewer dependents than their male co-workers and could fall back more easily on parental resources, perhaps because the peer culture and increased independence encouraged by factory labor stirred boldness and inspired experimentation.[32]

The fact of women's initiative and participation in collective action is instructive. Even more intriguing is the gender-based symbolism of their protest style. Through dress, language, and gesture, female strikers expressed a complex cultural identity and turned it to their own rebellious purposes.

Consider, for instance, Trixie Perry and a woman who called herself "Texas Bill." Twenty-eight-year-old Trixie Perry was a reeler in the Glanzstoff plant. She had apparently become pregnant ten years before, had married briefly and then divorced, giving her son her maiden name. Her father was a butcher and a farmer, and she lived near her family on the edge of town. Trixie later moved into Elizabethton. She never remarried but went on to have several more children by other men. Texas Bill's background is more elusive. All we know is that she came from out of state, lived in a boardinghouse, and claimed to have been married twice before she arrived in town. These two friends were ringleaders on the picket line. Both were charged with violating the injunction, and both were brought to trial.[33]

Trixie Perry took the stand in a dress sewn from red, white, and blue bunting and a cap made of a small American flag. The prosecuting attorney began his cross-examination:

"You have a United States flag as a cap on your head?"

"Yes."

"Wear it all the time?"

"Whenever I take a notion."

"You are dressed in a United States flag, and the colors?"

"I guess so, I was born under it, guess I have a right to."

The main charge was that Perry and her friend had drawn a line across the road at Gap Creek and dared the soldiers to cross it. Above all they were accused of taunting the National Guard. The defense attorney, a fiery local lawyer playing to a sympathetic crowd, did not deny the charges. Instead, he used the women to mock the government's case. Had Trixie Perry threatened a lieutenant? "He rammed a gun in my face and I told him to take it out or I would knock it out." Had she blocked the road? "A little thing like me block a big road?" What had she said to the threat of a tear gas bomb? "That little old fire cracker of a thing, it won't go off."[34]

Texas Bill was an even bigger hit with the crowd. The defense attorney called her the "Wild Man From Borneo." A guard said she was "the wildest human being I've ever seen." Texas Bill both affirmed and subverted her reputation. Her nickname came from her habit of wearing "cowboy" clothes. But when it was her turn to testify, she "strutted on the stand" in a fashionable black picture hat and a black coat. Besides her other transgressions, she was accused of grabbing a soldier's gun and aiming it at him. What was she doing on the road so early in the morning? "I take a walk every morning before breakfast for my health," Texas replied with what a reporter described as "an assumed ladylike dignity."[35]

Witnesses for the prosecution took pains to contradict Texas Bill's "assumed ladylike dignity." A guardsman complained that she called him a "'God damned yellow son-of-a-bitch,' and then branched out from that." Texas offered no defense: "When that soldier stuck his gun in my face, that did make me mad and I did cuss a little bit and don't deny it." Far from discrediting the strikers, the soldiers' testimony added to their own embarrassment and the audience's delight. In tune with the crowd, the defense attorney "enjoyed making the guards admit they had been 'assaulted' . . . by 16- and 18-year-old girls."[36]

Mock gentility, transgressive laughter, male egos on the line—the mix made for wonderful theater, and proved effective in court as well. The judge reserved maximum sentences for three especially aggressive men; all the women and most of the men were found not guilty or were lightly fined. In the end even those convictions were overturned by the state court of appeals.[37]

Trixie Perry and Texas Bill certainly donned the role of "disorderly woman." Since, presumably, only extraordinary circumstances call forth feminine aggression, women's assaults against persons and property constitute a powerful witness against injustice. At the same time, since women are considered less rational and taken less seriously than men, they may meet less resistance and be punished less severely for their crimes.[38]

But Trixie Perry and Texas Bill were not just out of line in their public acts; they also led unconventional private lives. It was this erotic subtext that most horrified officialdom and amused the courtroom crowd. The only extended discussion of the strike that appears in the city council minutes resulted in a resolution that read in part:

> WHEREAS, it has come to [our] attention . . . that the moral tone of this community has been lowered by reason of men and women congregating in various houses and meeting-places in Elizabethton and there practicing lewdness all hours of the night, in defiance of morality, law and order. . . .
>
> NOW, THEREFORE, BE IT RESOLVED, that the police force of the City arrest and place in the City Jail those who are violating the laws by practicing lewdness within the City of Elizabethton. . . .[39]

Union representatives apparently shared, indeed anticipated, the councilmen's concern. Worried by rumors that unemployed women were resorting to prostitution, they had already announced to the press that 25 percent of the strikers had been sent back to their hillside homes, "chiefly young single girls whom we want to keep off the streets." The townsmen and the trade unionists were thus united in drawing a line between good women and bad, with respectability being measured not only by chastity but by nuances of style and language as well.[40] In the heat of the trial, the question of whether or not women—as workers—had violated the injunction took second place to questions about their status as women, as members of their sex. Had they cursed? Had they been on the road at odd hours of the day or night? Was Texas Bill a lady or a "wild man from Borneo"? Fearing that "lewd women" might discredit the organizing drive, the organizers tried to send them home. To protect the community's "moral tone," the city council threatened to lock them up.

There is nothing extraordinary about this association between sexual misbehavior and women's labor militancy. Since strikers are often young single women who violate gender conventions by invading public space customarily reserved for men (and sometimes frequented by prostitutes)—and since female aggressiveness stirs up fears of women's sexual power—opponents have often undercut union organizing drives by insinuations of prostitution or promiscuity. Fearing guilt by association, "respectable" women stay away.[41]

What is impressive here is how Trixie Perry and Texas Bill handled the dichotomy between ladyhood and lewdness, good girls and bad. Using words that, for women in particular, were ordinarily taboo, they refused deference and signaled disrespect. Making no secret of their sexual experience, they combined flirtation with fierceness on the picket line and adopted a provocative courtroom style. And yet, with the language of dress—a cap made of an American flag, an elegant wide-brimmed hat—they claimed their rights as citizens and their place in the female community.

Moreover, that community upheld their claims. The defense attorney chose unruly women as his star witnesses, and the courtroom spectators enthusiastically cheered them on. The prosecuting attorney recommended dismissal of the charges against all the women on trial except Trixie Perry, Texas Bill, and a "hoodlum" named Lucille Ratliffe, on the grounds that the rest came from "good families." Yet in the court transcripts, few differences can be discerned in the behavior of good girls and bad. The other female defendants may have been less flamboyant, but they were no less sharp-tongued. Was Vivian King a member of the UTW? "Yes, and proud of it." Had she been picketing? "Yes, proud of that." What was a young married woman named Dorothy Oxindine doing on Gap Creek at five o'clock in the morning? "Out airing." Did Lena May Jones "holler out 'scab'"? "No, I think the statement made was 'I wouldn't be a scab' and 'Why don't you come and join our organization.'" Did she laugh at a soldier and tell him his gun wouldn't shoot? "I didn't tell him it wouldn't shoot, but I laughed at him . . . and

told him he was too much of a man to shoot a lady."[42]

Interviewed over fifty years later, strike participants still refused to make invidious distinctions between themselves and women like Trixie Perry and Texas Bill. Bessie Edens was a settled, self-educated, married woman. But she was also a self-described "daredevil on the picket line," secure in the knowledge that she had a knife hidden in her drawstring underwear. To Edens, who came from a mountain hamlet called Hampton, the chief distinction did not lie between herself and rougher women. It lay between herself and merchants' wives who blamed the trouble on "those hussies from Hampton." When asked what she thought of Trixie Perry and Texas Bill, she answered simply, "There were some girls like that involved. But I didn't care. They did their part."[43]

Nettie Reece, who lived at home with parents who were "pretty particular with [their] daughters," shared Bessie Edens's attitude. After passing along the town gossip about Trixie Perry, she was anxious to make sure her meaning was not misconstrued. "Trixie was not a woman who sold her body," she emphasized. "She just had a big desire for sex. . . . And when she had a cause to fight for, she'd fight." Reece then went on to establish Perry's claim to a certain kind of respectability. After the strike Perry became a hard-working restaurant cook. She was a good neighbor: "If anybody got sick, she was there to wait on them." The children she bore out of wedlock did well in life, and they "never throwed [their mother] aside."[44]

Industrialization, as we know, changed the nature of work, the meaning of time. In Carter County it entailed a shift of economic and political power from the countryside to the town. At issue too were more intimate matters of fantasy, culture, and style.

Implicit in the conflict were two different sexual systems. One, subscribed to by union officials and the local middle class, mandated chastity before marriage, men as breadwinners, and women as housewives in the home. The other, rooted in a rural past and adapted to working-class life, recognized liaisons established without the benefit of clergy or license fees and allowed legitimacy to be broadly construed. It was unfamiliar with—or pragmatic about—prostitution. It circumscribed women's roles without investing in abstract standards of femininity. It was, in short, a society that might produce a Trixie Perry or defend "hussies from Hampton" against the snubs of merchants' wives.

This is not to say that the women of Elizabethton were simply acting on tradition. On the contrary, the strikers dressed the persona of the disorderly woman in unmistakably modern garb. Women's behavior on the witness stand presupposed a certain sophistication: A passing familiarity allowed them to parody ladyhood and to thumb a nose at the genteel standards of the town. Combining garments from the local past with fragments of an expansive consumer culture, the women of Elizabethton assembled their own version of a brash, irreverent Jazz Age style.

By the early 1920s radios and Model Ts had joined railroads and mail-order catalogs as conduits to the larger world. Record companies had discovered hill-country music and East Tennessee's first country-music stars were recording hits that transformed ballad singing, fiddle playing, and banjo picking into one of America's great popular-music sounds. The banjo itself was an Afro-American instrument that had come to the mountains with the railroad gangs. Such cultural interchanges multiplied during the 1920s as rural traditions met the upheavals of industrial life. The result was an explosion of musical creativity—in the hills of Tennessee no less than in New York City and other cosmopolitan centers.[45] Arriving for work in the rayon plants, young people brought with them the useable past of the countryside, but they quickly assimilated the speeded-up rhythms of a changing world.

Work-related peer groups formed a bridge between traditional loyalties and a novel youth culture. Whether married or single, living with parents or on their own, women participated in the strike in same-sex groups. Sisters boarded, worked, and demonstrated together. Girlfriends teamed up in groups or pairs. Trixie Perry and Texas Bill were a case in point. But there were others as well. Nettie Reece joined the union with her parents' approval but also with her whole school girl gang in tow. Ethel and M. C. Ashworth, ages eighteen and seventeen, respectively, came from Virginia to work in the plants. "Hollering and singing [in a] Ford touring car," they were arrested in a demonstra-

tion at Watauga Point. Ida and Evelyn Heaton boarded together on Donna Avenue. Evelyn Heaton was hit by a car on the picket line, swore out a warrant, and had the commander of the National Guard placed under arrest. After the strike she was blacklisted, and Ida attended the Southern Summer School.[46]

The sudden gathering of young people in the town nourished new patterns of heterosociability, and the strike's erotic undercurrent surfaced not only in Trixie Perry's "big desire for sex" but also in the behavior of her more conventional peers. The loyalties of the national guardsmen were divided, but their sympathy was obvious, as was their interest in the female strikers. Most of the Elizabethton women were in their teens or early twenties, the usual age of marriage in the region, and the strike provided unaccustomed opportunities for courtship. Rather than choosing a neighbor they had known all their lives, under watchful parental eyes, women flirted on the picket lines or the shop floor. Romance and politics commingled in the excitement of the moment, flowering in a spectrum of behavior—from the outrageousness of Trixie Perry to a spate of marriages among other girls.

What needs emphasis here is the dynamic quality of working-class women's culture—a quality that is sometimes lost in static oppositions between modernism and traditionalism, individualism and family values, consumer and producer mentalities. This is especially important where regional history has been so thoroughly mythologized. Appalachian culture, like all living cultures, embraced continuity and discontinuity, indigenous and borrowed elements.[47] As surely as Anna Weinstock—or Alabama's Zelda Fitzgerald—or any city flapper, the Elizabethton strikers were "new women," making their way in a world their mothers could not have known but carrying with them values handed down through the female line.

Two vignettes may serve to illustrate that process of grounded change.

Flossie Cole's mother, known by everyone on Stoney Creek as "Aunt Tid," was Sheriff Moreland's sister, but that didn't keep her from harboring cardplayers, buckdancers, and whiskey drinkers in her home. Aunt Tid was also a seamstress who "could look at a picture in a catalog and cut a pattern and make a dress just like it." But like most of her friends, Cole jumped at the chance for store-bought clothes: "That first paycheck, that was it . . . I think I bought me some new clothes with the first check I got. I bought me a new pair of shoes and a dress and a hat. Can you imagine someone going to a plant with a hat on? I had a blue dress and black shoes—patent leather, honey, with real high heels—and a blue hat." Nevertheless, before Cole left home in the morning for her job in the rayon plant, Aunt Tid made sure that around her neck—beneath the new blue dress—she wore a bag of asafetida, a strong-smelling resin, a folk remedy to protect her from diseases that might be circulating in the town.[48]

Second, there is visual evidence: a set of sixteen-millimeter films made by the company in order to identify—and to blacklist— workers who participated in the union. In those films groups of smiling women traipse along the picket line dressed in up-to-date clothes.[49] Yet federal conciliator Anna Weinstock, speaking to an interviewer forty years later, pictured them in sunbonnets, and barefooted. "They were," she explained, "what we would normally call hillbillies": women who "never get away from their shacks."[50] This could be seen as the treachery of memory, a problem of retrospection. But it is also an illustration of the power of stereotypes, of how cultural difference is registered as backwardness, of how images of poverty and backwardness hide the realities of workingclass women's lives.

The strike, as we know, was defeated. Participants were blacklisted. The Great Depression settled over the mountains, rekindling reliance on older ways of making do. Flossie Cole, for instance, had been new to factory labor, but she was no stranger to women's work. While her brothers had followed their father's lead to the coal mines, she had pursued the two most common occupations of the poorest mountain girls: agricultural labor and domestic service. "We would hire out and stay with people until they got through with us and then go back home. And when we got back home, it was workin' in the corn or wash for people." When Cole lost her job after the strike she went back to domestic service, "back to the drudge house," as she put it.[51]

Young women had poured eagerly into the rayon mills, drawn at least in part by the promise of independence, romance and adventure. As hard times deepened, such motives paled beside stark necessity. Two statistics make the point: The percentage of Carter County women who were gainfully employed held steady through the thirties. But by the end of the period a larger proportion than before worked as servants in other people's homes. When Flossie Cole went "back to the drudge house," she had plenty of company.[52]

Still, despite subsequent hardships, the spirit of the 1920s flickered on. Setting out to explore the strike through oral-history interviews, we expected to find disclaimers or silences. Instead, we heard unfaded memories and no regrets. "I knew I wasn't going to get to go back, and I didn't care," said Bessie Edens. "I wrote them a letter and told them I didn't care whether they took me back or not. I didn't! If I'd starved I wouldn't of cared, because I knew what I was a'doing when I helped to pull it. And I've never regretted it in any way. . . . And it did help the people, and it's helped the town and the country."[53] For those, like Edens, who went on to the Southern Summer School or remained active in the union, the strike was a pivot around which the political convictions and personal aspirations of a lifetime turned. For them, there were intangible rewards: a subtle deepening of individual power, a belief that they had made history and that later generations benefited from what they had done.

The strike, of course, made a fainter impression on other lives. Women's rebelliousness neither redefined gender roles nor overcame economic dependency. Their desire for the trappings of modernity could blur into a self-limiting consumerism. An ideology of romance could end in sexual danger or a married woman's burdensome double day. Still, the women of Elizabethton left a legacy. A norm of female public work, a new style of sexual expressiveness, the entry of women into public space and political struggles previously monopolized by men—all these pushed against traditional constraints even as they created new vulnerabilities. The farm daughters who left home for the rayon plants pioneered a new pattern of female experience, and they created for their post-World War II daughters an environment far different from the one they, in their youth, had known. It would be up to later generations to wrestle with the costs of commercialization and to elaborate a vision that embraced economic justice and community solidarity as well as women's liberation.

NOTES

This study began as a collaborative endeavor with Sara Evans of the University of Minnesota, who helped to gather many of the interviews on which I have relied. Rosemarie Hester and Jennifer Dowd also joined me on trips to the mountains, and I benefited from their companionship, ideas, and research. I owe a special debt to Christopher Daly, Lu Ann Jones, Robert Korstad, James Leloudis, and Mary Murphy, with whom I have co-written *Like a Family: The Making of a Southern Cotton Mill World* (Chapel Hill, 1987).

1. Dan Crowe, *Old Town and the Covered Bridge* (Johnson City, Tenn., 1977), pp. 32, 71; Florence (Cole) Grindstaff interview by Jacquelyn Hall, July 10, 1981 (in Hall's possession).

2. For this strike wave, see Tom Tippett, *When Southern Labor Stirs* (New York, 1931); James A. Hodges, "Challenge to the New South: The Great Textile Strike in Elizabethton, Tennessee, 1929," *Tennessee Historical Quarterly* 23 (Dec. 1964):343–57; . . .

3. Contemporary observations include, *Knoxville News Sentinel*, May 17, 1929; Florence Kelley, "Our Newest South," *Survey*, June 15, 1929, pp. 342–44; . . .

4. Anne Firor Scott, "On Seeing and Not Seeing: A Case of Historical Invisibility," *Journal of American History* 71 (June 1984):7–8.

5. Natalie Zemon Davis, *Society and Culture in Early Modern France* (Stanford, 1975), pp. 124–51. . . .

6. Michel Foucault, *Power/Knowledge: Selected Interviews and Other Writings, 1972–1977*, trans. and ed. Colin Gordon (New York, 1980), p. 81.

7. Joseph Leeming, *Rayon: The First Man-Made Fiber* (Brooklyn, 1950), pp. 1–82; Jesse W. Markham, *Competition in the Rayon Industry* (Cambridge, Mass., 1952), pp. 1–38, 97, 186, 193, 209.

8. Bruce Roberts and Nancy Roberts, *Where Time Stood Still: A Portrait of Appalachia* (New York, 1970); William Goodell Frost, "Our Contemporary Ancestors in the Southern Mountains," *Atlantic Monthly* 83 (March 1899):311; Arnold J. Toynbee, *A Study of History*, 2 vols. (New York, 1947), II:312; . . .

9. For this preindustrial economy, and its transformation, see Eller, *Miners, Millhands, and Mountaineers*, pp. 3–38, 86–127. . . .

10. *Mountaineer*, Dec. 28, Dec. 31, 1887.

11. U.S. Department of the Interior, Census Office, *Report on the Productions of Agriculture as Returned at the Tenth Census* (June 1, 1880) (Washington, 1883), pp. 84–85, 132, 169; U.S. Department of Commerce, Bureau of the Census, Fourteenth Census of the *United States Taken in the Year 1920: Agriculture*, vol. VI, pt. 2 (Washington, [D.C.] 1922), pp. 446–47.

12. Holly, "Elizabethton, Tennessee," pp. 123, 133–38, 156, 198; U.S. Congress, Senate, Committee on Manufactures, *Working Conditions of the Textile Industry in North Carolina, South Carolina, and Ten-*

nessee, 71 Cong., 1 sess., May 8, 9, and 20, 1929, p. 95; Henry Schuettler interview by Hall, n.d. [1981] (in Hall's possession).

13. Thirteenth Census of the United States, 1910, Manuscript Population Schedule, Carter County, Tenn., district 7; ibid., district 15; ibid., district 10; ibid., district 12.

14. Grindstaff interview.

15. *Scraps of Work and Play*, Southern Summer School for Women Workers in Industry, Burnsville, N.C., July 11-Aug. 23, 1929, typescript, pp. 21–22, 24, box 111, American Labor Education Service Records (Martin P. Catherwood Library, New York State School of Industrial and Labor Relations, Cornell University, Ithaca, N.Y.); Bessie Edens interview by Mary Frederickson, Aug. 14, 1975, pp. 1–2, 31–32, Southern Oral History Program Collection, Southern Historical Collection (Wilson Library, University of North Carolina at Chapel Hill) [hereafter SOHP].

16. Edens interview, Aug. 14, 1975, p. 32; Grindstaff interview.

17. Nettie Reece [pseud.] interview by Hall, May 18 and 19, 1983 (in Hall's possession).

18. *Knoxville News Sentinel*, May 13, 1929; *American Bemberg Corporation* v. *George Miller, et al.*, East Tennessee District Supreme Court, Jan. 29, 1930, record of evidence, typescript, box 660 (Tennessee State Library and Archives, Nashville) [hereafter Record of Evidence]. . . .

19. *Knoxville News Sentinel*, Mar. 14, 1929; Christine (Hinkle) Galliher and Dave Galliher interview by Hall, Aug. 8, 1979, pp. 8–9, SOHP; Tom Tippett, "Southern Situation," speech typescript, meeting held at the National Board, May 15, 1929, p. 3, box 25, Young Women's Christian Association Papers, Sophia Smith Collection (Smith College, Northampton, Mass.); Tom Tippett, "Impressions of Situation at Elizabethton, Tenn., May 10, 11, 1929," typescript, p. 1, ibid.

20. *Knoxville News Sentinel*, Mar. 20, Mar. 29, 1929; "Instructions for Adjustment of Wage Scale for Girl Help," Mar. 15, 1929, Records of the Conciliation Service, RG 280 (National Archives); Committee of Striking Workers[,] Members of United Textile Workers of America to the Honorable Herbert Hoover, Apr. 16, 1929, ibid; "Preliminary Report of Commissioner of Conciliation," Apr. 16, 1929, ibid.

21. Dr. J. A. Hardin to Hon. H. H. Horton, May 16, 1929, box 12, Governor Henry H. Horton Papers (Tennessee State Library and Archives); *Knoxville News Sentinel*, May 6, May 10, May 12, May 14, May 19, May 24, 1929.

22. Edens interview, Aug. 14, 1975, pp. 40, 49; Galliher interview, 33; *Knoxville News Sentinel*, Mar. 15, May 16, 1929.

23. *Knoxville News Sentinel*, May 27, 1929; Ina Nell (Hinkle) Harrison interview by Hall, Aug. 8, 1979, p. 2, SOHP; Mary Heaton Vorse, "Rayon Strikers Reluctantly Accept Settlement," press release, May 27, 1929, box 156, Mary Heaton Vorse Papers, Archives of Labor and Urban Affairs (Walter P. Reuther Library, Wayne State University, Detroit, Mich.).

24. "Rays of Sunshine in the Rayon War," *Literary Digest*, June 8, 1929, p. 12; *Charlotte Observer*, June 2, 1929; *Raleigh News and Observer*, May 24, 1929.

25. Edens interview, Aug. 14, 1975, pp. 43–44; Myrtle Simmerly interview by Hall, May 18, 1983 (in Hall's possession); Ollie Hardin interview by Hall and Sara Evans, Aug. 9, 1979 (in Hall's possession); Effie (Hardin) Carson interview by Hall and Evans, Aug. 6, 1979, p. 41 SOHP; Holly, "Elizabethton, Tennessee," 306–7.

26. James Myers, "Field Notes: Textile Strikes in the South," box 374, Archive Union Files (Martin P. Catherwood Library); *Raleigh News and Observer,* Mar. 15, 1929.

27. Hoffmann, "Mountaineer in Industry," 2–5; Robert (Bob) Moreland and Barbara Moreland interview by Hall, July 11, 1981 (in Hall's possession); *Knoxville News Sentinel,* Mar. 15, 1929; Honard Ward interview by Hall, n.d. [1981] (in Hall's possession).

28. *Knoxville News Sentinel,* May 15, 1929; Reece interview; . . .

29. For the argument that precisely because they are "left behind" by the economic developments that pull men into wage labor, woman-centered families may harbor alternative or oppositional values, see Mina Davis Caulfield, "Imperialism, the Family, and Cultures of Resistance," *Socialist Revolution* 4 (Oct. 1974):67–85; . . .

30. Bessie Edens, "Why a Married Woman Should Work," in *Scraps of Work and Play,* pp. 30–31; Edens interview, Aug. 14. 1975, pp. 14, 21, 34–35; Bessie Edens interview by Hall, Aug. 5, 1979 (in Hall's possession); Millie Sample, "Impressions," Aug. 1931, box 9, American Labor Education Service Records.

31. Mirion Bonner, "Behind the Southern Textile Strikes," *Nation.* Oct. 2, 1929, pp. 351–52; "Scraps From Our Lives," in *Scraps of Work and Play,* pp. 5–11; . . .

32. Corbin, *Life, Work, and Rebellion,* pp. 92–93; Louise A. Tilly, "Paths of Proletarianization: Organization of Production, Sexual Division of Labor, and Women's Collective Action," *Signs* 7 (Winter 1981):400–17; . . .

33. *Elizabethton Star,* Nov. 14, 1953, Jan. 31, 1986; Reece interview; Carson interview, 25; Nellie Bowers interview by Hall, May 15, 1983 (in Hall's possession); *Knoxville News Sentinel,* May 17, May 18, 1929.

34. Record of Evidence.

35. *Knoxville News Sentinel,* May 17, 1929.

36. Ibid.; Record of Evidence.

37. *American Bemberg Corporation* v. *George Miller, et al.,* minute books "Q" and "R," Chancery Court minutes, Carter County, Tenn., July 22, 1929 (Carter County Courthouse, Elizabethton, Tenn.); *American Bemberg Corporation* v. *George Miller, et al.,* Court of Appeals, #1, Sept. 5, 1930 (Supreme Court and Courts of Appeal, State of Tennessee, Knoxville).

38. Davis, *Society and Culture in Early Modern France,* pp. 124–51; Laurel Thatcher Ulrich, *Good Wives* (New York, 1982), pp. 191–97.

39. Elizabethton City Council, Minutes, May 23, 1929, Minute Book, vol. 5, pp. 356–57 (City Hall, Elizabethton, Tenn.).

40. *Knoxville News Sentinel,* May 5, 1929; Myers, "Field Notes." . . .

41. See, for instance, Alice Kessler-Harris, "The Autobiography of Ann Washington Craton," *Signs* 1 (Summer 1976):1019–37.

42. *Knoxville News Sentinel,* May 18, 1929; Record of Evidence.

43. Edens interview, Aug. 5, 1979.

44. Reece interview, May 19, 1983.

45. Charles K. Wolfe, *Tennessee Strings: The Story of Country Music in Tennessee* (Knoxville, 1977), pp. 22–90; Barry O'Connell, "Dick Boggs, Musician and Coal Miner," *Appalachian Journal* 11 (Autumn-Winter 1983–84):48.

46. *Miller's Elizabethton, Tenn., City Directory,* 1930; Reece interview; Record of Evidence; *Knoxville News Sentinel,* May 16, May 17, 1929; . . .

47. David E. Whisnant, *All That Is Native and Fine: The Politics of Culture in an American Region* (Chapel Hill, 1983), p. 48.

48. Grindstaff interview; Moreland interview.

49. *Knoxville Journal,* Apr. 22, 1929; sixteen-millimeter film (1 reel), ca. 1929, Helen Raulston Collection, Archives of Appalachia (East Tennessee State University, Johnson City); sixteen-millimeter film (20 reels), ca. 1927–1928, Bemberg Industry Records (Tennessee State Library and Archives). . . .

50. Anna Weinstock Schneider interview by Julia Blodgett Curtis, 1969, pp. 161, 166, 172–3, 177, Anna Weinstock Schneider Papers, box 1 (Martin P. Catherwood Library).

51. Grindstaff interview.

52. Bureau of the Census, *Fifteenth Census of the United States: 1930. Population,* vol. III, pt. 2 (Washington, [D.C.], 1932), p. 909; U.S. Department of Commerce, Bureau of the Census, *Sixteenth Census of the United States: 1940. Population,* vol. II, pt. 6 (Washington, [D.C.], 1943), p. 616.

53. Edens interview, Aug. 14, 1975, p. 50. . . .

BLANCHE WIESEN COOK

Eleanor Roosevelt as Reformer, Feminist, and Political Boss

Despite the divisions over an equal rights amendment, many women who had been enthusiastic reformers, suffragists, and feminists continued their political activism during the 1920s. Few did so more effectively than Eleanor Roosevelt.

A woman of limitless energy, compassion, and humanitarian zeal, Eleanor Roosevelt was the most active and controversial First Lady in the nation's history. A fascinating figure, her ability to change never ended. She began her adult life a shy, insecure woman who had imbibed the racism and anti-Semitism of the privileged world to which she was born. She ended her life a feminist and a political champion of civil rights, civil liberties, social justice, and world peace—a woman whose activism was played out on a world stage.

This transformation was well underway by the 1920s. Indeed, it had been accelerated when Franklin Delano Roosevelt was paralyzed by polio in 1921 and Eleanor began serving as his representative in the political arena. But as Blanche Cook makes clear in the following essay, Eleanor was no mere surrogate. A political activist, she was a shrewd analyst of the political scene whose observations remain timely. At the end of the twentieth century, political observers continue to seek remedies to women's prolonged political marginality. Even if women repeat the gains made in the 1992 Congressional elections each election year, it will take another seventy-four years before parity is achieved in Congress.

What did ER think women needed to do in order to make their votes meaningful? What advice did she give to those who wished to see women achieve numerical parity as officeholders? How did she respond to those who distrusted political activity in a woman as unfeminine? What advice do you think she would offer to those who seek real political power in the interests of social justice?

Eleanor Roosevelt began her career as the foremost political woman of the twentieth century convinced that women and men enter politics for different reasons: Men enter politics to pursue their own careers; women are motivated by a desire to change society, to improve the daily conditions of life. Impressed by the women she worked with, she came to believe that women's public activities would determine America's national future. Not a prewar suffragist herself, she fully appreciated the suffragists' century of struggle, and the grassroots strategy that ultimately triumphed.

She believed that fundamental change required active and committed women who were willing to go door to door, block by block, and educate people on an individual basis about the real needs and conditions of society. She saw the need for newsletters and information bulletins. ER was one of the first

From *Eleanor Roosevelt, Volume I, 1884–1933* by Blanche Wiesen Cook. Copyright © 1992 by Blanche Wiesen Cook. Used by permission of Viking Penguin, a division of Penguin Putnam, Inc. Notes have been renumbered and edited.

women activists to realize that little would be achieved without a mimeograph machine, and persuaded New York's League of Women Voters to purchase one on 3 October 1922.[1] Above all, ER understood that information and organization required local clubs and political centers, a network of women active in every town and village connected to one another through meetings, debates, round-table discussions, luncheons, dinner parties, and personal friendships.

During the 1920s, there were four centers of political power for women in New York State: the League of Women Voters, ... the Women's Trade Union League (WTUL), ... the Women's Division of the New York State Democratic Committee, ... and the Women's City Club, an umbrella organization dedicated to social reform and municipal affairs. Most of the two thousand members of the club were professional women—attorneys, physicians, educators, consumer activists, unionists, businesswomen, writers, artists, advertising agents, architects, engineers, printers, accountants, volunteer activists, saleswomen, office workers, and bankers—and many of them were active also in the WTUL and the League of Women Voters. Here ER met and worked with every activist political woman in New York—social workers like Lillian Wald, Mary (Molly) Dewson, and Mary Simkhovitch; labor reformers such as Frances Perkins and Belle Moskowitz; Marie Jennie Howe, the Unitarian minister who created the women's social club Heterodoxy.

There were many and labyrinthine connections.[2] But a small number of women really pulled the network together. They served on the governing councils of each organization and decided on policy and strategy. ER rapidly became a leader of this group, which was made up largely of her own circle of Democratic women. She helped to raise funds, edited newsletters, moderated panels, participated in debates, presented information, toured the state on behalf of candidates and causes, and represented New York at national conventions of political women. To pursue the women's agenda, for six years ER, Nancy Cook, Marion Dickerman, Elinor Morgenthau, and Caroline O'Day went "Trooping for Democracy." In every weather and in every season, they toured New York State in their Democratic blue roadster, which they had bought together, or in

O'Day's chauffeured Packard. They toured every county to demand an expanded public-housing program, improved sanitation and sewerage control, frequent and comfortable public transit, new parks and public playgrounds, school lunches and nursing facilities, unemployment insurance, workers' compensation, occupational-safety-and-health legislation, the eight-hour day, protective laws for women workers, mandatory-education laws, child-labor legislation, pure food-and-milk legislation, the right of women to serve on juries, and equal representation of women on all committees of the Democratic Party. ...

Throughout the 1920s, articles about ER and her political work appeared almost weekly in *The New York Times*. She was the subject of news accounts, columns, editorials, profiles in the Sunday *Magazine* section, and letters to the editor. Her public appearances were national news. ... [However] in her memoirs ER called the chapter devoted to the 1920s, the decade of the most robust political activity she undertook on her own, "Private Interlude."[3] Since she could hardly have meant by that an absorption in private or domestic affairs, one must conclude that this period in her life seemed in retrospect private in the sense that it was hers to do with as she pleased. She neither campaigned for FDR [who was recuperating from polio] nor served as his surrogate. He was preoccupied with recovery; she was preoccupied with politics. She became famous not as FDR's wife, but as a major political force to be reckoned with.

Yet, the more she achieved, the more she was acclaimed and celebrated in her own right, the more she sought to reassure FDR that she was doing it all for him. On 6 February 1924, for example, ER wrote him a long, rambling letter full of detail about her activities. But she concluded by reminding her husband that she was merely his temporary stand-in.[4] She had been asked to sponsor or attend several memorial services for President Wilson, who died on 3 February. She agreed, though she understood they only wanted FDR's name. She aimed neither to compete with her husband nor to upstage him. Only slowly and with considerable reluctance did ER admit that she was genuinely pleased by her public activities. Much more often she professed a selfless lack of interest in her own work and her own career, and thereby contributed to our distorted image of her public self. While she was First Lady, she wrote that she was pushed into politics reluctantly—and solely in support of her husband. She never acknowledged her own joy in the game, or her own skills at manipulating the cards. . . .

[For example] in her 6 February 1924 letter to FDR where she minimized her activities, she reported that she, Caroline O'Day, and Nancy Cook had been to a "remarkable dinner" of "600 women from Albany and nearby and all workers!" They saw Governor Al Smith, who asked them to lobby for his new reform program, and ER spent several days in Albany, working out the details. But there was still one piece of additional news, she noted almost as an afterthought: Cordell Hull, the Democratic Party's National Committee chairman in 1924, had invited ER—currently finance chair of the Women's Division—to head a platform committee for women to present their demands at the June convention in New York. She was delighted, though she gave no hint of that to FDR: "I'm up to my eyes in work for the convention preparations and trying to raise our budget which is going to be an endless job." ER even rejected FDR's praise for her work, the words of which are now lost along with most of his correspondence during this period: "You need not be proud of me dear. I'm only being active till you can be again. . . ."[5]

When one considers the disparity between ER's denial and the reality of her daily activities, one pauses to wonder what motivated her decision to trivialize both her work and her commitment to it. Her need to minimize her efforts and to reassure her husband that she was in fact no threat, and no competition to his primary place in the political arena, is a sturdy testimony to the proverbial double standard that was and remains the burden of political women. . . .

ER was embattled on several fronts in 1924. On 9 April, she wrote FDR that she wished he were at home to advise her "on the fight I'm putting up on a delegate and 2 alternates at large." The fight was classic: Would the female or male party leaders get to name the women delegates? Forty-nine county chairwomen had already selected and endorsed their representatives when Tammany boss Charles Murphy claimed it his privilege to name the delegates. ER, resolute and ready for a fight, wrote: "I imagine it is just a question of

which [Murphy] disliked most—giving me my way or having me give the papers a grand chance for a story by telling [all] at the women's dinner . . . and by insisting on recognition on the floor of the convention & putting the names in nomination!" Clearly, ER had already decided to do full battle: "There's one thing I'm thankful for—I haven't a thing to lose and for the moment you haven't either."[6]

The New York Times featured ER's fight for women's equality at the state convention in an article titled "Women Are in Revolt." It was the "only inharmonious note" of the convention: the women supported Smith, but demanded their right to choose their own representatives. "Mrs. Franklin D. Roosevelt . . . slated to be one of the four delegates-at-large, led the fight for the women." She said:

> We have now had the vote for four years, and some very ardent suffragists seem to feel that instead of gaining in power the women have lost. . . .
> I have been wondering whether it occurs to the women as a whole that, if they expect to gain the ends for which they fought, it is not going to be sufficient simply to cast a ballot. . . . They must gain for themselves a place of real equality and the respect of the men. . . . The whole point in women's suffrage is that the Government needs the point of view of all its citizens and the women have a point of view which is of value to the Government. . . .[7]

ER was in the vanguard of those feminists who protected and promoted women's issues and the equal representation of women within the party's committees. She demanded that women be represented on county committees "in equal numbers" and be listed among those nominated for office in all primary elections. . . .

ER's efforts were victorious. She was named chair of a committee that negotiated the women's right to name their own delegates and alternates. Their meetings with Smith and other party leaders "established a precedent," and ER felt encouraged: "We go into the campaign feeling that our party has recognized us as an independent part of the organization."

But it was only a preliminary victory. The women's political movement had become a significant element within the Democratic Party. It was feminist and bold. And the entrenched male power brokers hated it. They sought at every turn to set up roadblocks, brake its momentum, and destroy it. A daily and nasty battle ensued, fought meanly and through subterfuge. For example, women who finally achieved membership status on a committee often found the doors to the meetings locked, or the meetings moved to secret places. Other apparent victories were no sooner announced than betrayed.

In March 1924, the Democratic National Committee proudly announced that it was "the first political group to seek women's views on important questions of peculiar interest to them so that these social legislation planks as incorporated in the national Democratic platform may represent their ideas." And, with considerable public relations fanfare, the leadership announced it had asked Eleanor Roosevelt to chair the women's platform committee.[8]

ER agreed, and determined to base the recommendations for needed social-welfare legislation on the "requests of all women's organizations in the country." She appointed a panel of activist experts. . . . The committee endorsed the League of Nations, and called for the creation of a federal department of education, equal pay for women workers, and the ratification of the child-labor amendment. It called for a forty-eight-hour workweek, wages commensurate with the cost of living and health care, the creation of employment bureaus and the means to ensure "healthy and safe working conditions."

But in June, their three months' effort was rudely rebuffed by the Resolutions Committee at the convention. For hours ER and her coworkers sat outside the locked doors of the all-male Resolutions Committee and waited to be heard. At dawn the men voted twenty-two to eighteen, for the third and last time, to reaffirm their refusal even to hear the women's proposals. ER wrote that at the convention of 1924 she saw "for the first time where the women stood when it came to a national convention. I shortly discovered that they were of very little importance. They stood outside the door of all important meetings and waited." She spent most of her time during the deadlocked, heat-filled convention—every day the temperature topped one hundred degrees Fahrenheit—trying to seem calm. "I sat and knitted, suffered with the heat and wished it would end." One day, [comedian] Will Rogers noticed ER and asked: "Knitting in the names

of the future victims of the guillotine?" ER was tempted to respond that she was "ready to call any punishment down on the heads of those who could not bring the convention to a close."[9]

The 1924 convention was a setback for the women, and a disaster for the Democrats. But for the Roosevelts 1924 represented another turning point. Both ER and FDR were widely perceived as the most significant contributors to the Democratic convention. The women's political community acknowledged ER as a major leader. Personally, she was informed and toughened by her new understanding of the way male bastions of power actually worked. And during the convention, FDR's reputation as a national figure soared. In fact, the only bright moment of the divided and frequently violent convention—a convention dominated by Al Smith and his chief opponent, William Gibbs McAdoo, who was now frankly associated with the Ku Klux Klan—occurred when FDR presented the nominating speech for Smith. [Although Smith lost the presidential nomination,] . . . ER agreed to help run Al Smith's campaign for re-election as New York's governor—against Republican nominee Theodore Roosevelt, Jr.

ER's willingness to support Al Smith in the face of the continued rebuffs and indignities experienced by the organized political women throughout 1924 was more than a testimony to her belief that Smith was serious about social reform. It was a demonstration of her own conviction that women needed to work systematically and earnestly within the power structure if they were to achieve political change. Votes for women could be rendered meaningless unless women organized to take over specific areas of party activity, specific areas of real power. Now was the time "to prove our strength and demand respect."[10]

ER appreciated that this meant working under duress with frequently hostile allies, who would attempt to undermine every victory. She spoke directly of male hostility to women in politics. In an interview in *The New York Times* published on 20 April 1924, she described male contempt for politically involved women. Men would say: "You are wonderful. I love and honor you. . . . Lead your own life, attend to your charities, cultivate yourself, travel when you wish, bring up the children, run your house. I'll give you all the freedom you wish and all the money I can but—leave me my business and politics." This, ER urged, women must not allow. "Women must get into the political game and stay in it." Women together must build up new institutions of alternative power "from the inside."[11]

She had seconded Smith's nomination at the New York State convention with vigor, and with a thrust at her cousin TR, Jr., that finally and forever alienated the two branches of the family. How could Smith not win, she asserted, since the Republicans, by their useless nomination of TR, "did everything to help him"? She campaigned throughout the state in an extraordinary vehicle rigged up with a steam-spouting teapot to signify TR, Jr.'s involvement in the Teapot Dome scandal. [The scandal involved the transfer of oil-rich public lands to private oil companies by the Secretary of the Interior, Albert B. Fall. The Wyoming land called Teapot Dome was sold to Harry Sinclair. Although Fall went to prison, the national oil reserves remained in the hands of Sinclair and other developers.] In county after county she systematically dismissed her cousin as a reasonably nice "young man whose public service record shows him willing to do the bidding of his friends." . . . [12]

ER was delighted by Smith's victory, and entirely pleased with the success of her "rough stunt."[13] Indeed, she was so proud of the teapot, which was of her own design, that she drove it to Connecticut, evidently to give her Aunt Bye a glimpse of what the fuss was all about. Aunt Bye was frankly dismayed by her niece's unseemly display of raw political muscle: "Alas and lackaday! Since politics have become her choicest interest all her charm has disappeared, and the fact is emphasized by the companions she chooses to bring with her. . . ."[14]

However much ER's political vigor, new friends, and public prominence might disturb the older members of her family, she herself greeted every new controversy with verve. Eleanor Roosevelt had become a feminist [as well as a politician]. She fought for women's rights steadfastly and with determination; she championed equality in public and private matters; and she herself used the word "feminist." But during the 1920s, the bitterly divisive Equal Rights Amendment ripped the women's movement apart, obscuring for decades the full dimensions of historical feminism—and ER's leadership role with it. . . .

The ERA-protectionist division resulted from a conflicting understanding of what was possible in an unrestrained capitalist economy. In 1923, despite years of progressive action, there was still no limitation on the number of hours or the conditions of work for women or men; and ER and the protectionist feminists—all of whom wanted protective legislation for all—sincerely believed that it was possible to achieve a fair and just administration of a forty-eight-hour workweek by demanding it for women *first*. Equal-rights feminists sincerely believed that shorter hours for women first would result in the loss of jobs for women, who were not as valued as men workers and were not paid on a par with them, and who were therefore required by economic need to work longer hours merely to survive. Although both sides agreed that women worked in a brutal economy that achieved profits by demanding the longest possible hours for the least possible pay, the battle between them raged in bitter tones of acrimony. The protectionists believed the ERA women were elitists and careerists who cared only for privileged and professional women and were ignorant of and unconcerned about the poor. The ERA activists believed the protectionists were old-fashioned reformers who refused to see that, until women were acknowledged equal in law, all reforms to protect women were frauds that could only work against them. . . .

Eleanor Roosevelt too tended to consider the ERA proponents self-serving aristocrats who cared little and understood less about the needs of the poor. She was drawn toward the vision of reform created by that earlier generation of community activists, unionists, and radicals led by Florence Kelley, Jane Addams, Lillian Wald, Rose Schneiderman, and Dr. Alice Hamilton, [who] regarded the ERA as a fantasy that endangered their life's work. . . .

As Eleanor Roosevelt's influence grew, and as her confidence increased, she threw herself into a range of social initiatives aimed at strengthening government protection for women and children. She fought for the Child Labor Amendment, increased support for the Children's Bureau and the Women's Bureau, and worked to raise state matching funds for the $1.25-million Sheppard-Towner Act to establish maternity and pediatric clinics and a health-care program for mothers and infants. A great victory for social feminists, who had campaigned for years to decrease the grim rate of infant mortality in the United States, the Sheppard-Towner Act was attacked as "Sovietism," and a dangerous precedent leading to birth control and governmental programs of "social hygiene." ER and Narcissa Vanderlip were among the leaders of New York's crusade to raise the enabling funds.

To charges that the law was unconstitutional and not economical, Vanderlip countered: "If it is constitutional to use federal funds to save hogs from cholera, and cows from tuberculosis, it is constitutional to use them to save babies and their mothers from death."[15]

Every issue involving women was of concern to ER.... She called for equal political education for girls and for boys, and noted with pride that "Girls nowadays may be rivals of their brothers in school, sports, and business." But ER lamented they "lag behind in a knowledge and interest in government." She gave as examples her own daughter, Anna, and Governor Smith's daughter Emily, whom she had overheard complaining that politics dominated their fathers' conversations. ER contrasted this attitude with the one that prevailed among "flappers of politically prominent families in England. British daughters not only take a keen interest in their fathers' careers but go out to help in the political battle." She cited the good works of Ishbel MacDonald and Megan Lloyd George in particular, and concluded that, if "our American girls are not to be left behind, something must be done to stimulate their interest in civic responsibilities." She thought that daughters of politicians should at least want to be able "to outtalk their fathers."[16]

Eleanor Roosevelt's own sense of responsibility took her beyond strong words to vigorous deeds. In 1926, she made headline news when she participated in a mass picket demonstration of three hundred women in support of striking paper-box makers. Eight notable women "of prominence" were arrested for ignoring a police order "to move on," and charged with "disorderly conduct," including ER, Margaret Norrie, Mrs. Samuel Bens, Marion Dickerman, Evelyn Preston, and Dorothy Kenyon.[17]

ER was proud of the achievements of women. She honored their daring and their vision. She considered women flyers marvelously courageous, and she promoted women in flight. She herself wanted to fly, and she did.... [18] Her friend Amelia Earhart gave her preliminary lessons, and ER actually took and passed the physical examination. But FDR persuaded her that he had sufficient worries without her flying above the clouds at top speed. FDR's opposition to flying was genuine. In 1920, he was horrified when his mother flew from London to Paris, and asked her never to go aloft again. Evidently both women acquiesced to his fear; but ER always regretted not becoming a pilot, because, she said, she liked to be in control of her own mobility.

Increasingly, ER's interests became international [ist as well as feminist and reformist]. [In 1923, Edward Bok, the former publisher of *Ladies' Home Journal,* had offered a prize of $50,000 to a practical plan that would allow the United States to do its share to preserve world peace without making compulsory the nation's involvement in any future European wars. ER had agreed to serve on the prize committee at the request of Esther Lape, a college professor, journalist, researcher, and publicist whom she much admired. The winning plan recommended the United States' immediate adherence to the Permanent Court of Internal Justice and cooperation with (though not membership in) the League of Nations. When Bok, Lape, ER, and their allies proceeded to promote U.S. entrance into the World Court, Senate isolationists charged them with being a tool of foreign radicals who were trying to manipulate public opinion and legislative action. Investigation by the FBI, the first of many, did not deter ER. She continued to work for the League and for U.S. entrance into the World Court.] In October 1927, she hosted a meeting of four hundred women at Hyde Park to launch a women's peace movement and support the Kellogg-Briand Treaty to outlaw war.... For the next ten years, ER was to be one of the most prominent antiwar women in the United States, associated with both Jane Addams's Women's International League for Peace and Freedom, and Carrie Chapman Catt's National Conference on the Cause and Cure of War. ER [also] devoted considerable space in the *Women's Democratic News* to issues of war and peace.... Wherever she went, or whatever her announced topic, whenever ER spoke as the decade of the 1920s drew to a close, she spoke at least in part about world peace. Long before the war clouds gathered her message was urgent: "The time to prepare for world peace is during the time of peace and not during the time of war."[19]

By 1928, the year FDR ran for governor of New York, Eleanor Roosevelt had become a major political force. For six years, she had served as finance chair of women's activities of the New York Democratic State Committee. She was vice-chair of the Woman's City Club of New York, chair of the Non-Partisan Legislative Committee, editor and treasurer of the *Women's Democratic News*, a member of the board of directors of the Foreign Policy Association and the City Housing Corporation. In fact, in 1928, ER was one of the best-known and highest-ranking Democrats in the United States. She was named director of the Bureau of Women's Activities of the Democratic National Committee, and in July asked to head a Woman's Advisory Committee to develop Al Smith's presidential campaign organization.

In 1928, ER held, therefore, the most powerful positions ever held by a woman in party politics. In matters of "turfing," which we now recognize as more than symbolic, she demanded and received equality for the women political organizers: Their offices had the same floor space their male counterparts had, and equal comfort. There were windows, carpets, plants; the accommodations were light and airy. *The New York Times* reported that the space allotted to women in the national headquarters of the Democratic party was "said to be the largest headquarters ever occupied by a women's political organization." ER's rooms and those of John J. Raskob, then Democratic national chairman, were "identical in size and location."[20]

Throughout the 1920s ER worked to ensure that this equality involve more than floor space. In September 1926, after a bitter struggle for equal representation for women within the New York State Democratic Party, the party convention elected Caroline O'Day vice-chair of the State Committee, and women were voted equal representation with men in 135 of 150 Assembly districts.... [21] But she quickly realized that equal representation had

as yet very little to do with equal power. Increasingly distressed by the manipulations of her male colleagues, ER argued that women needed to take tougher, more direct measures.

In April 1928, she published a boldly feminist article in *Redbook.* "Women Must Learn to Play the Game as Men Do" was a battle cry that urged women to create their own "women bosses" in order to achieve real power:

> Women have been voting for ten years. But have they achieved actual political equality with men? No ... In small things they are listened to; but when it comes to asking for important things they generally find they are up against a blank wall....
>
> Politically, as a sex, women are generally "frozen out" from any intrinsic share of influence....
>
> The machinery of party politics has always been in the hands of men, and still is. Our statesmen and legislators are still keeping in form as the successors of the early warriors [who gathered] around the camp-fire plotting the next day's attack.... [22]

ER's tone was outraged and unrelenting: Women went into politics with high hopes and specific intentions. They were courted and wooed. But when they demanded and expected real power, they were rebuffed....

Although only a few years before ER had contended that women did not go into politics for personal gain, or the customary party reward for their work, by 1928 she expressed dismay that the hardworking women who devoted their time and energy to the political game continued to go unrewarded: "Men who work hard in party politics are always recognized, or taken care of in one way or another. Women, most of whom are voluntary workers ... are generally expected to find in their labor its own reward...."

Then there was the matter of political office. Party leaders "will ask women to run for office now and then, sometimes because they think it politic and wise to show women how generous they are, but more often because they realize in advance their ticket cannot win in the district selected. Therefore they will put up a woman, knowing it will injure the party less to have a woman defeated, and then they can always say it was her sex that defeated her. Where victory is certain, very rarely can you get a woman nominated...."

ER was proud of the many women

throughout the United States who had been elected to public office.... But, ER asked: "Does this indicate any equal recognition or share in political power?" She answered with a resounding no: There were instead infinite "examples ... of women who were either denied a nomination or who were offered it only when inevitable defeat stared the party leaders in the face." ER suggested a reason for this situation: Public men dislike women in public life. "Beneath the veneer of courtesy and outward show of consideration universally accorded women, there is a widespread male hostility—age-old perhaps—against sharing with them any actual control."

To alter this, she urged women to "elect, accept and back" women bosses on every level of party management, in "districts, counties and states. Women must organize just as men organize." ER did not believe in a separate woman's party. "A woman's ticket could never possibly succeed. And to crystalize the issues on the basis of sex-opposition would only further antagonize men, congeal their age-old prejudices, and widen the chasm of existing differences." Rather, within the party, women needed to select, promote, and elect women bosses to positions of leadership and authority—where they could, with equality and independence and above all the assurance that they had the backing of their women's constituency, fight it out with the men who routinely denied power to women.

ER was aware that the word "boss" might "shock sensitive ears." She did not mean by "boss" some sleazy and easy-to-buy politician, but, rather, a "high-minded leader." And she chose the word deliberately, "as it is the word men understand." She explained in detail her conviction that, "if women believe they have a right and duty in political life today, they must learn to talk the language of men. They must not only master the phraseology, but also understand the machinery which men have built up through years of practical experience. Against the men bosses there must be women bosses who can talk as equals, with the backing of a coherent organization of women voters behind them."

Tough-minded and direct, ER was also critical of women who refused to take the business of politics seriously or to consider their own political work a matter of fundamental urgency and significance: "If we are

still a negligible factor, ignored and neglected, we must be prepared to admit in what we have ourselves failed." ER believed that too many women refused to work; to take themselves and their visions seriously; and too many women lacked knowledge and refused to "take the pains to study history, economics, political methods or get out among human beings." ...

ER explained, in conclusion, that women could only achieve real power by serious organization, unlimited study, endless work. Male hostility to women was only partly responsible for women's failure to achieve power. Women seemed to ER reluctant to claim power. She dismissed the attitude of those women who professed "to be horrified at the thought of women bosses bartering and dickering in the hard game of politics with the men." " ... [But] politics cannot be played from the clouds," [she insisted.] She understood that the task was hard and that the role of women in public life was difficult. Women's lives, to begin with, ER noted, were always "full of interruptions." There were the home, the children, the meals to prepare, the dinner parties to arrange. She was aware of the double standards and the double-job burdens. And so, she argued, women have to be more organized, more methodical, and, yes, more hard-working than men. She was adamant: "Women must learn to play the game as men do."

ER's earlier years in Albany and Washington, and her lifelong association with politicians and their ways, had accustomed her to the vagaries and strategies of power. Silence on the sidelines never achieved a thing, and was always interpreted as consent. The more she spoke out, the more she recognized her impact. She was ready to become—indeed, had already become—the very "political boss" about whom she wrote.

ER's *Redbook* article hit the stands with rather a splash. It resulted in several *New York Times* articles, including a *Magazine* interview by S. J. Woolf, "A Woman Speaks Her Political Mind," ... [which] was entirely favorable to ER, [but] revealed an ever-present double standard: ER was a mother, a teacher, and a homemaker, Woolfe wrote, who never allowed her public or political activities to

interfere with her devotion to her home, nor has she sacrificed her private life in any respect to her public activities. She is the mother of five children and their upbringing has been her first consideration. She believes that a woman fitted to serve her community or her country can show that fitness best in the management of her own home. . . .

Mrs. Roosevelt is tall and has an engaging smile. There is something about that smile that is reminiscent of her illustrious uncle, while the droop in the outer corner of her eyes likewise reminds one of the former President. There is nothing about her that marks her as a woman in public life. Her manner is that of the young suburban mother. She is the strongest argument that could be presented against those who hold that by entering politics a woman is bound to lose her womanliness and her charm.

She is the type of mother . . . interested in civic betterment, who believes that that finds its beginning in the home.[23]

Woolf's article was a clear indication of what was expected of ER if she were to maintain credibility and acceptance as a woman in public life. Among her colleagues and friends, she might depart from such prescriptions. But publicly ER understood and always worked within the limitations of her time and her marriage. Publicly she denied to the end of her life that she ever had, or ever wanted, real political power. She acknowledged that she worked for those issues that she believed in, but not once did she profess to enjoy the game. She never publicly acknowledged that it satisfied her own interests, served her own needs, or that she delighted even in the rough-and-tumble of the deals and battles. Nevertheless, she did express dismay whenever she or other women were bypassed or blithely ignored and men took credit for their efforts and ideas. And she hated it when she was given no specific job to do, or was not encouraged to participate in a way she deemed appropriate. . . . [Her dilemma was reflected in her response to the 1928 election when Al Smith finally ran for president and her husband for governor of New York.]

ER's initial response to Smith's defeat and FDR's victory was complex. For over nine months, she had worked daily and imaginatively for the Smith campaign. ER hated to lose. It was not merely Smith's personal loss, or her own, but the continued defeat on the national level of all the social programs she championed. . . . ER was eager to continue the

battle, but in terms of her own work, she considered FDR's victory a mixed blessing. She feared that FDR's election to office meant that she would have to withdraw from public life. To reporters, her remarks were restrained, even ungracious: "If the rest of the ticket didn't get in, what does it matter?" "No, I am not excited about my husband's election. I don't care. What difference can it make to me?"[24] In retrospect, she wondered if she had "really wanted Franklin to run. I imagine I accepted his nomination and later his election as I had accepted most of the things that had happened in life thus far; one did whatever seemed necessary and adjusted one's personal life to the developments in other people's lives."[25]

There was in 1928 no accepted place for a political wife, except in the background. ER had grown accustomed to a different role. She was a publisher, an editor, a columnist; she debated on the radio and before large audiences; her opinions were forthright and specific. She had a following, and people relied on her views and depended on her leadership. . . . There was no turning back. Yet neither was there any precedent for this new reality. History presented no other couple similarly equal in spirit, commitment, and ambition—giant personalities, powerful egos, inspiring and commanding presences. Was ER seriously meant to become again the dutiful wife at home with the children, . . . while her husband and all their friends were engaged in the work she most enjoyed? It was impossible. She could not abide the thought. She resented even contemplating it. And so the Roosevelt partnership departed yet again from tradition. . . . She would do it all—she would be the governor's wife, and she would pursue her own agenda.

NOTES

1. New York League of Women Voters, *Weekly News*, 22 Oct. 1922.

2 Elizabeth Israels Perry, "Training for Public Life: ER and Women's Political Networks in the 1920s," and Susan Ware, "ER and Democratic Politics: Women in the Postsuffrage Era," both in *Without Precedent: The Life and Career of Eleanor Roosevelt*, eds. Joan Hoff-Wilson and Marjorie Lightman (Bloomington: Indiana University Press, 1984), pp. 28–45, 46–60.

3. Eleanor Roosevelt, *This I Remember* (New York: Harper & Brothers, 1949), p. 32.

4. ER to FDR, 6 Feb. 1924, Franklin Delano Roosevelt Library [FDRL].

5. Ibid.

6. ER to FDR, 9 April 1924, FDRL.

7. *New York Times*, 15 April 1924.

8. Ibid., 31 March 1924.

9. Ibid., 11 June 1924 and 23 June, 1924. Also Eleanor Roosevelt, *This Is My Story* (New York: Garden City Publishing Company, 1937), pp. 354–55.

10. *New York Times*, 14 April 1924.

11. Interview with ER by Rose Feld, Ibid., 20 April 1924.

12. *New York Times*, 27 Sept. 1924.

13. ER, *This I Remember*, pp. 31–32.

14. Anna Roosevelt Cowles to Corinne Alsop, Alsop Family papers, Houghton; quoted in Geoffrey C. Ward, *A First-Class Temperament: The Emergence of Franklin Roosevelt* (New York: Harper & Row, 1989), p. 701n.

15. Vanderlip on Sheppard-Towner, quoted in

Hilda R. Watrous, *Narcissa Cox Vanderlip*, League of Women Voters' pamphlet (New York: Foundation for Citizenship Education, 1982), p. 31.

16. *New York Times*, 26, 27 May 1927.

17. *New York Times*, 9 Dec. 1926.

18. *New York Times*, 1, 6 June 1929.

19. *New York Times*, 15 Oct. 1927; 8 Dec. 1927; 2 Nov. 1929.

20. *New York Times*, 19 July 1928; 4 Aug. 1928.

21. *New York Times*, 28 Sept. 1926.

22. For this quotation and those in the following paragraphs, see "Women Must Learn to Play the Game as Men Do," *Redbook* (April 1928): 71–72ff.

23. *New York Times Magazine*, 8 April 1928.

24. Quoted in Joseph P. Lash, *Eleanor and Franklin* (New York: W. W. Norton, 1971), p. 320.

25. ER, *This I Remember*, p. 46.

JACQUELINE JONES

Harder Times: The Great Depression

The chronic scarcity of jobs that characterized the Appalachian South where the Elizabethton strike occurred became a national phenomenon in the 1930s. As the Great Depression tightened its hold on the economy, the plight of America's working people generated protest in the farm belt as well as industrial centers. Government aid eventually alleviated some of the suffering while New Deal legislation and a revitalized labor movement brought improved working conditions. Nevertheless many workers, agricultural as well as industrial, struggled daily to survive. They, especially, remained at the mercy of any employers who would hire them.

African Americans were especially vulnerable. Jacqueline Jones's study of black women reminds us once again of the extent to which race and class shape women's experience. Consider the difference that race made in both the job opportunities available to women in the 1930s and the debate about whether married women should work. Observe how the experience of black domestics demonstrated the power of race and class to override "the bonds of womanhood." Note, too, how the speed-ups generating such dissatisfaction among the textile workers in the 1920s described by Hall were extended in the 1930s to private household service.

High unemployment rates among their husbands and sons forced many white wives to enter the labor market for the first time in the 1930s.[1] But black men experienced even higher rates of joblessness, causing their wives to cling more desperately to the positions they already had, despite declining wages and deteriorating working conditions. During the Great Depression, most black women maintained only a precarious hold on gainful employment; their positions as family breadwinners depended upon, in the words of one social worker, "the breath of chance, to say nothing of the winds of economic change."[2] Unemployment statistics for the 1930s can be misleading because they do not reveal the impact of a shifting occupational structure on job options for women of the two races. Just as significantly, the relatively high rate of black females' participation in the labor force obscures the highly temporary and degrading nature of their work experiences. Specifically, most of these women could find only seasonal or part-time employment; racial and sexual discrimination deprived them of a living wage no matter how hard they labored; and they endured a degree and type of workplace exploitation for which the mere fact of having a job could not compensate. During the decade, nine out of ten black women workers toiled as agricultural laborers or domestic servants. Various pieces of federal legislation designed to protect and raise the purchasing power of workers (most notably the National Industrial Recovery Act [1933], the Social Security Act [1935], and the Fair Labor Standards Act [1938]) exempted these two groups of workers from their provisions. In essence, then, no more than 10 percent of gainfully employed black women derived any direct benefit from the new federal policies related to minimum wages, maximum hours, unemployment compensation, and social security.[3]

Despite the rapid decline in a wide variety of indicators related to production and economic growth in the early 1930s, and despite the sluggishness of the pre-1941 recovery period, the numbers and kinds of job opportunities for white women expanded, as did their need to help supplement household income. The clerical sector grew (as it had in the 1920s) and would continue to do so in the 1940s, and in the process attracted more and more women into the work force and employed a larger proportion of all white women workers. (The percentage of white women who were gainful workers steadily increased throughout the period 1920 to 1940 from 21.3 to 24.1 percent of all adult females.) Recent historians have stressed the "benefits of labor segregation" for

women, arguing that, at least during the early part of the depression decade, unemployment in the male-dominated industrial sector was generally greater than in the female-dominated areas of sales, communications, and secretarial work. But this was a race-specific phenomenon. In a job market segmented by both race and sex, black women had no access to white women's work even though (or perhaps because) it was deemed integral to both industrial capitalism and the burgeoning federal bureaucracy. In 1940 one-third of all white, but only 1.3 percent of all black, working women had clerical jobs. On the other hand, 60 percent of all black female workers were domestic servants; the figure for white women was only 10 percent. . . . [4]

KITCHEN SPEED-UPS: DOMESTIC SERVICE

Contemporary literary and photographic images of a stricken nation showed dejected white men waiting in line for food, jobs, and relief. Yet observers sensitive to the racial dimensions of the crisis provided an alternative symbol—that of a middle-aged black woman in a thin, shabby coat and men's shoes, standing on a street corner in the dead of winter and offering her housecleaning services for 10 cents an hour. If the migrant labor camp symbolized the black agricultural worker's descent into economic marginality, then the "slave markets" in northern cities revealed a similar fate for domestic servants.

"The 'mart' is but a miniature mirror of our economic battle front," wrote two investigative reporters in a 1935 issue of the NAACP's monthly journal, *The Crisis*. A creature of the depression, the slave market consisted of groups of black women, aged seventeen to seventy, who waited on sidewalks for white women to drive up and offer them a day's work. The Bronx market, composed of several small ones—it was estimated that New York City had two hundred altogether—received the most attention from writers during the decade, though the general phenomenon recurred throughout other major cities. Before 1929, many New York domestics had worked for wealthy white families on Long Island. Their new employers, some of them working-class women themselves, paid as little as $5.00 weekly for full-time laborers to wash windows and clothes, iron (as many as twenty-one shirts a shift), and wax floors. The black women earned radically depressed wages: lunch and 35 cents for six hours of work, or $1.87 for an eight-hour day. They had to guard against various ruses that would deprive them of even this pittance—for example, a clock turned back an hour, the promised carfare that never materialized at the end of the day. As individuals they felt trapped, literally and figuratively pushed to the limits of their endurance. A thirty-year-old woman told federal interviewer Vivian Morris that she hated the people she worked for: "Dey's mean, 'ceitful, an' 'ain' hones'; but what ah'm gonna do? Ah got to live—got to hab a place to steh," and so she would talk her way into a job by boasting of her muscle power. But some days groups of women would spontaneously organize themselves and "run off the corner" those job seekers "who persist[ed] in working for less than thirty cents an hour."[5]

Unlike their country cousins, domestics contended directly with white competitors pushed out of their factory and waitressing jobs. The agricultural labor system served as a giant sieve; for the most part, displaced farm families went to the city rather than vying for the remaining tenant positions. The urban economy had no comparable avenues of escape; it was a giant pressure cooker, forcing the unemployed to look for positions in occupations less prestigious than the ones they held formerly or, in the event of ultimate failure, to seek some form of charity or public assistance. A 1937 Women's Bureau survey of destitute women in Chicago revealed that, although only 37 percent of native-born white women listed their "usual occupation" as domestic service, a much greater number had tried to take advantage of employers' preferences for white servants before they gave up the quest for jobs altogether and applied for relief. Meanwhile, the 81 percent of black women who had worked in service had nowhere else to go. Under these circumstances, the mere act of hiring a black woman seemed to some to represent a humanitarian gesture. In 1934 an observer of the social-welfare scene noted approvingly, with unintentional irony, that "From Mistress Martha Washington to Mistress Eleanor Roosevelt is not such a long time as time goes. There may be some significance in the fact that the household of the first First Lady was manned by Negro servants and the present First Lady has followed her example."[6]

The history of domestic service in the 1930s provides a fascinating case study of the lengths to which whites would go in exploiting a captive labor force. Those who employed live-in servants in some cases cut their wages, charged extra for room and board, or lengthened on-duty hours. But it was in the area of day work that housewives elevated labor-expanding and money-saving methods to a fine art. General speed-ups were common in private homes throughout the North and South. Among the best bargains were children and teenagers; in Indianola, Mississippi, a sixteen-year-old black girl worked from 6 A.M. to 7 P.M. daily for $1.50 a week. In the same town a maid could be instructed to do her regular chores, plus those of the recently fired cook, for less pay than she had received previously. (A survey of Mississippi's domestics revealed that the average weekly pay was less than $2.00.) Some women received only carfare, clothing, or lunch for a day's work. Northern white women also lowered wages drastically. In 1932 Philadelphia domestics earned $5.00 to $12.00 for a forty-eight- to sixty-seven-hour work week. Three years later they took home the same amount of money for ninety hours' worth of scrubbing, washing, and cooking (an hourly wage of 15 cents).[7]

The deteriorating working conditions of domestic servants reflected the conscious choices of individual whites who took advantage of the abundant labor supply. Social workers recorded conversations with potential employers seeking "bright, lively" domestics (with the very best references) to do all the cooking, cleaning, laundry, and childcare for very little pay, because, in the words of one Pittsburgh woman, "There are so many people out of work that I am sure I can find a girl for $6.00 a week." Indeed, at times it seemed as if there existed a perversely negative relationship between expectations and compensation. An eighty-three-year-old South Carolina black woman, Jessie Sparrow, resisted working on Sundays because, she told an interviewer in 1937, "when dey pays you dat little bit of money, dey wants every bit your time." A southern white man demonstrated his own brand of logic when he "admitted as a matter of course that his cook was underpaid, but explained that this was necessary, since, if he gave her more money, she might soon have so much that she would no longer be willing to work for him."[8]

The field of domestic service was virtually unaffected by national and state welfare policies. In the 1930s Women's Bureau officials tried to compensate for this inaction with a flurry of correspondence, radio and luncheon-meeting speeches, and voluntary guidelines related to the "servant problem." In her talks on the subject, bureau head Mary Anderson tried to appeal to employers' sense of fairness when she suggested that they draw up job descriptions, guard against accidents in the workplace, and establish reasonable hours and wages. But the few housewives privy to Anderson's exhortations were not inclined to heed them, especially when confronted by a seemingly accommodating "slave" on the street corner. Consequently, black domestic workers in several cities, often under the sponsorship of a local Young Women's Christian Association, Urban League branch, or labor union, made heroic attempts to form employees' organizations that would set uniform standards for service. However, they remained a shifting, amorphous group immune to large-scale organizational efforts. For example, founded in 1934 and affiliated with Building Service Union Local 149 (AFL), the New York Domestic Workers Union had only 1,000 (out of a potential of 100,000) members four years later. It advocated two five-hour shifts six days a week and insisted, "last but not least, no window washing." Baltimore's Domestic Workers Union (in the CIO fold) also welcomed members of both races and remained a relatively insignificant force in the regulation of wages and working conditions. Without adequate financial resources, leaders like New York's Dora Jones labored to organize women who "still believe in widespread propaganda that all unions are rackets." As a result, efforts by domestics to control wage rates informally through peer pressure or failure to report for work as promised represented spontaneous job actions more widespread and successful than official "union" activity.[9]

During the depression, a long life of work was the corollary of a long day of work. Black women between the ages of twenty-five and sixty-five worked at consistently high rates; they simply could not rely on children or grandchildren to support them in their old age.

The Federal Writers Project interviews with former slaves recorded in the late 1930s contain hundreds of examples of women in their seventies and eighties still cooking, cleaning, or hoeing for wages on a sporadic basis in order to keep themselves and their dependents alive. An interviewer described the seventy-seven-year-old widow Mandy Leslie of Fairhope, Alabama, as "a pillar of strength and comfort to several white households" because she did their washing and ironing every week. Living alone, her children gone, this elderly woman boiled clothes in an iron pot heated by a fire, and then rubbed them on a washboard and hung them on lines so they could be ironed the following day. Such was the price exacted from black women for the "strength and comfort" they provided whites.[10]

NOTES

1. Lois Scharf, *To Work and to Wed: Female Employment, Feminism, and the Great Depression* (Westport, Conn.: Greenwood Press, 1980), pp. 107–8. . . .

2. Marion Cuthbert, "Problems Facing Negro Young Women," *Opportunity* 14 (Feb. 1936):47–49.

3. U.S. Department of Commerce, Bureau of the Census, *The Labor Force*, Pt. 1, U.S. Summary, p. 90; Mary Elizabeth Pidgeon, "Employed Women Under N.R.A. Codes," United States Department of Labor, Women's Bureau, *Bulletin*, no. 130 (1935); "Women at Work: A Century of Industrial Change," United States Department of Labor, Women's Bureau, *Bulletin*, no. 161 (1939). . . .

4. Alice Kessler-Harris, *Out to Work: A History of Wage-Earning Women in the United States* (New York: Oxford University Press, 1982), pp. 250–72; Ruth Milkman, "Women's Work and Economic Crisis: Some Lessons of the Great Depression," *Review of Radical Political Economics* 8 (Spring 1976):73–97; Winifred D. Wandersee, *Women's Work and Family Values, 1920–1940* (Cambridge, Mass.: Harvard University Press, 1981), pp. 84–102; U.S. Dept. of Commerce, Bureau of the Census, *The Labor Force*, Pt. 1, U.S. Summary, p. 90.

5. Ella Baker and Marvel Cooke, "The Bronx Slave Market," *Crisis* 42 (Nov. 1935):330, 340; Vivian Morris, "Bronx Slave Market," Dec. 6, 1938, Federal Writers Project, Negro Folklore Division (New York), p. 1, Archive of Folk Song, Manuscript Division, Library of Congress, Washington, D.C. . . .

6. Harriet A. Byrne and Cecile Hillyer, "Unattached Women on Relief in Chicago, 1937," United States Department of Labor, Women's Bureau, *Bulletin*, no. 158 (1938); Elmer Anderson Carter, "The Negro Household Employee," *Woman's Press* 28 (July–Aug. 1934):351.

7. John Dollard, *Caste and Class in a Southern Town* (New Haven, Conn.: Yale University Press, 1937), pp. 107–8; Jean Collier Brown, "The Negro

Woman Worker," United States Department of Labor, Women's Bureau, *Bulletin*, no. 165 (1938); pp. 3–4, 7; Charles T. Haley, "To Do Good and Do Well: Middle-Class Blacks and the Depression, Philadelphia, 1929–1941" (Ph.D. diss., State University of New York at Binghamton, 1980), p. 59. . . .

8. Harold A. Lett, "Work: Negro Unemployed in Pittsburgh" *Opportunity* 9 (Mar. 1931):79–81; "Women Workers in Indianapolis," *Crisis* 37 (June 1930):189–91; *The American Slave: A Composite Autobiography*, ed. George Rawick, 41 vols., Series 1, Supp. Series 1 and 2 (Westport, Conn.: Greenwood Press, 1972, 1978, 1979), Series 1, *South Carolina Narratives*, pt. IV, vol. 3, p. 146; Hortense Powdermaker, *After Freedom: A Cultural Study in the Deep South* (New York, 1939), pp. 117–18.

9. "The Domestic Worker of Today," Radio Talk by Miss Mary Anderson, Sept. 21, 1932, Station WJAY, sponsored by Cleveland Parent Teachers Association, Speeches No. 112 (Box 71), Women's Bureau Collection, Department of Labor Archives, Record Group 86, National Archives, Washington, D.C.; Dora Jones quoted in "The Domestic Workers'

Union," in *Black Women in White America: A Documentary History*, ed. Gerda Lerner, (New York, 1972), pp. 231–34. On the New York union, see Evelyn Seeley, "Our Feudal Housewives," *The Nation* 46 (May 28, 1938):613–15; on Baltimore, see article reprinted from *Baltimore Afro-American*, Oct. 1936, in *The Black Worker: A Documentary History from Colonial Times to the Present*, vol. 6, *The Era of Post-War Prosperity and the Great Depression, 1920–1936*, eds. Philip S. Foner and Ronald L. Lewis (Philadelphia: Temple University Press, 1981), pp. 184–85; Roderick N. Ryon, "An Ambiguous Legacy: Baltimore Blacks and the CIO, 1936–1941," *Journal of Negro History* 65 (Winter 1980):29. For evidence of the Urban League's efforts in this area, see "Program of Mass Meeting of General House Work Employees, Sept. 21, 1933 (St. Louis)" in Correspondence—Household (Domestic) File, General Correspondence Prior to 1934 (Box 926), Women's Bureau Collection, RG 86, National Archives.

10. Rawick, ed., *American Slave, Alabama Narratives*, vol. 6, p. 251.

JUDY YUNG

Coping with the Great Depression in San Francisco's Chinatown

---

If race made a difference in the impact of the Great Depression, so did ethnicity and, even more important, class. Judy Yung's essay focuses on the women of San Francisco's Chinatown. She puts their experience in a comparative perspective that allows us to see how Chinese-American women fared in contrast to other ethnic groups. Chinese-American families, she makes clear, suffered many of the same hardships that befell other families. And Chinese-American women exerted the same effort and ingenuity to hold their families together in the face of economic adversity.

Despite the commonalities within a single ethnic community, note the difference class made. In what ways did the New Deal help many of Chinatown's women? In what sense did the opportunities available to them actually increase during the 1930s?

Compared to their men and the rest of the country, Chinese women in San Francisco were relatively unaffected by unemployment. Following the national pattern—in which the unemployment rate for men, who were concentrated in hard-hit production jobs, was

Excerpted from "Long Strides: The Great Depression, 1930s," chap. 4 of *Unbound Feet: A Social History of Chinese Women in San Francisco* by Judy Yung (Berkeley and Los Angeles: The University of California Press, 1995). Copyright © 1995 by Judy Yung. Reprinted by permission of the author. Notes have been renumbered and edited.

almost twice as high as for women, who tended to work in protected clerical and service occupations—Chinese immigrant men who had been chiefly employed as seasonal workers, laundrymen, and cooks were the first to lose their jobs. Immigrant women, however, who worked primarily in the garment industry, continued to find employment. This situation made some immigrant wives the breadwinners, albeit marginal ones, during a time when their husbands were unemployed and relief funds were either unavailable or inadequate to support their families. While a significant number of urban black and white working-class families experienced discord and disintegration during this time, Chinese women were able to keep their families together by providing them with emotional support, stretching family means, and tapping resources in the community. And while the reversal of gender roles proved controversial in many parts of the nation, the social status of Chinese women in San Francisco was elevated as a result of their indispensable contributions. . . .

The stories of Law Shee Low and Wong Shee Chan (my maternal grandaunt) illustrate how the depression affected Chinese immigrant women with large families, as well as the strategies some women employed to cope with the hard economic times. Law recalled, "Those were very poor and tough years for us. When my uncle who became penniless died and we were all asked to help with the funeral expenses, we could only afford to give a few dimes. We were so poor, we wanted to die." Her husband, who had been working twelve hours a day at a Chinatown restaurant for $60 a month, lost his job. For a brief period, he lived and worked in the city of Vallejo. "Just made $40 at a restaurant. He gave me $20 and kept $20 for himself. I sewed and made another $30 or $40. So we struggled on." When he was laid off again, she became the chief wage earner. There was still sewing to keep them going, and her husband helped her sew at home and did the shopping. But when even sewing became scarce for a spell, they had to dip into their small savings and seek outside help. "Joe Shoong [the owner of a large garment factory and Law's clansman] was giving out rice, so my husband went and carried back a fifty-pound sack. Food was cheap then. A dime or two would buy you some *sung* [vegetable or meat dishes to go with the rice]."[1]

With an unemployed man and four dependents in the house, the family qualified for free milk and food rations from the federal government. And when FERA established a much-needed nursery school in Chinatown, two of their children were among the first to enroll.

Wong Shee Chan recalled similar hard times. Betrothed when ten years old and married at seventeen to my great-grandfather Chin Lung's eldest son, Chin Wing, she was admitted to the United States in 1920 as a U.S. citizen's wife. They initially farmed land that Great-Grandfather had purchased in Oregon but, soon after, returned to San Francisco and worked at Chin Lung's trunk factory on Stockton Street. In 1932, Great-Grandfather decided to retire to China to avoid the depression, leaving what business assets he had left to his sons. Chin Wing tried to maintain the trunk factory, but to no avail. The family had to pawn Grandaunt's jewelry in order to make ends meet. "Those were the worst years for us," recalled Grandaunt, who by then had six children to support. "Life was very hard. I just went from day to day." They considered themselves lucky when they could borrow a dime or a quarter. "A quarter was enough for dinner," she said. "With that I bought two pieces of fish to steam, three bunches of vegetables (two to stir-fry and the third to put in the soup), and some pork for the soup."[2] For a brief period, while her husband was unemployed, the family qualified for federal aid; but after he went to work as a seaman, Grandaunt was left alone to care for the children. She had to find work to help support the family. Encouraged by friends, she went to beauty school to learn how to be a hairdresser. At that time, there were sixteen beauty parlors in Chinatown—the only businesses in the community to be run by Chinese women.[3] After she passed the licensing examination, which she was able to take in the Chinese language, Grandaunt opened a beauty parlor and bathhouse in Chinatown, working from 7 A.M. to 11 P.M. seven days a week. She kept the children with her at the shop and had the older ones help her with the work. Thus she was able to keep the family together and make it through the depression.

Women across the country likewise found ways to "make do." When their husbands and sons became unemployed, many white women entered the labor market for the first time, finding work in female-dominated occupations—clerical work, trade, and services. In the decade between 1930 and 1940, the number of married women in the labor force increased nearly 50 percent despite mounting public pressure that they not compete with men for jobs. Often, in fact, it was not men who were edged out of jobs by white women, but black women—particularly domestic workers—who were already at the bottom of the labor ladder. Concentrated in the marginal occupations of sharecropping, household service, and unskilled factory work, black women suffered the highest unemployment rate among all groups of women. Most other working-class women were able to keep a tenuous hold on their jobs in the industrial and service sectors even as their husbands became unemployed. Women's marginal wages thus often kept whole families alive. Women also learned to cut back on family expenditures, substituting store-bought items with homemade products. They planted gardens, canned fruits and vegetables, remade old clothing, baked bread, raised livestock, rented out sleeping space, and did odd jobs. Pooling resources with relatives and neighbors provided mutual assistance in terms of shared household duties and child care. As a last resort, some women turned to prostitution. And among those who qualified, many went on relief.[4] . . . No doubt, Chinese women experienced their share of emotional stress during the depression, but because of cultural taboos against divorce they found other ways to cope [with the marital discord and family conflict that led to a rising divorce rate nationally]. My grandaunt Wong Shee Chan recalled a number of occasions when her unemployed husband took his frustrations out on her. "I remember buying two sand dabs to steam for dinner," she said. "Because he didn't like the fish, he flipped the plate over and ruined the dinner for the entire family. Even the children could not eat it then. See what a mean heart he had?"[5] Having promised her father that she would never disgrace the Wong family's name by disobeying or divorcing her husband, she gritted her teeth and carried on. But when the situation at home became unbearable, Grandaunt would go to the Presbyterian Mission Home for help. "She went there a couple of times, and each time it got ironed out and she came home," recalled her

eldest daughter, Penny. . . . This pragmatic approach to life, kindled by personal initiative and a strong sense of obligatory self-sacrifice in the interest of the family, helped many Chinese immigrant women through the hardships that they faced. . . .

The adverse impact of the depression was also blunted by the benefit that Chinese immigrant women and their families drew from federal legislation and programs. Many of the New Deal programs discriminated against women and racial minorities in terms of direct relief, jobs, and wages. One-fourth of the NRA codes, for example, established lower wage rates for women, ranging from 14 to 30 percent below men's rates. Relief jobs went overwhelmingly to male breadwinners, and significant numbers of female workers in the areas of domestic service, farming, and cannery work were not covered by the Fair Labor Standards Act or Social Security Act. Black, Mexican, and Asian women who were concentrated in these job sectors were thus denied equal protection from labor exploitation and access to insurance benefits. Moreover, under federal guidelines, Mexican and Asian aliens could not qualify for WPA jobs and were in constant fear of deportation.[7] Nevertheless, considering their prior situation, Chinese women had more to gain than lose by the New Deal. For the first time, they were entitled to public assistance. At least 350 families were spared starvation and provided with clothing, housing, and medical care to tide them over the depression. In addition, more than fifty single mothers qualified for either Widow Pension Aid or Aid to Dependent Children.[8] The garment industry—which employed most of the Chinese immigrant women—was covered by the NRA. At the urging of the International Ladies' Garment Workers' Union (ILGWU), sweeps through Chinatown were periodically made to ensure the enforcement of the new minimum-wage levels, work hours, banned child labor law, and safety standards.[9] NRA codes, however, were insufficient to change sweatshop conditions in Chinatown, as employers circumvented or nullified the imposed labor standards through speed-ups and tampered records. Only when workers took matters into their own hands, as in the case of the 1938 National Dollar Stores strike, were employers forced to comply with federal labor laws.

The New Deal did have a positive impact on the living environment of Chinese families. A 1935 study of Chinatown's social needs . . . indicated that housing was woefully substandard, playground space and hours of operation inadequate, and health and day child care sorely lacking.[10] Federal programs, staffed by Chinese American social workers in cooperation with churches and community organizations, were instituted to deal with these specific problems. Families were moved out of tenement houses to apartments and flats close by. Playground hours were extended and street lighting improved. Immigrant mothers learned about American standards of sanitation and nutrition, particularly the importance of milk in their diet, and had access to birth control and health care at the newly established public clinic in the community. They were also entitled to attend English and job-training classes and . . . enroll their children in nursery school. As a result, not only did some immigrant women receive direct relief, but their overall quality of life was somewhat improved by the New Deal. . . .

Jane Kwong Lee, one of the few Chinese women who fulfilled this role of the modern woman in the 1930s, [was an example]. After becoming the mother of two and upon graduation from Mills College, she decided to go back to work, even though her husband still had his meat market in Oakland. "To stay home and take care of my children was, of course, my primary concern," she wrote in her autobiography, "but in the midst of the depression period, it was necessary for me to seek employment."[11] Unable to find work in white establishments because of racism, Jane finally secured a part-time job at the Chinese YWCA, at a time when bilingual community workers were sorely needed. It was her responsibility to make home visits and to provide assistance to immigrant women regarding immigration, health and birth control, housing, domestic problems, and applications for government relief. Until she was offered a full-time job as coordinator two years later, she also taught at a Chinese school in the evenings. How did she manage it all?

In these two years of my life, I actually divided my attention in three different directions—my family, the YWCA, and the Chinese Language School. Aside from providing the necessary care for my children, I did not have any other worries for my family as they were healthy; my husband left for work in the East Bay every morning without asking me to prepare breakfast and came home after work to look after the children. I considered myself lucky to have his cooperation in raising two normal children and maintaining a normal family life.

With her husband's support and cooperation, Jane was able to raise a family and devote herself to her work at the YWCA, which she called "my JOB, in capital letters."[12] Because of her leadership skills and hard work, the YWCA soon broadened its services, grew in membership, moved into a new building, and garnered the respect and support of the community. . . .

Jane's dedication and effectiveness as a community leader did not go unnoticed. Whereas the community had once disapproved of women in the public arena, she found that her role as a female activist was respected by the Chinatown establishment. Once her bilingual speaking abilities and organizational skills became known, she was courted by Chinatown churches and invited to speak before the Chinese Six Companies and other Chinatown organizations. . . . Even as she was proving useful to the community, she was paving the way for other bilingual social workers, who were sought after by agencies with federal funding to expand their services. Already a prominent figure in the community, Jane was asked to serve on the civil service examination board that helped hire the first Chinese-speaking social workers for the city.

NOTES

1. Law Shee Low, an interview with the author, October 30, 1989.
2. Wong Shee Chan, an interview with the author, March 5, 1982.
3. California State Emergency Relief Administration, "Survey of Social Work Needs of the Chinese Population of San Francisco, California," 1935, hereafter cited as CSERA 1935 Survey, p. 12; and Pardee Lowe, "The Good Life in Chinatown: Further Adventures of a Chinese Husband and His American Wife Among His Own People," *Asia* 37 (February 1937):128.
4. See Jeane Westin, *Making Do: How Women Survived in the Thirties* (River Grove, Ill.: Follett Press, 1976); Ruth Milkman, "Women's Work and the Economic Crisis: Some Lessons from the Great Depression," in *A Heritage of Her Own: Toward a New Social History of American Women*, ed. Nancy F. Cott and Elizabeth Pleck (New York: Simon and Schuster, 1979), pp. 520–28; Jacqueline Jones, *Labor of Love, Labor of Sorrow: Black Women, Work, and the Family*

from Slavery to the Present (New York: Basic Books, 1985), pp. 221–30; and Rosalinda M. Gonzalez, "Chicanas and Mexican Immigrant Families, 1920–1940: Women's Subordination and Family Exploitation," in *Decades of Discontent: The Women's Movement, 1920–1940,* ed. Lois Scharf and Joan M. Jensen (Westport, Conn.: Greenwood Press, 1983), p. 70.

5. Wong Shee Chan, interview.

6. Penny Chan Huey, an interview with the author, November 21, 1988.

7. On how the New Deal discriminated against women and racial minorities, see Lois Scharf, *To Work and to Wed: Female Employment, Feminism, and the Great Depression* (Westport, Conn.: Greenwood Press, 1980), chap. 6; Alice Kessler-Harris, *Out to Work: A History of Wage-Earning Women in the United*

States (New York: Oxford University Press, 1982), pp. 262–71; Jones, *Labor of Love,* chap. 6; Julia K. Blackwelder, *Women of the Depression: Caste and Culture in San Antonio* (College Station, Tex.: Texas A & M University Press, 1984), chap. 7.

8. Ethel Lum, "Chinese During the Depression," *Chinese Digest,* Nov. 22, 1935; and CSERA 1935 Survey, pp. 40–41.

9. *CSYP [Chung Sai Yat Po],* July 11, 1933; July 11, 1934; March 13, 1935; March 6, 1939; *Chinese Times,* February 16, 17, 1936; and *San Francisco News,* April 26, 1936, p. 1.

10. See CSERA 1935 Survey.

11. J. Lee, "A Chinese American," pt. 11, p. 81.

12. Ibid., p. 91.

ALICE KESSLER-HARRIS
Providers: Gender Ideology in the 1930s

Whatever their ethnic or racial background, women to whom the depression had dealt a severe blow poured out their troubles in letters to the Roosevelts. This outpouring owed much to the fireside chats that brought the President's voice into every home that had a radio, thereby establishing a new sense of connection between the Chief Executive and the American citizenry. Eleanor Roosevelt's well-known sympathy for ordinary people, especially the needy, was another factor. Women in particular felt comfortable writing to her, as well as to Secretary of Labor Frances Perkins, who, like the First Lady, had enjoyed a long career as a social reformer.

Historian Alice Kessler-Harris has used letters to the Roosevelts and to various members of the administration to explore what both gender and jobs meant in the lives of working people. She finds that letter writers had a clear sense of justice that was often at odds with the realities of the free market. They also assumed that the administration and Congress had a responsibility to intervene to repair injustice—an assumption that reveals the sea-change in attitudes toward government that occurred in the 1930s. Perhaps most important, given the attention that many have attached to the concept of separate spheres, is the extent to which these letter writers resisted thinking in terms of a public/private dichotomy: indeed, they refused to separate the two.

What do Kessler-Harris's findings suggest about attitudes toward working women, more particularly married women? How did women themselves feel about this issue? How does her evidence complicate answers to these questions? What can we conclude about gender ideology in the 1930s and the utility of the concept of separate spheres on the basis of this essay?

Dorothea Lange was working for the Farm Security Administration in the mid-1930s. Along with her colleagues Russell Lee and Roy Stryker, she documented the problems of farm tenancy in images that would become classic. This photograph was taken at a pea-picker's camp in Nipomo, California. Later Lange recalled, "I saw and approached the hungry and desperate mother, as if drawn by a magnet. I do not remember how I explained my presence or my camera to her, but I do remember she asked me no questions. I made five exposures, working closer and closer. . . . I did not ask her name or her history. She told me her age, that she was thirty-two. She said that they had been living on frozen vegetables from the surrounding fields, and birds that the children killed. She had just sold the tires from their car to buy food. There she sat in that lean-to tent with her children huddled around her, and seemed to know that my picture might help her, and so she helped me. There was a sort of equality about it." (Quoted in Milton Meltzer, Dorothea Lange: A Photographer's Life [New York: Farrar Straus Giroux, 1978]. Photograph courtesy of the Library of Congress.)

On May 10, 1933, Earl Leiby of Akron, Ohio, wrote to Franklin Delano Roosevelt, president of the United States:

> You are probably aware of the fact that homes are being wrecked daily due to the fact that married women are permitted to work in factories and offices in this land of ours. You and we all know that the place for a wife and mother is at home, her palace. The excuse is often brought up that the husband cannot find employment. It is the writers' belief that if the women were expelled from places of business, . . . these very men would find employment. These same women's husbands would naturally be paid a higher salary, inasmuch as male employees demand a higher salary than females.[1]

Like other people who chose the early months of a new administration to pass on suggestions for relief to the president, Mr. Leiby was convinced that the solution to three long years of economic depression lay in a return to old values. For him, as for others, a restoration of women and men to their appropriate spheres would return peace and prosperity to the land. But if Leiby's belief in a particular form of domesticity was widespread, it was not universal.

Consider the following letter from Mrs. Blanche Crumbly, a weaver of McDonough, Georgia, who wrote to FDR on October 26, 1933. The letter, written in pencil on lined foolscap paper, protested the failure of her textile mill employers to pay her an expected $12 a week. "I am sending you my checks to show you what I made," she wrote.

> I want to let you see that they didn't pay me enough. I worked eight hours a day and you will see they have me marked up forty hours a week and didn't pay twelve dollars and by law they were supposed to pay twelve dollars whether you operated one machine or not but I worked in the weave shop and run five looms so I want you to see that I get my money that is due me for I am just a poor woman and was working trying to make some money but they didn't pay enough to keep me working so I want you to write right back to me and let me know what you can do.[2]

Nothing in this letter speaks to the values of domesticity. If the subtext has the ring of humility, the message is insistent and demanding. Mrs. Crumbly wants action, not on the basis of her place in the household, but as a matter of workplace justice. She had worked in the weave shop running five looms; she had earned her pay; she was a poor woman who needed the money.

These letters seem to reflect opposing positions on the issue of domesticity: the first assumes its inevitability and explicitly validates it; the second fails even to acknowledge its existence, much less its role in shaping the labor force. From the perspective of the first letter writer, the world appears to be structured around the household whose effective regulation would have a salutary effect on the economy. In that of the second, work and wages are central—their just resolution by state agencies is demanded independently of the writer's household role. Taken together, these letters raise questions about the validity of the notion of separate spheres—a notion that has dominated American women's history for the past two decades. . . . [and about whether] gender adequately reflects the ways that ordinary women and men self-identify in a given historical period or at a given phase of their lives. . . . The depression of the 1930s provides an ideal place to examine these questions because its atypicality opens working people's world views to public examination.

The previous decade had witnessed a dramatic rise in the proportion of married workers among wage-earning women, heightening public concern about the breakdown of the traditional family among some sectors while encouraging others to claim that female wage work helped hold families together.[3] Increased concern preceded and was sharply exacerbated by a fearsome and rising tide of unemployment that engulfed the country beginning in the winter of 1929. In the period between the election of FDR in November 1932 and his inauguration four months later, nearly a quarter of the labor force was unemployed, and emergency conditions prevailed everywhere. The result was an unprecedented discussion of who was and was not entitled to work.

One of the nation's first and most immediate responses was to exclude the spouses of wage earners from the labor force. Pressure was brought on employers to fire married women; states passed laws discriminating against married women teachers; and the federal government responded by passing section 232 of the National Economy Act, which allowed only one partner in a marriage to draw a federal salary.[4] But though public pressure continued, neither the numbers nor the proportion of married women working declined in response. We now understand this to have been a function of the desperate straits in which families found themselves when they were driven from the land, or when the traditional bread winner, generally male, lost his job or was reduced to a few hours a week of work. As family need pushed women into the labor market, they were simultaneously pulled by a segregated labor market whose aggregate demand for female workers recovered more quickly than for males. The result was that women who needed to support families in whole or part either continued to work or went out to work for the first time.[5] Self-evident need, however, seemed invisible to many.

So great was sentiment against married women holding jobs that it provoked hundreds of letters to President Roosevelt, Eleanor Roosevelt, the National Recovery Administration code authorities, Secretary of Labor Frances Perkins, and the Women's Bureau of the Department of Labor. Beginning in 1932 and reaching a crescendo in the spring of 1933, writers suggested that married women with employed husbands had no right to work and ought to be forcibly ejected from jobs. The letters came from single and married women, from widows, and from men of all kinds. Many were nearly illiterate. Most were handwritten, sometimes in pencil. Some were written on the letterheads of apparently prosperous businesses, others on foolscap. They complained of injustices done, asked for help, and offered solutions to the depression crisis.

My reading of these letters is not scientific in any sense. It could not be, for the letters themselves represent no known sample of the population, and the context that motivated them is often obscure. . . . Nonetheless, they offer a spectacular opportunity to explore the meanings of work as they appear in a spontaneous outburst. The letters tell us about much more than gendered responses under emergency conditions. They speak to a sense of social order that is much more consistent than the contradictions implied by a superficial reading. Read carefully and together, they illuminate a moral code that transcends gendered identification and simultaneously affirms it.

These letters appear at first to reflect the significance of the concept of separate spheres in the daily lives of their authors, though they offer no immediately apparent distinctions between those written by men and women. Many of both sexes insist, like Earl Leiby, on "a woman's place," suggesting that the historian's interpretation and the common wisdom were not far apart. "Have all women stop working," wrote an East St. Louis, Illinois, resident. "Put them back in their homes where they belong and then there would not be enough men to fill the jobs. Then we would have better homes, more children, a more contented people, and a better place to live in every way."[6] . . . Such perceptions are not gender specific. Miss B. Wohlmaker of Brooklyn wrote to Franklin Delano Roosevelt, "I have heard so much about prosperity. I don't think it will ever return as long as married women are taking the Bread and Butter out of the men who have familys to support."[7]

The common wisdom, then, is that women have a primary domestic role while men are responsible for earning their family's living. . . . But a closer examination reveals that the domestic role is far from a separate sphere. Concerns over both work and family life converged in a widely shared conception of justice that neither contradicted a felt perception of role difference nor entirely depended on it. Rather, images of justice seem to have been shaped by the impact of the material world. The letters reveal an integration of wage work and family life that belies the dualistic paradigms of work and domesticity typically utilized by historians. They present instead a perception of social reality far more unified than that embodied within a notion of separate spheres.

The first thing revealed by these letters is the sharp distinction made by those who believed work to be an individual right and the vast majority who did not. Women who pleaded for their jobs or angrily declared their rights to have been violated tended to claim rights as citizens. Thus, twenty-eight married women dismissed by New York State after thirteen or more years in civil service jobs protested the injustice "of depriving us as individuals of our right to security under the Civil Service Law."[8] . . . The female assistant postmaster of Deerfield, Michigan, wrote to Frances Perkins: "I can't see why if we women are American Citizens why we haven't just as much right to work as anybody. I would have written to the Post Master General but woman to woman I thought you would understand better."[9]

A predepression world of job opportunity, where ambition might be rewarded, could afford to make room for personal goals for both men and women. . . . In the depression world, the concept that a job was a right of citizenship appeared to be selfish. It was not characteristic of either the working or the nonworking poor before or after the depression. In contrast to the official stance of the Department of Labor under Frances Perkins and of the Women's Bureau, most of those who put pen and pencil to paper did so to argue that work was the prerogative of those who needed to support themselves and their families. In the code of honor of working people, jobs belonged to providers.[10] Though this typically meant married men, the scales of justice encompassed widows, single women, and married women with unemployed or disabled husbands as well. And while ambivalence reigned about the rights of single men, males with other means of support were clearly excluded. As one writer explained the priorities, "The idea is to first place to work all men who have dependents, then girls who have dependents. The remaining jobs to be given to those not having dependents."[11]

The idea appeared to be self-evident because it did not begin with the depression. Such comments affirm ideas of justice among the working poor that certainly antedate economic crisis. Those who continued to work, like Blanche Crumbly, clearly thought of themselves as providers. Their work was part of a long tradition in which wages were seen as part of their contribution to family well-being. As the Women's Bureau of the Department of Labor put it in 1924, married women worked "for one purpose and generally speaking, for one purpose only—to provide necessities for their families or to raise their standard of living."[12] Among communities of textile workers in the South and among some immigrant women in the North, wage work for wives had long been part of a pattern of shared family support. Thus, one New Hampshire textile worker told an interviewer that she, not her husband, had been the first to return to work after a 1922 strike. She offered two reasons. First, "fall was coming and we didn't have any money. We didn't know how we were going to live." Second, "I was afraid he would be hurt by the pickets."[13] During the depression women like this resisted removal from the

work force, not out of ideological commitment, but because they clearly did not feel themselves to be the selfish, neglectful women described in many of the letters.

Such tacit acknowledgment of shared responsibility enables us to make sense of the general hostility that surrounded married women's work while it simultaneously explains how a Blanche Crumbly functioned outside the orbit of apparently traditional roles. The role of provider served to legitimate the roles of women, married and single, who earned wages; but it did not prevent them from being turned into targets by those men and women who perceived married women as unfair competitors. Single women, widowed and divorced mothers, and the wives of unemployed workers constituted a large proportion of the cacophonous complainants.

Indeed, other women were often the most virulent advocates of removing married women from jobs. Identifying not with their sex but with their work/family positions, they complained on behalf of others like them. "How can the youth of our land eliminate married women from working and taking from us every means of support, every hope, every chance for morality and high standards?" asked a young, single woman from Bellingham, Washington.[14] "If there were not so many married women working who have husbands working and no family, we single women might stand a better show in getting a job," wrote another.[15] A mother from Redonda [sic] Beach, California, asserted, "It keeps our Boys and Girls from getting work and they are the ones that need it."[16] . . . Widow women did not fail to assert their provider roles in justification of a demand for a job. One textile worker, fired because she was unable to make the minimum rate of production, pleaded for her job back: "I am a widow with one child to support with no job no fuel and no provision and House Rent to pay."[17]

If women self-identified not only as women but as young people, family supporters, parents, and dependents, they were vulnerable to any who threatened their family lives, whether such people were male or female. Men and women translated their sense of grievance to all who seemed to undermine the provider role, including most especially farmers, country people, anyone who did not live in their town, foreigners, and nameless racketeers. The free-flowing relationships of these categories appears in the following letter to Frances Perkins. After first insisting that married women ought to "be compelled by law to give up their positions to single girls and married men," the writer went on to complain about foreigners along with married women holding "most of our city and country positions and consuming 90% of the welfare money."[18] In other words, males who had other means of support faced the same criticism as married women. This was especially true in communities (like the textile mills of the Piedmont) where family wage work was the norm rather than the exception. . . . Mrs. Lee A. Crayton, a twelve-year veteran of the Cannon mills, wrote: "Our greatest obstacle though, at the present time is the country people. They come to the Textile mills in the winter and work for less money than the people in the city can afford to work for as the country man owns his home, raises practically all of his groceries. He can afford to work for less money than the people in the city who has to depend on the textile mills for their living."[19]

At issue here is a question broader than gender but in which gender participates and to some extent becomes the scapegoat. A careful reading of these letters suggests that while the perspective of domesticity was certainly an available angle of vision, it was not the only perspective that guided the attack on married women workers. Where, then, is the outrage rooted? . . . For the men and women who complained that jobs were going to the undeserving, conceptions of dignity did not lie in equal opportunity, or in equality, but rather in the intertwined reality of their own complex images of themselves and in their expectations of family life.

At one level what was at issue was whether the free market (which gave employers the prerogative of hiring most cheaply) would prevail over indigenous standards of justice. This is apparent in the various levels of exasperation with which writers asked why the government couldn't take control of the situation. "Why not issue an order that all married women whose husbands are employed be dropped from payrolls? Why not issue an order that all men drawing retired pay be dropped from payrolls?" read one letter to Hugh Johnson [the head of the National Recovery Administration] in its entirety.[20] Another letter writer asked of the

president, "Why can't you forbid these great corporations and all others with few exceptions employing women to do men's work."[21] . . .

Whether leveled at government, at employers, or at workers, these queries reflected impatience with the failure of those in power to understand their perspective. Freedom of choice and free enterprise were clearly not the major concerns of most letter-writers. A Liberty, Missouri, man touched the core when he asked whether the employers of working women were living up to the NRA: "I can see no justice in their practices and many of the good citizens of this town are of the same opinion."[22] . . . "Did it ever occur to you," asked a Swansea, Massachusetts, resident, "the number of husbands and wives who are employed and receiving a revenue . . . my idea is that just one in a family namely either man or wife should be employed."[23] . . .

In expressing their skepticism about the capacity of the market to sustain what seemed to be elementary notions of justice, writers conflated public and private spheres. Indeed, one of the most striking things about these letters is their consistent inability or unwillingness to separate the two. The family may have been the private domain of individuals, but male and female workers interpreted its survival and protection as a public duty. In a situation such as the depression, the most intimate details of one's life became a public issue; the idea of a distinct domestic sphere scarcely existed. Most letter writers translated work into wages—wages that held the capacity to sustain or undermine the moral precepts thought to reside in the family. Thus, the income produced by work constituted the glue that melded the family, that joined public and private together. Like some modern epoxies, it had to be mixed just right.

While few doubted that only an adequate income could preserve family values, most correspondents feared that an income that was either too low or too high would yield moral disaster for the individual, the family, and the community as a whole. They spoke of "necessity" wages as opposed to "luxury" wages. Depriving families of the first—the result of allowing the wrong people to hold jobs—would yield moral degeneration. It encouraged the "less strong in character" to spend their time "loafing and resorting to crime for a living."[24] . . . It could result in . . . "forcing many young girls on the streets because they have to get along the best they can."[25]

But the relatively high income—the luxury wage—of the dual income family was perceived as no less threatening to an individual's character and equally responsible for private and public moral degeneration. "All over the country," wrote a self-described "unemployed young woman," "women marry and immediately return to their jobs, instead of endeavoring to live within their husband's income and living a domesticated life, building a home, etc."[26] Even worse, "The women consistently dodge motherhood and go home after their work is done with a paper carton in one hand and a can opener in the other."[27] ...

Differing conceptions of how men and women were thought to spend their incomes exacerbated public concern about the nation's future. A male who worked would, in the popular parlance, "spend his income to the support of his family while the woman spends for permanent waves, lip sticks. But those things do not pay the grocer and all the other bills that father is expected to pay walking up and down the street looking and praying for something to do. The woman comes home says she works for her money and she will do as she pleases with it which is a fact."[28] If a boy gets a job, "he marries, buys a home, a car, a radio, etc. But a girl— its cosmetics and finery, the loss often of modesty and refinement, drifting farther and farther from matrimony, in most cases."[29]

Distinctions about what the wage was likely to buy constituted the easiest way of determining what was fair. A wage ought not to be frittered away on luxuries while its absence prevented others from sustaining the provider role. As a Washington, D.C. lawyer put it, "I do not believe these women are making as good use of the money they receive as would be made of it if it was paid to the husbands of other women who are desperately in need of employment and whose wives are staying at home looking after the home and children."[30] But the sentiment was not male alone. A single woman wrote that she knew of "any number of married women who work just in order that they might have fine furniture, clothes and a nice automobile, while we single women must go without the necessities of life."[31] ...

Encoded in these comments is the sense that the individual rights to which the ideology of a free labor market theoretically entitled all workers were not, in practice, available to some. But nobody took the ideology to task. Neither the realities of the segregated labor market, nor the economic desperation that drove most of those who sought jobs, protected wage-earning married women. They were blamed for acting unfairly. They were taking jobs from men and from single women; they were destroying the moral fiber of men and reducing men's respect for women. They were responsible for the delinquency of children and for the disintegration of the family. The continuing depression was laid at their feet—the future of the nation placed in their hands. These messages, as the letters convey, were deeply held and virulently argued. They mitigated against a continuing demand for female equality and help to explain why the assertion of individual rights, which brought the nation to such a pass, appears to be unfair.

Public opinion contrasted sharply with the responses of government representatives that, even when they acknowledged the legitimacy of the search for justice, repeatedly affirmed the role of the free market. Typically, A.R. Forbush, chief of the Correspondence Division of the NRA, replied to complainants, "It is not a function of the National Recovery Administration to tell an employer whom he may or may not employ."[32] ... Many of the married women who earned wages would not have disagreed with these sentiments. Understanding their self-image as providers should give us some insight into workplace behavior, into the sense of justice on which women will act. ... Mrs. Blanche Crumbly protested the insufficient $12 a week, but she quit because "they didn't pay enough to keep me working." A year or two later, under other circumstances, she might have joined the organizing drive of the Congress of Industrial Organizations.

While the felt injustice of married women working cannot be read as other than hostility, it takes on a different cast when seen from the perspective of work, rather than that of separate spheres. In the light of domesticity, it is a conservative plea for a return to traditional roles. In the light of workplace concerns, it becomes a demand for justice: for cooperation and sharing, and, arguably, for a different kind of market system. Articulated by both men and women, the injustice of wage work for those with alternate sources of incomes or for those without dependents was an idea that might have been conceived in, and sustained by, domesticity, but it took on a larger resonance in the prevailing climate of industrial distress. In practice, it was not gender neutral, and yet it reflects a conception of work-related roles that transcends a simple division into separate spheres.

What appears at first reading to be a defense of separate spheres and an affirmation of female domesticity contains a more complex statement about social reality. The letters articulate a vision of social order in which the provider role is related to both family and individual life cycle and in which men and women provide in different ways. They suggest a perception of jobs as a public resource to be disposed of fairly; and though there are clearly job hierarchies that are gender specific, the letters assume a pool of work that is available to be divided among the deserving. The definition of *deserving* rested primarily on the need to support oneself and others and only secondarily, in so far as the need was perceived as gender dependent, on sex. The letters reveal an inability or unwillingness to separate public and private values and an acknowledgment that dignity for both men and women lay in the preservation of both work possibilities and household order.

In challenging the moral authority of employers to hire who and where they please, they explicitly confront the neoclassical rationale that is said to organize the labor market and that demanded that the cheapest appropriate labor be sought and hired. Public opinion, gauged by this correspondence, insisted that this was wrong: letter writers repeatedly affirmed that the only appropriate criterion for hiring and firing was family need. While built-in assumptions about which sex most often had greater needs confirmed existing gender lines, gender difference did not add up to separate spheres. Rather, it seems to have constituted a coherent set of understandings from which to question the privileges of industrial power.... It ... encourages us to ask different kinds of questions. Among whom and under what conditions do gendered perceptions take the first place? What functions did gendered perceptions serve in particular times and places? Where did they impart a conservative outlook? Where did they lead to change?

But most important of all, in moving us from the dichotomous framework of separate spheres, a complex approach to gender as a part of everyone's world view enables us to interpret the past without the distortion of a single "difference" that becomes an overwhelming explanatory variable when the behavior of men and women is at issue. Gendered identity remains a critically important source of consciousness and behavior. As part of a historically contingent nexus that includes race, class, and ethnicity, it shapes the behavior of historical actors and frames the interpretations of historians. And, depending on its form, variety, and congruence in a particular historical setting, it can promote solidarity, consensus, disinterest, or conflict. But rarely in the same ways.

NOTES

1. Earl A. Leiby to FDR, May 10, 1933, National Archives, Record Group 174: General Records of the Department of Labor, Chief Clerk's Files, Entry 167/838, Box 183. (Hereinafter referred to as NA RG 174. All quotations are cited as in the original. Changes in the letters have been made only for the purposes of clarity.)

2. Blanche Crumbly to FDR, October 26, 1933, National Archives, Record Group 9: Records of the National Recovery Administration. (Hereinafter referred to as NA RG 9.) Entry 398: Records relating to employee complaints in the textile industry, Box 5, File: Bibb Manufacturing Co., Macon, Ga. (Hereinafter referred to as NA RG 9, Entry 398.)

3. Warren Susman, "The Culture of the Thirties," in *Culture and Commitment: The Transformation of American Society in the Twentieth Century* (New York: Pantheon, 1984); U.S. Department of Labor, Women's Bureau, *Women Workers and Family Support*, Bulletin no. 49 (Washington, D.C.: Government Printing Office, 1925).

4. Lois Scharf, *To Work and to Wed: Female Employment, Feminism, and the Great Depression* (Westport, Conn.: Greenwood Press, 1980); Susan Ware, *Holding Their Own: American Women in the 1930s* (Boston: Twayne, 1982).

5. The Women's Bureau estimated that 1,603 federal employees lost their jobs between June 30, 1932, and December 31, 1934. U.S. Department of Labor, Women's Bureau, "Gainful Employment of Married Women" (mimeographed pamphlet, 1936), Martin Catherwood Library, Cornell University, American Association for Labor Legislation Collection, Box: Women.

6. E. E. Jett to FDR, June 23, 1933, NA RG 174, Entry 167/838, Box 183. Jett described his letter as "the bravest thing I have ever tried" and concluded it with, "Will you reply to this, PLEASE."

7. June 15, 1933, NA RG 174, Entry 167/838, Box 183.

8. Women's Bureau, "Gainful Employment of Married Women," 17.

9. Mrs. C. C. Beach to Frances Perkins, April 27, 1933, NA RG 174, Entry 167/838, Box 183.

10. The empirical work of Judith Buber Agassi, which explores worker attitudes in the 1970s, indicates that the stance still prevails: *Comparing the Work Attitudes of Women and Men* (Lexington, Mass.: D. C. Heath, 1982), especially chap. 5 and 10.

11. William Einger of Cincinnati, Ohio, to FDR, April 9, 1933, NA RG 174, Entry 167/838, Box 183.

12. Mary Winslow, *Married Women in Industry*, Women's Bureau Bulletin no. 38 (Washington, D.C.: Government Printing Office, 1924), 6.

13. Tamara Hareven, *Family Time and Industrial Time: The Relationship between Family and Work in a New England Community* (Cambridge, England: Cambridge University Press, 1982), 78; Jacquelyn Dowd Hall et al., *Like a Family: The Making of a Southern Cotton Mill World* (Chapel Hill: University of North Carolina Press, 1987), chap. 2.

14. Miss Thelma Pontney to FDR, June 30, 1933, NA RG 174, Entry 167/838, Box 183.

15. Miss Clara Rossberg of St. Paul, Minn., to FDR, May 18, 1933, NA RG 174, Entry 107/838, Box 183.

16. Mrs. C. M. Rogers to FDR, April 4, 1933, in ibid.

17. Mrs. Georgia Ervin of Columbus, Ga., to FDR, August 8, 1933, NA RG 9, Entry 398, Box 5, File: Bibb Manufacturing Co.

18. Jno Brogan of Pittsburgh, Pa., to Frances Perkins, July 12, 1933. And see M. B. Henley to the president, May 18, 1933. . . . NA RG 174, Entry 167/838, Box 183.

19. Mrs. Lee A. Crayton to NRA, February 16, 1934. See also S. J. Gwynn to Hugh Johnson, June 7, 1934. Both in NA RG 9, Entry 398, Box 8, File: Cannon Mills, Plant No. 6, Concord, N.C.

20. R. A. Gailey of Monitor, Wash., to Gen. Hugh Johnson, August 9, 1933, NA RG 9, Entry 23, PI 44, Box 491.

21. Sam Raspy of Anderson, Ind., to FDR, May 21, 1933, NA RG 174, Entry 167/838, Box 183.

22. Frank Dale to Hugh Johnson, September 21, 1933, NA RG 9, Entry 23, Box 491.

23. Joseph Gildard to FDR, January 31, 1935, NA RG 9, Entry 23, Box 491.

24. Frances S. Key-Smith of Washington, D.C., to Vice-President Charles Curtis, November 12, 1931, NA RG 174, Entry 167/838, Box 183. He is a lawyer.

25. Henley to FDR, May 18, 1933. . . .

26. Murray to FDR, July 18, 1933.

27. Mrs. Beatrice Hobart Steely of Beverly Hills, Calif., to FDR, May 5, 1933, NA RG 174, Entry 167/838, Box 183.

28. Sam Raspy to FDR, May 21, 1933.

29. A. H. Davenport of Tampa, Fla., to FDR, May 22, 1933, NA RG 174, Entry 167/838, Box 183.

30. Frances S. Key-Smith to Charles Curtis, November 12, 1931.

31. Rossberg to FDR, May 18, 1933.

32. Forbush to Wanda Dabkowski, April 10, 1934, NA RG 9, Entry 23, Box 491.

BETH BAILEY AND DAVID FARBER
Prostitutes on Strike: The Women of Hotel Street during World War II

On a Sunday afternoon the nation listened as radio announcers spoke in shocked tones of the Japanese attack on Pearl Harbor. The date was December 7, 1941. World War II would transform these then remote, ethnically diverse islands no less than the mainland as the military made Hawaii its midpoint stopover in the Pacific. For those returning from combat as well as for those going into it, the place to go in Honolulu was Hotel Street.

The following essay focuses on the women of Hotel Street, more particularly the sex workers who populated its brothels. Note the conditions of work, the complicity and concerns of military authorities, and the conflict between the military and the local

Excerpted from "Hotel Street: Prostitution and the Politics of War" by Beth Bailey and David Farber, in *Radical History Review* 52 (Winter 1992):54–77. Copyright © 1992 by MARHO: The Radical Historian's Organization, Inc. Reprinted by permission of Cambridge University Press. Notes have been renumbered and edited.

police, who acted as agents of the local elite. Note, too, the way the prostitutes maneuvered to improve their lives. How did the Hotel Street prostitutes inadvertently serve to undermine Hawaii's racial hierarchy? In what other respects did their strategy foreshadow that of postwar civil rights activists?

Hotel Street was the center of Honolulu's eponymous vice district, through which some 30,000 or more soldiers, sailors, and war workers passed on any given day during most of World War II. . . . On Hotel Street, some of the most complex issues in America's history came together. Systems of race and of gender (complicated by both sex and war) structured individual experience and public policy. At the same time, the story of Hawaii's vice district revolves around the changing role of the State, as it asserted its interests in counterpoint to local elites. For most of the war Hawaii was under martial law, ruled by a military governor. Even if not fully by intention, agents of the federal government—ironically in the form of the military and martial law—emerged as limited guarantors of equality and created openings for social struggle. . . . A critical part of this struggle for power centered on prostitution and its control. . . .

Hotel Street was more than just brothels, but it was the brothels, for most of the men, that gave the district its identity and its dark magic. During the war years fifteen brothels operated in this section of Chinatown, their presence signaled by neatly lettered, somewhat circumspect signs (" The Bronx Rooms," "The Senator Hotel," "Rex Rooms") and by the lines of men that wound down the streets and alleyways. The brothels were not new; they had developed along with Honolulu's status as a port city, and had, in recent years, served both the growing military population and the plantation workers who came to town on paydays.[1]

Prostitution was illegal in Hawaii. Nonetheless, it existed as a highly and openly regulated system, involving the police department, government officials, and the military. Red-light districts in Honolulu had survived a Progressive Era campaign to close them down, and flourished in the face of the World War II–era May Act until late 1944, when an emerging new political elite succeeded in closing the houses.[2]

Some of the reasons for the brothels' survival are found in Hawaii's multiracial and multicultural society. To many of the people who made up the islands' varied population, prostitution was not a "social evil." And many of the islands' white elite, the "respectable" people who would have provided the necessary pressure to have the brothels closed down, approved of a regulated system of prostitution. The brothels, many believed, kept the predominately lower-class white soldiers and sailors and especially the overwhelmingly male and dark-skinned population of plantation workers [who lived in communities with few women] away from the islands' respectable women, who were, by their definition, white.[3] The head of the Honolulu Police Commission (which was comprised solely of leading white businessmen) said it directly: too many men in and around Honolulu were "just like animals."[4] An editorial in *Hawaii*, a magazine published and supported by the *haole* elite, explained further: "If the sexual desires of men in this predominately masculine community are *going to be satisfied*, certainly not one of us but would rather see them satisfied in regulated brothels than by our young girls and women— whether by rape, seduction or the encouraging of natural tendencies. . . ."[5] The brothels, they thought, helped keep the peace.

The military was pleased with the system, for regulated prostitution kept venereal disease rates relatively low in Hawaii. During World War II, this consideration became especially important. Like any other illness, venereal disease hurt the war effort by cutting into military manpower. At the end of World War I more men left military service with a contagious venereal disease than had been wounded in battle. While the military officials in Hawaii *never* said publicly and directly that they supported regulated vice districts, the military participated fully in the regulation process, putting houses off limits to the men if they broke rules that would compromise venereal disease control, and setting up prophylaxis stations in Honolulu. Each brothel had a sign in its waiting room reminding the men where the "pro" stations were and why it was important for them to make use of the service. The prophylaxis stations were free and open to all—civilian and military—and the Hotel Street stations could handle 1,500 men an hour.[6]

The police department, while to some extent acting on behalf of the *haole* elite, also benefited from the system. Like most police departments, the Honolulu police understood that shutting down the vice district would not end prostitution. Police officials believed that unregulated, dispersed prostitution would more likely be rife with pimps, procurers, and other men who used violence to enforce their criminal order on both the prostitutes and their customers, thus creating much unpleasantness for the police department. In Honolulu, the chief of police personally decided who might open a brothel and who would suffer penalties. The department, according to several sources, received steady payoff money to overlook the varied forms of vice that accompanied the quasi-legal acts of prostitution.[7]

The central charge of the police department was to keep the district orderly and to keep the prostitutes out of sight of respectable Honolulu. The majority of official Honolulu prostitutes were white women recruited through San Francisco. Both police and madams preferred it that way, for women from the mainland had fewer choices but to go along with the system. Each prostitute arriving from the mainland was met at the ship by a member of the vice squad. After she was fingerprinted but before she received her license, she was instructed in the rules that would govern her stay on Hotel Street:

She may not visit Waikiki Beach or any other beach except Kailua Beach (a beach across the mountains from Honolulu).

She may not patronize any bars or better class cafés.

She may not own property or an automobile.

She may not have a steady "boyfriend" or be seen on the streets with any men.

She may not marry service personnel. She may not attend dances or visit golf courses.

She may not ride in the front seat of a taxicab or with a man in the back seat.

She may not wire money to the mainland without permission of the madam.

She may not telephone the mainland without permission of the madam.

She may not change from one house to another. She may not be out of the brothel after 10:30 at night.[8]

... To break these rules was to risk a beating at the hands of the police and possible removal from the islands.

Before the war, few white women served in the houses for more than six months before they returned to the West Coast. The Honolulu service, while lucrative, was not paradise. A few months was often all a woman could take. Some probably earned what money they had hoped for and left the trade. One "sporting girl," writing at the time, said that the police forced prostitutes to leave the islands after about six months "whether the girl's record was up to standard or not . . . [because] she got to know too much in that length of time." Once a prostitute left Hawaii the police prohibited her from returning for a year.[9]

Not all the prostitutes in the Hotel Street district were white. At the Bronx, which was one of the largest houses during the war years, approximately twenty-five prostitutes worked. About half were white women from the mainland and the other half local women. Five of the women were Hawaiian or part Hawaiian. Two were Puerto Rican. The Bronx also had six Japanese prostitutes, which was highly unusual and probably due to Tomi Abe, the Japanese-American woman who ran the Bronx during the war. Most of the madams were white women from the mainland, with names like "Norma Lane," "Peggy Staunton," and "Molly O'Brian." The owners of the buildings in which the brothels operated were almost all Chinese or Chinese American, but almost none were actively involved in running the brothels.[10]

A less fully regulated set of brothels existed across the river—a very narrow river—from the Hotel Street district. Brothels such as the "Local Rooms" were staffed by local women [of color] only, and charged lower prices. Despite their cheaper rates these brothels were much less popular, for their venereal disease rates were astronomical. Men referred to the prostitutes as "white meat" or "dark meat."

During the war, most of the brothels only served white men. Before the war, the brothels had also maintained a color line, but of a more complicated sort. The major Hotel Street brothels used a two-door system, one for whites (almost all of whom were soldiers and sailors) and the other for local men. This segregated system, in a city where segregation was not commonplace, was aimed at the servicemen. Many were Southern, most had been raised with racist beliefs. Some did not like to think of colored men preceding them in the vagina or mouth of a prostitute. Because the district was rough, and the men likely to be drunk and easily moved to violence, segregation was deemed the safest policy.

With the influx of servicemen and war workers following Pearl Harbor, demand for prostitutes soared. With so many white men lining up outside the brothels, the two-door policy was abandoned for the duration and men of color were simply not served. A couple of brothels in the district did not observe a color line and were open to all who could pay. But almost always the men of color had to pay more.

The color line, as far as the white servicemen and war workers saw it, ran only in one direction. While they did not want to share prostitutes with men of color, some white men preferred the "exotic" women.

While the regulated brothels of Hotel Street had been lucrative, thriving businesses through the 1920s and 1930s, the war changed the scale of success. War conditions presented an amazing economic opportunity to the sex workers of Hotel Street. During the war, approximately 250 prostitutes were registered with the Honolulu Police Department—as "entertainers." They paid $1 a year for their licenses, and could make $30,000–$40,000 a year when the average working woman was considered fortunate to make $2,000. The houses took in over $10 million each during the war years, and the twenty-five to thirty madams who ran and/or owned them each took away between $150,000 and $450,000 every year. As a group, the prostitutes and madams of Hotel Street were incredibly successful economically.

But the conditions of sale, "$3 for 3 minutes," suggests how hard they must have worked. Most houses enforced a quota for each woman of 100 men a day, at least twenty days out of every month. The risks of sexually transmitted diseases were extremely high; in 1943, 120 professional prostitutes were hospitalized 166 times for a contagious venereal disease. A bad dose put the woman into the hospital—she had to go—for at least two weeks.[11]

Some women could accept the physically brutal and health-threatening conditions. They fixed their attention on the payoff. Others found the life, the numbers of men, and the social contempt degrading. Many sought distance from what they did by shooting morphine or by smoking opium. . . . Opiates gave them back some of the feelings of inviolability their roles as prostitutes worked to take from them.

During the war, even more than before, the women of Hotel Street did their best to exercise as much practical control as they could over their punishing livelihood and over the men who paid them for their services. First of all, the brothels were all owned and operated by women. The prostitutes maximized their economic control by allowing no pimps and there were no behind-the-scenes male owners. Even the doorkeepers at the brothels were women, often powerfully built women of Hawaiian descent. While the brothels existed for men, women controlled access.

The men who wanted sex had to wait in line, sometimes for hours, and in full public view. Because the curfew limited brothel hours, all of this took place only during daylight hours. From souvenir shops and beauty parlors and upstairs windows, the older Chinese women of the district watched and laughed at the lines of white men. Lines were generally quiet, but the shoeshine boys kidded the men who seemed visibly nervous, and quite a few of the men were drunk. But those who fortified themselves with drink faced a further obstacle: the women who kept door at the brothels rejected any man they did not trust to behave properly or to perform quickly. Adeline Naniole, the Hawaiian woman who kept door at the Bronx through part of the war, kept out any man who seemed too drunk. . . . "I don't think you can make business," she would say.[12]

Inside, the system was streamlined for maximum efficiency and control. At the head of the hall that led to the prostitutes' cubicles, a madam stood behind a money booth. Some of the booths were caged; there was no pretense that the houses offered gracious entertainment. The madam collected $3, almost always in singles, and gave the man a token, usually a poker chip. He then waited for an available woman.[13] . . .

Even in the sex act, most men felt little control. That was partly due to the setup: in the interest of time, women rotated from room to room; thus, no time was lost in cleaning up and waiting for the man to dress. When a man's turn came, he went into a cubicle—a regular room divided in half by a flimsy sheet of plywood or wall board that reached only two-thirds of the way to the ceiling. The room was bare except for a single cot, a table with a wash bowl, and a wastebasket. Sometimes, if the maids had been overwhelmed by the pace of business, soiled towels littered the floor. Often the man undressed and waited alone while the prostitute finished up in the cubicle on the other side of the half wall. The man could hear what went on the other side, and he knew that he would be heard in turn.

As time was money, and three minutes was the limit, prostitutes used various strategies to control the sex act itself. After quickly inspecting and washing the man's genitals (as a patron of other brothels described the routine):

> She'd lay on her back and get you on top of her so fast, you wouldn't even know you'd come up there on your own power. She'd grind so that you almost felt like you had nothing to do with it. Well, after that, she had you. She could make it go off as quickly as she wanted to. . . .[14]

About a quarter of the men chose fellatio, a fact that worried the senior shore-patrol officer in charge of the district, for he believed that "it is not a far cry from such sex perversions ["buccal coitus," he termed it] to homosexual acts."[15] The women, their minds on the lines outside their doors and always seeking control, seemed to prefer fellatio—it was quicker. For many of the men, sexually inexperienced and fresh from months at sea or long weeks in a battle zone, three minutes was more than enough. As one veteran recalls, "They put it in and they're gone. Sometimes they're gone washing off in the pail. . . ."[16]

Despite the impersonal efficiency of the system, it could break down. One regular customer told his favorite, a half-Chinese, half-Mexican prostitute, at the end of a three-minute session, "Judy, you're the bummest fuck I ever had." As he tells it, she was so angry she spent the rest of the night proving him a liar—for free. It meant a lot; he named his daughter after her.[17] . . .

In the houses, men's money bought women's sexual favors; that was undeniable, and to that extent the men commanded and

controlled the women. Women's bodies were commodified. Yet the system was structured to emphasize the women's control over the men. Standing in line, facing the doorkeeper, taking one's place in the day's quota of 100 anonymous acts: none of those experiences served to confirm a sense of male power or control. . . .

While the prostitutes and madams asserted control within the brothels during the war, it is perhaps more significant that they also attempted to challenge the larger system of controls and regulations within which they lived. After the Pearl Harbor attack the Hotel Street district, like much of the city, was shut down for a few weeks. Soon after the houses reopened, with the troops pouring through Honolulu and the men's pay upped from the prewar scale, the women raised their fee to $5 for three minutes. As they saw it, market conditions had changed.

Word of the price hike immediately reached Frank Steer, at that point an army major who had come to the islands in September 1940 to head the military police. Steer . . . served during the war as provost marshall under the state of martial law imposed on Hawaii after the Japanese attack. Under martial law, he had final authority over matters of vice. . . . Steer had no problem with the existence of brothels, but he did have a problem with the price hike. Raising prices on the fighting men was bad for morale and, as he saw it, unfair. Steer ordered the prices dropped: "The price of meat is still three dollars," he told the madams, and they backed down. They trusted Steer, and they knew he was their ally against the dictates of the police department. But though the prices returned to normal, Hotel Street business would not.

Right after the attack on Pearl Harbor, the women of the houses had rushed to the hospitals and temporary facilities set up for the burned and wounded men. Some of those who came to help were turned away when they admitted their occupations or gave their addresses—the official reason was fear of infection. But more than a few prostitutes nursed the men and did what they could to help. The madams turned over the brothels' living quarters to the overflow of wounded, and for a few days Hotel Street looked like a Red Cross annex.[18]

With their beds filled—and with normal lines of authority disrupted—the women took a chance. They moved out of the district and out of the shadows. They bought and leased houses all around Honolulu—up the rises (mountain slopes), down by the beaches, in fashionable neighborhoods. They told anyone who asked that the district was too risky, that it was a firetrap if the Japanese came back. The explanation was not just a cover; many on the islands believed invasion was imminent. Several prostitutes passed up the promised boom times and joined other women, longtime residents and wives of army and navy officers, who arranged passage on the 20 December special evacuation transport bound for San Francisco.

For several weeks, even as the brothels reopened and long after the wounded had moved out of the prostitutes' living quarters, no one seemed to pay any attention to the women's quiet movement out of the district. The women of Hotel Street, long subject to the dictates of the vice squad, had reason to hope that those days were over.[19]

At first, the women who had moved out of the district attracted little attention; gradually that changed. One businesswoman worked out a lucrative scheme: through an agent, she would buy a house in a fashionable neighborhood and then make clear to her neighbors what her line of work was. The investments paid off handsomely and rapidly, as the neighbors banded together to buy her out—at a premium.[20]

Other women, their minds less on business than on pleasure, simply began to enjoy their earnings. They flouted the rules—rules that had not been officially relaxed—appearing in "respectable" public places, having "wild" parties, doing as they wished. The military police, under martial law holding more authority than the civilian police, let such behavior pass.[21]

The police, especially their chief, William Gabrielson, were outraged at the new order of things. Prostitutes had invaded every neighborhood. Hawaii's carefully calibrated social stratification was being mocked. Mainland whores—white women—were out in public, demonstrating how little difference white skin had to mean in the way of moral superiority or some sort of "natural" right to rule the majority of Hawaii's people of darker hues. Already the hordes of working-class white soldiers, sailors, and war workers had damaged

the equilibrium that gave stability to the island's ruling white elite. Now the white prostitutes made a mockery of the whole racist and racialist system. Their too-public presence signaled to all who watched that one set of controls was being challenged. The prostitutes' rejection of hierarchy seemed a foreshadowing of what could happen on a larger scale politically, economically, and culturally after the war. Worse yet, supporting the new laissez-faire approach to the prostitutes was General Emmons, the military governor. . . .

For General Emmons, and for Major Steer, maintaining orderly troops, low rates of venereal diseases, and a reasonably high morale superseded long-range thinking about racial or ethnic boundaries and the elite's postwar control of the islands. . . . The men, judging by the hundreds of thousands of them who went up and down the Hotel Street brothel stairs in the months after the Pearl Harbor attack, wanted prostitutes. The regulated brothels supplied the prostitutes and ensured that they were relatively disease-free (the Hawaii military district had the lowest venereal disease rates in the armed forces). The prostitutes had nursed the wounded and given over their rooms after Pearl Harbor. They had accepted the command not to raise their prices. Many high-ranking military officers believed that "any man who won't fuck, won't fight"; they saw the women of Hotel Street as important to morale and to maintaining a manly spirit among the "boys."[22] All in all, Emmons, Steer, and others who played a role in enforcing martial law believed that keeping the prostitutes safe from needless harassment and hypocritical near-bondage was a commonsense way of keeping the more or less disease-free houses operating smoothly under what were obviously extraordinary conditions.

The matter came to a head quickly. In April of 1942, chief of police Gabrielson ordered his men to evict four prostitutes living together in a house in Waikiki, one of the areas most strictly off-limits to prostitutes in the prewar years. Waikiki before the war was not the bustling tourist center it would become. It was an exclusive resort for the well-to-do, and Jews and people of color knew better than to try to stay in any of its three luxurious hotels. Although a mixture of Hawaii's ethnic/racial groups lived in its residential section, Waikiki was carefully maintained as a respectable area.

The war had changed Waikiki: tourism halted for the duration, and servicemen had taken over even one of the exclusive hotels. At least a few of the Hotel Street prostitutes saw an opportunity in wartime Waikiki—for pleasure, if not for profit.

When Gabrielson's man told the women to leave, they complained to Captain Benson of the military police, who seemed well acquainted with their affairs. He told them that the police did not run things anymore, and that his commander did not care where they lived as long as they did not ply their trade outside the Hotel Street district. All this was relayed to Gabrielson, whose angry queries were met with official but vague statements that the military police would take care of such issues in the future.[23]

Gabrielson, angry but thinking strategically, issued Administrative Order No. 83, acknowledging the military control of vice in Honolulu. He then had the memo leaked to the Honolulu *Star-Bulletin.* He wanted to watch the military squirm.

To reiterate what must have slipped many minds in the face of the public and highly regulated system, prostitution was illegal in Honolulu. It was also outlawed through the federal-level May Act, which ... stated that the federal government would, where local officials were unwilling or unable to do the job themselves, stamp out prostitution aimed at the servicemen. The May Act was not just window-dressing; it was rigorously enforced throughout the country. Though most of the military administration in Hawaii preferred the regulated brothels to what they saw as the alternative, more dangerous system, no one wanted to take the credit for running the brothels and breaking federal law—least of all General Emmons, the military governor of Hawaii. . . .

In a letter to Police Chief Gabrielson . . . Emmons made his position clear:

> I desire to inform you that your understanding regarding the responsibility for vice conditions in the City and County of Honolulu is in error. . . . No directive had been issued to the Police Department in any way limiting its responsibility for any phase of law enforcement. . . . Cancel Administrative Order No. 83.

Chief Gabrielson, with pleasure, resumed control. But the issue had been settled only on the administrative level. The MPs and the vice squad continued to skirmish, with the vice squad trying to round the women up and return them to their living quarters in the quarter, and the MPs undermining those efforts whenever possible. The MPs told the women they were within their rights.

The women of Hotel Street were caught in the middle. They did not want to go back to the prewar order. It was one thing to choose to service 100 men a day, but it was another to abide by rules that denied them their basic freedoms. They framed the issues that way, and they went on strike.[24]

For close to three weeks in June of 1942 a group of prostitutes walked a picket line outside the police department headquarters, which was just a few blocks from the district. The police headquarters also housed Major Steer and his MPs. The women carried placards protesting their treatment and the rules that restricted their freedoms. This strike was not for better pay but for better treatment, for fuller rights of citizenship.

While no documentation of their specific arguments at that time exists, a clear line of reasoning appears in an angry appeal to Honolulu's citizens written by a prostitute in the fall of 1944. In it, she asserted her right to freedom of movement and to adequate police protection, basing her claims on a traditional liberal concept of citizenship. "We pay some of the highest taxes in this town," she wrote. "Where, I ask you, are the beneficial results of our taxes?"

This woman and many of her coworkers believed they were doing vital war work. In addition to the obvious but controversial contributions, the prostitutes had acquitted themselves well after the Pearl Harbor attack and had been willing participants in war-bond drives. One madam had received a special citation from Secretary of the Treasury Henry Morganthau for selling $132,000 in war bonds, most of them, no doubt, to fellow sex workers. The prostitutes believed their good citizenship and patriotism should be recognized as such.[25]

The striking prostitutes gambled that the military police would keep the police department from using force against them and that their military supporters would back them up. What they did took courage, for they had no public allies.

Establishment Hawaii did its best to

ignore the strike, and the newspapers carried not a single word about it. General Emmons, however, saw the situation as both embarrassing and serious, and moved quickly to resolve it. . . . Though he had the power under martial law to order the police to do as he wanted, he instead argued his case in what one participant called a "constructive and cooperative" manner. His arguments were simple and straightforward, avoiding the complicated terrains of morality and the political order and focusing instead on the women's working conditions. He said that "the girls are overworked and need periods of rest; that their work is not during daylight hours; that formerly they could go to the Coast for a rest and could be replaced by new girls arriving by steamer; that this is not possible today." Emmons also offered, on behalf of the military, to take over the unpleasant task of ensuring that the women had their regular medical checkups and inspecting the houses for breaches of the sanitary code. The police department, he assured all concerned, would have the right to enforce all other laws and regulations that applied to the women. The police commission and Chief Gabrielson, who really had little choice in the matter, accepted the compromise. The prostitutes ended their strike. Their right to appear in public and to live outside the brothels, while fragile, was won.[26]

Ultimately, the struggle over Hotel Street was not played out in terms of gender, or even with the prostitutes as players. As the prostitutes had seen an opportunity in the context between the military government and the police department, which acted as an agent of the traditional *haole* elite, so too another group saw an opportunity in the divided lines of authority. During the war years a new elite was taking shape, drawn largely from the more liberal range of the *haole* community. By mid-1944, with Hawaii completely out of harm's way and Allied victory seemingly a matter of time, some in Hawaii had begun to look to the future, toward statehood and economic development.

In trying to orchestrate Hawaii's future and maneuver toward statehood, [they] worried about ungovernable prostitutes and regulated brothels. Open prostitution somehow seemed to confirm mainland stereotypes of Hawaii as a primitive, licentious place populated by dark-skinned "natives." . . . One of

the [group's] earliest goals was to demolish the unbridled vice district.

The Social Protection Committee of the Honolulu Council of Social Agencies [which] led the way in fighting the regulated brothel system . . . resembled the kind of well-educated, modern reformers who had closed down regulated brothel systems in dozens of American cities during the Progressive Era.[27] On 1 August 1944, the committee issued a bulletin, "Prostitution in Honolulu," that described (in absolutely untitillating prose) the Hotel Street system. The bulletin included a map that showed where every known prostitute in Honolulu lived. The message was clear: the prostitutes live in YOUR neighborhood.[28] . . .

As military control waned, the first phase of the antiprostitution campaign went into effect. All prostitutes were ordered to vacate houses in residential areas and to move back into the district, to the houses in which "they carry on their trade." News of this dictate was carried in the Honolulu newspapers.[29]

One month after the prostitutes had been ordered back into the district, Governor Stainback joined the antiprostitution campaigns, . . . in part, as [a way of] attack[ing] military control [and, in part, as an effort to link] interests with the progressive elite. . . . On 21 September 1944, in one of his first major reversals of military policy, Governor Stainback ordered the regulated brothels shut down. The Social Protection Committee had maneuvered very cleverly, using their greatest weapon: publicity, or at least the threat of publicity. In letters to Admiral Nimitz, Admiral Furlong, and General Richardson, the committee asked whether each supported the system of regulated brothels. The admirals and the general replied, in writing, that they did not support the system. This was, of course, official policy, even though military practice was quite different. When Stainback closed the brothels, the military offered no resistance. A public debate about the issue, in the face of a determined campaign by an influential group of citizens, was not something anyone in the armed forces could weather. The leaders of the Social Protection Committee knew that.[30]

The actual closing of the brothels went smoothly. On 22 September three uniformed members of the vice squad visited the brothels during working hours, between 11 A.M. and 1:30 P.M. The madams had already heard about the governor's order issued the day before and so had the customers. Business had virtually come to a halt in most houses. The vice-squad officers informed the madams that after 2 P.M. any acts of prostitution committed on their premises would subject them to arrest. The prostitutes were told not to practice their trade, in the houses or elsewhere, and to move out of the district as soon as possible.

According to newspaper reports, many of the prostitutes welcomed the end of an era, and not without humor. One greeted the announcement that she could not longer "practice prostitution" with the old witticism, "I don't practice, I'm an expert." Another woman, wearing "an abbreviated red apron, short-short skirt and a pair of cowboy riding boots," gave a loud "whoopie" at the news. Madams took the news in a variety of ways. . . . But in general the[y] seemed to feel they had little about which to complain. One, and probably not the most successful, had voluntarily paid taxes on an income of $383,000 in 1943. . . . No one had expected the wartime boom to last; most prostitutes and madams had only meant to make the most money they could while it lasted. With the new clampdown in effect, some prostitutes left Honolulu as soon as they could arrange transportation back to the mainland. [Others continued to work outside of brothels.] . . .

The struggle of the Honolulu prostitutes, in retrospect, was charged not only by the usual issues surrounding illicit sex trade and lines of authority, but by concerns specific to prestatehood Hawaii. The women who made such claims on the citizens of Hawaii were white women, and their public presence and vocal demands called into question all the associations of race and gender and the ideology of the purity of white women to be defended against the sexual threat of colored races that were implicit and sometimes explicit in underpinning Hawaii's social structure. In the history of prostitution in America, many have justified the "sacrifice" of lower-class women to "protect" the purity of women of the middle and upper classes. The system in Hawaii was in many ways similar, except that race played a crucial role, and the racial lines were more complex in Hawaii than on the mainland. The public struggles—and yes, excesses—of these "impure" white women called the whole ideological system into question.

At least in small part the system had been dependent on the complicity of the white prostitutes. The prostitutes were seen as a means to keep the low-status white service personnel and the plantation workers sexually satisfied. It was crucial to the system that the prostitutes not claim any public role in Hawaii. In fact, in exchange for a great deal of money, the prostitutes (despite their white skin) were supposed to accept total pariah status. They were not to live or visit outside the vice district; they were supposed to remain silent and hidden. They could amass capital but they could not exercise their economic power in Hawaii. They were required to return to the mainland. But with their strike and with the aid of the military government, the prostitutes had demanded—and in part had gotten—the rights economic power normally guaranteed in the United States. . . .

The prostitutes' strike was only one small and indirect part of a larger movement toward a more pluralistic postwar society in Hawaii. But it is especially significant because it brought together issues of race and gender in such a way that it worked to undermine the ideology of racial superiority. White prostitutes demanded full rights of citizenship, and while the very public fact of their race had, in some small way, helped to undermine Hawaii's racial hierarchy, their race was not sufficient to guarantee their rights. Instead, the public power they were able to display for a short while in wartime Hawaii depended on the utility the federal authorities found in them.

The prostitutes' temporary victory—their ability to emerge from the dangerous shadows and to operate as legitimate, fully protected war workers—could not have happened without the intervention of the State, in the form of the military government. The concern of the federally authorized participants was not with the rights of prostitutes (though several seemed to have some respect or liking for members of the profession), but with winning the war. [What that] intervention . . . signaled [was] the increased and continuing willingness of the federal government to impose its nationally minded agendas upon local entities. . . . The ways in which socially marginal groups like the prostitutes of Hotel Street could succeed in furthering their struggles by publicly aligning themselves with the relatively autonomous federal government's often mercurial concerns would become an ever-more critical characteristic of social change movements in the postwar years.

NOTES

1. Herman Gist, interviewed by David Farber, Germantown, Md., Dec. 1989.

2. Barbara Meils Hobson, *Uneasy Virtue: The Politics of Prostitution and the American Reform Tradition* (New York: Basic Books, 1987).

3. Memo from Commissioner Houston to the Honolulu Police Commission, "Abatement of Houses of Prostitution in the City and Country of Honolulu" (n.d. [1 Sept. 1941?]), Lawrence M. Judd Papers ([hereafter cited] LJ), Hawaii State Archives (HA).

4. Quoted by James Cummings in a letter to Dr. Theodore Richards, 11 July 1944, "Prostitution" file, Governor Stainback Papers, HA.

5. "Why Talk about Prostitution," *Hawaii* (31 July 1944):5.

6. Eric A. Funnel, "Venereal Disease Control: A Bedtime Story," *Hawaii Medical Journal* (Nov.–Dec. 1942): 67–71; Hobson, *Uneasy Virtue*.

7. Frank Steer interviewed by David Farber, Kailua, Oahu, Hawaii, June 1989; Brian Nicol, "Interview with Col. Frank Steer," *Honolulu* (Nov. 1981):83.

8. Jean O'Hara, "My Life as a Honolulu Prostitute," (n.p. [Nov. 1944?]), Hawaii Collection of the University of Hawaii (HC-UH), pp. 15–16.

9. Ibid., pp. 15–18.

10. Letter to Governor Stainback by Senator Alice Kamokila Campbell, 5 Feb. 1945, "Prostitution" folder, Governor Stainback Papers (GS), HA.

11. Social Protection Committee, *Prostitution in Honolulu, Bulletin* 1 (1 Aug. 1944):2–3.

12. Quote from former brothel employee Adeline Naniole, interviewed by Vivian Lee, 2 March 1979, Women Workers in Pineapple, Ethnic Studies Oral History Project, University of Hawaii, p. 769; interviews with Colonel Steer, Herman Gist, and Robert Cowan.

13. Dr. G. Gary Schram, "Suppressed Prostitution," *Honolulu Advertiser* (6 Oct. 1944); interviews with "C" (July 1990, by telephone); Herman Gist, Elton Brown (Nov. 1990, by telephone).

14. Ruth Rosen, *The Lost Sisterhood* (Baltimore: Johns Hopkins University Press, 1982), p. 96.

15. Lt. Commander Carl G. Stockholm, "The Effects of Closing Houses of Prostitution on the Navy" (paper given at the Meeting of the Social Protection Committee), 7 Feb. 1945, HC-UH.

16. Elton Brown, telephone interview, Nov. 1990.

17. Ibid.

18. "Hotel Street Harry," *Midpacifican* (15 Aug. 1943):10; Frank Steer interview, June 1989; Peggy Hickok, "In the Midst of War," *Hawaii* (30 June 1942):17.

19. O'Hara, "My Life."

20. "Hotel Street Harry," *Midpacifican* (15 Jan. 1944):10; Naniole, p. 771; and "Police Clamp Lid on Houses," *Honolulu Advertiser* (24 Sept. 1944):1.

21. O'Hara, p. 41.

22. Elizabeth Fee, "Venereal Disease: The Wage of Sin?" in Kathy Peiss and Christina Simmons, *Passion and Power* (Philadelphia: Temple University Press, 1989), p. 189.

23. 014.12 Civil Authorities, Decimal File 1941–45, RG 338, MGH, National Archives.

24. Colonel Steer's assistant in "Memoranda of Conference with Major Slattery...." May 1945, office of Interior Secretary, Research and Historical Sector, RG338, NA.; J. Garner Anthony, *Hawaii Under Army Rule*, p. 440.

25. O'Hara, "My Life," p. 47.

26. 014.12 Civil Authorities, Decimal File 1941–45, RG 338 MGH, NA.

27. "Prostitution" file, Governor Stainback Papers, HA; Lawrence H. Fuchs, *Hawaii Pono: A Special History* (New York: Harcourt Brace, 1961), p. 279, 286–88; Hobson, *Uneasy Virtue*.

28. Social Protection Committee, "Prostitution in Hawaii" (1 Aug. 1944).

29. "Residential Areas Banned Prostitutes," *Honolulu Advertiser* (20 July 1944).

30. Dr. Charles L. Wilbar Jr., "The Effects of Closing Houses of Prostitution on Community Health," (paper given at the Meeting of the Social Protection Committee), 7 Feb. 1945, 2–3, HC-UH; and "Prostitution" file, GS, HA.

VALERIE MATSUMOTO
Japanese-American Women during World War II

On no group of U.S. citizens did the war have greater impact than upon Japanese Americans. Fearful of a Japanese fifth column on American shores, military and civilian leaders urged Franklin Roosevelt to issue an executive order removing Americans of Japanese decent on the West Coast to relocation camps inland. Despite the fact that a vast majority of the nearly 120,000 Japanese Americans in the United States were citizens with the same rights and obligations as any other citizen, the president succumbed to pressure and issued Executive Order 9066 in February 1942, which ultimately resulted in the establishment of ten concentration camps in remote areas of the West. Forced to leave their homes and businesses at great financial cost, both Japanese-born parents, the Issei, and their American-born children, the Nisei, faced the trauma of removal and the shame of implied disloyalty. Not until 1990 would the nation acknowledge the magnitude of its offense and begin providing financial redress for survivors of the camps.

The following essay explores what life in the camps was like for women and the efforts of younger ones to reconstruct a life after internment.

The life here cannot be expressed. Sometimes, we are resigned to it, but when we see the barbed wire fences and the sentry tower with floodlights, it gives us a feeling of being prisoners in a "concentration camp." We try to be happy and yet oftentimes a gloominess does creep in. When I see the "I'm an American" editorial and write-ups, the "equality of race etc."—it seems to be mocking us in our faces. I just wonder if all the sacrifices and hard labor on [the] part of our parents has gone up to leave nothing to show for it?
Letter from Shizuko Horiuchi,
Pomona Assembly Center, May 24, 1942

Overlying the mixed feelings of anxiety, anger, shame, and confusion [of the Japanese Americans who were forced to relocate] was resignation. As a relatively small minority caught in a storm of turbulent events that destroyed their individual and community security, there was little the Japanese Americans could do but shrug and say, "*Shikata ga nai,* " or "It can't be helped," the implication being that the situation must be endured. The

phrase lingered on many lips when the Issei, Nisei [second generation], and the young Sansei (third generation) children prepared for the move—which was completed by November 1942—to the ten permanent relocation camps organized by the War Relocation Authority: Topaz, Utah; Poston and Gila River, Arizona; Amache, Colorado; Manzanar and Tule Lake, California; Heart Mountain, Wyoming; Minidoka, Idaho; Denson and Rohwer, Arkansas.[1] Denson and Rohwer were located in the swampy lowlands of Arkansas; the other camps were in desolate desert or semi-desert areas subject to dust storms and extreme temperatures reflected in the nicknames given to the three sections of the Poston Camp: Toaston, Roaston, and Duston.

The conditions of camp life profoundly altered family relations and affected women of all ages and backgrounds. Family unity deteriorated in the crude communal facilities and cramped barracks. The unceasing battle with the elements, the poor food, the shortages of toilet tissue and milk, coupled with wartime profiteering and mismanagement, and the sense of injustice and frustration took their toll on a people uprooted, far from home.

The standard housing in the camps was a spartan barracks, about twenty feet by one hundred feet, divided into four to six rooms furnished with steel army cots. Initially each single room or "apartment" housed an average of eight persons; individuals without kin nearby were often moved in with smaller families. Because the partitions between apartments did not reach the ceiling, even the smallest noises traveled freely from one end of the building to the other. There were usually fourteen barracks in each block, and each block had its own mess hall, laundry, latrine, shower facilities, and recreation room. . . . The even greater lack of privacy in the latrine and shower facilities necessitated adjustments in former notions of modesty. There were no partitions in the shower room, and the latrine consisted of two rows of partitioned toilets "with nothing in front of you, just on the sides".[2] . . . A married woman with a family wrote from Heart Mountain:

Last weekend, we had an awful cold wave and it was about 20° to 30° below zero. In such a weather, it's terrible to try going even to the bath and latrine house. . . . It really aggravates me to hear some politicians say we Japanese are being coddled, for *it isn't so!!* We're on ration as much as outsiders are. I'd say welcome to anyone to try living behind barbed wire and be cooped in a 20 ft. by 20 ft. room. . . . We do our sleeping, dressing, ironing, hanging up our clothes in this one room.[3]

After the first numbness of disorientation, the evacuees set about making their situation bearable, creating as much order in their lives as possible. With blankets they partitioned their apartments into tiny rooms and created benches, tables, and shelves as piles of scrap lumber left over from barracks construction vanished; victory gardens and flower patches appeared. . . .

Despite the best efforts of the evacuees to restore order to their disputed world, camp conditions prevented replication of their prewar lives. Women's work experiences, for example, changed in complex ways during the years of internment. Each camp offered a wide range of jobs, resulting from the organization

of the camps as model cities administered through a series of departments headed by European American administrators. The departments handled everything from accounting, agriculture, education, and medical care to mess hall service and the weekly newspaper. The scramble for jobs began early in the assembly centers and camps, and all able-bodied persons were expected to work.

Even before the war many family members had worked, but now children and parents, men and women all received the same low wages. In the relocation camps, doctors, teachers, and other professionals were at the top of the pay scale, earning $19 per month. The majority of workers received $16, and apprentices earned $12. The new equity in pay and the variety of available jobs gave many women unprecedented opportunities for experimentation, as illustrated by one woman's account of her family's work in Poston:

First I wanted to find art work, but I didn't last too long because it wasn't very interesting . . . so I worked in the mess hall, but that wasn't for me, so I went to the accounting department—time-keeping—and I enjoyed that, so I stayed there. . . . My dad . . . went to a shoe shop . . . and then he was block gardener. . . . He got $16. . . . [My sister] was secretary for the block manager; then she went to the optometry department. She was assistant optometrist; she fixed all the glasses and fitted them. . . . That was $16.[4]

As early as 1942, the War Relocation Authority began to release evacuees temporarily from the centers and camps to do voluntary seasonal farm work in neighboring areas hard hit by the wartime labor shortage. The work was arduous, as one young woman discovered when she left Topaz to take a job plucking turkeys:

The smell is terrific until you get used to it. . . . We all wore gunny sacks around our waist, had a small knife and plucked off the fine feathers.

This is about the hardest work that many of us have done—but without a murmur of complaint we worked 8 hours through the first day without a pause.

We were all so tired that we didn't even feel like eating. . . . Our fingers and wrists were just aching, and I just dreamt of turkeys and more turkeys.[5]

Work conditions varied from situation to situation, and some exploitative farmers refused to pay the Japanese Americans after they had finished beet topping or fruit picking. One worker noted that the degree of friendliness on the employer's part decreased as the harvest neared completion. Nonetheless, many workers, like the turkey plucker, concluded that "even if the work is hard, it is worth the freedom we are allowed." . . .

Like their noninterned contemporaries, most young Nisei women envisioned a future of marriage and children. They—and their parents—anticipated that they would marry other Japanese Americans, but these young women also expected to choose their own husbands and to marry "for love." This mainstream American ideal of marriage differed greatly from the Issei's view of love as a bond that might evolve over the course of an arranged marriage that was firmly rooted in less romantic notions of compatibility and responsibility. The discrepancy between Issei and Nisei conceptions of love and marriage had sturdy prewar roots; internment fostered further divergence from the old customs of arranged marriage. In the artificial hothouse of camp, Nisei romances often bloomed quickly. As Nisei men left to prove their loyalty to the United States in the 442nd Combat Team and the 100th Battalion, young Japanese Americans strove to grasp what happiness and security they could, given the uncertainties of the future. Lily Shoji, in her "Fem-a-lites" newspaper column, commented upon the "changing world" and advised Nisei women: "This is the day of sudden dates, of blind dates on the up-and-up, so let the flash of a uniform be a signal to you to be ready for any emergency. . . . Romance is blossoming with the emotion and urgency of war."[6]

In keeping with this atmosphere, camp newspaper columns like Shoji's in *The Mercedian, The Daily Tulean Dispatch's* "Strictly Feminine," and the *Poston Chronicle's* "Fashionotes" gave their Nisei readers countless suggestions on how to impress boys, care for their complexions, and choose the latest fashions. These evacuee-authored columns thus mirrored the mainstream girls' periodicals of the time. Such fashion news may seem incongruous in the context of an internment camp whose inmates had little choice in clothing beyond what they could find in the Montgomery Ward or Sears and Roebuck mail-order catalogues. These columns, however, reflect women's efforts to remain in touch with the world outside the barbed wire fence; they reflect as well women's attempt to maintain morale in a drab, depressing environment. "There's something about color in clothes," speculated Tule Lake columnist "Yuri"; "Singing colors have a heart-building effect. . . . Color is a stimulant we need—both for its effect on ourselves and on others."[7] . . .

RESETTLEMENT: COLLEGE AND WORK

Relocation began slowly in 1942. Among the first to venture out of the camps were college students, assisted by the National Japanese American Student Relocation Council, a nongovernmental agency that provided invaluable placement aid to 4,084 Nisei in the years 1942–46.[8] Founded in 1942 by concerned educators, this organization persuaded institutions outside the restricted Western Defense zone to accept Nisei students and facilitated their admissions and leave clearances. A study of the first 400 students to leave camp showed that a third of them were women.[9] Because of the cumbersome screening process, few other evacuees departed on indefinite leave before 1943. In that year, the War Relocation Authority tried to expedite the clearance procedure by broadening an army registration program aimed at Nisei males to include all adults. With this policy change, the migration from the camps steadily increased.[10]

Many Nisei, among them a large number of women, were anxious to leave the limbo of camp and return "to normal life again."[11] . . . An aspiring teacher wrote: "Mother and father do not want me to go out. However, I want to go so very much that sometimes I feel that I'd go even if they disowned me. What shall I do? I realize the hard living conditions outside but I think I can take it."[12] Women's developing sense of independence in the camp environment and their growing awareness of their abilities as workers contributed to their self-confidence and hence their desire to leave. Significantly, Issei parents, despite initial reluctance, were gradually beginning to sanction their daughters' departures for education and employment in the Midwest and East. One Nisei noted: "[Father] became more broad-minded in the relocation center. . . . At first he didn't want me to relocate, but he gave in. . . . He didn't say I could go . . . but he helped me pack, so I thought, 'Well, he didn't say no.'"[13]

The decision to relocate was a difficult one. . . . Many internees worried about their acceptance in the outside world. The Nisei considered themselves American citizens, and they had an allegiance to the land of their birth. . . . But evacuation had taught the Japanese Americans that in the eyes of many of their fellow Americans, theirs was the face of the enemy. Many Nisei were torn by mixed feelings of shame, frustration, and bitterness at the denial of their civil rights. . . . "A feeling of uncertainty hung over the camp; we were worried about the future. Plans were made and remade, as we tried to decide what to do. Some were ready to risk anything to get away. Others feared to leave the protection of the camp."[14]

Thus, those first college students were the scouts whose letters back to camp marked pathways for others to follow. May Yoshino sent a favorable report to her family in Topaz from the nearby University of Utah, indicating that there were "plenty of schoolgirl jobs for those who want to study at the University."[15] Correspondence from other Nisei students shows that although they succeeded at making the dual transition from high school to college and from camp to the outside world, they were not without anxieties as to whether they could handle the study load and the reactions of the European Americans around them. One student at Drake University in Iowa wrote to her interned sister about a professor's reaction to her autobiographical essay, "Evacuation": "Today Mr.—, the English teacher that scares me, told me that the theme that I wrote the other day was very interesting. . . . You could just imagine how wonderful and happy I was to know that he liked it a little bit. . . . I've been awfully busy trying to catch up on work and the work is so different from high school. I think that little by little I'm beginning to adjust myself to college life."[16] . . . Lillian . . . Ota, a Wellesley student, reassured [her interned friends contemplating college:] "During the first few days you'll be invited by the college to teas and receptions. Before long you'll lose the awkwardness you might feel at such doings after the months of abnormal life at evacuation centers."[17] Although Ota had not noticed "that my being a 'Jap' has made much difference on the campus itself," she offered

cautionary and pragmatic advice to the Nisei, suggesting the burden of responsibility these relocated students felt, as well as the problem of communicating their experiences and emotions to European Americans.

It is scarcely necessary to point out that those who have probably never seen a nisei before will get their impression of the nisei as a whole from the relocated students. It won't do you or your family and friends much good to dwell on what you consider injustices when you are questioned about evacuation. Rather, stress the contributions of [our] people to the nation's war effort.[18] . . .

Armed with [such] advice and drawn by encouraging reports, increasing numbers of women students left camp.[19] . . . The trickle of migration from the camps grew into a steady stream by 1943, as the War Relocation Authority developed its resettlement program to aid evacuees in finding housing and employment in the East and Midwest. . . . [But] leaving camp meant [more changes.] Even someone as confident as Marii Kyogoku . . . found that reentry into the European American-dominated world beyond the barbed wire fence was not a simple matter of stepping back into old shoes. Leaving the camps—like entering them—meant major changes in psychological perspective and self-image.

I had thought that because before evacuation I had adjusted myself rather well in a Caucasian society, I would go right back into my former frame of mind. I have found, however, that though the center became unreal and was as if it had never existed as soon as I got on the train at Delta, I was never so self-conscious in all my life.

Kyogoku was amazed to see so many men and women in uniform and, despite her "proper" dining preparation, felt strange sitting at a table set with clean linen and a full set of silverware.

I felt a diffidence at facing all these people and things, which was most unusual. Slowly things have come to seem natural, though I am still excited by the sounds of the busy city and thrilled every time I see a street lined with trees, I no longer feel that I am the cynosure of all eyes.[20] . . .

Many relocating Japanese Americans received moral and material assistance from a number of service organizations and religious groups, particularly the Presbyterians, the Methodists, the Society of Friends, and the Young Women's Christian Association. One such Nisei, Dorcas Asano, enthusiastically described to a Quaker sponsor her activities in the big city:

Since receiving your application for hostel accommodation, I have decided to come to New York and I am really glad for the opportunity to be able to resume the normal civilized life after a year's confinement in camp. New York is really a city of dreams and we are enjoying every minute working in offices, rushing back and forth to work in the ever-speeding subway trains, counting our ration points, buying war bonds, going to church, seeing the latest shows, plays, operas, making many new friends and living like our neighbors in the war time. I only wish more of my friends who are behind the fence will take advantage of the many helpful hands offered to them.[21]

The Nisei also derived support and strength from networks—formed before and during internment—of friends and relatives. The homes of those who relocated first became way stations for others as they made the transition into new communities and jobs. In 1944, soon after she obtained a place to stay in New York City, Miné Okubo found that "many of the other evacuees relocating in New York came ringing my doorbell. They were sleeping all over the floor!"[22] Single women often accompanied or joined sisters, brothers, and friends as many interconnecting grapevines carried news of likely jobs, housing, and friendly communities. . . .

For Nisei women, like their non-Japanese sisters, the wartime labor shortage opened the door into industrial, clerical, and managerial occupations. Prior to the war, racism had excluded the Japanese Americans from most white-collar clerical and sales positions, and, according to sociologist Evelyn Nakano Glenn, "the most common form of nonagricultural employment for the immigrant women (Issei) and their American-born daughters (Nisei) was domestic service."[23] The highest percentage of job offers for both men and women continued to be requests for domestic workers. In July 1943, the Kansas City branch of the War Relocation Authority noted that 45 percent of requests for workers were for domestics, and the Milwaukee office cited 61 percent.[24] However, Nisei women also found jobs as secre-

taries, typists, file clerks, beauticians, and factory workers. By 1950, 47 percent of employed Japanese American women were clerical and sales workers and operatives; only 10 percent were in domestic service.[25] The World War II decade, then, marked a turning point for Japanese American women in the labor force. . . .

[Improved opportunities could not compensate for the] uprooting [of] communities and [the] severe psychological and emotional damage [inflicted upon Japanese Americans by internment.] The vast majority returned to the West Coast at the end of the war in 1945—a move that, like the initial evacuation, was a grueling test of flexibility and fortitude. Even with the assistance of old friends and service organizations, the transition was taxing and painful; the end of the war meant not only long-awaited freedom but more battles to be fought in social, academic, and economic arenas. The Japanese Americans faced hostility, crude living conditions, and a struggle for jobs. Few evacuees received any compensation for their financial losses, estimated conservatively at $400 million, because Congress decided to appropriate only $38 million for the settlement of claims.[26] It is even harder to place a figure on the toll taken in emotional shock, self-blame, broken dreams, and insecurity. One Japanese American woman still sees in her nightmares the watchtower searchlights that troubled her sleep forty years ago.

The war altered Japanese American women's lives in complicated ways. In general, evacuation and relocation accelerated earlier trends that differentiated the Nisei from their parents. Although most young women, like their mothers and non-Japanese peers, anticipated a future centered on a husband and children, they had already felt the influence of mainstream middle-class values of love and marriage and quickly moved away from the pattern of arranged marriage in the camps. There, increased peer group activities and the relaxation of parental authority gave them more independence. The Nisei women's expectations of marriage became more akin to the companionate ideals of their peers than to those of the Issei.

As before the war, many Nisei women worked . . . , but the new parity in wages they received altered family dynamics. And though they expected to contribute to the family economy, a large number did so in settings far from the family, availing themselves of opportunities provided by the student and worker relocation programs. In meeting the challenges facing them, Nisei women drew not only upon the disciplined strength inculcated by their Issei parents but also upon firmly rooted support networks and the greater measure of self-reliance and independence that they developed during the crucible of the war years.

NOTES

1. Many of the Japanese community leaders arrested by the FBI before the evacuation were interned in special all-male camps in North Dakota, Louisiana, and New Mexico. Some Japanese Americans living outside the perimeter of the Western defense zone in Arizona, Utah, etc., were not interned.

2. Chieko Kimura, personal interview, Apr. 9, 1978, Glendale, Arizona.

3. Shizuko Horiuchi to Henriette Von Blon, Jan. 24, 1943, Henriette Von Blon Collection, Hoover Institution Archives ([hereafter] HIA).

4. Ayako Kanemura, personal interview, Mar. 10, 1978, Glendale, Arizona.

5. Anonymous, Topaz Times, Oct. 24, 1942, p. 3.

6. Lily Shoji, "Fem-a-lites," The Mercedian, Aug. 7, 1942, p. 4.

7. "Yuri," "Strictly Feminine," Sept. 29, 1942, p. 2.

8. From 1942 to the end of 1945 the Council allocated about $240,000 in scholarships, most of which were provided through the donations of the church and the World Student Service Fund. The average grant for student for was $156.73, which in that area was a major contribution towards the cost of higher education. Source: National Japanese American Student Relocation Council, Minutes of the Executive Committee Meeting, Philadelphia, Pennsylvania, Dec. 19, 1945.

9. Robert O'Brien, The College Nisei (Palo Alto: Pacific Books, 1949), pp. 73–74.

10. The disastrous consequences of the poorly conceived clearance procedure had been examined by Wilson and Hosokawa, pp. 226–27, and Girdner and Loftis, pp. 342–43.

11. May Nakamoto to Mrs. Jack Shoup, Nov. 20, 1943, Mrs. Jack Shoup Collection, HIA.

12. Toshiko Imada to Margaret Cosgrave Sowers, Jan. 16, 1943, Margaret Cosgrave Sowers Collection, HIA.

13. Ayako Kanemura, personal interview, Mar. 24, 1978, Glendale, Arizona.

14. Mine Okubo, Citizen 13660 (New York: Columbia University Press, 1946), p. 66.

15. Topaz Times, Oct. 24, 2942, p. 3.

16. Masako Ono to Atsuko Ono, Sept. 28, 1942, Margaret Cosgrave Sowers Collection, HIA. Prior to the war, few Nisei had college experience: the 1940 census lists 674 second-generation women and 1,507 men who had attended or who were attending college.

17. Lillian Ota, "Campus Report," Trek (Feb. 1943), p. 33.

18. Ota, pp. 33–34.

19. O'Brien, p. 84.

20. Marii Kyogoku, Resettlement Bulletin (July 1943), p. 5.

21. Dorcas Asano to Josephine Duveneck, Jan. 22, 1944, Conard-Duveneck Collection, HIA.

22. Miné Okubo, Miné Okubo: An American Experience, exhibition catalogue (Oakland: Oakland Museum, 1972), p. 84.

23. Evelyn Nakana Glenn, "The Dialectics of Wage Work: Japanese American Women and Domestic Servants, 1905–1940," Feminist Studies 6, no. 3 (Fall 1980):412.

24. Advisory Committee of Evacuees, Resettlement Bulletin (July 1943), p. 3.

25. 1950 United States Census, Special Report.

26. Susan M. Hartmann, The Home Front and Beyond, American Women in the 1940s (Boston: Twayne Publishers, 1982), p. 126. There is some debate regarding the origins of the assessment of evacuee losses at $400 million. However, a recent study by the Commission on Wartime Relocation and Internment of Civilians has estimated that the Japanese Americans lost between $149 million and $370 million in 1945 dollars, and between $810 million and $2 billion in 1983 dollars. See the San Francisco Chronicle, June 16, 1983, p. 12.

SARA EVANS
"Rosie the Riveter": Women and War Work during World War II

World War II, like the depression, affords another occasion to explore attitudes toward working women. The manpower shortages created by the war meant that women could move into industry, experiencing new vocational opportunities and a lessening of discrimination based on marital status, age, and race. The response was overwhelming. Rosie the Riveter, as these wartime workers were dubbed, soon became a kind of icon signifying that women were doing the job and doing it well.

Demobilization provided an opportunity to make these changes permanent, overturning the prewar sexual division of labor known as job segregation. Management could have continued the wartime redefinition of what had previously been "men's jobs" and "women's jobs." Labor could have insisted that union rules concerning job seniority apply to women members. To have done so would have meant that once men discharged from the military were rehired, wartime women workers, who had been terminated against their wishes, would be next in line by virtue of seniority as new jobs became available. If male unionists feared that reemploying Rosie would give employers an opportunity to replace male labor with less expensive female labor, they could have pressed more vigorously for equal pay for the same work and for work of comparable skill and difficulty. In sum, the potential existed for real change. Women in the workplace might finally be treated as workers rather than as women.

As Sara Evans's account suggests, that potential was not realized. What role did gender play? In what sense did it trump class in working-class families that would have benefited from women's pay? Why were the efforts of women to hold onto their jobs largely futile? Which unions were most supportive of women workers? How do you respond to the conclusion that the war ultimately had little impact on women's workforce participation? Evans also indicates that World War II marked the end of an ascendent women's network that had been a presence in government and an advocacy group for women in earlier decades. Why was this the case? What has happened with respect to the factors that Sklar identified as being key to explaining the presence and power of progressive women in the political arena in the early years of the twentieth century?

... The most powerful, immediate effects of the attack on Pearl Harbor and President Roosevelt's call for a Declaration of War were the surge of patriotism and the creation of new jobs. At the end of the 1930s, 25 percent of American workers remained unemployed, but now suddenly jobs were everywhere. Employers scrambled to find enough workers at the same time the government drafted young men into the armed services. Manpower was at a premium. . . .

By 1942 the economy had absorbed avail-

Frances Green, Peg Kirchner, Ann Waldner, and Blanche Osborne emerging from their 4-engine Flying Fortress. They were among the 1,074 Women's Airforce Service Pilots (WASPs) who flew noncombat missions during World War II. Although several died in the line of duty, WASPs were not eligible for military insurance or for G.I. benefits. At the end of the war the WASPs were disbanded; not until 1978 were the survivors offered veteran's status. (Courtesy the U.S. Army Museum)

able supplies of male workers and there was widespread recognition that only the employment of women could meet industrial demand. U.S. Employment Service surveys reported marked shifts that year in employers' willingness to hire women. Between January and July, employers raised their estimates of the proportion of new jobs for which women would be acceptable from 29 to 55 percent.[1] One of the primary reasons given for refusal to hire women was the opposition of male workers who periodically walked out rather than work with, or for, a woman. However, with fewer men in the factories and increased demands for industrial output, employers saw fit to tap the pool of female workers. By 1943 *Fortune* magazine noted, "There are practically no unmarried women left to draw upon. . . . This leaves, as the next potential source of industrial workers, the housewives." . . .[2]

To entice women into the factories while allaying anxieties about the consequences of change, the government mounted a major propaganda campaign aided and abetted by the active cooperation of the media and industrial advertisers. Indeed, the mobilization of women for industrial work illustrates an extraordinary degree of governmental intervention in the economy and in molding values and attitudes achieved during the war. Through the War Production Board, the administration determined what would be produced and how scarce resources would be used. The War Manpower Commission allocated the labor supply. The War Labor Board intervened in labor disputes to prevent strikes or other disruptions. And the Office of War Information coordinated publicity and propaganda campaigns. Once the War Manpower Commission decided to recruit female workers, including married women, the War Labor Board indicated its intention to rule that women working in previously male jobs should be paid at the male rate, and the Office of War Information generated recruitment posters and pamphlets and established guidelines for fiction, features, and advertising in the mass media. The response was immediate.

"Rosie the Riveter" became a national heroine, gracing magazine covers and ads that emphasized women's civic and patriotic duty to work in the defense industry in no way undermined their traditional femininity. In Seattle, Washington, Boeing Aircraft placed large ads urging women to come to work. They displayed "pretty girls in smart slack outfits showing how easy it is to work on a wiring board."[3] Propaganda films such as *Glamour Girls of '43* assured women that industrial tasks and machines mimicked household work:

> Instead of cutting the lines of a dress, this woman cuts the pattern of aircraft parts. Instead of baking cake, this woman is cooking gears to reduce the tension in the gears after use. . . . After a short apprenticeship, this woman can operate a drill press just as easily as a juice extractor in her own kitchen.[4]

Similarly, a group of 114 electric companies extolled the "modern magic" of electricity: "She's 5 feet 1 from her 4A slippers to her spun-gold hair. She loves flower-hats, veils, smooth orchestras—and being kissed by a boy who's now in North Africa. *But, man, oh man, how she can handle her huge and heavy press!*"[5]

Labor shortages affected the military as well, and from the outset of the war women's organizations demanded that women be allowed to serve their country. The result was the creation in 1942 and 1943 of women's branches in the army (WACs), the navy (WAVES), the Coast Guard (SPARS), and the marines (MCWR) in addition to the army and navy nursing corps. Close to three hundred fifty thousand women served in these various branches and an additional thousand flew commercial and air force transport planes for the Women's Airforce Service Pilots (WASP). As in the case of women in industry, glamorized service-women appeared everywhere in the media, looking for all the world like Joan Crawford or Katharine Hepburn with their squared shoulders and sophisticated smiles. In another version these "girls" or "gals" peeked prettily out from under their sailor hats, looking too cute to be threatening. A Sanforized ad in 1942 epitomized the latter with a headline "Maidens in Uniform" and the following verse:

> Oh, aren't we cute and snappy
> in our cover-alls and slacks?
> And since the tags say "Sanforized"
> we'll stay as cute as tacks![6]

In retrospect, such reassurance seems excessive. The breakdown in the sexual division of labor was clearly limited to the war effort from the start. In the armed services women's work sustained the traditional values and labor force segregation of the civilian world. Most women worked in clerical and supply areas or as nurses. Each of the services avoided placing women in positions where they might give orders to men and prohibited overseas duty as long as they could (1943 for WACs and 1944 for WAVES). They also prohibited the enlistment of women with children, actively persecuted lesbians, and segregated black women.

Similarly, though women entered manufacturing industries in large numbers, many new jobs such as riveting and wiring aircraft were simply redefined from male to female work. Women were hired in far greater numbers in light industry than in heavy, and they often found themselves confined to entry-level and lower-skilled positions. In addition, many areas of growth were in jobs like clerical work and teaching previously defined as female. As the numbers of female clerical workers grew by 85 percent they dominated the field more than ever, raising their proportion of all clerical workers from 50 to 70 percent. A nation-wide teacher shortage induced many localities to withdraw prohibitions on the employment of married women thus increasing the numbers of female teachers as well.[7]

Discrimination against women in traditionally male blue-collar jobs continued in spite of the crisis. Employers were reluctant to invest in training women for skilled work, as they presumed women workers were only temporary. And for the most part, they flatly refused to hire black women. When they tried to lower the wages of women workers holding formerly male jobs, however, unions protested vigorously. Even if unions were less than enthusiastic about their new female members, unions were unambiguous about protecting the wages they had fought for and they worried that lower wages for women might create an incentive for industries to retain female workers after the war. As a result they waged the first effective battles for equal pay for equal work.

Practical obstacles lay in the paths of most working women as well. Critical shortages of housing and transportation limited their options. Government agencies in Washington, D.C., for example, suddenly expanded their clerical labor force to meet wartime demands. In 1942 the Pentagon opened with office space for 35,000 workers, the largest office building in the world. Yet as thousands of young women flooded into Washington, D.C., to fill clerical jobs in the swelling federal bureaucracy, they doubled and tripled up in shabby boardinghouses and tiny rooms, unable to find decent places to live. Their conditions, however, were probably easier to bear than those of industrial workers' families crushed into prefab housing and tiny apartments in places like Detroit and Mobile. Single young women on government wages quickly learned the value of cooperative housekeeping. "The result was a whole collection of strangely-bonded female groups."[8]

Mothers of small children found virtually no help. When the Federal Works Agency finally decided in 1943 to fund day-care centers for defense workers, their efforts met only a tiny proportion of the demand. Newspapers ran stories of infants locked in cars parked in employee lots, young children shut up in apartments most of the day, and juvenile delinquents. Local communities tried to address the problems. More than 4,400 communities had established child care and welfare committees by the summer of 1943, but their efforts paled in comparison to the need. Most women relied on family members, but a Women's Bureau survey in 1944 found that 16 percent of mothers in war industries had no child-care arrangements at all.[9] The federal government never considered measures like those in Britain which relieved the double burdens of working mothers with time off for shopping; extended shopping hours; and restaurants offering inexpensive, take-home prepared food. As a result of these stresses, women workers' absenteeism was 50 percent higher than that of men and their turnover was twice as high.[10]

Nevertheless, the government campaign to fill defense needs with women workers was hugely successful. Six million women who had never worked outside the home joined the labor force during the war years while millions more shifted from agricultural, domestic, or service work to industrial work. Their profile represented a marked shift toward older and married women from the traditional young and single worker, and most of them did not want their new status to be temporary. When questioned about their future intentions, women in defense industries indicated an overwhelming preference for retaining their jobs after the war.[11] If the stresses of managing home and workplace were acute, the gains were also real. For the first time, women had access to high-paying industrial jobs requiring specialized skills and affording status. Black women, though blocked from higher-level industrial jobs, began to enter the female jobs which had previously been virtually all white, such as clerical work and nursing, and significantly reduced their reliance on domestic service. In Detroit in 1942 and 1943 black women demonstrated for jobs and housing with the support of the UAW. Two busloads of women finally stormed a Ford plant to call attention to discriminatory hiring. Perhaps most important, half the rural black female labor force left the countryside and found employment in cities.[12]

From the beginning, business owners and government planners worried that women might not willingly give up higher paying industrial jobs once they had access to them. . . . Surveys of women workers confirmed planners' fears.... [But] government and media propaganda consistently reassured Americans that while women would do their civic duty for the duration, they would certainly return to their traditional roles once the emergency was over....

Unions reflected the prejudices of their constituents, especially fears that women would displace male workers at lower rates of pay. In the beginning, unions objected strenuously when women were hired, frequently to the point of going on strike. "Women don't know how to be loyal to a union," said a skilled craftsman. "They're born, and they grow up, dirty dealers. There isn't a straight one among 'em."[13] Once the War Labor Board announced its intention to rule that women must be paid at male rates for the same work, unions expressed their willingness to support women workers and accept them as members. Because unions began to see organizing women as the key to protecting jobs and wage rates in previously all male work settings, and because the War Labor Board protected labor's right to organize, the unionization of women as well as men made enormous strides during the war. The number of organized women grew between 1940 and 1944 from eight hundred thousand to three million, and the female proportion of organized labor from 11 to 23 percent.[14] ...

At the end of the war women knew that they, as well as men, had made victory possible. The outpouring of energy and patriotic emotion had given a new dimension to citizenship and to their sense of self. Yet there was no way to institutionalize such emotions when public life itself was so thoroughly dominated by the state. The political focus of wartime activity had only one purpose—victory. There was little to debate either about means or ends. Only military and technocratic experts could know what was needed to mobilize and direct the massive resources of America. Women's duty was simply to respond, to do what was necessary "for the duration," and to maintain the family as the essential foundation for democracy.[15]

As a result, the exhilaration of wartime communal effort had neither structural nor ideological support for continuation after the war. At the same time, the changes, even if temporary, were shocking and deeply unsettling, and their consequences must be read far into the postwar era.

As men were mustered out of the army, women were mustered out of the factories; both were sent home to resume increasingly privatized lives. What the war had accomplished, with a reinvigorated economy and pent-up consumer demand, was a new expectation that most Americans could enjoy the material standard of living promised by the consumer economy in peace. The purpose of work outside the home was to procure the resources to sustain this standard of living (which now included a private house; appliances such as a refrigerator, stove, and vacuum cleaner; and a car). The female task was to oversee the quality of this private life, to purchase wisely, and to serve as an emotional center of the family and home....

The UAW Women's Bureau held a conference for women union leaders in April 1945 to discuss the postwar situation. Union women expressed great concern that seniority must operate in a nondiscriminatory way so that women would have equal opportunity when postwar layoffs came. Two delegates reported that their unions had surveyed women workers regarding their work needs. "In one shipyard, 98 percent of the women want to continue working in shipyards or at least continue working in those skills which they have been able to pick up there. Many of them worked in service industries before the war." Another survey in a New York manufacturing industry indicated that 82 percent of the women intended to continue working.... Even if four out of five industrial women workers preferred to keep their jobs, few had much choice. When military orders ceased, industries shut down to prepare for reconversion, laying off women workers. For a moment unemployment was high again and everyone feared the return of the depression. Plants reopened rapidly, however, and for the most part they refused to rehire women regardless of their skills or seniority rights. In the Detroit auto industry after the war, the proportion of women in the work force fell from 25 to 7.5 percent and women's share of work in durable goods industries throughout the nation dropped 50 percent.[16]

Women who went to the U.S. Employment Service were incredulous to discover that the only jobs available to them paid only half what they had made in war industries. Skilled industrial jobs were no longer open to them.

One union organizer reported that [women were] told. "No, these jobs are for men; women can't do them."[17] As one woman complained: "They say a woman doesn't belong behind a factory machine or in any business organization. But who will support me, I ask? And who will give my family the help they have been getting from me? No one has thought to ask me whether or not I need my job."[18]

Women fought back, staging picket lines protesting their exclusion. But they met with little sympathy or support even from their unions. . . . Only a few spaces remained where the ideals of women's rights and female equality could be kept alive. Among the most important of these were the Women's Bureau of the United Auto Workers, [the United Electrical Workers], and the continued activities of the YWCA and other religious women's organizations. . . .

The impact of World War II on women cannot easily be measured in the immediate postwar era. . . . Millions of women left the labor force, voluntarily and involuntarily; the women who stayed represented an increase in labor force participation consistent with previous trends. In other words, one could argue that the war itself made little difference. Ideologically, wartime propaganda justified the erosion of gender boundaries "for the duration" and no more. The intense pressure on women to return to domesticity coincided with the wishes of a younger cohort of women and men to focus on their private lives. This privatization promised a dramatically new level of isolation within the family as bulldozers began to reshape the landscape in preparation for growing suburbs.

At the same time, there were some long-term consequences of the changes in women's behavior during the war. Even though the trends the war exaggerated, toward the employment of older, married women, were clearly in place before the war, only the expanding economy created during and after the war could have allowed those trends to continue. As a result, the war removed some of the legal and cultural barriers to the employment of married women. Laws, for example, against married women teachers were removed in several states, and the equal pay for equal work standard was adopted by many unions and by eleven states.

The longer-term consequence of a gener-ation of women shaped by their wartime experiences. . . . can only be inferred, but its importance should not be underestimated. The mothers of the baby boom generation experienced a moment of independence and cultural validation (whether personally or vicariously) during the war years; this may well have shaped the mixed messages they gave their daughters who loudly proclaimed the rebirth of feminism two decades later. . . . In between, however, lay the contradictory and illusion-filled decade of the 1950s.

NOTES

1. "USES Reports Changing Employer Attitudes," *Employment Security Review* 9, no. 12 (December 1942): 12–13.

2. "The Margin Now Is Womanpower," *Fortune* 27 (February 1943): 99, 100.

3. Ibid., 100.

4. Quoted in Ruth Milkman, "Redefining 'Women's Work,'" *Feminist Studies* 8 (Summer 1982): 341.

5. *Saturday Evening Post* 215 (June 12, 1943): 55.

6. In Carol Wald, *Myth America: Picturing Women 1865–1945* (New York: Pantheon Books, 1975), 168.

7. Susan M. Hartmann, *The Homefront and Beyond: American Women in the 1940s* (Boston: Twayne Publishers, 1982), 88.

8. Personal communication from Anne Firor Scott.

9. Mary Schweitzer, "World War II and Female Labor Force Participation Rates," *Journal of Economic History* 40 (March 1980), 93.

10. Nelson Lichtenstein, *Labor's War at Home: The CIO in World War II* (Cambridge: Cambridge University Press, 1982), 124.

11. Karen Anderson, *Wartime Women: Sex Roles, Family Relations, and the Status of Women during World War II* (Westport, Conn.: Greenwood Press, 1981), 162–64.

12. Alice Kessler-Harris, *Out to Work* (New York: Oxford University Press, 1982), 279; Jacqueline Jones, *Labor of Love, Labor of Sorrow* (New York: Basic Books, 1985), chap. 7.

13. Katherine Archibald, "Women in the Shipyard," *Radical America* 9 (July-August 1975): 139–45, quote on 143.

14. Ruth Milkman, *Gender at Work* (Urbana: University of Illinois Press, 1987), 85.

15. See Sonya Michel, "American Women and the Discourse of the Democratic Family in World War II," in *Behind the Lines: Gender and the Two World Wars*, ed. M. R. Higonnet, et al. (New Haven, Conn.: Yale University Press, 1987), 154–67.

16. Hartmann, *Homefront*, 92.

17. "Women Union Leaders Speak," U.S. Women's Bureau Union Conference, April 18–19, 1945 (Washington, D.C.: U.S. Department of Labor, 1945), 14; also Will Jones, "Women Workers Spurn

Peace Jobs," *Minneapolis Tribune*, 15 September 1947, 7.

18. Mary Smith in Ruth Young and Catherine Filene Shouse, "The Woman Worker Speaks," *Independent Woman* 24 (October 1945): 274.

19. See Sara M. Evans and Barbara J. Nelson, *Wage Justice: Comparable Worth and the Paradox of Technocratic Reform* (Chicago: University of Chicago Press, 1988), chap. 2.

LAURA MCENANEY

Atomic Age Motherhood: Maternalism and Militarism in the 1950s

If at the end of the war Rosie the Riveter was sent home to have babies in the newly emerging suburbs, she was not expected to disappear entirely into domesticity. Defense planners had another role in mind—and with good reason, they believed. The explosion of the atomic bomb, followed by the increase in tensions between the U.S.S.R. and the U.S., left Americans feeling vulnerable. The Cold War could become hot and the Soviet military establishment could well choose to direct this new weapon of mass destruction at the nation's cities. Living in the shadow of nuclear war required preparedness. If the American people were to survive an atomic attack, the family bomb shelter must be stocked in advance. A wide array of social services with which women had traditionally been identified would have to be provided for survivors. Civil defense, in short, was women's business.

Which women responded to the government's call, why, and with what consequences for themselves and the nation are matters Laura McEnaney explores in this essay. *Maternalism*, she explains, is a term applied to various generations of women activists, most notably the reformers of the late nineteenth and early twentieth century whose activism on behalf of women and children helped to lay the foundation for the welfare state. These women were able to justify their public activism for progressive purposes as an extension of their maternal responsibilities for children and family. Activism in the peace movement was also couched in maternalist rhetoric. As Crystal Eastman wrote to Jane Addams in 1915, women, as mothers or potential mothers, "have a more intimate sense of the value of human life"; therefore, "there can be more meaning and passion in the determination of a woman's organization to end war than in an organization of men and women with the same aim."*

What made maternalism such an appealing umbrella for a wide variety of activists to use in the Cold War years? How is it consistent with the upsurge in domesticity at the end of World War II? What, according to McEnaney, were the consequences of

---

*Crystal Eastman to Jane Addams, January 16, 1915, Woman's Peace Party Papers, Swarthmore College Peace Collection, Swarthmore, Penn.

Prepared especially for *Women's America*, this essay is drawn from *"Civil Defense Begins at Home": The Militarization of Cold War Political Culture* by Laura McEnaney (Princeton: Princeton University Press, forthcoming). Copyright © Laura McEnaney.

merging maternalism and militarism? Should both the women who embraced civil defense and those who rejected it in the interests of pacifism be termed maternalists? Does McEnaney agree with Eastman that women, whether for reasons that are innate or cultural, are more inclined to pacificism?

In 1953, just after the Soviet Union had exploded its own hydrogen bomb, defense official Katherine Howard argued that the arms race "cannot help but add to the household responsibilities of the average wife and mother. She must now assume a further and more serious awareness of her public duties as a citizen."[1] Howard was one of several female administrators hired by the Federal Civil Defense Administration (FCDA) to educate the average wife and mother about her new atomic-age responsibilities, which were one part maternal and one part military. This convergence of defense and domesticity is only fathomable if one understands how the atomic bomb, and the more powerful hydrogen bombs that followed, changed profoundly the rules of modern warfare, bringing civilians perilously close to ground zero. Nuclear weapons demanded a rewrite of old war scripts, blurring distinctions between soldier and civilian, protector and protected. Amidst a highly ideological war against communism and an escalating arms race, defense planners refashioned the World War II notion of fighting *for* the American family into a new ideal that positioned the family at the very center of the battle. President Eisenhower himself acknowledged the family as "a new element . . . in the total strength of the nation."[2] According to FCDA scenarios, nuclear families fought and won nuclear wars, providing the material protections the federal government said it could not or would not fund, as well as the symbolic unity and moral authority deemed critical to winning psychological victories over communism.

The decision to make nuclear preparedness a family matter once again pressed American women into service for national defense, only this time not as Rosie the Riveter but as nonemployed wives and mothers who infused their culturally prescribed family guardianship with paramilitary purpose. In the FCDA's lexicon, the duties of domesticity and those of Cold War citizenship were one and the same; the performance of domestic obligations was the very enactment of patriotic public service, "a direct answer to the

sword rattling of Mr. Khrushchev."[3] Civil defense, said Howard, was "merely a prudent extension" of a woman's maternal responsibilities.[4] Government planners cultivated this feminization of nuclear defense together with a battalion of female volunteers, mostly from large national women's organizations. The FCDA hoped that female recruits could rescue an underfunded national program, and club women hoped to enhance their political status in an era when citizenship had highly military meanings. Both groups endorsed "home protection" based on the notion that women's so-called "special knowledge" and "natural" feminine traits could be harnessed for war. But this merger of the maternal and the military entangled female civil defense activists in broader ideological systems and processes—anti-communism and militarism—which proved injurious to postwar political culture and only narrowly accommodating of club women's interests.

Civil defense came to life as the uneasy U.S.–Soviet wartime alliance, or "shotgun marriage," as Walter LaFeber puts it, deteriorated in an economic and military standoff. U.S. and Soviet leaders jockeyed for position to reconstruct the postwar world, relying on nuclear weapons for diplomatic advantage. Nuclear fear became part of the postwar cultural landscape. Indeed, "war and national security became consuming anxieties," resulting in what one historian has wryly called a "national insecurity state."[5] Civil defense emerged in 1950 as an anxious response to the Soviet acquisition of the atomic bomb, and as one of an array of new Cold War security programs designed to contain communism abroad and at home. It was unique in the sense that it was neither entirely military nor entirely civilian, and because it was the only defense agency entirely dependent on mass participation to enact its policies. It was a paramilitary program situated in the sizable gap between the military priorities of the defense establishment and the cultural ideals of the postwar populace.

The FCDA's invitation to families to build national security "from the basement up" reflected a larger, gradual process of "militarization," or the encroachment of military ideas, values, and structures into civilian life.[6] Civil defense was the domestic analogue of the militarization of foreign policy. The FCDA told citizens that military readiness, whether abroad or at home, was the basis of national security, and that ordinary people now had to share the burdens of defense. Early in the decade, congressional hostility toward FCDA funding proposals, which opponents depicted as "New-Deal style big government," steered FCDA planners away from a more collective, publicly funded civil defense system and toward a privatized, family-centered model based on "self-help." This meant that families had to adopt military hierarchies, training styles, and psychologies into their daily routines and build their own basement or backyard fallout shelters to protect themselves from Soviet attack. And this adaptation was not just "for the duration"; the open-ended commitments of the Cold War implied a permanent realignment of family priorities around military interests.

This militarization of family life created an opening for women's participation, but female entry into the world of paramilitary defense did not occur without political struggle. In the fall of 1941, well before the first atomic bomb had been deployed, a controversy emerged about the extent to which civil defense should involve highly physical and daring acts of rescue, identified as "protective" services performed by men, or whether it should provide so-called "nonprotective" social welfare services, reminiscent of those organized by women's groups during the previous world war. The head of the wartime Office of Civil Defense (OCD), New York City's Mayor Fiorello La Guardia, assailed nonprotective activities as "sissy stuff," preferring helmeted volunteers performing heroic feats. Pressured by his OCD colleagues and citizens to expand volunteer opportunities, La Guardia appointed Eleanor Roosevelt to expand the OCD's volunteer ranks.[7]

Characteristic of her social welfare interests, however, the First Lady believed the "sissy stuff" was in fact the core of an effective civil defense program. Although she certainly shared her husband's belief that civil defense had a political purpose—to build popular support for his planned intervention in the European war—she also saw civilian

defense as a kind of civilian offense, a program that attacked the travails of the home front through social provision, such as nutrition programs, consumer education, and youth activities. Where La Guardia saw the need for neighborhood militias, Roosevelt envisioned neighborhood social service networks to aid needy noncombatants.

Her vision was ultimately a casualty of larger political struggles between conservative opponents of the New Deal and liberal activists like herself. After only months in office, partisan critics attacked her ideas as "frivolous." They used her hiring of a professional dancer (to direct youth fitness programs) as an occasion to hurl wild accusations that she was turning a national defense effort into a haven for "fan dancers" and "striptease artists," preying on nascent fears that the war would erode family and moral restraints on teen behavior. La Guardia's call for a protective militia of civilian-soldiers was a way to masculinize civil defense by coupling it with the regular military, an association that would surely boost its toughness quotient and distance it from anything remotely feminine.[8]

The fallout from the La Guardia–Roosevelt conflict hovered over FCDA officials in 1950 as they began to mold an appropriate character for their defense program. Now confronting much more powerful weapons, they knew that atomic-age civil defense had to project a sober and steely presence commensurate with the level of the threat. As one congressman remarked, "The tin hats and sand buckets of the last war would seem rather pathetic in the awful glare of an atomic blast."[9] Planners also worried that Eleanor Roosevelt's approach had linked civil defense too closely with childish morale-building activities, "not a happy association," as one remarked.[10] Initially, their deliberations remained internal, but a vast network of local and national women's organizations, including the General Federation of Women's Clubs, the Girl Scouts, the National Association of Business and Professional Women, and the Democratic and Republican Party women's caucuses, lobbied President Truman and the FCDA to find a place for women in the nationalist struggle against communism. These activists dragged the debate about the proper personality of civil defense into public view in order to shape its gender meanings in their own interests.

They succeeded in creating a space for women in a paramilitary program by shaping its core identity in a way that made them indispensable to it. Club members pressured the FCDA to define preparedness as "home protection" and a "welfare problem," knowing that women's culturally defined roles as homemakers and their long-standing involvement in "social housekeeping" would secure them a place in civil defense. Their proposals received a hospitable hearing because they were compatible with the swiftly changing needs of the FCDA. As planners mulled over attack scenarios, they began to realize that recovery from attack would indeed require a vast array of welfare services at levels well beyond what state and local governments could provide. Because of women's historic involvement in social welfare provision, FCDA administrators saw an advantage in using female volunteers, who could presumably furnish first aid, set up soup kitchens, and care for orphaned children with little or no training. Moreover, as the stinginess of congressional funding necessitated family self-help, housewives increasingly seemed a natural resource for civil defense. Thus, women's groups abetted this feminization of preparedness, even as factors outside of their policy grasp were redefining it as a family and welfare matter. As female reformers had done before them, these activists gendered civil defense policies and programs to accommodate and justify their participation.

Female activists carved out their niche in civil defense in ways that are hard to untangle because their arguments for inclusion were contradictory and drew on differing historical traditions of women's mobilizations. As maternalists, they (even the childless among them) celebrated motherhood as a force for political change, often invoking nineteenth-century notions of women's moral superiority. At the same time, however, they advanced some feminist arguments about the necessity for equal professional opportunities in the male world of defense policymaking. Their earliest organizing efforts were dedicated to jettisoning what Washington Post columnist Malvina Lindsay called the "substitution approach," the World War II pattern of pressing women into service only as stand-ins for men. Such a policy, she argued, gave women only a tenuous place in national defense and would ultimately prevent

them from assuming the kind of "partnership with men that atomic defense demands."[11] Martha Sharp, the first female civil defense administrator, echoed these comments and also attacked the notion of a special "woman's committee," an idea Truman floated to get "the feminine viewpoint" on mobilization issues. Sharp thought such committees could be relegated too easily to the periphery: "When you start segregating women, you are in trouble," she wrote.[12]

But female administrators and activists desired inclusion to express their differences, or "special aptitudes and concerns," as Sharp called them.[13] Traversing familiar philosophical ground about whether women were essentially the same as or different from men, female activists argued that barring women from equal access to policymaking would "deprive the Nation of what special contributions they might make."[14] General Federation president Dorothy Houghton argued that "the influence of women [was] one of the most potent forces" for home defense.[15] Katherine Howard (who replaced Sharp after Eisenhower's election) insisted that "the special knowledge of women must be consulted" for civil defense to succeed at the grass roots.[16] These arguments reprised women's political theorizing from earlier epochs. For example, as Nancy Cott has shown, suffrage activists similarly expressed "an equal rights goal that ... sought to give women the same capacity as men so they could express their differences. ..." Neither club women nor female FCDA officials saw anything irreconcilable about their assertions; they expected to be simultaneously treated as men's equals and appreciated for their uniquely feminine contributions. As Cott points out, women activists have historically been able to "voice these two arguments almost in the same breath," without being tripped up by their potentially contradictory meanings.[17]

Along with their ongoing efforts to attain equal opportunities outside the home, female activists worked to redefine the meaning of women's work within it. As they feminized civil defense, they militarized women's housework. Routine chores, such as house-cleaning, cooking, and consumption, now had a survivalist function. The FCDA acknowledged that "Keeping up with the housework and Junior and the international situation—in addition to Mom's 1,001 other duties" did not leave much time for learning what Eisenhower called "the new language of atomic warfare," but officials reassured women that they could practice atomic housewifery without extraordinary effort.[18] In a sense, home protection literature was indistinguishable from the litany of "expert" advice in the postwar era that counseled women to perform their domestic chores with care and precision. The FCDA recommended meticulous "fireproof housekeeping," for, as Howard claimed, "the highest military authorities in our country stressed the fact that good housekeeping is one of the best protections against fire in an atomic blast."[19] Along with house-cleaning, shelter preparation was an area in which "a homemaker's ingenuity . . . [would] be tested."[20] Maintaining the fallout shelter required both prudent decision-making and creativity in order to stock the right mixture of survival tools and the family's favorite foods. Print and television media disseminated the FCDA's gospel of atomic housekeeping by providing free advertising. CBS Television broadcast a two-week educational program on family defense, praised by the *New York Times* as an "admirable new television series for the housewife" that enabled her "to become versed in the needs of civil defense without leaving her home."[21] But FCDA planners also expected women to advertise civil defense through neighborhood gossip. As Sharp remarked, "Women's tongues were . . . more effective weapons of national defense than their hands."[22]

This militarized elaboration of postwar domesticity was more than a one-note sermon on the glory of traditional femininity, for it was too malleable to be interpreted and applied in the same way by its female adherents. In fact, it accommodated an articulation of women's rights even as it extolled domestic obligation. Members of the General Federation and the National Association of Business and Professional Women wanted to be paid for their services on planning boards if men were being compensated for the same work. Sharp and Howard grumbled about sexist employment policies and office cultures within the FCDA and complained about men's intransigence in certain programs. All female activists decried the notion that Cold War politics were "men's concerns," arguing that women could and should understand international affairs as well as men. At times the investment in proving

women's equality in security matters took on bizarre dimensions imaginable only in the atomic age. Jean Fuller, Howard's successor at the FCDA, was one of several "helmeted housewives" invited to witness an atomic blast in the Nevada desert, and she used her experience to prove "that women can stand the shock and strain of an atomic explosion just as well as men."[23]

Still, these longings for representation and professional validation never strayed far from home. World War II may have unleashed a set of expectations that these women could not repress, but conventional gender ideologies reemerged after the war and remained stubbornly in the cultural mainstream. Home protection campaigns, for example, often took the form of morality tales about "good" and "bad" mothers. One FCDA pamphlet warned: "Unless you, a responsible American woman, take action you are gambling with the safety of your family . . . and your country."[24] There was also a hint of anxious reassurance in FCDA propaganda about the fact that this postwar mobilization would not rearrange gender roles, however temporarily and superficially this had occurred during World War II. As Howard described her task, "I have dedicated myself to the *perpetuation* of household responsibilities, not to their abandonment" (emphasis hers).[25] In the end, female activists evinced some feminist impulses, but they eschewed an overt identification with organized feminism, such as it existed in the shadow of McCarthyism and the feminine mystique.

While the most visible and organized female support for nuclear preparedness came from club women who organized myriad home defense programs of their own, it is impossible to know how "unorganized" women responded to the FCDA's calls for family militarization. Planners hoped that women would comprise 60 percent of the seventeen million volunteers needed. Government reports show that about four and a half million people participated in civil defense (or 2 to 3 % of population), but it is difficult to know how many were female because the FCDA's statistics did not differentiate by sex. Further complicating the matter was the fact that "participation" could mean a range of behaviors, from simply ordering a pamphlet to maintaining family food rations in one's newly built shelter. Public interest in general was fickle and sporadic, with moments of overzealous voluntarism that exposed the incoherence of the FCDA's own planning and periods of inactivity to the point of invisibility.

What is clear is that the FCDA's assumptions about the ability of women to participate ignored the changes in women's labor and family patterns already under way. More women entered the paid labor force in the 1950s, especially married women with children, but civil defense officials and activists—male and female alike—envisioned a nonemployed militia of housewives available around the clock. This assumption likely reflected the fact that the female civil defense network was situated in the mainstream of party politics and the women's club movement, both of which were divided along the axes of race and class. The largely white and prosperous composition of the network rarely, if ever, acknowledged women outside of the conventional family configurations that are now the stuff of popular nostalgia. This wishful thinking about the simplicity of postwar family life certainly simplified the task of creating a nuclear defense scheme for some 160 million people, but it did little to cultivate active female constituents.

Clear explanations for women's tepid support of civil defense remain difficult for the historian, in part because some of the deepest impacts of homefront militarization lay in the public's moods and views, which are as hard to discern today as they were for FCDA planners and activists to mold. Theories that advance women's supposedly innate or culturally influenced pacifism are inadequate, even though peace movements have long enjoyed women's support and a maternalist-pacifist movement emerged in this decade to challenge the militarism represented by civil defense.[26] Contrary to female activists' claims to "special concerns," women behaved quite like men in the shadow of the bomb; as Cold War citizens and taxpayers, they generally endorsed the arms race and its premises, but as private citizens, they rejected a level of household militarization that required the rearrangement of daily life around national security threats. As the FCDA's own director admitted, "constant readiness requires constant apprehension, which Americans refuse to have."[27]

Together, FCDA administrators and club women forged a militarized maternalism, a hybrid of Cold War militarism, domesticity, and female reform traditions. The conventional gender and family politics prescribed by the postwar feminine mystique did not constrain female activism in this case. As historians continue to reveal the variances between women's experiences and the preachments of the mystique, it is important to remember that both liberal-progressive and conservative women revised and adapted its tenets to suit their interests. Female civil defense activists, after all, used the same maternalist-domestic ideology to support the Cold War state as their pacifist opposition did to challenge it, proving that "the cult of domestic, feminine values may be militarist as well as pacifist."[28]

Yet, even as it enabled female activism, militarized maternalism discouraged any potentially feminist activism. The emphasis on home protection through patriotic motherhood tightly circumscribed the kind of political roles female activists (in and out of the FCDA) could assume, making their place tenuous and conditional in a national security mobilization that valorized masculine toughness. Furthermore, their support for civil defense represented an endorsement of the Cold War's most conservative and toxic manifestations. At no point did they ponder the excesses of domestic anti-communism that preparedness encouraged. Most importantly, though their attempt to make nuclear weapons familiar by making them *familial* pried open a space for women in the national security state, it also aided strategists in their domestication of nuclear weapons. This troubling disassociation of the ultimate weapon of mass destruction from war and militarism has outlasted the Cold War itself.

NOTES

1. Katherine Howard, transcript of "Women as Atomic Age Citizens," *Negro Women* 20 (August 1953), Katherine Graham Howard Papers (hereafter cited as KGH Papers), Box 13, Dwight D. Eisenhower Library, Abilene, Kansas (hereafter cited as DDEL).

2. Transcript of recorded statement of President Eisenhower opening National Civil Defense Week, 9 September 1956, Files of Special Assistant Relating to Office of Coordinator of Government Public Service Advertising, James M. Lambie Jr. Records, Box 27, DDEL.

3. Katherine Howard, untitled speech, n.d., KGH Papers, Box 6, DDEL.

4. Katherine Howard, "Home of the Brave," speech presented to the National Amvets Auxiliary, 3 September 1953, Indianapolis, Indiana, KGH Papers, Box 1, DDEL.

5. Michael Sherry, *In the Shadow of War: The United States Since the 1930s* (New Haven, 1995), ix–xii; H. W. Brands, "The Age of Vulnerability: Eisenhower and the National Insecurity State," *American Historical Review* 94 (October 1989): 963–989.

6. Sherry, *In the Shadow of War*, ix–xii and Prologue; John R. Gillis, ed., *The Militarization of the Western World* (New Brunswick, N.J., 1989); Cynthia Enloe, *Does Khaki Become You? The Militarisation of Women's Lives* (London, 1983), 6–10.

7. Robert Miller, "The War That Never Came: Civilian Defense, Mobilization, and Morale During World War Two" (Ph.D. diss., University of Cincinnati, 1991).

8. Eleanor Roosevelt's civil defense activities and controversies are documented in Miller, chap. 2.

9. Congressman Chet Holifield quoted in the *Washington Post*, 21 May 1950.

10. William Gill to Paul Larsen, 29 June 1950, National Security Resources Board, Records of the Office of Civil and Defense Mobilization (hereafter cited as NSRB/OCDM), RG 304, Box 1, National Archives, Washington, D.C. (hereafter cited as NA).

11. *Washington Post*, 15 July 1950.

12. Harry Truman to Stuart Symington, 9 September 1950; handwritten note by Martha Sharp, n.d., in Office of Defense Mobilization, NSRB, Office File of Martha Sharp, RG 304 (hereafter cited as Sharp Office File), Box 39, NA.

13. Martha Sharp, "Women and Civil Defense," speech presented to the Women and Civil Defense Conference, 4 October 1950, Washington, D.C., Sharp Office File, Box 32, NA.

14. *Washington Post*, 15 July 1950.

15. Radio transcript, "Handbook for Life: Atomic Bomb Do's and Don'ts, Part 3," Mutual Broadcasting System, Inc., p. 5, 11 November 1950, Sharp Office File, Box 34, NA.

16. Katherine Howard, speech presented to the New England Conference of Federated Women's Clubs, 17 September 1950, Bretton Woods, New Hampshire, KGH Papers, Box 4, DDEL.

17. Nancy Cott, "Feminist Theory and Feminist Movements: The Past Before Us," in *What Is Feminism? A Re-Examination*, eds. Juliet Mitchell and Ann Oakley (New York, 1986), 49–62.

18. "Civil Defense News for Women," vol. 1, no. 3, July 1953, Defense Civil Preparedness Agency, Office of Civil Defense, Publication Office, Publication History Files, 1950–1962, RG 397, Box 4, NA.

19. FCDA, *Survival Under Atomic Attack* (Washington, D.C., 1950); FCDA, *Firefighting for Householders* (Washington, D.C., 1951); Katherine Howard, "Civil Defense at Home and Abroad," speech presented to the Massachusetts Society of Colonial Dames of America, 31 March 1955, Boston, Massachusetts, KGH Papers, Box 5, DDEL.

20. Radio script, United Press Service, 6 April 1954, KGH Papers, Box 9, DDEL.

21. *New York Times*, 28 February 1951.

22. Sharp, "Women and Civil Defense."

23. *Los Angeles Times*, 6 May 1955.

24. FCDA, *Women in Civil Defense* (Washington, D.C., 1952).

25. Katherine Howard, "Civil Defense Progress," *Armed Forces Chemical Journal* (May–June 1954), KGH Papers, Box 13, DDEL.

26. Dee Garrison, "'Our Skirts Gave Them Courage': The Civil Defense Protest Movement in New York City, 1955–1961," in *Not June Cleaver: Women and Gender in Postwar America, 1945–1960*, ed. Joanne Meyerowitz (Philadelphia, 1994), 201–226.

27. Minutes of Cabinet Meeting, 29 July 1955, Dwight Eisenhower Papers as President, Ann Whitman File, Box 5, DDEL.

28. Joanne Meyerowitz, "Beyond the Feminine Mystique: A Reassessment of Postwar Mass Culture, 1946–1958," *Journal of American History* 79 (March 1993): 1455–1482; Margaret R. Higonnet and Patrice L.-R. Higonnet, "The Double Helix," in *Behind the Lines: Gender and the Two World Wars*, ed. Margaret Randolph Higonnet et al. (New Haven, 1987), 44.

ESTELLE FREEDMAN
Miriam Van Waters
and the Burning of Letters

Miriam Van Waters belonged to that elite group of women reformers that included Florence Kelley and Eleanor Roosevelt. She was also part of a transitional generation, having grown up in an era when many educated women seeking public careers rejected marriage and family for a woman-centered existence. The female networks they created enhanced their public as well as private lives, providing professional mentors and allies and personal relationships that were supportive and intimate. Even if the intimacy extended to sexual expression, couples often lived together for extended periods attracting little comment. Prior to the 1920s, many people simply assumed that these were the intense female friendships described in Carroll Smith-Rosenberg's essay "The Female World of Love and Ritual" (part II). Tolerance lessened markedly, however, with the pathologizing of homosexuality in the 1920s.

As Estelle Freedman makes clear, Miriam Van Waters was very much aware of the new construction of lesbianism as deviant behavior. As the head of a women's correctional institution and a leading reformer in her field, she was also highly informed about the increasing attention to prison lesbianism. How she understood her own sexuality is the subject of this sensitive and perceptive essay.

Van Waters's problems were compounded by the fact that as a penal administrator, she was on the public payroll during the heyday of domestic containment. In Cold War America, lesbianism, like unwed motherhood, represented the dangers of female sexuality and intolerable deviations from the family norm. Used since the 1920s to label and stigmatize nonconforming women, especially feminists, "lesbian" in the 1950s came to signify an aggressive deviance that verged on criminality.

Why did Van Waters resist labeling her long-term romantic partnership with Geraldine Thompson as a lesbian relationship? In what sense was class a factor?

On a clear June morning in 1948, the controversial prison reformer Miriam Van Waters made a painful and momentous decision. For months she had been embroiled in a political struggle with conservative state officials who wished to dismiss her as the liberal superintendent of the Massachusetts Reformatory for Women. Local newspapers headlined the claims that Van Waters coddled prisoners, hired ex-inmates, and condoned homosexual behavior in prison. Investigators from the Department of Corrections interrogated her staff and seized inmate files as evidence.

As she sat before a glowing fireplace in her home that June morning, Miriam Van Waters fueled the blaze with some of her most precious possessions. "The Burning of Letters continues," she wrote in her journal that day. "One can have no personal 'life' in this battle, so I have destroyed many letters of over 22 years." Van Waters had met her patron and romantic partner, Geraldine Thompson, twenty-two

From "The Burning of Letters Continues" by Estelle Freedman in *Journal of Women's History*, 9.4. Reprinted by permission of the author and Indiana University Press. Notes have been renumbered and edited.

years earlier. Since the late 1920s they had corresponded almost daily, sharing their thoughts, their activities, and their love during the weeks between their regular visits with one another. All but a few of the daily letters Thompson had addressed to her "Old Sweet," her "Dearest Dearest Love," went up in flames that day. As she burned the letters, Van Waters recorded her sense of loss: "They might have been inspiration, history, joy, style—to me in 'old age.'" Instead, she resolved to keep their message within herself. "The letters are bone and sinew now in my carnage. Doubtless my character has been formed by them."[1] . . .

[To understand] Van Waters's conscious effort to conceal her relationship with Thompson, [we need to understand how Van Waters understood her own sexuality. Did she identify herself as lesbian? What would she have known about same-sex relationships?] . . .

In the early twentieth century, highly-educated women such as Miriam Van Waters might be exposed to published literature that clearly named both male and female homosexuality. Only a generation earlier, even romantic female friends and women who passed as men perceived their experiences within frameworks largely devoid of sexual references. The "female world of love and ritual" mapped by historian Carroll Smith-Rosenberg allowed same-sex attractions to "pass" as sexually innocent, whether they were or not. Beginning in the late nineteenth century, a modern conception of homosexuality emerged, articulated first as a form of gender inversion and later as an expression of erotic desire.[2] Gradually an explicitly sexual language characterized the literature on same-sex relationships. Helen Horowitz' insightful interpretation of M. Carey Thomas provides a good example of the transition. In the 1870s, Thomas' reading of romantic and pre-Raphaelite poets afforded her an initial and asexual framework for understanding passion between women; after the 1890s, however, the Oscar Wilde trial and the availability of works by sexologists such as Richard von Krafft-Ebing allowed Thomas to name sexual acts between women as well. . . .

As a graduate student at Clark University between 1910 and 1913, Van Waters easily discovered the scholarly literature on sexuality. She read Havelock Ellis, Krafft-Ebing, and some Sigmund Freud, as well as the work of her advisor, psychologist G. Stanley Hall. Her own writing recognized the power of sexuality and stressed the importance of sex education and the strategy of channeling youthful energies into recreation and social service. She also became curious about gender identity and same-sex relationships, as a questionnaire she designed reveals. The survey of adolescent girls asked, for example, "did you wish to be a boy?" and was your first "love for some one you knew closely, or for some distant person . . . or for some older woman or girl friend?" A separate questionnaire for teachers asked if "crushes" between girls were "based on mutuality of interest and inclination; or are they more likely to exist between 'masculine,' and excessively 'feminine' types?"[3] The questions suggest Van Waters' interest in whether same-sex attractions correlated with gender identity, an inquiry prompted in part by Ellis' notion of sexual inversion, which associated "mannish" women with lesbianism.

Although Van Waters never conducted this survey, her intellectual curiosity about gender nonconformity and its relationship to homosexuality recurred in her doctoral dissertation, "The Adolescent Girl among Primitive People." At this time she consciously rejected Freudian interpretations of sexuality and adopted Ellis' language of inversion—albeit without the pathological notions of deviant sexuality. Her views also reflected the cultural relativism of Franz Boas. After describing institutionalized gender-crossing among North American Indians, for example, Van Waters concluded that "among primitive peoples, a useful and appropriate life-role is commonly furnished the inverted individual. . . . It is quite possible that modern policy could profitably go to school to the primitive in this regard."[4] Similarly, in an appendix on contemporary American approaches to adolescent delinquents, Van Waters analyzed the case of a cross-dressing young woman accused of being a "white slaver" because she brought girls to her rooms at night. Reluctant to label the girl a "true homosexual," she reported that "it is impossible for her to earn an honest and adequate living while dressed as a woman," and claimed that sympathy for women of the underworld rather than sexual proclivities accounted for her behavior.[5]

During her subsequent career working in juvenile and adult female reformatories, Van Waters retained a liberal tolerance for homosexuality, even as she increasingly incorporated Freudian views of sexual psychopathology. When she discussed the management of "'crushes' and sentimental attachment" among reformatory inmates in her 1925 book, *Youth in Conflict,* she advised that a trained social worker could draw out the girl and replace unhealthy attachments with healthy ones through a beneficial "transference." A harsher passage reflected conservative medical views of sex and gender when she labeled as the most perverse juvenile case she had encountered a narcissistic girl whose "emotional life will be self-centered or flow toward those of her own sex," and who would "never wish to live the biologically normal life."[6]

Despite these published critiques of unhealthy homosexual attachments, as superintendent of the Framingham, Massachusetts, reformatory for women from 1932 to 1957, Miriam Van Waters consistently resisted the labeling of prison relationships as homosexual. Her liberal administration emphasized education, social welfare services, psychiatric counseling, and work opportunities outside prison for the three to four hundred women inmates, the large majority of whom were young, white, Catholic, and working-class. Although the criminological literature then identified black women in prison as the aggressors in interracial sexual relationships, Van Waters and her staff did not draw a racial line around prison homosexuality. Rather, they tried to distinguish between "true homosexuality" and temporary attractions. They believed the former could be detected by the Rorschach test; in the absence of such "positive evidence" they assumed that only the boredom of prison routine stimulated "unnatural" interest in same-sex relationships. Thus an active program of classes and clubs attempted to channel the energies of both black and white prisoners into what the staff considered healthier recreations. Even when staff discovered two women in bed together—of any racial combination—they hesitated to label them as homosexual.

Van Waters' tolerance of prison homosexual liaisons contributed to the conservative assault on her administration in the 1940s. In 1949, when the Commissioner of Corrections dismissed Van Waters from office, he charged:

That you have known of and failed to prevent the continuance of, or failed to know and recognize that an unwholesome relationship has existed between inmates of the Reformatory for Women which is called the "doll racket" by inmates and some officer personnel; the terms "stud" and "queen" are used with implied meanings, and such association has resulted in "crushes", "courtships", and homosexual practises [*sic*] among the inmates in the Reformatory.[7]

During several months of public hearings, Van Waters successfully defended her policies, in part by minimizing the existence of homosexuality at the reformatory, in part by deferring to psychiatric authorities when asked about homosexual tendencies among inmates. Typical of her strategic evasion was this response to hostile interrogation about whether certain acts or personal styles revealed homosexual tendencies:

That, sir, is so distinctly a medical and technical question that I would not presume to answer it. One of the first things we are taught is that a homosexual tendency must be distinguished from a homosexual act. A homosexual tendency may be completely repressed and turned into a variety of other expressions, including a great aversion to emotion.[8]

By invoking the power of psychiatry, Van Waters acknowledged the shifting meaning of homosexuality—from an act to an identity. At the same time, she tried to avoid a labeling process that would mark close friends, mannish women, and those who had crushes on other inmates as confirmed homosexuals, a category she reserved for a treatable psychopathological condition that posed problems only when characterized by aggressive sexual behaviors.

Whether consciously or not, Van Waters' testimony represented a form of resistance to the use of accusations of homosexuality to discredit nonconforming women. Rather than sacrifice some "mannish" women or close female friends by calling them either "homosexuals," "latent homosexuals," or "women with homosexual tendencies," she firmly opposed labeling. At the same time, like psychologists of the period, she did so by accepting a definition of true homosexuality as pathology. In the 1950s, partly in response to her reading of the Kinsey Reports, and partly in the wake of the accusations about prison lesbianism during her dismissal hearings, Van Waters' public lectures urged greater tolerance. Homosexuality, she explained, could be "found in all levels of society," in all types of people. Her emphasis, however, was on treatment. Once revealed through use of the Rorschach test, she believed, homosexual tendencies could be reversed with the aid of psychiatry.[9]

In short, for Miriam Van Waters, lesbianism was a curable social problem not unlike alcoholism. Although she initially encountered lesbianism among working-class, immigrant, and black reformatory inmates, she recognized that it occurred within other groups, as well. Rather than emphasizing a heterosexual solution, Van Waters placed great faith in "healthy" female bonding as an alternative to lesbianism. In this sense, whether or not she had internalized modern medical categories, she strategically invoked an earlier discourse of sexually innocent and nurturing female friendships as a corrective to the increasing stigmatization of women's love for women as a form of perversion.

When Superintendent Van Waters evaded the labeling of homosexuality during her dismissal hearings, she also sidestepped implicit questions about her own sexual identity. In her personal life, Van Waters had refused to label her love for a woman as a form of homosexuality, despite her long-term romantic partnership with Geraldine Thompson, a New Jersey philanthropist who was known publicly only as a wealthy benefactor and a supporter of Van Waters' reforms. So, too, she hesitated to assume that other women who appeared to fit the medical definition really were homosexuals, a term she reserved for women's pathological, though curable, sexual aggression toward other women.[10]

What of her internal consciousness of her own sexuality? The private story of Miriam Van Waters' own relationships with women both parallels and contradicts her public pronouncements. Beginning in adolescence, she fell deeply in love with other women and, for the most part, preferred their company to the attentions of male suitors. Never a sexual prude, Van Waters recognized the importance of the erotic, especially within the poetry and fiction she wrote in her late twenties. But she also placed great stock in the power of sublimation for harnessing erotic energy into expression as art, spirituality, or public service. Thus, upon reading Radclyffe Hall's *The*

Well of Loneliness in 1929, Van Waters commented in her journal that had Stephen Gordon's parents been more loving, instead of becoming a lesbian Gordon might have "run a girls camp," become a high school counselor, or supervised a juvenile protective agency, all activities remarkably similar to those Van Waters chose.[11]

The detailed introspective journals Van Waters kept as an adult provide further clues about her subjective experience of sexuality, despite the frequently coded and intentionally obscure nature of her writing. Tantalizing passages in Van Waters' journals made little sense to me until late into my research, when I gained access to a cache of personal papers that had not been deposited in the archives. Literally locked away within a rusting trunk and forgotten in an attic, that cache included passionate letters from two of Van Waters' ardent admirers: one set from Hans Weiss, a young Swiss social worker who wished to marry Van Waters; the other, a year's worth of daily letters from Geraldine Thompson, the older, wealthy, married philanthropist whose subsequent correspondence Van Waters burned in 1948. Working with both the journals and the "courtship letters," as I called them, I learned how Van Waters struggled to balance the erotic, the emotional, and the spiritual in each of these relationships.

Despite significant differences between the Weiss and Thompson correspondence—his letters were more erotic, hers more spiritual; he was more emotionally demanding, she longed to be of service to her beloved—I was struck by the consistency in Van Waters' response to her male and female suitors. In each case, she remained publicly silent, restrained in her responses to passion, and conflicted about making any lifelong commitment. The two relationships did present separate challenges to Van Waters' sexuality. The younger, less established Weiss frequently articulated his erotic longings; in response, Van Waters struggled to incorporate physical passion while subsuming it to her ideal of a spiritualized romantic friendship. The older, wealthier, and more powerful Thompson longed for "the Justice of the Peace and church bells" to signify their commitment; in response, Van Waters feared the dependency that could result from their union.[12]

In both cases, the management of passion was a recurrent theme for Miriam Van Waters.

Although her journals were characteristically obscure about sexual experiences, one passage written after a visit with Weiss alluded to an unidentified young "Beloved" with whom she had experienced both a spiritual epiphany and a "yielding to love." In one entry, she recalled a candlelit scene in which her "hands were flung up by a strong clasp of young hands on my wrists—and with another soul—I plunged down a glittering waterfall immeasurably high, and sunk at last—into a pool—where two floated in weariness and content."[13] More typical, however, was her insistence on limiting their intimacy. "As a lover I yield to no one in sustained worship," she wrote in her journal. To Weiss she explained that their spiritual union transcended the need for physical proximity, suggesting that unrequited love could yield the "deepest spiritual gain."[14] By 1930, she had successfully encouraged Weiss to wed someone else; she had already informed him of another, unnamed attraction.

The Thompson courtship, begun during the late 1920s, overlapped with the waning of Van Waters' intimacy with Weiss. Both women valued romantic and spiritual intimacy, and neither wrote explicitly about their sexual experiences. Yet Van Waters left hints about her consciousness of lesbianism and her continuing management of erotic impulses. In 1930, she read an article about Katherine B. Davis' 1929 study of female sexuality, which found that a quarter of unmarried women college graduates acknowledged a sexual component within their intense emotional relationships with other women. Van Waters starred the point that these were normal, not pathological, women, as if to differentiate her experience from the perversions she had earlier identified among juvenile delinquents. As in her relationship with Weiss, however, Van Waters continued to place limits on erotic expression. Thus when Thompson expressed a desire "to 'catch your soul's breath' in kisses," Van Waters questioned the impulse in her journal: "What one calls appetite—satisfaction of warmth needs—hunger needs—is not just that.... In maturity some times in some circumstances—to feed hunger fully—is to lose hunger. There are other ways of quenching the fire—and all must be escaped." Professionally she had recommended channeling youthful sexual energies, whether heterosexual or homosexual. But her personal ideal suggested

not simply sublimation but rather that desire could be maintained best by leaving it largely unfulfilled. While staying at Thompson's home, she again alluded to the value of control: "The secret of life is manifested in hunger—it can't safely be quenched—neither by denial, nor complete feeding, nor running away, nor escape—but by a new way."[15]

Whether or not she discovered this "new way" of managing desire, by the time she and Thompson pledged their love at the end of 1930, Van Waters recognized that she had crossed some line. "The object which arouses love—cannot be foreseen or controlled," she wrote in her journal. "All we know is—that same force which engulfs us, and makes us ready for service to husband and children—some times—to some persons—flows out to a man, woman, child, animal, 'cause,' idea." Van Waters did not, however, acknowledge her love publicly nor claim a lesbian identity. When Geraldine longed to "shout about" their love so that her family would "know what life through you is giving me," Miriam counseled discretion.[16] Similarly, when an acquaintance who lived openly with another woman later asked Van Waters in public about the ring she wore—a gift from Thompson—Van Waters seethed at the impudence of this inquiry into her private life. Perhaps her status as a civil service employee, and as the guardian and later adoptive mother of a child, made Van Waters more cautious than her independently wealthy partner, Thompson. Equally likely, Van Waters struggled to reconcile her passion with the psychological construction of lesbianism she had already formed.

Another cryptic journal entry suggests how powerfully that psychological construction influenced her. In a dream, she wrote, she had enjoyed a feeling of "Understanding" that derived in part from "the recent Rorshak [sic] and integration." Van Waters used the Rorschach test to detect "innate homosexuality" among inmates; in 1938, a trusted friend administered the test to her and the results made Van Waters feel confident and optimistic. One line in this passage was crossed out heavily in pencil, especially over someone's name, but the entry continued, "Geraldine and I shall learn together."[17] In my reading, the Rorschach test proved to Van Waters that she was not an innate homosexual, thus freeing her of the deviant label and, ironically, granting her permission to integrate her love for Thompson, without adopting a lesbian identity.

Why, then, the burning of letters? Even if Van Waters did not consider herself a lesbian, the world around her was not as thoroughly convinced. Although her close associates insisted to me that the relationship was much too spiritual to have been homosexual, Van Waters' partnership with Geraldine Thompson made her increasingly vulnerable to the insinuations of her political opponents.

In the conformist atmosphere after World War II, accusations of Communism, often conflated with homosexuality, fueled an attack on liberalism. Thus, in 1948, claims that Van Waters tolerated homosexuality at the Massachusetts women's reformatory facilitated her dismissal from office. Aside from the widely publicized claims about the "doll racket" among inmates, rumors about Van Waters' sexuality circulated underground, though never in print. For example, Eleanor Roosevelt—a friend of Thompson and supporter of Van Waters—learned of the whispering campaign when she received several "vile" letters that were so disturbing that she destroyed most of them. Similarly, a hostile postcard sent to supporters referred to Van Waters as "supt. (or Chief Pervert)" of the reformatory.[18] It was at this time that Van Waters burned most of Thompson's correspondence, carefully locking away only that one year of "courtship" letters.

Despite the private insinuations that led her to burn Thompson's letters, Van Waters survived the attempt to fire her. The publicity surrounding prison lesbianism during her hearings, however, contributed to a national preoccupation with homosexuality and to the naming of lesbianism as a social threat. No matter how confident Van Waters may have been that she was not a lesbian, outside observers often assumed that she was. Late in my research, after years of waiting to receive Van Waters' FBI file, I found a 1954 document that seemed to place an official government seal upon Van Waters' identity. While carrying out surveillance on Helen Bryan, a suspected Communist sympathizer with whom Van Waters had a romantic friendship later in life, a local FBI informant read the correspondence between the two women. Shocked by the "unusual" nature of the letters, which contained "numerous repeated terms of endear-

ment and other statements," he came to "the definite opinion that Dr. van waters and bryan are Lesbians."[19] It was to prevent just such a conclusion from being drawn that Van Waters had earlier burned Thompson's letters.

That identity formation is often a social as much as an individual phenomenon is further revealed by a final anecdote from my research on Van Waters, a coda of sorts that brings the story into the 1990s. My book completed, I turned to the task of acquiring permission to quote from sources, including Geraldine Thompson's courtship letters. With trepidation I sent the permission form to Thompson's eldest surviving granddaughter, who soon called to discuss the request. Her initial words, "I will not grant permission," struck further terror in me, until I absorbed the completion of her sentence: "I will not grant permission to repeat any lies; I want the truth." Too much had been concealed in her family, she explained, too much smoothed over. By the end of our conversation, she had told me with confidence that her grandmother had been a lesbian and that she was sure that Thompson and Van Waters were lovers, for they had shared a bed during family vacations. "Do you know what we grandchildren called Miriam when she came to visit?" she asked. "Grammy Thompson's yum-yum." She gladly granted permission to quote when I seemed willing to reveal "the truth."[20] . . .

Van Waters came of age in a transitional moment, when the social possibilities for romantic and sexual love between women increased, but also while medical labeling pathologized these relationships. As an educated, professional woman, exposed to such sexologists as Ellis and Freud, she was both conscious of the erotic and aware of the psychopathic label then attached to same-sex relationships. At the same time, Van Waters was attracted to women; she was able to live outside of heterosexual institutions; and she could and did take advantage of the opportunity to establish a partnership with another woman, even as she fiercely resisted lesbian identification.

Perhaps the fear of losing her job, and her social standing, kept Van Waters from identifying as a lesbian. But her rejection of lesbianism as an identity was not merely self-serving, for she just as fiercely resisted the labeling of working-class prison inmates as lesbians, and during her dismissal hearings in 1949 she more or less placed her class and race privilege on the line to defend these women from such charges. In the end, it was Van Waters' privileges—combined with her distinguished career of service and her upper-class political connections—that protected her from public disgrace. The working-class women she tried to protect would forge their own public lesbian identity, one that equally rejected the pathological discourse of the early twentieth century.

. . . To contemporary feminists, who value our own historically constructed ideal of the openly lesbian sexual subject, Van Waters seems anything but progressive. Yet if we are serious about . . . recognizing women's historical agency, we have to be willing to accept it when beliefs, and possibly behaviors, go against the grain of a "progressive" narrative that embraces categories we have claimed for ourselves. And we must keep in mind that this narrative rests heavily upon a highly class- and race-specific lesbian identity constructed since the 1960s, one that depathologized white, middle-class women's love for women but simultaneously failed to recognize a range of other sources of identity. . . . [Ultimately] Miriam Van Waters' case suggests the ways that some women could simultaneously internalize, resist, manipulate, and ignore the cultural constructions of sexuality in their times. Above all, her story reminds us to look beyond our sources, to read both silences and speech, and, at times, to accept the historical integrity of elusive personal identities.

NOTES

1. Miriam Van Waters Journal (hereafter MVW Journal), 16 June 1948, 19 June 1948, and 22 June 1948, file 220v, Anne Gladding-Miriam Van Waters Papers, Schlesinger Library, Radcliffe College (hereafter Gladding-MVW Papers). A handful of surviving letters were scattered through Van Waters' correspondence in the papers she donated to the Schlesinger Library. Miriam Van Waters Papers, For a full account of her life, see Estelle B. Freedman, *Maternal Justice: Miriam Van Waters and the Female Reform Tradition* (Chicago: University of Chicago Press, 1996).

2. MVW to parents, 10 October 1911, file 42 (misdated, probably 9 October 1911), MVW Papers; MVW, "Topical Syllabus No. 44 (A) and No. 44 (B) [for teachers], Psychology of Adolescence," 15 November 1911, Box 37, file 464, G. Stanley Hall Papers, Clark University, Worcester, Massachusetts.

3. MVW, "The Adolescent Girl among Primitive People," *Journal of Religious Psychology* 6, no. 4

(1913): 375–421, and 7, no. 1 (1914): 75–120 (esp. pt. 1, 377–78 and pt. 2, 102–5). Her advisor, Alexander Chamberlain, had been Franz Boas' first doctoral student at Clark.

4. MVW, "Adolescent Girl," pt. 2, 108–12.

5. MVW, *Youth in Conflict* (New York: New Republic, 1925), 35–36.

6. McDowell to MVW, 7 January 1949, file 201, MVW Papers.

7. John O'Connor, "Van Waters Rejects Inmate Sex Charge," *Boston Herald,* 1 January 1949, 1.

8. MVW, Boston University lecture transcript, 24 October 1951 (in possession of author).

9. Rumors about Van Waters' sexuality are discussed in MVW to Ethel Sturges Dummer, 26 September 1948, file 825, Ethel Sturges Dummer Papers, Schlesinger Library, Radcliffe College; and in letters from a former inmate to MVW, 1 June 1948, file 195, and from Harry R. Archbald to MVW, 7 February 1949, file 203, both in MVW Papers. For a full discussion of Van Waters' interpretation of lesbian identity and the political response to rumors of her own homosexuality, see Freedman, *Maternal Justice,* esp. chaps. 9, 12, 14, and 15.

10. MVW Journal, 30 March 1929, file 208, Gladding-MVW Papers. MVW's phrasing suggests an ambivalence about the experience of marriage and reproductive, as opposed to social, motherhood: Gordon, she wrote might have been "anything—everything in fact but a stupid wife and mother—Wife she co[uld] have been and mother too."

11. See, for example, Geraldine Thompson (GT) to MVW, 31 October 1930, 4 November 1930, and 14 November 1930, file 261, Gladding-MVW Papers.

12. MVW Journal, 28 June 1928, file 206, Gladding-MVW Papers; compare Hans Weiss' (HW) sweet memory of "what you did for me when you had the tremendous courage of giving yourself to me." HW to MVW, 24 July 1930, file 279, Gladding-MVW Papers.

13. MVW Journal, 19 February 1928, 14 June 1928, file 206, and 23 November 1928, file 208; HW to MVW, 7 August 1930, file 280, all in Gladding-MVW Papers. For complex reasons, Van Waters refused to consider marrying Weiss. Aside from the emotional distance she kept, the formal obstacle to their marriage was his "tremendous longing for a home and for children." He accepted "the cruel reality" that he could not have this with her, for like many professional women, she had chosen career over marriage. Although some women reformers did try to combine the two, having a job and children would be too physically taxing for her and, given her history of tuberculosis, possibly life-threatening. HW to MVW, 19 January 1929, file 276, Gladding-MVW Papers.

14. MVW to Edna Mahan, 20 July 1930, file 253, Gladding-MVW Papers; and Katherine B. Davis, *Factors in the Sex Life of Twenty-Two Hundred Women* (New York: Harper and Row, 1929), 312, 295, 280. The data showed that 28 percent of the women's college graduates and 20 percent of those from coeducational schools recognized sexual components in their relations; in addition, almost equal numbers had enjoyed intense emotional attachments that involved kissing and hugging.

15. GT to MVW, 31 October 1930, file 261, 10 November and 6 November 1930, file 262, all in Gladding-MVW Papers; MVW Journal, 27 September 1930, and 11 June 1931, file 211, Gladding-MVW Papers.

16. MVW Journal, 27 September 1930, and GT to MVW, 13 November 1930, file 262, both in Gladding-MVW Papers.

17. On Rorschach, see, for example, Inmate record, 21 February 1949, file 251, MVW Journal, 11 June 1938, 213v, Gladding-MVW Papers; MVW Journal, vol. 5, 26 June 1938, MVW Papers.

18. Eleanor Roosevelt (ER) letter, 19 December 1948, file 200; GT to Dorothy Kirchwey Brown, 4 January 1949, file 201; ER to GT, n.d., in response to an enclosed letter from GT dated 5 January 1949, all in Box 3820, ER Papers. ER to GT, 13 January 1949, file 8, Friends of Framingham Papers (hereafter FOF Papers), Schlesinger Library, Cambridge, Massachusetts; Miriam Clark Nichols to ER, 18 January 1949, file 8, FOF Papers (the letter was reprinted in The Civil Service Reporter [8 February 1949]: 5); George Hooper to Friends of Framingham, 1 January 1949, file 8, FOF Papers.

19. SAC, Boston (100-15782) to Director, FBI (100-206852), "Office Memorandum," Re: Helen Reid Bryan, 20 January 1954, declassified 12 April 1994 pursuant to Freedom of Information Act Request (emphasis in original).

20. Telephone interview with Geraldine Boone, 17 February 1995; and Boone to author, 6 March 1995.

SUSAN K. CAHN

"Mannishness," Lesbianism, and Homophobia in U.S. Women's Sports

Miriam Van Waters, like many white middle-class women who loved other women, chose not to acknowledge her lesbianism. To do so would have meant acknowledging an affiliation with working-class lesbians. Their butch-femme roles and bar culture, like the aggressive prison lesbian, had been so thoroughly pathologized in the 1950s as to seem quite alien to women of a different class and culture. Others made a different choice. Some even tried to organize to gain rights, only to discover subsequently that the Daughters of Bilitis had been infiltrated with informants who were supplying names to the FBI and CIA. In an era when sexual conformity was seen as essential to national security, it is hardly surprising that *all* women engaged in any same-sex activity were suspect. Women athletes were particularly vulnerable.

In the following article, Susan Cahn explores the suspicions and the reality behind those suspicions in women's athletics. Note the persistence of concerns about feminine sexuality, whether heterosexual or homosexual, throughout the history of women's sports. What measures did colleges and universities take to protect women's sports from charges of lesbianism? What was the price of such actions? Since those athletes who were lesbian could no more afford to proclaim their sexual identity publicly than Van Waters, why does Cahn argue that athletics nonetheless afforded them social and psychic space to affirm their identity and find community? Do you agree?

This article is reprinted from *Feminist Studies*, Volume 19, Number 2 (Summer 1993): 343–68, by permission of the publisher, Feminist Studies, Inc. Notes have been renumbered and edited.

In 1934, *Literary Digest* subtitled an article on women's sports, "Will the Playing Fields One Day Be Ruled by Amazons?" The author, Fred Wittner, answered the question affirmatively and concluded that as an "inevitable consequence" of sport's masculinizing effect, "girls trained in physical education to-day may find it more difficult to attract the most worthy fathers for their children."[1] The image of women athletes as mannish, failed heterosexuals represents a thinly veiled reference to lesbianism in sport. At times, the homosexual allusion has been indisputable, as in a journalist's description of the great athlete Babe Didrikson as a "Sapphic, Brobdingnagian woman" or in television comedian Arsenio Hall's more recent witticism, "If we can put a man on the moon, why can't we get one on Martina Navratilova?"[2] More frequently, however, popular commentary on lesbians in sport has taken the form of indirect references, surfacing through denials and refutations rather than open acknowledgment. When in 1955 an *Ebony* magazine article on African American track stars insisted that "off track, girls are entirely feminine. Most of them like boys, dances, club affairs," the reporter answered the implicit but unspoken charge that athletes, especially Black women in a "manly" sport, were masculine manhaters, or lesbians.[3]

The figure of the mannish lesbian athlete has acted as a powerful but unarticulated "bogey woman" of sport, forming a silent foil for more positive, corrective images that attempt to rehabilitate the image of women athletes and resolve the cultural contradiction between athletic prowess and femininity. As a stereotyped figure in U.S. society, the lesbian athlete forms part of everyday cultural knowledge. Yet historians have paid scant attention to the connection between female sexuality and sport.[4] This essay explores the historical relationship between lesbianism and sport by tracing the development of the stereotyped "mannish lesbian athlete" and examining its relation to the lived experience of mid-twentieth-century lesbian athletes.

I argue that fears of mannish female sexuality in sport initially centered on the prospect of unbridled heterosexual desire. By the 1930s, however, female athletic mannishness began to connote heterosexual failure, usually couched in terms of unattractiveness to men, but also suggesting the possible absence of heterosexual interest. In the years following World War II, the stereotype of the lesbian athlete emerged full blown. The extreme homophobia and the gender conservatism of the postwar era created a context in which longstanding linkages among mannishness, female homosexuality, and athletics cohered around the figure of the mannish lesbian athlete. Paradoxically, the association between masculinity, lesbianism, and sport had a positive outcome for some women. The very cultural matrix that produced the pejorative image also created possibilities for lesbian affirmation. Sport provided social and psychic space for some lesbians to validate themselves and to build a collective culture. Thus, the lesbian athlete was not only a figure of discourse but a living product of women's sexual struggle and cultural innovation.

The athletic woman sparked interest and controversy in the early decades of the twentieth century. In the United States and other Western societies, sport functioned as a male preserve, an all-male domain in which men not only played games together but also demonstrated and affirmed their manhood.[5] The "maleness" of sport derived from a gender ideology which labeled aggression, physicality, competitive spirit, and athletic skill as masculine attributes necessary for achieving true manliness. This notion found unquestioned support in the dualistic, polarized concepts of gender which prevailed in Victorian America. However, by the turn of the century, women had begun to challenge Victorian gender arrangements, breaking down barriers to female participation in previously male arenas of public work, politics, and urban nightlife. Some of these "New Women" sought entry into the world of athletics as well. On college campuses students enjoyed a wide range of intramural sports through newly formed Women's Athletic Associations. Off-campus women took up games like golf, tennis, basketball, swimming, and occasionally even wrestling, car racing, or boxing. As challengers to one of the defining arenas of manhood, skilled female athletes became symbols of the broader march of womanhood out of the Victorian domestic sphere into once prohibited male realms.

The woman athlete represented both the appealing and threatening aspects of modern womanhood. In a positive light, she captured the exuberant spirit, physical vigor, and brazenness of the New Woman. The University of Minnesota student newspaper proclaimed in 1904 that the athletic girl was the "truest type of All-American coed."[6] Several years later, *Harper's Bazaar* labeled the unsportive girl as "not strictly up to date," and *Good Housekeeping* noted that the "tomboy" had come to symbolize "a new type of American girl, new not only physically, but mentally and morally."[7]

Yet, women athletes invoked condemnation as often as praise. Critics ranged from physicians and physical educators to sportswriters, male athletic officials, and casual observers. In their view, strenuous athletic pursuits endangered women and threatened the stability of society. They maintained that women athletes would become manlike, adopting masculine dress, talk, and mannerisms. In addition, they contended, too much exercise would damage female reproductive capacity [interfering with menstruation and causing reproductive organs to harden or atrophy]. And worse yet, the excitement of sport would cause women to lose [sexual] control, . . . unleash[ing] nonprocreative, erotic desires identified with male sexuality and unrespectable women. . . . These fears collapsed into an all-encompassing concept of "mannishness," a term signifying female masculinity . . .

The public debate over the merits of women's athletic participation remained lively throughout the 1910s and 1920s. On all sides of the issue, however, the controversy about sports and female sexuality presumed heterosexuality. Neither critics nor supporters suggested that "masculine" athleticism might indicate or induce same-sex love. And when experts warned of the "amazonian" athlete's possible sexual transgressions, they linked the physical release of sport with a loss of hetero sexual *control*, not of *inclination*.

In the 1930s, however, the heterosexual understanding of the mannish "amazon" began to give way to a new interpretation which educators and promoters could not long ignore. To the familiar charge that female athletes resembled men, critics added the newer accusation that sport-induced mannishness disqualified them as candidates for heterosexual romance. In 1930, an *American Mercury* medical reporter decried the decline of romantic love, pinning the blame on women who

entered sport, business, and politics. He claimed that such women "act like men, talk like men, and think like men." The author explained that "women have come closer and closer to men's level," and, consequently, "the purple allure of distance has vamoosed."[8] . . . Although the charges didn't exclusively focus on athletes, they implied that female athleticism was contrary to heterosexual appeal, which appeared to rest on women's difference from and deference to men.

The concern with heterosexual appeal reflected broader sexual transformations in U.S. society. Historians of sexuality have examined the multiple forces which reshaped gender and sexual relations in the first few decades of the twentieth century. Victorian sexual codes crumbled under pressure from an assertive, boldly sexual working-class youth culture, a women's movement which defied prohibitions against public female activism, and the growth of a new pleasure-oriented consumer economy. In the wake of these changes, modern ideals of womanhood embraced an overtly erotic heterosexual sensibility. At the same time, medical fascination with sexual "deviance" created a growing awareness of lesbianism, now understood as a form of congenital or psychological pathology. The medicalization of homosexuality in combination with an antifeminist backlash in the 1920s against female autonomy and power contributed to a more fully articulated taboo against lesbianism. The modern heterosexual woman stood in stark opposition to her threatening sexual counterpart, the "mannish" lesbian.[9]

By the late 1920s and early 1930s, with a modern lesbian taboo and an eroticized definition of heterosexual femininity in place, the assertive, muscular female competitor roused increasing suspicion. It was at this moment that both subtle and direct references to the lesbian athlete emerged in physical education and popular sport. Uncensored discussions of intimate female companionship and harmless athletic "crushes" disappear from the record, pushed underground by the increasingly hostile tone of public discourse about female sexuality and athleticism. Fueled by the gender antagonisms and anxieties of the Depression, the public began scrutinizing women athletes—known for their appropriation of masculine games and styles—for signs of deviance.

Where earlier references to "amazons" had signaled heterosexual ardor, journalists now used the term to mean unattractive, failed heterosexuals. Occasionally, the media made direct mention of athletes' presumed lesbian tendencies. A 1933 *Redbook* article, for example, casually mentioned that track and golf star Babe Didrikson liked men just to horse around with her and not "make love," adding that Babe's fondness for her best girlfriends far surpassed her affection for any man.[10] The direct reference was unusual; the lesbian connotation of mannishness was forged primarily through indirect links of association. . . .

Tentatively voiced in the 1930s, these accusations became harsher and more explicit under the impact of wartime changes in gender and sexuality and the subsequent panic over the "homosexual menace." In a post-World War II climate markedly hostile to nontraditional women and lesbians, women in physical education and in working-class popular sports became convenient targets of homophobic indictment.

World War II opened up significant economic and social possibilities for gay men and women. Embryonic prewar homosexual subcultures blossomed during the war and spread across the midcentury urban landscape. Bars, nightclubs, public cruising spots, and informal social networks facilitated the development of gay and lesbian enclaves. But the permissive atmosphere did not survive the war's end. Waving the banner of Cold War political and social conservatism, government leaders acted at the federal, state, and local levels to purge gays and lesbians from government and military posts, to initiate legal investigations and prosecutions of gay individuals and institutions, and to encourage local police crackdowns on gay bars and street life. The perceived need to safeguard national security and to reestablish social order in the wake of wartime disruption sparked a "homosexual panic" which promoted the fear, loathing, and persecution of homosexuals.[11]

Lesbians suffered condemnation for their violation of gender as well as sexual codes. The tremendous emphasis on family, domesticity, and "traditional" femininity in the late 1940s and 1950s reflected postwar anxieties about the reconsolidation of a gender order shaken by two decades of depression and

war. As symbols of women's refusal to conform, lesbians endured intense scrutiny by experts who regularly focused on their subjects' presumed masculinity. Sexologists attributed lesbianism to masculine tendencies and freedoms encouraged by the war, linking it to a general collapsing of gender distinctions which, in their view, destabilized marital and family relations.[12]

Lesbians remained shadowy figures to most Americans, but women athletes—noted for their masculine bodies, interests, and attributes—were visible representatives of the gender inversion often associated with homosexuality. Physical education majors, formerly accused of being unappealing to men, were increasingly charged with being uninterested in them as well. The 1952 University of Minnesota yearbook snidely reported: "Believe it or not, members of the Women's Athletic Association are normal" and found conclusive evidence in the fact that "at least one . . . of WAA's 300 members is engaged."[13]

The lesbian stigma began to plague popular athletics too. . . . The career of Babe Didrikson, which spanned the 1920s to the 1950s, illustrates the shift. In the early 1930s the press had ridiculed the tomboyish track star for her "hatchet face," "door-stop jaw," and "button-breasted" chest. After quitting track, Didrikson dropped out of the national limelight, married professional wrestler George Zaharias in 1938, and then staged a spectacular athletic comeback as a golfer in the late 1940s and 1950s. Fascinated by her personal transformation and then, in the 1950s, moved by her battle with cancer, journalists gave Didrikson's comeback extensive coverage and helped make her a much-loved popular figure. In reflecting on her success, however, sportswriters spent at least as much time on Didrikson's love life as her golf stroke. Headlines blared, "Babe Is a Lady Now: The World's Most Amazing Athlete Has Learned to Wear Nylons and Cook for Her Huge Husband," and reporters gleefully described how "along came a great big he-man wrestler and the Babe forgot all her man-hating chatter."[14] . . . The challenge for women athletes was not to conquer new athletic feats, which would only further reduce their sexual appeal, but to regain their womanhood through sexual surrender to men.

Media coverage in national magazines and metropolitan newspapers typically focused on the sexual accomplishments of white female athletes, but postwar observers and promoters of African American women's sport also confronted the issue of sexual normalcy. In earlier decades, strong local support for women's sport within Black communities and the racist gender ideologies that prevailed outside Black communities may have weakened the association between African American women athletes and "mannish" lesbianism. Historically, European American racial thought characterized African American women as aggressive, coarse, passionate, and physical—the same qualities assigned to manliness and sport.[15] Excluded from dominant ideals of womanhood, Black women's success in sport could therefore be interpreted not as an unnatural sexual deviation but, rather, as the natural result of their reputed closeness to nature, animals, and masculinity.[16] . . . Moreover, stereotypes of Black females as highly sexual, promiscuous, and unrestrained in their heterosexual passions further discouraged the linkage between mannishness and lesbianism. . . .

Although Black athletes may initially have encountered few lesbian stereotypes . . . circumstances in the broader society eventually pressed African American sport promoters and journalists to address the issue of mannish sexuality. The strong postwar association of sports with lesbianism developed at the same time as Black athletes became a dominant presence in American sport culture. . . . Therefore, while there was no particular correlation between Black women and lesbianism, the association of each with mannishness and sexual aggression potentially linked the two. . . . In the late 1950s, Black sport promoters and journalists joined others in taking up the question of sexual "normalcy." One Black newspaper in 1957 described tennis star Althea Gibson as a childhood "tomboy" who "in later life . . . finds herself victimized by complexes."[17] The article did not elaborate on the nature of Gibson's "complex," but lesbianism is inferred in the linkage between "tomboys" and psychological illness. This connotation becomes clearer by looking at the defense of Black women's sport. Echoing *Ebony's* avowal that "entirely feminine" Black female track stars "like boys, dances, club affairs," in 1962 Tennessee State University track coach Ed Temple asserted, "None of my girls have any trouble getting boy friends. . . . We don't want amazons."[18]

Constant attempts to shore up the heterosexual reputation of athletes can be read as evidence that the longstanding reputation of female athletes as mannish women had become a covert reference to lesbianism. By midcentury, a fundamental reorientation of sexual meanings fused notions of femininity, female eroticism, and heterosexual attractiveness into a single ideal. Mannishness, once primarily a sign of gender crossing, assumed a specifically lesbian-sexual connotation. In the wake of this change, the strong cultural association between sport and masculinity made women's athletics ripe for emerging lesbian stereotypes. This meaning of athletic mannishness raises further questions. What impact did the stereotype have on women's sport? And was the image merely an erroneous stereotype, or did lesbians in fact form a significant presence in sport? . . .

The image of the mannish lesbian athlete had a direct effect on women competitors, on strategies of athletic organizations, and on the overall popularity of women's sport. The lesbian stereotype exerted pressure on athletes to demonstrate their femininity and heterosexuality, viewed as one and the same. Many women adopted an apologetic stance toward their athletic skill. Even as they competed to win, they made sure to display outward signs of femininity in dress and demeanor. They took special care in contact with the media to reveal "feminine" hobbies like cooking and sewing, to mention current boyfriends, and to discuss future marriage plans.[19]

Leaders of women's sport took the same approach at the institutional level. In answer to portrayals of physical education majors and teachers as social rejects and prudes, physical educators revised their philosophy to place heterosexuality at the center of professional objectives. . . . Curricular changes implemented between the mid-1930s and mid-1950s institutionalized the new philosophy. In a paper on postwar objectives, Mildred A. Schaeffer explained that physical education classes should help women "develop an interest in school dances and mixers and a desire to voluntarily attend them."[20] To this end, administrators revised coursework to emphasize beauty and social charm over rigorous exercise and health. They exchanged old rationales of fitness and fun for promises of trimmer waistlines, slimmer hips, and prettier complexions. . . . Some departments also added co-educational classes to foster "broader, keener, more sympathetic understanding of the opposite sex."[21] Department heads cracked down on "mannish" students and faculty, issuing warnings against "casual styles" which might "lead us back into some dangerous channels."[22] They implemented dress codes which forbade slacks and men's shirts or socks, adding as well a ban on "boyish hair cuts" and unshaven legs.[23]

Popular sport promoters adopted similar tactics. Martialing sexual data like they were athletic statistics, a 1954 AAU poll sought to sway a skeptical public with numerical proof of heterosexuality—the fact that 91 percent of former female athletes surveyed had married.[24] Publicity for the midwestern All-American Girls Baseball League included statistics on the number of married players. . . . Behind the scenes, teams passed dress and conduct codes. For example, the All-American Girls Baseball League prohibited players from wearing men's clothing or getting "severe" haircuts.[25] That this was an attempt to secure the heterosexual image of athletes was made even clearer when league officials announced that AAGBL policy prohibited the recruitment of "freaks" and "Amazons."[26]

In the end, the strategic emphasis on heterosexuality and the suppression of "mannishness" did little to alter the image of women in sport. The stereotype of the mannish lesbian athlete grew out of the persistent common-sense equation of sport with masculinity. Opponents of women's sport reinforced this belief when they denigrated women's athletic efforts and ridiculed skilled athletes as "grotesque," "mannish," or "unnatural." Leaders of women's sport unwittingly contributed to the same set of ideas when they began to orient their programs around the new feminine heterosexual idea. As physical education policies and media campaigns worked to suppress lesbianism and marginalize athletes who did not conform to dominant standards of femininity, sport officials embedded heterosexism into the institutional and ideological framework of sport. The effect extended beyond sport to the wider culture, where the figure of the mannish lesbian athlete announced that competitiveness, strength, independence, aggression, and physical intimacy among women fell outside the bounds of womanhood. As a symbol of female deviance, she served as a powerful reminder to all women to toe the line of heterosexuality and femininity or risk falling into a despised category of mannish (non-women) women. . . .

[But] was the mannish lesbian athlete merely a figure of homophobic imagination, or was there in fact a strong lesbian presence in sport? When the All-American Girls Baseball League adamantly specified, "*Always appear in feminine attire* . . . MASCULINE HAIR STYLING? SHOES? COATS? SHIRTS? SOCKS, T-SHIRTS ARE BARRED AT ALL TIMES," and when physical education departments threatened to expel students for overly masculine appearance, were administrators merely responding to external pressure?[27] Or were they cracking down on women who may have indeed enjoyed the feel and look of a tough swagger, a short haircut, and men's clothing? And if so, did mannishness among athletes correspond to lesbianism, as the stereotype suggested? In spite of the public stigmatization, [is it probable that] some women may have found the activities, attributes, and emotions of sport conducive to lesbian self-expression and community formation?

As part of a larger investigation of women's athletic experience, I conducted oral histories with women who played competitive amateur, semiprofessional, and professional sports between 1930 and 1970. The interviews included only six openly lesbian narrators and thirty-six other women who either declared their heterosexuality or left their identity unstated.[28] Although the sample is too small to stand as a representative study, the interviews . . . and scattered other sources indicate that sport, particularly softball, provided an important site for the development of lesbian subculture and identity in the United States.[29] Gay and straight informants alike confirmed the lesbian presence in popular sport and physical education. Their testimony suggests that from at least the 1940s on, sport provided space for lesbian activity and social networks and served as a path into lesbian culture for young lesbians coming out and searching for companions and community.

Lesbian athletes explained that sport had been integral to their search for sexual identity and lesbian companionship. Ann Maguire, a softball player, physical education major, and top amateur bowler from New England, recalled that as a teenager in the late 1950s,

> I had been trying to figure out who I was and couldn't put a name to it. I mean it was very—no gay groups, no literature, no characters on "Dynasty"—I mean there was just nothing at that time. And trying to put a name to it. . . . I went to a bowling tournament, met two women there [and] for some reason something clicked and it clicked in a way that I was not totally aware of.

She introduced herself to the women, who later invited her to a gay bar. Maguire described her experience at age seventeen:

> I was being served and I was totally fascinated by the fact that, oh god, here I am being served and I'm not twenty-one. And it didn't occur to me until after a while when I relaxed and started realizing that I was at a gay bar. I just became fascinated. . . . And I was back there the next night. . . . I really felt a sense of knowing who I was and feeling very happy. Very happy that I had been able to through some miracle put this into place.[30] . . .

For women like Maguire, sport provided a point of entry into lesbian culture.

The question arises of whether lesbians simply congregated in athletic settings or whether a sports environment could actually "create" or "produce" lesbians. Some women fit the first scenario, describing how, in their struggle to accept and make sense out of lesbian desire, sport offered a kind of home that put feelings and identities into place. For other women, it appears that the lesbian presence in sport encouraged them to explore or act on feelings that they might not have had or responded to in other settings. Midwestern baseball player Nora Cross remembered that "it was my first exposure to gay people. . . . I was pursued by the one I was rooming with, that's how I found out." She got involved with her roommate and lived "a gay lifestyle" as long as she stayed in sport. Dorothy Ferguson Key also noticed that sport changed some women, recalling that "there were girls that came in the league like this . . . yeah, gay," but that at other times "a girl came in, and I mean they just change. . . . When they've been in a year they're completely changed. . . . They lived together."[31]

The athletic setting provided public space for lesbian sociability without naming it as such or excluding women who were not les-

bians. This environment could facilitate the coming-out process, allowing women who were unsure about or just beginning to explore their sexual identity to socialize with gay and straight women without having to make immediate decisions or declarations. Gradually and primarily through unspoken communication, lesbians in sport recognized each other and created social networks. Gloria Wilson, who played softball in a mid-sized midwestern city, described her entry into lesbian social circles as a gradual process in which older lesbians slowly opened up their world to her and she grew more sure of her own identity and place in the group.

> A lot was assumed. And I don't think they felt comfortable with me talking until they knew me better. Then I think more was revealed. And we had little beer gatherings after a game at somebody's house. So then it was even more clear who was doing what when. And then I felt more comfortable too, fitting in, talking about my relationship too—and exploring more of the lesbian lifestyle, I guess.[32]

In an era when women did not dare announce their lesbianism in public, the social world of popular sport allowed women to find each other as teammates, friends, and lovers. But if athletics provided a public arena and social activity in which lesbians could recognize and affirm each other, what exactly was it that they recognized? This is where the issue of mannishness arises. Women athletes consistently explained the lesbian reputation of sport by reference to the mannishness of some athletes. . . . Suspected lesbians were said to "act like a man, you know, the way they walked, the way they talked, the things they did."

Such comments could merely indicate the pervasiveness of the masculine reputation of athletes and lesbians. However, lesbian narrators also suggested connections, although more complicated and nuanced, between athletics, lesbianism, and the "mannish" or "butchy" style which some lesbians manifested. None reported any doubt about their own gender identification as girls and women, but they indicated that they had often felt uncomfortable with the activities and attributes associated with the female gender. They preferred boyish clothes and activities to the conventional styles and manners of femininity.

Several spoke of . . . their relief upon find-ing athletic comrades who shared this sensi-bility. Josephine D'Angelo recalled that as a lesbian participating in sport, "you brought your culture with you. You brought your arm swinging . . . , the swagger, the way you tilted or cocked your head or whatever. You brought that with you." She explained that this style was acceptable in sports: "First thing you did was to kind of imitate the boys because you know, you're not supposed to throw like a girl." Although her rejection of femininity made her conspicuous in other settings, D'An-gelo found that in sport "it was overlooked, see. You weren't different than the other kids. . . . Same likeness, people of a kind."[33]

These athletes were clearly women play-ing women's sports. But in the gender system of U.S. society, the skills, movements, clothing, and competition of sport were laden with impressions of masculinity. Lesbianism too crossed over the bounds of acceptable femi-ninity. Consequently, sport could relocate girls or women with lesbian identities or feel-ings in an alternative nexus of gender mean-ings, allowing them to "be themselves"—or to express their gender and sexuality in an unconventional way. This applied to hetero-sexual women as well, many of whom also described themselves as "tomboys" attracted to boyish games and styles. As an activity that incorporated prescribed "masculine" physical activity into a way of being in the female body, athletics provided a social space and practice for reorganizing conventional meanings of embodied masculinity and femininity. *All* women in sport gained access to activities and expressive styles labeled masculine by the dominant culture. However, because lesbians were excluded from a concept of "real wom-anhood" defined around heterosexual appeal and desire, sport formed a milieu in which they could redefine womanhood on their own terms. . . .

However, the connections among les-bianism, masculinity, and sport require quali-fication. Many lesbians in and out of sport did not adopt "masculine" markers. And even among those who did, narrators indicated that butch styles did not occlude more traditionally "feminine" qualities of affection and tender-ness valued by women athletes. Sport allowed women to combine activities and attributes perceived as masculine with more conven-

tionally feminine qualities of friendship, coop-eration, nurturance, and affection. Lesbians particularly benefited from this gender con-figuration, finding that in the athletic setting, qualities otherwise viewed as manifestations of homosexual deviance were understood as inherent, positive aspects of sport.[34] Aggres-siveness, toughness, passionate intensity, expanded use of motion and space, strength, and competitiveness contributed to athletic excellence. With such qualities defined as ath-letic attributes rather than psychological abnormalities, the culture of sport permitted lesbians to express the full range of their gen-dered sensibilities while sidestepping the stigma of psychological deviance. For these reasons, athletics, in the words of Josephine D'Angelo, formed a "comforting" and "com-fortable" place.[35]

Yet lesbians found sport hospitable only under certain conditions. Societal hostility toward homosexuality made lesbianism unspeakable in any realm of culture, but the sexual suspicions that surrounded sport made athletics an especially dangerous place in which to speak out. Physical educators and sport officials vigilantly guarded against signs of "mannishness," and teams occasionally expelled women who wore their hair in a "boyish bob" or engaged in obvious lesbian relationships. Consequently, gay athletes avoided naming or verbally acknowledging their sexuality. Loraine Sumner explained that "you never talked about it. . . . You never saw anything in public amongst the group of us. But you knew right darn well that this one was going with that one. But yet it just wasn't a topic of conversation. Never."[36] Instead, les-bian athletes signaled their identity through dress, posture, and look, reserving spoken communication for private gatherings among women who were acknowledged and ac-cepted members of concealed communities.

Although in hindsight the underground nature of midcentury lesbian communities may seem extremely repressive, it may also have had a positive side. Unlike the bars where women's very presence declared their status as sexual outlaws, in sport athletes could enjoy the public company of lesbians while retaining their membership in local com-munities where neighbors, kin, and coworkers respected and sometimes even celebrated their athletic abilities. The unacknowledged, indefinite presence of lesbians in sport may have allowed for a wider range of lesbian experience and identity than is currently acknowledged in most scholarship. For instance, among women who did not identify as lesbian but were sexually drawn to other women, sport provided a venue in which they could express their desires without necessarily having articulated their feelings as a distinct sexual identity. The culture of sport provided space for some women to create clearly delineated lesbian identities and communities, at the same time allowing other women to move along the fringes of this world, operating across sexual and community lines without a firmly differentiated lesbian identity.

Women in sport experienced a contradictory array of heterosexual imperatives and homosexual possibilities. The fact that women athletes disrupted a critical domain of male power and privilege made sport a strategic site for shoring up existing gender and sexual hierarchies. The image of the mannish lesbian confirmed both the masculinity of sport and its association with female deviance. Lesbian athletes could not publicly claim their identity without risking expulsion, ostracism, and loss of athletic activities and social networks that had become crucial to their lives. Effectively silenced, their image was conveyed to the dominant culture primarily as a negative stereotype in which the mannish lesbian athlete represented the unfeminine "other," the line beyond which "normal" women must not cross.

The paradox of women's sport history is that the mannish athlete was not only a figure of homophobic discourse but also a human actor engaged in sexual innovation and struggle. Lesbian athletes used the social and psychic space of sport to create a collective culture and affirmative identity. The pride, pleasure, companionship, and dignity lesbians found in the athletic world helped them survive in a hostile society. The challenge posed by their collective existence and their creative reconstruction of womanhood formed a precondition for more overt, political challenges to lesbian oppression which have occurred largely outside the realm of sport.

NOTES

1. Fred Wittner, "Shall the Ladies Join Us?" *Literary Digest* 117 (19 May 1934):43.

2. Jim Murray, *Austin American Statesman* (n.d.), Zaharias scrapbook, Barker Texas History Center ([hereafter] BTHC), University of Texas, Austin; Arsenio Hall Show, 1988.

3. "Fastest Women in the World," *Ebony* 10 (June 1955):28.

4. Helen Lenskyj, *Out of Bounds: Women, Sport, and Sexuality* (Toronto: Women's Press, 1986); Yvonne Zipter, *Diamonds Are a Dyke's Best Friend: Reflections, Reminiscences, and Reports from the Field on the Lesbian National Pastime* (Ithaca: Firebrand Books, 1988).

5. J. A. Mangan and Roberta J. Park, eds., *"Fair Sex" to Feminism: Sport and the Socialization of Women in the Industrial and Post-Industrial Era* (London: Frank Cays, 1987).

6. 1904–5 Scrapbooks of Anne Maude Butner, Butner Papers, University of Minnesota Archives, Minneapolis (UMA).

7. Violet W. Mange, "Field Hockey for Women," *Harper's Bazaar* 44 (Apr. 1910):246; Anna de Koven, "The Athletic Woman," *Good Housekeeping* 55 (Aug. 1912):150.

8. George Nathan, "Once There Was a Princess," *American Mercury* 19 (Feb. 1930):242.

9. This is an extremely brief and simplified summary of an extensive literature. For a good synthesis, see Estelle Freedman and John D'Emilio, *Intimate Matters: A History of Sexuality in America* (New York: Harper & Row, 1988), chaps. 8–10.

10. William Marston, "How Can a Woman Do It?" *Redbook* (Sept. 1933):60.

11. John D'Emilio, *Sexual Politics, Sexual Communities: The Making of a Homosexual Minority in the United States, 1940–1970* (Chicago: University of Chicago Press, 1983), pp. 9–53; Alan Berube, *Coming Out Under Fire: The History of Gay Men and Women in World War Two* (New York: Free Press, 1990).

12. Donna Penn, "The Meanings of Lesbianism in Post-War America," *Gender and History* 3 (Summer 1991):190–203; Wini Breines, "The 1950s: Gender and Some Social Science," *Sociological Inquiry* 56 (Winter 1986):69–92.

13. Gopher Yearbook (1952), p. 257, UMA.

14. Paul Gallico, *Houston Post*, 22 Mar. 1960; Pete Martin, "Babe Didrikson Takes Off Her Mask," *Saturday Evening Post* 20 (Sept. 1947):26–27.

15. Paula Giddings, *When and Where I Enter: The Impact of Black Women on Race and Sex in America* (New York: William Morrow, 1984), chaps. 1, 2, 4; Patricia Hill Collins, *Black Feminist Thought: Knowledge, Consciousness, and the Politics of Empowerment* (Boston: Unwin Hyman, 1990), chaps. 4, 8.

16. Elizabeth Lunbeck, "'A New Generation of Women': Progressive Psychiatrists and the Hypersexual Female," *Feminist Studies* 13 (Fall 1987): 513–43.

17. *Baltimore Afro-American*, 29 June 1957.

18. "Fastest Women in the World," pp. 28, 32; *Detroit News* 31 (July 1962):1.

19. Patricia Del Rey, "The Apologetic and Women in Sport," in Carole Oglesby, ed., *Women and Sport* (Philadelphia: Lea & Febiger, 1978), pp. 107–11.

20. Mildred A. Schaeffer, "Desirable Objectives in Post-war Physical Education," *Journal of Health and Physical Education* 16 (Oct. 1945):44–47.

21. "Coeducational Classes," *Journal of Health, Physical Education, and Recreation* 26 (Feb. 1955):18. For curricular changes, I examined physical education records at the universities of Wisconsin, Texas, and Minnesota, Radcliffe College, Smith College, Tennessee State University, and Hampton University.

22. Dudley Ashton, "Recruiting Future Teachers," *Journal of Health, Physical Education, and Recreation* 28 (Oct. 1957):49.

23. The 1949–50 Physical Training Staff Handbook at the University of Texas stated, "Legs should be kept shaved" (p. 16). Box 3R213 of Department of Physical Training for Women Records, BTHC.

24. Roxy Andersen, "Statistical Survey of Former Women Athletes," *Amateur Athlete* (Sept. 1954):10–11.

25. All-American Girls Baseball League (AAGBL) 1951 Constitution, AAGBL Records.

26. Morris Markey, "Hey Ma, You're Out!" (n.d.), 1951 Records of the AAGBL; and "Feminine Sluggers," *People and Places* 8 (1952), AAGBL Records.

27. AAGBL 1951 Constitution, AAGBL Records.

28. The sample included forty-two women, ranging in age from their forties to their seventies, who had played a variety of sports in a range of athletic settings in the West, Midwest, Southeast, and Northeast. The majority were white women from urban working-class and rural backgrounds.

29. Zipter, *Diamonds Are a Dyke's Best Friend;* Lillian Faderman, *Odd Girls and Twilight Lovers: A History of Lesbian Life in Twentieth-Century America* (New York: Columbia University Press, 1991), pp. 154, 161–62.

30. Ann Maguire, interview with the author, Boston, 18 Feb. 1988.

31. Nora Cross (pseudonym), interview with the author, 20 May 1988; Dorothy Ferguson Key, interview with the author, Rockford, Ill., 19 Dec. 1988.

32. Gloria Wilson (pseudonym), interview with the author, 11 May 1988.

33. Josephine D'Angelo, interview with the author, Chicago, 21 Dec. 1988.

34. Joseph P. Goodwin, *More Man Than You'll Ever Be! Gay Folklore and Acculturation in Middle America* (Bloomington: Indiana University Press, 1989), p. 62.

35. D'Angelo interview.

36. Loraine Sumner, interview with the author, West Roxbury, Mass., 18 Feb. 1988.

AMY SWERDLOW

Ladies' Day at the Capitol: Women Strike for Peace versus HUAC

In the years surrounding World War I, women played a significant role in the peace movement, often justifying their activism in maternalist rhetoric. As mothers and potential mothers, they had a responsibility to save children from the horrors of war. Nearly half a century later, American women would again invoke their role as mothers to urge the end of nuclear testing on behalf of the world's children. The women's peace movement, which Swerdlow explores in the following article, coalesced at a time when the Cuban Missile Crisis had brought the United States and the Soviet Union to the brink of war. It also occurred during a period when virtually any form of political protest was automatically labeled by its critics as "communist inspired." Although the most virulent phase of McCarthyism had subsided by 1962, the machinery of repression was still intact; the women's peace movement was promptly investigated by the House Un-American Activities Committee.

This article is reprinted from *Feminist Studies*, Volume 8, Number 3 (Fall 1982): 493–520, by permission of the publisher, Feminist Studies, Inc. Notes have been edited.

The assumption that women found their true happiness in domesticity could be carried to extremes; here the film star Joan Crawford posed for a publicity photograph that showed her engaged in household tasks. She does not look very happy. (Photograph courtesy of the Museum of Modern Art/Film Stills Archive)

Note the prior involvement of some of the women strikers in radical and liberal causes. Combine this information with Evans's point about the persistence of concern about the status of women workers in key unions such as the UE and UAW in the aftermath of World War II. Add the growing attention on the part of liberal women to the race reconciliation. How does our view of the Cold War years change? Does this suggest that some women may have retained a willingness to criticize and subvert dominant power relationships? Might minority women be especially eager to fight injustice?

Note how participants in the peace strike countered committee tactics by manipulating traditional gender stereotypes. Who were these women? How can their emergence as political activists be explained?

In mid-December of 1962 in the Old House Office Building of the United States Congress, a confrontation took place between a recently formed women's peace movement called Women Strike for Peace (WSP) and the House Committee on Un-American Activities (HUAC). The confrontation took place at a HUAC hearing to determine the extent of Communist party infiltration into "the so-called 'peace movement' in a manner and to a degree affecting the national security."[1] This three-day battle of political and sexual adversaries, which resulted in a rhetorical victory for the women of WSP and a deadly blow to the committee, occurred only twenty-five years ago.[2] It is a moment in the history of peace movements in the United States in which women led the way by taking a more courageous and principled stand in opposition to cold war ideology and political repression than that of their male counterparts.[3] However, in keeping with the historical amnesia which besets both the history of women and radical movements in America, the WSP-HUAC struggle is largely forgotten.[4]

This article seeks to reconstruct the WSP-HUAC confrontation and the reasons it took the form it did. By analyzing the ideology, consciousness, political style, and public demeanor of the WSP women as they defended their right as mothers "to influence the course of government," we can learn a great deal about the strengths and weaknesses of women's movements for social change that build on traditional sex role ideology and on female culture.[5]

WSP burst upon the American political scene on November 1st, 1961, when an estimated fifty thousand women in over sixty cities across the United States walked out of their kitchens and off their jobs in a one-day women's strike for peace. As a radioactive cloud from a Russian nuclear test hung over the American landscape, these women strikers staged the largest female peace action in the nation's history.[6] In small towns and large cities from New York to California, the women visited government officials demanding that they take immediate steps to "End the Arms Race—Not the Human Race."[7] Coming on the heels of a decade noted for cold war consensus, political conformity, and the celebration of female domesticity, this spontaneous women's initiative baffled both the press and the politicians. The women seemed to have emerged from nowhere. They belonged to no unifying organizations, and their leaders were totally unknown as public figures.

The women strikers were actually responding to a call from a handful of Washington, D.C., women who had become alarmed by the acceleration of the nuclear arms race. So disheartened were they by the passivity of traditional peace groups, that they had sent a call to women friends and contacts all over the country urging them to suspend their regular routine of home, family, and job to join with friends and neighbors in a one-day strike to end the nuclear arms race.[8]

The call to strike spread rapidly from Washington through typical female networks: word of mouth and chain letter fashion from woman to woman, from coast to coast, through personal telephone calls, and Christmas card lists. Contacts in Parent Teacher Associations (PTAs), the League of Women Voters, church and temple groups, as well as the established peace organizations such as the Women's International League for Peace and Freedom (WILPF) and the Committee for a

Sane Nuclear Policy (SANE), also spread the word.

The nature of the strike in each community depended entirely on what the local women were willing, and able, to do. Some marched, others lobbied local officials, a few groups took ads in local newspapers. Thousands sent telegrams to the White House and to the Soviet embassy, calling upon the two first ladies of the nuclear superpowers, Jacqueline Kennedy and Nina Khrushchev, to urge their husbands on behalf of all the world's children to "stop all nuclear tests— east and west." Amazed by the numbers and composition of the turnout on November 1st, *Newsweek* commented:

> They were perfectly ordinary looking women, with their share of good looks; they looked like the women you would see driving ranch wagons, or shopping at the village market, or attending PTA meetings. It was these women by the thousands, who staged demonstrations in a score of cities across the nation last week, protesting atomic testing. A "strike for peace," they called it and—carrying placards, many wheeling baby buggies or strollers—they marched on city halls and Federal buildings to show their concern about nuclear fallout.[9]

The strikers' concern about the nuclear arms race did not end with the November 1st actions. Within only one year, the one-day strike for peace was transformed by its founders and participants into a national women's movement with local groups in sixty communities and offices in ten cities. With no paid staff and no designated leaders, thousands of women in different parts of the country, most of them previously unknown to each other, managed to establish a loosely structured communications network capable of swift and effective direct action on both a national and international scale.

From its inception, the WSP movement was a non-hierarchical participatory network of activists opposed both to rigid ideologies and formal organizational structure. The WSP women called their format simply "our unorganization." It is interesting to note that the young men of Students for a Democractic Society (SDS), a movement founded in the same year as WSP, more aware of their place in the radical political tradition, more aware of the power of naming, and more confident of their power to do so, named their loose structure

"participatory democracy." Eleanor Garst, one of the Washington founders, explained the attractions of the un-organizational format:

> No one must wait for orders from headquarters—there aren't any headquarters. No one's idea must wait for clearance through the national board. No one waits for the president or the director to tell her what to do—and there is no president or director. Any woman who has an idea can propose it through an informal memo system; if enough women think it's good, it's done. Those who don't like a particular action don't have to drop out of the movement; they just sit out that action and wait for one they like. Sound "crazy"?—it is, but it also brings forth and utilizes the creativity of thousands of women who could never be heard from through ordinary channels.[10]

The choice of a loose structure and local autonomy was a reaction to hierarchical and bureaucratic structures of traditional peace groups like WILPF and SANE to which some of the early leaders belonged. These women perceived the WILPF structure, which required that all programmatic and action proposals be cleared with state and national offices, as a roadblock to spontaneous and direct responses to the urgent international crisis.[11] The willingness of the Washington founders to allow each group to act in the way that suited its particular constituency was WSP's greatest strength and the source of the confidence and admiration that women across the country bestowed on the Washington founders. Washington came to be considered the WSP national office not only because it was located in the nation's capital, but also because the Washington group was trusted by all.

There was also another factor militating against a traditional membership organization. Only the year before the WSP strike, Linus Pauling, the Nobel Laureate in physics and opponent of nuclear testing, had been directed by the Senate Internal Security Subcommittee to turn over the names of those who had helped him gather signatures on a scientists' antinuclear petition. The commandeering of membership lists was not an uncommon tactic of political intimidation in the 1950s. Membership lists of radical organizations could therefore be a burden and responsibility. As they served no purpose in the WSP format, it was a sensible strategy to eliminate them. Another benefit was that WSP never had to assess accurately its numerical strength, thus allowing its legend to grow even when its numbers did not.

From its first day onward, WSP tapped a vast reservoir of moral outrage, energy, organizational talent, and sisterhood—female capacities that had been submerged and silenced for more than a decade by McCarthyism and the "feminine mystique." Using standard pressure group tactics, such as lobbying and petitioning, coupled with direct demonstrative action and civil disobedience, executed with imagination and "feminine flair," the WSP women succeeded in putting women's political demands on the front pages of the nation's newspapers, from which they had largely disappeared since the days of the suffrage campaign. WSP also managed to influence public officials and public policy. At a time when peace marchers were ignored, or viewed as "commies" or "kooks," President John F. Kennedy gave public recognition to the women strikers. Commenting on WSP's first antinuclear march at the White House, on January 15, 1962, the president told the nation that he thought the WSP women were "extremely earnest."

> I saw the ladies myself. I recognized why they were here. There were a great number of them, it was in the rain. I understand what they were attempting to say, therefore, I consider their message was received.[12]

In 1970, *Science* reported that "Wiesner (Jerome Wiesner, Pres. Kennedy's Science Advisor) gave the major credit for moving President Kennedy toward the limited Test Ban Treaty of 1963, not to arms controllers inside the government but to the Women Strike for Peace and to SANE and Linus Pauling."[13]

Although WSP, in its first year, was well received by liberal politicians and journalists, the surveillance establishment and the right-wing press were wary. They recognized early what the Rand Corporation described obliquely as the WSP potential "to impact on military policies."[14] Jack Lotto, a Hearst columnist, charged that although the women described themselves as a "group of unsophisticated wives and mothers who are loosely organized in a spontaneous movement for peace, there is nothing spontaneous about the way the pro-Reds have moved in on our mothers and are using them for their own purposes."[15] On the

West Coast, the *San Francisco Examiner* claimed to have proof that "scores of well-intentioned, dedicated women . . . were being made dupes of by known Communists . . . operating openly in the much publicized Women Strike for Peace demonstrations."[16]

That WSP was under Federal Bureau of Investigation (FBI) surveillance from its first public planning meeting in Washington in October 1961, is abundantly evidenced in the forty-three volumes of FBI records on WSP which have been made available to the movement's attorneys under the provisions of the Freedom of Information Act. The records show that FBI offices in major cities, North, East, South, and West—and even in such places as Mobile, Alabama; Phoenix, Arizona; and San Antonio, Texas; not known for WSP activities—were sending and receiving reports on the women, often prepared in cooperation with local "red squads."[17]

Having just lived through the Cuban Missile Crisis of October 1962, WSP celebrated its first anniversary in November with a deep sense of urgency and of heightened political efficacy. But, as the women were making plans to escalate their commitment and their protests, they were stopped in their tracks in the first week of December by HUAC subpoenas to thirteen women peace activists from the New York metropolitan area, as well as Dagmar Wilson of Washington, D.C., the WSP national spokesperson.[18]

It is difficult today to comprehend the emotions and fears such a summons could invoke in individuals and organizations. Lillian Hellman's *Scoundrel Time* gives a picture of the tension, isolation, and near hysteria felt by an articulate and prominent public figure, as she prepared her defense against the committee in 1953.[19] By 1962, cold war hysteria had abated somewhat, as the United States and the USSR were engaged in test ban negotiations, but HUAC represented those forces and those voices in American politics that opposed such negotiations. As a congressional committee, it still possessed the awesome power of an agency of the state to command headlines; cast suspicion; and by labeling individuals as subversives, to destroy careers, lives, and organizations.

The HUAC subpoenas gave no indication of the subject of the hearings, or of their scope. So there was, at first, some confusion about whether it was the WSP connection or other aspects of the subpoenaed women's political lives that were suspect. To add to the confusion, it was soon discovered that three of the women called were not even active in WSP. They were members of the Conference of Greater New York Peace Groups, an organization founded by New Yorkers who had either been expelled from, or who had willingly left, SANE because of its internal red hunt. Of these three women, two had already been named by the committee informers as communists in previous HUAC hearings. One of these women, Elizabeth Moss, had achieved considerable notoriety when she was identified by accused Russian spy William Remington as his mother-in-law and a card-carrying communist. Given these circumstances it was clear that the WSP leadership had some important decisions to make regarding their response to the HUAC hearings. There were two important questions to be faced. First, as WSP had no official membership list, would the movement embrace any woman working for peace even if she were not directly involved in WSP activity? Second, would WSP disavow its members who had past or present communist affiliations, and if WSP did not disavow them, would the movement lose its following and its effectiveness?

The key to WSP unity in the face of the "communist issue" which had divided and disrupted peace, labor, and even civil liberties organizations in the previous decade, was the fact that WSP had previously decided to handle forthrightly and in advance of any attack, the issue of communist inclusion. WSP had, even before the HUAC hearings, decided to reject political screening of its members, deeming it a manifestation of outdated cold war thinking. This decision, the women claimed, was based not on fear or expediency, but on principle. The issue of accepting communists in the movement was brought to the floor of the first national WSP conference in June 1962 by the Los Angeles coordinating council. A prepared statement by the Los Angeles group declared: "Unlike SANE and Turn Toward Peace, WSP must not make the error of initiating its own purges." Treating the issue of communist membership as a question of personal conscience, the Los Angeles group asked, "If there are communists or former communists working in WSP, what difference does that

make? We do not question one another about our religious beliefs or other matters of personal conscience. How can we justify political interrogation?" The Los Angeles statement continued, "If fear, mistrust and hatred are ever to be lessened, it will be by courageous individuals who do not hate and fear and can get together to work out tolerable compromises."[20] The argument that "this is a role women would be particularly equipped to play," won over the conference and resulted in the inclusion of a section in the WSP national policy statement which affirmed, "we are women of all races, creeds and political persuasions who are dedicated to the achievement of general and complete disarmament under effective international control."[21]

An emergency meeting of about fifty New York area "key women," along with Dagmar Wilson and other representatives from Washington, was called a few days after the HUAC summonses began to arrive.[22] The first decision made at this meeting was that WSP would live up to the national policy statement that had been arrived at six months earlier and make a reality of the phrase, "We are women of all . . . political persuasions." Following from this decision it was clear that WSP would support and embrace every woman summoned before HUAC, regardless of her past or present affiliations, as long as she supported the movement's campaign against both Russian and American nuclear policies. This meant that in addition to supporting its own women, the three women not active in WSP would also come under the movement's protection if they so desired. They would be given access to the same lawyers as the WSP activists. They would not be isolated or attacked either for their affiliations or for the way they chose to conduct themselves at the hearing. This decision was in sharp contrast to the action taken by SANE in 1960 when it expelled a leading member of its New York chapter after he invoked the Fifth Amendment at a Senate Internal Security Subcommittee hearing, and then refused to tell Norman Cousins, a cochairman of SANE, whether or not he had ever been a communist.[23]

The decision made by the New York and Washington women not "to cower" before the committee, to conduct no internal purges, to acknowledge each woman's right to act for peace and to conduct herself according to the dictates of her conscience was bold for its day. It was arrived at within the movement, by the women themselves, without consultation with the male leaders of traditional peace and civil liberties groups, many of whom disagreed with this WSP policy.[24] It was based not only on the decision to resist the demonology of the cold war, but also on a sense of sisterhood, on feelings of identification with and empathy for the women singled out for attack. Even the subpoenaed women themselves turned for counsel and support more to each other and the WSP leadership than to their families and lawyers. Working together at a feverish pace, night and day for three weeks, writing, phoning, speaking at rallies, the key women seemed to be acting as if they were a family under attack, for which all personal resources, passions, and energies had to be marshaled. But the family, this time, was "the movement" and it was the sisters, not the fathers, who were in charge.

In response to the subpoenas, a massive campaign was organized for the cancellation of the hearings and for support of WSP from national organizations and public figures. An anti-HUAC statement was composed in New York and Washington which spoke so well to the concerns and the consciousness of "the women" that it succeeded in unifying a movement in shock. The WSP statement on the HUAC inquisition was quoted widely by the press, used by local groups in ads and flyers, in letters to editors, and in speeches. "With the fate of humanity resting on a push button," the statement declared, "the quest for peace has become the highest form of patriotism."[25] In this first sentence, the women set the ground rules for their confrontation with the committee: it was going to be a contest over which group was more patriotic. But the test of "Americanism," according to the WSP rules, was the extent of one's dedication to saving America's children from nuclear extinction. Addressing the issue of communism in the movement, WSP declared: "Differences of politics, economics or social belief disappear when we recognize man's common peril . . . we do not ask an oath of loyalty to any set of beliefs. Instead we ask loyalty to the race of man. The time is long past when a small group of censors can silence the voice of peace." These words would be the WSP *leitmotif* in the Washington hearings. The women were say-

ing, once again, as they had throughout their first year, that for them, the arms race, cold war ideology, and cold war politics, were obsolete in the nuclear age, as was the committee itself. This is the spirit Eric Bentley caught and referred to when he wrote: "In the 1960s a new generation came to life. As far as HUAC is concerned it began with Women Strike for Peace."[26]

The WSP strategy against HUAC was innovative. An organizing memorandum from the Washington office declared, "the usual response of protest and public statements is too traditional and ineffectual. . . . Let's Turn the Tables! Let's meet the HUAC challenge in the Good New WSP way!"[27] The "new way" suggested by women all over the country was to insist that WSP had nothing to hide. Instead of refusing to testify, as radicals and civil libertarians had done in the 1950s, large numbers of WSP participants volunteered to "talk." Approximately one hundred women sent wires to Representative Francis Walter, chairman of HUAC, offering to come to Washington to tell all about their movement. The offers were refused by HUAC. But this new WSP tactic pointed up the fact that the committee was less interested in securing information than in exposing and smearing those it chose to investigate. Some WSP groups objected to the free testimony strategy on the grounds that there was a contradiction between denying the right of the committee to exist, and at the same time offering to cooperate with it. But these groups were in a minority. Carol Urner of Portland, Oregon, spoke for all those who volunteered to testify, making it clear that she would not be a "friendly witness." "I could not, of course, divulge the names of others in the movement," she wrote to Representative Walter. "I suppose such a refusal could lead one to 'contempt' and prison and things like that . . . and no mother can accept lightly even the remote possibility of separation from the family which needs her. But mankind needs us too. . . ."[28]

Only three weeks' time elapsed between the arrival of the first subpoenas from HUAC and the date of the Washington hearings. In this short period, the WSP key women managed to develop a legal defense, a national support system for those subpoenaed, and a broad national campaign of public protest against the committee. The women's performance at the hearings was so original, so winning, and so "feminine" in the traditional sense, that it succeeded in capturing the sympathy and the support of large sections of the national media and in strengthening the movement instead of destroying it.

The hearings opened on December 11, 1962, at 10:00 A.M. in the caucus room of the Old House Office Building of the United States Congress in Washington, D.C. Fear, excitement, and exhilaration were in the air as each WSP woman in the audience looked around to see every seat in the room occupied by sisters who had come from eleven states, some from as far as California, in response to a call for their presence from the national leadership. Clyde Doyle, chairman of the subcommittee of HUAC conducting the WSP hearings, opened with a statement of their purpose. Quoting from Lenin, Stalin, Khrushchev, and Gus Hall, he explained:

> Communists believe that there can be no real peace until they have conquered the world.... The initiated Communist, understanding his Marxist-Leninist doctrine, knows that a Moscow call to intensify the "fight for peace" means that he should intensify his fight to destroy capitalism and its major bastion, the United States of America.[29]

The WSP women in the audience rose as one as the committee called its first witness, Blanche Posner, a retired schoolteacher who was the volunteer office manager for New York WSP. The decision to rise with the first witness, to stand *with* her, was spontaneous. It was proposed only a few minutes before Posner was called, as a note from an unknown source was circulated around the room. Posner refused to answer any questions about the structure or personnel of WSP. She resorted to the Fifth Amendment forty-four times, as the press pointed out in dozens of news stories covering the first day of the hearings. They also reported the way in which Posner took matters into her own hands, lecturing the committee members as though they were recalcitrant boys at DeWitt Clinton High School in the Bronx, where she had taught. Talking right through the interruptions and objections raised by the chairman and by committeee counsel, Alfred Nittle, Posner declared:

> I don't know, sir, why I am here, but I do know why you are here, I think ... because you don't quite understand the nature of this movement.

This movement was inspired and motivated by mothers' love for children.... When they were putting their breakfast on the table, they saw not only the wheaties and milk, but they also saw strontium 90 and iodine 131.... They feared for the health and life of their children. That is the only motivation.[30]

Each time Posner resorted to the Fifth Amendment, she did it with a pointed criticism of the committee or a quip that endeared her to the women in the hearing room who needed to keep their spirits up in the face of charges that Posner had been identified by an FBI informer as a Communist party member while working in New York City as a schoolteacher. One prize exchange between Nittle and Posner led to particularly enthusiastic applause and laughter from WSP women. Nittle asked, "Did you wear a colored paper daisy to identify yourself as a member of the Women Strike for Peace?" Posner answered, "It sounds like such a far cry from communism it is impossible not to be amused. I still invoke the Fifth Amendment."[31]

Most of the witnesses were called because the committee believed it had evidence to link them with the Communist party through identification by FBI informers or the signing of party nominating petitions. But the strategy backfired with Ruth Meyers, of Roslyn, Long Island. She stepped forward, according to Mary McGrory's report in the Washington (D.C.) *Evening Star*, "swathed in red and brown jersey, topped by a steeple crowned red velvet hat," and "she was just as much of a headache to the committee as Posner had been."[32] There was much sparring between Meyers and the committee about the nature and structure of WSP. "Are you presently a member of a group known as Women Strike for Peace?" Nittle asked. "No, sir, Women Strike for Peace has no membership," Meyers answered. Nittle then asked, "You are familiar, I understand, with the structural organization of Women Strike for Peace as evidenced by this plan?" Meyers replied, "I am familiar to the extent of the role that I play in it. I must say that I was not particularly interested in the structure of Women Strike for Peace. I was more involved in my own community activities.... I felt that structure, other than the old telephone, has not much of what I was interested in." Nittle then proceeded to deliver what he believed would be the coup de grâce for Meyers. "Mrs. Meyers," he barked, "it appears from the public records that a Ruth Meyers, residing at 1751 East 10th Street, Brooklyn, New York, on July 27, 1948, signed a Communist Party nominating petition. . . . Are you the Ruth Meyers who executed that petition?" Meyers shot back, "No, sir." She then examined the petition carefully, and announced, "I never lived in Brooklyn, and this is not my signature."[33] Although the official transcript does not contain this statement, many, including the author, remember that she added, "My husband could never get me to move there." This female remark brought an explosion of laughter and applause. Meyers also invoked the Fifth Amendment. As she left the witness stand, Meyers received a one-minute ovation for humor, grace, and mistaken identity. In the corridor outside the caucus room in front of the TV cameras, she told reporters that she had never been a Communist. "But I'll never acknowledge the Committee's right to ask me that question."[34]

Another witness, Lyla Hoffman, chose to tell the committee of her past communist affiliation, asserting that she had left the Communist Party, but would not cooperate in naming names or in citing the cause of her resignation. In a statement written after the hearings Hoffman explained, "I felt that it was high time to say, 'What difference does it make what anyone did or believed many years ago? That's not the problem facing humanity today.' But I had to say this in legal terms." She found it very difficult to do so, as the committee was interested only in whether she was a genuine anticommunist or a secret fellow-traveler.[35] Hoffman invoked the Fifth Amendment.

The witnesses that followed Posner, Meyers, and Hoffman, each in her own style, invoked whatever legal and rhetorical strategy her conscience and her situation dictated. They lectured the committee eloquently and courageously on the danger of nuclear holocaust, on women's rights and responsibility to work for peace. In attempting to explain the nonstructured format of WSP, several witnesses suggested that the movement was too fluid and too unpredictable to be comprehended by the masculine mind.

In their most optimistic projections, the WSP women could not have predicted the overwhelmingly favorable press and public response they would receive, and the support and growth for the movement that would

result from the HUAC episode. From the outset, the WSP leadership understood that HUAC needed the press to make its tactics of intimidation and punishment work. So, WSP played for the press—as it had done from its founding—and won! The Washington and New York leadership knew that it had two stories; both were developed to the hilt. The first was "motherhood under attack" and the second was the age-old "battle of the sexes." The contest between the sexes, according to the WSP version, involved female common sense, openness, humor, hope and naiveté versus male rigidity, solemnity, suspicion, and dark theories of conspiracy and subversion. The WSP women, in their middle-class, feminine, political style turned the hearings into an episode of the familiar and funny "I Love Lucy," rather than the tragic and scary inquisition of Alger Hiss.

For the first time, HUAC was belittled with humor and treated to a dose of its own moral superiority. Headlines critical of the committee and supportive of WSP were featured on the front pages of prominent newspapers from coast to coast. The *Chicago Daily News* declared: "It's Ladies' Day at Capitol: Hoots, Howls—and Charm; Congressmen Meet Match." Russell Baker's column was headed "Peace March Gals Make Red Hunters Look Silly" and a *Detroit Free Press* story was entitled, "Headhunters Decapitated." A cartoon by Herblock in the *Washington* (D.C.) *Post* of December 13th showed three aging and baffled committee members: One is seated at the hearing table. One is holding a gavel. Another turns to him and says, "I Came in Late, Which Was It That Was Un-American—Women or Peace?"[36] A story in the *Vancouver* (B.C.) *Sun* of December 14 was typical of many other reports:

> The dreaded House Un-American Activities Committee met its Waterloo this week. It tangled with 500 irate women. They laughed at it. Klieg lights glared, television cameras whirred, and 50 reporters scribbled notes while babies cried and cooed during the fantastic inquisition.

Bill Galt, author of the *Vancouver Sun* story, gave a blow-by-blow description of WSP civil disobedience in the Old House Office Building:

> When the first woman headed to the witness table, the crowd rose silently to its feet. The irri-

tated Chairman Clyde Doyle of California outlawed standing. They applauded the next witness and Doyle outlawed clapping. Then they took to running out to kiss the witness. . . . Finally, each woman as she was called was met and handed a huge bouquet. By then Doyle was a beaten man. By the third day the crowd was giving standing ovations to the heroines with impunity.[37]

The hearings were a perfect foil for the humor of Russell Baker, syndicated columnist of the *New York Times*.

If the House Un-American Activities Committee knew its Greek as well as it knows its Lenin, it would have left the women peace strikers alone. . . . Instead with typical male arrogance it has subpoenaed 15 of the ladies, . . . spent several days trying to show them that women's place is not on the peace march route, and has come out of it covered with foolishness.

Baker, a liberal columnist, understood the committee's purpose and also the "drama of the absurd" that WSP had staged to defeat that purpose. "The Committee's aim was simple enough," Baker pointed out,

their sleuths studying an organization known as Women Strike for Peace had learned that some of the strikers seemed to have past associations with the Communist Party or its front groups. Presumably if these were exposed, right thinking housewives would give up peace agitation and go back to the kitchen.

The committee had reckoned without female logic, according to Baker:

How could WSP be infiltrated, witness after witness demanded, when it was not an organization at all? . . . Try as he might, Alfred Nittle, the committee counsel, never managed to break through against this defense.[38]

The *Detroit Free Press* commented: "The House Committee can get away with attacking college students in California, government flunkies who are forced to shrive their souls to save their jobs, and assorted misguided do-gooders. But when it decides to smear an estimated half-million angry women, it's in deep trouble. We wish them nothing but the worst."[39]

Mary McGrory in the *Washington* (D.C.) *Evening Star* played up the difference between the male, HUAC perceptions and those of the female, WSP:

"Why can't a woman be like a man?" sings Henry Higgins in *My Fair Lady*. That is precisely the

question the House Committee on Un-American Activities is asking itself today. . . . The committee is trying to find out if the ladies' group is subversive. All it found out was that their conduct in the caucus room certainly was.

"The leader of the group kept protesting that she was not really the leader at all," McGrory observed. Pointing out that few men would deny being leaders, or admit they didn't know what was going on, Mary McGrory reported that:

Dagmar Wilson of Washington, when asked if she exercised control over the New York chapter merely giggled and said, "Nobody controls anybody in the Women Strike for Peace. We're all leaders."

Characterizing Wilson's appearance as the "coup de grâce in the battle of the sexes," McGrory noted that the ladies had been using the Congress as a babysitter, while their young crawled in the aisles and noisily sucked their bottles during the whole proceedings. With a mixture of awe and wonder McGrory described how the ladies themselves, as wayward as their babies, hissed, gasped, clapped entirely at will. When several of their number took the Fifth Amendment, to McGrory's surprise, the women applauded, and

when Mrs. Wilson, trim and beguiling in red wool, stepped up to take the stand, a mother with a baby on one hip worked her way through the crowd and handed her a bouquet of purple and white flowers, exactly as if she were the principal speaker at a ladies' luncheon.

McGrory caught the flavor of Wilson's testimony which was directed not only at the committee, but also at her sisters in the audience. She reported that when Mr. Nittle asked whether the New York chapter had played a dominant role in the group, Wilson replied, "Other cities would be mortified if you said that."

"Was it," Mr. Nittle wanted to know, "Mrs. Wilson's idea to send delegates to a Moscow peace conference?" "No," said Mrs. Wilson regretfully, "I wish I'd thought of that." When Mr. Nittle pursued the question of whose idea it was to send observers to Moscow, Dagmar Wilson replied, "This is something I find very difficult to explain to the masculine mind."

And, in a sense, it was. "Mr. Nittle pressed forward to the clutch question," one, according to McGrory, "that would bring a man to his knees with patriotic protest: 'I would like to ask you whether you would knowingly permit or encourage a Communist Party member to occupy a leadership position in Women Strike for Peace." Wilson replied:

> Well, my dear sir, I have absolutely no way of controlling, do not desire to control, who wishes to join in the demonstrations and the efforts that women strikers have made for peace. In fact, I would also like to go even further. I would like to say that unless everybody in the whole world joins us in this fight, then God help us.

"Would you knowingly permit or welcome Nazis or Fascists?" asked Mr. Nittle. Mrs. Wilson replied, "if we could only get them on our side."[40] Mr. Doyle then thanked Wilson for appearing and being so helpful. "I want to emphasize," he said,

> that the Committee recognizes that there are many, many, many women, in fact a great great majority of women, in this peace movement who are absolutely patriotic and absolutely adverse to everything the Communist Party stands for. We recognize that you are one of them. We compliment you on your leadership and on your helpfulness to us this morning.

Dagmar Wilson tried to get the last word: "I do hope you live to thank us when we have achieved our goal." But Doyle replied, "Well, we will."[41]

The way in which WSP, a movement of middle-class, middle-aged, white women, mobilized to meet the attack by a feared congressional committee was energetic and bold, politically nontraditional, pragmatic rather than ideological, moralistic and maternal. It was entirely consistent with the already established program, tactics, rhetoric, and image of this one-year-old movement, labeled by the University of Wisconsin's student newspaper as "the bourgeois mother's underground."[42]

Were these courageous women who bowed to traditional notions of female behavior merely using the politics of motherhood for political advantage? Or had they internalized the feminine mystique? It is useful to examine the backgrounds of the WSP women in seeking to understand their use of their own female culture to legitimate a radical critique of national, foreign, and military policies. The WSP key women were mostly in their late thirties to mid forties at the inception of the

movement in 1961. Most of them, then, had come into adulthood in the late 1930s and early 1940s. They were students or workers in the years of political ferment preceding World War II. Many had married just before, during, or right after the war. The majority of these women participated in the postwar baby boom, the rise of middle-class affluence, and the privatism and consumerism connected with suburban life. It was during the 1950s that they made their adjustment to family, parenting, community, and consensus politics.

As a movement born out of, and responding to, the consciousness of the 1950s, WSP projected a middle-class and politically moderate image. In an article celebrating WSP's first anniversary, Eleanor Garst, one of WSP's early image makers, proclaimed:

> Breaking all the rules and behaving with incredible disorder and naivete, "the women" continue to attract recruits until the movement now numbers hundreds of thousands.... Furthermore, many of the women behaving in these unaccustomed ways are no odd-ball types, but pillars of the community long courted by civic organizations. Others—perhaps the most numerous—are apolitical housewives who have never before lifted a finger to work for peace or any other social concern.[43]

Although the movement projected an image of political innocence and inexperience, WSP was actually initiated by five women who were already active members of SANE. The women—Dagmar Wilson, Jeanne Bagby, Folly Fodor, Eleanor Garst, and Margaret Russell—had gravitated toward each other because of their mutual distaste for SANE's internal red hunt, which they felt contributed to an escalation, rather than an end to cold war hysteria. Perhaps, more important, they shared a frustration over the slow pace with which the highly structured SANE reacted to international crises. They also resented the reluctance of SANE's male leadership to deal with "mother's issues" such as the contamination of milk by radioactive fallout from nuclear tests.

Dagmar Wilson was forty-five years old, and a political novice when she was moved to call a few friends to her home in the late summer of 1961 to discuss what could be done about the nuclear crisis. At this meeting WSP was born. Wilson was at that time a successful freelance children's book illustrator, the mother of three daughters and wife of

Christopher Wilson, a commercial attaché at the British embassy. Wilson had been born in New York City, had moved to Germany as a very young child, and had spent most of her adult years in England where her father, Cesar Searchinger, was a well-known broadcast correspondent for the Columbia Broadcasting System and the National Broadcasting Company.

Wilson came to the United States prior to World War II, held a variety of professional jobs as an artist and teacher, and finally became a freelance illustrator. She worked in a studio at home, so as to be available to her children and to ensure a smooth-running household. Despite the fact that Wilson was so successful an artist that one of her children's books had become a best-seller, she nevertheless identified herself as a housewife.

> My idea in emphasizing the housewife rather than the professional was that I thought the housewife was a downgraded person, and that we, as housewives, had as much right to an opinion and that we deserved as much consideration as anyone else, and I wanted to emphasize . . . this was an important role and that it was time we were heard.[44]

A gifted artist, an intelligent person of good sense, good grace, and charm, Wilson possessed the charisma of those who accurately represent the feelings and the perceptions of their constituency, but excel them in passion and the capacity for creative articulation. Having been most of her life a "nonjoiner" Wilson was, as the *New York Times Magazine* reported in a feature story in May 1962, a "political neophyte."[45] Because Wilson had not been involved in U.S. radical politics of the 1940s, she was free from the self-conscious timidity that plagued those who had been involved in leftist organizations and who feared either exposure or a repetition of the persecution and the political isolation they had experienced in the 1950s.

Among the women who met at Wilson's house to plan the emergency peace action was Eleanor Garst, whose direct, friendly, practical, yet passionate political prose played a powerful role in energizing and unifying the WSP women in their first year. It was she who drafted the call for November 1st, and later helped create most of the anti-HUAC rhetoric.

Garst came from a conservative Baptist background. She recalls that everything in her upbringing told her that the only thing a woman should do was to marry, have babies, care for her husband and babies, and "never mind your own needs." Despite this, Garst was the only one of the inner circle of Washington founders, who in 1961 was a completely self-supporting professional woman, living on her own. She was the mother of two grown children. At the time of the founding of WSP, Garst was employed as a community organizer for the Adams Morgan Demonstration Project, administered by American University, working to maintain integrated neighborhoods in Washington, D.C. She had become a pacifist in her early childhood after reading about war in novels and poems. Her husband, a merchant seaman, refused to be drafted prior to World War II, a decision that he and Eleanor made together without consulting any other pacifists because they knew none. They spent their honeymoon composing an eighty-page brief against peacetime conscription.

After the war, Garst became a professional political worker, writer, and peace activist on the West Coast before coming to Washington. She had been a founder of the Los Angeles SANE and editor of its newsletter. A forceful and easy writer, Garst had already been published in the *Saturday Evening Post, Reporter, Ladies' Home Journal,* and other national publications when she was asked to draft the letter that initiated the successful November 1st strike.

Folly Fodor, a leading figure in the founding group, had come to Washington in 1960 to follow her husband's job with the U.S. Labor Department. She joined SANE on her arrival in Washington and had been elected to the board. Thirty-seven years old at the time of the founding of WSP, Fodor was the mother of two. Folly Fodor was not new to politics. She was the daughter of parents who had been involved in liberal-to-communist political causes and had herself been a leader in political organizations since her youth. As an undergraduate at Antioch College, in Yellow Springs, Ohio, Folly Fodor had become active in the Young People's Socialist League, eventually becoming "head of it," as she put it. In retrospect she believes she spent too much time fighting the communists on campus, and "never did a goddamn thing." Fodor had been chairperson of the Young Democrats of California and as a Democrat she had clandestinely supported Henry Wallace in 1948. During the mid-1950s, after the birth of her second child, Fodor organized a mother's group to oppose nuclear testing. So Fodor, like Garst, was not new to radical causes, to peace activity, or to women's groups. She was ready and eager for a separate women's peace action in the fall of 1961.

Two other women who founded WSP, Jeanne Bagby and Margaret Russell, were also already active in the peace cause at the time of the founding of WSP. Bagby was a frequent contributor to *Liberation* magazine. Together the founders possessed research, writing, organizing, and speaking talents that were not unusual for women active in a variety of community, civic, and church groups in the 1950s. All the founders shared a conviction that the men in the peace movement and the government had failed them and that women had to take things into their own hands.

But what of the thousands of women who joined the founders? What was their social and political background and their motivation to take to the streets in peace protest? Elise Boulding, a sociologist and longtime pacifist activist, who became involved in the WSP communications network right after November 1st, decided to try to find out. During the six months in which Boulding edited the *Women's Peace Movement Bulletin,* an information exchange for WSP groups, she kept asking herself whether the WSP women were really political neophytes as they claimed, or "old pros with a well defined idea of some kind of world social order?" Using the resources of the Institute for Conflict Resolution in Ann Arbor, Michigan, where she was working, and with the help of WSP colleagues in Ann Arbor, she composed a questionnaire that was sent to every eighth name on the mailing lists of forty-five local groups. By the fall of 1962, shortly before the summonses from HUAC, 279 questionnaires had been returned from thirty-seven localities in twenty-two states. According to Boulding, the respondents represented a cross-section of the movement—not only leaders.[46]

Boulding found that the overwhelming majority of the WSP women were well-educated mothers, and that 61 percent were not employed outside the home. But she concluded that the women who went out on strike for peace on November 1, 1961, and stayed on

in the movement in the following months, appeared to be a more complex and sophisticated group than the "buggy-pushing housewife" image the movement conveyed. She characterized the early WSP participants as "largely intellectual and civic-minded people, mostly of the middle class"—very much like the Washington founders themselves.[47]

Most of the women strikers had been liberals, radicals, or pacifists in the 1940s. Although few had been political leaders of any kind, they shared the 1940s belief that society could be restructured on humanistic lines through the direct political action of ordinary people. Dorothy Dinnerstein described the psychological process of depoliticization and privatization that many politically active people experienced in the 1950s. Many radicals, according to Dinnerstein, spent the 1950s in a state of moral shock, induced by the twin catastrophes of Stalinism and McCarthyism. They lost their capacity for social connectedness and, "in this condition they withdrew from history—more or less totally, more or less gradually, more or less blindly into intensely personalistic, inward-turning, magically thing-and-place-oriented life." According to Dinnerstein they withdrew their passion from the larger human scene and sought to invest in something less nightmarish, more coherent and mentally manageable.[48] What the WSP women withdrew into, with society's blessing and encouragement, was the domestic sphere, the management of family, children, home, and local community. Many, when their school-aged children no longer required full-time care, were propelled into the PTAs, League of Women Voters, Democratic party politics, church, synagogue, or cultural activities by their earlier social, political, and humanitarian concerns.

It took the acceleration of nuclear testing by both the capitalist United States and the socialist USSR to convince the WSP women of something they already suspected: that there was no political force in the world acting morally and humanely in the interest of the preservation of life. It took a series of international crises, the example of the civil rights sit-ins, and the Aldermarston antibomb marches in Britain to give the WSP women both the sense of urgency, and of possibility, that are the necessary ingredients for a political movement. Once out in the political arena, the women found that their moral outrage, their real fear for their children's future, and their determination never to be pushed back into the non-political domestic sphere, made them unafraid of a mere congressional committee before which others had quaked.

The women who were drawn to WSP certainly took the job of motherhood seriously. They had willingly chosen to sacrifice careers and personal projects to raise society's children because they had been convinced by the post-Freudians that the making of human beings is a far more important vocation than anything else; and that the making of human beings was a sex-specific vocation requiring the full-time duties of a resident mother.[49] But where the WSP women differed from the majority of their middle-class cohorts was that they saw motherhood not only as a private function, but also as a contribution to society in general and to the future. When they built on their rights and responsibilities to act politically in defense of the world's children, they were invoking not only their maternal consciousness, but their social conscience as well. They were women of heart, emotion, ingenuity, wit, and guile, but they were also serious political thinkers and activists. They chose to rely on their femininity, as most women did in the fifties and early sixties, to create whatever space and power they could carve out for themselves.

The Birmingham (England) Feminist History Group in an article, "Feminism as Femininity in the Nineteen Fifties?" suggests that feminism of the fifties seemed to be more concerned with integrating and foregrounding femininity than in transforming it in a fundamental way.[50] The conduct of WSP before the House Committee on Un-American Activities follows this pattern. The WSP women were not concerned with transforming the ideology of femininity, but rather with using it to enhance women's political power. But in so doing they were transforming that ideology and foreshadowing the feminism that emerged later in the decade.

Very much in the way that the concept of Republican motherhood was used in the late eighteenth century to justify the demand for women's education, and the cult of true womanhood was built upon to project women into the ante-bellum reform movements, WSP used the feminine mystique of the 1950s to legitimize women's right to radical dissent from foreign and military policies. In the repressive political climate of the early 1960s, WSP relied heavily upon sex role stereotypes to legitimize its opposition to cold war policies. But by emphasizing the fact that the men in power could no longer be counted on for protection in the nuclear age, WSP implied that the traditional sex-gender contract no longer worked. And by stressing global issues and international sisterhood, rather than domestic responsibilities, WSP challenged the privatization and isolation of women which was a key element of the feminine mystique. Most important, by performing in relation to HUAC with more courage, candor, and wit than most men had done in a decade of inquisitions, WSP raised women's sense of political power and self-esteem. One of the negative effects for WSP of relying so heavily on the politics of motherhood to project its political message was that it alienated a new generation of younger women who admired the movement's stand for peace, but saw its acquiescence to sex role stereotypes as regressive. In the late 1960s these younger women insisted upon working for peace not as wives, mothers, and sisters, but as autonomous persons.

Sara Evans, in *Personal Politics,* points out that those few young women in the civil rights movement who first raised feminist issues within the movement had to step *outside* the sex role assumptions on which they were raised in order to articulate a radical critique of women's position.[51] For WSP it was obviously different. The founders and leaders of WSP certainly did not step outside the traditional sex role assumptions; rather, they stood squarely upon them, with all their contradictions. By using these contradictions to present a radical critique of man's world, WSP began the transformation of woman's consciousness and woman's role.

NOTES

1. U.S. Congress, House, Committee on Un-American Activities, *Communist Activities in the Peace Movement (Women Strike for Peace and Certain Other Groups), Hearings before the Committee on Un-American Activities on H.R. 9944.* 87th Cong., 2d. sess., 1962, p. 2057.

2. Historians and political opponents of HUAC agree that the WSP hearing marked the beginning of the end of the committee's power. Eric Bentley

called the WSP-HUAC confrontation, "the fall of HUAC's Bastille." See Eric Bentley, *Thirty Years of Treason* (New York: Viking Press, 1971), p. 951....

3. In May 1960, Senator Thomas Dodd, vice-chairman of the Senate International Security Sub-committee, threatened SANE with congressional investigation if it did not take steps to rid itself of communist infiltrators. SANE responded by voting to exclude all those with communist sympathies. Whole chapters that did not go along with internal red hunts were expelled, as was Henry Abrams, a leading New York activist who refused to tell the Senate committee whether or not he was a communist. Turn Toward Peace also rejected communists or former communists. See Milton S. Katz, "Peace, Politics, and Protest: SANE and the American Peace Movement, 1957–1972" (Ph.D. diss., St. Louis University, 1973), pp. 109–130....

4. The way in which WSP's militant role in the peace movement has been either ignored or trivialized by journalists, peace movement leaders, and historians is illustrated by the following examples. Mary McGrory in her syndicated column described a WSP visit to the White House in the following manner: "This week's Cinderella story has to do with Women Strike for Peace, which after 15 years of drudgery in the skullery of anti-war activity has been invited to the White House" (*New York Post*, 8 Mar. 1977, p. 27). Dave Dellinger, one of the most prominent of the male leaders of the 1960s peace movement, devoted about 10 lines to WSP in a 317-page book on the history of the civil rights and peace movements from 1965 to 1973. He described WSP as a group fearful of engaging in civil disobedience in the 1967 "Mobilization March on the Pentagon." Nowhere in the book did Dellinger mention that nine months earlier 2,500 WSP women broke through police barricades to bang their shoes on the Pentagon doors which had been shut in their faces. See Dave Dellinger, *More Power Than We Know* (Garden City, N.Y.: Anchor Press, 1975)....

5. For a symposium on the relationship of feminism, women's culture, and women's politics, see Ellen DuBois, Mari Jo Buhle, Temma Kaplan, Gerda Lerner, and Carroll Smith-Rosenberg, "Politics and Culture in Women's History: A Symposium," *Feminist Studies* 6 (Spring 1980):26–64....

6. The figure of fifty thousand claimed by the Washington founders after November 1st was accepted in most press accounts and became part of the WSP legend. It was based on reports from women in sixty cities and from newspapers across the country....

7. "End the Arms Race—Not the Human Race" was the central slogan of the November 1st "strike": "Help Wanted" flyer, 25 Oct. 1961, Washington, D.C. See WSP Document Collection in custody of the author. (Mimeographed.)

8. "Dear—, Last night I sat with a few friends in a comfortable living room talking of atomic war." Draft of call to strike by Eleanor Garst, Washington, D.C., 22 Sept. 1961. WSP Document Collection. (Mimeographed.)

9. *Newsweek*, 13 Nov. 1961, p. 21.

10. Eleanor Garst, "Women: Middle-Class Masses," *Fellowship* 28 (1 Nov. 1962):10–12.

11. Minutes of the WILPF National Executive Committee stated: "Each branch taking direct action should clear with the National Action Projects Committee. The committee should have, and send out to branches, a list of approved action and a list of the organizations with which we formally cooperate." Women's International League for Peace and Freedom, Minutes of the National Executive Committee meeting of 28–29 Sept. 1961. Swarthmore College Peace Collection, DG 43, Series A-2, Box 18, p. 5.

12. "Transcript of the President's News Conference on World and Domestic Affairs," *New York Times*, 16 Jan. 1962, p. 18.

13. *Science* 167 (13 Mar. 1970):1476.

14. A. E. Wessel, *The American Peace Movement: A Study of Its Themes and Political Potential* (Santa Monica: Rand Corporation, 1962), p. 3.

15. *New York Journal American*, 4 Apr. 1962, p. 10.

16. *San Francisco Examiner*, 21 May 1962, p. 10.

17. The FBI files on WSP are located in the offices of the Washington, D.C., law firm of Gaffney, Anspach, Shember, Klimasi, and Marx. These contain hundreds of documents from security officers in major cities to the director of the FBI and from the directors to the security officers. For instance, as early as 23 Oct. 1961, one week before the November 1st strike, the Cleveland office of the FBI already identified one of the WSP planning groups as communist. (FBI Document 100-39566-8)....

18. Those subpoenaed were (in order of appearance) Blanche Posner, Ruth Meyers, Lyla Hoffman, Elsie Neidenberg, Sylvia Contente, Rose Clinton, Iris Freed, Anna Mackenzie, Elizabeth Moss, Ceil Gross, Jean Brancato, Miriam Chesman, Norma Spector, and Dagmar Wilson. Spector never testified; she was excused due to illness. *Hearings before Committee on Un-American Activities*, p. iii.

19. Lillian Hellman, *Scoundrel Time* (Boston: Little, Brown & Co., 1976), p. 99.

20. Los Angeles WISP, Statement I, Ann Arbor Conference, June 9–10, 1962 (WSP Document Collection); ...

21. "WSP National Policy Statement," *Women Strike for Peace Newsletter*, New York, New Jersey, Connecticut, Summer 1962, pp. 1–2.

22. "Key women" was the name used by WSP for those women who were part of the national and local communications network. They were the ones who were called upon to initiate actions or who called upon others to do so.

23. Katz, "Peace, Politics, and Protest," pp. 122–26.

24. Homer Jack, "The Will of the WISP versus the Humiliation of HUAC," transcript of a talk on Radio Station WBAI, New York, 28 Dec. 1962 (WSP Document Collection).

25. The anti-HUAC statement by WSP was composed by the New York and Washington leadership in their usual collaborative fashion, with no pride or claim of authorship, so it is difficult to know which group wrote what part. It was distributed through official WSP channels via the national office in Washington.

26. Bentley, *Thirty Years of Treason*, p. 951.

27. Women Strike for Peace, Washington, D.C.

to "Dear WISP's," 6 Dec. 1962 (WSP Document Collection).

28. Carol Urner to Representative Francis Walter reprinted in the *Women's Peace Movement Bulletin* 1 (20 Dec. 1962):5.

29. *Hearings before Committee on Un-American Activities*, pp. 2064–65.

30. Ibid., p. 2074.

31. Ibid., p. 2085.

32. Mary McGrory, "Prober Finds 'Peacemakers' More Than a Match," *Washington* (D.C.) *Evening Star*, 12 Dec. 1962, p. A-1.

33. *Hearings before Committee on Un-American Activities*, pp. 2095, 2101.

34. McGrory, "Prober Finds 'Peacemakers' More Than a Match," p. A-1.

35. Lyla Hoffman, undated typewritten statement (WSP Document Collection).

36. Thirty-seven favorable news stories, columns and editorials were reprinted in a hastily prepared WSP booklet, published less than two weeks after the hearings. . . .

37. *Vancouver* (B.C.) *Sun*, 14 Dec. 1962, p. 2.

38. "The Ladies Turn Peace Quiz into Greek Comedy," *Detroit Free Press*, 16 Dec. 1962, p. 1.

39. *Detroit Free Press*, 13 Dec. 1962, p. A-8.

40. Mary McGrory, "Nobody Controls Anybody," *Washington* (D.C.) *Evening Star*, 14 Dec. 1962, pp. A-1, A-9.

41. *Hearings before Committee on Un-American Activities*, p. 2201.

42. *Madison* (Wis.) *Daily Cardinal*, 14 Dec. 1962, p. 2.

43. Garst, "Women: Middle-Class Masses," pp. 10–11.

44. Interview with Dagmar Wilson, Leesburg, Va., Sept. 1977.

45. *New York Times Magazine*, 6 May 1962, p. 32.

46. On a WSP activity measure, 38 percent rated themselves as "very active," 10 percent as "active," and 42 percent rated themselves as "not active," or only "slightly active." The profile of the majority of the WSP participants that emerged was indeed that of middle-class, well-educated housewives. . . .

Thirty-eight percent of the women who responded claimed to belong to no other organizations, or at least did not record the names of any organizations in response to questions concerning other community activities. Forty percent of the women were active in a combination of civic, race relations, civil liberties, peace, and electoral political activity. Only 11 percent were members of professional organizations. . . .

47. Ibid., p. 15.

48. Dorothy Dinnerstein, *The Mermaid and the Minotaur: Sexual Arrangements and Human Malaise* (New York: Harper Colophon Books, 1976), pp. 259–62.

49. Ashley Montagu, "The Triumph and Tragedy of the American Woman," *Saturday Review*, 27 (Sept. 1958):14; . . .

50. "Feminism as Femininity in the Nineteen Fifties?" Birmingham (England) Feminist History Group, *Feminist Review*, no. 3 (1979):48–65.

51. Sara Evans, *Personal Politics: The Roots of Women's Liberation in the Civil Rights Movement and the New Left* (New York: Alfred A. Knopf, 1979), p. 23.

DANIEL HOROWITZ
Betty Friedan and the Origins of Feminism in Cold War America

The years immediately after World War II were marked by a resurgent domesticity. The average age at marriage of women dropped sharply—by the end of the 1950s it was 20. Women's age at the birth of their first child also dropped precipitously; the number of children per family increased sharply. The proportion of women in college fell in comparison to men; many others dropped out of college to marry or because they saw no advantage in increased education.

Daniel Horowitz, "Rethinking Betty Friedan and *The Feminist Mystique*: Labor Union Radicalism and Feminism in Cold War America." *American Quarterly*, vol. 48 (1998): 1–42. Copyright © 1996 by The American Studies Association. Reprinted by permission of the Johns Hopkins University Press. Notes have been renumbered and edited.

In 1963 Betty Friedan published *The Feminine Mystique,* a searing indictment of the triviality and frustrations of a resurgent domesticity. She wrote in the voice of an author who located herself in the middle-class suburbs and whose ethnicity was unmarked. The problem she described was one, she said, "that has no name."

> The problem lay buried, unspoken, for many years in the minds of American women. It was a strange stirring, a sense of dissatisfaction, a yearning that women suffered in the middle of the twentieth century in the United States. Each suburban wife struggled with it alone. As she made the beds, shopped for groceries, matched slipcover material, ate peanut butter sandwiches with her children, chauffeured Cub Scouts and Brownies, lay beside her husband at night—she was afraid to ask even of herself the silent question—"Is this all?" . . . In the fifteen years after World War II, this mystique of feminine self-fulfillment became the cherished and self-perpetuating core of contemporary American culture. Millions of women lived their lives in the image of those pretty pictures of the American suburban housewife, kissing their husbands goodbye in front of the picture window, depositing their station wagons full of children at school, and smiling as they ran the new electric waxer over the spotless kitchen floor.

Friedan urged women to give thought to "the unfeminine problems of the world outside the home," to reclaim education and practical work in the world; not to concede to men the sole right "to make the major decisions." Her book became a long-lived bestseller and the subject of much controversy. Some women objected that as wives and mothers and perhaps community activists they enjoyed a lifestyle that benefited their families and communities and provided them with freedom and a sense of self-worth. But most of the response was favorable: a wide range of backgrounds applauded her articulation of their own dissatisfactions. In Red Oak, Iowa, Mary Louise Smith found in Friedan's book inspiration to demand more than envelope stuffing jobs in the local Republican Party; in 1976 she would be the first and only woman to chair the Republican National Committee.*

But as Daniel Horowitz explains in the essay that follows, Friedan's analysis emerged not only from her experience of suburban life but also from her experience in left-wing politics and in the labor movement—experiences she did not mention in *The Feminine Mystique.* The execution of Ethel and Julius Rosenberg for spying in 1952 frightened many progressive Jewish organizations lest they be tainted as Communist sympathizers; they would subsequently be inhospitable to reformers from the left.** The House Un-American Activities Committee investigations that Swerdlow describes continued in the late 1950s and early 1960s. Many elements of Cold War politics and culture may have contributed to the choices she made as she developed her voice.

In 1951, a labor journalist with a decade's experience in protest movements described a trade union meeting where rank-and-file women talked and men listened. Out of these conversations, she reported, emerged the realization that the women were "fighters—that they refuse any longer to be paid or treated as some inferior species by their bosses, or by any male workers who have swallowed the bosses' thinking."[1] The union was the UE, the United Electrical, Radio and Machine Workers of America, the most radical American union in the postwar period and in the 1940s what historian Ronald Schatz . . . has called "the largest

*See Mary Louise Smith's interview in *More Strong-Minded Women: Iowa Feminists Tell Their Stories,* ed. Louise Noun (Ames: Iowa State University Press, 1992), pp. 147–156.

**Stanley Svonkin, *Jews Against Prejudice: American Jews and the Fight for Civil Liberties* (New York: Columbia University Press, 1997).

communist-led institution of any kind in the United States."[2] In 1952 that same journalist wrote a pamphlet, *UE Fights for Women Workers*, that the historian Lisa Kannenberg, unaware of the identity of its author, has called "a remarkable manual for fighting wage discrimination that is, ironically, as relevant today as it was in 1952." At the time, the pamphlet helped raise the consciousness of Eleanor Flexner, who in 1959 would publish *Century of Struggle*, the first scholarly history of American women. In 1953–54, Flexner relied extensively on the pamphlet when she taught a course at the Jefferson School of Social Science in New York on "The Woman Question." Flexner's participation in courses at the school, she later said, "marked the beginning of my real involvement in the issues of women's rights, my realization that leftist organizations—parties, unions—were also riddled with male supremacist prejudice and discrimination."[3] The labor journalist and pamphlet writer was Betty Friedan.

In 1973 Friedan remarked that until she started writing *The Feminine Mystique* (1963), "I wasn't even conscious of the woman problem." In 1976 she commented that in the early 1950s she was "still in the embrace of the feminine mystique."[4] Although in 1974 she revealed some potentially controversial elements of her past, even then she left the impression that her landmark book emerged only from her own captivity by the very forces she described. Friedan's portrayal of herself as so totally trapped by the feminine mystique was part of a reinvention of herself as she wrote and promoted *The Feminine Mystique.* Her story made it possible for readers to identify with its author and its author to enhance the book's appeal. However, it hid from view the connection between the union activity in which Friedan participated in the 1940s and early 1950s and the feminism she inspired in the 1960s. In the short term, her misery in the suburbs may have prompted her to write *The Feminine Mystique;* a longer term perspective makes clear that the book's origins lie much earlier—in her college education and in her experiences with labor unions in the 1940s and early 1950s.[5] . . . Friedan's life provides evidence of. . . . continuity. . . . between the struggle for justice for working women in the 1940s and the feminism of the 1960s. This connection gives feminism and Friedan, both long under

attack for a lack of interest in working class and African American women, a past of which they should be proud. . . . Moreover, a new reading of *The Feminine Mystique* sheds light on the remaking of progressive forces in America, the process by which a focus on women and the professional middle and upper middle classes supplemented, in some ways replaced a focus on unions. Finally, an examination of *The Feminine Mystique* reminds us of important shifts in the ideology of the left: from an earlier economic analysis based on Marxism to one developed in the 1950s that also rested on humanistic psychology, and from a focus on the impact of conditions of production on the working class to an emphasis on the effect of consumption on the middle class.

In print and in interviews, Friedan has offered a narrative of her life that she popularized after she became famous in 1963.[6] A full biography might begin in Peoria, where Bettye Naomi Goldstein was born February 4, 1921 and grew up with her siblings and their parents: a father who owned a jewelry store and a mother who had given up her position as a society editor of the local paper to raise a family.[7] My analysis of Friedan's political journey starts with her years at Smith College, although it is important to recognize Friedan's earlier sense of herself as someone whose identity as a Jew, a reader, and a brainy girl made her feel freakish and lonely.[8]

As an undergraduate, she has suggested, her lonely life took a turn for the better. "For the first time," she later remarked of her years in college, "I wasn't a freak for having brains." Friedan has acknowledged that she flourished at Smith, with her editorship of the student newspaper, her election to Phi Beta Kappa in her junior year, and her graduation *summa cum laude* among her most prominent achievements. She has told the story of how Gestalt psychology and Kurt Koffka (one of its three founders) were critical in her intellectual development.[9]

Friedan has described the years between her graduation from Smith in 1942 and the publication of her book twenty-one years later as a time when the feminine mystique increasingly trapped her. In her book and in dozens of speeches, articles, and interviews beginning in 1963, she mentioned a pivotal moment in her life, one that she felt marked the beginning of the process by which she succumbed. She told how, while in graduate school at Berkeley in the year after her graduation from college, the university's offer of a prestigious fellowship forced her to make a painful choice. Her first serious boyfriend, a graduate student who had not earned a similarly generous award, threatened to break off the relationship unless she turned down her fellowship. "I never could explain, hardly knew myself, why" she turned away from a career in psychology, she wrote in 1963. She decided to reject the fellowship because she saw herself ending up as an "old maid college teacher" in part because at Smith, she said, there were so few female professors who had husbands and children.[10] The feminine mystique, she insisted, had claimed one of its first victims.[11]

After leaving Berkeley, the copy on the dust jacket of The Feminine Mystique noted, Friedan did some "applied social-science research" and free-lance writing for magazines. Friedan's biography in a standard reference book quotes her as saying that in the 1940s, "for conscious or unconscious reasons," she worked at "the usual kinds of boring jobs that lead nowhere."[12] This story continues in 1947 with her marriage to Carl Friedan, a returning vet who would eventually switch careers from theater to advertising and public relations. She has told of how she gave birth to three children between 1948 and 1956 and the family moved to the suburbs, with these experiences making her feel trapped. Friedan's picture of her years in the suburbs is not one of contentment and conformity.[13] Though she acknowledged her role in creating and directing a program that brought together teenagers and adult professionals, Friedan portrayed herself as someone who felt "freakish having a career, worried that she was neglecting her children."[14] In an oft-repeated story whose punch line varied, Friedan recounted her response to the census form. In the space where it asked for her occupation, she put down "housewife" but remained guilty, hesitant, and conflicted about such a designation, sometimes pausing and then adding "writer."[15]

Friedan laced The Feminine Mystique with suggestions of how much she shared with her suburban sisters. In the opening paragraph, she said that she realized something was wrong in women's lives when she "sensed it first as a question mark in my own life, as a wife and mother of three small children, half-guiltily, and therefore half-heartedly, almost in spite of myself, using my abilities and education in work that took me away from home." Toward the end of the paragraph, when she referred to "a strange discrepancy between the reality of our lives as women and the image to which we were trying to conform," she suggested that she experienced the feminine mystique as keenly and in the same way as her readers. Using the second person plural, she wrote that "all of us went back into the warm brightness of home" and "lowered our eyes from the horizon, and steadily contemplated our own navels." Her work on newspapers, she wrote in The Feminine Mystique, proceeded "with no particular plan." Indeed, she claimed that she had participated as a writer in the creation of the image of the happy housewife.[16]

Friedan asserted she embarked on a path that would lead to The Feminine Mystique only when, as she read over the responses of her college classmates to a questionnaire in anticipation of their fifteenth reunion in 1957, she discovered what she called "The Problem That Has No Name," the dissatisfaction her suburban peers felt but could not fully articulate. When she submitted articles to women's magazines, Friedan said, editors changed the meaning of what she had written or rejected outright her suggestions for pieces on controversial subjects. Then at a meeting of the Society of Magazine Writers, she heard Vance Packard recount how he had written The Hidden Persuaders (1957) after Reader's Digest turned down an article critical of advertising. Friedan decided to write her book.[17]

In "It Changed My Life": Writings on the Women's Movement (1976), a book that included a 1974 autobiographical article, Friedan suggested some of what she had omitted from earlier versions of her life.[18] Perhaps responding to attacks on her for not being sufficiently radical, she acknowledged that before her marriage and for several years after she participated in radical activities and worked for union publications.[19] She and the friends with whom she lived before marrying considered themselves in "the vanguard of the working-class revolution," participating in "Marxist discussion groups," going to political rallies, and having "only contempt for dreary bourgeois capitalists like our fathers." Without getting much more specific, Friedan noted that right after the war she was "very involved, consciously radical. Not about women, for heaven's sake!" but about African Americans, workers, the threat of war, anti-communism, and "communist splits and schisms." This was a time, Friedan reported briefly, when, working as a labor journalist, she discovered "the grubby economic underside of American reality."[20]

"I was certainly not a feminist then—none of us," she remarked in the mid-1970s, "were a bit interested in women's rights." She remembered one incident, whose implications she said she only understood much later. Covering a strike, she could not interest anyone in the fact that the company and the union discriminated against women. In 1952, she later claimed, pregnant with her second child, she was fired from her job on a union publication and told that her second pregnancy was her fault. The Newspaper Guild, she asserted, was unwilling to honor its commitment to grant pregnancy leaves. This was, Friedan later remembered, as she mentioned her efforts to call a meeting in protest, "the first personal stirring of my own feminism, I guess. But the other women were just embarrassed, and the men uncomprehending. It was my own fault, getting pregnant again, a *personal* matter, not something you should take to the union. There was no word in 1949 for 'sex discrimination.'"[21]

Though in the 1970s Friedan suggested this more interesting version of her life in the 1940s and 1950s, she distracted the reader from what she had said. She began and ended the 1974 piece with images of domestic life. Even as she mentioned participation in Marxist discussion groups, she talked of how she and her friends read fashion magazines and spent much of their earnings on elegant clothes. Describing what she offered as a major turning point in her life, she told of how, after campaigning for Henry Wallace in 1948, all of a sudden she lost interest in political activity. The 1940s and 1950s were a period, she later asserted, when she was fully exposed to what she would label the feminine mystique as she learned that motherhood took the place of career and politics. She gave the impression of herself in the late 1940s as a woman who embraced domesticity, motherhood, and housework, even as she admitted that not everything at the time resulted from the feminine mystique.[22]

In her 1974 article Friedan filled her descriptions of the late 1940s and 1950s with a sense of the conflicts she felt over her new roles, as she surrendered to the feminine mystique with mixed emotions. She reported how wonderful was the time in Parkway Village, Queens, a period when she experienced the pleasure of a spacious apartment, edited the community newspaper, and enjoyed the camaraderie of young marrieds. Yet, having read Benjamin Spock's *Child and Baby Care,* she felt guilty when she returned to work after a maternity leave. With her move to a traditional suburb, she said, the conflicts intensified. She spoke of driving her children to school and lessons, participating in the PTA, and then, when neighbors came by, hiding "like secret drinking in the morning" the book she was working on.[23]

Accomplishing practical, specific tasks around the house and in local politics was "somehow more real and secure than the schizophrenic and even dangerous politics of the world revolution whose vanguard we used to fancy ourselves." Friedan remarked that by 1949 she realized that the revolution was not going to happen in the United States as she anticipated, in part because workers, like others, wanted kitchen gadgets. She reported that she found herself disillusioned with what was happening in unions, in Czechoslovakia, and in the Soviet Union, despite the fact that cries about the spread of Communism merely provided the pretext for attacks on suspected subversives. In those days, she continued, "McCarthyism, the danger of war against Russia and of fascism in America, and the reality of U.S. imperial, corporate wealth and power" combined to make those who once dreamed of "making the whole world over uncomfortable with the Old Left rhetoric of revolution." Using the first person plural as she referred to Margaret Mead's picture in *Male and Female* (1949) of women fulfilled through motherhood and domesticity, Friedan wrote, "we were suckers for that apple." It hardly occurred to any of those in her circle, who themselves now wanted new gadgets, that large corporations profited from marketing household appliances by "overselling us on the bliss of domesticity."[24]

The new information Friedan offered in 1974 did not dislodge the accepted understanding of how she became a feminist . . . [Yet] what the written record reveals of Friedan's life from her arrival at Smith in the fall of 1938 until the publication of *The Feminine Mystique* makes possible a story different from the one she has told. To begin with, usually missing from her narrative is full and specific information about how at college she first developed a sense of herself as a radical.[25] Courses she took, friendships she established with peers and professors, events in the United States and abroad, and her campus leadership all turned Friedan from a provincial outsider into a determined advocate of trade unions as the herald of progressive social change, a healthy skeptic about the authority and rhetorical claims of those in power, a staunch opponent of fascism, a defender of free speech, and a fierce questioner of social privilege expressed by the conspicuous consumption of some of her peers.[26]

What and with whom she studied points well beyond Gestalt psychology and Koffka.[27] Though Friedan acknowledged the importance of James Gibson, she did not mention his activity as an advocate of trade unions.[28] Moreover, her statement that at Smith there were few role models is hard to reconcile with the fact that the college had a number of them; indeed she took courses from both James Gibson and Eleanor Gibson, husband and wife and parents of two children, the first of them born in 1940.[29] As a women's college, and especially one with an adversarial tradition, Smith may well have fostered in Friedan a feminism that was at least implicit—by enabling her to assume leadership positions and by encouraging her to take herself seriously as a writer and thinker.

In the fall of her junior year, Friedan took an economics course taught by Dorothy W. Douglas, Theories and Movements for Social Reconstruction. Douglas was well known at the time for her radicalism.[30] In what she wrote for Douglas, and with youthful enthusiasm characteristic of many members of her generation, Friedan sympathetically responded to the Marxist critique of capitalism as a cultural, economic, and political force.[31]

Friedan also gained an education as a radical in the summer of 1941 when, following Douglas's suggestion, she participated in a writers' workshop at the Highlander Folk School in Tennessee, an institution active in helping the CIO organize in the South. The school offered a series of summer institutes for fledgling journalists which, for 1939 and 1940

(but not 1941), the communist-led League of American Writers helped sponsor. For three years beginning in the fall of 1939, opponents of Highlander had sustained a vicious redbaiting attack, but a FBI investigator found no evidence of subversive activity.[32] In good Popular Front language, Friedan praised Highlander as a truly American institution that was attempting to help America to fulfill its democratic ideals. She explored the contradictions of her social position as a Jewish girl from a well-to-do family who had grown up in a class-divided Peoria, gave evidence of her hostility to the way her parents fought over issues of debt and extravagance, and described the baneful influence of the mass media on American life. Though she also acknowledged that her Smith education did "not lead to much action," she portrayed herself as someone whose radical consciousness relied on the American labor movement as the bulwark against fascism.[33]

At Smith Friedan linked her journalism to political activism. She served as editor-in-chief of the campus newspaper for a year beginning in the spring of 1941. The campaigns she undertook and the editorials she wrote reveal a good deal of her politics. Under Friedan's leadership, the newspaper's reputation for protest was so strong that in a skit a fellow student portrayed an editor, perhaps Friedan herself, as "a strident voice haranguing from a perpetual soap-box.[34] While at Smith, a Peoria paper reported in 1943, Friedan helped organize college building and grounds workers into a union.[35] Under her leadership, the student paper took on the student government for holding closed meetings, fought successfully to challenge the administration's right to control what the newspaper printed, campaigned for the relaxation of restrictions on student social life, censured social clubs for their secrecy, and published critiques of professors' teaching.[36] In response to an article in a campus humor magazine that belittled female employees who cleaned the students' rooms and served them food, an editorial supported the administration's censorship of the publication on the grounds that such action upheld "the liberal democratic tradition of the college."[37]

The editorials written on her watch reveal a young woman who believed that what was involved with almost every issue—at Smith, in the United States and abroad—was the struggle for democracy, freedom, and social justice.

Under Friedan's leadership the editors supported American workers and their labor unions in their struggles to organize and improve their conditions. . . . The inequality of power in America, the editorial argued in good social democratic terms, "has to be admitted and dealt with if democracy is to have meaning for 95% of the citizens of this country."[38]

Above all, what haunted the editorials was the spread of fascism and questions about America's involvement in a world war. In April of 1941, the editors made it clear that the defeat of fascism was their primary goal and one that determined their position on questions of war or peace. In the fall of 1941, after the German invasion of the Soviet Union during the preceding summer, the editors increasingly accepted the inevitability of war even as they made it clear that they believed "fighting fascists is only one part of fighting fascism."[39] Some Smith students responded with redbaiting to the newspaper's anti-fascism and reluctance to support intervention wholeheartedly, accusing the editorial board of being dominated by communists, at a time when the Party reached its greatest membership in the years after Pearl Harbor while the United States and the Soviet Union were allies. Though one editor denied the charge of communist influence, like many newspapers at American colleges in these years, on the paper's staff were students attracted to the political analysis offered by radical groups. In the fall of 1940 one columnist argued against lumping communists and Nazis together, remarking that communism was not a "dark terror" but "a precarious scheme worked out by millions of civilized men and women."[40]

When America entered the war in December of 1941, the editors accepted the nation's new role loyally, albeit soberly. The central issue for them was how American students, especially female ones, could "contribute actively to the American cause." . . .

Friedan's experiences at Smith cast a different light on her decision to leave Berkeley after a year of graduate school. The editorials she and her peers had written immediately after Pearl Harbor revealed an impatience to be near the action. A 1943 article in the Peoria paper reported that Friedan turned down the fellowship because "she decided she wanted to work in the labor movement—on the labor press."[41] . . . Off and on from October 1943

until July 1946 she was a staff writer for the Federated Press, a left-wing news service that provided stories for newspapers, especially union ones, across the nation.[42] Here Friedan wrote articles that supported the aspirations of African Americans and union members. She also criticized reactionary forces that, she believed, were working secretly to undermine progressive social advances.[43] As early as 1943, she pictured efforts by businesses, coordinated by the National Association of Manufacturers (NAM), to develop plans that would enhance profits, diminish the power of unions, reverse the New Deal, and allow businesses to operate as they pleased.[44]

At Federated Press, Friedan also paid attention to women's problems. Right after she began to work there, she interviewed UE official Ruth Young, one of the clearest voices in the labor movement articulating women's issues. In the resulting article, Friedan noted that the government could not solve the problem of turnover "merely by pinning up thousands of glamorous posters designed to lure more women into industry." Neither women, unions, nor management, she quoted Young as saying, could solve problems of escalating prices or inadequate child care that were made even more difficult by the fact that "women still have two jobs to do." Action of the federal government, Friedan reported, was needed to solve the problems working women faced.[45]

She paid special attention to stories about protecting the jobs and improving the situation of working women, including married ones with children.

For about six years beginning in July, 1946, precisely at the moment when the wartime Popular Front came under intense attack, Friedan was a reporter for the union's paper *UE News*.[46] At least as early as 1943, when she quoted Young, Friedan was well aware of the UE's commitments to equity for women.[47]

. . . In 1949–50, union activists who followed the recommendations of the Communist Party . . . advocated the automatic granting of several years of seniority to all African Americans as compensation for their years of exclusion from the electrical industry. If the UE pioneered in articulating what we might call affirmative action for African Americans, then before and during World War II it advocated what a later generation would label comparable worth. Against considerable resistance from within its ranks, the UE also worked to improve the conditions of working-class women in part by countering a seniority system which gave advantage to men.[48] After 1949, with the UE out of the CIO and many of the more conservative union members out of the UE, women's issues and women's leadership resumed the importance they had in the UE during World War II, when it had developed, Ruth Milkman has written, a "strong ideological commitment to gender equality."[49]

Beginning in 1946, Friedan [also] witnessed the efforts by federal agencies, congressional committees, major corporations, the Roman Catholic Church, and the CIO to break the hold of what they saw as the domination of the UE by communists. The inclusion of a clause in the Taft-Hartley Act of 1947, requiring union officers to sign an anticommunist affidavit if they wished to do business with the National Labor Relations Board, helped encourage other unions to challenge the UE, whose leaders refused to sign.[50] Internecine fights took place within the UE, part of a longer term fight between radicals and anticommunists in its ranks. . . . Before long, . . . the UE was greatly weakened: in 1949, its connection with the CIO was severed and the newly-formed and CIO-backed IUE recruited many of its members. Membership in UE, numbering more than 600,000 in 1946, fell to 203,000 in 1953 and to 71,000 four years later.[51]

At UE News, from her position as a middle-class woman interested in the lives of the working class, Friedan continued to articulate a progressive position on a wide range of issues. She again pointed to concerted efforts, led by big corporations under the leadership of the NAM, to increase profits, exploit labor, and break labor unions.[52] In 1951, she contrasted the extravagant expenditures of the wealthy with the family of a worker who could afford neither fresh vegetables nor new clothes.[53] Friedan also told the story of how valiant union members helped build political coalitions to fight Congressional and corporate efforts to roll back gains workers made during the New Deal and World War II.[54] She drew parallels between the United States in the 1940s and Nazi Germany in the 1930s as she exposed the way HUAC and big business were using every tactic they could to destroy the UE.

Friedan hailed the launching of the Progressive Party in 1948.[55] She exposed the existence of racism and discrimination, even when they appeared among union officials and especially when directed against Jews and African Americans. Praising heroic workers who struggled against great odds as they fought monopolies, Friedan, probably expressing her hopes for herself, extolled the skills of a writer "who is able to describe with sincerity and passion the hopes, the struggle and the romance of the working people who make up most of America."[56]

Throughout her years at UE News, Friedan participated in discussions on women's issues, including the issue of corporations' systematic discrimination against women. Going to factories to interview those whose stories she was covering, she also wrote about working women, including African Americans and Latinas.[57] In the worlds Friedan inhabited in the decade beginning in 1943, as the historian Kathleen Weigand has shown, people often discussed the cultural and economic sources of women's oppression, the nature of discrimination based on sex, the special difficulties African American women faced, and the dynamics of discrimination against women in a variety of institutions, including the family.[58] Moreover, for the people around Friedan and doubtlessly for Friedan herself, the fight for justice for women was inseparable from the more general struggle to secure rights for African Americans and workers.[59] As she had done at the Federated Press, at UE News in the late 1940s and early 1950s she reported on how working women struggled as producers and consumers to make sure their families had enough to live on.[60]

Friedan's focus on working women's issues resulted in her writing the pamphlet, UE Fights for Women Workers, published by the UE in June of 1952.[61] She began by suggesting the contradiction in industry's treatment of women as consumers and as producers. "In advertisements across the land," Friedan remarked, "industry glorifies the American woman—in her gleaming GE kitchen, at her Westinghouse laundromat, before her Sylvania television set. Nothing," she announced as she insightfully explored a central contradiction women faced in the postwar world, "is too good for her—unless" she worked for corporations, including GE, or Westinghouse, or Sylvania.[62]

The central theme of the piece was how, in an effort to improve the pay and conditions of working women, the UE fought valiantly against greedy corporations that sought to increase their profits by exploiting women. Friedan discussed a landmark 1945 National War Labor Board decision on sex-based wage discrimination in favor of the UE. Remarking that *"fighting the exploitation of women is men's business too,"* she emphasized how discriminatory practices corporations used against women hurt men as well by exerting downward pressure on wages of all workers. To back up the call for equal pay for equal work and to fight against segregation and discrimination of women, she countered stereotypes justifying lower pay for women: they were physically weaker, entered the work force only temporarily, had no families to support, and worked only for pin money. She highlighted the "even more shocking" situation African American women faced, having to deal as they did with the "double bars" of being female and African American.[63] Friedan set forth a program that was, Lisa Kannenberg has noted, "a prescription for a gender-blind workplace."[64]

The conditions under which she left Federated Press and *UE News* are not entirely clear. In May of 1946, during her second stint at Federated Press, she filed a grievance with the Newspaper Guild, saying she had lost her job in June of 1945 to a man she had replaced during the war. Later she claimed she was "bumped" from her position "by a returning veteran." There is evidence, however, that Friedan had to give up her position to a man who returned to the paper after two years in prison because he refused to serve in the military during what he considered a capitalists' war.[65] Friedan later claimed that she lost her job at the UE during her second pregnancy because the labor movement failed to honor its commitment to maternity leaves. Yet a knowledgeable observer has written that when the union had to cut the staff because of the dramatic drop in its membership, something that resulted from McCarthyite attacks, Friedan "offered to quit so another reporter," a man with more seniority, could remain at *UE News.*[66] Although her experience with unions may have provided a negative spur to her feminism, it also served as a positive inspiration. Friedan was indebted to the UE for major elements of her education about

gender equity, sex discrimination, and women's issues.

The reason Friedan left out these years in her life story is now clear. Her stint at the *UE News* took place at the height of the anti-communist crusade, which she experienced at close quarters. When she emerged into the limelight in 1963, the issue of affiliation with communists was wracking SANE, SDS, and the civil rights movement. In the same years, HUAC was still holding hearings, the United States was pursuing an anti-communist war in Vietnam, and J. Edgar Hoover's FBI was wiretapping Martin Luther King, Jr., ostensibly to protect the nation against communist influence. Had Friedan revealed all in the mid-1960s, she would have undercut her book's impact, subjected herself to palpable dangers, and jeopardized the feminist movement, including the National Organization for Women (NOW), an institution she was instrumental in launching. Perhaps instead of emphasizing continuities in her life, she told the story of her conversion in order to heighten the impact of her book and appeal to white middle-class women. Or . . . Friedan may have come to believe a narrative that outlived the needs it originally fulfilled.

Until 1952, almost everything Friedan published as a labor journalist appeared under the name Betty Goldstein, though she had married in 1947. When she emerged as a writer for women's magazines in 1955, it was as Betty Friedan. Aside from indicating her marital status, the change in name was significant. It signaled a shift from an employee for a union paper who wrote highly political articles on the working class to a free-lance writer for mass circulation magazines who concentrated on the suburban middle class in more muted tones [and in the 1950s became a suburbanite herself. In 1957, the Freidans moved into an] eleven-room Victorian house, which they bought with the help of the GI Bill and some money Friedan inherited from her father.[67]

What Friedan wrote for mass circulation women's magazines [during those years] belies her claim that she had contributed to what she later attacked in *The Feminine Mystique.*

Sylvie Murray has demonstrated that Friedan drafted, but was unable to get into print, articles that fully celebrated women's political activism, expressed skepticism about male expertise, and described blue collar and lower middle-class families, not generic middle-class ones. Yet Friedan was able to sell articles that went against the grain of the cold war celebration by criticizing middle-class conformity.... Friedan critiqued suburban life by drawing a dismal picture of those who conformed, by offering alternatives to conventional choices, and by exploring the strength of cooperative communities.[68] She drew portraits of American women that opposed the picture of the happy, suburban housewife who turned her back on a career in order to find satisfaction at home.[69] Friedan also portrayed women accomplishing important tasks as they took on traditionally feminine civic roles, thus implicitly undercutting the ideal of the apolitical suburban housewife and mother.[70]

In one particularly revealing piece, Friedan prefigured some of the issues she later claimed she only began to discover when she started to work on The Feminine Mystique. In "I Went Back to Work," published in Charm in April 1955, she wrote that initially she did not think highly of housework or of housewives and was guilty about what she was doing. Eventually she decided that her commitment to being a good mother was not "going to interfere with what I regarded as my 'real' life." Finding it necessary to be away from home for nine hours a day in order to work, she solved the problem of child care by hiring "a really good mother-substitute—a housekeeper-nurse." In the end, Friedan had no regrets about her decision or apparently about her privileged position. She believed her work outside the home improved her family's situation and acknowledged that her "whole life had always been geared around creative, intellectual work" and "a professional career."[71]

In what ways, then, was Friedan a captive of the feminine mystique? There is no question but that she was miserable in the suburbs. Her emphasis on her captivity may have expressed one part of her ambivalence. Yet, though she claimed that she shared so much with her suburban, white, middle-class sisters in the postwar world, during much of the two decades beginning in 1943 Friedan was participating in left-wing union activity, writing articles that went against the grain of cold war ideology, and living in a cosmopolitan, racially integrated community. During most of the time between her marriage in 1947 and the publication of The Feminine Mystique, Friedan combined career and family life. As a woman who worked with her at Federated Press later noted, at the time Friedan and her female colleagues expected to have professional careers.[72] Caution about the predominantly suburban origins of her book is also in order because Friedan's move to suburban Rockland County in 1956 preceded by only a few months her initial work on the survey for her reunion that was so critical to The Feminine Mystique.[73]

To be sure, in the postwar world Friedan experienced at first hand the trials of a woman who fought against considerable odds to combine marriage, motherhood, and a career.[74] Yet in critical ways her difficulties did not stem from the dilemmas she described in her book: lack of career and ambition, a securely affluent household, and absence of a political sensibility. Friedan experienced psychological conflicts over issues of creativity in writing and motherhood.[75] Researching and writing her free-lance articles was a laborious process.[76] She had three young children, hardly felt comfortable in the suburbs, had no local institutions to provide a supportive environment for an aspiring writer, and continually faced financial difficulties. Her income from writing articles was unpredictable, a situation exacerbated by the pressure she was under to help support the household and justify the expenses for child care. Tension persisted between the Friedans over a wide range of issues, including who was responsible for earning and spending the family's income. Moreover, she was in a marriage apparently marked by violence.[77]

Friedan was largely right when she said "all the pieces of my own life came together for the first time in the writing" of The Feminine Mystique. The skills as a journalist she had developed beginning as a teenager stood her in good stead as she worked to make what she had to say accessible to a wide audience. Her identity as a Jew and an outsider gave her a distinctive perspective on American and suburban life. Her years at Smith boosted her confidence and enhanced her political education. Her life as a wife and mother sensitized her to the conflicts millions of others experienced but could not articulate. Her education as a psychologist led her to understand the gestalt, the wholeness of a situation, and to advocate self-fulfillment based on humanistic psychology. Above all, her work as a labor journalist and activist provided her with the intellectual depth, ideological commitments, and practical experiences crucial to her emergence as a leading feminist in the 1960s.

Why did a woman who had spent so much energy advocating political solutions focus in *The Feminine Mystique* largely on adult education and self-realization and turn social problems into psychological ones? How did a woman who had fought to improve the lives of African Americans, Latinas, and working-class women end up writing a book that saw the problems of America in terms of the lives of affluent, suburban white women?[78]

Even at the time, at least one observer, Gerda Lerner, raised questions about what Friedan emphasized and neglected. Active in the trade union movement in the 1940s, present at the founding meeting of NOW, and after the mid-1960s one of the nation's leading historians of women, in February 1963 Lerner wrote Friedan. "I have just finished reading your splendid book and want to tell you how excited and delighted I am with it. . . . You have done for women," she remarked as she referred to the author who had warned about the destruction of the environment, "what Rachel Carson did for birds and trees." Yet, Lerner continued:

I have one reservation about your treatment of your subject: you address yourself solely to the problems of middle class, college-educated women. This approach was one of the shortcomings of the suffrage movement for many years and has, I believe, retarded the general advance of women. Working women, especially Negro women, labor not only under the disadvantages imposed by the feminine mystique, but under the more pressing disadvantages of economic discrimination. To leave them out of consideration of the problem or to ignore the contributions they can make toward its solution, is something we simply cannot afford to do. By their desperate need, by their numbers, by their organizational experience (if trade union members), working women are most important in reaching *institutional* solutions to the problems of women.[79]

The dynamics of Friedan's shifts in attention from working-class to middle-class women are not entirely clear. At some point after May 1953, when she followed the proceedings at the UE conference on the problems of women workers, Friedan turned away from working-class and African American women,

something that undercut the power of *The Feminine Mystique*. An important question is whether the shift from her UE radicalism and focus on working-class women was a rhetorical strategy designed for the specific situation of *The Feminine Mystique* or part of a longer-term deradicalization. Until her personal papers are fully open and extensive interviewing is carried out, and perhaps not even then, we may not know the dynamics of this change. Issues of the 1940s, and the fights by radicals for justice for women and African Americans in setting the stage for the reemergence of protests in the 1960s.

NOTES

1. Betty Goldstein, "UE Drive on Wage, Job Discrimination Wins Cheers from Women Members," *UE News*, 16 Apr. 1951, 6. My interview of Friedan in 1987 first brought to my attention the possibility of this alternative story, as did the research my colleague, Helen L. Horowitz, carried out in the late 1980s. The appearance of the article by Joanne Meyerowitz in 1993, cited below, added an important piece of evidence. Because Friedan has denied me permission to quote from her unpublished papers and has not responded to my request that she grant me an opportunity to interview her or to have her respond to my questions, I have not been able to present as full and perhaps as accurate a story as I wished to do.

2. Ronald W. Schatz, *The Electrical Workers: A History of Labor at General Electric and Westinghouse, 1923–60* (Urbana, Ill., 1983), xiii.

3. Lisa Kannenberg, "The Impact of the Cold War on Women's Trade Union Activism: The UE Experience," *Labor History* 34 (spring-summer 1993): 318; Jacqueline Van Voris, interview with Eleanor Flexner, Northampton, Mass., 16 Oct. 1982, 70–71, Eleanor Flexner Papers, Schlesinger Library, Radcliffe College, Cambridge, Mass. [hereinafter cited as FP-SLRC]; [Eleanor Flexner], "The Woman Question," Syllabus for course at Jefferson School of Social Science, 1953–54, 1, 2, 5. For information on Flexner. I am relying on Ellen C. DuBois, "Eleanor Flexner and the History of American Feminism," *Gender and History* 3 (spring 1991): 81–90. On the Jefferson School, see Annette T. Rubinstein, "David Goldway," *Science and Society* 54 (winter 1990–91): 386–89; Daniel F. Ring, "Two Cultures: Libraries, the Unions, and the 'Case' of the Jefferson School of Social Science," *Journal of Library History* 20 (1985): 287–88.

4. Betty Friedan, "Up From the Kitchen Floor," *New York Times Magazine*, 4 Mar. 1973, 8; Betty Friedan, *"It Changed My Life": Writings on the Women's Movement* (New York, 1976), 304.

5. For evidence of the continuing importance of Friedan and her book, see, for example, Elaine T. May, *Homeward Bound: American Families in the Cold War Era* (New York, 1988), 209–17, 219 and Joanne

Meyerowitz, "Beyond the Feminine Mystique: A Reassessment of Postwar Mass Culture, 1946–1958," *Journal of American History* 79 (Mar. 1993): 1455–82. For textbooks, see John M. Faragher et al., *Out of Many: A History of the American People* (Englewood Cliffs, N.J., 1994), 2:865, 943: James A. Henretta et al., *America's History*, 2d ed. (New York, 1993), 2:909, 910, 911, 968; William H. Chafe, *The Unfinished Journey: America Since World War II*, 3d ed. (New York, 1995), 124, 330, 433. A widely-used reader in American women's history contains a selection from Friedan's book, introducing its author as "a suburban housewife": Linda K. Kerber and Jane S. De Hart, *Women's America: Refocusing the Past*, 4th ed. (New York, 1995), 512.

6. For biographical information, in addition to what Friedan has said in print, I am relying on Kathleen Wilson, "Betty (Naomi) Friedan," *Contemporary Authors*, New Revision Series (New York, 1995) 45: 133–36; David Halberstam, *The Fifties* (New York, 1993), 592–98; Marilyn French, "The Emancipation of Betty Friedan," *Esquire* 100 (Dec. 1983): 510, 512, 514, 516, 517; Jennifer Moses, "She's Changed Our Lives: A Profile of Betty Friedan," *Present Tense* 15 (May–June 1988): 26–31; Lyn Tornabene, "The Liberation of Betty Friedan," *McCall's* 98 (May 1971): 84, 136–40, 142, 146; Paul Wilkes, "Mother Superior to Women's Lib," *New York Times Magazine*, 29 Nov. 1970, 27–29, 140–43, 149–50, 157; Marcia Cohen, *The Sisterhood: The True Story of the Women Who Changed the World* (New York, 1988), 25, 54–71, 83–84, 89–99; Lisa Hammel, "The 'Grandmother' of Women's Lib," *New York Times*, 19 Nov. 1971, 52; Friedan, *Changed My Life*, 5–16; Jacqueline Van Voris, interview of Betty Friedan, New York, N.Y., 17 Apr. 1973, College Archives, Smith College, Northampton, Mass. [hereinafter cited as CA-SC]; Daniel Horowitz, interview of Betty Friedan, Santa Monica, Calif., 18 Mar. 1987. As late as 6 Nov. 1995, the date she sent me a letter denying me permission to quote from her unpublished papers, Friedan reiterated key elements of her story: I am grateful to Rachel Ledford for reporting to me on Friedan's 6 Nov. 1995 talk at the Smithsonian Institution, Washington, D.C. Ironically, two biographies aimed at children provide fuller stories than do other treatments (for instance, they are the only published sources I have been able to locate that make clear that Friedan worked for the UE): Sondra Henry and Emily Taitz, *Betty Friedan: Fighter for Women's Rights* (Hillside, N.J., 1990) and Milton Meltzer, *Betty Friedan: A Voice for Women's Rights* (New York, 1985).

7. This article is based on considerable but hardly exhaustive examination of the available written record. When other researchers examine the Friedan papers (including those to which access is restricted) and are able to carry out extensive interviews, they will be able to offer a fuller exploration of several issues, especially the shifts in Friedan's commitments as a radical at a time of great factionalism, when and how the feminine mystique did or did not trap her, how she interpreted the research on which *The Feminine Mystique* relied, and the pressures Friedan faced from her publisher to shape her 1963 book in certain ways.

8. An examination of what Friedan wrote for her high school paper reveals someone less lonely than she has often portrayed herself: see articles by Friedan in *Peoria Opinion* from the fall of 1936 until the spring of 1938. For one political piece that reveals an early anti-fascism, see Bettye Goldstein, "Long, Coughlin, Roosevelt in 'It Can't Happen Here,'" *Peoria Opinion*, 18 Sept. 1936, 8.

9. Friedan, quoted in Wilkes, "Mother Superior," 140; Betty Friedan, *The Feminine Mystique* (New York, 1963), 12.

10. Friedan, *Feminine Mystique*, 70; Friedan, quoted in Wilkes, "Mother Superior," 140. On the paucity of role models at Smith, see Van Voris, Friedan interview.

11. Horowitz, interview.

12. Dust jacket of 1963 copy of *The Feminine Mystique*, author's possession. See also, "About Betty Friedan . . . ," biographical note accompanying Betty Friedan, "How to Find and Develop Article Ideas," *The Writer* 75 (Mar. 1962), 13.

13. Friedan, quoted in "Betty Friedan," *Current Biography Yearbook 1970*, ed. Charles Moritz (New York, 1971), 146; Betty Friedan, "New York Women: Beyond the Feminine Mystique," *New York Herald Tribune*, 21 Feb. 1965, 7–15, women's liberation, biographics, individuals, box 4, folder 31, clippings on Betty Friedan, Sophia Smith Collection, Smith College [hereinafter referred to as SSC-SC]; Wilkes, "Mother Superior," 141; Friedan, quoted in Wilkes, "Mother Superior," 141; Tornabene, "Liberation," 138; and Friedan, "Kitchen Floor," 8.

14. Tornabene, "Liberation," 138. See Betty Friedan, "The Intellectual Pied Pipers of Rockland County," unpublished paper, written in 1960–61, FP-SLRC, carton 9, folder 347, Friedan Collection, Schlesinger Library, Radcliffe College, Cambridge, Mass. [hereinafter cited as BF-SLRC; unless otherwise noted, the references are to collection 71–62 . . . 81-M23].

15. Rollene W. Saal, "Author of the Month," *Saturday Review*, 21 Mar. 1964, women's liberation, biographies, individuals, box 4, folder 31, SSC-SC; *Hackensack Record*, 2 May 1963, Class of 1942 folders, Betty Goldstein folder, CA-SC; Friedan, "Kitchen Floor," 8.

16. Friedan, *Feminine Mystique*, 9, 20, 66, 70, 186–87.

17. Horowitz, interview: Betty Friedan, "Introduction to the Tenth Anniversary Edition" of *Feminine Mystique* (New York, 1974), 1–5. For early articles with the themes that would emerge in the book, see Betty Friedan, "I Say: Women are *People* Too!" *Good Housekeeping* 151 (Sept. 1960): 59–61, 161–62; Betty Goldstein Friedan, "If One Generation Can Ever Tell Another," *Smith Alumnae Quarterly*, Feb. 1961, 68–70.

18. The 1974 article, which in the book was called "The Way We Were—1949," was originally published with some relatively unimportant differences, but with a more revealing title, as Betty Friedan, "In France, de Beauvoir Had Just Published 'The Second Sex,'" *New York* 8 (30 Dec. 1974–6 Jan. 1975): 52–55. In Horowitz, interview, which covered mainly the years up to 1963, Friedan discussed her move to a radical politics even as she emphasized captivity by the feminine mystique beginning in the Berkeley years. Though Friedan has revealed a good

deal about her life, to the best of my knowledge she has not acknowledged in print the full range of reasons she left Berkeley, that she worked for the UE, her authorship of the 1952 pamphlet, and her leadership of the rent strike. Moreover, she has insisted that in the late 1940s and early 1950s, she had interest neither in a career nor in women's problems.

19. I am grateful to Judith Smith for helping me to think through this and other issues.

20. Friedan, *Changed My Life*, 6, 8–9.

21. Friedan, *Changed My Life*, 6, 9, 16; Halberstam, *Fifties*, 593; French, "Emancipation," 510. Horowitz, interview, dates the firing in 1952. In the immediate postwar years, the term "feminist" often referred to women who were Republicans, independent businesswomen, and professionals.

22. Friedan, *Changed My Life*, 5, 6–7, 8–9, 15, 16. She gave 1949 as the turning point because she had been asked to do a piece in 1974 on what had happened a quarter of a century earlier: Horowitz, interview.

23. Friedan, *Changed My Life*, 14–16.

24. Friedan, *Changed My Life*, 12, 16.

25. Cohen, *Sisterhood*, 63 and Wilkes, "Mother Superior," 140 briefly draw a picture of Friedan as a college rebel but to the best of my knowledge, the politics of that rebellion have remained largely unknown.

26. This summary relies on unsigned editorials that appeared under Friedan's editorship, which can be found in *SCAN* [*Smith College Associated News*] from 14 Mar. 1941 to 10 Mar. 1942, p. 2. Although members of the editorial board held a wide range of opinions. I am assuming that as editor-in-chief Friedan had a significant role in shaping editorials. Friedan placed four editorials in her papers: "They Believed in Peace," "Years of Change and Unrest," "Behind Closed Doors," and "Answer No Answer": carton 7, folder 310, BF-SLRC.

27. For the article she published on the basis on her honors thesis, see H. Israel and B. Goldstein, "Operationism in Psychology," *Psychological Review* 51 (May 1944): 177–88.

28. See James J. Gibson, "Why A Union For Teachers?" *Focus* 2 (Nov. 1939): 3–7.

29. I am grateful to Margery Sly, Archivist of Smith College, for providing this information. She has also pointed out that teaching at Smith in Friedan's years were several married, female faculty members who had children and that Harold Israel and Elsa Siipola, two of Friedan's mentors, were married but without children.

30. In 1955 Douglas took the Fifth Amendment before HUAC as she was redbaited, accused of having been a member of a communist teachers union in the late 1930s. I am grateful to Margery Sly and Jacquelyn D. Hall for providing this information on Douglas. See also, Betty Friedan, "Was Their Education UnAmerican?" unpublished article, 1953 or 1954, carton 11, folder 415, BF-SLRC, 3. For Friedan's continued use of Marxist analysis, see Friedan, *It Changed My Life*, 110.

31. Bettye Goldstein, "Discussion of Reading Period Material," paper for Economics 319, 18 Jan. 1941, carton 1, folder 257, BF-SLRC, 1, 2, 4, 8. See also "Questions on *Communist Manifesto*" and

"Questions on Imperialism," papers for Economics 319, carton 1, folder 257, BF-SLRC.

32. John M. Glen, *Highlander: No Ordinary School, 1932–1962* (Lexington, Ky., 1988), 47–69. I am grateful to Professor Glen for a letter in which he clarified the timing of the League's sponsorship. Meltzer, *Friedan*, 20 says that Friedan's economics professor pointed her to Highlander but identifies that professor as a male; since the only economics course Friedan took was from Douglas, I am assuming that it was she who urged her student to attend the workshop. Meltzer thinks that is a reasonable assumption: Milton Meltzer, phone conversation with Daniel Horowitz, 24 Sept. 1995.

33. Bettye Goldstein, "Highlander Folk School—American Future," unpublished paper, 1941, carton 6, folder 274, BF-SLRC; Goldstein, "Learning the Score," 22–24.

34. "Epilogue of Failure," *SCAN*, 10 Mar. 1942, 2.

35. "Betty Goldstein, Local Girl, Makes Good in New York," clipping from Peoria newspaper, probably 10 Dec. 1943 issue of *Labor Temple News*, carton 1, folder 86, BF-SLRC.

36. "Behind a Closed Door," *SCAN*, 3 Oct. 1941, 2; "Declaration of Student Independence," *SCAN*, 5 Dec. 1941, 1–2; "SCAN Protests Against Censorship," *SCAN*, 5 Dec. 1941, 1; "A Few Hours More," *SCAN*, 10 Oct. 1941, 2; "Review of Philosophy Courses," *SCAN*, 10 Mar. 1942, 2.

37. "The Tatler Suspension," *SCAN*, 7 Nov. 1941, 2; for the article in question see "Maids We Have Known and Loved," *Tatler*, Oct. 1941, 9, 21. When the administration moved against *SCAN*, over a different incident, the editors changed their minds about the earlier suspension of the *Tatler: SCAN*, 5 Dec. 1941, 1–2.

38. "Education in Emergency," *SCAN*, 15 Apr. 1941, 2; "The Right to Organize," *SCAN*, 21 Oct. 1941, 2; "Comment," *SCAN*, 14 Nov. 1941, 2; Filene's advertisement, *SCAN*, 21 Oct. 1941, 2. Bettye Goldstein, "For Defense of Democracy," *Smith College Monthly* 1 (Oct. 1940): 11, 12, 28 is a passionate defense of democracy and a warning about the possibility of American fascism.

39. "They Choose Peace," *SCAN*, 22 Apr. 1941, 2; for the minority opinion, see "The Case for Intervention," *SCAN*, 2 May 1941, 2; "War Against Fascism," *SCAN*, 24 Oct. 1941, 2. Placing the editorials written on Friedan's watch in the national context of student politics makes clear that after the Nazi-Soviet pact the student movement was more active and radical at Smith than elsewhere. In addition, the commitment of Friedan and her fellow editors to anti-fascism and their reluctance to embrace interventionism fully after the German invasion of the Soviet Union suggests that they dissented from the Communist Party position. On the national context see Robert Cohen, *When The Old Left Was Young: Student Radicals and America's First Mass Student Movement, 1929–1941* (New York, 1993), especially 315–37.

40. J. N., "The Red Menace," *SCAN*, 14 Oct. 1941, 2; Neal Gilkyson, "The Gallery," *SCAN*, 21 Oct. 1941, 2.

41. "Betty Goldstein, Local Girl," Meltzer, *Friedan*, 21 provides explanations for Friedan's decision that do not rely on the standard story.

42. To date her work for the Federated Press, see Betty Friedan, job application for Time Inc., 1 July 1951, carton 1, folder 61, BF-SLRC. For information on the Federated Press, see Doug Reynolds, "Federated Press," *Encyclopedia of the American Left*, ed. Mari Jo Buhle, Paul Buhle, and Dan Georgakas (New York, 1990), 225–27.

43. Betty Goldstein, "Negro Pupils Segregated, Parents Strike; Issue Headed for Courts," Federated Press, 15 Sept. 1943, carton 8, folder 328, BF-SLRC; Betty Goldstein, "Peace Now: Treason in Pious Garb," Federated Press, 16 Feb. 1944, carton 8, folder 328, BF-SLRC; Betty Goldstein, "Well-Heeled 'White Collar League' Seen as Disguised Native Fascist Threat," Federated Press, 16 Mar. 1944, carton 8, folder 328, BF-SLRC.

44. Betty Goldstein, "Big Business Getting Desperate, Promising Postwar Jobs," Federated Press, 19 Nov. 1943, carton 8, folder 328, BF-SLRC; Betty Goldstein, "NAM Convention Pro-War—For War on Labor, New Deal, Roosevelt," Federated Press, 14 Dec. 1943, carton 8, folder 328, BF-SLRC; Betty Goldstein, "Details of Big Business Anti-Labor Conspiracy Uncovered," Federated Press, 11 Feb. 1946, carton 8, folder 328, BF-SLRC. For the larger story, see Elizabeth A. Fones-Wolf, *Selling Free Enterprise: The Business Assault on Labor and Liberalism, 1945–60* (Urbana, 1994).

45. Betty Goldstein, "Pretty Posters Won't Stop Turnover of Women in Industry," Federated Press, 26 Oct. 1943, and Ruth Young quoted in same, carton 8, folder 328, BF-SLRC.

46. Job application, 1951.

47. For information on women in the UE see Schatz, *Electrical Workers*; Ruth Milkman, *Gender at Work: The Dynamics of Job Segregation by Sex During World War II* (Urbana, 1987); Kannenberg, "Impact"; Lisa A. Kannenberg, "From World War to Cold War: Women Electrical Workers and Their Union, 1940–1955," M.A. thesis, University of North Carolina, Charlotte, 1990. Robert H. Zieger, *The CIO, 1935–1955* (Chapel Hill, N.C., 1995), 253–93 assesses the role of communists in the CIO, including the UE and discusses the vagueness of the line between sympathy and Party membership in unions like the UE; Ronald L. Filippelli and Mark McCulloch, *Cold War in the Working Class: The Rise and Decline of the United Electrical Workers* (Albany, N.Y., 1994) charts the attack on the UE and discusses the issue of communist presence in the UE.

48. Schatz, *Electrical Workers*, 30, 89, 116–27, 129–30.

49. Milkman, *Gender at Work*, 77–78; see also Kannenberg, "Impact," esp. 311, 315. Nancy B. Palmer, "Gender, Sexuality, and Work: Women and Men in the Electrical Industry, 1940–1955," Ph.D. diss., Boston College, 1995, more skeptical of women's gains in the UE, focuses on how the construction of gender in labor unions, including UE, limited women's advances: see esp. chap. 4.

50. Zieger, *CIO*, 251.

51. This summary relies on Schatz, *Electrical Workers*, 167–240. The 1946 quote is from Harry Block in Schatz, *Electrical Workers*, 181. For the impact of the attack on UE on women's issues, see Kannenberg, "From World War to Cold War," 95.

52. Betty Goldstein, "NAM Does Gleeful War Dance to Profits, Wage Cuts, Taft Law," *UE News*, 13 Dec. 1947, 4. What follows relies on the more than three dozen articles signed by Betty Goldstein in the *UE News* from the fall of 1946 until early 1952.

53. Betty Goldstein, "A Tale of 'Sacrifice': A Story of Equality in the United States, 1951," *March of Labor*, May 1951, 16–18, carton 8, folder 334, BF-SLRC. This also appeared in *UE News*, 12 Mar. 1951, 6–7.

54. Betty Goldstein, "It'll Take a Strong Union To End Winchester Tyranny," *UE News*, 7 Dec. 1946, 9; Betty Goldstein, "Fighting Together: We Will Win!" *UE News*, 31 May 1947, 5, 8: Betty Goldstein, "Labor Builds New Political Organization To Fight for a People's Congressman," *UE News*, 23 Aug. 1947, 4.

55. Betty Goldstein, "People's Needs Forgotten: Big Business Runs Govt.," *UE News*, 12 May 1947, 5; Betty Goldstein, "In Defense of Freedom! The People Vs. the UnAmerican Committee," *UE News*, 8 Nov. 1947, 6–7; Betty Goldstein, "They Can't Shove the IBEW Down Our Throats," *UE News*, 4 Sept. 1948, 6–7; Betty Goldstein, "UnAmerican Hearing Exposed as Plot By Outsiders to Keep Grip on UE Local," *UE News*, 22 Aug. 1949, 4; Betty Goldstein, "New NAM Theme Song: Labor-Management Teamwork," *UE News*, 9 Jan. 1950, 5; Betty Goldstein, "Plain People of America Organize New Political Party of Their Own," *UE News*, 31 July 1948, 6–7.

56. B. G., review of Sinclair Lewis, *Kingsblood Royal*, *UE News*, 6 Sept. 1947, 7; B. G., review of the movie "Gentleman's Agreement," *UE News*, 22 Nov. 1947, 11; B. G., review of movie "Crossfire," *UE News*, 9 Aug. 1947, 8–9; Betty Goldstein, "CIO Sold Out Fight for FEPC, T-H Repeal, Rep. Powell Reveals," *UE News*, 17 Apr. 1950, 4; B. G., review of Fielding Burke, *Sons of the Stranger, UE News*, 24 Jan. 1948, 7.

57. These two sentences rely on James Lerner, interview. For treatments of the relationship between communism and women's issues, see Ellen K. Trimberger, "Women in the Old and New Left: The Evolution of a Politics of Personal Life," *Feminist Studies* 5 (fall 1979): 432–61; Van Gosse, "'To Organize in Every Neighborhood, in Every Home': The Gender Politics of American Communists Between the Wars," *Radical History Review* 50 (spring 1991): 109–41; Kannenberg, "From World War to Cold War"; and Kathleen A. Weingand, "Vanguards of Women's Liberation: The Old Left and the Continuity of the Women's Movement in the United States, 1945–1970s," Ph.D. diss., Ohio State University, 1995. For her coverage of Latinas, see Betty Goldstein, "'It's a Union That Fights for All the Workers,'" *UE News*, 3 [?] Sept. 1951, 6–7.

58. Though she does not discuss Friedan's situation, the best treatment of the prominent role of women's issues in radical circles in the 1940s and 1950s is Weigand, "Vanguards." In working on *The Feminine Mystique*, Friedan may have been influenced by writings she may have encountered in the 1940s, such as Mary Inman, *In Women's Defense* (Los Angeles, 1940) and Betty Millard, "Woman Against Myth," *New Masses*, 30 Dec. 1947, 7–10 and 6 Jan. 1948, 7–20. There is evidence that Friedan was well

aware of *New Masses*. Under a pseudonym, she published two articles in *New Masses:* Lillian Stone, "Labor and the Community," *New Masses* 57 (23 Oct. 1945): 3–5; Lillian Stone, "New Day in Stamford," *New Masses* 58 (22 Jan. 1946): 3–5. In identifying Friedan as the author, I am relying on a 22 Sept. 1995 conversation with Kathy Kraft, an archivist at the Schlesinger Library and on a letter in carton 49, folder 1783, BF-SLRC.

59. Chinoy, interview.

60. Betty Goldstein, "Price Cuts Promised in Press Invisible to GE Housewives," *UE News*, 1 Feb. 1947, 7; Betty Goldstein, "Union Members Want to Know—WHO Has Too Much Money to Spend," *UE News*, 26 Mar. 1951, 8.

61. [Betty Goldstein], *UE Fights for Women Workers*, UE Publication no. 232, June 1952 (New York, 1952). To authenticate her authorship, I am relying on the following: Horowitz, interview; James Lerner, interview; Betty Friedan, postcard to author, late August, 1995; Meltzer, *Friedan*, 25. Meltzer, who knew Friedan in the 1940s, discusses her work on women's issues at the UE. Friedan may also have written *Women Fight For a Better Life!* (New York, 1953): see Friedan, postcard.

62. [Goldstein], *UE Fights*, 5.

63. [Goldstein], *UE Fights*, 9–18, 26–27, 38.

64. Kannenberg, "Impact," 318.

65. Betty Goldstein to Grievance Committee of Newspaper Guild of New York, 23 May 1946, carton 8, folder 330, BF-SLRC; Friedan, *Changed My Life*, 9; Mim Kelber, phone conversation with Daniel Horowitz, 16 Sept. 1995, identified the man as James Peck; obituary for James Peck, *New York Times* 13 July 1993, B7.

66. Meltzer, *Friedan*, 29. For additional perspectives on Friedan's departure from the *UE News*, see Kelber, conversation and James Lerner, interview, Lerner, who had more seniority than Friedan, worked for the UE for more than 40 years, eventually becoming managing editor of *UE News*. He shared an office with Friedan during her years at *UE News* and has noted that the union protected Friedan's position during her first pregnancy: James Lerner, interview.

67. To date these moves, I am relying on a number of sources, including Betty Friedan to Mrs. Clifford P. Cowen, 5 Aug. 1957, carton 7, folder, 313, BF-SLRC; Friedan, "New York Women"; "About the Author," in "New York Women"; "Friedan," *Current Biography*, 146; *Smith College Bulletin*.

68. Betty Friedan, "Two Are an Island," *Mademoiselle* 41 (July 1955): 88–89, 100–101; Betty Friedan, "Teenage Girl in Trouble," *Coronet* 43 (Mar. 1958): 163–68; Betty Friedan. "The Happy Families of Hickory Hill," *Redbook*, Feb. 1956, 39, 87–90; Stone, Marian and Harold Stone [fictitious names], as told to Betty Friedan, "With Love We Live. . . ." *Coronet* 42 (July 1957): 135–44. For another article on a suburban development that relied on cooperation, see Betty Friedan, "'We Built a Community for Our Children,'" *Redbook*, Mar. 1955, 42–45, 62–63. Friedan's papers contain information on scores of articles that she was working on; this analysis focuses on those actually published. Sylvie Murray's "Suburban Cit-

izens: Domesticity and Community Politics in Queens, New York, 1945–1960," Ph.D. diss., Yale University, 1994 ably contrasts the adversarial politics of Friedan's unpublished pieces with the milder tone of her published ones; on the difficulty of getting into print articles on women who were not middle-class, I am relying on Sylvie Murray, phone conversation with Daniel Horowitz, 9 Oct. 1995.

69. Betty Friedan, "The Gal Who Defied Dior," *Town Journal*, Oct. 1955, 33, 97–98; Betty Friedan, "Millionaire's Wife," *Cosmopolitan*, Sept. 1956, 78–87; Betty Friedan, "New Hampshire Love Story," *Family Circle*, June 1958, 40–41, 74–76. An influential book on the origins of 1960s feminism begins with a discussion of Friedan's magazine articles without seeing how they might connect parts of her career: Sara Evans, *Personal Politics: The Roots of Women's Liberation in the Civil Rights Movement and the New Left* (New York, 1979), 3.

70. Betty Friedan, "Now They're Proud of Peoria," *Reader's Digest* 67 (Aug. 1955): 93–97.

71. Betty Friedan, "I Went Back to Work," *Charm*, Apr. 1955, 145, 200.

72. Kelber, conversation.

73. Parkway Village had some suburban characteristics and was marketed on the basis of its suburban qualities: Murray, conversation. Yet Friedan has made it clear that she was happy there: Friedan, *Changed My Life*, 14. Moreover, being in Parkway Village did not involve inhabiting a single-family home or living individualistically among conformists.

74. Especially crucial but nonetheless elusive is the period from May 1953, when she appears to have ended her union work, and 1955, when her first article appeared in a woman's magazine.

75. Friedan, "How to Find and Develop Article Ideas," 12–15 has some discussion of these conflicts.

76. This becomes clear through an examination of her files on her free-lance work, especially when compared with the files of Vance Packard in the same years.

77. Wilkes, "Mother Superior," 141. On violence in the marriage, see also Tornabene, "Liberation," 138; Cohen, *Sisterhood*, 17–18; Meyer, "Friedan," 608; Myra MacPherson, "The Former Mr. Betty Friedan Has Scars to Prove It," probably 1971, newspaper article from unidentified source, women's liberation, biographies, individuals, box 4, folder 31, clippings on Betty Friedan, SSC-SC.

78. On this problem, see Elizabeth V. Spelman, *Inessential Woman: Problems of Exclusion in Feminist Thought* (Boston, 1988).

79. Gerda Lerner to Betty Friedan, 6 Feb. 1963, box 20a, folder 715, BF-SLRC; quoted with permission of Gerda Lerner. For information on Lerner's participation in the labor movement, the Congress of American Women, and at the founding meeting of NOW, I am relying on Daniel Horowitz, phone conversation with Gerda Lerner, 18 Oct. 1995; Amy Swerdlow, "The Congress of American Women: Left-Feminist Peace Politics in the Cold War," in *U.S. History as Women's History: New Feminist Essays*, ed. Linda K. Kerber, Alice Kessler-Harris, and Kathryn Kish Sklar (Chapel Hill, 1995), 306.

CATHERINE E. RYMPH
Neither Neutral nor Neutralized: Phyllis Schlafly's Battle against Sexism

Betty Goldstein Friedan and Phyllis Stewart Schlafly seem, at first glance, to be polar opposites: Freidan, left-liberal and Jewish, whose name would become synonymous with a resurgent feminism in the late 1960s, and Schlafly, politically conservative and Catholic, who would emerge in the early 1970s as a symbol of antifeminism. Yet the two have much in common. Separated in age by only three years, both were the first child born to their respective families. Both grew up during the Depression years in Illinois and were valedictorians of their high school class. Both attended academically rigorous colleges where they excelled, both did some postgraduate work, and both held interesting jobs before marrying. Both women had children—Friedan three and Schlafly six—whom they reared in suburbia along with the millions of other middle-class families caught up in the resurgent domesticity of the postwar years. Yet neither of these energetic and intelligent women found domesticity sufficient.

In this perceptive essay, which tells us much about the role of women in the major political parties in the post-suffrage decades, Catherine Rymph examines Schlafly's political activism within the Republican Party in the 1950s and 1960s. How does she explain the fact that a woman so aware of sexism within the Party became an antifeminist rather than a feminist? How does Rymph's essay complicate the pattern, exemplified by other figures in this book, that female education, activism, and empowerment lead to the embrace of progressive causes and often feminism?

During the late 1960s many politically active women became frustrated that their role within political organizations was to make coffee and copies. Responding to the sexism of the New Left, young middle-class women began demanding their own voice within the civil rights and antiwar movements, ultimately launching the women's liberation movement, one component of what came to be known as second-wave feminism.[1] At the same time, a similar scenario unfolded within a very different political organization and with very different results. In 1967, over 1,000 conservative Republican women, led by Phyllis Schlafly, rebelled against the mainstream GOP they believed was ignor-ing and belittling them. Eventually Schlafly and her followers developed an organized and influential opposition to feminism.

As a leader in the battle against the Equal Rights Amendment (ERA), Schlafly emerged in the 1970s as a champion of the "pro-family" politics that has profoundly influenced American politics in recent decades. Socially conservative herself, the issues that initially moved Schlafly politically were traditional ones: antistatism, anti-communism, and pro-defense. Schlafly's evolution into a leader of socially conservative women had its roots in her frustrations with the Republican Party. She was an ideological conservative within a party domi-

Prepared especially for *Women's America*. Copyright © 1998 Catherine E. Rymph. Drawn from Catherine E. Rymph, "Forward and Right: The Shaping of Republican Women's Activism, 1920–1967," Ph.D. diss., University of Iowa, 1998.

nated by moderates and an ambitious woman within a party dominated by men.

Phyllis Stewart was born August 15, 1924, in St. Louis. Her Catholic parents, who valued education for their daughters, sent Phyllis to a Catholic girls' school. She graduated from Washington University at St. Louis in 1944, winning a scholarship for graduate work at Radcliffe. After receiving her master's degree in political science, she worked for a year in Washington, D.C., before returning to St. Louis, where she began volunteering for the Republican Party and working at a bank. In 1949, she married lawyer Fred Schlafly, with whom she shared a passionate interest in conservative politics.[2]

Family responsibilities did not prevent Phyllis Schlafly from pursuing her political interests. In 1952, already a mother, she ran unsuccessfully for Congress against an incumbent Democrat.[3] Afterwards, Schlafly continued her political activism in the ways that were available to women at the time—as a party volunteer. Party women at the local level (often organized into women's partisan clubs) rang doorbells, registered voters, distributed leaflets, and babysat for voting mothers on election day. As good partisans, women were expected to be loyal to their party even when they disagreed with a particular candidate or position. This apparent self-censorship actually reflected a plan for gaining inclusion. Republican women themselves, in the National Federation of Republican Women (NFRW), had promoted this strategy, beginning in the late 1930s. They believed that only by proving themselves to be loyal workers, indispensable to Party successes, would they eventually gain access to political influence. By the 1950s, the Republican Party had developed a system of grassroots organizing that depended on women's voluntarism. Yet little corresponding access to political influence followed.[4]

Schlafly distinguished herself from other women party workers by displaying exceptional drive and political interest. Not content to continue stuffing envelopes in the precincts, Schlafly took on those larger roles available to her—through leadership in the party's women's organizations. In the late 1950s, she served on the NFRW's national Kitchen Cabinet (a plan to encourage women's interest in the issues facing President Eisenhower's cabi-

net) and in 1960 became president of the Illinois Federation of Republican Women.[5]

In the 1950s, Schlafly remained a loyal party activist, despite becoming increasingly frustrated that leaders of her party were advocating policies she found too liberal. In 1964 she described her history of party activism as that of a steadfast partisan, promoting good government, and trying to persuade women to work for the party. When a candidate she supported was not nominated, she nonetheless campaigned in her state for the party's choice "just as enthusiastically and energetically" as if her candidate had been on the ballot.[6] She eventually grew disenchanted with the arguments for party loyalty, however, coming to believe that only if the party put forward truly conservative candidates would it be victorious.

Schlafly was not the only Republican to become frustrated with her party during the 1950s. In 1960, conservative Republicans across the country tried to capture control of the party when they sought to win the presidential nomination for Arizona Senator Barry Goldwater. Goldwater had emerged in recent years as a leader of the party's right wing, whose adherents were displeased with Eisenhower's domestic, foreign, and economic policy agendas. Insisting that any growth in government threatened freedom, Goldwater objected in principle to many programs supported by Eisenhower Republicans, including federal aid to education, federal housing programs, and federal enforcement of desegregation orders in the South. In the area of foreign policy, Goldwater insisted that the U.S. should not be satisfied with its policy of containing communism to those areas where it had existed since the end of World War II. Instead, he argued, the United States should be seeking victory over its communist enemies abroad.[7] Conservative renegades failed in 1960 to win the nomination for Goldwater. Shortly after the convention, however, several who had worked together in the Young Republicans began plans to draft Goldwater to make a serious run for the GOP nomination in 1964. To this end, they sought to unite various sources of conservative sympathy into an outpouring of support (outside traditional party leadership) for a Goldwater presidential bid.

Although not a part of this initial group, Schlafly, too, was an enthusiastic supporter of Goldwater. In 1964, she produced a small, self-

Phyllis Schlafly demonstrated the domestic ideal by posing cooking her husband's breakfast the morning after her 1952 primary victory. (St. Louis Globe-Democrat *photo. Courtesy, The Collections of the St. Louis Mercantile Library at the University of Missouri-St. Louis)*

published book, *A Choice Not an Echo,* which promoted Goldwater's candidacy and ushered Schlafly onto the national political stage. Written in a simple, polemical style, Schlafly's book purported to document a plot by a cabal of "kingmakers" to control the selection of presidential candidates. The "kingmakers," according to Schlafly, were a group of financial, political, and press elites with a vested interest in centralized government and internationalist foreign policy, who periodically met in secret to "make important plans they do not reveal to the public." Since 1936, these "kingmakers," Schlafly alleged, had manipulated the Republican National Conventions into nominating non-conservative candidates.[8]

In her book, which was panned by critics, Schlafly concluded that Goldwater was the obvious choice for conservatives. Schlafly's book had none of the careful, reasoned tone promoted by party loyalists. But many conservatives at the grass-roots level were sympathetic to Schlafly's charges that the Republican Party was ruled by a secret, elite group, unresponsive to the concerns of ordinary people. Although never officially endorsed by Goldwater or his campaign staff, Schlafly's book became an important piece of campaign literature for the candidate. Its first edition, printed in May 1964, sold 600,000 copies. A second edition printed in June sold another million, requiring a third printing in August. Through the popularity of her book, Schlafly built a name for herself among alienated grass-roots conservatives in general, and among women in particular. She developed a vast, loyal following among grass-roots women, many of whom were members of the NFRW. In the spring of 1964, she was elected 1st Vice-President of that organization.

Efforts to create a groundswell of support for Goldwater were successful; the Arizona senator received the presidential nomination despite a general lack of support among party insiders. He failed to win over the American public as a whole, however. His rigid anti-statism struck many as racist, his aggressive anti-communism as war-mongering. Goldwater and the GOP received a crushing defeat from American voters in 1964. After the elections, Republican insiders tried to recoup and rebuild the party. A study issued in early 1965 by the Ripon Society (a moderate Republican organization) urged, among other things, the

"unequivocal dissociation" of the GOP from "irrational and irresponsible extremist elements."[9] To remain in positions of influence, Goldwater backers would have to demonstrate their willingness to mellow their views in the interest of the party.

The NFRW had been one of the most crucial centers of Goldwater support during the campaign. The GOP leadership now believed it essential that the NFRW, with its thousands of party volunteers, come back into the loyal Republican fold. Although she had been a Goldwater supporter, NFRW President Dottie Elston now threw her weight behind party unity. She worked hard to rebuild the NFRW and the GOP, emphasizing the necessity that "we submerge any thoughts or acts which would divide our Party."[10] In terms of the post-1964 goals of party regulars, Elston was an ideal leader to have at the helm of the NFRW.

Elston's second term as NFRW president was scheduled to end in September 1966, however. A major contender for the position of Elston's successor was the NFRW's 1st Vice-President, Phyllis Schlafly. Schlafly was now well known nationally and commanded a large and devoted following within the NFRW. Schlafly was also skeptical of arguments supporting compromise for the sake of party unity. As columnists Rowland Evans and Robert Novak editorialized, many in the party foresaw "disaster" if "nature [took] its course" and Schlafly were elected NFRW president.[11] By the fall of 1965, signs of what Schlafly identified as a conspiracy by Republican National Committee (RNC) Chairman Ray Bliss and Dottie Elston to keep her out of NFRW leadership had already emerged. At that time the decision was made to postpone the date and to change the site of the convention where the NFRW elections would take place (both moves seen as unfavorable to Schlafly).

The NFRW's Nominating Committee announced Gladys O'Donnell of California as its official candidate for president in March 1967. O'Donnell, who had been a Goldwater supporter, was by no means a liberal (although Schlafly would characterize her as such). Like Elston, however, O'Donnell was now pledged to bring harmony to the party, and to return the NFRW to its previous role as a neutral, educational arm of the party, loyally performing volunteer tasks.[12] Schlafly did not accept the choice of O'Donnell as candidate. Schlafly stated publicly that "custom and courtesy" dictated that she, as NFRW 1st Vice-President, be "invite[d] to serve as president." On April 5, she announced her own candidacy and set out to discredit O'Donnell as well as the process by which she was nominated.[13]

Over 3,000 women attended the NFRW convention in May 1967, where the election was held. Tears were shed, contentious memos circulated, and insults traded in the press. The final vote of the convention delegates was 1,910 (56%) for O'Donnell and 1,494 (44%) for Schlafly.[14] Schlafly considered her performance remarkable in light of the forces mobilized against her. Despite the RNC's efforts to diminish Schlafly's support at the convention and the NFRW's obvious bias in favor of O'Donnell, Schlafly had lost by only slightly more than 500 votes. She did not accept defeat. Convinced that she was the choice of a majority of NFRW members, she publicly accused the RNC and Elston of election irregularities.

Her bid for the NFRW presidency left Schlafly further disillusioned with the party and with traditional NFRW strategies for integrating women substantively into the GOP. In December 1967, Schlafly published a new book, *Safe—Not Sorry*, in which she devoted an entire chapter to exposing the scheme, as she saw it, to deny her the NFRW presidency.[15] The discussion of behind-the-scenes chicanery and Schlafly's hyperbolic tone were similar in style to her other self-published books, including *A Choice Not an Echo*. In discussing her fight for the NFRW presidency, however, Schlafly did not limit her charges to accusations that liberals were attempting to purge conservatives from the NFRW. She also saw a shameful effort to squelch women's independent voices:

> They [the liberals] were joined by all those who feel it is to their own interests to keep Republican women neutralized. The Republican Party is carried on the shoulders of the women who do the work in the precincts, ringing doorbells, distributing literature, and doing all the tiresome, repetitive campaign tasks. Many men in the Party frankly want to keep the women doing the menial work, while the selection of candidates and the policy decisions are taken care of by the men in the smoke-filled rooms.[16]

For Schlafly the RNC campaign against her belittled all Republican women because the RNC implied that it would not permit NFRW women to choose their own leaders.

Schlafly's use of the word "neutralized" exposed the weaknesses of NFRW strategies for integrating women into the party. The NFRW, since its founding in the late 1930s, had presented itself as a division of the RNC that would remain "neutral" in inter-party conflicts. The "neutrality" of Republican club women was offered in exchange for the hope that women would eventually move into leadership positions. In 1967, Schlafly suggested that far from a strategy of empowerment, promises of "neutrality" (or impartiality) effectively "neutralized" (or obliterated) Republican women's voices. Schlafly boldly articulated what countless other Republican women leaders had been suggesting—albeit more timidly and diplomatically—for years: women were carrying a critical share of the work of political organizing for the party, yet male political leaders were unwilling to give women a voice commensurate with their contributions.

Schlafly's defeat was not a simple case of sexism, as her version of events might suggest. It is impossible to state unequivocally whether GOP regulars sought to silence Schlafly's supporters because they were conservatives, because they were ideologues, because they were outsiders, or because they were women. Among Schlafly's supporters at the NFRW, all of these identities converged.

The issues surrounding the Schlafly-O'Donnell election are best understood within the context of the long disagreement among Republican women, dating back to 1920, over how women best could achieve power within the party. Should women try to prove themselves to be neutral party loyalists, not allied with any party faction, and thereby hope to win the trust of male party leaders? Or should they mobilize and articulate an independent agenda within the party? In 1967, on the eve of the eruption of second-wave feminism, these two viewpoints openly conflicted for the first time. Ironically, it was the party loyalists in the NFRW who went on to embrace mainstream feminist principles. The NFRW, under Gladys O'Donnell, endorsed the ERA as it emerged as a major issue in the early 1970s.[17] Within ten years, the independent Schlafly would become the United States' most famous anti-feminist.

After her defeat in 1967, Schlafly took her supporters aside and threatened to form a "grassroots organization made up of just plain old American women and mothers who believe in the cause of constitutional government and freedom." In August 1967, three months after the NFRW's convention, Schlafly began a monthly newsletter of her opinions on current events, *The Phyllis Schlafly Report*, which she sent to 3,000 of her NFRW supporters. Schlafly also set up the Eagle Trust Fund (a precursor of Eagle Forum) as a means of collecting donations sent to her in support of the issues she publicized through her newsletter. In October 1968, Schlafly began holding yearly national political training conferences for women where Schlafly's followers learned strategies for defeating liberal candidates for local political and party offices.[18]

Schlafly initially focused her attention on mobilizing women behind the conservative issues she traditionally had pursued, such as support for free enterprise and nuclear weapons. Not until 1972 would she hit on the issue that would propel her and her followers into the political limelight. *The Phyllis Schlafly Report* in February 1972 was devoted entirely to challenging conventional wisdom that the ERA was a logical reform whose time had come. Initially uninterested in the issue, Schlafly eventually was persuaded to look into the ERA. Once Schlafly came out against the Amendment, the number of people receiving the *Phyllis Schlafly Report* increased from 3,000 to 35,000 as her movement grew to embrace fundamentalist Christian women who previously had not been involved in politics.[19]

Schlafly's opposition to the ERA reflected her social conservatism. The ERA violated her religious traditions by threatening to disrupt what she understood to be the proper functioning of families. Schlafly, a devout Catholic, was sincere in these arguments. But her opposition also was deeply rooted in the anti-statist Goldwater movement, and in grass-roots resentment against political elites. The ERA's second section, which empowered the federal government to enforce the amendment's provisions, suggested an increase in federal power anathema to Schlafly's long-held opposition to big government. In the 1970s, organized feminism (which appeared to represent both the disruption of families as well as the enlargement of government and which was becoming influential in both political parties) was among the most prominent of the "elites" that Schlafly targeted.

Connecting Schlafly's opposition to the ERA to her anti-statism and anti-elitism offers an important reminder that current debates about feminism are not only about the proper roles of men and women. Certainly they are that. However, these debates typically are embroiled also in conflicts over the proper role and size of government. Mainstream feminism is today associated by many (non-social) conservative critics with what they identify as the failures of New Deal/Great Society liberalism: welfare, government regulation, identity politics, and affirmative action. Discrediting those policies and discrediting feminism typically go hand in hand.

Detailing these aspects of Schlafly's past also addresses what many have found to be contradictions in Schlafly's anti-feminism. Certainly Schlafly's biography is that of one who believes that women should be politically involved. For Schlafly, women's political power means the ability to have socially conservative women's voices heard. These voices are understandably right wing. Furthermore, women's political power, according to Schlafly, is properly exercised altruistically for the benefit of family, community, and country, rather than selfishly (as Schlafly understands feminists' calls for power).[20] One can disagree unequivocally with Schlafly's conclusions, yet recognize that her positions are not necessarily any more contradictory than those of suffragists who had argued in the early part of the century that political rights would enable them to better fulfill their home and family duties. Calls for the empowerment of women can mean profoundly different things depending on behalf of which issues such calls are made.

NOTES

1. See Sara Evans, *Personal Politics: The Roots of Women's Liberation in the Civil Rights Movement and the New Left* (New York, 1979).
2. Biographical information is taken from Carol Felsenthal, *Phyllis Schlafly: The Sweetheart of the Silent Majority* (Chicago, 1981), 9–102.
3. Ibid., 151–162.
4. Catherine E. Rymph, "Forward and Right: Shaping Republican Women's Activism, 1920–1967" (Ph.D. diss., University of Iowa, 1998).
5. National Federation of Republican Women (hereafter cited as NFRW) News Release, 15 April

1955, box 142, Kitchen Kabinet Press Release; Washington Newsletter [supplement], April 1956, box 103, Nominating Committee—1956, NFRW records, Dwight D. Eisenhower Presidential Library, Abilene, Kan.

6. Phyllis Schlafly, *A Choice Not an Echo* (Alton, Ill., 1964), 117–118.

7. Mary C. Brennan, *Turning Right in the Sixties: The Conservative Capture of the GOP* (Chapel Hill, N.C., 1995), 31–33; Robert Alan Goldberg, *Barry Goldwater* (New Haven, 1995), 162.

8. Schlafly, *A Choice Not an Echo*, 25–26.

9. "Ripon Society Offers Twelve 'First Steps' for Rebuilding Republican Party," Ripon Society Press Release, 18 January 1965; The Ripon Society, "Election '64: A Ripon Society Report," 19 January 1964, copy in Mary Louise Smith papers, Louise Noun–Mary Louise Smith Iowa Women's Archives, University of Iowa Libraries, Iowa City.

10. Report by Mrs. Dorothy A. Elston, transcripts of Republican National Committee Executive Session, 28 June 1965, Republican Party Papers part I, series B, reel 7, frame 282.

11. "Bliss Learning That the Center Sometimes Is the Storm Center," *Los Angeles Times*, 2 July 1965, II, 5.

12. Gladys O'Donnell, Build! [newsletter of the NFRW] July–August 1966, box 118, Republican party—Women's Organizations and Activities—NFRW, misc. (1967–1977), Mary Louise Smith papers.

13. "Goldwater Denies Mrs. Schlafly Is Target of Purge Attempt," *St. Louis Post-Dispatch*, 6 April 1967.

14. "Mrs. O'Donnell Elected to Head GOP Federation," *Los Angeles Times*, 7 May 1967.

15. Like Schlafly's other books, *Safe—Not Sorry* contains numerous footnotes to back up her charges, but also demonstrates Schlafly's penchant for quoting selectively and occasionally out of context.

16. Schlafly, *Safe—Not Sorry*, 168–169.

17. Gladys O'Donnell to All Club Presidents, 11 May 1970, binder labeled "1970–71," uncatalogued records of the NFRW, Alexandria, Va.

18. Mary McGrory, "G.O.P. Gals Storm," 10 May 1967, *Cedar Rapids* [Iowa] *Gazette* [editorial]; "Bitter Fight Sees GOP Women Tap Coalition Choice," *Washington Post*, clipping in box 118, NFRW Biennial Convention—1967, Mary Louise Smith papers; "Mrs. O'Donnell Elected to Head GOP Federation," 7 May 1967; "Loser Decides to Stay in Republican Women Federation," 17 May 1967; "GOP Woman Foresees End to Bloodletting," *Los Angeles Times*, 30 June 1967.

19. Felsenthal, *Sweetheart of the Silent Majority*, 269–271.

20. Both Jane De Hart and Rebecca Klatch have noted that socially conservative women often use their belief in the different roles of men and women and the moral superiority of women to justify public roles for women. De Hart and Klatch also point out that socially conservative women see men's and women's interests fundamentally at odds and exhibit a distrust of men. It is for these reasons that these women oppose reforms such as the ERA that would seem to relieve men of the responsibility of caring for their wives and families. These women have a keen sense of their own interests within the traditional, religiously based gender systems in which they live. Rebecca Klatch, "The Two Worlds of Women of the New Right," in *Women, Politics, and Change*, Louise Tilly and Patricia Gurin, eds. (New York, 1990), 543–545; Jane Sherron De Hart, "Gender on the Right: Meanings Beyond the Existential Scream," *Gender and History* 3 (1991), 246–67.

DOCUMENTS: Making the Personal Political: Fighting Injustice

> *Pauli Murray, "I had entered law school preoccupied with the racial struggle . . . but I graduated an unabashed feminist as well. . . ."*

Pauli Murray was a remarkable woman. Born into a family that blended slaves, slave-owning whites, Cherokee Indians, freeborn African Americans—a family whose history she would later celebrate in her book *Proud Shoes*—she grew up an orphan in her grandparents' home in Durham, North Carolina. Bright and energetic but poor, Murray graduated from the city's segregated schools in 1926. In a display of characteristic determination, she applied to Hunter College in New York City. Rejected because she was so poorly prepared, she moved in with a cousin, enrolled in high school in New York, and entered Hunter a year later. The struggle to find work and stay in school in the midst of the Great Depression was so intense, however, that Murray, already suffering from malnutrition, nearly succumbed to tuberculosis. Shortly after her graduation from Hunter in 1933, she found brief sanctuary in Camp Tera, one of the handful of women's camps established by the New Deal as a counterpart to the men's Civilian Conservation Corps, and then as an employee of remedial reading and workers' education projects funded by the WPA.

"World events were breeding a new militancy in younger Negroes like me," she would write; "One did not need Communist propaganda to expose the inescapable parallel between Nazi treatment of Jews in Germany and the repression of Negroes in the American South. Daily occurrences pointed up the hypocrisy of a United States policy that condemned Fascism abroad while tolerating an incipient Fascism within its own borders." In 1938, she applied to the law school at the University of North Carolina at Chapel Hill, attracted by the work of its sociologists on race relations and farm tenancy. Many law school students supported her admission, as did Frank Porter Graham, the president of the university, but state law mandated her rejection because of race.

Torn between her writing and law, Murray threw herself into working for social justice. Her involvement in the unsuccessful struggle to obtain clemency for Odell Waller, a black sharecropper whose right to be tried by a representative jury had been denied because Virginia called to jury service only those who had paid a poll tax, brought her to the attention of Leon Ransom of Howard University Law School in Washington, D.C. When Howard University offered her a scholarship in 1941, she entered law school "with the single-minded intention of destroying Jim Crow."

The following selections from her autobiography include an account of Murray's discovery of sexism amidst her battle with racism during her years at Howard University,

Excerpted from "Writing or Law School?," "Jim Crow in the Nation's Capital," and "Don't Get Mad, Get Smart" in *Song in a Weary Throat: An American Pilgrimage* (New York: Harper & Row, 1987), pp. 183–85, 205–9, 238–45, 361–62. Reprinted courtesy of the Schlesinger Library, Radcliffe College.

and her leadership, eighteen years before the famous sit-ins in Greensboro, North Carolina, of a successful sit-in to desegregate a restaurant in Washington, D.C. Perhaps more than any other single person, Murray linked the civil rights movement with the federal quest for equity for women. After the establishment of New Deal wages and hours legislation, liberals began to recognize that the old protective labor laws (see pp. 325–26) were increasingly "protecting" women from better-paying "men's" jobs, just as the label of "privilege" was sustaining many inequalities, among them unequal access to professions and permissive rather than mandatory jury service (see pp. 517–21). As early as 1947, Pauli Murray had begun to call discrimination on the basis of sex a system of "Jane Crow." In a biting and deeply personal essay published in *Negro Digest* entitled "Why Negro Girls Stay Single," Murray insisted that the "minority status" of women is suffered "despite their numerical size," and "independently of race, religion or politics." As a staff member of John F. Kennedy's Commission on the Status of Women in 1962, Murray grew firm in her conviction that "Jane Crow" and "Jim Crow" were twin evils. She welcomed the passage of the Civil Rights Act of 1964, with its notable Title VII outlawing employment discrimination on the basis of sex as well as race. With a colleague, Mary Eastwood, she wrote what would become a classic essay, "Jane Crow and the Law." The arguments made there would help make it possible for the Supreme Court to rule in 1971 that discrimination on the basis of sex was discrimination, not privilege.

Murray would go on to have an extraordinary legal career as a champion of racial and gender justice, serving on the National Board of the American Civil Liberties Union. In January 1977, she became one of the first women to be ordained as an Episcopal priest. Not long after, she was invited to celebrate her first Holy Eucharist in the Chapel of the Cross in Chapel Hill, the same church where the daughter of a prominent slaveholding family had many years before brought for baptism an infant whose father was her own lawyer brother, and whose mother was her own servant, Harriet. The infant was Pauli Murray's grandmother. On that occasion, "all the strands of my life came together," Murray wrote in an autobiography aptly subtitled "Activist, Feminist, Lawyer, Priest, and Poet." For Pauli Murray, the personal was indeed political.

Ironically, if Howard Law School equipped me for effective struggle against Jim Crow, it was also the place where I first became conscious of the twin evil of discriminatory sex bias, which I quickly labeled Jane Crow. In my preoccupation with the brutalities of racism, I had failed until now to recognize the subtler, more ambiguous expressions of sexism. In the all-female setting of Hunter College, women were prominent in professional and leadership positions. My awareness of the additional burden of sex discrimination had been further delayed by my WPA experience. Hilda Smith, national director of the WPA Workers' Education Project, was a woman, my local project director and my immediate supervisor were both women, and it had not occurred to me that women as a group received unequal treatment. Now, however, the racial factor was removed in the intimate environment of a Negro law school dominated by men, and the factor of gender was fully exposed.

During my first year at Howard there were only two women in the law school student body, both of us in the first-year class. When the other woman dropped out before the end of the first term, I was left as the only female for the rest of that year, and I remained the only woman in my class for the entire three-year course. While I was there, not more than two or three women enrolled in the lower classes of the law school. We had no women on the faculty, and the only woman professional on staff was . . . the registrar, who had graduated from the law school many years earlier.

The men were not openly hostile; in fact, they were friendly. But I soon learned that women were often the objects of ridicule disguised as a joke. I was shocked on the first day of class when one of our professors said in his opening remarks that he really didn't know why women came to law school, but that since we were there the men would have to put up with us. His banter brought forth loud laughter from the male students. I was too humiliated to respond, but though the professor did not know it, he had just guaranteed that I would become the top student in his class. Later I began to notice that no matter how well prepared I was or how often I raised my hand, I seldom got to recite. It was not that professors deliberately ignored me but that their freewheeling classroom style of informal discussion allowed the men's deeper voices to obliterate my lighter voice, and my classmates seemed to take it for granted that I had nothing to contribute. For much of that first year I was condemned to silence unless the male students exhausted their arguments or were completely stumped by a professor's question.

My real awakening came several months after school began, when I saw a notice on the official bulletin board inviting "all male students of the First Year Class" to a smoker at the residence of Professor Leon A. Ransom. The exclusion of women from the invitation was so pointed that I went to Dr. Ransom's office to seek an explanation. He told me blandly that Sigma Delta Tau, a legal fraternity limited to male students and members of the legal profession, had established a chapter at the law school and that the purpose of the smoker was to look over first-year men for likely prospects. Through their association with experienced lawyers these young men would enhance their professional development. I had not yet become aware of the sexist bias of the English language, and recalling that the national professional English "fraternity" to which I had been elected while in college included both sexes, I asked Dr. Ransom, "What about us women?"

To my surprise, Dr. Ransom merely chuckled and said that if we women wanted an organization we could set up a legal sorority. Angrily, I said it was ridiculous to speak of a legal sorority for two women, but he did not seem concerned about our plight. I left Dr. Ransom's office feeling both bewildered and betrayed, especially because he was one of the most liberal professors on the university campus and had always treated me as a person. He had encouraged me to come to law school and used his influence to have me awarded a scholarship. Yet he did not seem to appreciate fully that barring women from an organization purporting to promote professional growth had the same degrading effect upon women as compelling us as Negroes to sit in the back of a bus or refusing to admit black lawyers to white bar associations. The discovery that Ransom and other men I deeply admired because of their dedication to civil rights, men who themselves had suffered racial indignities, could countenance exclusion of women from their professional association aroused an incipient feminism in me long before I knew the meaning of the term "feminism." . . .

The fact that an accident of gender exempted me from military service and left me free to pursue my career without interruption made me feel an extra responsibility to carry on the integration battle. Many other Howard University women were feeling a similar responsibility, which was heightened by the dramatic leave-taking of sixty-five Howard men, who marched off campus in a body to report for military duty. We women reasoned that it was our job to help make the country for which our black brothers were fighting a freer place in which to live when they returned from wartime service.

From the nightly bull sessions in Truth Hall a plan of action emerged. . . . It was designed to attract the widest possible support from all segments of the university community, with direct action reserved for the last of a series of steps. My role as student "legal adviser" was to make sure that our proposed actions were within the framework of legality so as not to arouse the official disapproval of the university administration. . . . Although we were engaged in serious business, our planning sessions were fun and challenged our power of imagination. The fact that we were doing something creative about our racial plight was exhilarating and increased our self-esteem. The Direct Action subcommittee attracted some of the leading students on campus, for it was important that those undertaking unorthodox activities maintain academic excellence. Also, we proceeded cautiously, aware that a misstep would compromise our goal. Instead of rushing precipitously into "hostile" territory, a group of students surveyed public eating places in the neighboring, mostly Negro community on Northwest U Street that still catered to the "White Trade Only." One of the most notorious of these lily-white establishments was the Little Palace Cafeteria, located at the busy intersection of Fourteenth and U streets, N.W., and run by a Mr. Chaconas. Because of its strategic location, the Little Palace had long been a source of mortification for countless unsuspecting Negroes, who entered it assuming that at least they would be served in the heart of the Negro section of the city.

The Little Palace Cafeteria was selected as our first target. For a week prior to our move against the cafeteria we held campus pep rallies and drummed up support for our effort through noon-hour broadcasts from the tower of Founder's Library. We decorated hot-chocolate cups and used them around campus as collection cans to solicit the funds we needed for paper, postage, and picket signs. We held a midweek Town Hall meeting and brought in experienced political leaders . . . to lead a forum on civil rights legislation and methods of achieving it. We conducted classes on the legal aspects of picketing and disorderly conduct in the District of Columbia, spent hours in small groups discussing public decorum, anticipating and preparing for the reactions of the black public, the white public, white customers, and white management respectively. We stressed the importance of a dignified appearance, and the subcommittee directed that all participants dress well for the occasion. We also pledged ourselves to exemplary nonviolent conduct, however great the provocation.

Finally, on April 17, a rainy Saturday afternoon, we assembled on campus and began to leave the Howard University grounds in groups of four, about five minutes apart, to make the ten-minute walk to the Little Palace Cafeteria. The demonstration was limited to a carefully selected group of volunteers—less than twenty students—who felt confident they could maintain self-restraint under pressure. As each group arrived, three entered the cafeteria while the fourth remained outside as an "observer." Inside, we took our trays to the steam table and as soon as we were refused service carried our empty trays to a vacant seat at one of the tables, took

out magazines, books of poetry or textbooks, notebooks and pencils, and assumed an attitude of concentrated study. Strict silence was maintained. Minutes later the next group arrived and repeated the process. Outside, the observers began to form a picket line with colorful signs reading "Our Boys, our Bonds, our Brothers are Fighting for YOU! Why Can't We Eat Here?"; "We Die Together—Why Can't We Eat Together?"; "There's No Segregation Law in D.C. What's Your Story, Little Palace?" Two pickets carried posters (prepared for the War Manpower Commission by the Office of War Information) depicting two workers—one black and the other white—working together as riveters on a steel plate. The inscription on the poster read "UNITED WE WIN!"

My heart thumped furiously as I sat at a table awaiting developments. The management was stunned at first, then after trying unsuccessfully to persuade us to leave, called the police. Almost immediately a half-dozen uniformed officers appeared. When they approached us we said simply, "We're waiting for service," and since we did not appear to be violating any law, they made no move to arrest us.

After forty-five minutes had passed and twelve Negro students were occupying most of the tables of the small cafeteria, Chaconas gave up and closed his restaurant eight hours earlier than his normal closing time. Those of us who were inside joined the picket line and kept it going for the rest of the afternoon. Chaconas told reporter Harry McAlpin, who covered the demonstration for the *Chicago Defender:* "I'll lose money, but I'd rather close up than practice democracy this way. The time is not ripe." When Juanita Morrow, a journalism student, interviewed Chaconas several days later, he admitted that he had lost about $180 that Saturday afternoon and evening, a considerable sum for a small business.

Actually, the incident did not arouse the furor we had feared but revealed the possibilities for change. When told why the place was closed and being picketed, a white customer named Raymond Starnes, who came from Charlotte, North Carolina, said, "I eat here regularly, and I don't care who eats here. All I want is to eat. I want the place to stay open. After all, we are all human." Another white bystander, asked what he thought of the students' action, replied, "I think it's reasonable.

Negroes are fighting to win this war for democracy just like whites. If it came to a vote, it would get my vote."

When Chaconas opened his place on Monday morning, our picket line was there to greet him, and it continued all day. Within forty-eight hours he capitulated and began to serve Negro customers. We were jubilant. Our conquest of a small "greasy spoon" eating place was a relatively minor skirmish in the long battle to end segregation in the nation's capital—a battle that was ended by a Supreme Court decision ten years later—but it loomed large in our eyes. We had proved that intelligent, imaginative action could bring positive results and, fortunately, we had won our first victory without an embarrassing incident. (One other small restaurant in the area was desegregated that spring before final examinations and summer vacation interrupted our campaign.)

Significantly, the prominent role of women in the leadership and planning of our protest was a by-product of the wartime thinning of the ranks of male students. Twelve of the nineteen Howard University demonstrators at the Little Palace on April 17 were female. . . . Many of those young women who had joined together to defy tradition would continue to make breakthroughs in their respective fields after their college days. . . . The youngest member of that little band of demonstrators, Patricia Roberts, carried the impact of her civil rights experiences from Howard University to the cabinet level of the federal government, [Patricia Roberts Harris served as President Carter's Secretary of Housing and Urban Development from 1977 to '79]. . . .

I had entered law school preoccupied with the racial struggle and single-mindedly bent upon becoming a civil rights attorney, but I graduated an unabashed feminist as well. Ironically, my effort to become a more proficient advocate in the first struggle led directly into the second through an unanticipated chain of events which began in the late fall of my senior year.

One day Dean Hastie called me into his office to discuss what I planned to do after graduation. To my utter surprise, he spoke of the possibility of my returning to teach at the law school after a year of graduate study, and with that possibility in mind he recommended that I apply for a Rosenwald fellowship. For a number of reasons, "graduate study" meant to me "graduate study at Harvard University." At least half of the Howard Law School faculty had studied at Harvard, both Hastie and Ransom held doctorates from its law school, and it had become a tradition at Howard to groom an exceptionally promising law graduate for a future faculty position by sending him to Harvard "to put on the gloss" of a prestigious graduate degree in law. My greatest rival in the preceding class, Francisco Carniero, who had graduated with top honors and as Chief Justice of the Court of Peers, was now completing his year of graduate law there. We had run neck and neck in courses we took together, he topping me by a couple of points in one and I topping him in another.

Naively unaware of Harvard's policy toward women, I was stunned when my schoolmates began kidding me. "Murray," someone said, "don't you know they're not going to let you into Harvard?" Harvard, it became clear, did not admit women to its law school.

Then my hopes were raised by a rumor which circulated around campus that Harvard was opening up to women students. Accordingly, when filling out my application to the Rosenwald Fund, I wrote in the space provided for choice of law school: "I should like to obtain my Master's degree at Harvard University, in the event they have removed their bar against women students. If not, then I should like to work at Yale University or at any other University which has advanced study in the field of labor law." I also wrote to the secretary of Harvard Law School, requesting confirmation or denial of the rumor I had heard. The answer was prompt. On January 5, 1944, the secretary's office wrote back: "Harvard Law School . . . is not open to women for registration."

This verdict was disappointing, of course, but with all the other preoccupations of my senior year, the matter probably would have rested there if I had not won the Rosenwald fellowship or at least if the names of the award winners had not been published nationwide. The announcement, made in late spring, listed me among fifteen white Southerners and twenty-two Negroes (including such notables as E. Franklin Frazier, Adelaide Cromwell Hill, Chester Himes, Rayford W. Logan, Dorothy Porter, and Margaret Walker) who received awards "for creative talent or distinguished scholarship." Mine was the only award in the field of law, and all the news stories reported that I was to do graduate study in labor law at Harvard University.

I was embarrassed to receive congratulatory messages from a number of people who were either unaware of Harvard's restrictive policy or assumed I had broken the barrier. At the same time, some of the men at Howard stepped up their banter, not without a touch of malicious glee. Until then I had been able to lick my wounds in private, but the public disclosure of my dilemma mortified me and presented a challenge I could not pass over lightly. If my schoolmates expected me to dissolve into tears under their stinging gibes, they were disappointed. I simply sat down and wrote a letter of application to Harvard Law School, which was duly processed, and I received a written request for my college transcript and a photograph.

In due course there came from Professor T. R. Powell, who chaired Harvard Law School's Committee on Graduate Studies, a letter that must have been dictated with an impish smirk. As nearly as I can recall, it ran: "Your picture and the salutation on your college transcript indicate that you are not of the sex entitled to be admitted to Harvard Law School." To appreciate the impact of this letter upon me, it is only necessary to remember the similar letter of rejection I had received in 1938 from the dean of the graduate school of the University of North Carolina in Chapel Hill: "Under the laws of North Carolina and under the resolutions of the Board of Trustees of the University of North Carolina, members of your race are not admitted to the University."

The personal hurt I felt now was no different from the personal hurt I had felt then. The niceties of distinction that in one case rejection was based upon custom and involved my sex and in the other was grounded in law and involved my race were wholly irrelevant to me. Both were equally unjust, stigmatizing me for a biological characteristic over which I had no control. But at least in the case of racial rebuffs long experience had taught me some coping mechanisms and I did not feel alone in that struggle. The fact that Harvard's rejection was a source of mild amusement rather than outrage to many of my male colleagues who were ardent civil rights advocates made it all the more bitter to swallow.

The harsh reality was that I was a minority within a minority, with all the built-in disadvantages such status entailed. Because of the considerable snobbery that—even apart from race and sex—existed in the highly competitive field of law, one's initial entry into the profession was profoundly affected by the law school one attended. This was particularly true for anyone who had ambitions to teach law. Since in my case the most common hurdles— lack of funds and a poor scholastic record— did not apply, I felt the injustice of the rejection even more strongly. I knew that however brilliant a record I had made at Howard, among my teaching colleagues I would never be considered on equal academic footing with someone who could boast of Harvard training. I also knew that the school of my second choice, Yale, had suspended its graduate program in law during the wartime emergency. [Professors William H.] Hastie and [Leon] Ransom, my law school mentors, understood my academic dilemma and were quietly supportive of my decision to pursue the Harvard matter further. Dr. [Caroline] Ware, whose great-great-grand-father Henry Ware had been the first dean of Harvard Divinity School and who grew up surrounded by the Harvard tradition, identified with me wholly in my fight. The only one of five generations of Phi Beta Kappas in her family not to take a Harvard degree, she held a Ph.D. from Radcliffe.

Then began the disheartening effort to budge a sluggishly corpulent bureaucracy on which my protests and appeals made about as much impression as a gnat on an elephant's hide. Harvard, being a private institution, was immune from legal attack and thus I had only the force of reason and logic with which to plead my case. A letter to Professor Powell asking what procedure to follow in appealing the law school's policy brought the information that the law school was bound by the rule of the Harvard Corporation not to admit women, and any appeal from that ruling would have to be submitted to the Corporation through its secretary, A. Calvert Smith.

Since my exclusion from Harvard was based solely on gender, my appeal necessarily was strongly feminist in tone:

> I have met a number of women and have heard of many more who wished to attend Harvard and yet were refused. This fight is not mine, but

that of women who feel they should have free access to the very best of legal education. . . .

Women are practicing before the Supreme Court, they have become judges and good lawyers, they are represented on the President's Cabinet and greater demand is being made for women lawyers in administrative positions as the men move into the armed forces. They are proving themselves worthy of the confidence and trust placed in them. . . . They are taking an intelligent view toward the political events at home and abroad, and statistics show they are in the majority of the voting population this year. A spot-check on memory would indicate there are only four important places they are not now holding—(1) As graduates of Harvard University, (2) as President of the United States, (3) as a member of the United States Supreme Court, and (4) as workers in the mines. Although [by admitting women] Harvard might lose in the sense of a loss of tradition, it might gain in the quality of the law school student personnel.

Meanwhile, two influential (if wholly unanticipated) male supporters sympathetic to the rights of women materialized. One was President Franklin D. Roosevelt! I had sent copies of the correspondence with Harvard to Mrs. Roosevelt, suggesting that the President might be amused at this attempt to storm the walls of his alma mater, never dreaming it would evoke more than a chuckle on his part. FDR was not merely amused; he actually wrote a letter on my behalf to President James B. Conant of Harvard University.

It would take more than one of that institution's most illustrious graduates to overturn a three-hundred-year tradition of male exclusiveness, however. President Conant's reply, sent on to me by FDR's secretary, only confused the issue. The letter assured President Roosevelt that I was free to do graduate work at Radcliffe, and even sent along a Radcliffe catalogue—never mind the obvious fact that Radcliffe did not offer graduate courses in law. I was flattered that the President of the United States had intervened on my behalf, but I was no nearer my goal. Mrs. Roosevelt was unequivocally in my corner, and wrote me a note saying: "I loved your Harvard appeal."

Lloyd K. Garrison, who was to become a lifelong friend and sponsor, was my second unexpected supporter. Mr. Garrison, former dean of the University of Wisconsin School of Law, was then a member of the National War Labor Board, which he later chaired. He was also a member of the Harvard Board of Overseers. I first met him through an ambitious undertaking of our student organization, the First Annual Court of Peers Dinner, jointly sponsored by the faculty and the Student Guild of Howard University School of Law. Mr. Garrison was our guest speaker, and as chief officer of the Student Guild it was my function to preside over the dinner and sit next to him at the speakers' table.

The great-grandson of abolitionist William Lloyd Garrison, Lloyd K. Garrison bore a striking resemblance to his famous ancestor and had inherited his commitment to human freedom. Unlike the fiery nineteenth-century Garrison, however, Lloyd K. Garrison combined a gentleness of disposition with a tough-minded pragmatism. . . . He was intensely interested in my effort to get into Harvard but warned me that I did not have a chance against the arch-conservative Harvard Corporation. Under the circumstances he encouraged me to follow an alternative plan for graduate study elsewhere, in the meantime pressing my appeal.

A. Calvert Smith informed me that the Harvard Corporation would review my appeal on July 10, by which time I had already applied to Boalt Hall [School] of Law, University of California at Berkeley, one of the few schools in the country whose wartime faculty of distinguished scholars remained relatively intact. On July 12, Mr. Smith wrote me to say that since I was asking, in effect, for a change in the long-established practice of the law school not to admit women, and since the conditions of admission to any department were in general set up by the faculty governing that department, "Whether or not women should be admitted to the Law School is . . . a decision for the Faculty of the Law School." Mr. Smith indicated that since no recommendation from the faculty of the law school was then before the Corporation, "it does not feel itself in a position to take any action on your application."

By sidestepping my appeal, the Harvard Corporation had rid itself temporarily of an annoying question, but it had also called into play a theory about the significance of individual action I had once announced half-seriously to Dr. Ware: "One person plus one typewriter constitutes a movement." If I could not compel admission to Harvard, at least I could raise the issue in such a way that its law school would be unable to avoid it. I was also learning the process of patiently following whatever administrative procedure was available even when there was every reason to believe the result would be futile.

My next letter was addressed to the Faculty of the Harvard Law School, summarizing the correspondence to date and requesting a meeting of the faculty "to reconsider my application and to decide whether it will recommend a change of the policy now in practice." I included a copy of my appeal to the Harvard Corporation and closed on a humorous note:

> [G]entlemen, I would gladly change my sex to meet your requirements but since the way to such change has not been revealed to me, I have no recourse but to appeal to you to change your minds on this subject. Are you to tell me that one is as difficult as the other?

As I had learned in the case of the University of North Carolina, correspondence could accomplish little more than stir up interest among a few key individuals and keep the issue flickering feebly. At the suggestion of Dr. Ware, I wrote to Judge Sarah T. Hughes of the United States District Court of Texas, who also chaired the Committee on Economic and Legal Status of Women. She replied that this was not a matter her committee had considered, but she said, "I shall be glad to discuss the problem at the next meeting which is in September," and asked that I keep her informed. After I left Washington, Dean Hastie wrote: "My best information on the Harvard situation is that the faculty is sharply divided on the matter of admitting women and will probably take the position that no action should be taken while a majority of the permanent faculty are on leave for war work." Lloyd K. Garrison's analysis prepared me for the inevitable. He wrote:

> From what I could pick up in Cambridge, my guesses are:
> (1) That the corporation will do nothing unless the Law School takes the initiative in asking that the rules be changed to admit women.
> (2) That the Law School will do nothing . . . , certainly not until Dean Landis gets back next fall and probably not then.
> (3) That this is due to combination of long tradition, an excessively high enrollment which has become an increasing headache [and]
> (4) A touch of some undefinable male egoism, which is, I think, rather particularly strong

in and around Boston as compared let us say with the middle west where we take our co-education for granted.

At my last meeting on the Board of Overseers [at Harvard] there was a great debate as to whether women should be admitted to the Medical School and, so I was told (I had to leave the meeting early), the proposal mustered only two votes out of a dozen. . . .

I was in California when the faculty of the Harvard School of Law met on August 7, 1944, and took action on my petition for review. A few days later, Acting Dean E. M. Morgan informed me of their decision. His letter said in part:

> In October, 1942, the Faculty thoroughly considered a proposal to request the University authorities to change the general rule. The first proposition was to admit women only during the emergency. This was almost immediately and unanimously rejected. The second proposal was for a permanent policy admitting women on exactly the same basis as men. This was debated by the Faculty at intervals for about three months, and the views of all members fully considered. There was much difference of opinion, but it was finally unanimously voted that no action looking to a change in the present practice be taken until after the emergency and after the School has returned to normal conditions with its full Faculty in residence. At that time the question will be debated anew. Accordingly it has been necessary to deny all applications for admission by women.
> At its meeting on August 7, the Faculty determined to abide by its previous decision.

Having lost my first battle against "Jane Crow," I was somewhat comforted to learn indirectly that the effort was not entirely wasted. That fall when I registered at the University of California's Boalt Hall [School] of Law, I was surprised to discover that news of the Harvard affair had traveled across country, and I was greeted with the remark, "So you're the woman who caused the Harvard Law School faculty to split 7-7 on your application." I also learned later of Harvard's announcement that women would be admitted to its medical school in 1945.

Fortunately, my controversy with Harvard was unresolved when I graduated from Howard in June, and it did not affect the high excitement of the ceremonies. Aunt Pauline came from Durham and Uncle Lewis Murray from Baltimore, each filled with proprietary pride and vying to share the honor of a niece who had "turned out so well." The high point of Aunt Pauline's visit was having tea at the White House with Mrs. Roosevelt. Then on Commencement Day an unexpected recognition electrified the huge outdoor gathering. Harry McAlpin, a reporter for the *Pittsburgh Courier,* captured the mood of the occasion in a story headlined "Flowers from the First Lady." He wrote:

> Flowers—a huge bouquet of them—delivered near the close of the Howard University commencement exercises last Friday, overshadowed all the previous proceedings of the impressive occasion. They were from Mrs. Roosevelt, wife of the President of the United States. They were for brilliant, active, strong-willed Pauli Murray, graduate cum laude of the Howard Law School.

According to McAlpin—no stranger to hyperbole—the arrival of the flowers overshadowed the commencement address . . . [and] the conferring of honorary degree[s]. . . .

Actually, the flowers had been delivered to the law school a half hour before the ceremonies began. When I came in to get my cap and gown, I glanced at them admiringly. . . . When someone finally made me realize it was my name on the card, I removed it, suggesting the flowers be placed on the platform for all the graduates to share. A few minutes later, the sight of University Secretary . . . parading across campus with the spectacularly beautiful display only moments before the academic procession began created an extra touch of excitement and added a special luster to the pageantry of the event. . . .

My intense involvement with the early stirrings of the resurgent feminist movement called on all my professional skills and kept me so busy I had no time to become demoralized. In 1965 and 1966, Title VII was the principal issue that fueled the movement, especially among business and professional women, as we battled against public attitudes ranging from ridicule to disregard of the new law. The Equal Employment Opportunity Commission (EEOC), charged with administration of the statute, was one of the chief offenders in that respect. A warning of what women might expect came shortly after the law went into effect, on July 2, 1965. EEOC Chairman Franklin D. Roosevelt, Jr., declared

in his first public statement that "the whole issue of sex discrimination is terribly complicated," and indicated that the Commission had not yet come to grips with most of the problems involved. Along with this lukewarm approach, Chairman Roosevelt announced the appointment of his seven key aides who would head the EEOC staff, giving a further clue to official indifference toward women's issues. All seven appointees to the staff were men, and not one of them had functioned on the President's Commission on the Status of Women or any of its study committees that had canvassed sex-based discrimination in employment. The prevailing attitude of the EEOC staff (with a few exceptions) seemed to be that of its executive director, Herman Edelsburg, who stated some months later at New York University's Annual Conference on Labor that the sex provision of Title VII was a "fluke" and "conceived out of wedlock." The newly appointed EEOC deputy general counsel had recently published a lengthy law review article on Title VII, offering an unduly restrictive interpretation of the sex provision as a prohibited ground of discrimination.

Only two of the EEOC's five commissioners responded sympathetically to representations made by women's groups: Richard Graham, a Republican appointed for a term of one year, who had been given responsibility for reviewing cases of sex discrimination, and Aileen Clarke Hernandez, the lone female member of the Commission, an honor graduate of Howard University and a former official of the International Ladies' Garment Workers' Union, with extensive experience in the administration of the California fair employment practices law. No pressure group existed to press for implementation of women's employment rights under the statute, and members of our feminist network who had fought to keep the word "sex" in Title VII were powerless to do more than sound an alarm. . . .

In the absence of organized group actions, we had to rely upon maximizing our individual efforts. Mary Eastwood and I coauthored a law review article entitled "Jane Crow and the Law: Sex Discrimination and Title VII," setting forth ways in which the Fifth and Fourteenth amendments and the sex provisions of Title VII could be interpreted to accord women equality of rights. We equated the evil of antifeminism (Jane Crow) with the evil of racism (Jim Crow), and we asserted that "the rights of women and the rights of Negroes are only different phases of the fundamental and indivisible issue of human rights." Published in the *George Washington Law Review* in December 1965, at a time when few authoritative legal materials on discrimination against women existed, our article broke new ground and was widely cited.

Hoyt *v.* Florida, *1961*; Taylor *v.* Louisiana, *1975*

When Pauli Murray surveyed the American landscape in 1962 for examples of sex discrimination, jury service was the first contemporary example to which she turned. Jury service was, she thought, the issue that most clearly illustrated widespread "confusion" about whether women had been oppressed by the law and required emancipation, or favored by the law and permitted easy exemption from an onerous duty.

Some members of the founding generation had believed that service on juries is a more significant aspect of citizenship than voting; voting, after all, is complete in a moment, while service on juries requires extended periods of time, debate, and deliberation among the jurors, and ultimately the exercise of judgment, which can result in important consequences—including the death sentence—for an accused fellow citizen. The Constitution promises an "impartial" jury drawn from "the district wherein the crime shall have been committed." The conditions of impartiality are not spelled out; the Constitution promises neither "a jury of one's peers," nor one drawn from a "cross-section" of the community. It is tradition that has linked the concept of the jury with "peers," neighbors, and the community in which the crime is committed and from which the jury is chosen.

When women achieved the vote in Wyoming in 1869, it seemed to follow that they could hold office and serve on juries, but after only a few years the objection of male voters and officeholders was so severe that the law was changed to exclude them.

In some states, the achievement of jury service followed painlessly on the heels of suffrage. In Iowa, Michigan, Nevada, and Pennsylvania, where statutes defined as competent jurors "all qualified electors . . . of good moral character, sound judgment, and in full possession of the senses of hearing and seeing, and who can speak, write and read the English language," the admission of women to the electorate automatically defined them as competent jurors. When these interpretations were tested in state courts, judges usually upheld them. Not all state courts, however, thought it was obvious that "electors" could be properly construed to mean women as well as men. In 1925 the Illinois Supreme Court ruled that because only men had been voters in 1874 when the jury statute had been passed, the terms "legal voters" and "electors" referred only to male persons. Not until 1939 did the Illinois state legislature permit women to serve on juries.

Hoyt v. *Florida* 368 U.S. 57 (1961); *Taylor* v. *Louisiana* 419 U.S. 522 (1975); *J.E.B.* v. *Alabama ex rel. T.B.* No. 92–1239 (April 19, 1994). For a full treatment of the history of women and jury service, see Linda K. Kerber, *No Constitutional Right to Be Ladies: Women and the Obligations of Citizenship* (New York: Hill and Wang, 1998), ch. 4.

In most states, new statutes were required. By 1923, eighteen states and the territory of Alaska had arranged for women to serve on juries. But then the momentum ran out; subsequently the issue had to be debated afresh in each state. A few states continued to exclude women completely, but most developed some form of "voluntary" jury service, in which women could be called to serve but could easily decline. In Florida, no women at all served on juries until 1949, when the legislature passed a law providing that women who wished to be eligible could go to their county courthouses and register their willingness to have their names placed in the jury pool.

When Gwendolyn Hoyt came to trial in Tampa in 1957, charged with manslaughter for killing her husband, only 218 women of the more than 46,000 women voters in Hillsborough County had registered to serve; the jury commissioner placed only 10 of those women's names in a pool of 10,000 names. It was no surprise that she was tried—and found guilty—by an all-male jury. It took the six-man jury only twenty-five minutes to convict Gwendolyn Hoyt of second-degree murder; on January 20, 1958, she was sentenced to imprisonment at hard labor for thirty years.

Hoyt appealed, first to the Florida Supreme Court, and then to the U.S. Supreme Court, which heard the case in 1961. Hoyt claimed temporary insanity, brought on by her suspicions of her husband's infidelity, his rejection of her offer of reconciliation, and her own vulnerability to epilepsy. She believed that women would understand her distress better than would men. Her lawyers did not claim that a fair jury was required to have women as members; rather, they claimed that a fair jury would have been drawn at random from a list of names from which women had not been excluded. Hoyt claimed that in order to have enjoyed the right to a trial by a jury of her peers, other women would have to be obligated to serve on juries. To grant other women the privilege of easy avoidance of jury duty, she and her lawyers thought, was to diminish Hoyt's right to a fair trial. The prosecution argued, instead, that if men and women were truly equal, Hoyt should have no objection to being judged by men.

MR. JUSTICE JOHN MARSHALL HARLAN:

At the core of appellant's argument is the claim that the nature of the crime of which she was convicted peculiarly demanded the inclusion of persons of her own sex on the jury. She was charged with killing her husband . . . in the context of a marital upheaval involving, among other things, the suspected infidelity of appellant's husband, and culminating in the husband's final rejection of his wife's efforts at reconciliation. It is claimed, in substance, that women jurors would have been more understanding or compassionate than men in assessing the quality of appellant's act and her defense of "temporary insanity." No claim is made that the jury as constituted was otherwise afflicted by any elements of supposed unfairness.

. . . [T]he right to an impartially selected jury assured by the Fourteenth Amend-

ment . . . does not entitle one accused of crime to a jury tailored to the circumstances of the particular case, whether relating to the sex or other condition of the defendant, or to the nature of the charges to be tried. It requires only that the jury be indiscriminately drawn from among those eligible in the community for jury service, untrammelled by any arbitrary and systematic exclusions. . . . The result of this appeal must therefore depend on whether such an exclusion of women from jury service has been shown.

. . . Florida's [law] does not purport to exclude women from state jury service. Rather, the statute "gives to women the privilege to serve but does not impose service as a duty." It accords women an absolute exemption from jury service unless they expressly waive that privilege. . . . [W]e [cannot] . . . conclude that

THEY AUGUR NO GOOD FOR LOVE SLAYERS

When New York State passed a voluntary jury service law for women in 1937, hundreds of women lined up to register. The New York World Telegram *treated the story as cute; the caption identifying these women read: "Women jurors registering in the Hall of Records, and do they like it!" Dorothy Kenyon, a feminist attorney who had fought for fifteen years for mandatory jury service, welcomed the new statute as a first step: "This gives a new lease of life to the jury system." In the 1960s, Kenyon and Pauli Murray would lead the efforts of the American Civil Liberties Union to establish equitable jury service throughout the nation. (Courtesy of the Library of Congress)*

Florida's statute is . . . infected with unconstitutionality. Despite the enlightened emancipation of women from the restrictions and protections of bygone years, and their entry into many parts of community life formerly considered to be reserved to men, woman is still regarded as the center of home and family life. We cannot say that it is constitutionally impermissible for a State, acting in pursuit of the general welfare, to conclude that a woman should be relieved from the civil duty of jury service unless she herself determines that such service is consistent with her own special responsibilities.

II

. . . Finding no substantial evidence whatever in this record that Florida has arbitrarily undertaken to exclude women from jury service . . . we must sustain the judgment of the Supreme Court of Florida.

JUSTICES WARREN, BLACK, AND DOUGLAS:

We cannot say from this record that Florida is not making a good faith effort to have women perform jury duty without discrimination on the ground of sex. Hence we concur in the result, for reasons set forth in Part II of the Court's opinion.

Why do you think Warren, Black, and Douglas wrote a separate concurring opinion? To what extent was the Court's opinion based on arguments from equality? on arguments from difference?

When Ruth Bader Ginsburg began to work on the ACLU's Women's Rights Project (see *Frontiero* v. *Richardson*, pp. 545–46), she was committed to persuading the Supreme Court to reverse its decisions on several major cases that had sustained sex discrimination; one of those cases was *Hoyt*. Not until 1975, in a case arising in Louisiana, a state in which women were still required to file a written declaration of their desire to be subject to jury service, was *Hoyt* reversed by the Supreme Court. Billy Taylor, convicted of rape and kidnapping, successfully appealed his conviction on the grounds that women had been systematically excluded from the jury pool. His lawyers drew an analogy between his experience and the Court's decision three years before that a white man was entitled to have a jury from which blacks had not been systematically barred. The majority opinion upheld Taylor's claim. It made extensive use of an opinion written by Justice William O. Douglas in 1946. What did Douglas mean when he said, "the two sexes are not fungible"? Do you agree?

MR. JUSTICE BYRON R. WHITE DELIVERED THE OPINION OF THE COURT:

The Louisiana jury-selection system does not disqualify women from jury service, but in operation its conceded systematic impact is that only a few women, grossly disproportionate to the number of eligible women in the community, are called for jury service. In this case, no women were on the venire from which the petit jury was drawn. . . .

The State first insists that Taylor, a male, has no standing to object to the exclusion of women from his jury. . . . Taylor was not a member of the excluded class; but there is no rule that claims such as Taylor presents may be made only by those defendants who are members of the group excluded from jury service. In [1972] . . . a white man [successfully] challenged his conviction on the ground that Negroes had been systematically excluded from jury service. . . .

We are . . . persuaded that the fair-cross-section requirement is violated by the systematic exclusion of women, who in the judicial district involved here amounted to 53 percent of the citizens eligible for jury service. . . . This very matter was debated in *Ballard* v. *U.S.* [1946]. . . . The . . . view that an all-male panel drawn from various groups in the community would be as truly representative as if women were included, was firmly rejected:

> . . . who would claim that a jury was truly representative of the community if all men were intentionally and systematically excluded from the panel? The truth is that the two sexes are not fungible; a community made up exclusively of one is different from a community composed of both; the subtle interplay of influence one on the other is among the imponderables. . . . The exclusion of one may indeed make the jury less representative of the community than would be true if an economic or racial group were excluded. [Justice William O. Douglas, 1946]

. . . It is untenable to suggest these days that it would be a special hardship for each and every woman to perform jury service . . . it may be burdensome to sort out those who should be exempted from those who should serve. But that task is performed in the case of men, and the administrative convenience in dealing with women as a class is insufficient justification for diluting the quality of community judgment represented by the jury in criminal trials.

The decision in *Taylor* addressed only the problem of who is included in the panels from whom jurors are chosen. Not until 1994 did the Supreme Court rule that the Fourteenth Amendment's equal protection clause prohibits the use of peremptory jury challenges on the basis of gender. Overturning a paternity suit in which a woman challenged virtually all the men in the jury pool, leaving an all-female jury to decide on her claims for child support, the majority held "that gender, like race, is an unconstitutional proxy for juror competence and impartiality."*

*J.E.B. v. *Alabama* 511 U.S. 127 (1994).

Civil Rights Act, Title VII, 1964

The Civil Rights Act of 1964 was a comprehensive law of enormous significance. It was a complex statute, twenty-eight printed pages long and divided into eleven major sections, or *Titles.* Title I dealt with voting rights; Title III with the desegregation of public facilities; Title V established a Commission on Civil Rights. Title VII defined a long list of practices that would be forbidden to employers and labor unions, obliged the federal government to undertake an "affirmative" program of equal employment opportunity for all employees and job applicants, and created an Equal Employment Opportunity Commission (EEOC) to monitor compliance with the law.

Title VII was notable in that it outlawed discrimination on the basis of gender as well as race. Sex was added to the categories "race, color, religion and national origin" by Congressman Howard Smith, a conservative Democrat from Virginia, who was a vigorous opponent of civil rights legislation. He introduced his motion after urging from Republican supporters of the National Women's Party, who had been lobbying for an Equal Rights Amendment whether or not it would undermine protective labor legislation, and who wanted to equate discrimination on the basis of race and discrimination on the basis of sex. The debate on Smith's motion was filled with misogyny; Smith joked that his amendment would guarantee the "right" of every woman to a husband. But it passed, supported by conservative members who were more comfortable voting for a civil rights bill if there was something in it for white women.

The Equal Employment Opportunity Commission, which began to operate in the summer of 1965, anticipated that virtually all its complaints would come from blacks. They were surprised to discover that 25 percent of the complaints received during the

U.S. Statutes at Large, 78:253–66. For a discussion of the circumstances of the passage of Title VII, see Jo Freeman, "How 'Sex' Got into Title VII: Persistent Opportunism as a Maker of Public Policy," *Law and Inequality* IX (1991): 163–84.

first year were from women. In the course of responding to these complaints, both the commission and the courts were driven to a more subtle analysis of female job categories and work patterns. Section 703(e)1 required that employers wishing to define a job category by sex had to show that sex was a "bona fide occupational qualification"; it was not enough to say that men or women had traditionally filled any given job.

In the decade that followed, most states developed their own versions of Title VII, establishing laws that prohibited sex discrimination in employment. The federal statute was amended in 1972 and again in 1978; on both occasions the EEOC was given substantial additional powers and responsibilities. The three major areas of EEOC activity are: (1) furnishing assistance to comparable state agencies, (2) furnishing advice to employers and labor unions about compliance, and (3) enforcing compliance by conciliation and by legal action. In 1978 Congress passed the Pregnancy Discrimination Act, which amplified the definition of sex to include pregnancy, childbirth, or related medical conditions. EEOC has been willing to view sexual harassment as a form of sex discrimination but has not endorsed the concept of comparable worth.

Sec. 703.(a) It shall be an unlawful employment practice for an employer—

(1) to fail or refuse to hire or to discharge any individual, or otherwise to discriminate against any individual with respect to his compensation, terms, conditions, or privileges of employment, because of such individual's race, color, religion, sex, or national origin; or

(2) to limit, segregate, or classify his employees in any way which would deprive or tend to deprive any individual of employment opportunities or otherwise adversely affect his status as an employee, because of such individual's race, color, religion, sex, or national origin.

(b) It shall be an unlawful employment practice for an employment agency to fail or refuse to refer for employment, or otherwise to discriminate against, any individual because of his race, color, religion, sex, or national origin, or to classify or refer for employment any individual on the basis of his race, color, religion, sex, or national origin.

(c) It shall be an unlawful employment practice for a labor organization—

(1) to exclude or to expel from its membership, or otherwise to discriminate against, any individual because of his race, color, religion, sex, or national origin;

(2) to limit, segregate, or classify its membership, or to classify or fail or refuse to refer for employment any individual, in any way which would deprive or tend to deprive any individual of employment opportunities, or would limit such employment opportunities or otherwise adversely affect his status as an employee or as

an applicant for employment, because of such individual's race, color, religion, sex, or national origin; or

(3) to cause or attempt to cause an employer to discriminate against an individual in violation of this section. . . .

(e) Notwithstanding any other provision of this title, (1) it shall not be an unlawful employment practice for an employer to hire and employ employees, for an employment agency to classify, or refer for employment any individual, for a labor organization to classify its membership or to classify or refer for employment any individual, or for an employer, labor organization, or joint labor-management committee controlling apprenticeship or other training or retraining programs to admit or employ any individual in any such program, on the basis of his religion, sex, or national origin in those certain instances where religion, sex, or national origin is a bona fide occupational qualification reasonably necessary to normal operation of that particular business or enterprise. . . .

Sec. 705.(a) There is hereby created a Commission to be known as the Equal Employment Opportunity Commission, which shall be composed of five members, not more than three of whom shall be members of the same political party, who shall be appointed by the President by and with the advice and consent of the Senate. . . .

(g) The Commission shall have power—

(1) to cooperate with and, with their consent, uti-

lize regional, State, local, and other agencies, both public and private, and individuals; . . .

(3) to furnish to persons subject to this title such technical assistance as they may request to further their compliance with this title or an order issued thereunder;

(4) upon the request of (i) any employer, whose employees or some of them, or (ii) any labor organization, whose members or some of them, refuse or threaten to refuse to cooperate in effectuating the provisions of this title, to assist in such effectuation by conciliation or such other remedial action as is provided by this title;

(5) to make such technical studies as are appropriate to effectuate the purposes and policies of this title and to make the results of such studies available to the public;

(6) to refer matters to the Attorney General with recommendations for intervention in a civil action brought by an aggrieved party under section 706, or for the institution of a civil action by the Attorney General under section 707, and to advise, consult, and assist the Attorney General on such matters. . . .

FELICIA KORNBLUH

A Human Right to Welfare?
Social Protest among Women
Welfare Recipients after World War II

In the Cold War years, racial justice became a new and compelling terrain for progressive white women; for black women it had always been an imperative. In the aftermath of the historic Supreme Court decision banning school segregation, black and white women in Southern cities such as Atlanta and Little Rock worked to keep public schools open so as to begin the process of integration. By the 1960s, the civil rights movement elicited the involvement of young college-age women of both races and the leadership of remarkable older African-American women such as Fannie Lou Hamer and Ella Baker.

Rights talk was contagious. As the focus of the civil rights movement shifted from the South to the urban areas of the North, it became increasingly clear to national leaders of both races that there could be no racial justice without economic justice. It was in this context that the Johnson administration declared its war on poverty.

As Martin Luther King turned his attention to the poor, so did another civil rights activist, George Wiley. Wiley's focus was on a particular segment of the poor—those on welfare. In his quest for welfare rights, he found allies in a new breed of "poverty lawyers" who mounted a legal campaign to persuade the Supreme Court that there was a constitutional right to welfare. But the story of the welfare rights movement was never just the story of a litigation strategy that ultimately failed. The National Welfare Rights Organization (NWRO) that Wiley formed was intended to mobilize the poor at the grassroots level. While the organization was interracial, its rank-and-file members were overwhelmingly black and female. Most were recipients of funds through the government program known as Aid to Families with Dependent Children (AFDC), which had its origins in mothers' pensions. (Mothers' pensions were government stipends paid to eligible widows to enable them to stay at home and care for their children.) As was the case with mothers' pensions, AFDC was means-tested and involved supervision of recipients by social workers.

This mobilization of welfare mothers, especially poor African-American women, marked a first in American history. As these women marched on local welfare offices and ultimately on the national capital under the banner of "Mother Power," they demonstrated that maternalism knew no color. The realities of welfare that brought these women into the NWRO, how they understood their goals and "rights," and what tactics they used to achieve them is the focus of Felicia Kornbluh's essay.

To what extent did the consumerism that had permeated American culture since the end of World War II influence NWRO members' definition of "basic needs"? How were these relatively powerless women attempting to reconfigure basic American understanding of rights and obligations? Do you see any continuities in their understanding of welfare and that of the earlier generation of elite black welfare reformers about whom Linda Gordon wrote? To what extent do their concerns remain relevant?

Welfare gives us enough for food and rent and second-hand clothes for us and our children, and in some states, not even enough for food. But food and rent is not all of life. Why shouldn't we be able to buy perfume once in a while—or a ring—or even a watch? Every woman wants and needs some of these things—particularly when we see all other women having them. If we put money in the collection plate at church, we're taking food out of our children's mouths. Our children drop out of school because they don't have decent clothes, let alone the things that other children take for granted—enough school supplies, money for a class trip, a graduation suit or dress.

—Mrs. Juliet Greenlaw,
Indiana State Representative,
National Welfare Rights
Organization, 1968[1]

Between 1963 and 1973 a grass-roots movement of welfare recipients changed the political conversation about welfare in the United States. This movement has not received much attention in history books, including accounts of 1960s organizing and histories of women.[2] However, for several years it captured public attention, inspired heated debates, and compelled both national and local government officials to recognize the perspectives of some of their poorest constituents. The welfare rights effort crossed paths with other social change campaigns, including those of white feminists, black civil rights activists, and members of the New Left who organized against the Vietnam War. Welfare rights activists differed from their counterparts in the other movements in their intense focus on economic inequality and their lack of faith in the private labor market to fill the gaps between the material needs of poor people and their resources.

Beginning in 1967, a National Welfare Rights Organization (NWRO) with headquarters in Washington, D.C., represented this movement and coordinated many of its activities. At its height in 1969, NWRO membership reached approximately 25,000 welfare recipients and other poor people. Thousands more participated in actions sponsored by NWRO's local affiliates or organized for welfare rights with unaffiliated groups.[3] By 1971, NWRO encompassed 540 local Welfare Rights Organizations (WROs), located primarily in big cities in the Northeast, Midwest, and California. A majority of welfare rights activists were African-American women. Smaller numbers were Puerto Rican, Chicana/o, Native American, or white. Perhaps 10% of them were men.[4] Although low-income mothers with children predominated in the movement, smaller numbers of senior citizens, disabled people, public housing tenants, and tenant farmers—recipients of such government programs as Aid to

Johnnie Tillmon addressing a Mother's Day March on Washington, circa 1968 or 1969. George Wiley sits directly behind her, on the left; Ethel Kennedy looks on. (Courtesy State Historical Society of Wisconsin. Whi (x3) 52064. Lot 5025)

Families with Dependent Children (AFDC), Old Age Assistance, Aid to the Disabled, food stamps, and Indian Welfare—rallied to the cry of rights for clients of the welfare state.

These activists made four primary arguments about why they had a right to welfare. First, they argued that access to welfare in times of need was part of their inheritance as American citizens. Second, they argued that as women of color, welfare was essential to their equality—a means to narrow the economic gap between themselves and those Mrs. Juliet Greenlaw in the epigraph identified as "all other women." Third, some welfare rights activists claimed that they deserved benefits because they did the difficult, but socially necessary, work of raising young children. Fourth, many others argued that they deserved benefits because they were human beings who possessed a "right to live." This "right to live" encompassed not only a right to base survival, but also a right to the goods and services that signified normality in postwar America, including many of the things that Greenlaw

pointed out: "[D]ecent clothes" or "money for a class trip" for school-aged children, and for adult women, not only "food and rent" but also "perfume . . . a ring—or even a watch."

As part of the argument that they possessed a "right to live" in modern terms, activists criticized the welfare system for underestimating the needs of families. They fought welfare authorities over the contents of the welfare budget, the breakdown of welfare families' needs that formed the basis of their biweekly welfare grants. They also fought over the assessments that case workers and other welfare authorities made of what they called the "basic" and "special needs" of clients— charging in general that clients' basic needs were more profound, and their special needs more frequent, than welfare officials recognized.[5] Welfare rights activists utilized loopholes in the rules that governed welfare practice, legal challenges, and confrontational tactics to gain what they saw as the material substance of their human rights from reluctant welfare administrations.

"I SHOULD AT LEAST BE TREATED LIKE A HUMAN BEING": BUDGETS AND NEEDS

The welfare budget of a public assistance recipient in the 1960s was a complex entity. Although all recipients had the same right to aid as specified under the federal program AFDC, states and localities had wide discretion in the way they administered the program. They, in turn, directed caseworkers to calculate the budget of each individual or family separately, based on the caseworker's understanding of the particular situation.[6] Caseworkers had one major guide in making their determinations, the Welfare Manual that the local department issued to all employees. The manual was full of details about the basic welfare budget—scaled to family size and children's ages, dependent upon whether the people in question received AFDC, Home Relief,[7] or Old Age Assistance,[8] on what they paid for rent, and on whether they had a washing machine or needed to pay separately for laundry.[9] The manual also detailed the numerous goods welfare departments expected families to have to bring them "up to standard." These were the "basic needs" that welfare administrators thought all families required as a prerequisite before they could provide for their families with the biweekly grant. In New York City, welfare officials determined that an "adequate basic supply" of clothing that would bring an adult woman "up to standard" included:

1 hat	2 cotton dresses
1 "dressy dress"	3 pairs of panties
1 girdle	2 pairs of stockings, etc.[10]

The manual contained specified appropriate "unit prices" for each of the items, for both regular and large sizes. The basic supply of furniture and household equipment that would bring a family "up to standard" included:

Living Room:

Couch ("spring on legs with new cotton linters mattress")

"Table—drop leaf or extension (wood)"

Kitchen:

"Dinette set (table and 4 chairs)"

"Linoleum (new)"

Cooking Equipment:

"Paring knife"

"Egg beater, rotary type"

"Fruit reamer, glass"[11]

In addition to these "basic needs," Welfare Manuals itemized various "special needs" that welfare clients might encounter, which the welfare department might pay for on a one-time-only basis or under certain circumstances. These ran the gamut from a special diet for a diabetic welfare recipient, to transportation to a doctor's visit, to baby-sitting or child care help for an "overburdened mother" who was certified as such by a Case Supervisor.[12] The total amount a family or individual received in the welfare check was to be a combination of its basic budget, plus any "basic needs" that the welfare department was meeting to bring the case "up to standard," plus payment to fulfill various "special needs," *minus* amounts earned from employment; received in gifts, alimony, or child support; or due the welfare department because of a prior overpayment.

Although Welfare Manuals stipulated an enormous array of consumer goods (from a fruit reamer to a "dressy dress") that families were supposed to receive to bring them "up to standard," welfare departments almost never brought their clients fully up to standard. Neither did they fully meet recipients' "special needs." They were able to maintain wide gaps between what they theoretically maintained welfare clients should have and what they in fact offered these clients by tightly controlling the information in the manual.

The welfare rights movement exploited the ambiguities of this system. The first strategic objective of most WROs was to get hold of the Welfare Manual. Next, WRO members sought collectively to make welfare departments narrow the gap between manual and reality, by making good on their stated standards for "basic" and "special needs"—that is, by distributing enormous quantities of cash or in-kind benefits to recipients. Often the WRO would distribute a simple one-page flier to all of its members asking them to check off the things they did not have, but which the welfare department claimed every family needed if it was to survive on a welfare budget. Members would submit these "basic needs" forms to welfare departments together in large batches.

Complaints and protests about the welfare budget were widespread within the welfare rights movement. In Columbus, Ohio, for example, an AFDC recipient and movement poet named Mary Spurlock did her own rendition of the welfare budget. Whereas welfare administrators presented budgets as adequate to cover the food and other expenses of thirty families, Spurlock associated the welfare budget with terms such as "Wanting," "Envy," "Losing," "Begging," "Underfed," and "Tears."[13] On the occasion of a Sunday morning welfare rights protest at the church of the Governor of Ohio, Spurlock contributed "Ten Welfare Commandments," which pointed up many of the things she believed should be included in welfare cost accounting:[14]

1— Thou shall give thy children what they need—but don't spend over 73c. a day.
2— Thou shall have furniture—if glue will hold it together.
3— Thou shall live in a real nice house—in the slums.
4— Thou shall clothe thy children—as long as their clothes are rags.
5— Thou shall send thy children to school but don't give them any supplies.
6— Thou shall feed thy children—but don't give them meat.
7— Thou shall not buy any underclothes—no one sees them.
8— Thou shall not give thy children spending money—let them beg.
9— Thou shall not ride a bus up-town—Walk!
10— Thou shall not get sick—just die.[15]

Spurlock registered her protest at the low figures the Ohio welfare department budgeted for items such as clothing, especially underclothes ("no one sees them"), transportation ("Walk!") and food. The official symbol of the Columbus Welfare Rights Organization was an empty horn of plenty, turned upside down, perhaps symbolizing how little welfare recipients such as Spurlock believed they received from the bounty of postwar America.[16]

Welfare activists also had more discrete complaints regarding needs that welfare budgets failed to cover. Mrs. Andrea Keyes, an NWRO member from Meriden, Connecticut, expressed her concerns about welfare cuts in her state in a letter to the NWRO staff in Wash-

ington. "With a total of $6.41 left monthly after expenses," she asked, "where will I get the money to buy women's monthly needs, clothing for my sons & myself, household needs, and appliance repairs[?] I feel that I should at least be treated like a human being."[17] In New York City, a neighborhood activist lampooned the hypocrisy he saw in the welfare department's suggestions to recipients about how to attain a healthy diet:

> The heighth of bureaucratic idiocy has finally been reached.... The D[epartment of] W[elfare] has large, beautiful, colored posters in the various centers, illustrating many food items, with the advice to welfare clients that in order to maintain a balanced healthy diet, the pictured items should become a part of their daily fare.
>
> With the price of fruits and vegetables today ... and with the present welfare allotments (would you believe $1.12 cents a day for a single man?) to follow the DW advice would call for a more than tripling of food allotments [in the budget] ...
>
> Welfare recipients can't even afford the paper the poster is made of, let alone the items pictured.[18]

The implication here was that welfare department employees did not understand consumer prices as well as did recipients themselves. Moreover, it suggested that welfare employees constructed budgets ("would you believe $1.12 cents a day for a single man?") that made it impossible for recipients to have such ordinary amenities as fresh fruits and vegetables.

Welfare recipients complained about specific goods that they felt they needed, but that welfare departments denied or called into question. Mrs. Eliza Williams, a WRO leader, wrote in 1969 to Health, Education, and Welfare Secretary Robert Finch. She complained that some of her elderly neighbors "have been badly mistreated by the Welfare department." As for one, Mr. Moses Hemingway, Williams explained: "He is in need of clothing, has to go to the hospital and he doesn't have any pajamas ... This is what the elderly has to go through. This is their last plea for their rightly needs. If you can't help then the next step is to demolish the whole Welfare program."[19] In a letter she mailed to New York City Mayor John Lindsay and other officials, AFDC recipient Annie Frett complained: "There is no protection for people on welfare who trie [sic] to help themselves, or justice." She wrote of the welfare department's refusal to help her move to what she considered a decent apartment and its reluctance to help pay her bills, and then asked:

> WHAT LAW OR RULE IS THERETHAT SAYS THAT A NEGRO WOMAN MUST USE ONE BOX OF SANITARY NAPKINS A MONTH AND NO MORE/? I WAS QUESTIONED BY A [CASE] WORKE[R] ABOUT THAT.[20]

Frett appears to have reached the end of her tether with a welfare department that she saw as denying her the basics in terms of shelter, utilities, and even personal hygiene.

LEGAL APPEALS: THE CASE OF THE CHROME DINETTE

When welfare recipients such as Annie Frett, Eliza Williams, or Andrea Keyes were dissatisfied with the decisions of their local welfare departments, they could formally appeal the decisions. These appeals were also available to welfare rights groups that were dissatisfied with the responses they received to collective requests for "basic" and "special needs." From the early 1960s through the early 1970s, both individual welfare recipients and organized welfare rights organizations made increasing use of these appeals, called "Fair Hearings." Fair hearings became a particularly effective backup tool for protests over the budgeting decisions of local welfare departments. When caseworkers and welfare department directors failed to fulfill clients' stated needs, dragged their heels on responding to clients' requests, or refused requests without explanation, the clients could always appeal. At least initially, the hearings were costly to welfare departments in terms of money, bureaucratic attention, and negative publicity. Often welfare departments chose to fulfill clients' demands for new budgets, or "basic" and "special needs," rather than pay these costs.

The role of fair hearings as backups to efforts by welfare recipients to compel welfare departments to meet what they saw as their needs appears in the case of Margaret Hayes. This case also illustrates the degree to which battles over such needs amounted to battles between welfare recipients and welfare department personnel over the question of who would determine the specifics of welfare fam-

ilies' needs. Margaret Hayes was an NWRO activist from Newport News, Virginia, and a recipient of supplementary welfare benefits, which she received in addition to her salary as a school bus driver.[21] Hayes requested a grant to fulfill her "basic need" for a dinette set. Department personnel agreed to pay for a dinette, but determined that the reasonable set cost $100, while the one Mrs. Hayes wanted cost almost three times more. Hayes decided to accept the $100 and to find the rest of the money for the furniture she wanted from another source, but welfare officials refused to give her the money. She brought a fair hearing, which she lost. She then appealed to the Commonwealth of Virginia's Director of Welfare and Institutions to reopen the case. The official summary of Mrs. Hayes's fair hearing notes that she:

> Stated that she was … informed by [case] worker, Supervisor and Superintendent that the estimates [she obtained] were too high and that the agency would sanction a chrome [dinette] set in the price range of $100.00. Stated that she would not accept a chrome set (would not say why), that she wanted a wood set and this was the reason for her appeal. Stated that the agency has "lowered her dignity" by not giving her a check for the furniture so that she could buy the kind of set she wanted to suit her specifications.
>
> Appellant stated that she had read the Manual and in her opinion the estimates for a wooden set were not unreasonable … Appellant queried Superintendent as to what her check would be if she didn't work at all. Stated that if she didn't get a wood dinette set of her own choice she would go to "Richmond" [i.e., to the Commonwealth Welfare Department], that she was sick and tired of getting the "run around" by the Local Department.
>
> Agency representative attempted to explain to appellant that the need for a dinette set was recognized, but that the agency was obligated to authorize those items sold for a reasonable price … That the Department kept a file on local sales and that chrome dinette set could be bought for approximately $100.00.[22]

The conflict between Margaret Hayes and the authorities in Newport News emerged from the context of a welfare system that gave the authority to define clients' needs to local officials and not to the clients themselves. As much as it concerned the dinette set, Hayes's appeal may have concerned her claim as a mother, and a welfare recipient with rights, to define her material needs. What "'lowered her dignity'" in particular may have been the department's insistence that she buy only the set her caseworker thought was offered "for a reasonable price"—especially since "in her opinion the estimates" she obtained "for a wooden set were not unreasonable." In correspondence to the Virginia Director of Welfare and Institutions, Hayes further explained her position:

> The furniture which I desired to purchase costs more than the $100 which the Department feels welfare recipients should be satisfied with. I told my caseworker that if $100 was all that the Department would allow, then I would accept the $100 and apply it toward the dining set of my choice . . . In your letter you say that the State Board found that the $100 offered by the welfare was not acceptable to me. This is not true. The whole question is whether the Department will give me the $100 not whether I will accept it.[23]

In response, an welfare official advised Mrs. Hayes that when she found "a dinette set of your choice which will not cost more than the amount of $100.00, we believe the local agency will be willing to reconsider your request."[24] The welfare departments, at both the county and state levels, were as fixed in their position as Mrs. Hayes was in hers. As much as she considered it a component of her dignity to choose the furniture she wanted instead of settling for what "the Department feels welfare recipients should be satisfied with," welfare administrators apparently considered it imperative that Hayes buy what they considered "reasonable" merchandise instead of using public money to do what she liked in the consumer marketplace.

Beyond their needs for basic food and clothing, welfare rights activists who mobilized in the 1960s saw as part of their human rights a range of additional goods and services that would help round out their lives. For Juliet Greenlaw it was "perfume" or "a watch," for Mary Spurluck a little meat in her children's diets, and for Margaret Hayes a wood dinette set that represented the material minimum for being "a human being" in the affluent United States. These and other public assistance recipients did what few poor people had ever done before: They formed a national movement that placed its own political perspectives on the public agenda.

The essence of this perspective was an insistence that the recipients of public benefits had rights—rights as Americans, rights as people of color who had never yet enjoyed the fruits of full citizenship, rights as mothers, and rights as human beings. Unlike the women who formed the nucleus of the feminist movement of the 1960s, they did not ask for greater access to the wage labor market. Unlike virtually all parties to the welfare reform debates of the years since then, welfare rights activists did not generally believe that they needed to work outside their homes in order to justify receiving welfare. In light of these later debates, the political vision of the welfare rights movement seems almost irremediably far off. However, while the historical moment that shaped the welfare rights movement will not come again, remembering the concerns that welfare recipients voiced at the high-water mark of their political influence may help us imagine alternatives to the narrowness that has prevailed when welfare policy proceeded as though their perspectives did not matter.[25]

Notes

1. Mrs. Juliet Greenlaw, "Statement of National Welfare Rights Organization to the Democratic Platform Hearing," August 16, 1968, from Box 2101, file titled "Demo Platform August 19, 1968," NWRO papers, Moorland-Spingarn Research Center, Howard University.

2. Exceptions include such histories of black women as Paula Giddings, *When and Where I Enter: The Impact of Black Women on Race and Sex in America* (New York, 1984), 312–13; Jacqueline Jones, *Labor of Love, Labor of Sorrow: Black Women, Work, and the Family from Slavery to the Present* (New York, 1985), 306–7; and such histories of social welfare as Michael Katz, *In the Shadow of the Poorhouse: A Social History of Welfare in America* (New York, 1986), 253–54, and James Patterson, *America's Struggle Against Poverty 1900–1980* (Cambridge, Mass., 1981), 153, 180–81, 195–96.

3. Thirty thousand was the official membership figure that NWRO leaders utilized most frequently. However, my study of NWRO records reveals somewhat lower figures. See National Welfare Rights Organization, "Table, Annual Membership Figures, by State, for 1968, 1969, 1970, 1971," n.d., "Table, WROs and Members, by State, for 1967, 1968, and 1969, through 5/27," and "Membership Report for August, 1969," all in Box 8, Folder 4, George Wiley papers, State Historical Society of Wisconsin (SHSW).

4. "1971 Membership Lists, by Region," no author, Box 1971, file titled "Regional Group Lists—1971," NWRO Papers, Moorland-Spingarn Research Center, Howard University.

5. For the complicated politics of needs and rights see Nancy Fraser, "Struggle Over Needs: Outline of a Socialist-Feminist Critical Theory of Late-Capitalist Political Culture," in *Women, The State, and Welfare*, ed. Linda Gordon (Madison, Wis., 1990), 199–225. I am also indebted to Jeremy Waldron's suggestion that needs and rights are not competing, but complementary, and that meaningful social and political struggle can involve battles over needs within a framework of rights.

6. For the origins of such "differential diagnoses" in the social work theories of the early twentieth century, see Linda Gordon, "Social Insurance and Public Assistance: The Influence of Gender in Welfare Thought in the United States, 1890–1935," *American Historical Review* 97 1 (February 1992): 19–54.

7. Home Relief was, and is, the term in many states for the assistance program for adults who have no children or who do not qualify for AFDC for some other reason. Home Relief is not a federal program, but is funded and administered exclusively by the states. The same program is known in some states as General Assistance.

8. Old Age Assistance (OAA) was a federal program for the low-income elderly who were not covered by the Old-Age Insurance program (what we usually call "Social Security"). Created by the Social Security Act of 1935, OAA was supplanted in 1974 by Supplementary Security Insurance (SSI), which was designed to serve both disabled and elderly people; unlike OAA, which, like AFDC, had combined state–federal administration, SSI was to be funded and administered entirely by the federal government.

Frances Fox Piven argues that the welfare rights movement should be given credit for the creation of SSI, which had all the features that NWRO sought in a welfare program while not covering the people who formed the bulk of the NWRO membership (discussion with the author, City University of New York Graduate Center, December 5, 1995).

9. Social Service Employees Union (SSEU), New York City, "Tables of Minimum Standards from Information Found in the Handbook for Case Units in Public Assistance," n.d., "Basic Budget" (no page), Box 2010, file titled "SSEU-NY," NWRO papers. At the time that NWRO was most active, SSEU was an independent union of welfare caseworkers, which had on its staff a liaison to the welfare activists. For discussion see Daniel J. Walkowitz, *The Muddle of the Middle Classes* (Chapel Hill, N.C., 1997). SSEU probably drew up these tables specially for NWRO or its New York affiliate, the Citywide Coordinating Committee of Welfare Rights Groups.

10. Basic clothing chart, "Woman," no page, in SSEU manual, in ibid.

11. "Household Furnishings and Equipment (not included in the regular check)," no page, in SSEU manual, in ibid. Former Lindsay Administration official Charles Morris, who generally treats the welfare rights movement with disdain, also emphasizes the variations from client to client in welfare grants, adding that welfare codes "stipulated living conditions in such detail—for example, a kitchen should have a fruit reamer—that almost everyone could qualify for additional special grants to meet standards." Charles Morris, *The Cost of Good Intentions: New York City and the Liberal Experiment, 1960–1975* (New York, 1980), 69.

12. SSEU manual, p. 13, in Box 2010, file titled "SSEU-NY," NWRO papers.

13. Mary Spurlock, "Welfare Budget," from Columbus Welfare Rights Organization pamphlet, "Got Welfare Problems? Join WRO," n.d., Box 2167, file titled "Columbus WRO," NWRO papers.

14. I borrow the idea of "cost accounting" from Nell Irvin Painter, "Soul Murder and Slavery: Toward a Fully Loaded Cost Accounting," in *U.S. History as Women's History: New Feminist Essays*, ed. Linda K. Kerber, Alice Kessler-Harris, and Kathryn Kish Sklar (Chapel Hill, N.C., 1995), 125–46.

15. Mary Magdalene Spurlock, "Ten Welfare Commandments," from the Ohio Steering Committee for Adequate Welfare, "Notice for the Ohio Crusade for Adequate Welfare," November 5, 1967, Box 2167, file titled "Ohio Steering Committee for Adequate Welfare," NWRO papers.

16. "The [Columbus] WRO has adopted as its symbol an empty horn of plenty circled by the words 'Welfare: a right—not a privilege,'" from Ohio Steering Committee for Adequate Welfare, *Adequate Welfare News*, January 9, 1967, 3, from Box 2167, file titled "Ohio Steering Committee for Adequate Welfare," NWRO papers.

17. Letter from Mrs. Andrea Keyes, Meriden, Connecticut, to the National Welfare Rights Organization, Washington, D.C., October 13, 1971, Box 1971, file titled "Connecticut," NWRO papers.

18. [Henry Pollack], "Mama, What's a Strawberry?" *Newsletter, West Side Welfare Council, The Voice of Poverty Midst Plenty*, vol. 1, no. 5, September 1966: 3, Box 2167, file titled "Upper West Side Council," NWRO papers. Home economists on the staffs of local welfare departments drew up schedules of standard prices for goods, as well as of the retinue of goods that constituted consumption by the normal American family.

19. Letter from Mrs. Eliza Williams, Co-chairman, Waterbury Welfare Rights Organization, Waterbury, Conn., to Secretary of Health, Education and Welfare Robert Finch, Washington, D.C., June 3, 1969, Box 2017, file titled "Letters of Complaint," NWRO papers.

20. Letter from Annie Frett, Brooklyn, New York, to Mayor Lindsay, [New York City Welfare] Commissioner Ginsberg, and [New York State Welfare] Commissioner Louch[heim], August 28, 1967, Fox 47, Folder 118, papers of the Scholarship, Education, and Defense Fund for Racial Equality (SEDFRE), SHSW.

21. In a 1969 membership tally, Hayes appeared as the contact person for the Newport News WRO, which had a total of 36 members. Membership list, 1969, in Box 1952, file titled "Local Groups—WRO," NWRO papers.

22. Summary of Appeal, Case of Margaret Beatrice Hayes, May 20, 1970, 5–6, Box 2063, file titled "Margaret Hayes," NWRO papers. For similar issues raised in a Fair Hearing, see Fair Hearing

Transcript, Case of Joanne Smitherman, October 24, 1967, 80–82, in Box 49, Folder 1, SEDFRE papers. Smitherman, a Harlem welfare rights activist, spoke in the hearing of her right to keep "[d]emitasse cups and saucers . . . goblets and wine glasses."

23. Letter from Mrs. Margaret Hayes, Newport News, Va., to Mr. Otis L. Brown, Director, Department of Welfare and Institutions, Richmond, Va., August 12, 1970, in ibid.

24. Letter from (Miss) Mary Kilcullen, Assistant to the Chief, Bureau of Assistance and Service Programs, Commonwealth of Virginia Department of Welfare and Institutions, Richmond, Va., to Mrs. Margaret Hayes, August 27, 1970, in ibid.

25. This is not to suggest that welfare recipients in more recent years have not tried to make their voices heard in the making of social policy. For discussions of more recent efforts among college students who are also welfare recipients, see my article "Class Dismissed: Welfare Recipients Fight to Stay in College," *In These Times,* October 5, 1997: 18–20. For a more general discussion of the relationship between welfare rights and contemporary politics, see my "The Goals of the National Welfare Rights Movement: Why We Need Them Thirty Years Later," *Feminist Studies* 24/1 (Spring 1998): 65–78.

DOCUMENTS: Making the Personal Political: Becoming a Feminist

> *Jessie Lopez de la Cruz, "The first woman farmworker organizer out in the fields"*

As the twentieth century progressed, Chicana women of the American Southwest were forced to follow their men in search of work, abandoning communal village life. Joined by migrants from Mexico, they found jobs in factories, service work, and in the fields. Although entire families were incorporated into wage labor in the fields of Colorado and California, women, who had fewer job opportunities than men, gradually lost the power base and economic autonomy that had sustained them in their communal villages. They did not lose their resourcefulness or their determination to improve their working conditions, as the following account makes clear.

The movement of Jessie de la Cruz from farmworker to union organizer to community leader and Chicana spokeswoman to membership on the California Commission on the Status of Women is an example of one woman's determination to make the personal political. Contrary to popular stereotypes, Latina women have a tradition of activism. The best-known example is provided by the miners' wives at Silver City whose exploits on the picket line are documented in the classic film *Salt of the Earth*. Historians have recently added other examples: Mexican American women in textile factories and canneries who fought, often unsuccessfully, to gain the benefits for themselves and their families that unions could provide. Their efforts were preceded by those Cuban American women a continent away whose labor militancy and political activism in turn-of-the-century Florida further demonstrates the continuous intertwining of family and work, of home, factory, and field in the lives of many immigrant women as well as their willingness to fight economic and political oppression.

CHILDHOOD

My grandmother was born in Mexico in Aguas Calientes, near Guadalajara. She was raised by a very strict father and she married at thirteen. That was the custom. The girls, as soon as they were old enough to learn cooking and sewing, would get married. She had my mother and my oldest brother when she and my grandfather came across. My grandfather worked for the railroad laying the ties and tracks. Then he worked for a mining company. And after that we moved to Anaheim. We lived in a big four-bedroom house my grandfather built. With my grandparents and their children, three children of my mother's sister who had died, and the three of us, that made a big crowd.

My grandfather would get up Sunday mornings and start the fire in a great big wood-burning stove. He would wrap us up in blankets and seat us around that stove on chairs and say, "Now, don't get too close to the stove. Take care of the younger children." Then he would go out to the store and get

Reprinted by permission of The Feminist Press at the City University of New York, from Ellen Cantarow with Susan Gushee O'Malley and Sharon Hartman Strom, *Moving the Mountain: Women Working for Social Change.* Copyright © 1980 by Ellen Cantarow, Susan Gushee O'Malley, and Sharon Hartman Strom.

bananas and oranges and cereal that he'd cook for us to eat, and milk, and he would feed us Sunday mornings. . . .

Then my grandfather had an accident. The middle finger of his right hand was crushed and he couldn't work for about two weeks. When he went back he was told that he'd already been replaced by another worker. So he was out of a job. He decided we'd better go on and pick the crops. We had done that before, during the summer. But this time we went for good.

We came North. The families got together; the women would start cooking at night, boiling eggs and potatoes and making piles of tortillas and tacos, and these lunches would be packed in pails and boxes. There was as much fruit as they could get together, and roasted pumpkin seeds. My uncle had a factory where he made Mexican candy in East Los Angeles. And he used to give us a lot of pumpkin seeds. So my mother dried these, and she roasted and salted them for the trip to keep the drivers awake. We'd start in a car caravan, six or seven families together, one car watching for the other, and when it got a little dark they'd pull onto the roadside and build a fire and start some cooking to feed us. Then they'd spread blankets and quilts on the ground and we would sleep there that night. The next morning the women and older children would get up first and start the breakfast. And we smaller children, it was our job to fold the blankets and put them back in the cars and trucks. Then my brothers and the men would check the cars over again, and after breakfast all the women would wash the dishes and pack them, get 'em in the cars, and we'd start again.

We'd finally get to Delano and would work there a little. If work was scarce we would keep on going till San Jose. I did the same thing my mother and my grandfather and my uncles did, picking prunes on our hands and knees off the ground, and putting them in the buckets. We were paid four dollars a ton and we had to fill forty boxes to make it a ton. They made us sign a contract that we would stay there until all the prunes were picked. When we would finish the prunes, in early September, we would start back. And stop on the way to Mendota to pick cotton.

When I was about 13, I used to lift a 12-foot stack of cotton weighing 104 or 112 pounds. When you're doing this work, you get to be an expert. I could get that sack and put it on my shoulder, and walk with that sack for about a city block or maybe a little less, to where the scale was. I could hook this sack up on the scale, have it weighed, take it off the hook and put it back on my shoulder and walk up a ladder about eight feet high and dump all that cotton in the trailer.

My brothers taught me how to do it. When I first started picking cotton, they had to untie their sack and go on my side of the row and help me put this sack on my shoulder; so they taught me how to do it when it was full. It's stiff. My brother said, "Just walk over it, pick up one end, and sort of pull it up, up, and then bend down, and when the middle of the sack hits your shoulder, you just stand up slowly. Then put your arm on your waist and the sack will sit on your shoulder and you can just walk with it." At 13, 14 I was lifting 104 and 112 pounds. I weighed 97, I guess!

As a child I remember we had tents without any floors. I think it was Giffen's Camp Number Nine. I remember the water coming from under the tent at night to where we were sleeping. My brothers would get up with shovels and put mud around the tent to keep the water out. But our blankets and our clothes were always damp during the winter. . . .

In thirty-three we came up North to follow the crops because my brothers couldn't find any work in Los Angeles during the Depression. I remember going hungry to school. I didn't have a sweater. I had nothing. I'd come to school and they'd want to know, "What did you have for breakfast?" They gave us a paper, to write down what we had! I *invented* things! We had eggs and milk, I'd say, and the same things the other kids would write, I'd write. There weren't many Mexican people at school, mostly whites, and I'd watch to see what they were writing or the pictures that they'd show. You know: glasses of milk, and toast, and oranges and bananas and cereal. I'd never had *anything*. . . .

COURTSHIP AND MARRIAGE

When I was a girl, boys were allowed to go out and have friends and visit there in camp, and even go to town. But the girls—my mother was always watching them. We couldn't talk to nobody. If I had a boyfriend he had to send me letters, drop notes on his way or send them along with somebody. We did no dating. If girls came to visit at my house, my grandmother sat right there to listen to what we were talking about. We weren't allowed to speak English because she couldn't understand. . . . We were allowed nowhere except out to the field, and then we always worked between my two older brothers. The only one they trusted was Arnold. He's the one I married! I was fourteen when I met Arnold, in 1933. We lived next door to his family, which was a big one. . . .

Arnold and I got married in 1938 in Firebaugh, where we'd all moved. We had a big party with an orchestra: some of Arnold's friends played the violin and guitar. But we had no honeymoon. On the second day after our wedding, he went back to his job—irrigating. I'd get up at four o'clock in the morning to fix his breakfast and his lunch. He'd start the fire for me. I did the cooking in his mother's kitchen. In the morning I'd get up and run across and I'd fix his breakfast and his lunch and he'd go off and I'd go back to bed. There was no women's liberation at the time! I felt I was overworked in the house. . . . But I felt, "What can she (her mother-in-law) do without the help I'm giving her?" I felt sorry for her. She'd worked very hard and she had so many children, and had to wash her clothes in a tub with a rock board and do the ironing by heating the irons on top of the stove. All of us had to do this, but not many families had eight or nine little children.

I cooked with her until May. But I kept after Arnold: "I want my own kitchen!" So in May we drove all the way into Fresno. We got a few spoons and plates and pots and skillets and I started my own housekeeping. I still went to his mother's to help her during the day when Arnold was working. But I cooked in my own stove.

After I was married, sometime in May, my husband was chopping cotton and I said, "I want to go with you."

"You can't. You have to stay at home!"

"I just feel like going outside somewhere. I haven't gone anyplace. I want to at least go out to the fields. Take another hoe and I'll help you." I went, but only for one or two days. Then he refused to take me. He said, "You have to stay home and raise children." I was pregnant with my first one. "I want you to rest," he said. "You're not supposed to work. You worked ever since I can remember. Now

that you're married, you are going to rest." So I stayed home but I didn't call it rest doing all the cooking for his mother.

Arnold was raised in the old Mexican custom—men on the one side, women on the other. Women couldn't do anything. Your husband would say, "Go here," you'd do it. You didn't dare go out without your husband saying you could. . . .

After a time I said, "I have really had it. Why do you have to go with your friends all the time when I'm being left alone?"

"Well, what's wrong with that? You can go visit my mother." I said, "Big deal, you want me to visit your mother and help make some tortillas." So he finally started giving me money, five or six dollars. He'd say, "My mother's going to Fresno. If you want to go with them you can go." Or he would say, "Donna Genoveva," a friend of ours, "is going to Fresno and she said you can come along." I'd get my two kids ready early in the morning and we'd go to Fresno or to visit her husband, who was up in the mountains in the hospital for TB. One day I just said, "Why do I have to depend on other people to take me out somewhere? I'm married, I have a husband—who should be taking me out." The next time he was home and said, "Here's the money," I said, "I don't want to go." He let it go at that and I did too, I didn't say another word. The following weekend he said, "Do you want to go to a show? My mother's going. They're going to Fresno." I said, "No." Then about the third time this happened he said, "Why don't you want to go anymore?"

"I do, I do want to go. I want to go somewhere, but not with anyone else. I want to go with you." So then he started staying home and he'd say, "Get ready, we're going into Fresno." And both of us would come in, bring the children, go to a show and eat, or just go to the park.

Arnold would never teach me how to drive. One day I asked him to. We were on a ditch bank about eight feet wide. He says, "Get on the driver's side. Now turn around and go back." I got out. I said, "You do it! Just tell me you don't want me to learn if that's what you want." Then in 1947 I asked my sister, Margaret, and she showed me. We practiced in a field. After a few times she said, "Hey! You know how to drive! Let's go into town so you can buy your groceries."

So one day I said to Arnold, "I'm going out to get the groceries."

"Who's going to take you?"

"Me. I'm going to do the buying from now on."

I stopped working toward the last months of my pregnancies, but I would start again after they were born. When I was working and I couldn't find somebody I would take them with me. I started taking Ray with me when he wasn't a year old yet. I'd carry one of those big washtubs and put it under the vine and sit him there. I knew he was safe; he couldn't climb out. Arnold and I would move the tub along with us as we worked. I hated to leave him with somebody that probably wouldn't take care of him the way I could.

In 1944 we moved to a labor camp in Huron and we stayed there 'til 1956. But before that we had a single-room cabin. I used to separate the bed section from the kitchen by nailing blankets or pieces of canvas to divide. We had our bed and another bed for the children. All the boys slept in the bed and the girl slept with us in our bed. During the night Bobby being the youngest of the boys would wake up and be scared and he always ended up in our bed! It was pretty crowded, but what could you do? I was always nailing orange crates on the walls to use as cupboards for dishes. . . .

There was a lot of sickness. I remember when my kids got whooping cough. Arnold was sick, too, he was burning hot. During this time instead of staying in my own cabin at night I'd go to my mother-in-law's. The children would wake up at night coughing and there was blood coming out of their noses. I cried and cried, I was afraid they'd choke. I went to the clinic and they told me the children had whooping cough. That cough lasted six months.

It was like that for all of us. I would see babies who died. It was claimed if you lifted a young baby up fast, the soft spot would cave in and it would get diarrhea and dehydrate and die. After all these years, I know it wasn't that that killed them. It was hunger, malnutrition, no money to pay the doctors. When the union came, this was one of the things we fought against.

FIELD WORK

From 1939 until 1944 we stayed at Giffen's Camp Number Three. We were still following the crops. We would go out to pick cotton or apricots or grapes here near Fresno or we would go father north to Tracey to pick peas. When there was no work chopping or picking cotton we'd go to Patterson or San Jose to pick apricots. Arnold did the picking and I did cutting for the drying-out in the sheds. . . .

We always went where we wanted to make sure the women and men were going to work because if it were just the men working it wasn't worth going out there because we wouldn't earn enough, to support a family. We would start early, around 6:30 A.M., and work for four or five hours, then walk home and eat and rest until about 3:30 in the afternoon when it cooled off. We would go back and work until we couldn't see. Then we'd get home and rest, visit, talk, then I'd clean up the kitchen. I was doing the housework and working out in the fields, and taking care of the kids. I had two children by this time. . . .

The hardest work we did was thinning beets. You were required to use a short-handled hoe. The cutting edge is about seven to eight inches wide and the handle is about a foot long. Then you have to be bent over with the hoe in one hand. You walk down the rows stooped over. You have to work hard, fast, as fast as you can because you were paid by the row, not by the hour. . . .

I used a short-handled hoe in the lettuce fields. The lettuce grows in a bed. You work in little furrows between two rows. First you thin them with the hoe, then you pick off the tops. My brothers-in-law and Arnold and I and some other friends worked there picking the tops off the lettuce. By the time they had taken up one row I had taken up two. The men would go between the two beds and take one row and break the little balls off. But I took two rows at a time, one with each hand. By the time I finished my two rows at the other end, it was close to a mile long, and my brother-in-law had only taken one row part-way. He said, "I'm quitting! If Jessie can beat me at this kind of work, I'm no good at it." So he never came back. About three or four other men wouldn't go back to work because they were beaten by a woman. They said, "I'm ashamed to have a woman even older than I am work faster than I can. This is women's job." I said, "Hey! What do you mean? You mean the men's job is washing dishes and baking tortillas?" They said working out in the fields was women's work because we were faster at it!

Out in the fields there were never any restrooms. We had to go eight or ten hours without relief. If there wasn't brush or a little ditch we were forced to wait until we got home! Just the women. The men didn't need to pull their clothes down. Later, when I worked for the Farmworkers, in a hearing, I said, "I was working for Russell Giffen, the biggest grower in Huron. These big growers have a lot of money because we earned all that money for them. Because of our sweat and our labor that we put on the land. What they do instead of supplying restrooms and clean water where we can wash our hands, is put posts on the ground with a piece of gunny sack wound around them." That's where we went. And that thing was moved along with us. It was just four stakes stuck in the ground and then there was canvas or a piece of gunny sack around it. You would be working and this restroom would be right there. The canvas didn't come up high enough in front for privacy. We made it a practice to go two at a time. One would stand outdoors and watch outside that nobody came along. And then the other would do the same for the one inside.

LA CAUSA

One night in 1962 there was a knock at the door and there were three men. One of them was Cesar Chavez. And the next thing I knew, they were sitting around our table talking about a union. I made coffee. Arnold had already told me about a union for the farmworkers. He was attending their meetings in Fresno, but I didn't. I'd either stay home or stay outside in the car. But then Cesar said, "The women have to be involved. They're the ones working out in the fields with their husbands. If you can take the women out to the fields, you can certainly take them to meetings." So I sat up straight and said to myself, "*That's* what I want!"

When I became involved with the union, I felt I had to get other women involved. Women have been behind men all the time, always. In my sister-in-law and brother-in-law's families the women do a lot of shouting and cussing and they get slapped around. But that's not standing up for what you believe in. It's just trying to boss and not knowing how. I'd hear them scolding their kids and fighting their husbands and I'd say, "Gosh! Why don't you go after the people that have you living like this? Why don't you go after the growers

that have you tired from working out in the fields at low wages and keep us poor all the time? . . . Then I would say we had to take a part in the things going on around us. "Women can no longer be taken for granted— that we're just going to stay home and do the cooking and cleaning. It's way past the time when our husbands could say, 'You stay home! You have to take care of the children. You have to do as I say.'"

Then some women I spoke to started attending the union meetings, and later they were out on the picket lines.

I was well-known in the small towns around Fresno. Wherever I went to speak to them, they listened. I told them about how we were excluded from the NLRB in 1935, how we had no benefits, no minimum wage, nothing out in the fields—no restrooms, nothing. I'd ask people how they felt about all these many years they had been working out in the fields, how they had been treated. And then we'd all talk about it. They would say, "I was working for so-and-so, and when I complained about something that happened there, I was fired." I said, "Well! Do you think we should be putting up with this in this modern age? You know, we're not back in the 20s. We can stand up! We can talk back! It's not like when I was a little kid and my grandmother used to say, 'You have to especially respect the Anglos, "Yessir," "Yes, Ma'am!"' That's over. This country is very rich, and we want a share of the money those growers make of our sweat and our work by exploiting us and our children!" I'd have my sign-up book and I'd say, "If anyone wants to become a member of the union, I can make you a member right now." And they'd agree!

So I found out that I could organize them and make members of them. Then I offered to help them, like taking them to the doctor's and translating for them, filling out papers that they needed to fill out, writing their letters for those that couldn't write. A lot of people confided in me. Through the letter-writing, I knew a lot of the problems they were having back home, and they knew they could trust me, that I wouldn't tell anyone else about what I had written or read. So that's why they came to me.

I guess when the union found out how I was able to talk to people, I was called into Delano to one of the meetings, and they gave me my card as an organizer. I am very proud to say I was the first woman organizer out in the fields organizing the people. There have been Dolores Huerta and others, but they were in cities organizing the people, and I was the first woman farmworker organizer out in the fields. . . .

It was very hard being a woman organizer. Many of our people my age and older were raised with old customs in Mexico: where the husband rules, he is the king of his house. The wife obeys, and the children, too. So when we first started it was very, very hard. Men gave us the most trouble—neighbors there in Parlier! They were for the union, but they were not taking orders from women, they said. When they formed the ranch committee at Christian Brothers—that's a big wine company, part of it is in Parlier—the ranch committee was all men. We were working under our first contract in Fresno County. The ranch committee had to enforce the contract. If there are any grievances they meet with us and the supervisors. But there were no women on that first committee.

That year, we'd have a union meeting every week. Men, women, and children would come. Women would ask questions and the men would just stand back. I guess they'd say to themselves, "I'll wait for someone to say something before I do." The women were more aggressive than the men.

When the first contract was up, we talked about there being no women on the ranch committee. I suggested they be on it, and the men went along with this. And so women were elected.

The women took the lead in calling for picketing and we would talk to the people. It got to the point that we would have to find them, because the men just wouldn't go and they wouldn't take their wives. So we would say, "We're having our picket line at the Safeway in Fresno, and those that don't show up are going to have to pay a five dollar fine." We couldn't have four or five come to a picket line and have the rest stay home and watch T.V. In the end, we had everybody out there. . . .

At White River Farms one morning very early, we were out there by the hundreds by the road, and these people got down and started working out there in the grapes. We were asking them not to work, telling them that there was a strike going on. The grower had two guards at the entrance and there was

a helicopter above us. At other White River Farm ranches they had the sheriff, the county police, everybody. But there were pickets at three different ranches and where we were picketing there wasn't anybody except these two guards. So I said, "Hey! What about the women getting together and let's rush 'em!" And they said, "Do you think we could do that?" And I said, "Of course we can! Let's go in there. Let's get 'em out of there any way we can." So about fifty of us rushed. We went under the vines. We had our banners and you could see them bobbing up and down, up and down, and we'd go under those rows on our knees and roll over. When the scabs saw us coming they took off. All of them went and they got on the bus. The guards had guns that they would shoot, and something black like smoke or teargas would come out. That scared us, but we still kept on. After we saw all those workers get back on the busses, we went back. Instead of running this time, we rolled over and over all the way out. The vines are about four feet tall, and they have wire where you string up the vines. So you can't walk or run across one of these fences. You have to keep going under these wires. When I got out there on the road they were getting these big, hard dirty clods and throwing them at us. And then the pickets started doing the same thing. When the first police car came, somebody broke the windshield. We don't know if it was the scabs or someone on the picket lines, but the picketers were blamed.

When we women ran into the fields we knew we'd be arrested if they caught us. But we went in and we told the scabs, "If you're not coming out we're gonna pull you out!"

In Kern County we were sprayed with pesticides. They would come out there with their sprayers and spray us on the picket lines. They have these big tanks that are pulled by a tractor with hoses attached and they spray the trees with this. They are strong like a water hose, but wider. When we were picketing they came out there to spray the pickets. They had goons with these big police dogs on leashes.

One of the things the growers did to break our strikes was to bring in "illegal aliens." I would get a list of names of the scabs and give them to the border patrol. At that time you see, we were pitted against each other, us and the people from Mexico, so it was either us or them. When I went to the border patrol office

I'd go in and say, "Can I come in?" They'd say, "You can't come in. This is a very small office." They kept telling us they were short of men. But every time I went there, there were all of them with their feet up on the desks in their air-conditioned office. They told me they were under orders not to interfere with labor disputes. So I called Bernie Sisk's office and talked to them about it. Then I came home and called a lot of students who'd been helping us, and other people, and the next morning there we were at the border patrol. I said, "We're paying our tax money, but not for you to sit here while the illegal aliens are being used to break our strike."

While we were in Parlier, I was put in charge of the hiring hall. My house was right next to the office, and I had an extension to the office phone in my house. I could do the housework and take care of the children, but I could take care of the office, too. Before the contract, the hiring hall was just a union office where people came to learn about the union. When they got the first contracts we began dispatching people out to work. The hiring hall was also a place where people could meet and talk. A lot of people were migrants who needed to get to know each other. The people who were there all the time were against the migrants. I said, "We have to get these people together. We can't be divided." I was at the hall all day. People would drop by and I'd introduce them.

The second year we had a contract I started working for Christian Brothers. The men were doing the pruning on the grape vines. After they did the pruning the women's crew would come and tie the vines. (That was something we got changed; we made them give pruning jobs to women.) I was made a steward on the women's crew.... the first time we were paid when I started working, during the break the supervisor would come out there with our checks. It was our fifteen minute break, which the contract gave us the right to. We had to walk to the other end of the row; it took us about five minutes to get there, the rest of the fifteen to get our checks, and walk back, and we'd start working. This happened twice. The third time I said, "We're not going to go after our check this time. They always come during our break and we don't get to rest." So when we saw the pickup coming with the men who had the checks I said, "Nobody move. You just sit here." I walked

over to the pickup. I said to the man inside, "Mr. Rager, these women refuse to come out here on their break time. It's their time to rest. So we're asking you, if you must come during our rest period, you take the checks to these ladies." From that day on, every payday he would come to us. That was the sort of thing you had to do to enforce the contract.

I became involved in many of the activities in the community—school board meetings, city council meetings, everything that I could get into. For example I went to fighting for bilingual education at Parlier, went to a lot of meetings about it and spoke about it. Parlier is over 85 percent Chicano, yet during that time there were no Chicanos on the school board, on the police force, nowhere. Now it's changed: we fought to get a Chicano mayor and officials. But then I was asking people, "Why are we always asked to go to the public school for our meetings? Why can't they come over to our side of town in Parlier?" So we began having meetings in *la colonia* at the Headstart Center, and there we pushed for bilingual education.

Fresno County didn't give food stamps to the people—only surplus food. There were no vegetables, no meat, just staples like whole powdered milk, cheese, butter. At the migrant camp in Parlier the people were there a month and a half before work started, and since they'd borrowed money to get to California they didn't have any food. I'd drive them into Fresno to the welfare department and translate for them and they'd get food, but half of it they didn't eat. We heard about other counties where they had food stamps to go to the store and buy meat and milk and fresh vegetables for the children. So we began talking about getting that in Fresno. Finally we had Senate hearings at the Convention Center in Fresno. There were hundreds of people listening. I started in Spanish, and the Senators were looking at each other, you know, saying, "What's going on?" So then I said, "Now, for the benefit of those who can't speak Spanish, I'll translate. If there is money enough to fight a war in Vietnam, and if there is money enough for Governor Reagan's wife to buy a $3000 dress for the Inauguration Ball, there should be money enough to feed these people. The nutrition experts say surplus food is full of vitamins. I've taken a look at that food, this corn meal, and I've seen them come up and down, but you know, we don't call them vitamins, we call them weevils!" Everybody began laughing and whistling and shouting. In the end, we finally got food stamps.

Ellen Willis, "I see men who consider themselves dedicated revolutionaries, yet exploit their wives and girl friends shamefully without ever noticing a contradiction. . . ."

In January 1968, Ellen Willis went to Washington to take part in a demonstration against the Vietnam war and for black liberation, which was staged to coincide with Richard Nixon's inaugural as president. At the demonstration, women in the group had asked to make a statement about their subordinate position within the New Left and on behalf of their own liberation. When they tried to make what they described as a "moderate, pro-movement statement," Willis reports, men in the audience "booed, laughed, catcalled and yelled enlightened remarks like 'Take her off the stage and fuck her.'" Instead of reprimanding the hecklers (as was done during an unpopular speech by a black GI), male organizers hurried the women off the stage.

On her return to New York, Willis wrote an article entitled "Women and the Left" (*Notes from the Second Year*, n.v. [1970]:55–56), in which she argued that the New Left was dominated by men and its theory, priorities, and strategy reflected male interests. Radical men would not take women seriously, she insisted, unless "we build an independent movement so strong that no revolution at all is possible without our cooperation."

The article elicited criticism in the form of letters-to-editor, one of which Willis answered. Although the editor chose not to publish her reply, it is a cogent statement of the thinking of young women who would come to be known as radical feminists.

Dear Wanda,

I was disturbed by your comments on my *Guardian* article, not because you disagreed but because you accused me of not thinking seriously. . . .

You say "the basic misperception is that our enemy is man, not capitalism." I say, the basic misperception is the facile identification of "the system" with "capitalism." In reality, the American system consists of two interdependent but distinct parts—the capitalist state, and the patriarchal family. Engels, in *Origin of the Family, Private Property and the State*, explains that the material basis of history is twofold: the means of production of commodities, and the means of production of new human beings. The social organization for the production of commodities is the property system, in this case the capitalist state. The social organization for the production of new human beings is the family system. And within the family system, men function as a ruling class, women as an exploited class. Historically, women and their children have been the property of men (until recently, quite literally, even in "advanced" countries). The mistake many radicals make is to assume that the family is simply part of the cultural superstructure of capitalism, while actually both capitalism and the family system make up the material substructure of society. It is difficult to see this because capitalism is so pervasive and powerful compared to the family, which is small, weak, and has far less influence on the larger economic system than vice versa. But it is important for women to recognize and deal with their exploited position in the family system, for it is primarily in terms of the family system that we are oppressed *as women*. Of course capitalism also exploits us, but the way in which it exploits us is primarily by taking advantage of, turning to its own purposes, our subordinate position in the family system and our historical domination by man, which stems from a time when the family system was all-powerful and the state did not yet exist. If you really *think* about our exploitation under capitalism—as cheap labor and as consumers—you will see that our position in the family system is at the root. This does not mean we shouldn't fight capitalism. Unless the power of the corporate state is broken, there can be no revolution in the family system. Furthermore, to attack male supremacy (i.e., man's class dominance in the family system) consistently inevitably means attacking capitalism in vulnerable areas. But if we simply work to destroy capitalism, without working to destroy male supremacy on all levels, we will find that the resulting revolution is only vicarious. . . .

So much for ideology. Now for some practical politics. Our position here is exactly analogous to the black power position, with male radicals playing the part of white liberals. White liberals (and radicals, too, before they got wise to themselves) made exactly the same argument you're making. "Racism affects us too, we should work together, divisions between us only help the common enemy." (Incidentally, I thought you were being a little disingenuous in saying there are no "women's

issues." A women's issue—or a black issue—means, in the accepted usage, a way in which women are oppressed because they are women, or blacks because they are black. This doesn't mean that men, and whites, are not affected by such issues.) Blacks answered, "We can't work together because you don't understand what it is to be black; because you've grown up in a racist society, your behavior toward us is bound to be racist whether you know it or not and whether you mean it or not; your ideas about how to help us are too often self-serving and patronizing; besides, part of our liberation is in thinking for ourselves and working for ourselves, not accepting the domination of the white man in still another area of our lives. If you as whites want to work on eliminating your own racism, if you want to support our battle for liberation, fine. If we decide that we have certain common interests with white activists and can form alliances with white organizations, fine. But we want to make the decisions in our own movement." Substitute man-woman for black-white and that's where I stand. With one important exception: while white liberals and radicals always understood the importance of the black liberation struggle, even if their efforts in the blacks' behalf were often misguided, radical men simply do not understand the importance of our struggle. . . . All around me I see men who consider themselves dedicated revolutionaries, yet exploit their wives and girl friends shamefully without ever noticing a contradiction. Anyone who was at that incredible rally in Washington knows it will be a long time before the majority of men, even those on the Left that should be closest to us, grasp that we have a grievance, and that we are serious. When they do grasp this, then we can talk about working together.

Sincerely,
Ellen Willis

Jennie V. Chavez, "It has taken . . . a long time . . . to realize and speak out about the double oppression of Mexican-American women."

Jennie Chavez, like thousands of young women of color, joined liberation movements in the 1960s and early 1970s. Whether they were part of the Black Power movement, the Chicano movement, the Native American movement, or the Asian American movement, these young militants found themselves in a position similar to that of Ellen Willis in the New Left. Women's views were dismissed. Efforts to raise the issue of their treatment in the movement were ridiculed. Even worse, their commitment to the cause was questioned.

In this account of her experience in the Chicano movement, Chavez describes the resistance she faced when, recognizing the double oppression of Mexican American women, she organized "Las Chicanas." Incipient feminists, these women of color recognized early on that gender was not the only factor subordinating women. What insights does she have into power relationships between Mexican Americans and Anglos as well as between men and women within her own ethnic group? Note her disdain for the consumer goods that signal middle-class status. What evidence is there to suggest that Chavez and her Chicana generation had also been affected by the sexual revolution of the 1960s?

As one of the first members of the United Mexican America Students [UMAS] when it got started in 1969 on the UNM [University of New Mexico] campus, I was given special attention, being fairly attractive and flirtatious. But as soon as I started expounding my own ideas the men who ran the organization would either ignore my statement or make a wisecrack about it and continue their own discussion. This continued for two years until I finally broke away because of being unable to handle the situation. I turned to student government. There I was considered a radical racist Mexican militant, yet with the Chicano radicals I was considered a sellout. I was caught in the middle, wanting to help but with neither side allowing me.

The summer of 1970, after the Cambodia crisis, I traveled extensively, "getting my head together," [and formed] Las Chicanas the following December. [The result was that I] caught more shit than I knew existed from both males and females in the movement. Some felt

I was dividing the existing UMAS; some were simply afraid of displeasing the men. Some felt that I was wrong and my ideas were "white," and still others felt that their contribution to LaCausa or El Movimiento was in giving the men moral support from the kitchen. It took two months of heartbreak on both sides for the organization to be recognized as valid. Now, however, because a few women were willing to stand strong against some of the macho men who ridiculed them, called them white and avoided them socially, the organization has become one of the strongest and best-known in the state.

It has taken what I consider a long time for [Chicanas] to realize and to speak out about the double oppression of the Mexican-American woman. Chicanas traditionally, have been tortilla-makers, baby-producers, to be touched but not heard. In order to someday obtain those middle-class goods (which in my eyes oppress more people than they liberate from "drudgery") our women have not only been

Excerpted from "Women of the Mexican American Movement" by Jennie V. Chavez in *Chicana Feminist Thought: The Basic Historical Writings,* edited by Alma M. Garcia (New York: Routledge, 1998), pp. 36–39. Courtesy *Mademoiselle.* The order of some sentences and paragraphs has been altered in the editing of the original version to maximize clarity.

working at slave jobs for the white society as housemaids, hotel maids and laundry workers, but have tended also to the wants of a husband and many children—many children because contraceptives have been contrary to the ethnic idea of La Familia (with all its sociopolitical economic implications).

As the social revolution for all people's freedoms has progressed, so Chicanas have caught the essence of freedom in the air. The change occurred slowly. Mexican-American women have been reluctant to speak up, afraid that they might show up the men in front of the white man—afraid that they may think our men not men. Now, however, the Chicana is becoming as well-educated and as aware of oppression, if not more so, as the Mexican-American male.

The women are changing their puritanical mode of dress, entering the professions of law, business, medicine and engineering. They are no longer afraid to show their intellect, their capabilities and their potential. More and more they oppose the Catholic Church, to which a large majority of our ethnic group belongs, challenging its sexual taboos as well as the idea that all Catholic mothers must be baby-producing factories, and that contraceptives are a sin.

Out of the workshop on "Sex and La Chicana" at the first National Mujeres Por la Raza conference in Houston, Texas came the following resolutions:

(1) that Chicanas should develop a more healthy attitude toward sex and get rid of the misconceptions about its "evil," thus allowing ourselves to be as aggressive as men: (2) that we object to the use of sex as a means of exploiting women and for commercial purposes: (3) that no religious institution should have the authority to sanction what is moral or immoral between a man and a woman.

As the new breed of Mexican-American women, we have been, and probably will continue to be, ridiculed by our men for attempting the acrobatics of equality. We may well be ostracized by La Familia for being vendidos, sell-outs to the "white ideas" of late marriage, postponing or not wanting children and desiring a vocation other than tortilla-rolling, but I believe that this new breed of bronze womanhood, as all women today, will be a vanguard for world change.

Naturally, there are liberated Chicanos who respect and treat women as equals, but they are so few that at this point I still have to generalize. Mexican-American men, as other men of oppressed groups, have been very reluctant to give up their machaismo [exaggerated assertion of masculinity] because it has been a last retention of power in a society which dehumanizes and mechanizes them. But now they are comprehending the meaning of carnalismo (brotherhood) in the feminine gender as well . . . a new revolution within a revolution has begun.

Equal Rights Amendment, 1972

An equal rights amendment, with wording slightly different from that passed by Congress in 1972, was sponsored in 1923 by the National Woman's Party. It seemed to party members the logical corollary to suffrage. But that amendment was vigorously opposed by the League of Women Voters and other progressive reformers, lest it undermine the protective legislation for which they had fought so hard.

An equal rights amendment was introduced regularly in Congress virtually every year thereafter, but it received little attention until after World War II. In 1950 and 1953 it was passed by the Senate but ignored by the House.

By 1970 much protective legislation had been applied to both men and women. It was possible to support an equal rights amendment without risking the undoing of labor law reforms. The hope that the Supreme Court would apply the Fourteenth Amendment's "equal protection of the laws" clause to cases involving discrimination on the basis of sex as firmly as it applied the clause to cases involving racial discrimination had not been fulfilled. When the current Equal Rights Amendment was introduced in 1970, it was endorsed by a wide range of organizations, some of which had once opposed it; these organizations included groups as disparate as the United Automobile Workers and the Woman's Christian Temperance Union. Its main sponsor in the House was Martha Griffiths of Michigan; in the Senate, Birch Bayh of Indiana.

The ERA was passed by Congress on March 22, 1972, and sent to the states for ratification. There was much initial enthusiasm; within two days six states had ratified. But the pace of ratification slowed after 1975, and only thirty-five of the needed thirty-eight states had ratified it by 1978. (Four state legislatures voted to rescind ratification, although the legality of that move was open to question.) In October 1978 Congress extended the deadline for ratification to June 30, 1982; the extension expired with no additional ratifications. The amendment was reintroduced in Congress in 1983 but has not been passed.

Section 1. Equality of rights under the law shall not be denied or abridged by the United States or by any State on account of sex.

Section 2. The Congress shall have the power to enforce, by appropriate legislation, the provisions of this article.

Section 3. The amendment shall take effect two years after the date of ratification.

Title IX, Education Amendments of 1972

In 1972, women received 9 percent of the M.D. degrees awarded by universities in the United States, 7 percent of the law degrees, and 15 percent of the doctoral degrees. Women were 2 percent of college varsity athletes. It was common practice to encourage women students into specialties marked as appropriate for women: teaching rather than scientific research, for example, or nursing rather than medicine. In athletics, it was usual practice for the travel budgets of male athletic teams to be paid for from student fees (paid by both women and men), while women's teams received 0.5 percent of the school's athletic budgets and there were no athletic scholarships for women. Women's teams often had to raise their own travel funds, sometimes from bake sales and raffles. Title IX of the Education Amendments of 1972 was brief but far-reaching.

No person in the United States shall, on the basis of sex, be excluded from participation in, be denied the benefits of, or be subjected to discrimination under any education program or activity receiving Federal financial assistance . . .

Each Federal department and agency which is empowered to extend Federal finan-

Title IX of Public Law 92–318 (1972) and subsequent amendments. See also *Hearing on Title IX of the Education Amendments of 1972 Before the Subcommittee on Post Secondary Education . . . of the Committee on Economic and Educational Opportunities*, 104th Congress, House of Representatives, 1st Session, May 9, 1995, Serial No. 104–31.

cial assistance to any education program or
activity, by way of grant, loan, or contract . . . is authorized and directed to effectuate the provisions of . . . this title with respect

to such program or activity by issuing rules,
regulations, or orders of general applicability
which shall be consistent with achievement of
the objectives of the statute . . .

Title IX was enforced by the Office of Civil Rights and by the Department of Education. Enforcement was gradual; two years after the passage of Title IX it was estimated
that colleges offered athletic scholarships to 50,000 men and fewer than 50 women. Not
until 1975 were there full federal regulations applying to secondary schools and colleges
and universities; other regulations were subsequently developed. Although Title IX
applies to all elements of university programs, its impact on athletic programs had high
visibility, and has been followed attentively by the public and the press. Equality in athletics has been taken by much of the public as the marker of equality in higher education in general. Participation in athletics has been linked to benefits to health and to self-
confidence and self-esteem.

Title IX regulations require that the total amount of athletic financial assistance
awarded to men and women be proportionate to their respective participation rates in
intercollegiate athletic programs. They require that male and female athletes receive
equivalent benefits, treatment, services, and opportunities; *identical* benefits and opportunities are not required. It does not require that all teams be coeducational, or that the
same number of teams be provided for men and women, or that men's teams be cut in
order for the institution to come into compliance with the law.

In the years since the passage of Title IX, the number of women participating in
NCAA intercollegiate athletics has more than tripled (from 31,850 in 1971, to 105,530 in
1994), while the number of men participants has continued to grow (from 172,450 in
1971 to 190,650 in 1994). But argument continues about what constitutes equitable treatment: Is it fair for men to hold the great majority of athletic scholarships (an imbalance
largely credited to the size of men's football and basketball teams)? Is it fair for a university to support a women's varsity rowing team but not a men's varsity rowing team?
What is the proper relationship between women's sports and men's sports? Between
women's sports and men's "minor" sports? Perhaps most significantly, what is the wise
relationship between expenditures on athletics and expenditures on academic programs?

Title IX also provides that "no person shall, on the basis of sex . . . be subjected
to discrimination under any education program." In 1999 the Supreme Court responded
to the appeal of the fifth-grade girl who had been subjected to explicit sexual teasing by
a classmate. He attempted to touch her breasts and genital area, he told her "I want to
get into bed with you," and he rubbed his body against her in the hallway. Her grades
plummeted as she lost the ability to concentrate on her studies. Although she and her
mother complained repeatedly to teachers and the principal, no action was taken. The
Court ruled that school districts may be liable for damages when administrators are
indifferent to repeated and known acts of student-to-student sexual harassment, during school hours and on school grounds. (*Davis* v. *Monroe County Board of Education*, 119
S. Ct. 1661). The case raised the question of responsibility of schools to provide a harass-
ment-free environment (cf. *Meritor Savings Bank* v. *Vinson*, pp. 543–44). Critics charged
that remedies should have been sought, if at all, against the offending student, not
against the school administration. Do you agree?

Frontiero *v.* Richardson, *1973*

Sharron A. Frontiero was an Air Force officer who was dismayed to discover that she could not claim dependent's benefits for her husband on the same terms that her male colleagues could for their wives. She and her husband brought suit, claiming that statutes requiring spouses of female members of the uniformed services to receive more than half of their support from their wives to be considered dependents, while all spouses of male members were treated as dependents, violated the due process clause of the Fifth Amendment and the equal protection clause of the Fourteenth Amendment.

Until 1971, the Supreme Court had never ruled that discrimination on the basis of sex was a violation of the equal protection clause of the Fourteenth Amendment. So long as a legislature had a "reasonable" basis for making distinctions between men and women, discriminatory laws were upheld. Between 1971 and 1975, in a stunning series of decisions, the Supreme Court placed the burden of proof that discrimination on the basis of sex was reasonable on those who tried to discriminate. Ruth Bader Ginsburg was a 38-year-old law professor working with the American Civil Liberties Union in 1971 when the Court accepted her argument that an Idaho law requiring that fathers, rather than mothers, always be preferred as executors of their children's estates was unconstitutional. (*Reed* v. *Reed* 404 U.S. 71 [1971].)

The ACLU set up a Women's Rights Project in 1973 with Ginsburg at its head to follow up on the implications of the *Reed* decision. Ginsburg wrote the brief and managed the argument in *Frontiero;* it was one of a brilliant series of cases that she argued in the early 1970s. With her colleagues, she helped persuade the Court that a wide range of discriminatory practices were illegal. Her career as a litigator would lead to her appointment as a judge on the U.S. Court of Appeals in 1980 and, in 1993, to her appointment to the U.S. Supreme Court.

The Supreme Court ruled in favor of the Frontieros in a complex decision that used statistical information about woman's place in the work force in a manner reminiscent of the Brandeis Brief. Speaking for three of his colleagues Justice William J. Brennan, Jr., prepared a historically based argument, explaining the distance American public opinion had traveled since the *Bradwell* case (see *Bradwell* v. *Illinois*, pp. 242–43). He drew analogies between discrimination on the basis of race, which the court subjected to strict scrutiny, and discrimination on the basis of sex.

In concurring with Brennan's opinion, three justices observed that although they agreed with the Frontieros in this particular case, they were not yet persuaded that sex ought to be regularly treated as a "suspect category." Only when—or if—the Equal Rights Amendment were passed could the Court be sure that the public agreed that discrimination on the basis of sex ought to be evaluated as critically as discrimination on the basis of race. Note that the facts in *Frontiero* relate to discrimination against the husband of the wage earner, not directly against a woman. It is the family of the wage earner that is discriminated against. A similar case, also argued by Ginsburg, is *Weinberger* v. *Weisenfeld* (420 U.S. 636 [1975]), in which the husband of a dead woman suc-

---

411 U.S. 677. See also *Craig* v. *Boren* 429 U.S. 190 (1976).

cessfully demanded survivor's benefits equal to those available to widows. Ginsburg and her colleagues stressed that both men and women benefited from gender-blind equal treatment under the law.

MR. JUSTICE WILLIAM J. BRENNAN, JR. DELIVERED THE OPINION OF THE COURT:

The question before us concerns the right of a female member of the uniformed services to claim her spouse as a "dependent." . . .

At the outset, appellants contend that classifications based upon sex, like classifications based upon race, alienage, and national origin, are inherently suspect and must therefore be subjected to close judicial scrutiny. We agree. . . .

There can be no doubt that our Nation has had a long and unfortunate history of sex discrimination. Traditionally, such discrimination was rationalized by an attitude of "romantic paternalism" which, in practical effect, put women, not on a pedestal, but in a cage. Indeed, this paternalistic attitude became so firmly rooted in our national consciousness that, 100 years ago, a distinguished Member of this Court was able to proclaim. . . . "The natural and proper timidity and delicacy which belongs to the female sex evidently unfits it for many of the occupations of civil life." . . .

It is true, of course, that the position of women in America has improved markedly in recent decades. Nevertheless, it can hardly be doubted that, in part because of the high visibility of the sex characteristic, women still face pervasive, although at times more subtle, discrimination in our educational institutions, in the job market, and perhaps most conspicuously, in the political arena. . . .

Moreover, since sex, like race and national origin, is an immutable characteristic determined solely by the accident of birth, the imposition of special disabilities upon the member of a particular sex because of their sex would seem to violate "the basic concept of our system that legal burdens should bear some relationship to individual responsibility. . . . " And what differentiates sex from such non-suspect statuses as intelligence or physical disability, and aligns it with the recognized suspect criteria, is that the sex characteristic frequently bears no relation to ability to perform or contribute to society. . . .

. . . over the past decade, Congress has itself manifested an increasing sensitivity to sex-based classification. In Tit[le] VII of the Civil Rights Act of 1964, for example, Congress expressly declared that no employer, labor union, or other organization subject to the provisions of the Act shall discriminate against any individual on the basis of "race, color, religion, sex, or national origin." Similarly, the Equal Pay Act of 1963 provides that no employer covered by the Act "shall discriminate . . . between employees on the basis of sex." . . .

With these considerations in mind, we can only conclude that classifications based upon sex, like classifications based upon race, alienage, or national origin, are inherently suspect, and must therefore be subjected to strict judicial scrutiny. Applying the analysis mandated by that stricter standard of review, it is clear that the statutory scheme now before us is constitutionally invalid. . . .

MR. JUSTICE LEWIS F. POWELL, JR., WITH WHOM THE CHIEF JUSTICE AND MR. JUSTICE HARRY A. BLACKMUN JOIN, CONCURRING IN THE OPINION:

I agree that the challenged statutes constitute an unconstitutional discrimination against servicewomen . . . but I cannot join the opinion of Mr. Justice Brennan, which would hold that all classifications based upon sex . . . are "inherently suspect and must therefore be subjected to close judicial scrutiny." . . . The Equal Rights Amendment, which if adopted will resolve the substance of this precise question, has been approved by the Congress and submitted for ratification by the States. If this Amendment is duly adopted, it will represent the will of the people accomplished in the manner prescribed by the constitution. . . . It seems to me that this reaching out to pre-empt by judicial action a major political decision which is currently in process of resolution does not reflect appropriate respect for duly prescribed legislative processes.

Roe *v*. Wade, *1973*; Planned Parenthood
of Southeastern Pennsylvania *v*. Casey, *1992*

The Comstock Law had been echoed by a series of anticontraception and antiabortion laws throughout the country. James Mohr observes, "Every state in the Union had [by 1900] an antiabortion law of some kind on its books . . . except Kentucky, where the state courts outlawed the practice anyway."* In 1962 the ethics of abortion became a pressing problem when it was revealed that thalidomide, a drug extensively used in Europe and occasionally in the United States, resulted in the birth of thousands of babies with phocomelia (deformed or missing arms and legs). Sherry Finkbine, an Arizona woman who had taken the drug, demanded a legal abortion. Although her doctors supported her, the county medical society refused to approve the procedure, and, lacking confidence that she and her doctors would be spared immunity from prosecution, she fled to Sweden, where abortion was legal.

Her plight, and her challenge to hospital practice, helped to shift public opinion, both within the medical profession, which would subsequently be instrumental in advocating liberalization of abortion legislation, and among women's groups, who began to articulate dismay that women were generally denied access to safe abortion services. Estimates of the number of illegal abortions performed each year before 1973 range from 200,000 to 1,200,000; it is estimated that 200 women died each year as a result. Abortion was virtually the only medical procedure to which middle-class women did not have access. The issue was less intense for black women's groups; working-class minority women lacked a wide range of medical services, and abortion was only one among many which they needed. Thus at the beginning of the reinvigorated women's movement of the late 1960s, black and white women were divided about the place that access to legal abortion should hold in their list of priorities for legal change.

In 1970, Alaska, Hawaii, New York, and Washington legalized abortion. Texas law, like the law of most states, continued to prohibit abortion except for the purpose of saving the mother's life. In 1970, Norma McCorvey, a single pregnant woman, known as Jane Roe to protect her privacy, brought a class action suit challenging the constitutionality of that law as a violation of her right to liberty as guaranteed by the due process clause of the Fourteenth Amendment.

The Supreme Court's decision in *Roe* v. *Wade* marked a sharp change from long-established practice. As the opening lines of the majority decision make clear, the justices were aware they were making a sensitive and important decision.

MR. JUSTICE HARRY A. BLACKMUN DELIVERED THE OPINION OF THE COURT:

We forthwith acknowledge our awareness of the sensitive and emotional nature of the abortion controversy, of the vigorous opposing views, even among physicians, and of the deep

---

*James C. Mohr, *Abortion in America: The Origins and Evolution of National Policy, 1800–1900* (New York: Oxford University Press, 1978), pp. 229–30.

410 U.S. 113; 112 S. Ct. 2791.

and seemingly absolute convictions that the subject inspires. One's philosophy, one's experiences, one's exposure to the raw edges of human existence, one's religious training, one's attitudes toward life and family and their values, and the moral standards one establishes and seeks to observe, are all likely to influence and to color one's thinking and conclusions about abortion.

In addition, population growth, pollution, poverty, and racial overtones tend to complicate and not to simplify the problem.

Our task, of course, is to resolve the issue by constitutional measurement, free of emotion and of predilection. We seek earnestly to do this. . . .

The principal thrust of the appellant's attack on the Texas statutes is that they improperly invade a right, said to be possessed by the pregnant woman, to choose to terminate her pregnancy. Appellant would discover this right in the concept of personal "liberty" embodied in the Fourteenth Amendment's Due Process Clause; or in personal, marital, familial and sexual privacy said to be protected by the Bill of Rights . . . or among those rights reserved to the people by the Ninth Amendment. . . .

It perhaps is not generally appreciated that the restrictive criminal abortion laws in effect in a majority of States today are of relatively recent vintage. Those laws, generally proscribing abortion or its attempt at any time during pregnancy except when necessary to preserve the pregnant woman's life, are not of ancient or even of common-law origin. Instead, they derive from statutory changes effected, for the most part, in the latter half of the nineteenth century. . . . At common law, at the time of the adoption of our Constitution, and throughout the major portion of the nineteenth century . . . a woman enjoyed a substantially broader right to terminate a pregnancy than she does in most states today. . . .

When most criminal abortion laws were first enacted, the procedure was a hazardous one for the woman. This was particularly true prior to the development of antisepsis. . . . Abortion mortality was high. . . . Modern medical techniques have altered this situation. Appellants . . . refer to medical data indicating that abortion in early pregnancy, that is, prior to the end of the first trimester, although not without its risk, is now relatively safe. Mortality rates for women undergoing early abortions, where the procedure is legal, appear to be as low as or lower than the rates for normal childbirth. Consequently, any interest of the State in protecting the woman from an inherently hazardous procedure . . . has largely disappeared. . . . The State has a legitimate interest in seeing to it that abortion, like any other medical procedure, is performed under circumstances that insure maximum safety for the patient. . . .

The Constitution does not explicitly mention any right of privacy. In a line of decisions, however . . . the Court has recognized that a right of personal privacy, or a guarantee of certain areas or zones of privacy, does exist under the Constitution. . . . This right . . . whether it be founded in the Fourteenth Amendment's concept of personal liberty . . . or . . . in the Ninth Amendment's reservation of rights to the people, is broad enough to encompass a woman's decision whether or not to terminate her pregnancy. . . . We . . . conclude that the right of personal privacy includes the abortion decision, but that this right is not unqualified and must be considered against important state interests in regulation. . . .

. . . the State does have a important and legitimate interest in preserving and protecting the health of the pregnant woman . . . and . . . it has still *another* important and legitimate interest in protecting the potentiality of human life. These interests are separate and distinct. Each grows in substantiality as the woman approaches term, and, at a point during pregnancy, each becomes "compelling."

With respect to the State's important and legitimate interest in the health of the mother, the "compelling" point, in the light of present medical knowledge, is at approximately the end of the first trimester. This is so because of the now-established medical fact . . . that until the end of the first trimester mortality in abortion may be less than mortality in normal childbirth. It follows that . . . for the period of pregnancy prior to this "compelling" point, the attending physician, in consultation with his patient, is free to determine, without regulation by the State, that in his medical judgment, the patient's pregnancy should be terminated.

. . . For the state subsequent to approximately the end of the first trimester, the State, in promoting its interest in the health of the mother, may, if it chooses, regulate the abortion procedure in ways that are reasonably related to maternal health.

For the state subsequent to viability, the State in promoting its interest in the potentiality of human life may, if it chooses, regulate, and even proscribe, abortion except where it is necessary, in appropriate medical judgment, for the preservation of the life or health of the mother.

Our conclusion . . . is . . . that the Texas abortion statutes, as a unit, must fall. . . .

In the years before 1973, when abortion was generally illegal, commonly performed in the private offices of doctors and unlicensed practitioners without emergency medical support, and generally without anesthesia, death from abortion was substantial. In 1985, it was estimated that only two deaths occurred from illegal abortion and only six deaths resulted from legal abortion.

The issues that were raised by *Roe* v. *Wade* have not been fully settled and are not likely to be easily resolved, touching as they do on basic religious and ethical beliefs. Because only women become pregnant, and because there is no obvious parallel to pregnancy in male experience, arguments about abortion are less easily made on the equal treatment grounds that served women's rights activists well in *Frontiero* (see *Frontiero* v. *Richardson*, pp. 545–46). and other similar cases. Advocates must ask what equal treatment would mean for men and women, who are differently situated in relation to abortion.

In the 1980s, a number of states tested what boundaries would be considered reasonable limits on the abortion rights sustained in Roe. In 1980, the Supreme Court upheld the "Hyde Amendment" by which Congress refused to fund even medically necessary abortions for indigent women (*Harris* v. *McRae*, 448 U.S. 297). This decision was not the focus of massive public protest, and it was replicated in the laws of many states. An effort to defeat the Hyde Amendment failed in Congress in 1993, but some states did revise their practice, covering some abortions for indigent women, usually in the case of rape or incest.

Missouri legislators developed further the position that the state could deny any form of public support or facilities for the performance of abortions. A 1986 law prohibited the use of public employees and facilities to perform or assist abortions not necessary to save the life of the mother and also prohibited the use of public funds for counseling a woman in abortion decisions not necessary to save her life. It included a preamble that claimed that the life of each human being begins at conception and a provision that required that medical tests of fetal viability—tests whose efficacy was disputed—be performed before any abortion on a fetus estimated to be twenty weeks or more in gestation. Since 97 percent of all late abortions (done at an estimated sixteen-week gestational age) were performed at a single hospital in Kansas City that, although private, received public aid and was located on public property, the practical impact of the law was great.

In deciding *Webster* v. *Reproductive Health Services* in July 1989, by a 5–3 vote, the Supreme Court majority claimed that the conclusions of *Roe* had not been changed.* Missouri law left a pregnant woman free to terminate her pregnancy so long as neither public funds nor facilities were used for it; this was, the Court majority said, a "value judgment" favoring childbirth over abortion. But the majority raised a general question

---

*William L. Webster, Attorney General of Missouri v. Reproductive Health Services, 109 Sup. Ct. 3040 (1989).

about *Roe.* "[T]he rigid Roe framework," wrote Chief Justice Rehnquist in the majority opinion, "is hardly consistent with the notion of a Constitution cast in general terms, as ours is, and usually speaking in general principles, as ours does. The key elements of the *Roe* framework—trimesters and viability—are not found in the text of the Constitution or in any place else one would expect to find a constitutional principle . . . the result has been a web of legal rules that . . . [resemble] a code of regulations rather than a body of constitutional doctrine." Justice Anthony Scalia concurred, adding that in his view, *Roe* should have been overturned; abortion is, he thought, a field in which the Court "has little proper business since the answers to most of the cruel questions posed are political and not juridical." He was appalled at efforts to bring the pressure of public opinion to bear on the decisions of the Court, notably the March on Washington of some 200,000 people that had been sponsored by pro-choice groups shortly before the *Webster* case was argued in April 1989.

Justice Harry A. Blackmun, who had written the Court's opinion in *Roe,* now wrote a bitter dissent for the minority. He denied that Rehnquist's opinion left *Roe* "undisturbed." Rather it challenged a large body of legal precedent that had established a "private sphere of individual liberty," which although not explicitly specified in the Constitution had long been taken to have been implied by the Fourth Amendment guarantee against unreasonable searches. The right to privacy had been invoked in the 1960s when the Court protected the sale and use of birth control devices; the *Webster* decision, Blackmun feared, bypassed "the true jurisprudential debate underlying this case: . . . whether and to what extent . . . a right to privacy extends to matters of childbearing and family life, including abortion." Justice John Paul Stevens argued that the preamble's claim that life begins at conception was a religious view, and to write it into law was to ignore First Amendment requirements for the separation of church and state. Finally, Blackmun argued that the state had a distinct interest in maintaining public health, and that as safe and legal abortions became more difficult to get, an increase in deaths from illegal abortions could be predicted. "For today," he concluded, "the women of this Nation still retain the liberty to control their destinies. But the signs are evident and very ominous, and a chill wind blows."

The Court's decision in *Webster* left many questions open. If states could deny public funds for abortions, what other limitations was it reasonable for state legislatures to impose? Was it reasonable to require a waiting period? Was it reasonable to require minors to get the consent of one parent? of both parents? The Court had ruled in 1976 that a state could not require a married woman to get her husband's consent before having an abortion (*Planned Parenthood* v. *Danforth,* 428 U.S. 52 [1976]); could a state require a married woman to *notify* her husband?

In 1988 and 1989 Pennsylvania amended its Abortion Control Act of 1982 extensively, requiring a twenty-four-hour waiting period and the provision of "certain information" twenty-four hours before the abortion is performed. Minors were required to have the consent of one parent, and married women to have notified their husbands, although it was possible for a court to waive that requirement and all requirements could be waived in the event of a "medical emergency." Because most of the Justices had made public substantial reservations about the decision in *Roe,* it seemed to many observers not unreasonable to predict that the Court would uphold the entire Pennsylvania statute and, possibly, overturn *Roe* v. *Wade*. Instead, a majority organized by Justices Sandra Day O'Connor, Anthony Kennedy, and David Souter, joined by Harry Blackmun and John Paul Stevens, wrote a complex opinion, which began with a ringing affirmation of *Roe*. But O'Connor, Kennedy, and Souter also made it clear that they shared Rehnquist's skepticism of the trimester framework of *Roe*. How does the majority think the principle of equal protection of the laws should be applied in abortion decisions?

Note the comments on coverture at the end of the majority opinion; this statement marks the first explicit recognition by the Court of the end of coverture.

Why do the dissenting Justices think *Roe* should be overturned?

PLANNED PARENTHOOD OF SOUTHEASTERN PENNSYLVANIA V. CASEY

JUSTICES O'CONNOR, KENNEDY, SOUTER:

Liberty finds no refuge in a jurisprudence of doubt. Yet 19 years after our holding that the Constitution protects a woman's right to terminate her pregnancy in its early states . . . that definition of liberty is still questioned. . . . After considering the fundamental constitutional questions resolved by *Roe*, principles of institutional integrity, and the rule of *stare decisis* [the principle that decisions of previous courts should be let stand unless there is overwhelming reason to change them], we are led to conclude this: the essential holding of *Roe* v. *Wade* should be retained and once again reaffirmed. . . . Constitutional protection of the woman's decision to terminate her pregnancy derives from the Due Process Clause of the Fourteenth Amendment. It declares that no State shall "deprive any person of life, liberty, or property, without due process of law." . . . It is a premise of the Constitution that there is a realm of personal liberty which the government may not enter. We have vindicated this principle before. Marriage is mentioned nowhere in the Bill of Rights and interracial marriage was illegal in most States in the 19th century, but the Court was no doubt correct in finding it to be an aspect of liberty protected against state interference by the substantive component of the Due Process Clause in *Loving* v. *Virginia* 388 U.S. 1 (1967). . . .

Men and women of good conscience can disagree, and we suppose some always shall disagree, about the profound moral and spiritual implications of terminating a pregnancy, even in its earliest stage. Some of us as individuals find abortion offensive to our most basic principles of morality, but that cannot control our decision. Our obligation is to define the liberty of all, not to mandate our own moral code. . . .

Our law affords constitutional protection to personal decisions relating to marriage, procreation, contraception, family relationships, child rearing, and education. . . . These matters, involving the most intimate and personal choices a person may make in a lifetime, choices central to personal dignity and autonomy, are central to the liberty protected by the Fourteenth Amendment. At the heart of liberty is the right to define one's own concept of existence, of meaning, of the universe, and of the mystery of human life. Beliefs about these matters could not define the attributes of personhood were they formed under compulsion of the State. The woman's right to terminate her pregnancy before viability is the most central principle of *Roe* v. *Wade*. It is a rule of law and a component of liberty we cannot renounce.

On the other side of the equation is the interest of the State in the protection of potential life. The *Roe* Court recognized the State's "important and legitimate interest in protecting the potentiality of human life." . . . That portion of the decision in *Roe* has been given too little acknowledgment and implementation by the Court in its subsequent cases. . . . Though

112 S. Ct. 2791 (1992).

the woman has a right to choose to terminate or continue her pregnancy before viability, it does not at all follow that the State is prohibited from taking steps to ensure that this choice is thoughtful and informed. Even in the earliest stages of pregnancy, the State may enact rules and regulations designed to encourage her to know that there are philosophic and social arguments of great weight that can be brought to bear in favor of continuing the pregnancy to full term. . . . We reject the trimester framework, which we do not consider to be part of the essential holding of *Roe*. . . . Measures aimed at ensuring that a woman's choice contemplates the consequences for the fetus do not necessarily interfere with the right recognized in *Roe* . . . not every law which makes a right more difficult to exercise is, ipso facto, an infringement of that right. . . .

. . . We . . . see no reason why the State may not require doctors to inform a woman seeking an abortion of the availability of materials relating to the consequences to the fetus. . . . Whether the mandatory 24-hour waiting period is . . . invalid because in practice it is a substantial obstacle to a woman's choice to terminate her pregnancy is a closer question. [We do not agree with the District Court] that the waiting period constitutes an undue burden. . . . [From Part D: We have already established the precedent, and] we reaffirm today, that a State may require a minor seeking an abortion to obtain the consent of a parent or guardian, provided that there is an adequate judicial bypass procedure. . . .

. . . Pennsylvania's abortion law provides, except in cases of medical emergency, that no physician shall perform an abortion on a married woman without receiving a signed statement from the woman that she has notified her spouse that she is about to undergo an abortion. The woman has the option of providing an alternative signed statement certifying that her husband is not the man who impregnated her; that her husband could not be located; that the pregnancy is the result of spousal sexual assault which she had reported [or that she fears bodily harm from him.] A physician who performs an abortion on a married woman without receiving the appropriate signed statement will have his or her license revoked, and is liable to the husband for damages.

. . . In well-functioning marriages, spouses discuss important intimate decisions such as whether to bear a child. But there are millions of women in this country who are the victims of regular physical and psychological abuse at the hands of their husbands. . . . Many may have a reasonable fear that notifying their husbands will provoke further instances of child abuse [or psychological abuse]. . . .

. . . [A]s a general matter . . . the father's interest in the welfare of the child and the mother's interest are equal. Before birth, however, the issue takes on a very different cast. It is an inescapable biological fact that state regulation with respect to the child a woman is carrying will have a far greater impact on the mother's liberty than on the father's. [That is why the Court has already ruled that when the wife and husband disagree on the abortion decision, the decision of the wife should prevail.]

. . . There was a time, not so long ago, when a different understanding of the family and of the Constitution prevailed. In *Bradwell* v. *Illinois* [see pp. 242–43], three Members of this Court reaffirmed the common-law principle that "a woman had no legal existence separate from her husband." . . . Only one generation has passed since this Court observed that "woman is still regarded as the center of home and family life," with attendant "special responsibilities" that precluded full and independent legal status under the Constitution (*Hoyt* v. *Florida* [pp. 517–21]). These views, of course, are no longer consistent with our understanding of the family, the individual, or the Constitution. . . . [The Pennsylvania abortion law] embodies a view of marriage consonant with the common-law status of married women but repugnant to our present understanding of marriage and of the nature of the rights secured by the Constitution. Women do not lose their constitutionally protected liberty when they marry.

CHIEF JUSTICE REHNQUIST, WITH WHOM JUSTICE WHITE, JUSTICE SCALIA, AND JUSTICE
CLARENCE THOMAS JOIN:

The joint opinion . . . retains the outer shell of *Roe* v. *Wade* . . . but beats a wholesale retreat from the substance of that case. We believe that *Roe* was wrongly decided, and that it can and should be overruled consistently with our traditional approach to *stare decisis* in constitutional cases. We would . . . uphold the challenged provisions of the Pennsylvania statute in their entirety. . . . [B]y foreclosing all democratic outlet for the deep passions this issue arouses, by banishing the issue from the political forum that gives all participants, even the losers, the satisfaction of a fair hearing and an honest fight, by continuing the imposition of a rigid national rule instead of allowing for regional differences, the Court merely prolongs and intensifies the anguish.

We should get out of this area, where we have no right to be, and where we do neither ourselves nor the country any good by remaining.

Abortion is an issue of concern to men as well as to women. It is an issue on which women and men hold a wide variety of views. Among the questions raised are:

1. What are the limits of a woman's right to make her own reproductive decisions?
2. Should the unborn be afforded legal rights?
3. What rights does the father have? In 1976 the Supreme Court held that a state could not require a married woman to get her husband's consent before having an abortion (*Planned Parenthood* v. *Danforth*, 428 U.S. 52 [1976]). Is the husband's claim of a role in an abortion decision a reinstatement of the old law of coverture?
4. What rights does the community have to set general policy? What are the appropriate limits of government intervention? The state may not require a woman to conceive a child; can the state require a woman to bear a child?
5. Will any of these rights change as improvements are made in the technology for the discovery of birth defects and genetic abnormalities, for the implantation of embryos, and for caring for premature infants at earlier ages?

FAYE D. GINSBURG

Women Divided:
Abortion and What It Means to Be Female

Abortion, as we have seen, was commonly used in the first half of the nineteenth century by women, married as well as unmarried, middle and upper class as well as working class, when other methods of fertility control were unreliable or unavailable. When

Excerpted from chapters 9–10 of *Contested Lives: The Abortion Debate in an American Community* by Faye D. Ginsburg (Berkeley: University of California Press, 1989). Copyright © University of California Press, 1991. Reprinted by permission of the author and publisher.

in the post–Civil War decades states began to impose restrictions on abortion, they did so primarily at the urging of the newly established American Medical Association. Concerned about the health risks posed for pregnant women, "regular" physicians were also eager to put out of business "irregular" caregivers (abortionists and midwives), thereby securing for themselves a monopoly on medical practice. One hundred years later, the medical profession once again sought changes in abortion policy, this time urging liberalization of state laws in the wake of technological advances that made possible early detection of fetal abnormalities and medically safe abortion procedures. Although nonmedical factors played a role in these policy decisions, especially in the earlier effort to criminalize abortion, physicians, not women, were the chief participants in the abortion debate until the 1960s.

That situation changed dramatically with *Roe* v. *Wade,* the 1973 Supreme Court decision liberalizing abortion restrictions (see pp. 547–49). Women mobilized in large numbers both in opposition to and support of the Court's decision as the abortion debate "went public." The growing intensity of that debate suggests that much is at stake for both sides.

Faye Ginsburg has examined both pro-choice and pro-life activists in Fargo, North Dakota, using extensive oral interviews in order to understand the abortion struggle from the viewpoint of the women most actively engaged in it. While her North Dakota sample may not be representative of activists nationwide, her findings are illuminating. Listening carefully to activists, trying to make sense out of their lives, she discovered that for women on both sides, positions on abortion are closely associated with their sense of identity, life choices, and life experience. Both groups believe they are working for the best interests of women.

From her discerning analysis of these women's narratives, what can you conclude about the two sides? Are there significant socioeconomic or religious differences? Do they have different understandings of gender, sexuality, and reproduction? Do they differ in their views of women's economic dependency? How do they view feminism? How well does each side understand the other? What really is at issue in the abortion debate?

The women activists who organized the pro-choice efforts to defend the Fargo abortion clinic in 1981 were born, for the most part, between 1942 and 1952. They represent a range of backgrounds in terms of their natal families, and their current household, conjugal, and work arrangements differ. However, in all their stories, the strong commitment to pro-choice activism was connected to particular personal and political experiences: on the one hand, they all drew connections to specific life-cycle events, generally having to do with experiences and difficulties around sexuality, pregnancy, and childbearing, including the choice not to have children. On the other hand, the social unrest of the late 1960s and early 1970s, and the women's movement in particular, are critical turning points in their plots as

they define themselves oppositionally in relation to the culture. For some, their encounter with these social movements as young adults was experienced as a moment of "conversion" from ideas and values with which they had been raised. For others it was expressed more as an "awakening" of some truth felt but never fully realized.

The central figure of the current controversy in Fargo is Kay Bellevue, the woman who opened the abortion clinic in 1981. Kay grew up in the Midwest, the oldest of seven children, the daughter of a Baptist minister and a woman who was a homemaker and part-time worker in the public school system. As is the case for most of the pro-choice activists, Kay began her narrative with the biographical "reasons" that, in her view, made her different. The plot begins with this early sense of differentiation, the source of identification with a key family member who served as a model for what she sees as her later oppositional stance toward the culture.

> I always perceived myself as different from other kids. As a preacher's kid, whether it was true or not, I always felt people expected me to be perfect and to behave in a ladylike manner. . . . My dad was always interested in what was going on politically and took a keen interest in the antiwar movement and rights for blacks. I was the apple of his eye and he's always been proud of the things I've done. My dad's a real independent person and I see a lot of that in me.

Although she stopped going to church when she got married—something she feels could stigmatize her in a community noted for its church attendance—Kay nonetheless connects her activism to religious principles of social justice learned in her natal family. Again, like other pro-choice women, the stress on caring and nurturance as part of their concern is prominent.

> I have always acted on what to me are Judeo-Christian principles. The Ten Commandments plus love thy neighbor. I was raised by my family to have a very very strong sense of ethics and it's still with me. I have a strong concern about people and social issues. I've had a tough time stomaching what goes on in the churches in the name of Christianity. I've found my sense of community elsewhere. . . . It's very distressing to me that [people,] particularly the people opposed to abortion, will attempt to say their moral beliefs are the only correct ones. . . . I think pro-choice people have a very strong basis in theology for the caring, loving perspective they have on abortion as do the antiabortion people have a basis in theology for their strong, loving caring perspective about the fetus.

In her senior year of college, Kay got pregnant and married and soon after moved to Denver where her husband was pursuing graduate studies. Like almost *all* of the women activists, regardless of their position on abortion, Kay's transition to motherhood was an event surrounded by ambivalence. Although her behavior was not, in fact, that different from that of many right-to-life women—for example, as a young mother she worked part-time and became involved in community associations—Kay's *interpretation* of her actions stresses the limitations of motherhood. Kay's

plot turns on her unexpected reaction to her assigned and chosen role as mother.

> I enjoyed being home, but I could never stay home all the time. I have never done that in my life. After being home one year and taking care of a kid, I felt my mind was a wasteland. And we were so poor we could almost never go out together.

Dividing childcare with her husband and babysitter, Kay started substitute teaching and taking classes. In her early twenties, she became active in a local chapter of La Leche League, an international organization promoting breastfeeding and natural childbirth. She marks this as a key event. Her quote demonstrates how, through her activities, she refigured both her social world and her initial dissonant experience of childbirth into a critique of the medical system's treatment of women.

> My first child had not been a pleasant birth experience so I went [to La Leche] and I was really intrigued. There were people talking about this childbirth experience like it was the most fantastic thing you'd ever been through. I certainly didn't feel that way. I had a very hard labor. I screamed, I moaned. . . . My husband thought I was dying.
>
> So anyway, this group introduced me to a whole different conception of childbirth and my second experience was so different I couldn't believe it.
>
> And the way I came to feminism was that through all of this, I became acutely aware of how little physicians who were supposed to be doctors for women actually knew about women's bodies. So I became a real advocate for women to stand up for their rights, starting with breastfeeding.

In many ways, her concerns are not so different than those articulated by her neighbors and fellow citizens who so vehemently oppose her work. Not surprisingly, for both groups of women, voluntary work for a "cause" was an acceptable and satisfying way of managing to balance the pleasures and duties of motherhood with the structural isolation of that work as it is organized in America. La Leche League, for example, is a group where one stands an equal chance of running into a pro-life or pro-choice woman. In Kay's case, she met a woman who introduced her to feminism, a critical twist in the plot that sets it in tension with the "story."

> Through La Leche League, I made a really good friend and she had read Judith Holes's book. *The*

Rebirth of Feminism. It was at the time when, well feminism in New York was several years into its development, but in the Midwest, it certainly was not, so she and I started talking about some things I had never thought about and that was my introduction to the whole feminist perspective.

. . . Kay's growing sense of consciousness concerning the way women's reproductive needs were mishandled by the medical profession crystallized during her third pregnancy. She remembers being influenced in particular by the Sherry Finkbine case.

She was trying to get an abortion in the country because she was carrying a thalidomide child. At that time, I had never had any connection to abortion and as I read these stories, I began to feel very strongly that this woman had the right to make this decision and who in the world has the right to tell someone that they have to bring a deformed child into the world. I just remember feeling that so very strongly. So the funny thing is, when I look back on it, from my involvement with La Leche League and my strong feelings about a woman's right not to have a child, I felt strongly enough that this was important to me when I chose my physician, even though I had no experience with abortion in any way shape or form.

In 1972, Kay moved to Fargo with her husband and children. She continued as a leader in La Leche and got pregnant again. Kay marks this period as one of crisis. Her parents were divorcing and one of her children was having problems.

Then I ended up having an abortion myself. My youngest was eighteen months old and I accidentally got pregnant. We had four small kids at the time and we decided if we were going to make it a family unit, we had all the stress we could tolerate if we were going to survive.

Kay went to a clinic in another state for her abortion and, due to complications, stayed in touch with the staff there. A year later, they gave Kay's name to a NARAL [National Abortion Right Action League] organizer who was looking for people to start chapters in the Upper Midwest.

I talked it over with my husband and he said "Kay, what are you asking me? This is your choice. You do what you want to do."

In her life story Kay consistently linked her activism to a commitment to maintaining strong family ties, whether it concerned her public role or her personal decisions regarding abortion. This was, in part, a self-conscious response to right-to-life claims that pro-choice advocates are opposed to marriage, family, and children. This stereotype, to which most of the pro-choice women in Fargo were extremely sensitive, may account for the lack of open public support for pro-choice efforts in Fargo, even among feminists and liberals. Kay's comments below indicate . . . her resentment of the casting of pro-choice by right-to-life advocates as being "antifamily" . . .

I think it's easy for them to stereotype us as having values very different than theirs and that's not the case at all. Many of the people who get abortions have values very similar to the antiabortion people. The right-to-life people don't know how deeply I care for my own family and how involved I am since I have four children and spent the early years of my life working for a breastfeeding organization.

The perspective that abortion is "destroying the family" is a very, very narrow one. In my experience, people who have made the choice to have an abortion made it because they want a strong family. How bringing an unwanted child into a family strengthens it is something I have never been able to understand.

. . . By 1977, Kay was providing abortion referrals from her home and was growing increasingly disturbed at the lack of abortion services for women in the area. Two years later, when Kay was asked to be on the national board of NARAL, she met Sharon and with her help began plans in earnest to open a clinic in Fargo.

In making the shift from activist to professional, Kay has faced new frustrations. As plans for the clinic progressed, and right-to-life groups began to mobilize to stop it, Kay became increasingly worried that something she wanted so badly and had worked for so long to achieve would fall through. Since the clinic opened, facing protesters has become an almost regular part of Kay's work. Pickets are there weekly on the day that abortions are performed. The reward of her work, not surprisingly, comes from the moments that remind her of the initial impulse that sent her off on the trajectory of pro-choice activism in the first place, her desire to make safe and legal abortions available to women who need them.

The very most satisfying thing of all has been when the patients are ready to leave here and they come up and put their arms around me or one of my staff people and say, "Thank you so much. You don't know what a difference this has made to my life. I expected something very different, [but] everyone here was so warm and so caring and nonjudgmental." And that in itself is a real reward.

The scenario Kay evokes in this "ideal" compliment indicates her goal is not simply the provision of safe abortion services but also the creation of a medical environment for women that is nurturant, warm, and caring. . . .

> I just can't say no to things that are important to me. . . . most things that have to do with women's issues. And I can't really pick one over the other. The abortion issue is more important to me probably because it affected me personally in so many ways, so many times. I just feel it's a duty.

Sitting in the cramped kitchen of Sherry's modest two-story house, I remember a description of her given by another activist as "every Fargo woman's ideal. Slim, blonde, attractive with a decent job and a husband who travels a lot." Dressed in faded jeans and a man's shirt, Sherry looks and sounds unpretentious. She finds the images others have of her disturbing, a misreading of her life. Her marriage is a rocky one and she describes her work as an office administrator as "a ridiculous job I hate with men who are impossible to deal with." She is trying with difficulty to maintain the life course that was expected of her—marriage, family, children, church, and community—while accommodating experiences of the last decade that have taken her in different directions. In her plot, it is the progressive sense of dissonance from an "ideal female biography" that led her, eventually, to political activism.

Sherry was the first of two girls born to a couple who met at the utility company where they worked their whole lives. She describes herself as having been a dutiful daughter, attending Lutheran church activities four times a week until she was seventeen, and as a teenager more interested in fun than politics. Like the other pro-choice women, she marks her contact with the social movements of the late 1960s as a time when she began to look at things differently, the roots of a view of the world that she feels differentiates her from right-to-life women.

When I left high school and got to college, the whole hippie generation, the campus unrest, the Vietnam war made a lot of people question. . . . You have to answer things for yourself. . . . I realized it's dangerous to believe in something beyond being able to ask a question. I don't feel the right-to-life position is invalid. I understand what they're saying. And if they honestly believe life begins at conception, I don't see any other choice for them. It only makes me angry that they don't realize other people don't believe that. And that they can't determine what's gonna happen in other people's lives.

I mean people react in ways that you don't expect them to all the time, every day. Who am I to say they're right or wrong?

The unexpected events in Sherry's life in the late 1960s and early 1970s are almost a catalog of what right-to-life activists call "the hard cases," the most persuasive of the pro-choice arguments, beginning with the horror of illegal abortion.

> I never thought about abortion at all until my first year in college. In high school, I believed no one had sex, so I didn't. And then my friends started getting pregnant. We had no sex education. I had friends with whom I went to have abortions before it was legal. One got pregnant at my eighteenth birthday party and I felt this incredible sense of responsibility.
>
> The first time, I went to Winnipeg to a woman's home. I sat out in the living room and looked out the window for the police. I was sure she was going to die. It was really terrifying. It wasn't subject I could discuss with them and say, "I don't think you should do this." . . . It was their decision and they were my friends and I cared about them. It was a growing up story for all of us. I just about flunked out of college because of it.

Angered by this personal encounter with the inequities women faced in reproduction, Sherry became interested in feminism and a passive pro-choice supporter. In 1976, she married and began teaching in the local parochial school and, to her surprise, was pregnant within a year. The child was very much desired, but there were unexpected complications.

> It wasn't a pregnancy I planned. I was teaching and my husband was beginning as a salesman so our financial position wasn't great. It didn't occur to me to have an abortion. I would work it out no matter what I had to do. Finally, my daughter was born and I was thrilled. For about

thirty seconds. And then the doctor said, "There's something wrong here. There's an opening in the spine." I don't know if I can explain the feelings that I had. . . . I didn't know if I really had had a baby, and then, the doctor came in and told us our daughter was born with spina bifida. She would never have been able to control her bowels or her bladder. She would never have been able to walk. And all of a sudden we heard her start to choke and the hospital social worker said, "Don't worry it's going to be all right," and I said, "No it's not. It's never going to be all right again." And we just stood there and watched our daughter die. And what I can say mostly about that time is that I don't feel anyone has the right to force me to go through that again.

Sherry's characterization of the pro-choice and pro-life positions reflect critical differences in their philosophies of human nature and show how these abstractions are integrated into individual experience. . . . She is critical of the pro-life belief that people should behave in the present according to ideals of a future society in which abortion would be considered unnecessary. From the pro-choice point of view, life is seen as essentially problematic. Abortion is understood as an act of compassion, a way of helping women solve dilemmas according to the solutions they themselves have decided upon in difficult circumstances.

I think it's really more important that you do good things and you care about people. Sometimes those of us who already exist are more important. Even if someone who is anti-choice said I was well intentioned but misguided . . . well. I think, then how could you possibly be found wanting when it came to Judgment Day?

In this way, Sherry and her colleagues see their activism as part of a broader goal for improving the conditions of women's lives in conditions of sexual inequality. . . .

In the plots of their life stories, pro-choice activists stress their work and activities outside the home over motherhood, but always in terms of the values of caretaking that are identified with motherhood and domesticity. Thus, their defense of abortion rights is linked to a larger goal of (re)producing on a larger social scale what they would call female cultural values and what I am calling nurturance. This is apparent in the way their life stories uphold

nurturance as a valued quality that is considered natural to women as well as the basis of their cultural authority; however, they reject it as an attribute that might confine them to childbearing, caretaking, and domesticity.

In most cases, the narrator portrays as unusual her involvement in the breaking of the boundaries between home and the workplace, arenas conventionally held apart in American culture. Her plot traces her convictions and behavior to a sequence of biographical encounters that emphasize her differentiation from cultural expectations of an ideal female biography: in the plot of a pro-choice life story, these events might include an unusual birth or childhood, identification with iconoclastic and outspoken family members, the experience of life-cycle events related to reproduction that brought her to question the institutions and received wisdom she had always known, and a conversion like encounter with the social movements of the late 1960s. For almost every pro-choice activist, this historical moment is deployed in the plot of her narrative as a transitional marker. Its central meaning for the narrator is shaped by the fact that this encounter occurred, in most cases, when the speaker was a young adult, . . .

. . . In the repeated insistence that their activism is not for personal gain or individual indulgence but serves the interests of women and social justice. . . . nurturance takes on a broad definition: although it is viewed as rooted in particular female experience, it is seen as a guide to action and a goal for social change in general. In other words, nurturance is understood as an oppositional stance to a world that is viewed as materialistic, male defined, and lacking in compassion. Activists express this stance as a desire to create generative, loving, or at least tolerant relationships between family, friends, members of the community, people in the workplace, and even the nation as a whole. . . .

Like their pro-choice colleagues, right-to-life activists also express a concern for the preservation of what I am calling nurturance, but their interpretation differs. Although nurturance is understood to be a source of cultural value and female authority, as it is in the pro-choice narratives, it is linked more directly to biological reproduction. In all the stories of pregnancy and birth told by right-to-life women, the ambivalence of the speaker toward that condition is invoked and then overcome, either through reference to her own or her mother's experience. . . . Paradoxically, despite the stress of this link to the physical body, nurturance as a characteristic on mothering and the domestic domain is not seen as a natural moral quality but one that is achieved.

Like the pro-choice life stories, the pro-life narratives reveal how these activists are continually reworking ideologies about the place of women in American culture so that they are contextualized in their historically specific experiences of everyday life. However, for many pro-life activists who came of age in the 1970s and left the work force to have children, this encounter with feminism is worked into the plot as a misguided identity they have transcended.

. . . Peggy Jones is a devout Catholic woman, born in 1942 and raised on a farm in a family of nine. Her narrative begins with a recollection of her initial difference from her mother on the issue of abortion when she was a teenager. Her comment that "so much has changed since then" indicates the twist in the plot marking her conversion to the pro-life position. She was persuaded by the pictures of aborted fetuses.

> You know, when I was in my teens, I remember my mother saying she was against abortion, how it could lead to euthanasia and I always used to disclaim that and say, "Oh mother, you're so out of date." I can just hear myself saying that. And so much has changed since then.
>
> I remember in 1972 when there was that referendum here and I bought a book, *The Handbook on Abortion*, and I remember being shocked by the pictures of the aborted babies. My own children were five and two, so that was even more shocking to have gone through pregnancy and know that it's a life and all that.

I first met Peggy at the Fargo parochial high school where she had programmed a day of events on the tenth anniversary of the 1973 *Roe* v. *Wade* decision legalizing abortion. On that occasion, as coordinator of the pro-life section of the local Catholic diocese, she introduced the play she had written based on the Supreme Court testimony. The staging, with the teachers cast as Justices, costumed in choir robes and seated at long tables draped with cloth, was meant to mimic the decorum of the high court but seemed to me to resemble more closely a tableau vivant of the Last Supper. What impressed me was that Peggy had retained in her stage version the most compelling speeches in defense of abortion argued before the court, a recognition of an opposing point of view I had not expected.

Peggy greeted me at her office wearing loden green corduroy trousers and jacket, a white turtleneck sweater, with her red hair in a short stylish cut. Her manner reinforced my earlier impression of her as an open, intelligent, and compassionate person. Peggy is one of the small number of pro-life activists in Fargo from the same group from which much of the pro-choice support is drawn—women born between 1940 and 1945.

In the narratives of the right-to-life women of this age group, their concern with abortion reflected issues prominent for them at this point in their life cycles: they are contemplating the changes ahead as they move back into the paid work force and out of a decade or more spent as full-time mothers and homemakers. They are evaluating their marriages in relation to these shifts, particularly as they witness marital trouble among many of their peers. They worry over the effect on their teenage children of the ubiquitous temptations of the American adolescent subculture that have made their way into Fargo life. This last concern was one of the first that Peggy mentioned when I asked her why she became active in the pro-life movement.

> Well, I didn't get that involved until the last two years. And one thing I feel keenly about now, and it's probably because my oldest son is fifteen and a freshman in high school, but I just firmly believe that the more we can talk to high-school-age students about what abortions are, and the realities of abortion and its alternatives, that there are people who care. . . . I've personally been speaking in the schools now for these last two years.
>
> I guess I see abortion as being linked in terms of . . . well, if we can respect ourselves enough that we can say no to outside pressures kids are getting today, and I know they are tremendous, then we can feel good enough about ourselves that if we become pregnant, its OK to go through with that. I think a lot of it has to do with the fact that we don't feel good enough. . . . We're pushed from the outside. I mean every magazine you pick up today talks about sexuality and 98 percent of the teens have had sex by the time they're

nineteen. So you think you're some kind of freak if you don't.

As lay pro-life coordinator for the Catholic Church, Peggy was involved with public education and made it her personal goal to develop outreach programs to high schools, along with keeping up on legislation, staying in contact with other national, state, and local right-to-life groups, and maintaining ties with parishes throughout the area, each of which has its own pro-life contact. Peggy, like many other right-to-life women, sees the abortion issue as inseparable from a need for sex education that goes beyond "explaining the plumbing," an obligation that she feels should be shared jointly by family, school, church, and state.

I always considered our generation would certainly be open about talking with our kids about sex, and I've tried to be with my family. I think part of the problem is we haven't talked nearly enough about being responsible for our actions. You spill a glass of water then you wipe it up. There are natural and logical consequences. That's the risk. It's like getting in the car. One of the risks you take is having an accident.

Peggy worries especially that abortion fosters a sense of irresponsibility for the reproductive consequences of sexual activity and makes a concerted effort to discuss these things with her son. She prides herself that now (after practicing by talking to her plants) they can sit at the kitchen table and discuss wet dreams, or the sudden mood shifts of his thirteen-year-old sister.

When Peggy finished high school in a small town north of Fargo at age seventeen "it was assumed you would get married and have kids." Within two years, Peggy did just that, marrying a man she met at her job as a grocery clerk. He now works in middle management for a utility company. She is grateful that it took her two years (even without birth control) to get pregnant so that they had time to get to know each other "before the kids came." Since then, they have had two and adopted a third, a biracial child.

In their late twenties, the Joneses became actively involved in church-sponsored marriage reform movements, starting with an activity called Marriage Encounter. Initiated by the Catholic Church, it has become quite popular in the Fargo—Moorhead area (and

throughout the country) and is now imitated by other denominations. In Peggy's view, the energy they have put into their marriage through these activities (including pro-life work) has enabled them to focus on common goals as a couple and helped them keep their marriage together through what they recognize can be a very stressful period in the family cycle. In her narrative, "women's growth" is seen as particularly dangerous to the survival of marriages.

We've noticed, my husband and I, with our friends, that now that we're all through our thirties, there's been a heck of a lot of growth, especially for the women. A lot of us have gone back to work or to school. A lot of our friends, about five couples this last year, are experiencing serious marital difficulties because of [the woman's] growth. My husband and I just really care about each other and how the other is growing and I think our spiritual life together has helped us a lot too, the time we spend in prayer together, that's given us hope when it's been tough. Gosh, I just think that our own marriage is a lot healthier than it was ten years ago. We're a lot more willing to compromise and talk things out.

As was the case for most of the right-to-life women I worked with, successful marriages are seen as the product of much time and effort.

While the move from motherhood to marketplace was absorbing these women in their late thirties, those born a decade later were facing the opposite transition. Sally Nordsen is part of a group of women born between 1952 and 1958 who made up the majority of Fargo's activists involved in the fight against the clinic and were the most dedicated members. Like most of the other pro-life women of this group, Sally went to college where she met her husband who now works in wholesale marketing. They married soon after her graduation; she worked for seven years as a social worker. In her late twenties, she got pregnant and decided to leave the work force in order to raise her children. This is a critical element in her plot, a difficult passage. Although she regards the choice as a positive one, it was nonetheless marked by ambivalence.

I had two days left of work before my resignation was official but Dick was born earlier than expected. So I left the work on my desk and never went back to it. There were so many things that were abrupt. When I went into the hospital it was raining, and when I came out it was snowing. A change of seasons, a change of work habits, a new baby in my life. It was hard. I was so anxious to get home and show this baby off. And when I walked in the door, it was like the weight of the world and I thought, "What am I going to do with him now?" Well, these fears faded.

So it was a change. When Ken would come home, I would practically meet him at the door with my coat and purse cause I wanted to get out of there. I couldn't stand it, you know. And that's still the case sometimes. But the joys outweigh the desire to go back to work.

Like other pro-life activists, Sally is articulate about the difficulties of motherhood, the work involved, and her acceptance of that identity despite the hardships. Balancing motherhood with voluntary work provides a temporary resolution for the difficulties of this period in her life cycle, much as it did for some of the pro-choice activists. In contrast to the pro-choice narrators, however, Sally stresses her need to be at home.

I had some hobbies at one time (laughs) but with the pro-life work and my family and church—it's really all I've been able to manage. And there have been times when I've just spread myself too thin. And the kids are the ones that suffer if I get too involved. . . .

I first met Sally during a health fair at the local shopping mall where she and a neighbor spent the day at a pro-life information table handing out literature to passersby. For those who stopped, she explained the life of the unborn with the aid of plastic models of fetal development loaned by a sympathetic obstetrician. Later, at her home, she explained how she became "converted" to the right-to-life cause. A reevaluation of the meaning of her continuing belief in "women's rights" and "freedom" are critical to this twist of her plot.

When the abortion chamber came to town, it just hit me that I was responsible for this. I was walking in front of the clinic and all of a sudden, many things just came crashing down, you might say, about my attitudes and values and things. . . .

I go around acting like I had to be the champion for women's rights. But I honestly have a hard time with some of the screaming that goes on because some of those women also feel that abortion is one of those rights and they call it reproductive freedom. To me, yes, it is your freedom to choose to reproduce or not to reproduce. But once that's done, you've already made that

choice. So when those things get lumped together with women's rights, like equal pay, I get really upset. There are some things, such as abortion, that can actually be destructive to other people. If we are so right, let's not repeat the same mistakes that other people have made. Let's not repeat the mistakes that men have been making.

Her statement was interrupted briefly by a crying child, the younger of her two boys aged three and one who, until this moment, had been snoozing amid recently abandoned toys in a comfortable heap on the floor with the family husky.

Sally is extremely warm, with an engaging and available sense of humor even in the presence of two demanding toddlers. Her blonde hair, blue eyes, and broad bone structure bear testimony to her second-generation Norwegian heritage. Her clothes—old jeans and a turtleneck—are the daily uniform of a young mother. For Sally and the other pro-life activists her age, the move from wage labor to motherhood occurred in the late 1970s or more recently. This critical moment in their life histories intersected a paradoxical moment for American feminism. Much of what the prior cohort of feminist activists of the 1960s and 1970s had struggled for appeared to have been achieved. Sally's developing plot indicates the hidden toll of feminism's rapid successes. In her narrative, she progressively differentiates herself from feminist rhetoric that was so powerful ten years earlier yet did not reflect her experience in the late 1970s.

Some of these things I equated with being a free woman were not necessarily good and did not necessarily have to do with freedom. Women's rights were important to me. But sometimes I acted as if I was downtrodden. I have a husband who respects me completely, who shares in the work around the house. I have no reason to complain. I didn't live in a home where I was belittled for being female.

Women like Sally who have decided to leave the work force for a "reproductive phase" of their life cycle are keenly aware of the disjunction of their choice with the images that surround them. . . .

In my work, I saw a lot of people who were part of the middle class and then because of a divorce or having a child out of wedlock, they became part of the welfare system. I saw how really necessary, how many reasons there were to really maintain that relationship. There's a very real world out there. I feel sorry for men that they can't have the same feelings I do about pregnancy. But in the situation of a woman, where all of a sudden after twenty years of a marriage, she has nothing, and he at least has a business or a job or whatever . . . women just have a different kind of investment in the marriage situation.

Ironically, the same sort of cases are used by pro-choice activists who attribute the viewpoints of their opponents to ignorance of the difficulties many women face. Almost all of the Fargo pro-life activists were aware of these stereotypes and addressed them in a dialectical fashion, using them to confirm their own position. [One pro-lifer,] for example, expressed it in the following way:

If you take the pro-life stand, you're labeled as being against anything else that women stand for. And ironically, it's mostly women in our movement. The pro-choice people say about us. "Well, they must have feelings but they're so put down they can't make up their own minds, you know." And they think we're just saying what we do because that's what men have taught us. Well, if the men have taught us, why aren't the men helping us?

To write off the views of a Sally or [Peggy] as naive is as much a misreading as are their claims that pro-choice women are unconcerned with raising families. They, along with other right-to-life activists, are well aware of the fragility of traditional marriage arrangements and recognize the lack of other social forms that might ensure the emotional and material support of women with children or other dependents. . . .

The collective portrait that emerges from these stories is much more complex than the stereotype that portrays pro-life women as reactionary housewives and mothers passed by in the sweep of social change. They are astute, alert to social and political developments, and on many issues are not antifeminist. They approve of and endorse women seeking political power and economic equity. . . . Most held or had held jobs and some had careers. In the marriage relationships I observed, husbands helped out regularly in domestic duties and were pragmatically and emotionally supportive of their wives' political work.

What is striking in the narratives is how most of these women had assimilated some version of feminist thought and woven it into their life choices. The plot of almost every story hinges on how the narrator either repudiated or reorganized these ideas into a right-to-life framework. Sally's narrative of how her ideas have changed as she joined the pro-life movement is illustrative.

You're looking at somebody who used to think the opposite. I used to think that sex outside of marriage was fine. Now I see I don't believe that anymore. I believe when you practice sex outside of marriage you are taking all kinds of chances, including walking out on each other and not having to accept the responsibility of children or whatever. And to me, once you engage in the act of sex, it's a big emotional commitment. If my boyfriend walked out on me I would be devastated. I think the world preaches you can have it all . . . doing lots of things without getting caught and I guess over the last few years, I've really changed my mind about a lot of things. And when I see the abortion clinic, there's proof positive to me that my values are right and an innocent human being is paying the price for all this.

It is this sort of negotiation of feminism into their life story that distinguishes the younger right-to-life women in particular, although it is present in more muted form with older activists. . . . Rather than simply defining themselves in opposition to what they understand feminist ideology and practice to be, many, like Sally, claim to have held that position, and to have transcended it. Sally, for example, describes her former "liberated" ideas about sexuality and heterosexual relationships as a repression of her true self.

I think there was part of me that never fully agreed. It wasn't a complete turnaround. It was kind of like inside you know it's not right but you make yourself think it's OK. When I was in college, I loved to read Cosmopolitan magazine, all kinds of magazines and I thought, "This is the kind of life I was meant to lead." You know, I think part of it is rebellion.

This sort of appropriation of other identities by rejection occurs in political rhetoric as well; for example, a pro-life lecture popular in 1984 Fargo is entitled, "I Was a Pro-Choice Feminist, but Now I'm Pro-Life."

What the pro-life women consider feminism to be is another issue. The point here is that in their narratives they assert the prior alliance; this assertion is usually described as a period of (ideological) separation from the narrator's mother. The "conversion" to the pro-life position often follows a first birth or pregnancy; this becomes the basis, in the plot, for a reexamination of the previously held position. Thus, they narratively subsume their opponents' ideology into their own and thus claim authority over it.

Their position on abortion is not defined simply by repudiation of the other. In their narratives, their commitment to the right-to-life cause is connected to experiences of pregnancy and motherhood. The plots of these "procreation stories" told by right-to-life women hang on the ambivalence of the mother toward that condition, which is invoked and then transcended. In this way, the narrator becomes a mother not automatically but by *effort*. In the context of legal abortion, pro-life activists reframe the transition to motherhood as an achieved rather than a natural state. At the same time, the heroic cast of these "procreation" stories offers an embedded critique, the challenge of nurturance to the values of materialism and competitive individualism that they see as negative social forces.

Much in the same way that pro-choice women embraced feminism, this younger cohort of pro-life women find in their movement a particular symbolic frame that integrates their experience of work, reproduction, and marriage with the shifting ideas of gender and politics that they encounter around them. It is not that they discovered an ideology that "fit" what they had always been. Their sense of identification evolves in the very process of voicing their views against abortion. . . .

. . . While [both pro-choice and pro-life] activists' actions and "life scripts" are cast against each other, both provide ways for managing the structural opposition in America between wage work and parenthood that still shapes and differentiates the lives of most women from men in this culture. Nurturance, reformulated to mesh with different historical and biographical experiences, is prominent in both positions as a source of both female authority and a critique of "masculine" values. As the historian Linda Gordon points out.

> [Right-to-lifers] fear a completely individualized society with all services based on cash nexus relationships, without the influence of nurturing women counteracting the completely egoistic principles of the economy, and without any forms in which children can learn about lasting human commitments to other people. Many feminists have the same fear.

Additionally, nurturance provides a link in the narratives that ties critical moments in the narrator's life course—the transition to motherhood—to the central philosophical questions of each side: the pro-life concern with the protection of nascent life, and the pro-choice concern with the rights and obligations of women to whom the care of that nascent life is culturally assigned. The plots constructed by women on each side suggest different interpretations of the place of procreation in women's lives, and the place of women in reproducing the culture.

DOCUMENTS: Equality and Military Service

> "*We were the first American women sent to live and work in the midst of guerrilla warfare . . .*"

The American ships and planes that went to Vietnam carried women as well as men. There were approximately 10,000 military women and more than 13,000 Red Cross women, as well as smaller numbers of women foreign service officers, staff of the U.S. Agency for International Development, and employees of the USO. In 1980, Congress authorized a memorial to be built "in honor and recognition of the men and women of the Armed Forces of the United States who served in Vietnam." The competition for the design of the memorial was won by 21-year-old Maya Lin, an undergraduate architecture student at Yale. The memorial stands today in Washington, visited by millions of people each year. They leave offerings as at a shrine: flowers, photographs, mementos.

The design of the memorial—whose black granite walls bear the names of 58,000 Americans who died, including eight women—was controversial from the beginning. Many veterans groups insisted on a more traditional, representational design. In 1984 an additional statue that depicted three soldiers was placed in a grove of trees nearby. When the additional statue failed to include the figure of a woman, women veterans began to urge the addition of another statue honoring the women who had served.

In 1988 Congress authorized a statue recognizing women, to be constructed on federal property at the Vietnam Veterans Memorial from funds (like those of the other memorials) raised from private donations. The comments that follow were made at hearings conducted by Senator Dale Bumpers of Arkansas, chair of the Senate Subcommittee on Public Lands, National Parks and Forests.

Each of the veterans had complex memories of their experience in Vietnam, twenty years before. How do the women explain the meaning of their service? How is Robert Doubek's testimony affected by concerns about class, race, and gender?

Both Karen Johnson's testimony and the arguments of the Supreme Court in *Rostker* v. *Goldberg* (pp. 568–70) address the issue of whether men and women have an equal obligation to serve in the military. Do you think men and women have an equal obligation to serve in the military in time of war, as Karen Johnson believes? Does that obligation extend to service in combat? Does the exclusion of women from combat suggest that American society attaches greater value to women's lives than men's? What other factors might also be relevant in explaining the exclusion of women from combat?

Vietnam Women's Memorial. Hearing Before the Subcommittee on Public Lands, National Parks and Forests of the Committee on Energy and Natural Resources, United States Senate 100th Congress, 2nd session. February 23, 1988, pp. 89–90, 99–100, 108–9, 124–25.

STATEMENT OF DONNA-MARIE BOULAY, CHAIRMAN, VIETNAM WOMEN'S MEMORIAL PROJECT

Mr. Chairman, people who serve in wars have unique experiences. War was never meant to be. War makes death. Day after day, even hour after hour, we lived and worked amidst the wounded, the dead, and the dying.

I arrived in Vietnam at the end of February 1967. A few days later I was assigned to triage for the first time. The medevac helicopters brought twelve soldiers into our emergency room. Ten were already dead. Two were bleeding to death.

Mr. Chairman, our daily duty was to care for the badly wounded, the young men whose legs had been blown off, whose arms had been traumatically amputated, whose bodies and faces had been burned beyond recognition.

We eased the agony of a young marine, his legs amputated, his wounds dangerously infected. We worked hard to stop the bleeding of a sailor who had been shot in his liver. He died three days after, in immense pain.

We cared for a young Army lieutenant from New York named Pat who had been admitted with a badly mangled leg and later evacuated to Japan, like many of the other seriously wounded soldiers we treated. I do not know whether Pat's leg was saved. I hope so. Pat was a good soldier.

Mr. Chairman, "Pat" is not short for "Patrick." Pat is a nurse. Patty was a nurse. She was stationed at the 24th Evacuation Hospital in Long Binh.

We were the first American women sent to live and work in the midst of guerrilla warfare. The month-long Tet offensive was especially frightening. The Viet Cong blew up the ammunition dump down the street, causing a wall in our unit to collapse on some patients.

VC snipers shot at us. The North Vietnamese Army artillery roared throughout the nights. Those of us not at work huddled in our bunkers, wondering if we would survive until dawn.

At work, listening to the thundering sounds around us, we tried to keep our hands from shaking, the fear out of our voices and off of our faces, so that the wounded would not see or hear it.

Women served in Vietnam in many capacities. We served as personnel specialists, journalists, clerk-typists, intelligence officers, and nurses. There was no such thing as a generic woman soldier, as there was no such thing as a generic male soldier. Men served as mechanics, engineers, pilots, divers, and infantrymen.

The design of the men's statue at the Veterans Memorial was selected, according to Frederick Hart, the sculptor, because they "depict the bonds of men at war and because the infantry bore the greatest burden."

Mr. Chairman, we are proposing that the design for the women's statue be that of a nurse who served in Vietnam. The statue of a nurse is so compatible with the existing trio of figures because the nurses' experience so closely parallels the experience of the infantrymen—the intensity, the trauma, the carnage of war.

The statue design which we are proposing is an easily recognizable symbol of healing and hope, consistent with the spirit and the experience of the Vietnam Veterans Memorial. . . .

STATEMENT OF KAREN K. JOHNSON, LITTLE ROCK, AR

I was born in Petersburg, Virginia. My father was in the military. He was killed in France on November the 11th, 1944.

I was raised in Oklahoma. I graduated from college in 1964 and explored the military as a career and joined the Army in 1965.

My family was very patriotic because of the trials and tribulations that we had to go through because of being raised without a father. Considering that everyone in my family had experienced all that patriotism, when I said that I was going to join the Army it was not a new thought, even though I was the first woman to have joined.

My family felt that all Americans owed their country any sacrifice needed for the national good, regardless of their race or sex, that patriotism should be a blind emotion, and it should be accepted by our country without any thought or qualm as to who offered such patriotism.

Consequently, after I served in Germany from 1966 to 1968, when my country asked me to go overseas again to Vietnam, I went. I served in Vietnam from July of 1970 to March of 1972, for a total of 20 months in country.

When I tell people these facts, they always ask me, was I a nurse, that I did not see any combat, and that I must have volunteered. When I tell them that I was awarded a Bronze Star, they ask me what for.

For 18 years I have answered these questions with several long-winded explanations which were really an apology for my Vietnam service, because I was not a nurse and I was not a combat soldier, and there were many others who had served who the public much better understood their service in their traditional roles.

I have kept silent on what I did in Vietnam because it was easier than making the apologies or trying to educate my listener. I know now that I have done many Vietnam veterans a great disservice by my silence. Thanks to the support of the Arkansas Vietnam Veterans, my husband and my grandchildren, I have made my last apology, felt my last twinge of embarrassment, and I will not remain silent to the detriment of my comrades in arms.

I am a veterans' veteran and I am proud of it. I was not a nurse. I saw very little full-fledged combat, and when my country called I went willingly. I see no disgrace in answering such a call or in volunteering to serve in the United States Army.

I served as the Command Information Officer of the United States Army, Vietnam Headquarters, located at Long Binh. However, my job entailed finding out what Army troops were doing, photographing those troops, writing news reports, and printing the internal publications to keep the troops informed.

I could not do that from Long Binh. I traveled all over Vietnam. Wherever there were Army troops, I went, too. I have flown in attack helicopters, been shot at in jeeps, and I went over the Hay Van Pass in several convoys.

Whatever it took to get the news out to the troops is what I and my staff did, and we did it very well. "Uptight Magazine," one of our publications, was awarded the Thomas Jefferson Award for the outstanding military publication in its field, an award that was given to me by "Time Magazine."

Our office published a twice-daily news bulletin, a weekly Long Binh paper, the weekly "Army Reporter," "Uptight Magazine Quarterly"; and "Tour 364," the history of the war, was updated every six months so that troops rotating home had a written history of their service. We were also responsible for the free distribution of "Stars and Stripes" to ensure that every U.S. military personnel serving in Vietnam had daily access to a newspaper.

There were a lot of obstacles to resolve to make all of this happen. My staff made it happen every day for 20 months, in 12 hour shifts, seven days a week, including Christmas, when we worked harder because we were responsible for making Operation Jingle Bells work so that the troops could see Bob Hope.

I am here today to tell you that I am very proud of that staff, and especially of Spec. 5 Steven Henry Warner, who gave his life so the American soldier could be the best informed and most motivated soldier in the world. I do not believe they would want me to apologize for our service or the fact that Steve Warner gave his life as a journalist and not as a combat soldier.

If there is any apology owed, it is the one I owe my staff for not standing up for them for the last 18 years because I did not like the questions my admission to being a Vietnam veteran elicited because I was a woman, something not well understood by the American public.

Their service and mine should be given equal recognition with all who served, not diminished because of the non-traditional position I held.

I come before you today to ask you to legislate equal dignity for the women who served their country by answering the call to arms. The Vietnam Women's Memorial would do much to give women veterans a new sense of self-respect and it will make a strong public statement that bias, prejudice, or ignorance of the sacrifices that women veterans have made for their country will no longer be tolerated.

Today the flag that covered my father's casket when he was put to final rest in 1948 lies in front of me, because I have always wanted him to be proud of me, his only child. And I believe he would be proudest of me today when I say, after 18 long years of silence: I was an American soldier; I answered my country's call to arms; and I am an American veteran, a title I should be able to share with equal dignity with all who have served before me and will serve after me. . . .

STATEMENT OF ROBERT W. DOUBEK . . .

Mr. Chairman, my name is Robert W. Doubek of Washington, D.C. I am a Vietnam veteran.

I am employed in the private sector. I was a founder of the Vietnam Veterans Memorial Fund. I served as its Executive Director and Project Director. I was responsible for building the memorial. I did the work. In recognition of my achievement, I was nominated for a Congressional Gold Medal which was a bill passed by the Senate on November 14, 1985.

The fact is that women are not represented by the Vietnam Veterans Memorial. The fact is also that the memorial does not represent anyone. It is not a legislative body. It is a symbol of honor, and as such, it is complete as a tribute to all who served their country in the Vietnam War.

It is a basic rule of common sense that mandates that something which is not broken should not be fixed. The genius of the wall is its equalizing and unifying effect. All veterans are honored, regardless of rank, service branch, commission, sex, or any other category. The names of the eight women casualties take their rightful places of honor. To ensure that this fact is never overlooked, the inscription on the first panel of the wall states that the memorial is in honor of the men and women of the Armed Forces. The reason I know this is because I was instrumental in drafting the inscription.

In 1982, politics required that we add a figurative sculpture as a more specific symbol of the Vietnam veteran. Even with the heroic and dangerous service rendered by other combatants such as Air Force and Navy pilots, Navy swiftboat crews, and the life saving efforts of nurses, helicopter pilots and medics, there was only one possible choice of what category would be literally depicted to symbolize the Vietnam veteran, and that could only be the enlisted infantrymen, grunts. They account for the majority of names on the wall; they bore the brunt of the battle. The fact is all grunts were men.

The addition of a statue of a woman or of any other category, for that matter, would reduce the symbolism of the existing sculpture from honoring or symbolizing the Vietnam veterans community as a whole to symbolizing only enlisted infantrymen. This in turn would open a Pandora's box of proliferating statuary toward the goal of trying to depict every possible category. The National Park Service has already received requests for a statue to literally depict Native Americans and

even for scout dogs, and in fact, I want to say that the figure for Native American casualties was 225.

The addition of a statue solely on the basis of gender raises troubling questions about proportion. Is gender of such overriding importance among veterans that we should have a specific statue to women who suffered eight casualties, and none for the Navy which suffered over 2,500, nor for the Air Force which suffered over 2,400? Is gender of such importance to outweigh that some 90 percent of the women who served in Vietnam in the military were officers [nurses were commissioned officers], while over 87 percent of all casualties were enlisted? . . . Approval . . . would set the precedent that strict literal depiction of both genders is an absolute requirement of all military related memorials. What about the new Navy memorial? Will Congress mandate an additional figure at the Iwo Jima Memorial?

STATEMENT OF COL. MARY EVELYN BANE, USMC (RETIRED), ARLINGTON, VA

Mr. Chairman, my name is Mary Evelyn Bane. I live in Arlington, Virginia, and I have lived in the Washington metropolitan area for a total of almost 19 nonconsecutive years. I retired in 1977 from a 26-year career in the United States Marine Corps in the grade of colonel. I never served in Vietnam, only a few women Marines did, and they were in Saigon, but I was in active service during the entire period of the war there. My career was in personnel management and, like most Marine officers, I had a variety of assignments and experiences, including two tours at our famous or infamous Parris Island training recruits, and an assignment with the Joint Staff in France. All of my male Marine colleagues did serve in Vietnam, many of them more than once, and some of their names are on the Vietnam Veterans Memorial.

I am opposed to the installation of a statue of a woman at the site of the VVM for both artistic and philosophical reasons, artistically, because it is at odds with the design as well as the theme of the memorial. . . . [and] philosophically simply because I am a woman. This may seem unfathomable to the statue's proponents, but perhaps I can explain. From the beginning of my chosen career in what most will agree is a macho outfit, I tried hard to be the best Marine I was capable of being. When I was commissioned, fewer than 1 percent of the officers in the Marine Corps were female. Women were assigned to women's billets, and restricted to a handful of occupational specialties considered appropriate for women. Over the years, through the combined efforts of many, many people, of which I am happy to say I am one, the concept of how women could and should serve their country has changed. The huge increase in the military's population required by the Vietnam War hastened the changes.

Nevertheless, in 1973 when I, then a lieutenant colonel, was assigned as the Marine Corps member of a Department of Defense ad hoc group studying the recruitment and processing of non-prior service personnel, the Civil Service GS-15 chair of the group complained to the Commandant of the Marine Corps that he had not appointed a real Marine.

My point here is that sex is an accident of birth. I chose to be a Marine and worked hard at it, and spent a career combatting discrimination based on sex. I feel every service person should be recognized for what he or she accomplished as a soldier, sailor, Marine or airman. The Vietnam Veterans Memorial recognizes American military members for their service in Vietnam, irrespective of sex, rank, service, race, or occupational specialty. To single out one of these criteria for special recognition in the form of a statue on the site of the Vietnam Veterans Memorial would not only violate the integrity of the design, but would be discriminatory.

Rostker *v.* Goldberg, *1981*

Classical republican tradition linked political identity with property holding and military obligation. In the United States, the obligations of male citizens include military service; the obligations of female citizens do not. Although women had been employed by the army and navy as nurses, not until World War II were they involved in military service in substantial numbers. Women's sections of the Army, Navy, and Air Force accepted volunteers under strict regulations which excluded them from combat duty, limited the numbers who could be accepted and the rank to which they could rise (until 1967 no woman could serve in a command position), and offered fewer fringe benefits than were received by servicemen of the same rank (see *Frontiero* v. *Richardson*, pp. 545–46). Partly in response to the Vietnam War, many of these restrictions were eased; in 1976 women were admitted to West Point, Annapolis, and the Air Force Academy.

When President Jimmy Carter recommended the resumption of peacetime selective service registration in 1980, he proposed registering women as well as men. The president and his supporters on the Armed Services Committees of the Senate and the House sought to separate the issue of registration, the actual draft, and the use of women in combat. They argued that decision on whether women would actually be drafted (and, if so, whether mothers would be exempted) and whether women would be placed in combat positions could be left for future debate. They also argued that registration did

---

101 Sup Ct. 2646. For extended comment see Linda K. Kerber, *No Constitutional Right to Be Ladies: Women and the Obligations of Citizenship* (New York: Hill and Wang, 1998), ch. 5.

not necessarily mean that one would be drafted, for men who planned to request exemption as conscientious objectors were still required to register.

Opponents insisted that the issues were linked: if the sexes were treated equally in registration, it would be impossible to reject equity in future treatment. Since the primary goal of Selective Service was to identify combat-ready men, opponents also argued that if women were not used in combat there was no need to register them. In the course of debate contrasting ideas of the role of women in American society were expressed.* This debate overlapped with the debate on the Equal Rights Amendment, taking place at the same time; probably the single most effective argument used by opponents of the ERA was that it would involve women in the draft. In the end, Congress approved registration for men but not for women.

The Military Selective Service Act of 1980 was challenged by a group of men who argued that they had been denied the equal protection of the laws guaranteed by the Fifth Amendment. The Carter administration was now placed in the odd position of having to defend the statue it had opposed.

Note the reasoning of the Supreme Court and its emphasis on the exclusion of women from combat positions. Although the argument was not offered in *Rostker*, some men have argued that if women are drafted but not placed in combat positions, the likelihood that any specific man would be assigned to a noncombat job diminishes and men are therefore placed at greater risk for combat assignments. Moreover, some men in similar situations, such as police or prison guards, have demanded the exclusion of women on the grounds that women can not back men up effectively in physical confrontation; thus giving women equal opportunity to become prison guards actually increases the risks to men. Yet another perspective is offered by the legal historian Leo Kanowitz, who argues that "the equanimity with which men's exclusive liability for military service is regarded by the general population, even during times of violent combat . . . [suggests] the philosophy that a man's life is less precious than that of a woman." Do you agree?

MR. JUSTICE WILLIAM H. REHNQUIST DELIVERED THE OPINION OF THE COURT:

The question presented is whether the Military Selective Service Act . . . violates the Fifth Amendment to the United States Constitution in authorizing the President to require the registration of males and not females. Whenever called upon to judge the constitutionality of an Act of Congress—"the gravest and most delicate duty that this Court is called upon to perform," . . . the Court accords "great weight to the decisions of Congress."

. . . This case is quite different from several of the gender-based discrimination cases we have considered in that . . . Congress did not act "unthinkingly" or "reflexively and not for any considered reason." . . . The question of registering women for the draft not only received considerable national attention and

was the subject of wide-ranging public debate, but also was extensively considered by Congress in hearings, floor debate, and in committee. Hearings held by both Houses of Congress in response to the President's request for authorization to register women adduced extensive testimony and evidence concerning the issue. . . . the decision to exempt women from registration was not the "accidental byproduct of a traditional way of thinking about women. . . ."

Women as a group, however, unlike men as a group, are not eligible for combat. The restrictions on the participation of women in combat in the Navy and Air Force are statutory. . . . The Army and Marine Corps preclude the use of women in combat as a matter

*See the *Congressional Record,* June 10, 1980.

of established policy. . . . The existence of the combat restrictions clearly indicates the basis for Congress' decision to exempt women from registration. The purpose of registration was to prepare for a draft of combat troops. Since women are excluded from combat, Congress concluded that they would not be needed in the event of a draft, and therefore decided not to register them. . . . This is not a case of Congress arbitrarily choosing to burden one of two similarly situated groups, such as would be the case with an all-black or all-white, or an all-Catholic or all-Lutheran, or an all-Republican or all-Democratic registration. Men and women, because of the combat restrictions on women, are simply not similarly situated for purposes of a draft or registration for a draft. . . . The Constitution requires that Congress treat similarly situated persons similarly, not that it engage in gestures of superficial equality.

MR. JUSTICE BYRON WHITE, DISSENTING:

I assume . . . that excluding women from combat positions does not offend the Constitution . . . [but] I perceive little, if any, indication that Congress itself concluded that every position in the military, no matter how far removed from combat, must be filled with combat-ready men.

MR. JUSTICE THURGOOD MARSHALL, DISSENTING:

The Court today places its imprimatur on one of the most potent remaining public expressions of "ancient canards about the proper role of women." It upholds a statute that requires males but not females to register for the draft, and which thereby categorically excludes women from a fundamental civic obligation.

LINDA BIRD FRANCKE
Women in the Gulf War

In 1990, women made up 11 percent of the all-volunteer armed forces. They were placed in positions on patrol ships and stationed on the fringes of the defense perimeter. They were also placed in "combat support" units; in the Panama invasion of 1989 Army captain Linda Bray led a military police unit in an exchange of fire while conducting what had been expected to be a routine police mission. Five women were killed in the Gulf War of 1991 and, as Linda Bird Francke describes in the essay that follows, two were taken prisoner. Two women pilots based on the *U.S.S. Enterprise* flew successful combat missions in the Arabian Gulf in December 1998. What implications, if any, do these developments have for the reasoning of the Supreme Court in *Rostker?*

On January 30, 1991, almost two weeks into the air war against Iraq, NBC's Pentagon correspondent Fred Francis made one of his twice daily calls to Riyadh, Saudi Arabia. Iraqi troops were battling U.S., Qatari and Saudi troops for control of the Saudi border town of Khafji. In what would prove to be the fiercest battle of the war, three hundred Iraqis and eleven Marines would be killed. But the news tip Francis got from an Army colonel in Riyadh set up the dynamic the Pentagon feared most. "We've got a white female missing and probably snatched by the Iraqis," the colonel told Francis. "Holy shit, do we have problems now."

Francis hurried down the hall in the Pentagon to Defense Department spokesman Pete Williams's office to confirm the tip. "Pete got on the phone and called Powell's office," recalls Francis. "Powell's office confirmed it and I went on the air with it. It was boom-boom-boom. There was no hesitation at all." NBC's bombshell led the evening news: an American servicewoman attached to an Army transportation company was missing near Khafji in the northern Saudi desert.

The news was particularly ominous in concert with the Iraqi announcement shortly thereafter that a "number of male and female transcripts" had been captured. The Iraqi government's assurance that any female prisoners would receive "good treatment in accordance with the spirit of lofty Islamic laws" was questionable in light of the stories circulating about the Iraqi brutality toward women in Kuwait.

The Pentagon was less concerned about the well-being of the missing servicewoman than it was about the effect of a female prisoner of war on the national psyche. Fifty years had passed since the nurses had been captured by the Japanese and they had been officers. The servicewoman, who was soon identified as Melissa Rathbun-Nealy, a twenty-year-old Army truck driver with the 233rd Transportation Company, would be the first enlisted American woman to be captured by an enemy in history.

If indeed she had been captured, there was concern that the Iraqis would publicly exploit her, potentially eroding public support for the conflict during the buildup to the ground war. Such speculation about the negative effect of female POWs on the "national will" had circulated for years, though there

had been no such erosion over the nurses in World War II.

The unanswerable question lay in the potential propaganda visuals of women POWs being marched through the streets of Baghdad, women being among the downed, battered Allied pilots captured by the Iraqis and displayed on Iraqi television in January, a woman's face replacing the swollen, scratched face of captured Navy pilot Jeffrey Zaun which ran on the cover of *Newsweek*. Similar images of blindfolded American diplomatic hostages in Iran had helped bring down Jimmy Carter's presidency in 1980. The political effect of women POWs was incalculable.

"Will it cause such a public outcry that our leaders will be forced to terminate the conflict under less than desirable terms and in spite of any national goals which may not have been attained?" Air Force Major Wayne Dillingham had written the year before the Gulf war. "Or, in the alternative, will the outcry incite us to conduct reprisal-type operations which, in turn, may unnecessarily escalate the conflict?"[1]

Perhaps that is why the Pentagon professed not to know what had happened to Specialist Rathbun-Nealy and her co-driver, Specialist David Lockett, or how they had ended up in Khafji. The scuttlebutt going around the Pentagon involved a sexual tryst. "They thought they'd gotten lost for the purpose of being alone," says a Pentagon observer. "They still do." And a new round of military gender politics began.

Instead of declaring Rathbun-Nealy and Lockett as POWs or missing in action, the Army's accounting of their disappearance merely classified them as DUSTWUN, or duty status whereabouts unknown, a low-level categorization that simply meant the Army had no idea where they were or what had happened to them. "They found her truck and she and a man in her truck had disappeared," Pentagon spokesman Lieutenant Colonel Douglas Hart would say a year after the fact. "We make no assumptions."

Leo Rathbun, Rathbun-Nealy's father, was convinced the Pentagon was covering up his daughter's capture. All the evidence pointed toward her and her partner being taken prisoner by the Iraqis. Not only had Iraq reported "female transcripts" captured, but on February 10, ten days after Rathbun-Nealy's disappearance, NBC News reported that a captured Iraqi said he had transported two American prisoners—a white woman and a black man—to the city of Basra.

"There was never any doubt that they'd been taken prisoner, never a question among reporters covering the story that she was believed by senior leadership to be missing and a POW," says Fred Francis.

But the Pentagon stuck to its low-level story. "The [rescuers] found the truck she was in and it appeared to be an accident," insisted Lieutenant Colonel Hart. "So we couldn't say what the reasons were. The truck wasn't blown up or anything. It couldn't be proven that they had engaged the enemy, so to speak."

Rathbun hounded the Pentagon to have Melissa declared either MIA or POW. Not only was he worried that his daughter might be left behind when the war ended because she wasn't on an official list, he also wanted her to get whatever benefits were due her. "I told them, if she survives this thing and gets home, she won't receive any MIA or POW benefits because you bastards won't say she is one, even if you know she really is," says Rathbun.

It wasn't until February 14, two weeks after Rathbun-Nealy and Lockett had disappeared, that the Rathbuns got an official accounting of their daughter's disappearance. The bare facts in the Army casualty report noted only that Melissa was "last seen" on January 30, 1991, when the two trucks in her convoy "took a wrong turn." When Melissa's truck "became stuck in the sand trying to turn around," the second truck "went for assistance." A Marine Corps patrol found her 22-wheel vehicle "in the vicinity of Ras Al Khafji, Saudi Arabia," but "could not locate the soldier."[2]

The more telling details were in the Army letter accompanying the casualty report and came from the truck drivers who had been following Rathbun-Nealy and Lockett in the second truck. By their account, the young soldiers had thought they were heading back to their base when they were headed toward the fighting in Khafji. Their error became apparent when the two trucks maneuvered around a freshly destroyed Saudi tank partially blocking the road north of Khafji only to be met by two explosions and "the sound of debris hitting their vehicle." Seeing "what they perceived to be enemy troops" ahead near the archway into Khafji, the soldiers tried to turn

their 22-wheel trucks around to escape. The second truck made it, but Rathbun-Nealy and Lockett's lead truck crashed into a wall. The last sight the escaping soldiers had of Rathbun-Nealy and Lockett was of the pair still sitting in their crippled truck as Iraqi soldiers approached. When a rescue party of Marines arrived soon thereafter, they found the truck with a flat tire and its engine still running, but "no trace of Melissa or Specialist Lockett."

More clues to Rathbun-Nealy's status in the Army letter came from Saudi interrogation reports of Iraqi soldiers captured during the battle for Khafji. An Iraqi lieutenant told Saudi interrogators he had "witnessed the capture of an American male and female" and that "both had been injured." The "white female," he reported, had "sustained an injury to her arm." Two other Iraqi prisoners of war told their Saudi interrogators what had already been reported by NBC News: the POWs had seen a "white female and a black male" near the city of Basra in southern Iraq.

Based on these reports, the Army notified the Rathbuns, the Army was changing Melissa's status from duty status whereabouts unknown to missing, which put her under the jurisdiction of the National Prisoner of War Information Center. The Army stopped short, however, of declaring Melissa a POW or even MIA, a designation reserved for personnel missing involuntarily as a result of "hostilities directed against the United States."[3] "While there are indications that Melissa and Specialist Lockett may have been captured, the reports received are unconfirmed and unsubstantiated," read the letter from the Army chief of POW/MIA Affairs.[4]

The Army's letter made Leo Rathbun even more furious. Not only had it taken the Army two weeks to at least declare his daughter missing, he was convinced that the Pentagon was denying her POW or MIA status because of her gender. "Bush was afraid of adverse publicity with a woman captured," he says.

The Defense Department denied the charge of gender politics. "There was a long delay in declaring them MIA and I can't remember exactly the reason," says Pete Williams, who joined NBC News after the war. "I don't recall that it was a sensitivity about women. No one ever told me, 'let's hold off on this because she's a woman.'"

But Rathbun-Nealy's presumed capture

was all about gender politics. While the Pentagon was playing down her military status, the civilian sector was playing up her sexual status. Though the International Red Cross had predicted that any U.S. woman taken POW would be treated in accordance with the Geneva Conventions and shown the respect afforded women in the Iraqi culture, Rathbun-Nealy became a presupposed rape victim.[5]

Historically, no U.S. servicewomen had been sexually molested as POWs, including the nurses in the Pacific and Lieutanant Reba Whittle, an Army flight nurse who was captured by the Germans in September 1944 after her hospital plane was shot down. The North Vietnamese had not molested Monika Schwinn, a German nurse who had endured forced marches, disease and near starvation in her three and a half years of captivity in Vietnam, including a stint in 1973 as the only woman prisoner at the infamous "Hanoi Hilton."[6] But Rathbun-Nealy's projected sexual molestation overshadowed all other concerns about her disappearance, including her reported injuries.

"I was asked by a reporter what I thought about that little girl's chances of being mistreated in Iraq," says former World War II POW Sally Millett. "I said I would doubt that. I would be inclined to think that she would be treated quite well. The Muslims aren't that mean. And they don't hate women any more or as much as American men hate women."

Rathbun-Nealy as symbolic rape victim was seized on by both sides of the growing debate about women in combat. The National Organization for Women adopted the position of [the female students at the Defense's survival, evasion, resistance, and escape (SERE) schools] in trying to preempt any reaction that would jeopardize servicewomen's future roles. "We don't think rape is a problem peculiar to women," said NOW vice president Rosemary Dempsey only four day after Melissa vanished. "Men also are victims of rape and sodomy. We'd strongly hope all POWs would be treated in accord with the Geneva Convention and would consider any kind of brutalization affecting either sex equally horrible."[7]

Conservatives were just as quick to adopt the position of SERE's male students in order to limit the future utilization of servicewomen. "It's not a good idea to try to obliterate concerns about a woman's reproductive system

and the kinds of humiliation she could be forced to endure," said Jean Yarborough, a professor at Bowdoin College who used the POW issue to question the combat support jobs women had held for almost twenty years. Phyllis Schlafly, president of the Eagle Forum, added: "It's absolutely ridiculous to have women in combat. It's an embarrassment to our country."[8]

While the debate raged in Washington over her reproductive organs and her official status, the twenty-year-old truck driver was very much a POW in the Gulf. Suffering from shrapnel wounds and a bullet through the upper arm, she had been taken first to a prison cell in Basra, then on to a prison in Baghdad. She was, in fact, safer from sexual abuse in Baghdad than were her fellow female soldiers in the field. At least twenty-five servicewomen were sexually assaulted in the Gulf, while Rathbun-Nealy had only one minor and brief sexual incident as a POW. En route by truck from Khafji to Baghdad, she would tell her father, one of her guards had reached over and touched her breasts. When she slapped him, he stopped and did not try again.

Her guards in Baghdad were sympathetic. One, an Arab Christian, gave her a crucifix and another, an Iraqi with relatives in Detroit, gave her a rosary. An English-speaking officer took a particular shine to her, chasing away the Iraqis who gawked at her in her cell and bringing her food. "I'm probably the only POW who gained weight in prison," she would say after her release. Instead of abusing her, the Iraqi officer ended up proposing to her. "She told him she was already married and that her country didn't allow multiple husbands," says her father.

On March 4, 1991, Melissa Rathbun-Nealy was among the first group of U.S. POWs to be exchanged for Iraqi POWs. She was still officially listed as missing by the Army, though U.S. pilots flying over Baghdad had reported seeing her in her prison compound. The Pentagon's stubbornness, whether calculated or not, would make the first television pictures of Rathbun-Nealy still wearing Iraq's yellow prisoner-of-war uniform doubly sweet to Leo Rathbun. "I called that jackass in the Pentagon at 3 a.m. in the morning," says Rathbun. "'Now, you asshole, will you declare her a prisoner of war?'"

The World War II nurses, who themselves had still been classified as missing a year and a half into their three-year captivity, were more impressed by Rathbun-Nealy's bearing, regardless of what she had endured. "When she came off the plane, she had her head up and her hair combed and she walked like a real American woman," says former Navy nurse Mary Nelson. "I was so proud of her."

The nurses were equally proud two days later when a civilian jet chartered by the International Red Cross flew the last load of fifteen U.S. POWs from Baghdad to Riyadh. Among them, with both her arms in slings, was Army Flight Surgeon Major Rhonda Cornum. No one knew yet that Cornum's weeklong experience as a POW would be reduced to a single incident and prove pivotal in the debate over women in combat.

On February 27, 1991, the last day of the four-day ground war, "Doc" Cornum and seven other crew members were flying low and fast over the Iraqi desert in a Black Hawk search-and-rescue helicopter. Accompanied by two Apache attack helicopters and directed by an AWACS radar plane overhead, they were answering an emergency call to retrieve a downed and injured Air Force pilot. "He was worth getting before the Iraqis got to him," says Cornum, who was planning to jump out of the helicopter to quickly stabilize the pilot on the ground before he was loaded and whisked away. "He was flying a mission for the Army. He was the highest decorated guy in the Air Force. And he was my husband's classmate at the Air Force Academy."

The Black Hawk crew was startled when the seemingly empty desert suddenly erupted into flashes of green light and the crack of anti-aircraft guns. "It was as if we were a lawn mower that had run over a beehive, and the bees were coming up to sting," Cornum wrote later in her Gulf war memoir.[9] While the door gunners sprayed return machine-gun fire, the protective infantrymen aboard the Black Hawk pushed Cornum to the floor. In misguided chivalry they covered her body with theirs, thus pinning Cornum in a direct line with the Iraqi fire coming from below.

The last words Cornum heard after the Black Hawk took a thunderous hit came from a pilot yelling, "We're going in." By the time she regained consciousness on the desert floor

and saw five Iraqi officers looking down at her, both her arms had been broken between the elbow and the shoulder, a bone in her little finger had been shot away, the ligaments in her right knee were torn beyond repair and she had lost half the blood in her body from a bullet lodged in her shoulder. Even at that, Cornum was lucky. She was one of three crew members to be taken prisoner. The other five crew members—the two pilots, one of the door gunners and two of the infantrymen—died in the crash.

As Cornum's Iraqi captors led her by the hair from one command bunker to the next in their desert compound, she was well aware she had not had any prisoner-of-war training. SERE school was reserved primarily for high-flying aircraft crews whose return to earth by parachute made them prime targets for enemy capture. Army helicopters flew so fast and low in combat that the crews didn't even wear parachutes and were more or less expected to die if their helicopters went down.

The Code of Conduct was also just a dim thirteen-year-old memory to Cornum from Officer Basic Course. What little she remembered came from old war movies and from her husband, Kory, who had been a SERE instructor at the Air Force Academy. She did know that under the terms of the Geneva Conventions, a flight surgeon shouldn't be taken prisoner of war at all. But she had purposely left her medical identity card behind. Not only did she think it would do her little good if she were captured on a combat search-and-rescue mission, she also didn't want to be treated any differently from the rest of the crew. Forced to kneel on her one good leg in the enemy compound with a gun pressed into the back of her head, Cornum, thirty-six, was as much a POW as the surviving twenty-year-old infantryman kneeling beside her.

For the next seven days Cornum was shuttled blindfolded between Iraqi bunkers in the desert, the Baath Party office and a health clinic in Basra, a military hospital and a final cell in Baghdad. Like Melissa Rathbun-Nealy, she had only one, though very unpleasant, sexual incident. On her first night of captivity, as she and the young infantryman, Troy Dunlap, were being transported to Basra in the back of a truck, an Iraqi guard suddenly unzipped her flight suit and started kissing and mauling her. "I was manually molested, anally and vaginally," Cornum would tell me later. While Dunlap sat helplessly on the other side of the truck, only Cornum's broken arms and screams of pain kept the Iraqi from consummating the assault. "I would have gotten raped but he couldn't get my flight suit off," says Cornum.

Cornum was not physically molested again. Indeed, her experience in captivity seems a benchmark in international cross-gender sensitivity. With her broken arms dangling and tied in front of her Cornum persuaded her next Iraqi guards to cut off her flight suit with a knife and pull down her underpants so she could go to the bathroom. They then voluntarily reclothed her in a blue wool bathrobe. "All three of them averted their eyes, or looked me straight in the eye, so I would know they weren't leering," Cornum wrote later.

In Basra, she depended on Dunlap and, later, other male POWs not only to feed and clothe her, but also for the most intimate help. "I had my period and they helped me go to the bathroom and remove the tampons and all that stuff," says Cornum. "It was bad planning to have my period. I'm not sure what good planning would be, but it just happened that way. I didn't want to die of toxic shock out there. I wanted to make it home."

On the fifteen-hour bus ride with other blindfolded POWs to Baghdad on her fourth day of captivity, Cornum developed chills and a fever from blood poisoning and had to manipulate her broken finger to drain the pus. She was cheered, however, when she looked out from under her blindfold and saw the name tag on a fellow prisoner with a broken leg: it was the Air Force pilot she and her crew had been on their way to save.

At home, Cornum's father was as worried about his daughter as Leo Rathbun was about his. In the brave new world of role reversals, Cornum's father was sending furious telegrams to George Bush and Norman Schwarzkopf saying, "You've lost my daughter. What are you going to do about it?" while his daughter was in Baghdad listening to Troy Dunlap being interrogated and beaten. "Shouting. Silence. Whap, the sound of a hand across Troy's face," Cornum writes. "I felt terrible, helpless."

But Norrington's prognosis turned out to be correct. [Giles Norrington was a Navy com-

bat reconnaissance pilot and a former POW in Vietnam.] While the U.S. prisoners in Cornum's group could hear each other's interrogation, they were interrogated separately. Cornum braced for the worst when she was brought in for her interrogation and saw Dunlap sitting on a chair with his head between his knees and tied with a rope to his boots before he was led away. But whether it was her obvious injuries, her status as a medical officer or her gender, she was not beaten.

Norrington was also correct in predicting that a woman would be more apt to answer the interrogator's questions. But Cornum deliberately gave the wrong answers. After lying about such inquiries as to what direction her helicopter had been headed when it was shot down (straight north, she had answered, instead of due east), she was abruptly dismissed by the interrogating officer. "Was that it? Was it over?" Cornum would write. "The officer said nothing."

Her release came just as abruptly. On March 5, day 7 of her captivity, Cornum was awakened at 3 a.m. in her military hospital room, blindfolded and taken by bus to a cement block of cells somewhere in Baghdad. A guard threw a pair of sneakers and a plastic bag into her cell containing a yellow suit with the words PW stenciled on the pocket. She was then reblindfolded and bused to another location. But this time when the blindfolds were removed, she and at least twenty other yellow-suited prisoners were in the lobby of a luxury hotel. "You are safe. You are now in the custody of the International Committee of the Red Cross," someone called out. "It's over and you are going home." Not until the Red Cross plane left Iraqi airspace the next day, however, and entered the air over Saudi Arabia, did the POWs erupt into cheers.

Cornum and Rathbun-Nealy came home to the same disproportionate attention which was showered on all servicewomen in the Gulf. Rathbun-Nealy, who had been missing for over a month, had become an international celebrity. In France, a photograph of the twenty-year-old truck driver ran on the cover of *Paris-Match*. The president of Italy sent her a huge bouquet of flowers and she was declared an honorary citizen of an Italian town named Melissa. Newspapers around the world carried her photo on the front page and a special edition of *Life* magazine ran a cover photograph of Norman Schwarzkopf hugging her in Riyadh. "Survivor of 32 Too Many Arabian Nights, Melissa Rathbun-Nealy Heads Home from Baghdad" ran a story in *People.*

The attention upset Rathbun-Nealy, who was just one of the ten prisoners of war released on March 4. "She was very embarrassed that she was considered a hero. 'I just got stuck on the sand,'" she told her father. "She literally disappeared as much as she could. She didn't want publicity."

But Saddam Hussein and his armed forces had given U.S. servicemen a gift. By taking Rathbun-Nealy and Cornum prisoners of war, by not exploiting them for propaganda as they had the captured male pilots, by returning Rathbun-Nealy in apparent good health and Cornum in better shape than she was when she was shot down, the Iraqi forces had reassured the American public about the viability of women in combat.

For all the trepidation and the Pentagon over women POWs, the public had not overreacted. "Women did get captured," says Pete Williams, "but I don't recall at the time any more great public outrage about that other than the general mistreatment of American POWs by the Iraqis."

Cornum did not reveal the groping episode in her press interviews. Both she and Rathbun-Nealy did tell the SERE agency about their respective incidents in their POW debriefings, but no one else. Like her female counterparts at SERE school, Cornum resented the issue of sexual abuse being seen solely as a woman's issue. "None of the male POWs asked me whether I got molested. I didn't ask any of the guys, either," says Cornum. "The only people who asked were inquisitive reporters." Cornum insisted her feelings of helplessness listening to Troy Dunlap being beaten were no different from his feelings when she was being molested on the truck. "I don't think Troy liked it," she says. "But I didn't like it when they beat him up, either."

It was religion, Cornum told me, that was far more of a danger to her fellow male POWs in Iraq than her gender was to her. "If we're going to pick people to send to war based on cultures, we should have taken out all the Jewish soldiers and left them home," she says. "The Iraqis asked me my religion, but they made all the male POWs drop their pants so they could see if they were circumcised. These guys had to do a lot of talking to convince the Iraqis that circumcision was an American tradition, not Jewish, or they would have shot them. No question of that."

It would be another year before Cornum's episode in the back of the truck would become public knowledge and deemed so explosive in the debate over women in combat that it merited a front-page story in the *New York Times.* Lost in the public frenzy over the sexual groping was the far greater slight to Cornum.

For her voluntary participation in the search for the downed pilot, for all the injuries she suffered in the downing of the Black Hawk, she alone among the surviving crew did not get a medal for the search-and-rescue mission in Iraq. The Army refused to admit she had been in combat. "I got put in for a Distinguished Flying Cross and a Bronze Star," says Cornum. "Everyone else on my mission got a DFC. I got nothing."

The World War II nurses were not surprised. For their service under constant shelling in the Pacific and their three years of internment by the Japanese, the nurses, too, had come home to public, but not military recognition. "The eighty-four women were all but ignored when they came back," says Giles Norrington, the ex-Vietnam POW. "There were press things, to be sure. But the military ignored them. The history books, and that's what really counts, ignored them." ...

[But] the Gulf war marked the end of women's invisibility in the military. The women who died or were taken prisoners of war, combined with the seemingly painless rout of the enemy, elevated women's military contribution and cemented their new public status. [Congress established a Presidential Commission on the Assignment of Women in the Armed Forces; it held hearings in the summer of 1992.]

Female prisoners of war had dominated the combat debate from the moment Hays Parks, chief of the Army's International Law Branch, testified on June 8, 1992, that each of the Army women taken prisoner of war in the Gulf had been "treated more favorably than their U.S. and Coalition male counterparts," though each had been the "victim of indecent assaults."[10]

Five former prisoners of war had given testimony later the same day, including three men held in Vietnam, a World War II Navy nurse interned by the Japanese and Desert Storm POW Major Rhonda Cornum. The commissioners had not asked the male POWs to elaborate on the torture they had endured which had left one unable to lift his arm above the height of his shoulder. Elaine Donnelly zeroed in on Cornum, however, demanding to know the nature of her "indecent assault." Cornum's reply, that she had been "violated manually, vaginally and rectally" the year before in Iraq, had provided an emotional argument against women in combat and generated public interest in the hearings for the first time.[11]

"Sexual Assaults of Female POW's Withheld from Panel," read the story headline in *USA Today.* "Women in War: Ex-Captive Tells of Ordeal" read the front-page story in the *New York Times*.[12] While male POWs had traditionally been viewed as heroes, Cornum had become a victim.

The cultural divide over female POWs was the most graphic to come out of the presidential commission. The female pilots monitoring the commission had been furious at Donnelly for invading Cornum's privacy. "Mrs. Donnelly's disgraceful conduct was an attempt to exploit Major Cornum's courage to further her well-known political agenda oposing women in combat," WMA [Women Military Advisors] president Rosemary Mariner wrote to the *Washington Times*.[13] Commissioner Mimi Finch was angry that Donnelly had pressed Cornum for details about her treatment as a POW, but not the male POWS. "Why didn't they call in Jeffrey Zaun and ask him what it was like or what made him talk?" said Finch. "It just seemed very sexist that Cornum would be asked that question and nobody else would."

Cornum had been the least disturbed. "Getting raped or abused or whatever is one more bad thing that can happen to you as a prisoner of war. There's about four hundred bad things I can think of and it's not the worst of them," Cornum had testified, calling her incident an "occupational hazard." The other female POW, Army truck driver Melissa Rathbun-Nealy, dismissed her designation as a "victim of indecent assault." A letter sent on her behalf to the presidential commission reiterated that she "at all times steadfastly maintained that she was not the victim of sex-

ual abuse and continues to so maintain this position."[14]

But another "difference" had been identified between servicemen and servicewomen, another perceived threat to unit cohesion. "There is no question in my mind that I would certainly lean toward giving the enemy something if I knew they were raising hell with a fellow female prisoner," former Vietnam POW and Air Force Colonel Norman McDaniel testified.[15]

The POW issue became a matter of white male "values" in their protectionist arguments against women in combat. "I am not prepared to see America's mothers and daughters paraded down the streets of Baghdad and subjected to abuse, when it's not necessary," testified Rhonda Cornum's battalion commander, Lieutenant Colonel William Bryan. "Now those are my values as an American citizen."[16]

"Values" would motivate General Maxwell Thurman's commision vote against the female pilots. "No people want women to get victimized," Thurman would tell me. "Even if the pilots want to get victimized, we don't want to get them victimized. You follow me? It's not our American value system." The word "values" was never attached to the American concept of equal opportunity or individual choice or the meritocracy in which the military took such pride, but was being denied women.

The POW issue was never about women, but about men. In the commission's final report to the president, every argument against women in combat would revolve around the pain women's capture would cause, not to the women themselves but to their male colleagues. "The mistreatment of women taken as POWs could have a negative impact on male captives," read one rationale against women in ground combat. "The presence of women might cause additional morale problems for male prisoners," read an argument against women in combat aircraft.[17]

The philosophical battle over women in combat was so incendiary that the conservative bloc staged a walkout in the midst of the commission's final votes in November. "The Fadeout Five," as the Navy Times called them, demanded, and would get, their own section in the final report titled "Alternative Views: The Case Against Women in Combat," written before a single vote on combat had been taken. . . . One white male commissioner would cite the Scriptures, the Bible, God and his identity as a "Christian" in his combat case against women.[18]

The presidential commission voted resoundingly against women in ground combat, and even called on Congress to enact a new combat exclusion law shielding the Army and Marine Corps from women and a hypothetical draft. (During the Vietnam War, 99.7 percent of draftees had gone to the Army or Marine Corps; during the Korea War, 100 percent, presumably as ground combat troops.) For extra insurance against women, the commission voted to retain the DOD's "Risk Rule" that supposedly distanced women in support roles from combat and against the nonissue of requiring women to register for the draft.[19]

By one vote, the commission voted to lift the combat exclusion law against women on Navy combat vessels, save for submarines and amphibious ships. By the same margin, they voted to reinstate the combat exclusion law against women pilots. The deciding vote against the pilots was based on menstruation.[20]

"I'd like to know, is it true or false that flight schedules are adjusted for menstrual cycles?" asked Commissioner Charles Moskos, who would author the controversial "Don't Ask, Don't Tell" policy for gays in the military.[21]

A chorus of noes came from the pilots in the back of the room.

No, confirmed Commissioner Meredith Neizer.

Commissioner Finch, an Army helicopter pilot, explained that aviators, male or female, had the discretion to adjust their peacetime flight schedules if they hadn't slept well, had hangovers or felt under the weather so as not "to sacrifice the aircraft or themselves." "I do not believe menstruation in any way, shape or form is an issue here," she said.

But pilots' menstrual cycles continued to be a prime concern to the white male commissioners. Commissioner Darryl Henderson, an expert on male cohesion, suggested that during "the highest rate of flow," one study showed that women had an increased susceptibility to decompression sickness and hypoxia.

Commissioner Hogg questioned "menstrual considerations" as well, but reported he had heard it might be a problem for a forty-five-year-old woman pilot, but not for younger women.

The pilots sitting in the back of the room were incredulous at the turn the debate had taken. After nine months of military testimony about their qualifications as aviators, the hundreds of hours they had spent in the air in the Gulf refueling fighter planes and ferrying combat troops, the lives lost like Marie Rossi's, it had all come down to making men feel bad if women were taken prisoners of war and their menstrual periods. [Marie Rossi was an Army pilot and company commander who was killed in the Gulf War.]

The Clinton administration threw out the presidential commission recommendations on combat in April 1993. Adopting the DEOMI approach to diversity and replacing the defining category of gender with individual qualifications, Secretary of Defense Les Aspin removed the Risk Rule as "no longer appropriate," and ordered the services to open combat cockpits to women and the eager, post-Tailhook Navy to seek congressional repeal of the 1948 law against women on combat ships.[22] In 1994 the Navy opened combat ships to women and the Army, under pressure from its black male secretary, Togo D. West Jr., muscled the white male club of the Army into opening over 32,000 new jobs to women. Only Army and Marine units engaged in direct combat with an enemy—infantry, armor and much of field artillery—remained closed to women.

NOTES

1. Wayne E. Dillingham, "The Possibility of American Military Women Becoming POWs: Justification for Combat Exclusion Rules?" *Federal Bar News & Journal*, May 1990, p. 228.

2. Department of the Army, "Report of Casualty D-0702," Feb. 11, 1991.

3. Response to a Freedom of Information Act request from the U.S. Total Army Personnel Command, Alexandria, VA, July 26, 1993.

4. Letter to Mr. and Mrs. Leo Rathbun from the POW/MIA Division of the U.S. Total Army Personnel Command, Alexandria, VA, Feb. 14, 1991, from Lt. Col. J. G. Cole, chief, POW/MIA Affairs.

5. "Panel One Report to the Presidential Commission," p. 92.

6. Monika Schwinn, "Break Your Teeth on Me," *Der Spiegel*, March 26, 1973, pp. 46–57, from the library archives at Fort Belvoir, VA.

7. Joyce Price, "NOW Cites Woman POW," *Washington Times*, Feb. 4, 1991.

8. Ibid.

9. Rhonda Cornum as told to Peter Copeland, *She Went to War: The Rhonda Cornum Story* (Novato,

CA: Presidio, 1992), p. 9. The quotations in the next paragraphs are from pp. 13, 54, 174, 113, 115, and 162.

10. Testimony of Hays Parks, chief of the International Law Branch of the International and Operational Law Division Office of the Judge Advocate General, USA, to the presidential commission, June 8, 1992, Washington, DC.

11. Testimony of Rhonda Cornum to the presidential commission, June 8, 1992.

12. Laurence Jolidonin, "Sexual Assaults of Female POW's Withheld from Panel," *USA Today*, June 11, 1992. Elaine Sciolino, "Women in War: Ex-Captive Tells of Ordeal," *New York Times*, June 29, 1992, p. A1.

13. Letter from Cmdr. Rosemary Mariner to the *Washington Times*, June 28, 1992.

14. Letter to the presidential commission, June 11, 1992.

15. Air Force Col. Norman McDaniel was one of the prisoners of war giving testimony to the presidential commission on June 8, 1992.

16. Testimony of Lt. Col. William Bryan, USA, attack helicopter battalion commander, U.S. Army Aviation Center, to the presidential commission, Aug. 7, 1992, Los Angeles.

17. "Issue K: Ground Combat," "Issue L: Combat Aircraft," presidential commission report, pp. 25, 28.

18. George Wilson, "Opinion/Commentary," *Navy Times*, Nov. 30, 1991, Commissioner Ronald D. Ray, Commissioner Statements in the presidential commission report, p. 116.

19. Presidential commission report, pp. 24–27, 22, 36, 40, 41.

20. "Issue M: Combatant Vessels," presidential commission report, p. 31.

21. Commissioners' discussion and vote on women in combat cockpits, Nov. 3, 1992.

22. Memorandum from Secretary of Defense Les Aspin to the Secretaries of the Army, Navy and Air Force, the chairman of the Joint Chiefs of Staff, and the Assistant Secretaries of Defense for Personnel and Readiness and Reserve Affairs, Jan. 13, 1994.

DOCUMENT: Reliving the Immigrant Experience

> *Fu Lee, "After working so hard under such horrendous working conditions, we should at least get our pay."*

Defeat in South Vietnam and the exodus of Americans put the lives of large numbers of South Vietnamese in jeopardy. Since many of those fleeing had aided the U.S. during the Vietnam War, the United States offered them political asylum. Their arrival was part of a larger influx of Asian immigrants to the West Coast from China, Korea, and the Philippines. The most impoverished of these Asian newcomers, like their Latin American counterparts, encountered conditions in the U.S. strikingly similar to those faced by earlier generations of immigrants from eastern and southern Europe. Indeed, a quick reading of the follow account of Fu Lee's work experience suggests that it might have been written in the 1890s. The date is actually 1993.

Fu Lee's story serves as an important reminder that on the eve of the twenty-first century economic oppression persists, working environments are often hazardous, and union or collective bargaining protections do not exist for many employees.

Note Fu Lee's efforts to remedy her plight. That she turned for help to an organization of more established Asian-American women is a characteristic pattern among immigrants. Fu Lee's efforts and the efforts of those who assisted her place these women in the company of many other activists encountered in this volume.

Hello, my name is Fu Lee. I am forty-one years old, married, and I have a nine-year-old daughter. I have been living in Oakland Chinatown since I left Hong Kong twelve years ago. . . .

I worked as a seamstress at Lucky Sewing Co. for two years. Before that, I worked as a seamstress at other similar sweatshops. All of the workers worked long hours, ten to twelve hours a day and six to seven days a week. We were paid by the piece, which sometimes was below the minimum wage. Overtime pay was unheard of. You may think sewing is an easy job, but it requires a lot of skill. For fancy dresses, with laces, tiny buttons, and tricky fabric patterns, you really have to concentrate so you don't make any mistakes. My wage was never enough money for our family to live on.

We always worried about our daughter getting sick because we had no health insurance.

My eyes hurt from straining under poor lighting; my throat hurt because of the chemical fumes from the fabric dye. Sometimes, I would wear surgical masks so I don't have to breathe in all the dust from the fabric. My back never stopped hurting from bending over the sewing machine all day. Our boss was like a dictator. He was always pushing us to work faster. There was a sign in the shop that said, "No loud talking. You cannot go to the bathroom." When we did talk loudly or laugh during work, he would throw empty boxes at us and tell us to go back to work. When there was a rush order, we had to eat lunch at our work station.

Last year, my employer closed his shop

Excerpted from *Immigrant Women Speak Out on Garment Industry Abuse: A Community Hearing Initiated by Asian Immigrant Women Advocates,* May 1, 1993, Oakland, California, AIWA, 310 8th Street, Suite 301, Oakland, CA 94607 in *Making More Waves: New Writings by Asian-American Women,* edited by Elaine H. Kim, Lilia V. Villanueva and Asian American Women United of California (Boston: Beacon Press, 1997). Reprinted with permission.

Asefa Patel, age sixteen, and her sister Hafsalo visit the Flushing branch of the Queens Borough Public Library three or four times a week, "sometimes for school and sometimes for fun." The library has materials in Spanish, Chinese, Korean, Hebrew, Hindi, Urdu, Gujarati, and Russian; the hunger of young women for learning is as strong as it was in Rose Schneiderman's day. (Courtesy Nancy Siesel/New York Times)

The Vietnam War created hundreds of thousands of refugees; among them were these Hmong women, shown filling out tax forms in Seattle. Photo by Nancy D. Donnelly, from her book, Changing Lives of Refugee Hmong Women *(Seattle: University of Washington Press, 1994). (Courtesy of the University of Washington Press and Nancy D. Donnelly)*

and left us holding bad paychecks. We found out that he had filed for bankruptcy and had no intention of paying us our meager wages. The twelve Chinese seamstresses including myself were so mad. After working so hard under such horrendous working conditions, we should at least get our pay.

With the help of Asian Immigrant Women Advocates, we began searching for ways to get our pay.

DOCUMENTS: Feminists Name New Harms

Meritor Savings Bank *v.* Mechelle Vinson et al., *1986*

The term "sexual harassment" was unknown before the mid-1970s. One legal scholar has written, "the term was invented by feminist activists, given legal content by feminist litigators and scholars, and sustained by a wide-ranging body of scholarship generated largely by feminist academics." Another legal scholar observes "[f]or the first time in history, women have defined women's injuries in a law."*

Consider Part 1 of Section 703 of Title VII of the Civil Rights Act of 1964 (pp. 521–23). The authors of the statute were defining economic injuries, and for more than a decade the Equal Employment Opportunity Commission supported only economic claims of sex discrimination. But working women had long put up with behavior that, beginning in the 1970s, they began to say was also sex discrimination: supervisors who referred to all women as "whores," whether or not in joking tones; workplaces that had cheesecake or frankly pornographic calenders on the walls; and, worst of all, covert or explicit pressure to have sex with supervisors or employers for fear of losing their jobs if they refused.

Legal scholar Catharine MacKinnon gave names to two forms of sexual harassment: (1) "quid pro quo": when sexual submission to a supervisor becomes, either implicitly or explicitly, a condition of employment; and (2) "offensive working environment": when the conduct of a supervisor, co-employee, or client unreasonably interferes with an individual's work or creates an intimidating and hostile workplace. By the late 1970s, many behaviors that men had described as flirting, and that women had "put up with" because they saw no alternative, could be named and challenged. In 1980, the EEOC published an official set of guidelines describing behavior it would challenge as sexual harassment, even if the actors claimed they were merely flirting or "joking around."

In 1986, a unanimous Supreme Court for the first time formally recognized sexual harassment as a violation of Title VII. Catharine MacKinnon was one of the attorneys for Mechelle Vinson, who complained that she had been hired in 1974 as a teller-trainee by a vice president of Meritor Savings Bank and was steadily promoted for four years until she became assistant branch manager. During those four years, however, she had a sexual relationship with the man (Mr. Taylor) who had hired her; when she tried to decline his attentions, he exposed himself to her, and even forcibly raped her.

Vinson claimed that she had been the victim of both "quid pro quo" and offensive environment forms of sexual harassment. Vinson told the court "that because she was

---

*Martha Chamallas, "Writing About Sexual Harassment: A Guide to the Literature," *UCLA Women's Law Journal* IV (1993):37–38; Catharine MacKinnon, *Feminism Unmodified: Discourses on Life and Law* (Cambridge, Mass.: Harvard University Press, 1987) p. 105; Vicki Schultz, "Reconceptualizing Sexual Harassment," *Yale Law Journal* 107 (1998):1683–1805.

477 U.S. 57 (1986).

afraid of Taylor she never reported his harassment to any of his supervisors and never attempted to use the bank's complaint procedure." But when she was fired for what the bank claimed was excessive use of sick leave, she sued the bank, claiming sexual harassment and asking for punitive damages. The bank claimed that "any sexual harassment by Taylor was unknown to the bank and engaged in without its consent or approval."

A unanimous Court agreed with Vinson. What analogies do they see with race discrimination? Why do they hold Meritor Bank guilty as well as Mr. Taylor? Taylor argued that Vinson wore sexually provocative clothing. How much responsibility do you think the victim of sexual harassment should be expected to take for avoiding the harassment?

JUSTICE WILLIAM REHNQUIST:

This case presents important questions concerning claims of workplace "sexual harassment" brought under Title VII of the Civil Rights Act of 1964 . . . [Vinson] argues . . . that unwelcome sexual advances that create an offensive or hostile working environment violate Title VII. Without question, when a supervisor sexually harasses a subordinate because of the subordinate's sex, that supervisor "discriminate[s]" on the basis of sex. [Meritor Bank] does not challenge this proposition. It contends instead that in prohibiting discrimination with respect to "compensation, terms, conditions, or privileges" of employment, Congress was concerned with what petitioner describes as "tangible loss" of "an economic character," not "purely psychological aspects of the workplace environment."

We reject petitioner's view. First, the language of Title VII is not limited to "economic" or "tangible" discrimination. The phrase "terms, conditions, or privileges of employment" evinces a congressional intent "to strike at the entire spectrum of disparate treatment of men and women" in employment. . . . As

the Court of Appeals for the Eleventh Circuit wrote . . . in 1982: "Sexual harassment which creates a hostile or offensive environment for members of one sex is every bit the arbitrary barrier to sexual equality at the workplace that racial harassment is to racial equality. Surely a requirement that a man or woman run a gauntlet of sexual abuse in return for the privilege of being allowed to work and make a living can be as demeaning and disconcerting as the harshest of racial epithets."

. . . [W]e reject the . . . view that the mere existence of a grievance procedure and a policy against discrimination, coupled with respondent's failure to invoke that procedure, must insulate petitioner from liability. . . . the bank's grievance procedure apparently required an employee to complain first to her supervisor, in this case Taylor. Since Taylor was the alleged perpetrator, it is not altogether surprising that respondent failed to invoke the procedure and report her grievance to him. . . . [W]e hold that a claim of "hostile environment" sex discrimination is actionable under Title VII. . . .

A wave of attention to sexual harassment in the workplace took place after the fall of 1991, when hearings on the nomination of Clarence Thomas to the Supreme Court were interrupted by the charges of Anita Hill that he had sexually harassed her a decade earlier. Ironically, their encounter had taken place within the EEOC itself, where Thomas had been director and Hill had been a lawyer on his staff. In response, Thomas charged that he was himself victimized by the media attention. Adrienne Davis and Stephanie Wildman observe, "in a stunning sleight of hand, [Thomas] managed to convince all involved, including the Senate, that white racism, rather than a Black woman, had accused him of harassment."* Thomas's nomination to the Supreme Court was confirmed by the Senate.

Over the years since the *Meritor* decision, increasing numbers of workers have filed sexual harassment complaints, and a massive body of doctrine has developed on the details of the law's protection. In 1998 the Supreme Court ruled that harassment based on an employee's homosexuality could constitute sex discrimination, and that male-on-male harassment could be a cause of action (*Oncale* v. *Sundowner Offshore Services, Inc.*). The definition of an "offensive working environment" remains under debate. Legal theorist Vicki Schultz has proposed:

> Many of the most prevalent forms of harassment are actions that are designed to maintain work—particularly the more highly rewarded lines of work—as bastions of masculine competence and authority. Every day, in workplaces all over the country, men uphold the image that their jobs demand masculine mastery by acting to undermine their female colleagues' perceived (or sometimes even actual) competence to do the work. The forms of such harassment are wide-ranging. They include characterizing the work as appropriate for men only; denigrating women's performance or ability to master the job; providing patronizing forms of help in performing the job; withholding the training, information, or opportunity to learn to do the job well; engaging in deliberate work sabotage; . . . isolating women from the social networks that confer a sense of belonging . . . much of the time, harassment assumes a form that has little or nothing to do with sexuality but everything to do with gender.**

*Adrienne D. Davis and Stephanie M. Wildman, "The Legacy of Doubt: Treatment of Sex and Race in the Hill-Thomas Hearings," *Southern California Law Review* 65 (1992):1367.

**Schultz, p. 1687.

Violence Against Women Act, 1994

The Violence Against Women Act was part of a comprehensive Violent Crime Control and Law Enforcement Act passed in 1994. It was pathbreaking in establishing a new right: "All persons within the United States shall have the right to be free from crimes of violence motivated by gender." It defined a range of crimes against women as violations of their federal civil rights, crimes subject to federal remedies, so that a victim of a violent crime motivated by gender may bring a civil lawsuit in federal or state court, seeking money damages or an injunction.

42 U.S.C. § 13981 (1994).

(a) PURPOSE.—Pursuant to the affirmative power of Congress to enact this subtitle under section 5 of the Fourteenth Amendment to the Constitution, as well as under section 8 of Article I of the Constitution, it is the purpose of this subtitle to protect the civil rights of victims of gender motivated violence and to promote public safety, health, and activities affecting interstate commerce by establishing a Federal civil rights cause of action for victims of crimes of violence motivated by gender.

(b) RIGHT TO BE FREE FROM CRIMES OF VIOLENCE.—All persons within the United States shall have the right to be free from crimes of violence motivated by gender (as defined in subsection (d)).

(c) CAUSE OF ACTION.—A person (including a person who acts under color of any statute, ordinance, regulation, custom, or usage of any State) who commits a crime of violence motivated by gender and thus deprives another of the right declared in subsection (b) shall be liable to the party injured, in an action for the recovery of compensatory and punitive damages, injunctive and declaratory relief, and such other relief as a court may deem appropriate.

(d) DEFINITIONS.—For purposes of this section—

(1) the term "crime of violence motivated by gender" means a crime of violence committed because of gender or on the basis of gender, and due, at least in part, to an animus based on the victim's gender; and

(2) the term "crime of violence" means—

(A) an act or series of acts that would constitute a felony against the person or that would constitute a felony against property if the conduct presents a serious risk of physical injury to another, and that would come within the meaning of State or Federal offenses described in section 16 of title 18, United States Code, whether or not these acts have actually resulted in criminal charges, prosecution, or conviction and whether or not those acts were committed in the special maritime, territorial, or prison jurisdiction of the United States; and

(B) includes an act or series of acts that would constitute a felony described in subparagraph (A) but for the relationship between the person who takes such action and the individual against whom such action is taken.

The statute redefines domestic violence and sexual assault as infractions of the civil rights of the victim. It overrides the inadequate remedies that persist in many states. (For example, several states exempt cohabiting companions from rape laws, or permit defendants to introduce allegations of victims' past sexual behavior.) It provided federal penalties for sex crimes, including the sexual exploitation and other abuses of children, established a National Domestic Violence Telephone Hotline, and authorized public expenditures for increased security in public transportation systems and in national and urban parks. This statute also provides support for rape prevention and education programs, and for state and local government programs to improve the prosecution of domestic violence and child abuse cases. It created federal criminal penalties for anyone who travels across state lines with the intent to injure their spouse or intimate partner and then intentionally commits a crime of violence causing bodily injury.

The constitutionality of the the law was challenged in a case brought before the Court of Appeals for the Fourth Circuit (which includes Maryland, Virginia, West Virginia, North Carolina, and South Carolina). The appeals court ruled in March 1999 that Congress had reached too far in its interpretation of its right to regulate interstate commerce and that the Violence Against Women Act was a sweeping intrusion into matters traditionally reserved for the states. The ruling, which applies only to those states within the Fourth Circuit, is likely to be appealed to the Supreme Court.*

*Bronzonkala v. Virginia Polytechnic Institute 169 F. 3d 820 (1999).

Congresswoman Bella Abzug addressing a crowd in New York City in 1972. (Copyright © 1972 by Diana Mara Henry)

CONCLUSION

The New Feminism
and the Dynamics of Social Change

Jane Sherron De Hart

Fifty years after gaining the right to vote, women who had been suffragists and women young enough to be their great-granddaughters embarked on a new feminist movement. Referred to as feminism's second wave to distinguish it from an earlier surge occurring around 1910, this new movement was vigorous, diffuse, and highly controversial. It was, in fact, many movements. Some were predominantly white and acquired the labels liberal, radical, socialist, and cultural feminism. Others consisted largely of women of color who identified themselves variously as Black, Chicana, Asian American, Native American, or U.S. Third World Feminists. One cannot make simplistic assumptions about which variant an individual woman might embrace. (For example, Pauli Murray, an African American lawyer and writer, would have been more likely to describe herself as a liberal feminist rather than a Black feminist.) Nor can one assume that only women embraced this new feminism or that all women did so. "As an *ism* (an ideology), feminism presupposed a set of principles not necessarily belonging to every woman—nor limited to women," wrote historian Nancy Cott of first wave feminism.[1] Her observation also applies to second wave feminism. Some men, but not all women, embraced those principles and joined this renewed struggle to dismantle gender hierarchy. For those who did so, the goal became not mere formal equality, but genuine liberation. Their objective: to change not only laws and institutions, but values, patterns of behavior, personal relationships, and ultimately themselves.

The feminism explored in this essay is sometimes referred to as mainstream feminism. Emerging out of liberal and radical feminism, it has been a predominantly white phenomenon. In order to understand its origins and agendas, its opponents, and most important, its potential for changing society, it is necessary to examine the long-term economic and social changes that created an environment within which this strand of the movement could emerge. It is important also to appreciate the ferment of the 1960s, much of it initiated by African Americans, that provided white mainstream feminism with its ideological core, vitality, and impetus. To explore such origins is also to explore the extent to which these feminists confronted issues that their ideological foremothers had left unresolved.

UNFULFILLED EXPECTATIONS

By winning the vote in 1920, many women believed that the decisive battle in the long struggle for sexual equality had been won. The atmosphere was electric with a sense of achievement and expectation generated by the euphoria of the moment. The fact that enfranchisement had come on the heels of other reforms identified with women seemed evidence of their growing influence. Congress had passed legislation to protect women in industry, outlaw child labor, and enact prohibition—measures important to those who believed that women and children were the primary victims of exploitative employment and alcohol-related abuse. Champions of women's rights also celebrated gains in education and employment. Since 1900 female enrollment had shot up 1,000 percent in public colleges and universities and nearly 500 percent in private ones. As ambitious graduates gained access to advanced training, the proportion of women in the professions climbed by 1920 to an unprecedented 11.9 percent.[2] During World War I women in record numbers had moved into skilled jobs and administrative positions formerly held by men.

These very real achievements had been won by a movement that was successful only so long as large numbers of women remained committed to each other and to common goals. This collective commitment had secured the vote and corrected some of the wrongs associated with women's exclusion from full participation in the public sphere of ballot box and marketplace. Few suffragists and reformers, however, were any more prepared to confront the barriers to equality in the domestic sphere of family than they were to dismantle racial barriers. Most women as well as men still accepted as one of the few unchanging facts of life the conviction that woman's primary duty was to be "helpmate, housewife, and mother." Feminists who hoped to provide additional, complementary, or alternative possibilities gradually found themselves a diminishing minority. Since their understanding of the many kinds of change yet required to ensure full emancipation was shared by so few women, enfranchisement failed to create a bloc of female voters prepared to use the ballot to remove additional barriers to equality. Some found issues of class, race, and ethnicity more compelling factors in the voting booth than the need to improve women's status. Many Southern women, white as well as black, could not vote because they could not pay the poll tax—a hurdle that would loom even higher in the depression years of the 1930s. The collective power of the "woman's vote" through which suffragists had hoped to achieve further gains never fully materialized in the decade ahead.

Part of the reason for this failure lay in the physical and emotional fatigue of the suffragists themselves. The fight for the ballot, compounded by the stress of World War I, had taken its toll. As one suffragist explained: "After we [got] the vote, the crusade was over. It was peacetime and we went back to a hundred different causes and tasks that we'd been putting off all those years. We just demobilized."[3] For those who still had the energy, there were new causes. Pacifism and disarmament acquired an added urgency not only for pre-war pacifists such as Crystal Eastman and Jane Addams but also for more recent enthusiasts such as suffragist leader Carrie Chapman Catt, who established the National Conference on the Cause and Cure of War. Other women, whose feminist sympathies and political activism had been tenuous even in the yeasty reformist milieu of the progressive era, gradually yielded to the political conservatism of the 1920s. They could not be effectively mobilized for protest even when the Supreme

Court in 1922 and 1923 invalidated two of the major legislative gains of the pre-war women's movement—minimum wages for women and the abolition of child labor. Younger women who might have become new recruits found old visions of female equality less exciting than the quest for personal fulfillment associated with the relaxed social and sexual mores and affluence of the new consumer culture.

As these and other disappointments mounted, divisions developed within the movement itself. The organizations most responsible for winning the vote, the National American Woman Suffrage Association (NAWSA) and its militant offshoot, the Congressional Union, had regrouped under new names. The Congressional Union, under Alice Paul's leadership, became the National Woman's Party. It enrolled between four and five thousand members, many of them professional women, whose first priority was improvement of women's status. Many NAWSA members moved in a different direction, finding their way into the new League of Women Voters created in 1919 to educate women for citizenship. The League represented the persistence of a broad progressive impulse along with the commitment to the advancement of women. Its bipartisan concern for "good government" and legislation protecting women and children made it the more broadly reformist of the two organizations. Disagreement over tactics during the suffrage campaign continued in the debate over the next tactic in the struggle for equality. The Woman's Party advocated a constitutional amendment to guarantee equality before the law. The League and other organizations—such as the General Federation of Women's Clubs, the Women's Trade Union League, the Young Women's Christian Association, and the American Association of University Women—preferred to deal with the many discriminatory aspects of the law through a state-by-state effort to change specific statutes.

The League's preference derived in part from fears that an equal rights amendment would jeopardize legislation regulating hours, wages, and working conditions for thousands of unskilled, nonunionized female workers. Their health and safety, insisted the League, required the special protection of government. The courts, having denied this legislation to men on the ground that such laws interfered with their "freedom of contract," permitted it to women workers only because of their traditional role as mothers. Women workers, opponents of the amendment argued, could ill afford to surrender concrete gains for the abstract principle of equality.

By the end of the 1920s the League and its allies could point to a few transitory gains in the area of maternal and infant health care and to the easing of legal strictures affecting marriage, divorce, property holding, and contracts. But they failed to shake the unswerving conviction of Woman's Party loyalists that the key to equality lay in amending the Constitution. As a result of these disagreements, intense and acrimonious debate persisted throughout years of fragmentation and frustration. Feminism as an organized mass movement virtually disappeared. To be sure, a loose network of individuals and organizations continued to work to improve the status of women; however, only the Woman's Party, unwavering in its single-minded advocacy of an equal rights amendment, persistently wore the feminist label as a badge of honor. Modest gains in the postsuffrage decades could not obscure the fact that the fundamental circumstances of most women's lives remained little changed.[4]

For working-class women, especially women of color, life was still one of constant toil—on farms, in factories and mills, or in other women's homes. The factory job that had promised escape from poverty or the drudgery of farm work or the servility of domestic service often carried with it new problems. To be sure, increases in productivity during the 1920s allowed a handful of companies to initiate a five-day workweek, the eight-hour day, or a two-week annual vacation with pay. But low wages, long hours, frequent lay-offs, monotony, noise, dirt, and danger still characterized many industrial jobs, especially in the nonunionized South. Moreover, wage work brought no escape from domestic duties.

Middle-class white women fared better than their working-class counterparts. More advantaged economically, they had easier access to birth control devices and to the educational and professional opportunities that would equip them to function in the world outside the home. Yet if progress is measured by achievements in professional, commercial, and political life, middle-class women made few gains in the postsuffrage decades. The proportion of women attending colleges and universities actually declined between 1920 and 1960, as did the proportion of women on college faculties. By 1960 only 4 percent of the lawyers and judges in this nation were women, only 6 percent of the medical doctors, and less than 1 percent of the architects. Percentages, of course, can be misleading in that they indicate a share rather than absolute numbers.[5] In the final analysis, however, there was no escaping the fact that access had not meant parity, even for the most privileged. In certain areas of business, notably real estate, women had increased in both numbers and percentage. But a seat on the Stock Exchange was as difficult to come by as a seat on the president's cabinet. Boards of directors of major corporations were a male preserve. So, too, the higher echelons of government. The number of women elected to Congress throughout this entire forty-year period totaled a mere three in the Senate and forty-four in the House. The number of female cabinet members was a scant two.[6]

UNRESOLVED ISSUES

The discrepancy between early feminists' expectations and the actual accomplishments of women in the postsuffrage decades is a measure of how effectively internal and external barriers interacted to bind white women especially to the traditional pattern of domesticity. That so many rejected the new possibilities of public life for the old expectations of a private one when the former *seemingly* offered more challenging and potentially rewarding options is testimony both to the power of cultural constraints that undermined real freedom of choice and to the reality of external barriers that ensured inequality in the workplace. Although women themselves may have thought they chose "freely," few were actually in a position to do so. Most had grown up in an atmosphere of profound conditioning that from infancy through adulthood assigned individuals of each sex social roles defined essentially by gender.

The cumulative impact of this socialization shaped young women's sense of themselves as females and the options open to them by the time the more fortunate reached college. There, as in high school, the curriculum reinforced established patterns. Students taking home economics courses learned about the tasks that awaited them as consumer, homemaker, and mother. By the 1940s and 1950s many sociology courses portrayed the "normal" family as one based on a sexual division of labor and "sex-determined" behavioral characteristics. If the campus served as an environment within which to pursue a husband rather than an independent intellectual life or preprofessional training, that acknowledged a basic reality. Getting a man, especially one with bright prospects, was itself a vocational objective, one preferable to others.

The reason was that in a labor force segregated by sex as well as race and ethnicity positions filled predominantly by women carried little pay and prestige—to the financial detriment of the few males involved as well as the many females. Fields such as business, engineering, architecture, law, medicine, science, and university teaching were only slightly open to women. Female applicants to professional schools were usually confronted with admission quotas limiting the number of women, often to 5 percent. University faculties frequently assumed that female students would marry, get pregnant, and drop out, or, if they did graduate, never practice the profession for which they had been trained. Those young women who persisted, ultimately receiving the Ph.D. or the M.D., could expect continued discrimination in hiring, pay, or promotion once their active work life began.

They also had to face the problem of combining work and family in a society governed by traditional assumptions relating to both. Many business and professional women in the early years of the twentieth century solved the problem by staying single. Successive generations, less attracted to that option, had to find husbands willing to have a spouse pursue an active work life outside the home in an era in which a working wife was thought to reflect poorly on a man's ability to provide for his family. Those who were able to do so had to contend with still other problems. Nagging fears that successful careers were inconsistent with marital happiness—at least for women—found reinforcement in Hollywood movies, women's magazines, and scholarly studies. The conventional assumption that an achieving woman would lose "her chance for the kind of love she wants" was criticized by the anthropologist Margaret Mead in 1935 to no avail.[7] In a society in which the normative ideology of middle-class Americans reinforced such assumptions, women whose personal and professional lives provided refutation were simply too few to make a difference.

Parenting complicated the situation even further, creating practical problems and compounding internal anxieties. To be a lawyer and a father in America was to be "normal"; to be a lawyer and a mother was to be "deviant" because motherhood was assumed to be a full-time occupation, especially in middle-class circles. How to cope with the physical and psychological demands of family while simultaneously meeting the performance criteria and competitive pressures of work challenged even the most dedicated and resourceful woman. Pregnancy and child care leaves, tax benefits for child care expenses, public day care centers with strong programs to encourage physical and intellectual growth: these measures had become well established in advanced European nations such as Sweden. But they were never fully incorporated into the structure of American society during the first three-quarters of this century.

Families, too, were ill prepared to accommodate the special needs of women who worked outside the home. With kin networks often scattered about in distant cities and towns, it was difficult to find a grandparent or aunt who could take care of children during an emergency. Husbands, even when supportive in principle, often proved reluctant in practice to assume additional responsibilities at home. The assumption that family responsibilities would not interfere with work efficiency was built into the very structure of their jobs, as was the expectation that the corporate manager, for example, would have at his disposal a wife who could devote significant time and energy to the needs of *his* career.

For the vast majority of middle-class women the problems of combining a professional career and family were simply too great. Moreover, their social position was such that most of the working women they knew—clerks, waitresses, domestics—were lower-middle- and working-class people. *Not* working for pay outside the home indicated the high status so important to millions of Americans. As internal constraints and external constraints reinforced each other, most middle-class women concluded that they would have a better chance for security and status as wives and mothers than as workers.

There were, to be sure, achieving women whose lives were not defined only by domesticity—Helen Keller, Amelia Earhart, Mary McLeod Bethune, and Eleanor Roosevelt. But this was a culture that, while celebrating the "exceptional woman" and urging all women to work for community betterment, endlessly extolled the joys of the housewife-mother who lovingly tended her garden and a bumper crop of children. Even the heroines hawked by Hollywood in the 1950s fell into two categories: sex objects and wives. Gone were the brainy, resourceful, independent working women of an earlier era; depicted in their stead were lonely, frustrated neurotics whose unhappiness signaled the futility of sacrificing home and children for career.

THE GROWING GAP BETWEEN IDEOLOGY AND REALITY

The apparent retreat from feminism into domesticity after 1920 hid a more complex reality. Impersonal economic, scientific, and demographic forces were subtly undermining old patterns and assumptions. Although in themselves these new developments did not produce a resurgence of feminism, they did add impetus to the growing gap between conventional attitudes and changing conditions. This in turn lent credibility to a feminist critique of society.

One of the economic realities of modern America has been that many women were never fully in their "place"—the home. They have long been part of a paid labor force (see graph on percentage of men and women in the labor force, 1890–2000, on page 620). Their numbers increased significantly throughout the twentieth century. Even during the depression the proportion of women in the work force remained constant, hovering around 25 percent. This occurred despite the fact that many employers, including local school boards and the federal civil service, sought to deny employment to married women, assuming, often mistakenly, that their husband's earnings were adequate to support the family and that, as working women, they took jobs away from other men with families to support. But if hard times forced some women back into the home, others were forced out. Many mothers desperately needed even meager wages to keep the family afloat at a time when one out of every five children in this country was not getting enough nourishing food to eat.

As the nation shifted from fighting economic depression to waging global war, women responded by the millions to patriotic appeals to get a war job so as to bring their men home sooner. Between 1940 and 1945 the proportion of women in the work force rose to 37 percent. Money as well as patriotism was involved. The women who flocked to factories were beneficiaries of New Deal legislation governing wages and hours for both sexes. They also benefited from the Congress of Industrial Organizations' (CIO) successful unionization effort during the 1930s and became the first generation of female industrial employees to receive good wages. Not surprisingly many were reluctant to return home when "Rosie the Riveter," that symbol of women war workers, was told to put down her riveting machine at the return of peace. Forced out of well-paying "male" jobs, many women returned to low-paying "female" jobs in restaurants, laundries, shops, and offices.

Some did not. Remaining in union jobs, they became activists within those unions, lobbying union leaders and public officials and creating cross-class alliances with other women's organizations on behalf of their goals. Those goals were not only progressive, but in many respects feminist. Specifically, they called for the right to wage work (equal access to employment regardless of marital status, sex, race, or age); the right to higher wages (equal pay for equal work, and reevaluating the worth of female-dominated jobs so that pay equity could be achieved by women and men doing different but comparable work in terms of skill level and other criteria); and finally the right to combine wage work and family life (maternity leaves, sex-based limits on hours, family allowances, guaranteed income, and the family wage for men.) Indeed, historian Dorothy Cobble argues, they constituted a kind of labor feminism that persisted from the 1940s to the 1960s. But if the ideas and activism of these labor women helped shape the modern workplace, they initially made little impact on either dominant cultural norms or public attitudes.

When asked whether married women whose husbands made enough to support them should be allowed to hold jobs if they wanted to, the majority of Americans responded with a resounding no.[8] Yet as white-collar and clerical jobs expanded rapidly in the post-war years, so did the number of working women.[9]

By 1960 some 40 percent of American women were employed in full- or part-time jobs. Moreover, those who worked outside the home were no longer predominantly young, single, or poor. Nearly half were mothers of school-age children; many of them were middle class. When asked why they worked most responded that they regarded their jobs as an extension of family responsibilities as well as a matter of economic need. A second salary made possible a family vacation, a large home better suited to the children's needs, savings for college tuition, or simply a color television set for the family room. During the period when all America seemed about to become one great shopping mall, the definition of economic need was clearly changing. But even if one allows for a rising level of expectations consistent with the consumer culture of the 1950s as well as a higher inflation rate, the fact remains that, while rhetoric still conformed to the old domestic ideology, the growing presence of women in the work force did not.

The gap between the old ideology of home and family and the new reality of office and work widened still further as medical advances resulted in improved birth control devices and longer life expectancy. Referring to the extent to which women's lives had been determined by their reproductive role, Sigmund Freud had observed that "anatomy is destiny." But as women gained the ability to control "destiny"—to decide whether to have children, when, and how many—they were no longer victims of biological processes (see graph on American birth rates on page 619). Use of condoms and diaphragms, widespread especially among middle-class couples, made birth control a reality even before the introduction in 1960 of an oral contraceptive—"the pill." As medical science also devised new weapons against disease, the non-childbearing years during which one could expect to function as a healthy, active adult increased accordingly.

The implications were enormous. That they were not immediately grasped is not surprising for a generation seeking in the private world of home and family the security unavailable in a public world wracked successively by economic depression, world war, and the threat of global annihilation. Throughout the 1950s, family experts emphasized the importance of early marriage and motherhood if the "atomic age" family were to be a bulwark of morality and stability. Specialists in marketing techniques continued to fuse the role of homemaker and mother with that of consumer, stressing that true feminine fulfillment lay in maternity, domesticity, and purchase of the "right" products. Yet by glorifying women as homemakers and mothers at precisely the same time important changes were occurring that served to undermine those roles, advertisers, like the family experts, were unwittingly helping to sharpen the dissonance between the domestic myth and the new reality of many women's lives.

The gap between reality and the dominant ideology, often present for many minority women, now existed for women who were both white and middle class. It was a gap that could be ignored initially because it was a "bad fit"—a size six foot in a five-and-one-half shoe—a small discomfort with which people thought they could live. Yet even as more women felt the pinch, they still had difficulty seeing themselves as permanent members of the work force. Many seemed reluctant to join unions or press for equal treatment in the workplace, perhaps because they saw themselves as supplementary breadwinners or as housewives whom misfortune had trapped in monotonous, low-paying jobs.[10] Or perhaps they knew that most unions tended to marginalize women, denying them equal access to positions of leadership within the union and excluding gender equality as a demand in collective bargaining agendas.[11] That so many women continued to see themselves and their work primarily as serving family needs is hardly surprising in a culture in which their rights to participate in the labor force was contested and homemaking was described as "the most important and difficult profession any woman can have."[12] But the bad fit was there. So, too, was the unfairness of unequal pay for the same or comparable work, the low value placed on jobs women performed, the double burden of housework and wage work. Those women who felt the growing discomfort needed a new way of looking at things that would allow them to examine afresh the condition of their lives, moving from endurance of painful inequities to confrontation and change. They needed, in short, a feminist consciousness.

THE CREATION OF A FEMINIST CONSCIOUSNESS

Although labor union women and black women had fashioned their own distinctive feminism, one that emphasized women's self-definition and rights as well as obligations to family and community, mainstream feminism emerged as a mass movement in the 1960s as different groups and a new generation acquired a feminist consciousness. In the vanguard were educated, middle-class women whose diverse experiences had sharpened their sensitivity to the fundamental inequality between the sexes at a time when America had been thrust into the throes of self-examination by a movement for racial equality. Some were young veterans of the civil rights movement and the New

Left, steeped in a commitment to equality and the techniques of protest. Others were young professionals increasingly aware of their secondary status. Still others were older women who in their long careers as professionals or as activists had used organizations such as the American Civil Liberties Union (ACLU), the Young Women's Christian Association (YWCA) and the United Auto Workers (UAW) to fight sex-based discrimination. Included, too, were those whose outwardly conformist lives belied an intense awareness of the malaise of domesticity and the untenably narrow boundaries of their prescribed roles. To explore how they came self-consciously to appraise women's condition as one demanding collective action is to explore the process of radicalization that helped to create a new feminist movement.

In its early state, a major component of that movement consisted of two different groups—women's rights advocates and women's liberationists. Although the differences between the two groups began to blur as the movement matured, initial distinctions were sharp. Women's rights advocates were likely to have been older, to have had professional training or work experience, to have been more inclined to form or join organized feminist groups. Reform oriented, these organizations used traditional pressure group tactics to achieve changes in laws and public policy that would guarantee women equal rights. Emphasis on "rights" meant extending to women in life outside the home the same "rights" men had, granting them the same options, privileges, and responsibilities that men enjoyed. There was little suggestion initially of personal or cultural transformation.

Women's liberationists were younger women, less highly educated, whose ideology and political style, shaped in the dissent and violence of the 1960s, led them to look at women's predicament differently. Instead of relying upon traditional organizational structure and lobbying techniques, they developed a new style of politics. Instead of limiting their goals to changes in public policy, they embraced a transformation in private, domestic life as well. They sought liberation from ways of thinking and behaving that they believed stunted or distorted women's growth and kept them subordinate to men. Through the extension of their own personal liberation they hoped to remake the male world, changing it as they had changed themselves. For women's liberationists as for women's rights advocates, however, the first step toward becoming feminists demanded a clear statement of women's position in society, one that called attention to the gap between the egalitarian ideal and the actual position of women in American culture. There also had to be a call to action from women themselves, *for* women, *with* women, *through* women. Redefining themselves, they had to make being a woman a political fact; and, as they did so, they had to live with the radical implications of what could only be called a rebirth.

The Making of Liberal Feminists: Women's Rights Advocates

For some women, the process of radicalization began with the appointment of a Presidential Commission on the Status of Women in 1961. Presidents, Democrat and Republican, customarily discharged their political debt to female members of the electorate, especially to those who had loyally served the party, by appointing a few token women, usually party stalwarts, to highly visible posts. John Kennedy was no exception. He was, however, convinced by Esther Peterson, the highest-ranking woman in his administration, that the vast majority of women would be better served if he also appointed a commission charged with investigating obstacles to the full participation of women in society. Peterson, who was assistant secretary of labor and head of the Women's Bureau, believed that the report of such a commission could sensitize the public to barriers to equality just as her own experience as a labor organizer had sensitized her to the particular problems confronting women workers. Citizens thus informed could then be mobilized on behalf of governmental efforts at reform.[13] Accordingly, the commission was appointed with Eleanor Roosevelt serving as chair until her death a year later. Its report, *American Women* (1963), was conservative in tone, acknowledging the importance of women's traditional roles within the home and the progress they had made in a "free democratic society." Acknowledging also that women were an underutilized resource that the nation could ill afford to ignore, the report provided extensive documentation of discriminatory practices in government, education, and employment, along with substantial recommendations for change.[14] Governors, replicating Kennedy's move, appointed state commissions on the status of women. In these commissions hundreds of men and women encountered further evidence of the economic, social, and legal disabilities that encumbered the nation's "second sex." For some, the statistics were old news; for others, they were a revelation.

Aroused by growing evidence of "the enormity of our problem," members of state commissions gathered in Washington in 1966 for the Third National Conference of the Commissions on the Status of Women. Individuals who were coming to know and rely on one another as they pooled their growing knowledge of widespread inequities, they were a network in the making. They were also women who wanted something done. This time they encountered a situation that transformed at least some of those present into activists in a new movement for women's equality. The catalyst proved to be a struggle involving Representative Martha Griffiths and the Equal Employment Opportunity Commission (EEOC), the federal agency in charge of implementing the Civil Rights Act of 1964.

Despite the fact that the law proscribed discrimination on the basis of sex as well as race, the commission refused to take seriously the problem of sexual discrimination. The first executive director of EEOC, believing that "sex" had been injected into the bill by opponents seeking to block its passage, regarded the sex provision as a "fluke" best ignored. Representative Griffiths from Michigan thought otherwise. The inclusion of sex discrimination, while used by civil rights opponents to sabotage the bill, had been initiated by the venerable and elitist National Woman's Party. Support was also strong among women in the House whom Griffiths had mobilized. While liberals had initially objected, fearing that so encumbering a bill would prevent passage of much-needed legislation on behalf of racial equality, Griffiths had prevailed. Without the sex provision, she had reminded her colleagues, the Civil Rights Act would give black women advantages that white women were denied. A racist appeal that revealed the exclusivity of Griffiths's vision of sisterhood, it had worked. Once the bill passed she was determined to see the new law enforced in its entirety. When EEOC failed to do so, she lambasted the agency for its inaction in a biting speech delivered on the House floor only days before the Conference of the Commissions on the Status of Women met.

Griffiths's concern was shared by a group of women working within EEOC. Echoing an argument made the year before by a black trade unionist in the Women's Bureau,[15] they insisted that the agency could be made to take gender-related discrimination more seriously if women had a civil rights organization as adept at applying pressure on their behalf as was the National Association for the Advancement of Colored People (NAACP) on behalf of blacks. Initially the idea was rejected. Conference participants most upset by EEOC's inaction decided instead to propose a resolution urging the agency to treat sexual discrimination with the same seriousness it applied to racial discrimination. When the resolution was ruled inappropriate by conference leaders, they were forced to reconsider. After a whispered conversation over lunch they concluded the time for discussion of the status of women was over. It was time for action. Before the day was out twenty-eight women had paid five dollars each to join the National Organization for Women (NOW), including author Betty Friedan, who happened to be in Washington at the time of the conference.[16]

Friedan's presence in Washington was auspicious; her involvement in NOW, virtually inevitable. The author of a brilliant polemic published in 1963, she not only labeled the resurgent domestic ideology of recent decades but exposed the groups perpetuating it. Editors of women's magazines, advertising experts, Freudian psychologists, social scientists, and educators—all, according to Friedan, contributed to a romanticization of domesticity she termed "the feminine mystique." The result, she charged, was the infantilization of intelligent women and the transformation of the suburban home into a "comfortable concentration camp."[17] Harsh words, they rang true to those who found the creativity of homemaking and the joys of motherhood vastly exaggerated. Sales of the book ultimately zoomed past the million mark.

By articulating heretofore inarticulated grievances, *The Feminine Mystique* had advanced a process initiated by more dispassionate investigations of women's status and the discriminatory practices which made that status inferior. That process was the collective expression of discontent. It is not surprising that the voices initially heard were those of women who were overwhelmingly white, educated, and middle or upper middle class. College women who regarded themselves the equals of male classmates by virtue of intellect and training were, as Jo Freeman points out, more likely to develop expectations they saw realized by their male peers but not, in most cases, by themselves. The frustrations were even greater for women with professional training. The very fact that many had sought advanced training in fields not traditionally "female" meant that they were less likely to find in traditional gender roles the identity and self-esteem such roles provided other women. Moreover, when measuring themselves against fellow professionals who happened to be men, the greater rewards enjoyed by their white male counterparts seemed especially galling. Privileged though they were, such women *felt* more deprived in many cases than did those women who were in reality less privileged. By 1966 this sense of deprivation had been sufficiently articulated and shared and the networks of like-minded women sufficiently developed so that collective discontent could be translated into collective action. The formation of NOW signaled a feminist resurgence.[18] The three hundred men and women who gathered in October for the organizational meeting of NOW included mainly professionals, some of them veterans of commissions on the status of women as well as a few feminist union activists, notably Dorothy Haener. Adopting bylaws and a statement of purpose, they elected officers, naming Friedan president. Her conviction that intelligent women needed purposeful, generative work of their own was reflected in NOW's statement of purpose, which attacked "the traditional assumption that a woman has to choose between marriage and motherhood on the one hand and serious participation in industry or the professions on the other." Determined that women should be allowed to develop their full potential as human beings, the organization's goal was to bring them into "full participation in the mainstream of American society NOW, exercising all the privileges and responsibilities thereof in truly equal partnership with men." To that end NOW developed a Bill of Rights, adopted at its 1967 meeting, that exhorted Congress to pass an equal rights amendment to the Constitution, called on EEOC to enforce antidiscrimination legislation, and urged federal and state legislators to guarantee equal and unsegregated education. To ensure women control over their reproductive lives, these new feminists called for removal of penal codes denying women contraceptive information and devices as well as safe, legal abortions. To ease the double burden of working mothers, they urged legislation that would ensure maternity leaves without jeopardizing job security or seniority, permit tax deductions for child care expenses, and create public, inexpensive day care centers. To improve the lot of poor women, they urged reform of the welfare system and equality with respect to benefits, including job-training programs.[19]

Not content simply to call for change, NOW leaders, following the lead of equality advocates within the labor movement, worked to make it happen. Using persuasion, pressure, and even litigation, they, with other newly formed women's rights groups such as the Women's Equity Action League (WEAL), launched a massive attack on sex discrimination. By the end of the 1960s NOW members had filed legal suits against newspapers listing jobs under the headings "Help Wanted: Male" and "Help Wanted: Female," successfully arguing that such headings discouraged women from applying for jobs they were perfectly capable of doing. Building on efforts begun in the Kennedy administration such as the passage of the Equal Pay Act, they pressured the federal government to intensify its commitment to equal opportunity. They urged congressmen and labor leaders to persuade the Department of Labor to include women in its guidelines designed to encourage the hiring and promotion of blacks in firms holding contracts with the federal government. They persuaded the Federal Communications Commission to open up new opportunities for women in broadcasting. Tackling the campus as well as the marketplace, WEAL filed suit against more than three hundred colleges and universities, ultimately securing millions of dollars in salary raises for women faculty members who had been victims of discrimination. To ensure that women receive the same pay men received for doing the same work, these new feminists lobbied for passage of a new Equal Employment Opportunity Act that would enable EEOC to fight discrimination more effectively.

NOW also scrutinized the discriminatory practices of financial institutions, persuading them to issue credit to single women and to married women in their own—not their husband's—name. WEAL, in turn, filed charges against banks and other lending institutions that refused to grant mortgages to single women, or in the case of married couples, refused to take into account the wife's earnings in evaluating the couple's eligibility for a mortgage. Colleges and universities that discriminated against female students in their sports programs came under fire, as did fellowship programs that failed to give adequate consideration to female applicants.

While NOW and WEAL attacked barriers in industry and education, the National Women's Political Caucus (NWPC) focused on government and politics. Formed in 1971, the caucus was initiated by Friedan, New York congresswomen Bella Abzug and Shirley

Chisholm—both outspoken champions of women's rights—and Gloria Steinem, soon to become founding editor of the new mass-circulation feminist magazine *Ms.* Abzug, a lawyer and veteran activist for peace and civil rights, and Chisholm, the first black woman elected to Congress, were especially concerned about the small numbers of women in government. Accordingly the caucus concentrated on getting women elected and appointed to public office while also rallying support for issues such as the Equal Rights Amendment (see pp. 542–43). Meanwhile, women in the professions, aware of their small numbers and inferior status, began to organize as well. Physicians, lawyers, and university professors fought for equal opportunity in the meetings of such over-whelmingly male groups as the American Medical Association, the American Association of University Professors, and the American Historical Association.[20] Union women also mobilized. In 1974, three thousand women from fifty-eight unions attended the founding convention of the Coalition of Labor Union Women (CLUW), resolving to fight for equality in the workplace and within organized labor.

Collectively such protests served notice that more women were becoming radical-ized. The particular combination of events that transformed these women into feminists varied with the individual. A southern legislator, describing the process that brought home the reality of her own second-class citizenship, wrote:

> As a State Senator, I succeeded in getting Mississippi women the right to sit on juries (1968); the opposition's arguments were appalling. When women began hiring me in order to get credit, I became upset at the discrimination I saw. After I was divorced in 1970, I was initially denied a home loan. The effect was one of the worst traumas I've suffered. Denial of a home loan to one who was both a professional and a member of the legislature brought things to a head.[21]

Although the number of women who understood what it meant to be the "second sex" were still only a tiny minority, they were nonetheless a minority whose energy, talents, and experience enabled them to work for changes necessary to ensure equal rights. And they were gaining important allies in liberal organizations. The American Civil Liber-ties Union (ACLU) was a case in point. Best known for its defense of civil liberties, the ACLU put its considerable resources behind a newly created Women's Rights Project, headed by Ruth Bader Ginsberg, then a professor at Columbia School of Law. Her task was to devise a litigation strategy designed to persuade the Supreme Court (of which she is now a member) that gender discrimination in the law was unconstitutional. Since even the liberal Warren Court had been unable to move beyond judicial paternalism and gender stereotypes, the challenge was formidable. But Ginsberg had "high hopes for significant change," as, no doubt, did strategically placed feminists in trade unions, foundations, and other organizations whose support helped legitimate this fledgling movement.[22]

The Making of Radical Feminists: Women's Liberationists

The process of radicalization that transformed some individuals into liberal feminists occurred simultaneously—but in different fashion and with somewhat different results—among a younger generation of women who were also predominantly white and middle class. Many of them veterans of either the civil rights movement or of the New Left, these were the activists who would initially become identified as women's liberationists. Differing in perspective as well as style, they would ultimately push many of their older counterparts beyond the demand for equal rights to recognition that true emancipation would require a far-reaching transformation of society and culture.

The experiences awakening in this 1960s generation a feminist consciousness have been superbly described by Sara Evans in her book, *Personal Politics*.[23] "Freedom, equality, love and hope," the possibility of new human relationships, the importance of participatory democracy—letting the people decide—were, as Evans points out, part of an egalitarian ideology shared by both the southern-based Student Nonviolent Coordinating Committee (SNCC) in its struggle for racial equality and the Students for Democratic Society (SDS) in its efforts to mobilize an interracial organization of the urban poor in northern ghettos. Membership in both organizations—"the movement"—thus reinforced commitment to these ideals among the women who joined. In order to translate ideals into reality, however, young, college-age women who had left the shelter of middle-class families for the hard and dangerous work of transforming society found themselves doing things that they would never have thought possible. Amidst the racial strife of the South, they joined picket lines, created freedom schools, and canvassed for voter registration among blacks, often enduring arrest and jailing. SDS women from affluent suburbs entered decaying tenements and were surrounded by the grim realities of the ghetto. They trudged door-to-door in an effort to reach women whose struggle to survive made many understandably suspicious of intruding strangers. In the process, not only did these young activists achieve a heightened sense of self-worth and autonomy, they also learned the skills of movement building and the nuts and bolts of organizing.

Particularly important was the problem of getting people, long passive, to act on their own behalf. SDS women began by encouraging ghetto women to come together to talk about their problems. This sharing of experiences, they believed, would lead these women to recognize not only that their problems were common but that solutions required changes in the system. In the process of organizing, the organizers also learned. They began to understand the meaning of oppression and the valor required of those who fought it. They found new role models, Evans suggests, in extraordinary southern black women whose courage seemed never to waver in the face of violence and in those welfare mothers of the North who confronted welfare bureaucrat and slum lord after years of passivity.

But if being in the movement brought a new understanding of equality, it also brought new problems. Men who were committed to equality for one group were not necessarily committed to equality for another group. Women in SNCC, as in SDS, found themselves frequently relegated to domestic chores and treated as sex objects, denied most leadership positions, and refused a key voice in the formulation of policy. Moreover, the sexual freedom that had been theirs as part of the cultural revolution taking place in the 1960s soon began to feel more like sexual exploitation as they saw their role in the movement spelled out in the draft resister's slogan: "Girls Say Yes to Guys Who Say No." Efforts to change the situation were firmly rebuffed. When SNCC leader Stokely Carmichael joked that the only "position for women in SNCC is prone," he encapsulated views which, while not his own, reflected all too accurately the feelings of males in the New Left as well as many in SNCC.[24]

By 1967 the tensions had become so intense that white women left the movement to organize on behalf of their own "liberation." Black women, whose own tradition of feminism was venerable, stayed. Fully aware of the double jeopardy involved in being both black and female, many would embrace varieties of feminism that reflected their own problems and priorities. In the meantime, however, racial equality remained their top concern.

The women who left did not leave empty-handed. As radicals, they were impatient with liberalism, critical of capitalism, and profoundly suspicious of authority. Accustomed to challenging prevailing ideas and practices, they had acquired a language of protest, an organizing tactic, and a deep-seated conviction that the personal was political. How that legacy would shape this burgeoning new feminist movement became evident as small women's liberation groups began springing up spontaneously in major cities and university communities across the nation.

STRUCTURE, LEADERSHIP, AND CONSCIOUSNESS-RAISING

Initially, at least, the two branches of mainstream feminism seemed almost to be two different movements, so unlike were they in structure and style. Linked only by newsletters, notices in underground newspapers, and networks of friends, women's liberation groups rejected both traditional organizational structure and leadership. Unlike NOW and the other women's rights groups associated with liberal feminism, they had no central headquarters, no elected officers, no bylaws. There was no legislative agenda and little of the activism that transformed the more politically astute women's rights leaders into skilled lobbyists and tacticians. Instead this younger generation of feminists, organizing new groups wherever they found themselves, concentrated on a kind of personal politics rooted in movement days. Looking back on male-dominated meetings in which, however informal the gathering, a few highly verbal, aggressive men invariably controlled debate and dictated strategy and left less articulate and assertive women effectively excluded, they recalled the technique they had used in organizing the poor. They remembered how they had encouraged those women to talk among themselves until the personal became political, that is, until problems which, at first glance, seemed to be personal were finally understood to be social in cause—rooted in society rather than in the individual—and political in solution. Applying this same process in their own informal "rap groups," women's liberationists developed the technique of "consciousness-raising." Adopted by women's rights groups such as local chapters of NOW, consciousness-raising sessions became one of the most important innovations of mainstream feminism.[25]

The immediate task of the consciousness-raising session was to bring together in a caring, supportive, noncompetitive setting women accustomed to relating most intimately not with other women but with men—husbands, lovers, "friends." As these women talked among themselves, exchanging confidences, reassessing old options, and mentally exploring new ones, a sense of shared problems began to emerge. The women themselves gradually gained greater understanding of how profoundly their lives had been shaped by the constraints of culture. Personal experience with those constraints merged with intellectual awareness of women's inferior status and the factors that made it so. By the same token, new understanding of problems generated new determination to resolve them. Anger, aggression, and frustration formerly turned inward in unconscious self-hatred began to be directed outward, becoming transformed into new energy directed toward constructive goals. If society and culture had defined who women were through their unconscious internalization of tradition, they could reverse the process, and, by redefining themselves, redefine society and culture. Or, to put it another way, if woman was a *social construct*—the product not so much of biology, but of what people in a particular society and culture believed to be the implications of biology—then women themselves would re-create the construct. At work was a process of discovery so radicalizing that the individuals undergoing it ultimately emerged in a very real sense as different people. Now feminists, these were women with a different understanding of reality—a new "consciousness," a new sense of "sisterhood," and a new commitment to change.

Consciousness-raising was an invigorating and sometimes frightening experience. As one young woman wrote, "This whole movement is the most exhilarating thing of my life. The last eight months have been a personal revolution. Nonetheless, I recognize there is dynamite in this and I'm scared shitless."[26] "Scared" or not, such women could no longer be contained. Veterans of one rap group fanned out, creating others, often with arresting names such as Cell 16, the Furies, Redstockings, or simply Radical Women.

Since consciousness-raising groups functioned best when the group was homogeneous, women of color and lesbians sometimes felt unwelcome. Nonetheless, groups mushroomed, providing the movement with increased numbers and added momentum, as did the formation of black, Chicana, and Asian-American organizations. For the minority-group women, being feminists took special courage because it meant facing accusations of having deserted the liberation struggles of their own racial and ethnic communities. Whatever their background, women's liberationists were faced with an additional challenge, articulating theoretically as well as personally what "oppression," "sexism," and "liberation" really meant: in short, developing a feminist ideology.

TOWARD A FEMINIST IDEOLOGY: OPPRESSION, SEXISM, AND CHANGE

To explain the significance of the discovery that woman is a *social construct* and that subordination was built into that construct was no simple process. The concept itself was complex. Moreover, women's rights advocates who were essentially pragmatic were more interested in practical results than in theoretical explanations. Even among women's liberationists who were far more theoretically oriented and ideologically fractious, intellectual perspectives reflected differences in politics, experience, temperament, style, and sexual preference. Manifestos, position papers, and books began to pile up as liberationists searched for the historical origins of female oppression. Those whose primary loyalty was still to the New Left—soon dubbed "politicos"—attributed women's oppression to capitalism. Others, who would come to be known as socialist-feminists, insisted that both male supremacy and capitalism were responsible for women's subordination and that feminists must be allied with, but apart from, the left. Still other liberationists argued that male supremacy, not class or race, was the more fundamental and universal form of oppression and that women as a group constituted an oppressed class. Known as radical feminists, their emphasis on the primacy of gender would prevail, although it would be ultimately challenged by feminists of color, who insisted on multiple forms of oppression. In the meantime, however, radical feminists' identification of the family as the basic unit in the system of oppression led to new debates among radical feminists themselves. If marriage as an intersexual alliance divided women, leading them to identify with the oppressor from whom they derived economic advantages rather than each other, ought marriage to be abolished? If so, what new structure should take its place? Pushing the logic of this position, lesbian feminists argued that the ultimate rejection of male domination required not just the rejection of marriage, but the rejection of sexual intimacy with men. Heterosexuality, they insisted, was at the very core of patriarchy. Other feminists disagreed. Family, while a source of gender hierarchy, could also be a site of support. Moreover, collective struggle against male supremacy did not mean rejecting the men with whom one was intimately connected; the challenge ought to be to make them allies.

Other radical feminists, seeking to desexualize lesbianism, argued that sexual behavior—who one slept with—was less important than being "woman identified." They pointed to sex-based role differentiation as a source of oppression, arguing that work and family roles should be restructured in ways that would encourage greater mutuality and fulfillment for both sexes. Others argued that personality—men and women's psychic identity—were also overly differentiated by sex. Only by merging role and personality characteristics of both sexes within each individual could androgynous men and women be developed and real liberation achieved.[27]

Given the great variety of perspectives and positions even among women's liberationists alone, it is impossible to talk about a feminist ideology to which all those who identified with the women's movement subscribed. The ascendancy of radical feminism among women's liberationists in the early 1970s and the eventual embrace of many of their insights by liberal feminists, however, does make it possible to talk about a common conceptual framework shared by mainstream feminists. Most believed that *gender hierarchy* is a primary factor essential to any understanding of why women *as a group* suffer from an unequal distribution of power and resources in a society. They agreed that men have been the dominant sex and that women as a group are subordinate. While not all mainstream feminists were comfortable talking about a *system* of oppression or even using the word "oppression," they were quick to list the many areas where inequities were—and still are—evident.

At the top of the list was the economy. Men, they agreed, are more likely to be economically independent than women because the latter work within the home where their labor has no monetary value and/or outside the home in sex-segregated jobs for wages too meager to ensure economic self-sufficiency. Society and culture also provided numerous examples of the higher status, greater options, and greater power conferred upon men by virtue of their sex. Just as traditional male roles provide access to power and independence, whereas female roles do not, so, feminists pointed out, masculine values define what attributes are admired and rewarded. The very fact that strength, competence, independence, and rationality are considered masculine values, that they are more highly regarded by both sexes, *and* that they constitute the standard by which mental health is judged these new feminists found revealing indeed. The problem, they insisted, is not simply that the qualities themselves, intrinsically neither "male" or "female," are the product of gender socialization. It is the preference, conscious and unconscious, for whatever society regards as "masculine" that is so persistent and so objectionable—a preference feminists termed *sexism*.

Sexism, they believed, is persistent, pervasive, and powerful. It is internalized by women as well as men. It is most dramatically evident in the programmed-to-please women who search for happiness through submissiveness to men and in the men who use their power to limit women's options and keep them dependent. It is also evident in a more subtle fashion among women who emulate male models and values, refusing to see those aspects of women's lives that are positive and life-affirming, and among men who are unaware of the unconscious sexism permeating their attitudes and actions. Internalized in individuals, sexism is also embedded in institutions—the family, the education system, the media, the economy, politics, law, organized religion, language, and sexual morality.

Given the pervasiveness of sexism, many feminists saw no possibility for real equality short of transformation not only of individuals but also of social institutions and cultural values. Even what was once seen as the relatively simple demand of women's rights advocates for equal pay for equal work no longer looked so simple. What seemed to be a matter of obtaining equal rights *within* the existing system in reality demanded changes that *transform* the system. Involved was:

> a reevaluation of women as workers, of women as mothers, of mothers as workers, of work as suitable for one gender and not for the other. The demand implies equal opportunity and thus equal responsibilities. It implies a childhood in which girls are rewarded for competence, risk taking, achievement, competitiveness and independence—just like boys. Equal pay for equal work means a revision in our expectations about women as equal workers and it involves the institutional arrangements to make them so.

"There is nothing small here," a feminist scholar observed.[28] And indeed there was not.

FEMINISM IN ACTION

How feminists chose to enact their new commitment varied. For some the changes consisted largely of private actions—relationships renewed, careers resumed. Others, preferring public statements, used flamboyant methods to dramatize their newfound understanding of the subtle ways in which society defined and thereby confined women. As part of the confrontational politics of the 1960s, radical feminists picketed the 1968 Miss America contest, protesting the commercialization of beauty and our national preoccupation with bust size and "congeniality" rather than brain power and character. (In the process they were dubbed "bra burners," despite the fact that no bras were burned.) Activists pushed their way into all-male bars and restaurants as a way of forcing recognition of how these bastions of male exclusivity were themselves statements about "man's world/woman's place." They sat in at the offices of *Ladies' Home Journal* and *Newsweek* protesting the ways in which the media's depiction of women perpetuated old stereotypes at the expense of new realities. Others focused on abortion, mindful that mishandled illegal abortions claimed the lives of an estimated ten thousand women each year. Organizing "speakouts," they talked publicly about their own humiliating and dangerous encounters with the netherworld of abortion, thereby transforming this heretofore taboo and explosive subject into a matter of public debate and an issue of women's rights. Feminist lawyers, no less convinced that forcing a woman to bear a child against her will was a violation of her fundamental rights, used their legal skills to advance the cause of abortion law repeal in the courts.

Still other feminists chose to work for social change in a different fashion. They created nonsexist day care centers, wrote and published nonsexist children's books, monitored sex stereotyping in textbooks, lobbied for women's studies programs in high schools and colleges, and founded women's health clinics. They formed rape crisis centers so that rape victims could be treated by caring females; they agitated for more informed, sympathetic treatment on the part of hospital staffs, the police, and the courts. They created shelters for battered women, insisting that physical abuse was not a private family matter but a social problem requiring a public response. Feminist scholars used their talents to recover and interpret women's experience, opening new areas for research and in the process furthering change.

Feminist legislators, especially black Congresswoman Shirley Chisholm, sponsored legislation to extended minimum wage coverage to domestic workers. Other lawmakers sponsored bills, not always successful, to help housewives to secure some form of economic recognition for work performed, to enable women workers to obtain insurance that would give them the same degree of economic security afforded male coworkers, and to protect them from violence, which is the most blatant form of male oppression.

Trade union feminists, concerned with their dual identity as women and as wage workers, struggled to keep the needs of working women in the forefront. Black feminists, by their own admission "the most pressed down of us all," focused on issues of special concern to many minority women: media depictions of black women, racially coded credit policies, public housing, household workers' rights, and welfare and prison reform. Their sisters on the left in the Third World Women's Alliance, convinced that imperialism as well as sexism, racism, and classism oppressed women, organized demonstrations of solidarity with the women of Cuba and Vietnam. Actions, like voices, differed. Such diversity, however, was basic to the movement.[30]

FEMINISM: THE PUBLIC IMPACT

In a society in which the media create instant awareness of social change, feminism burst upon the public consciousness with all the understated visibility of a fireworks display on the Fourth of July. The more radical elements of the movement, with their talk of test tube conception, the slavery of marriage, and the downfall of capitalism, might be dismissed out of hand. But it was hard to ignore 50,000 women parading down New York's Fifth Avenue, the presence of *Ms.* magazine on newsstands, feminist books on the best-seller lists, women in hard hats on construction jobs, or the government-mandated affirmative action programs that put them there. It was harder still to ignore the publicity that accompanied the appointment of women to the Carter cabinet, the enrollment of coeds in the nation's military academies, and the ordination of women to the ministry. A Harris poll of December 1975 reported that 63 percent of the women interviewed favored most changes designed to improve the status of women, although some were quick to insist that they were not "women's libbers." Black

The Torch Relay, opening the International Women's Year Conference, Houston, Texas, 1977.
The torch, brought by runners from Seneca Falls to Houston, symbolized the link between those
early feminists who drafted the Declaration of Sentiments and their contemporary counterparts
who assembled to present new proposals designed to achieve the still-elusive goal of equality.
From left to right: Billie Jean King, Susan B. Anthony II, Bella Abzug, Sylvia Ortiz, Peggy Kok-
ernot, Michele Cearcy, Betty Friedan. (Copyright © 1978 by Diana Mara Henry)

women, recognizing that equality is indivisible, viewed feminism even more positively
than did their white counterparts, although the feminists among them preferred their
own organizations.[31]

Evidence of changing views was everywhere. The list of organizations lined up in
support of ratification of the Equal Rights Amendment included not only such avowedly
feminist groups as NOW, WEAL, and NWPC as well as longtime supporters such as
the National Woman's Party and the National Federation of Business and Professional
Women's Clubs, but also well-established women's organizations such as the General
Federation of Women's Clubs, the American Association of University Women, the
League of Women Voters, the National Council of Jewish Women, the National Council of Negro Women, and the YWCA.

Even more potent evidence that feminism had "arrived" was the 1977 International
Women's Year Conference in Houston. Before more than two thousand delegates from
every state and territory in the United States and twenty thousand guests, three First
Ladies—Lady Bird Johnson, Betty Ford, and Rosalynn Carter—endorsed the Equal
Rights Amendment and the goals of the Houston Conference, their hands holding a
lighted torch carried by women runners from Seneca Falls where, in 1848, the famous
Declaration of Sentiments had been adopted. Confessing that she once thought the

women's movement belonged more to her daughters than to herself, Lady Bird Johnson added, "I have come to know that it belongs to women of all ages." Such an admission, like the presence of these three women on the platform, proclaimed a message about feminists that was boldly printed on balloons throughout the convention hall: "We Are Everywhere."[32]

OPPOSITION TO FEMINISM

For some women the slogan was not a sign of achievement but of threat. Gathered at a counter-convention in Houston were women who shared neither the critique nor the goals of the movement. They were an impressive reminder that social change generates opposition and that opposition to feminism had crystalized in the struggle for ratification of the Equal Rights Amendment. ERA—as the amendment is called—simply stated: "Equality of rights under the law shall not be denied or abridged by the United States or by any State on account of sex." First suggested in 1923 as the logical extension of suffrage, the amendment had long been opposed by those who feared it would be used to strike down laws intended to protect women in the workplace. By the 1960s, those concerns no longer applied. Prodded by NOW, Congress once again turned its attention to a constitutional amendment removing sexual bias from common, statutory, and constitutional law. After a massive lobbying effort by women's rights advocates and their allies, the Senate finally joined the House and sent ERA to the states for ratification by a lopsided vote of eighty-four to eight in 1972. Almost immediately twenty-one states rushed to ratify. Within a year, however, opponents of ratification had begun a counterattack that ultimately stalled the number of ratified states at thirty-five, three short of the needed three-fourths majority when the deadline for ratification expired on June 30, 1982. Opponents even induced some ratifying states to rescind their approval. Early successes indicated a majority of Americans favored ERA—but not a large enough majority.

Opposition to ERA is starkly paradoxical. A constitutional amendment proposed especially to benefit women was opposed by women. The paradox is resolved in part by remembering that many Americans who claim to believe in equality become profoundly apprehensive when the principle is identified with specific governmental policies they consider to be intrusive and unreasonable. When supporters of ERA said that implementation of a constitutional ban on sex discrimination would be left to the Supreme Court, conservatives of both sexes were reminded that this was the same Supreme Court that had not only mandated racial integration, but prohibited prayer in the public schools and struck down bans on birth control, abortion, and pornography. Court-enforced sexual equality, like racial equality, many people believed, would further diminish the power of state and local governments and the right of individuals to live as they chose. As one women wrote her U.S. senator: "*Forced* busing, *forced* mixing, *forced* housing. Now *forced* women! No thank you!"[33]

Such logic also illuminates antiratificationist charges, mystifying to ratificationists, that ERA would destroy the family. Although ERA supporters correctly pointed out that the amendment had nothing to do with private relationships, social conservatives were not convinced; they had seen what a federal agenda in feminist hands looked like at the International Women's Year Conference in Houston. A meeting subsidized by the U.S. government had endorsed not only women's rights and ERA, but government-sponsored child care, federal funding of abortions for poor women, contraception for minors without parental consent, and gay rights. If Big Brother or, more appropriately, Big Sister, had her way in Washington, women might well be forced to live in the kind of post-ERA world invoked by anti-ERA spokeswoman Phyllis Schlafly—a world in which mothers, no longer financially able to remain at home, would be forced to surrender their children to government-sponsored daycare centers. There child-care personnel would supplant parental authority and family identification with loyalty to the state.

The danger, as anti-ERA women saw it, was not just to family, but to women themselves. Feminists believed that theirs was a struggle for justice and liberation—liberation from economic inequities, social roles, and cultural values that denied rights and limited autonomy. To require *all* women to endure constraints dictated not by biology (sex) but by culture (gender) was, from the standpoint of feminists, to deny freedom and self-determination to half the population simply because they were born female. To women who did not believe they were oppressed, feminists' efforts at liberation, especially the rhetoric of radical feminists, appeared *not* as an attack on traditional gender categories, but rather an assault on familar patterns that provided security, identity, and meaning. Fusing feminism and ERA, an antiratificationist begged her senator not to vote for the amendment, insisting that she did not want to be liberated. "My husband," she wrote, "works for me and takes care of me and our three children, doesn't make me do things that are hard for me (drive in town), loves me and doesn't smoke, drink, gamble, run around or do anything that would upset me. I do what he tells me to do. I like this arrangement. *It's the only way I know how to live.*" Insisted another: "I am a widow, have three children, and work to make ends meet. I am still against ERA. I am a woman—and want to be treated as a woman."[34]

When ERA supporters responded that treating women as individuals legally rather than classifying them by sex had nothing to do with the division of labor between husbands and wives, social etiquette, or the masculinization of women, their reassurances fell on deaf ears. The free-floating anxiety aroused by the enormity of the social change inherent in feminism had acquired concrete focus in ERA. Opponents' predictions of the terrible consequences that would result from ratification of the amendment were not so important as the function such statements served—an indictment of what Schlafly called the "unisex" society and an affirmation of traditional gender categories. For women living in a world in which personal identity, social legitimacy, economic viability, and moral order were rooted in traditional gender categories, calling those categories into question in the name of gender-neutral law meant that feminists must want men and women to be "the same." Finding it difficult to separate gender from sex—to see gender as a social construction—ERA opponents could only conclude that this latest drive for equality was not only absurd ("you can't fool Mother Nature") but dangerous. By rallying women to this danger, Schlafly revealed that the issue was not whether women should stay at home minding the children and cooking the food—Schlafly herself did not do that. The issue was the *meaning* of sexual differences between men and women.

In the early years of the movement, both radical and liberal feminists minimized those differences, believing reproductive control and work in the public sector have made women's lives more like men's. Antifeminists inflated those differences. Their response is a measure both of their belief that women are "eternal in their attributes and unchanged by events" and their anger and distress at changes that had already occurred.[35] It is a reminder, too, of how far the feminist movement has still to go to achieve the reforms sought by women's rights advocates, much less its more far-reaching goals.

NEW PROGRESS AND OLD PROBLEMS

There were gains to be sure. New reproductive freedom came in 1973 with the Supreme Court's liberalization of abortion laws that removed the danger of the illegal, back-alley abortions so long the recourse of desperate women. Sexual preference and practice became less an occasion for denial of civil rights and more a matter of individual choice. Evidence of expanding educational and employment opportunities seemed to be everywhere. Women assumed high-level posts in government, the judiciary, the military, business, and labor. In a new batch of female "firsts," Sandra Day O'Connor assumed a seat on the Supreme Court, NASA's Sally Ride zoomed into space, and Geraldine Ferraro won the vice-presidential slot on the 1984 Democratic ticket. From an expanding population of female college graduates, younger women moved in record numbers into professional school, dramatically changing enrollment patterns in such fields as law, medicine, and business. Their blue-collar counterparts, completing job training programs, trickled into the construction industry and other trades, finding in those jobs the decent wage that had eluded them as waitresses, hairdressers, salesclerks, or domestics. Political participation also increased. Women emerged from years of lobbying for ERA with a new understanding of the political process. (So, too, did their opponents.) More female candidates filed for office and more female politicians worked themselves into positions of power. Revision of discriminatory statutes, while by no means completed, brought a greater measure of legal equality. A heightened public consciousness of sexism ushered in other changes. School officials began admitting boys to home economics classes, girls to shop. Some employers transformed maternity leaves into child-care leaves, making them available to fathers as well as mothers. Liberal religious leaders talked of removing gender-related references from prayer books.

Such gains, while in some cases smacking of tokenism, are not to be minimized. Most required persistent pressure from feminists, from government officials, and often from both. They were by no means comprehensive, however. As in the case of the civil rights movement, the initial beneficiaries of the feminist movement were predominantly middle-class, often highly educated, and relatively young. The increase in the number of single women, the older age at which women married for the first time, the declining birth rate—changes characteristic of the entire female population during the 1970s—were especially characteristic of a younger generation of career-oriented women.[36] But even for these women and their partners, financial as well as personal costs were sometimes high: couples living apart for some portion of the week or year in order to take advantage of career opportunities; married women devoting virtually all of their salaries to domestic and child-care costs, especially during their children's preschool years. Perhaps the personal recognition, independence, and sense of fulfillment associated with career success made the costs "affordable"—especially given the alternatives.

The women who stood to gain most from the implementation of feminists' efforts to change the nation's economic and social structure were not those who were young, talented, and educated but those who were less advantaged. Yet by the 1990s the latter could with good reason argue that two decades of feminist activity had left their lives little changed in ways that really count. While the number of women in the work force continued to rise from less than 20 percent in 1920 to a projected 87 percent by 2000, working women in the 1970s and 1980s saw the gap between male and female income remain virtually unchanged. By 1998 female workers earned 76 cents for every dollar earned by males, although the gap has substantially narrowed among younger women. Part of the explanation for this persistent gap lies in pay inequities.[37] More fundamental, however, is the continuation of occupational segregation and the undervaluation of work done by women. Around 80 percent of all working women still cluster in gender-segregated occupations in which wages are artificially low. That women made up two-thirds of all minimum-wage workers in the United States is, therefore, hardly surprising.[38]

With the dramatic rise in the number of female-headed households—33 percent of all working mothers are their family's breadwinners—the continuation of this occupational ghetto has disturbing implications not only for women workers but also for their children. Female heads of households, often lacking both child-care facilities and skills that would equip them for better-paying jobs if such jobs were available, earn enough to enable less than two-thirds to stay above the poverty level. Their struggle for economic survival is shared by other women, especially older women—widows or divorcées whose years of housework have left them without employment skills. Indeed divorce often contributes to the problem, for with the breaking up of a marriage, the standard of living for most women falls dramatically. The fact that child support, if awarded, is frequently inadequate, unpaid, and uncollectible further exacerbates the economic plight of those women who have custody of their children. Thus, ironic as it may seem, the decade that witnessed the revival of the feminist movement also saw the feminization of poverty. By the end of the 1970s, two out of every three poor persons in the United States were female. If this trend continues at the present rate, it is estimated that by the year 2000 the poverty population will be composed entirely of women and their children.[39]

Ironic, too, given the feminist insistence that child-care and household responsibilities should be shared by working spouses, is the persistence of the double burden borne by women working outside the home. Working women continue to do 80 to 90 percent of the chores related to running a household, with husbands and children "helping out." For all the talk about the changing structure of family roles, major shifts have occurred slowly, even in households in which women were informed and engaged enough to be familiar with current feminist views.[40] Although some fathers, especially among the middle class, have become more involved in parenting, the primary responsibility for children still remains the mother's.[41] And working mothers still receive little institutional help despite the fact that by 1990 over half of all mothers with children under six worked outside the home.[42] Without a fundamental rethinking of both work and family, women will continue to participate in the labor force in increasing numbers. Many, however, will remain in its lower echelons as marginal members.

In sum, economic and demographic change has been the basis of important changes in attitudes and behavior. As a result, life is more challenging for many women, but the feminization of poverty reminds the nation of its failures. We have yet to see the new social policies necessary to create the egalitarian and humane society envisioned by feminists. Indeed, in the climate of political conservatism of the 1980s feminists had to fight hard to maintain gains already won. The reproductive freedom of poor women had already been eroded by limitations on federal funding of abortions, and the reproductive freedom of all women had been threatened by congressional advocates of the Human Life Bill. Although that bill never received the votes necessary to become law, an increasingly conservative Supreme Court dealt reproductive rights a further blow. The 1989 *Webster* and the 1992 *Planned Parenthood* decisions, while not overturning the right to an abortion, upheld the right of states to limit access. With reproductive rights now a contested issue in state legislatures, the struggle to keep abortion legal and unrestricted has escalated dramatically.[43]

During the 1980s legislation mandating equal opportunity in education and employment was also weakened by the courts and assaulted by the Reagan and Bush administrations, whose budget cuts further hampered EEOC's antidiscrimination efforts. There were also cuts in funds for Title IX, which seeks to ensure sex equality on campus; cuts in grants for traditionally female programs such as nursing; and cuts in Small Business Administration funding for programs benefiting women. Day care centers, battered women's shelters, and legal aid centers had their work curtailed by budget cuts as well. Also under attack was comparable worth, a policy designed to reduce pay inequities by evaluating skills, effort, and responsibilities associated with jobs traditionally held mainly either by men or by women so that pay could be equalized for jobs that are indeed comparable. Defeat of the Equal Rights Amendment left determination of the meaning of discrimination in the law to Supreme Court justices with varying understandings of legal equality.

The election of 1992 brought to the White House a pro-choice president and a feminist First Lady, new feminist legislators to Capital Hill, and the subsequent appointment of a pioneer feminist litigator to the Supreme Court. The gains of the 1990s, however, were accompanied by sharp reminders of the elusiveness of full equality. The Supreme Court opened the doors of Virginia Military Institute and The Citadel to women and clarified the law on sexual harassment, while Congress offered block grants to states outlawing marital rape. Yet that same Congress passed a welfare reform law that presupposes a society in which there is full employment, living wages, child care, and health care for all. While some women may be able to make the transition from welfare to employment, many more are likely to find themselves in an ever-deepening economic crisis without the safety net that offered them a modicum of security in the past. Meanwhile, a robust economy accelerated the flow of women into the workplace, where they now constitute 55 percent of the labor force, increasingly own their own businesses, and earn more than previously—one in five women in the U.S. earns more than her husband. (See graph on women in the workforce on page 620.) Yet the wage gap remains, especially for less skilled workers, who are disproportionately women of color. Lower pay usually means lower or no benefits and smaller pensions upon retirement. Meanwhile, the war on affirmative action threatens the educational and occupational mobility of black and Hispanic women in particular. Whatever their occupational level, few working mothers are spared a high degree of stress. Unlike their European and Japanese counterparts, women in the U.S.

continue to make do with only brief time off for childbirth and a patchwork quilt of child care that is as good as they can afford, and frequently not good enough. (See graph on maternity and parental leave entitlements on page 625.)[44]

Gains in other areas have also come with reminders of parity yet to be achieved. Americans can now point to two female Supreme Court justices and a female Secretary of State; however, women are proportionately underrepresented in Congress, where in 1998 they constitute only 12.6 percent of the House of Representatives and a mere 9 percent of the Senate—a sharp contrast to the Nordic countries, where women have attained near parity in parliament. At the state level, women's electoral victories made headlines; however, they currently hold only two of the fifty governorships and barely more than 20 percent of the seats in state legislatures. (See graph on women in political power on page 626.)[45] In the military, women won combat medals in the Gulf War even as the armed services gained new notoriety as a continuing site of gender warfare and sexual harassment. Medals were also scooped up by the nation's female athletes at the Olympic games. Yet the celebration of the twenty-fifth anniversary of Title IX, which mandated equity in college and university athletic programs, was tempered by a new study revealing that the money spent by N.C.A.A. colleges on women's programs was dwarfed by that spent on men's—$663,000 on average was budgeted for women and $2.4 million for men.[46] On another twenty-fifth anniversary, pro-choice women celebrated the survival of *Roe* v. *Wade* while mourning an Indiana teenager who died from an illegal abortion after her state mandated parental consent.[47] Even feminism itself is not exempt from this mixed tally. At the end of the twentieth century, American women enjoy the gains of the feminist movement and women and men alike believe it has improved women's lives; nonetheless, the number of women who consider the label "feminist" to be an insult has increased since 1992.[48]

THE EVOLUTION AND FUTURE OF FEMINISM

This seemingly contradictory view of feminism reminds us is that social change is complex and results from the interplay of many factors. Nowhere is this truer than in the women's movement. The swiftness with which a resurgent feminism captured the imagination of millions of American women dramatized the need for change. The inability of feminists to win ratification of ERA dramatized the limits of change. The irony of the polarization, however, was that the failure of ERA did not and could not stop feminism in its tracks and that antifeminist women, in mobilizing to fight the amendment, were themselves assuming a new role whether they acknowledged that fact or not. They organized lobbies, political action committees, and conventions; they also ran for and won public office. Where feminists have led, antifeminists would not be too far behind, defining themselves within the context of change they could not stop. But the rhetoric of liberation that had been so important to the awakening and maturation of women in the 1970s seemed by the 1980s to be less appealing. Women could happily benefit from the achievements of feminism without understanding or embracing its critique of style. Transformational politics seemed to have given way to a bevy of career women armed with a copy of *Savvy* or *Working Woman*, "dressed for success," and busily playing "games their mothers never taught them" with scant realization, as one observer noted, that "only a decade ago they would never have been allowed to play."[49] Commentators, speculating that feminism had become careerism, pronounced the movement dead.

Although press speculation was off the mark, feminism had changed. By the mid-seventies, radical feminism had given way to cultural feminism. The appeal that alternative institution-building held for cultural feminists in the conservative eighties was understandable. But the kind of valorization of the female reflected in the search for lost matriarchies and goddess worship seemed to radical and liberal feminists to represent not only female separatism but a retreat from political struggle. Both seemed alien to women whose aim had been to transcend gender, not reaffirm it. Valorization of female difference was also at the heart of still newer varieties of feminism such as eco-feminism: women as natural nurturers were presumed to be uniquely concerned with ecological ruin. If eco-feminism focused on issues that radical and liberal feminists of the 1960s would have regarded as broad human issues rather than distinctively feminist ones, the groups themselves functioned as a sharp reminder that second wave feminism had always been an ideologically pluralistic, decentralized, and structurally amorphous movement. Indeed diversity is a source of strength—a point made with renewed intensity in the 1980s by women of color. Their insistence that racism, classism, and sexism are multiple and interlocking forms of oppression has served to remind mainstream feminists that women speak in different voices from multiple historical, cultural, racial, economic, and sexual locations. The need to move beyond totalizing notions of "sisterhood," recognizing the extent to which women have themselves been oppressors of other women, requires of mainstream feminism further transformation. There can be no mistaking black poet and feminist Audre Lorde's meaning when she asked, "What woman here is so enamored of her own oppression that she cannot see her heelprint upon another woman's face?"[50] If feminism is to become genuinely egalitarian and multicultural, mainstream feminists who bear the greater responsibility for that transformation will have much to do.

Meanwhile the movement continues to expand even in the midst of antifeminist backlash as women continue to make the connection between the personal and political as they confront in their own lives or the lives of others the trauma of sexual harassment, job discrimination and sexual violence. For every woman who disdains the label "feminist," there is another who proclaims, as does the young Anastasia Higgenbotham: "The one word all phallocrats most fear (and well they should), I wear like a badge of honor, my pride, my work, my glowing, spiked tiara."[51] It is on this youngest generation of feminists that the future of feminism depends. They understand that the battle against gender inequality is not over. Indeed, a resurgent Right has made it abundantly clear that older gender patterns have not lost their force and that contemporary efforts to secure women's full emancipation can be challenged, even interrupted. Yet the dynamics of change are such that all women—not merely feminists—will find that they have to forge a definition of self that extends beyond the definitions of the past.

NOTES

1. Nancy F. Cott, *The Grounding of Modern Feminism* (New Haven, 1987), p. 3.
2. William H. Chafe, *The Paradox of Change: American Women in the 20th Century* (New York, 1991), pp. 99–100.
3. Marion K. Sanders, *The Lady and the Vote* (Boston, 1956), p. 142.

4. For new studies of feminism in the postsuffrage decades, see Nancy F. Cott. *The Grounding of Modern Feminism* (New Haven, 1987), and Leila J. Rupp and Verta Taylor, *Survival in the Doldrums: The American Women's Rights Movement, 1945 to the 1960s* (New York, 1987).

5. For a discussion of statistics relating to women in professional as well as attitudes of college-educated women to careers, see Frank Stricker, "Cookbooks and Law Books: The Hidden History of Career Women in Twentieth Century America," *Journal of Social History* 10 (1976):1–19.

6. Excluded are women who were appointed to congressional office simply to finish out the term of a deceased husband. Among these forty-seven in Congress, however, are women who were initially appointed or elected in a special election to fill the seat of a deceased incumbent, often a husband, and who went on to win election to a subsequent term—or terms—on their own. Figures were compiled from Rudolf Engelbart, *Women in the United States Congress, 1917–1972* (Littleton, Colo., 1974).

7. Margaret Mead, "Sex and Achievement," *Forum* 94 (1935):303.

8. According to a Gallup Poll, 86 percent of American people objected to married women working; according to a *Fortune* poll, 67 percent. See Hadley Cantril, *Public Opinion, 1935–1946* (Princeton, 1951), p. 1047, and "The Fortune Survey: Women in America," *Fortune* 34 (1946):8. For the impact of the cold war on the resurgent domesticity of women, see Elaine Tyler May, *Homeward Bound: American Families in the Cold War Era* (New York, 1988).

9. For a much more detailed analysis, see Valerie Kincade Oppenheimer. *The Female Labor Force in the United States: Demographic and Economic Factors Governing Its Growth and Changing Composition* (Berkeley, 1970).

10. For a perceptive discussion of this issue, see Leslie Woodcock Tentler, *Wage-Earning Women: Industrial Work and Family Life in the United States, 1900–1930* (New York, 1979), pp. 180–85.

11. Nancy F. Gabin, *Feminism in the Labor Movement: Women and the United Auto Workers, 1935–1975* (Ithaca, N.Y., 1990), p. 4.

12. Quoted in Marguerite Wykoff Zapoleon, *The College Girl Looks Ahead to Her Career Opportunities* (New York, 1956), p. 9. See also Ashley Montagu, "The Triumph and Tragedy of the American Woman," *Saturday Review* 41 (1958):14.

13. Cynthia E. Harrison, "A 'New Frontier' for Women: The Public Policy of the Kennedy Administration," *Journal of American History* 67 (1980):630–46.

14. U.S. President's Commission on the Status of Women. *American Women* (Washington, D.C., 1963).

15. Gabin, *Feminism in the Labor Movement*, p. 188.

16. For events leading to the founding of NOW, see Jo Freeman, *The Politics of Women's Liberation: A Case Study of an Emerging Social Movement and Its Relation to the Social Policy Process* (New York, 1975), pp. 53–55; and Cynthia Harrison, *On Account of Sex: The Politics of Women's Issues, 1945–1968* (Berkeley, 1988), pp. 192–209.

17. Betty Friedan, *The Feminine Mystique* (New York, 1963).

18. Freeman, *Politics of Women's Liberation*, pp. 35–37.

19. National Organization of Women, Statement of Purpose, 1966, reprinted in *Up from the Pedestal*, ed. Aileen S. Kraditor (Chicago, 1968), pp. 363–64; National Organization of Women, Bill of Rights. 1967, reprinted in *Sisterhood Is Powerful: An Anthology of Writings on the Women's Liberation Movement*, ed. Robin Morgan (New York, 1970), pp. 512–14.

20. Freeman, *Politics of Women's Liberation*, chap. 3; Maren Lockwood Carden. *The New Feminist Movement* (New York, 1974), chaps 8–10: also Gayle Graham Yates. *What Women Want The Ideas of the Movement* (Cambridge, Mass., 1975). chap. 2; Gabin, *Feminism in the Labor Movement*. p. 226.

21. Quoted in Carolvn Hadley, "Feminist Women in the Southeast," *Bulletin of the Center of the Study of Southern Culture and Religion* 3 (1979):10.

22. Quoted in "Ruth Bader Ginsurg," *1994 Current Biography*, p. 214.

23. Sara Evans, *Personal Politics: The Roots of Women's Liberation in the Civil Rights Movement and the New Left* (New York, 1979); see also Evans, "Tomorrow's Yesterday: Feminist Consciousness and the Future of Women," in *Women of America: A History*, ed. Carol Ruth Berkin and Mary Beth Norton (Boston, 1979), pp. 390–415. The following paragraphs rely heavily on this essay and on Evans's *Personal Politics*.

24. Mary King, one of the authors of the manifesto protesting the treatment of women in SNCC, insists that Carmichael was personally responsive to their concerns if others were not. See Mary King, *Freedom Song* (New York, 1987), pp. 450–52.

25. Carden, *New Feminist Movement*, chaps. 5–7, and Yates, *What Women Want*, chap. 3.

26. Quoted in Evans, "Tomorrow's Yesterday," p. 407.

27. The literature is extensive, beginning with Simone de Beauvoir, *The Second Sex*, trans, and ed. by H. M. Parshley (New York, 1961). Kate Millett, *Sexual Politics* (Garden City, N.Y., 1970); Shulamith Firestone. *The Dialectic of Sex: The Case for a Feminist Revolution* (New York, 1970); Germaine Greer, *The Female Eunuch* (New York, 1970); Juliet Mitchell, *Women's Estate* (New York, 1971); Evelyn Reed, *Problems of Women's Liberation: A Marxist Approach* (New York. 1971); Mary Daly, *Beyond God the Father: Toward a Philosophy of Women's Liberation* (New York, 1968); Carolyn Heilbrun, *Toward a Recognition of Androgyny* (New York, 1973). Anthologies include *Sisterhood Is Powerful*, ed. Robin Morgan; *The Black Woman: An Anthology*, ed. Toni Cade (New York, 1970); *Liberation Now: Writings from the Women's Liberation Movement*, eds. Deborah Babcox and Madeline Belkin (New York, 1971). The best historical treatment of radical feminism is Alice Echols, *Daring to Be Bad: Radical Feminism in America, 1967–1975* (Minneapolis, 1989).

28. Judith M. Bardwick, *In Transition: How Feminism, Sexual Liberation and the Search for Self-Fulfillment Have Altered America* (New York, 1979), p. 26.

29. For a fuller discussion of what is meant by the term *emancipation*, see Gerda Lerner's statement in "Politics and Culture in Women's History," *Feminist Studies* 6(1980):50.

This characterization of black feminists is from Patricia Hayden, Donna Middleton, and Patricia Robinson. "A Historical and Critical Essay for Black Women." in *Voices from Women's Liberation*, ed. Leslie B. Tanner (New York, 1971), pp. 316–24. For the differing concerns of black feminists. see Carol Kleiman, "When Black Women Rap, the Talk Sure is Different," *Chicago Tribune*, June 1, 1975, sec. 5, p. 13. Information on the Third World Women's Alliance is based on my research in its papers, which are located in the Records of the National Congress of Negro Women, Bethune Museum and Archives, Washington, D.C.

30. The phrase is that of Patricia Haden, Donna Middleton, and Patricia Robinson in "A Historical and Critical Essay for Black Women," in *Voices from Women's Liberation*, ed. Leslie B. Tanner (New York, 1971), pp. 316–324. On the Third World Women's Alliance, see Third World Women's Alliance Papers, in the National Association of Negro Women's Collection, Mary McLeod Bethune Council House, Washington, D.C.

31. Louis Harris, "Changing Views on the Role of Women," *The Harris Survey*, Dec. 11, 1975.

32. Caroline Bird and the Members and Staff of the National Commission on the Observance of International Woman's Year, *What Women Want: From the Official Report to the President, the Congress, and the People of the United States* (New York, 1979), p. 68 for Johnson's statement.

33. Violet S. Devieux to Senator Sam J. Ervin, Jr., Mar. 23, 1972, Samuel J. Ervin Papers, #3847 Southern Historical Collection, Library of the University of North Carolina at Chapel Hill. For a fuller analysis of the significance of the struggle over ERA and the debate over feminism, see Donald G. Mathews and Jane S. De Hart, *Sex, Gender, and the ERA: A State and the Nation* (New York, 1990).

34. See also De Hart, "Gender on the Right: Meanings Behind the Existential Scream," *Gender and History* 3 (1991):246–67.

35. This apt characterization is William Chafe's; see *The Paradox of Change*, p. 209.

36. See U.S. Bureau of the Census, *Statistical Abstract of the United States: 1997* (117th ed.). (Washington, D.C., 1997), pp. 160, 397–398; and *USA Today*, June 5, 1998, p. B1.

37. For a fuller discussion, see *Women's Work, Men's Work: Sex Segregation on the Job*, eds. Barbara F. Reskin and Heidi I. Hartmann (Washington, D.C., 1986).

38. Diane Pearce, "The Feminization of Poverty: Women, Work, and Welfare," *Urban and Social Change Review* 11 (1978):28–36; Barbara Ehrenreich and Francis Fox Piven, "The Feminization of Poverty: When the 'Family Wage System' Breaks Down," *Dissent* 31 (1984):162–70; Leonore J. Weitzman, *The Divorce Revolution and the Unanticipated Consequences for Women and Children in America* (New York, 1985).

39. *The American Woman, Status Report 1988–1989*, ed. Sara E. Rix (New York, 1988), p. 151.

40. Arlie Hochshild, *Second Shift: Working Parents and the Revolution at Home* (New York, 1989).

41. *New York Times*, April 15, 1998, p. A16.

42. *The American Woman, 1990–1991: A Status Report*, ed. Sara E. Rix (New York, 1990), p. 380.

43. For a fuller account of court decisions affecting women during the 1980s, see Jane Sherron De Hart, "Equality Challenged: Equal Rights and Sexual Difference," *Journal of Policy History* 6 (1994):40–72.

44. For further workforce data in a comparative perspective, see the special supplement of *The Economist* (July 18, 1998), pp. 3–16.

45. For data on women governors and state legislators, see CAWP Fact Sheet: Women in Elective Office in 1997, compiled by the Center for the American Woman and Politics, Eagleton Institute for Politics, Rutgers University; New Brunswick, N.J.

46. *New York Times*, June 16, 1997, p. A1.

47. On the celebration of *Roe*, see "NARAL News" 28:2 (Fall, 1997): 1.

48. *New York Times*, December 12, 1997, p. A3.

49. Quoted in Verta Taylor, "The Future of Feminism in the 1980s: A social Movement Analysis," in *Feminist Frontiers*, eds. Laurel Richardson and Verta Taylor (Reading, Mass., 1983), p. 442.

50. The quote is from Audre Lorde, *Sister Outsider* (Trumansburg, N.Y., 1984), p. 60. See also Angela Y. Davis, *Women, Race, and Class* (New York, 1981). For a more theoretical discussion, see Patricia Hill Collins, *Black Feminist Thought: Knowledge, Consciousness, and the Politics of Empowerment* (New York, 1990); and Nancie Caraway, *Segregated Sisterhood: Racism and the Politics of American Feminism* (Knoxville, Tenn., 1991).

51. Quoted in *Listen Up: Voices From the Next Feminist Generation*, ed. Barbara Findlen (Seattle, 1995), p. 6.

GRAPHS AND TABLES

American Birth Rates, 1800–2000

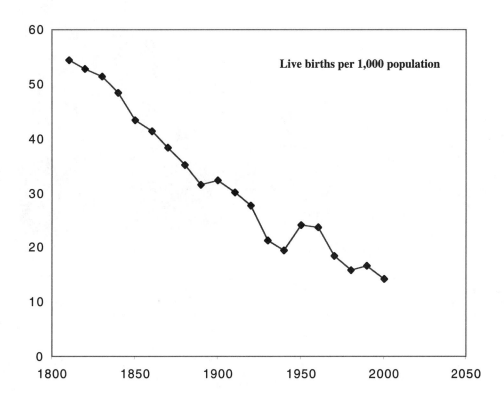

Live births per 1,000 population

Sources: 1800 to 1970: *Historical Statistics of the United States, Colonial Times to 1970*, Part 1, U.S. Department of Commerce, Bureau of the Census, (Washington, D.C., 1975), p. 49. 1980 to 1990: Advance Report of Final Natality Statistics, 1994; *Monthly Vital Statistics Report; vol. 44, no. 11, supp.* p. 28 (Hyattsville, Maryland, 1996). Projections for the year 2000: *Annual Projections and Components of Change for the United States: 1995 to 2050 (Middle Series), Part A. Total Population*, U.S. Department of Commerce, Bureau of the Census, (Washington, D.C.), accessed via internet on 8/27/98 at *http://www.census.gov/prod/1/pop/p25–1130*. Note that statistics until 1920 are for white population only.

Men and Women in the American Labor Force, 1890–2000

LABOR FORCE PARTICIPATION IN THOUSANDS

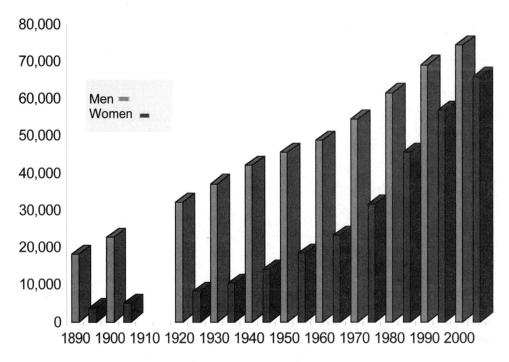

Sources: 1890–1970: *Historical Statistics of the United States, Colonial Times to 1970*, Part 1, U.S. Department of Commerce, Bureau of the Census (Washington, D.C., 1975), p. 131. 1980–2000: *Statistical Abstract of the United States, 1997*, U.S. Department of Commerce, Bureau of the Census (Washington, D.C., 1997), p. 397. Note that figures for the year 2000 are projections and that figures for 1910 are not available.

Bachelor's and Doctoral Degrees Earned by Men and Women, 1879–1880 through 2004–2005

BACHELOR'S DEGREES:

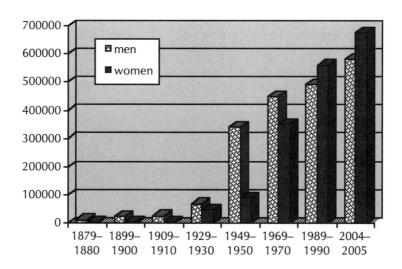

DOCTORAL DEGREES:

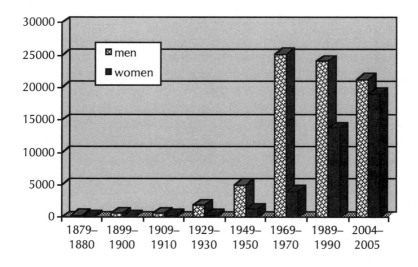

Source: *Statistical Handbook on Women in America, 2nd Edition*, Cynthia M. Taeuber, compiler and editor (Pheonix, 1996), p. 307. Note that figures for 2004–2005 are projections.

"Women's" Work: Persistence of Occupational Segregation in the U.S.

Of all jobs in given occupations, the proportion
filled by women, 1970 to 1990.

Occupation	1970	1990
Bartender	27%	57%
Chemist	17	29
Doctor	11	22
Economist	14	44
Farmer	7	17
Industrial engineer	3	27
Lawyer, judge	6	27
Librarian	84	85
Nurse	91	94
Police, detective	5	13
Psychologist	43	59
Public official	24	59
Secretary	98	98
Teacher	74	74

Source: *New York Times;* April 27, 1995, p. A12. Copyright © 1995 by *The New York Times*. Reprinted by permission.

The New Norm: Women in the Workforce in Comparative Perspective

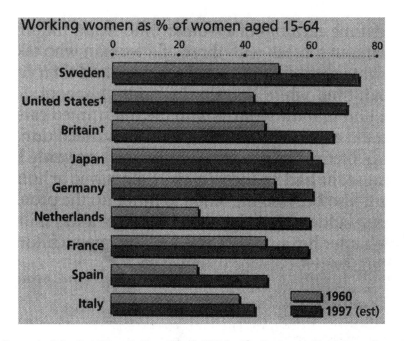

Working women as % of women aged 15-64

Source: *The Economist*, July 18, 1998, p. 7. Copyright © 1998 by The Economist Newspaper Group, Inc. Reprinted with permission. Further reproduction prohibited. www.economist.com

Who Needs Babies?: Declining Birth Rates in Comparative Perspective

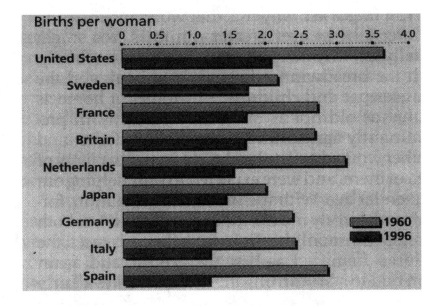

Births per woman

	1960	1996
United States		
Sweden		
France		
Britain		
Netherlands		
Japan		
Germany		
Italy		
Spain		

Source: *The Economist*, July 18, 1998, p. 4. Copyright © 1998 by The Economist Newspaper Group, Inc. Reprinted with permission. Further reproduction prohibited. www.economist.com

How Family-Friendly?: Maternity and Parental-Leave Entitlements in Comparative Perspective

	Maternity leave	% of previous pay on maternity leave	Parental leave*	Mother/father
Britain	14–18 weeks	90% initially	—	—
France	16–26 weeks	100%	3 years	Entire leave transferable
Germany	14 weeks	100%	3 years	Entire leave transferable
Italy	22 weeks	80%	6 months	Entire leave transferable
Japan	14 weeks	60%	1 year	Entire leave transferable
Netherlands	16 weeks	100%	1 year	6 months non-transferable
Spain	14 weeks	100%	3 years	Entire leave transferable
Sweden	14 weeks	75%	1 year	Transferable except for 30 days
United States	12 weeks**	0	—	—

*Previous job preserved; pay varies by country, mostly minimal. **Available to either parent.

Source: *The Economist*, July 18, 1998, p. 13. Copyright © by The Economist Newspaper Group, Inc. Reprinted with permission. Further reproduction prohibited. www.economist.com

Gendered Politics: Persistence
of Disproportionate Representation
of Women in Comparative Perspective

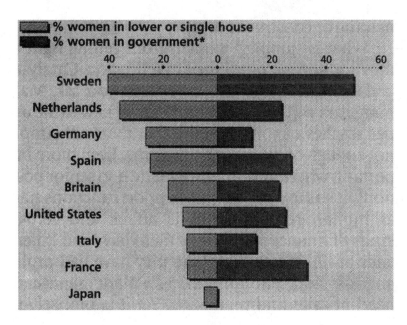

*Cabinet level.
Source: *The Economist,* July 18, 1998, p. 9. Copyright © 1998 by The Economist Newspaper Group, Inc. Reprinted with permission. Further reproduction prohibited. www.economist.com

FURTHER READING

Full citations of works preceded by an asterisk may be found in the credit lines for the appropriate selections in this volume or in the initial citation listed below.

PART I: TRADITIONAL AMERICA, 1600–1820

Biology

James Axtell, ed., *The Indian Peoples of Eastern America: A Documentary History of the Sexes* (New York, 1981), is organized in terms of life cycle and includes sections on birth, puberty, marriage, and death. Elaine Foreman Crane has edited *The Diary of Elizabeth Drinker*, 3 vols. (Boston, 1991), and a single-volume edition, *The Diary of Elizabeth Drinker: The Life Cycle of an Eighteenth Century Woman* (Boston, 1994); both include extensive comments on Drinker's experience of childbearing and motherhood. The intersection of biology and economics is revealed in Laurel Thatcher Ulrich's insightful study of a woman who delivered nearly 900 infants safely in a record comparable to that achieved in modern medical practice: *A Midwife's Tale: The Life of Martha Ballard Based on Her Diary 1785–1812* (New York, 1990). See also Daniel Scott Smith and Michael S. Hindus, "Premarital Pregnancy in America, 1640–1971: An Overview and Interpretation," *Journal of Interdisciplinary History* 5(1975):537–70.

Economics

Julia Cherry Spruill, *Women's Life and Work in the Southern Colonies* (Chapel Hill, N.C., 1938), is rich in descriptive detail and still repays reading. Carole Shammas, "The Domestic Environment in Early Modern England and America," *Journal of Social History* 31 (1980): 3–24, clarifies the economics of household management. For a thoughtful introduction to work that occupied most women much of the time, see Susan Burrows Swan, *Plain and Fancy: American Women and Their Needlework 1750–1850* (New York, 1977).

A special issue of the *Pennsylvania Magazine of History and Biography* (January 1983) has useful essays on the economic aspects of colonial women's lives; see especially Jean R. Soderland, "Black Women in Colonial Pennsylvania," pp. 49–68, and Sharon V.

Salinger, "'Send No More Women': Female Servants in Eighteenth-Century Philadelphia," pp. 29–48. For women's lives in the Chesapeake, the place to begin is Lois Green Carr and Lorena Walsh, "The Planter's Wife: The Experience of White Women in Seventeenth-Century Maryland," *William and Mary Quarterly*, 3d ser., 34 (1977):542–71. Richard S. Dunn, "A Tale of Two Plantations: Slave Life at Mesopotamia in Jamaica and Mount Airy in Virginia, 1799–1828," *William and Mary Quarterly*, 3d ser., 34 (1977):32–65, is a comparative study that provides a detailed reconstruction of the work lives of enslaved women and emphasizes the pressures under which they lived. On the law, see Elizabeth Bowles Warbasse's classic *The Changing Legal Rights of Married Women 1800–1861* (New York, 1987 [1960]), Marylynn Salmon, *Women and the Law of Property in Early America* (Chapel Hill, N.C., 1986), and Cornelia Hughes Dayton, *Women Before the Bar: Gender, Law and Society in Connecticut, 1639–1789* (Chapel Hill, N.C., 1995).

Politics

Religious and political concerns often mingled, especially in New England; see Jane Kamensky, *Governing the Tongue: The Politics of Speech in Early New England* (New York, 1998). Elaine G. Breslaw, *Tituba, Reluctant Witch of Salem: Devilish Indians and Puritan Fantasies* (New York, 1996) offers fine detective work, tracing the Indian slave Tituba to her early life in Barbados and exploring the multiethnic traditions of the occult. For more on witchcraft, in addition to *Carol Karlsen's *Devil in the Shape of a Woman*, see Elizabeth Reis, *Damned Women: Sinners & Witches in Puritan New England* (Ithaca, N.Y., 1997), Paul Boyer and Stephen Nissenbaum, *Salem Possessed: The Social Origins of Witchcraft* (Cambridge, Mass., 1974), and John Demos, *Entertaining Satan: Witchcraft and the Culture of Early New England* (New York, 1982). For white women who chose to stay with the Indians who captured them, see James E. Seaver, ed., *A Narrative of the Life of Mrs. Mary Jemison* (Syracuse, 1990 [1823]), and John Demos, *The Unredeemed Captive: A Family Story from Early America* (New York, 1994).

Ideology

For a general overview, see *Carol Berkin, *First Generations*, and *Mary Beth Norton, *Founding Mothers and Fathers*. For striking examples of the ways in which some representative colonial women interpreted their own lives, see Anne Firor Scott, "Self Portraits: Three Women," in *Uprooted Americans: Essays to Honor Oscar Handlin*, ed. Richard Bushman et al. (Boston, 1979). For the very high rates of literacy among New England women, see William J. Gilmore, *Reading Becomes a Necessity of Life: Material and Cultural Life in Rural New England, 1780–1835* (Knoxville, Tenn., 1989). For women's religious practices and understandings, see Catherine A. Brekus, *Strangers and Pilgrims: Female Preaching in America 1740–1845* (Chapel Hill, N.C., 1989), Susan Juster, *Disorderly Women: Sexual Politics and Evangelicalism in Revolutionary New England* (Ithaca, N.Y. 1994), and Janet Wilson James, ed., *Women in American Religion* (Philadelphia, 1980), especially Mary Maples Dunn, "Saints and Sisters: Congregational and Quaker Women in the Early Colonial Period."

For the interaction of biology, economics, politics, and ideology in the colonial era, see Kathleen Brown, *Good Wives, Nasty Wenches and Anxious Patriarchs: Gender, Race, and Power in Colonial Virginia* (Chapel Hill, N.C., 1996), and Elaine Foreman Crane, *Ebb Tide in New England: Women, Seaports, and Social Change, 1630–1800* (Boston, 1998). Crane extends her narrative into the Revolutionary era, engaging arguments made in Linda K. Kerber, *Women of the Republic: Intellect and Ideology in Revolutionary America* (Chapel Hill, N.C., 1980), Mary Beth Norton, *Liberty's Daughters: The Revolutionary Experience of American Women, 1750–1800* (Boston, 1980), and Ronald Hoffman and Peter J. Albert, eds., *Women in the Age of the American Revolution* (Charlottesville, Va., 1989). For the debate over the relationship of women to the state, see Carroll Smith-Rosenberg, "Discovering the Subject of the 'Great Constitutional Discussion' 1786–1789," *Journal of American History* 79 (1992): 841–73 and Linda K. Kerber, *No Constitutional Right to Be Ladies: Women and the Obligations of Citizenship* (New York, 1998), ch. 1.

PART II: THE MANY FRONTIERS
OF INDUSTRIALIZING AMERICA, 1820–1880

Biology

For an important overview, see John D'Emilio and Estelle B. Freedman, *Intimate Matters: A History of Sexuality in America* (New York, 1980), esp. Parts I and II; for childbirth, see Judith Walzer Leavitt, *Brought to Bed: Childbearing in America, 1750 to 1950* (New York, 1986). See also Carl N. Degler, *At Odds: Women and the Family in America from the Revolution to the Present* (New York, 1980), especially chapters 2–9, as well as *James Mohr, Abortion in America.* For the relationship of women to the health reform movement, see Susan E. Cayleff, *Wash and Be Healed: The Water Cure Movement and Women's Health* (Philadelphia, 1987). For problems characteristic of one region, see Sally G. McMillen, *Motherhood in the Old South: Pregnancy, Childbirth and Infant Rearing* (Baton Rouge, La., 1990).

Economics

Dorothy Sterling, ed., *We Are Your Sisters: Black Women in the Nineteenth Century* (New York, 1984), includes many well-selected documents of the working lives of black women, slave and free (it also includes documents that have much bearing on politics and ideology), as does Gerda Lerner, ed., *Black Women in White America* (New York, 1972). Willie Lee Rose, ed., *A Documentary History of Slavery in North America* (New York, 1976), and John Blassingame, ed., *Slave Testimony: Two Centuries of Letters, Speeches, Interviews and Autobiographies* (Baton Rouge, La., 1977), should also be consulted.

Deborah Gray White, *Ar'n't I A Woman?: Female Slaves in the Plantation South* (New York, 1985), and *Jacqueline Jones, *Labor of Love, Labor of Sorrow*, are basic introductions to the history of women and slavery. The most authoritative of the many editions of Harriet A. Jacobs, *Incidents in the Life of a Slave Girl* [Linda Brent] *Written By Herself*, ed. Lydia Maria Child (1860), is the one prepared with notes and a new introduction by Jean Fagen Yellin (Cambridge, Mass., 1987). Melton McLaurin, *Celia, A Slave* (Athens, Ga., 1991), is a compelling account of the trial of a woman charged with murder. Elizabeth Keckley, *Behind the Scenes, or Thirty Years a Slave, and Four Years in the White House* (reprinted New York, 1988), includes her experiences during the Civil War and her friendship with Mary Todd Lincoln.

Many elderly women who had been slaves when young were interviewed by the Federal Writers' Project in the 1930s. Selected interviews appear in B. A. Botkin, ed., *Lay My Burden Down: A Folk History of Slavery* (Chicago, 1945), and Ira Berlin et al. eds., *Remembering Slavery: African Americans Talk About Their Personal Experiences of Slavery and Freedom* (New York, 1998).

For women's work in the domestic economy, see Nancy F. Cott, *The Bonds of Womanhood: "Woman's Sphere" in New England 1780–1835* (New Haven, 1977), ch. 1. Widowhood is an economic category as well as a demographic one; see Lisa Wilson, *Life After Death: Widows in Pennsylvania 1750–1850* (Philadelphia, 1992). For analyses of the interrelationship between biology, economics, politics, and gender, see Joan Jensen, *Loosening the Bonds: Mid-Atlantic Farm Women, 1750–1850* (New Haven, 1986), and *Jeanne Boydston, *Home and Work*. For domestic work and the maintenance of gendered roles in a frontier context, see John Mack Faragher's *Women and Men on the Overland Trail* (New Haven, 1979), and *Sugar Creek: Life on the Illinois Prairie* (New Haven, 1988), and Paula Petrik's *No Step Backward: Women and Family on the Rocky Mountain Mining Frontier, Helena Montana 1865–1900*.

For the impact of industrialization on working women, see Thomas Dublin, *Women at Work: The Transformation of Work and Community in Lowell, Massachusetts, 1826–1860* (New York, 1979), Judith A. McGaw, *Most Wonderful Machine: Mechanization and Social Change in Berkshire Papermaking, 1801–1885* (Princeton, 1987); and Mary H. Blewett, *Men, Women and Work: Class, Gender and Protest in the New England Shoe Industry, 1780–1910* (Urbana, Ill., 1988). A classic memoir is Lucy Larcom, *A New England Girlhood* (1889, reprint New York, 1961); for a classic study, see Helen Sumner, *History of Women in Industry in the United States* (Washington, D.C., 1910).

For the feminization of schooling, see Richard M. Bernard and Maris A. Vinovskis, "The Female School Teacher in Ante-Bellum Massachusetts," *Journal of Social History* X(1977):332–45, and the important essays on teaching in Anne Firor Scott, *Making the Invisible Woman Visible* (Urbana, Ill., 1984). For gender and power in the schools, see Myra H. Strober and David Tyack, "Why Do Women Teach and Men Manage? A Report on Research on Schools," *Signs* V(1980):494–503.

For the origins of the first work force in which women and men worked side by side, see Cindy Sondik Aron, *Ladies and Gentlemen of the Civil Service: Middle Class Workers in Victorian America* (New York, 1987). For entry into the professions, see Mary Roth Walsh, *"Doctors Wanted, No Women Need Apply": Sexual Barriers in the Medical Profession 1835–1975* (New Haven, 1977); Regina Morantz-Sanchez, *Sympathy and Science: Women Physicians in America* (New York, 1985); Susan Reverby, *Ordered to Care: The Dilemma of American Nursing, 1850–1945* (Cambridge, Mass., 1987); and Margaret Rossiter, *Women Scientists in America: Struggles and Strategies to 1940* (Baltimore, 1982).

Politics

Nancy Isenberg, *Sex and Citizenship in Antebellum America* (Chapel Hill, N.C., 1998), links antislavery reform and political change; see also Elizabeth Varon, *We Mean to Be Counted: White Women and Politics in Antebellum Virginia* (Chapel Hill, N.C., 1998). Estelle Freedman, *Their Sisters' Keepers: Women and Prison Reform in Nineteenth-Century America* (Ann Arbor, 1981), introduces an important reform movement. Gerda Lerner, *The Grimké Sisters from South Carolina: Rebels Against Slavery* (Boston, 1967), is a readable biography that suggests the way in which abolitionism could lead to a concern for women's rights, a theme more recently pursued in Jean Fagen Yellin, *Women and Sisters: Antislavery Feminists in American Culture* (New Haven, 1990), and Dorothy Sterling, *Ahead of Her Time: Abby Kelley and the Politics of Antislavery* (New York, 1991). Sojourner Truth's *Narrative* of her life, prepared by Olive Gilbert, has been thoughtfully edited by Margaret Washington (New York, 1993). Biographies of Truth involve challenging detective work; see Carlton Mabee, *Sojourner Truth: Slave, Prophet, Legend* (New York, 1993), and Nell Irvin Painter, *Sojourner Truth: A Life, a Symbol* (New York, 1996).

Ellen Carol DuBois, *Feminism and Suffrage: The Emergence of an Independent Women's Movement in America, 1848–1869* (Ithaca, N.Y., 1978), stresses the radicalism of the demand for suffrage. Nancy Hewitt, *Women's Activism and Social Change: Rochester, New York, 1822–1872* (Ithaca, N.Y., 1984), and Lori Ginzberg, *Women and the Work of Benevolence: Morality and Politics in the Nineteenth Century United States* (New Haven, 1990), incisively examine reformers' tactics and underlying strategies. For an overview of women's organizations at the local and national levels, see Anne Firor Scott, *Natural Allies: Women's Associations in American History* (Urbana, Ill., 1991). For women's participation in a variety of public sectors, see Mary Ryan, *Women in Public: Between Banners and Bullets, 1825–1880* (Baltimore, 1990).

The Selected Papers of Elizabeth Cady Stanton and Susan B. Anthony, ed. Ann D. Gordon (New Brunswick, N.J., 1997), makes unusually compelling reading; Stanton had a wicked wit. Selections from the correspondence between Stanton and Anthony and some of their more notable testimony and speeches are conveniently available in Ellen Carol DuBois, ed., *Elizabeth Cady Stanton, Susan B. Anthony: Correspondence, Writing and Speeches* (New York, 1981). Six massive volumes of the basic sources on the suffrage movement have been conveniently abridged in *A Concise History of Woman Suffrage: Selections from the Classic Work of Stanton, Anthony, Gare and Harper*, ed. Mari Jo Buhle and Paul Buhle (Urbana, Ill., 1978). Gerda Lerner examines the process of women's politicization in *The Creation of Feminist Consciousness: From the Middle Ages to 1870* (New York, 1993).

There are many memoirs of women's participation in the Civil War, among them *Belle Boyd in Camp and Prison*, ed. Sharon Kennedy-Nolle (Baton Rouge, La., 1998); Susie King Taylor, *A Black Woman's Civil War Memoirs*, ed. Patricia W. Romero and Willie Lee Rose (New York, 1988); *Civil War Nurse: The Diary and Letters of Hannah Ropes*, ed. John R. Brumgardt (Knoxville, Tenn., 1980); Sarah Emma Edmonds, *Nurse and Spy in the Union Army* (Hartford, 1865); Louisa May Alcott, *Hospital Sketches* (New York, 1863); and Mary A. Livermore, *My Story of the War* (Hartford, 1865). For the perspective of a Southern woman on the home front, see the compelling *Mary Chestnut's Civil War* ed. C. Vann Woodward (New Haven, 1981). Catherine Clinton and Nina Silber, eds., *Divided Houses: Gender and the Civil War* (New York, 1992), is a collection of recent work; see also Catherine Clinton, *Tara Revisited: Women, War, and the Plantation Legend* (New York, 1995), George C. Rable, *Civil Wars: Women and the Crisis of Southern Nationalism* (Urbana, Ill., 1989), and *Drew Gilpin Faust, *Mothers of Invention*.

Compelling new interpretations of the Reconstruction era, which link economics, politics, and ideology in complex ways, have recently been published: see Laura Edwards, *Gendered Strife and Confusion: The Political Culture of Reconstruction* (Urbana, Ill., 1997); Lee Ann Whites, *The Civil War as a Crisis in Gender: Augusta, Georgia 1860–1890*

(Athens, Ga., 1995); and Martha Hodes, *White Women, Black Men: Illicit Sex in the Nineteenth Century South* (New Haven, 1997).

Ideology

"The Cult of True Womanhood" was given its name in an essay with the same title by Barbara Welter, *American Quarterly* 18 (1966):151–74. A challenging interpretation of some of the same sources is offered by Gerda Lerner in her classic essay, "The Lady and the Mill Girl," which appears in *The Majority Finds Its Past: Placing Women in History* (New York, 1979), ch. 2.

The relationship of women's roles to a developing economy is brilliantly dissected in Mary P. Ryan, *Cradle of the Middle Class: The Family in Oneida County, New York, 1970–1865* (Cambridge, Mass., 1981), and *Women in Public: Between Banners and Ballots 1825–1880* (Baltimore, 1990). The social construction of gender is insightfully explored in Carroll Smith-Rosenberg, *Disorderly Conduct: Visions of Gender in Victorian America* (New York, 1985), and Lee Chambers-Schiller, *Liberty, A Better Husband: Single Women in America: The Generations of 1780–1840* (New Haven, 1984). For the intersections of gender, class, and sexuality in a major city, see Christine Stansell, *City of Women: Sex and Class in New York* (New York, 1986); Timothy Gilfoyle, *City of Eros: New York City, Prostitution and the Commercialization of Sex 1790–1920* (New York, 1992); and Patricia Cline Cohen, *The Murder of Helen Jewett: The Life and Death of a Prostitute in Nineteenth-Century New York* (New York, 1998). For efforts to control domestic violence, see Elizabeth H. Pleck, *Domestic Tyranny: The Making of American Social Policy Against Family Violence from Colonial Times to the Present* (New York, 1987). For radical experiments in changing gender roles, see Maren Lockwood Carden, *Oneida: Utopian Community to Modern Corporation* (Baltimore, 1969).

For changes in the legal construction of gender, see Norma Basch, *In the Eyes of the Law: Women, Marriage and Property in Nineteenth Century New York* (Ithaca, N.Y., 1982); Ellen Carol DuBois, "Outgrowing the Compact of the Fathers: Equal Rights, Woman Suffrage, and the United States Constitution, 1820–1878," *Journal of American History* 74 (1987):836–62; Peter Bardaglio, *Reconstructing the Household: Families, Sex and the Law in the Nineteenth Century South* (Chapel Hill, N.C., 1995); and Amy Dru Stanley, *From Bondage to Contract: Wage Labor, Marriage and the Market in the Age of Slave Emancipation* (Cambridge, Eng., 1998).

In *The Free Women of Petersburg: Status and Culture in a Southern Town* (New York, 1984), Suzanne Lebsock examines the interconnection of biology, economics, politics, and ideology in a single city. The relationship of poor Southern white women to state power is analyzed in Victoria Bynum, *Unruly Women: The Politics of Social and Sexual Control in the Old South, 1840–1865* (Chapel Hill, N.C., 1992). Elizabeth Fox-Genovese, *Within the Plantation Household: Black and White Women of the Old South* (Chapel Hill, N.C., 1988), is an effort to treat mistresses and enslaved women as part of the same social order; see also Nell Irvin Painter, ed., *The Secret Eye: The Journal of Ella Clanton Thomas, 1848–1889* (Chapel Hill, N.C., 1990).

Women's claims to intellectual authority are examined in Mary Kelley, "Reading Women/Women Reading: The Making of Learned Women in Antebellum America," *Journal of American History* 83 (1996):401–24, and *Private Woman, Public Stage: Literary*

Domesticity in Nineteenth-Century America (New York, 1984). See also Annette Kolodny, *the Land Before Her: Fantasy and Experience of the American Frontiers, 1630–1860* (Chapel Hill, N.C., 1984). The making of marriages is evaluated in Ellen K. Rothman, *Hands and Hearts: A History of Courtship in America* (New York, 1984). For the way in which religious beliefs affected women's roles and behavior, see Joan Jacobs Brumberg, *Mission for Life: The Story of the Family of Adoniram Johnson* (New York, 1980).

PART III: THE MANY FRONTIERS
OF INDUSTRIALIZING AMERICA, 1880–1920

For overviews of minority women, see Karen Anderson, *Changing Woman: A History of Racial Ethnic Women in Modern America* (New York, 1997); *Judy Yung, *Unbound Feet* (Berkeley, 1995); Vicki L. Ruiz, *From Out of the Shadows: Mexican Women in 20th Century America* (New York, 1995); *Jacqueline Jones, *Labor of Love, Labor of Sorrow*; and *We Specialize in the Wholly Impossible: A Reader in Black Women's History*, ed. Darlene Clark Hine, Alma King, and Linda Reed (Brooklyn, 1995). For overviews with a regional focus, see *Writing the Range: Race, Class, and Culture in the Women's West*, ed. Elizabeth Jameson and Susan Armitage (New York, 1997); Christine Anne Farnham, *Women of the American South: A Multicultural Reader* (New York, 1997); and Huping Ling, *Surviving on the Gold Mountain: A History of Chinese American Women and Their Lives* (Ithaca, N.Y., 1998).

Biology and Sexuality

Biology and ideology interacted in the medical treatment of women, a subject much discussed in scholarly articles. See, for example, Carroll Smith-Rosenberg and Charles Rosenberg, "The Female Animal: Medical and Biological Views of Woman and Her Role in Nineteenth-Century America," *Journal of American History* 60 (1973): 332–56. For differing interpretations of Sanger and the birth control movement, see Linda Gordon, *Woman's Body, Woman's Right: Birth Control in America* (New York, 1977); James Reed, *From Private Vice to Public Virtue: The Birth Control Movement and American Society Since 1830* (New York, 1978); David M. Kennedy, *Birth Control in America: The Career of Margaret Sanger* (New Haven, 1970); and Ellen Chesler, *Woman of Valor: Margaret Sanger and the Birth Control Movement in America* (New York, 1992). For an overview of women's sexuality during this period, see *Carl N. Degler, *At Odds*, chaps. 11–12, and *John D'Emilio and Estelle B. Freedman, *Intimate Matters*, chaps. 8–10. See also *Powers of Desire: The Politics of Sexuality*, ed. Anne Snitow, Christine Stansell, and Sharon Thompson (New York, 1983), and *Passion and Power: Sexuality in History*, ed. Kathy Peiss and Christina Simmons (Philadelphia, 1989). For developments in childbirth, see *Judith Walzer Leavitt, *Brought to Bed*, chaps. 3–6. For abortion, see Leslie J. Reagan, *When Abortion Was a Crime: Women, Medicine, and the Law, 1867–1973* (Berkeley, 1997). Another issue that is biologically related and also intersects with ideology and the state is the physical abuse of women's bodies in situations of domestic violence. See Linda Gordon, *Heroes of Their Own Lives: The Politics and History of Family Violence, Boston, 1880–1960* (New York, 1988), chap. 8; *Elizabeth Pleck, *Domestic Tyranny*, chap. 6; and David Peterson Del Mar, *What Trouble I Have Seen: A History of Violence Against Wives* (Cambridge, Mass., 1998).

Economics

Housework engaged all women, except for the most privileged. See Ruth Schwartz Cowan, *More Work for Mother: The Ironies of Household Technology from the Open Hearth to the Microwave* (New York, 1983), chaps. 4–6, and Susan Strasser, *Never Done: A History of American Housework* (New York, 1982), chaps. 1–12. Farm women had additional burdens, as described in Deborah Fink, *Agrarian Women: Wives and Mothers in Rural Nebraska, 1880–1940* (Chapel Hill, N.C., 1992), Nancy Grey Osterud, *Bonds of Community: The Lives of Farm Women in Nineteenth Century New York* (Ithaca, N.Y., 1991), and Marilyn Irvin Holt, *Linoleum, Better Babies, and the Modern Farm Woman, 1890–1930* (Albuquerque, 1995).

Whether women worked outside the home and at what jobs depended on economic need and work options as well as family expectations. How family expectations and work options interacted with different ethnic groups is explored in a variety of studies. See, for example, *Tera W. Hunter, *To 'Joy My Freedom;* *Jacqueline Jones, *Labor of Love, Labor of Sorrow,* chaps. 4–5; Virginia Yans-McLaughlin, *Family and Community: Italian Immigrants in Buffalo, 1880–1930* (Ithaca, N.Y., 1977); Louise Lamphere, *From Working Daughters to Working Mothers: Immigrant Women in a New England Industrial Community* (Ithaca, N.Y., 1989); *Sara Deutsch, *No Separate Refuge;* Janet A. Nolan, *Ourselves Alone: Women Immigrants from Ireland* (Lexington, N.Y., 1989); and Susan A. Glenn, *Daughters of the Shtetl: Life and Labor in the Immigrant Generation* (Ithaca, N.Y., 1990).

For a general study of working-class women who found work options in industry, see Leslie Woodcock Tentler, *Wage-Earning Women: Industrial Work and Family Life in the United States, 1900–1930* (New York, 1979), and Ardis Cameron, *Radicals of the Worst Sort: Laboring Women in Lawrence, Massachusetts, 1860–1912* (Urbana, Ill., 1993). For those finding new opportunities in other areas, see Patricia A. Cooper, *Once a Cigar Maker: Men, Women, and Work Culture in American Cigar Factories, 1900–1919* (Urbana, Ill., 1987); Ileen A. DeVault, *Sons and Daughters of Labor: Class and Clerical Work in Turn-of-the-Century Pittsburgh* (Ithaca, N.Y., 1990); Miriam Cohen, *Workshop to Office: Two Generations of Italian Women in New York City, 1900–1950* (Ithaca, N.Y., 1993); and Susan Porter Benson, *Counter Cultures: Saleswomen, Managers, and Customers in American Department Stores: 1890–1940* (Urbana, Ill., 1986). Shoplifters rather than shopworkers are the focus of Elaine Abelson's *When Ladies Go A-Thieving: Middle-Class Shoplifters in the Victorian Department Store* (New York, 1989). Prostitution also provided jobs whether women entered such work voluntarily or, as many did, involuntarily, as demonstrated in Ruth Rosen's *Lost Sisterhood: Prostitution in America, 1900–1918* (Baltimore, 1982), and Benson Tong's *Unsubmissive Women: Chinese Prostitutes in Nineteenth-Century San Francisco* (Norman, Okla., 1994).

How working-class women used their leisure and whether leisure activities contributed to individual and/or collective self-improvement are issues explored by *Kathy Peiss, *Cheap Amusements,* and Elizabeth Ewen, *Immigrant Women in the Land of Dollars: Life and Culture on the Lower East Side, 1890–1925* (New York, 1985). For efforts to improve the economic well-being of working-class women through unionization, see *Annelise Orleck, *Common Sense and a Little Fire;* Susan Levine, *Labor's True Woman: Carpet Weavers, Industrialization, and Labor Reform in the Gilded Age* (Philadelphia, 1984); Nancy Schrom Dye, *As Equals and as Sisters: Feminism, the Labor Movement and the Women's Trade Union League of New York* (Columbia, Mo., 1980); Elizabeth A. Payne, *Reform, Labor, and Feminism: Margaret Dreier Robins and the Women's Trade Union League* (Urbana, Ill., 1988);

Stephen H. Norwood, *Labor's Flaming Youth: Telephone Operators and Worker Militancy, 1878–1923* (Urbana, Ill., 1990); as well as selected essays in *Women, Work, and Protest: A Century of U.S. Women's Labor History,* ed. Ruth Milkman (Boston, 1985). On the larger issue of working-class consciousness, see Sarah Eisenstein, *Give Us Bread but Give Us Roses: Working Women's Consciousness in the United States, 1890 to the First World War* (London, 1983).

Better educated, middle-class women also discovered new opportunities for employment in a variety of new professions. See, for example, Barbara Melosh, *The Physician's Hand: Work, Culture, and Conflict in American Nursing* (Philadelphia, 1982); Susan M. Reverby, *Ordered to Care: The Dilemma of American Nursing 1850–1945* (Cambridge, Mass., 1987); Darlene Clark Hine, *Black Women in White: Racial Conflict and Cooperation in the Nursing Profession, 1890–1950* (Bloomington, Ind., 1989); *Regina Morantz-Sanchez, *Sympathy and Science* (New York, 1985); Gloria Moldow, *Women Doctors in Gilded Age Washington: Gender, Race, and Professionalization* (Urbana, Ill., 1987); *Margaret W. Rossiter, *Women Scientists in America;* Virginia G. Drachman, *Sisters in Law: Women Lawyers in Modern American History* (Cambridge, Mass., 1998); and Adrienne Fried Block, *Amy Beach, Passionate Victorian: The Life and Works of the American Composer, 1867–1944* (New York, 1998). See also Barbara Miller Solomon, *In the Company of Educated Women: A History of Women and Higher Education in America* (New Haven, 1985), and Dee Garrison, *Apostles of Culture: The Public Librarian and American Society, 1876–1920* (New York, 1979). For new opportunities provided by office work, see Margery W. Davies, *Woman's Place Is at the Typewriter: Office Work and Office Workers, 1879–1930* (Philadelphia, 1982), Lisa M. Fine, *The Souls of Skyscrapers: Female Clerical Workers in Chicago, 1890–1930* (Philadelphia, 1990), Sharon Strom Hartman, *Beyond the Typewriter: Gender, Class, and the Origins of Modern American Office Work, 1900–1930* (Champaign, Ill., 1992), and Cindy Sondik Aron, *Ladies and Gentlemen of the Civil Service* (New York, 1998). Black women found new work in the professions as well as entrepreneurial opportunities in the new beauty business, as did white women. See Stephanie J. Shaw, *What a Woman Ought to Be and to Do: Black Professional Women Workers During the Jim Crow Era* (Chicago, 1995), and Kathy Peiss, *Hope in a Jar: The Making of America's Beauty Culture* (New York, 1998). On the first generation of working women to live alone, see Joanne J. Meyerowitz, *Women Adrift: Independent Wage Earners in Chicago, 1880–1930* (Chicago, 1988).

For an important overview of this changing work force, see Alice Kessler-Harris, *Out to Work: A History of Wage-Earning Women in the United States* (New York, 1982), secs. 2–3; Lynn Y. Weiner, *From Working Girl to Working Mother: The Female Labor Force in the United States, 1820–1920* (Chapel Hill, N.C., 1985), chap. 3; and Claudia Goldin, *Understanding the Gender Gap: An Economic History of American Women* (New York, 1989). On the application of gender analysis to labor history, see Ava Baron, "Gender and Labor History: Learning from the Past, Looking at the Future," in *Work Engendered: Toward a New History of American Labor* (Ithaca, N.Y., 1991), pp. 1–46.

Politics

There is increasing literature on female political activism in the decades before women could vote. Paula Baker examines the intimate relationship between gender and politics in "The Domestication of Politics: Women and American Political Society, 1780–1920," *The American Historical Review* 89 (June 1984): 620–48. Studies of the temperance movement include Ruth Bordin, *Woman and Temperance: The Quest for Power and Liberty, 1873–1900* (Philadelphia, 1980); Barbara Epstein, *The Politics of Domesticity: Women, Evangelism, and Temperance in Nineteenth-Century America* (Middletown, Conn., 1981); and Ian Tyrrell, *Woman's World, Woman's Empire: The Woman's Christian Temperance Union in International Perspective, 1880–1930* (Chapel Hill, N.C., 1991). On women's clubs, see Karen Blair, *The Clubwoman as Feminist: True Womanhood Redefined, 1868–1914* (New York, 1980); Theodora Penny Martin, *The Sound of Our Own Voices: Women's Study Clubs, 1860–1910* (Boston, 1987); Anne Ruggles Gere, *Intimate Practices: Literacy and Cultural Work in U.S. Women's Clubs, 1880–1920* (Urbana, Ill., 1997). On black women's clubs, see Anne Miess Knupfer, *Toward a Tenderer and a Nobler Womanhood: African American Women's Clubs in Turn-of-the-Century Chicago* (New York, 1996). Leila J. Rupp, *Worlds of Women: The Making of an International Women's Movement* (Princeton, 1998), examines the internationalization of the movement.

Women's voluntary associations and philanthropy are examined in Prescilla Murolo, *The Ground of Womanhood: Class, Gender, and Working Girls' Clubs, 1884–1928* (Champaign, Ill., 1996); Anne Firor Scott, *Natural Allies: Women's Associations in American History* (Urbana, Ill., 1991); Elizabeth Hayes Turner, *Women, Culture and Community: Religion and Reform in Galveston 1880–1923* (New York, 1997); and Kathleen D. McCarthy, *Lady Bountiful Revisited: Women, Philanthropy, and Power* (New Brunswick, N.J., 1990). McCarthy also explores women's philanthropic involvement in the art world in *Women's Culture: American Philanthropy and Art, 1830–1930* (Urbana, Ill., 1991).

Women missionaries are the subject of Jane Hunter's *The Gospel of Gentility: American Women Missionaries in Turn-of-the-Century China* (New Haven, 1989) and of Peggy Pascoe's *Relations of Rescue: The Search for Female Moral Authority in the American West, 1874–1939* (New York, 1990). Social purity advocates are the focus of Alison M. Parker, *Purifying America: Women, Cultural Reform, and Pro-Censorship Activism, 1873–1933* (Urbana, Ill., 1997).

For black women's activism, see Paula Giddings, *When and Where I Enter: The Impact of Black Women on Race and Sex in America* (New York, 1984); Evelyn Brooks Higginbotham, *Righteous Discontent: The Women's Movement in the Black Baptist Church, 1880–1920* (Cambridge, Mass., 1993); Susan L. Smith, *Sick and Tired of Being Sick and Tired: Black Women's Health Activism in America, 1890–1950* (Philadelphia, 1995); Judith Weisenfeld, *African American Women and Christian Activism: New York's Black YWCA 1905–1945* (Cambridge, Mass., 1998); and *Glenda E. Gilmore, *Gender and Jim Crow.*

The most famous group of reformers were the settlement house women, whose political activism is skillfully probed in Kathryn Kish Sklar's "Hull House in the 1890s: A Community of Women Reformers," *Signs* (1985): 658–77 and her *Florence Kelley and the Nation's Work: The Rise of Women's Political Culture, 1830–1900* (New Haven, 1995). On Jane Addams, see Allen Davis, *American Heroine: The Life and Legend of Jane Addams* (New York, 1973), and *The Social Thought of Jane Addams*, ed. Christopher Lasch (New York, 1965).

On the relationships between social service and the new profession of social work, see Clarke A. Chambers, *Seedtime of Reform: Social Service and Social Action, 1918–1933* (Ann Arbor, 1967), and Robyn Muncy, *Creating a Female Dominion in American Reform, 1890–1935* (New York, 1991). For a first-hand account of many facets of female activism by a pioneer in industrial medicine, see *Alice Hamilton: A Life in Letters*, ed. Barbara Sicherman (Cambridge, Mass., 1984).

On delinquent girls and the women reformers, see *Regina G. Kunzel, *Fallen Women, Problem Girls*, chaps. 1–4; Ruth M. Alexander, *The "Girl Problem": Female Sexual Delinquency in New York, 1900–1930* (Ithaca, N.Y., 1995); and Mary E. Odum, *Delinquent Daughters: Protecting and Policing Adolescent Female Sexuality in the United States, 1885–1920* (Chapel Hill, N.C., 1995). On courts and correctional institutions, see Elizabeth J. Clapp, *Mothers of All Children: Women Reformers and the Rise of Juvenile Courts in Progressive-Era America* (University Park, Pa., 1998), and Anne M. Butler, *Gendered Justice in the American West: Women Prisoners in Men's Penitentiaries* (Urbana, Ill., 1997).

Female activists and social scientists also had an impact on other social policies, as is demonstrated in Ellen Fitzpatrick, *Endless Crusade: Women Social Scientists and Progressive Reform* (New York, 1990); Theda Skocpol, *The Political Origins of Social Policy in the United States* (Cambridge, Mass., 1992); Molly Ladd-Taylor, *Mother-Work: Women, Child Welfare, and the State, 1890–1930* (Urbana, Ill., 1994); Joanne L. Goodwin, *Gender and the Politics of Welfare Reform: Mother's Pensions in Chicago, 1911–1929* (Chicago, 1997); and Linda Gordon, *Pitied but Not Entitled: Single Mothers and the History of Welfare, 1890–1935* (New York, 1994).

The peace movement and the socialist movement also attracted dedicated activists. On peace movement participation, see Carrie A. Foster, *The Women and the Warriors: The U.S. Section of the Women's International League for Peace and Freedom, 1915–1946* (Syracuse, N.Y., 1995); see also Catherine Foster, *Women for All Seasons: The Story of the Women's International League for Peace and Freedom* (Athens, Ga., 1989). Participation in the socialist movement and its politics was also an important part of the process of political socialization for women, as is ably documented by Mari Jo Buhle in *Women and American Socialism, 1870–1920* (Urbana, Ill., 1983).

Biographies of radicals include Candace Falk, *Love, Anarchy and Emma Goldman: A Biography* (New York, 1989); Dee Garrison, *Mary Heaton Vorse: The Life of an American Insurgent* (Philadelphia, 1989); Janice R. MacKinnon and Stephen R. MacKinnon, *Agnes Smedley: The Life and Times of an American Radical* (Berkeley, 1987); and Helen C. Camp, *Iron in Her Soul: Elizabeth Gurley Flynn and the American Left* (Pullman, Wash., 1995).

The classic history of suffrage, Eleanor Flexner's *Century of Struggle: The Woman's Rights Movement in the United States* (Cambridge, Mass., 1958), should be supplemented with *Ellen Carol DuBois, *Harriot Stanton Blatch and the Winning of Woman Suffrage;* Sara Hunter Graham, *Women Suffrage and the New Democracy* (New Haven, 1996); and Suzanne Marilley, *Woman Suffrage and the Origins of Liberal Feminism, 1880–1920* (Cambridge, Mass., 1996). New books on African American women and suffrage include Rosalyn Terborg-Penn, *African-American Women in the Struggle for the Vote, 1850–1920* (Bloomington, Ind., 1998); *African American Women and the Vote, 1837–1935*, ed. Anne D. Gordon with Bettye Collier-Thomas et al. (Amherst, Mass., 1997). For illuminating regional studies, see Marjorie Spruill Wheeler's *New Women of the New South: The Leaders of the Woman Suffrage Movement in the Southern States* (New York, 1993), and Elna Green, *Southern Strategies: Southern Women and the Woman Suffrage Question* (Chapel Hill, N.C., 1997). On anti-suffragists, see Susan E. Marshall, *Splintered Sisterhood: Gender and Class in the Campaign Against Woman's Suffrage* (Madison, Wis., 1997).

On the Woman's Party, see Christina A. Leonardi, *From Equal Suffrage to Equal Rights: Alice Paul and the National Woman's Party, 1910–1928* (New York, 1986). For women's involvement in other political parties, see Robert J. Dinkin, *Before Equal Suffrage: Women in Partisan Politics from Colonial Times to 1920* (Westport, Conn., 1995), and Michael Goldberg, *An Army of Women: Gender and Politics in Gilded Age Kansas* (Baltimore, 1997).

Ideology

*Carroll Smith-Rosenberg, *Disorderly Conduct,* extends its sophisticated and nuanced treatment of gender ideology and social change into the early twentieth century. On ideology and education, see Devon A. Mihesuah, *Cultivating the Rosebuds: The Education of Women at the Cherokee Female Seminary, 1851–1928* (Urbana, Ill., 1993); Barbara Miller Solomon, *In the Company of Educated Women* (New Haven, 1985); Helen L. Horowitz, *Alma Mater: Design and Experience in the Women's Colleges from Their Nineteenth Century Beginning to the 1930s* (New York, 1984); Lynn D. Gordon, *Gender and Higher Education in the Progressive Era* (New Haven, 1990); and Dorothy C. Holland and Margaret A. Eisenhart, *Educated in Romance: Women, Achievement, and Culture* (Chicago, 1990). The way ideology affected both attitudes toward divorce and the debate on changing divorce laws is evident in Glenda Riley, *Divorce: An American Tradition* (New York, 1991). The effect of ideology on changing standards of beauty is explored in Lois Banner, *American Beauty* (New York, 1983). The intersection of ideology and technology is explored in Virginia Scharff, *Taking the Wheel: Women and the Coming of the Motor Age* (New York, 1991). For insight into contemporary feminist thought, see Ann J. Lane, *To "Herland" and Beyond: The Life and Work of Charlotte Perkins Gilman* (New York, 1990), and Nancy F. Cott, *A Woman Making History: Mary Ritter Beard Through Her Letters* (New Haven, 1991).

PART IV: MODERN AMERICA, 1920–2000

For overviews of the period, see William H. Chafe, *The Paradox of Change: American Women in the 20th Century* (New York, 1991), and Rosalind Rosenberg, *Divided Lives: American Women in the Twentieth Century* (New York, 1992). On minority women, see *Karen Anderson, *Changing Woman;* *Judy Yung, *Unbound Feet;* Vicki L. Ruiz, *From Out of the Shadows;* and *Christine Anne Farnham, *Women of the American South.*

Biology and Sexuality

On sexuality, see *John D'Emilio and Estelle B. Freedman, *Intimate Matters,* chaps. 11–15. On the development of homosexual subcultures, see John D'Emilio, *Sexual Politics, Sexual Communities: The Making of a Homosexual Minority in the U.S., 1940–1970* (Chicago, 1983); also Allan Berube, *Coming Out Under Fire: Gay Men and Women in World War II* (New York, 1990). For recent scholarship on gay and lesbian studies, see Eric Marcus, *Making History: The Struggle for Gay and Lesbian Equal Rights, 1945–1990: An Oral History* (New York, 1992), and Lillian Faderman, *Odd Girls and Twilight Lovers: A History of Lesbian Life in Twentieth-Century America* (New York, 1991). On birth control and the black community, see Jessie M. Rodrique, "The Black Community and the Birth Control Movement," in *Kathy Peiss and Christina Simmons, eds., *Passion and Power.* For infertility and childbirth, see Elaine Tyler May, *Barren in the Promised Land: Childless Americans and the Pursuit of Happiness* (New York, 1995) and *Judith Walzer Leavitt, *Brought to Bed,* chaps. 7–8. On single pregnancy, see Rickie Solinger, *Wake Up Little Susie: Single Preg-*

nancy and Race Before Roe v. *Wade* (New York, 1992), and Kristen Luker, *Dubious Conceptions: The Politics of Teenage Pregnancy* (Cambridge, Mass., 1996). The role of the state in relation to both reproductive freedom and domestic violence cuts across biology, ideology, and politics. On abortion and fetal politics, see Rosalind Pollack Petchesky, *Abortion and Woman's Choice: The State, Sexuality and Reproductive Freedom* (New York, 1984); Leslie J. Reagan, *When Abortion Was a Crime: Women, Medicine, and the Law 1867–1973* (Berkeley, 1997); and Cynthia Daniels, *At Women's Expense: State Power and the Policies of Fetal Rights* (Cambridge, Mass., 1993).

On battering, see *Elizabeth Pleck, *Domestic Tyranny,* chaps. 7–10, and David Peterson Del Mar, *What Trouble I Have Seen: A History of Violence Against Wives.* Eating disorders and aging also involve the intersection of biology and ideology, as is demonstrated in *Joan Jacob Brumberg's *Fasting Girls* and Lois Banner's *In Full Flower: Aging Women, Power and Sexuality: A History* (New York, 1992), chaps. 7–9.

Economics

For an overview, see *Alice Kessler-Harris, *Out to Work,* and *Lynn Y. Weiner, *From Working Girl to Working Mother,* chaps. 4–6. On the interaction of family expectations for more recent immigrant women, see Donna Gabaccia, *From the Other Side: Women, Gender, and Immigrant Life in the U.S., 1820–1990* (Bloomington, Ind., 1994). For the 1930s, see Lois Scharf, *To Work and to Wed: Female Employment, Feminism and the Great Depression* (Westport, Conn., 1980), and Winifred Wandersee, *Women's Work and Family Values, 1920–1940* (Cambridge, Mass., 1981). Women who engaged in paid labor in the home are the focus of *Homework: Historical and Contemporary Perspectives on Paid Labor at Home,* ed. Eileen Boris and Cynthia R. Daniels (Urbana, Ill., 1989). The impact of technology on farm women's work is described in Katherine Jellison, *Entitled to Power: Farm Women and Technology, 1913–1963* (Chapel Hill, N.C., 1993). Southern textile workers are the focus of Jacquelyn Dowd Hall et al., *Like a Family: The Making of a Southern Cotton Mill World* (Chapel Hill, N.C., 1987).

For additional employment opportunities provided in the military, law enforcement, and construction, see Leisa D. Meyer, *Creating G.I. Jane: Sexuality and Power in the Women's Army Corps During World War II* (New York, 1996); Molly Merryman, *Clipped Wings: The Rise and Fall of the Women Air Force Service Pilots (WASPS) of World War II* (New York, 1998); Dorothy Moses Shulz, *From Social Worker to Crime Fighter: Women in United States Municipal Policing* (Westport, Conn., 1995); Janis Appier, *Policing Women: The Sexual Politics of Law Enforcement and the LAPD* (Philadelphia, 1998); and Susan Eisenberg, *We'll Call You If We Need You: Experiences of Women Working Construction* (Ithaca, N.Y., 1998).

On women and labor unions, see Dorothy Sue Cobble, *Dishing It Out: Waitresses and Their Unions in the Twentieth Century* (Urbana, Ill., 1991); Nancy F. Gabin, *Feminism in the Labor Movement: Women and the United Auto Workers, 1935–1975* (Ithaca, N.Y., 1990); and Elizabeth Faue, *Community of Suffering and Struggle: Women, Men, and the Labor Movement in Minneapolis, 1915–1945* (Chapel Hill, N.C., 1991). On Hispanic women and unionization, see Vicki L. Ruiz, *Cannery Women, Cannery Lives: Mexican Women, Unionization, and the California Food Processing Industry, 1930–1950* (Albuquerque, 1987). For the particular problems facing black women, see *Jacqueline Jones, *Labor of Love, Labor of Sorrow,* chaps. 6–7; Dolores Janiewski, *Sisterhood Denied: Race, Class, and Gender in a New South Commu-*

nity (Philadelphia, 1985); Elizabeth Clark-Lewis, *"This Work Hada' End": The Transition from Live-in to Day Work* (Memphis, 1985); and Phyllis Palmer, *Domesticity and Dirt: Housewives and Domestic Servants in the United States, 1920–1945* (Philadelphia, 1990).

Karen Anderson explores women's work as part of a larger study of women's status during World War II in *Wartime Women: Sex Roles, Family Relations and the Status of Women during World War II* (Westport, Conn., 1981), as does Susan M. Hartmann in *The Home Front and Beyond: American Women in the 1940s* (Boston, 1982). Job segregation in two key industries is the focus of Ruth Milkman's *Gender at Work: The Dynamics of Job Segregation by Sex During WWII* (Urbana, Ill., 1997). On wage equity, see *Alice Kessler-Harris, *A Woman's Wage*, chaps. 4–5. Discrimination in the professions is examined in such studies as Mary Roth Walsh's *Doctors Wanted, No Women Need Apply: Sexual Barriers in the Medical Profession, 1835–1975* (New Haven, 1977). The challenge of combining marriage, family, and career is perhaps best explored in biographies such as Joyce Antler's *Lucy Sprague Mitchell: The Making of a Modern Woman* (New Haven, 1987).

Politics

On the impact of suffrage, see Kristi Anderson, *After Suffrage* (Chicago, 1996). The activities of politically active women in the aftermath of suffrage were first probed in J. Stanley Lemons, *The Woman Citizen: Social Feminism in the 1920s* (Urbana, Ill., 1975). More recent works include Felice Gordon's *After Winning: The Legacy of New Jersey Suffragists 1920–1946* (New Brunswick, N.J., 1986) and Nancy F. Cott's rich and persuasive *The Grounding of Modern Feminism* (New Haven, 1987). For black women's activism, see *Paula Giddings's *When and Where I Enter*, and Jacqueline Anne Rouse, *Lugenia Burns Hope: Black Southern Reformers* (Athens, Ga., 1989). On women reformers' continued concern for industrial conditions, see Claudia Clark, *Radium Girls: Women and Industrial Health Reform, 1910–1935* (Chapel Hill, N.C., 1997). The political activism of conservative women is the focus of Kathleen M. Blee, *Women of the Klan: Racism and Gender in the 1920s* (Berkeley, 1991), and Glen Jeansonne, *Women of the Far Right: The Mother's Movement and World War II* (Chicago, 1990).

Important biographies of activists and/or politicians include Jacquelyn Dowd Hall's *Revolt Against Chivalry: Jessie Daniel Ames and the Women's Campaign Against Lynching* (New York, 1974); Christie Miller, *Ruth Hanna McCormick: A Life in Politics, 1880–1944* (Albuquerque, 1992); Susan Ware, *Partner and I: Mollie Dewson, Feminism, and New Deal Politics* (New Haven, 1987); * Blanche Weisen Cook, *Eleanor Roosevelt*; Ingrid Scobie, *Center Stage: Helen Gahagen Douglas, A Life* (New York, 1992); and Patricia L. Schmidt, *Margaret Chase Smith: Beyond Convention* (Orono, Me., 1996).

Although the 1950s have traditionally been considered a period in which female activism was largely dormant, more recent studies suggest that there were important exceptions. See for example, Susan Lynn, *Progressive Women in Conservative Times: Racial Justice, Peace, and Feminism, 1945 to the 1960s* (New Brunswick, N.J., 1992), and *Not June Cleaver: Women and Gender in Postwar America, 1945–1960*, ed. Joanne Meyerowitz (Philadelphia, 1994). For black women's involvement in the civil rights movement, see *Women and the Civil Rights Movement: Trailblazers and Torchbearers, 1941–65*, ed. Vicki L. Crawford, Jacqueline Anne Rouse, and Barbara Woods (Brooklyn, 1990); *The Montgomery Bus Boycott and the Women Who Started It: The Memoir of Jo Ann Gibson Robinson*, ed. David

Garrow (Knoxville, Tenn., 1987); Joy James, *Race, Women and Revolution: Ella Baker and Black Female Radicalism* (Cambridge, Mass., 1999); and Belinda Robnett, *How Long? How Long?: African American Women in the Struggle for Civil Rights* (New York, 1997). On peace activism, see Harriet Hyman Alonso, *The Women's Peace Movement and the Outlawry of War, 1921–1942* (Knoxville, Tenn., 1990), and Amy Swerdlow, *Women Strike for Peace: Traditional Motherhood and Radical Politics in the 1960s* (Urbana, Ill., 1993). On women's influence on diplomatic policy, see Edward P. Crapol, *Women and American Foreign Policy: Lobbyists, Critics, and Insiders* (Wilmington, Del., 1992), and Rhodri Jeffreys-Jones, *Changing Differences: Women and the Shaping of American Foreign Policy, 1917–1994* (New Brunswick, N.J., 1995).

For the roots of feminist resurgence, see Leila Rupp and Verta Taylor, *Survival in the Doldrums: The American Women's Rights Movement, 1945 to the 1960s* (New York, 1987); Cynthia Harrison, *On Account of Sex: The Politics of Women's Issues, 1945–1968* (Berkeley, 1988); *Nancy F. Gabin, *Feminism in the Labor Movement;* and Sara Evans, *Personal Politics: The Roots of Women's Liberation in the Civil Rights Movement and the New Left* (New York, 1979). On the rise and demise of radical feminism, see Alice Echols, *Daring to Be Bad: Radical Feminism in America, 1965–1975* (Minneapolis, 1989). On black and Chicana feminism, see Patricia Hill Collins, *Black Feminist Thought: Knowledge, Consciousness, and the Politics of Empowerment* (New York, 1990), and *Chicana Feminist Thought: The Basic Historical Writings,* ed. Alma M. Garcia (New York, 1997). For overviews of the impact of the feminist movement, see Winfred D. Wandersee, *On the Move: American Women in the 1970s* (Boston, 1988), and Susan M. Hartmann, *From Margin to Mainstream: American Women and Politics Since 1960* (Philadelphia, 1989).

For studies of two highly contested policy issues that mobilized women politically, see Kristin Luker, *Abortion and the Politics of Motherhood* (Berkeley, 1984), and Donald G. Mathews and Jane Sherron De Hart, *Sex, Gender, and the ERA: A State and the Nation* (New York, 1990). Another policy issue of importance is presented in Mary Francis Berry, *The Politics of Parenthood: Child Care, Women's Rights and the Myth of the Good Mother* (New York, 1993).

Ideology

On the intersection of gender and fundamentalism, see Betty A. DeBerg, *Ungodly Women: Gender and the First Wave of American Fundamentalism* (Minneapolis, 1990). Gender representation during the Great Depression is the focus of Barbara Melosh's *Engendered Studies: Manhood and Womanhood in the New Deal Public Art and Theater* (Washington, D.C., 1991). On feminist ideology, see Rosalind Rosenberg, *Beyond Separate Spheres: Intellectual Roots of Modern Feminism* (New Haven, 1984), and * Nancy F. Cott, *The Grounding of Modern Feminism.* For anti-feminist ideology and its impact during the years since World War II, see Elaine Tyler May's *Homeward Bound: American Families in the Cold War Era* (New York, 1988), and Rebecca Klatch, *Women of the New Right* (Philadelphia, 1988). For the intersection of ideology, sexuality, and sports, see Susan E. Cayleff, *Babe: The Life and Legend of Babe Didrikson Zaharias* (Urbana, Ill., 1995), and Susan K. Cahn, *Coming on Strong: Gender and Sexuality in Twentieth Century Women's Sports* (Cambridge, Mass., 1994).

Reference Works

Important references containing excellent short biographies and a brief bibliography for many of the women appearing in this book are *Notable American Women, 1607–1950: A Biographical Dictionary*, ed. Edward T. James, Janet Wilson James, and Paul Boyer, 3 vols. (Cambridge, Mass., 1971); *Notable American Women: The Modern Period*, ed. Barbara Sicherman and Carol Hurd Green, (Cambridge, Mass; 1980); *Black Women in America: An Historical Encyclopedia*, ed. Darlene Clark Hine, 2 vols (Brooklyn, 1993); and *Jewish Women in America: An Historical Encyclopedia*, ed. Paula Hyman and Deborah Dash Moore, 2 vols. (New York, 1997). An annually updated reference, first published in 1987, which surveys all aspects of the status of women in the United States, is the series sponsored by the Women's Research and Education Institute in Washington, D.C., *The American Woman: A Status Report*.

DOCUMENTARY FILMS

A number of films both complement and supplement material in *Women's America*. This list is not comprehensive; it includes films, new and old, that we, our students, and our colleagues have found interesting and informative.

A Midwife's Tale (1998, 88 min., color) presents a delicate enactment of the book by the same name by Laurel Thatcher Ulrich. A rare account of a woman's life in Northern New England in the years of the early republic. Produced by Laurie Kahn-Leavitt. PBS Video. (Blue Berry Hill Productions, 112 Bailey Road, Watertown, MA 02172.)

Hearts and Hands: A Social History of Nineteenth Century Women and Quilts (1987, 63 min., color) is a beautifully crafted and absorbing documentary that explores the lives of anonymous and notable women as they intersected with the major movements and events of the nineteenth century. See the companion book, *Hearts and Hands: The Influence of Women and Quilts on American Society* by Pat Ferrero, Elaine Hedges, and Julie Silber. (Hearts and Hands Media Arts, 372 Frederick St., San Francisco, CA 94117; 415-664-9623.)

The Women of Hull-House (1992, 18 min., b/w, color) describes the work of Florence Kelley, Julia Lathrop, Grace and Edith Abbott, and founders Jane Addams and Ellen Gates Starr, and the thirteen-building complex that served as a focal point for education, urban research, and social reform in Chicago during the early twentieth century. (Jane Addams's Hull House Museum, the University of Illinois at Chicago, 800 South Halsted Street, Chicago, IL 60607-7017.)

Ida B. Wells: A Passion for a Justice (1990, 53 min., color) examines the personal and intense career of slave-born African-American journalist and activist Ida B. Wells from her militant opposition to lynchings and discrimination to her determined support for the NAACP and the women's suffrage movement. This excellent film is particularly effective at showing how her activism was shaped by both her sex and race. (William Greaves Productions, 230 55th St., 26th Floor, New York, NY 10019.)

One Woman, One Vote (1995, 1 hr., 46 min., b/w) documents the seventy-year bat-tle for woman suffrage, which finally culminated in the ratification of the Nineteenth Amendment to the Constitution in 1920. This excellent film portrays the movement's leaders, among them Susan B. Anthony, Elizabeth Cady Stanton, Lucy Stone, and Alice Paul, who dedicated much of their lives to the suffrage struggle. Interspersed are use-ful comments from historians. (PBS Video, 1320 Braddock Place, Alexandria, VA 22314, Educational Film Center; 800-424-7963.)

A portrayal of the Bryn Mawr Summer School, which flourished between 1921 and 1938, *The Women of Summer* (1975, 55 min., color) documents the effort to expose blue-collar women to humanistic study in such a way as to empower them to go back to their own communities as leaders. Duplicated in the South, these summer schools for women workers were part of the worker's education movement. Their impact on some of the alumnae is conveyed in archival footage, oral histories, and clips of many of the women leaders who served to link Progressivism and the New Deal. (Film-Makers Library, Inc., 133 E. 58th Street, New York, NY 10022; 212-355-6545.)

Beginning in 1911, *You May Call Her Madam Secretary* (1986, 58 min., b/w, color) follows New Dealer Frances Perkins from teaching to settlement house work to FDR's Cabinet as Secretary of Labor, documenting effectively the continuity between Pro-gressivism and the New Deal. (Vineyard Video Productions, Elias Lane, West Tisbury, MA 02575.)

Based on Alice Lynch's account of the labor movement in the 1930s, *Union Maids* (1976, 50 min., b/w) depicts the personal experiences of three women who were labor organizers in Chicago during this period. (New Day Films, 22 Riverside Drive, Wayne, NJ 07470; 201-663-0212.)

The story of the Women's Emergency Brigade, *With Babies and Banners* (1979, 45 min., color) is an account of women's critical role in the General Motors sitdown strike in Flint, Michigan, in 1937, which was the key to the success of the Congress of Indus-trial Organizations' drive for industrial unionism. (New Day Films, 22 Riverside Drive, Wayne, NJ 07470; 201-663-0212.)

The Life and Times of Rosie the Riveter (1980, 65 min., color) presents the powerful and moving reminiscences of five women who welcomed the challenges and higher pay provided by new jobs in industry during World War II and details their loss of oppor-tunities at the war's end when women were told to return home. (Clarity Educational Productions, Box 315, Franklin Lakes, NJ 07414.)

Never Turn Back: The Life of Fannie Lou Hamer (1983, 58 min., color) is an informa-tive and powerful documentary that follows the career of black activist Fannie Lou Hamer from her early life as a sharecropper in Sunflower County, Mississippi, to national prominence as a civil rights leader and founding member of the Mississippi Freedom

Democratic party in the 1960s. (Rediscovery Production, 2 Half Mill Common, West-port, CT 06880; 203-226-4489.)

Focusing solely on Mexican-American/Chicana women, *Adelante, Mujeres* (1992, 30 min., b/w, color) provides a brief history from colonial Mexico to the present. Women are presented in their work and family roles and as community and union activists. (National Women's History Project, 7738 Bell Road, Windsor, CA 95492.)

Other films containing important segments on women include:

Eyes on the Prize: Fighting Back (1986, 60 min., color) examines the explosive inte-gration of the public schools in Little Rock, Arkansas, and the courage of the young black girls who had to go past angry white mobs to enter the schools. (PBS Video, 1320 Braddock Place, Alexandria, VA 22314; 800-424-7963.)

America's War on Poverty: My Brother's Keeper (1995, 60 min., color) has a useful seg-ment on the National Welfare Rights Organization that captures the determination of these predominantly black welfare mothers. (PBS Video, 1320 Braddock Place, Alexan-dria, VA 22314, 800-424-7963.)

INDEX